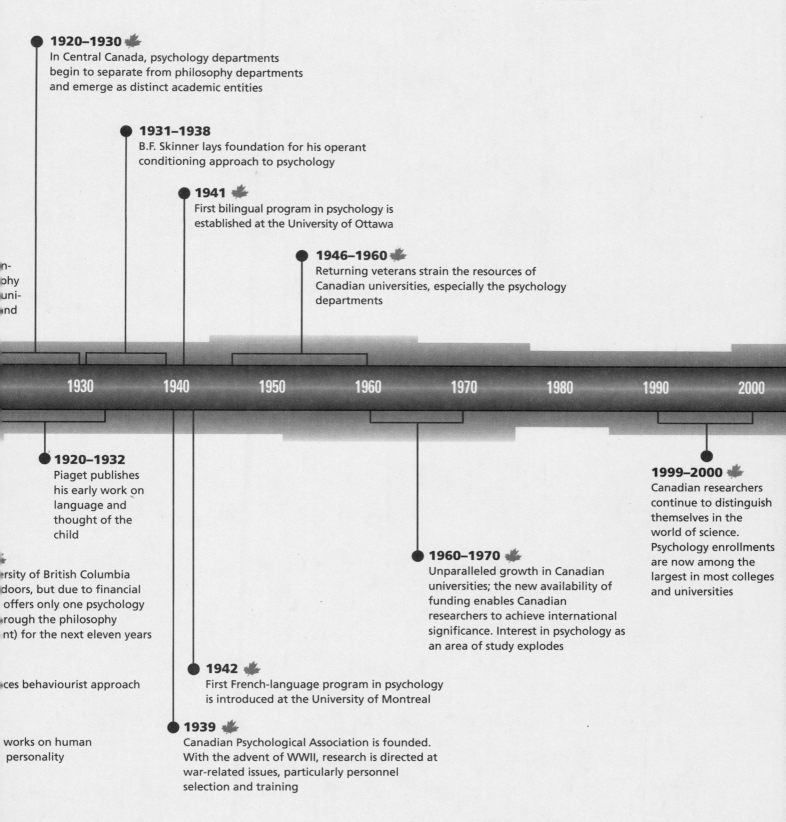

1920–1930
In Central Canada, psychology departments begin to separate from philosophy departments and emerge as distinct academic entities

1931–1938
B.F. Skinner lays foundation for his operant conditioning approach to psychology

1941
First bilingual program in psychology is established at the University of Ottawa

1946–1960
Returning veterans strain the resources of Canadian universities, especially the psychology departments

n-
ohy
uni-
nd

1930   1940   1950   1960   1970   1980   1990   2000

1920–1932
Piaget publishes his early work on language and thought of the child

rsity of British Columbia
doors, but due to financial
offers only one psychology
rough the philosophy
nt) for the next eleven years

ces behaviourist approach

works on human
personality

1960–1970
Unparalleled growth in Canadian universities; the new availability of funding enables Canadian researchers to achieve international significance. Interest in psychology as an area of study explodes

1999–2000
Canadian researchers continue to distinguish themselves in the world of science. Psychology enrollments are now among the largest in most colleges and universities

1942
First French-language program in psychology is introduced at the University of Montreal

1939
Canadian Psychological Association is founded. With the advent of WWII, research is directed at war-related issues, particularly personnel selection and training

Psychology

Third Canadian Edition

Robert A. Baron
Rensselaer Polytechnic Institute
With the special assistance of Michael J. Kalsher

Bruce Earhard
Dalhousie University

Marcia Ozier
Dalhousie University

Toronto

Canadian Cataloguing in Publication Data

Baron, Robert A.
    Psychology

3rd Canadian ed.
Includes bibliographical references and index.
ISBN 0-205-30677-2

1. Psychology. I. Earhard, Bruce. II. Ozier, Marcia, 1937– . III. Title.

BF121.B37 2001   150   C00-930573-4

Copyright © 2001 Pearson Education Canada Inc., Toronto

ISBN 0-205-30677-2

Vice President, Editorial Director: Michael Young
Acquisitions Editor: Jessica Mosher
Marketing Manager: Judith Allen
Developmental Editors: Dawn du Quesnay, Lise Dupont
Production Editors: Matthew Christian, Avivah Wargon
Copy Editor: Lisa Berland
Production Coordinator: Wendy Moran
Page Layout: Joan Wilson
Photo Research: Susan Wallace-Cox
Art Director: Mary Opper
Interior Design: Sarah Battersby
Cover Design: Sarah Battersby
Cover Image: Thom Sevalrud

1 2 3 4 5   05 04 03 02 01

Printed and bound in the U.S.A.

Contents at a Glance

Contents

Preface

Why Psychology Matters:

Reflections of Robert Baron— Long-Term Believer

Psychology, I have long believed, is much more than a scientific field or a collection of findings and principles: It is also an invaluable perspective for understanding ourselves, other people, our relationships with them, and just about everything else that really matters to most of us most of the time. It is, in short, an eminently useful field, with important practical benefits for anyone wise enough to use it, or at least to adopt it as a personal framework. So, it's no exaggeration to state that I strongly believe in the theme of this edition: *making psychology part of your life.*

To The Instructor

At the beginning of this 21st century, an instructor in introductory psychology has many choices when selecting a textbook. Is the present text simply another standard offering? We think not. This is now the third edition of *Psychology*, by Baron, Earhard, and Ozier, and again it has been specifically tailored to meet the needs of students being introduced to psychology in Canada.

Robert A. Baron

In this edition, as before, we continue to recognize fully that much of the past history of our discipline happened elsewhere, and the contemporary research that continues to enrich our understanding of human behaviour occurs all around the world. We have made every effort to ensure that the traditional coverage of problems, theories, findings, and practices in this text is complete. However, we also recognize that most introductory psychology texts are standard U.S. editions. The illustrations, demographics, place names, historical figures, and current events are set below the 49th parallel for American students. In their introduction to psychology, students studying from those books become educated also in the culture, history, and institutions of the United States. We thought that, if our students were going to have exposure to those kinds of things in their intro psychology textbooks, we might as well use the opportunity to include some information about Canada.

Thus, since its first edition, this text has been different. Here, you will find Canadian place names, ethical codes, public figures, history, law, demographics, institutions, culture and language, even Canadian athletes and entertainers at relevant points throughout the book — but only where appropriate. There are charts, graphs, images, and illustrations drawn from Canadian sources.

Bruce Earhard

Recently, a number of other "Canadian" texts have appeared on the Canadian scene. We welcome the company. The result will be better books. In one case, however, almost all that "Canadian" has meant is the inclusion of a photo of some U.S. hockey players! We don't agree with tokenism of that kind. And we are pleased that, in their review of "Canadian" Psychology, Adair et al (1996) singled out our text as a "thoroughly retooled" revision . . . adapted specifically for a Canadian audience.

Here is one more reason we think that is important. Psychology came later to Canada than to the United States, and different significant figures populate the early Canadian landscape. Ethical codes, and the legal system within which they operate, are not the same in Canada and in the United States. Deinstitutionaliza-

Marcia Ozier

tion of mental patients and community service organizations available to deal with these changes have been different in Canada. We believe our students should know something about the development and practice of psychology in Canada and should understand the differences and why they occurred.

The three Canadian editions of our book reflect our experience that students studying psychology in Canada are attentive, comfortable, and responsive to material presented in a context that is directly relevant to themselves. We believe that our students will be better equipped to make psychology a part of their lives if it is put in a Canadian context, and as a result, acquire and retain the material more easily and more permanently.

Our confidence in this approach was strengthened early by a survey of introductory psychology students at Dalhousie University. We asked them to indicate anonymously, in writing, whether they preferred an American text similar to the one they were currently using or a comparable text that used Canadian demographics, place names, illustrations, and examples and singled out, where possible, significant contributions of Canadian researchers. Of 399 students, 337 expressed a preference for a Canadian edition. We continue to receive much positive feedback from students and their professors on this particular point. We are now told by those teaching second-year classes that their students are asking them for Canadian context!

The third edition of *Psychology* is special in many respects. Notwithstanding the wide acceptance of the first two editions, we decided the third time round to make certain that ours was not only the best Canadian adaptation but also the most current. Perhaps it was the spirit of the millennium. At any rate, this revision has taken a full twenty months of work. The first set of changes was made as the result of wide consultation with reviewers from across this country. The content and the organization of each chapter were adjusted in response to their suggestions. For example, the biological perspective on personality was added and the art program for the brain and behaviour chapter much expanded. The chapter on learning received attention from expert reviewers, one of whom now says that "Chapter 5 was a pleasure to read — of the five (chapters) I reviewed, this was the most cohesive, informative, and well-written."

The second set of changes included the additional coverage of evolutionary psychology, genetics and neuroscience, and other new material in the U.S. edition under revision. Concurrently, the contemporary scene in Canadian psychology was incorporated into every chapter.

Introducing students to psychology can be one of the most pleasurable assignments in post-secondary academic life. We have found that to be the case and we hope, with the support of this textbook, you will have that experience as well.

Bruce Earhard and Marcia Ozier
Halifax, June 2000

New to This Edition

Here is some of the news, on a chapter-by-chapter basis.

Chapter 1

Coverage of the historical background of psychology has been extended to include consideration of Structuralism and Functionalism. A new section describing the character and growing significance of evolutionary psychology has been added.

Consideration of scientific methodology has been extended to include information about the importance of operational definitions. The coverage of ethical issues has been lengthened to include special consideration of special factors that must be taken into account in carrying out research studies involving young children.

Chapter 2

The exciting innovation in Chapter 2 is the expansion of the art program. Every effort has been made to provide students with a visual image of the structures they are studying. The material in every section has been made current—for example, the section on how drugs work and drug addiction. There is a new Research Process box on Treating Addiction at the Synapse. There is extended coverage of the effects of brain damage, including very new information about how the brain deals with humour and music. In connection with traumatic brain injury, this edition has a new section on basic research into the recovery of damaged nerve cells.

Chapter 3

The question is raised as to whether natural selection may determine the range of physical stimuli to which different species are sensitive. New information is provided about visual priming effects illustrating how our responses and reactions may be influenced by stimuli that do not register consciously. The section dealing with eye movements has been expanded to include the consequences of stabilizing images on the retina. The section on colour vision has been expanded and a new diagram has been added to simplify explanation of the role opponent-process mechanisms play in colour vision. A detailed consideration of how a variety of products of modern technology can contribute to hearing loss is provided in the Making Psychology Part of Your Life section.

Chapter 4

Here are some topics relevant to states of consciousness which have been introduced or expanded in the third edition: evolution and consciousness, resetting circadian rhythms with melatonin pills and bright light, brain activity during sleep, REM deprivation, sleep deprivation in long-haul truck drivers, different types of insomnia, treatment of sleep disorders, the neodissociation theory of hypnosis, genetics and alcoholism, legalization of marijuana in B.C. for therapeutic use, sexual fantasies, meditation, and the positive and negative aspects of self-awareness or self-consciousness.

Chapter 5

To the satisfaction of experts in the field of learning, this chapter has received long and specific attention as to the clarity of the extensive terminology, detailed explanations, and many examples. With the help and direction of the reviewers, we think we have made this learning chapter as reader friendly and as interesting as is humanly possible. In addition to the incorporation of current findings throughout, the content of the Making Psychology Part of Your Life feature is new: punishment in the real world. There are new details about "alcoholic myopia" and procrastination in animals, for example.

Chapter 6

The section dealing with the structure of human memory has been updated. The coverage of working memory, its character, function, and role in the human memory process has been much enlarged. The Research Process section now details the various different techniques that contemporary researchers use to study memory. Additional information about the development and detection of false memories has been added. The role schema play in memory construction and distortion has been extended and clarified. New information has been introduced about a recent vaccine that may be an important new tool in the struggle to control Alzheimer's disease.

Chapter 7

A new Research Process section has been introduced to explain how psychologists use reaction time, evoked potentials, and event-related brain potentials to study the brain processes that underlie cognitive processes. Additional elaboration of hindsight bias (I could have predicted that) studies and the illusionary knowledge (I always knew that) effect has been provided. Added also is information about how the study of decision making in natural situations can sometimes alter conclusions drawn from laboratory studies. New figures have been introduced to illustrate trial and error problem solving and lateral thinking processes. Material dealing with artificial intelligence and neural networks has been updated, and the chapter ends with a new section on evolution, language, and thought.

Chapter 8

In this chapter on development in childhood, all sections have been updated and a number of topics have been newly introduced or expanded. Some of these deal directly with information processing in cognitive development. For example there are new studies on children's strategies for retaining information and achieving cognitive efficiency, on adult contributions of mental scaffolding, and on metacognition and theory of mind. Others deal with early social understanding of facial expressions, childhood friendship, and attachment.

Chapter 9

The changes in this chapter include several recent advances in our understanding of adolescents and adults. These include: pseudomaturity, two kinds of subjective age, risk-taking, multiracial teens, adolescent resilience, adult attachment, and developmental regulation and other cognitive changes that occur as a consequence of aging. The Making Psychology Part of Your Life feature on career planning has been revised significantly, making it as relevant as possible to current conditions.

Chapter 10

In this revision, you will find new information about both motivation and emotion as the research had progressed in the three years since the last edition. Some of the topics that we have introduced or changed are the biological basis of eating behaviour and genetic factors in the long-term regulation of body weight. You will find the results of cross-cultural comparisons of body image in Canadian ethnic groups. Research in anger and aggression has been updated with new material about the brain, alcohol consumption and aggression, as well as gender differences and new data on the inhibition of aggression under the influence of alcohol. There are new pieces on power and affiliation. In the sections on emotion, there is new material on the relationship between mood and cognition, memory and decision-making, and the hemispheric specialization for emotional valence and emotional intensity, as well as new data on how people tell genuine from false pain.

Chapter 11

Gardner's section on the domains of intelligence has been updated. Consideration of Sterberg's Triarchic Theory has been clarified and streamlined. A new figure demonstrating the types of performance tasks used on intelligence tests has been added. The treatment of intelligence test validity has been rewritten to make it more readily comprehensible to students. The Key Concept page has been revamped. A new figure on gender differences in verbal abilities has been introduced. The section on the role genetic factors play in intelligence has been extended to include the historical work of Galton as well as contemporary genetic assessment studies.

Chapter 12

The section on Freud has been updated with new references, and the figure illustrating his levels of consciousness has been revised for greater clarity. An extensive new section on biological approaches to personality, including Personality and the Biology of Arousal, Genetics and Personality, and Evolution and Personality, has been added. New figures illustrating the role of genetic factors play a prominent role in this new section.

Chapter 13

There have been many interesting findings recently in the area of Health Psychology. Of course this chapter continues to provide students with the fundamentals of health, stress, and coping. In this edition, beliefs and their effects on health, also personality factors (optimism/pessimism), and the biological reasons for unhealthy eating appear, as well as expanded attention to the factors important in the promotion of healthy lifestyles. Other expanded issues include the biological basis and treatment of nicotine addiction and the genetic basis for alcoholism as determined by specially-engineered mice. Sections of special interest to students include a new section on gender and coping with stress. The Canadian Focus feature has been brought up to date and expanded to include new data about the psychological well-being of peacekeepers from other countries as well. The Research Process feature is new and the focus is upon laboratory and fields studies of alcohol intoxication and HIV/AIDS prevention.

Chapter 14

This chapter has been heavily revised to put increased emphasis on the biological perspective. Biological determinants of the various different mental disorders are detailed wherever possible. A new, much more detailed discussion of childhood disorders has been added. New comprehensive tables outlining the structure of DSM-IV have been introduced. Sections dealing with Suicide, Anxiety, and Dissociative Identity Disorders have been updated and lengthened.

Chapter 15

A new section has been added to reflect current concern about empirically validating various forms of psychotherapy. Additional detail has been provided about the processes involved in evaluating and comparing various therapies. A new section weighing the pros and cons of drug therapy and psychotherapy has been added. A section on the need for cultural sensitivity in the practice of psychotherapy has been also introduced.

Chapter 16

These are a few of the topics which have been updated or newly introduced to students: attribution, athletes and the self-serving bias, automatic vigilance and evolution, heuristic processing of social information, counterfactual thinking, how genetics contribute to attitudes, early development of prejudice, misattribution of arousal, complaining as a compliance tactic, mood and attraction, reciprocity in attraction and love, evolution and love and jealousy. The Canadian Focus feature is now directed towards understanding Canadian multiculturalism from the perspective of social psychology. It is now about immigrants, ethnic groups, attitudes, attitude change and ambivalent attitudes. Also, the section on Applied Social Psychology has been revised and now includes a section on decision-making in groups.

And those are just some of the enhancements we have made to the content of the text in this edition.

Features

This new edition retains many of the features from the first and second editions designed to reinforce the overall theme of making *the science of* psychology part of your life. The most important of these features are as follows.

Chapter Openers   Chapters open with a lead-in based on a story from a Canadian newspaper, showing how psychological principles relate to what is going on in the real world. There is at least one from every province and territory, including stories from the *Winnipeg Free Press, Regina Leader Post, Victoria Times Colonist* and *The Telegram* of St. John's, Newfoundland. For example, the lead-in to Chapter 12 from the *Moncton Times and Transcript* asks the question: Why do genetic clones have individual differences in personality? The point of these vignettes is to encourage students to see the relevance between what they learn in class, what they learn from the textbook, and the world in which they live.

Making Psychology Part of Your Life   These special sections illustrate how readers can actually apply the information presented in each chapter to their own lives. For example, Chapter 1 provides students with information about the most efficient and effective way to commit information to memory, and how to prepare for quizzes and examinations.

Canadian Focus   Special sections outline distinctive contributions in applications, problem analysis, and research made by psychologists in Canada. For example, the Canadian Focus box in Chapter 3 looks at unique case studies of two individuals with injury to visual areas of the brain, undertaken by M. Goodale of the University of Western Ontario. These studies shed important light on how the visual system monitors different aspects of our visual experience. Canadian Focus boxes also highlight material with special relevance to Canadians, such as "Peacekeeper Stress" or special techniques to treat mental disorders in the far North.

The Research Process Research fuels the progress of psychology. Much effort has gone into making students aware of this fact, and to emphasizing the variety of different research tools and techniques that are employed in contemporary psychology. In the introductory chapter, we have provided a thorough discussion of scientific method and basic research techniques. In virtually all remaining chapters special Research Process sections illustrate unique research approaches to the particular domain of psychology covered in that chapter. Our overall goal is to show:

- How psychologists use research to answer important questions about human behaviour.
- The range of approaches that can be taken in asking and answering basic questions about human behaviour.
- How the findings of psychological research are interpreted and contribute to the development of accurate theories.

Perspectives on Diversity Presented as a major section within each chapter and integrated into the narrative, this feature takes into account the growing interest among psychologists in cultural diversity, and the fact that most readers of this text are likely to encounter increasing cultural diversity themselves in the years ahead. Understanding the role of cultural and ethnic factors in behaviour, therefore, is crucial to applying psychology to everyday life.

Key Terms Key Terms are identified in bold letters throughout the text. These terms are concepts that play a crucial role in material being covered. Definitions of Key Terms are provided in margin areas adjacent to the relevant section of the text. This serves to clarify the meaning of important terms, and allows students an opportunity to review the significant concepts contained in a section before moving to the next section, or before a quiz. Key Terms also appear in chapter's Summary and Review section (with page references) and in the end-of-book Glossary.

Key Questions Key Questions are posed at the end of major sections in every chapter. They are designed to make readers stop and think about the major points covered in the section. They provide the reader with an opportunity to determine instantly whether he or she has grasped the core concerns of the section. Each chapter ends with a listing of Key Questions and correct answers. This offers students the opportunity to test their retention of central issues covered in the chapter.

Critical Thinking Questions A series of Critical Thinking Questions now appears at various points in each section. These questions are designed to encourage students to ponder about important issues and themes relevant to material covered in the chapter. A *separate* series of Critical Thinking Questions appears at the end of each chapter in the Summary and Review section.

Key Concept Pages The special Key Concept pages are concise, graphically appealing, visually memorable summaries of important psychological concepts. They are designed to accomplish two goals:

- To illustrate concepts and principles that students often find difficult to understand (for example, the fact that correlation does not equal causation, in Chapter 1).
- To summarize and integrate topics covered in the text (for example, contrasting theories of emotion in Chapter 10).

Summary and Review   Each chapter ends with a useful Summary and Review section, which provides answers to the Key Questions posed in the chapter, a list of Key Terms with page references, additional Critical Thinking Questions, and a short list of Weblinks.

Critical Thinking Questions   More Critical Thinking Questions appear at the end of each chapter. These questions — distinct from the critical thinking questions that appear at the end of major sections — are designed to stimulate critical thinking, an important goal for any psychology text.

Weblinks   This feature links students to a whole world of psychology resources. Researched and tested for quality, relevant sites are listed at the end of each chapter in the Summary and Review sections.

Supplementary Materials

A complete teaching and learning package accompanies this text. The key elements are described below.

Learning Aids for Students

- The *Study Guide* for *Psychology,* Third Canadian Edition (ISBN 0-205-30745-0), offers a comprehensive, carefully structured learning guide to all of the important concepts in this text. Organized around chapter learning objectives, it includes a variety of book-specific exercises, review sections, and exercises to strengthen readers' critical thinking and application skills. In addition, the study guide contains practice tests for each chapter.

- *Companion Website.* The Pearson Education Canada Companion Website (www.pearsoned.ca/baron) is easy to navigate and is organized to correspond to the chapters in this textbook. It features an Online Study Guide with practice tests, dynamic, interactive learning activities, and links to related websites, student discussions, and polls and surveys. The *InterActivities* expand and update the book itself, providing additional opportunities to take psychology beyond the classroom and make it a meaningful part of the reader's life.

Additional supplements for students include:

- *Psychologically Speaking: A Self-Assessment*, by Craig P. Donovan and Peter C. Rosato, Allyn & Bacon, ISBN 0-205-16364-5

- *Tools of Critical Thinking: Metathoughts for Psychology,* by David A. Levy, Allyn & Bacon, ISBN 0-205-26083-7

- *Psychology and Culture*, edited by Walter Lonner and Roy Malpass, Allyn & Bacon, ISBN 0-205-14899-9

- *Evaluating Psychological Information: Sharpening Your Critical Thinking Skills,* Second Edition, by James Bell, Allyn & Bacon, ISBN 0-205-28635-6

- *Studying Psychology: A Manual for Success,* by Robert T. Brown, Allyn & Bacon, ISBN 0-205-13027-5

Supplements for Instructors

- The *Instructor's Resource Manual* is designed to encourage student involvement in the classroom and understanding of the textbook. It includes teaching suggestions, examples, demonstrations, visual aids, learning objectives, critical thinking exercises, and more. The *Instructor's Resource Manual* provides step-by-step instructions, as well as ready-to-duplicate handouts for over 150 activities and demonstrations. It also includes detailed notes on lecture launchers, Chapter-at-a-Glance tables that show how to organize the many supplementary materials available for each chapter, Transparency Masters, and an array of additional teaching aids.

- The *Test Item File*, available in both print and computerized format, contains over 2600 true/false, matching, multiple choice, and essay questions. Pearson Test Manager is a test generator designed to allow the creation of personalized exams. Test questions can be added to the Test Item File and existing questions can be edited using a personal computer. The Test Manager also offers an On-Line Testing System, which is the most efficient, time-saving examination aid on the market, allowing the instructor to administer, correct, grade, record, and return computerized exams over a variety of networks.

- *Psychology Presentation Software*, accessible through the internet at www.abacon.com/ppt/, is a series of presentations designed to enhance lecture presentations. The presentation software provides detailed outlines of key points, supported by charts, graphs, diagrams, and other visuals.

- *Digital Media Archive CD-ROM for Psychology, 2.0 Version* offers an array of media products to help liven up your classroom presentations. The Digital Media Archive provides charts, graphs, tables, and figures electronically on one, cross-platform CD-ROM. The archive also provides video and audio clips, along with electronic images, that can easily be integrated into your lectures.

Please see your Pearson Education Canada sales representative for information about these ancillaries.

Acknowledgments

The third Canadian edition of *Psychology* has turned out to be the most effortful and all-consuming project yet in this series. We acknowledge freely the collaboration of many other people — family and friends — who sustained us with their enthusiasm and their support and their patience over the years it took. Here are some other folks whose most important contributions were essential.

First, there are our colleagues in psychological science who contributed, through their publications and prepublications, their hypotheses, their results, and their conclusions, their specific advice, and in some cases their faces as well. To them again we proclaim our admiration and our gratitude.

Second, we were blessed again with amazing student researchers. For this edition we relied upon the remarkable accuracy of Leslie Newhook for the hundreds of new references in the bibliography, Darren Cargill, Lisa Aldridge, and Peter Duke for superb assistance with library research, Leanna Rutherford for her magical ability to read two manuscripts at the same time, Blaine Mullins for help with newspaper searches, and to the very special Ophelia She, who managed to do what was needed even before we knew it had to be done!

Third, there are the people connected with Pearson Canada. Dawn du Quesnay is a most talented and tireless Developmental Editor *par excellence*, whose good taste is evident all through this edition. Lisa Berland is the remarkable and gifted freelance editor whose sharp eye, intelligence, and goodness sustained us during the last ten critical weeks. Avivah Wargon, production editor, took over the project at the last minute, and her very special attention to detail was most helpful. Nicole Lukach and Lise Dupont were there when we needed them. There were also professionals at Pearson with whom we had little or no direct contact but whose wonderful contributions we recognize in the photographs, the art, the design, and the production of this textbook.

We recognize with special thanks the cooperation of Robert A. Baron and others at Allyn & Bacon (USA). Also acknowledged here are Beverly Fehr of the University of Winnipeg for her work on Chapter 16 of the second edition, Don Sharpe of the University of Regina for the Instructor's Manual and Test Item File, and Emir Andrews of Memorial University for the Study Guide. We also thank the many reviewers, listed alphabetically here, who gave us their advice on this edition: Dr. Mike Boyes, University of Calgary; Dr. Annabel Evans, Concordia University College of Alberta; Dr. Mark Hammer, Carleton University; Dr. Andrew Howell, Grant MacEwan Community College; Dr. Alison Kulak, Concordia University College of Alberta; Dr. Doug McCann, York University; Dr. Stuart McKelvie, Bishop's University; Dr. Myriam Mongrain, York University; Dr. Robert Moore, Campion College - The University of Regina; Dr. Marcia Moshé, Ryerson Polytechnic University; Dr. Nancy Ogden, Mount Royal College; Dr. Russ Powell, Grant MacEwan Community College; Dr. Susan Sajna-Hebert, Lakehead University; Dr. Tony Simmonds, Memorial University of Newfoundland; Dr. Shelagh Towson, University of Windsor; Dr. Gillian Wark, Simon Fraser University; Dr. Lee Woodson, Kwantlen College; and Dr. Sandra Wright, University of Saskatchewan.

Fourth, there are the librarians: at the Killam, McDonald Science, Weldon Law, and Kellog Medical libraries at Dalhousie; and at St. Mary's University, Mount Saint Vincent University, Halifax Regional Library (main branch reference room), the Nova Scotia legislature, and Statistics Canada in Halifax; and Mark Robertson at York University.

Fifth, there are the associations and societies that provided information for one or more of the three editions: The Addiction Research Foundation (Toronto); the Canadian Heart and Stroke Foundation (Nova Scotia); the Nova Scotia, Ontario, and British Columbia Head Injury Associations; the Canadian Mental Health Association (Nova Scotia); the Canadian Cancer Society (Nova Scotia Division); the American Cancer Society (Washington, D.C., and Portland, Oregon); AIDS Nova Scotia and AIDS Canada; Sport Nova Scotia; the National Eating Disorder Information Centre; the Nova Scotia Heart Health Program; and the Nova Scotia Department of Health, Drug Dependency Services. We appreciate the help we received from the staff at the Ontario Psychological Association and the Registry of Ontario Psychologists.

Sixth, there are Canada's newspapers which contributed the material for the vignettes. Most helpful were the Web sites of the *Ottawa Citizen* and the *Montreal Gazette.*

To The Student

Using This Book: A Note on Its Features

Are all textbooks alike? Not at all. Textbooks, like individuals, are all unique and reflect the experience, perspectives, and goals of their authors. The goals for this book have already been outlined: to provide you with a broad yet integrated overview of the findings of modern psychology, and to call your attention to how you, personally, can benefit from this knowledge. To achieve these goals, a number of special features have been incorporated into this book. These will be briefly described at this point so that you'll have a better idea of what's coming and an awareness of how to make maximum use of these features.

First, several steps have been taken to make the text easier to read and more convenient to use. Each chapter begins with an outline and ends with a summary. Within the text, key terms are printed in **boldface type like this** and are accompanied by a definition in the margin. These terms are also defined in a glossary at the end of the book. In addition, important principles that lie at the very heart of our field are highlighted in the margins under the headings Key Questions and Critical Thinking Questions. If you take the time to stop and answer these questions you will be off to a good start in developing an understanding of the important issues dealt with in this, your first course in psychology. All figures and tables have been made as clear as possible, and most contain special labels and notes designed to help you interpret them. Concepts that we have found many students have difficulty dealing with have been given special consideration on Key Concept pages which provide an extensive elaboration of these ideas in an attractive graphic format.

Second, an attempt has been made, wherever possible, to include references to experiences, situations, and problems that will get you thinking about ways in which the topics and materials discussed are relevant to your own experiences — ways in which you can make psychology a part of your life. You will encounter them repeatedly throughout the book.

Third, this version of the text has been augmented and improved to meet the needs of Canadian students. Wherever possible, Canadian demographics are cited and reference is made to Canadian places, traditions, and cultures. Our objective is to present modern developments in psychology in a Canadian context. The point is not to exaggerate the role of Canadian traditions or the contributions of Canadian psychologists; rather, it is to offer you, as a student studying in Canada, an opportunity to appreciate and understand the degree to which the study of psychology flourishes in Canada, and to gain some insight into the scope, diversity, and character of psychological research carried out at various Canadian institutions.

Fourth, this text includes several types of special sections that you should find both interesting and informative. Sections labelled The Research Process discuss active lines of research in psychology — current efforts by psychologists to understand specific aspects of behaviour. They are designed to help you understand how research actually unfolds in psychology and to provide you with practice in critical thinking. Canadian Focus boxes appear in all chapters. These will outline distinctive contributions in applications, problem analysis, and research made by Canadian psychologists, and give you a sense of the enormous variety of problems being dealt with, and the significant contributions being made, by contemporary Canadian practitioners and researchers. Sections headed Perspectives on Diversity appear in many chapters. These examine the impact of ethnic and cultural factors on many aspects of behaviour and bring into focus psychology's growing concern about multicultural issues. Finally, all chapters conclude with a section titled Making Psychology Part of Your Life. These sections indicate how you can personally apply the information presented in this text to enhance your own life.

What can you expect to take away with you from the book and your first course in psychology? We think the most valuable thing that you can take away is the *ability to think critically*. The basic principles in critical thinking are laid out in Chapter 1, and subsequent chapters build and emphasize these principles further. Once you acquire the basic principles of scientific inquiry, and understand the various errors in thinking that these principles are designed to guard against, we believe you will continue to think in this fashion about problems, issues, and experiences that you have to deal with in everyday life. It is our hope and expectation that long after you have forgotten much of the content of this book, you will retain one thing of enduring value — the ability to think critically.

Special Request to Readers of This Book   Please let us know how you like the book and how we can make it better. Here are our e-mail addresses:

bearhard@is.dal.ca
mozier@is.dal.ca

Where to find ...

Key Concepts

Making Psychology Part of Your Life

Canadian Focus

The Research Process

Perspectives on Diversity

The Pearson Education Canada

companion Website...

Your Internet companion to the most exciting, state-of-the-art educational tools on the Web!

The Pearson Education Canada Companion Website is easy to navigate and is organized to correspond to the chapters in this textbook. The Companion Website comprises five distinct, functional features:

1) **Customized Online Resources**

2) **Online Interactive Study Guide**

3) **Interactivities**

4) **Communication**

5) **Table of Contents**

Explore the five areas in this Companion Website. Students and distance learners will discover resources for indepth study, research, and communication, empowering them in their quest for greater knowledge and maximizing their potential for success in the course.

A NEW WAY TO DELIVER EDUCATIONAL CONTENT

1) Customized Online Resources

Our Companion Websites provide instructors and students with a range of options to access, view, and exchange content.

- **Syllabus Manager** provides *instructors* with the option of creating online classes and constructing an online syllabus linked to specific modules in the Companion Website.

- **Your Profile** enables *students* to customize the sending of results to various recipients, and also to customize how the material is sent, e.g., as HTML, as text, or as an attachment.

- **Help** includes an evaluation of the user's system and a tune-up area that makes updating browsers and plug-ins easier. This new feature will enhance the user's experience with Companion Websites.

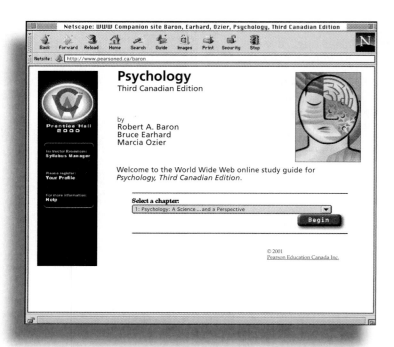

www.pearsoned.ca/baron

Pearson
Education
Canada

2) Online Study Guide

Interactive Study Guide modules form the core of the student learning experience in the Companion Website. These modules are categorized according to their functionality:

- Objectives
- Review 1
- Review 2
- Glossary
- Net Search

The Review modules provide students with the ability to send answers to our grader and receive instant feedback on their progress through our Results Reporter. Coaching comments and references back to the textbook ensure that students take advantage of all resources available to enhance their learning experience.

Net Search allows you to search the Internet based on key words specified in the Companion Website.

3) Interactivities

This area features dynamic, interactive learning activities; links to related Websites; student discussions; and polls and surveys.

4) Communication

Companion Websites contain the communication tools necessary to deliver courses in a **Distance Learning** environment. **Message Board** allows users to post messages and check back periodically for responses. **i-Chat** allows users to discuss course topics in real time, and enables professors to host on-line classes.

Communication facilities of Companion Websites provide a key element for distributed learning environments. There are two types of communication facilities currently in use in Companion Websites:

- **Message Board** – this module takes advantage of browser technology providing the users of each Companion Website with a national newsgroup to post and reply to relevant course topics.

- **i-Chat** – enables instructor-led group activities in real time. Using our chat client, instructors can display Website content while students participate in the discussion.

5) Table of Contents

Click here to view a detailed table of contents.

Note: Companion Website content will vary slightly from site to site depending on discipline requirements.

The Companion Website for this text can be found at:

www.pearsoned.ca/baron

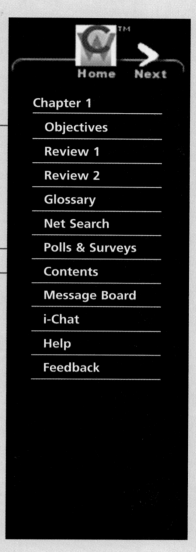

Home   Next

Chapter 1

Objectives

Review 1

Review 2

Glossary

Net Search

Polls & Surveys

Contents

Message Board

i-Chat

Help

Feedback

PEARSON EDUCATION CANADA

26 Prince Andrew Place
Don Mills, Ontario M3C 2T8

To order:
Call: 1-800-567-3800
Fax: 1-800-263-7733

For samples:
Call: 1-800-850-5813
Fax: (416) 299-2539
E-mail:
phabinfo_pubcanada@pearsoned.com

Psychology:
A Science ... and
a Perspective

CHAPTER OUTLINE

2000 and Beyond

What did Dr. Tomorrow, a seventy-nine-year-old Vancouverite, have to say about the year 2000 and beyond? According to a column in the *Ottawa Citizen*, he predicted that change—more rapid than our species has ever known—will come upon us.

For example, in the future, we will be able to see, hear, smell, and touch remotely—all around the world. There will be an explosion of new products. Indeed, Dr. Tomorrow reports that Sony Corporation developed five new products every single day of 1999. Age will not count in the same way. So called "granny-hackers" will make novel and important contributions to the world of business.

In order to survive in the years to come, Dr. Tomorrow predicts that, instead of strength, intelligence, race, age, or country of origin, *natural selection will favour those of us who are most adaptable to change*. And the key to that kind of adaptability will be knowledge. We will be a global village of the "knows" and the "know-nots."

With Chapter 1 of this introduction to psychology, you begin your quest for knowledge about psychological science. Here you will find much information that will contribute towards your own personal adaptability in the future.

Source: Enman, C. 2000 and Beyond. *Ottawa Citizen.*

Psychologists seek to obtain scientific information on virtually every imaginable aspect of human behaviour.

Why study psychology? If this question is put to a class of students, three reasons are typically advanced. Most students claim that they are interested in psychology and they want to gain a better understanding of why people and other organisms behave the way they do. A smaller (but substantial) number of students usually concede that they are taking psychology because they have an urge to find out something more about themselves and the processes that have shaped and molded them. A still smaller, third group of students will generally admit that they are studying psychology simply because a slot in their timetable needed to be filled and space was available in the class. All too often, students in this group will confess that they have no interest in psychology and that they harbour doubts about whether they will learn anything of value.

We would like to believe that this book will offer something of value to students studying psychology for any of the above reasons. For those who are interested in learning about why people and other animals behave the way they do, it will provide an overview of a vast array of findings—useful and intriguing information about virtually every imaginable aspect of human behaviour. Those students wanting more information about why they behave the way they do should find much insightful information about the factors that shape and mold their behaviour. Finally, we believe that the material covered, and the issues considered, should have enough intrinsic interest and relevance to convince even those disinterested souls who find themselves studying psychology because it happened to fit their timetable that they made the right decision—even if it was for the wrong reason.

The goal of this first chapter is to provide you with the background material you need to construct a framework that will help you to organize and understand new information about psychology as it is presented. To make the material covered familiar and meaningful to you, we will use, wherever possible, Canadian examples, practices, and statistics. Let's begin with an overview of this chapter.

We have a number of tasks to accomplish in this chapter. First, we'll provide some background information about psychology and where it came from. Then we'll define the field, say a few words about its roots, and describe its scope as we begin a new century. Next, we'll provide some information about the training of psychologists, and various specialties in which they work. After that, we'll turn to the *scientific method* and explain how psychologists—and for that matter you—can use it. Included here will be a discussion of *critical thinking*, a careful, cautious, and open-minded approach to thinking about human behaviour and many other topics. These discussions will be followed by an examination of the major *research methods* psychologists use in their efforts to add to our knowledge of human behaviour. While careful research helps to answer one set of questions, the process of conducting such research raises another set of questions—ethical issues relating to the research itself. These complex issues will be considered in another major section of this chapter. Let's start with a look at how the discipline developed.

Psychology: How It Developed and What It Is

How did the field of psychology come to exist? In movies and television shows, scientists are sometimes represented as magnificent loners—geniuses who work in isolation and develop major breakthroughs out of their own creative spirit. While this sometimes occurs, another pattern is more frequent: Progress flows naturally from what went before. Modern psychology is no exception to this general rule. When it emerged as an independent field of study in the late nineteenth century, it had important roots in several other disciplines, ranging from philosophy on the one hand to biology and physiology on the other.

Philosophy and Science: The Dual Roots of Modern Psychology

From philosophy came two key ideas: *empiricism*, the view that knowledge can be gathered through careful observation, and *rationalism*, the view that knowledge can be gained through logic and careful reasoning. These ideas provided an intellectual framework which, when joined with rapid advances occurring in natural sciences, gave birth to the idea of a field of study that would use scientific methods to study human behaviour (see Figure 1.1). Especially important in this process were scientific advances in the field of *physiology*—the branch of biology that studies the functions of living organisms—which were directly related to the emergence of psychology. For example, during the late nineteenth century, Johannes Muller described how signals were conducted by nerves within the body, Hermann von Helmholtz reported findings on how receptors in the eyes and ears receive and interpret sensations from the outside world, and Gustav Fechner demonstrated that seemingly hidden mental events, such as sensations, could be precisely measured. These advances led inevitably to the position that *the methods of science should be used as a basis for studying human behaviour.* A famous figure in the history of psychology—Wilhelm Wundt—was an ardent supporter of this position. In addition, he was also an impressive—and persuasive—figure. Indeed, so convincing was Wundt that, in 1879, he managed to "sell" his colleagues at the University of Leipzig (Germany) on the validity of an independent science of psychology. We'll never know whether they fully accepted Wundt's beliefs, but they did provide the funding for the first laboratory for psychological research. By 1879, then, the idea of an independent, science-based psychology had taken shape and was spreading throughout the academic world. What was this new field like? And how did it develop in the decades that followed? Let's take a brief look at these important issues.

Wilhelm Wundt (1832–1920)

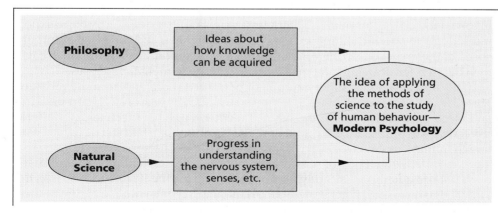

Figure 1.1
The Dual Roots of Psychology

Psychology emerged as an independent field of study when ideas from philosophy (about how valid knowledge of the natural world can be obtained) were applied by scientists in other fields to the task of understanding human behaviour.

Early Battles Over What Psychology Should Study: Structuralism, Functionalism, and Behaviourism

Although Wundt held firmly to the idea of a scientific field of psychology, his conception of what this science should involve was quite different from that held by most psychologists today. Wundt believed that psychology should study *consciousness*—what goes on inside our minds. This approach was known as **structuralism** because it focused on the elements and structure of the human consciousness. Wundt centred his research on analyzing the sensations, feelings, and images we all have into their basic elements, largely through the method of *introspection*, in which individuals describe what is going on in their own minds.

Structuralism's focus on identifying the elements and structure of consciousness was soon challenged by William James and other psychologists who felt that their new field should focus not on the structure of consciousness, but on its functions. Their approach, **functionalism,** was strongly influenced by Darwin's theory of natural selection. Functionalists argued that since consciousness is a uniquely human characteristic, it must serve important functions for us—otherwise it would never have evolved. With this thought in mind, James and other functionalists focused on understanding the functions of consciousness—how it helps human beings cope with the challenging and changing world around them. This gave a practical slant to the research conducted by functionalists, who began to focus on such topics as child development and the relative benefits of various educational practices.

It has sometimes been suggested that given enough time, functionalism would have evolved into an approach quite similar to modern psychology: functionalists appeared to be largely on the right track. They never got the chance, however, because both structuralism and functionalism fell victim to the onslaught of a new wind that swept through the academic halls of psychology—**behaviourism,** the view that psychologists should study only what can be *observed*—overt behaviour. The most radical spokesperson for behaviourism was John B. Watson. Watson argued forcefully that only observable, overt activities can be measured in a scientific manner. Thus, only these should be part of a scientific field of psychology. In contrast, Watson held, "internal" events such as thoughts, images, feelings, and intentions are unmeasurable, and so should not be part of the new science.

So compelling were the arguments offered by Watson and other behaviourists, such as B.F. Skinner, that their conception of psychology defined the field for more than forty years—right up until the 1960s. The 1960s seemed to be a time of major change in many respects, and psychology was no exception to this general pattern. During that decade, it expanded its scope to recapture the mental events that Watson and others had written off as outside the proper domain of psychology. Why did this shift take place? Again, the answer seems to involve a convergence of several independent trends. During the 1960s, advances in technology provided new or improved techniques for studying mental events—for instance, techniques that involved the use of computers. Computers, for example, made it possible to expose individuals to specific stimuli in a very precise manner, and then to measure the speed of their reactions to them, again with great precision. Such information could then be used for drawing inferences about underlying mental processes.

In a similar manner, other equipment permitted rapid and accurate measurement of subtle internal changes in bodily states, such as heart rate, blood pressure, and electrical activity within the brain. Together, these new technologies offered psychologists important new tools for measuring what had been, in the past, largely unmeasurable.

Next, a growing body of scientific findings on such mental processes as memory had been quietly, but steadily, accumulating during the 1940s and 1950s. As this knowledge increased, it generated important new insights into the nature of these processes. When this growing body of knowledge was combined with the new research techniques described earlier, the result was something many psychologists

John B. Watson
(1878–1958)|

Structuralism: An early view suggesting that psychology should focus on conscious experience and on the task of analyzing such experience into its basic parts.

Functionalism: An early view of psychology suggesting that psychology should study the ways in which the ever-changing stream of conscious experience helps us adapt to a complex and challenging world.

Behaviourism: The view that psychology should study only observable behaviour.

describe as the *cognitive revolution*—a tremendous surge in interest, within psychology, in the task of studying mental events or, as psychologists prefer to term them, *cognitive processes*. You'll see the results of this "revolution" in later chapters, where we'll focus on many aspects of cognition, such as perception, dreams, moods, attitudes, problem solving, and memory.

As a result of the events described above, most psychologists now define their field as follows: **Psychology** is the science of behaviour and cognitive processes. This is the view we'll adopt in this book, and as will soon be clear, it is one that permits psychologists to study virtually every aspect of human behaviour and human experience. Why? Because by the term *behaviour*, psychologists mean any observable action or reaction by a living organism—everything from overt actions (anything we say or do), through subtle changes in the electrical activity occurring deep within our brains. If it can be observed and measured, then it fits within the boundaries of "behaviour." Similarly, by the term *cognitive processes* psychologists mean every aspect of our mental life—our thoughts, our memories, mental images, how we reason, make decisions and judgments, and so on. One final point: although our definition mentions both behaviour and cognitive processes, we'll use the term "behaviour" to represent both, simply to avoid repeated use of the phrase "behaviour and cognitive processes" over and over again.

Computers and the Study of Cognitive Processes

Because they allow for very precise control over the presentation of stimulus materials and the precise measurement of the speed of responding to these materials, computers provide psychologists with a powerful new tool for studying mental (cognitive) processes—events early behaviourists felt were beyond the scope of psychology.

Modern Psychology

We have provided a very general overview of psychology and its historical development. It is now time to point out some general themes that cut across the psychological landscape. One such grand issue or theme is the question of *stability versus change*: To what extent do we remain stable over time, and to what extent do we change? We'll meet this question repeatedly in this book, as we address changes over time in cognitive abilities, physical functioning, personality, and other aspects of behaviour (e.g., Cohen & Reese, 1994).

A second, and closely related theme, centres around the following question: To what extent are various aspects of our behaviour determined by inherited tendencies, and to what extent are they learned—shaped by experience with the world around us? This is usually known as the *nature–nurture* question, and we'll meet it repeatedly in the coming chapters. Does aggression stem primarily from innate tendencies, or is it the result of experience and "triggers" in a current situation? Is intelligence inherited, or shaped by early experience? Are differences in the behaviour of women and men due to biological factors, or mainly to the impact of contrasting child-rearing experiences and society's beliefs about gender differences? This is only a small sampling of the questions we'll examine relating to this major theme. As you'll soon see, growing evidence indicates that the answer to this question is definitely *not* one suggesting that either environment or heredity dominates; rather, many aspects of behaviour seem to represent the result of complex interactions between these factors. That question, then, is not "Which one dominates?" but rather "To what extent do nature and nurture influence specific forms of behaviour—and how?" Nature versus nurture remains a key issue in modern psychology. We will see shortly that a developing interest in how evolution influences our behaviour is causing many psychologists to look anew at the nature versus nurture issue. Indeed it has resulted in a new field of study termed **evolutionary psychology.**

The easiest way to introduce the third theme is to ask a question. Answer quickly: Would you eat a piece of chocolate shaped exactly like a spider, bulging eyes, long hairy legs, fangs, and all? If you experienced some reluctance, you are like many

Psychology: The science of behaviour and cognitive processes.

Evolutionary Psychology: A branch of psychology that studies the adaptive problems humans have faced over the course of evolution and the behavioural mechanisms that have evolved in response to these environmental pressures.

people in this situation. But now ask yourself, *why* would you be reluctant to do so? The chocolate has no relationship to a real spider in any manner. So, why would the fact that it resembles one cause you to hesitate? The answer, in most general terms, is straightforward—in many cases, we are *not* completely rational! We know very well what the logical response or reaction would be, but our reason is overridden by our emotions. This is one illustration of a third "grand theme" you'll find in your study of psychology: *rationality versus irrationality*. Sometimes we do seem to operate in a largely rational manner, making decisions and reaching conclusions in accordance with the laws of logic (perhaps, as a computer would proceed). But in many others, we behave in a manner that is *not* consistent with the "cold light of logic." Have you ever been over-optimistic in estimating how long it would take you to complete a task? Have you ever lashed out at someone else not because of something they did or said, but mainly because you were feeling rotten? If so, then you already have first-hand experience with the less-than-completely rational side of human behaviour. This is another theme to which we'll return again and again in this book, as we examine such issues as decision making, eye-witness testimony, and social perception (how we perceive other persons and make judgments about them).

Be on the watch for these three "grand themes"—they are central issues that have captured the attention of psychologists for decades, and with which experts in the field will still be wrestling well into the next century.

Perspectives of Modern Psychology

Psychologists could examine the behaviour shown here from many different perspectives—behavioural, cognitive, biological, social and cultural, psychodynamic, and evolutionary. Each perspective would add to our understanding of these events. (See Table 1.1 on page 9 for a description of these perspectives.)

KEY PERSPECTIVES IN PSYCHOLOGY: THE MANY FACETS OF BEHAVIOUR Consider the following scene in a Vancouver arena. Canada's most popular figure skater, Elvis Stojko, moves onto the ice. An enthusiastic crowd of smiling and shouting fans are immediately on their feet applauding vigorously as he moves toward the centre of the arena. The music begins slowly and he moves forward. As the pulse of the music accelerates, he bursts into motion, his arm and body movements aggressively mirroring the rhythm of the music. He sails down the ice—a cocky, strutting dynamo—delighting the crowd with an amazing series of toe loops, lutzes, triple flips, and triple axels. As he slows to a finish, the crowd once again rises to give him a standing ovation.

What would a psychologist have to say about this performance? A great deal—because the event can be viewed from many different perspectives. What are these different perspectives? One, known as the *behavioural* perspective, would emphasize the overt behaviours occurring—the pattern of Stojko's movement in rhythm with the music, and the different kinds of reactions these various movements provoke in the audience.

Another, the *cognitive* perspective, would focus on cognitive factors in this situation: What are Stojko's thoughts, as he gauges and calculates his speed and position in performing his routine in synchrony with the music? How does he decide on a musical selection? How does he mentally map out and choreograph his performance?

A third perspective on this situation would emphasize the *biological factors* that play a role in it. What are the emotions of Stojko as he faces the crowd and moves through his routine? What are the emotions of the crowd, and how are these reactions reflected in their blood pressure, heart rate, and other bodily states?

A fourth perspective would focus on the *social* and *cultural* factors that play a role. What is it that makes figure skating so popular in North American and European cultures? What is it about the performance that attracts people in such large numbers?

Yet another perspective that could be adopted by a psychologist observing this incident would focus on factors within the personality of the skater. This *psychodynamic* perspective might ask: What aspects of his personality and motives—conscious or unconscious—led Stojko to choose such an occupation?

Finally this incident could also be examined by focusing on the question of whether, and to what extent, Stojko's performance is influenced by *evolutionary factors*. For example, a psychologist working within this *evolutionary perspective* might ask: What is it that we as a species find so fascinating when a gifted individual visually interprets a melodic rhythm through the movement of his or her body? Does our interest have its roots in our early tribal history when, for countless generations, dance was one of the few ways people of the period could express themselves creatively?

The key point to remember is that human behaviour is extraordinarily complex, and it is influenced by many different factors. Thus, any aspect of behaviour can be examined from many different perspectives. All can add to our understanding of behaviour, so all will be represented throughout this book. (Table 1.1 summarizes these contrasting perspectives.)

KEY PERSPECTIVES IN PSYCHOLOGY: THE GROWING INFLUENCE OF EVOLUTIONARY PSYCHOLOGY   In outlining key perspectives in psychology, we made reference to the fact that one can view behaviour in term of an evolutionary perspective. Although many have insisted on the importance of considering evolutionary factors in explaining behaviour, the influence of this approach on mainstream psychology has been limited (Plotkin, 1997). There is evidence that this is changing, and psychologists are becoming increasingly aware that many aspects of behaviour require taking into account evolutionary forces that have shaped and molded us and the other animals. A flood of new publications in both psychology (e.g., Pinker, 1997;

TABLE 1.1

Major Perspectives of Modern Psychology

As shown here, psychology studies behaviour from many different perspectives.

Perspective	Description
Behavioural	Focuses on overt behaviour.
Cognitive	Focuses on cognitive processes such as memory, thought, and reasoning.
Biological	Focuses on the biological events and processes that underlie behaviour.
Socio-Cultural	Focuses on all aspects of social behaviour and on the impact of cultural factors on behaviour.
Psychodynamic	Focuses on personality and on the role of hidden, often unconscious, processes on behaviour.
Evolutionary	Focuses on the possible role of inherited tendencies in various aspects of behaviour.

Plotkin, 1997) and philosophy (e.g., Dennett, 1995) argue compellingly for the relevance of evolution to virtually every area and issue in psychology. Perhaps the most telling harbinger of the growing influence of evolutionary psychology is the fact that the first textbook in evolutionary psychology written specifically for an undergraduate audience is now on bookstore shelves (Buss, 1999).

What is evolutionary psychology? It is more than just a way of looking at things. It involves accepting the fact that we are products of natural selection. It involves understanding how natural selection works, and it involves using this understanding to determine how our evolutionary history influences the way we behave and think. Evolutionary psychology is rooted in Darwin's theory of natural selection. There are three basic components: variation, selection, and inheritance. *Variation* refers to the fact that organisms in any given species can vary in many different ways. Variations are instrumental in determining how effective an individual member of a species is in dealing with the struggle for survival. Some variations give the individual an "edge" or a selective natural advantage over other members of its species in meeting the challenges of life, and in successfully mating. If the advantage a variation gives can be passed on genetically to the individual's offspring, then the variation and the advantage it confers will, over many generations, spread throughout the gene pool of the species and become an inherent characteristic of the species.

To illustrate further, consider a species of herbivores dwelling in an area where edible vegetation is scarce, and an inedible vegetation flourishes. If a chance adaptation occurs making a member of the herbivore species tolerant of the bad taste, and able to digest the normally inedible vegetation, then that individual will have access to a food resource denied to other members of the species and have a much higher chance of surviving and reproducing. If the digestive tolerance can be passed on genetically, that individual's progeny will be similarly advantaged. Over many generations the advantageous adaptation will gradually spread through the gene pool, and the entire species will be able to feed upon the previously inedible vegetation. See Figure 1.2 for a summary of this process.

Although the logic associated with natural selection is straightforward, a couple of things should be kept in mind. It is important to recognize that there is no grand design or plan directing evolutionary change. There is no striving for complexity or higher order development. Evolution is a blind and accidental

Figure 1.2
Evolution: An Overview

As shown here, evolution involves three major components: variation, inheritance, and selection.

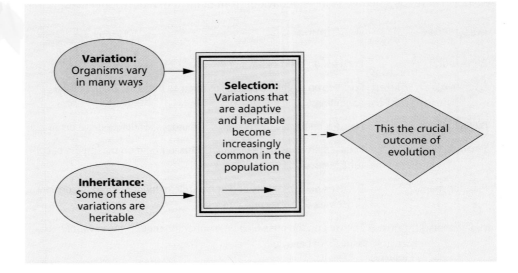

process. The crucial issue is always whether differences among individuals in a species are sufficient to provide some with a greater chance of survival and reproduction, and whether an advantage can be transmitted genetically to descendants. It must be acknowledged also that there is always a delicate balance between the environment and the species living in that environment. Environmental change can snuff out an initially advantageous adaptation. Consider our previous example of an adaptation that allowed consumption of abundant but previously inedible plants. It was stated that over many, many generations, this adaptation would spread through the gene pool. If this vegetation was wiped out by climatic changes in temperature or moisture, the ability to consume this vegetation would confer no advantage, and that adaptation's spread through the gene pool would be arrested. Other adaptations that might offer a survival advantage more suited to the changed environment would be favoured.

The position that changes in our biochemistry, physiology, and anatomy are hammered out on the evolutionary anvil seems inarguable. But what about the way we think and behave? Are they, too, influenced by evolutionary pressures? Evolutionary psychologists believe so. They point out that our line of development split off from that of the chimpanzees about five million years ago, and that over this time period all those personal qualities that give depth and dimension to our life—our feelings, emotions, attractions, our behaviour toward our mates and kin, and even the way we think about problems have been shaped and formed by natural selection. Evolutionary psychologists offer many illustrations of these effects (e.g., Crawford & Krebs, 1998).

Consider what men find attractive in women. Buss (1999) reports that the features that attract men to women are relatively consistent across cultures: full lips; luxuriant hair; clear, smooth skin and eyes; and a firm muscle tone. Also important is an energetic activity level and an animated facial expression. Why do men find these features attractive? Buss argues that through natural selection men have become sensitized to these features because they indicate fertility and high reproductive potential. Being specifically attracted to potential sexual partners who are fertile and have a high reproductive potential increases the likelihood that descendants will ensue and the male's genes will endure in the gene pool.

Consider what women find attractive in men. According to the evolutionary perspective, women are attracted to men who have ambition, social status, and financial resources; who are strong, healthy, and athletic; who share the same values; and who appear prepared to make a long-term commitment. The reason women find these attributes attractive is that child-bearing and child-rearing require a very large investment in time and care. In the past, men with these attributes have been best able to provide the support, protection, and security to ensure the survival of any offspring that may ensue from courtship.

Such claims may appear to perpetuate a disconcertingly stereotyped and outmoded view of female dependency. Advocates of the evolutionary viewpoint would accept that the contemporary viewpoint does differ from that of the distant past. The position that they would take is that natural selection pressures become entrenched over very long time spans and over many, many generations, and these pressures cannot be automatically altered by a change in the contemporary perspective of gender roles. They would also point out that by opening the door on the evolutionary perspective, and by becoming aware of the nature and character of natural selection pressures, resistance and change do become possible (Buss, 1999).

Finally, consider the human disposition to be very fearful in certain situations and circumstances. Darwin (1877) suspected the common fears of children such as the fear of strangers and the dark might be expressions of inherited tendencies carried forward from our distant past. He suggested that children who were cautious about approaching strangers and entering dark areas were more likely to survive to adulthood and have descendants. More recently Seligman and others have speculated that common phobias have a similar origin (Seligman & Hager, 1992). People with phobias tend to seek help because they have become fearful of certain things and situations. Most common phobias are to natural objects or events that were, and still are, dangerous: animals such as snakes and insects, heights, being in very closed or very crowded open places from which escape is difficult, open wounds, and blood. Seligman's argument, like Darwin's, is that in primeval times, it was advantageous for people to avoid these objects and situations, and those that had a disposition to do so were more likely to survive and reproduce. This sensitization has endured and remains with us. Thus full-fledged phobias to these objects and events continue to be easily established.

These examples allow you to get a feel for the character of the evolutionary approach to psychology. Advocates of evolutionary psychology are fond of pointing out that Darwin predicted that the time would come when his theory would provide a wholly new foundation for psychology, and they think that time has arrived. Critics are less certain (see Horgan, 1995). Some think the explanations offered by evolutionary psychologists are sometimes no more than reinterpretation of known facts in a manner consistent with the theory of natural selection, and are troubled by what they see as the theory's limited ability to generate new, counter-intuitive predictions. Controversy over the interpretive prowess of evolutionary psychology will continue. It is difficult, however, to cast off the conclusion that much of the way we currently think and act has been shaped and determined by the pressure of evolution.

Multicultural and Gender Issues

Psychology has changed markedly since its early origins in Wundt's laboratory, and the world has also changed. Psychology used to be primarily a North American- and European-based field, and it was an overwhelmingly male-dominated profession. This is no longer the case. Psychology studies are pursued in virtually every country in the world, and the major figures are no longer exclusively male. At least half of the psychologists in the United States are now women. In Canada, the role of women is even more pronounced. The 1996 census shows that the majority of those listing psychology as a profession are women, and they outnumber men 8785 to 5215. This pattern is not likely to change: the most recent statistics show Canadian women receiving graduate degrees in psychology outnumber men 1105 to 464.

It is worth noting that women psychologists did not achieve full professional stature in Canada without a struggle. As late as the early 1970s, program committees of the Canadian Psychological Association were reluctant to support presentation and discussion of issues relating to the psychology of women, gender issues, and sex-role stereotyping at annual meetings. Editors of journals controlled by the association were similarly reluctant to publish papers on these issues (Pyke, 1992; Pyke & Stark-Ademac, 1981).

What changed these attitudes? An important first step occurred when a group of women from York University organized their own independent "underground" symposium in Montreal, to be held at the same time as the regular association meeting in 1972. The symposium proved popular and signalled, as Kimball (1986) notes, that women members of the association were no longer going to remain silent about women's issues. By the late 1970s, convention programming issues had been resolved and a permanent Status of Women Committee had been established. Other changes also followed. Journal policies were changed to eliminate sexist language, and women began to gain representation on journal editorial boards and on committees of the association in numbers more in keeping with their membership in the association. In recent years, more and more women have been assuming senior administrative functions.

It is clear the representation of women in the various domains of psychology has increased enormously; it is less clear whether there has been change in the ethnic composition of professional psychologists that mirrors dramatic changes in the ethnic composition of the Canadian population. Around the time of Confederation, most Canadians were of either British or French background. Canada is now no longer primarily an English and French country. No single group is a majority in the country as a whole (Dreidger, 1989; Kerr & Ram, 1994).

Although the profession may not reliably reflect the ethnic diversity of the country, there is a growing tendency to assume a **multicultural perspective.** That is, increasing attention is being paid to the concerns of different ethnic groups and to all aspects of cultural diversity (e.g., Smith & Bond, 1993). This attention has taken the form of an increased volume of research on the effects of ethnic and cultural factors on many aspects of behaviour, which you will find emphasized at various points in this book in special **Perspectives on Diversity** sections. Indeed, there is hardly an area of psychology in which research on such issues is not currently being conducted. In addition, growing concern with multicultural diversity on the part of psychologists has led to the formulation of ethical guidelines in both Canada and the United States emphasizing the need to pay particular attention to ethnic and cultural factors in carrying out all professional and research activities. The code of ethics of the Canadian Psychological Association requires that psychologists "engage in self-reflection regarding how their own values, attitudes, experience and social context (e.g., culture, ethnicity, colour, religion, gender, sexual orientation, physical and mental ability level, age, and socioeconomic status) influence their actions, interpretations, choices, and recommendations" (Canadian Psychological Association, 1991).

Multiculturalism: A Fact of Modern Life

Cultural diversity has always been a fact of life in Canada, and the field of psychology has begun to reflect this.

Multicultural Perspective: In modern psychology, a perspective that takes note of the fact that many aspects of behaviour are strongly influenced by factors related to culture and ethnic identity.

K E Y   QUESTIONS

- What ideas and trends converged to give rise to an independent, science-based field of psychology?

- What is the definition of psychology?

- What are the three "grand issues" about behaviour with which psychology must grapple?

- What are the key differences between the various perspectives adopted by psychologists—the behavioural, cognitive, biological, socio-cultural, psychodynamic, and evolutionary?

- How do psychologists take account of cultural diversity in their research and in providing psychological services?

Critical Thinking

Suppose some aspect of behaviour made individuals highly attractive to the opposite sex but also shortened their lives so that they died before they were fifty. According to evolutionary psychology, would this behaviour become increasingly common or would it die out?

Psychologists: Who They Are and What They Do

Now that you know something about the nature and scope of psychology, let's turn, briefly, to two related issues: Who psychologists are and what they actually do.

Who: The Training of Psychologists

The terms *psychiatrist* and *psychologist* are quite similar, so it is not surprising they are often confused. Psychiatrists are physicians who, after completing medical studies, specialize in the treatment of mental disorders. In contrast, psychologists receive their training in graduate programs of psychology, where they earn both a master's degree and, in most cases, a Ph.D.—a process that takes approximately an additional five to six years of study after completing an undergraduate program. Graduate programs in psychology typically require extensive training in statistics, research methods, and related fields such as biology, neuroscience, and in the case of some programs, industrial and personnel management.

Clearly psychologists and psychiatrists receive different kinds of training. Are there reasons for confusion other than a similarity in name? One reason may be that many psychologists specialize in the diagnosis, study, and treatment of psychological (mental) disorders. This means that they focus on many of the same problems and perform many of the same activities as psychiatrists. In fact, members of the two fields often work closely together in the same mental health facilities. Given that only some psychologists focus on mental disorders, the two fields overlap only partially and, in fact, remain largely independent.

What: Subfields of Psychology

What exactly do psychologists do? Most people tend to say "conduct therapy" or "help people with problems." This is only a partial truth. Almost half of all psychologists in North America are *clinical* or *counselling* psychologists, who do indeed focus on mental problems and disorders. However, there are many other specialties within psychology, so in reality psychologists do many different things and investigate a wide range of topics. A brief description of some of psychology's major subfields is shown in Table 1.2. As you can see from even a brief glance at this table, psychologists specialize in studying many different forms of behaviour, and perform their work in many different settings. To gain an idea of the proportion of psychologists working in various subfields, see Figure 1.3, which shows the percentage of licensed Ontario psychologists employed in different specialty areas.

It should be noted that whatever their specific subfield, many psychologists engage in *research*—they work hard to acquire new information about human behaviour and cognitive processes. The specific content of this research varies from subfield to subfield. For example, a *clinical psychologist* might study such topics as the effects of depression on memory (Backman, Hill, & Forsell, 1996), while a child psychologist—one who specializes in studying the behaviour and development of children—might investigate the effects of stress early in life on children's later language development (e.g., Hura & Echols, 1996). Moreover, while some psychologists engage in *basic research*—research designed to increase our understanding of basic psychological processes (for example, memory or learning), other psychologists focus on *applied research*—research designed to deal with practical problems.

K E Y QUESTIONS

▪ How does the training of psychologists differ from that of psychiatrists?

▪ What are the major subfields of psychology? What aspects of behaviour do they study?

TABLE 1.2

The Major Subfields of Psychology

As shown here, psychologists specialize in studying many different aspects of behaviour.

Subfield	Description
Clinical Psychology	Studies diagnosis, causes, and treatment of mental disorders.
Counselling Psychology	Assists individuals in dealing with many personal problems that do not involve psychological disorders.
Developmental Psychology	Studies how people change physically, cognitively, and socially over their entire lifespan.
Educational Psychology	Studies all aspects of the education process.
Experimental psychology	Studies all basic psychological processes, including perception, learning, and motivation.
Cognitive Psychology	Investigates all aspects of cognition—memory, thinking, reasoning, language, decision making, etc.
Industrial/Organizational Psychology	Studies all aspects of behaviour in work settings.
Psychobiology	Investigates the biological bases of behaviour.
Social Psychology	Studies all aspects of social behaviour and social thought—how we think about and interact with others.

Source: American Psychological Association, 1994.

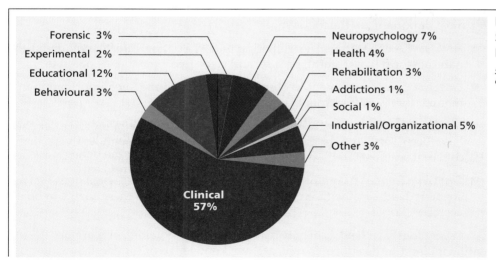

Figure 1.3
Specialty Areas of Licensed Psychologists in Ontario

Source: Based on membership lists of the College of Psychologists of Ontario.

Psychology and the Scientific Method

In a sense, we are all psychologists. From time to time, we all think about our own feelings and actions and those of other people. Such informal efforts to make sense out of human behaviour have continued for thousands of years—probably since our species first emerged on earth. As a result, we have at our disposal not only our own experience and observations, but also the collected thoughts of countless philosophers, poets, and writers. This fact leads to an obvious—and important— question: Is the knowledge provided by psychology different, in any important way, from this accumulated "wisdom of the ages"? Or is it simply "more of the same"—the result of doing on a full-time basis what most of us do only occasion- ally? The answer is that knowledge gathered by psychologists *is* different from that provided by intuition and common sense; it is both more accurate and more useful than knowledge of behaviour acquired through informal means. Why is this so? Primarily because in their quest for greater understanding of human behaviour, psychologists rely heavily on the *scientific method*. We'll now look at the scientific method and consider the advantages of adopting this approach in attempting to un- derstand human behaviour.

The Scientific Method: Its Basic Nature

To many people, the term *science* conjures up images of white-coated individuals working around mysterious equipment in impressive laboratories. On the basis of such images, they assume that this term applies only to fields such as chemistry, physics, or biology. Actually, however, the word *science* refers to a special approach for acquiring knowledge—an approach involving the use of several systematic meth- ods for gathering information, along with an adherence to several key values or stan- dards. Viewed in this light, the phrase *scientific method* refers simply to using these methods and adopting these values and standards in efforts to study virtually any topic—any aspect of the natural world around us. Since as human beings, we, too, are part of the natural world, the scientific method can certainly be applied to study- ing human behaviour and cognition. It is this adoption of the scientific method that makes psychology a science—and that makes the information it acquires so valuable.

Since the actual procedures used to gather data by means of the scientific method are described in detail in a later section, we'll concentrate here on the val- ues and standards that are essential components of the scientific method. Among the most important are the following:

■ *Accuracy*: A commitment to gathering and evaluating information about the natural world in as careful, precise, and error-free a manner as possible.

■ *Objectivity*: A commitment to obtaining and evaluating such information in a manner that is as free from bias as humanly possible.

■ *Skepticism*: A commitment to accepting findings as accurate only after they have been verified over and over again, preferably, independently by many different scientists.

■ *Open-mindedness*: A commitment to changing one's views—even ones that are strongly held—in the face of new evidence that shows these views to be in- accurate.

Psychology, as a field, is deeply committed to these values, and applies the sci- entific method in its efforts to increase our knowledge of human behaviour and cognitive processes. It is primarily for this reason that it makes sense to describe psychology as a science. In short, it "plays by the rules," and so qualifies fully as a scientific field.

Although it is relatively easy to state the standards listed above, it is quite an- other matter to put them into practice. *Skepticism* is, perhaps, the easiest to attain because it is built into all fields of science: scientists, psychologists included, learn as part of their training to say "show me!" before accepting any statements or conclusions as true. *Accuracy* can be enhanced by using only the best measuring instruments available—whether these are sophisticated equipment for measuring internal bodily reactions such as blood pressure, or special tests designed to measure various aspects of personality (see Chapter 12). Implementing the values of *objectivity* and *open-mindedness,* however, requires special training—and special forms of self-discipline.

Scientists, like everyone else, have personal views on various issues—including the ones they study. And like everyone else, they prefer to have their views confirmed rather than refuted. As you can readily see, this poses a potential problem any time a scientist's personal views are relevant to some aspect of her or his research. The danger is that the scientist may be tempted to conduct the research in such a manner, or to interpret the results in such a way, as to confirm these views. Such errors do not have to be conscious or overt to occur; as we'll see in later chapters, our personal views can sometimes influence our judgments or perceptions in subtle ways (see Chapter 7). So, all scientists—including psychologists—must always be on guard against the possibility that their own views and preferences will interfere, to some degree, with their objectivity and open-mindedness.

One way scientists endeavour to guard against letting their own views influence their conclusions is to use operational definitions to define the concepts that they employ during the course of their investigations. An **operational definition** is a clear, precise statement of the operations that are used to measure the concept. To illustrate, suppose a psychologist is investigating whether a new drug elevates mood. Mood is a complicated psychological concept. We all have an intuitive sense of what this concept means, but this is not sufficient. Science requires us to move beyond intuition to objective description. By requiring a researcher to explicitly define mood in terms of a measuring operation, for example, scores on a particular type of assessment scale, the researcher is forced to declare publicly exactly how he or she is using the term. Other researchers can then judge the adequacy of the measuring procedure and replicate the research to seek additional confirmation of the findings—should they choose to do so.

THE ROLE OF THEORY IN THE SCIENTIFIC METHOD   There is one more aspect of the scientific method we should consider before concluding this discussion. In their research, scientists seek to do more than simply describe the natural world—they also want to be able to *explain* it. For example, a chemist is not content merely to describe what happens when two chemicals are brought into contact with one another—she or he also wants to be able to explain *why* this reaction took place. Similarly, a psychologist studying memory is not content to merely describe the extent to which individuals forget various kinds of information; the psychologist also wants to be able to explain *why* such forgetting occurs, and the nature of forgetting itself (which we'll examine in detail in Chapter 6). The scientific method therefore, involves the construction of **theories**—frameworks for explaining various events or processes. The procedures involved go something like this:

1. On the basis of existing evidence, a theory that reflects this evidence is formulated.

2. This theory, which consists of some basic concepts and statements about how these concepts are related, helps to organize existing information and makes predictions about observable events. For example, it might predict the conditions under which certain forms of behaviour will occur.

3. These predictions, known as **hypotheses**, are then tested by actual observations—by further research.

4. If results of new observations are consistent with the theory, confidence in its accuracy is increased. If they are not, the theory is modified and further tests are conducted.

Is Psychology Scientific?
All psychological researchers, regardless of the techniques they use, are firmly committed to the scientific method and to the values of science.

Operational Definition: A clear and precise statement of the procedures that are used to measure a psychological concept.

Theories: Frameworks in science for explaining various phenomena. Theories consist of two major parts: basic concepts and assertions concerning relationships between these concepts.

Hypothesis: In psychology, a prediction about behaviour that is to be investigated in a research project.

5. Ultimately, the theory is either accepted as accurate, or rejected as inaccurate. Even if it is accepted as accurate, however, it remains open to further refinement as additional research is conducted.

This may sound a bit abstract, so perhaps a concrete example will help. Imagine that a psychologist has formulated a theory to explain the fact that people often seem to become trapped into "throwing good money after bad"; that is, once they have made a decision, they feel compelled to stick with it, even if it has turned out badly. Thus, they continue to invest time, effort, and money in a losing course of action. (This is known as *escalation of commitment* and we'll examine it in more detail in Chapter 7.) A theory designed to explain this effect might go something like this: People get trapped in bad decisions because once they have made them, they feel a strong need to justify these decisions to others. Since admitting they made a mistake runs counter to this need, they find it very hard to escape from such situations. Predictions derived from this theory would now be tested. For instance, one prediction might be that if people have to justify their initial decision publicly, explaining it to others, they will find it especially hard to escape from the trap of escalating commitment. If, in contrast, they don't have to justify their initial decision in this public manner, they may find it easier to escape.

Research would then be conducted to test these hypotheses. If research findings are consistent with such predictions, confidence in the theory would be strengthened; if they are not, confidence in the theory would be reduced, and it might be changed or, ultimately, rejected. This process, which lies at the core of the scientific method, is illustrated in Figure 1.4. Many different theories relating to important aspects of human behaviour will be described in later chapters. And as each is presented, we'll comment on the current state of evidence relating to these theories. So, you'll soon encounter many examples of this process as it actually operates in psychology.

Figure 1.4
The Role of Theory in Psychological Research

Once a theory has been formulated, predictions derived from it are tested through research. If these predictions are confirmed, confidence in the theory's accuracy is increased. If they are not confirmed, confidence in the theory's accuracy is reduced. The theory may then be modified so far as to generate new predictions, or, ultimately, be rejected.

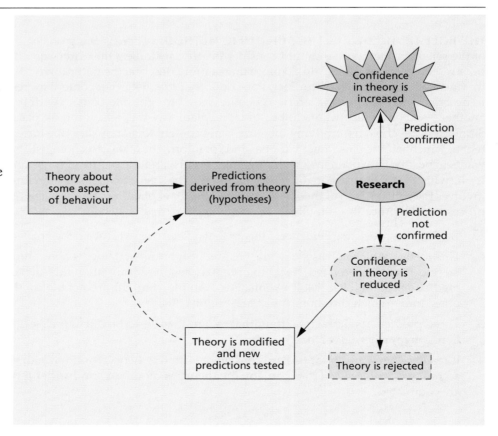

Advantages of the Scientific Method

By now, you are probably convinced that using the scientific method can be difficult. If that's so, you may be wondering, then why bother? Doesn't common sense or the accumulated wisdom of the ages provide us with the answers and insights we want? Unfortunately, the answer is *no*. Common sense, or what is sometimes called "folk psychology," provides a good starting point—it often gives us interesting "food for thought." But by itself, it is far from enough. In fact, on close examination, the suggestions it offers often turn out to be inconsistent and contradictory. For example, consider the following statement: "Absence makes the heart grow fonder." Do you agree? Is it true that when people are separated from those they love, they miss them and so experience increased attachment to them? Many people would answer "Yes, that's right. Let me tell you about what happened when I was separated from my lover…" But now, consider the following statement: "Out of sight, out of mind." (Variation: "When I'm not near the boy/girl I love, I love the boy/girl I'm near.") How about this statement? Does it make sense? Is it true that when people are separated from those they love they quickly find another object for their affections? Again, many people would agree. As you can see, these two views—both part of "common sense," are contradictory. The same is true for many other informal observations about human behaviour; here are two more examples:

- "Birds of a feather flock together" versus "Opposites attract."
- "Haste makes waste" versus "He who hesitates is lost."

Other examples could be listed, but the conclusion that should be drawn is very apparent: Common sense often paints a confusing and inconsistent picture of human behaviour.

This is not the only reason why we must be wary of common sense, however. Another, and more important one, relates to the fact that unlike Mr. Spock or Data of *Star Trek* fame, we are *not* perfect information-processing machines. On the contrary, as we'll note over and over again in this book (see Chapters 6, 7, and 16), re-echoing the "grand issue" of rationality versus irrationality, our thinking is subject to several forms of errors that can lead us badly astray. Because of this fact, we simply cannot rely on informal observation, common sense, or intuition to provide us with accurate information about human behaviour. Let's take a brief look at several of the sources of potential error.

THE CONFIRMATION BIAS: THE TEMPTATION TO VERIFY OUR OWN VIEWS
Earlier, we noted that people generally prefer to have their views confirmed rather than refuted. Don't you? Now, consider what this means when we attempt to use informal observation as a source of knowledge about human behaviour. Since we prefer to have our views confirmed, we tend to notice and remember mainly information that lends support to these views—information that confirms what we already believe. This tendency is known as the **confirmation bias,** and the results of many studies indicate that it is a powerful one (e.g., Greenwald & Pratkanis, 1988; Johnson & Eagly, 1989). When it operates, it places us in a kind of closed system, where only evidence that confirms our existing views and beliefs "gets inside"; other information is often noticed (e.g., Bardach & Park, 1996), but it is quickly rejected as false. Clearly, then, the confirmation bias is one tendency that can lead us to serious errors in our efforts to understand others or ourselves.

Confirmation Bias: The tendency to pay attention primarily to information that confirms existing views or beliefs.

Availability Heuristic: A cognitive rule of thumb in which the importance or probability of various events is judged on the basis of how readily they come to mind.

THE AVAILABILITY HEURISTIC: EMPHASIZING WHAT COMES TO MIND FIRST Quick— are there more words in English that start with the letter *k* (e.g., king) or more words in which *k* is the third letter (e.g., awkward)? If you answered "More words that begin with the letter *k*," you are like most people. In fact, though, this answer is wrong: more words have the letter *k* in the third position. What's responsible for this type of error? A mental shortcut known as the **availability heuristic**. This shortcut, which is designed to save us mental effort, suggests that the easier it is to bring something to mind, the more frequent or important it is. In the case of our example, we find it much easier to bring to mind words that start with *k* than those that have *k* as the third letter. Hence we assume that there must be more words that begin with *k* than have *k* as a third letter. This shortcut makes good sense in many cases because events or objects that are common *are* usually easier to think of than ones that are less common. But relying on availability in making judgments can also lead to important errors, as we just illustrated (e.g., Schwarz et al., 1991). In short, because the ease with which we can bring information to mind strongly influences our judgments, we can't rely on informal observation—and our memories—to reach sound conclusions about human behaviour. Only careful research using the scientific method can accomplish this task.

MOOD EFFECTS: HOW WE FEEL OFTEN INFLUENCES THE WAY WE THINK
One day, you wake up feeling absolutely great—you are on top of the world. Another day, you wake up feeling miserable—you are in the depths of despair. Will these contrasting *moods*—your current feelings—influence the way you think? Research on this topic leaves little room for doubt. When you are in a good mood, you will tend to think happy thoughts, remember happy events, and view everything around you in a positive light. In contrast, when you are in a bad mood, you will tend to think unhappy thoughts, remember sad events, and view everything around you negatively (e.g., Forgas, 1995). Not surprisingly, these effects of mood can strongly influence your thinking about—and conclusions concerning—human behaviour. And often, it appears, we are quite unaware of the presence or magnitude of such effects (e.g., Isen & Baron, 1991).

As we'll see in later chapters (for instance, Chapters 7 and 16), there are many other tendencies in the way in which we think that can, potentially, lead us astray (see Figure 1.5 for a summary of the ones we've discussed). The main point, though, should already be clear: Because our thinking is subject to many potential sources of bias, we really can't rely on informal observation as a basis for valid conclusions about human behaviour. And this, of course, is where the scientific method enters the picture. It is specifically designed to keep these and other potential sources of bias in check. By adopting this method, therefore, psychologists vastly increase the probability that their efforts to attain valid information about human behaviour will be successful. It is this commitment to the scientific method, more than anything else, that sets psychology apart from other efforts to understand human behaviour—efforts ranging from the speculations of novelists and poets to the predictions of fortune-tellers and astrologers. Science, of course, is not the only road to truth—many would argue that philosophy and religion offer others. Still, psychologists firmly believe that where human behaviour is concerned, science is the surest and most useful.

KEY *QUESTIONS*

- Why can psychology be considered to be a scientific field?

- What values or guidelines are central to the scientific method and what is the role of theories in the scientific method?

- What's wrong with using informal observation and common sense as guides to understanding human behaviour?

- What sources of potential error in our own thinking often lead us astray with respect to conclusions about behaviour?

- How does the scientific method help to reduce or eliminate such errors?

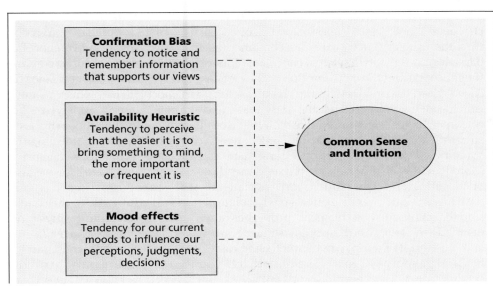

Figure 1.5
Aspects of Cognition That Reduce the Value of Common Sense and Intuition

The three tendencies described here are only a few of the factors that make it risky to rely on common sense and intuition as useful guides for understanding human behaviour.

The Scientific Method in Everyday Life

You may be thinking to yourself: The scientific method may be the soundest way to investigate human behaviour, but is it of any practical use to someone who is not going to be a psychologist or a researcher? The answer is that it can be a very useful navigational aid in piloting your way through the problems encountered in everyday life. Understanding the basic methods of science allows you the opportunity to think critically about things. What do we mean by critical thinking? **Critical thinking** refers to thinking that is *critical* in the sense of the basic meaning of this word: thinking that is *discerning* and wise. In essence, critical thinking is thinking that avoids blindly accepting conclusions or arguments, and instead, closely examines all assumptions, carefully evaluates existing evidence, and cautiously assesses all conclusions.

Perhaps the best way of illustrating critical thinking, and giving you some practice in it, is by means of a concrete example. Consider the following headline: "Is It the Chocolate—or Are You Really in Love?" Dramatic headlines like this one were common introductions to articles in the late 1980s and 1990s reporting that people who ate a lot of chocolate experienced positive feelings—waves of euphoria similar to those they had experienced when they fell in love. Other reports, which also seemed to support a link between chocolate and love, cited findings indicating that persons who were depressed by romantic rejections strongly craved chocolate. To put the icing on the cake, so to speak, chemical analyses of chocolate indicated that it contains substances like serotonin and dopamine, which play a role in "pleasure" or "reward" centres deep in the brain (we'll discuss these in Chapter 2.)

Many people read these findings and came to believe that there might be something to the notion that chocolate is indeed the "food of love." This provided them with an additional incentive to consume a highly favoured food. Unfortunately for chocolate-lovers, this was only part of the scientific story. Other research on chocolate soon indicated that it also contains substances that are anything but "feel-good" chemicals: caffeine and at least one substance known to play a role in migraine headaches. Moreover, other findings indicated that chocolate addicts didn't necessarily feel better after eating chocolate. In fact, they more frequently noted that eating chocolate made them feel good for a few minutes, but then left them feeling depressed. Finally, in still other studies (Rozin & Michener, 1996), persons who reported strong cravings for chocolate were fed either regular chocolate

Critical Thinking: Careful assessment of available evidence in order to evaluate claims and statements in an objective and reasoned manner.

bars, white chocolate bars (which have none of the chemical ingredients of whole chocolate), or special tasteless capsules of cocoa. Chocolate is derived from cocoa, thus the tasteless cocoa capsules contained all the chemicals found in chocolate bars. Results indicated that real chocolate (dark or white in colour) reduced cravings for chocolate, but the consumption of the tasteless cocoa capsules did not. Since the cocoa capsules contained all the chemicals found in chocolate bars, this was fairly conclusive evidence against the view that the chemicals themselves played a key role in chocolate's supposed effects. What does thinking critically about this issue suggest? That while there may be a link between chocolate and pleasant feelings for some people, the evidence concerning such a relationship is far from conclusive. Moreover, if such a link exists, it may depend more on people's liking for the taste of chocolate (and their tendency to associate this with other positive feelings) than with any specific chemical effects of chocolate on the brain. Jumping to the conclusion that chocolate has "magical" properties or will enhance romantic feelings is not justified—no matter how strongly some people would like to make this leap.

This simple example involving feelings associated with chocolate consumption has a single purpose. It is offered to provide you with an illustration of how critical thinking, with its emphasis on caution, skepticism, and careful evaluation of *all* existing evidence (not just the findings we prefer!) works. In short, critical thinking is thinking that mirrors the key values of the scientific method. In actual practice, critical thinking involves following guidelines such as these:

- Never jump to conclusions; gather as much information as you can before making up your mind about any issue.

- Keep an open mind; don't let your existing views blind you to new information or new conclusions.

- Always ask "How?" as in "How is this evidence gathered?"

- Be skeptical; always wonder about why someone is making an argument, offering a conclusion, or trying to persuade you.

- Never be stampeded into accepting some view or position by your own emotions—or by arguments and appeals designed to play upon them.

- Be aware of the fact that your own emotions can strongly influence your thinking, and try to hold such effects to a minimum.

Acquiring the ability to think critically is very important. To help you think critically, we will provide special "Critical Thinking" questions in each chapter—questions designed to get you to think about the big issues raised in that chapter. The goal, of course, is to give you practice in thinking critically—carefully, cautiously, and systematically—about your own behaviour and that of others. The habit of thinking in this manner will be one of the key benefits you'll take away with you from this book, and your first course in psychology.

K E Y *QUESTIONS*

- What is critical thinking?

- What role does it play in psychology?

- What benefits can it provide for your everyday life?

Research Methods in Psychology

Now that we've looked at what modern psychology is and described both the scientific method and its relation to critical thinking, it's time to turn to another, closely related issue. How do psychologists actually perform the task of adding to our knowledge of human behaviour? (Remember: *behaviour* means everything people do, feel, experience, or think.) In this section, we'll examine three basic procedures used by psychologists in their systematic study of human behaviour: *observation* (sometimes termed *description*), *correlation*, and *experimentation*.

Observation

One basic technique for studying behaviour—or any other aspect of the natural world—involves carefully observing it as it occurs. Such observation is not the kind of informal observation we all practise from childhood on. Rather, in science, it is accompanied by careful, accurate measurement. For example, scientists studying the formation of tornadoes may drive hundreds of miles in order to be present at spots where tornadoes are likely to form. They don't do this because they like to put themselves in danger, but rather because they wish to engage in careful observation of the physical events that unfold as tornadoes actually form. The use of such **systematic observation** takes several different forms in the study of behaviour.

Systematic Observation: One Way of Studying the World Around Us

Psychologists sometimes observe human behaviour in the locations where it normally occurs. For example, recent studies have used such methods to study how and when people touch each other in public places.

NATURALISTIC OBSERVATION: OBSERVING BEHAVIOUR WHERE IT NORMALLY OCCURS Almost everyone finds the giant panda of China fascinating. Here, at least in outward appearance, is a teddy bear come to life. For many years, zoos throughout the world sought eagerly to add these appealing animals to their collections. Unfortunately, these efforts usually produced disappointing results. The pandas seemed to pine away in captivity, and adamantly refused to mate. Given the small and declining number of pandas present in the wild, all of this seemed to spell disaster for a species most people would very much like to preserve. Could anything be done to change this situation? There seemed only one way to find out: observe the pandas in their natural habitat to learn more about their behaviour and about what could be done to save them from extinction. In short, this seemed to be a situation in which research should be conducted through **naturalistic observation**—systematic study of behaviour in natural settings. Fortunately, efforts along these lines (Schaller, 1986) have added greatly to our knowledge of giant pandas. Scientists have spent months observing pandas in the mountainous regions of western China where they live and, from such study, have extracted information about their diet and mating habits that may prove useful in assuring their survival.

   As this example suggests, naturalistic observation is often used to study animal behaviour. However, it is sometimes applied to human beings as well. For example, an ingenious study of this type conducted by Murdoch and Pihl (1988) observed the behaviour of male patrons drinking beer or liquor in randomly selected Montreal bars. Information on the type of drinks the patrons consumed and the aggressiveness of their reactions to others offered intriguing insights into the effects of alcohol on behaviour in at least one setting.

Systematic Observation: A basic method of science in which the natural world, or various events or processes in it, are observed and measured in a very careful manner.

Naturalistic Observation: A research method in which various aspects of behaviour are carefully observed in the settings where such behaviour naturally occurs.

The Giant Panda

In recent years, naturalistic observation has been used effectively to gain valuable information about the habits of the giant panda. This knowledge is crucial if pandas are to be saved from extinction.

Case Method: A method of research in which detailed information about individuals is used to develop general principles about behaviour.

Survey Method: A research method in which large numbers of people answer questions about aspects of their views or their behaviour.

Sampling: With respect to the survey method, refers to how people who participate in a survey are selected.

It should be added that sometimes the data obtained through naturalistic observation are relatively informal, and this can reduce their scientific value. However, the fact that subjects are studied in natural settings and so are likely to act in the ways they normally do is an important advantage that makes this method useful in some contexts.

CASE STUDIES: GENERALIZING FROM THE UNIQUE Human beings are unique: we each possess a distinctive combination of traits, abilities, and characteristics. Given this fact, is it possible to learn anything about human behaviour from detailed study of one or perhaps a few persons? Several famous figures in the history of psychology contended that it is. They adopted the **case method**, in which detailed information is gathered on specific individuals. This information is then used to formulate principles or reach conclusions that, presumably, apply to much larger numbers of persons—perhaps to all human beings. By far the most famous practitioner of the case method was Sigmund Freud, who used a small number of cases as the basis for his entire theory of personality. (We'll discuss Freud's theories in Chapter 12.)

Is the case method really useful? In the hands of talented researchers it does seem capable of providing insights into various aspects of human behaviour. Moreover, when the behaviour involved is very unusual, the case method can be quite revealing. In Chapters 3 and 6, we'll describe how several unique cases have added greatly to our understanding of both perception and memory. The use of the case study method has been especially influential in the study of memory. By studying the pattern of memory losses, psychologists have been able to piece together a more complete picture of how memories are stored in the brain (e.g., Squire, 1991). Much can be learned from the case method—especially when it is applied to persons who are unique in some manner. However, there are drawbacks. First, if the persons *are* unique, it may be inappropriate to generalize from them to other human beings. Second, because researchers using the case method often have repeated and prolonged contact with the persons they study, there is the real risk that they will become so committed and involved with these persons that they lose their scientific objectivity. These potential difficulties have to be kept in mind when using the case study procedure and in assessing reports based on this approach.

SURVEYS: THE SCIENCE OF SELF-REPORT At the opposite end of the scale where systematic observations are concerned, is the **survey method**. Here, instead of focusing in detail upon a small number of individuals, a very limited sample of the behaviour of large numbers of persons is obtained, usually through their responses to questionnaires. Surveys are used for many purposes—to assess attitudes toward specific issues (for example, toward health reform measures or to a blended sales tax), to measure voting preferences prior to elections, and to assess consumer reactions to new products.

Surveys are sometimes repeated over long periods of time in order to track shifts in public opinion or actual behaviour. For example, some surveys of job satisfaction—individuals' attitudes toward their jobs—have continued for several decades. And changing patterns of sexual behaviour have been tracked by the Kinsey Institute since the 1940s.

The survey method offers several advantages. Information can be gathered about thousands or even hundreds of thousands of persons with relative ease. Further, since surveys can be constructed quickly, public opinion on new issues can be obtained very quickly. However, in order to be useful as a research tool, surveys must meet certain requirements. First, if the goal is to use the results to predict some event (for example, the outcome of an election), special care must be devoted to the issue of **sampling**—how the persons who will participate in the survey are selected. Unless these persons are representative of the larger *population* for which predictions are to be made (for example, from a sample of voters to the entire voting public), serious errors can result.

Yet another issue that must be carefully addressed with respect to surveys is this: The way in which surveys are worded can exert strong effects on the outcomes obtained. For example, when asked to indicate how satisfied they are with their jobs, more than 85 percent of persons questioned indicate that they are "Satisfied" or "Very Satisfied." When asked whether they would choose the same job or career again, however, less than 50 percent indicate agreement! So, as experts in the survey method well know, it's often true that the way you ask the question determines the answer you get.

In sum, the survey method can be a useful approach for studying some aspects of human behaviour—especially positive and negative reactions toward almost anything—but the results obtained are accurate only to the extent that issues relating to sampling and wording are carefully addressed.

Correlation

At various times, you have probably noticed that some events appear to be related to each other: as one changes the other also appears to change. For example, perhaps you have noticed that when dark clouds appear in the sky, storms often follow. Or, if you listen to the evening news, you may have noticed that when interest rates rise, the stock market often falls and the sales of new homes tend to decrease. Such relationships, if they actually exist, are known as **correlations.** Psychologists and other scientists refer to such changeable aspects of the natural world as *variables*, since they can take different values.

From the point of view of science, the existence of a correlation between two variables can be very useful. This is so because when a correlation exists, it is possible to predict one variable from information about one or more other variables. The ability to make such *predictions*—to forecast future events from present ones—is one important goal of science. Psychologists often attempt to make predictions about human behaviour. To the extent that such predictions can be made accurately, important benefits can be obtained. For instance, consider how useful it would be if we could predict, from current information, such future outcomes as a person's success in school or various occupations, effectiveness as a parent, life expectancy, or likelihood of developing a serious mental disorder.

The discovery of correlations between variables allows us to make such predictions. In fact, the stronger such correlations are, the more accurate the predictions that can be made. These basic facts constitute the foundation for another important method of research—the **correlational method**. In this method, psychologists or other scientists attempt to determine whether, and to what extent, different variables are related to each other. This involves making careful observations of each variable, and then performing appropriate statistical analyses to determine whether and to what extent they are correlated—to what extent changes in one are related to changes in the other. Correlations range from –1.00 to +1.00, and the greater their departure from zero, the stronger the correlation in question. Thus, a correlation of –.67 is stronger than one of –.18. Similarly, a correlation of +.52 is stronger than one of +.29. Positive correlations indicate that as one variable increases, the other increases too. For instance, the greater the number of hours students study for their psychology tests, the higher their grades tend to be. The fact that this relationship is not perfect suggests that the correlation between these two variables—studying and grades—is less than 1.00. Negative correlations indicate that as one variable increases, the other decreases. For example, if personal health declines as the level of stress individuals experience increases, then a negative correlation may exist between these two variables. (The Appendix, beginning on p. 687, provides more information about correlations and how they are computed.)

Psychologists often use correlations in their research. In fact, they often search for relationships between variables in order to be able to make accurate predictions about important aspects of behaviour. As a means of illustrating this method of research, let's consider a concrete example.

Correlations: A tendency for one aspect of the world (or one variable) to change with another aspect of the world (or variable).

Correlational Method of Research: A research method in which investigators observe two or more variables to determine whether, and to what extent, changes in one are accompanied by changes in the other.

THE CORRELATIONAL METHOD OF RESEARCH: AN EXAMPLE Imagine that a researcher wished to test the following *hypothesis* (a prediction derived from a theory): the more positive individuals' moods are, the more likely they are to help others. How could research on this hypothesis be conducted by the correlational method? While there are many possibilities, a very basic approach would involve devising some means of measuring both variables (some way of assessing individuals' current moods and some way of assessing their willingness to help others) and then determining whether these two variables are related to each other. For example, individuals who have agreed to participate in the research could be asked to rate their current mood on a simple scale ranging from one (very negative) to five (very positive). Then they could be asked if they are willing to make a small donation to a charity (this would serve as a measure of their willingness to help). If being in a good mood does lead to increased helping, it would be observed that the better individuals' current moods, the more likely they are to make a donation.

One key advantage of the correlational method is that it can be used in both natural settings and the laboratory. For instance, a psychologist wishing to test the hypothesis that being in a good mood leads to greater helping could conduct a study at a large shopping mall. Here, passers-by would be stopped and asked to rate their mood. Then their behaviour as they pass someone soliciting funds for a charity would be observed. If being in a good mood is indeed related to helping, the psychologist might observe that the happier people are, the more likely they are to make a donation. In other words, the psychologist would observe a positive correlation between these two variables. Research conducted in natural settings is known as *field research.* It is often very useful because it studies behaviour in the settings where it usually occurs. In contrast, *laboratory research* is conducted in special settings that may differ, in many respects, from natural ones. However, as we'll see below, laboratory settings, too, offer important advantages.

In addition to its usefulness in natural settings, the correlational method also offers several other advantages. It is often highly efficient and can yield a large amount of interesting data in a relatively short time. Moreover, it can be extended to include many different variables at once. Thus, in the study we have just described, information on the age and gender of shoppers at the mall could also be obtained. Then appropriate statistical analyses could be conducted to determine whether these variables are also related to helping. It is often the case that success at prediction improves as more variables are brought into the picture, so correlational research often includes measures of many different variables that, psychologists have reason to believe, may be related to each other.

While the correlational method of research offers many advantages, it also suffers from one major drawback: The findings it yields are generally not conclusive with respect to cause-and-effect relationships. That is, the fact that two variables are correlated, even highly correlated, does not guarantee that there is a causal link between them—that changes in one cause changes in the other. Rather, in many cases, the fact that two variables are correlated simply reflects the fact that both are caused by a third variable.

For example, suppose that our researcher finds a positive correlation between individuals' ratings of their own moods and the likelihood that they will donate to a charity. Does this mean that being in a good mood causes people to help others? Common sense suggests that this is so, but other possibilities also exist. For instance, it may be the case that people in a good mood have more money in their pockets—that's one reason they are in a good mood! If this is so, then the relationship between mood and helping uncovered in this research may be misleading. Both mood and helping are actually related to a third factor—personal funds available at the moment! The important point is that even strong correlations between two variables do not necessarily mean that one causes the other. See the **Key Concept** on page 27 for a look at correlational research and the problems that may arise when establishing correlational relationships.

▶

Key Concept — *Why Correlation Does Not Equal Causation*

The fact that two variables are correlated—even strongly correlated—does not necessarily mean that one causes the other. This is true because both variables may actually be related to—or caused by—a third variable. Following are two examples.

Observation: As weight increases, income increases.

Possible Interpretations:

1. Weight gain causes increased income.

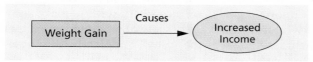

2. As people grow older, they tend to gain weight and also earn higher incomes.

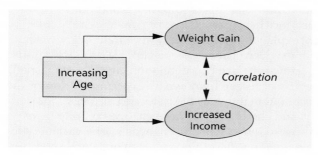

Observation: The more television people watch, the more likely they are to have a heart attack.

Possible Interpretations:

1. Watching television causes heart attacks.

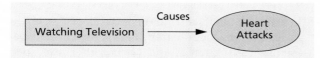

2. People who watch lots of television don't like to exercise; lack of exercise causes heart attacks.

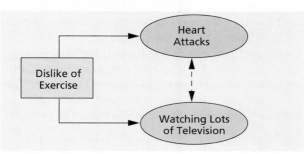

▶ **The Experimental Method**

As we have just seen, the correlational method of research is very useful, and it helps psychologists reach one important goal of science—being able to make accurate predictions. But it is less useful from the point of view of reaching yet another goal—*explanation*. This is sometimes known as the "why" question because it relates to the fact that scientists do not merely wish to describe the natural world and relationships between variables in it; they want to be able to *explain* these relationships too. For example, while it is interesting and valuable to know that people who possess certain personality traits are more likely than others to suffer heart attacks, it is even more valuable to understand *why* this is so. What is it about these traits that cause such persons to experience heart attacks?

In order to attain the goal of explanation, it is usually important to know something about *causality*—the extent to which changes in one variable produce or cause changes in one or more others. How can such causal relationships be established? Primarily through another method of research known as **experimentation** or the **experimental method**. Experimentation involves the following strategy: one variable is changed systematically, and the effects of these changes on one or more other variables are carefully measured. If systematic changes in one variable produce changes in one or more others (and if additional conditions we'll soon consider are also met), it is possible to conclude with reasonable certainty that there is indeed a causal relationship between these variables: changes in one do indeed cause changes in the other. Because the experimental method is so valuable in answering this kind of question, it is frequently the method of choice in psychology. But bear in mind that there is no single "best" method of research. Rather, psychologists—like all other scientists—choose the research method that is most appropriate for studying a given topic.

EXPERIMENTATION: ITS BASIC NATURE In its most basic form, the experimental method involves two key steps: (1) the presence or strength of some variable believed to affect behaviour is systematically altered, and (2) the effects of such alterations (if any) are carefully measured. The logic behind these steps is as follows: If the variable that is systematically changed does indeed influence some aspect of behaviour, then individuals exposed to different levels or amounts of that factor should differ in terms of their behaviour. For instance, exposure to a relatively low amount of the variable should result in one level of behaviour, while exposure to a higher amount should result in a different level, and so on.

The factor systematically varied by the researcher is termed the **independent variable**, while the aspect of behaviour studied is termed the **dependent variable.** In a simple experiment, then, different groups of participants are exposed to contrasting levels of the independent variable (such as low, moderate, and high). Their behaviour is then carefully measured to determine whether it does in fact vary with these changes in the independent variable. If it does—and if two other

Experimentation (the Experimental Method): A research method in which one variable is systematically changed to determine whether it has an effect on one or more other variables.

Independent Variable: The variable that is systematically altered in an experiment.

Dependent Variable: The aspect of behaviour that is measured in an experiment.

conditions described below are also met—the researcher can tentatively conclude that the independent variable does indeed cause changes in the aspect of behaviour being measured.

To illustrate the basic nature of experimentation in psychological research, let's return to the topic we considered earlier: the possible effects of being in a good mood on willingness to help others. How could this be studied by means of the experimental method? One possibility is as follows. The researcher would assign participants to one of three conditions: a low positive mood, a high positive mood, and a control condition. The psychologist would then systematically vary events known, from past research, to induce different levels of positive mood states in the two mood conditions. For instance, the experimenter might ask participants to perform a series of tasks and give subjects in the low positive mood condition some mild positive feedback by commenting favourably on their work, and give subjects in the high positive mood condition a great deal of positive feedback by highly praising their work. In contrast to the positive mood condition, subjects in the control condition would be asked to perform similar tasks and would receive neutral feedback—comments designed to have no effect on their current mood. The control situation thus provides a baseline against which to measure the effects of low and high mood induction procedures in the other two conditions.

Following exposure to one or the other of these conditions, participants would be given an opportunity to help another person. For instance, they could be asked by a confederate of the researcher posted just outside the door of the laboratory building to make a donation to a charity. If results now looked like those in Figure 1.6, the researcher could conclude—tentatively—that being in a good mood does indeed increase helping. It's important to remember that in this case, efforts have been made to directly change participants' moods (by giving them varying amounts of positive feedback); in the correlational study, participants' current moods were simply measured—no effort was made to change them. By the way, research very much like this has been performed, and results indicate that this hypothesis *is* correct: the better people's current moods, the more willing they are to help others (e.g., Baron, 1997; Levine et al., 1994). And one last point is worth mentioning. In a real experimental study, investigators would have administered tests to assess the mood of each participant before and after commenting on their work to confirm that the positive feedback procedure used did actually alter subjects' mood state.

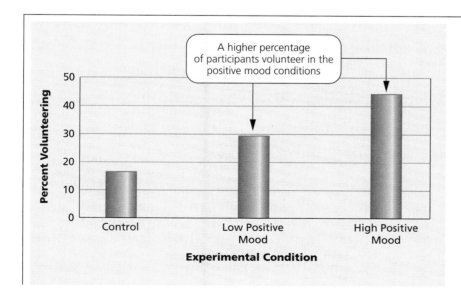

Figure 1.6
Experimental Research:
A Simple Example

Participants in the low and high mood conditions are exposed to procedures designed to put them in positive mood states. They might receive, respectively, a modest and a large amount of praise for their work on a task, while participants in the control condition would not be exposed to this procedure. All participants would be given an opportunity to help with a donation to a charity as they leave the building. If the above pattern of results is obtained, it would provide some support for the hypothesis that the better your mood is, the more likely you are to help others.

EXPERIMENTATION: TWO REQUIREMENTS FOR ITS SUCCESS   Earlier, reference was made to two additional conditions that must be met before a researcher can conclude that changes in an independent variable have caused changes in a dependent variable. Let's consider these now. The first involves what is termed **random assignment of participants to experimental and control conditions**. This means that all participants in an experiment must have an equal chance of being exposed to each level of the independent variable. The reason for this rule is simple: If participants are *not* randomly assigned to each condition, it may later be impossible to determine whether differences in their behaviour stem from differences they brought with them to the study, from the impact of the independent variable, or from both. For example, imagine that in the study just described, all participants assigned to the positive mood conditions were members of a religious group that emphasizes the importance of helping others, while those in the control group were not members of this church. Why did those in the positive mood condition engage in more helping? Because they were in a better mood than the persons in the control group? Because of their strong religious convictions? Because of both factors? As you can readily see, we can't tell. If, in contrast, the members of this religious group had been randomly distributed across the three different conditions, their greater willingness to help would have been equally represented in the groups. Thus, any differences between the groups could still be attributed to the independent variable. So, as you can see, it is crucial that all participants have an equal chance of being assigned to all experimental conditions; if they are not, the potential value of an experiment may be seriously reduced.

The second condition essential for successful experimentation is that (insofar as possible) all other factors that might also affect participants' behaviour aside from the independent variable must be held constant. To see why this is so, consider what will happen if, in the study on mood and helping, persons in the positive mood condition are exposed to a stronger plea to contribute to charity than those in the control condition. Again, more people in the positive mood condition volunteer. What is the cause of this result? The fact that people in this condition are in a better mood? The stronger plea for help from the person requesting a donation? Both factors? Once again, we can't tell—and since we can't tell, the value of the experiment as a source of new information about human behaviour is reduced. In situations like this, the independent variable is said to be *confounded* with another variable—one that is not under systematic investigation in the study. When such confounding occurs, the findings of an experiment may be largely meaningless (see Figure 1.7).

Random Assignment of Participants to Experimental and Control Conditions: Assuring that all research participants have an equal chance of being assigned to each of the experimental and control conditions.

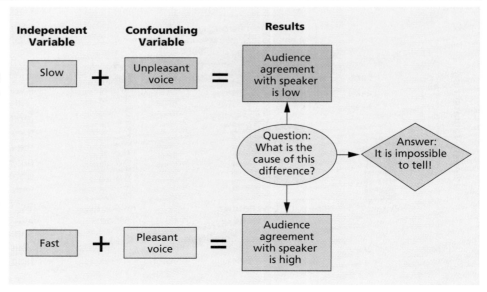

Figure 1.7
Confounding of Variables: A Fatal Flaw in Experimentation

In an imaginary study designed to investigate the effects of speed of speech on persuasion, the person who speaks quickly has a pleasant, cultivated voice, while the person who speaks slowly has an irritating voice. As a result, two variables—speed of speech and pleasantness of speech—are *confounded*. Because of this fact, it is impossible to interpret the results.

But why, you may now be wondering, would a researcher make such a muddle of his or her own study? Why would this person make different kinds of requests for help in the two conditions? The answer, of course, is that the researcher certainly wouldn't do this on purpose. But suppose that the researcher's assistant who makes the request for donations believes firmly in the hypothesis under test. This may have a subtle effect on his or her behaviour. The assistant may ask for participants' help a bit more fervently in the positive mood conditions. The result: more helping does indeed occur in the positive mood condition, but this is due, at least in part, to the fact that the assistant makes stronger or more persuasive requests in this condition. In order to avoid such potential problems, which are known as **experimenter effects** (unintended effects, by researchers or their assistants, on participants' behaviour), many experiments in psychology employ a **double-blind procedure** in which the research personnel who have contact with participants do not know the hypothesis under investigation. Since they lack this knowledge, the likelihood that they will influence results in the subtle ways just described is reduced. We'll describe other procedures used by psychologists to reduce factors that might interfere with the accuracy or validity of their results in the **Research Process**, special sections appearing in each chapter.

In sum, experimentation is, in several respects, the "crown jewel" among psychology's methods for answering questions about behaviour. When it is used with skill and care, it yields results that help us not only to answer complex questions about human behaviour, but also to understand the causes of such behaviour. Thus, in one sense, experimentation is psychology's ultimate answer to the question "Why?" (See Table 1.3 for an overview of the major research methods we have considered.)

Experimenter Effects: Unintentional influence exerted by researchers on research participants.

Double-Blind Procedure: Procedure in which neither the people collecting data nor research participants have knowledge of the experimental or control conditions to which they have been assigned.

TABLE 1.3

Research Methods Used by Psychologists

As shown here, psychologists use several different research methods. Each offers a complex mixture of advantages and disadvantages—so the guiding rule is to use the best and most appropriate method for studying a particular research question.

Method	Description	Advantages	Disadvantages
Systematic Observation	Systematic study of behaviour in natural settings.	Behaviour is observed in the settings where it normally occurs.	Cannot be used to establish cause-and-effect relationships; often costly and difficult to perform.
Case Method	Detailed study of a small number of persons.	Detailed information is gathered; individuals can be studied for long periods of time.	Generalizability of results is uncertain; objectivity of researcher may be compromised.
Surveys	Large numbers of persons are asked questions about their attitudes or views.	Large amount of information can be acquired quickly; accurate predictions of large-scale trends can sometimes be made.	Generalizability may be questionable unless persons surveyed are a representative sample of a larger population.
Correlational Research	Two or more variables are measured to determine if they are related in any way.	Large amount of information can be gathered quickly; can be used in field as well as laboratory settings.	Difficult to establish cause-and-effect relationships.
Experimentation	The presence or strength of one or more variables is varied.	Cause-and-effect relationships can be established; precise control can be exerted over other (potentially confounding) variables.	Results can be subject to several sources of bias (e.g., experimenter effects); generalizability can be doubtful if behaviour is observed under highly artificial conditions.

Interpreting Research Results

Once an experiment has been completed, researchers must turn to the next crucial task: interpreting the results. Suppose that in the study we have been discussing, results indicate that people in a good mood do indeed offer more help than those in a neutral mood. How much confidence can we place in these results? In other words, are the differences observed real ones—ones that would be observed if the study were repeated again with other participants? This is a crucial question, for unless we can be confident that the differences are real, the results tell us little about human behaviour.

One way of dealing with this question, of course, would be to repeat the study over and over again. This would work, but as you can imagine, it would be quite costly in terms of time and effort. Another approach is to use **inferential statistics**. This is a special form of mathematics that allows us to evaluate the likelihood that a given pattern of findings, such as differences in the behaviour of experimental groups, is due to chance alone. Thus, to determine whether the findings of a study are indeed real (are unlikely to have occurred by chance alone), psychologists perform appropriate statistical analyses on the data they collect. If these analyses suggest that the likelihood of obtaining the observed findings by chance is low (usually, fewer than five times in a hundred), the results are described as being *significant*. Only then are they interpreted as being of value from the point of view of understanding some aspect of behaviour.

It's important to realize that the likelihood that a given pattern of findings is a chance event is *never* zero. This probability can be very low—one chance in ten thousand, for instance—but it can never be zero. For this reason, actual replications of results by different researchers in different laboratories are usually necessary before the findings of any research project can be accepted with confidence. In other words, the basic scientific principle of **replication** is still important, even when inferential statistics are used to evaluate research findings.

META-ANALYSIS AND THE SEARCH FOR AN OVERALL PATTERN   Suppose that a specific hypothesis has been tested in many different studies. If all yield similar results, confidence in the accuracy of the hypothesis would be quite strong. But sometimes a different pattern emerges: some studies yield one result and others yield a different pattern. What happens then? How can we combine the results of all these different experiments in order to determine whether, overall, there is support for the hypothesis? One answer involves a very powerful statistical technique known as **meta-analysis** (e.g., Bond & Smith, 1996). This procedure allows us to combine the results of many different studies in order to estimate both the direction and magnitude of the effects of independent variables. The procedures are mathematical in nature, so they eliminate potential sources of error that might arise if we attempted to examine the findings of existing studies in a more informal manner (for example, by doing a simple "box count" to see how many studies offer support for the hypothesis and how many do not). Meta-analysis largely eliminates the all-too-human tendency to seek confirmation of our views or preferences. Overall, then, meta-analysis is a very valuable tool for psychological research, and we'll refer to it at several points in this book.

Inferential Statistics: Statistical procedures that provide information on the probability that an observed event is due to chance, and that permit us to determine whether differences between individuals or groups are ones that are likely or unlikely to have occurred by chance.

Replication: A basic scientific principle requiring that the results of an experiment be repeated before they are accepted with confidence.

Meta-Analysis: Statistical procedures for combining the results of many studies in order to determine whether their findings provide support for specific hypotheses.

K E Y QUESTIONS

- What is the basic nature of experimentation?
- Why must participants in an experiment be randomly assigned to different conditions?
- What is confounding of variables in an experiment?

■ What are experimenter effects and what is the double-blind procedure?

■ What are inferential statistics, and how do they help psychologists interpret the findings of their research?

■ What is meta-analysis, and what role does it play in interpreting the findings of many studies dealing with the same aspect of behaviour?

Critical Thinking

Human behaviour is influenced by a very large number of factors. Given this fact, can confounding of variables ever be completely prevented in psychological research? If not, does this necessarily reduce the value of the results?

Ethical Issues in Psychological Research

The phrase "psychological research" has an ominous ring for some people. When they hear it, they visualize unsettling scenes in which all-knowing psychologists somehow force unwary subjects to reveal their deepest secrets and wildest fantasies. Do such concerns have any basis in fact?

Given that it is dangerous to gloss over a complex and serious issue, the answer is a firm *no*. Virtually all psychological research conducted today is performed in accordance with ethical principles acceptable both to society and to science. Indeed, in Canada, the conduct of psychological research is monitored at a variety of levels. The Canadian Psychological Association has a code of ethical standards to which members must adhere. In addition, provincial licensing boards have special ethical codes governing psychologists in private practice. Further, government granting agencies such as the National Science and Engineering Research Council, the Medical Research Council, and the Social Science and Humanities Research Council all require careful ethical review of the research projects they support. These standards seek to guarantee the safety, privacy, and well-being of all research participants and are strictly enforced in universities and other organizations in which research takes place.

Despite such precautions, however, two ethical issues deserving of our attention persist. One has to do with the use of deception—withholding information about a study from research participants or, in some cases, giving false information about it. The other has to do with the use of animals in psychological research.

Deception

Let's return to the study we discussed earlier—one designed to investigate the effects of being in a good mood on helping. Suppose that before the start of the study, the researcher explained this hypothesis to research participants. Would this influence the results? The chances are high that it would. Some persons might decide to "help" the researcher by confirming the hypothesis: they would agree to the later request for help for this reason. Others, in contrast, would decide to play "devil's advocate," and refuse to help just to disprove the hypothesis. In either case, of course, any possibility of learning something about human behaviour would vanish; the study would largely be a waste of time.

In situations like this, many psychologists believe that it is necessary to withhold information about a study from participants, or even to give them misleading information, on a temporary basis. The reason behind such procedures, which are known as **deception**, is obvious: Researchers believe that if participants have complete information about the purposes and procedures of a study, their behaviour will be changed by this information, and the results will be invalid.

While this reasoning is sound, the use of deception also raises important ethical issues. Is it appropriate for psychologists to withhold information from research

Deception: Withholding information about a study from participants. Deception is used in situations in which the information that is withheld is likely to alter participants' behaviour.

participants, or even to mislead them? Although the issue remains somewhat controversial, most psychologists have concluded that such procedures are permissible, provided that two basic principles are followed. The first of these is known as **informed consent**, and requires that research participants be provided with information about all the events and procedures a study will involve before agreeing to participate in it, and that they be informed that they are completely free to leave at any time.

The second principle is known as **debriefing**, and it requires that research participants be given full information about all aspects of the study after they have participated in it. These procedures assure that participants in psychological research leave with a full understanding of its purpose, and that they receive any information that was temporarily withheld from them.

Existing evidence suggests that informed consent and thorough debriefing go a long way toward eliminating any adverse effects of temporary deception (Mann, 1994; Sharpe, Adair, & Roese, 1992). However, despite such findings and the fact that most persons who have experienced temporary deception as part of a research project feel that it is justified (e.g., Smith & Richardson, 1985), some psychologists still object to its use (e.g., Rubin, 1985). These critics feel that the use of such procedures diminishes participants' faith in science generally, and in psychology in particular. They feel that such procedures may sometimes leave research participants with negative feelings centring around such thoughts as "How could I have been fooled so easily?" and "Why didn't I figure out what was really happening?" The prevalent feeling is that psychologists must vigilantly protect the rights of those who are prepared to participate in research projects. Canadian ethical codes certainly take a serious view of the use of deception. The code of the Canadian Psychological Association forbids the use of deception in service activities. Deception is countenanced in research only if no alternative procedure is available and no negative effects can be predicted, or such predicted negative effects can be offset.

Informed Consent: Participants' agreement to take part in a research project after they are provided with information about the nature of such participation.

Debriefing: Providing participants in psychological research with complete and accurate information about a study after they have taken part in it.

Animal Research: The Debate

Research with animals is only a small part of psychological research, but it is invaluable for exploring many topics, including learning, attachment, and social behaviour.

Research with Animals

While most research conducted by psychologists involves human participants, some studies (about 8 percent) are performed with animals (Beckstead, 1991). Why do psychologists conduct such research? There are several reasons. First, psychologists may want to find out something about the behaviour of a particular species. For example, they may want to learn about the mating behaviour of an endangered species so that its numbers can be increased through breeding programs. Second, psychologists conduct research on animals in order to examine the generality of basic principles of behaviour—for example, certain forms of learning. Does learning occur in much the same manner across many different species, or does the unique evolutionary history of each species alter this process in important ways? Research conducted with several species can help answer such questions.

The most important reason for conducting research with animals, however, is the one that raises significant ethical issues: some research exposes participants to conditions or treatments that could not be performed with human beings. For obvious ethical and legal reasons, researchers cannot perform operations on healthy people in order to study the role of various parts of their brains in key aspects of behaviour. Similarly, researchers cannot place human beings on diets lacking in important nutrients in order to determine how this affects their development. In these and many other cases, there appears to be no choice: if the research is to be conducted, it must be conducted with animals.

But is it appropriate to subject helpless rats, pigeons, and monkeys to such treatment? This is a complex issue, on which different persons have sharply contrasting views. On the one hand, supporters of animal rights contend that the procedures employed in research with animals often expose them to harsh or cruel treatment, and argue that such research is unethical. Psychologists respond to such criticism in two ways. First, they note that such procedures are not commonly used in their research. In those instances where invasive procedures are used, there is careful peer review of the scientific merit of the project, and ethical review of procedures to be employed. Second, psychologists note that research with animals has contributed to human welfare in many important ways. For example, it has led to such benefits as improved means for treating emotional problems, controlling high blood pressure, and reducing chronic pain. In addition, psychological research with animals has increased our understanding of the neural mechanisms underlying memory loss, senility, and various addictions (Miller, 1985). Many persons would contend that these benefits far outweigh the minimal risks to animals participating in psychological research.

Animal research practices in Canada are largely regulated by the Canadian Council on Animal Care, a broad-based committee with representatives from humane societies, professional associations (including the Canadian Psychological Association), governments, and granting agencies. It was formed in an effort to establish uniform treatment practices in all Canadian research institutions, and it specifies, in detail, procedures to be followed in the care and treatment of research animals. Although compliance is not mandated by law, public institutions almost invariably follow its guidelines (Bowd, 1990).

Do such benefits justify research with animals? Clearly, this is a value judgment outside the realm of science. However, many psychologists believe that if every possible precaution is taken to minimize harm or discomfort to subjects, the potential benefits do outweigh the very real costs. It is for you as an individual to decide whether—and in what circumstances—you agree.

Ethical Issues in the Practice of Psychology

While psychologists often face complex ethical issues in their research, this is not the only source of ethical dilemmas in psychology. Such issues also arise as psychologists practise their profession—for instance, as they deliver psychological services to clients. A survey of practising psychologists (Pope & Vetter, 1992) indicates that, as you might well expect, there are many different situations in which ethical issues or dilemmas arise. The most frequent of these centre on questions of *confidentiality*—situations in which psychologists receive information from their clients that professional ethics require them to hold confidential, but which they also feel obligated to reveal to legal authorities. For example, one psychologist reported a distressing situation in which a client reported being raped but could not get police to believe her story. Shortly afterward, another client of the same psychologist admitted committing this crime (Pope & Vetter, 1992, p. 399). Clearly, the psychologist faced a difficult ethical dilemma. What would *you* do in the same situation? (We don't know how this dilemma was resolved because the psychologist chose to keep the decision itself confidential.)

The confidentiality issue is especially complicated in Canada. In the United States, a large number of states have laws according privileged communication status to psychologist–client relationships; psychologists in Canada have no such protection. Moreover, according to Canadian law, certain information (such as information about child abuse) must be reported to authorities, even when the psychologist believes that reporting this information is not in the best interest of the client. There are those who argue that, rightly or wrongly (depending on the circumstances), this is tantamount to converting a therapist into a police informant. Others see reporting in such circumstances as the only appropriate course of action.

Without question, special care has to be taken in dealing with young children in therapeutic and research settings. A study of children's understanding by Abramovitch, Freedman, Thoden, and Nicolick (1991) revealed that a majority of children as young as five to seven years can explain what is expected of them in a research setting, but a very substantial proportion do not fully understand they can refuse to answer questions or decline to participate—even if they are informed that they have this right. A further disconcerting fact was that almost all the very young children and a majority of older children in the ten to twelve year range did not accept the assurance of confidentiality and assumed their parents would have access to information about their performance. As Abramovitch et al. note, a disbelief in confidentiality may cause children to be less forthcoming when sensitive issues are dealt with in research or therapeutic sessions. It is unfortunately not possible to deal with all the legal and ethical issues in this chapter. (A good summary of the confidentiality issue in Canada is provided by Cram and Dobson, 1993; and Walters, 1995)

Another frequent ethical concern involves situations in which psychologists find themselves in dual or conflicted relationships with clients. That is, the psychologist's professional role as healer is somehow inconsistent with other relationships he or she may have with a client. One of the most troublesome situations of this type centres on sexual issues. It is estimated that 7 to 11 percent of male therapists and 2 to 4 percent of female therapists have contact of an intimate nature with their patients (Carr & Robinson, 1990). It is not always the therapist that initiates intimacy. Weinberger (1989) describes a case in which a male client became sexually infatuated with his female therapist. This not only threatened to shatter the normal professional distance that has to be maintained in a therapeutic setting but also began to disrupt the therapist's personal life. The patient repeatedly attempted to meet with the therapist outside of the office and to talk with her by telephone at night and on weekends. Only with great difficulty was the therapist able to convince the patient to transfer to another case worker. The code of ethics of the Canadian Psychological Association forbids sexual relationships between therapists and clients, but such attraction still occurs and the results can be very distressing and detrimental to the welfare of all concerned.

These are just a few of the ethical dilemmas and problems faced by psychologists in their efforts to assist individuals. Many others, ranging from concerns over providing expert testimony in criminal trials to the use of advertising to build one's practice, exist as well.

KEY QUESTIONS

- What is deception and why do many psychologists use it in their research?
- What ethical issues are raised by research with animals?
- What ethical dilemmas do psychologists often face in their work?

making Psychology Part of Your Life

How to Study Psychology—or Any Other Subject—Effectively

Among the topics that psychologists know most about are learning, memory, and motivation. The following tips will provide you with some useful information about how to study effectively.

- *Begin with an overview.* Research reported in Chapter 6 will show you that information in memory is structured and organized. Studies indicate that it is easier to retain information if it can be placed within a conceptual framework (i.e., if it is clear how different pieces of information or topics relate to one another). When you begin to study, examine the outline at the start of each chapter and thumb through the pages once or twice. That way, you'll know what to expect and will already have an initial framework for organizing the information that follows.

■ *Eliminate distractions.* In order for information to be entered into memory, you have to carefully attend to it. You will find in Chapter 2 that it is very hard to divide attention and attend to more than one thing at a time. This means that you should eliminate distractions—anything that will draw your attention away from the materials you are trying to learn. Studying has to be done in a quiet place. So turn off the radio and television, and let your answering machine take your phone messages. We guarantee it will take you less time to cover the materials you want to study.

■ *Don't do all your studying at once.* All-nighters may seem to work, but in fact, they are very inefficient. You will find in Chapter 6 that retention is much better when such learning is spaced out over time, rather than when it is crammed into a single long session. Try to spread your study sessions out. This will give you greater return for less overall effort.

■ *Use your problem solving skills to set challenging—but attainable—goals.* Studying is an exercise in applied problem solving. In Chapter 7 you will learn that one of the first stages in problem solving is identifying and understanding the goal. Your goal should be to do well on each and every quiz, and to do that you will have to develop a study program. Make note of when your quizzes will occur, and work out a sequence of study sessions that will ensure you will have mastered all the material. Set a concrete goal for each study session—for example, "I'll read twenty pages, learning all the key terms printed in **dark type**, and review my class notes." Set challenging goals, but ones you can attain. Challenging goals encourage us to "stretch"—to do a little bit more. But if they are impossible to attain, they may cause us to despair—and to give up along the way!

■ *Reward yourself for progress.* You will find in Chapter 5 that rewards are crucial determinants of performance. It is most often the case that rewards are awarded externally by organizations or others, but we can provide our own rewards. We can pat ourselves on the back for reaching goals we've set or for other accomplishments, and this can take many different forms: eating a favourite dessert, watching a favourite TV program, visiting friends.

■ *Engage in active—not passive—studying.* It is possible to sit in front of a book or a set of notes for hours without accomplishing very much. In order to learn and remember, you must think about the materials you are reading, ask yourself questions about it, and relate this new information to things you already know. The **Key Questions** sections in each chapter are designed to help you think about material in this way. You will discover in Chapter 6 that this form of elaborative rehearsal—thinking about the material and relating it to other material in memory—results in much better retention that simply reading it over and over.

Summary and Review

Key Questions

Psychology: How It Developed and What It Is

■ **What ideas and trends converged to give rise to an independent, science-based field of psychology?** Ideas from philosophy suggesting that knowledge can be gathered through careful observation, and through careful reasoning, combined with advances in other sciences, led to the idea of a scientific field of psychology.

■ **What is the definition of psychology?** Psychology is defined as the science of behaviour and cognitive processes.

■ **According to structuralism, functionalism, and behaviourism, what should psychology study?** These three early schools of psychology suggested that it should study the structure of consciousness, the functions of consciousness, or observable behaviour, respectively.

■ **What are the three "grand issues" about behaviour with which psychology must grapple?**   These three issues are stability versus change, nature versus nurture, and rationality versus irrationality.

■ **What are the key differences between the various perspectives adopted by psychologists—the behavioural, cognitive, biological, social and cultural, psychodynamic, and evolutionary?**   The behavioural perspective focuses on observable aspects of behaviour. The cognitive perspective focuses on the nature of cognitive processes. The biological perspective focuses on the biological processes underlying behaviour. The social and cultural perspective focuses on social interaction and various aspects of culture. The psychodynamic perspective suggests that many aspects of behaviour stem from hidden forces within our personalities. The evolutionary perspective focuses on the role of inherited tendencies in behaviour.

■ **How do psychologists take account of cultural diversity in their research and in providing psychological services?**   In their research, psychologists attempt to study the impact of cultural and ethnic factors on various aspects of behaviour. In providing psychological services, they attempt to assure that testing, therapy, and all aspects of psychological practice are sensitive to cultural and ethnic differences.

Psychologists: Who They Are and What They Do

■ **How does the training of psychologists differ from that of psychiatrists?**   Psychologists receive Ph.D. or PsyD. degrees in academic departments of psychology. Psychiatrists are medical doctors who specialize in the diagnosis and treatment of mental disorders.

■ **What is evolutionary psychology and how does it contribute to our understanding of human behaviour?**   This is a new branch of psychology suggesting that evolutionary processes have played a substantial role in shaping the way in which human beings think and behave.

■ **What are the major subfields of psychology? What aspects of behaviour do they study?**   There are many subfields of psychology including cognitive psychology, developmental psychology, social psychology, psychobiology, and industrial/organizational psychology.

Psychology and the Scientific Method

■ **Why can psychology be considered to be a scientific field?**   Psychology can be considered to be a scientific field because in their research, psychologists employ the scientific method.

■ **What values or guidelines are central to the scientific method?**   Values central to the scientific method include accuracy, objectivity, skepticism, and open-mindedness.

■ **What are theories and what is their role in the scientific method?**   Theories organize existing knowledge and make predictions that can be tested in actual research. Evidence gathered in research is used to refine a theory and, ultimately, can lead to its acceptance as accurate or its rejection as false.

■ **Why is common sense such an uncertain guide to understanding human behaviour?**   Common sense and intuition are not accurate guides to understanding human behaviour because they often point to inconsistent or contradictory conclusions, and because they are subject to many forms of bias.

■ **What sources of potential error in our own thinking often lead us astray with respect to conclusions about behaviour?**   Important sources of error include the confirmation bias (our tendency to pay more attention to evidence that confirms our views than to evidence that refutes them), our reliance on mental shortcuts known as heuristics, and effects of our current moods on our thinking, judgments, and decisions.

■ **How does the scientific method help to reduce or eliminate such errors?**   The scientific method insists that researchers adhere to the values of accuracy, objectivity, skepticism, and open-mindedness.

The Scientific Method in Everyday Life

■ **What is critical thinking?**   Critical thinking is thinking that avoids blindly accepting conclusions or arguments, and instead, closely examines all assumptions, carefully evaluates existing evidence, and cautiously assesses all conclusions. In short, it is thinking that mirrors the key values of the scientific method.

■ **What role does critical thinking play in psychology?**   Psychologists are trained to think critically about all aspects of human behaviour and to adopt this approach in their research.

■ **What benefits can critical thinking provide for your everyday life?**   Thinking critically can help you to think in a more sophisticated and useful way about your own behaviour and that of others. It can be used to make reasonable and accurate assessments of claims you may encounter in various media sources.

Research Methods in Psychology

■ **What is the basic nature of naturalistic observation, the case method, and the survey method?**   Naturalistic observation involves observing various aspects of behaviour in natural settings. The case method involves collecting detailed information about individuals in order to develop general principles about behaviour. In the survey method, large numbers of persons answer questions about aspects of their behaviour or their personal views on various issues.

■ **What is the correlational method of research and what are some advantages it offers?**   In the correlational method of research, efforts are made to determine whether relationships (correlations) exist between variables—that is, whether changes in one variable are accompanied by changes in another. The correlational method is easily adapted to studying behaviour in natural settings and can yield large amounts of information quickly. It can also be used to study relationships between many different variables.

■ **Why don't even strong correlations between variables provide evidence that one causes changes in the other?**   Correlations do not assure the existence of a causal link because changes in both variables may stem from a third variable. Thus, the two variables that are correlated may not influence each other directly.

- **What is the basic nature of experimentation?** Experimentation is a research method in which one variable is systematically changed to determine whether it has an effect on one or more other variables.

- **Why must participants in an experiment be randomly assigned to different conditions?** Participants in an experiment must be randomly assigned to different conditions because only then is it possible to determine whether differences between the conditions stem from the independent variable or from differences among participants.

- **What is confounding of variables in an experiment?** Confounding occurs when one or more variables other than the independent variable are permitted to vary across the conditions of an experiment.

- **What are experimenter effects and the double-blind procedure?** Experimenter effects refer to unintentional influence exerted by researchers on research participants. In the double-blind procedure, experimenters who interact with research participants do not know the hypothesis under investigation. As a result, the likelihood of experimenter effects is reduced.

- **What are inferential statistics, and how do they help psychologists interpret the findings of their research?** Inferential statistics are mathematical procedures that allow researchers to assess the likelihood that the results of

their research occurred by chance. Only when the probability that results occurred by chance is quite low (for example, less than five times in a hundred), do psychologists accept the results of their research as being informative.

- **What is meta-analysis, and what role does it play in interpreting the findings of many studies dealing with the same aspect of behaviour?** Meta-analysis is a statistical procedure for combining the results of many different experiments. Through meta-analysis, it is possible to determine whether, across all the studies considered, an independent variable has exerted significant effects upon behaviour.

Ethical Issues in Psychological Research

- **What is deception and why do many psychologists use it in their research?** Deception involves temporarily withholding information about an experiment from research participants. It is often used in psychological research because knowledge about the purposes of an experiment many affect participants' behaviour in it.

- **What ethical issues are raised by research with animals?** Research with animals raises questions concerning the possibility that they may be exposed to painful or dangerous conditions. Such conditions are very rare in psychological research. Moreover, offsetting any potential risk to animal subjects is the potential contribution of such research to human welfare.

Key Terms

Availability Heuristic (p. 19)
Behaviourism (p. 6)
Case Method (p. 24)
Confirmation Bias (p. 19)
Correlational Method of Research (p. 25)
Correlations (p. 25)
Critical Thinking (p. 21)
Debriefing (p. 34)
Deception (p. 33)
Dependent Variable (p. 28)
Double-Blind Procedure (p. 31)

Evolutionary Psychology (p. 7)
Experimental Method (p. 28)
Experimentation (p. 28)
Experimenter Effects (p. 31)
Functionalism (p. 6)
Hypotheses (p. 17)
Independent Variable (p. 28)
Inferential Statistics (p. 32)
Informed Consent (p. 34)
Meta-Analysis (p. 32)
Multicultural Perspective (p. 13)

Naturalistic Observation (p. 23)
Psychology (p. 7)
Operational Definition (p. 17)
Random Assignment of Participants to Experimental and Control Conditions (p. 30)
Replication (p. 32)
Sampling (p. 24)
Structuralism (p. 6)
Survey Method (p. 24)
Systematic Observation (p. 23)
Theories (p. 17)

Critical Thinking Questions

Appraisal

Most psychologists view their field as being scientific in nature. Do you agree? If so, explain why you accept this view.

Controversy

Do you think that there is such a thing as "human nature"—tendencies or preferences that are unique to human beings and not other animals that might result from differences in evolutionary history?

Making Psychology Part of Your Life

Suppose that one day you read a news story suggesting that results of a survey indicated that 40 percent of women and 30 percent of men have little or no interest sex. How could you use critical thinking to interpret this report? What kind of questions would you ask about the source of the data, how the study was conducted, and background (e.g., age) of the participants?

Weblinks

*Check out our Companion Website at **www.pearsoned.ca/baron** for additional Websites, activities, and more.*

Mind and Body

serendip.brynmawr.edu/exhibitions/Mind/Table.html

The history of psychology from the 17th century to the 20th century is the subject of this site. René Descartes and mind/body dualism, the rise of experimental psychology, and psychology in the United States are among the topics covered.

Guidelines for Ethical Conduct in the Care and Use of Animals

www.apa.org/science/anguide.html

These guidelines for ethical conduct in the care and use of animals in research were developed by the American Psychological Association's Committee on Animal Research and Ethics.

Critical Thinking in Psychology

gateway1.gmcc.ab.ca/~digdonn/psych104/think.htm

At this site are some useful tutorials that teach students to ask testable questions and to distinguish between experimental and correlational evidence.

Canadian Psychological Association

www.cpa.ca

This is the homepage for the Canadian Psychological Association. Follow the link "For students" to connect to various kinds of information, including details about graduate study in psychology.

Classics in the History of Psychology

www.yorku.ca/dept/psych/classics/

This Website from York University provides a search engine which will lead you to more facts about many of the historic figures you meet in this introduction to psychology and some of their original papers also.

Daily Calendar of Events in the History of Psychology

www.cwu.edu/~warren/calendar/datepick.html

Here you will find a calendar. Click on any day of any month and you will find events in the History of Psychology that occurred on that date.

The History of Psychology

www.unb.ca/web/units/psych/likely/psyc4053.htm

This award-winning Website from the University of New Brunswick has crozzles, puzzles, and cartoons that will help you test your knowledge of psychology and a great link to headlines in the history of psychology from 1650 to 1950.

Chapter 2

Biological Bases of Behaviour

CHAPTER OUTLINE

Luxury Lobes

The report in *The Toronto Star* noted that 800 scientists from 33 countries had gathered to share their new research about the frontal lobes of the human brain. One speaker called the frontal lobes the "luxury cortex" because it is not necessary for survival. Without the frontal lobes, we can still eat, breathe and flee from danger—as can all other animals. Other parts of the brain support those functions.

However, with the frontal lobes we can think, plan, remember, and be conscious of doing those things. For that reason, "The science of the frontal lobes is really the science of ourselves."

Presentations at the conference included the results of studies not only of normal, but also of abnormal brain structure and function. For example, injury to a region of the frontal lobe that sits just above the eyes may result in dramatic personality changes and criminal behaviour.

What is the structure of the human brain? What is its composition? How does it function—produce speech, movement, music? What happens when foreign substances—drugs for example—get into the brain? What is the effect of brain damage—in sports or in automobile accidents? Can brain damage be repaired? As you work through Chapter 2—Biological Bases of Behaviour—you will find those questions and some of the exciting answers being offered by contemporary psychological science.

Source: Talaga, T. (2000, March 24). Rethinking the Brain. *The Toronto Star.*

> **All of our thoughts, feelings, and behaviours originate from basic biological processes—more specifically, from the brain.**

How is it that human beings dream and plan, feel joy and hunger, fall in and out of love, read and understand this page, and remember events that took place ages ago? That question is about the relationship between biology, brain, and behaviour. The simple answer is this: All of our thoughts, feelings and behaviours originate from basic biological processes—more specifically, from the brain. The complex answer is being put together by thousands of researchers—all over the world. These researchers work in *biopsychology,* the study of biology and behaviour; *neuropsychology,* the study of brain, brain damage, and behaviour; and *neuroscience,* the general term applied to any research on how brain cells work.

The human brain is the most complex organ of all—and the most mysterious. Its abilities—reading, feeling, understanding, computing, deciding, planning, strumming, slam-dunking, tasting, sleeping, predicting, and, in essence, living are without equal. Rapid advances in technology over the past several decades have enabled scientists to look inside the nervous systems of living people to study these processes directly, and exciting new discoveries are taking place—at an astonishing pace.

Research into brain and behaviour has vital practical applications. For example, statistics tell us that about five million Canadians suffer from some kind of brain damage; often that is traumatic brain injury as the result of an automobile accident. Those injuries have not only a serious emotional impact on the individual, their family and friends, but also a significant economic impact on society. For those reasons, Canada's federal government has established a network of over one hundred scientists at sixteen different universities to develop new research in this field. Their shared goal is to discover how the nervous system works and how it might be made to recover from damage. Many of them have training and expertise in psychology.

Although the last decade was designated the "Decade of the Brain," it was in 1949 that a remarkable book called *The Organization of Behaviour: A Neuropsychological Theory* was published. Its author, D.O. Hebb, a Nova Scotian who spent his scientific career at McGill University, changed the direction of psychology and his ideas became very influential in brain science. Hebb predicted that, in order to understand human behaviour, it would be necessary to understand the nervous system and its functions. This sounds reasonable today, but fifty years ago it was considered radical. In those days, the contribution of biology to individual behaviour was deliberately ignored!

Donald Hebb
1904–1985

Hebb recognized, however, that human behaviour could never be explained entirely by knowledge of how the brain functions. Rather, he acknowledged that our physical, psychological, social, and emotional *experiences* affect the state of our nervous system, and thus the ways in which we behave. Research by biopsychologists confirms that in many circumstances environmental factors can offset the effects of nature.

Hebb was not the first to suggest that behaviour is a product of brain function. That idea already had a long history. A full 2400 years before Hebb, the Greek physician Hippocrates had concluded, "From the brain, and from the brain only, arise our pleasures, joys, laughter and jests, as well as our sorrows, pains, griefs, and fears. Through [the brain], in particular, we think, see, hear, and distinguish the

ugly from the beautiful, the bad from the good, the pleasant from the unpleasant."
Hippocrates, however, lacked both knowledge of the principles of scientific investigation and the know-how to test his ideas scientifically. Today, because of rapid
advances in technology, researchers can actually construct computer images of the
nervous systems of human beings, while they are awake and following instructions, in order to see how the brain's structure and function relate to behaviour.

In this chapter, we begin our study of brain–behaviour relationships by examining the design of neurons, the building blocks of the nervous system, and the
way they work. That information is important because research about how neurons function—and especially how they communicate with one another—provides important insights into important topics in psychology today: for example,
how drugs work and how they make us act the way they do, and how serious
mental illnesses develop. Next, we will consider the nervous system, devoting
special attention to the human brain. Discussion of the structure and function of
the brain will lead us to several special topics, including the unique abilities of the
two sides of the brain, and how the brain processes music and language. After this,
we will turn briefly to the endocrine system—the internal glands regulated by the
nervous system that are vital in emotional behaviour—and review the role genetic
factors play in normal behaviour and in physical and mental disorders. Finally, we
will look at treatment of brain injury and the contributions of basic research to advances in that area.

Neurons

How do the words "Wake up—you are late for your exam!" produce feelings of
anxiety and a mad scramble to get to class? In other words, how can information
reaching our ears produce the panic and the hurried actions related to it? The answer involves the activity of **neurons**—cells within our bodies that are specialized
for the tasks of receiving and processing information, and moving us around.

Neurons: Their Basic Structure

Scientists estimate that the human brain may contain 100 billion neurons, or more.
Neurons are tremendously varied in appearance. Yet most consist of three basic
parts: (1) **dendrites,** (2) a *cell body,* and (3) an **axon.** Dendrites carry information toward the cell body, whereas axons carry information away from it. Thus, neurons
are one-way channels of communication. Information moves from dendrites to the
cell body and then on along the axon to its terminals. A simplified diagram of a neuron is shown in Figure 2.1.

In some neurons the axon is bare, but in many others, wrapped around the
axon is a sheath of fatty material known as *myelin.* The myelin sheath is not continuous, however. Rather, it is interrupted at regular intervals by small gaps. Both
the sheath and the gaps play an important role in the neuron's ability to keep information shielded and to transmit news rapidly. Damage to the myelin sheath can
have a serious effect on behaviour. In diseases such as *multiple sclerosis* (MS), progressive deterioration of the myelin results in jerky, uncoordinated movement in
the affected person.

The myelin sheath is made up of the other cells found within the nervous system: **glial cells.** Glial cells actually outnumber neurons by about ten to one and
serve several other functions in our nervous system. They occupy some of the
empty space between neurons and thus provide structure and support. They perform basic housekeeping chores, such as cleaning up the by-products of chemical
activities within neurons. They also help form the *blood-brain barrier*—the structure
that prevents certain substances in the bloodstream from entering the brain.

Neurons: Cells specialized for
communicating information, the
basic building blocks of the nervous system.

Dendrites: The parts of neurons that conduct action potentials toward the cell body.

Axon: The part of the neuron
that conducts the action potential away from the cell body.

Glial Cells: Cells in the nervous
system that surround, support,
and protect neurons.

Figure 2.1
Neurons: Their Basic Structure

Neurons appear in many forms, but all possess the basic structures shown here: dendrites, a cell body, and an axon (with axon terminals).

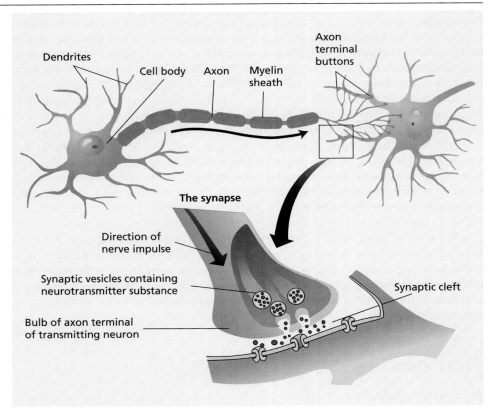

Near its end, the axon divides into several small branches. These branches end in **axon terminals**, which closely approach, but do not actually touch, other cells (other neurons, muscle cells, or gland cells). The space between an axon terminal and another neuron is known as the **synapse**. The way in which neurons communicate across this break is described below.

Neurons: Their Basic Function

As we consider how neurons function, two questions arise: (1) How does information travel from point to point within a single neuron, and (2) how is information transmitted from one neuron to another or from neurons to other cells of the body?

COMMUNICATION WITHIN NEURONS: ELECTRICAL TRANSMISSION   The answer to the first question is complex. When a neuron is in its resting state, there is an electrical charge (−70 millivolts) across the cell membrane. This electrical charge is due to the fact that several types of ions (positively or negatively charged particles) exist in different concentrations outside and inside the cell. As a result, the interior of the cell has an electric charge that is slightly negative relative to the outside. This *resting potential* does not occur by accident; the neuron works to maintain the resting potential by actively pumping positively charged ions out while retaining negatively charged ions in greater concentrations inside the cell.

Stimulation of the neuron, usually by chemical messages from other neurons, produces **graded potentials,** a type of electrical transmission. Because graded potentials tend to weaken quickly, they typically move neural information over short distances, usually along dendrites toward a neuron's cell body. An important feature of graded potentials is that their magnitude varies in proportion to the size of

Axon Terminals: Structures at the end of axons that contain transmitter substances.

Synapse: The gap between the axon of one neuron and other neurons, muscles, or glands.

Graded Potential: A basic type of signal within neurons that results from external physical stimulation of the dendrite or cell body. Unlike the all-or-nothing nature of action potentials, graded potentials vary in proportion to the size of the stimulus that produced them.

the stimulus. Thus, a loud sound or a bright light produces graded potentials of greater magnitude than a softer sound or a dim light.

If the overall pattern of graded potentials reaching the cell body from all of these other cells is of sufficient magnitude—that is, if it exceeds the *threshold* of the neuron in question—complex biochemical changes occur in the cell membrane, and a nerve impulse called an **action potential** is generated. Since neurons typically receive information from thousands of other cells, it is the overall pattern of graded potentials reaching the cell body that determines whether or not an action potential will occur. In one sense, then, neurons are *decision-making* cells, firing only when the pattern of information reaching them is just right. (Please see the Key Concept on page 48 for more detail.)

During an action potential, some types of *positively charged ions* are allowed to enter the axon briefly through specialized pores called *ion channels*. This influx of positive ions reduces and then eliminates the resting potential. Indeed, for a brief period of time, the interior of the cell becomes positively charged relative to the exterior.

After a very brief period (1 or 2 milliseconds), the neuron actively pumps positive ions back out and allows other ions to re-enter through their own ion channels. As a result, the resting potential is restored, and the cell is ready to "fire" once again. We call these swings in electric charge—from negative to positive and back again—the action potential. It is the passage of this electrical disturbance along the length of the axon membrane that is the basic transmission within the nervous system.

Unlike the graded potentials, the action potential is an *all-or-none response*. Either it occurs at full strength or it does not occur at all; there is nothing in between. Also, the speed of conduction of an action potential is very rapid, especially in neurons possessing a myelin sheath. That is because, the action potential along myelinated axons jumps from one gap in the myelin sheath to another, skipping along the length of the axon. (These gaps are called **nodes of Ranvier.**) Speeds along myelinated axons can reach 450 kilometres an hour. The Key Concept on page 48 illustrates information transmission in the nervous system.

COMMUNICATION BETWEEN NEURONS: SYNAPTIC TRANSMISSION Earlier we saw that neurons closely approach, but do not make physical contact with other neurons. How, then, does the message being transmitted by the action potential cross the gap? Existing evidence points to the following answer.

When a neuron "fires," the action potential travels along the axon and arrives at the axon terminals. Within the axon terminals are many containers of chemicals called **synaptic vesicles**. Arrival of the action potential causes these vesicles to approach the cell membrane, fuse with it, and then empty their contents into the synapse (see Figure 2.2). Some of the molecules thus released—known as **neurotransmitters**—cross the synaptic gap and reach special receptor sites in the dendrites of other cells.

These receptor sites are complex protein molecules into which transmitter substances fit—like chemical keys into locks. Specific transmitters can deliver signals only at certain locations on certain cell membranes, and this introduces precision into the nervous system's complex communication system (see Figure 2.3). Upon binding to their receptors, neurotransmitters produce their effects either directly or indirectly (that is through other substances called neuromodulators).

Directly or indirectly, neurotransmitters produce one of two effects. If their effects are *excitatory*, they *depolarize* the membrane of the second cell—decrease the negative charge—making it more likely that cell will fire (see Figure 2.4). That is *neural excitation.* Or the transmitter substances may be *inhibitory*. In this case, they *hyperpolarize* the membrane of the second cell—increase the negative charge—making it less likely that the cell will fire. That is *neural inhibition.*

What happens to a used neurotransmitter after synaptic transmission has occurred? Either these molecules are taken back for recycling into the axon

Action Potential: A rapid shift in the electrical charge across the cell membrane of neurons. This disturbance continues along the axon membrane and communicates information within neurons.

Nodes of Ranvier: Small gaps in the myelin sheath surrounding the axons of many neurons.

Synaptic Vesicles: Structures in the axon terminals that contain neurotransmitters.

Neurotransmitters: Chemicals, released by axon terminals, that carry information across the synapse.

Key Concept

Communication in the Nervous System: Putting It All Together

Communication in the nervous system depends on the movement of positively and negatively charged ions across the membrane that surrounds the neuron.

As shown in the diagram, a resting neuron has a slight negative charge (−70 millivolts) across the cell membrane—that is, the inside is negative relative to the outside. The nervous system expends a great deal of energy to maintain this state of readiness. This is because the neuron's cell membrane is not a perfect barrier. Rather, it leaks a little, allowing some particles to slip in and others to slip out.

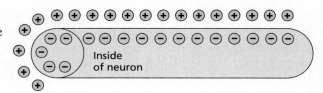

Steps in the Transmission Mechanism

1. When the neuron is stimulated either by an external stimulus or by another neuron, positively charged particles enter the membrane through specialized ion channels, thereby momentarily changing the neuron's charge from negative to positive. Movement of this disturbance along the membrane constitutes the action potential.

Action Potential

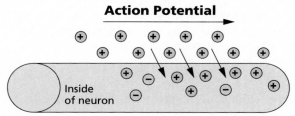

2. After a brief period, positively charged particles are pumped back outside the neuron's membrane via the ion channels.

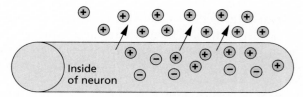

3. As a result of this active process, the inside of the neuron's membrane regains the negative charge (−70 millivolts) relative to the outside, and the cell is ready to "fire" once more. The passage of this electrical disturbance along the cell membrane serves as the basis for communication in the nervous system.

Figure 2.2
Synaptic Transmission: An Overview

The axon terminals found on the ends of axons contain many *synaptic vesicles*. When an action potential reaches the axon terminal, these vesicles move toward the cell membrane. Once there, the vesicles fuse with the membrane and release their contents (*neurotransmitters*) into the synapse.

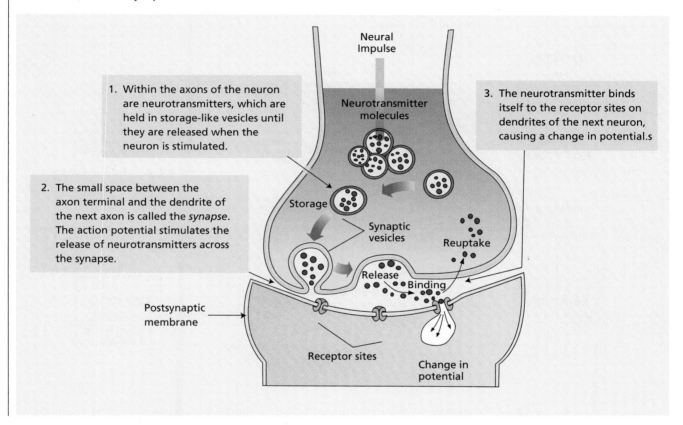

Neural Impulse

1. Within the axons of the neuron are neurotransmitters, which are held in storage-like vesicles until they are released when the neuron is stimulated.

2. The small space between the axon terminal and the dendrite of the next axon is called the *synapse*. The action potential stimulates the release of neurotransmitters across the synapse.

3. The neurotransmitter binds itself to the receptor sites on dendrites of the next neuron, causing a change in potential.s

Neurotransmitter molecules

Storage

Synaptic vesicles

Reuptake

Release

Binding

Postsynaptic membrane

Receptor sites

Change in potential

Figure 2.3
Neurotransmitter Keys

Neurotransmitters are the keys to synaptic transmission. It is as though the neurotransmitter is the master key capable of unlocking each of the several receptor subtype locks. Some drugs are capable of mimicking the natural neurotransmitter's action at one of the receptor subtypes. Thus, such drugs act as submaster keys at only one of the locks.

Source: Stephen M. Stahl (1996). Essential Psychopharmacology, p. 49. Reprinted with the permission of Cambridge University Press.

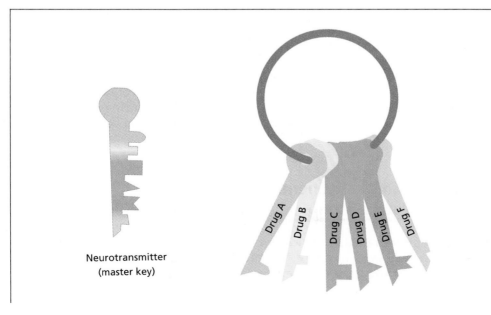

Drug A

Drug B

Drug C

Drug D

Drug E

Drug F

Neurotransmitter (master key)

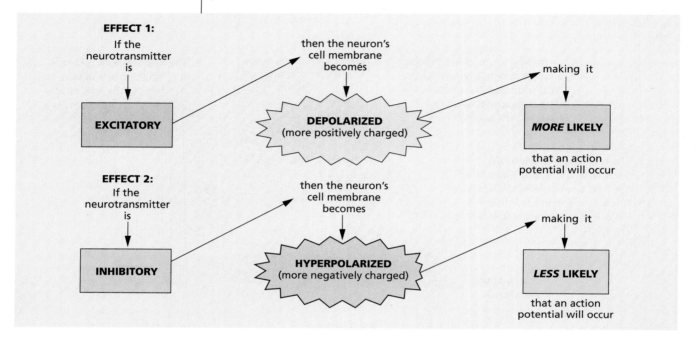

Figure 2.4
Neurotransmitters: Their Basic Effects

Neurotransmitters exert one of two basic effects on neurons. If the neurotransmitter is *excitatory*, the neuron's cell membrane becomes depolarized (the charge becomes more positive), increasing the likelihood that an action potential will occur. In contrast, if the neurotransmitter is *inhibitory*, the cell membrane of the neuron becomes hyperpolarized (the charge becomes more negative), thereby decreasing the likelihood that an action potential will occur.

terminals of the neuron that released them—a process known as *re-uptake*—or they are deactivated by various enzymes in the synapse and then returned. The used neurotransmitter must be cleared away; otherwise, reactivation will occur when it should not.

At any given moment, neurons receive complex patterns of excitatory and inhibitory influences from many neighbours—perhaps as many as 100 000. Whether a neuron conducts an action potential or not depends on the total pattern or summation of this input. Moreover, the effects of excitatory and inhibitory input can accumulate over time. Thus, if a neuron has received weak stimuli in succession over a brief period of time, these sources of excitation may combine to reach the threshold for generating an action potential. As we will see further on, it is this intricate web of neural activity that generates the richness and complexity of our conscious experience.

Neurotransmitters: Chemical Keys to the Nervous System

The fact that transmitter substances produce either excitation or inhibition might suggest that there are two types of neurotransmitters. In fact, there are at least nine universally recognized neurotransmitters, and forty or more substances that appear to function as neurotransmitters. Several known neurotransmitters and their functions are summarized in Table 2.1.

TABLE 2.1

Neurotransmitters: A Summary

The neurons have been found to communicate by means of many different neurotransmitters. This table presents several known neurotransmitters, their locations, and their known or supposed effects on the body.

Neurotransmitter	Location	Effects
Acetylcholine	Found throughout the central nervous system, in the autonomic nervous system, and at all neuromuscular junctions.	Involved in movement, learning, and memory.
Norepinephrine	Found in neurons in the autonomic nervous system.	Principally involved in control of alertness and wakefulness.
Dopamine	Produced by neurons located in a region of the brain called the substantia nigra.	Involved in movement, attention, and learning. Degeneration of dopamine-producing neurons is linked to Parkinson's disease. Too much dopamine has been linked to schizophrenia.
Serotonin	Found in neurons in the brain and spinal cord.	Plays a role in the regulation of mood and in the control of eating, sleep, and arousal. Has also been implicated in the regulation of pain and in dreaming.
GABA (gamma-amino butyric acid)	Found throughout the brain and spinal cord.	GABA is the major inhibitory neurotransmitter in the brain. Abnormal levels of GABA have been linked to sleep and eating disorders.

Although the specific role of many transmitter substances is only becoming clear, several have been studied extensively. For example, *acetylcholine* is an important neurotransmitter found throughout the nervous system. Acetylcholine is the neurotransmitter at junctions between motor neurons (neurons that carry instructions about movement) and muscle cells. Thus, anything that interferes with the action of acetylcholine can have dramatic effects on normal control of movement. These effects may vary from total paralysis to muscular convulsions. Acetylcholine is also believed to play a role in attention, arousal, and memory processes (Quirion, 1993). Scientists believe that the severe memory loss characteristic of **Alzheimer's disease**—a profound disorder that has the potential to become "the plague of the twenty-first century"—results from the degeneration of cells that produce acetylcholine. On autopsy, researchers find unusually low levels of this substance in the brains of former Alzheimer's patients (Coyle, Price, & DeLong, 1983).

The neurotransmitter *dopamine* serves as a good example that too little, or too much, of a good thing can often have profound effects—at least where neurotransmitters are concerned. In **Parkinson's disease**, another progressive and ultimately fatal nervous-system disorder, there is a gradual increase of tremors and muscle rigidity, followed by trouble maintaining balance and difficulty initiating movements. The symptoms of Parkinson's disease are the result of progressive degeneration of dopamine-producing neurons in an area of the brain essential for normal motor function. Michael J. Fox has made public that he has this disease. Unfortunately, too much dopamine can also have negative effects. High levels of dopamine have been found in persons with *schizophrenia*, a severe psychological disorder that we will consider again in Chapter 14.

Alzheimer's Disease: An illness primarily afflicting individuals over the age of sixty-five and involving severe mental deterioration, including retrograde amnesia.

Parkinson's Disease: A progressive and ultimately fatal nervous-system disorder, characterized by a gradual increase of tremors and muscle rigidity, followed by trouble maintaining balance and difficulty initiating movements.

Endorphins: Neurotransmitters as Pain Relievers?

Endorphins are released by the body in response to pain and may also intensify positive bodily sensations, as in the "jogger's high."

Agonist: A drug that mimics the action of a neurotransmitter.

Antagonist: A drug that reduces the impact of a neurotransmitter.

ENDORPHINS During the 1970s, researchers studying the effects of morphine and other opiate drugs learned that there are special receptor sites for these drugs within the brain (Hughes et al., 1975). Since morphine and opiates are not natural to the brain, this was indeed a puzzle. Why should such receptor sites exist? The answer was this: Within the brain there are naturally occurring substances that, in their chemical structure, closely resemble morphine. These substances, known as *endorphins*, seem to act as neurotransmitters, stimulating those same receptor sites naturally.

Why should the brain produce such substances? Research suggests that endorphins are released in response to pain and so help reduce sensations of pain that might otherwise interfere with our ongoing behaviour (Fields & Basbaum, 1984). They are our "natural painkillers." Release of endorphins as a result of injury on the playing field or the hockey rink is one reason athletes are able to continue to play despite serious injuries. Similar reasons explain the lack of immediate pain experienced by some soldiers injured in battle. The release of endorphins may also serve to intensify positive sensations—for example, the "jogger's high" many people experience after vigorous exercise.

In short, it appears that we possess our own internal system for moderating unpleasant sensations and magnifying positive ones. The effects of morphine and other opiates stem, at least in part, from the fact that these drugs exploit the receptor sites of this natural system.

Research efforts are now aimed at identifying drugs that will alter synaptic transmission for practical purposes. In the Research Process section, you will find out how psychologists are using their understanding of synaptic transmission to battle alcohol and other drug addictions. As we will see later, it is very possible that understanding the process of synaptic transmission will lead researchers to successful treatment of several psychological disorders. First, however, it is necessary for us to understand how drugs work.

HOW DRUGS WORK IN THE BRAIN Drugs are big business—*very* big business—and the medical portion of this huge industry is by no means the whole picture. Each day, all over the world, hundreds of millions of people take drugs not only for health reasons, but also to change the way they feel. People use drugs to combat insomnia and to fight fatigue, to calm jittery nerves or increase their energy, to chase away the blues, or—perhaps most questionable of all—simply to get high.

Understanding how drugs affect the nervous system, and thereby also affect behaviour, has helped us develop techniques for treating harmful drug effects, especially drug addictions (Self, 1998). In addition, however, knowledge of various drugs and their effects on synaptic transmission has also proved valuable for helping to combat disease, control pain, prolong life as in AIDS, and determine the causes of serious psychological disorders. For example, studies of antidepressant drugs are shedding new light on the neural basis of the serious psychological problem of depression itself (e.g., Linesman, 1989; McNeal & Cimbolic, 1986), as well as on anorexia nervosa and bulimia (Kennedy & Garfinkel, 1992), and on chronic low back pain (Sullivan et al., 1992). In these and other ways, basic knowledge about how neurons function has turned out to be of considerable practical value. This information is already making substantial contributions to the enhancement of human health and well-being.

Whatever our motives for taking them, many drugs affect us by altering the process of synaptic transmission. They produce their effects—including the pleasure that many addicts crave—by using the biochemical events that occur when one neuron communicates with another. If a particular drug *mimics* (i.e., copies the effect of) a specific neurotransmitter, it is said to be an **agonist** of the neurotransmitter. If a drug interferes with or *inhibits* the impact of a neurotransmitter, it is said to be an **antagonist** of the neurotransmitter. The specific ways in which drugs can function as agonists or antagonists in synaptic transmission are summarized in Figure 2.5. Here are some examples of some drugs that influence behaviour in these ways (Kalivas & Samson, 1992).

Figure 2.5
How Drugs Influence Synaptic Transmission

Various drugs produce their effects either by mimicking (agonistic) or by interfering with (antagonistic) the operations of specific transmitter substances.

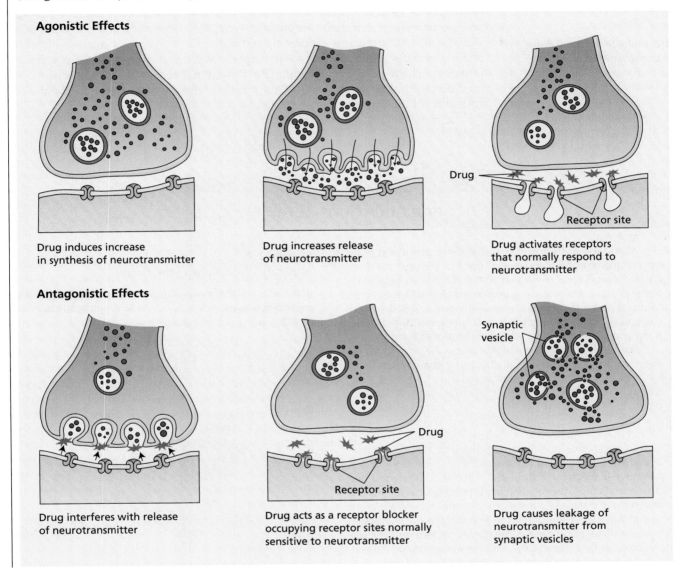

Agonistic Effects

Drug induces increase in synthesis of neurotransmitter

Drug increases release of neurotransmitter

Drug activates receptors that normally respond to neurotransmitter

Antagonistic Effects

Drug interferes with release of neurotransmitter

Drug acts as a receptor blocker occupying receptor sites normally sensitive to neurotransmitter

Drug causes leakage of neurotransmitter from synaptic vesicles

Nicotine, a drug found in tobacco, influences neural receptors sensitive to acetylcholine. Nicotine is an agonist of acetylcholine; it excites post-synaptic receptors for acetylcholine and so acts as a mild stimulant. Morphine and heroin are also neurotransmitter agonists. These drugs engage the receptor sites that normally fit endorphins and opiate peptides. In that way, they mimic the effects of those naturally occurring substances, lessening pain and stress and producing a drug-induced feeling of wonderful well-being.

Several drugs, including cocaine and amphetamines, enhance the impact of natural neurotransmitter substances (Wise & Bozarth, 1987). Cocaine and amphetamines inhibit re-uptake of the neurotransmitters *dopamine* and *norepinephrine* (Roberts, 1993; Phillips & Fibiger, 1990) and prolong their action. As a result, the neurotransmitter molecules remain in the synapse and continue to reactivate other neurons. This is one reason why individuals taking such drugs often experience feelings of tremendous excitement and energy.

Other drugs—for example atropine and curare—are antagonists. Atropine is used by eye doctors to dilate the pupils of your eyes so that they can examine the insides of your eyeballs. Atropine occupies receptors that normally respond to acetylcholine, thus interfering with normal synaptic transmission. As a result, the pupils do not respond to messages delivered by the acetylcholine, and remain dilated. Curare is a poison used for hunting by native people in South America. Curare occupies acetylcholine receptors at synapses between neurons and muscles. When shot with an arrow or dart tipped with this substance, an animal loses its ability to move. Total paralysis soon results—including paralysis of the respiratory muscles, which may prove fatal. The **Research Process** section describes one method psychologists use to study the effects of drugs on the brain and behaviour and some of the findings they have made.

Intracranial Self-Stimulation:
A procedure in which animals provide their own electrical brain stimulation.

The Research Process:
Treating Addictions at the Synapse

Understanding how to treat drug addiction is an important scientific and social goal of current research (Adlaf, Ivis, Smart, & Walsh, 1995). How can psychologists tell how drugs such as cocaine or alcohol work in the brain? The methods that have been developed to study this question are among the most ingenious. Here is a description of one of those advances in methodology.

The development of one tool to assess the way drugs act as rewards in the brain actually began by chance. At McGill University in the 1950s, researchers James Olds and Peter Milner were studying whether electrical stimulation of a particular area of the rat brain would improve learning (see Figure 2.6). Quite by accident, a microelectrode they placed in the brain of one of their subjects missed its mark. In retrospect, this was fortunate because the effects produced by the misplaced electrode were profound. When given weak electrical stimulation each time it entered one corner of its cage, the rat soon began to come back for more on a regular basis. As a result, the researchers asked: What would happen if we deliberately implanted a microelectrode in those brain areas—the limbic system and the hypothalamus (see Figure 2.6)—and permitted the rats to provide their own brain stimulation by pushing a lever?

Tests of the new procedure, called **intracranial self-stimulation** or ICS, revealed dramatic results: Subjects would press a lever for ICS hundreds, even thousands, of times—until they literally collapsed from exhaustion (Olds, 1973; Olds & Milner, 1954). In contrast, when microelectrodes were placed in other areas of the brain, subjects would press the lever once, then avoid it altogether. Olds and Milner concluded that they had discovered discrete "pleasure" and "pain" centres within the brain.

Since then, researchers have determined that these brain centres are connected in *naturally-occurring reward circuits* located deep within the brain. One structure in this network is a set of long axons that connects the midbrain with the forebrain—called the *medial forebrain bundle* (Phillips & Fibiger, 1989; Wise, 1998). Weak electrical stimulation of this structure produces consistently

Figure 2.6
Apparatus for Studying the Brain

With the aid of this device (known as *stereotaxic apparatus*) psychologists can place tiny electrodes within the brains of animals with great precision.

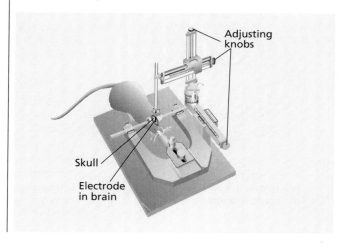

Adjusting knobs

Skull

Electrode in brain

higher rates of lever pressing for ICS than stimulation in other, adjacent areas. Why does that happen? Perhaps it is because levels of dopamine—a neurotransmitter in this system—also rise after self-stimulation (Phillips & Fibiger, 1989).

We now know that some drugs—opiates, for example—affect these naturally-occurring reward circuits deep within the brain (e.g., Wise, 1998). Rats readily learn to press a lever for small injections of cocaine or morphine, and injections of these drugs into the brain in the median forebrain bundle increase rats' lever pressing for ICS (Goeders, Lane, & Smith, 1984). Apparently, these substances enhance the pleasure rats derive from ICS.

Does exposure to drugs affect the reward circuitry of the brain while it is still developing? Researchers have

▶ found that cocaine exposure produces fundamental changes in the reward mechanisms of the brains of adolescent animals, particularly involving dopamine (Philpot & Kirsten, 1999). That finding has important implications for the brains of human adolescents who begin to experiment with drugs in their teen years.

How do we use these findings to counteract addictive drugs? Here is an example. Reid and his colleagues (1996) used the ICS procedure to test whether an opiate antagonist (naltrindole) would block the rewarding effects of a highly-addictive recreational drug called MDMA (ecstasy). In humans, repeated exposure to MDMA causes users to be more impulsive and more psychologically disturbed than control subjects (Morgan, 1998). Reid first trained rats to press a lever for ICS. Then the rats received injections of MDMA—either alone or in combination with naltrindole. As predicted, MDMA alone increased rats' lever pressing for ICS. In contrast, MDMA plus naltrindole did not. Please note, however, that these results are preliminary; naltrindole may not be the drug of choice to treat addictions in people because it may have negative effects on the immune system.

Other findings confirm also that when activity of dopamine or other naturally occurring neurotransmitters in the medial forebrain bundle is inhibited, opiates lose much of their appeal (Phillips, Spyraki, & Fibiger, 1982; Reneric & Bouvard, 1998). The results of this kind of research (e.g., Hubbell & Reid, 1995), show that an understanding of synaptic transmission during intracranial self-stimulation can be helpful in the search for treatments that will promote recovery from drug addiction.

Although many of the results described here are from animal studies, some success in research with human subjects has been reported. Based on the success of previous animal research, Volpicelli and his colleagues (1992) administered the drug naltrexone (another opiate antagonist) to people suffering from alcohol dependence. This study found that participants who received naltrexone had much weaker cravings for alcohol than those in a control group. They also reported that they drank less alcohol and—most importantly—were less likely to resume drinking after the study had ended.

K E Y QUESTIONS

- What is biopsychology?

- What does a neuron do and what are its parts?

- What are action potentials and graded potentials? How do neurons communicate with one another?

- What are the effects of neurotransmitters?

- How do drugs produce their effects? What are agonists? Antagonists?

The Nervous System

Neurons are the building blocks, and the **nervous system** is the structure they form. Since this system regulates our internal bodily functions and permits us to react to the external world in countless ways, it deserves very careful attention. In this section you will learn about the basic structure of the nervous system and find also several techniques psychologists use to study its complex functions.

Major Divisions of the Nervous System

While the nervous system functions as an integrated whole, it is often described as having two major divisions—the **central nervous system** and the **peripheral nervous system**. Figures 2.7 and 2.8 diagram these and other parts of the nervous system.

THE CENTRAL NERVOUS SYSTEM (CNS) The CNS consists of the brain and the spinal cord. The spinal cord runs through a column of hollow bones known as *vertebrae*. You can feel these by moving your hand up and down the middle of your back.

Nervous System: The complex structure that regulates bodily processes and is responsible, ultimately, for all aspects of conscious experience.

Central Nervous System: The brain and the spinal cord.

Peripheral Nervous System: The division of the nervous system that connects internal organs and glands, as well as voluntary and involuntary muscles, to the central nervous system.

Figure 2.7
Central and Peripheral Nervous Systems

The nervous system is divided into the *central nervous system (CNS)*, consisting of the brain and spinal cord, and the *peripheral nervous system (PNS)*, the system of neurons that carries messages between the CNS and the body's sensory receptors, muscles, and internal organs.

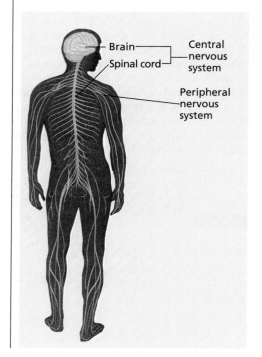

Brain
Spinal cord

Central nervous system

Peripheral nervous system

Somatic Nervous System: The division of the peripheral nervous system that connects the brain and spinal cord to voluntary muscles.

Autonomic Nervous System: The division of the peripheral nervous system that connects internal organs, glands, and involuntary muscles to the central nervous system.

Sympathetic Nervous System: The portion of the autonomic nervous system that readies the body for expenditure of energy.

Parasympathetic Nervous System: The portion of the autonomic nervous system that readies the body for restoration of energy.

The spinal cord has two major functions. First, it carries sensory information to the brain and relays motor instructions from the brain to muscles and glands. Second, it plays a key role in various protective *reflexes*. Withdrawing your hand from a hot object and blinking your eye in response to a rapidly approaching object are examples of common reflex actions. In their simplest form, reflexes are neural circuits that carry information from various sensory receptors to the spinal cord where connections are made with motor neurons, which in turn relay instructions to muscles, thus producing reflex action. Reflexes may seem really simple, but please take note—they are usually much more complex. For example, the information may be sent from the sensory to the motor neurons indirectly, via *interneurons*. Hundreds or even thousands of neurons may influence a reflex, and input from certain areas of the brain may modify the behaviour as well. Nevertheless, spinal reflexes offer an obvious advantage: They permit us to react to potential dangers much more rapidly than if the information had to travel all the way to the brain first.

THE PERIPHERAL NERVOUS SYSTEM (PNS)   The PNS consists primarily of nerves—bundles of axons from many neurons—that connect the central nervous system with sense organs and with muscles and glands throughout the body. These *spinal nerves* serve all of the body below the neck. The *cranial nerves* carry sensory information from receptors in the eyes and ears and other sense organs above the neck. They also carry instructions from the brain to the muscles of the face, neck, and head.

The peripheral nervous system has two subdivisions: the **somatic nervous system** and **autonomic nervous system**. The somatic nervous system connects the central nervous system to voluntary muscles throughout the body. Thus, when you engage in almost any voluntary action, such as when you shake your bon-bon, portions of your somatic nervous system are involved. In contrast, the autonomic nervous system connects the central nervous system to internal organs and glands and to muscles over which we have little voluntary control—for instance, the muscles in our digestive system.

Still, we cannot stop dividing things here. The autonomic nervous system, too, consists of two distinct parts. The first is known as the **sympathetic nervous system**. In general, this system prepares the body for using energy, as in vigorous physical actions. Stimulation of this system increases heartbeat, raises blood pressure, releases sugar into the blood for energy, and increases the flow of blood to muscles. The second portion of the autonomic system, known as the **parasympathetic nervous system,** operates in the opposite manner: It stimulates processes that conserve the body's energy. Activation of this system slows heartbeat, lowers blood pressure, and diverts blood away from skeletal muscles (e.g., muscles in the arms and legs) and to the digestive system. Figure 2.9 summarizes the structure and many of the functions of the autonomic nervous system.

At first glance it might appear that these two parts of the autonomic system compete with each other head-on. In fact, this is far from the case. The sympathetic and parasympathetic systems actually function in a coordinated manner by taking turns, for instance, at various stages of sexual intercourse. Otherwise, there would be a lot of discomfort. That happens, for example, after a person eats a large meal on a warm day: the parasympathetic system stimulates digestion and, at the same time, the sympathetic system increases sweating in order to eliminate excess heat.

While the autonomic nervous system plays an important role in regulating internal bodily processes, it does so mainly by transmitting information to and from the central nervous system. Thus, the CNS, ultimately, has all the information to run the show.

Figure 2.8
Major Divisions of the Nervous System

The nervous system consists of several major divisions.

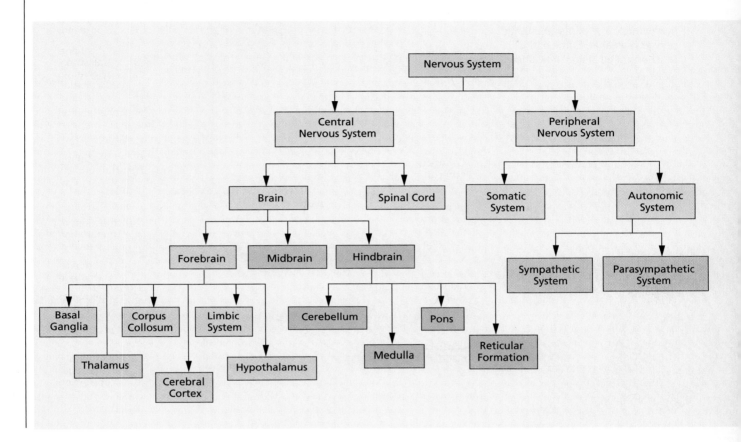

How the Nervous System Is Studied

Suppose that you are a psychologist interested in creating a map of the brain, one that identifies the brain structures involved in various behaviours. How do you obtain the information to construct your map? There is no simple way, but there are now many ingenious methods.

OBSERVING THE EFFECTS OF BRAIN DAMAGE   Any event that interferes with normal brain function is likely to result in changed behaviour. One of the earliest sources of information for researchers was clinical observation of people who had suffered damage to their brain through disease, accident, or even vitamin deficiencies. Then, following their death—sometimes years later—researchers examined these brains to identify the location and extent of the injury and make inferences about how normal brains work.

One of the most dramatic cases of severe brain injury occurred to a railroad worker named Phineas Gage during the late 1800s. Gage suffered severe damage to his brain when an explosion drove a metal rod completely through his skull (see next page). Amazingly, he survived the blast—but was never again the same person. Gage could no longer control his emotions and frequently exhibited fits of rage. Inspection of Phineas Gage's brain after his death showed extensive damage to the part of the brain involved in the control of emotions—a clear illustration of the relationship between the brain, brain damage, and behaviour.

Figure 2.9
The Autonomic Nervous System

The autonomic nervous system consists of two major parts: the sympathetic and parasympathetic nervous systems. Some of the functions of each are shown here.

Source: From Wilson et al., *Abnormal Psychology: Integrating Perspectives,* © 1996 by Allyn and Bacon. Reprinted by permission.

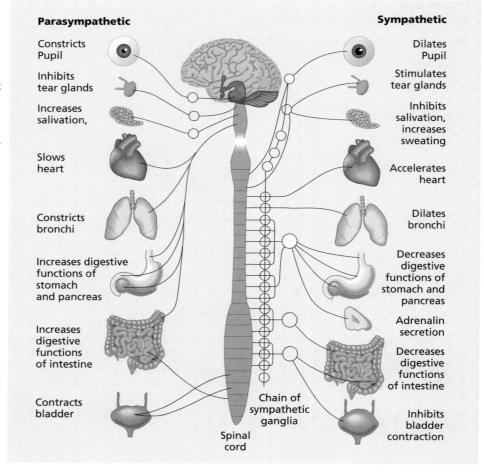

Parasympathetic

Constricts Pupil
Inhibits tear glands
Increases salivation,
Slows heart
Constricts bronchi
Increases digestive functions of stomach and pancreas
Increases digestive functions of intestine
Contracts bladder

Sympathetic

Dilates Pupil
Stimulates tear glands
Inhibits salivation, increases sweating
Accelerates heart
Dilates bronchi
Decreases digestive functions of stomach and pancreas
Adrenalin secretion
Decreases digestive functions of intestine
Inhibits bladder contraction

Chain of sympathetic ganglia
Spinal cord

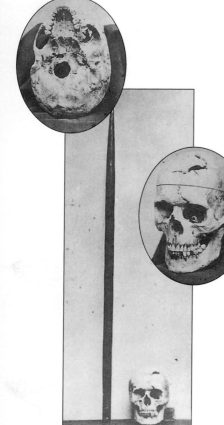

The Effects of Brain Damage: The Case of Phineas Gage

Psychologists still marvel that Phineas Gage was able to survive the blast that hurled the tamping rod depicted above through his skull.

Brain damage often results from other unhappy events. Automobile accidents and gun-shot wounds are two major causes. Depending upon the nature of the accident and how the brain and spinal chord were involved, the symptoms of brain damage may include confusion, loss of consciousness, memory problems, emotional disturbances, and/or paralysis. These cases are serious and unfortunate, but they do provide researchers with information as to how brain damage to particular brain structures affects behaviour, and with indirect clues as to how normal brains work. That information may then turn into knowledge about how to maximize the quality of life of the injured individual.

Other changes in the nervous system that result in behaviour deficits include tumours and infections. Tumours are abnormal growths of masses of nerve cells that press upon brain structures and affect their functions. Infection may occur when bacteria attack the linings of the brain as in *meningitis.* The brain is sensitive also to poisons in the environment—for example, mercury—that may be in the air we breathe.

Nervous system diseases produce changes in behaviour. These include epilepsy, in which unusual electrical events in the brain produce seizures during which convulsions may occur, and multiple sclerosis, in which the myelin covering of axons in the nervous system degenerates causing gradual loss of motor coordination. Alzheimer's disease is most common in elderly individuals who gradually lose their ability to remember until they do not recognize even their closest relatives. As Alzheimer's disease progresses, hard *plaques,* which are clumps of degenerating neurons, and *tangles* of protein within neurons collect in the brain. Under these circumstances, it is no surprise that the functions of the brain deteriorate.

Some brain injuries are very specific and produce very limited changes in how the person acts or what they can still do. These cases provide important information to brain researchers. For example, damage to the visual cortex may result in a blind spot in a particular part of the external world. This gives us evidence about how the environment is mapped by the visual system. Damage to the auditory cortex may result in an individual being unable to recognize or discriminate environmental noises such as car horns and doorbells from each other. These data give us an insight into how the sounds we hear are organized in the brain

In a related approach, researchers operate on different brain structures of laboratory animals and then carefully observe and examine the behavioural effects. For example, scientists might damage or destroy a portion of the brain assumed to be important in eating, in order to find out whether such procedures influence subjects' later eating habits. The basic assumption here is that if a particular structure plays a role in a specific kind of behaviour, then damage to that area should affect the behaviour in question.

Psychologists have also mapped the brain's functions by using minute quantities of drugs to damage specific brain sites or to stimulate or anesthetize specific sets of neurons. If, for example, a drug that anesthetizes neurons is introduced into an area of the brain believed to play a role in speech production, we might expect the person's ability to speak to decrease while the drug's effects persist.

ELECTRICAL RECORDING AND BRAIN STIMULATION Biopsychologists also study the nervous system by observing the electrical activity of the brain in the awake organism. Recording the electrical activity of the entire brain by means of electrodes placed on the skull is a procedure called **electroencephalography,** or **EEG.** EEG studies have examined specific responses of the brain to various external conditions. For example, Fowler and Lindeis (1992) used the EEG to demonstrate that, in a low oxygen environment, reactions to odd sounds and sights slow down. In other cases, fine electrodes are precisely implanted in specific brain locations of animals to record the activity of single neurons or groups of neurons. In addition, accurately implanted electrodes can be used to stimulate specific areas of the brain electrically, like in intracranial self-stimulation, for example, to determine their particular role in various forms of behaviour.

In a related procedure, scientists study brain activity using *event-related potentials* (or *ERPs*) while people perform various cognitive tasks such as remembering and problem solving. ERPs allow us to detect abnormal brain activity as well, and therefore they may be useful in the diagnosis of various nervous system disorders, such as Alzheimer's disease (Polich, 1993).

IMAGES OF THE LIVING BRAIN: MRIS, SQUIDS, AND PETS Perhaps the most exciting methods of investigation of brain function, however, are those that provide detailed images of the living brain's structures and functions. One of these techniques is **magnetic resonance imaging,** or **MRI** (see Figure 2.10). MRI is a way of creating an image of an individual's internal state—that is, of examining the subject's biochemical and physical well-being—without actually invading the body or the brain. At the Institute for Biodiagnostics, established in Winnipeg by the National Research Council of Canada, and at about thirty other centres across the country, MRI technology is being used to advance our knowledge of the basic biology of the body and of disease—for example, to pinpoint tumours and to diagnose injuries.

Here is how MRI works: Hydrogen atoms, which are found in all living tissue, emit measurable waves of energy when exposed to strong magnetic fields. In MRI, these waves are measured and transformed by computer into images of cross-sections of the brain. MRI scanning uses no radioactive substances. It is a way of studying how the brain works that has no known risk.

MRI images are impressively clear and therefore extremely useful in diagnosing many brain disorders. In basic research, MRI may be used to compare the

Electroencephalography (EEG): A technique for measuring the electrical activity of the brain via electrodes placed at specified locations on the skull.

Magnetic Resonance Imaging (MRI): A method for studying the intact brain in which images are obtained by exposure of the brain to a strong magnetic field.

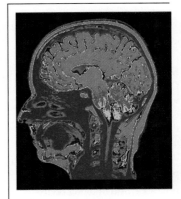

**Figure 2.10
MRI: A High-Tech Tool to Peek Inside the Brain**

Magnetic resonance imaging provides detailed images of the brain and is especially useful in diagnosing brain disorders.

Figure 2.11
SQUID: Images of the Living Brain

SQUID is a recently developed imaging device that operates by detecting minute changes in magnetic fields in the brain.

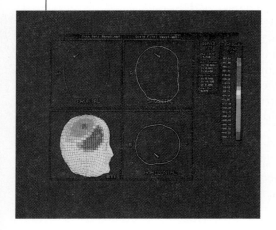

SQUID (Superconducting Quantum Interference Device): An imaging device that captures images of the brain through its ability to detect tiny changes in magnetic fields in the brain.

Positron Emission Tomography (PET): An imaging technique that detects the activity of the brain by measuring glucose utilization or blood flow.

average size of various brain structures in patients with particular disorders, such as epilepsy (Watson, et al., 1992). *Functional MRI* displays detailed images of the brain in action. For example, functional MRI has revealed where the brain plans and produces movements.

A second imaging device is called **SQUID**—short for **superconducting quantum interference device**. Here is how SQUID works: When neurons fire, they produce electrical currents that flow along the axon of the cell. Those currents give rise to weak magnetic fields, which the SQUID is able to detect. A supercomputer can then interpret and image that information (see Figure 2.11). Researchers have used SQUID to locate various brain functions—for example, to create a map of the brain's responses to different musical notes. This SQUID brain map closely resembles the way keys on a piano are arranged. One tiny group of cells reacts to middle C, an adjacent group to C sharp, and so on.

A third high-tech method used by neuroscientists to snoop on the working brain is **positron emission tomography,** or **PET**. PET scans use the rate of blood flow to various areas of the brain, and the rate at which glucose (the fuel of the brain) is used, to produce an image of relative levels of activity in different brain locations. With that information, scientists have been able to map the parts of a person's brain involved in activities such as reading, listening to music, and performing other mental activities such as solving math problems or moving their fingers. Since abnormal cells metabolize glucose at a higher rate than normal, PET has come to be a diagnostic tool in the detection of cancer and of heart problems such as blocked arteries. PET has also been used to identify which AIDS patients will benefit from particular kinds of drugs.

PUTTING BRAIN-IMAGING DEVICES TO WORK These devices are useful in solving both practical problems and basic puzzles in research. In one study (Fiez & Petersen, 1993; Posner & McCandliss, 1993), researchers asked participants to give an appropriate verb for each of several nouns (e.g., baseball–throw; money–spend). The subjects did that task at three different times: before they had practised the task (*naive* condition); after they had practised with the same set of nouns (*practised* condition); and following practice with the task, but with a new set of nouns (*novel* condition). The brain delegated language-processing tasks to different structures—based on past practice. Higher cortical activity was observed during the naive and novel conditions. These data imply that when we undertake a novel or complex task, much cortical activity is required. Later, as we master a task, less cortical activity is required and responsibility is shifted to other brain regions.

Brain imaging techniques are now helping to determine what the differences might be between male and female brains (Nopoulos & Andreasen, 1999). Also, as we will see in Chapter 14, they have contributed to our understanding of people with *obsessive-compulsive disorder* who have unwanted thoughts and irresistible urges to perform in ritualistic behaviours. Their PET scans show higher than normal activity in several areas of the brain, including a brain region involved in impulse control and response inhibition—the frontal lobe (see Figure 2.12). After successful treatment, the PET scans of these patients' brains indicate that activity in these areas has decreased. This illustrates the use of PET scans to monitor the progress of treatment. Imaging techniques may also reveal how the brain works under normal circumstances—even when we think of ourselves (Craik et al., 1999; Levine et al., 1998).

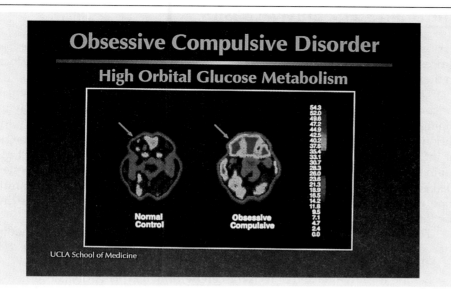

Figure 2.12
PET Scanners: A Useful Device for Detecting Mental Disorders

PET scans provide colour-coded maps of the brain's activity. These PET scans show the brain activity of a normal person (left) and of a patient with obsessive-compulsive disorder (right). Note the increased brain activity in the frontal area of the brain on the right.

Source: Courtesy of Lewis Baxter, UCLA: from Resnick, 1992.

KEY *QUESTIONS*

- What structures comprise the central nervous system? What is the function of the spinal cord?

- What two systems make up the peripheral nervous system? What are the roles of these two systems?

- What are the functions of the sympathetic and parasympathetic nervous systems?

- How do psychologists study the nervous system?

- How are PET scans used to study the activity of the brain?

Critical Thinking

Suppose that research clearly identified certain parts of the brain that, when they malfunction, cause people to engage in violence. Would it be ethical to perform operations on such people to repair these malfunctioning areas?

The Brain

If there can be said to be a "governing organ" of the body, it is definitely the brain. And what an amazing structure it is! The brain is the envy of computer scientists. No computer, no matter how huge or advanced, is currently capable of storing seemingly unlimited amounts of information for years, rewriting its own programs in response to new input and experience, and simultaneously controlling a vast number of complex internal processes and external activities. As far as we can tell now, no computer will reproduce the emotional experience, imagery, insight, flexibility, and creativity of the human brain.

The brain is a complex structure and can be described in many different ways. Often, though, it is said to have three major divisions: the first concerned with basic bodily functions and survival, the second with motivation and emotion, and the third with such complex activities as language, planning, foresight, and reasoning (Luria, 1973).

The Brain Stem: Survival Basics

Medulla: A brain structure concerned with the regulation of vital bodily functions such as breathing and heartbeat.

Pons: A portion of the brain through which sensory and motor information passes, and which contains structures relating to sleep, arousal, and the regulation of muscle tone and cardiac reflexes.

Reticular Activating System: A structure within the brain concerned with sleep, arousal, and the regulation of muscle tone and cardiac reflexes.

Cerebellum: A part of the brain concerned with the regulation and coordination of basic motor activities.

Midbrain: A part of the brain containing primitive centres for vision and hearing. It also plays a role in the regulation of visual reflexes.

Let us begin with the basics: the structures in the brain that regulate the bodily processes we share with many other life forms on earth. These structures are located in the *brain stem,* which sits at the top of the spinal cord.

The **medulla** and the **pons** are the first two of these parts of the brain stem. Major sensory and motor pathways pass through these structures on their way up to higher brain centres or down to muscles or glands in other parts of the body. In addition, the medulla and the pons contain a special central core—a dense network of interconnected neurons. This is the **reticular activating system,** a part of the brain that plays a key role in sleep and arousal. The reticular activating system is also concerned with many other seemingly unrelated functions, such as muscle tone, cardiac and circulatory reflexes, and attention (Pinel, 1993). Thus, referring to the RAS as a single "system" may be misleading.

The medulla also contains several *nuclei*—collections of neuron cell bodies—that control vital functions such as breathing, heart rate, and blood pressure, as well as reflexes such as coughing and sneezing.

Behind the medulla and pons is the **cerebellum**. It is primarily concerned with coordination and synchronization of muscular activities. Damage to the cerebellum results in jerky, poorly coordinated movement. The cerebellum also plays a role in nonmotor cognitive activities, such as memory and learning (e.g., Daum et al., 1993; Lalonde & Botez, 1990; Woodruff-Pak & Papka, 1999). Also involved in movement are subcortical structures called the *basal ganglia* (see Figure 2.13).

The brainstem structure above the medulla and pons is the **midbrain**. It contains an extension of the reticular activating system as well as primitive centres concerned with vision and hearing: the *superior colliculi* (vision) and the *inferior colliculi* (audition). The midbrain nuclei play a role in other brain functions, such as pain perception and the guidance of movement by sensory input from vision, hearing, and touch.

Figure 2.13
The Basal Ganglia

The basal ganglia subcortical structures, found deep within the brain, are involved in the regulation and control of movement.

Source: From Lefton, Psychology, Sixth Edition, © 1997 by Allyn and Bacon. Reprinted by permission.

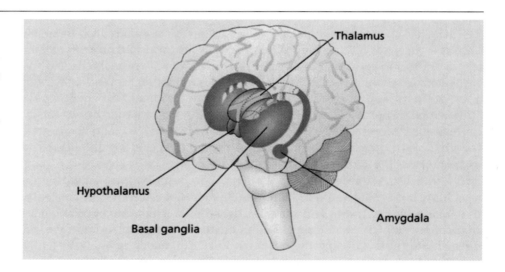

The Hypothalamus, Thalamus, and Limbic System

Ancient philosophers identified the heart as the centre of our emotions. While this poetic belief is still reflected on many valentine cards, modern science indicates that it is wrong. If there is indeed a centre for appetites, emotions, and motives, it actually lies deep within the brain in several interconnected structures.

Perhaps the most fascinating of these is the **hypothalamus**. Less than one cubic centimetre in size, this tiny structure exerts a profound influence on our behaviour. First, it regulates the autonomic nervous system, thus influencing a range of reactions, from sweating and salivating to altering blood pressure. Second, it plays a key role in *homeostasis*—the maintenance of the body's internal environment at optimal levels. Third, the hypothalamus plays a role in the regulation of eating and drinking, primarily through its influence on metabolism. Animals that have suffered damage to the ventromedial hypothalamus tend to increase their food intake; their bodies store calories as fat much more than is normally the case. As a result, they must keep eating to maintain sufficient stores of available energy in their blood to meet immediate requirements (Gray & Morley, 1986; Powley et al., 1980).

Damage to the lateral hypothalamus *reduces* food intake, perhaps because of a more general reduction in responsiveness to *all* sensory input. In other words, subjects with lesions in the lateral hypothalamus lose interest in many stimuli, including food and drink. The results of more recent investigations reveal a more sharply defined role for the lateral hypothalamus—coordination between the needs of the body's internal state (including thirst and hunger), and the prefrontal cortex—the structure responsible for planning and initiating behaviour (Winn, 1995). Thus, when damage is confined strictly to cells of the lateral hypothalamus, the older parts of the brain may detect the need to eat or drink, but this information does not reach the prefrontal cortex. As a result, the animal fails to act to satisfy its need. (See Chapters 10 and 14 for further discussion of eating disorders.)

The hypothalamus also plays a role in other forms of motivated behaviour such as mating and aggression. This structure exerts its influence, at least in part, by regulating the release of hormones from the **pituitary gland**, which we will consider in more detail further on.

Above the hypothalamus, quite close to the centre of the brain, is the **thalamus**. Of course, like all other brain parts, there is a left thalamus on the left side of your brain and a right thalamus on the other side. The thalamus has sometimes been called the great relay station of the brain, and with good reason: It receives input from all of our senses except olfaction (smell), performs preliminary analyses, and then directs those messages to various parts of the brain.

Finally, there is a set of structures that together are known as the **limbic system** (see Figure 2.14). Whether it should even be considered a unitary system is unclear, but several of the subcortical structures have been studied a great deal, most notably the *amygdala* and the *hippocampus*. For example, the amygdala is important for remembering whether to approach or avoid an object in the environment, and whether that object is for eating (like a burger—that may be a veggie burger) or not (like wood chips). That information comes from our *past* experience. The hippocampus provides information about our *current* experience to other structures that are engaged in the creation of new memory traces. The structures that make up the limbic system play an important role in motivated behaviours such as feeding, fleeing, fighting, and sex.

The Cerebral Cortex

The **cerebral cortex**—the thin outer covering of the brain (see Figure 2.15)—is responsible for our impressive capacity to assemble, combine, and transform information about the external world (gathered by the senses) into behaviour—that is, into action.

Hypothalamus: A small structure deep within the brain that plays a key role in the regulation of the autonomic nervous system and of several forms of motivated behaviour such as eating and aggression.

Pituitary Gland: An endocrine gland that releases hormones to regulate other glands and several basic biological processes.

Thalamus: A structure deep within the brain that receives sensory input from other portions of the nervous system and then transmits this information to the cerebral cortex and other parts of the brain.

Limbic System: Several structures deep within the brain that play a role in emotional responding and behaviour.

Cerebral Cortex: The outer covering of the cerebral hemispheres.

Figure 2.14
Principal Structures of the Limbic System

The limbic system is a set of subcortical structures that plays an important role in emotion and motivated behaviour.

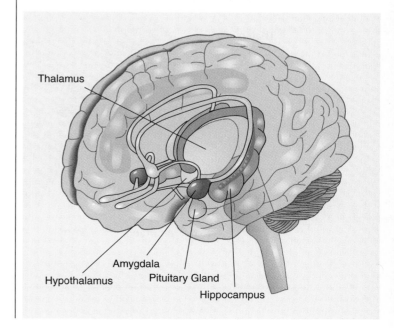

Thalamus

Hypothalamus   Amygdala   Pituitary Gland   Hippocampus

Figure 2.15
The Human Brain

These diagrams show the lateral (side) view of the left hemisphere and the medial (middle) view of the right hemisphere of the human brain.

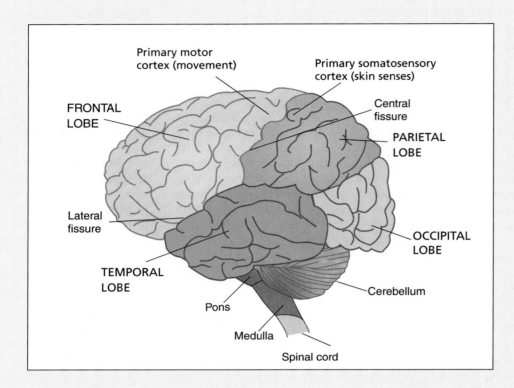

LATERAL VIEW

Left Hemisphere

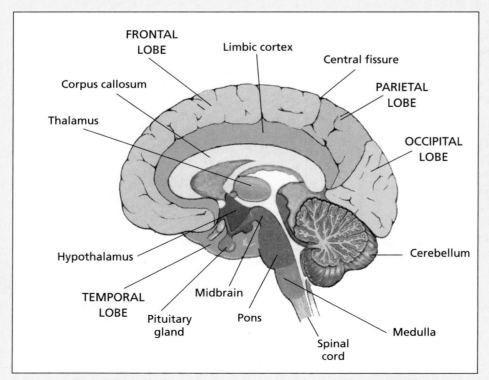

MEDIAL VIEW

Right Hemisphere

The cerebral cortex contains billions of neurons, each connected to many thousands of others. Because it is composed mostly of brownish-grey cell bodies, it is often referred to as "grey matter." Beneath the cortex are myelin-sheathed axons connecting the neurons of the cortex with those of other parts of the brain. The large concentrations of myelin give this tissue an opaque appearance, and hence it is often referred to as "white matter." It is important to note that the cortex is divided into two nearly symmetrical halves, the *cerebral hemispheres*. Thus, the structures described above and below appear in both the left and the right cerebral hemispheres. As we will soon see, however, this similarity in appearance is not entirely matched by similarity in function—the two hemispheres are also specialized in the functions they perform.

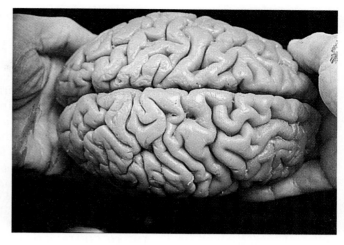

Hemispheres of the Brain
View from above showing the two nearly symmetrical halves of the brain.

The cerebral hemispheres are folded into many ridges and grooves, and this greatly increases their surface area. Each hemisphere is usually described as having four regions or lobes, divided by the largest of these grooves or *fissures*. The three fissures are: the lateral, the central, and the longitudinal. The four lobes are: the frontal, parietal, occipital, and temporal. We will discuss each one in detail next.

THE FRONTAL LOBE The rear boundary of the **frontal lobe** is the deep *central fissure*. Lying along this fissure, just within the frontal lobe, is the *motor cortex*, an area concerned with the control of body movements. Typically, the right motor cortex controls the movement of the left limbs; the left motor cortex controls the movement of the right limbs. The connections of this strip of cortex were revealed by the renowned Montreal neurosurgeon Wilder Penfield, who founded the Montreal Neurological Institute in 1935 and became world-famous for his maps of the brain (e.g., Penfield & Boldrey, 1937; Penfield & Rassmusson, 1950). Damage to a particular location in this area of the motor cortex often results in a loss of control over fine movements, especially independent movements of the fingers of the contralateral hand—that is, the hand on the side of the body opposite to the injured motor cortex.

Wilder Penfield
1891–1976

Much research had been done on the front third of this lobe (called the prefrontal cortex) and on its involvement in the planning, timing, sequencing, and flexibility of behaviour, the control of impulses, and the management of interference (Miller & Cummings, 1999; Stuss & Benson, 1984). One of the prefrontal areas has been linked to memory over short intervals (Goldman-Rakic,1998) and patients who have brain damage in that area are poor at remembering the location of a visual target if they have to remember that information for 30 seconds or more (Ptito et al., 1995). Damage to the right frontal lobe is most disruptive to the appreciation of humour—to smiling or laughing at jokes and understanding what is funny (Shammi & Stuss, 1999). You can see three different measures used in Shammi and Stuss's study in Figure 2.16 (see next page). Notice how difficult these humour tests were for patients with damage to the right frontal lobe!

THE PARIETAL LOBE Across the central fissure from the frontal lobe is the **parietal lobe.** The anterior portion of the parietal lobe contains the *somatosensory cortex*, to which information from the skin senses—touch, temperature, pressure, and possibly pain—is sent.

One of the most amazing phenomena in psychology is "the phantom limb," attributable in large part to this area of the parietal lobe. In some cases of accident or injury, individuals may lose a limb or part of a limb. Almost all of these people have the impression that their lost limb is still part of their body, even though they can see that it has been removed. Moreover, the pain that they experienced in connection with that limb persists after the operation (this is "phantom limb" pain).

Frontal Lobe: The portion of the cerebral cortex that lies in front of the central fissure.

Parietal Lobe: A portion of the cerebral cortex, lying behind the central fissure, that plays a major role in the skin senses: touch, temperature, pressure.

Figure 2.16
Appreciation of Verbal Humorous Statements

Three tests of humour showing that patients with right frontal lesions were significantly impaired in comparison to four other groups of subjects.

Source: Shammi and Stuss, 1999. Reproduced by permission of Oxford University Press.

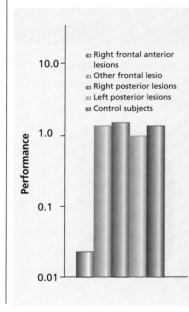

Occipital Lobe: The posterior portion of the cerebral cortex, involved in vision.

Temporal Lobe: The lobe of the cerebral cortex that is involved in audition.

Researchers have suggested that the set of neurons in the brain that represents our body-self continues to signal the presence of the limb (Melzack, 1999), so that the sensory memory of the limb and its pain continues to exist (Katz, 1992; Katz & Gagliese, 1999), even though the limb is really gone.

Damage to the posterior (rear) area of the parietal lobe produces a variety of defects, depending in part on whether the injury has occurred to the left or the right cerebral hemisphere. If the damage involves the left hemisphere, individuals may be no longer able to point to various parts of their body. That is, they no longer "know," for example, where their limbs are. For some patients, putting on clothes is quite a chore, with the left arm ending up in the right pant leg, and so on. If damage occurs in the right hemisphere, individuals may neglect the left side of space. For example, a person may eat only what is on the right side of a dinner plate and neglect the food on the left, write on the right side of a page and not the left, and make up or shave the right side of the face and not the left.

THE OCCIPITAL LOBE   The **occipital lobe** is located at the back of the brain. Its primary functions are visual, and it contains a sensory area that receives input from the eyes. Damage to this area may produce a scotoma—that is, a "hole"—in the person's field of vision: Objects in a particular location cannot be seen, but the rest of the visual field is unaffected. A notable case is that of B.K., a Canadian professor of psychology who, in 1986, suffered an occipital stroke. This is how B.K. described his own experience: "I arose early on the morning of Jan. 9 in order to prepare a lecture. Upon rising, I walked into the kitchen in the dark and turned the lights on. My first reaction was that the lighting was rather dim, and that one of the kitchen lights must have burned out. I proceeded to open a can of cat food, and, in so doing, I was startled to discover that I could not see my left hand" (Kolb, 1990). B.K. found that he had a large "scintillating" scotoma in the left visual field (the left side of space). The scotoma shrank over the next two months and remained about the same thereafter, although B.K. reported that his reading speed and eye-hand coordination continued to improve. As evidence that he has adjusted to his new visual world, B.K. continues his distinguished scientific work and his tennis, squash, and badminton as well.

It is a pathway from the visual cortex to the parietal lobe that provides essential information for visually guided actions, such as picking up something you see (Goodale et al., 1992), because vision and movement must work together for us to reach toward objects in the visual world. When accurate aiming is required, other areas of the frontal lobe get involved too (Whishaw et al., 1992). These functions may be damaged independently. For example, a patient in London, Ontario, who suffered brain damage from breathing too much carbon monoxide, lost the ability to tell what she was looking at, but retained the ability to aim her arm and grasp it (Goodale et al., 1991). You can read more about how it is that this patient can grasp what she cannot see in Chapter 3.

THE TEMPORAL LOBE   Finally, the **temporal lobe** is located along the side of each hemisphere. The location makes sense, for this lobe is concerned primarily with hearing. It is to an area on the upper surface of this lobe that sensory input from the ears is first sent. Damage to the left temporal lobe can result in different symptoms from damage to the right. When such injuries occur in the left hemisphere, people may lose the ability to understand spoken words. When damage is restricted to the right hemisphere, they may lose the ability to recognize other kinds of sounds—for example, melodies, tones, or rhythms. Remarkably, in some patients, increases in creativity, particularly in visual artistic skills, follow damage to the anterior temporal lobe (Miller et al., 1998).

Notice that the primary regions of the brain that either directly control motor movements (*motor cortex*) or receive direct sensory input (*sensory cortex*) account for only 20 to 25 percent of the cortex's area. The remainder is known as the *association cortex*. As its name suggests, this region is assumed to play a role in integrating the activities in the various sensory systems and in translating sensory input into programs for motor output. Thus, the association cortex is involved in complex cognitive activities such as speaking, reading, writing, and spelling.

K E Y *QUESTIONS*

- What structures comprise the brain stem? What are their functions?

- What are the functions of the hypothalamus and thalamus?

- What is the role of the cerebral cortex?

Lateralization of the Cerebral Cortex

A simple visual inspection of the two halves of the human brain would lead a casual observer to conclude that they are mirror images of one another. Yet the cerebral hemispheres of the human brain are quite different, at least with respect to what they do. This means the brain shows a considerable degree of **lateralization of function.** That should not surprise you too much—the two sides of our bodies look the same, yet they often serve different purposes. For example, think of the contribution each hand makes when you tie up your sneakers. We rely on our two hands and feet differently, and on our two eyes and two ears differently, usually favouring one over the other for certain tasks (e.g., Coren, 1993; Porac, 1993) and on our two brain hemispheres as well.

Each hemisphere is specialized for the performance of somewhat different tasks (see Figure 2.17). Language is one of the most obvious of these. In most people, though not all, the left hemisphere performs verbal activities such as speaking, reading, writing, and the detailed analysis of information. The right hemisphere has special responsibility for the perception of space and the comprehension and communication of emotion. Many studies employing diverse methods and procedures support these basic conclusions.

One important centre internationally for these studies is McMaster University, where Sandra Witelson (1991) has assembled a large collection of brain samples—a "brain bank," so to speak. These were "living donations," thus Witelson was able to collect much behavioural data (for example, about verbal skills, memory, and general intelligence) in advance of obtaining the brain samples post mortem. This collection of brain samples is a valuable resource for researchers into brain-behaviour relations all over the world.

In the next sections you will read about two major categories of studies about lateralization of brain function. First you will find the results of investigations of individuals whose brains are intact, and then you will learn about individuals whose cerebral hemispheres have been isolated from each other during brain surgery.

Sandra Witelson
McMaster University

Research with Intact Individuals

Convincing evidence for lateralization of function in the cerebral hemispheres has been provided by research employing the drug *sodium amytal*. When injected into an artery, this drug quickly anesthetizes (i.e., deactivates) the cerebral hemisphere on the side of the injection. During the few minutes before the anesthesia passes, the patient can be tested on a number of different tasks. Recent reports that have used this procedure have investigated differences in brain organization of men and women (Strauss et al., 1992), memory (McGlone & MacDonald, 1989), awareness of partial paralysis (Dywan et al., 1995), multiple-personality disorder, and obsessive-compulsive disorder (Ross & Anderson, 1988). When the right hemisphere is anesthetized, participants can—with their left hemisphere—recite letters of the alphabet or days of the week, name familiar objects, and repeat sentences. In contrast, when the left hemisphere is anesthetized and only the right hemisphere is available, participants have difficulty performing such tasks.

Lateralization of Function: Specialization of the two hemispheres of the brain for the performance of different functions.

Figure 2.17
Lateralization of Brain Function

Scientists have shown that in most humans one cerebral hemisphere, usually the left, is specialized for processing speech and language, and for sequential analysis. The other hemisphere, usually the right, specializes in spatial tasks, in musical and artistic talent, in the recognition of faces, and in other mental processes that require "all at once" or holistic analysis.

Source: Wood and Wood, The World of Psychology. Copyright © 1993 by Allyn and Bacon. Reprinted by permission.

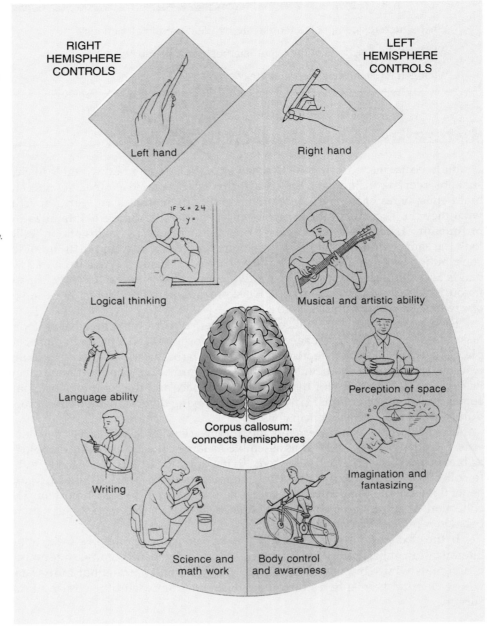

Additional evidence for lateralization of brain function is provided by studies using the PET scan. When individuals speak or work with numbers, activity in the left hemisphere increases. In contrast, when they work on spatial perceptual tasks—for instance, when they compare various shapes—activity increases in the right hemisphere (e.g., Springer & Deutsch, 1985). Interestingly, while individuals are making up their minds about something, EEG activity is higher in the left than in the right hemisphere (Cacioppo, Petty, & Quintanar, 1982). However, once logical thought is over and a decision has been made, heightened activity occurs in the right hemisphere.

Research results point also to differences between the left and right hemispheres in the recognition of emotions and the ability to communicate emotional states. Several studies (e.g., Bryden, Ley, & Sugarman, 1982) find that the right hemisphere is faster than the left at recognizing signs of emotional arousal in the facial expressions of other people (see Figure 2.18).

In a relevant study (Lalande et al., 1992), post-stroke patients performed three tasks. First, they pointed to the appropriate emotion name (on a list) when they heard a sentence read in a neutral emotional tone. That was to see if they understood the emotional sense of a spoken sentence from the words only. Second, they identified the emotion being conveyed when all that they heard was a humming sound of the sentence being produced. Third, they identified the tone of the sentence when the words were said clearly, both when the tone was consistent with the meaning of the sentence and when it was not. Those patients with damage to the right hemisphere were significantly impaired when they had to rely on the emotional tone of voice for the correct response. One result of this study is shown in Figure 2.19, in which you can see the clear relationship between right- and left-hemisphere damage and verbal content and emotional tone.

Figure 2.18
Evidence for Superiority of the Right Hemisphere in the Expression of Emotions

Which photo shows the most intense emotion? Most people choose the one on the right, which is constructed from mirror images of the *left* side of the face—the side controlled by the right cerebral hemisphere. In contrast, the photo on the left is constructed from mirror images of the *right* side of the face—the side controlled by the left hemisphere. It seems to show less intense emotion.

Source: Sackheim and Gur, 1978.

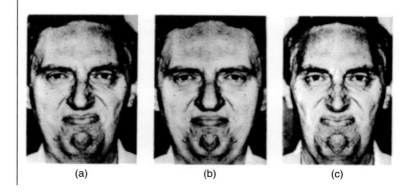

(a)　　　　(b)　　　　(c)

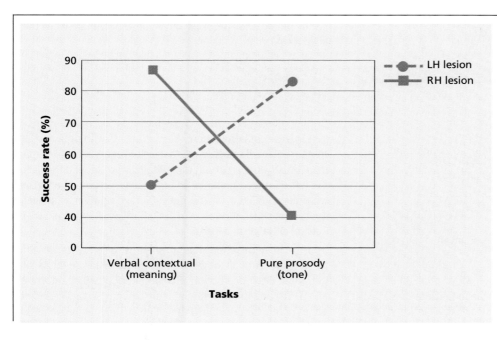

Figure 2.19
The Relationship Between Right- and Left-Hemisphere Damage and Content and Tone of Speech

When the right hemisphere is down (RH-lesion), the problem is identifying emotions from the *tone* of speech; when the left hemisphere is down (LH-lesion), the problem is identifying emotions from the *meanings* of words.

Source: Lalande, Braun, Charlbois, and Whitaker, 1992. Copyright © 1992 by Academic Press. Reproduced by permission of the publisher.

Why does such specialization exist? From an evolutionary perspective, the answer might be this: Rapid emotional responding increased our chances of survival. What is the connection here? There is scientific evidence that emotional expressions appear sooner on the left side of the face, which is controlled by the right hemisphere (e.g., Hauser, 1993). This suggests that the right hemisphere responds to emotion-provoking events more quickly than the left. This, in turn, contributes to rapid recognition of potential dangers or threats and speedy responding with behaviour patterns that were evolved over millions of years to preserve life and prevent death. Because of specialization of the two hemispheres, we can respond in a quicker "gut-level" manner. Of course, sometimes that may be a mistake, and so we also have nervous system capability to "override" those reactions.

Some investigators find, however, that both hemispheres play roles in the emotions we experience (Springer & Deutsch, 1997)—that is, that the left hemisphere is more active during positive emotions, whereas the right is more active during negative ones (Miller, 1987). Thus, individuals suffering from the intense negative feelings of depression often show higher activity in the frontal lobes of their right hemispheres. Since the two hemispheres work together, of course, and the matter is complex, the contribution of each hemisphere to our comprehension and expression of emotion remains a matter for continuing research.

For information on the role of both hemispheres, see the **Canadian Focus** section.

Canadian Focus

Music: The Brain at Work

Jimi Hendrix said, "Music is a safe kind of high." If that strikes you as an overstatement, observe the faces of the fans at concerts by performers like Sarah McLachlan, the Tragically Hip, and many others. Historically, evidence of written music goes back at least 5000 years. In every culture, music is central to human lives and we come by that honestly. Music is the product of the human brain at work.

What makes music a subject of contemporary psychological research? From ancient times to the present, music has been a way for people to communicate personal (and political) feelings—publicly. Through music we arouse emotions (our own and those of others), and we unite socially with other people—to sing our national anthem, to dance together, to play musical instruments in groups, or to overcome. Music analyzers are already present in the brains of very young infants and may be fundamental to early bonding between caregiver and child (Schellenberg & Trehub, 1996; Trehub et al., 1996).

Over the last twenty years or so, researchers working in Canada have led the investigation into how the brain perceives and produces music (e.g., Peretz, 1997; Zatorre et al., 1998). At the McConnell Brain Imaging Unit and the Medical Cyclotron Unit of the Montreal Neurological Institute, MRI and PET scans have confirmed the following conclusion. There is a special neural network for music that includes visual, auditory, space, and motor brain areas, as well as emotional systems. This special neural network enables us to read music somewhat independently of reading words. In fact, brain damage that affects our ability to *speak* may leave us still able to *sing* a song—not only the melody, but also the words.

Here are some of the questions psychologists have asked about music and the brain, and some of the answers they have found.

Where does the brain do music? Patients with brain damage have been studied by Robert Zatorre and others at McGill University and Isabelle Peretz and her colleagues at the University of Montreal. These patients have provided many clues to how music perception is organized in the brain—particularly in the right hemisphere. When patients with right and left temporal-lobe damage were tested for recognition of songs, the words (with or without the melody) were most difficult for the left-damaged patients; the melodies (without the words) were most difficult for the right-damaged patients, as were the rhythms (Penhune et al., 1999; Samson & Zatorre, 1991; Zatorre & Halpern, 1993).

The left hemisphere has a different role—it provides the lyrics. That is not all, however. The left hemisphere has a role in perfect pitch perception (Schlaug et al., 1995; Zatorre et al., 1998) and in the sequential processing of music—the order of notes, for example (Patel et al., 1997). Moreover, both right and left hemisphere-damaged patients are impaired when it comes to making judgments like "Was that a waltz or a march?"—leading the researchers to speculate that tempo

Isabelle Peretz
University of Montreal

judgment requires both sides of the brain to function normally (Liegeois-Chavel et al., 1998).

These recent findings have led researchers to conclude that language and music are *not* completely separate faculties (Patel & Peretz, 1997). Thus, we think of the two hemispheres as co-operating in various ways in the perception of music—as in every other kind of behaviour.

What happens in the brain when you imagine music? A report called "Hearing in the Mind's Ear" told the results of three new studies using PET imaging to find out which brain structures are engaged when we imagine auditory events, including music (Zatorre et al., 1996). The results supported the idea that when we hear music and when we imagine music, some of the very *same* brain structures are engaged.

How do we remember music? Although our memory for music is very good, and recognizing familiar tunes is easy for most of us, there is the case of C.N., a woman who suffered damage to both left and temporal lobes and lost her recognition memory for music, although all of her other abilities remained intact. This case supports the conclusion that there is "a perceptual memory that is specialized for music" (Peretz, 1997).

How does the brain make music? When we make music, the notes, melody, rhythm, harmony, loudness, quality, and emotion, along with the skilled breathing, lip, and hand movements, are all put together (synthesized) by the brain. When brain damage occurs, one or more of those functions may become defective, while the others remain intact. That was illustrated dramatically by patients who were unable to tell the difference between melodies, but continued to be able to discriminate among different rhythms. Those results led to the conclusion that the special brain subsystems for music include one for the temporal pattern—the rhythm of notes, and another for the melodic pattern—the pitch of the notes (Hébert & Peretz, 1997).

What is special about the brains of trained musicians? The MRI scans of highly trained musicians reveal a thicker *corpus callosum*, which is the bundle of millions of nerve fibres that connects the two hemispheres of the brain (Schlaug et al., 1995). Musicians who began their training before the age of seven had the greatest advantage in the size of the bridge between the hemispheres. How does that work? This huge bundle of neural transmission lines may contribute to musical skill by allowing the rapid flow of information from one hemisphere to another, thus allowing the coordination of the right and left hand movements required by skilled musicians.

What is the link between music and emotion? Some music we find joyful, sorrowful, angry, calming—and even thrilling. Why is that so? That is a most complicated question. Here is what we do know. Human beings are very quick to make judgments about the emotional message of a piece of music. In a series of six experiments, investigators tested the judgments of normal listeners on whether classical musical excerpts were intended to convey a happy or a sad mood. These normal subjects made accurate judgments within as little as half of a second! In comparison, it took them about two seconds, on average, to identify a very common tune, for example, "Happy Birthday to You" (Peretz et al., 1998).

Brain-damaged patients who cannot recognize music can identify its emotional impact or report how music made them feel (Peretz, 1997; Peretz et al., 1998). These cases make the same point that extensive brain damage can spare emotional appreciation of music. Note, however, that the emotional response to the music is a product of not only the sound patterns in the music itself, but also the characteristics of the person listening. So when you and your roommate listen to the same song on the radio, one of you may feel uplifted and one of you may feel downhearted (Sloboda, 1991).

What does the musical soundtrack contribute to a motion picture? In the earliest days of the film industry, music was introduced to drown out the noise of the projector. Now, according to Annabel Cohen at the University of Prince Edward Island, the soundtrack has a number of special functions: to provide meaning, arouse emotions, elicit particular moods, establish attitudes towards characters, and draw attention to particular events on screen and filter out any distractions that may occur. In addition, music can provide continuity by playing through transitions in the film and facilitate memory by playing certain themes in association with specific characters as they appear. Finally, Cohen suggests that music in film allows us to suspend our disbelief and engage in the film as though it were virtual reality (Cohen, 2000a; Cohen, 2000b).

Why do we like some pieces of music better than others? We have known since about the turn of the last century that human beings like music that is familiar to them (Meyer, 1903). By presenting the same music over and over again, we can increase liking. That is probably not surprising to those who promote the music of particular artists on the radio or television! But what is it about the brain processing of music that results in increased liking? For the answer to that question we await the results of future research (Peretz et al., 1998).

Now that we know something about music, a primary responsibility of the right hemisphere, it is important to remind ourselves that it is the whole brain that produces and comprehends music or language, or any other brain work—not just one set of structures or another.

When we perceive, produce, and recall music, and respond emotionally to their tunes, we use a network of specialized brain structures—located primarily within the right hemisphere.

Language and the Cerebral Cortex

One of the most remarkable evolutionary advances in the human brain is the ability to produce and comprehend language. Where and how does the brain handle language? Here first is an early explanation and then a newer one (Peterson et al., 1989).

THE NEURAL BASIS OF LANGUAGE Writing in the mid-nineteenth century in France, neurosurgeon Paul Broca suggested that an area of the left frontal lobe, just in front of the primary motor cortex, played a key role in the *production of speech*. He noted that damage to this area left people still able to understand speech, but less able to produce it. Broca concluded, *"On parle avec l'hémisphère gauche."* Damage to Broca's area may produce a condition known as Broca's aphasia, in which speech is slow, effortful, and limited.

Some years later, in 1874, another physician, Karl Wernicke, suggested that a second area (in the left temporal lobe just behind the primary auditory cortex) also played a key role in language. Wernicke had noticed that, after damage to this region, people could produce fluent speech, but their *speech comprehension* was defective. In other words, they could not understand what was said to them—or what they themselves were saying.

Almost one hundred years later, Norman Geschwind combined these theories into the **Wernicke-Geschwind theory** (Geschwind, 1972). His idea was that both areas of the cortex identified by Broca and Wernicke, as well as the pathways connecting them and several other regions of the cerebral cortex are engaged in the production and comprehension of language.

Was Geschwind correct? The evidence is mixed. On the one hand, when people have language-related problems, brain imaging techniques reveal that often it is Broca's or Wernicke's areas that have been damaged. On the other hand, when the crucial parts of the cortex are removed for medical reasons, some patients show little disruption in their language skills (Rasmussen & Milner, 1975). It remains for future research to show us how these data may be reconciled.

Research with Split-Brain Participants

Under normal conditions, the two hemispheres of the brain communicate with each other primarily through the **corpus callosum**. The corpus callosum is a massive structure, consisting of more than 200 million nerve fibres, dedicated to the transmission of neural messages back and forth between the two cerebral hemispheres. There are a few other connections or bridges between the hemispheres, but these are very much smaller.

On occasion, however, the corpus callosum may be absent from birth (Lassonde et al., 1995) or disconnected as a result of damage (Jason & Pajurkova, 1992). Sometimes it is necessary to cut this link between the hemispheres deliberately—for example, in order to prevent the spread of epileptic seizures from one hemisphere to the other. Careful study of individuals who have undergone such surgery (and of animals as well) has provided intriguing information about the lateralization of brain function (Corballis & Sergent, 1992; Sperry, 1968).

Here is a demonstration. A man whose corpus callosum has been cut is seated and told to fix his eyes on a central point on a screen. Then simple words such as *tenant* are flashed across the screen so that the letters *ten* appear to the left of the central point and the letters *ant* appear to the right. Because of the way our visual system is constructed, stimuli presented in the *left* part of space arrive in the *right* hemisphere of the brain; items on the *right* side of space arrive in the *left* hemisphere (see Figure 2.20).

Wernicke-Geschwind Theory: A theory of how the brain processes information relating to speech and other verbal abilities.

Corpus Callosum: A band of nerve fibres connecting the two hemispheres of the brain.

Figure 2.20
Some Intriguing Effects of Severing the Corpus Callosum

A man whose corpus callosum has been cut stares at a central point on a screen (left drawing). Simple words such as TENANT are flashed across the screen so that the letters TEN appear to the left of the central point and the letters ANT appear to the right. Because of the way our visual system is constructed, stimuli presented on the *right* side of the visual field of each eye stimulate only the *left* hemisphere. When asked "What do you see?" (middle drawing), the man answers: "Ant." But when asked to *point* to the word he saw with his left hand (right drawing) he points to the TEN in the word TENANT. These findings provide evidence for lateralization of function in two cerebral hemispheres.

Source: Carlson, 1999, p. 291.

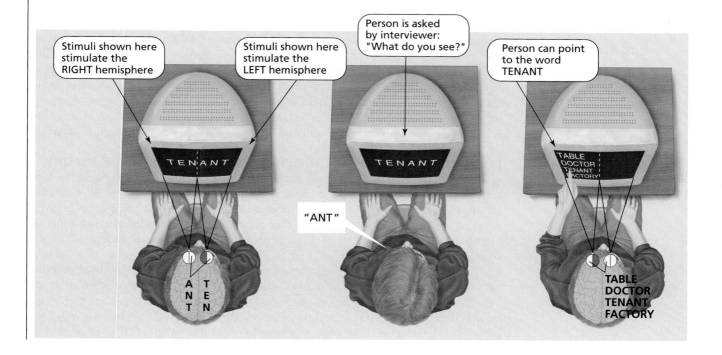

Which word do you think the split-brain subject reports seeing? If you said "ant," you are correct since only the left hemisphere can answer verbally. However, when asked to *point* to the word he saw on a list of words with his left hand, he points to the word *ten*. So the right hemisphere had indeed seen and recognized this stimulus; it simply could not say the word. In a recent report, researchers described a patient who could *say* the words they presented to her left hemisphere but not those presented to her right hemisphere. Nevertheless, she could *write* the words presented to her right hemisphere—with her left hand. It seemed fair to conclude from this evidence that "spoken and written language output can be controlled by independent hemispheres" (Baynes et al., 1998).

Here is a recent example that shows a clear advantage for the right hemisphere. Researchers presented pictures of faces to split-brain monkeys. The faces were either right side up or upside down. Performance was better when the upright faces were presented and more disrupted when the upside-down faces were presented—to the right hemisphere. The conclusion was that monkeys—like humans—use the right hemisphere's global approach for making discriminations between faces (Vermeire & Hamilton, 1998).

Another illustration of this difference is a study of memory for faces in a study by Metcalfe, Funnell, and Gazzaniga (1995). They found that the right hemisphere of a split-brain subject was better able to recognize which faces had been seen before and which were new. The left hemisphere made more errors in this judgment. Metcalfe and the others suggested that the left hemisphere not only records the details of specific events, but also constructs and stores an interpretation of these events. That extra information may make it more difficult for the left hemisphere to tell whether it has seen a stimulus before or not. In contrast, the right hemisphere is not so analytic. It stores a more direct representation of the to-be-remembered information, from which it is easier to recognize previously seen stimuli. These speculations do fit the data but more research is needed before we can conclude that they are correct.

What happens when the split cerebral hemispheres are provided with different information? In one study, pictures of two different objects were presented on a screen. One picture was presented only in the left visual field (to the right hemisphere), while the other was presented only in the right (to the left hemisphere). Participants were then asked to reach into two bags simultaneously, pick the objects they were shown, and name the items in their hands. Almost invariably, they named the object shown to the right visual field, which, of course, stimulated the verbal left hemisphere. Imagine their surprise when, on looking in their hands, they found that they actually held two different objects. These data raise interesting questions about how these separate systems are able to produce a unified consciousness—the unity that we feel about ourselves and our own unique identity.

PUTTING THE BRAIN BACK TOGETHER: MULTIPLE RESOURCE THEORY In some ways, the two hemispheres of the brain are different in structure and in function. Those differences are often striking (Zaidel, 1994). However, the way in which responsibility for brain function is divided between the two hemispheres is not always easy to predict. Some information-processing tasks require the combined efforts of both hemispheres of the brain; others may be carried out independently by the right or left hemisphere.

Several investigations suggest that whether the two sides of the brain collaborate on a particular task is based on efficiency—that is, on the relative costs and benefits of interhemispheric cooperation (Hellige, 1993). One relevant factor may be the difficulty of the task; performance on cognitively difficult tasks is enhanced by cooperation *between* the brain's hemispheres, while simple tasks are carried out more efficiently *within* a single hemisphere (Banich & Belger, 1990).

This may be how the brain delegates its resources in situations involving *one* task. But how about more complex situations involving multiple tasks? After all, most often, daily life involves doing two or more things at once. Recent evidence suggests that the brain delegates its resources not only between its two hemispheres but also *within* each hemisphere (Boles, 1992). Each side of the brain contains multiple cognitive resources. It *is* possible to do two things at once—however, Boles's data say that tasks should not require the same cognitive resource in the same hemisphere.

KEY *QUESTIONS*

How are the left and right hemispheres of the brain specialized for the performance of different tasks?

What evidence supports the existence of hemispheric specialization?

Why is it possible to perform more than one activity at once, such as listening to the radio while driving?

The Endocrine System

The hypothalamus plays a key role in the activities of important glands. These are the **endocrine glands**, which release chemicals called **hormones** directly into the bloodstream. Hormones exert profound effects on a wide range of processes relating to basic bodily functions. Of special interest to psychologists are *neurohormones*, which interact with and affect the nervous system. Neurohormones, like neurotransmitters, influence neural activity. However, because they are released into the circulatory system rather than into synapses, they exert their effects more slowly, at a greater distance, and often for longer periods than neurotransmitters. The locations of the major endocrine glands are shown in Figure 2.21. Table 2.2 summarizes the major endocrine glands and their effects.

The relationship between the hypothalamus and the endocrine glands is complex. Basically, though, the hypothalamus exerts its influence through the *pituitary gland* (refer to Figure 2.21). This gland is located just below the hypothalamus and is closely connected to it. The pituitary is sometimes described as the body's master gland, for the hormones it releases control and regulate the actions of other endocrine glands.

The pituitary is really two glands in one, the *posterior pituitary* and the *anterior pituitary*. It is the anterior pituitary that releases the hormones that regulate the activity of other endocrine glands. One such hormone, ACTH, stimulates the outer layer of the adrenal gland, the *adrenal cortex*, causing it to secrete cortisone. Cortisone, in turn, affects cells in many parts of the body. The pituitary also secretes

Endocrine Glands: Glands that secrete hormones directly into the bloodstream.

Hormones: Substances secreted by endocrine glands that regulate a wide range of bodily processes.

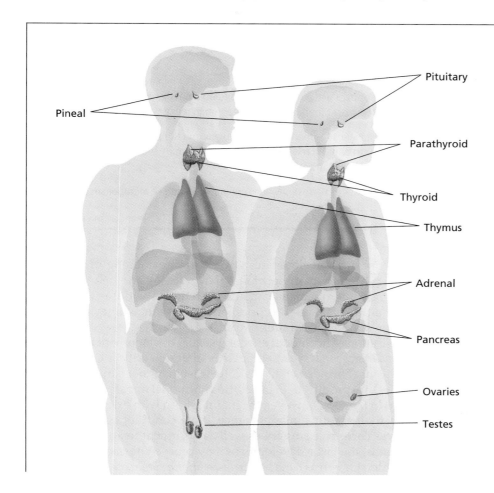

Figure 2.21
Location of the Endocrine Glands

Endocrine glands are found in several locations throughout the body. The hormones they produce exert important effects on many bodily functions.

TABLE 2.2

The Endocrine System: A Summary of Its Major Effects

Hormones of the endocrine glands and their major roles in bodily processes.

Gland	Effects or Functions It Regulates
Adrenal Glands	
Adrenal medulla	Produces epinephrine or norepinephrine. Both play an important role in reactions to stress (e.g., increased heartbeat, raised blood sugar).
Adrenal cortex	Produces hormones that promote release of sugar stored in the liver. Also regulates the excretion of sodium and potassium.
Gonads	
Ovaries	Produce hormones responsible for secondary sex characteristics of females (e.g., breast development); also regulate several aspects of pregnancy.
Testes	Produce hormones responsible for secondary sex characteristics of males (e.g., beard growth); also affect sperm production and male sex drive.
Pancreas	Produces hormones (e.g., insulin) that regulate metabolism.
Parathyroid	Produces hormones that regulate levels of calcium and phosphate within the body (these substances play an important role in the functioning of the nervous system).
Pituitary Gland	
Anterior	Controls activity of gonads; regulates timing and amount of body growth; stimulates milk production in females.
Posterior	Releases hormones that control contractions of the uterus during birth and the release of milk from mammary glands; also regulates excretion of water.
Thyroid	Produces thyroxin, which regulates the rate of metabolism and controls growth.

hormones that affect sexual development, govern the functioning of the sexual glands (by regulating the amount of hormones they release), and help control basic bodily functions relating to metabolism and excretion. The posterior pituitary releases hormones that regulate re-absorption of water by the kidneys and, in females, the production and release of milk.

A dramatic illustration of hormones affecting sexual development is a disorder known as *congenital adrenogenital syndrome* or CAS. In this condition, excessive levels of adrenal androgens (hormones that typically exist in higher concentrations in males than in females) are produced. In males, this hormonal imbalance accelerates the onset of puberty. In females, however, the infant is born with external sexual organs that are distinctly masculine in appearance. If her condition is recognized at birth and she receives corrective surgery as well as hormonal treatment to reduce her levels of androgens, the girl's development may proceed normally.

In another disorder, known as *adrenogenic insensitivity syndrome*, the cells of genetic males lack receptors for androgens. Although such people lack the internal female organs, they are born with genitalia that are distinctly female. As noted by Money and Ehrhardt (1972), their childhood play, goals, sexual behaviour, and maternal interests all conform to patterns traditionally seen among females.

Together, these syndromes highlight the contribution of the endocrine glands, and the hormones they secrete, to physical and cognitive development. As we will see in Chapter 8, the development of *gender identity*—individuals' recognition of their sex and the effects of such recognition on later development—is also influenced by many social and environmental variables. Nevertheless, the endocrine glands and their various different hormones are central to our biopsychological well-being.

Hormones and Behaviour

Gonadal hormone levels remain fairly constant in males, but change in a rhythmic manner in young to middle-aged females. This is the *menstrual cycle*, which occurs regularly over about twenty-eight days. As you know, this pattern is related to shifts in fertility.

Because there are shifts in gonadal hormones during the course of this cycle, these shifts may be related in some way to behaviour or emotions. And, indeed, there are women who report that their moods, energy level, and even sexual desire shift over the course of their menstrual cycle. For some women, these changes are most pronounced in the days just before the start of menstruation—an effect known as the *premenstrual syndrome* (PMS) (Hopson & Rosenfeld, 1984). Are these changes strictly hormonal? Perhaps, but research evidence suggests that in many cases the effects may be smaller and less clear-cut than is often assumed. In fact, it appears that in many cases, reports of shifts in mood, energy, and symptoms may relate to *beliefs* about such changes, not just the hormonal changes themselves. This point is illustrated by a revealing study by McFarland, Ross, and De-Courville (1989).

These researchers asked women at the University of Waterloo to rate (each day for several weeks) various physical discomforts (e.g., headaches, backaches, or cramps) and mood states (e.g., crying, anxiety, or tension). Their beliefs about the physical and psychological impact of menstruation were assessed separately. Later, all of the subjects were asked to recall their *ratings* for a particular day two weeks previous. For half the subjects, that was a day they had been menstruating; for the others, it was not. The results of the recall of the original ratings were these: "The more a woman believed menstruation to have a negative influence on her, the more negatively she recalled her menstrual symptoms." Memories for ratings of days on which they had not been menstruating were not biased in this way.

These findings by no means imply that shifts in hormonal levels have no influence on moods or behaviour; on the contrary, such effects do occur (Pinel, 1993). However, the results obtained by McFarland and her colleagues indicate that the psychological and physical impact of hormones can be influenced by expectations, beliefs, and other cognitive factors. For more information on the possible role of biological factors in sex differences, see **Perspectives on Diversity**.

Perspectives on Diversity

Biological Bases of Gender Differences

WHY ARE THERE DIFFERENCES IN THE ways that men and women think, feel, and behave? Are those differences due to social and cultural factors only, or do differences between male and female brains contribute as well? During the past several decades, attention has focused upon the social and cultural differences between the sexes. Thanks to the evolution in socialization, education, and employment practices, gender-related differences *have narrowed* somewhat.

Hormones: Shaping Gender-Specific Behaviours

Researchers are studying the effects of basic biological processes—including hormonal influences—on the development of sex-typed behaviours among children.

Nevertheless, there continue to be differences in certain cognitive behaviours of males and females (e.g., Law, Pellegrino, & Hunt, 1993). On the one hand, on average, men score slightly higher on tests of spatial ability. On the other hand, women, on average, have a slight advantage over men on tests of verbal ability. These findings have led to new research questions. Are there differences in the sizes of brain structures between men and women. If so, are those related to the ways in which men and women think?

After correcting for body size differences, men's brains are, on average, about 100 grams heavier than women's (Ankney, 1992). At present, we do not know what those extra grams of brain weight are good for, though we do know that more brain does not mean more intelligence (McGlone, 1993). However, let us look at one particular part of the brain, the *corpus callosum*, which has been the focus of much recent attention.

The rear third of the corpus callosum carries messages from the temporal–parietal–occipital junction of one hemisphere to that of the other. As you may have guessed, that region of the corpus callosum is very much involved in cognitive processing of language. On average, men have a smaller corpus callosum in this region (though it is larger elsewhere) and they do less well on tests of verbal ability. These findings do not prove that differences in brain structure are the cause of the cognitive differences observed in this or any other study. Still, they do raise interesting questions about sex differences in brain structure and differences in behaviour.

What, then, is the biological basis for sex differences in brain structure? Because the brains of male and female fetuses develop in different environments within the mother's womb, particularly with respect to the male and female hormones present, it should not surprise us to find out that there are differences between male and female brains. These differences may influence not only the development of the central nervous system, but also some gender-related behaviours much later on.

As evidence, take for example the study of Berenbaum and Hines (1992) in which the participants were boys and girls between the ages of three and eight—including some girls with congenital adrenogenital syndrome (CAS). Berenbaum and Hines observed their subjects' preferences with respect to three types of toys: traditional boys' toys, girls' toys, and toys that were gender-neutral. The preferences of the CAS girls closely matched those of boys. Since there were no differences among the parents in their efforts to encourage their children to behave in gender-specific ways, these results suggest that early biological processes may play a significant role in complex behaviours that emerge much later in childhood.

KEY QUESTIONS

- How does the endocrine system influence aspects of our behaviour?

- What role does the endocrine system play in shaping gender-specific behaviours?

- Are there sex differences in brain size? In cognitive abilities?

Heredity and Behaviour

Heredity: Biologically inherited characteristics.

The basic theme of this chapter is straightforward: behaviour is the product of complex biological processes. It makes sense, then, to consider the relationship between **heredity**—biologically determined characteristics—and behaviour (Wright, 1999). After all, many aspects of our biological nature are inherited, so in an indirect way, and always through the filter of our experience and environmental factors, heredity can indeed influence behaviour.

Genetics: Some Basic Principles

Every cell of the body contains a set of biological blueprints that enables it to perform its essential functions. This information is contained in **chromosomes**, strand-like structures found in the nuclei of all cells. Chromosomes are composed of deoxyribonucleic acid, DNA. In turn, DNA is made up of several simpler components arranged in the form of a double helix. Chromosomes contain thousands of **genes**—segments of DNA that serve as basic units of heredity. Our genes, working in complex combinations with each other, with our environment, and with our experiences, ultimately determine our biological makeup.

Most cells in the human body contain forty-six chromosomes, arranged in pairs (see Figure 2.22). When such cells divide, the chromosome pairs split; then, after the cells have separated, each chromosome replicates itself so that the full number is restored. This kind of cell division is known as **mitosis**. In contrast, sperm and ova, the male and female sex cells, or *gametes*, contain only twenty-three chromosomes each. Thus, when they join to form a fertilized ovum from which a new human being will develop, the full number (forty-six) is attained. For each of us, then, half of our genetic material comes from our mother and half from our father.

These basic mechanisms explain why blood relatives resemble one another more than those who are unrelated, and also why the closer the family tie between individuals, the more similar they tend to be physically—because of the greater proportion of chromosomes and genes that family members share. And since genes determine many aspects of physical appearance, similarity increases with closeness of relationship. Thus, siblings tend to be more alike than cousins. In the case of *identical* or *monozygotic twins*, a single fertilized egg splits in two and forms two children. Because identical twins share all of their genes, they look alike. Often, they are remarkably similar in other respects as well, including their religious beliefs, their television-viewing preferences, their grief responses (e.g., Segal & Bouchard, 1993), and even their risk for divorce. The explanation for these kinds of differences, however, remains uncertain.

Remarkable progress has been made toward identifying the genetic basis of a variety of *physical and mental disorders*. For example, researchers recently discovered the gene that causes **Huntington's disease,** a rare neuromuscular disorder. People afflicted with Huntington's disease experience a gradual onset of uncontrollable, jerky movements in their limbs. The children of those affected have a 50 percent chance of inheriting the gene that causes this disorder. Ironically, the symptoms usually appear after the age of forty, long after many parents have their children. Although scientists are not yet sure how the gene actually causes the disease, and there is not yet a cure, it is now possible to detect its presence before the onset of symptoms and, more importantly, in time for parents to choose whether they wish to risk passing the gene on to their offspring.

Merely possessing a particular gene does not ensure that a specific effect will follow. Genes do not control behaviour or other aspects of life directly—they exert their influence only indirectly, through chemical reactions in the body and the brain. These reactions may depend on certain environmental conditions. For example, consider

Figure 2.22
DNA: Mapping Our Genetic Heritage

Chromosomes are composed of DNA (deoxyribonucleic acid). Each human cell contains twenty-three pairs of chromosomes. The twenty-third pair determines sex. In males, the twenty-third pair contains one X and one Y chromosome (shown here); in females, the twenty-third pair contains two X chromosomes.

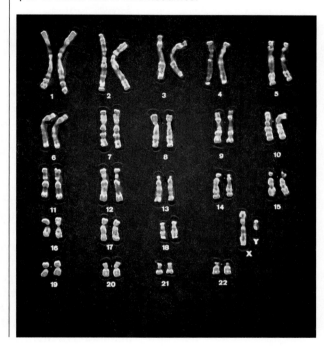

Chromosomes: Threadlike structures containing genetic material, found in every cell of the body.

Genes: Biological "blueprints" that shape development and all basic bodily processes.

Mitosis: Cell division in which chromosome pairs split and then replicate themselves so that the full number is restored in each of the cells produced by division.

Huntington's Disease: A genetically based fatal neuromuscular disorder characterized by the gradual onset of jerky, uncontrollable movements.

Identical Twins

Identical twins not only look alike but are surprisingly similar in a variety of psychological aspects as well. Studies of identical twins separated at birth have yielded valuable information about the importance of genetic and environmental influences on behaviour.

phenylketonuria (PKU), a genetically based disorder in which the body lacks the enzyme necessary to break down *phenylalanine,* a substance present in many foods. Affected individuals on a normal diet tend to accumulate phenylalanine in their bodies. This in turn interferes with normal development of the brain: mental retardation, seizures, and hyperactivity follow (Nyhan, 1987). Altering environmental conditions, however, can prevent this chain of events. Hospitals now routinely screen infants' blood for high levels of phenylalanine. If PKU is detected during the first few weeks of life, babies placed on a diet low in phenylalanine do not develop the PKU symptoms (Archer et al., 1988). Dietary restrictions can be relaxed in late childhood after brain development is mostly complete (Clarke et al., 1987).

Psychologists have long known that there is an increased *risk of divorce* among the children of divorced parents, and data reported recently by McGue and Lykken (1992) indicate that genetic factors may play a role in this outcome. Briefly, they found that if one identical (monozygotic) twin was divorced, the probability that her or his twin would also divorce was higher than among nonidentical (dizygotic) twins. This suggests that there may be inherited tendencies that contribute to the likelihood of divorce. We will consider what these might be in a more detailed discussion of this study (see Chapter 9).

Disentangling Genetic and Environmental Effects

At this point you might be wondering, "How do psychologists tell which aspects of behaviour are determined by inheritance and which by experience?" This question has been the source of debate among psychologists for many years and is often referred to as the *nature–nurture controversy*, an issue we will consider now, and again in later chapters.

Here is one perspective on heredity and environment incorporated into their theory by evolutionary psychologists. Fundamentally, what we have evolved over millions of years and what we pass on from generation to generation is the potential to behave in certain human ways. For example, all normal people express themselves in language. We infer from this that we inherit the potential to acquire language, but the particular language we do acquire is a product of that potential developing in a particular linguistic environment. Similarly, we all possess beliefs, and we assume therefore that we inherit the potential to believe, but the particular beliefs that we acquire depends upon the environment in which we develop. In other words, we inherit the biological "hardware" for language and beliefs, but experience loads the experiential "software" we use onto that hardware. In this final section we will examine several aspects of heredity that appear to be relevant to understanding the biological basis of behaviour.

Phenylketonuria (PKU): A genetically based disorder in which a person lacks the enzyme to break down phenylalanine, a substance present in many foods. The gradual buildup of phenylalanine contributes to subsequent outcomes that include retardation.

As you continue, however, keep in mind that most human traits are determined by more than one gene. In fact, hundreds of genes, acting in concert with environmental forces, may be involved in shaping complex physical or cognitive abilities (Lerner, 1993; McClearn et al., 1991). There is not one gene for poetry or music or for personality characteristics such as persistence, curiousity, or specific abilities—to focus attention and exclude distractions, for example. There is not one gene that makes one person average and another a genius or particularly talented (Howe et al., 1998; Lykken, 1998). Rather, complex human behaviours require contributions of many genes. Furthermore, genetics and environment must interact to produce human behaviour.

Efforts to assess the interaction of heredity and the environment in complex forms of behaviour have often involved comparisons between identical twins who were separated early in life and raised in contrasting environments. As we have already noted, since such twins have identical genes, any differences between them must be due to contrasting experiences and environments. And to the extent that identical twins behave alike, despite being raised in different environments, there are genetic contributions to such behaviours. Research of this type (e.g., Bouchard, 1987; Bouchard et al., 1990) has yielded some surprising findings. Even identical twins reared in very different environments show great similarities in behaviour (Lykken et al., 1992).

Perhaps the most startling evidence was provided by researchers who asked thirty-four sets of identical twins to complete standard measures of job satisfaction (Arvey et al., 1989). Each twin pair (average age forty-two) had been separated in infancy. Since then, each sibling in each pair had always lived in a different home and led a different life. Despite all this, and despite the fact that the siblings held different jobs, there were significant similarities in their rated job satisfaction. The higher the satisfaction reported by one twin, the higher the satisfaction reported by the other. Moreover, this statistical relationship occurred even when adjustments were made for possible similarities in the twins' jobs. (Of course, if they held similar jobs, then it would not be surprising for them to report similar levels of satisfaction). These researchers suggested that tendencies to be positive and enthusiastic—characteristics already known to have a biological basis and to be partly determined by genetic factors—may explain these data (Tellegen et al., 1988).

In other words, because of genetic factors, some people inherit the tendency to experience positive moods more often than others, and these positive moods contribute to their level of satisfaction with their work. Whatever the biochemical mechanism involved here, it seems clear that there may be a genetic component in many aspects of behaviour, including sexual orientation, as discussed in **Perspectives on Diversity**.

Perspectives on Diversity

Sexual Orientation: Brain Matters

DETERMINING THE CAUSES OF BEHAVIOUR can be a complicated business. Doing so requires careful examination of both environmental and biological factors. Is a person's sexual orientation determined genetically? Or does it stem from powerful influences in our environment? These and similar questions form the basis of one of the most public issues of our times—sexual orientation.

A number of studies have reported neuroanatomical and neurochemical differences between homosexual and heterosexual persons (Gladue, 1994). Differences have been detected in levels of sex-related hormones and their precursors (Banks & Gartrell, 1995; Collaer & Hines, 1995) as well as in several brain structures (e.g., LeVay, 1991; Swaab, Gooren, & Hofman, 1995), For example, the size and shape of the suprachiasmatic nucleus, an area of the brain involved in coordinating hormonal functions, are somewhat different between homosexual and heterosexual men, but strikingly similar between homosexual men and heterosexual women.

Researchers have also studied twins to determine whether homosexuality is an inherited trait. The rationale? If homosexuality has a genetic component, then the chances that if one twin is gay, the other is too—the concordance for homosexuality—should be highest among identical twins. That seems to be the case. In one study, 52 percent of the identical twins were both gay, compared to 22 percent of the nonidentical twins and 11 percent of the adopted brothers (Bailey & Pillard, 1991). A similar pattern of results was obtained for a group of homosexual women (Bailey et al., 1993).

Scientists have also tried to locate a possible homosexual gene directly (Turner, 1995). In an intriguing study, Hamer and colleagues (1993) traced a group of gay men's family histories and discovered a relatively high incidence of homosexuality among the men's mothers' male relatives—a clear signal that the gene might be located on the X chromosome (the only chromosome inherited exclusively from the mother).

Nevertheless, the evidence for the biological basis of homosexuality is mixed. Some studies report differences; others do not. Moreover, even in instances in which consistent differences are discovered, the question of how these differences in structure or neurochemistry are linked to specific behaviours remains to be seen (Byne, 1995; Swaab, Gooren, & Hofman, 1995). Therefore, some researchers continue to maintain that sexual orientation is the product of biological and environmental factors (Bem, 1996). You will read more about those theories in Chapter 10.

KEY *QUESTIONS*

- How do genetic factors influence behaviour?
- What are some examples of genetically based diseases?
- What evidence supports the possibility that genetic factors influence aspects of our behaviour?

Critical Thinking
List other human potentials that come to mind besides language and beliefs. List the experience that applies to each one.

making **Psychology** *Part of Your Life*

Traumatic Brain Injury: Consequences and Rehabilitation

*E*ach year there are about 40 000 cases of traumatic brain injury in Canada. Traumatic brain injury (TBI) is permanent damage to the nervous system, particularly to the brain, as a result of a severe blow to the head. Most of those cases result from vehicle accidents and could have been prevented. There are also less common causes of traumatic brain injury: falls, illness, assault, and work-related. Some cases are sports-related. One of the rarest is *dementia pugilistica*—disordered brain function in boxers who have been punched in the head too many times.

What are the consequences of TBI? Traumatic brain injury has serious emotional, cognitive, and social consequences. Even a mild head injury may produce subtle deficits in brain function for many years after the original incident (Segalowitz et al., 1996). A common *emotional* reaction, found in 70 percent of patients, is irritability—a tendency to get annoyed easily. This shows itself in a lower tolerance for stress. Another common reaction is impulsivity—that is, a tendency to act without considering consequences. Typically these patients are apathetic, but they may also explode in anger or act

▶

silly. In some cases, there may be episodes of destructive behaviour.

There are *cognitive* changes also—confused thinking, difficulty remembering, forgetting, inability to acquire new knowledge, poor judgment, and faulty reasoning. In a large sample of high school and university students in Ontario, there were subtle differences in attention, reading, or speech for those with TBI (Segalowitz & Lawson, 1995). After suffering a traumatic brain injury, patients may process information more slowly (Stuss et al., 1989), and their memory—for example, of where they learned something or who told them—may be poor, especially if they were in a coma for an extended period of time (Dywan et al., 1993).

The subjects in one recent study were professional soccer players in Holland (Matser et al., 1998). They were compared with elite noncontact sport athletes of about the same age (twenty-four years old). The soccer players had more difficulty with memory, planning, and visual perception. Furthermore, the more concussions a player had had and the more "heading" of the ball a player had done, the worse was his performance on the psychological tests.

Individuals with mild TBI often survive with their self-awareness intact. Thus they recognize that they have specific problems with thinking and remembering. That understanding may intensify their emotional reactions and increase their anxiety levels (McAllister & Flashman, 1999). Other traumatic brain injury patients have serious *social* problems. They act inappropriately in social situations and they do not recognize their own misbehaviours. Also, they seem unable to learn from their experiences with other people or to improve. They resent those who try to help them change, and they act accordingly.

Of course, each case is different and, therefore, prediction is difficult. For instance, the consequences of traumatic brain injury may be focal—that is, localized to a particular brain structure. In such cases, it may be possible to predict with some accuracy what behavioural disturbances will occur. However, brain damage is often diffuse, extending to many regions throughout the brain. When that is the case, psychologists and other health professionals are unable to predict exactly which psychological disturbances are likely to follow. This, in turn, makes the design of effective treatments for individual patients a real challenge (Armstrong, 1991). The most general statement we can make about the consequences of TBI is that the more severe the injury, the more difficult the adjustment afterwards (Tate & Broe, 1999).

What are the treatments for TBI? The behaviour changes that follow a traumatic brain injury affect not only the patient personally, but also relationships with his or her family, friends, employer, co-workers, and others (Stambrook et al., 1989). For this reason, a treatment team, including neuropsychologists, physical, occupational, and speech therapists, and specialist social workers, is usually called on to design a rehabilitation program that accommodates the unique changes that have taken place within the patient (Armstrong, 1991).

There will likely be a neuropsychological assessment to determine the strengths that remain and the deficits that have resulted from the trauma (Stuss & Buckle, 1992). A number of functions of the frontal lobes (arousal, planning, attention and memory, initiation, inhibition and social monitoring) are examined to provide a measure of the degree to which these behaviours have been disturbed by brain damage in adult and adolescent brain-injured individuals (e.g., Dywan & Segalowitz, 1996).

Donald T. Stuss
University of Toronto and Rotman Institute

The rehabilitation plan may include physical, occupational, and speech therapy. Vocational assessment may be necessary, as well as retraining (e.g., Park et al., 1999). Preparation must begin for occupations in which the individual may reasonably expect to succeed. Because brain-injured people often feel frustrated by their inability to think ahead, it is important that rehabilitation take place in a carefully structured environment, which will allow them to attend to one thing at a time and reduce potential sources of confusion.

Often the success of rehabilitation depends upon how firmly patients believe they have the ability to determine their own progress (MacFarlane, 1999). At the University of Manitoba, researchers found that if victims believe they are helpless, their lives become much more restricted than they might have been (Moore & Stambrook, 1995). Their confidence in the difference they themselves can make—and their belief in themselves—are very important to their own rehabilitation.

More and more people are turning to protective headgear to guard themselves and their children against traumatic brain injury.

▶

▶ Family members are also involved. Their expectations are discussed, and they are taught not only how to help when difficulties occur, but also how to cope (themselves) with the stresses of becoming caregivers to individuals whose behaviour may have changed dramatically (Moore et al., 1991). Psychological counselling may be in order; marital or family therapy may be needed. The most effective treatment begins soon after injury, involves family members actively, and continues consistently through time.

Thanks to our understanding of the complex interactions between biological processes and behaviour, psychologists can improve the quality of the lives of those who suffer a traumatic brain injury. It is important to realize, however, that at present, the best we can do is help people deal with their disabilities effectively. We cannot restore their former physical and cognitive strengths.

How does basic research contribute to recovery from TBI? Recovery of the nervous system after damage is a hot topic in contemporary neuroscience research. Much basic research is now being performed on the mechanisms of recovery of function after brain damage, both in people (e.g., Goodale et al., 1990) and in animals (e.g., Kolb, 1999). Here is some of the knowledge we have to date. We know that when neurons are damaged, eventually they deteriorate and die—in systematic ways. The first deterioration occurs from the cut end of an axon back to the cell body; that is *retrograde degeneration*. After that, the other cut end of the axon towards the synaptic endings deteriorates. That is called *anterograde degeneration* and it may occur not only in the injured axon but also in neurons further forward. It is the responsibility of glial cells within the central and the peripheral nervous systems to remove the residue of the damaged tissue.

Can damaged neurons recover? The answer is yes and no. Yes, there may be regeneration in the peripheral nervous system. No, neurons in the central nervous system do not recover. This difference is not linked to differences in the neurons in those places, but to differences in the capabilities of the glial cells to promote regrowth of the damaged axons. Glial cells in the peripheral nervous system produce substances that encourage growth of new axons; in the central nervous

system they obstruct regeneration (Pinel, 2000). Although damaged central nervous system neurons do not recover, the axons of healthy neurons *around* the damaged area sprout more endings and form new synapses, thus making new connections (Kolb & Whishaw, 1998).

Bryan Kolb
University of Lethbridge

Many of the animal experiments compare recovery of function in young animals with recovery in mature animals. For example, at the University of Lethbridge, Kolb and Whishaw (1991) showed that brain damage inflicted on adult rats affected their ability to navigate in space; however, in adult rats who were damaged as infants but tested as adults, spatial navigation was satisfactory. In another study, Kolb and Gibb (1991) compared the effects of enriched and isolated housing conditions on rats with damaged brains. They found that the enriched environment had a positive effect on brain-damaged animals; there were increases in their brain weight and other neuronal changes, similar to those that occurred in normal rats.

Neurotransplantation is one new radical approach that promises some success. In rats, for example, we know that transplantation of healthy sections of neural tissue may produce improvement in the ability of the brain to function normally. Ultimately, the neural tissue may come from a different animal, or even from a different part of the same animal. Indeed, when we look to the distant future, it may ultimately be possible even to transplant replacement parts into the central nervous system!

These are the kinds of basic studies that may one day in the far future make it possible to recover from traumatic brain injuries. According to Think First Saskatchewan, a provincial organization in Saskatchewan involved with brain trauma, however, our primary goal must be the *prevention* of brain injury. Therefore, volunteers in this organization and many others like it across Canada—some of whom are young people who have suffered permanent brain injuries—are actively engaged in promoting safety by bringing safety instruction to the schools.

Summary and Review

Key Questions

Neurons

■ **What is biopsychology?** Biopsychology is the branch of psychology concerned with discovering the biological processes that give rise to our thoughts, feelings, and actions.

■ **What does a neuron do and what are its parts?** Neurons are cells specialized for receiving, processing, and moving information. They are made up of a cell body, an axon, and one or more dendrites.

■ **What are action potentials and graded potentials? How do neurons communicate with one another?** Action potentials are rapid changes in the electrical properties of the cell membranes of neurons. They constitute a basic mechanism by which information travels through the nervous system. Graded potentials occur in response to a physical stimulus or stimulation by another neuron; they weaken quickly and their strength is directly proportional to the intensity of the physical stimulus that produced them. Neurons communicate across the gaps (synapses) that separate them by means of neurotransmitters.

■ **What are the effects of neurotransmitters?** Neurotransmitters produce one of two effects: Excitatory effects cause a depolarization in the nerve cell membrane, making it more likely that a graded potential will be generated; inhibitory effects hyperpolarize the cell membranes, making it less likely that the cell will fire.

■ **How do drugs produce their effects?** Many drugs produce their effects by influencing synaptic transmission.

■ **What are agonists? Antagonists?** Agonists are drugs that mimic the impact of neurotransmitters at specific receptors; drugs that inhibit their impact are termed antagonists. Growing evidence suggests that knowledge of neurotransmitter systems can be applied to solve important practical problems, including drug and alcohol abuse and certain mental disorders.

The Nervous System

■ **What structures comprise the central nervous system? What is the function of the spinal cord?** The central nervous system includes the brain and the spinal cord. The spinal cord carries sensory information from receptors of the body to the brain via afferent nerve fibres and carries information from the brain to muscles and glands via efferent nerve fibres. It also plays an important role in reflexes.

■ **What two systems make up the peripheral nervous system? What roles do they play?** The peripheral nervous

system consists of the somatic and autonomic nervous systems. The somatic nervous system connects the brain and spinal cord to voluntary muscles throughout the body; the autonomic nervous system connects the central nervous system to internal organs and glands and to muscles over which we have little voluntary control.

■ **What are the functions of the sympathetic and parasympathetic nervous systems?** The sympathetic nervous system prepares the body for using energy, whereas the parasympathetic nervous system activates processes that conserve the body's energy.

■ **How do psychologists study the nervous system?** Psychologists use several methods for studying the nervous system, including observing the effects of brain damage, electrical or chemical stimulation of the brain, and several modern imaging techniques.

■ **How are PET scans used to study the activity of the brain?** PET scans have been used to show how the brain's activities change as people perform various mental activities and to detect brain activity differences between normal persons and persons with mental disorders, such as obsessive-compulsive disorders. PET scans reveal that the brain expends less energy as it masters a task.

The Brain

■ **What are the structures that comprise the brain stem? What are their functions?** The brain stem—including the medulla and the pons—is concerned primarily with the regulation of basic bodily functions. The cerebellum, however, may be involved in higher cognitive processes, such as learning.

■ **What are the functions of the hypothalamus and thalamus?** The hypothalamus is a brain structure involved in the regulation of motivated behaviour and emotion. The thalamus serves as a relay station; directing afferent messages to appropriate brain regions.

■ **What is the role of the cerebral cortex?** The cerebral cortex is the hub for higher mental processes such as thinking, planning, reasoning, and memory.

■ **How is language processed in the brain?** The Wernicke-Geschwind model suggests that language processing may be localized in specific regions of the brain. Support for this model comes from studies in which brain imaging devices have been used to scan the brains of individuals suffering from language-related problems. These studies usually report damage to either Broca's or Wernicke's area.

Lateralization of the Cerebral Cortex

■ **How are the left and right hemispheres of the brain specialized for the performance of different tasks?** In most persons, the left hemisphere specializes in verbal activities and in logical thought and analysis. The right hemisphere specializes in the comprehension and communication of emotion and in the synthesis of information. The right hemisphere may be more accurate in recalling certain types of stored information.

■ **What evidence supports the existence of hemispheric specialization?** Evidence for hemispheric specialization has been obtained from studies of people with intact brains and from research on split-brain individuals.

■ **Why can you perform more than one activity at once, such as listening to the radio while driving?**
Within each hemisphere of the brain, cognitive processes may operate independently allowing us to do two tasks at once—as long as the tasks do not depend on the same cognitive resource.

The Endocrine System

■ **How does the endocrine system influence aspects of our behaviour?** Hormones released by the endocrine glands exert far-reaching effects on bodily processes and, in turn, on important aspects of behaviour.

■ **What role does the endocrine system play in shaping gender-specific behaviours?** Genetically based hormonal disturbances such as CAS may play a role in shaping gender-specific behaviours.

■ **Are there sex differences in brain size? In cognitive abilities?** Some evidence suggests a relationship between sex differences in the size of regions of the corpus callosum and sex differences in several cognitive abilities, including verbal fluency and language lateralization. However, most differences in cognitive abilities are small and the differences *within* each sex are usually larger than the differences *between* men and women.

Heredity and Behaviour

■ **How do genetic factors influence behaviour?** Genetic factors influence behaviour via genes—"biological blueprints" located on chromosomes. Genes do not control behaviour or other aspects of life directly. Instead, genes exert their influence indirectly through their influence on chemical reactions in the brain or other organs.

■ **What are some examples of genetically based diseases?** Two well-known genetically based diseases are Huntington's disease and phenylketonuria (PKU). The mental retardation that often accompanies PKU can be prevented by avoiding foods containing phenylalanine.

■ **What evidence supports the possibility that genetic factors influence aspects of our behaviour?** Research comparing identical twins raised apart suggests that genetic factors play a role in many aspects of behaviour.

Key Terms

Action Potential (p. 47)
Agonist (p. 52)
Alzheimer's Disease (p. 51)
Antagonist (p. 52)
Autonomic Nervous System (p. 56)
Axon (p. 45)
Axon Terminals (p. 46)
Central Nervous System (p. 55)
Cerebellum (p. 62)
Cerebral Cortex (p. 63)
Chromosomes (p. 79)
Corpus Callosum (p. 72)
Dendrites (p. 45)
Electroencephalography (EEG) (p. 59)
Endocrine Glands (p. 75)
Frontal Lobe (p. 65)
Genes (p. 79)
Glial Cells (p. 45)

Graded Potential (p. 46)
Heredity (p. 78)
Hormones (p. 75)
Huntington's Disease (p. 79)
Hypothalamus (p. 63)
Intracranial Self-Stimulation (p. 54)
Lateralization of Function (p. 67)
Limbic System (p. 63)
Magnetic Resonance Imaging (MRI) (p. 59)
Medulla (p. 62)
Midbrain (p. 62)
Mitosis (p. 79)
Nervous System (p. 55)
Neurons (p. 45)
Neurotransmitters (p. 47)
Nodes of Ranvier (p. 47)
Occipital Lobe (p. 66)
Parasympathetic Nervous System (p. 56)

Parietal Lobe (p. 65)
Parkinson's Disease (p. 51)
Peripheral Nervous System (p. 55)
Phenylketonuria (PKU) (p. 80)
Pituitary Gland (p. 63)
Pons (p. 62)
Positron Emission Tomography (PET) (p. 60)
Reticular Activating System (p. 62)
Somatic Nervous System (p. 56)
SQUID (Superconducting Quantum Interference Device) (p. 60)
Sympathetic Nervous System (p. 56)
Synapse (p. 46)
Synaptic Vesicles (p. 47)
Temporal Lobe (p. 66)
Thalamus (p. 63)
Wernicke-Geschwind Theory (p. 72)

Critical Thinking Questions

Appraisal

Throughout this chapter, we have seen that our thoughts, feelings, and actions all stem from basic biological processes. Do you think that all of our conscious experience can be reduced to electrochemical events? If so, why? If not, offer an alternative view.

Controversy

Scientists are now able to tinker with the genetic code of our species. For example, it is now possible to determine whether there are genetic abnormalities in the sperm and/or egg. What ethical issues does this raise? What are your views on this issue?

Making Psychology Part of Your Life

Perhaps you know someone who has suffered traumatic brain injury. Now that you understand the difficult path such a person faces during rehabilitation, what are some ways in which you can use the information in this chapter to improve the TBI patient's quality of life?

Weblink

Check out our Companion Website at www.pearsoned.ca/baron for additional Websites, activities, and more.

The Whole Brain Atlas

www.med.harvard.edu/AANLIB/home.html

Maintained by Keith A. Johnson, M.D., and J. Alex Becker, this fascinating site includes a neuroimaging primer, an atlas of the normal brain, and sections on cerebrovascular disease (stroke), degenerative and infectious diseases of the brain, and brain tumours.

Brain Ventricles: Our Internal Lake

www.epub.org.br/cm/n02/fundamentos/ventriculos_i.htm

Here you will find lots of diagrams of the brain spaces that contain cerebrospinal fluid. Follow the link to hydrocephalus to find many diagrams and a clear explanation of what happens when there is excess CSF.

The External Architecture of the Brain

www.epub.org.br/cm/n01/arquitet/architecture_i.htm

At this address you will find many illustrations of the cerebral cortex and the layered structure of the outside covering of the brain. You will read also about brain function as it is related to cortical organization.

Neurons: Our Internal Galaxy

www.epub.org.br/cm/n07/fundamentos/neuron/rosto_i.htm

Here there are animated illustrations of neurons and the way in which they work. You will even find a Gallery of Neurons from different locations within the brain.

Concussion in Sports: Return to Play Guidelines

www.obia.on.ca/retnplay.html

These are guidelines, approved by the Canadian Hockey Association, for return to sports after concussion. On this Website of the Ontario Brain Injury Association you will find other information about traumatic brain injury as well.

Chapter 3

Sensation and Perception:

Making Contact with the World around Us

CHAPTER OUTLINE

Remote Smell

"You smell iSmell"—an article with that title in *The Telegram* (St. John's, Newfoundland) predicts that, by December, people playing computer video games will be able not only to see and hear what is going on, but also to smell it. For example, when the game takes you to a jungle or on a mad automobile ride, you will be able to smell the vegetation or the burn of the rubber on the road.

By turning smells into digital codes, it may be possible in the future to send the smell of chocolate or flowers by e-mail or to create advertisements that include odours as well as visual images and words. In addition to clip art and clip sounds, our word processing software may come with clip smells!

Why would this make any difference to us? Because vision, hearing, smell, taste, and touch are sensory systems that monitor the external environment for us. The real world that each of us experiences is constructed from the information gathered by these sensory modalities. In Chapter 3, you will learn about all of those and about how they contribute to the reality we experience— whether that be in the fantasy world of video games or in real life.

You smell iSmell. 2000, March 4. *The Telegram*, p. 25.

Making sense of the world around us is a complicated business.

Have you ever wondered why certain smells trigger scenes long since forgotten? Why does bath water that initially "scalds" us feel soothing only moments later? Do you know why the moon appears large on the horizon, but smaller overhead? Do you believe in ESP? If you've wondered about phenomena like these, then you're already aware that making sense of the world around us is a complicated business. Indeed, the mystery of how we sense and interpret events in our environment constitutes one of the oldest fields of study in psychology. Careful psychological research conducted over several decades has shown that we do not understand the external world in a simple, automatic way. Rather, we actively construct our interpretation of sensory information through several complex processes.

Understanding the information conveyed to us by our various senses is a complicated process. To clarify how we do it, psychologists distinguish between two key concepts: sensation and perception. The study of **sensation** is concerned with the initial contact between organisms and their physical environment. It focuses on describing the relationship between various forms of sensory stimulation (including electromagnetism, sound waves, and pressure) and how these inputs are registered by our sense organs (the eyes, ears, nose, tongue, and skin). In contrast, the study of **perception** is concerned with identifying the processes through which we interpret and organize sensory information to produce our conscious experience of objects and object relationships. It is important to remember that perception is not simply a passive process of decoding incoming sensory information. If this were the case, we would lose the richness of our everyday stream-of-conscious experiences. We actively elaborate the sensory information registered on our receptors. Suppose we glance outside our window on a winter's day. Initially, we might see only trees and parked cars. A more detailed inspection might reveal that there is still a little snow left on the ground, that a woman is walking her dog in the distance, and perhaps that the door on the house across the road is painted a hideous yellow colour. The information provided by our senses remains constant during our brief inspection of the scene, but our perceptual representation of the scene becomes increasingly complex as our scrutiny continues.

The dual processes of sensation and perception play a role in virtually every topic we will consider in later chapters. For this reason, we will devote careful attention to them here. We'll begin by exploring in detail how the receptors for each sensory system convert raw physical energy into an electrochemical code. As we'll soon note, our sensory receptors are exquisitely designed to detect various aspects of the world around us. As part of our discussion, we'll consider the degree to which environmental circumstances, and internal subjective states, can influence our registration of sensory information—and whether cultural factors can affect the sensation of pain. Next, we'll turn our attention to the active process of perception. Here, we'll focus on how the brain integrates and interprets the constant flow of information it receives from our senses.

Sensation: Input about the physical world provided by our sensory receptors.

Perception: The process through which we select, organize, and interpret input from our sensory receptors.

Constructing the World Around Us: The "Active" Role of Perception

As illustrated by the *mis*-perception depicted in this cartoon, how we see ourselves and the world around us is the result of complex processes occurring within the nervous system.

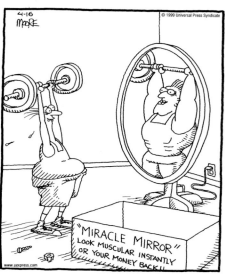

In our discussion of perception, we'll also consider roles heredity and experience play in configuring our perceptual processes. Finally, we'll attempt to determine if there is evidence to support one highly speculative perceptual domain—that of extrasensory perception or *psi.*

Sensation: The Raw Materials of Understanding

The sight of a breathtaking sunset, the taste of ice-cold lemonade on a hot day, the piercing sound of heavy metal music, the soothing warmth of a steamy bath ... exactly how are we able to experience these events? As you may recall from Chapter 2, all of these sensory experiences are based on complex processes occurring within the nervous system. This fact highlights an intriguing paradox: Although we are continually bombarded by various forms of physical energy, including light, heat, sound, and smells, our brain cannot directly detect the presence of these forces. Rather, it can only respond to intricate patterns of action potentials conducted by neurons, special cells that receive, move, and process sensory information. Thus, a critical question is how the many forms of physical energy impacting our sensory systems are converted into signals our nervous system can understand.

Highly specialized cells known as **sensory receptors**, located in our eyes, ears, nose, tongue, and elsewhere, are responsible for accomplishing this coding task. The sights, sounds, and smells that we experience are actually the product of **transduction**, a process in which the physical properties of stimuli are converted into neural signals that are then transmitted to our brain via specialized sensory nerves. To illustrate how our nervous system makes sense out of the surging sea of physical energies in our environment, we'll begin by focusing on two critical concepts: *thresholds* and *sensory adaptation.*

Sensory Thresholds

Although we are immersed in sensory information, we thrive rather than drown. Our bodies seem so well prepared to deal with this ocean of information that if, for some reason, the flow of sensory input is diminished, we sometimes hallucinate to fill the void. To illustrate, consider the complex visual hallucinations that some people experience when their eyesight deteriorates. This disorder is called Bonnet's syndrome after Charles Bonnet, who described the elaborate hallucinations reported by his grandfather, who, although well in all other respects, was losing his sight. Schulz and Melzack (1991) of McGill University attribute these hallucinations to spontaneous internal patterns of neural activity generated by the visual system in the face of diminished external sensory stimulation.

Although we are normally bombarded by sensory information, there are times when it is important for us to discern the faintest of sensations. What is the slightest amount of stimulation that our sensory systems can detect? In other words, how much physical stimulation is necessary in order for us to experience a sensation? Actually, surprisingly little for most aspects of sensation. We can hear a watch tick six metres away in a quiet room; we can smell a single drop of perfume in an empty three-room apartment; and on a clear, dark night, we can see a dim candle 48 kilometres away (Galanter, 1962).

Despite the remarkable efficiency of our receptors, they do not register all the information available in the environment at any given moment. We are able to smell and taste certain chemicals but not others, we hear sound waves only at certain frequencies, and our ability to detect light energy is restricted to a relatively narrow band of wavelengths. As Coren, Ward, and Enns (1999) of the University of British Columbia point out, the range of physical stimuli that we and other

Sensory Receptors: Cells specialized for the task of transduction—converting physical energy (light, sound) into neural impulses.

Transduction: The translation of a physical energy into electrical signals by specialized receptor cells.

species can detect seems to be designed in a way that maximizes survival potential. Thus it is not surprising that our auditory system is best at detecting sound frequencies that closely match those of human speech—given the importance of language to human existence.

ABSOLUTE THRESHOLDS For more than a century, psychologists have conducted studies to determine the level of sensitivity in each sensory system. To do this, they have used a variety of procedures called *psychophysical methods*. These procedures allow psychologists to determine the smallest magnitude of a stimulus that can be reliably discriminated from no stimulus at all 50 percent of the time; this is called the **absolute threshold.** To understand how absolute thresholds for our sensory systems have been explored, consider the following example. Suppose researchers at the Moose Jaw Chewing Gum Company have discovered a new way to make the flavour in gum last forever. The process is simple and inexpensive but has a minor flaw: A critical ingredient, substance SOUR, escapes detection in low concentrations, but in larger concentrations makes the gum taste terrible.

To determine the absolute threshold for detection of SOUR, Moose Jaw researchers select several concentrations; the lowest is clearly below threshold (nobody tastes the SOUR), and the highest causes the tasters to spit out the gum. Then volunteers chew many samples of gum with different concentrations of SOUR. The concentration at which the volunteers detect SOUR 50 percent of the time is the absolute threshold; it follows that the concentration of SOUR in the final product should fall *below* this level.

SOME COMPLICATIONS OF ABSOLUTE THRESHOLDS We often assume there is a direct relationship between the presence of a physical stimulus and the resulting sensation. Thus, given a stimulus of sufficient intensity, we should always be able to detect its presence. Unfortunately, as shown in the SOUR example, this relationship is not so simple. Why? One reason is that our sensitivity to stimuli changes from moment to moment. A stimulus we can detect at one time will not necessarily be detected by us later. For this reason, psychologists have arbitrarily defined the absolute threshold as that magnitude of physical energy we can detect 50 percent of the time.

Although this definition takes account of fluctuations in our sensitivity to various stimuli, it does not explain *why* such fluctuations occur. There are actually several reasons. First, our bodies are constantly adjusting in order to maintain their internal environment at optimal levels, a state termed *homeostasis*. It is not surprising that as a result of these adjustments, the sensitivity of our sensory organs to external stimuli also varies. Second, motivational factors such as the rewards or costs associated with detecting various stimuli play a role. For example, the outcome of the SOUR study might have been different if the participants had been faced with the prospect of being fired for a "wrong" decision.

Signal detection theory suggests that complex decision mechanisms are involved whenever we try to determine if we have or have not detected a specific stimulus (Swets, 1992). For instance, imagine that you are a radiologist. While scanning a patient's X-ray, you think you detect a faint spot on the film, but you're not quite sure. What should you do? If you conclude that the spot is an abnormality, you must order more scans or tests—an expensive and time-consuming alternative. If further testing reveals an abnormality, such as cancer, you may have saved the patient's life. If no abnormality is detected, though, you'll be blamed for wasting resources and unnecessarily upsetting the patient. Alternatively, if you decide the spot is *not* an abnormality, there's no reason to order more tests. If the patient remains healthy, then you've done the right thing. If the spot is really cancerous tissue, however, the results could be fatal.

Absolute Threshold: The smallest amount of a stimulus that we can detect 50 percent of the time.

Signal Detection Theory: A theory suggesting that there are no absolute thresholds for sensations. Rather, detection of stimuli depends on their physical energy and on internal factors such as the relative costs and benefits associated with detecting their presence.

Your decision in this scenario is likely to be influenced by the rewards and costs associated with each alternative. Because of the potentially deadly consequences, you may be tempted to order more tests, even if the spot on the X-ray is extremely faint. But what if you are new in the field and you have just gone deeply into debt buying a house for your growing family? The fear of making a decision that could jeopardize your position may weigh more heavily in the balance; you may avoid reporting the spot unless you are quite certain you saw it.

In summary, deciding whether we have detected a given stimulus is not always easy. These decisions often involve much more than a simple determination of the relationship between the amount of physical energy present in a stimulus and the resulting psychological sensations.

DIFFERENCE THRESHOLDS: ARE TWO STIMULI THE SAME OR DIFFERENT? A good cook tastes a dish, then adds salt to it, then tastes it again to measure the change. This suggests another basic question relating to our sensory capacities: How much change in a stimulus is required before a shift can be noticed? Psychologists refer to the amount of change in a stimulus required for a person to detect it as the **difference threshold**. Obviously, the smaller the change we can detect, the greater our sensitivity. In other words, the difference threshold is the amount of change in a physical stimulus necessary to produce a **just noticeable difference (jnd)** in sensation. As it turns out, our ability to detect differences in stimulus intensity depends on the magnitude of the initial stimulus; we easily detect even small changes in weak stimuli, but we require much larger changes before we notice differences in strong stimuli. If you are listening to your favourite tunes at a low sound intensity, even small adjustments to the volume are noticeable. But if you are listening to very loud music, much larger changes are required before a difference is apparent. As you might guess, we are also more sensitive to changes in some types of stimuli than to changes in others. For example, we are able to notice very small shifts in temperature (less than 1 degree Celsius) and in the pitch of sounds (a useful ability for people who tune musical instruments), but we are somewhat less sensitive to changes in loudness or in smells.

STIMULI BELOW THRESHOLD: CAN THEY HAVE AN EFFECT? For decades, **subliminal perception** has been a source of controversy. Subliminal perception first captured the public's attention in the 1950s when a marketing executive announced he had embedded subliminal messages like "Eat popcorn" and "Drink Coke" into a then popular movie. Supposedly, the embedded messages were flashed on the screen in front of movie audiences so briefly (a fraction of a second) that audience members were not aware of them (Brean, 1958). Although the executive later confessed to the hoax (no messages were actually presented), many people remained convinced that subliminal messages can be powerful sources of persuasion.

During the 1980s, public attention was again drawn to the issue of subliminal perception, this time in response to concerns over backward masking, a procedure in which "evil" messages are recorded backward and embedded into songs on rock albums. In a highly publicized trial, subliminally embedded messages were alleged to be instrumental in the suicides of two young men. The judge in the case eventually dismissed the charges, citing a lack of evidence that the messages actually *caused* the shootings, (*Vance et al. v. Judas Priest et al.*, 1990).

An important question raised by these incidents is whether we can sense or be affected by stimuli that remain outside our conscious awareness (Greenwald, 1992; Merikle, 1992). The most direct answer to this question seems to come from studies that have used a technique called *visual priming*. In a typical experiment,

Difference Threshold: The amount of change in a stimulus required before a person can detect the shift.

Just Noticeable Difference (jnd): The smallest amount of change in a physical stimulus necessary for an individual to notice a difference in the intensity of the stimulus.

Subliminal Perception: The presumed ability to perceive a stimulus that is below the threshold for conscious experience.

Phillip Merikle
University of Waterloo

participants are "primed" with brief exposures (less than one-tenth of a second) to words or simple pictures. The duration of the exposure is long enough to be detected by the nervous system, but too brief for people to be consciously aware of its presence. Participants have great difficulty naming the visual "primes," but their reactions to stimuli presented subsequently (e.g., words or pictures) do seem to be affected (Merikle & Daneman, 1998). Indeed, systematic research has demonstrated that subliminally presented visual stimuli can measurably influence our evaluation of ambiguous stimuli (Murphy & Zajonc, 1993), and our evaluation of words (Greenwald et al., 1996). For example, people primed with the word *happy* tend to rate the target word *kiss* as more pleasant than persons primed with the word *vomit*. The results of these studies suggest that the priming stimuli, despite their brief duration, are registered at some level within the nervous system. (Psychologists also use priming to study certain aspects of memory; see Chapter 6.)

New research is beginning to reveal how subliminal stimuli—stimuli sufficiently intense to be registered by the nervous system, but outside our conscious awareness—are processed by the brain. In one recent study, Bar and Biederman (1998) primed participants by presenting very brief exposures of pictures of common objects. Participants were required to name each object as it was presented. As expected, they performed poorly on this task, correctly naming about 13 percent of the objects shown. After a delay of 15 minutes, and other intervening presentations, a second equally brief presentation of either the identical objects, or similar objects, occurred (for example, they might view a kitchen chair on the first presentation, but an office chair the second time). The second presentation was made at either the same or a different location. The participants viewing the same objects in their original location showed an approximately three-fold increase in naming accuracy. Viewing the same objects at different locations also resulted in a significant, albeit less pronounced, increase in naming accuracy. Naming accuracy for similar objects did not increase. These data suggest that subliminal visual primes manage to partially activate visual representational centres, and that traces of this activation can endure for a substantial period of time and serve to facilitate subsequent recognition of an object.

Do recent research findings mean that subliminal messages can influence what we do and how we act? The answer is no. Although we have seen that they can influence our affective assessment of a stimulus under rather highly constrained laboratory conditions, and they can facilitate recognition, there is no evidence that subliminal messages can impel or motivate us to directly think or act in a particular manner or fashion. Contrary to claims of promoters of self-help materials that promise subliminal suggestion can assist people in losing weight, stopping smoking, increasing their intelligence, or improving their sex life, the evidence indicates this does not happen (Greenwald, et al., 1991; Urban, 1992).

Sensory Adaptation

Nova Scotia is very nearly surrounded by the Atlantic Ocean. Anyone putting a toe in the ocean water on a Nova Scotia beach is in for a shock—it's cold! This does not stop native Nova Scotians, and some brave tourists, from plunging in for a swim on warm summer days … and claiming to enjoy the experience. The initial shock of the icy water is traumatic, but eventually it feels refreshing. This type of experience illustrates the process of **sensory adaptation**—the fact that our sensitivity to an unchanging stimulus tends to decrease over time. When we first encounter a stimulus, like icy water, our temperature receptors fire vigorously. Soon, however, they fire less vigorously, and through the process of sensory adaptation, the water begins to feel just right.

Sensory adaptation has some practical advantages. If it did not occur, we would constantly be distracted by the stream of sensations we experience each day.

Sensory Adaptation: Reduced sensitivity to unchanging stimuli over time.

We would not adapt to our clothing rubbing our skin, to the feel of our tongue in our mouth, or to bodily processes such as eye blinks and swallowing. However, sensory adaptation is not always beneficial and can even be dangerous. For instance, after about a minute our sensitivity to most odours drops by nearly 70 percent. Thus, in situations where smoke or harmful chemicals are present, sensory adaptation may actually reduce our awareness of existing dangers. In general, though, the process of sensory adaptation allows us to focus on changes in the world around us, and that ability to focus on and respond to stimulus change is usually what is most important for survival.

Now that we've considered some basic aspects of sensation, let's examine in detail each of the major senses.

Sensory Adaptation

Have you ever jumped into the icy waters of a mountain lake, or the chilly ocean off the coast of Nova Scotia? At first the water feels freezing, but later it feels refreshing. This is an example of sensory adaptation.

KEY QUESTIONS

- What is the primary function of our sensory receptors?
- What does the term *absolute threshold* refer to, and why is signal detection theory important?
- What is a difference threshold?
- Can subliminal messages affect what we do or how we act?
- What is the role of sensory adaptation in sensation?

Vision

Light, in the form of energy from the sun, is part of the fuel that drives the engine of life on earth. Thus, it is not surprising that we possess exquisitely adapted organs for detecting this stimulus: our eyes. Indeed, for most of us, sight is the most important way of gathering information about the world. Figure 3.1 shows a simplified diagram of the human eye.

The Eye: Its Basic Structure

How is light energy converted into signals our brain can understand? The answer lies in the basic structure of the eye. It is in the eye that light energy is converted into a neural code understandable to our nervous system. Light rays first pass through a transparent protective structure called the **cornea** and then enter the eye through the **pupil,** a round opening whose size varies with lighting conditions: the less light present, the wider the pupil opening (see Figure 3.1). These adjustments are executed by the **iris,** the coloured part of the eye, which is actually a circular muscle that contracts or expands to let in varying amounts of light. After entering through the pupil, light rays pass through the **lens,** a clear structure whose shape adjusts to permit us to focus on objects at varying distances. When we look at a distant object, the muscles of the lens relax, allowing it to become thinner and flatter; when we look at a nearby object, those muscles contract, making the lens thicker and rounder. Light rays leaving the lens are projected on the **retina** at the back of the eyeball. As illustrated in Figure 3.2, the lens bends light rays in such a way that the image projected onto the retina is actually upside down and reversed; nevertheless the brain interprets this information in such a way the world seems upright and objects and people are positioned correctly.

Cornea: The curved, transparent layer through which light rays enter the eye.

Pupil: An opening in the eye, just behind the cornea, through which light rays enter the eye.

Iris: The coloured part of the eye that adjusts the amount of light that enters by constricting or dilating the pupil.

Lens: A curved structure behind the pupil that bends light rays, focusing them on the retina.

Retina: The surface at the back of the eye containing the rods and cones.

Figure 3.1
The Human Eye

The photoreceptors of the retina connect to higher brain pathways through the optic nerve. Light filters through layers of retinal cells before hitting the receptors (rods and cones), which are located at the back of the eye and pointed away from the incoming light. The rods and cones pass an electrical impulse to bipolar cells. Rods assist in night vision; cones are necessary for day vision, colour vision, and fine discrimination. Rods and cones relay the impulse to the ganglion cells. The axons of the ganglion cells form the fibres of the optic nerve.

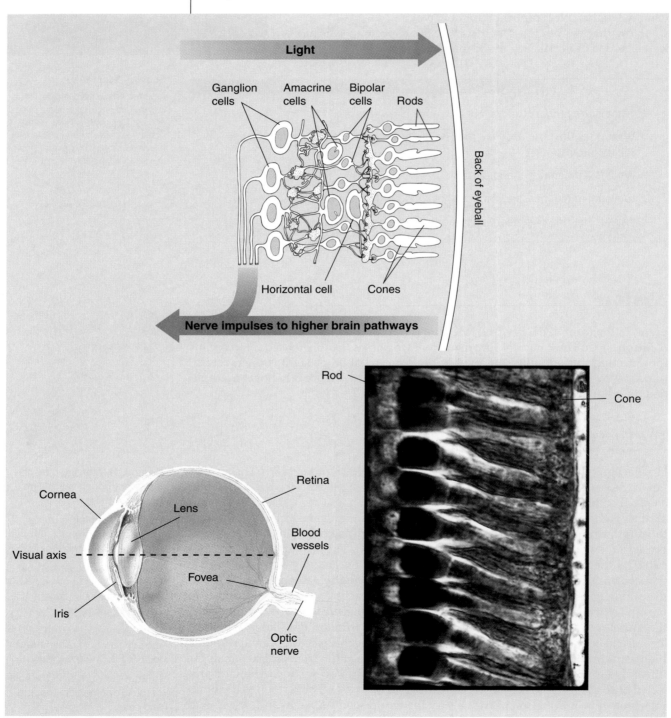

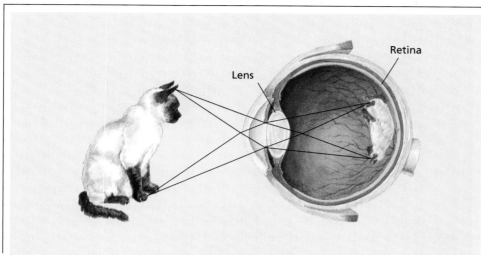

Figure 3.2
The Upside-Down and Reversed Image Projected onto Our Retina

The lens of our eye bends light rays entering our eye so that the image projected onto our retina is actually upside down and reversed: The light from the top of an object is projected onto receptors at the bottom of the retina, and light rays from the left side of an object are projected onto receptors on the right side of the retina. Our brain interprets this information so that we can see the object correctly.

The retina is actually a postage-stamp-sized structure that contains two types of light-sensitive receptor cells: about 6.5 million **cones** and about 100 million **rods**. Cones, located primarily in the centre of the retina in an area called the **fovea**, function best in bright light and play a key role both in colour vision and in our ability to notice fine detail. In contrast, rods are found only outside the fovea and function best under lower levels of illumination, so they help us to see in a darkened room or at night. At increasing distances from the fovea, the density of cones decreases and the density of rods increases. When stimulated, the rods and cones transmit neural information to other neurons called *bipolar cells*. These cells, in turn, contact other neurons, called *ganglion cells*. Axons from the ganglion cells converge to form the **optic nerve** and carry visual information to the brain. Interestingly, no receptors are present where this nerve exits the eye, so there is a **blind spot** at this point in our visual field. Try the exercise in Figure 3.3 to check your own blind spot.

Cones: Sensory receptors in the eye that play a crucial role in sensations of colour.

Rods: One of the two types of sensory receptors for vision found in the eye.

Fovea: The area in the centre of the retina in which cones are highly concentrated.

Optic Nerve: A bundle of nerve fibres that exit the back of the eye and carry visual information to the brain.

Blind Spot: The point in the back of the retina through which the optic nerve exits the eye. This exit point contains no rods or cones and is therefore insensitive to light.

Light: The Physical Stimulus for Vision

At this point we will consider some important facts about light, the physical stimulus for vision. First, the light that is visible to us is only a small portion of the

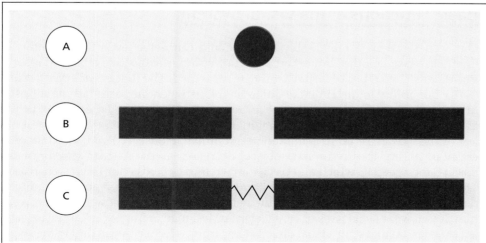

Figure 3.3
The Blind Spot

To find your blind spot, close your left eye and focus your right eye on the "A." Slowly move the page toward and away from your right eye until the dark spot on the right disappears. The image of this dot is now being projected onto the blind spot—the region of the retina where the nerve fibres group together and leave the eye. There are no rods or cones in this area of the retina. Now, follow the same procedure for "B" and "C." What do you see?

Figure 3.4
The Electromagnetic Spectrum

Visible light occupies only a narrow band in the entire spectrum.

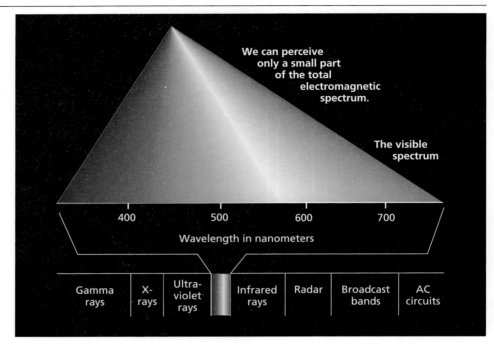

electromagnetic spectrum. This spectrum ranges from radio waves at the slow or long-wave end to cosmic rays at the fast or short-wave end (see Figure 3.4). Visible light occupies only a narrow band in the entire spectrum.

Second, certain physical properties of light contribute to our psychological experiences of vision. **Wavelength**, the distance between successive peaks and valleys of light energy, determines what we experience as **hue** or colour. As shown in Figure 3.4, as wavelength increases from about 400 to 700 nanometres (a nanometre is one-billionth of a metre), our sensations shift from violet through blue (shorter wavelengths), green, yellow, orange (medium wavelengths), and finally red (longer wavelengths). The intensity of light—the amount of energy it contains—is experienced as **brightness**. The extent to which light contains only one wavelength, rather than many, determines our experience of **saturation**; the fewer the number of wavelengths mixed together, the more saturated or "pure" a colour appears. For example, the deep red of an apple is highly saturated, whereas the pale pink of an apple blossom is low in saturation.

Basic Functions of the Visual System

Our visual system is remarkably sensitive and can detect even tiny amounts of light. However, another important aspect of vision is acuity, the ability to resolve fine details. Two types of visual acuity are measured. The first is *static visual acuity (SVA)*, our ability to discriminate different objects when they are stationary or static, as on the familiar chart at an eye doctor's office. The second measure of acuity is *dynamic visual acuity (DVA)*, our ability to resolve detail when either the test object or the viewer, or both, is in motion (Houfman, House, & Ryan, 1981). In general, our ability to discriminate objects decreases as the *angular velocity* of the object—the speed at which an object's image moves across our retina—increases. This aspect of our visual capacity is important in, for example, a goalie's ability to detect a puck fired at the corner of the net by a player flying down the ice toward him. If you wear eyeglasses or contact lenses designed to improve your visual acuity, chances are that your visual deficit stems from a slight abnormality in the shape of your eye. If your eyeball is too long, you suffer from **nearsightedness**, in which

Wavelength: The peak-to-peak distance in a sound or light wave.

Hue: The colour that we experience due to the dominant wavelength of a light.

Brightness: The physical intensity of light.

Saturation: The degree of concentration of the hue of light. We experience saturation as the purity of a colour.

Nearsightedness: A condition in which the visual image of a distant object is focused slightly in front of the retina rather than directly on it. Therefore, distant objects appear fuzzy or blurred, whereas near objects can be seen clearly.

you see near objects clearly but distant objects appear blurry. This occurs because the image entering your eye is focused slightly in front of the retina rather than directly on it. Similarly, in **farsightedness**, your eyeball is too short and the lens focuses the image behind the retina.

Another aspect of visual sensitivity is **dark adaptation**, the increase in sensitivity that occurs when we move from bright light to a dim environment, such as a movie theatre. The dark-adapted eye is about 100 000 times more sensitive to light than the light-adapted eye. Actually, dark adaptation occurs in two steps. First, within five to ten minutes, the cones reach their maximum sensitivity. After about ten minutes, the rods begin to adapt; they complete this process in about thirty minutes (Matlin & Foley, 1992).

Eye movements also play a role in visual acuity. To appreciate the importance of the ability to move your eyes, just imagine how inefficient it would be to read a book or play your favourite sport if your eyes were stuck in one position. In order to change the direction of your gaze, you would have to move your entire head.

Eye movements are of two basic types: *version movements*, in which the eyes move together in the same direction, and *vergence movements*, in which the lines of sight for the two eyes converge or diverge. As we'll discover later in this chapter, vergence movements are crucial to our ability to perceive distance and depth. Three types of version movements are *involuntary movements, saccadic movements,* and *pursuit movements.*

At the end of this sentence, stop reading and stare at the last word for several seconds. Did your eyes remain motionless or did they tend to move about? The eye movements you probably experienced were *involuntary*; they occurred without your conscious control. These movements ensure that the stimuli reaching our rods and cones are constantly changing. Like other sensory receptors, those in our retina are subject to the effects of sensory adaptation; if involuntary movements did not occur we would lose our capacity to see an object by fixing our gaze upon it for more than a few seconds. This can be readily demonstrated though the use of special contact lens devices such as those developed at McGill in the1960s (Pritchard, 1961). These devices cause the image of the object of regard to hold a fixed position on the retinal surface no matter how the eye moves The result is that the image of the object fades rapidly in and out—directly mirroring the process of receptor adaptation and recovery.

Saccadic movements are fast, frequent jumps by the eyes from one fixation point to the next. These movements serve to cause objects of interest to fall on the foveal area of the eye where they can be seen most clearly. Saccadic movements are apparent in reading or driving. Careful research has shown that both the size of the jumps and the region seen during each fixation affect the amount of information we glean while reading (Just & Carpenter, 1987; McConkie et al., 1989; McConkie & Zola, 1984). Moreover, the saccadic movements of good readers move smoothly across the materials being read; those of poor readers are shorter and move backward as well as forward (Schiffman, 1990). Finally, *pursuit movements* are smooth eye movements used to track moving objects, as when you watch a plane fly overhead and out of sight.

Colour Vision

A world without colour would be sadly limited, for colour—vivid reds, glowing yellows, restful greens—is a crucial part of our visual experience. For many people, though, some degree of colour deficiency is a fact of life. Nearly 8 percent of males and 0.4 percent of females are less sensitive than the rest of us either to red and green or to yellow and blue (Nathans, 1989). And a few individuals are totally colour blind, experiencing the world only in varying shades of white, black, and grey. Intriguing evidence on how the world appears to people suffering from colour

Farsightedness: A condition in which the visual image of a nearby object is focused behind rather than directly on the retina. Therefore, close objects appear out of focus, while distant objects are seen clearly.

Dark Adaptation: The process by which the visual system increases its sensitivity to light under low illumination.

Saccadic Movements: Quick movements of the eyes from one point of fixation to another.

Figure 3.5
A Simple Test of Colour Vision

What do you see in this circle? People who have normal colour vision see the number 5; those who have a colour weakness may not.

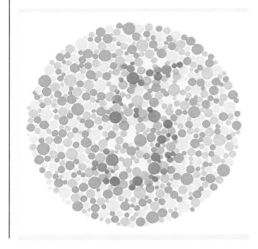

Trichromatic Theory: A theory of colour perception suggesting that we have three types of cones, each primarily receptive to particular wavelengths of light.

Negative Afterimage: A sensation of complementary colour that we experience after staring at a stimulus of a given hue.

Opponent-Process Theory: A theory that describes the processing of sensory information related to colour at levels above the retina. The theory suggests that we possess six types of neurons, each of which is either stimulated or inhibited by red, green, blue, yellow, black, or white.

weakness has been gathered from rare cases in which individuals have normal colour vision in one eye and impaired colour vision in the other (e.g., Graham & Hsia, 1958). For example, one such woman indicated that to her colour-impaired eye, all colours between red and green appeared yellow, while all colours between green and violet seemed blue. See Figure 3.5 to check your own colour vision.

There are two leading theories to explain our rich sense of colour. The first, **trichromatic theory**, suggests that we have three different types of cones in our retinas, each of which is maximally sensitive, though not exclusively so, to a particular range of light wavelength—a range roughly corresponding to blue (450–500 nanometres), green (500–570 nanometres), or red (620–700 nanometres). Careful study of the human retina suggests that we do possess three types of receptors, although as Figure 3.6 shows, there is a great deal of overlap in each receptor type's sensitivity range (DeValois & DeValois, 1975; Rushton, 1975).

According to trichromatic theory, our ability to perceive colours results from the joint action of the three receptor types. Thus, light of a particular wavelength produces differential stimulation of each receptor type, and it is the overall pattern of stimulation that produces our rich sense of colour. This differential sensitivity may be due to genes that direct different cones to produce pigments sensitive to blue, green, or red (Nathans, Thomas, & Hogness, 1986).

Trichromatic theory, however, fails to account for certain aspects of colour vision, such as the occurrence of **negative afterimages**—sensations of complementary colours that occur after one stares at a stimulus of a given colour. For example, after you stare at a green object, if you shift your gaze to a neutral background, sensations of red will follow. Similarly, after you stare at a yellow stimulus, sensations of blue will follow. (Figure 3.7 demonstrates negative afterimage.)

The **opponent-process theory** addresses phenomena like afterimages more effectively than the trichromatic theory. It does so by introducing the idea that there are special-purpose *opponent-process cells* in the retina and in post-retinal brain centres that further elaborate information conveyed by the three different types of cones in the retina. Although opponent-process theory suggests that six kinds of cells play a role in regulating our black-and-white and colour experience (DeValois & DeValois, 1975), a relatively clear picture of the operations involved can be obtained by considering three of the six different opponent-process cell types. What has to be kept in mind is that an opponent-process cell is unique in that the same cell can transmit two different signals to higher cortical colour-processing centres—depending on whether it is excited or inhibited. Examples of the two main types of colour opponent-process cells are illustrated in Figure 3.8. As may be seen, one of the cells, the Y− B+ cell, signals the presence of yellow when it receives inhibitory input from red and green receptors, and signals the presence of blue if it receives excitatory input from the blue receptor. The other G− R+ cell signals the presence of green if it receives inhibitory input from green receptors, and the presence of red if it receives excitatory input from red receptors. A third type of opponent-process cell, the black-white achromatic cell, captures brightness and determines whether the colour we are seeing is rich and pure, or faded and washed out. Opponent-process theory is particularly useful in explaining the occurrence of negative afterimages (Jameson & Hurvich, 1989). The idea is that if one component of an opponent pair is stimulated to the point of exhaustion, the other component of the pair becomes dominant. Thus, if the satiating stimulus was green, the afterimage seen would be red.

The opponent-process and trichromatic theories have competed for many years. We now know that both are necessary to explain our impressive ability to respond to colour. Trichromatic theory explains how colour coding occurs in the cones of the retina, whereas opponent-process theory accounts for processing in higher-order nerve cells (Coren & Ward; 1989; Hurvich, 1981; Matlin & Foley, 1992).

Processing Visual Information

Our rich sense of vision does not result from the output of single neurons, but instead from the overall pattern of our sensory receptors. In other words, there is more to vision than meets the eye. But how, then, do the simple action potentials of individual neurons contribute to our overall conscious experience? To help answer this question, let's consider how the brain "generates" our visual world.

At one time it was believed that visual scenes in our environment were impressed onto our retinas, much like images on photographic plates, and transmitted directly to the brain. We now know this view is incorrect. In reality, the rich tapestry of our visual experience is generated by a progressive elaboration of information inherent in the light falling upon the retinal surface. Our understanding of the initial stages of this process was greatly advanced by the Nobel Prize-winning series of studies conducted by Hubel and Wiesel (1979). These researchers conducted studies on **feature detectors**—neurons at various levels in the visual cortex that respond primarily to stimuli possessing certain features. Their work revealed the existence of three types of feature detectors. One group of neurons, known as **simple cells**, responds to bars or lines presented in certain orientations (horizontal, vertical, and so on). A second, higher-order group of **complex cells** responds most strongly to moving stimuli such as a vertical bar moving from left to right, or a tilted bar moving from right to left. Finally, a still higher-order group of **hypercomplex cells** respond to even more complex features of the visual world, such as length, width, and even aspects of shape, like corners and angles. These cells may fail to respond to a thin bar moving from right to left, but may respond strongly to a thick bar moving from lower to higher regions of the visual field. Or they may respond to a shape containing a right angle but fail to respond to one containing an acute angle. Higher-order cells receive their input from lower-order cells. The basic notion is that the brain processes visual information hierarchically. According to this view, critical aspects or features of the visual world are detected by groups of neurons that send their results to other groups of neurons for further analysis, and this process continues through many stages. At each successive stage in this multi-stage process, an increasingly complex representation of the visual information falling on the retina is generated.

What has to be realized is that the light falling on our retinas is full of information about the world around us. In fact, there is so much information, and so little time to interpret it, that the visual system must pluck out information about salient aspects of our environment (e.g., form, motion, depth, and colour) simultaneously. The current point of view is that information about the various salient properties of the visual domain is extracted by relatively separate and distinct

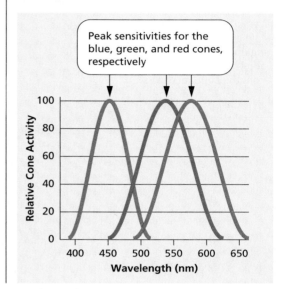

Figure 3.6
Three Types of Receptors Contribute to Our Perception of Colour

Colour vision appears to be mediated by three types of cones, each maximally (but not exclusively) sensitive to wavelengths corresponding to blue, green, and red.

Source: Adapted from MacNichol, 1964.

Feature Detectors: Neurons at various levels within the visual cortex that respond primarily to stimuli possessing certain features.

Simple Cells: Cells within the visual system that respond to linear shapes presented in certain orientations (horizontal, vertical, etc.).

Complex Cells: Neurons in the visual cortex that respond to stimuli moving in a particular direction and having a particular orientation.

Hypercomplex Cells: Neurons in the visual cortex that respond to complex aspects of visual stimuli, such as width, length, and shape.

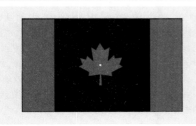

Figure 3.7
Demonstration of a Negative Afterimage

Stare at the object on the left for about one minute. Then shift your gaze to the blank space at the right. Do you see a negative afterimage?

Figure 3.8
The Role of Opponent Processing in Colour Vision

Cone cells from the retina convey information to opponent-process cells to post-retinal brain centres. Opponent-process cells provide higher cortical colour-processing centres with more precise information about the character of colours that are present, depending upon whether they are excited or inhibited by input they receive from the cone receptors.

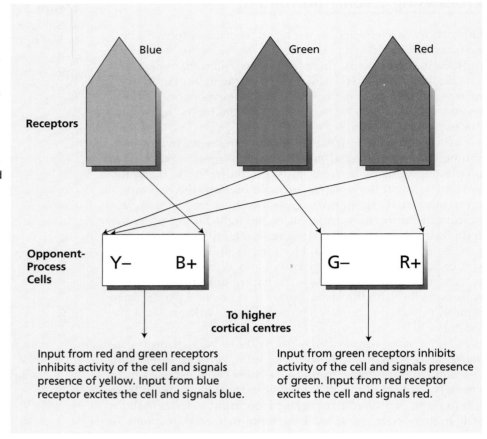

processing systems within the visual system. Information from the various specialized systems is finally assembled to produce the coherent and flowing scenes that constitute perception of the world around us (Zeki, 1993).

If there are separate and distinct processing systems for salient aspects of the visual world such as shape, form, depth, movement, and colour, one would expect that brain injury could selectively disable one system or more and leave the others untouched. This is what is found. A remarkable case reported by Zihl, von Cramon, and Mai (1983) describes a woman who became unable to perceive movement, but was otherwise unimpaired. As would be expected, she had great difficulty coping with everyday tasks. She could not pour herself a glass of juice because she was unable to follow the movement of the liquid filling the cup. She was also unable to cope with traffic on a busy street because she could not see the movement of the cars. She would see an approaching car initially at a substantial distance and then, suddenly, it would appear in front of her. She was unable to discern the intervening movement of the car.

It is likely that there are separate and distinct processing systems for many more visual functions than shape, form, motion, and colour. Some thirty distinct visual areas have been identified using a wide variety of different brain imaging techniques (Felleman & Van Essen, 1991), and it is known that some very selective visual deficits can occur after brain injury. In **prosopagnosia,** for example, there is selective loss of the ability to identify faces—including the patient's own face, but no difficulty in identifying other visual objects. **Blindsight,** is another rare condition that results from damage to the primary visual cortex. Persons with blindsight are able to respond to certain aspects of visual stimuli, such as colour or movement, as if they could see; yet, paradoxically, they are completely unaware of the stimuli

Prosopagnosia: A rare condition in which brain damage impairs a person's ability to recognize faces.

Blindsight: A rare condition resulting from damage to the primary visual cortex in which individuals report being blind, yet respond to certain aspects of visual stimuli as if they could see.

and deny having "seen" anything (Gazzaniga et al., 1994; Weiskrantz, 1995). See the **Canadian Focus** feature for some useful additional insight into the position that there are separate and distinct processing systems for different visual functions.

From all of this, what overall conclusions can be drawn about how the visual system works? First, the visual system seems to be highly selective; certain types

Canadian Focus

Grasping What Cannot Be Seen: A Case Study

Mel Goodale
University of Western Ontario

Case studies of individuals with brain injury have repeatedly provided researchers with important information about how visual information is processed. Sometimes case studies provide unexpected insights into the functioning of the visual system. A particularly interesting example is provided in a series of reports by Melvyn Goodale of the University of Western Ontario (Goodale, 1996; Goodale, Milner, Jakobson, & Carey, 1991).

We typically assume we must consciously understand the visual world in order to interact with it. If, for example, you were asked to explain how you would go about picking up a letter opener on your desk, you would probably reply that you would look at the letter opener, discern its shape and orientation, then move your hand toward the letter opener adjusting the position of your fingers and wrist during the movement so as to be able to grasp it appropriately. The act of reaching for and grasping an object appears to require conscious attention to the shape, size, and orientation of the sought-after object ... or does it?

Goodale began to wonder whether picking up an object depended on being consciously aware of the shape and size of the object after observing a patient in one of his research projects. The patient, known as D.F., is a woman of above-average intelligence whose visual system has been selectively damaged by carbon monoxide poisoning. Her visual system is able to register visual information, but she is unable to make sense of, or understand, what she is seeing. When presented with common objects or simple forms, she cannot identify, or describe, what she is being shown. What is surprising is that she has no difficulty in reaching out and directly grasping the very object that she is unable to identify. Goodale observed that during the course of her reaching movement, her hand and wrist position seemed to automatically adjust so as to ensure that the object would be gripped appropriately. This suggested that at some level D.F. had to be registering information about the size and orientation of the object.

To examine D.F.'s abilities more fully, Goodale carried out a series of studies. In the first study, Goodale presented pairs of domino-type forms to D.F. and normal-sighted control sub-

jects. The forms used all had the same surface area but differed markedly in shape, some being square and others extremely rectilinear. In some trials the two forms presented were identical, and in others the two forms presented were very different in shape. The task was simple: decide whether the two forms were identical or different in shape. Normal-sighted control subjects had no difficulty reporting whether the forms presented were the same or different, but D.F. was unable to perform above chance level on this task, indicating that she was not capable of consciously discerning the shape of the forms presented.

A second study was carried out to demonstrate that D.F. was also unable to discriminate the size of these same forms. A single form was presented within reaching distance of both D.F. and control subjects. Their task was to look at the form presented and estimate by adjusting the distance between their index finger and their thumb the width of the form. Control subjects had no difficulty with this task but D.F. was quite unable to perform the task, confirming that she was unaware of both the size as well as the shape of forms presented to her.

A final test required D.F. and control subjects to reach out and pick up the various forms. Special devices were attached to the thumbs and index fingers of both D.F. and the control subjects, and these devices allowed continuous monitoring of any changes in the position of the subjects' index fingers and thumbs as they reached out to pick up the forms. Computer analysis showed that on this task, D.F. and the control subjects did not differ. D.F. appropriately adjusted the distance between her index finger and thumb so as to precisely capture the form well before she came into contact with it.

How can the seeming contradiction between D.F.'s inability to recognize or describe an object in front of her, and her ability to reach out and pick up that same object (automatically adjusting her grasp during the act of reaching to compensate for its size and orientation), be explained? Goodale contends that there are two visual systems involved in the processing of visual information about the location, size, and orientation of objects. One system, which he refers to as the *ventral system,* is held responsible for consciously cataloguing and describing the properties of objects. The other, which he refers to as the *dorsal system,* is held responsible for visually regulating our bodily interactions with objects. Injuries to D.F.'s ventral system prevent her from becoming cognitively aware of the visual properties of objects she is aware of in front of her, but her intact dorsal system allows her to reach out and appropriately adjust her grasp to capture objects she cannot describe. Goodale's position is much strengthened by the discovery of a second patient, R.V., with an apparently intact ventral system and damaged dorsal system. This patient's behaviour is exactly opposite to D.F.'s. R.V. can readily identify and provide a detailed description of an object in front of her, but she is unable to appropriately adjust her hand to pick up that object until she comes into physical contact with it.

Why are Goodale's findings important? They are important because they correct a common assumption that there is just one central visual system that is responsible for monitoring each and every aspect of our visual experience. Goodale's findings support the view that there are many functionally independent systems working in parallel to extract visual information and regulate behaviour.

of visual features stand a greater chance of reaching the brain and undergoing further processing. Second, cells that are equipped to detect certain features of the external world likely constitute the building blocks for the production of the complex visual shapes and forms of everyday existence. Third, visual information is processed hierarchically: groups of neurons that register critical features of the visual world convey this information to other neurons for further analysis and elaboration, and this process continues through many stages. Fourth, there are a multitude of special-purpose processing systems that work in parallel to simultaneously extract information about significant aspects of our visual domain (as we saw in Goodale's study). Finally, it seems clear that the seemingly simple act of "seeing" is a complex process that requires integration across many levels and processing systems.

KEY QUESTIONS

- What are the basic structures of the eye and what is the physical stimulus for vision?

- What are the basic functions of the visual system?

- How do psychologists explain colour perception?

- Why is visual perception a hierarchical process?

- What are the basic building blocks of visual perception?

- What evidence suggests that separate and distinct processing systems work independently to extract information about important aspects of the visual world?

Critical Thinking

Are the same visual system structures that allow us to make sense of our sensory experience employed when we engage in other mental activities, such as mental imagery and dreaming?

Hearing

The clamour of laughing voices, the sound of a jet plane, the rustling of leaves, and that quintessential sound of the beginning of the twenty-first century—the ringing of a cell phone … clearly, we live in a world full of sound. And, as with vision, human beings are well equipped to receive many sounds in their environment. A simplified diagram of the human ear is shown in Figure 3.9; refer to it as you proceed through the discussion below.

Figure 3.9
The Human Ear

A simplified diagram of the human ear. Sound waves (alternating compressions and expansions in the air) enter through the external auditory canal and produce slight movements in the eardrum (tympanic membrane). This motion, in turn, produces movements in fluid within the cochlea. As this fluid moves, tiny hair cells shift their position, thus generating the nerve impulses we perceive as sound.

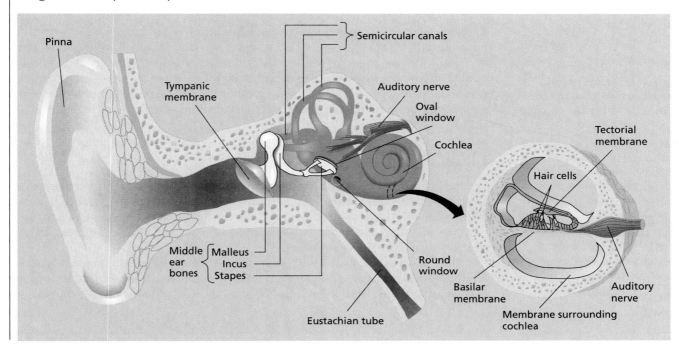

The Ear: Its Basic Structure

Try asking a friend, "When did you get your pinna pierced?" The response will probably be a blank stare. **Pinna** is the technical term for the visible part of our hearing organ, the *ear*. However, this is only a small part of the entire ear. Inside the ear is an intricate system of membranes, small bones, and receptor cells that transform sound waves into neural information for the brain. The *eardrum* (tympanic membrane), a thin piece of tissue just inside the ear, moves ever so slightly in response to sound waves striking it. When it moves, the eardrum causes three tiny bones within the *middle ear* to vibrate. The third of these bones is attached to a second membrane, the *oval window*, which covers a fluid-filled, spiral-shaped structure known as the **cochlea.** Vibration of the oval window causes movements of the fluid in the cochlea. Finally, the movement of fluid bends tiny *hair cells*, the true sensory receptors of sound. The neural messages they create are then transmitted to the brain via the *auditory nerve*.

Sound: The Physical Stimulus for Hearing

In discussing light, we noted that relationships exist between certain of its physical properties, such as wavelength and intensity, and psychological aspects of vision, including hue and brightness. Similar relationships exist for sound, at least with respect to two of its psychological qualities: *loudness* and *pitch*.

Pinna: The external portion of the ear.

Cochlea: A portion of the inner ear containing the sensory receptors for sound.

Sound waves are compressions of the air, or, more precisely, of the molecules that compose air. The greater the *amplitude* (magnitude) of these waves, the greater their loudness to us (see Figure 3.10). The rate at which air is expanded and contracted constitutes the *frequency* of a sound wave, and the greater the frequency, the higher the **pitch**. Frequency is measured in cycles per second, or hertz (Hz), and humans can generally hear sounds ranging from about 20 Hz to about 20 000 Hz. In **Making Psychology Part of Your Life** (see page 130), we'll explore how the loudness of your stereo headset and various other household devices can affect your hearing.

A third psychological aspect of sound, its **timbre**, refers to a sound's quality and depends on the mixture of frequencies and amplitudes that make up the sound. For example, a piece of chalk squeaking across a blackboard may have the same pitch and amplitude as a note played on a clarinet, but it will certainly have a different quality. In general, the timbre of a sound is related to its complexity—how many different frequencies it contains. However, other physical aspects of the source of the sound may be involved, too, so the relationship is not simple (refer to Figure 3.10).

Pitch Perception

When we tune a guitar or sing in harmony with other people, we demonstrate our ability to detect differences in pitch. Most individuals can easily tell when two sounds have the same pitch and when they do not. But how does a person manage to make such fine distinctions? Two explanations, based on two different mechanisms, seem to provide the answer.

Place theory (also called the *travelling wave theory*) suggests that sounds of different frequencies cause different places along the *basilar membrane* (the floor of the cochlea) to vibrate. These vibrations, in turn, stimulate the hair cells—the sensory

Pitch: The characteristic of a sound that is described as high or low. Pitch is mediated by the frequency of a sound.

Timbre: The quality of a sound, resulting from the complex makeup of a sound wave; timbre helps us to distinguish the sound of a trumpet from that of a saxophone.

Place Theory: A theory suggesting that sounds of different frequency stimulate different areas of the basilar membrane.

Figure 3.10
Physical Characteristics of Sound

Our perception of sounds is determined by three characteristics. *Loudness* depends on the amplitude, or height, of the sound waves; as amplitude increases, the sound seems louder. *Pitch* is determined by the frequency of the sound waves—that is, the number of sound waves that pass a given point per second. *Timbre* refers to the quality of the sound we perceive and is the characteristic that helps us distinguish the sound of a flute from the sound of a saxophone.

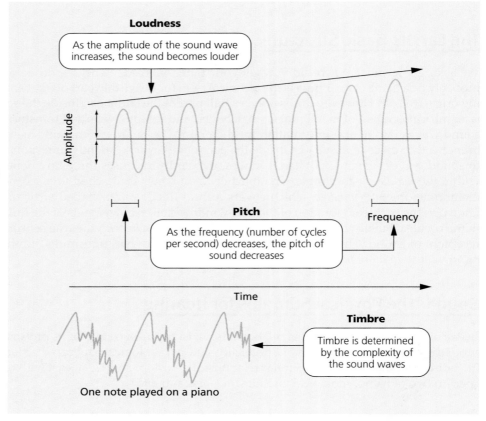

receptors for sound. Actual observations have shown that sound does produce pressure waves and that these waves peak, or produce maximal displacement, at various distances along the basilar membrane, depending on the frequency of the sound (Békésy, 1960). High-frequency sounds cause maximum displacement at the narrow end of the basilar membrane near the oval window, whereas lower frequencies cause maximum displacement toward the wider, farther end of the basilar membrane (see Figure 3.11). Unfortunately, place theory does not explain our ability to discriminate between sounds of very low frequency—of only a few hundred cycles per second—for which displacement on the basilar membrane is nearly identical. Another problem is that place theory does not account for our ability to discriminate sounds whose frequencies differ by as little as 1 or 2 Hz; basilar membrane displacement for these sounds is also nearly identical.

Frequency theory suggests that sounds of different pitch cause different rates of neural firing. Thus, high-pitched sounds produce high rates of activity in the auditory nerve, whereas low-pitched sounds produce lower rates. Frequency theory seems to be accurate up to sounds of about 1000 Hz—the maximum rate of firing for individual neurons. Above that level, the theory must be modified to include the *volley principle:* the assumption that neurons begin to fire in volleys. For example, a sound with a frequency of 5000 Hz might generate a pattern of activity in which each of five groups of neurons fires 1000 times in rapid succession—that is, in volleys.

Since our daily activities regularly expose us to sounds of many frequencies, both theories are needed to explain our ability to respond to this wide range of stimuli. Frequency theory explains how low-frequency sounds are registered, whereas place theory explains how high-frequency sounds are registered. In the middle ranges, between 500 and 4000 Hz, the range that we use for most daily activities, both theories apply.

Sound Localization

You are walking down a busy street filled with many sights and sounds. Suddenly a familiar voice calls your name. You instantly turn in the direction of this sound and spot one of your friends. How do you know where to turn? Research on **localization**—the ability of the auditory system to locate the source of a given sound—suggests that several factors play a role.

The first factor is the fact that we have two ears, placed on opposite sides of our head. As a result, our head creates a *sound shadow*, a barrier that reduces the intensity of sound on the "shadowed" side. Thus, a sound behind us and to our left will be slightly louder in our left ear. The shadow effect is strongest for high-frequency sounds, which have difficulty bending around the head and may produce a difference in intensity of 30 decibels or more in the ear farthest away (Phillips & Brugge, 1985). The placement of our ears also produces a slight difference in the time it takes for a sound to reach each ear. Although this difference is truly minute—often less than one millisecond—it provides an important clue to sound localization.

Figure 3.11
The Basilar Membrane

The cochlea is unwound and cut open to reveal the basilar membrane, which is covered with thousands of hair cells. Pressure waves in the fluid filling the cochlea cause oscillations to travel in waves down the basilar membrane, stimulating the hair cells.

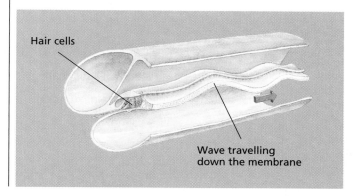

Hair cells

Wave travelling down the membrane

Sound Waves: The Physical Stimulus for Hearing

Like light, sound has a range of intensities—from very soft to very loud.

Frequency Theory: A theory of pitch perception suggesting that sounds of different frequencies, heard as differences in pitch, induce different rates of neural activity in the hair cells of the inner ear.

Localization: The ability of our auditory system to determine the direction of a sound source.

What happens when sound comes from directly in front or directly in back of us? At these times, we often have difficulty determining the location of the sound source, since the sound reaches both our ears at the same time. Head movements can help resolve a problem like this. By turning your head, you create a slight difference in the time it takes for the sound to reach each of your ears—and now you can determine the location of the sound and take appropriate action (Moore, 1982).

In summary, the human auditory system is ideally constructed to take full advantage of a variety of subtle cues. When you consider how rapidly we process and respond to such information, the whole system seems nothing short of marvellous in its efficiency.

K E Y QUESTIONS

- What is the physical stimulus for hearing?
- How do psychologists explain pitch perception?
- How do we localize sound?

Touch and Other Skin Senses

The skin is our largest sensory organ and produces the most varied experiences: everything from the pleasure of a soothing massage to the pain of an injury. Actually, there are several skin senses, including touch (or pressure), warmth, cold, and pain. Since there are specific sensory receptors for vision and hearing, it seems reasonable to expect this also to be true for the various skin senses as well—one type of receptor for touch, another for warmth, and so on. Microscopic examination reveals several different receptor types, which led early researchers to suggest that each receptor type produced a specific sensory experience. However, the results of research conducted to test this prediction were disappointing; specific types of receptors were *not* found at spots highly sensitive to touch, warmth, or cold. Other studies have also shown that many different types of receptors often respond to a particular stimulus. Therefore, the skin's sensory experience is probably determined by the total pattern of nerve impulses reaching the brain (Sherrick & Cholewiak, 1986).

Have you ever wondered why certain areas on your body are more sensitive than others? As it turns out, the receptors in skin are not evenly distributed; the touch receptors in areas highly sensitive to touch, such as the face and fingertips are much more densely packed than receptors in less sensitive areas, such as our legs. Additionally, areas of the skin with greater sensitivity also have greater representation in higher levels of the brain.

In most instances we discover the texture of an object through active exploration—using our finger tips or other sensitive areas of our body. Psychologists distinguish between *passive touch*, in which an object comes in contact with the skin, and *active touch*, in which we place our hand or other body part in contact with an object. We are considerably more accurate at identifying objects through active than through passive touch, in part because of feedback we receive from the movement of our fingers and hands when exploring an object (Matlin & Foley, 1997). Let's now turn to a discussion of how the sense of touch helps us experience pain.

Pain: Its Nature and Control

Pain plays an important adaptive role; without it, we would be unaware that something is amiss with our body or that we have suffered some type of injury. Determining the mechanisms for sensing pain has been particularly difficult, because unlike the other sensory processes that we have studied, pain sensation has no specific stimulus (Besson & Chaouch, 1987). However, sensations of pain do seem to originate in *free nerve endings* located throughout the body: in the skin, around muscles, and in internal organs.

Actually, two types of pain seem to exist. One can best be described as quick and sharp—the kind of pain we experience when we receive a cut. The other is dull and throbbing—the pain we experience from a sore muscle or an injured back. The first type of pain seems to be transmitted through large myelinated sensory nerve fibres (Campbell & LaMotte, 1983). As you may recall from Chapter 2, impulses travel faster along myelinated fibres, so it makes sense that sharp sensations of pain are carried via these fibres. In contrast, dull pain is carried by smaller, unmyelinated nerve fibres, which conduct neural impulses more slowly. Both fibre types synapse with neurons in the spinal cord that carry pain messages to the thalamus and other parts of the brain (Willis, 1985).

The discovery of the two pain systems described above, by researchers at McGill University in Montreal, led to the development of what is probably the most influential view of pain—the **gate-control theory** (Melzack, 1976). Gate-control theory suggests that there are neural mechanisms in the spinal cord that sometimes close, thus preventing pain messages from reaching the brain. Apparently, pain messages carried by the large fibres cause this "gate" to close, while messages carried by the smaller fibres—the ones related to dull, throbbing pain—cannot. This may explain why sharp pain is relatively brief, but an ache persists. The gate-control theory also helps to explain why vigorously stimulating one area to reduce pain in another sometimes works (Matlin & Foley, 1997). Presumably, tactics such as rubbing the skin near an injury, applying ice packs or hot-water bottles, and even acupuncture stimulate activity in the large nerve fibres, thus closing the spinal gate and reducing sensations of pain.

Endorphins, the opiate-like chemicals our body produces (discussed in Chapter 2), may also interact with the spinal gate to lessen sensations of pain (Akil et al., 1984; Millan, 1986). Researchers have found that certain areas of the spinal cord are highly enriched in opiate receptors and endorphin-containing neurons; thus, these substances may close the spinal gate by inhibiting the release of excitatory substances for neurons carrying information about pain (Neale et al., 1978; Snyder, 1977).

Gate-control theory has recently been revised to account for the importance of several brain mechanisms in the perception of pain (Melzack, 1993). For example, our emotional state at the time may interact with the onset of a painful stimulus to alter the intensity of pain we experience. The brain, in other words, may affect pain perception by transmitting messages that either close the spinal gate or keep it open. The result: When we are anxious (as many people are when sitting in a dentist's chair), pain is intensified; when we are calm and relaxed, pain may be reduced. In addition to emotional states, social and cognitive factors strongly influence our experience of pain.

An appreciation of the importance of cognitive factors can be gained by considering a recent study by Montgomery and Kirsch (1996). These researchers explored the possibility that placebos—chemically inert substances that a person is induced to believe will help them—would be effective in reducing perceptions of pain. Participants were told they would be involved in assessing the effectiveness of a new anesthetic. The new "anesthetic" was a neutral medicinal-smelling mixture dispensed in a bottle labelled as "Trivaricane: Approved for research purposes only." Researchers wearing surgical gloves applied it to one index finger of each participant. After a pause to allegedly allow the medication to take effect, equal intensities of a painful stimulus (pressure) were applied to both the treated and untreated index fingers of participants. The placebo was effective in reducing the participants' perceptions of pain; ratings of pain intensity and unpleasantness were

Ronald Melzack
McGill University

Gate-Control Theory: A theory suggesting that the spinal cord contains a mechanism that can block transmission of pain signals to the brain.

significantly lower for treated fingers than for untreated fingers. It is clear that cognitive expectations can play an important role in regulating the degree to which pain is experienced. Further information on the influence of cognitive factors on pain and how psychologists go about measuring these influences is provided in the **Research Process** section. After that, we will look at the perceptions of pain in different cultures in the **Perspectives on Diversity** section.

The Research Process:
How Psychologists Study the Effects of Negative Thinking on Pain Perception

We've already noted that cognitive processes play a significant role in pain perception. An aspect of cognition that seems particularly important is the degree to which pain-related thoughts and concerns about emotional distress pervade our mind while experiencing pain (Turk & Rudy, 1992). Those of us whose minds are flooded with such thoughts and concerns are termed *catastrophizers*. Research has shown that reducing or interrupting the disposition to catastrophize can greatly improve one's ability to cope with pain (Chaves & Brown, 1987; Turner & Clancy, 1986). The contention that negative thinking may affect our perception of pain seems reasonable enough, but how do we determine what a person is thinking and how do we relate a person's thoughts or feelings to their pain?

To try to clarify these issues, let's consider a recent study by Sullivan and his colleagues at Dalhousie University (Sullivan, Bishop, & Pivik, 1995). These researchers attempted to quantify the relationship between negative thoughts and pain. To accomplish their goal, the researchers first constructed the Pain Catastrophizing Scale (PCS)—a survey designed to measure people's negative thoughts about pain, such as the tendency to dwell on negative thoughts, to exaggerate the potential threat of painful stimuli, and to experience feelings of helplessness. High scores on the PCS reflect an increased tendency toward negative thoughts (catastrophizers), whereas low scores reflect a decreased tendency toward such thinking (non-catastrophizers). After completing the PCS, participants were subjected to a cold pressor test, a standard procedure used to induce intense, but temporary,

pain in laboratory settings. Participants immersed their arm in a container of icy water for about a minute—the point at which most people can no longer withstand the pain. At several points during the test, the researchers asked them to rate the pain they felt on a scale from 1 (no pain) to 10 (excruciating pain). Following the cold pressor test, participants were asked to report all the thoughts and feelings they experienced during their chilling experience. As shown in Figure 3.12, participants who

Figure 3.12
Negative Thinking and Pain

Participants who received high scores on the Pain Catastrophizing Scale—the catastrophizers—reported greater pain during the ice water immersion and more negative thoughts while in pain. These results underscore the role of cognitive processes in the perception of pain.

Source: Based on data from Sullivan et al., 1995.

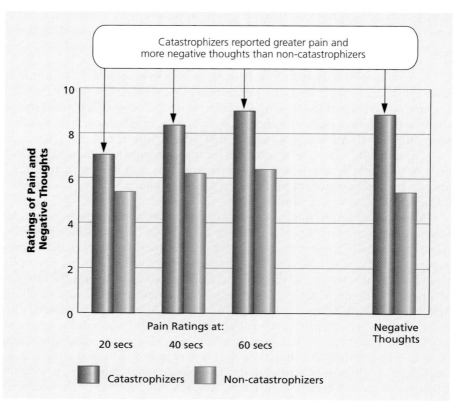

scored highest on the PCS—the catastrophizers—reported more negative thoughts while in pain than the non-catastrophizers. Further, although both groups reported increasing levels of pain over time, the catastrophizers reported more pain throughout the immersion period.

The results of this research have several significant implications. First, they demonstrate that there are ways to measure important aspects of our cognitive processes. Participants' scores on the PCS were strongly related to their ratings of pain and the extent to which they catastrophized (i.e, engaged in negative thinking about their pain). These results also suggest that the PCS may be a useful tool to predict who is likely to exhibit strong distress to painful medical procedures, such as chemotherapy. Identifying these persons before such procedures occur would enable

health professionals to help them cope more effectively with the pain these procedures often entail.

An increased recognition of the importance of the fact that pain stems from both physical and psychological causes has influenced the treatment of pain. In the past, people with persistent excruciating pain sought relief through potentially addictive drugs such as morphine, or measures as extreme as surgery to sever nerve pathways. A variety of less radical therapeutic procedures collectively termed *cognitive-behavioural procedures* (Novy, Nelson, Francis, & Turk, 1995; Turk, 1994) have emerged, and are often quite effective. These procedures are based on the fact that our thoughts, feelings, and beliefs—as well as our overt responses—before, during, and after painful episodes can dramatically influence our perceptions of pain (Turk & Rudy, 1992).

Perspectives on Diversity

Culture and the Perception of Pain

EUROPEAN EXPLORERS SUCH AS Jacques Cartier were amazed at the seeming indifference of the indigenous people to the torturous cold of a Canadian winter. They dressed much more lightly than Cartier and his men and seemed unaware of the pain of the cold that the explorers felt so keenly. Those of us who have grown accustomed to down jackets and central heating have a hard time believing that we could display the indifference to cold that so amazed Cartier.

At first glance, it is tempting to conclude that there are pronounced cultural differences in *pain thresholds*. However, there is no consistent experimental evidence to support such a notion (Zatzick & Dimsdale, 1990). Rather, observed cultural differences in the capacity to withstand pain (or not) seem to be perceptual in nature and to reflect the powerful effects of social learning (Morse & Morse, 1988). For example, honour and social standing among the Bariba of West Africa are tied closely to stoicism and the ability to withstand great pain (Sargent, 1984). Bariba men and women are expected to suffer pain silently. As you might expect, their language contains few words for the expression of pain. Additional environmental factors may also play a role in determining our perceptions of pain. For example, some evidence suggests that individuals exposed to harsh living or working conditions become more stoical than those who work or live in more comfortable circumstances (Clark & Clark, 1980). The most sensible conclusion is that differences in pain perception result from the powerful effects of social learning, not from physical differences.

Culture and Pain

Pain is a universal sensation, but pain perception can be strongly influenced by one's culture.

K E Y QUESTIONS

- What is the physical stimulus for touch?
- Where does the sensation of pain originate?
- What is the basis for cultural differences in pain perception?
- What role do cognitive processes play in the perception of pain?

Smell and Taste: The Chemical Senses

Although smell and taste are separate senses, we'll consider them together for two reasons. First, both respond to substances in solution—that is, substances that have been dissolved in a fluid or gas, usually water or air. That is why they are often referred to as the *chemical senses*. Second, in everyday life, smell and taste are interrelated.

How Smell and Taste Operate

SMELL   The stimulus for sensations of smell consists of molecules of various substances (odorants) contained in the air. Such molecules enter the nasal passages, where they dissolve in moist nasal tissues. This brings them in contact with receptor cells contained in the *olfactory epithelium* (see Figure 3.13). Human beings possess only about 10 million of these receptors. (Dogs, in contrast, possess more than 200 million receptors.) Nevertheless, our ability to detect smells is impressive. To appreciate this, consider a "scratch and sniff" smell survey that was done in which six different odours were embedded separately onto panels measuring about 4 by 3 centimetres. Amazingly, less than 30 grams of each odour was needed to place these smells onto 11 million copies of the survey (Gibbons, 1986; Gilbert & Wysocki, 1987).

Our olfactory senses are restricted, however, in terms of the range of stimuli to which they are sensitive, just as our visual system can detect only a small portion of the total electromagnetic spectrum. Our olfactory receptors can detect only substances with a molecular weight—the sum of the atomic weights of all atoms in an odorous molecule—between 15 and 300 (Carlson, 1994). This explains why we can smell the alcohol contained in a mixed drink, which has a molecular weight of 46, but cannot smell table sugar, which has a molecular weight of 342.

Figure 3.13
The Receptors for Smell

Receptors for our sense of smell are located in the olfactory epithelium, at the top of the nasal cavity. Molecules of odorous substances are dissolved in moisture present in the nasal passages. This brings them into contact with *receptor cells,* whose neural activity gives rise to sensations of smell.

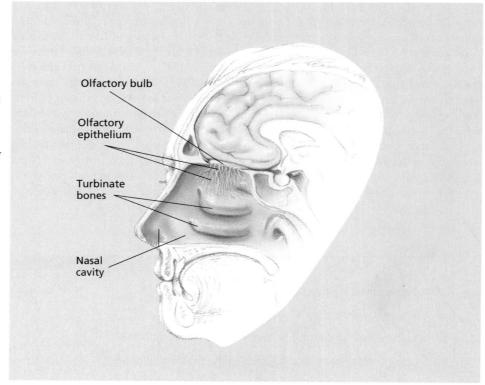

Olfactory bulb

Olfactory epithelium

Turbinate bones

Nasal cavity

Several theories have been proposed to explain how smell messages are interpreted by the brain. Stereochemical theory suggests that substances differ in smell because they have different molecular shapes (Amoore, 1970, 1982). Unfortunately, support for this theory has been mixed; nearly identical molecules can have extremely different fragrances, whereas substances with very different chemical structures can produce very similar odours (Engen, 1982; Wright, 1982). Other theories have focused on isolating "primary odours," similar to the basic hues in colour vision. But these efforts have been unsuccessful since there is often disagreement in people's perceptions of even the most basic smells.

A remaining explanation worth noting is the possibility that the brain's ability to recognize odours is based on the overall pattern of activity produced by the olfactory receptors (Sicard & Holley, 1984). According to this view, humans possess many different types of olfactory receptors, each one of which is stimulated to varying degrees by a particular odorant. This may, in turn, result in different patterns of output that the brain recognizes as specific odours. How the brain accomplishes this task is not yet known. We'll now turn to a discussion of the other chemical sense—taste.

TASTE The sensory receptors for taste are located inside small bumps on the tongue known as papillae. Within each papilla is a cluster of *taste buds* (see Figure 3.14). Each taste bud contains several receptor cells. Human beings possess about 10 000 taste buds. In contrast, chickens have only 24, while catfish would win any taste-bud-counting contest—they possess more than 175 000, scattered over the surface of their body. In a sense, they can "taste" with their entire skin (Pfaffmann, 1978).

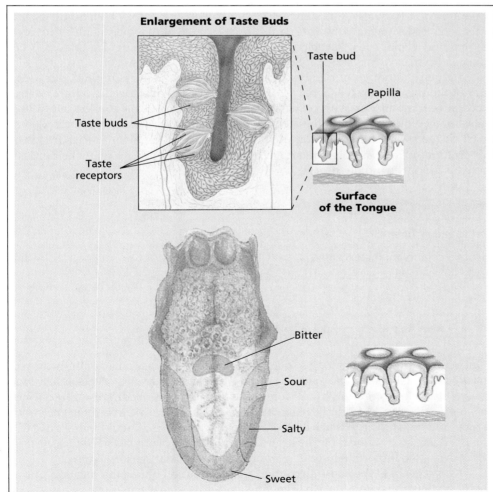

Enlargement of Taste Buds

Taste bud

Papilla

Taste buds

Taste receptors

Surface of the Tongue

Bitter

Sour

Salty

Sweet

Figure 3.14
Sensory Receptors for Taste

Taste buds are located inside small bumps on the surface of the tongue known as papillae. Within each taste bud are individual receptor cells. Also shown are the areas of the tongue most sensitive to the four basic tastes: sweet, salty, sour, and bitter.

People generally believe that they can distinguish a large number of flavours in foods. But in fact, there appear to be only four basic tastes: sweet, salty, sour, and bitter (refer to Figure 3.14). Why, then, do we perceive many more? The answer lies in the fact that we are aware not only of the taste of the food but of its smell, its texture, its temperature, the pressure it exerts on our tongue and mouth, and many other sensations. When these factors are removed from the picture, only the four basic tastes remain.

Smell and Taste: Some Interesting Findings

Perhaps because they are more difficult to study, smell and taste have received far less attention from researchers than vision and hearing. However, this does not imply that these senses are not important. Indeed, individuals who have lost their sense of smell (a state known as *anosmia*) often become deeply depressed; some even commit suicide (Douek, 1988).

Despite the relative lack of research, many interesting facts have been uncovered about smell and taste. For example, it appears that we are not very good at identifying different odours (Engen, 1986). When asked to identify thirteen common fragrances (such as grape, smoke, mint, pine, and soap), individuals were successful only 32 percent of the time. Even when brand-name products or common odours are used, accuracy is still less than 50 percent. Some research suggests that we lack a well-developed representational system for describing olfactory experiences (Engen, 1987). In other words, we may recognize a smell without being able to name the odour in question—a condition sometimes called the "tip of the nose" phenomenon (Lawless & Engen, 1977; Richardson & Zucco, 1989). Some experiments have shown that when odorants are associated with experimenter-provided verbal and visual cues, participants' long-term ability to recognize odours is enhanced (Lyman & McDaniel, 1986, 1987).

Actually, although our ability to identify specific odours is limited, our memory of them is impressive (Schab, 1991). Once exposed to a specific odour, we can recognize it months or even years later (Engen & Ross, 1973; Rabin & Cain, 1984). This may be due, in part, to the fact that our memory for odours is often coded as part of memories for more complex and significant life events (Richardson & Zucco, 1989). For example, the aroma of freshly made popcorn may elicit images of your favourite movie theatre.

KEY *QUESTIONS*

- What is the physical stimulus for smell?
- Where are the sensory receptors for taste located?

Kinesthesia and Vestibular Sense

One night, while driving along a solitary stretch of the Trans-Canada Highway, you notice flashing lights on the roadside ahead. You slow to a crawl and get a close look at the situation as you pass by. A Mountie is in the process of administering a sobriety test to the driver of a car he has pulled over. The driver's head is tilted back at an angle, and he is trying to touch each of his fingers to his nose, but is having great difficulty doing so. This example illustrates the importance of our *kinesthetic* and *vestibular senses*—two important but often ignored aspects of our sensory system.

Kinesthesia is the sense that gives us information about the location of our body parts with respect to each other and allows us to perform movements—from

Kinesthesia: The sense that gives us information about the location of our body parts with respect to each other and allows us to perform movements.

simple ones like touching our nose with our fingertips to more complex ones required for gymnastics, dancing, or driving an automobile. Kinesthetic information comes from receptors in joints, ligaments, and muscle fibres (Matlin & Foley, 1992). When we move, these receptors register the rate of change of movement speed as well as the rate of change of the angle of the bones in our limbs; then they transform this mechanical information into neural signals for the brain. We also receive important kinesthetic information from our other senses, especially vision and touch. To demonstrate how your kinesthetic sense system draws on other senses, try the following experiment: Close your eyes for a moment and hold your arms down at your sides. Now without looking, touch your nose with each of your index fingers—one at a time. Can you do it? Most people can, but only after missing their nose a time or two. Now, try it again with your eyes open. Is it easier this way? In most instances it is, because of the added information we receive from our visual sense.

Whereas kinesthesia keeps our brain informed about the location of our body parts in relation to each other, the **vestibular sense** gives us information about body position, movement, and acceleration—factors critical for maintaining our sense of balance (Schiffman, 1990). We usually become aware of our vestibular sense after activities that make us feel dizzy, like the rides at amusement parks that involve rapid acceleration or spinning.

The sensory organs for the vestibular sense are located in the inner ear (see Figure 3.15). Two fluid-filled **vestibular sacs** provide information about the body's position relative to the earth by tracking changes in linear movement. When our body accelerates (or decelerates) along a straight line, as when we are on a bus that is starting and stopping, or when we tilt our head or body to one side, hair cells bend in proportion to the rate of change in our motion. This differential bending of hair cells causes attached nerve fibres to discharge neural signals that are sent to the brain.

Three fluid-filled **semicircular canals**, also in the inner ear, provide information about rotational acceleration of the head or body along the three principle axes. Whenever we turn or rotate our head, the fluid in these canals begins to move and causes a bending of hair cells. Since these structures are arranged at right angles to each other, bending is greatest in the semicircular canal corresponding to the axis along which the rotation occurs.

Vestibular Sense: Our sense of balance.

Vestibular Sacs: Fluid-filled sacs in our inner ear that provide information about the positions and changes in linear movement of our head and body.

Semicircular Canals: Fluid-filled structures that provide information about rotational acceleration of the head or body around three principal axes of rotation.

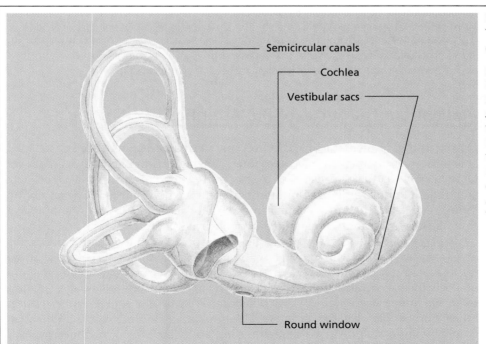

Semicircular canals

Cochlea

Vestibular sacs

Round window

**Figure 3.15
The Structures Underlying Our Sense of Balance**

Shown here are the organs of our kinesthetic and vestibular senses. Structures in the two *vestibular sacs* provide information about the positions of our head and body with respect to gravity by tracking changes in linear movement; those in the *semicircular canals* provide information about *rotational acceleration* around three principal axes.

BAR/3E/3.4P

The Vestibular Sense

A spinning ice skater provides an example of rotational acceleration around one of the three axes monitored in the semicircular canals.

Note that the vestibular system is designed to detect *changes* in motion rather than constant motion. For example, it helps us to detect the change in acceleration that accompanies takeoff in an airplane, but not the constant velocity that follows.

We also receive vestibular information from our other senses, especially vision—a fact that can produce queasy consequences if the information from these senses is in conflict (Jefferson, 1993). Developers of a realistic "Back to the Future" ride at Universal Studios in Florida discovered this fact when riders in their DeLorean simulator lost their cookies. Apparently, the visual effects were not synchronized with the movements the riders felt. Once reprogrammed, however, the simulator conveyed the developers' initial intent—the sensation of flying through space and time (Ebenholtz et al., 1994).

KEY *QUESTIONS*

■ What information does our kinesthetic sense provide to the brain?

■ What information does the vestibular sense provide to the brain?

Perception: Putting It All Together

Up to this point we have focused on the sensory processes that convert raw physical stimulation into usable neural codes. But you may be wondering how this array of neural action potentials contributes to the richness of conscious experience. Stop for a moment and look around you. Do you see a meaningless swirl of colours, brightnesses, and shapes? Probably not. Now turn on the radio and tune it to any station. Do you hear an incomprehensible babble of sounds? Certainly not (unless, of course, you've tuned to a foreign-language or heavy metal station). In both cases, you "see" and "hear" more than the raw sensations that stimulate the receptors in your eyes, ears, and other sense organs; you see recognizable objects and hear understandable words or music. In other words, transmission of sensory information from sensory receptors to the brain is only part of the process. Equally important is the process of perception—the way in which we select, organize, and interpret sensory input to achieve a grasp of our surroundings. The remainder of this chapter is about some of the basic principles that influence perception.

Perception: The Focus of Our Attention

Our attention, or mental focus, captures only a small portion of the stimuli available at a given moment. What determines where attention is focused? To a very large degree, we do. We can choose to selectively attend to almost any aspect of the stimulation bombarding us. Our attention can be wholly captured by an exciting movie on TV, but the unwelcome intrusion of a commercial shifts attention away from the television and we may suddenly notice the smell of dinner being prepared, or that the chair in which we are sitting or our position in the chair is uncomfortable—sensations that were outside our awareness only moments before. Our ability to selectively attend to certain aspects of our environment while relegating others to the background (Johnston & Dark, 1986) has obvious advantages. It allows us to maximize information extraction from a particular source while ignoring other sources of information around us. Without it, goal-directed thought or action would be impossible. When attention is directed by inner goals or concerns, its focus is said to be **endogenously controlled** (i.e., regulated from within).

Endogenously Controlled Attention: When attention is directed by inner goals or concerns.

Attention is not wholly directed to inner concerns. Were it so, we would be relatively short-lived. Concentrating exclusively on when you are going to find time to study for an impending psychology quiz, or how you are going to get through the rest of the month when you have next to nothing in the bank, could have disastrous results while trying to dart across a very busy thoroughfare. Fortunately, attention is usually automatically drawn to abrupt changes in the character of the stimulus field. An abrupt visual change produced by the movement of a fast-approaching car, or the sudden sound of an irate driver's horn, automatically attract attention. Reflexive stimulus changes driven by stimulus events external to us are said to be **exogenously controlled** (i.e., they are driven by stimulus events in the external environment).

Attention, then, always involves an interplay of both endogenous and exogeneous factors. We have to divide attention between inner concerns and important sources of information in the environment. Think back to the last time you were at a large crowded party with many conversations going on at once. Is it not the case that if you are intently listening to a titillating description of a friend's recent romantic escapade, the surrounding conversational babble seems to be blocked out? The ability to attend to one voice while blocking other voices is referred to as the *cocktail party phenomenon*. But rapt attention on the person to whom you are listening does not mean that you are completely indifferent to all other salient sounds in the environment. The sound of your name, or another particularly significant stimulus such as the voice of a person to whom you are strongly attracted, will very likely cause you to try and focus on that sound source even at the expense of losing some of the details of your friend's escapade (Moray, 1959).

There are circumstances in which it is almost impossible to divide attention. The best example of such a circumstance is the Stroop interference task, which has been widely used by experimenters (Stroop, 1935). It is easily demonstrated experimentally by presenting to subjects successively the two lists of names of common colours as shown in Figure 3.16.

There is a significant difference between the two lists. In one list, the ink with which a word is written is the same as the colour named, (i.e., the word *green* is printed in green ink); in the other list the word is always written in a colour other than that named by the word (the word *green* is printed in blue ink). The task is simple. Research subjects are required to start at the top of each list and proceed to state, as rapidly as possible, the different colours used in printing the words—ignoring, if possible, the printed words. As you may have expected, this is hard to do. It is difficult to focus exclusively on the colour of the ink when the word written in that ink names another colour. Subjects typically take much longer to state the colours of each word when the word is written in a colour other than that named by the word.

Attention is obviously crucial in determining what will be seen, or heard. What we want to focus on next are some long-established organizing factors in visual perception that can both divide and focus attention in interesting ways.

Exogenously Controlled Attention: When attention is directed by stimulus events in the external environment.

Figure 3.16
The Stroop Interference Task

Examine the two lists of colour names in the figure. In the list on the left, the ink in which each colour name is printed is the same as the colour named. In the list on the right, the ink in which a colour name is printed is different from the colour that is named. The Stroop interference task requires that you start at the top of each list and go down the list as rapidly as possible, naming only the *colour* in which each word is printed. It is easy to focus attention exclusively on the ink colour in the list on the left, and you will go through the list rapidly. In the list on the right, it is difficult to focus attention on the ink colour and ignore that different colour named by the word, and your progress through the list will be much slower.

Source: Based on Stroop, 1935.

RED	BLUE
GREEN	ORANGE
BLACK	BLACK
BLUE	BLUE
ORANGE	GREEN
GREEN	BLUE
ORANGE	RED
BLUE	BLUE

Perception: Some Organizing Principles

Look at the illustrations in Figure 3.17. Instead of random smatterings of black and white, you can probably discern a familiar figure in each. But how does our brain allow us to interpret these confused specks as a dog and a horseback rider? The process by which we structure the input from our sensory receptors is called *perceptual organization.* Aspects of perceptual organization were first studied systematically in the early 1900s by **Gestalt psychologists**—early German psychologists who were intrigued by certain innate tendencies of the human mind to impose order and structure on the physical world and to perceive sensory patterns as well-organized wholes rather than as separate, isolated parts (*Gestalt* means "whole" in German). These scientists outlined several principles that describe how we organize basic sensory input into whole patterns (gestalts). Some of these are described below. You could say that the Gestalt psychologists changed our perceptions about the nature of perception.

Figure 3.17
Perceptual Organization

Look carefully at each of the figures. What do you see? Our perceptual processes often allow us to perceive shapes and forms from incomplete and fragmented stimuli.

Figure 3.18
A Demonstration of Figure–Ground

What do you see when you look at this drawing? You probably see either a young woman or an old woman. Since this is an ambiguous figure, your perceptions may switch back and forth between these two possibilities.

FIGURE AND GROUND: WHAT STANDS OUT? By looking carefully at Figure 3.18, you can experience a principle of perceptual organization known as the **figure–ground relationship**. What this means, simply, is that we tend to divide the world around us into two parts: *figure,* which has a definite shape and a location in space; and *ground,* which has no shape, seems to continue behind the figure, and has no definite location. The figure–ground relationship helps clarify the distinction between sensation and perception. While the pattern of sensory information generated in our receptors remains constant, our perceptions shift between the two figure–ground patterns in Figure 3.18; thus, we may see either a young woman or an old woman, but not both. Note that the principles of perceptual organization apply to the other senses, too. For instance, consider how the figure–ground relationship applies to audition. During a complicated lecture, you become absorbed in whispered gossip between two students sitting next to you; the professor's voice becomes background noise. Suddenly you hear your name and realize the professor has asked you a question; her voice has now become the sole focus of your attention, while the conversation becomes background noise.

GROUPING: WHICH STIMULI GO TOGETHER?   The Gestaltists also called attention to a number of principles known as the **laws of grouping**—basic ways in which we group items together perceptually. Several of these laws, including a more recently discovered perceptual grouping principle called *common region*, are shown in the **Key Concept** on page 120 (Palmer, 1992). As you can see from this feature, laws of grouping do offer a good description of our perceptual tendencies. Once again it is worth pointing out that these principles do not just apply to vision. Bregman and Campbell (1971) of McGill University have demonstrated, in a much cited study, that a slowly presented and clearly heard alternating sequence of high- and low-pitched tones will be grouped into two separate, and seemingly simultaneous, sound streams—one high-pitched and the other low-pitched—if the rate of presentation is rapid. The implications of this, and many other studies of what are termed *auditory streaming* effects, are considered at length in Bregman's (1990) book on auditory streaming.

The principles outlined by Gestalt psychologists are not, however, hard-and-fast rules. They are merely descriptions of ways in which we perceive the world around us. Whether these principles are innate, as the Gestaltists believed, or learned, as some newer evidence suggests, is still open to debate. In any case, principles of perceptual organization are readily visible in the natural world, and they are effective in helping us organize our perceptual world.

Constancies and Illusions

Perception, we have seen, is more than the sum of all the sensory input supplied by our eyes, ears, and other receptors. It is the active selection, organization, and interpretation of such input. It yields final products that differ from raw, unprocessed sensations in important ways. Up till now, this discussion has focused on the benefits of this process. But perception, like any other powerful process, can be a double-edged sword. On the one hand, perception helps us adapt to a complex and ever-changing environment. On the other hand, perception sometimes leads us into error. To see how, let's consider *constancies* and *illusions*.

PERCEPTUAL CONSTANCIES: STABILITY IN THE FACE OF CHANGE   Try this simple demonstration. Hold your right hand in front of you at arm's length. Now, move it toward and away from your face several times. Does it seem to change in size? Probably not, but think about the size of the *image* of your hand that is registered on the surface of your retina as you move it back and forth. It undergoes enormous size change. The fact that your hand seems the same size regardless of whether it is close or far illustrates the principles of perceptual **constancies**—our tendency to perceive aspects of the world as unchanging despite changes in the sensory input we receive from them. The principle of **size constancy** relates to the fact that the perceived size of an object remains the same when the distance is varied, even though the size of the image it casts on the retina changes greatly. Under normal circumstances, such constancy is impressive. Consider, for example, what you see when you notice a friend walking toward you from several blocks away. Distant objects—cars, trees, people—cast tiny images on our retina. Yet we perceive them as being of normal size. Two factors seem to account for this tendency—distance invariance and relative size.

Laws of Grouping: Simple principles describing how we tend to group discrete stimuli together in the perceptual world.

Constancies: Our tendency to perceive physical objects as unchanging despite shifts in the pattern of sensations these objects induce.

Size Constancy: The tendency to perceive a physical object as having a constant size even when the size of the image it casts on the retina changes.

Key Concept *Figure–Ground and Laws of Grouping*

Figure-Ground

The tendency to view the world in two parts: *figure,* which has definite shape and location in space, and *ground,* background stimuli with no specific shape or location in space. In this reversing vase–face figure, there is a continual interchange between figure and ground areas.

Laws of Grouping

Law of Similarity
Tendency to form similar items into perceptual groups.

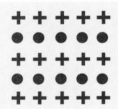

Law of Proximity
Tendency to form items that are close together into perceptual groups.

Law of Common Region
Tendency to percepually group objects if they occupy a region of space distinctively demarked by colour or contour.

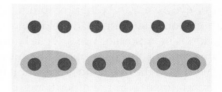

Law of Good Continuation
Tendency to perceive stimuli as part of a continuous pattern.

Law of Closure
Tendency to perceive objects as whole entities, despite the fact that some parts may be missing or obstructed from view.

Law of Simplicity
Tendency to perceive complex patterns in terms of simpler shapes. The complex form below could be a single irregularly shaped form. We tend to perceive it as a circle and triangle that overlap.

► The principle of *size–distance invariance* suggests that when estimating the size of an object, we take into account both the size of the image it casts on our retina and the apparent distance to the object. From these data we almost instantly calculate the object's size. Only when the cues that normally reveal an object's distance are missing do we run into difficulties in estimating the object's size (as we'll see in the discussion of illusions that follows). In the same way, we judge the **relative size** of an object by comparing it with objects of known size. This mechanism is especially useful for estimating the size of unfamiliar things.

But size is not the only perceptual feature of the physical world that does not correspond directly with the information transmitted by our sensory receptors. The principle of **shape constancy** refers to the fact that the perceived shape of an object does not alter as the image it casts on the retina changes. For example, all of us know that coins are round; yet we rarely see them that way. Flip a coin into the air: although you continue to perceive the coin as being round, the image that actually falls onto your retina constantly shifts from a circle to various forms of an ellipse.

The principle of **brightness constancy** refers to the fact that we perceive objects as constant in brightness and colour whatever the lighting conditions. Thus, we will perceive a sweater as dark green whether we are indoors or outdoors in bright sunlight. Brightness constancy apparently prevails because objects and their surroundings are usually lighted by the same illumination source, so changes in lighting conditions occur simultaneously for both the object and its immediate surroundings. As long as the changes in lighting remain constant for both object and surroundings, the neural message reaching the brain is unchanged. Brightness constancy breaks down, however, when changes in lighting are not equivalent for both the object and its surroundings (Sekuler & Blake, 1990).

Although most research on perceptual constancies has focused on size, shape, and brightness, constancy pervades nearly every area of perception, including our other senses. For example, imagine listening to elevator music while riding on an elevator en route to a dental appointment on the thirtieth floor of an office building. When one of your favourite oldies from the 1980s begins, you can't believe what they've done to "your song." Nonetheless, you are still able to recognize it, despite differences in its loudness, tone, and pitch.

Whatever their basis, perceptual constancies are highly useful. Without them, we would spend a great deal of time and effort re-identifying sensory information in our environment each time we experienced the information from a new perspective. The gap between our sensations and the perceptions provided by the constancies is clearly beneficial.

ILLUSIONS: WHEN PERCEPTION FAILS   We've seen that perception organizes sensory information into a coherent picture of the world around us. Perception can also, however, provide false interpretations of sensory information. Such cases are known as **illusions**, a term used by psychologists to refer to incorrect perceptions. Actually, there are two types of illusions: those due to physical processes and those due to cognitive processes (Matlin & Foley, 1992). Illusions due to distortion of physical conditions include *mirages*, in which you perceive things that aren't really there— like the water you often seem to see on the dry road ahead of you. Our focus, however, will be on the latter type of illusions—those involving cognitive processes.

Countless illusions related to cognitive processes exist, but most fall into two categories: illusions of *size* and illusions of *shape* or *area* (Coren et al., 1976). Natural examples of two well-known size illusions are presented in Figure 3.19, and as you can see, their effects are powerful. But why do illusions occur? What causes our interpretation of such stimuli to be directly at odds with physical reality? Recent evidence suggests that illusions generally have multiple causes (Schiffman, 1990). However, one explanation is provided by the *theory of misapplied constancy*, which suggests that when looking at illusions, we often interpret certain cues as suggesting that some parts are farther away than others. Our powerful tendency toward size constancy then comes into play, with the result that we perceptually distort the length of various lines. Experience and learning also play an import role in illusions.

Relative Size: A visual cue based on comparison of the size of an unknown object to one of known size.

Shape Constancy: The tendency to perceive a physical object as having a constant shape even when the image it casts on the retina changes.

Brightness Constancy: The tendency to perceive objects as having a constant brightness even when they are viewed under different conditions of illumination.

Illusions: Instances in which perception yields false interpretations of physical reality.

Figure 3.19
Illusions of Size

Natural examples of two powerful illusions of size. (A) The horizontal–vertical illusion stems from our tendency to perceive objects higher in our visual field as more distant. This illusion helps explain why the St. Louis Gateway falsely appears taller than it is wide (its height and width are actually equal). (B) In the Ponzo illusion, the object in the distance appears larger, although both objects are actually the same size.

A   B

Consider the vertical lines in the inside and outside corners shown in the two photos in Figure 3.20. They are exactly the same length, but the one on the right appears to be much longer than the one on the left. Why should this be so? The answer is that we have learned through experience that the angular arrangement of the floor and ceiling lines in the photo on the right indicate a distant inside corner of a room, whereas the angular roof and foundation lines of the structure on the left indicate a much closer outside corner of a building. The different impressions of distance, transmitted by these angular line arrangements, influence the perceived length of the vertical line. Constancy mechanisms in the brain conclude that if two lines occupy the same expanse on the retinal surface, and one is more distant than the other, the more distant line must be longer—and make us see it as so. It is important to note that the Muller-Lyer illusion is not confined to images of real-world objects. As may be seen in Figure 3.20, the addition of angular wing-like appendages represent the geometry of inside and outside corners to any given line can alter the perceived length of that line. Given that learning and experience play

Figure 3.20
The Müller-Lyer Illusion

(A) In the Müller-Lyer illusion, lines of equal length appear unequal; the line with the wings pointing outward looks longer than the line with the wings pointing inward. (B) Now carefully examine the vertical line in each of the photographs. Which line is longer? Most people perceive the vertical line in the photo on the right as longer, although careful measurement shows that the two lines are exactly the same length!

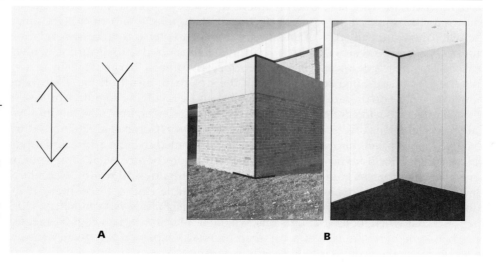

A   B

an important role in generating illusions, can these same factors diminish the effects of illusions? Only to a limited degree. Many visual illusions decline in magnitude following extended exposure—but they do not decline altogether (Greist-Bousquet, Watson, & Schiffman, 1990).

Another type of illusion is that of *shape* or *area*. If you've ever wondered why the moon looks bigger at the horizon (about 30 percent bigger!) than at its highest point in the sky, then you are familiar with the most famous area illusion—the *moon illusion*. Why does the moon illusion occur? In part, because when the moon is near the horizon, we can see that it is farther away than trees, houses, and other objects. When it is overhead at its zenith, such cues are lacking. Thus, the moon appears larger near the horizon because there are cues available that cause us to perceive that it is very far away. Once again, our tendency toward size constancy leads us astray.

Like illusions of size or area, shape illusions (see Figure 3.21) too can influence perception, sometimes with unsettling consequences. Consider a real-world example involving the *Poggendorf illusion* (see drawing A in Figure 3.21). In this illusion, a line disappears at an angle behind a solid figure, then reappears on the other side—at what seems to be the incorrect position. As reported by Coren and Girgus (1978), in 1965 two airplanes were about to arrive in New York City, and because of the Poggendorf illusion, they thought that they were on a collision course. Both pilots changed direction to correct for what they perceived as an error, and their planes thus collided. The result was four deaths and forty-nine injuries—all because of an illusion.

One final point: illusions are not limited to visual processes. Indeed, there are numerous examples of illusions involving our other senses, including touch and audition (Sekuler & Blake, 1990; Shepard, 1964). One well-known illusion that you can demonstrate for yourself is that of touch temperature. First place one hand in a container of hot water and the other hand in cold water. Then place *both* hands in a container of lukewarm water. What do you feel? Most people experience a dramatic difference in perceived temperature between the two hands; the hand initially placed in hot water feels the lukewarm water as cool, while the hand initially placed in cold water feels it as hot. How do we explain this illusion? When we touch an object, the temperature of the area of our skin in contact with it shifts toward that of the object's surface. So, when we perceive an object to be warm or cool, our experience stems partly from the temperature difference between the object and our skin, not solely from the actual temperature of the object.

Figure 3.21
Illusions of Area or Shape

Illusions of area or shape can be quite powerful. (A) In this drawing, known as the Poggendorf illusion, which of the three lines on the right continues the line on the left? Check your answer with a ruler. (B) In this drawing, are the horizontal lines straight or bent in the middle? Again, check for yourself. (C) Finally, in this drawing, are the letters tilted or vertical? When you check by connecting the corners of the letters and colouring them in, you'll see why sometimes you can't believe what you think you see.

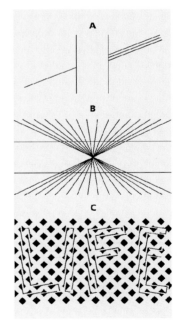

KEY QUESTIONS

- Why is selective attention important?
- What role do the Gestalt principles play in perceptual process?
- What are perceptual constancies?
- What are illusions?

Some Key Perceptual Processes

Perception is a practical process since it provides organisms with information essential to survival in their normal habitat. The specific nature of this information varies greatly with different species. For example, frogs must be able to detect small moving objects in order to feed on insects, whereas porpoises require sensory input that enables them to navigate turbulent and murky ocean waters. Nonetheless, it is probably safe to say that virtually all living creatures need information concerning (1) what's out there and (2) how far away it is. Humans are no exception to this general rule, and we possess impressive perceptual skills in both areas.

PATTERN RECOGNITION: WHAT'S OUT THERE? Our ability to read the words on this page depends on our ability to recognize small black marks as letters and collections of such marks as words. How do we accomplish this task? An early explanation for this phenomenon was the *template-matching theory*. According to this theory, we have many **templates**, or specific patterns, stored in our memories for various visual stimuli that we encounter. Thus, if a visual stimulus—say, a letter—matches one of the templates, we recognize it; if it does not, we search for another that does match. As you may have already guessed, this theory is impractical, since it requires that we store an almost infinite number of these templates in memory in order to be able to recognize even variants of the same letter. Additionally, the template-matching theory does not explain our ability to read at rates exceeding hundreds of words per minute or to recognize visual stimuli almost instantly, even when they're tilted or viewed upside down (Pinker, 1984).

A related but more viable explanation, referred to as *prototype-matching theory*, suggests that we automatically compare each letter (and perhaps word) to abstract representations of these stimuli in our memories. These representations are known as **prototypes**. According to this view, we would have a prototype in memory for each letter of the alphabet. A prototype is not an exact counterpart or template of a visual letter or form but an idealized "best" representation that develops as a consequence of many encounters with a given letter or form. Recognition depends on finding a match between a visual stimulus such as a letter and the prototype that represents that stimulus. Because we typically experience substantial variations in size, orientation, and perspective in our viewing of any visual form, the prototype that develops will be relatively tolerant of irregularities. Thus we would be able to recognize a letter even it were to be distorted. While some evidence supports this view (e.g., Rosch, Simpson, & Miller, 1976), the physiological details of this theory are not well developed (Matlin & Foley, 1992).

Two other approaches are the bottom-up and top-down theories of pattern recognition. As their names imply, these adopt somewhat opposite perspectives on the basic question of how we recognize patterns of visual stimuli. The *bottom-up approach* suggests that our ability to recognize specific patterns, such as letters of the alphabet, is based on simpler capacities to recognize and combine correctly lower-level features of objects, such as lines, edges, corners, and angles. Bottom-up theories suggest that pattern recognition is constructed from simpler perceptual abilities through a discrete series of steps (Hummell, 1994; Marr, 1982). One currently popular view on this topic suggests that a type of basic building block essential to pattern recognition consists of a group of three-dimensional components called *geons* (Biederman, 1987). According to Biederman, a small set of geons, when assembled according to specific rules, can be combined to form any object (see Figure 3.22). Thus, pattern recognition is accomplished by matching features of an object to geon representations of this information in memory. Although additional research is necessary to confirm the accuracy of this view of pattern recognition, it does help explain our efficiency at recognizing not only objects, but also complex scenes (Schyns & Oliva, 1994).

In contrast, the *top-down approach* emphasizes the fact that our expectancies play a critical role in shaping our perceptions. We often proceed in accordance with what our past experience tells us to expect, and therefore we don't always analyze every feature of most stimuli we encounter. Although top-down processing can be extremely efficient (think about the speed with which you can read this page), it can also lead us astray. Nearly everyone has had the experience of rushing over to another person who appears to be an old friend, only to realize he or she is actually a stranger. In such cases, our tendency to process information quickly from the top down can indeed produce errors.

Which of these theories is correct? Research indicates that both play a role in pattern recognition (Matlin & Foley, 1992). When we have strong expectations or we are in a familiar context, we often opt for speed and adopt a top-down approach. However, when dealing with unfamiliar situations or stimuli, bottom-up processing often dominates. In most situations, both processes are likely employed.

Templates: Specific patterns stored in our memories for various visual stimuli that we encounter.

Prototypes: Representations in memory of various objects or stimuli in the physical world; the best or clearest examples of various objects or stimuli in the physical world.

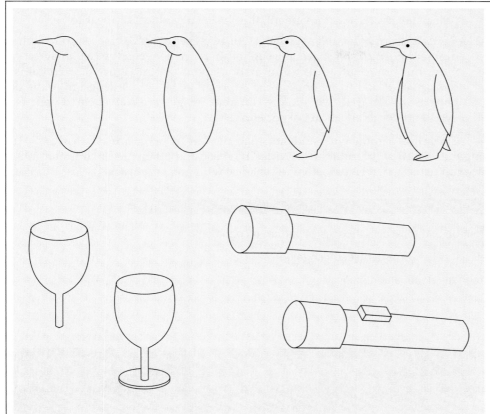

Figure 3.22
Geons: Basic Building Blocks of Object Recognition

Some evidence suggests that all objects can be assembled from a basic set of three-dimensional constituent components referred to as *geons*. Geons help explain our efficiency at recognizing the endless array of objects and scenes present in everyday life.

These figures illustrate the partial and complete geon structure of various objects.

Source: Biederman, I., 1987. Recognition by component: A theory of human image understanding. Psychological Review, 94, 115–147.

DISTANCE PERCEPTION: HOW FAR AWAY IS IT? Our ability to judge depth and distance is impressive because we make use of many different cues in forming such judgments. These cues are *monocular* or *binocular*, depending on whether they can be seen with only one eye or require the use of both eyes.

Monocular cues to depth or distance include the following:

1. *Size cues.* The larger the image of an object on the retina, the larger the object is judged to be; in addition, if an object is larger than other objects, it is often perceived as closer.

2. *Linear perspective.* Parallel lines appear to converge in the distance; the greater this effect, the farther away an object appears to be.

3. *Texture gradient.* The texture of a surface appears smoother as distance increases.

4. *Atmospheric perspective.* The farther away objects are, the less distinctly they are seen—smog, dust, haze, and so on get in the way.

5. *Overlap (or interposition).* If one object overlaps another, it is seen as being closer than the one it covers.

6. *Height cues.* Objects on the ground or in the sky are judged to be further away if they are seen to be close to the horizon.

7. *Motion parallax.* When we travel in a vehicle, objects far away appear to move in the same direction as the observer, whereas close objects move in the opposite direction. Objects at different distances appear to move at different velocities.

As you can see, much of our ability to perceive depth is based on the use of *monocular cues.* However, we also rely heavily on **binocular cues**—depth information based on the coordinated efforts of both eyes. Binocular cues for depth perception stem from two primary sources:

Monocular Cues: Cues to depth or distance provided by one eye.

Binocular Cues: Cues to depth or distance provided by the use of both eyes.

1. *Convergence.* In order to see close objects, our eyes turn inward, toward one another; the greater this movement, the closer such objects appear to be.

2. *Retinal disparity (binocular parallax).* Our two eyes observe objects from slightly different positions in space; the slight difference between the two images provides our brain with direct information about depth. Figure 3.23 contains a *stereogram.* If you fixate on it in the appropriate fashion, the design of the dot pattern is such that two slightly different images are conveyed to your two eyes, and depth effects are experienced.

These lists of monocular and binocular cues are by no means exhaustive. By using the wealth of information provided by these and other cues (Schiffman, 1990), we can usually perceive depth and distance with great accuracy.

KEY *QUESTIONS*

- What are the bottom-up and top-down theories of pattern recognition?

- What are geons? What is their role in object recognition?

- How are we able to judge depth and distance?

Figure 3.23
Retinal Disparity and Stereograms

Retinal disparity is the basis for perceiving 3-D images in stereograms. Hold the book right up to your nose and very, very slowly pull the book away from your face. Look through the image. Try not to blink and a 3-D picture will magically appear. What do you see? Hint: Do you like soccer?

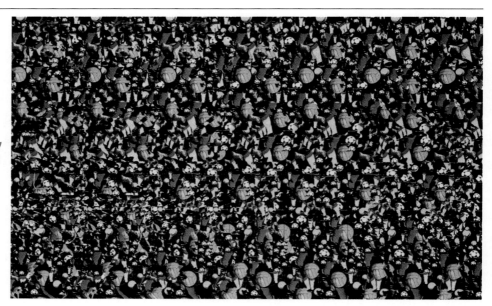

The Plasticity of Perception

Imagine a man blind from birth who is suddenly provided with sight through a miraculous operation. Will his visual world be the same as yours or mine? Will it be orderly and consistent with his expectations? Or will he experience a chaotic swirl of colours, brightnesses, and meaningless shapes? This question has often served as the basis for exploring the nature–nurture controversy. In other words, to what extent are aspects of perception learned or hereditary? Although there is a growing consensus among behavioural scientists that most, if not all, aspects of perception involve both (e.g., Turkheimer, 1998), we'll consider their separate contributions in the sections below.

Evidence That Perception Is Innate

Evidence that perception is innate stems from two lines of research. The first involves people like the one described above. A number of case studies provide information about people who were blind at birth because of cataracts (or who became blind because cataracts developed shortly after birth) and subsequently became able to see, after surgical removal of the cataracts (Von Senden, 1960). If perception is innate, then such individuals should be able to see clearly immediately after recovery from surgery. Can they? Unfortunately, the question does not have a clear yes or no answer, and one probably should not be expected. Many of these patients have less than perfect functioning visual systems. What does seem true is that, without exception, they have a hard time coping with the visual world, and typically have a difficult time discerning size, distance, and shape, but some aspects of vision are clearly innate. They can almost immediately differentiate figure from ground and detect and follow moving objects.

Further evidence of innate perceptual properties is provided by research with very young infants. Studies show that infants selectively prefer some visual forms over others within the first week of life (Fantz, 1961). Infants are especially responsive to human facial features. This is clearly demonstrated in a study by Valenza and her colleagues (1996), in which four-day-old infants were exposed to patterns that did or did not resemble a human face. They showed a pronounced preference for the face-like pattern. Other studies have shown that infants can imitate some facial expressions they see, such as the protrusion of a mother's tongue, within minutes of birth (e.g., Reissland, 1988). Why are newborns so sensitive to facial features? Valenza and her colleagues take the position that it is advantageous in evolutionary terms for newborns to "home-in" immediately on their primary source of care—and that consequently a preference for face-like stimuli is likely hard-wired in the brain

Evidence for the **Importance of Learning and Experience**

Although some aspects of perception appear to be innate, there is considerable evidence for the view that learning and experience play an important role in perception. It is true that newborn children have some quite remarkable discriminative capacities at birth, but there is an enormous gap between the act of discrimination and that of understanding—and that gap is filled by learning and experience. (See the section on perceptual development in Chapter 8 for more information.)

Perhaps the most compelling evidence indicating that early visual experience can have a profound effect on perceptual development is provided by animal studies. In these studies, animals are typically raised in impoverished visual environments, and later tested to assess the effect of such restricted experience on their visual abilities. A good example of such a study is a project undertaken at Dalhousie University by Muir and Mitchell (1974). They raised kittens in darkness except for brief periods, during which they were exposed to either horizontal or vertical stripes. When later transferred to a normal visual environment, it was clear that these animals had been markedly affected by the visual experience they had encountered during rearing. They were quite responsive to linear objects—such as a long black rod—if the rod was oriented in the same direction as the stripes to which they had been exposed during rearing. However, when the same rod was rotated ninety degrees, they appeared completely blind to it. After a substantial period of adjustment to a normal visual environment, these kittens continued to show enduring differences. For as long as six months after the rearing experience, they had difficulty "seeing" linear arrangements oriented differently from the ones they had been exposed to. Clearly, the early learning experience can influence the development of visual functions.

Darwin Muir
Queen's University

Additional evidence that learning and experience in perception can shape perceptual experience comes from studies in which human volunteers wear special goggles that invert their view of the world and reverse right and left. The participants at first have difficulty carrying out normal activities with their goggles on, but they soon adapt and do everything from reading a book to flying a plane (Kohler, 1962). These findings, and others, suggest that there is indeed a plasticity to perception and we may well learn to interpret a good deal of the information supplied by our sensory receptors.

TESTING THE LIMITS OF PERCEPTUAL PLASTICITY A particularly interesting study test of the limits of perceptual plasticity was undertaken by Stuart Anstis and his associates at York University in Toronto in the early 1990s (Anstis & Hutahajan, 1991; Anstis, 1992). In his study, Anstis used a video device that generated a negative image of the visual world: Black became white, white became black, and colours appeared in complementary hues—yellows were conveyed as blues, blues as yellows, and greens as reds or purples, and so on.

For three days Anstis viewed the world through this device, carefully closing or masking his eyes when away from the device so as not to interfere with the adaptive process. At first the world was very unsettling: The normally blue sky appeared as a dark yellow. Moving into bright sunshine caused a darkening of the visual world and produced white shadows. As night closed in, the world appeared as a "daylit snowscape." People had a strange appearance. A research assistant had black teeth, white hair, and dark-blue skin. The pupils of her eyes were white, her irises silvery white. Recognition of individuals was difficult, and facial expressions were difficult to read.

After three days, some adaptation had taken place. Gross movements became readily discernible. Shapes and shadows could be separated if the shadows were sharp-edged. (Fuzzy shadows were harder to interpret.) Some improvement in reading facial expressions had been acquired, but profound difficulties in face recognition remained. Even very familiar figures were hard to identify. Anstis reports watching an old movie in which Bob Hope danced, and being quite able to follow the movements but totally unable to recognize the person making them.

The Anstis study shows that it isn't enough to be exposed to all the necessary visual information. To be effective, that information has to be in a form that the visual system is programmed to read and interpret. Anstis had all the visual information that we have under normal viewing conditions; the only change he experienced was a reversal of colour and brightness. The fact that his visual system could adapt only to certain aspects of this reversal is informative with respect to the limits of perceptual plasticity. His inability to deal with the changes that colour and brightness reversal made to face recognition, and the difficulties he experienced in interpreting shading, suggest that there is something very special, and very difficult to change, about the way our system has evolved to cope with these aspects of our visual environment.

Must We Try to Resolve the Nature–Nurture Controversy?

The findings we've reviewed thus far offer no simple resolution to the nature–nurture issue; other studies involving both animals and humans are equally inconclusive. Some studies show that certain aspects of visual perception seem to be present without previous sensory experience, whereas other aspects develop only through experience with the external world (Wiesel, 1982). Virtually all psychologists now accept that both innate factors and experience are needed to provide a complete account of our perceptual abilities (e.g., Turkheimer, 1998).

In sum, there is no way that we can resolve the nature–nurture question. Perception is plastic in the sense that it can be, and often is, modified by our encounters with physical reality. But there are biological limits to that plasticity. The best we can do is try and tease out, through clever experimentation, the relative roles played by innate mechanisms and by learning and experience in various different perceptual phenomena.

K E Y *QUESTIONS*

- How are the concepts of nature and nurture related to perception?

Critical Thinking

If learning and experience play a role in perception, is it possible that individuals who suffer a selective injury to their visual system and develop defects such as prosopagnosia or blindsight can expect to recover at least some of the capacities they have lost? Is the likelihood of recovery better if the injury occurs early in life when the visual system is more plastic?

Extrasensory Perception

Have you ever wondered if we have a "sixth sense"? In other words, can we gain information about the external world without use of our five basic senses? Many persons believe we can and accept the existence of **extrasensory perception**—literally, perception without a basis in sensation. The first and most basic question we can ask about ESP is "Does it really exist?" This question has been recast by Bem and Honorton (1994) in terms of a hypothetical process known as **psi**. These researchers define psi as unusual processes of information or energy transfer that are currently unexplained in terms of known physical or biological mechanisms.

Psi: What Is It?

Parapsychologists, who study psi and other *paranormal events* (i.e., events outside our normal experience or knowledge), suggest that there are actually several distinct forms of psi (or ESP). One form of psi is *precognition*—the ability to foretell future events. Fortune-tellers and even stock market analysts often earn their living from their supposed ability to make such predictions. *Clairvoyance*, the ability to perceive objects or events that do not directly stimulate your sensory organs, is another form. While playing cards, if you somehow know which one will be dealt next, you are experiencing clairvoyance. *Telepathy*, a skill used by mind readers, involves the direct transmission of thought from one person to the next. Another phenomenon often associated with psi is *psychokinesis*, the ability to affect the physical world purely through thought. Bending spoons, moving objects with your mind, and performing feats of levitation (making objects rise into the air) are examples of psychokinesis.

Does Psi Really Exist?

The idea of a mysterious sixth sense is intriguing, and many people are passionately convinced of its existence (Bowles & Hynds, 1978). But does it really exist? Most psychologists are skeptical about the existence of psi for several reasons. The first, and perhaps the most important, reason for doubting its existence is the repeated failure to replicate instances of psi; that is, certain procedures yield evidence for psi at one time, but not at others. Indeed, one survey failed to uncover a single instance of paranormal phenomena that could be reliably produced after ruling out alternative explanations such as fraud, methodological flaws, and normal sensory

Extrasensory Perception (ESP): Perception without a basis in sensory input.

Psi: Unusual processes of information or energy transfer that are currently unexplained in terms of known physical or biological mechanisms. Included under the heading of psi are such supposed abilities as telepathy (reading others' thoughts) and clairvoyance (perceiving unseen objects or unknowable events).

Parapsychologists: Individuals who study psi and other paranormal events.

functioning (Hoppe, 1988). Moreover, it appears that the more controlled studies of psi are, the less evidence for psi they have provided (Blackmore, 1986).

Second, present-day scientific understanding states that all aspects of our behaviour must ultimately stem from biochemical events, yet it is not clear what physical mechanism could account for psi. In fact, the existence of such a mechanism would require restructuring our view of the physical world.

Third, much of the support for psi has been obtained by persons already deeply convinced of its existence. As we noted in Chapter 1, scientists are not immune to being influenced in their observations by their own beliefs. Thus, while studies suggesting that psi exists may represent a small sample of all research conducted on this topic, perhaps only the few experiments yielding positive results find their way into print; perhaps the many "failures" are simply not reported.

K E Y *QUESTIONS*

- How are the concepts of nature and nurture related to perception?

- How do most psychologists view the possibility of extrasensory perception, or psi?

Making **Psychology** *Part of Your Life*

The Sounds Of Silence: Hearing Loss Does Not Only Happen To "Other People"

*D*ata from a recent U.S. National Interview survey reveal that during the period 1971 to 1990, hearing problems among people between the ages of forty-five and sixty-four increased by 26 percent, and by 17 percent among persons between the ages of eighteen and forty-four. More alarming is the discovery of a similar trend among young persons between the ages of six and nineteen. Nearly 15 percent of persons in this age group showed evidence of premature hearing loss.

The cause appears to be noise from the toys and tools of modern living: car stereos and stereo headsets, electric blow-dryers, lawnmowers and leaf blowers, and even some children's toys. Although these devices are intended to enhance work performance or the pleasure we derive from recreational activities, there is growing concern they may damage our hearing. Raging rock concerts, well-known for their capacity to produce hearing loss among performing artists and their listeners, are being supplanted by advances in digital sound technologies that allow car owners to play their car stereos at more than 150 decibels. Another less well-known source of dangerous noise is associated with the deployment of automobile air bags. Widely recognized for their ability to lessen occupant injuries in the event

of a vehicle crash, these devices can permanently damage hearing since the sound that accompanies their activation may reach levels up to 170 decibels! Although very intense sounds, like the ones just described, can

Many of the tools used to enhance everyday life could actually be causing premature hearing loss.

produce permanent damage following a single exposure, most of the damage appears to be the result of long-term exposure to moderately intense sounds, such as regularly cranking up the volume of a stereo headset or working for long periods with or around noisy equipment (e.g., lawn mowers, industrial equipment).

Hearing loss is actually the result of damage to the ear's sensory receptors. In our discussion of how the ears respond to sound waves earlier in this chapter, we pointed out that hair cells line the floor of the basilar membrane. There are about 15 000 of these tiny hair cells, which bend in response to sound-induced mechanical vibrations relayed by the bones in the middle ear. Differential bending of the hair cells is converted to a neural code that is delivered to the brain and interpreted as sound. Normally, sound waves cause only temporary distortion of the hair

cells, but over time, the hair cells tend to lose their resilience, and hearing loss ensures. Long-term exposure to moderately intense sound appears to accelerate the loss of resiliency.

Unfortunately, the public remains largely unaware of the damage that modern technologies can inflict on the sensitive organs that give rise to hearing. This is due, at least in part, to the gradual nature of the decline. In other words, except in instances involving extremely intense sound, most hearing loss occurs only after years of exposure. So, the next time that you get the urge to "pump up the volume" of your portable headset or car stereo or think about NOT using protective equipment for your ears before mowing the lawn or working with noisy equipment, consider the long-term advantages of making correct decisions. The hearing you save may be your own.

Summary and Review

Key Questions

Sensation: The Raw Materials of Understanding

- **What is the primary function of our sensory receptors?** Sensory receptors transduce raw physical energy into neural impulses, which are then interpreted by our central nervous system.

- **What does the term *absolute threshold* refer to, and why is signal detection theory important?** The absolute threshold is the smallest magnitude of a stimulus that can be detected 50 percent of the time. Signal detection theory helps to separate sensitivity from motivational factors.

- **What is a difference threshold?** *Difference threshold* refers to the amount of change in a stimulus required for a person to detect it.

- **Can subliminal messages influence what we do or how we act?** There is no evidence that subliminal messages can impel us to think or act in a particular manner.

- **What is the role of sensory adaptation in sensation?** Sensory adaptation serves a useful function by allowing us to focus on important changes in our environment.

Vision

- **What are the basic structures of the eye and what is the physical stimulus for vision?** Light rays first pass through the cornea and then enter the eye through the pupil. Adjustments to lighting conditions are executed by the iris. The lens is a clear structure whose shape adjusts to permit us to focus on objects at varying distances. Light rays leaving the lens are projected onto the retina at the back of the eyeball. The physical stimulus for vision is electromagnetic wavelengths that stimulate the rods and cones in the retina.

- **What are the basic functions of the visual system?** The basic functions of the visual system include acuity, dark adaptation, and eye movements. Acuity refers to the ability to see fine details. Dark adaptation refers to the increase in sensitivity that occurs when we move from bright light to a dim environment. Various types of eye movements are crucial to our ability to track moving objects and to perceive distance and depth.

- **How do psychologists explain colour perception?** Our rich sense of colour stems from mechanisms at several levels of our nervous system. Two leading theories that explain how we perceive colour are the trichromatic theory and the opponent-process theory.

Why is visual perception a hierarchical process? Visual information is analyzed in successive stages. Each stage integrates and elaborates information received from preceding stages. The end product is a coherent and meaningful representation of the visual world.

What are the basic building blocks of visual perception? The basic building blocks of visual perception begin with feature detectors—neurons in the visual cortex that respond when particular types of stimuli, with characteristic features, are detected.

What evidence suggests that separate and distinct processing systems work independently to extract information about salient aspects of the visual world? Case studies show that our ability to respond to certain salient aspects of the visual world such as motion, shape, and colour can be selectively impaired without any general impairment in all other visual-processing operations.

Hearing

What is the physical stimulus for hearing? The physical stimulus for hearing is sound waves that stimulate tiny hair cells in the cochlea.

How do psychologists explain pitch perception? Place theory and frequency theory help explain how we perceive pitch.

How do we localize sound? The sound shadow created by our head causes sound to reach one ear slightly faster than the other. This small time difference helps us localize the source of sound.

Touch and Other Skin Senses

What is the physical stimulus for touch? The physical stimulus for touch is a stretching of, or pressure against, receptors in or near the skin.

Where does the sensation of pain originate? Sensations of pain originate in free nerve endings throughout the body.

What is the basis for cultural differences in pain perception? Cultural differences in pain perception appear to be the result of learning—not physical differences.

What role do cognitive processes play in the perception of pain? Negative thinking while in pain, referred to as *catastrophizing*, can increase the perceived intensity of pain.

Smell and Taste: The Chemical Senses

What is the physical stimulus for smell? The physical stimulus for sensations of smell are molecules that stimulate receptors in the nose.

Where are the sensory receptors for taste located? The sensory receptors for taste are located in papillae on the tongue.

Kinesthesia and Vestibular Sense

What information does our kinesthetic sense provide to the brain? Kinesthesia informs the brain about the location of body parts with respect to each other.

What information does the vestibular sense provide to the brain? The vestibular sense provides information about body position, movement, and acceleration.

Perception: Putting It All Together

Why is selective attention important? Selective attention reduces the interference from irrelevant sensory sources.

What role do the Gestalt principles play in perceptual processes? The Gestalt principles of perceptual organization help us to structure the input from our sensory receptors.

What are perceptual constancies? Perceptual constancies refer to our ability to perceive aspects of the world as unchanging despite variations in the information reaching our sensory receptors, such as size, shape, or brightness.

What are illusions? Illusion is a term used by psychologists to refer to errors in interpreting sensory information.

What are the bottom-up and top-down theories of pattern recognition? The bottom-up theory suggests that pattern recognition stems from our ability to recognize and combine basic visual features. In contrast, top-down theory emphasizes the role that expectations play in shaping our perceptions.

What are geons? What is their role in object recognition? Geons are basic three-dimensional forms that, when combined according to rules, can be used to produce any object. Some evidence suggests that geons are the basis of our representation of objects in memory.

How are we able to judge depth and distance? Judgments of depth and distance result from both binocular and monocular cues.

The Plasticity of Perception

How are the concepts *nature* and *nurture* related to perception? Both nature and nurture are important determinants of the ways we perceive the world around us. Nature refers to genetic influences on perception, whereas nurture refers to the relative effects of the environment and learning.

Extrasensory Perception

How do most psychologists view the possibility of extrasensory perception or psi? Most psychologists remain highly skeptical about its existence.

Key Terms

Absolute Threshold (p. 92)

Binocular Cues (p. 125)

Blind Spot (p. 97)

Blindsight (p. 102)

Brightness (p. 98)

Brightness Constancy (p. 121)

Cochlea (p. 105)

Complex Cells (p. 101)

Cones (p. 97)

Constancies (p. 119)

Cornea (p. 95)

Dark Adaptation (p. 99)

Difference Threshold (p. 93)

Endogenously Controlled Attention (p. 116)

Exogenously Controlled Attention (p. 117)

Extrasensory Perception (ESP) (p. 129)

Farsightedness (p. 99)

Feature Detectors (p. 101)

Figure–Ground Relationship (p. 118)

Fovea (p. 97)

Frequency Theory (p. 107)

Gate-Control Theory (p. 109)

Gestalt Psychologists (p. 118)

Hue (p. 98)

Hypercomplex Cells (p. 101)

Illusions (p. 121)

Iris (p. 95)

Just Noticeable Difference (jnd) (p. 93)

Kinesthesia (p. 114)

Laws of Grouping (p. 119)

Lens (p. 95)

Localization (p. 107)

Monocular Cues (p. 125)

Nearsightedness (p. 98)

Negative Afterimage (p. 100)

Opponent-Process Theory (p. 100)

Optic Nerve (p. 97)

Parapsychologists (p. 129)

Perception (p. 90)

Pinna (p. 105)

Pitch (p. 106)

Place Theory (p. 106)

Prosopagnosia (p. 102)

Prototypes (p.124)

Psi (p. 129)

Pupil (p. 95)

Relative Size (p. 121)

Retina (p. 95)

Rods (p. 97)

Saccadic Movements (p. 99)

Saturation (p. 98)

Semicircular Canals (p. 115)

Sensation (p. 90)

Sensory Adaptation (p. 94)

Sensory Receptors (p. 91)

Shape Constancy (p. 121)

Signal Detection Theory (p. 92)

Simple Cells (p. 101)

Size Constancy (p. 119)

Subliminal Perception (p. 93)

Templates (p. 124)

Timbre (p. 106)

Transduction (p. 91)

Trichromatic Theory (p. 100)

Vestibular Sacs (p. 115)

Vestibular Sense (p. 115)

Wavelength (p. 98)

Critical Thinking Questions

Appraisal

Many psychologists would agree that conscious experience is nothing more than the result of the brain's efforts to integrate information received from the senses. Do you agree? Why? If not, offer an alternative view.

Controversy

Visual priming studies show that subliminal stimuli—stimuli registered by our sensory organs, but that remain outside our conscious awareness—produce measurable effects on various aspects of cognition and behaviour. Based on this evidence, do you think there is any possibility that sublimi-

nal perception might, at some time, develop into a powe[r]
tool of persuasion?

Making Psychology Part of Your Life

On the basis of what you have learned about human s[ensory]
and perceptual processing in this chapter, specula[te on]
the character of sensory and perceptual experience[s in other]
organisms. Many animals rely on the chemical se[nses to a]
much greater degree than we do. Many animals a[re]
tuned to different parts of the visual and sound[spectrum.]
The senses provide our window on reality. Do di[fferent sen-]
sory systems shape different realities?

Weblinks

Check out our Companion Website at www.pearsoned.ca/baron for additional Websites, activities, and more.

Tutorials in Sensation and Perception

psych.hanover.edu/Krantz/sen_tut.html

This collection of tutorials in some fundamental concepts in sensory processes includes an interesting section about the use of visual information in art.

Subliminal Priming: Does It Work?

www.gettysburg.edu:8080/~s394566/Psych.html

This discussion of subliminal priming includes links to arguments on both sides of the debate about whether it works.

IllusionWorks

www.illusionworks.com/

This site contains a wonderful collection of illusions (optical and auditory) and articles, demonstrations, a reading list, and links to other illusions sites.

The Joy of Visual Perception

www.yorku.ca/research/vision/eye/how-to.htm

Here you will find a Web book entitled *The Joy of Visual Perception* created at York University. There are all kinds of graphic illustrations for difficult principles to enrich your study of this chapter. For example, follow the link to shape constancy and you will easily understand how this has to be the product of analysis in the brain.

Color Matters

www.colormatters.com/entercolormatters.html

Here is a Website about colour vision. Follow the links to find out the answer to all kinds of questions—for example, "What happens when a chicken sees red?"

Chapter 4

States of Consciousness

Awareness of Ourselves
in the External World

CHAPTER OUTLINE

Winter Blues

A report in the *Yellowknifer* asks, "Do you find yourself constantly feeling tense, continually high strung, carelessly teetering on the edge of complete mental breakdown?" That kind of anxiety—also intense depression—occurs commonly in the North during mid-winter.

Why would anxiety or depression be a seasonal thing? Why is it more common in the winter? One important reason is that our bodies operate according to certain biological rhythms. Changes in states of consciousness occur regularly and routinely, often in response to changes in the environment. Some of those rhythms occur every day—for example, sleep and waking are linked to the darkness of night and the light of day.

In the North, during the long nights and dark days of winter, the body's rhythms get out of synch with the changes in the environment and that causes changes in the way people feel and behave. Of course, that is true not only in the far North, but also anywhere with such seasonal changes in light and dark.

What is the purpose of these biological rhythms? How do they work? What can we do when they are out of order? Psychological science has much to offer to these puzzles, and you will know more about that as you proceed through Chapter 4.

Crabbe, S. 2000, February 11. Stressed out...Mental health week recognizes daily stress as this year's theme, *Yellowknifer*, p. A6.

> **We all experience different states of consciousness—levels of awareness of internal and external stimuli—every day.**

When do you feel more alert and energetic—in the morning or late in the afternoon? Do you daydream in class and later wonder what the professor said? While you brush your teeth, are you thinking neither about your brush nor your teeth? Do you drive for blocks without knowing what went by? If your answer to any of those questions is "Yes," you already know that there are **states of consciousness**—different levels of awareness that occur every day. These states vary in focus and in sensitivity—from the heightened awareness of a runner at the starting gate to the total lack of awareness of a patient in a state of coma. Every time you go to sleep or take some drug that affects the way you feel, you change your state of consciousness.

Being familiar with these shifts, however, does not necessarily help us understand them. Why are we more alert at some times during the day than at others? What happens when we fall asleep? What, precisely, are dreams? And how do various drugs affect our emotions, perceptions, and thinking? People have been wondering about these questions for many years (Hunt, 1995).

Given its obvious impact on all aspects of our behaviour, consciousness is clearly an important topic in psychology (Hameroff et al., 1996; Shear & Jevning, 1999). In contemporary psychology, consciousness is considered a function of the nervous system (Austin, 1998). For example, electrical activities of the brain as measured by EEG —*brain waves* as they are sometimes called—tell us about brain activity during changes in states of consciousness, such as changing from sleep to waking. Also, changes in consciousness result in observable differences in behaviour, as occur when we alter the chemistry of the nervous system with certain kinds of drugs—alcohol or LSD, for example.

How did consciousness evolve? Why are we able to recognize different levels of arousal and different states of awareness in ourselves? What is self-awareness? Those are questions being asked by contemporary theorists. One answer is this: The neural networks that make us conscious and aware evolved because they promoted survival. What is the evidence? First, some kinds of internal arousal states are positive and some are negative. We seek out circumstances that have provided pleasure and we likely benefit from that; we avoid circumstances that produce pain and predators, which contributes to our well-being also. Second, consciousness provides us with an understanding of ourselves—*self-awareness*—which is necessary for appreciating the differences between ourselves and other people. Awareness of other people and how they are feeling allows us to conduct ourselves appropriately in social situations and to engage in cooperative social ventures. Third, consciousness contributes to our remarkable human ability to create and understand complex ideas.

Much of current knowledge about how consciousness works will be summarized in this chapter. We will begin by considering the biological roots of consciousness: biological rhythms. These are naturally, regularly occurring, cyclical changes in many basic bodily processes and mental states (de Koninck, 1991). After that, we will turn to what is perhaps the most profound, regular shift in consciousness we experience: sleep. Then we will examine two external stimuli that sometimes produce altered states of consciousness—hypnosis and drugs. Finally, we will consider several aspects of normal, waking consciousness.

States of Consciousness:
Varying degrees of awareness of ourselves and the external world.

Biological Rhythms

Suppose that you must schedule an appointment for a very important interview. The interviewer has a number of time slots available; you can choose to meet with her at almost any time of day. What time would you select? Did you have any difficulty in making a choice? Probably not. Most of us are well aware of the fact that we are at our best—most alert, attentive, and energetic—at certain times of the day. Thus, all other things being equal, we will probably schedule the meeting for a time when we think we will most likely make a good impression (Monk & Folkard, 1983).

Regular shifts in alertness or energy are examples of **biological rhythms**—regular fluctuations in our bodily processes over time. Many of these fluctuations occur over the course of a single day and are known as **circadian** (from the Latin words for "around" and "day") **rhythms**. As we will soon see, such rhythms can affect us profoundly in many respects, at all ages. Other biological rhythms take place within shorter periods of time (e.g., Klein & Armitage, 1979); they are known as *ultradian rhythms*. For example, many people become hungry every two or three hours (at least while they are awake). Animals also develop cycles related to feeding (Mistlberger, 1996). And during sleep, periods of dreaming occur at roughly ninety-minute intervals. Finally, some biological cycles take longer than twenty-four hours, called *infraradian rhythms*. For example, each menstrual cycle spans approximately twenty-eight days.

Such rhythms often have a relationship to states of consciousness. Since circadian rhythms have received the most research attention, we will focus primarily on these, describing their basic nature, individual differences among them, and some of their practical implications.

Jet Lag

When our natural biological rhythms are interrupted, for example by changing time zones, we feel less alert, like these passengers on a transatlantic flight.

The Basic Nature of Circadian Rhythms

Most people are aware of fluctuations in their alertness, energy, and mood over the course of a day. Do such shifts reflect actual changes in underlying bodily states? There is much evidence that they do (e.g., Moore-Ede, Sulzman, & Fuller, 1982). Careful study has revealed that many bodily processes do indeed show daily cyclical changes. The production of various hormones fluctuates across the day; hormone levels are high at some times but much lower at others. For many people, core body temperature, blood pressure, and several other processes are highest in the late afternoon or evening and lowest in the early hours of the morning—although, as we will see below, there are large individual differences in these measures.

As you might expect, these cyclic fluctuations in basic bodily functions—and our subjective feelings of alertness—are related to task performance. In general, people do their best work when body temperature and other internal processes are at or near their personal peaks. For example, daily fluctuations in body temperature have a stronger impact on relatively simple tasks than on more complex cognitive ones (e.g., Daniel & Potasova,1989), as shown in Figure 4.1.

How Do Circadian Rhythms Work?

If bodily processes, mental alertness, and performance fluctuate regularly over the course of the day, there must be an internal biological mechanism for regulating such changes. In other words, we must possess a biological clock that *times* various circadian rhythms. While there is not yet total agreement on the nature of this clock, many scientists believe that it is located in a portion of the hypothalamus—

Biological Rhythms: Cyclic changes in bodily processes.

Circadian Rhythms: Cyclic changes in bodily processes occurring within a single day.

Figure 4.1
Circadian Rhythms, Body Temperature, and Task Performance

On a tapping task, performance rose and fell with daily changes in body temperature. However, there was no relationship between body temperature and performance on a more complex cognitive task.

Source: Based on data from Daniel and Potasova, 1989.

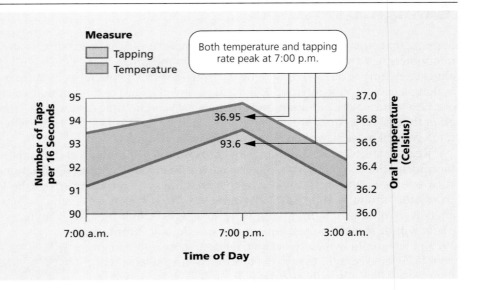

Suprachiasmatic Nucleus: A portion of the hypothalamus that seems to play an important role in the regulation of circadian rhythms.

Seasonal Affective Disorder (SAD): Depression typically experienced during the winter months, supposedly stemming from a lack of exposure to sunlight.

specifically, in the **suprachiasmatic nucleus** (Rusak, 1990). This nucleus responds to visual input from the eyes and either stimulates or inhibits activity in the pineal gland. The pineal gland, in turn, secretes *melatonin*, a hormone that exerts a far-reaching sedative effect, increasing fatigue and reducing activity.

Exposure to daylight stimulates the suprachiasmatic nucleus, and this in turn reduces the secretion of melatonin. In contrast, darkness enhances it. (See the **Canadian Focus** feature for more information on how amount of daylight affects us.) Evidence that the suprachiasmatic nucleus acts as a biological clock is provided by research indicating that when it is damaged, or when neural pathways connecting it to the eyes are destroyed, some circadian rhythms disappear. Some continue to work, however, so that there may be not just one but several biological clocks for different purposes, at different locations in the brain (Mistlberger, 1992; Mrosovsky, 1986).

Canadian Focus

Seasonal Sadness ... Let the Sunshine in!

Many Canadians feel down in winter, when the amount of sunlight is drastically reduced. You may feel that way too. Indeed, one might say that winter is a sad state of mind. However, for some of us, the reaction is more severe. The symptoms include recurring episodes of deep depression during winter, anxiety, withdrawal, decreased energy levels and sex drive, increased appetite, craving for carbohydrates, and weight gain. In that case, the depression may be winter **seasonal affective disorder**, or SAD. Research into the causes of SAD are being conducted in laboratories in Canada, including the Clarke Institute of the University of Toronto, (for example, Bagby et al., 1996), and the University of British Columbia in Vancouver (for example, Tam et al., 1995). Studies of animal behaviour indicate that winter depression may involve a disturbance in some circadian rhythms (Surridge et al., 1987), including those for body temperature, sleep–wakefulness, REM sleep, melatonin secretion, and levels of some neurotransmitters. Another finding is that people with SAD may have abnormal retinal sensitivity (too low or too high) to light. There is evidence for a genetic component to this disorder (Jang et al., 1998). Animals that hibernate in the winter—chipmunks, for example—may help us understand this type of depressive reaction (Mrosovsky, 1988).

Although you might think it is the cold temperature in winter that is getting you down, that does not seem to be the case. Rather, what is important is the amount of sunlight. Very cold but sunny places like Winnipeg or Calgary are better in this respect than somewhat warmer but duller spots. Of course, a sunny day has other positive effects as well. Compliance with a request from a stranger is one of these. For example, there is a positive relationship between whether there is sunshine and whether people will participate in a survey (Cunningham, 1979). More recently, Rind (1996) showed that even beliefs about sunshine affect behaviour. In his experiment, diners in a shielded room in a restaurant were told one of four reports about the weather outside: cold or warm, and rainy or sunny. Those who believed the weather was sunny gave significantly higher tips. Information about temperature had no such effect. Thus, beliefs about whether the skies are sunny can influence not only our mood, but also our behaviour.

The farther north one goes from the equator, the less sunlight there is in winter. In Inuvik, Northwest Territories, for example, in December the sun does not shine at all. It makes some sense to predict, then, that SAD will become more and more common the closer to the North Pole you get. The frequency of winter SAD at different latitudes has been studied (e.g., Rosen et al., 1990); these frequencies may vary from 1.4 percent of the population in southern Florida, to 8 percent in New Hampshire, to 12 percent in Edmonton, to an estimated 18 percent in Inuvik, the largest community in the Western Arctic.

The hormone melatonin plays an important role in the seasonal changes of our behaviour and our biology (Wher, 1997). Since lack of sunlight and too-high levels of melatonin during the day are both thought to be involved, the therapy for winter SAD may include resetting melatonin levels with melatonin pills taken at specific times (an experimental approach) or light therapy, or both.

According to research done at the Clarke Institute in Toronto, an antidepressant response occurs in at least half of winter SAD patients who are treated with light therapy (Lam, 1998). The light therapy may be provided by a bank of lights or by a helmet with a light visor that the SAD patient wears. There may be some temporary side effects of light therapy, such as "feeling wired," early in treatment (Levitt et al., 1993), and there is some concern for retinal damage if too-bright light is used. Antidepressant drugs also may help and some are known to change the response of the retina to light, which may be one of the ways they are effective in relieving this depression. Another possible explanation (Lam et al., 1996) is this: Light therapy may have an antidepressant effect by way of its influence upon levels of serotonin (a neurotransmitter related to mood state).

Those who live in Canada's north (Yukoners, for example) have created their own version of preventive light therapy. There, in winter, people use timers to turn on lights in the morning to mimic the dawn each day. Along the same lines, a new dawn simulator is being tested. This simulator emits low-intensity light in the early morning, while the patient is asleep, and tries to convince the brain to "pretend that it is spring." More generally, it may be no coincidence that many different ethnic and religious groups have holidays associated with lights that take place at the darkest time of the year.

Some patients suffer from a different seasonal disorder: summer SAD. The symptoms of summer and winter depression are quite opposite (Wehr et al., 1991). Indeed, symptoms consistent with winter SAD increase as latitude goes north and those consistent with summer SAD increase as latitude goes south (Rosen & Rosenthal, 1991).Where summer depressives most often report decreased appetite and insomnia, winter depressives most often report increased appetite and hypersomnia (excessive sleepiness). However, in June in Inuvik, where the sun does not set, patients also complain about summer SAD. They feel they have too much energy (hypomania) and are unable to slow themselves down. The more we understand biological rhythms, the better we will be able to solve the puzzle of these changes in mood over the course of the seasons and design treatments for them.

Another intriguing fact is that when left to its own devices, our internal biological clock seems to operate on a twenty-five-hour rather than a twenty-four-hour day. This is indicated by research in which volunteers have lived in caves or other environments totally removed from clocks, the rising and setting of the sun, and other cues we normally use to keep track of time. Under these conditions, most people shifted to a "day" of about twenty-five hours (Moore-Ede, Sulzman, & Fuller, 1982). In other words, each day they rose and went to sleep a little later, and all their activities shifted accordingly. Their basic bodily functions, too, shifted from a twenty-four-hour cycle to this slightly longer one. The implication of this for our usual activities seems to be negligible, but it is a factor in jet lag, since lengthening our day going west is easy, whereas shortening our day going east is difficult.

Perspectives on Diversity

Individual Differences in Circadian Rhythms

BEFORE READING FURTHER, please answer the questions in Table 4.1.

TABLE 4.1		

Are You a Lark or an Owl?

If you answer "Day" to eight or more of these questions, you are probably a morning person. If you answer "Night" to eight or more, you are probably a night person.

Please respond to each of the following items by circling either "Day" or "Night."

1. I feel most alert during the	Day	Night
2. I have most energy during the	Day	Night
3. I prefer to take classes during the	Day	Night
4. I prefer to study during the	Day	Night
5. I get my best ideas during the	Day	Night
6. When I graduate, I prefer to find a job during the	Day	Night
7. I am most productive during the	Day	Night
8. I feel most intelligent during the	Day	Night
9. I enjoy leisure-time activities most during the	Day	Night
10. I prefer to work during the	Day	Night

Source: Based on items from Wallace, 1993.

How did you score? If you answered "Day" to eight or more questions, chances are good that you are a morning person (a lark). If, instead, you answered "Night" to eight or more questions, you are probably a night person (an owl). Studies indicate that the two groups do differ. For example, morning people experience peaks in body temperature earlier in the day than night people (Wallace, 1993). Morning people have temperature peaks before noon; night people often experience those peaks in the evening around six p.m. or even later. Not surprisingly, morning people report feeling more alert and do better on many cognitive tasks early in the day. In contrast, night people report feeling more alert and do better on such tasks later in the day. The morning–evening difference in attention is evident at all ages (Intons et al., 1998) and there may be a genetic link (Hur et al., 1998), but experience also makes a difference. At Simon Fraser University, Mistlberger (1991) did make some hamsters into "night owls" and others into "early birds" by varying the times the animals exercised (i.e., in the late dark or in mid-light), or the times they were fed, or both.

That differences in alertness and bodily states translate into important effects on behaviour is indicated by a study conducted by Guthrie, Ash, and Bandapudi (1995). They had several hundred college students complete a questionnaire similar to the one in Table 4.1. On the basis of the replies, they classified the students as either morning or evening persons. Then, at the end of the semester, they obtained the students' grades in all their classes. As you can see from Figure 4.2, students classified as morning persons obtained higher grades in early morning classes than

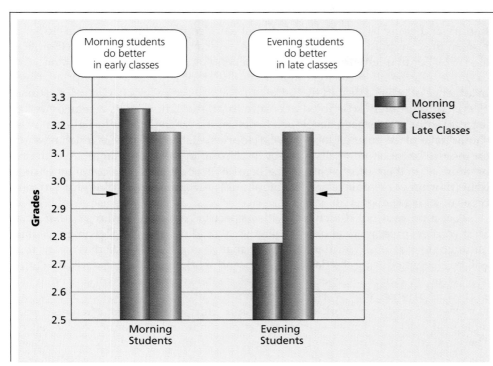

Figure 4.2
Circadian Rhythms and Grades

As shown here, students who were classified as being morning persons obtained higher grades in early morning classes than in later classes. In contrast, students classified as being night (evening) persons obtained higher grades in classes held later in the day than in early morning classes

Source: Based on data from Guthrie, Ash, and Banadpudi, 1995.

in later classes, and the opposite was also true. The practical implications of these findings seem clear: Determine whether you are a morning or night person, and then try—to the extent this is possible—to schedule your classes accordingly. There may be a benefit to your grade point average.

Disturbances of Circadian Rhythms

Under normal conditions, circadian rhythms pose no special problems. Unfortunately, though, there are circumstances in which circadian rhythms may get badly out of phase with our daily activities.

The first of these situations occurs as a result of modern travel—*jet lag*. When individuals cross several time zones, they often experience considerable difficulty in adjusting to their new location. They feel tired, dull, queasy, and generally out of sorts. The reason for this is clear: Their internal biological clocks are telling them it is one time, while the outside world is telling them something else. A recent survey showed that people who work in the airline industry, for example flight attendants on intercontinental flights, are just as likely as passengers are to get jet lag (Criglington, 1998).

This is particularly relevant to travel in Canada since the directions in which we go are most often east to west or west to east. For example, suppose you were flying from St. John's to Vancouver. If you left the east at 2:00 p.m. local time, you might arrive in the west about nine hours later. Back in Newfoundland it would be 11:00 p.m., just about time to hit the sack, perhaps. In B.C., however, it would be 6:30 p.m., still light, and a little early to go to sleep no matter what your brain was telling your body. This conflict between your internal clock and your external environment may produce jet lag. For most people, the disruption is less of a problem when we fly west, into a time zone where it is earlier, than when we fly east, into a time zone where it is later.

Current wisdom has it that to reduce the discomfort of jet lag—and to readjust your internal clock—immediately adopt the time on the external clock and behave accordingly. For a few days, that may mean eating at times when you do not feel hungry and going to bed when you do not feel sleepy until your internal clock adjusts to the external world. Exercise on the new timetable may also help (Shiota et al., 1996). For frequent fliers, there is new technology that may be of assistance. For example, alternately wearing a light visor and dark goggles at appropriate times in advance of travel can shift the setting of your biological clock (Gallo & Eastman, 1993). Appropriately scheduled exposure to bright light may be a remedy for jet lag, and software has been developed to determine when that bright-light exposure should take place during global travel (Houpt et al., 1996). There is much research on the use of melatonin pills to reset the circadian clock, but there are differing opinions as to their effectiveness (Czeisler, 1997). Some experts recommend bright light (morning or evening) and melatonin pills (evening or morning) for different types of jet lag (Lewy et al., 1998).

A second cause of difficulties with respect to circadian rhythms is *shift work*. Shift workers must work at times when they would normally be sleeping—usually midnight to 8:00 a.m. (Fierman, 1995). For many people in Canada that means they will be sleeping during the daylight hours and working when it is dark. In winter, that is true for more than one shift. To make matters worse, shift workers often face a schedule in which they work on one shift for a fairly short period (say a week), get two days off, and then work on another shift. Shift workers must often reset their biological clocks and may suffer serious personal and economic consequences. There are reports of high levels of fatigue and serious sleep disorders; increased rates of heart disease and ulcers; increased rates of automobile and industrial accidents; and increased use of alcohol, sleeping pills, and other drugs (Angerspach et al., 1980; Lidell, 1982; Meijmann et al., 1993). Nevertheless, the costs of modern industrial equipment make it almost a necessity to operate many factories around the clock. Airports, hospitals, police, and fire departments cannot close down at night.

Since shift work is a reality of modern life, can anything be done to lessen its potentially harmful effects? These are the findings of a recent study of disruptions in circadian rhythms that used an old research method—the diary approach—with new technology (Totterdell et al., 1995). Nurses were each given a pocket computer and asked to use it to report on specific aspects of their own behaviour, several times a day, for twenty-eight days. For example, when they received a signal, the nurses provided information about their sleep (e.g., when they went to sleep, when they woke up, the quality of their sleep, etc.), and their current moods (e.g., how cheerful, calm, and alert they felt). On work days, they also rated their own performance and their stress levels every two hours, and they tested their own mental alertness—for example, by completing a reaction-time task, which measured how quickly they responded to various stimuli—on the computer.

The findings of the diary approach suggested that the best solution to the negative effects of shift work might be to lengthen the time people spend on each shift (several weeks or months instead of just a week or two), and to recruit groups of employees who are willing to stay permanently on the night shift (Jamal & Baba, 1992). Implementation of these changes actually helped employees adjust better to changing shifts. In a study by Czeisler, Moore-Ede, and Coleman (1982), productivity increased, health improved, and rate of turnover (voluntary quitting) dropped appreciably. In other words, the work schedule that took account of the basic properties of the circadian system was much more effective than one that ignored them. Thus, basic knowledge about the nature of circadian rhythms points to some steps that might be of considerable help.

More recent efforts to help people cope with the stress of shift work have adopted a somewhat different approach—the one that is based on the role the suprachiasmatic nucleus plays in regulating circadian rhythms. Light exposure may be helpful (Boulos, 1998). In order to help night workers at nuclear power plants to stay awake in the early morning hours, one company has developed a lighting system that simulates the normal cycle of strengthening and weakening sunlight during the day (Noble, 1993). It is intended that these changes during the night shift will "trick" the visual system into reversing the times of peak alertness and drowsiness that are part of the normal circadian cycle. To help strengthen such effects, the workers wear dark glasses when they have to leave the light-controlled areas of the plant and they wear sunglasses when going home in the morning to avoid exposure to direct sunlight. The findings are encouraging with respect to increased alertness—and decreased errors.

The moral of this project is clear: Human beings are adaptive and can, to an extent, cope with almost any kind of work schedule. However, schedules designed to cooperate with rather than challenge employees' basic biological rhythms are almost certain to prove more cost effective, as well as more compassionate, in the long run.

K E Y QUESTIONS

■ What are biological rhythms? What are circadian rhythms?

■ How do morning people and night people differ?

■ What effects do jet lag and shift work have on circadian rhythms?

■ How do psychologists use diary studies to study circadian rhythms?

Critical Thinking

Suppose that you are an evening person but must make an important presentation early in the morning. What can you do to improve your own alertness—and performance?

Sleep

Which single activity occupies more of your time than any other? While you may be tempted to say "studying" or "working," think again. If you are like most people, the answer is probably **sleep**. Most human beings spend one-third of their lives asleep, and for some the proportion is even higher (Dement, 1975; Webb, 1975). Any activity that occupies so much of our time must be important, and the nature of sleep has been studied by psychologists for several decades (Antrobus & Bertini, 1992). What has this research revealed? What happens when we sleep and when we dream? And what are the functions of these behaviours? These are some of the questions we will now explore.

How Sleep Is Studied

We all agree that when we sleep, we are in a different state of consciousness than when we are awake. But what is sleep really like? This is a difficult question to answer, since during sleep we are far less aware of ourselves and our surroundings than at other times. For this reason, asking people about their own experience with sleep is not a very useful technique for studying it. Fortunately, there is another approach that is much more informative. As a person moves from a waking state to deep sleep, complex changes in electrical activity of the brain and the muscles of the body and the eyes occur. These electrical changes can be measured with great precision, and the resulting **electroencephalogram (EEG)** of brain activity, *electromyogram (EMG)* of muscle activity, and *electro-oculogram (EOG)* of eye activity reveal much about the nature of sleep.

In research on sleep, volunteers are fitted with electrodes so that researchers can record their brain activity as well as other changes in bodily functions such as respiration, muscle tone, heart rate, and blood pressure. The changes that occur as the volunteers fall asleep and continue sleeping are then studied. In this way researchers can obtain detailed information about the normal course of sleep.

Sleep: A process in which important physiological changes (including shifts in brain activity and slowing of basic bodily functions) are accompanied by major shifts in consciousness.

Electroencephalogram (EEG): A record of electrical activity within the brain. EEGs play an important role in the scientific study of sleep.

The Basic Nature of Sleep

What has sleep research revealed? When you are fully awake and alert, your EEG contains many *beta waves*, which are of relatively high frequency and low amplitude. As you enter a quiet, resting state (for example, just after getting into bed and turning out the light), these beta waves are replaced by **alpha waves**, which are of somewhat lower frequency but slightly higher amplitude. Prior to actually falling asleep, there is a transition period of chemical changes in the brain—a dream-like or *hypnogogic* state— that may take up to ten minutes. That may be why we use such phrases as "drifting off to sleep," which suggest that the onset of sleep is gradual, but it is actually quite sudden.

Sleep itself, however, is not a uniform type of activity. As you begin to fall asleep, increasingly large numbers of neurons begin firing together; that is, they fire in an increasingly *synchronized* manner. In contrast, desynchronized EEG activity occurs during wakefulness as many different populations of neurons carry out their own responsibilities.

EEG records obtained from thousands of volunteers in sleep research indicate that sleep can actually be divided into four different stages. As shown in Figure 4.3, each stage is marked by a pattern of activity that can be characterized by the frequency and the voltage of the electrical records. The transition from wakefulness to sleep occurs with the onset of Stage 1 sleep. During this stage, the EEG pattern becomes more and more mixed with the appearance of greater numbers of *theta* waves. Breathing slows, muscle tone decreases, and the body generally relaxes. At this point, individuals can still be easily awakened by external stimuli.

During Stage 2 sleep, theta waves continue and the brain emits occasional short bursts of rapid, high-voltage waves known as *sleep spindles* and slower K-complexes. It is thought that these events help us to remain asleep and enter deeper stages of sleep (Carlson, 1999). In Stage 2 also, sleepers are much more difficult to awaken. Stages 3 and 4 are marked by the increasing appearance of slow, high-amplitude **delta waves,** and by a further slowing of all major bodily functions (Dement, 1975). A departure from this pattern may be a sign of some disease or disorder, such as adolescent depression (Kutcher et al., 1992) or Alzheimer's disease (Petit et al., 1992).

Alpha Waves: Brain waves that occur when individuals are awake but relaxed.

Delta Waves: High-amplitude, slow brain waves that occur during several stages of sleep, but especially during Stage 4.

Figure 4.3
Sleep Stages

As an individual falls asleep, the electrical activity of the brain changes in an orderly manner. Note the contrasting patterns of activity shown before sleep begins and during each of the succeeding stages.

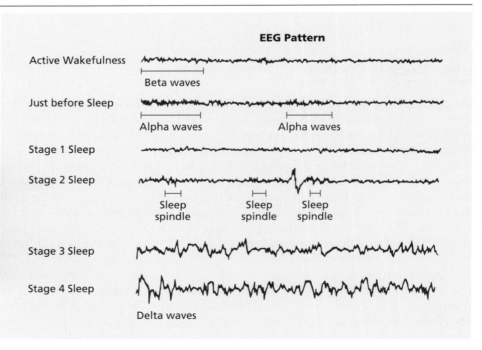

EEG Pattern

Active Wakefulness
Beta waves

Just before Sleep
Alpha waves   Alpha waves

Stage 1 Sleep

Stage 2 Sleep
Sleep   Sleep   Sleep
spindle   spindle   spindle

Stage 3 Sleep

Stage 4 Sleep

Delta waves

So far, the picture presented here probably sounds pretty consistent with your own subjective experience; you change from being awake to being more and more deeply asleep. About ninety minutes after sleep begins, however, several dramatic changes occur. First, most people enter a highly distinct phase known as **REM (rapid eye movement) sleep**. During this phase, the electrical activity of the brain changes; it now closely resembles that of people who are awake. Second, sleepers' eyes begin to move about rapidly beneath their closed eyelids. Third, there is an almost total suppression of activity in the body muscles, producing a temporary state of paralysis in the body. Yet at the same time, males may experience erections and females corresponding sexual changes. This combination of signs of activation and signs of profound relaxation has led some researchers to describe REM sleep as paradoxical; in several respects this description seems apt.

These observable shifts in brain activity are accompanied, in many cases, by one of the most fascinating phenomena of sleep: *dreams*. An individual awakened during REM sleep often reports dreaming. In some cases, eye movements during such sleep seem to be related to the content of dreams (Dement, 1974). It is as if the individual is following the action in a dream with his or her eyes. The relationship between rapid eye movement and dream content is uncertain, however, so it is best to view this as an intriguing but as yet unverified possibility.

Periods of REM sleep continue to cycle with the other stages of sleep throughout the night. The REM periods tend to increase in length toward morning, while the amount of time spent in Stage 4 tends to decrease (see Figure 4.4). Thus, while the first REM period may last only five to ten minutes, the final one—from which many people awake—may last thirty minutes or more (Hartmann, 1973; Kelly, 1991).

It is interesting to note that patterns of sleep do change somewhat with age. Newborn infants sleep sixteen hours a day or more, and spend about 50 percent of their time in REM sleep. Both figures drop rapidly, so that by the time we are teenagers, total sleep time has dropped to slightly more than eight hours, with REM sleep making up about 20 percent of this figure (less than two hours). Total sleep time continues to decrease as we grow older, dropping to six hours or less after age fifty; however, the proportion this time spent in REM sleep remains fairly constant (see Figure 4.5).

The research results support the conclusion that the states of consciousness that occur during sleep are produced by a network of sub-cortical structures distributed throughout the brain, including the brainstem, the thalamus, and the limbic system. These structures are neurally connected and seem to work by selective inhibition. For example, during waking hours the sleep centres are inhibited. Sleep

REM (Rapid Eye Movement) Sleep: A state of sleep in which brain activity resembling waking restfulness is accompanied by deep muscle relaxation and movements of the eyes. Most dreams occur during periods of REM sleep.

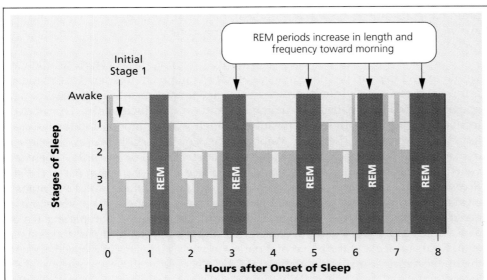

Figure 4.4
Time Spent in Various Stages of Sleep

Periods of REM sleep alternate with other stages of sleep during the night. The duration of the REM periods tends to increase toward morning, while the amount of time spent in Stage 4 decreases.

Figure 4.5
Changing Patterns of Sleep Over the Lifespan

Infants sleep sixteen hours a day or more and spend about half that time in REM sleep. Total sleep decreases as we grow older, dropping to only about six hours for persons over fifty. However, the proportion of REM sleep remains fairly constant.

Source: Based on data from Snyder and Scott, 1972.

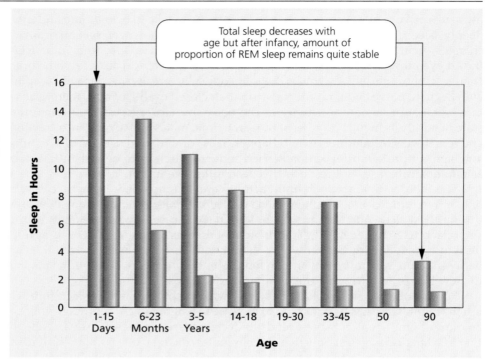

Total sleep decreases with age but after infancy, amount of proportion of REM sleep remains quite stable

and waking states require the activities of several different neurotransmitters to be in balance, as well. You will find out what happens when these are not quite as they should be later on in this chapter.

What Function Does Sleep Serve?

Any activity that fills as much of our lives as sleep must serve important functions. But what, precisely, are these? What do we gain from the hours we spend asleep? Several theories exist (Kreuger et al., 1995). One of these is the **recuperative theory**. It suggests that sleep provides the rest we require to recover from the wear and tear of the previous day's activities. More specifically, while repair of the body goes on during our waking hours—digestion and waste removal for example—repair of the brain happens during sleep (Horne, 1988). But what kinds of brain wear and tear are we talking about here? Possibilities being considered are cell repair, tissue growth, and neurotransmitter replenishment.

If we do need sleep to recover from the previous day's activities, then we would expect there to be consequences of not sleeping. On this point the evidence is mixed. In some individuals, prolonged sleep deprivation may produce attention and concentration impairments, irritability, and even hallucinations. The more effectively people sleep, the more positive are their waking moods and the less anxiety they experience (Berry & Webb, 1985). For others, however, prolonged deprivation of sleep does not seem to have much effect. For example, seventeen-year-old Randy Gardner wanted to earn a place in the *Guinness Book of World Records*, and he did. Randy stayed awake for precisely 264 hours and 12 minutes—eleven entire days! Although he had some difficulty staying awake, he remained generally alert and active throughout the entire period. After completing his ordeal, Randy slept fourteen hours and then, surprisingly, he returned to his usual eight hours of sleep. During that first period, it was as if his brain focused on making up the deprivation in slow-wave and REM sleep, without compensating for the losses in Stages 1 and 2 sleep. What was even more surprising, perhaps, was that there were no lasting physical or mental consequences of this long sleepless period.

Recuperative Theory: A theory suggesting that while repair of the body goes on during our waking hours, repair of the brain happens during sleep.

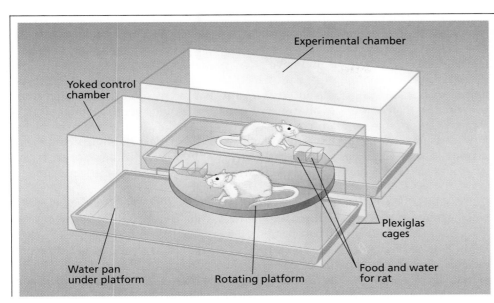

Figure 4.6
Studying the Effects of Sleep Deprivation: One Technique

As shown here, two animals are placed on a platform floating on water. Whenever one shows signs of falling asleep (e.g., as indicated by patterns of brain activity), the platform rotates, thus preventing the animal from sleeping. The other animal, too, is prevented from sleeping, but since this "yoked control" organism may have been awake anyway, its sleep is disturbed to a much smaller degree.

Rodgers and colleagues (1995) at the University of Toronto and of Western Ontario studied the effect of a forty-eight-hour period of sleep deprivation. During that time, the subjects in one sleep-deprived group did continuous physical work, while subjects in another sleep-deprived group did not. The continuous physical work consisted of repetitions of six different tasks that were chosen because together they involved all major muscle groups. For example, in Task 1 the study counted the number of sandbags carried over a distance of five metres in a half hour. In Task 6, the study counted the number of times a wheelbarrow was filled with top soil and pushed fifteen metres in a half hour. Before and after the forty-eight hours of sleep deprivation, physiological measures were taken of blood glucose, muscle contractions, and self-paced walking speed. Psychological measures assessed mood and perceived level of fatigue (from "very lively" to "ready to drop"). Here is the conclusion that was drawn on the basis of the results: "… although sleep-deprived individuals may have the physiological capacity to do the work, the interference of mood, perception of effort or even the repetitive nature of the tasks decreases the ability … to maintain a constant level of work output in a sleep-deprived state" (Rodgers et al., 1995, p. 34).

In several long-term studies, volunteer participants reduced their nightly sleep gradually—for example, by thirty minutes every two or three weeks. That continued until the volunteers did not want to reduce their sleep any further. Results indicate that most people can reduce their amount of sleep to about five hours per night (Mullaney et al., 1977) with no deterioration of their performance on various tasks, no negative shifts in mood, and no harmful effects on health. There is, however, a change in the sleep itself. After reducing their sleep to five hours or less, there is increased sleep efficiency. Sleep begins very quickly, and a higher proportion of time is spent in Stage 4 sleep. It is as if people compress their deep sleep requirements into the shorter period of time. In short, then, research on sleep deprivation does not help much with the question of whether we sleep for repair and restoration, but it does indicate that there is something special about deep Stage 4 sleep.

A second theory looks to circadian rhythms for the reason for why we sleep. According to **evolutionary theory,** sleep evolved to ensure that various species, including human beings, remain inactive during those times of day when they were not usually engaged in eating, drinking, or mating—activities necessary for survival. Sleep limits the use of energy to daytime activities, such as searching for food. Animals that hibernate, bats and squirrels for example, enter a state of reduced metabolism, brain activity, and breathing and their bodies cool down considerably in the winter when food is scarce.

Evolutionary Theory: A theory suggesting that sleep evolved to ensure that various species, including human beings, remain inactive during those times of day when they were not usually engaged in looking for food, eating, drinking, or mating—activities necessary for survival.

Third, we may have evolved the need to sleep so that we lie low when we are least safe. As one well-known sleep researcher (Webb, 1975) has put it, sleep is nature's way of keeping us quiet at night—a more dangerous time for our ancestors and for us as well. Animals that have many predators, sheep and goats for example, sleep less than animals like bats, which are relatively safe. However, every animal does have to sleep some and that means that the reason for sleeping is more complicated than a simple evolutionary hypothesis would suggest. Remarkably, in some species of marine mammals the two cerebral hemispheres take turns sleeping (Carlson, 1999). Why have they developed this pattern? Perhaps because as mammals, they are not as well-adapted to life in the water as other marine organisms, and so it is too dangerous for both hemispheres to sleep at the same time.

Carlyle Smith
Trent University.

DEPRIVATION OF REM SLEEP Selectively depriving individuals of REM sleep (by waking them up whenever their EEG indicates the onset of REM) increases the amount of REM sleep they have on subsequent nights (Webb & Agnew, 1967). Why might that be? Perhaps it has to do with the role that REM sleep has in remembering. Researcher Carlyle Smith (1995, 1996) at Trent University has studied REM sleep in animals. He suggests that, during REM sleep, changes necessary for the establishment of long-term spatial memories take place (Smith, 1998; Smith & Rose, 1997). There may be yet another special role for REM sleep—to eliminate unnecessary memories and other "mental clutter" from our brains (e.g, Crick & Mitchison, 1995).

Sleep Disorders

Do you ever have trouble falling or staying asleep? Almost 40 percent of adults report that they sometimes have this problem—generally known as **insomnia** (Bixler et al., 1979). Further, such problems seem to increase with age and are somewhat more common among women than men. Sleep researchers have identified different kinds of insomnia. Some people have difficulty falling asleep; that is *sleep-onset insomnia*. Others have difficulty staying asleep during the night; that is *sleep-maintenance insomnia*. Still others wake up too early in the morning; that is called *early-morning wakening*. In some cases, insomnia is a temporary response; in others, insomnia is chronic. The causes of insomnia vary. They include all kinds of stress, excitement, jet lag, shift change and other variations in circadian rhythms, pain, depression, stimulant drugs, and—as you will read further on—reliance on sleeping pills.

When the sleep habits of people who claim to be suffering from insomnia are carefully studied, it turns out that some of them sleep as long as people who do not complain of such problems (Empson, 1984). They have *pseudoinsomnia*. This does not necessarily imply that they are faking their disorder or complaining about a problem they do not really have (Trinder, 1988). The amount of sleep they get may be within normal limits (six and a half hours or more per night), but this may still not be enough to meet their individual needs. They may be short in a particular stage of sleep—Stage 4 or REM (Salin-Pascual et al., 1992). The quality of their sleep may be disturbed in ways not yet measured in research. Still, it does appear that many people who believe that their sleep is somehow inadequate may actually be getting as much sleep—and sleeping about as well—as others who do not report such problems.

For most people, sleep disturbances are temporary. For others, treatment at a sleep disorder clinic may be recommended. Canadian sleep disorder clinics can be found in cities like Ottawa, Toronto, and Vancouver. These are places where several approaches to the treatment of insomnia have been studied. Research has focused upon the effectiveness of melatonin (eg., Arendt et al., 1997), behaviour modification, group therapy, and substitution of drugs (eg., Jan & Espezel, 1995). All of these have been reported to work in some cases and not in others.

Insomnia: Disorder involving the inability to fall asleep or remain asleep.

Nevertheless, the following tactics have been found to be helpful if you suffer from insomnia:

1. Read something pleasant or relaxing just before going to bed.
2. Go to bed at the same time each night.
3. Avoid using your bed as a place to study or watch television.
4. Avoid coffee late in the day.
5. Avoid drinking alcohol at bedtime.
6. Exercise every day—but not just before going to bed.
7. Do not smoke.
8. Be reassured; at times almost everyone has trouble falling asleep.
9. If you find yourself tossing and turning, get up and read, work, or watch television until you feel drowsy. Lying in bed and worrying about your loss of sleep is definitely not the answer!

Sleepwalking: One Disorder of Slow-Wave Sleep

About 25 percent of children show one or more episodes of *somnambulism,* walking in their sleep.

By the way, despite what advertisements promise, sleeping pills—prescription as well as nonprescription—are not effective at inducing sleep, at least not in the long run. They may seem to be helping at first, but drug tolerance quickly develops so that larger and larger doses are soon needed. Also, some drugs used for this purpose interfere with REM sleep, and that can lead to different kinds of sleep disturbances.

Unfortunately, insomnia is far from the only problem associated with sleep. There are several other disorders of initiating and maintaining sleep. The most dramatic of these is **somnambulism**—sleepwalking. This is less rare than you might guess; almost 25 percent of children experience at least one sleepwalking episode (Empson, 1984). A second, related sleep disorder is **night terrors**. Here, children awaken from deep sleep with signs of intense arousal—such as a racing pulse and rapid respiration—and powerful feelings of fear. Yet they have no memory of any dream relating to these feelings. Night terrors occur primarily during Stage 4 sleep. Both somnambulism and night terrors appear to be related to disturbances of the autonomic nervous system, which plays a key role in regulating brain activity during sleep. In contrast, nightmares, which most of us experience at some point (most often as children) occur during REM sleep, during the late night or early morning, when REM sleep lasts longer. Most nightmares are vivid dreams and many include specific danger (Leung & Robson, 1993).

Another highly disturbing type of sleep disorder is **sleep apnea**. Those who suffer from sleep apnea actually stop breathing when they are asleep. Needless to say, this often causes them to wake up. Since this process can be repeated literally hundreds of times during the night, apnea can seriously affect the health of those who suffer from it, and various remedies are being tested (e.g., Bedard et al., 1993; Enns et al., 1995).

Have you ever felt yourself twitch suddenly as you were sleeping, or while falling asleep? If so, you have had a small taste of what people suffering from another sleep disorder—**nocturnal myoclonus**—experience. These individuals endure periodic and repeated episodes of body twitching all through the night. Little wonder that their sleep is greatly disturbed.

Finally, there are several disorders known as **hypersomnias**, in which people get too much sleep. The most serious of these is **narcolepsy**, a condition in which individuals suddenly fall directly into REM sleep during their daytime activities. Such attacks are sometimes accompanied by almost total paralysis and the person may suddenly fall down. These episodes are often triggered by a strong emotion—when the individual becomes excited or upset. Once there was a professor who suffered from narcolepsy. During a lecture he would sit down, lean forward, and suddenly be asleep—often in the middle of a sentence. Needless to say, he (and the students in his classes) found this disturbing. The impact of narcolepsy on the psychological and social life of the individual is serious (Broughton, 1992).

Somnambulism: A sleep disorder in which individuals actually get up and move about while still asleep.

Night Terrors: Extremely frightening dreamlike experiences that occur during non-REM sleep.

Sleep Apnea: Cessation of breathing during sleep.

Nocturnal Myoclonus: A sleep disorder in which individuals endure periodic and repeated episodes of body twitching all through the night.

Hypersomnias: Disorders involving excessive amounts of sleep or an overwhelming urge to fall asleep.

Narcolepsy: A sleep disorder in which individuals are overcome by uncontrollable periods of sleep during waking hours.

What causes such sleep disorders? With some people, insomnia seems to involve disturbances in the internal mechanisms that regulate body temperature. As noted in our discussion of circadian rhythms, core body temperature usually drops to low levels during sleep (and rises as we get ready to wake up). This lower temperature at night conserves energy and permits many bodily functions to proceed at reduced rates. In those suffering from insomnia, however, these mechanisms fail to operate normally, so that the body temperature remains relatively high (Sewitch, 1987).

Other causes of sleep disorders may involve disturbances of the biological clock within the hypothalamus (the suprachiasmatic nucleus). This clock interacts with other structures of the brain to regulate all circadian rhythms. A disturbance in these complex and delicately balanced mechanisms can result in a sleep disorder.

K E Y QUESTIONS

- How do psychologists study sleep?
- What are the major stages of sleep?
- What happens during REM sleep?
- What are the effects of sleep deprivation?
- What functions does sleep seem to play?
- What are some of the most common sleep disorders?
- What steps can you take to help get a good night's sleep every night?

Dreams

Without a doubt, the most dramatic aspect of sleep is that of **dreams**—those jumbled, vivid, sometimes enticing and sometimes disturbing images that fill the sleeper's mind. What are these experiences? Why do they happen? While psychologists are still seeking final answers to these puzzling questions, we already know much more about dreams than we did only a few decades ago (Koulack, 1992; Moffitt, 1993). Let us first consider some basic facts about dreams, and then turn to some answers to these questions—provided by psychological research.

DREAMS: SOME BASIC FACTS Try answering each of the following questions. Then consider the answers given, which reflect current knowledge about the nature of these encounters with the workings of our own nervous systems.

1. *Does everybody dream?* The answer seems to be *yes*. While not all people remember dreaming, EEG recordings and related data indicate that everyone experiences REM sleep. Moreover, if awakened during such periods, even people who normally do not recall dreaming may report vivid dreams.

2. *How long do dreams last?* Many people believe that dreams last only an instant, no matter how long they may seem. In fact, though, dreams seem to run on "real time": the longer they seem to last, the longer they really are (Dement & Kleitman, 1957).

3. *Can external events be incorporated into dreams?* Dement and Wolpert (1958) sprayed water on sleeping people who were experiencing REM sleep. Then they woke them up. In more than half the cases, participants reported water in their dreams. Nielsen (1993) applied pressure to either the right or the left leg of volunteers during their REM sleep. The subjects' dream reports included not only sensations of pressure or squeezing, but also effects of that pressure upon their posture and/or movement in the dream.

Dreams: Cognitive events, often vivid but disconnected, that occur during sleep. Most dreams take place during REM sleep.

4. *Do dreams foretell the future?* As you can probably guess, there is no scientific evidence whatsoever for this idea.

5. *Do dreams really express unconscious wishes?* Many people believe they do, but there is no convincing evidence.

6. *When people cannot remember their dreams, does this mean that they are purposely forgetting them, perhaps because they find the content too disturbing?* Probably not. Research on why people can or cannot remember their dreams indicates that this is primarily the result of what they do when they wake up—whether they lie quietly in bed, actively trying to remember the dream, or leap up and start the day's activities. While we cannot totally rule out the possibility of some kind of repression—that is, of active, motivated forgetting in dream amnesia—there is little evidence for it.

7. *What are lucid dreams?* Some people have the experience of being aware that they are dreaming while they are dreaming. Some researchers have suggested that lucid dreaming is a form of meditation in sleep because there are similarities between the EEG records in both states of consciousness (e.g., Gackenbach, 1992).

Now that we have considered some basic facts about dreams, let us turn to several different ideas about why we dream.

THE PSYCHODYNAMIC VIEW OF DREAMS Do dreams express unconscious wishes or impulses? This idea has existed for centuries, but it was made popular early in the twentieth century by Sigmund Freud. Freud wrote that in dreams we give expression to the thoughts, impulses, wishes, and desires we find unacceptable during our waking hours. Thus, we can dream about gratifying illicit sexual desires or about taking revenge on those who have made us angry, although we actively repress such thoughts during the day.

Freud maintained that no matter how vague, jumbled, or strange dreams may seem, they always contain important messages. Often these are disguised, either in the dreams themselves or in our memories of them. Therefore, he incorporated dream analysis into the treatment of his patients—who suffered from a wide range of psychological problems. Freud's reports of such dream interpretations make provocative reading—but, alas, there is no scientific evidence for their accuracy or for Freud's more general assertions about why we dream. In view of all this, psychologists are currently reluctant to accept Freud's view that dreams offer a unique means for exploring the unconscious. Instead, most accept one of the alternative views we will now consider.

THE PHYSIOLOGICAL VIEW OF DREAMS If dreams are not reflections of hidden wishes or impulses, what are they? According to the physiological view (Hobson, 1988; McCarley & Hobson, 1981), dreams are simply our subjective experience of random neural activity in the brain. Such activity may be ongoing information processing, or it may occur because a minimal amount of stimulation is necessary for the normal functioning of the brain and nervous system at all times. In other words, dreams may merely represent efforts by our thought processes to make sense out of the neural activity going on during REM sleep (Foulkes, 1985; Hobson, 1988). As Hobson has put it, the brain "is so … bent on the quest for meaning that it attributes and even creates meaning when there is little or none to be found in the data it is asked to process."

THE COGNITIVE VIEW OF DREAMS The third view takes these suggestions even further. The cognitive theory puts together two facts about REM sleep: First, during REM sleep, many areas of the cerebral cortex are highly active; and second, at the same time, there is massive suppression of sensory and motor systems. As a result, Antrobus (1991) reasons, the cortical structures or systems that normally regulate perception and thought have only their own output as input. It is this that is the basis for the images and ideas we interpret as dreams (see Figure 4.7).

Figure 4.7
Dreams: One Modern View

According to a model proposed by Antrobus (1991), dreams occur because during REM sleep, areas of the brain that play a key role in waking perception and thought are highly active while at the same time there is massive inhibition of input from sensory systems and muscles. As a result, the cortical systems that normally regulate perception and thought have only their own output as input. The interpretation of this activity forms the basis for dreams.

Source: Based on suggestions by Antrobus, 1991.

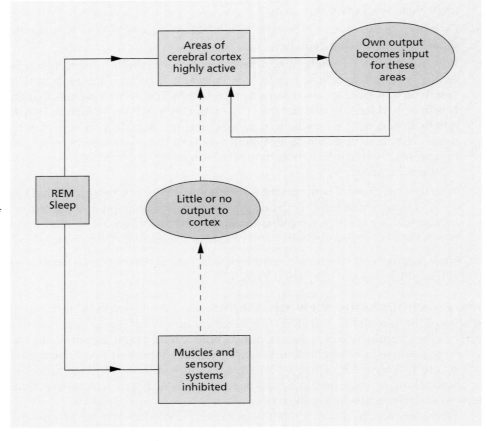

Does this mean that dreams are fundamentally meaningless? Not necessarily. Since dreams are our interpretations of the neural activity of our own brains, they are connected to our own experience. Some evidence for this comes from studies of people who are attempting to quit smoking or drinking. These folks often report having **dreams of absent-minded transgression**—DAMIT dreams, for short (e.g., Gill, 1985). In such dreams, people suddenly notice that they are smoking or drinking and that they have slipped back into this behaviour in an absent-minded or careless manner—without planning to do so. The smoking in these dreams is not pleasurable (Hajek & Belcher, 1991) and intense feelings of panic or guilt follow. In many cases, the dreamers wake up at that point feeling very disturbed. One year after the program, more of the DAMIT dreamers were still not smoking. Thus there is some evidence that the contents of dreams do have meaning—and may even influence the dreamers' behaviour while awake.

Dreams of Absent-Minded Transgression: Dreams in which people attempting to change their own behaviour, as in quitting smoking, see themselves unintentionally slipping into the unwanted behaviour, in an absent-minded or careless manner.

KEY *QUESTIONS*

- During what stage of sleep do dreams usually occur?

- Do most people dream? How long do dreams last?

- How do the psychodynamic, physiological, and cognitive views of dreams differ?

- What do dreams of absent-minded transgression tell us about the meaning of dreams?

Hypnosis

At one time in the past, every travelling fair and circus included at least one hypnotist among its performers. In front of hundreds of onlookers, the hypnotist would ask for volunteers and then put these people into what seemed to be a deep trance. Once they were hypnotized, the volunteers might be told to imagine that they were a rooster at dawn or a famous ballet dancer, and they would crow loudly or pirouette around the stage. Today, there are also performances like this, and **hypnosis** is advised by some practitioners: for pain control (in dentistry for example), to promote weight control, and in psychotherapy and rehabilitation of those with attention disorders (e.g., Barbasz & Barbasz, 1996).

Standard hypnosis usually begins with repeated suggestions by the hypnotist that the subject is feeling more and more tired, drowsy, sleepy. As a result, people relax progressively, in response to the hypnotic suggestions, and some enter an altered state of consciousness. What happens in the brain when hypnosis occurs? EEG recordings of hypnotized individuals resemble those of normal awake people, and are not like any of the sleep stages (Wallace & Fisher, 1987), but the differences depend upon the task set by the hypnotist (Crawford et al., 1998).

However, large individual differences exist in how people are affected by hypnosis. About 15 percent of adults are highly susceptible, and 10 percent are highly resistant to hypnosis. The rest are somewhere in between. According to research results, those who are susceptible to hypnosis tend to have good visual imagery and vivid, frequent fantasies, and to become deeply involved in sensory and imaginative experiences. They tend to be dependent on others and seek direction from them, and they expect to be influenced by hypnotic suggestions and believe that these will have a powerful effect on them (Lynn & Rhue, 1986; Silva & Kirsch, 1992). Their EEG records during hypnosis resemble those that occur in imagery, whereas the others resemble cognitive activity like mental arithmetic (Ray, 1997) and the indicators of focused attention are higher (De-Pascalis, 1999). The use of PET technology to study these differences has begun (Rainville et al., 1999).

The more an individual possesses these personality characteristics, the greater their susceptibility is to hypnosis. That is probably because such people can more readily imagine the suggestions of the hypnotist and (it follows) incorporate them into their own behaviour (Silva & Kirsch, 1992). There is little evidence that hypnosis-susceptible people obey the suggestions of the hypnotist intentionally.

Contrasting Views about Hypnosis

Systematic research has led to the formulation of two major theories of the nature of hypnosis.

THE SOCIAL-COGNITIVE OR ROLE-PLAYING VIEW The **social-cognitive theory** argues that hypnotized individuals are actually playing a *special social role*—that of hypnotic subject. Having seen movies and read stories about hypnosis, most people have an idea of what it supposedly involves. They believe that when hypnotized they will lose control over their own behaviour and be unable to resist strong suggestions from the hypnotist. When given instructions to behave in a certain way (or to experience specific feelings) they obey, since this is what they think should happen. Further, they often report experiencing the changes in perceptions and feelings that they expect to experience (e.g., Kirsch & Lynn, 1998; Lynn, Rhue, & Weekes, 1990; Spanos, 1991).

Hollywood: An Important Source of Our Beliefs about the Nature and Effects of Hypnotism

After watching countless movies with scenes like the one shown here, many people form clear ideas about what hypnotism involves and what, supposedly, will happen to them if they are ever hypnotized.

Hypnosis: An interaction between two persons in which one (the hypnotist) induces changes in the behaviour, feelings, or cognitions of the other (the subject) through suggestions. Hypnosis involves subjects' expectations and their attempts to conform to the role of the hypnotized person.

Social-Cognitive Theory: A theory of behaviour suggesting that human behaviour is influenced by many cognitive factors as well as by reinforcement contingencies, and that human beings have an impressive capacity to regulate their own actions.

This does not mean that those who undergo hypnosis engage in a conscious effort to fool other people. On the contrary, they sincerely believe that they are experiencing an altered state of consciousness and that they have no choice but to act and feel as the hypnotist suggests (Kinnunen, Zamansky, & Block, 1994). Thus, in an important sense, their behaviours and their experiences while hypnotized are genuine. These behaviours and experiences, however, reflect beliefs about hypnosis and the role of the hypnotic subject more than the special skills of the hypnotist or the effects of hypnosis on consciousness (see Figure 4.8).

THE NEODISSOCIATION THEORY The **neodissociation theory** relies on the phenomenon of *dissociation* to explain hypnosis. In general, dissociation is the division of consciousness into more than one state of awareness. In some rare cases, dissociation between different multiple personalities may occur; you will learn more about this in Chapter 14.

The neodissociation theory proposes that hypnosis induces a split or dissociation between two basic functions of consciousness: the executive function, through which we regulate our own behaviour, and a monitoring function, through which we observe it. According to Hilgard (1986, 1993), hypnosis disconnects these two aspects of consciousness, and creates a barrier (often referred to as *hypnotic amnesia*)—that prevents experiences during hypnosis from entering into normal consciousness. The result is that people who are hypnotized are in a special altered state of consciousness in which one part of their mind accepts suggestions from the hypnotist, while the other part—which Hilgard terms "the hidden observer"—observes what is going on, but does not participate. So, for example, if hypnotized persons are told to put their arms into icy water but instructed by the hypnotist that they will experience no pain, they will obey and will indeed report no discomfort.

> **Neodissociation Theory:** A theory of hypnosis suggesting that hypnotized individuals enter an altered state of consciousness in which consciousness is divided.

Figure 4.8
Evidence for the Social–Cognitive View of Hypnosis

Individuals who are hypnotized and told they will not be able to hear a sound rate it as lower in volume than they did initially. When some (those in a *demand instructions group*) are told that they have probably "slipped back into hypnosis," and probably won't be able to hear it again, they also rate it as lower. In contrast, those in a control condition who are *not* told they have "slipped back into hypnosis" rate the tone as louder. These findings suggest that some of the effects of hypnosis, at least, are due to individuals' beliefs about what they will experience or what the hypnotist wants them to do.

Source: Based on findings reported by Spanos and his colleagues in several studies.

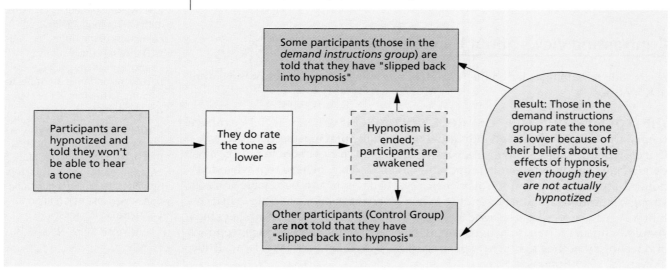

However, if asked to describe their feelings in writing, they may indicate that they did experience feelings of intense cold (Hilgard, 1979). On the basis of brain imaging data, some investigator argue that when hypnosis is used for pain suppression, there is active inhibition of attention that produces the dissociation between attention and awareness of pain (Crawford et al., 1998).

More recently, Bowers and his associates (e.g., Bowers, 1992; Woody & Bowers, 1994) have suggested that hypnotism does not necessarily split consciousness. Their idea is that, in the hypnotic trance, the control of the executive function over other aspects of consciousness is weaker than usual. In other words, the subject responding to the hypnotist's suggestions does so in an automatic manner that is not mediated by normal thought processes.

Which of these theories is correct? Existing evidence offers a mixed picture (e.g., Kirsch & Lynn, 1998; Noble & McConkey, 1995; Reed et al., 1996). While support for both views exists , most psychologists conclude that the unusual or bizarre effects observed under hypnosis can be explained by the hypnotized person's belief in hypnotism and by his or her efforts—not necessarily conscious—to behave in accordance with those expectations. Others have challenged this view. What kind of research findings support these different conclusions? For that information, see the **Research Process** box.

Nicholas P. Spanos
Carleton University
(1942–1994)

The Research Process:
Does Hypnosis Change Perception and Memory?

Under hypnosis, people may see and hear things that others do not, or deny that they heard or saw things that actually happened. Does hypnosis change our perceptions and our memories in some way? What are the current ideas about the dramatic events that occur on stage when an entertainer like Reveen plays Saskatoon, Brandon, Sherbrooke, or Thunder Bay?

As you already know, there are at least two theories here. One of these, the social–cognitive theory, proposes that how people behave under hypnosis is determined by the social demands of the situation. The neodissociation theory proposes that people under hypnosis enter a special state of consciousness in which they do or say, perceive or remember, things that they otherwise would not.

Hypnosis and Sensory Hallucinations

Does hypnosis really change what we see, hear, or feel? Well-known for their extensive research on this question, the late Nicholas Spanos and other researchers at Carleton University conducted numerous investigations into the apparent changes in perception that occur under hypnosis. For this, they used an ingenious experimental design. In one experiment, hypnotized subjects (Carleton undergraduate volunteers) were told that they were being shown a blank piece of paper. On the paper, however, there was a number *8*. After hypnosis was ended, those who said the paper they saw was blank were told that only fakers said that. Then they were given a chance to draw what had been on the paper. Of the fifteen subjects, fourteen drew the number *8* (Spanos, Flynn, & Gabora, 1989). Clearly, these students had seen what was on the

paper while they were hypnotized. In a subsequent study, subjects reported that, under hypnosis, they had used several different strategies not to see properly. For example, they unfocused their eyes, crossed their eyes, or looked above, below, or away from what was written on the paper (Spanos, Burgess, Cross, & MacLeod, 1992).

In another study, subjects heard the same clearly audible tone, three times. The first time they heard the tone, they rated how loud it sounded to them. Then they were hypnotized and given the hypnotic suggestion that they would not be able to hear the second tone. The second tone was presented, and again they rated its loudness. Before the third and final presentation, the hypnotic suggestion was cancelled. For some subjects, however, misinformation was added: They were told that they had probably slipped back into hypnosis and would not be able to hear the tone very well. Then the tone was played and all subjects rated it a third time.

The misinformed subjects rated the third tone as less loud than the others did. Was that because, under hypnosis, their hearing was somehow impaired? Not at all. Similar results have been obtained with individuals who reported little or no reaction to pain under hypnosis—for example, to placing their arms in icy water (Spanos, Perlini, Patrick, Bell, & Gwynn, 1990)—and with those who regressed into a past life under hypnosis (Spanos, Menary, Gabora, DuBreuil, & Dewhirst, 1991). From all of these results, it seems clear that what appear to be changes in the perceptual experiences of hypnotized people may really be changes in what these people *report* they experienced (Perlini et al., 1998).

On the other hand, dramatic findings offer support for the neodissociation view. In this research, hypnotized people were told that they have undergone a sex change—that they are now female if they were male, or male if they were female (e.g., McConkey, 1991) In one study, the three groups of subjects were exceptionally susceptible (virtuosos), highly susceptible, and low in susceptibility to hypnosis. Participants in the first two groups were hypnotized; participants in the third group (simulators) were not hypnotized, but they were told to simulate the reactions they would have if they had been hypnotized. Then participants in all three groups were told that they had undergone a sex change (Noble & McConkey, 1995). Following these procedures, all participants were asked to indicate their sex. As expected, almost all subjects in all three groups gave responses consistent with the hypnotic suggestion: they reported a sex change.

Here are the most remarkable results. When exceptionally susceptible subjects were examined by a "physician" and told that they had not undergone a sex change, they maintained that they had. Furthermore, more of those same subjects continued to insist they had had a sex change, even when they were looking their own images on a TV monitor—which showed them unchanged, of course. Finally, more of the subjects in this group changed their names to be consistent with a change in sex (see Figure 4.9).

Hypnosis and Memory

Can hypnotized people tell fact from fiction? Some investigators believe that the "extra" details recalled under hypnosis by eyewitnesses are distortions of memory. One recent finding (Dywan, 1998) is that hypnosis produces an "illusion of familiarity" that causes people under hypnosis to be more confident in what they think they remember, even when what they remember is incorrect!

Jane Dywan
Brock University

In another research method to examine memory and hypnosis, Murrey, Cross, and Whipple (1992) had students watch a videotape of a mock robbery. Then, under hypnosis, all of the students listened to an audiotape containing false details about the robbery. Later, they were asked to answer ten questions about the robbery that had been shown on the videotape.

Before the subjects actually answered the questions, however, some of them were offered an incentive to be as accurate as possible (a cash prize for the student with the most accurate set of answers). These students recalled the details of the robbery as they were on the original videotape. The students who were not offered the cash prize for accuracy reported the incorrect details they had heard on the audiotape. Clearly, the false details heard under hypnosis did not produce genuine changes in the memories of these students.

Why would subjects misrepresent what they saw, heard, felt, and remembered? Spanos argues that there are three kinds of pressures here: expectations and beliefs about how to behave under hypnosis; motivation to comply with the suggestions of the hypnotist; and concerns about how they are seen by those watching them.

In summary, then, psychologists have devised ingenious methods for studying this puzzling behaviour. From those methods we learn that hypnotism may produce changes in perception among some persons, particularly among those who are exceptionally susceptible to hypnotic suggestion. However, there are strong reasons to believe that the effects of hypnosis stem from pressures on hypnotized individuals to meet the expectations of the hypnotist, and to conform to their own beliefs—and those of others—concerning the powerful impact of hypnosis. Whichever theory you support, it is clear that the power of suggestion under hypnosis is indeed great. Nevertheless, hypnotism is certainly better understood in terms of expectations and beliefs than in terms of the supposedly mystical powers of hypnotists.

Figure 4.9
Hypnotism: Some Surprising Results

When people who are exceptionally susceptible to hypnotism (virtuosos) are told under hypnosis that they have undergone a sex change, they accept this suggestions and resist later efforts to change it.

Source: Based on data from Noble and McConkey, 1995.

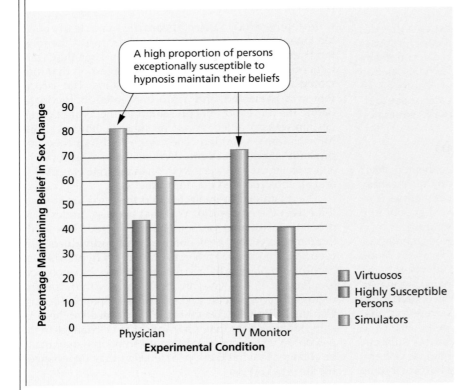

A high proportion of persons exceptionally susceptible to hypnosis maintain their beliefs

Consciousness-Altering Drugs

In Chapter 2, we saw that drugs are big business in our time. Each day, many millions of human beings use drugs to change the way they feel—to alter their moods or states of consciousness. You have probably taken a pill for a headache or coffee to keep you awake. Much of this use of consciousness-altering drugs is completely legal; indeed, many people take such drugs under a physician's supervision. In other instances, however, people turn to drugs that are illegal, or use legal ones to excess, contrary to medical advice. Drug use—and abuse—is clearly a contemporary social problem. In this final section, therefore, we will consider several issues relating to the use of consciousness-altering drugs.

Consciousness-Altering Drugs: Some Basic Concepts

First, what are **drugs**? One widely accepted definition is that they are compounds which, because of their chemical structure, change the structure or function of biological systems (Grilly, 1994; Levinthal, 1999). Thus, consciousness-altering drugs are drugs that produce changes in consciousness when introduced into the body (Wallace & Fisher, 1987).

Suppose you went to your family medicine cabinet and conducted a careful inventory of all the drugs present. Unless your family is very unusual, you would find quite a few. To the extent these drugs were prescribed by a physician and were used for medical purposes, taking them would probably be appropriate. The term **drug abuse**, therefore, is usually restricted to instances in which people take drugs purely to change their mood, and in which they experience impaired behaviour or social functioning as a result of doing so (Wallace & Fisher, 1987). Of course, alcohol is also a mind-altering drug, but not one that is normally used for medical purposes. You will read more about alcohol use and abuse on p. 162 and in various other chapters in this book.

Unfortunately, when people take consciousness-altering drugs on a regular basis, they often develop **dependence**—they come to need the drug and cannot function well without it. Two types of dependence exist. One, **physiological dependence**, occurs when the need for the drug is based on biological factors, such

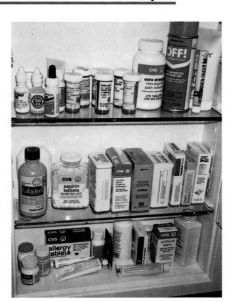

Drugs at Home

Does your medicine cabinet look like this one? Most people have a variety of consciousness-altering drugs in their home.

Drugs: Chemical substances that change the structure or function of biological systems.

Drug Abuse: Instances in which individuals take drugs to change their moods, and in which they experience impaired behaviour or social functioning as a result of doing so.

Dependence: Strong physiological or psychological need for particular drugs.

Physiological Dependence: Strong urges to continue using a drug based on biological factors such as changes in metabolism.

as changes in metabolism. This type of dependence is what is usually meant by the term *drug addiction*. However, people can also experience **psychological dependence**, in which case they experience a strong desire to continue using the drug even though, physiologically, their body does not need it. As we will soon see, several psychological mechanisms probably contribute to this dependence. Physiological and psychological dependence often occur together and magnify the individual's craving for and dependence on specific drugs.

Continued use of a drug over a prolonged period of time often leads to drug **tolerance**—a physiological reaction in which the body requires larger and larger doses in order to experience the same effects. Drug tolerance has been observed in connection with many different consciousness-altering drugs and often increases the dangers of these substances. In some cases, the use of one drug increases tolerance for a different drug; this is known as **cross-tolerance** (Pinel, 1993). In current research (e.g., Kim, Pinel, & Roese, 1992), experimenters at the University of British Columbia are testing ways in which one drug may be used in a positive way, to allow safe use of a second drug, which taken alone would have serious side effects.

Psychological Mechanisms Underlying Drug Abuse

On the face of it, drug abuse is a puzzle. Such recreational use of drugs carries considerable risk of harm and long-term drug abuse undermines physical and psychological health. Why, then, do so many people do drugs? Several different explanations have been proposed.

THE LEARNING PERSPECTIVE: REWARDING PROPERTIES OF DRUGS Several explanations link the use of consciousness-altering drugs to basic principles of learning—principles we will consider in detail in Chapter 5. One view suggests that the effects produced by these drugs are somehow rewarding. Specifically, the reward is the "good feeling" that is the consequence of taking the drug (Wise & Bozarth, 1987). Evidence in support of this idea comes from the many studies that have found that animals find these drugs rewarding, and will self-administer them if given the opportunity (e.g., Young & Herling, 1986). The rewarding effect of these drugs is linked to a particular brain structure—the *nucleus accumbens* (Self, 1998; White, 1996). Many addictive drugs trigger the release of the neurotransmitter dopamine in this nucleus, and prevention of dopamine release in the nucleus accumbens deprives these addictive drugs of their reinforcing properties (e.g., DiChiara, 1995).

On the other hand, these substances reduce negative feelings, such as stress, anxiety, or physical discomfort. Thus, people may take drugs to reduce negative feelings rather than simply to generate positive ones (Tiffany, 1990; Toneatto, 1995). This explanation is especially applicable to cases in which individuals have become physiologically dependent on a drug; the negative symptoms they experience when it is no longer used—known as withdrawal—may be a powerful incentive to obtain the drug again at all costs.

THE PSYCHODYNAMIC PERSPECTIVE: COPING WITH UNCONSCIOUS FEARS AND DESIRES As we saw in Chapter 1, the psychodynamic perspective views human behaviour as stemming from unconscious conflicts among hidden aspects of personality. This perspective points to another, and very different, explanation for drug abuse: Perhaps individuals use drugs to reduce or at least conceal the anxiety generated by such inner turmoil. While this is an intriguing idea, it is very difficult to test empirically. For this reason, it currently receives little attention from psychologists.

THE SOCIAL PERSPECTIVE: DRUG ABUSE AND SOCIAL PRESSURE A third perspective suggests that drug abuse can be understood largely in terms of social factors. According to this view, individuals—especially adolescents and young

Psychological Dependence: Strong desires to continue using a drug even though it is not physiologically addicting.

Tolerance: Habituation to a drug, causing larger and larger doses to be required to produce effects of the same magnitude.

Cross-Tolerance: Increased tolerance for one drug that develops as a result of taking another drug.

adults—use consciousness-altering drugs because it is the "in" thing to do. They see their friends using these substances and feel pressure—subtle or overt—to join in (Mann, Chassin, & Sher, 1987) in order to enhance their social "image." Evidence for this view has recently been reported by Sharp and Getz (1996).

Several hundred students completed a questionnaire about their use of alcohol, their motivation to gain others' liking, and how good they were at impression management—making a good impression on others. The results showed that people who reported using alcohol regularly were also strongly motivated to gain the liking of other people and see themselves as better at impression management than those who did not use alcohol frequently. These findings offer support for the view that some people use alcohol, and perhaps abuse it, for impression management—to help them look good.

You may well have experienced such pressure yourself; if so, you know how hard it can be to resist. We will examine these social influences in more detail in Chapter 16.

THE COGNITIVE PERSPECTIVE: DRUG ABUSE AS AUTOMATIC BEHAVIOUR

According to the cognitive perspective, over time the cognitive systems controlling many aspects of drug use become automatic. Once individuals have used a drug on a number of occasions, then, they may find themselves responding almost automatically to external cues—for example, to a specific place in which they have often enjoyed the drug, such as a bar (Davis & Tunks, 1990–91), or to specific sights and smells, such as the sight of people smoking or the aroma of a burning cigarette. Similarly, they may respond automatically to internal cues or emotions, such as wanting to celebrate or feeling tired or out of sorts. These external and internal cues may trigger drug use—on occasion without any strong urge to take a drug. To the extent this occurs, drug use becomes quick and relatively effortless, occurs without conscious intention, is difficult to inhibit, and may even take place in the absence of conscious awareness.

This is the basis of the cognitive explanation that has been offered by Tiffany (1990) to explain relapses during drug rehabilitation. In difficult times, people have to use more of their mental resources to deal with the stress (Bliss, 1989), thus leaving fewer resources to focus on continued abstinence. Indeed, studies at Concordia University confirm that stress causes relapse to heroin seeking in rats previously trained to self-administer heroin intravenously (Shaham & Stewart, 1995). Tiffany's theory offers important insights into the nature of relapse by human drug addicts during drug rehabilitation—as a cognitive response to stress. You will read more about automatic cognitive processing later on in this chapter.

K E Y QUESTIONS

- What are drugs? What is drug abuse?
- What are physiological and psychological dependence on drugs?
- How does the learning perspective explain drug abuse?
- How does the social perspective explain drug abuse?
- How does the cognitive perspective explain drug abuse?

An Overview of Consciousness-Altering Drugs

While many different drugs affect consciousness, most seem to fit under one of four major headings: *depressants, stimulants, opiates,* and *psychedelics and hallucinogens.* Please note that these categories are based on the psychological effects of various drugs, not their chemical nature. Several drugs can exert similar effects on mood or consciousness although they have fundamentally different chemical formulas, and some drugs with similar chemical formulas can exert very different psychological effects (Pinel, 1993).

DEPRESSANTS Drugs that reduce both behavioural output and activity in the central nervous system are called **depressants**. According to the reports of the Addiction Research Foundation in Toronto, perhaps the most common of these is **alcohol**, undoubtedly the most widely consumed drug in the world (Smart, 1991). Small doses of alcohol seem, subjectively, to be stimulating—they induce feelings of excitement. Larger doses, however, are depressant. They dull the senses so that pain, cold, and other forms of discomfort become less intense. This is why alcohol was widely used to deaden the pain of medical operations before more effective anesthetics became available.

Large doses of alcohol also interfere with coordination and normal functioning of our senses—often with tragic results for motorists—and may disrupt information processing. (Table 4.2 summarizes these effects.) Alcohol also lowers social inhibitions. After consuming large quantities of this drug, people often become more prone to engage in dangerous forms of behaviour as well as more generally unrestrained in their words and actions (e.g. Pihl, Lau, & Assad, 1997). Alcohol may produce its pleasurable effects by stimulating special receptors in the brain. Its depressant effects may stem from the fact that it interferes with the capacity of neurons to conduct nerve impulses, perhaps by affecting cell membranes directly.

Growing evidence suggests that alcohol abuse may have a strong genetic link. Two major patterns of alcohol abuse exist; one group of abusers can resist drinking alcohol for long periods of time, but if they do, cannot control themselves and go on true binges. In contrast, another group of abusers drinks consistently at high levels (steady drinkers); people in this group usually have a history of antisocial acts—fighting, lying, and so on. This second type of alcohol addiction seems to be passed on through heredity. For instance, in one large-scale study carried out in Sweden

Depressants: Drugs that reduce activity in the nervous system and therefore slow many bodily and cognitive processes. Depressants include alcohol and barbiturates.

Alcohol: The most widely consumed drug in the world.

TABLE 4.2

Behavioural Effects of Various Blood Alcohol Levels

Blood Alcohol Level (mg of alcohol/ml of blood)	Behavioural Effects
0.05	Lowered alertness, impaired judgment, release of inhibitions, good feeling
0.10	Slowed reaction times and impaired motor function, less caution
0.15	Large, consistent increases in reaction time
0.20	Marked depression in sensory and motor capability, decidedly intoxicated behaviour
0.25	Severe motor disturbance and impairment of sensory perceptions
0.30	In a stupor but still conscious—no comprehension of events in the environment
0.35	Surgical anesthesia; lethal dose for about 1 percent of the population
0.40	Lethal dose for about 50 percent of the population

(Sigvardsson, Bohman, & Cloninger, 1996) the participants were children who were adopted early in life. The focus was on the biological and the adoptive parents and whether one or other of them was alcoholic. Men whose biological fathers were steady drinkers were about seven times more likely to become steady drinkers, whether or not their adoptive fathers abused alcohol. These findings suggest that this kind of alcohol abuse is linked to heredity. On the other hand, binge drinking seems to be influenced by both heredity and environment. Adopted children with a biological parent who abused alcohol did not do so themselves—unless they were exposed to heavy drinking in their adoptive homes.

Barbiturates, which are contained in some sleeping pills and relaxants, are a second type of depressant. First manufactured in the late nineteenth century, these drugs depress activity in the central nervous system and reduce activation and mental alertness. How these effects are produced is not yet certain, but existing evidence suggests that barbiturates may reduce the release of excitatory neurotransmitters by neurons in many different locations.

Initially, high doses of barbiturates can produce feelings of relaxation and euphoria—a kind of drunkenness without alcohol. They often go on to produce serious confusion, slurred speech, memory lapses, and reduced ability to concentrate. Wide swings of emotion, from euphoria to depression, are also common. Extremely large doses can be fatal, because they result in paralysis of centres of the brain that regulate breathing. This is a real danger, since tolerance to barbiturates gradually develops, so that individuals find it necessary to take larger and larger doses to obtain the same effects.

Because some barbiturates induce sleep, people often try to use them to treat sleep disorders such as insomnia. However, these drugs do not seem to produce normal sleep. In particular, they suppress REM sleep, which may rebound after individuals stop taking the drugs.

STIMULANTS Drugs that produce effects opposite to those of depressants—feelings of energy and the desire for activity—are known as **stimulants**. **Amphetamines** and **cocaine** are stimulants. Others, in common use, include caffeine (found in coffee, tea, and many soft drinks) and nicotine (in tobacco). Drugs like cocaine and amphetamines raise the user's blood pressure, heart rate, and respiration—in effect, they mimic all the signs of activation or arousal that the sympathetic nervous system produces. They also yield short periods of pleasurable sensations, twenty to forty minutes long, during which the user feels incredibly powerful and energetic. When cocaine is heated and treated chemically, an even more powerful form, known as **crack** cocaine, is produced. Smoking crack produces an instant high, during which the individual experiences powerful feelings of energy, confidence, and excitement.

Statistics on the use of drugs in Grades 7, 9, 11, and 12 or 13, among university students, and in the adult population are gathered in several Canadian provinces (Adlaf et al., 1994; Adlaf et al., 1995; Gliksman et al., 1993; Poulin & Wilbur, 1996). In most parts of Canada, cocaine use is relatively rare, except among street youth (Smart & Adlef, 1992). In 1995, for example, in Ontario, fewer than four in every one hundred post-secondary students reported having used cocaine in the past year.

Both amphetamines and cocaine inhibit the re-uptake of the neurotransmitters dopamine and norepinephrine. As a result, neurons that would otherwise stop firing continue to respond. As the drug wears off, the user often experiences an emotional crash marked by strong anxiety, depression, and fatigue. This happens because the drug has stripped the body of its natural chemical supply.

Recent studies at the Addiction Research Foundation in Toronto have found that cocaine and nicotine use the same receiving sites in the brain (Shrier, 1994). That means we may ultimately be able to use a nicotine-like drug to help cocaine addicts kick their habit. Taking a different approach to rehabilitation of cocaine addiction, researchers at Carleton University are testing other compounds to determine which are able to reduce the reinforcing effects of cocaine in animals (Roberts

Barbiturates: Drugs that act as depressants, reducing activity in the nervous system and behaviour output.

Stimulants: Drugs that increase activity in the nervous system, including amphetamines, caffeine, and nicotine.

Amphetamines: Drugs that act as stimulants, increasing feelings of energy and activation.

Cocaine: A powerful stimulant that produces pleasurable sensations of increased energy and self-confidence.

Crack: A cocaine derivative that can be smoked. It acts as a powerful stimulant.

& Ranaldi, 1995). Yet a third tactic is using a drug to bind up the cocaine in the blood stream so that it cannot get to the brain and therefore cannot exert its influence upon the nervous system (Carrera et al., 1995).

OPIATES Among the most dangerous drugs in widespread use are the **opiates**, which include *opium, morphine, heroin,* and related synthetic drugs. Opium is derived from the opium poppy—remember the scene in *The Wizard of Oz* in which Dorothy falls asleep in a field of beautiful poppies? Morphine is produced from opium, and heroin is produced from morphine. Opiates produce lethargy and a pronounced slowing of almost all bodily functions. They also alter consciousness, producing a dreamlike state and, for some people, intensely pleasurable sensations. The costs associated with these sensations are high, however. Since tolerance for opiates such as heroin increases rapidly with use, physiological addiction can occur very quickly. The withdrawal symptoms are so painful that addicts will go to incredible lengths, and take incredible risks, to obtain a steady supply of the drug.

The brain normally produces substances closely related (in chemical structure) to the opiates—*opioid peptides* or *endorphins*—and contains special receptors for them (Phillips & Fibiger, 1989, 1992). This suggests one possible explanation for the discomfort opiate users experience during withdrawal. Regular use of opiates soon overloads endorphin receptors in the brain. As a result, the brain stops producing these substances. When the drugs are withdrawn, endorphin levels remain depressed. Thus, an important internal mechanism for regulating pain is disrupted (Reid, 1990).

PSYCHEDELICS AND HALLUCINOGENS The drugs with the most profound effects upon consciousness may well be the **psychedelics**, which alter sensory perception, and the **hallucinogens**, which generate sensory perceptions when there are no external stimuli.

The most widely used psychedelic drug is marijuana. In one study of about 500 undergraduates at Concordia College in Edmonton, it was found that while the overall rate of drug use was low, of the drugs used, marijuana was the most common (Campbell & Svenson, 1992).

Medicinal use of marijuana dates back to a Chinese guide to medicines written more than 4700 years ago. The world's earliest confirmed marijuana user was a pregnant teenager who lived 1700 years ago. Her skeleton was found near Jerusalem in 1993; she may have been given the drug as an anesthetic during childbirth (Mechoulam et al., 1993). Until this century, marijuana was advised for pain, headaches, cramps, and even ulcers. At the present time, some physicians suggest that marijuana prevents nausea associated with chemotherapy, reduces eye pressure in glaucoma, promotes weight gain in AIDS patients, decreases muscle spasms in multiple sclerosis, suppresses the immune system in organ transplant operations, and stabilizes mood in mood disorders (Grinspoon & Bakalar, 1998).

Since 1961, marijuana has been illegal under Canada's Narcotics Control Act. Illegal or not, it is grown and used as a recreational drug across the country and is the most common illicit drug. In the year 2000, it is a multimillion-dollar Canadian cash crop—particularly in British Columbia. In 1997 and 1998, judges in Ontario and B.C. found the production and use of marijuana for medicinal use to be legal. The principle here was an individual's right to an effective medicine. Nevertheless, the matter of the medicinal use of marijuana continues to be controversial (Gurley et al., 1998).

When smoked or eaten (e.g., baked in cookies or cakes), marijuana produces moderate arousal in the form of increased blood pressure and pulse rate; a perceived increase in the intensity of sounds, colours, tastes, and smells; and distorted judgment of time and distance. Other effects reported by some users (though not all) include reduced inhibitions, increased sexual pleasure (which may simply reflect increased sensitivity to all sensations), and feelings of relaxation.

Opiates: Drugs that induce a dreamy, relaxed state and, in some persons, intense feelings of pleasure. Opiates exert their effects by stimulating special receptor sites within the brain.

Psychedelics: Drugs that alter sensory perception and so may be considered mind-expanding.

Hallucinogens: Drugs that profoundly alter consciousness, such as LSD.

In the United States, many people believe that marijuana will turn them on sexually, and they report such effects. In India, in contrast, marijuana is believed to be a sexual depressant, and that is what users report. Similarly, in Jamaica, where marijuana is viewed as an appetite suppressant, users report that the drug has these effects. In North America, many people believe that marijuana will cause them to feel hungry, and especially to crave sweets, and this is what they experience. Clearly, then, the effects of marijuana are subtle and shaped, to an important degree, by an individual's expectations.

Marijuana smoke contains over 400 chemicals, many of which may affect the brain. The one that is psychoactive, and causes perceptual and other changes, is THC. Although THC is not found naturally in the body, it matches up with receptor sites in the brain, such as the hippocampus, cerebral cortex, and basal ganglia, and in other body locations, such as the spleen (which filters our complete blood supply every twenty-four hours). What these receptor sites normally do is a puzzle. But in 1992, a substance that uses the same receptors was discovered in pigs' brains. That substance was named anandamine ("bliss"), and it seems to have the same effects as THC in mice and hamsters. In humans, anandamine may relieve pain, control appetite and motor coordination, and regulate moods.

The use of marijuana poses certain dangers. First, the perceptual distortions it produces may result in tragedy—when users attempt to drive or to operate machinery, for example. Second, because it is illegal, marijuana purchasers never know exactly what they are getting. For example, a designer form of the drug may have ten times the usual THC content and produce terrifying paranoia. Third, long-term use of marijuana may result in shifts in the personality toward passivity and a general lack of motivation (Baumrind, 1984). Finally, some find that marijuana interferes with memory (Miller, Cornelius, & McFarland, 1978).

There have been few studies of the long-term effects of marijuana on individual users, or on children whose mothers used marijuana while pregnant (Fried, Watkinson, & Gray, 1992). Some research has reported few long-lasting adverse effects for users (e.g., Page, Fletcher, & True, 1988). However, Cynader and Chen at the University of British Columbia found that there are many more THC receptors in newborn kitten and monkey brains than in adults. This led them to suggest that exposure to the THC in marijuana smoke at a very young age may affect how well the brain will function throughout the person's life.

Moreover, there is some indication now that long-term use of marijuana can impair the immune system, thus making long-term user more susceptible to various diseases. Finally, since marijuana users inhale deeply, they expose their lungs to damage from a wide range of contaminants.

More dramatic effects are produced by hallucinogens—drugs that produce vivid hallucinations and other perceptual shifts. Of these, the most famous is **LSD** (lysergic acid diethylamide), or "acid." After taking LSD, many people report profound changes in perceptions of the external world. Objects and people seem to change colour and shape; walls may sway and move; and many sensations seem more intense than normal. There may also be a strange blending of sensory experiences known as *synesthesia*. Music yields visual sensations, while colours produce feelings of warmth or cold. These effects may sound exciting or even pleasant, but many others produced by LSD are quite negative. Objects, people, and even one's own body may seem distorted or threatening. Users may experience deep sorrow or develop intense fear of close friends and relatives. Perhaps worst of all, the effects of this drug are unpredictable; there is no way of determining in advance whether LSD will yield mostly pleasant or mostly unpleasant sensations. In fact, the same person may experience radically different effects at different times. Unless you are willing to gamble with your own health, therefore, LSD is a drug to avoid. An overview of various drugs and their effects is provided in the **Key Concept** feature on page 166.

LSD: A powerful hallucinogen that produces profound shifts in perception; many of these are frightening in nature.

Key Concept
Effects of Consciousness-Altering Drugs

Depressants

Reduce behavioural output and activity in the central nervous system.

Alcohol
- Deadening of pain
- Reduced coordination
- Interference with normal functioning of senses
- Reduced social inhibitions

Barbiturates
- Reduced mental alertness
- Sleep
- Confusion
- Euphoria
- Memory lapses, inability to concentrate
- Suppression of REM sleep

Stimulants

Induce feelings of energy and activation.

Amphetamines
- Elevation of blood pressure, heart rate, respiration
- Feelings of alertness and energy, followed by depression as effect wears off

Caffeine
- Mild feelings of increased alertness

- Mild diuretic effect (increased urination)

Cocaine and derivatives (including crack)
- Feelings of tremendous power and energy
- Intense pleasurable sensations
- Psychological dependence (cocaine)
- Powerful addiction (crack)

Opiates

Produce lethargy and pronounced slowing of almost all bodily functions; induce a dreamlike state and pleasurable sensations.

Opium
- Deadening of pain
- Induced dreamlike state
- Inducing of pleasurable sensations, feelings
- Highly addicting

Morphine
- Similar to opium but even more pronounced

Heroin
- Like opium and morphine, but pleasurable sensations are intensified
- Extremely addicting

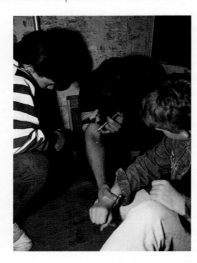

Psychedelics and Hallucinogens

Psychedelics alter sensory perception; sometimes viewed as mind-expanding. Hallucinogens generate sensory perceptions for which there are no external stimuli.

Psychedelics (e.g., marijuana)
- Moderate arousal
- Increased intensity of various stimuli
- Distortions in sense of time
- Diminished ability to judge distances
- Feelings of increased sexual pleasure, for some people
- Feelings of relaxation

Hallucinogens (e.g., LSD)
- Profound changes in perceptions of external world
- Blending of sensory experiences
- Objects seem to change shape
- Ordinary situations may become threatening or frightening
- Effects of drugs vary greatly on different people

Drug Effects and Other Influences

While specific drugs do generally produce the effects just described, their impact may vary, depending on many other factors.

First, the impact of drugs is often determined by expectations. If users expect a drug to produce certain effects (increase their sex drive, reduce their inhibitions, or put them in a good mood), these effects are much more likely to happen than if users do not anticipate them.

Second, a drug's effects depend on the user's physical state. Some people are naturally more tolerant of various drugs than others. Also, the influence of a specific drug may depend on whether the person taking it is fatigued or well rested, whether he or she has recently eaten, and many other factors.

Third, the effects of various drugs depend on previous experience. First-time users of alcohol or tobacco generally report very different reactions to these substances than people who have used them for quite some time. The same is true for many other drugs that alter mood or consciousness.

Finally, the influence of a given drug depends on which other drugs the user is also taking. In medicine, careful physicians consider the possibility of drug interactions before issuing prescriptions. People who take various illegal drugs, however, may fail to take such care—sometimes with tragic results.

In sum, the influence of drugs on feelings, behaviour, and consciousness is neither certain nor fully predictable. Many factors can determine the magnitude and direction of their effects. This is yet another reason why, where drugs are concerned, the byword should be caution.

K E Y *QUESTIONS*

- What are the effects of depressants?
- What are the effects of stimulants? Opiates? Psychedelics? Hallucinogens?
- What factors influence the behavioural effects of a given drug?

Waking States of Consciousness

As a new professor, one of the first things you learn about teaching university students is this: No matter what you are saying and no matter how you say it, only some members of the class are listening at any given time. While many are paying attention to your words, others are off somewhere in their own thoughts, daydreaming, making plans, and so on. Such fluctuations are a normal part of life, for during our waking hours, we shift frequently between contrasting states of consciousness. In this section we will focus on several of these recurring or routine changes.

Controlled and Automatic Processing

Have you ever tried to carry on conversations with two different people at once? If so, you already know a basic fact about human consciousness: Our cognitive resources or information-processing capacities are quite limited. We simply do not have the ability to focus on several different stimuli or events at once. Rather, we find it necessary to shift back and forth between events that we wish to make the centre of our current attention. If this is so, how do we manage to perform two or more activities at once—for example, brushing your teeth while thinking about the day's coming events? The answer seems to be that there are two contrasting ways of controlling ongoing activities—different levels of attention to, or conscious control over, our own behaviour (Logan, 1985, 1988).

Automatic Processing Requires Less Effort Than Controlled Processing—Unless We Think about It!

As Linus has just discovered, tasks we perform under automatic processing require little effort, unless we try to think about them! Directing attention to such tasks can actually interfere with their performance.

Source: United Feature Syndicate, 1990.

The first level is the kind of "automatic pilot" mentioned at the start of this chapter. Psychologists describe this as **automatic processing** because it is the performance of activities with relatively little conscious awareness. Such processing seems to make little demand on our cognitive resources. Thus, several activities, each under automatic control, can occur at the same time (Lamb et al., 1998; Shiffrin & Dumais, 1981; Shiffrin & Schneider, 1977). You are demonstrating automatic processing when you drive your car and listen to the radio at the same time. Automatic processing tends to develop with practice, as the components of the activity become well learned and become associated with specific stimuli.

In contrast, **controlled processing** requires more effortful and conscious control of behaviour. While it is occurring, you direct careful attention to the task at hand and concentrate on it. Obviously, processing of this type does use significant cognitive resources. As a result, tasks requiring controlled processing can usually only be performed one at a time. Automatic processing has been studied in memory and reading (Jacoby, Levy, & Steinbach, 1992; Jennings & Jacoby, 1993), in listening to music (Unyk, 1990), and in special populations (e.g., autistic children and those with attention-deficit-hyperactivity disorder).

Research on the nature of automatic and controlled processing suggests that they differ in several important ways. First, as you might guess, behaviours that have come under the control of automatic processing are performed more quickly and with less effort than those that require controlled processing (Logan, 1988, 1992; Newell & Rosenbloom, 1981). In addition, automatized acts, but not controlled ones, can be initiated without conscious intention; they are triggered in a seemingly automatic manner, by specific stimuli or events (Norman & Shallice, 1985). In fact, it may be difficult to inhibit automatized actions once they are initiated. If you ever played "Simon Says" as a child, you are well aware of this fact. After following many commands beginning "Simon says do this…," you probably also responded to the similar command "Do this…" (without the words "Simon says" in front of it) automatically.

Neither controlled nor automatic processing necessarily has an edge; both offer a mixed pattern of advantages and disadvantages. Automatic processing is rapid and efficient but relatively inflexible. Controlled processing is slower but is more flexible and open to change. Clearly, both have their place in our efforts to deal with information from the external world.

One final point: Automatic and controlled processing are not hard-and-fast categories. Rather, they represent the ends of a continuum. On any given task, individuals may be operating in a relatively controlled or a relatively automatic manner. It seems, however, that we have a strong tendency to adopt automatic processing whenever feasible. Given our limited capacity for attending to many simultaneous stimuli or for processing information generally (see Chapters 6 and 7), this tendency offers major benefits. At the same time, though, our readiness to use our automatic pilot can exact important costs. Whatever the balance between the relative pluses and minuses, the important point to remember is this: Even during waking activities, we can and often do shift back and forth between levels of awareness or states of consciousness.

Daydreams and Fantasies

Do you have moments during study time when your thoughts wander off somewhere into your own private world, so that your eyes are scanning the pages but

Automatic Processing: Processing of information with minimal conscious awareness.

Controlled Processing: Processing of information with relatively high levels of conscious awareness.

your mind is focused largely on other matters? Most people regularly have **day-dreams**—thoughts and images that we generate internally (Singer, 1975). When these daydreams become intense enough to affect our own emotions, they are sometimes called **fantasies** (e.g., Jones & Barlow, 1990). What are these daydreams and fantasies like, and what—if any—function do they serve?

THE CONTENT OF DAYDREAMS AND FANTASIES What was your last day-dream about? If you are like most people, it probably fit under one of the following headings: success or failure (you imagined receiving straight A's or failing an important test); aggression or hostility (you fantasized about getting back at someone who had angered or annoyed you); sexual or romantic fantasies; guilt (you tortured yourself once again over something you should or should not have done); or problem solving (you imagined yourself working on some task or solving some problem). Of course, many other daydream themes exist; these are merely the most common ones (e.g., Klinger, 1990).

While most people report daydreaming at least occasionally, there are large individual differences (Lynn & Rhue, 1986). While some report spending up to half their free time, others indicate that they rarely have fantasies or daydreams (Silva & Kirsch, 1992). Some young adults—mostly men—are *rolegamers,* and they report daydreaming more than some others (Rosenthal et al., 1998). Also, the intensity of such experiences also varies greatly. Some people report that their fantasies and daydreams are so vivid and life-like that they are almost real and they may even be confused with reality itself. If they are, and if such experiences are not readily controlled by those who have them, they may be **hallucinations**—vivid perceptual experiences that occur in the absence of an external stimulus. Such experiences are usually associated with severe psychological disorders, but they also sometimes occur among people who are not mentally ill (Bentall, 1990).

DAYDREAM SOURCES: INTERNAL AND EXTERNAL To a large extent, daydreams are self-induced; they are the result of turning our thoughts to images that are based on memory—or our imagination (Singer, 1975). However, there is evidence that daydreams can be influenced by external events. One such influence is television. The more television children watch, the more often they daydream. Most studies suggest that television encourages daydreaming among adults, too (e.g., McIlwrith et al., 1991). This may be because television provides the "raw materials"—vivid images and new information—from which people can construct their daydreams.

In contrast, however, television exerts a chilling effect on creative imagination. The more television children watch, the lower their creative imagination scores—as measured by teachers or by standard tests of creative imagination—for example, the less likely they are to generate different, novel, or unusual ideas (e.g., Singer et al., 1984; Valkenburg & van der Voort , 1994; Viemero & Paajanen, 1992). Why watching television has such consequences is not yet clear. Possibly it is because watching television is a passive process and the rapid pace leaves viewers little time to engage in their own thoughts, discourages the mental effort required for creative imagination, and reduces our capacity to cope creatively with unexpected situations or problems.

WHAT FUNCTION DO DAYDREAMS AND FANTASIES SERVE? If people spend a considerable amount of time engaging in daydreams and fantasies—changing their own consciousness—then these activities must serve some useful function. But what, precisely, do these activities accomplish? No clear-cut answer to this question has as yet emerged, but existing evidence points to several interesting possibilities.

First, daydreams and fantasies may serve as a kind of safety valve, permitting people to escape, however briefly, from the stresses and boredom of everyday life. Perhaps this is one reason why many students tend to daydream in class or while reading their textbooks.

Watching Television

Watching television is a passive process that leaves viewers little time to engage in their own thoughts, but may actually encourage daydreaming.

Daydreams: Imaginary scenes or events that occur while a person is awake.

Fantasies: Imaginary events or scenes that evoke emotions that a person experiences while awake.

Hallucinations: Vivid sensory experiences that occur in the absence of external stimuli yet have the full force of impact of real events or stimuli.

Second, daydreams and fantasies often provide us with a ready means of altering our own moods, primarily in a positive direction. If you have ever felt happier after a daydream filled with desirable activities and events, you are already familiar with these benefits (Forgas & Bower, 1988).

Third, it is possible that daydreams and fantasies help people find solutions to actual problems in their lives. By imagining various behaviours and the outcomes they may produce, we can examine potential courses of action carefully and from the safe perspective of our own mind. This can help us formulate useful plans of action. This is true not only for adults, but also for children who often use fantasy play as a way of working out intense feelings about difficult situations. In fantasy play, children work on fear, for example, and they develop emotional control (Gottman, 1986). They may pretend about being in an accident and going to the hospital or being lost and found.

Finally, fantasies may play an important role in the self-regulation of behaviour. By imagining negative outcomes, people become more likely to avoid dangerous or prohibited behaviours (Bandura, 1986). Similarly, by dreaming about potential rewards, people may enhance their own motivation and performance. In sum, fantasies and daydreams may be much more than a pleasant diversion; they may actually yield substantial benefits to those who choose to induce them.

SEXUAL FANTASIES As you now know, nearly everyone has daydreams, and there is growing evidence that, for most people, these sometimes are *sexual fantasies*—mental images that are sexually arousing or erotic (Leitenberg & Henning, 1995). In fact, more than 95 percent of both women and men report that they have had such fantasies at some time or other (e.g., Pelletier & Herold, 1988). While men report having more sexual fantasies each day than women, such fantasies are common for both genders. This does not mean that the content of sexual fantasies is identical for women and men, however. On the contrary, some gender differences do appear in this respect. For instance, men's erotic fantasies seem to contain more explicit visual imagery and anatomic detail, while women's fantasies contain greater reference to affection, more emotions, and a story line (e.g., Bond & Mosher, 1986).

Both women and men report that such fantasies increase their own arousal, and therefore their own sexual pleasure. Moreover, those who report frequent sexual fantasies also report engaging in greater sexual activity—and enjoying it more—than people who report fewer sexual fantasies (Leitenberg & Henning, 1995). Of course these are self-reports and must be interpreted as such. Nevertheless, sexual fantasies appear to be a normal part of sexual life for most persons. They become problematic when they focus on inappropriate partners (e.g., children) or unwelcome advances (e.g., sexual coercion).

INTRUSIVE THOUGHTS Some researchers distinguish between the daydreams and fantasies of normal people as described above and *intrusive thoughts*—cognitive intrusions that are sudden, unwanted, and uncharacteristic. They may be about sex or violence, but the thought of swerving into the next lane that comes into your head while driving is also an example (Byers et al., 1998). Intrusive thoughts occur commonly in normal people (Purdon & Clark, 1993) as well as in those with disordered thinking (Rachman, 1981).

Sexual cognitive intrusions have been studied in normal, unmarried, heterosexual university students at the University of New Brunswick by Sandra Byers and her colleagues (Byers et al., 1998; Byers et al., 2000; Renaud & Byers, 1999). These researchers differentiated between sexual thoughts that are positive, pleasant, and personally acceptable, and intrusive sexual thoughts that are negative, unpleasant, and uncharacteristic. The results revealed that men report a larger number of different sexual intrusive thoughts, but the most common one for both men and women in their study was the same: having sex in a public place. Furthermore, in some instances, sexual arousal accompanies these negative cognitive intrusions—more often for men than for women. These data contribute much to our understanding of internally generated thoughts and feelings of which we are conscious during our normal waking lives.

Self-Consciousness

What do you do when you pass a mirror? If you are like most people, you stop, however briefly, and examine your appearance. Now, while you stand in front of the glass, your thoughts are focused on you. Psychologists term this state **self-consciousness**. Here is one theory about the purpose of self-consciousness.

THE CONTROL THEORY OF SELF-CONSCIOUSNESS   Think for a moment about how the thermostat in your house or apartment works. It continuously compares the level of temperature you have set to the actual temperature in the room. When the temperature in the room is too cold or too hot, the thermostat adjusts a circuit that turns on your furnace or your air conditioner. In the **control theory of self-consciousness,** Carver and Scheier (1981, 1990) suggest that self-consciousness operates in a similar manner. Once we focus our attention on ourselves, we compare our current state with our goals. If the gap between reality and these goals is too large, we make adjustments. In this sense, self-consciousness is an important component in the self-regulation of our own behaviour.

Many psychologists draw a distinction between two forms of self-consciousness: *private self-consciousness* and *public self-consciousness* (e.g., Britt, 1992; Scheier & Carver 1986, 1987). We engage in private self-consciousness when we focus on the private aspects of the self—our own feelings, attitudes, and values. In contrast, our public self-consciousness focus is on public aspects of the self—how we think we appear to other people. When you look into a mirror or at a photograph of yourself, you almost certainly experience public self-consciousness; after all, you are seeing yourself (physically) the way others do. But if seeing your own reflection causes you to think about how you are feeling or about what kind of person you really are, you are engaged in private self-consciousness. In much of the research being done on self-awareness, the experimenters have subjects work in front of a mirror or with a camera aimed in their direction.

FACTORS THAT PRODUCE HEIGHTENED SELF-CONSCIOUSNESS   One factor that influences self-consciousness is the familiarity of a given situation. In general, the more familiar and comfortable with a situation people are, the greater their tendency to think about themselves, and so the greater their self-consciousness.

A second factor is mood. Research indicates that people who are feeling either happy or sad are more likely to focus their attention inward than those in a neutral mood, presumably because they wish to understand their feelings and the factors responsible for them (Conway et al., 1993; Salovey, 1992).

A third factor determining self-consciousness is the kind of person you are. Some people spend more time than others thinking about themselves—about their feelings and reactions, the kind of impression they are making on strangers. Do you know how you compare with others? To find out, answer the questions in Figure 4.10. These are items from a psychological test designed to measure both private and public self-consciousness (Scheier & Carver, 1986). Their revised self-consciousness scale has been translated and adapted by Pelletier and Vallerand (1991) at the University of Ottawa, for use with French Canadian highschool students, university students, and working adults. The items in the table measure private self-consciousness. People who score high on these items have a greater-than-average tendency to spend time thinking about themselves and their inner feelings or their reactions (Britt, 1992). Other items on the self-consciousness scale measure public self-consciousness.

Heightened Self-Consciousness

What do you do when you pass a mirror? If you are like most people, you glance at your reflection, thus experiencing increased awareness of yourself and your appearance.

Self-Consciousness: Increased awareness of oneself as a social object or of one's own values and attitudes.

Control Theory of Self-Consciousness: A theory suggesting that people compare their current behaviour and states with important goals and values. They then alter their behaviour to close any gaps they observe.

Figure 4.10
Private Self-Consciousness

Are you high in private self-consciousness? To find out, add the numbers you entered for items 1, 3, 4, 5, 6, and 8; then subtract the numbers you entered for items 2 and 7. The higher your score, the more you tend to be aware of your own inner feelings and reactions.

Source: Based on items from Britt, 1992.

Please indicate how characteristic or uncharacteristic of you each of these items is by placing a number in the blank space next to each.

0 = extremely uncharacteristic
1 = uncharacteristic
2 = neither characteristic nor uncharacteristic
3 = characteristic
4 = extremely characteristic

_____   1.   I'm always trying to figure myself out.

_____   2.   Usually, I'm not very aware of myself.

_____   3.   I think about myself a lot.

_____   4.   I'm often the subject of my own fantasies or daydreams.

_____   5.   I usually pay close attention to my inner feelings.

_____   6.   I'm aware of the way my mind works when I try to solve a problem or reason something out.

_____   7.   I never reflect on myself.

_____   8.   I frequently examine my own motives.

Choking Under Pressure: Self-Awareness May Play a Role

Sometimes even professional athletes like those shown here "choke under pressure"—they perform more poorly when the stakes are high than when performance is less important. Heightened self-awareness may play a role in such effects.

Choking Under Pressure: The tendency to perform less well at times when pressures for excellent performance are especially high.

THE EFFECTS OF SELF-CONSCIOUSNESS   That we often experience self-consciousness is obvious: This state is a regular part of daily life. But what are the effects of this inward focus? On the positive side, self-consciousness is necessary for insight to take place (Hixon & Swann,1993). On the negative side, sometimes self-consciousness causes **choking under pressure.** For example, athletes who do very well in practice, when pressure is low, may choke up during important games or contests. Why does that happen? First, the pressure, and consequently the arousal level of the player, may be high enough to interfere with performance. Second, heightened self-consciousness may contribute (Baumeister & Scher, 1988). Because many highly skilled activities are performed under automatic control, for example, keyboarding, once you have mastered this skill, it becomes automatic. That is, you no longer think about the keys, and doing so may slow you down and cause you to make errors. Similar effects occur in many other skilled activities, such as pitching a baseball or swinging a golf club. In addition, heightened self-awareness caused by a huge audience of cheering fans leads to precisely this kind of distraction.

The motivation for self-consciousness may also be positive or negative. When individuals focus on themselves, they can do so for two different motives (Trapnell & Campbell, 1999). First, such self-awareness can be motivated by curiosity—the positive desire to know oneself better; this is known as *reflection*. Second, self-awareness can be motivated primarily by fear—by concern over threats, perceived shortcomings, losses, or injustices one has experienced; this is known as *rumination*. Recent evidence has linked rumination, but not reflection, to several psychological problems. So, thinking about ourselves can produce psychological benefits or psychological costs, depending on the motivation behind this activity, and the topics on which we focus.

K E Y *QUESTIONS*

- What are daydreams? What are some of the major themes they contain?

- How are daydreams influenced by watching television?

- What is the difference between automatic processing and controlled processing?

- What is self-awareness and why do we sometimes enter this state of consciousness?

- What are some of the effects of self-awareness on our adjustment and performance?

Making **Psychology** *Part of Your Life*

Meditation: An Altered State of Consciousness

For centuries, travellers from the West who visited India returned with tales of the amazing feats performed by *yogis*—members of special religious orders who seemed to possess incredible powers. These people, it was reported, could walk barefoot over hot coals and lie on beds of nails without experiencing pain. Perhaps even more astounding, some seemed able to enter a self-induced trance in which they could bring their own heart to a virtual stop!

Were such reports actually true? Existing evidence is mixed, at best, but one fact is clear: there are techniques by which some individuals can alter their consciousness and enter a state in which their contact with and awareness of the external world is reduced (Shapiro, 1980). Several techniques for producing these changes exist, but of these, *meditation* is by far the most popular.

While some researchers have suggested that one can obtain similar effects simply by resting (Holmes, 1984), others contend that greater and more general shifts in physiological processes are produced by meditation (Benson & Friedman, 1985; Gackenbach, 1992) For example, in a classic study, Wallace and Benson (1972) found that during meditation people's oxygen consumption decreased, their heartbeat slowed, and they showed stronger alpha brain waves (see Figure 4.11). Those are the physiological signs of relaxation and reduced tension. More recently, brain wave and brain imaging techniques are contributing data about the patterns of neural activity in mediation versus normal consciousness (Lou, 1999; Lyubimov, 1999). There is additional evidence for physiological effects from people who do meditation and find it easier to give up the use of various drugs (Gelderloos et al., 1991), including marijuana, amphetamines, and barbiturates (Marzetta, Benson, & Wallace, 1972).

What are the benefits of meditating? Research designed to investigate the physiological effects of meditation suggests that there are various benefits: less tension, lower levels of anxiety (Eppley et al., 1989), an increased ability to express feelings freely (Greenberg, 1991), and reduction of stress (Collings, 1989). In an eight-week study of meditation-based stress reduction in premedical and medical students, Shapiro and colleagues (1998) found that participation in meditation reduced anxiety and psychological distress, which extended into the exam period. In business, transcendental meditation has been linked to improved health, job satisfaction, and efficiency as well as decreased absenteeism (Schmidt, 1996).

Can you enjoy these benefits yourself? Yes: meditation is a relatively simple technique and requires only a few minutes each day. Here are some basic steps:

1. **Find a quiet, isolated location.** Meditation does not require lots of time, but it does require you to find a quiet place where you can be alone for a while and focus your attention inward, away from the outside world.

2. **Choose an appropriate mantra.** Meditation derives historically from Buddhism and Hinduism. In its original form, a mantra came from religious

Meditation

Meditating is a relatively simple technique and requires only a few minutes each day.

writings. Your own mantra can be almost any word or phrase on which you can concentrate.

3. **Practise meditating**. Repeat your mantra silently, over and over again, and focus your attention only on this word. The hardest part of meditation is learning to keep your thoughts from slipping away from the mantra and back to the normal worries and concerns of everyday life. That is a skill you can acquire with practice.

4. **Continue meditating for fifteen to twenty minutes.** As you master the skill of focusing your attention on the mantra and screening out other distracting thoughts, gradually increase your period of meditation to fifteen or twenty minutes. Meditate in moderation, especially on days when you feel especially stressed.

Of course, meditation is not for everyone, and it does have detractors (Beyerstein, 1999; Persinger, 1993). If you find it difficult or unappealing, you should consider other techniques for gaining these benefits. If you do find meditation to your liking, however, you may wish to make it part of your daily life.

Figure 4.11
Physiological Changes During Meditation

During meditation, individuals experience changes in several basic physiological processes. Oxygen consumption decreases and the intensity of alpha waves increases.

Source: Based on data from Wallace and Benson, 1972.

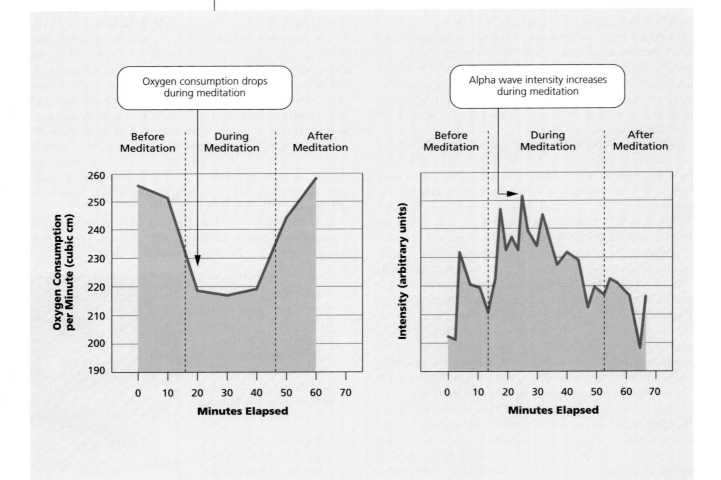

Summary and Review

Key Questions

Biological Rhythms

■ **What are biological rhythms? What are circadian rhythms?** Biological rhythms are regular fluctuations in our bodily processes. Circadian rhythms are biological rhythms that occur within a single day.

■ **How do "morning" people and "evening" people differ?** Morning people feel most alert and energetic early in the day. Evening people feel most alert and energetic late in the day.

■ **What effects do jet lag and shift work have on circadian rhythms?** Travel across time zones and shift work can produce disturbances in circadian rhythms. Knowledge of circadian rhythms suggests effective ways of countering such disturbances.

■ **How do psychologists use diary studies to study circadian rhythms and disruptions in them?** In diary studies, individuals record their own moods, physical states, and performance at regular intervals. Such information is useful in determining how various aspects of behaviour change over the course of a day or, sometimes, over longer periods of time.

Sleep

■ **How do psychologists study sleep?** Sleep is often studied by examining changes in the EEG—electrical activity in the brain—that occur as people sleep.

■ **What are the major stages of sleep?** There appear to be four major stages of sleep, each successive stage showing shifts in the EEG and reduced awareness of the outside world. In addition, there is another distinct phase of sleep—REM sleep.

■ **What happens during REM sleep?** During REM sleep the EEG shows a pattern similar to that of waking, but the activity of body muscles is almost totally suppressed. Dreams occur during REM sleep.

■ **What are the effects of sleep deprivation?** Although people undergoing sleep deprivation report feeling tired and irritable, they can function quite well even after long sleepless periods.

■ **What functions does sleep seem to play?** Growing evidence indicates that sleep serves important functions related to restoration of bodily resources and to basic circadian rhythms.

■ **What are some of the most common sleep disorders?** Insomnia is difficulty in falling asleep; somnambulism is walking in one's sleep; and narcolepsy is a tendency to fall suddenly into a deep sleep in the midst of waking activities.

■ **What steps can you take to help get a good night's sleep every night?** Steps that may help you get a good night's sleep include these: read something pleasant or relaxing just before going to sleep; arrange your schedule so you go to sleep at the same time each night; take a warm bath or have a massage before going to sleep; avoid coffee late in the day; exercise every day, but not just before going to sleep; do not smoke; do not nap during the day.

■ **During what stage of sleep do dreams usually occur?** Dreams occur during REM sleep.

■ **Do most people dream? How long do dreams last?** Almost everyone dreams. The longer dreams seem to be, the longer they last in actual time.

■ **How do the psychodynamic, physiological, and cognitive views of dreams differ?** The psychodynamic view, made famous by Freud, suggests that dreams reflect suppressed thoughts, wishes, and impulses. The physiological view suggests that dreams reflect the brain's interpretation of random neural activity that occurs while we sleep. The cognitive view holds that dreams result from the fact that many systems of the brain are active during sleep while input from muscles and sensory systems is inhibited.

■ **What are dreams of absent-minded transgression, and what do they tell us about the meaning of dreams?** In dreams of absent-minded transgression, individuals who are trying to change their own behaviour—for example, stop smoking or drinking alcohol—dream that they have performed the behaviours they wish to avoid in an absent-minded manner, without meaning to do so.

Hypnosis

■ **What is hypnosis?** Hypnosis involves a special type of interaction between two persons in which one (the hypnotist) induces changes in the behaviour, feelings, or cognitions of the other (the subject) through suggestions.

■ **How do the social–cognitive and neodissociation views of hypnosis differ?** The social–cognitive view suggests that the effects of hypnosis stem from the hypnotized person's expectations and his or her efforts to play the role of hypnotized subject. The neodissociation view suggests that the effects of hypnotism stem from a split in consciousness in which executive cognitive functions (those that allow us to control our own behaviour) are separated from other cognitive functions (those that allow us to observe our own behaviour).

■ **What evidence supports the social–cognitive view?** The social–cognitive view is supported by the finding that persons who are led to believe that they have "slipped back into hypnosis" but are not hypnotized often behave like those who have been hypnotized.

■ **Is there any evidence for the neodissociation view? If so, what is this evidence?** Some evidence offers support for the neodissociation view. For instance, it has been found that when persons who are highly susceptible to hypnosis are given the suggestion that they have undergone a sex change, they resist even very strong evidence that is contrary to this suggestion.

Consciousness-Altering Drugs

■ **What are drugs? What is drug abuse?** Drugs are substances that, because of their chemical structure, change the functioning of biological systems. Drug abuse involves instances in which people take drugs to change their moods, and in which they experience impaired behaviour or social functioning as a result of doing so.

■ **What are physiological and psychological dependence on drugs?** Physiological dependence involves strong urges to continue using a drug that are based on biological factors, such as changes in metabolism. Psychological dependence involves strong desires to continue using a drug even though it is not physiologically addicting.

■ **How does the learning perspective explain drug abuse?** The learning perspective suggests that these drugs have rewarding effects and they help to lessen stress, anxiety, and other negative feelings.

■ **How does the social perspective explain drug abuse?** The social perspective suggests that people abuse drugs because of strong social pressures to do so, or because they believe that doing so will enhance their social "image."

■ **How does the cognitive perspective explain drug abuse?** The cognitive perspective proposes that drug abuse may be at least in part an automatic behaviour triggered by the presence of external cues.

■ **What are the effects of depressants?** Depressants reduce both behavioural output and activity in the central nervous system. Important depressants include alcohol and barbiturates.

■ **What are the effects of stimulants? Opiates? Psychedelics? Hallucinogens?** Stimulants produce energy and activity. Opiates produce lethargy and pronounced slowing of many bodily functions, but also induce intense feelings of pleasure in some persons. Psychedelics such as marijuana alter sensory perception, while hallucinogens such as LSD produce vivid hallucinations and other bizarre perceptual effects.

■ **What factors influence the behavioural effects of a given drug?** A specific dose of a given drug may have very different effects for the same person at different times, depending on such factors as the person's expectations, physical state, and other drugs he or she has taken recently.

Waking States of Consciousness

■ **What are daydreams? What are some of the major themes they contain?** Daydreams are thoughts and images that we generate internally. Common themes in daydreams include success or failure, aggression or hostility, sexual or romantic fantasies, guilt, or problem solving.

■ **How are daydreams influenced by watching television?** Television seems to encourage daydreaming, perhaps by providing individuals with exciting images from which they can construct their daydreams. However, it seems to discourage *creative imagination*, that ability to generate many novel or unusual ideas.

■ **What is the difference between automatic processing and controlled processing?** In automatic processing, we perform activities without directing conscious attention to them. In controlled processing, we direct conscious attention to various activities.

■ **What is self-awareness and why do we sometimes enter this state of consciousness?** Self-awareness is a state of consciousness in which we turn our attention inward, toward ourselves. We enter this state because of situational factors (e.g., we pass a mirror), our affective states, or because we possess a predisposition to enter this state.

■ **What are some of the effects of self-awareness on our adjustment and performance?** If it takes the form of rumination (focus on our own flaws), self-awareness can have negative effects on our adjustment. Heightened self-awareness can lead to choking under pressure.

Key Terms

Alcohol (p. 162)

Alpha Waves (p. 146)

Amphetamines (p. 163)

Automatic Processing (p. 168)

Barbiturates (p. 163)

Biological Rhythms (p. 139)

Choking Under Pressure (p. 172)

Circadian Rhythms (p. 139)

Cocaine (p. 163)

Controlled Processing (p. 168)

Control Theory of Self-Consciousness (p. 171)

Crack (p. 163)

Cross-Tolerance (p. 160)

Daydreams (p. 169)

Delta Waves (p. 146)

Dependence (p. 159)

Depressants (p. 162)

Dreams (p. 152)

Dreams of Absent-Minded Transgression (p. 154)

Drugs (p. 159)

Drug Abuse (p. 159)

Electroencephalogram (EEG) (p. 145)

Evolutionary Theory (p. 149)

Fantasies (p. 169)

Hallucinations (p. 169)

Critical Thinking Questions

Appraisal

Today, most psychologists believe that states of consciousness can be studied in a scientific manner. Do you agree or disagree or do you feel that this is stretching the banner of science too far? Why do you hold the opinion that you do?

Controversy

Hypnotism is one of the most controversial topics of research. Many psychologists doubt that hypnosis represents an altered state of consciousness, while others believe that it does. There is evidence on both sides. What do you think? What kind of evidence would resolve this issue once and for all?

Making Psychology Part of Your Life

Now that you have some basic understanding of biological rhythms, states of consciousness, self-consciousness, and the nature of sleep, list three ways in which you can put this knowledge to practical use. For example, what could you do to improve your sleep? How could you change your own daily schedule so as to take advantage of high points in your own circadian rhythms?

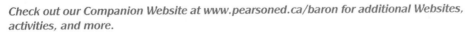

Weblinks

Check out our Companion Website at www.pearsoned.ca/baron for additional Websites, activities, and more.

Circadian Information Home Page

www.circadian.com/

Circadian Information, in Cambridge, Massachusetts, publishes the monthly newsletter *ShiftWork Alert,* the *Shiftworker Family Calendar,* the new monthly *Working Nights* newsletter, and other books and pamphlets about different aspects of shiftwork and fatigue management.

Sleep Home Pages

bisleep.medsch.ucla.edu/

The Sleep Pages provide a comprehensive resource for individuals who are involved in research on sleep or the treatment of sleep-related disorders. At this site are new abstracts and papers in the field, information about the Association of Professional Sleep Societies, the Bibliographic Electronic Databases of Sleep (BEDS), the Society for Light Treatment and Biological Rhythms, worldwide sleep laboratories and clinics, and a great deal more.

Chapter 5

Learning
How Experience Changes Us

CHAPTER OUTLINE

Pijariqpunga

In the *Nunsiaq News,* a columnist describes the adjustments she made to her behaviour as a child when her family moved to a new "neighbourhood" amongst the Netsilingmiut peoples. Their social behaviour was different from what she was used to, and quite traditional. For example, in her noisy family she was permitted to state her opinions out loud. In her new society, children were trained to be quiet in the company of adults—in order that they remain silent during a hunt.

She learned that in conversations among elders, the word *pijariqpunga,* meaning "That's all I have to say about that," indicated that a speaker was finished and someone else would then begin. If she was invited to speak, she was also allowed to express her own opinion without interruption—until she indicated that she was finished in the adult way.

How was this child able to adjust her behaviour to fit her new experience? She learned to do so by observing the ways of the people around her and by imitating what they did. Psychologists call this observational learning. That is only one of the ways we acquire new behaviours as a result of experience. In Chapter 5, you will find much more about this complex and fascinating area of psychological research.

Rachel Attituq Quitsualik. 2000, February 25. Lost in translation: Part one, *Nunsiaq News.*

> The learning process is crucial to all organisms, especially people, since it helps us adapt to changing conditions in the world around us.

Why do gamblers continue to put money into slot machines, even after losing a bundle? How do trained animals do their complicated routines? Does watching violence on television cause people to act aggressively? If questions like these make you wonder, then you will find much of interest in this chapter. The topic of learning is fundamental to all of psychology, because it is the way we change our behaviour as a result of our personal interactions with the world around us.

Learning is defined as any relatively permanent change in behaviour, or behaviour potential, produced by experience. Four points about this definition need further explanation. First, the term *learning* does not apply to temporary changes in behaviour such as those that result from fatigue, drugs, or illness. Second, it does not refer to changes that result from maturation—the many ways you change as you grow and develop. Third, learning may result from direct experience or from indirect observation of the behaviour of other people (Bandura, 1986). Fourth, the changes produced by learning are not always positive; people are as likely to acquire bad habits as good ones.

Being able to change as a result of experience is obviously adaptive not only for human beings but also for all other organisms. Brain mechanisms to provide for learning are present in the simplest nervous systems and in the most complex. Sea snails (aplysia) and earthworms learn to withdraw in anticipation of unpleasant stimuli (electric shock), and birds learn to sing somewhat different songs by listening to their parents sing. What changes occur in the nervous systems of these animals? We do not fully know the answer to that question. One suggestion is that novel experiences produce new networks of neurons.

Learning plays an important role in virtually everything we do: from driving a car to falling in love. Most psychologists believe, however, that there are basically three kinds of learning: *classical conditioning, operant conditioning,* and *observational learning.* We will begin with classical conditioning, which is the basis for learned fears—public speaking anxiety, for example. Next, we will turn to operant conditioning, and we will see how psychologists have applied current knowledge to encourage motorists to stop at pedestrian crosswalks. Finally, we will explore observational learning, a process by which people learn many complex behaviours—including sensitivity to the customs of other cultures—by imitation.

Classical Conditioning: Learning That Some Stimuli Signal Others

Consider the following situation: During a particularly hectic term, you find yourself with a timetable that leaves only a few minutes for lunch. A friend tells you about a vending area where she buys microwaveable popcorn. When the buzzer sounds and you open the door of the microwave, the delightful aroma of fresh popcorn rushes out and your mouth starts to water. After several days, however, your mouth waters immediately after you hear the buzzer, before you actually open the door to the microwave, before you can see or smell or taste or hear the popcorn. Assuming that your mouth does not normally water when you hear a buzzer—the buzzer to your alarm clock for example (after all, a buzzer is just a sound)—your

Learning: Any relatively permanent change in behaviour (or behaviour potential) resulting from experience.

response to this particular buzzer has changed as a result of classical conditioning. For an illustration of that process, see Figure 5.1.

Classical conditioning is quite common in everyday life and plays a role in the learning of fears, taste aversions, some aspects of sexual behaviour, racial or ethnic prejudice (Baron & Byrne, 1994), and even visual illusions (Allen & Siegel, 1993). Classical conditioning became the subject of careful study in the early twentieth century, when Ivan Pavlov, a Nobel Prize-winning physiologist from Russia, identified it as an important reason for why we behave the way we do. That is why classical conditioning is also called *Pavlovian conditioning.*

Pavlov's Early Work on Classical Conditioning

Pavlov's original research focused on the process of digestion in dogs. During his investigations he noticed a curious fact: The dogs in his studies often began to salivate when they saw or smelled food—before they actually tasted it. Some even salivated at the sight of the pan where their food was kept or when they saw or heard the person who usually brought it. This suggested to Pavlov that these **stimuli** had somehow become signals for the food itself: The dogs had learned that when these stimuli were present, food would soon follow.

Pavlov quickly recognized the potential importance of this observation and shifted the focus of his research accordingly. The procedures that he now developed were relatively simple. Dogs were placed in an apparatus similar to that shown in Figure 5.2. On conditioning trials, an originally neutral stimulus that previously had no effect on salivation—a bell, for example—was presented. Then

Stimuli: Physical events capable of affecting behaviour.

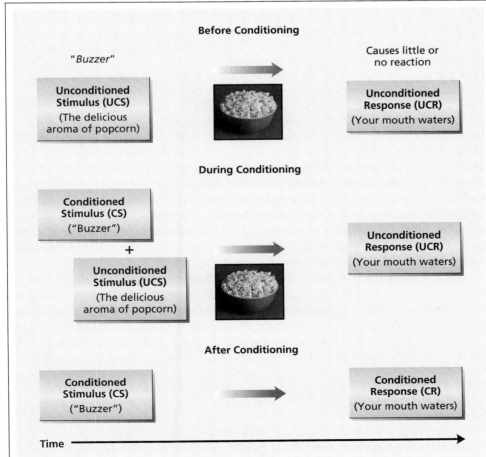

Figure 5.1
Classical Conditioning: A Simple Example

At first, the sound of the microwave's buzzer may startle you and cause you to look toward its source, but it will probably not cause you to salivate. However, after the buzzer has been paired with the aroma and taste of the popcorn on several occasions, you may find that you salivate to sound alone. This "mouth-watering" reaction is a result of classical conditioning.

Before Conditioning

"Buzzer"

Causes little or no reaction

Unconditioned Stimulus (UCS)
(The delicious aroma of popcorn)

Unconditioned Response (UCR)
(Your mouth waters)

During Conditioning

Conditioned Stimulus (CS)
("Buzzer")

+

Unconditioned Stimulus (UCS)
(The delicious aroma of popcorn)

Unconditioned Response (UCR)
(Your mouth waters)

After Conditioning

Conditioned Stimulus (CS)
("Buzzer")

Conditioned Response (CR)
(Your mouth waters)

Time

Figure 5.2
Pavlov's Apparatus for Studying Classical Conditioning

Pavlov used equipment similar to this in his early experiments on classical conditioning. He attached a tube to a dog's salivary gland, which had been surgically moved to the outside of the dog's cheek to allow easy collection of saliva. He then measured the number of drops of saliva that occurred naturally when a bell was sounded.

dried meat powder was put directly into the dog's mouth and the dog's mouth watered—that is, saliva was produced. That response, saliva in the mouth when food is present, is automatic; it occurs naturally and reliably. (You probably know yourself that when some tasty morsel of popcorn is put into your mouth, without your thinking about it, saliva begins to flow. You did not have to learn anything in order for that to happen. In that, we and Pavlov's dogs have much in common.)

Next, Pavlov measured the number of drops of saliva that occurred when a bell was sounded along with the presentation of food. Pavlov found that after repeated occasions when the bell was followed by the food, the dog's saliva increased as soon as the bell was sounded, indicating that it had learned to connect the originally neutral bell with the food.

The basic question for Pavlov was: Would the bell elicit a response when it was presented alone? The answer was clearly *yes*. After the originally neutral bell had been paired repeatedly with the meat powder, the dogs salivated when they heard its sound, even if the meat powder was no longer provided. Now let's look at the experiment carefully and define the terminology used to study classical conditioning.

Pavlov called the meat powder an **unconditioned stimulus (UCS).** When a UCS occurs, the response it produces happens naturally and automatically and without learning. Similarly, he called the response to the meat powder (the dog's salivation) an **unconditioned response (UCR)**—it also occurred without previous learning. He called the bell a **conditioned stimulus (CS),** because it produced salivation only after it had been paired with meat powder several times. In other words, the response to the bell was conditional upon the animal's experience. Finally, he called salivation in response to the bell a **conditioned response (CR),** because it required learning in order to occur. (Incidentally, Pavlov had another name for the conditioned salivation: "psychic secretion"!)

Note that the unconditioned stimulus and the conditioned stimulus in this experiment are the meat powder and the bell—two very different events. However, in this example (although not necessarily always) the unconditioned response and the conditioned response seem to be the same. In both cases, the response—the behaviour that is measured—is the production of saliva. But don't let this similarity confuse you into thinking that the UCR and the CR are the same thing. When the meat powder UCS is presented, the saliva occurs naturally and automatically, right away. When the bell CS is presented, the saliva does not occur until classical conditioning has taken place. Similarly, it takes several pairings of a microwave buzzer and hot buttery popcorn in order for your mouth to begin to water in advance of tasting the popcorn. Of course, classical conditioning is not limited to associations between salivation and various originally neutral events. Through classical

Unconditioned Stimulus (UCS): In classical conditioning, a stimulus that can elicit an unconditioned response the first time it is presented.

Unconditioned Response (UCR): In classical conditioning, the response elicited by an unconditioned stimulus.

Conditioned Stimulus (CS): In classical conditioning, the stimulus that is repeatedly paired with an unconditioned stimulus.

Conditioned Response (CR): In classical conditioning, the response to the conditioned stimulus.

conditioning we acquire many different responses—from anxiety about getting vaccinated to romantic feelings when we hear certain songs.

Furthermore, classical conditioning is not limited to one conditioned stimulus. Rather, if the original CS—let's say the bell—is preceded by another originally neutral event—let's say a light—after a number of trials, the light will elicit the conditioned salivation even though no meat powder has been provided at all! We call this procedure *second-order conditioning*. Here is how second-order conditioning might work in the real world. The sight of a predator becomes a feared object for a young animal through classical conditioning. That might happen as a result of the visible signs of fear in adult animals that occur when the predator comes into view. Then, the sound of the predator precedes its appearance, and that sound paired with the animal becomes a stimulus that evokes the fear response (Mazur, 1998). Thus, the pairing of the first CS (the sight of the predator) and the second CS (the sound of the predator) contribute to the survival of the young animal in the real world.

Some Basic Principles of Classical Conditioning

Let us turn now to the principles that govern the occurrence of classical conditioning.

ACQUISITION: THE TIME COURSE OF CLASSICAL CONDITIONING In most instances, classical conditioning is a gradual process in which an originally neutral stimulus gradually acquires the capacity to elicit a conditioned response—and thus becomes a CS. This process is called **acquisition** (see Panel A in Figure 5.3) The measurement of acquisition may be increases in the size or amount of the response— for example, the amount of saliva. Another measure used often is response delay: as learning proceeds, the length of time it takes for the CR to occur—after the CS has been presented—decreases.

Acquisition: The process by which a conditioned stimulus acquires the ability to elicit a conditioned response through repeated pairings of an unconditioned stimulus with the conditioned stimulus.

Figure 5.3
The Time Course of Conditioning

The strength of the conditioned response rapidly increases during acquisition (panel A). The process of extinction begins once the conditioned stimulus is no longer paired with the unconditioned stimulus (panel B). As shown in panels C and D, extinction can be disrupted through the processes of spontaneous recovery and reconditioning. Finally, although not shown in the figure, if no subsequent conditioned stimulus–unconditioned stimulus pairings occur, the conditioned response will decrease once again.

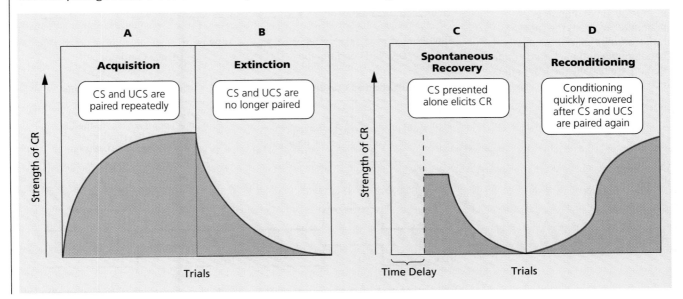

Conditioning proceeds steadily as the number of pairings between the CS and the UCS—the number of trials—increases. However, there is a limit to this effect. After a number of pairings of CS and UCS, the strength of the conditioned response reaches a maximum and remains stable after that.

Although psychologists initially believed that conditioning was determined primarily by the number of CS–UCS pairings, we now know that this process is affected by other factors. As shown in Figure 5.4, one factor that matters is *temporal arrangement* of the CS–UCS pairings (e.g., Davey & Biederman, 1991). Temporal means time-related, and refers to the point in time at which the conditioned stimulus occurs, relative to the unconditioned stimulus. The first two temporal arrangements shown, **delayed conditioning** and **trace conditioning,** are examples of *forward conditioning,* since the presentation of the unconditioned stimulus (shock) always follows the presentation of the conditioned stimulus (light). They differ, however, in that the CS and the UCS overlap to some degree in delayed conditioning, but not in trace conditioning. Two other temporal arrangements are **simultaneous conditioning,** in which the conditioned and unconditioned stimuli begin and end at the same time; and **backward conditioning,** in which the conditioned stimulus follows the unconditioned stimulus.

Delayed Conditioning: A form of forward conditioning in which the presentation of the conditioned stimulus precedes, but overlaps with, the presentation of the unconditioned stimulus.

Trace Conditioning: A form of forward conditioning in which the presentation of the conditioned stimulus precedes and does not overlap with the presentation of the unconditioned stimulus.

Simultaneous Conditioning: A form of conditioning in which the conditioned stimulus and the unconditioned stimulus begin and end at the same time.

Backward Conditioning: A type of conditioning in which the presentation of the unconditioned stimulus precedes and does not overlap with the presentation of the conditioned stimulus.

Figure 5.4
Temporal Arrangement of the CS and UCS Affects the Acquisition of a Conditioned Response

Four CS–UCS temporal arrangements commonly used in classical conditioning procedures are shown. Temporal means time-related: the extent to which a CS precedes or follows the presentation of an unconditioned stimulus. Delayed conditioning generally produces the most rapid learning. Simultaneous conditioning and backward conditioning are usually the least effective procedures.

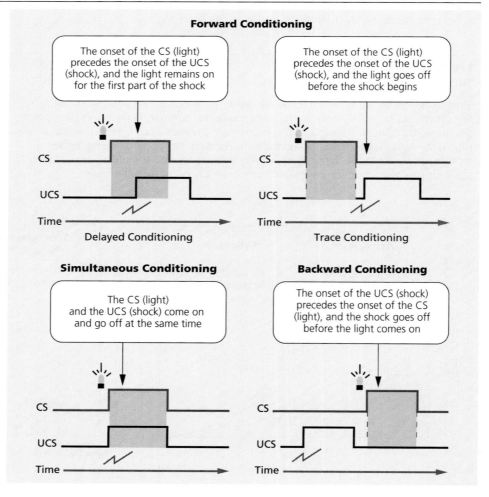

Research suggests that delayed conditioning is generally the most effective method for establishing a classically-conditioned response. This is because the CS often plays an important role in predicting forthcoming presentations of the unconditioned stimulus (Lieberman, 1990). Consider a real-life situation in which prediction is an important factor. You are taking a shower when suddenly the water turns icy cold. Your response—a startle reaction to the cold water—is an unconditioned response. Now imagine that just before the water turns cold, the plumbing makes a slight grinding sound. Because this sound occurs just before and overlaps with the onset of the icy water, delayed conditioning can occur. If this situation is repeated several times, you may acquire a startle reaction to the slight grinding sound; it serves as a conditioned stimulus. In contrast, suppose you do not hear the sound until after the water turns cold, as in backward conditioning, or until the precise instant at which it turns cold, as in simultaneous conditioning. In these cases, you will probably not acquire the startle reaction to the grinding sound because it provides no information useful in predicting the occurrence of the icy water.

Several other factors also appear to affect conditioning. In general, classical conditioning happens more quickly the higher the intensity is of either the CS or the UCS. However, it is not necessarily the absolute intensity of a stimulus that is most important to the conditioning process, but rather, the relative intensity or the degree of contrast with the background stimuli in the situation. In a classic study done at McMaster University in 1965, Kamin showed that conditioning is more likely when conditioned stimuli stand out relative to the background stimuli.

Conditioning also depends on the time interval between presentation of the two stimuli—the CS–UCS interval. Extremely short intervals—less than 0.2 seconds—rarely produce conditioning. In animal research, the optimal interval between the onset of the CS and the onset of the UCS usually seems to be between 0.2 and 2 seconds. Intervals longer than that make it difficult for animals to recognize the CS as a signal for some future event (Gordon, 1989; Wall et al., 1990), although there is an important exception, or, perhaps more correctly, an important extension to this rule, about which you will read shortly.

Similarly, familiarity can greatly affect conditioning. In a modern laboratory, many of the stimuli used are novel, but in the environment in which we live our lives from day to day, many of the potential stimuli are familiar. Thus our day-to-day experiences often teach us that certain conditioned stimuli, such as the background noise usually present in an office setting, or the odours ordinarily present in our homes, do not predict anything unusual. In other words, once we learn that these stimuli are largely irrelevant, future conditioning of them is more difficult (Baker & Mackintosh, 1977).

EXTINCTION: HOW CAN WE GET RID OF A CONDITIONED RESPONSE? Consider the following scenario. You are one of several executive assistants in the head office of a large supermarket chain. You and your co-workers have been working night and day to prepare a proposal crucial to the company's survival, and things are not going well. Over the past week, the president of the company has chewed you out at least a dozen times. Now, whenever you hear the unmistakable sound of his approaching footsteps, your heart starts racing and your mouth gets dry, even though he has not yet reached your office. Fortunately, this story has a happy ending—the company's directors are impressed with the proposal, and your boss is no longer angry when he enters your office. Will you continue to react strongly to his footsteps? Perhaps you will at first, but gradually his footsteps will elicit less and less of the original conditioned response. This decline and eventual disappearance of a conditioned response—in the absence of an unconditioned stimulus—is known as **extinction** (refer to Panel B in Figure 5.3). Extinction plays an important role, for if it did not occur, we would soon become walking collections of useless—but persistent—conditioned responses.

Extinction: The process through which a conditioned stimulus gradually loses the ability to elicit conditioned responses when it is no longer followed by the unconditioned stimulus.

The course of extinction, however, is not always entirely smooth. To see why, let us consider the behaviour of one of Pavlov's dogs. After many presentations of a bell (CS) in the absence of meat powder (UCS), the dog no longer salivates in response to the bell. In other words, extinction has occurred (refer to Panel B of Figure 5.3).

Suppose that after extinction, the experiment is interrupted: Pavlov is caught up in another project that keeps him away from his laboratory and the dog for some time. When he returns, will the sound of the bell, the CS, elicit salivation? The answer is yes, but the reaction will be weaker. The reappearance of the reaction after a time interval is referred to as **spontaneous recovery** (refer to Panel C of Figure 5.3). If the extinction procedure is allowed to continue again, with the sound of the bell occurring in the absence of meat powder—the animal will no longer salivate to the sound of the bell. Then if the CS (the bell) and the UCS (the meat powder) are again paired, salivation will return very quickly—a process termed **reconditioning** (refer to Panel D of Figure 5.3).

GENERALIZATION AND DISCRIMINATION: SIMILARITIES AND DIFFERENCES

Suppose that because of several painful experiences, a child has acquired a strong conditioned fear of hornets: Whenever he sees one or hears one buzzing, he shows strong emotional reactions and runs away. Will he also experience similar reactions to other flying insects, such as flies? He almost certainly will, because of a process called **stimulus generalization,** the tendency of stimuli similar to a conditioned stimulus to elicit similar conditioned responses (Honig & Urcuioli, 1981; Pearce, 1986). As you can readily see, stimulus generalization often serves a useful function. In this example, it may indeed save the boy from additional stings.

Many other species turn stimulus generalization to their advantage. For example, some totally harmless insects resemble more dangerous species in colouring and in this way ward off would-be predators. Similarly, some harmless frogs show markings highly similar to those of poisonous species, thus increasing their chances of survival as well. Although stimulus generalization can serve an important adaptive function, it is not always beneficial and in some cases can be dangerous. For example, because of many desirable experiences with parents and other adult relatives, a young child may become trusting of all adults through the process of stimulus generalization. Unfortunately, generalization in this instance will not be beneficial if it extends to certain strangers. You can understand why stimulus generalization can be maladaptive—even deadly.

Fortunately, most of us learn to avoid potential problems like these through **stimulus discrimination**—the process of learning to respond to certain stimuli but not to others. You have probably encountered many instances of stimulus discrimination. Perhaps this incident will serve as an example. About a year ago, the driver for a local pizza palace was badly bitten by a dog. Until that incident, he had no fear of dogs. Because he was so badly frightened by the attack, there was concern that his fear would generalize to dogs of all breeds—perhaps even to his own dog. Fortunately, because of stimulus discrimination, this did not happen. He becomes tense only when he encounters the breed of dog that bit him.

Spontaneous Recovery: Following extinction, return of a conditioned response upon reinstatement of CS–UCS pairings.

Reconditioning: The rapid recovery of a conditioned response to a CS–UCS pairing following extinction.

Stimulus Generalization: The tendency of stimuli similar to a conditioned stimulus to elicit a conditioned response.

Stimulus Discrimination: The process by which organisms learn to respond to certain stimuli but not to others.

K E Y *QUESTIONS*

- What is learning?
- What is classical conditioning?
- Upon what factors does acquisition of a classically conditioned response depend?
- What is extinction?
- What is the difference between stimulus generalization and stimulus discrimination?

Exceptions to the Rules of Classical Conditioning

When psychologists began the systematic study of learning around the turn of the last century, they noticed that some species could master certain tasks more quickly than others. Such findings sparked little interest, though, because early researchers saw their task as establishing general principles of learning—principles that applied equally well to all animals and to all stimuli. For several decades it was widely assumed that such universal principles existed. Now we know that idea is not quite correct. Not all organisms learn all associations between stimuli and responses with equal ease. There are exceptions to the traditional rules of classical conditioning and one of the clearest demonstrations of that is illustrated in the following example.

CONDITIONED TASTE AVERSIONS: BASIC IDEAS You are at a potluck supper, and to your delight someone has brought lasagna—a favourite dish of yours. Later that evening, you begin to feel dreadful. For the next two days you have a fever and cannot keep anything down. Consequently, months later, you still experience those same awful feelings whenever you see, smell, or even think about lasagna. You have developed a conditioned taste aversion.

Taste Aversion

Surveys show that taste aversions are quite common among humans, with most people reporting at least one (Logue, Logue, & Strauss 1983). Conditioned taste aversions may result from food poisoning, the painful aftereffects of overindulgence, or eating just before the onset of an illness like the flu (Garb & Stunkard, 1974). Interestingly, many people report that even when they know that what they ate or drank was not the cause of the illness, they still continue to have a taste aversion. This suggests that conditioned aversions to food and drink are unusually strong and can occur despite what we believe about the cause of the illness (Seligman & Hager, 1972).

Research also shows that these powerful associations differ from most of classical conditioning in several ways. First, a conditioned taste aversion may be established with a single CS–UCS pairing—that is, with one-trial learning. In contrast, many pairings are required for most Pavlovian conditioning. Second, conditioned taste aversions may occur when the CS is presented hours before the UCS. In contrast, most conditioning requires a CS–UCS interval of no more than a few seconds. For animals in their natural habitats, the fact that conditioned taste aversions may occur over long intervals is important for survival—to prevent them from eating and drinking dangerous and potentially toxic substances.

CONDITIONED TASTE AVERSIONS: STIMULI AND RESPONSES As well, not all stimuli are capable of establishing conditioned taste aversions (Garcia, Hankins, & Rusiniak, 1974). In their classic experiment, Garcia and Koelling (1966) allowed rats to drink sweetened water from a specially designed spout. Whenever the animals drank the water from the spout, a bright flashing light and a noisy clicking sound occurred. While they were drinking, half of the animals were exposed to X-rays that later made them feel sick and half of the animals received painful shocks to their feet. This is what the researchers found: The rats in the foot-shock group learned to avoid the light and the noise, but not the sweet water. The rats exposed to X-rays learned to avoid the sweet water, but not the light and noise (see Figure 5.5)

These results supported the following conclusions. Rats and other animals are predisposed to associate nausea and dizziness with something they have consumed (the sweet water), and to associate pain with something they have seen or heard (the bright light and clicking noise). Similar findings from many different studies (e.g., Braverman & Bronstein, 1985) suggest that acquisition of a conditioned response does not occur with equal ease to all stimuli. These findings make perfectly good sense in terms of the associations animals need to learn in order to avoid substances that are likely to make them ill and stimuli that may cause them pain as they struggle to sustain life in the natural world.

Figure 5.5

Biological Constraints and Characteristics of the CS and UCS Affect the Acquisition of a Conditioned Response

Rats quickly acquired an aversion to a flavoured water when it was followed by X-rays that made them ill, but they did not readily acquire an aversion to the flavoured water when it was followed by an electric shock. In contrast, rats learned to avoid a light–noise combination when it was paired with shock, but not when it was followed by X-rays. These findings indicate that classical conditioning cannot be established with equal ease for all stimuli and for all organisms.

Source: Based on data from Garcia and Koelling, 1966.

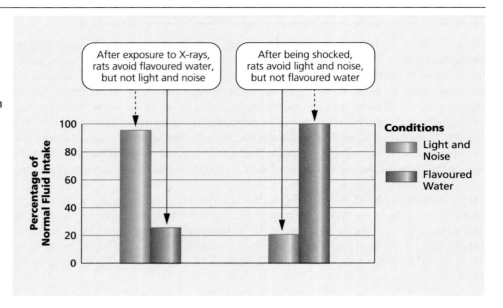

Important differences exist not only among stimuli, but also among species. Because of **biological constraints on learning,** conditioning that is readily accomplished by some species may occur slowly or not at all in others. Not surprisingly, the connections most readily learned by a particular species are the very ones it needs to survive in its normal habitat (Shettleworth, 1993). For example, since rats eat at night, and in many cases they do not see the food they eat, it is especially useful for rats to be able to associate specific tastes with illness hours or even days later. In contrast, because birds depend heavily on vision for finding food, it is more useful for birds to be able to form associations between the look of the food they consumed and later illness (Wilcoxon, Dragoin, & Kral, 1971).

Finally, conditioned taste aversions are extremely resistant to extinction. Indeed, some evidence suggests that everyday taste aversions may last a lifetime (Logue, 1979).

Some researchers think of a conditioned taste aversion as a learned fear of a new taste—*neophobia.* Therefore, attention has turned recently to the way in which the fear of tastes develops. At the University of British Columbia, researchers found that neophobia occurred in gerbils and hamsters when the flavour of their usual peanuts was changed—to sweet or bitter, for example (Wong & McBride, 1993). At Erindale College of the University of Toronto, undergraduates' willingness to eat "dangerous" food was determined by the taste. If the taste was OK, they were less likely to be neophobic (Pliner et al., 1993).

CONDITIONED TASTE AVERSIONS: PRACTICAL APPLICATIONS   Here are two practical applications of the findings of this research. First, because some treatments for cancer—radiation therapy and chemotherapy—often cause nausea or vomiting (Burish & Carey, 1986), cancer patients may acquire taste aversions to foods eaten before their therapy sessions. Several studies have in fact shown that conditioned taste aversions are common among patients receiving chemotherapy (Bernstein, 1978; Challis & Stam, 1972).

Radiation and chemotherapy patients take a number of steps to reduce the likelihood of developing a conditioned taste aversion. First, they arrange their meals so that the interval between their meals and chemotherapy is as long as possible. Second, they eat familiar foods and avoid new or unusual foods just before therapy. Because familiar foods have already been associated with feeling good, rather

Biological Constraints on Learning: Tendencies of some species to acquire some forms of conditioning less readily than other species do.

than feeling ill, it is less likely that cancer patients will acquire an aversion. Finally, since the strength of a conditioned response is related to the intensity of the conditioned stimulus, patients are advised to eat bland foods and avoid foods with strong flavours. These steps can minimize the development of conditioned taste aversions in these patients.

Second, our understanding of acquired taste aversions has been used to help Western ranchers in their efforts to prevent the loss of sheep and cattle to predators such as wolves and coyotes (Garcia, Rusiniak & Brett, 1977; Gustavson et al., 1974). By establishing in predators a conditioned taste aversion for cattle and sheep, ranchers have been able to save their livestock without actually having to kill wild animals. The predators eat bait that has been laced with a nausea-inducing drug and they become sick several hours later. As a result, they learn to avoid sheep or cattle in the future. This is not an ideal solution, however, because taste aversions established at one location may not occur in other places (Bonardi et al., 1990; Nakajima et al., 1995). This finding must also be taken into account when using this kind of learning to control predators. A solid understanding of processes like learned taste aversion—a clear exception to the traditional rules of classical conditioning—can be applied toward solving important real-life problems.

Learned Taste Aversions: Putting Classical Conditioning to Work

Classical conditioning has been used to solve many practical problems, including saving ranchers' livestock from predators.

K E Y QUESTIONS

- Where in the brain does classical conditioning take place?

- Is classical conditioning equally easy to establish with all stimuli for all organisms?

- How do we acquire conditioned taste aversions?

The Neural Basis of Learning

Now that we have discussed the basic principles of classical conditioning, let us turn to another question that has puzzled scientists for many years—what is the neural basis of this kind of learning? What happens—in the brain—during classical conditioning? The results indicate that the *cerebellum* (with its connections to other brain circuits) plays a significant role in learning. As you may recall from Chapter 2, the cerebellum is a structure in the brain best known for its role in helping us to maintain our sense of balance and coordinate movements.

What is the evidence that the cerebellum is engaged during classical conditioning? First, electrical recordings of the brains of laboratory animals show that the rate of neural firing of cells in the cerebellum predicts that a conditioned response is about to occur. Second, electrical stimulation of specific pathways into the cerebellum can elicit both conditioned and unconditioned responses. Finally, when structures in the cerebellum of laboratory animals are surgically removed, previously learned associations may be severely disrupted, and the ability to learn new associations eliminated altogether (Thompson & Krupa, 1994).

Studies of humans who have sustained damage to their cerebellum reveal a similar pattern of results. For example, careful research indicates that it is extremely difficult to establish conditioned responses with these persons. They blink normally (UCR) in response to a puff of air to the eye (UCS), indicating that their motor functions and ability to respond to external stimulation remains intact. However, efforts to establish a conditioned eye-blink (CR) response to, say, a light or a tone (CS) that has been paired with a puff of air to the eye, are usually unsuccessful (Daum & Shugens, 1996; Topka et al., 1993).

Related research has also revealed that the ability to acquire conditioned eye-blink responses seems to fade with age. Researchers believe that age-related declines in the number and efficiency of certain cells in the cerebellum may be the cause (Woodruff-Pak & Thompson, 1988). Other brain structures now known to be involved in eye-blink conditioning include the hippocampus, amygdala, and brain-stem areas that project to or receive information from the cerebellum (Myers et al., 1996; Steinmetz, 1999). Thus, systematic research with animals has resulted in nearly complete identification of the neural circuitry that underlies eye-blink classical conditioning (Thompson et al., 1997; Woodruff-Pak, 1999).

Because the fundamental neural circuitry underlying eye-blink classical conditioning is now well understood, researchers have begun to use this conditioning procedure to investigate a variety of basic processes in humans (e.g., Clark et al., 1999; Ivkovich et al., 1999) and including the biological correlates of certain mental disorders. A recent study by Tracy et al. (1999) suggests that some people may be biologically predisposed to establish associations between feelings of fear and anxiety and otherwise neutral objects. Clearly, these findings will help in understanding the origins of psychological disorders, and will be used in the design of prevention and treatment programs.

A Cognitive View of Classical Conditioning

During his early conditioning experiments, Pavlov (1927) observed a curious thing. A dog was conditioned to salivate to the sound of a metronome ticking. When the metronome was turned off, the dog sat in front of the metronome and proceeded to whine and beg. Why did that happen? This finding and several related ones point to the following conclusion: Regular pairing of a CS with a UCS provides an animal with valuable information about the way in which the environment works. That information is this: When a conditioned stimulus occurs, an unconditioned stimulus will follow shortly. Thus, as conditioning proceeds, subjects acquire an expectation that the CS will be followed by the UCS.

That expectations play a role in classical conditioning is supported by several types of evidence (Rescorla & Wagner, 1972). First, conditioning fails to occur when unconditioned and conditioned stimuli are paired at some times but not at others—that is, in a random manner. With random pairing, subjects cannot acquire any firm expectation that an unconditioned stimulus will indeed follow presentation of a conditioned stimulus. This means that for conditioning to occur, the CS–UCS pairing must be reliable.

Second, conditioning to one stimulus may be prevented by previous conditioning to another stimulus. This phenomenon is known as *blocking*. For example, suppose a dog is initially conditioned to salivate when a tone occurs. After repeated pairings with presentation of meat powder, the tone becomes a CS, capable of causing the dog to salivate. Then a second stimulus, a light, is added to the situation—appearing at the same time as the tone, just before the presentation of food. If classical conditioning occurs in an automatic manner, simply as a result of repeated pairings of a CS with a UCS, then the light too should become a CS: It should elicit salivation when presented alone. In fact, this does not happen. Why not? Again, an explanation in terms of expectancies is helpful. Since the meat powder is already predicted by the tone, the light provides no new information. Since it is of little predictive value to the subjects, it fails to become a CS. Figure 5.6 illustrates that point.

These findings suggest that classical conditioning involves much more than the formation of simple associations between specific stimuli. Indeed, modern views of classical conditioning conceive of it as a complex process in which organisms form rich representations of the relationships among a variety of factors—including many aspects of the physical setting (or context) in which the conditioned and unconditioned stimuli are presented (Rescorla, 1988; Swartzentruber, 1991). Pavlovian conditioning is "the learning of relations among events so as to allow the organism to represent its environment" (Furedy, 1992).

This cognitive perspective on classical conditioning has been extended in several ways. For example, one theory of stimulus generalization suggests that memory and other cognitive processes play an important role (Shettleworth, 1993). The idea here is this: During conditioning, organisms form a representation in memory of the stimuli that preceded the UCS. When they then encounter different stimuli at later times, they compare these with the information stored in memory. The greater the similarity between current stimuli and such memory representations, the stronger the response evoked. In short, both memory and active comparison processes play a role in what might at first seem to be an automatic function.

The suggestion that cognitive processes are important in human classical conditioning is not surprising. We all have expectations about which events go together or are likely to follow each other. But it may surprise you to learn that processes like memory and active comparison also occur in animals. There is growing evidence that animals, like humans, form mental representations of events in the world around them (Cook, 1993; Wasserman, 1993). We consider this topic again in Chapter 7.

Applications of Classical Conditioning

Many basic principles of classical conditioning were found originally by laboratory studies of animals. However, these principles have been put to many practical uses to help people—in all kinds of ways—combat learned fears and even save lives.

CLASSICAL CONDITIONING AND PHOBIAS One of the earliest applications was reported in a study, now a classic in psychology, conducted by John B. Watson and his assistant, Rosalie Raynor, in 1920. Watson and Raynor (1920) demonstrated that human beings can acquire strong irrational fears—**phobias**—through classical conditioning. In this study, an eleven-month-old child named Albert was shown a white laboratory rat. Albert's initial reactions to the rat were positive: He smiled and attempted to play with it. Just as he reached out for the rat, however, there was a loud noise right behind him. Albert jumped, obviously very upset by the startling noise. After several more pairings of the rat (CS) and the loud noise (UCS), Albert cried loudly and tried to crawl away whenever he saw the rat—even when there was no noise. Little Albert appeared to have acquired a phobia, not only for rats, but also for other animals, and other hairy objects—for example, men with beards.

You should note that the ethical principles that we apply today were not understood at that time. For example, Watson and Raynor neither sought nor obtained permission to experiment with the child who became the subject of their study. Moreover, there was no effort to follow the case or determine how best to deal with any lasting effects of the experiment, that is, there was no effort to undo what had been done to this subject.

Nevertheless, understanding how these kinds of phobias are learned has led to the development of several effective treatment procedures (Davey, 1992; Rachman, 1990). For example, in emotional **flooding,** a person suffering from a specific fear may be made to confront the fear-eliciting stimulus directly (e.g., Gordon, 1989). A person who has an irrational fear of heights might walk over a bridge—

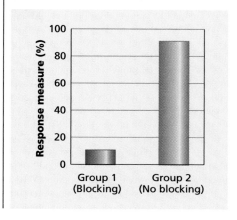

Figure 5.6
The Effect of Blocking

Two groups of animals showed different conditioned responses to a light. Group 1 was conditioned to the tone and then the tone–light combination. Group 2 was conditioned to the light only. The graph shows that conditioning to the light was blocked when the light plus tone had no more predictive power than the tone alone.

Source: After Kamin,1969, with permission of the author. Data from p. 283 of Predictability, Surprise, Attention, and Conditioning in Campbell and Church (Eds.), Punishment and Aversive Behaviour, *Appleton-Century-Crofts.*

Phobias: Intense, irrational fears of objects or events.

Flooding: Procedure for eliminating conditioned fears based on principles of classical conditioning. During flooding, an individual is exposed to fear-inducing objects or events. Since no unconditioned stimulus then follows, extinction of fears eventually takes place.

Classical Conditioning: A Human Example

John B. Watson and his graduate assistant Rosalie Raynor used classical conditioning to teach "Little Albert" to fear various small, furry objects. What ethical problems were involved in these studies?

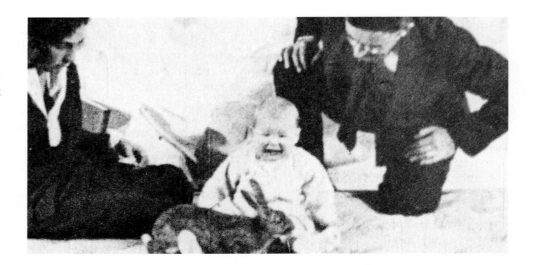

under careful supervision, of course. When no harm results, the person may lose the irrational fear. There are differences of opinion, however, with respect to the effectiveness of emotional flooding. In a 1993 study at the University of Alberta, Treit and his colleagues found that flooding did not help alleviate rats' fear of an elevated maze. In fact, after the "therapy," the rats avoided the feared maze even more.

An alternative application of these principles to the treatment of irrational fears is *systematic desensitization*—a progressive technique designed to replace anxiety with relaxation (Wolpe, 1958, 1969). A person undergoing this procedure is asked to describe fearful situations and to rank them in order of the intensity of the anxiety they produce. Then, starting with the least anxiety-producing situation, the person visualizes the fearful situation and relaxes. Gradually, the individual learns to relax while imagining situations that are increasingly more and more threatening. Because we do not experience anxiety if we are truly relaxed, systematic desensitization counters the anxiety of the irrational fear. This technique has been applied to numerous real problems, and is the clinical tool used in the treatment of fear of flying and fear of public speaking, for example (Banks et al., 1992). Chapter 15 will discuss these procedures in more detail.

CLASSICAL CONDITIONING AND DRUG OVERDOSE Knowledge of conditioning processes gained from basic research has also led to another contemporary application: an explanation for drug overdose. Research evidence suggests that some instances of drug overdose can be explained, at least in part, by principles of classical conditioning. For example, when a user does drugs in a particular place (such as in a particular room), the stimuli in that place become conditioned stimuli (Siegel, 1983, 1984). In that environment, a conditioned physiological response occurs that prepares the addict's body for the arrival of the drug.

To demonstrate the effect of that conditioned response in drug addiction, in one study (Siegel et al., 1982), rats received heroin on one day and placebo on another, in different environments. Then all subjects received a single high—potentially fatal—dose of heroin. Some animals received the high dose in the environment where they had been injected with heroin, and the others received it in the environment where they had been injected with the placebo. Mortality was highest among those receiving the injection in the environment previously associated with the placebo.

Why did that happen? Here is one explanation. Cues in the heroin environment served as conditioned stimuli and prepared the rats' bodies to counteract the effects of the potentially lethal injection; the placebo environment did not provide such cues for the rats in that condition (see Figure 5.7). Are there any human parallels to this finding? Indeed, human drug users who have nearly died following drug use commonly report that the environment in which they took the drug was not the usual one (Siegel, 1984).

Shepard Siegel
McMaster University

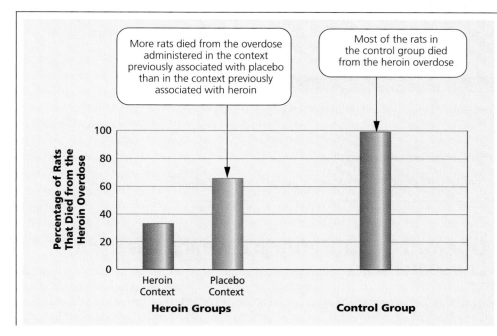

More rats died from the overdose administered in the context previously associated with placebo than in the context previously associated with heroin

Most of the rats in the control group died from the heroin overdose

Figure 5.7
Classical Conditioning Can Help Explain Deaths Following Drug Overdose

The results of this study lead to two conclusions: (1) Control group subjects—those with no previous experience with heroin— were more likely to die after receiving a potentially lethal dose of heroin than subjects with previous drug experience. (2) Subjects who received the potentially lethal dose of heroin in an environment previously associated with drug injections were more likely to survive than those who received the same injection in an environment not previously associated with the drug.

Source: Based on data from Siegel, Hinson, Krank, and McCully, 1982.

Siegel's findings may have practical implications for the treatment of drug addiction. Recent evidence has shown that the environments to which former drug users return often contain cues that may produce drug-related conditioned responses (Goodison & Siegel, 1995), such as withdrawal symptoms and drug cravings (Krank & Perkins, 1993). Knowledge of classical conditioning processes may ultimately help health professionals arrange environments that minimize relapse among former drug users.

Researchers are making progress towards that goal. By identifying the cues that trigger these classically conditioned responses and eliminating them in animal experiments, researchers have identified how cues that cause animals to relapse and seek drugs again affect the nervous system. There is new evidence in animal research about the way in which drugs that activate certain dopamine receptors can prevent drug relapse (Self, 1998).

CLASSICAL CONDITIONING OF THE IMMUNE SYSTEM It may be possible to affect the immune system—the body's response to disease— through classical conditioning (Ader et al., 1993; Husband et al., 1993). In one recent study, Alvarez-Borda and her colleagues (1995) used classical conditioning to enhance specific immune functions in rats. On conditioning day, rats in two groups were all given an injection of a substance known to elevate the levels of antibodies in their immune systems. Before the injection, rats in one group drank a distinctive beverage— saccharin-flavoured water. A second group of rats received plain water before the same injection. As expected, the injection enhanced the response of the immune system in both groups. Then, after the effects of the injection had worn off—more than a month later—the researchers tested to see if conditioning had taken place.

Half of the rats that drank the saccharin-flavoured water during conditioning were again given saccharin-flavoured water; the other half received plain water. Then levels of antibodies were measured in both groups. Here is what was found. Despite the fact that no injections were given to any of the animals during the intervening month, there was a significant increase in the level of antibodies in the rats that drank the saccharin-flavoured water—but not in the others. Although these results are very preliminary, and require replication in additional studies and testing with different species, they do suggest that classical conditioning of re-

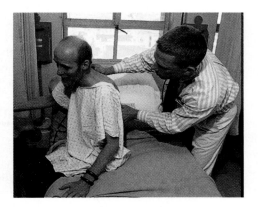

Classical Conditioning and the Immune System

Classical conditioning can exert powerful effects on the immune system, a discovery that may offer tremendous hope to people whose health is compromised due to depressed immune systems; for example, persons who are HIV-positive or have AIDS.

sponses of the immune system may occur. These results may eventually have relevance to those whose health is compromised by immune deficiency diseases, for example, those who are HIV-positive or who have AIDS.

K E Y *QUESTIONS*

▨ How do modern ideas about classical conditioning differ from earlier views?

▨ What is blocking?

▨ What is flooding? Systematic desensitization?

▨ How can classical conditioning principles solve some problems of everyday life?

Operant Conditioning: Learning Based on Consequences

Up to this point in the chapter, we have been considering one kind of conditioning—classical or Pavlovian. We now turn to a second kind: operant conditioning. Consider the case of young Jeff. Before starting the first grade, Jeff had always gotten his way. Although they knew it was wrong, his parents gave in to his demands because of his temper tantrums. Now it was the first day of school, and Jeff was already off to a bad start. Barely there an hour, he had already landed himself in the principal's office. Jeff's behaviour was unbearable—even in school.

Much to Jeff's surprise, his teacher did not react as he expected. In fact, each time Jeff misbehaved, he received "time out"—a few minutes in a quiet corner of the room, away from his classmates. At first Jeff tried his usual routine: He kicked and screamed all the way to the corner. The teacher's reaction remained consistent. She paid Jeffrey no attention during the time out—despite the fact that his tantrums worsened for a while. As the weeks went by, however, Jeff seemed to run out of steam. On days when he was well-behaved, the teacher smiled at him more and rewarded his good behaviour with sports cards or status jobs, like being in charge of the classroom VCR. After just a few weeks, Jeff's outbursts disappeared completely.

What happened here? The answer is probably obvious. Jeff's behaviours had new consequences, and so they changed. Behaviours that produced positive consequences became more frequent, while those that were ignored (or resulted in time out) became less frequent. When the consequences of his behaviours changed, Jeff's behaviour changed also. In short, the teacher had used the principles of **operant conditioning** to change Jeff's behaviour.

The Nature of Operant Conditioning

Operant Conditioning: A process through which organisms learn to repeat behaviours that yield positive outcomes or permit them to avoid or escape negative outcomes.

In situations involving operant conditioning, the probability that a given behaviour will reoccur depends on its consequences. We saw earlier that in classical conditioning, the stimulus occurs, followed by a response. In operant conditioning, a behaviour occurs and a consequence follows. Recognition that this is a kind of learning is credited to Edward Thorndike, a psychologist who lived early in the twentieth century. Thorndike found that, by trial and error, cats could learn to lift the latch on a box in which they were housed, and by lifting the latch escape the box, if they were fed afterwards. Thorndike then proposed the *law of effect*, which stated that learning depends upon the consequences for the animal of its behaviour. Around mid-century, that principle became the basis for a second theory of learning, called operant conditioning. This theory was made central to psychology by B.F. Skinner—in honour of whom operant conditioning is sometimes called *Skinnerian conditioning*.

In situations involving operant conditioning, the probability of a response changes, depending on the consequences that follow. Psychologists generally agree that there are four basic kinds of consequences: *positive* and *negative reinforcers,* events that strengthen the behaviours they follow; and *positive* and *negative punishers,* events that suppress the behaviours they follow.

Conditioned Reinforcers in Action

Conditioned reinforcers may be used in practical situations to reward behaviour.

REINFORCEMENT The goal of **reinforcement** is to increase the probability that a particular response will occur again. **Positive reinforcers** are desirable consequences that strengthen the responses they follow. Note that in the terminology of learning, it is a *response* that gets reinforced, not an animal or a person. Some positive reinforcers are related to basic biological needs. These are called *primary reinforcers,* and they include food when we are hungry, water when we are thirsty, and sexual pleasure. Other rewards acquire their ability to act as positive reinforcers through association with primary reinforcers. These are *conditioned reinforcers,* and they include money, prizes, status, grades, trophies, praise from others, and so on. These rewards become reinforcers indirectly, through association with primary reinforcers. Conditioned reinforcers have many practical uses.

Preferred activities can also be rewards used to reinforce behaviour. This is the **Premack principle.** If you recall hearing, "You must clean your room before you can watch TV," when you were growing up, then you are already familiar with this principle. Jeff's teacher could use the Premack principle and use a more preferred activity (like going out for recess) to reinforce a less preferred behaviour (like doing school work). As you can guess, the Premack principle is a powerful tool for changing behaviour.

Please note that a consequence that functions as a positive reinforcement on one occasion may have a different effect at another time or in another place. For example, food may serve as a positive reinforcer when you are hungry, but not when you are ill or just after you finish a large meal. Also, at least where people are concerned, many individual differences exist. A stimulus that functions as a positive reinforcement for one person may fail to act in a similar manner for somebody else. We will return to this important point later.

Negative reinforcers strengthen behaviours that allow us to escape aversive stimuli or even avoid them altogether. Thus, when we do something that allows us to escape from a bad situation or to avoid one in advance, our tendency to do that same thing under similar circumstances increases. For example, suppose Susan and Sally both have the first signs of a cold. Sally does nothing about it and develops a full-blown cold—sneezing, coughing, and fever. Her roommate convinces her to eat lots of hot chicken soup, and she seems to get better. Thus, as a consequence of eating the soup, she escapes the misery of the cold—and the likelihood that she will eat lots of hot chicken soup the next time she gets a cold is increased. Susan, on the other hand, sees the warning signs and immediately takes lots of Vitamin C, thereby avoiding the cold. It is more likely that the next time she feels a cold coming on, she will take Vitamin C again. Technically, her vitamin-taking behaviour is an avoidance response and that response has been strengthened because she avoided the aversive consequence: the misery of a cold.

Learning to avoid aversive situations is obviously an important contributor to personal survival. Early in human evolution, avoidance behaviour likely contributed to the preservation of life; for example, our ancestors learned to avoid places frequented by predators. In modern times, we stop at stop signs to avoid paying a fine; we pay our tuition on time in order to avoid the penalty charges; we hand in our papers by the due date in order to avoid being penalized; we change to snow tires in order to avoid wintertime accidents.

Reinforcement: The application or removal of a stimulus so as to increase the strength of a behaviour.

Positive Reinforcers: Stimuli that strengthen responses that precede them.

Premack Principle: The principle that a more preferred activity can be used to reinforce a less preferred activity.

Negative Reinforcers: Stimuli that strengthen responses that permit an organism to avoid or escape from their presence.

Negative reinforcement is quite common in our everyday lives. For example, imagine the following scene. On a particularly cold and dark winter morning, you are sleeping soundly in a warm, comfortable bed. Suddenly, the "alarm from hell" begins to wail from across the room. What do you do? If you get up to turn off the alarm (escape)—or, on subsequent mornings, get up early enough to shut off the alarm before it starts (avoidance)—your behaviour has been negatively reinforced. In other words, your tendency to perform actions that allow you to escape or avoid the sound of the alarm clock has been strengthened.

Another everyday example of negative reinforcement occurs when parents give in to their children's tantrums, especially in public places. Over time, the parents' tendency to give in may increase because doing so allows them to escape from the screaming. Thus, the likelihood that the parents will appease this child in the future increases every time that appeasement provides escape from the painful and embarrassing sound of the child screaming.

As you can see from these examples, both negative reinforcers and positive reinforcers are desirable outcomes, and they both increase the probability that the behaviour will reoccur at a future time. There are also two types of punishers: positive and negative. Let's turn to those now.

PUNISHMENT In contrast to reinforcement, the effect of **punishment** is to *decrease* the probability of a particular behaviour, so that it will no longer occur. In other words, in punishment, the consequence that follows behaviour is intended to stop an animal from behaving in a particular way. For example, if a rat turns right at a choice point in a maze and an electric shock or a loud noise occurs, the right turn response has been punished—in order that the animal not turn right in that place in the future. In the terminology of learning research, the consequence is called a *punisher*. It is important to note here that it is the response that gets punished, not the animal or the person.

As is the case with reinforcement, there are two kinds of punishers: positive and negative. When a **positive punisher** occurs, behaviour is followed by an aversive consequence. In such instances we learn not to behave in certain ways because a punisher will follow. This is what people typically understand punishment to mean. For example, following a disruptive outburst in the classroom, a teacher assigns a student twenty math problems as homework. The student learns not to burst out in class. The idea here is that we learn to suppress behaviours that are followed by positive punishers.

Contrary to what common sense seems to suggest, positive punishment is not the same as negative reinforcement. Positive punishment is meant to *decrease undesirable behaviours*. Negative reinforcement is meant to *increase desirable behaviours*. Here is an example to illustrate the difference.

Imagine that you are driving home in a hurry. Suddenly, you become aware of flashing lights and a siren. An RCMP officer has detected you speeding. You see how much the ticket will cost you; after paying that fine, you obey the posted speed limit. This is an example of how positive punishment works: An undesirable outcome follows your speeding. Consequently, the probability that you will exceed the speed limit decreases.

Now imagine that a year later you are again caught speeding. (Apparently the punishment suppressed your speeding behaviour only temporarily.) Because you are a past offender, the judge gives you a choice: attend a month-long series of driver education classes or lose your driver's license. This is an example of how negative reinforcement works: You attend the driver education classes to avoid an aversive outcome—the loss of your license.

Punishment: The application or removal of a stimulus so as to decrease the strength of a behaviour.

Positive Punisher: An aversive consequence that is delivered in order to suppress a target response.

What is negative punishment? A **negative punisher** is actually the loss of a desired outcome. As a result of that loss, the tendency to behave in certain ways decreases. Here are two examples. Parents frequently suppress certain teenage behaviours (such as fighting, talking back, missing curfew, drinking, and smoking) by suspending certain desirable privileges (access to the telephone, the family car, video games, or various social events). The loss of the desirable privilege is said to be the *response cost* of behaving in a particular manner.

A second common type of negative punisher is time out, as used by Jeff's teacher when she sent him to a quiet corner (see page 194). That is the kind of negative punisher you may have experienced as a youngster when you were "grounded to your room" for some reason or other. Thus, both positive and negative punishment involve aversive and undesirable consequences that are intended to suppress the behaviour they follow.

Punishment may be a quick fix, but as with all powerful methods of behaviour control, it has certain risks. Here are some of those. Many of the examples given below involve discipline of children by parents, but the same principles apply elsewhere.

Behaviour suppression by punishment is limited. The suppression of behaviour by punishment may be permanent, but it may also only be temporary. For example, a teen who is punished for using bad language in the presence of a parent may continue to curse and swear in the schoolyard nevertheless. When the threat of punishment is removed, often the compliance ends.

Punishment has emotional consequences. When a punisher is administered, the behaviour may change, but both child and parent feel hostile and angry towards each other. In future, they may feel anxious in each other's company. Those emotions may generalize from parent to anyone in authority—including teachers, coaches, crossing guards, and customs officers. Indeed, those feelings may become a feature of the child's adult personality and provide a basis for emotional expectations in social situations (Howe et al., 1998).

Punishment has general effects. For instance, criticism may affect not only the specific target behaviour but also behaviours that were not meant to change—creating children (and adults) who are generally timid and afraid to try anything new.

Punishment provides children with a poor example for how to behave. Through observational learning, children model their own aggressive behaviours after those of their parents. That was the original finding of University of Waterloo psychologists Richard Walters and Ross Parke in 1964, and it has been confirmed many times since then (e.g., Parke & Slaby, 1983). All over the world, children whose parents use physical punishment towards them behave more often in antisocial ways towards other children (Bandura & Walters, 1959; Dodge et al., 1994; Trickett & Kuczynski, 1986) and towards their own children when they become adults (Petretic-Jackson et al., 1995) as a result of parent-to-child transmission of attitudes towards physical punishment (Holden & Zambarano, 1992).

Punishment rewards the authority figure with temporary relief from the misbehaviour of the child, student, or employee. Thus punishment has negative reinforcer properties for the person delivering the punisher. That means that the frequency with which punishment will be used increases and the vicious cycle continues!

Punishment fails to teach the child how to behave otherwise. Scolding may tell the child what was done wrong, but often there is no indication of what other behaviours might be right in the same situation.

In view of all of these risks, is punishment an effective method of changing behaviour? There are different opinions, but psychological research supports this answer: It depends.

Negative Punisher: The loss of a desired outcome that occurs in order to suppress a target response.

If the goal is to assert power and to change behaviour quickly, punishment applied properly will do so. In cases where children put themselves in danger or inflict injury upon themselves, punishment may be the most effective way to control behaviour. Cases where this approach has been successful include a four-year-old autistic boy for biting and foot stomping, a handicapped seventeen-year-old girl for stealing and hoarding (Van Houten & Rolider, 1988), a severely retarded six-year-old boy for smearing feces, and a twenty-four-year-old schizophrenic male for aggressive and destructive behaviour (Rolider et al., 1991). In all these cases, however, punishment was one component of a treatment program, which included also reinforcement of appropriate behaviour.

Please see **Making Psychology Part of Your Life** on page 217 for some more information about the when, where, and how of punishment. Table 5.1 summarizes positive reinforcement, negative reinforcement, positive punishment, and negative punishment. The **Key Concept** illustration on page 199 summarizes the difference between negative reinforcement and punishment.

TABLE 5.1

Reinforcement and Punishment: An Overview

Positive and negative reinforcement are both procedures that strengthen behaviour. Positive and negative punishment are both procedures that weaken behaviour.

Procedure	Stimulus Event	Effects	Behavioural Outcome
Positive reinforcement	Application of a desirable stimulus (e.g., food, sexual pleasure, praise)	Strengthens responses that precede occurrence of stimulus	Organisms learn to perform responses that produce positive reinforcers
Negative reinforcement	Removal or postponement of an undesirable (aversive) stimulus (e.g., heat, cold, harsh criticism)	Strengthens responses that permit escape from or avoidance of stimulus	Organisms learn to perform responses that permit them to avoid or escape from negative reinforcers
Positive punishment	Application of an undesirable (aversive) stimulus	Weakens responses that precede occurrence of stimulus	Organisms learn to suppress responses that lead to unpleasant consequences
Negative punishment	Loss or postponement of a desirable stimulus	Weakens responses that lead to loss or postponement of reinforcement	Organisms learn to suppress responses that lead to loss or postponement of reinforcement

---

KEY QUESTIONS

- What is operant conditioning?
- What are examples of primary reinforcement? Of conditioned reinforcement?
- Which operant techniques strengthen behaviour? Weaken behaviour?
- How do negative reinforcement and punishment differ?

Critical Thinking

When, if ever, is punishment an appropriate consequence?

Key Concept

The Difference between Negative Reinforcement and Punishment

Negative reinforcement and punishment are definitely not the same. In fact, one of the few similarities between them is that both involve an aversive stimulus. The examples here illustrate ways in which negative reinforcement and punishment differ.

Negative Reinforcement

• Negative reinforcement motivates behaviour—organisms increase behaviours that allow them to escape or avoid aversive stimuli.

• In negative reinforcement, aversive stimuli *precede* the escape or avoidance response.

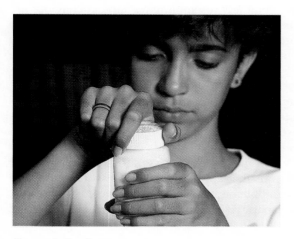

Escape behaviour
Organisms engage in behaviours (for example, taking an aspirin) that allow them to escape or terminate an undesirable, or aversive, event that has already occurred (such as a headache).

Avoidance behaviour
Sometimes, events in our environment (dark clouds in the sky) reliably signal an impending aversive event. These stimuli provide us with advance warning and motivate behaviour (such as using an umbrella) that allows us to avoid experiencing the aversive event (getting soaked) altogether.

Punishment

• Punishment decreases or suppresses behaviour—organisms decrease behaviours that produce aversive consequences.

• In punishment, an aversive stimulus *follows* a response and decreases the likelihood the response will occur again.

▶ Some Basic Principles of Operant Conditioning

As you learned in the first part of this chapter, in classical conditioning, certain stimulus events predict the occurrence of others, which then naturally trigger a specific response. Unconditioned responses are generally involuntary. They occur in response to a specific UCS, in an automatic manner—for example, salivation to the taste of food or blinking in response to a puff of air in the eye.

In operant conditioning, in contrast, we learn associations between particular behaviours and the consequences that follow them. The responses involved in operant conditioning are more voluntary and are made in a given environment. In order to understand the nature of operant conditioning, then, we must address two basic questions: Why are certain responses made in the first place? And once they occur, what determines how often they occur? The answers to those questions follow.

SHAPING, CHAINING, AND INSTINCTIVE DRIFT Many of the behaviours that we perform each day require little conscious effort on our part. In fact, we perform many of them flawlessly. But what about new forms of behaviour with which we are unfamiliar? How are these behaviours initially established?

The answer is a procedure known as **shaping.** When we shape behaviour, we define a target response, and subjects receive a reward for each small step towards that behaviour. At first, actions even remotely resembling the target behaviour are followed by a reward. Gradually, behaviours that are more and more similar to the target behaviour are required before the reward is given. These are called *successive approximations* and this method of training is called the method of successive approximations.

Here is an example that may help you to see how the method of successive approximations is applied in real life. When a baby suddenly blurts out the sound "Mmmuuhh," the parents are ecstatic; they immediately lavish attention and affection on the child and each time the baby repeats the sound; all the baby's other relatives do the same. Initially, then, the family responds enthusiastically to any sound the child makes. However, over time, the relatives gradually change so that they only behave excitedly over sounds that approximate actual words more and more closely. Here is a complex form of behaviour, the acquisition of new words, that is learned in part as a result of shaping. You might say that shaping is based on the principle that a little can eventually go a long way.

What about even more complex or unusual sequences of behaviour, such as the exciting water routines performed by dolphins and whales at a public aquarium? These behaviours involve a procedure called **chaining,** in which trainers establish a sequence, or chain, of responses, the last of which leads to a reward. Trainers usually begin by shaping the last response in the chain. When this terminal response is well established, the trainer shapes responses earlier and earlier in the chain— and that continues until the complete chain has been learned.

Shaping and chaining have important implications for human behaviour. For example, when working with a beginning student, a skilled ski instructor may use shaping techniques to establish basic skills, such as standing on the skis without falling down. At first, the instructor praises small improvements. As training progresses, however, the student may receive praise only when an entire sequence or chain of actions, such as skiing down a small slope, has been completed.

Shaping and chaining techniques can produce dramatic effects. But can they be used to establish virtually any form of behaviour in any organism? If you recall our earlier discussion of biological constraints on classical conditioning, you can probably guess the answer: no. Just as there are biological constraints on classical conditioning, there are constraints on operant learning based on consequences, or on shaping.

A Simple Demonstration of Shaping and Chaining

The dual processes of shaping and chaining help to explain the development of complex behaviour. Please note that *complex,* however, is a relative term—relative to the abilities and limitations of each organism.

Shaping: A technique in which closer and closer approximations of desired behaviour are required for the delivery of positive reinforcement.

Chaining: A procedure that establishes a sequence of responses, which lead to a reward following the final response in the chain.

Perhaps this is most clearly illustrated by the experience of two psychologists, Keller and Marian Breland (1961), who attempted to put their expertise in operant conditioning to commercial use by training animals to perform unusual tricks. At first, things went well. Using standard shaping techniques, the Brelands trained chickens to roll plastic capsules holding prizes down a ramp and then peck them into the hands of waiting customers; they also taught pigs to deposit silver dollars into a piggy bank.

As time went by, though, these star performers gradually developed some unexpected behaviours. The chickens began to seize the capsules and pound them against the floor, and the pigs began to throw coins onto the ground and root them about instead of making "deposits" in their bank. In short, despite careful training, the animals showed what the Brelands termed *instinctive drift*—a tendency to return to the type of behaviour they would show under natural conditions. Chickens, for example, naturally peck their food on the ground and pigs naturally root around for their food. Thus, notwithstanding the operant conditioning that had occurred, these animals reverted to their natural way of behaving when they were hungry. So operant conditioning, like classical conditioning, is subject to biological constraints. While the power of positive and negative reinforcers is great, natural tendencies are important, too, and can replace the learned responses over the course of time.

MAGNITUDE OF REWARD In most instances, operant conditioning proceeds faster as the magnitude of the reward that follows each response increases. But is magnitude the size of each reward or the number of rewards received? One study showed that if two groups of rats receive the same absolute amount of reward for each response, but one group receives this amount in a greater number of smaller pieces, the group receiving the most pieces will respond faster (Campbell, Batsche, & Batsche, 1972). This suggests that the rats preferred to receive smaller, more numerous rewards rather than larger, fewer rewards.

REWARD DELAY The effectiveness of rewards can be dramatically affected by reward delay—the amount of time that elapses before the reward is delivered. In general, having to wait for a reward affects operant conditioning, with longer delays producing poorer levels of performance. For example, in a study by Capaldi (1978), two groups of rats were rewarded on every trial. Although both groups received the same amount and quality of food reward, one group received the reward immediately, while the other group received the reward following a ten-second delay. As you might guess, subjects in the immediate-reward group performed better than subjects in the delayed-reward group. In another study, experimenters used a delay procedure and showed that rats' accuracy decreased systematically when reward was postponed over intervals that varied from 4, 15, 60, 120, to 600 seconds (Mumby, Pinel, & Wood, 1990).

In a typical study of reward delay in humans (Mazur, 1987), people are given a choice between a smaller reward available immediately, or a larger reward to be delivered after some period of time. If the wait for the larger reward is long, people usually choose the smaller-but-sooner alternative. However, if the smaller-but-sooner reward and the larger-but-later reward are both relatively far off in the future, people generally choose the larger-but-later alternative (Kirby & Herrnstein, 1995). Despite their wise original choice, however, as time passes and the time for the smaller reward draws nearer, impulsive tendencies seem to overcome the earlier rational decision to wait as long as it takes for the larger reward. Recognizing that may happen is the first step in controlling the impulse to take the smaller reward when you can have a larger one if you wait!

The effects of reward delay are also evident in humans. For example, children will often choose smaller, immediate rewards over rewards of greater value that they must wait to receive. That tendency is sometimes referred to as *impulsiveness*

(Logue, 1988). Are children more impulsive than adults? That was the question asked in one recent study by Green and his colleagues (1994). These researchers asked three groups of participants—sixth graders, college students, and older adults—to make a series of hypothetical choices between smaller amounts of money they could receive immediately, or larger amounts of money they could receive later. For example, a sample choice might be: "Would you prefer $1000 in five years or $650 right now?"

The results showed that there were clear differences between the groups: the sixth graders made significantly more impulsive choices than the college students, who in turn, made more impulsive choices than the older adults. Please note, however that adults, too, frequently engage in impulsive behaviour—even when the long-term consequences for their impulsiveness are deadly. Smokers and heavy drinkers, for instance, choose the immediate pleasures they derive from smoking or consuming alcoholic beverages over the potentially negative consequences they may suffer later on—for example, from diseases such as cancer (Rachlin, 1995).

Alcohol can impair behaviour and thought, limiting attention to the present situation and making it difficult to evaluate delayed consequences (Erlich & Earleywine, 1995). This is a result that researchers have called *alcoholic myopia*, which is another way of saying alcoholic shortsightedness (Steele & Josephs, 1990). For example, drinking the night before an exam may reduce the influence of delayed consequences, such as failing the next day's test, and may increase the influence of immediate gains, such as the company of friends or loud music. Researchers at the University of Lethbridge have found that when intoxicated people engage in risky behaviours—driving or unprotected sex—they are demonstrating alcoholic myopia also (MacDonald et al., 1995, 1996, 1998).

Opposite to impulsiveness is another kind of behaviour based on delay of reward: *procrastination*—putting off until tomorrow what should be done today. To illustrate this point, consider the choice procrastinators must make; they must decide between performing a less effortful task now or face a more effortful task later on. Although the most efficient decision in terms of time and effort is obvious—do the less effortful task now—research shows that people often choose the more delayed alternative, even if that means more work.

It may surprise you to discover that finding is true for animals as well. For example, in a recent study, Mazur (1996) placed pigeons in a situation in which they chose between two courses of action, both of which led to the same amount of food reinforcement. They could choose to perform a relatively easy task (eight key pecks on a coloured light) right away, or perform a more difficult task (up to thirty key pecks) that they could put off for a little while. Which option did they choose? Most pigeons chose to procrastinate—despite the fact it led to more work for the same amount of reward. Although these results seem counterintuitive in many respects, they do seem to provide an accurate reflection of the choices people sometimes make. We must wait for further research to know what would change procrastination in pigeons (and maybe in people too).

What are the practical implications of procrastination? At the start of a term, researchers identified procrastinators by their scores on standardized tests designed to measure this tendency All students were given a term paper to write and a deadline. Here are three of the findings of this research. First, students who were late in handing in the required paper did indeed score much higher on the procrastination scales. Second, since they received significantly lower grades, procrastinators did not benefit from any extra time that might have been available to absorb course-related information. Third, procrastinators reported higher levels of stress and illness at the end of the term, although they had lower levels at the beginning of the term. You can see those results in Figure 5.8. These findings suggest that the short-term pleasure of procrastinating may end up causing lower achievement and impaired health (Tice & Baumeister, 1997).

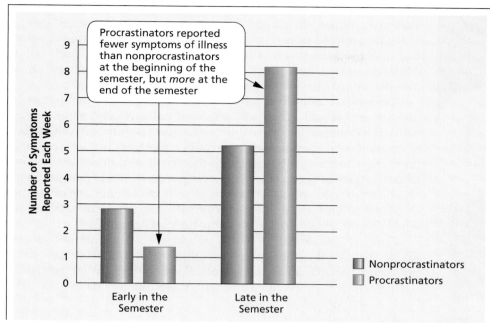

Procrastinators reported fewer symptoms of illness than nonprocrastinators at the beginning of the semester, but *more* at the end of the semester

Number of Symptoms Reported Each Week

Early in the Semester

Late in the Semester

Nonprocrastinators
Procrastinators

Figure 5.8
The Potential Negative Effects of Procrastination

The short-term benefits of procrastinating appear to be offset by the negative effects it exerts on our performance and health later on. Procrastinators reported fewer symptoms of illness at the beginning of the semester, compared to non-procrastinators. Late in the semester, when procrastinators were faced with impending deadlines, this relationship switched.

Source: Based on data from Tice and Baumeister, 1997.

SCHEDULES OF REINFORCEMENT: RULES FOR THE DELIVERY OF PAYOFFS

In real life, there is often some uncertainty about whether a reward will be forthcoming. Sometimes a given response yields a reward every time it occurs, but sometimes it does not. For example, sometimes smiling at someone you do not know will produce a return smile and additional desirable consequences. On other occasions, the same smile may produce a suspicious frown, or other kinds of rejection. Similarly, putting a loonie in a vending machine usually produces a can of something to drink. Sometimes, though, you merely lose the coin.

In these examples, the occurrence or non-occurrence of reinforcement seems to be random or unpredictable. In many other instances, though, it is governed by rules. For example, paycheques are delivered only on certain days of the month; free pizzas, coffee, or car washes are provided to customers who have purchased a specific amount. Do such rules—known as **schedules of reinforcement**—affect behaviour? Several decades of research by Skinner and other psychologists suggest that they do. Many different types of schedules of reinforcement exist (Ferster & Skinner, 1957; Honig & Staddon, 1977). We will consider several of the most important ones here.

The simplest timetable is called the **continuous reinforcement schedule,** in which a reward is delivered every time a designated response occurs. For example, if a rat receives a food pellet each time it presses a lever, or a small child receives a quarter each time she ties her shoes correctly, both are being delivered their rewards according to a continuous reinforcement schedule. As you might imagine, new behaviours are learned quickly when there is continuous reinforcement.

Another type of timetable is the *partial* (or *intermittent*) *reinforcement schedule,* which is so called because a reward is delivered only some of the times that a designated response occurs. There are four basic partial reinforcement schedules: Two of these are *interval schedules* according to which reward is delivered after an interval of time has passed; the other two are *ratio schedules* according to which reward is delivered after a number of responses has been made.

On the first of these four schedules, known as a **fixed-interval schedule,** the reinforcer occurs after a fixed amount of time has passed. That is, the first response made after the passage of a fixed amount of time gets rewarded. When placed on

Schedules of Reinforcement: Rules determining when and how reinforcements will be delivered.

Continuous Reinforcement Schedule: A schedule of reinforcement in which every occurrence of a particular behaviour is reinforced.

Fixed-Interval Schedule: A schedule of reinforcement in which a specific interval of time must elapse before a response will yield reinforcement.

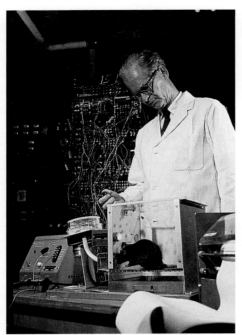

B.F. Skinner with His Skinner Box

In his experiments on animal behaviour and reinforcement, B.F. Skinner used a "Skinner box." Animals (such as the rat shown here) were placed in the device and were rewarded with food whenever they performed certain behaviours, such as pressing a lever.

schedules of this type, people generally respond at low rates immediately after reinforcement, and the rate of responding increases steadily as the time for the next reward approaches. A good example of behaviour on a fixed-interval schedule is provided by students' study habits. After a big exam, little if any studying takes place. As the time for the next one approaches, studying increases dramatically.

On a **variable-interval schedule,** the period of time that passes before a response will again yield a reward varies around some average value. For example, in some companies, supervisors monitor the calls of telemarketers at irregular intervals over a working day—for example, on average, after two hours. Since the employees never know when these checks will occur, they must perform consistently in order to obtain positive outcomes, such as praise, or to avoid negative ones, such as criticism. This steady rate of responding is precisely what results when reward is delivered on variable-interval schedules.

Random drug testing of individuals in safety-sensitive jobs—for example, airline pilots or machine operators at nuclear reactors—takes place on a variable interval schedule. Because they cannot predict the day on which the next test will occur, these individuals may be more likely to stay drug-free consistently.

On a **fixed-ratio schedule,** each reinforcer occurs after a fixed number of responses. For example, factory workers who are paid for every three garments completed are being rewarded according to a fixed-ratio schedule. Also, people who are paid by the dozen for bottles, cans, and other recyclables are being rewarded according to a fixed-ratio schedule. Generally, these schedules yield a high rate of response, though with a tendency toward a brief pause immediately after each reinforcer. The pauses occur as individuals take a slight breather after earning a reward.

On a **variable-ratio schedule,** each reinforcer occurs after a variable number of responses, but that number of responses varies around some average value. For example, payoffs of video lottery terminal (VLT) machines are preprogrammed so that the jackpot is delivered after a variable number of responses has taken place, that number varying around a preset average number of plays. Since animals confronted with a variable-ratio schedule cannot predict how many responses are required before reinforcement will occur, they usually respond at high and steady rates. The effect of variable-ratio schedules on human behaviour is readily apparent in gambling casinos and video arcades where high rates of responding occur. For a closer look at gambling-related behaviour, see the **Canadian Focus** box on page 205.

Variable-ratio schedules result in behaviours that are highly resistant to extinction—that persist for long periods of time even when reinforcement is no longer available. This persistence of behaviour is called the *partial reinforcement effect.* Many golfers are well acquainted with this effect; for each great shot they hit, they hit many more poor ones, yet they continue to play the game.

As summarized in Figure 5.9 and as was evident throughout the preceding discussion, different schedules of reinforcement produce distinct patterns of responding. Which schedules do we prefer? In Quebec, an analysis of arcade video games by Braun and Giroux (1989) found that the most popular games provided rewards on fixed-ratio, continuous reward schedules.

Variable-Interval Schedule: A schedule of reinforcement in which a variable amount of time elapses before a response will yield reinforcement.

Fixed-Ratio Schedule: A schedule of reinforcement in which reinforcement occurs only after a fixed number of responses have been emitted.

Variable-Ratio Schedule: A schedule of reinforcement in which reinforcement occurs after a variable number of responses have been performed.

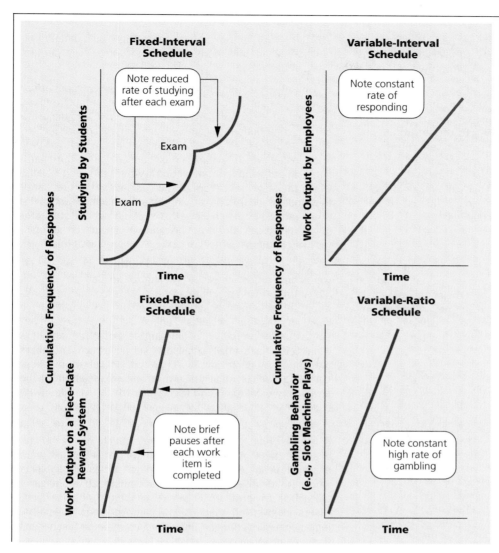

Figure 5.9
Schedules of Reinforcement: A Summary of Their Effects

Rates of responding vary under different schedules of reinforcement. The steeper each line in the graph, the higher the rate at which responses are performed.

Gambling: The Psychological Downside

Whether it is on bingo, horses, video lottery terminals, or slot machines, people learn to gamble according to the principles of the three kinds of learning you have studied in this chapter. There is evidence from research that operant conditioning, classical conditioning and observational learning each play a role. Canadian researchers Robert Ladouceur and his colleagues at Laval University have contributed much to our understanding of the psychology of gambling behaviour and to

the design of programs that will help gambling addicts stop gambling (e.g., Ladouceur, 2000).

Operant conditioning helps establish and maintain gambling behaviour. Because the rewards for gambling are delivered according to partial reinforcement schedules, the behaviour is

Robert Ladouceur
Laval University

resistant to extinction and will persist over periods of time during which no reward occurs. For many gamblers, then, betting continues even though they lose many times over—without a single win.

Classical conditioning is also involved in the maintenance of gambling behaviour. The pleasure associated with winning may become classically conditioned to the environmental cues in the casino (or in the corner grocery in some provinces). These conditioned stimuli then elicit the responses that were originally made to winning. When they return to those environments, gamblers are likely to fall back into their old habits. As with any other addiction, the behaviour continues—despite many unsuccessful attempts to recoup losses.

Researchers at McGill University in Montreal suggest that gambling is linked to observational learning also (Gupta & Derevensky, 1997). In their study, 86 percent of the subjects (nine to fourteen years old) who gambled regularly reported that they had gambled with members of their families. Watching family members gambling and being rewarded for gambling, these children learn that gambling is socially acceptable. Friends are also important influences and become more and more so as age increases.

Problem Gamblers For most of those who gamble, there are no serious consequences. However, it is estimated that about 1.2 million people living in Canada have a gambling problem, and about 60 000 of those are pathological gamblers. They have a chronic and progressive psychological disorder—an irresistible urge to gamble. That addiction is growing fastest in the age range from twelve to seventeen.

Not all kinds of gambling are equally addictive. Most seductive are the video lottery terminals (VLTs), which are also most easily accessible. VLTs are preprogrammed to deliver wins according to the most powerful schedule of partial reinforcement—the variable-ratio schedule. That means that they pay out after a preset number of turns, on average. That average can be changed often and, of course, it is never known to the players. Thus VLTs have become to gambling addiction what crack cocaine is to drug addiction. Those addicted to VLTs are much less likely to have had previous problems with gambling or other kinds of addictions. This compulsive behaviour is new to them.

The fact that people become addicted to gambling, as they do to nicotine, to alcohol, to heroin, and sometimes even to starving or jogging, suggests that there may be a biological basis to compulsive gambling. One study has identified *excitement* as the most important reinforcer for regular video-poker players (Dumont & Ladouceur, 1990). Perhaps the biochemical changes that accompany risk-taking provide the biological basis for reinforcement of gambling behaviour.

Other researchers have concluded, however, that problem gamblers have a deficit in impulse control (Vitaro et al., 1997). They prefer immediate reward. One study suggested that impulsivity, problem gambling, and substance use are linked. The authors suggested that "problem gambling and substance use develop simultaneously during adolescence and share a common impulse-control deficit" (Vitaro et al.,

1998, p. 185). In those cases, there might be a different biological explanation—perhaps a malfunction of the prefrontal lobes of the brain.

How else is learning involved in gambling behaviour? Here is another connection. Gamblers learn maladaptive ideas (thoughts, beliefs, and perceptions), and those also make important contributions to gambling behaviour (Ladouceur et al., 1996; Ladouceur et al., 1997). In spite of the fact that they know losing is the inevitable consequence of long-term gambling, many gamblers have contrary thoughts and beliefs, which they take with them to the casino. On the one hand, they understand they are playing a game of chance, but on the other hand, they also believe that skill is an important factor in whether you win or not. For example, when they gamble, they say to themselves: "I'm really getting good at this."

Although they understand that the machines deliver rewards on a random basis, they cling to the idea that there is a system for winning that can be discovered and used. Although they know it is simply superstition, they often have lucky charms (e.g., jewellery, coins). Although they understand that the probability of any single set of lottery numbers winning is infinitesimally small, they still have "lucky" numbers that they play each time. To change their behaviour, then, gambling addicts must unlearn erroneous ideas about the probability of winning and the way in which the odds work (Ladouceur et al., 1998; Sylvain et al., 1997).

Erroneous beliefs can be changed through the application of learning principles, but as with any addiction, it is difficult to kick the habit. A promising experimental treatment program has been designed and tested on older adolescent subjects who were identified as pathological gamblers (Ladouceur et al., 1994). The program includes five different modules. First, clients are given information about gambling and about pathological gambling. Second, they consider their mistaken ideas about gambling and are corrected. Third, they receive step-by-step training in how to approach their problems and how to solve them. Fourth, they receive training in social skills (how to communicate with others and how to assert themselves). Fifth, they are trained in relapse prevention. They identify situations in which they are at risk for relapse (e.g., times when they have money, are stressed, frustrated, lonely, or looking for excitement), and they learn what to do in those circumstances rather than return to gambling. By three to six months after beginning treatment, these adolescents were able to abstain from gambling and to continue to do so.

Treatments for pathological gambling may also include addiction counselling (e.g., Alberta Alcohol and Drug Abuse Commission), help lines (such as Recovery House in Antigonish), behaviour modification, support groups (Gamblers Anonymous), some drugs, and psychotherapy. Prevention programs for adolescents are being designed for use in the schools. These would make students aware of the risks associated with this kind of activity and how to deal with peer pressure to take up gambling. Given our current understanding of the development of gambling in childhood, it seems as though these programs should start in the early grades, perhaps even before age eight.

CONCURRENT SCHEDULES OF REINFORCEMENT AND THE MATCHING LAW

Psychologists readily admit that schedules of reinforcement do not fully account for the complex forms of human behaviour observed in everyday life (e.g., Hanisch, 1995; Pierce & Epling, 1994). Each day people are faced with alternatives, and they must choose one over the others. For example, on a given evening, students may choose between doing homework or other activities such as going out with friends, talking on the telephone, doing laundry, or watching TV. This describes a situation in which there are concurrent schedules of reinforcement—that is, there are two or more possible responses—each having its own schedule of reinforcement (Catania, 1992). This arrangement has been used to study choice behaviour in both animals and humans (e.g., Elsmore & McBride, 1994; Pierce & Epling, 1994).

To illustrate, let us consider a typical animal experiment involving a **concurrent schedule of reinforcement** in which a rat is free at any time to press lever A, lever B, or to press neither. Furthermore, the rat may distribute its presses between the two levers as it chooses. Now suppose the consequences of pressing each lever (e.g., food reward) are arranged according to distinct variable-interval schedules of reinforcement. How will the rat distribute its lever presses? The data say that the rate of responding on each lever will tend to match the rate of reinforcement each lever produces. In other words, the rat will distribute its behaviour between alternatives in such a way that maximizes the reinforcement it receives for its efforts. This phenomenon has been termed the *matching law* (Herrnstein, 1961).

The matching law has several important implications for human behaviour. First, it encourages researchers to view current behaviour as one response choice among many potential alternatives. Analyzing behaviour in this way may help psychologists improve their understanding of how people make choices in everyday life (e.g., Conger & Killeen, 1974). Second, research on the matching law helps explain why certain reinforcers are attractive at certain times, but not at others—for example, why cleaning your room is OK if you have nothing else to do, but pretty unattractive if you have better things to do. Finally, recognizing that people compare the value of a particular reinforcer with the values of other rewards available could lead to the development of more effective treatments. For instance, it may be possible to eliminate undesirable or destructive behaviour by increasing the relative attractiveness of rewards for desirable responses, instead of using punishment.

In these ways, consequences matter a great deal to how we behave. However, consequences are not the only determinants of behaviour. As we will see in the next section, stimuli that precede behaviour and signal the availability of certain consequences are also important.

SIGNALS ABOUT THE USEFULNESS (OR USELESSNESS) OF RESPONSES

Imagine that you are a rat in a Skinner box. Over the past few days, you have learned to press a lever in order to receive food pellets. One morning you notice the presence of a light in the box, which is turned on and off with some regularity. The light is actually a signal: You will be rewarded with food if you press the lever when the light is on, but not when the light is off. Over time, you learn to press the lever when the light is on but not when the light is turned off. In short, your lever-pressing behaviour is now a **discriminative stimulus** that has come under **stimulus control** of the light. You are obeying the light's signal as to whether to press the lever or not (Skinner, 1938).

Stimulus control has important implications for people—for example, as you found in Chapter 4, it can be an effective treatment for insomnia.

Concurrent Schedule of Reinforcement: A situation in which behaviours having two or more different reinforcement schedules are simultaneously available.

Discriminative Stimulus: Stimulus that signals reinforcement will occur if a specific response is made.

Stimulus Control: Consistent occurrence of a behaviour in the presence of a discriminative stimulus.

K E Y *QUESTIONS*

▨ What are shaping and chaining?

▨ How does reward delay affect operant conditioning?

continued

■ What are schedules of reinforcement?

■ When is the use of continuous reinforcement desirable?

■ What are concurrent schedules of reinforcement and the matching law?

■ What is a discriminative stimulus?

Critical Thinking

Describe some examples of stimulus control in your own life.

A Cognitive View of Operant Conditioning

Do thought processes play a role in operant conditioning as they do in classical conditioning? This continues to be a point on which psychologists disagree. Skinner and his supporters have contended that there is no need to introduce cognition into the picture. They maintain that, if we understand the nature of the reinforcement available in a situation and the schedules on which they are delivered, we can accurately predict behaviour. But many other psychologists—the majority, it seems—believe that no account of operant conditioning can be complete without attention to cognitive factors (e.g., Colwill, 1993). Several types of evidence support this conclusion.

LEARNED HELPLESSNESS First, and perhaps most dramatic, is the phenomenon known as **learned helplessness,** which occurs when nothing seems to work. In these aversive circumstances, no matter which response is made, there is no reward or escape. As a result, animals appear despondent; they seem literally to give up. Moreover, research findings suggest that there is a general expectation of helplessness that transfers across situations (Maier & Jackson, 1979). And here is the unsettling part: If the circumstances change so that some of their abandoned responses might work, the animals never discover that fact, because they have stopped trying altogether (Seligman, 1975; Tennen & Eller, 1977).

Research with human subjects suggests that learned helplessness starts with what we believe about how much control we have over our lives. When we begin to believe that we have no control, we stop trying (Dweck & Licht, 1980). For example, many disadvantaged children believe they have little control over their environment and even less hope of escaping it. As a result of learned helplessness, they may resign themselves to a lifetime of inactivity, denial, and isolation. However, not all people respond in this way, suggesting that other factors must also be involved. As we will note in Chapter 12, people differ in ways that make them more or less likely to develop learned helplessness (Minor, 1990; Minor et al., 1994).

Several studies indicate that people's beliefs about schedules of reinforcement may have greater effects on their behaviour than the schedules themselves (Kaufman, Baron, & Kopp, 1966). In one experiment, all subjects actually worked on the same schedule of reinforcement, but they were given three different sets of beliefs about the delivery of rewards. Those subjects who thought they were working on a variable-ratio schedule made the most responses: 259 per minute. Those who were told that they were working on a variable interval schedule made 65 responses per minute, and those told they would be rewarded on a fixed-interval schedule made 6 responses per minute. As suggested by Bandura (1986), behaviour may sometimes be more accurately predicted by beliefs than by the rewards people actually get. It may be, therefore, that a change in the way we think about ourselves and our abilities to change our circumstances is necessary in order to overcome learned helplessness.

Is there a biological link to learned helplessness? Recently, researchers have suggested genetic factors may be involved. One such factor is an inherited impairment

Learned Helplessness: Feelings of helplessness that develop after exposure to situations in which no effort succeeds in changing outcomes.

in the ability to experience pleasure, *hypohedonia*. According to Hamburg (1998), children who inherit hypohedonia do not experience the positive feelings that come from receiving a reward. This inherited defect may lead to perceptions of lack of control, helplessness, and depression.

THE CONTRAST EFFECT Some research findings show that our behaviour is influenced by the evaluation we make of a reward—relative to our experiences with previous rewards. Studies have shown that a shift in the amount of reward can influence learning dramatically. A shift in behaviour as a result of a shift in the amount of reward delivered is called the *contrast effect* (e.g., Crespi, 1942).

Here is an example of how the contrast effect works. When laboratory animals are shifted from receiving a small reward to receiving a larger reward, their performance increases to a level greater than that of subjects that have consistently received the larger reward. This increase in performance is known as a *positive contrast effect*. Conversely, when subjects shift from a large reward to a smaller reward, their performance decreases to a level lower than that of subjects that had received only the smaller reward—a *negative contrast effect*. However, both positive and negative contrast effects are transient. Thus, the elevated or depressed performances slowly give way to performance levels similar to those of control animals that have received only one level of reward.

This finding may help to explain some of our own very human behaviours. For example, following an unexpected raise in salary or a promotion, a person is initially elated, and productivity skyrockets—at least for a while. Then, after the novelty wears off, productivity levels out to that of other people already being rewarded at the same level.

TOLMAN'S COGNITIVE MAP: A CLASSIC STUDY AND CONTEMPORARY VIEWS Finally, let us consider the evidence that cognitive processes play an important role in animal learning. In a classic study by Tolman and Honzik (1930), rats were trained to run through a complicated maze. One group, the reward group, received a food reward in the goal box at the end of the maze on each of their daily trials. A second group, the no-reward group, never received a reward. The third group, the no-reward/reward group, did not receive a food reward until the eleventh day of training. As illustrated in Figure 5.10, rats in the reward group showed a steady improvement in performance, decreasing the number of errors they made in reaching the goal box. Rats in the no-reward group showed only a slight improvement in performance. Rats in the no-reward/reward group showed performance similar to those in the no-reward group—for the first ten days. Their performance improved dramatically immediately after the food reward was introduced. In fact, their performance was as good as that of rats who had been rewarded for their performance all along.

How do we account for these results? Tolman and others (e.g., Colwill & Rescorla, 1985, 1988) take these kinds of results as evidence that the animals had learned about the maze during the early no-reward trials. Tolman called that latent learning and he speculated that his rats may have formed a mental representation of the maze—that is, a *cognitive map*.

To examine the cognitive maps of animals, Marcia Spetch and others at the University of Alberta (e.g., Spetch & Grant, 1993) are investigating what pigeons know about their location in space and what they know about time. More specifically, they are trying to understand how it is that animals (such as many species of birds) use natural landmarks to guide them in their travels (Cheng & Spetch, 1998). For that purpose, Spetch has developed a touch-screen task, in which pigeons peck at an outdoor scene shown on a video monitor. The results show that, given the opportunity to use one, two, or three landmarks, pigeons choose only one. Different pigeons, however, choose different landmarks. Why does a particular pigeon choose a particular landmark? It may be that, even in pigeons, some matters are decided by individual taste.

Marcia Spetch
University of Alberta

Figure 5.10
The Role of Cognitive Processes in Learning

Performance for rats in the no-reward/reward group improved dramatically immediately after the introduction of the food reward. Because the improvement was so dramatic, these data suggest that the animals "learned" something during previous trials—even though they received no reward for their efforts. Tolman used this as evidence for the importance of cognitive processes in learning, suggesting that the rats may have formed a "cognitive map."

Source: Based on data from Tolman and Honik, 1930.

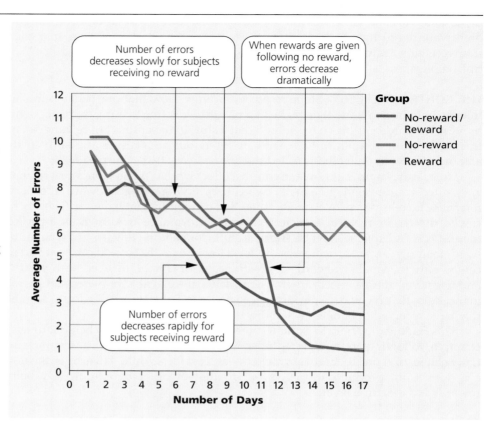

Other birds that store their food—chickadees, for example—remember a stimulus according to its location. That may be because they rely on spatial memories to locate their store of food (Brobeck & Shettleworth, 1995). The cognitive maps of bees and ants have also been studied (Wehner & Menzel, 1990). Bees choose individual flowers by flower size and flower depth (Harder, 1988). Although we do not yet fully understand their precise nature, one thing is clear: non-human species form mental representations that include spatial and temporal features of their environment (Poucet, 1993)—perhaps even memories of them as well.

Systematic research by Capaldi and his colleagues points also to the possibility that animals form memories of rewards they have received in the past (Capaldi, 1996; Capaldi et al., 1995). According to this view, distinctive reward events produce distinctive reward memories. Reward event memories apparently serve two important purposes. First, they serve as discriminative stimuli, directing the animal's behaviour by signalling when, or if, future responses will lead to reinforcement. Second, reward memories serve as a response-enhancing function. In other words, the memories of bigger rewards lead to greater increases in responding than memories of smaller rewards or non-reward. Thus memories are actively involved in learning according to operant conditioning principles.

Applications of Operant Conditioning

Because positive and negative reinforcement exert powerful effects on behaviour, procedures based on operant conditioning have been applied in many practical settings—so many that it would be impossible to describe them all here. These principles have been applied to address socially significant issues: crime, energy conservation and recycling, health, consumer affairs, and safety promotion (Geller, 1995, 1996; Green et al., 1987). In the **Research Process** section, you will find one method that has been applied successfully.

The Research Process:
Behaviour Analysis in Action: Graffiti

B.F. Skinner was a major proponent of the importance of operant conditioning. In his view, a complete understanding of behaviour requires knowledge of three kinds of information: (1) the characteristics of stimulus events that precede a particular response; (2) the characteristics of the response or behaviour itself; and (3) the reinforcing consequences that maintain the response (Skinner, 1969). These ideas led to the development of a branch of psychology called **applied behaviour analysis.** Below you will find examples of how the methods of behaviour analysis are applied to the problems of real life: graffiti. Here first, however, is a description of one particular research method that has been used successfully to promote positive changes in behaviour.

This research method is a four-step process. To remember the four steps, you can use the acronym "DO IT" (Geller, 1996). The first step in the process is to clearly *define* the target behaviours to be changed. Doing so allows researchers to develop procedures to *observe* how often the behaviours occur under existing (or baseline) conditions. Once a baseline measure of the behaviours has been obtained, researchers *intervene*—that is, they do something to change the target behaviours. For example, they may begin to reward behaviours they wish to increase, or withhold rewards from inappropriate behaviours they wish to decrease. Or, they may alter aspects of the physical environment to encourage or discourage certain behaviours from taking place. Finally, they *test* the impact of the intervention by observing and recording not only during the intervention, but also afterwards. This provides evidence of the intervention's immediate impact and its effectiveness over the longer term.

Here is an example to show how this research method was used to control graffiti.

Graffiti

Some people like to write messages in public places. Done with cans of spray paint, under the cover of darkness, graffiti art requires much practice and skill. Nevertheless, graffiti damages public property. This behaviour is costly in terms of repainting and refinishing; millions are lost to other social programs as a result. Moreover, the messages can be offensive to others. Is there any way that applied behaviour analysis can help? There are research programs that make a difference.

One study used the "DO IT" process to discourage people from marking up public places with graffiti (Watson, 1996). The goal was to reduce the amount of graffiti on the walls of three public washrooms in different buildings of a university campus. The university had had to repaint these rooms repeatedly.

The researchers began by objectively defining graffiti—the number of distinct markings on each wall. For example, letters and punctuation each counted as separate marks; a happy face was counted as five marks—one for the circle depicting the head and one each for the two eyes, nose, and mouth.

Next, they counted daily to determine a baseline level of occurrence. Figure 5.11 shows the cumulative number of markings observed in each bathroom across consecutive observation days. Then the researchers introduced an intervention. They taped a poster on the washroom wall that read: "A local licensed doctor has agreed to donate a set amount of money to the local chapter of the United Way for each day this wall remains free of any writing, drawings, or other markings. Your assistance is greatly appreciated in helping to support your United Way."

The poster was introduced into the three washrooms one after another rather than all at the same time. The reason was to insure that any changes observed in the occurrence of graffiti were due to the intervention (posting the signs) and not other unrelated factors. Following the introduction of the poster into the first washroom, graffiti

Graffiti in a Canadian City

Whether or not it is to your taste, graffiti such as this example found on a building in Scarborough, Ontario, is vandalism and is costly to clean up.

ceased to occur there, but continued to occur in the other two washrooms. Similarly, following the introduction of the poster into the second washroom, graffiti ceased to occur there, but continued to occur in the third. In short, this procedure—a multiple-baseline design—increases our confidence that the poster was the cause of any change in the amount of graffiti observed.

As shown in Figure 5.11, the intervention was successful. After the posters were introduced there was an abrupt change. No further marking occurred on any of the walls. Moreover, they remained free of graffiti at each of three monthly follow-ups, suggesting that the posters were a cost-effective solution to this problem.

Please note the following caution: the fact that the posters were useful in this setting does not insure the same outcome elsewhere. Nevertheless, the "DO-IT" process is a useful tool for systematically studying behaviour and the effects of behaviour-change interventions.

Figure 5.11
Applied Behaviour Analysis in Action

This graph shows the cumulative number of graffiti markings across observation days in three public washrooms. Before the intervention, a significant amount of graffiti was occurring in each bathroom. After the intervention, however, no more graffiti occurred. Follow-up observations showed that the walls of the washrooms remained graffiti-free three months later. Please note that the sequential introduction of the poster into each bathroom makes it more likely that the reduction in graffiti resulted from the contents of the posters, and not from other factors.

Source: Based on data from Watson, 1997.

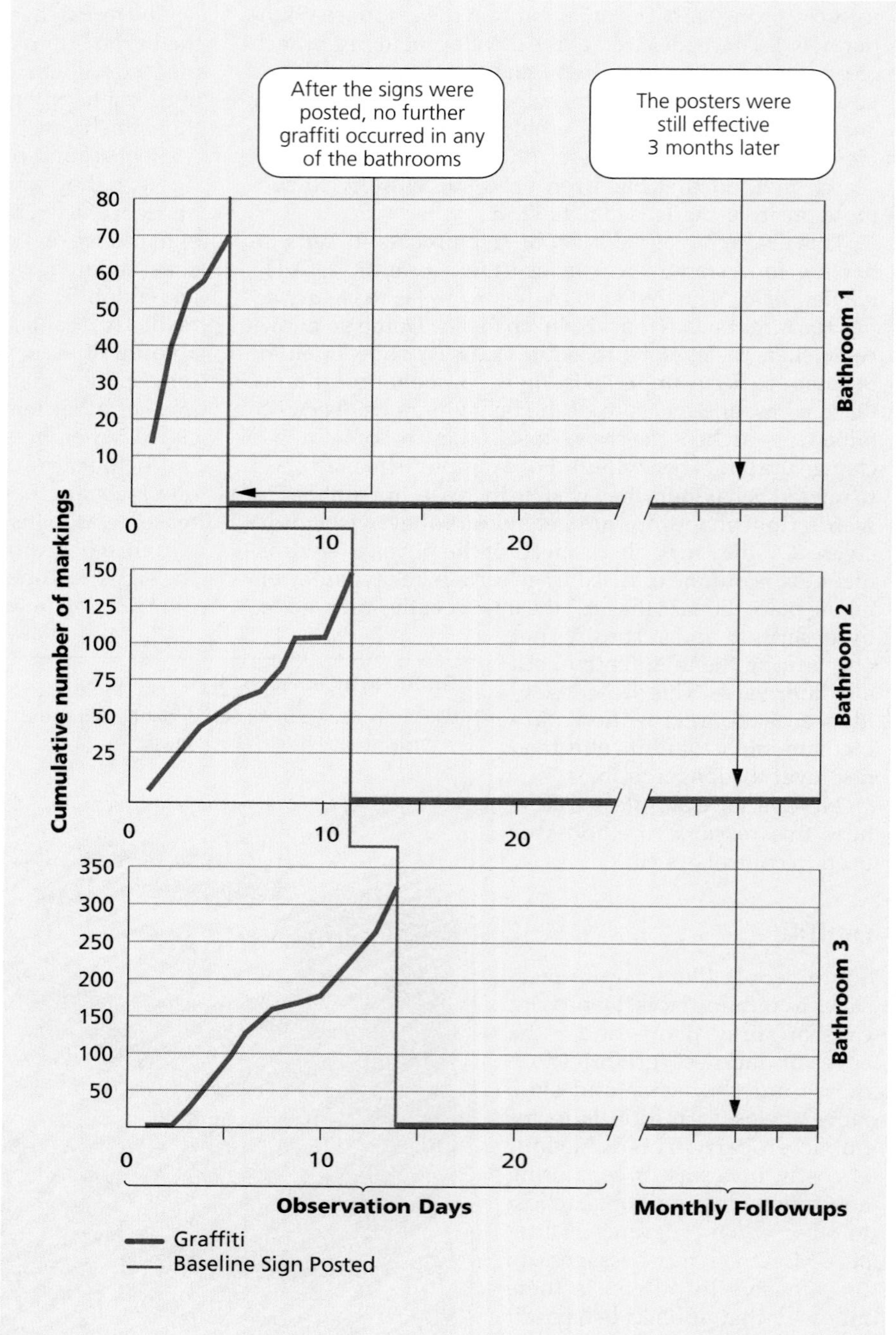

Applied Behaviour Analysis: A field of psychology that specializes in the application of operant conditioning principles to solve problems of everyday life.

In *computer-assisted instruction* (CAI) in education, students use sophisticated computer programs that provide immediate reinforcement of correct responses. The programs are paced according to each student's progress (Ross & McBean, 1995) and permit the student to hot link to special help in areas of weakness. CAI technology includes the use of computer-based simulation exercises that allow students to apply what they have learned in the classroom to solve problems under realistic conditions. With the colour graphics, synthesized speech, and other effects available on increasingly sophisticated equipment, CAI instruction may help add excitement and enhance motivation for learning (Kritch et al., 1995). Some evidence suggests that students may learn to take greater responsibility for their own performance under CAI because they view computers as impersonal and therefore fair.

In one program to improve safety, at crosswalks in St. John's, Fredericton, and Moncton, Malenfant and Van Houten (1989) studied the effects of various stimuli—among them signs, lines, and lighting—on pedestrian safety. One of these stimuli was a large sign displaying the percentage of motorists who yielded properly to pedestrians each week; the point of this was to provide motorists with feedback as to whether, as a group, they were improving or not. The program (based on operant conditioning principles) resulted in large increases in compliance by drivers and 50 percent fewer accidents.

Operant conditioning principles have been applied also to health. An example of this is *biofeedback*—a technique that teaches people to alter their own bodily responses such as skin temperature, muscle tension, blood pressure, and electrical activity of the brain. For example, a person suffering from high blood pressure is taught to recognize when increases and decreases occur. That is done by an apparatus that detects blood pressure changes and sounds a high tone when blood pressure goes up and a low tone when it goes down. Patients undergoing biofeedback use this feedback information to alter their own pressure level. After training, they are able to make the same changes happen—without the feedback from the tone. Biofeedback has been used to successfully treat a broad range of ailments, including headaches (Arena et al., 1995; Hermann et al., 1995), high blood pressure (Dubbert, 1995), muscle tics and chronic lower back pain (Newton et al., 1995; O'Connor et al., 1995), depression in alcoholics (Saxby & Peniston, 1995), marching endurance (Couture et al., 1994)—and even sexual dysfunction (Palace, 1995).

Operant conditioning principles have been applied also to self-injurious behaviour—a severe behaviour disorder in which people inflict injury on themselves (Lovaas, 1982). This occurs frequently in the developmentally handicapped and those with autism or brain damage. Common behaviours are head hitting, self-biting, severe scratching, eye gouging, and hair pulling (Maurice & Trudel, 1982). Using a unique observational assessment procedure, Iwata and his colleagues discovered that individuals engage in self-injury for a variety of reasons (Iwata et al., 1982)—to attract the attention of people around them or to avoid or terminate demands being made on them. For still others, these behaviours are performed for the feeling of it—for self-generated sensory stimulation. This principle was applied in the case of a ten-year-old boy who injured himself by slapping his own face. Van Houten (1993) reasoned that wrist weights would reduce the face slapping by making the action more effortful and by changing the sensory consequences—that is, changing the way it felt. The behaviour was modified using learning principles; in the five-month follow-up period, no face slapping occurred.

Finally, techniques of operant conditioning have been applied to work (Latham & Huber, 1992)—to improve the performance of retail clerks (Luthans, Paul, & Baker, 1981), the productivity of waiters (George & Hopkins, 1989), the success of work groups (Petty, Singleton, & Connell, 1992). and the effectiveness of managers (e.g., Komacki, 1986). That effective managers provide contingent rewards and punishments may sound like common sense, but it does not always come naturally in many work settings, where the consequences of good performance are more work, tougher challenges, and higher expectations. Clearly, work is one applied area that can benefit from research results in operant conditioning.

Observational Learning

You are at a formal dinner with a potential employer and other guests. Next to your plate are five different forks, including two of a shape you have never seen before. Which ones do you use for which courses? You have no idea. As the first course arrives, you decide to watch the others. Now, thank goodness, you can concentrate on the food (and the job).

Even if you have not had an experience quite like this, you probably have encountered situations in which you have acquired new information, forms of behaviour, or even abstract rules and concepts by watching other people. Such **observational learning** is a third major way we learn, and it is a natural part of human life (Bandura, 1977, 1986). Indeed, observational learning can play a role in almost every aspect of behaviour (Grusec & Goodnow, 1994), from learning to cook to accepting responsibilities to telling the truth. In these and countless other instances, we learn vicariously by watching the actions of other people and the consequences of their behaviour.

Observational learning occurs in fish, birds, and mammals (Robert, 1990; White & Galef, 1998). Eating and food selection are examples of this (Galef, 1996). For example, rats (when given a choice) preferred to eat the food that they had observed other rats chose. Of course, humans do that too (Hobden & Pliner, 1995). At one time or another, you have probably changed your order in a restaurant because someone else made another choice. Research shows that children copy their parents with respect to food aversions (Pliner, 1994) or other fears—yet another instance of observational learning.

That observational learning occurs in humans has been shown in hundreds of studies, many of them performed with children. Perhaps the most famous of these were the "Bobo doll" experiments conducted by Bandura and his colleagues (e.g., Bandura, Ross, & Ross, 1963). In this research, one group of nursery-school children saw an adult engage in aggressive actions against a large inflated Bobo doll. The adult, who was serving as a model—that is, setting an example—knocked the doll down, sat on it, insulted it verbally, and repeatedly punched it in the nose. Another group of children were exposed to a model who behaved in a quiet, non-aggressive manner.

Later, both groups of children were placed in a room with several toys, including a Bobo doll. Those children who had seen the aggressive adult model often imitated the behaviour they had seen. They too punched the toy, sat on it, and even made comments similar to those the model had made. In contrast, children in the control group rarely, if ever, demonstrated such actions. While you may not find these results surprising, they may be significant in relation to the enduring controversy over whether children acquire new aggressive behaviours through exposure to violent video games, television programs, and movies. We will return to this issue soon. For the moment, consider the nature of observational learning itself.

Albert Bandura
Bandura's research on observational learning changed the way we think about the effects of experience on human behaviour.

Observational Learning: The acquisition of new information, concepts, or forms of behaviour through observation of other people.

Some Basic Principles of Observational Learning

Given that observational learning exists, what do we know about how we learn new ways of behaving by observing others? According to Bandura (1986) four factors are most important.

First, in order to learn through observation, it is essential to direct attention to appropriate *models*—that is, to other people performing an activity. As you might expect, you do not choose such models at random. Rather, you focus the most attention on people who are attractive to you—on people who possess signs of status or success, and on people whose behaviour seems relevant to your own needs and goals (Baron, 1970).

Second, you must be able to *remember* what the people have said or done. Only if you can retain some representation of their actions in memory can you perform similar actions at later times or acquire useful information from them.

Third, these memory representations must be converted into appropriate actions by using *production processes.* Production processes depend on two things: your own physical abilities—if you cannot perform the behaviour in question, having a clear representation of it in memory is of little use—and your capacity to monitor your own performance and adjust it until it matches that of the model.

Finally, *motivation* plays a role. We often acquire information through observational learning but do not put it into use. You may have no need to learn a particular response (for example, to learn to tie a bowline or a reef knot if you have no plans to use one yourself). Or the observed behaviours may involve a high risk of punishment or be repugnant to you personally (for example, an ingenious way of cheating on an exam). Only if the information or behaviour acquired is useful will observers be motivated to actually learn what they observe. Figure 5.12 summarizes the factors affecting observational learning.

Figure 5.12
Key Factors in Observational Learning

Observational learning is affected by several factors or subprocesses. The most important of these are summarized here.

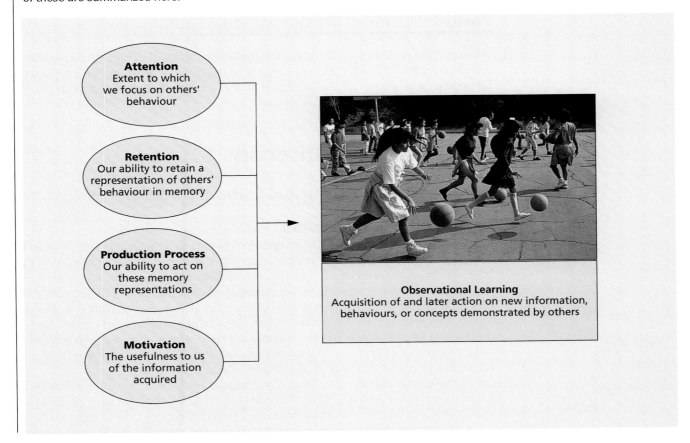

Negative Examples of Observational Learning

As you can see, observational learning is a complex process—far more complex than mere imitation—and it plays an important role in many aspects of behaviour. This point is perhaps most forcefully illustrated by a question that has persisted for half a century: How does what we watch television or in movies—and now in video games—affect the way we behave? By the time they enter junior high, many Canadian teens have already seen 100 000 violent acts and 8000 murders (Biddy & Postersky, 1992). Many of the most popular video games involve players in gruesome acts of violence, such as decapitating with spine attached ("Mortal Kombat") or "fragging" opponents into brightly coloured fountains of blood and chunks of meat ("Quake III") or running over helpless pedestrians as you steal brand new cars ("Grand Theft Auto 2").

What do we learn by observing all of that? Researchers have demonstrated that aggressive behaviour may be learned through observation (Baron & Richardson, 1994; Weigman & van-Schie, 1998). When children and adults are exposed to new ways of aggressing against others, they may add these new behaviours to their repertoire. Later, when angry, irritated, or frustrated, they may put these acquired behaviours to actual use.

Of course, media violence has other effects as well. It conveys the message that violence is an acceptable means of handling interpersonal difficulties. It may convince viewers that violence is more common in real life than it is (Berkowitz, 1984). And it may also lessen emotional reactions to the harm produced—that is, *desensitization* may occur—so that the painful consequences become less upsetting or objectionable (Thomas, 1982). The overall impact for many people may be an increased tendency to act aggressively (Eron, 1987). For at least these reasons, the potential influence of TV and video violence on behaviour seems worthy of careful attention.

Positive Examples of Observational Learning

Research has also studied the potential real-life benefits of observational learning for other areas of life, such as peer tutoring. Also, as we will see in **Perspectives on Diversity,** observational learning can help us to communicate better with people from different cultures.

Perspectives on Diversity

Observational Learning and Cultural Diversity

AS THE WORLD MOVES TOWARD a global economy and freer trade, companies everywhere are facing a difficult challenge. They must prepare their employees to communicate effectively with people from other cultures (Adler & Bartholomew, 1992; Feldman & Tompson, 1993). This is true also within Canada, where cultural diversity is the norm everywhere. For example, in one company in Richmond, B.C., fifty different ethnic backgrounds and nationalities are represented in the workforce of 820. Diversity is a challenge also when Canadians move to work in one part of the country from another. Social workers who moved from southern Canada to the Yukon required a period of adjustment and recovery—depending upon their personal history and their individual attitudes (Zapf, 1993).

Communication across cultures is difficult, sometimes, because behaviours that are acceptable and encouraged in one country or one culture may be offensive and intolerable to people from another. Dramatic differences in language, customs, dress, climate, and lifestyle may lead to unintended slights. Indeed, ignorance of these differences has long been cited as the biggest cause of misunderstandings between people from different cultures (Harris, 1979). These misunderstandings may arise from a matter as simple as the making of eye contact—which is taken as a positive gesture in Canada, but improper in some parts of Asia.

In early efforts to prepare employees for cross-cultural assignments (Fielder et al., 1971), trainees received factual information (government, religion, customs, weather, and so on). More recently, however, companies that conduct business abroad have begun to use techniques of observational learning to teach appropriate, sensitive, and consistent behaviour in cross-cultural interactions. In cross-cultural training programs like these (Black & Mendenhall, 1990), trainees first watch films in which models exhibit the correct behaviours in a problem situation. Then they participate in role-playing exercises to test their knowledge. Finally, they receive constructive feedback regarding their performance. These programs are available also to many other groups who may have reason to serve the diverse Canadian public—for example, members of the RCMP, student loan officers, judges, and teachers at all grade levels.

Are these programs effective? In one study (Harrison, 1992), results showed that participants who received both forms of training—information and behavioural modelling—performed best on measures of culture-specific knowledge and on a behavioural test. Thus, observational learning at first enables us to perform behaviours appropriate to our own cultures, but later helps us adapt to the demands of a diverse and rapidly changing world.

KEY QUESTIONS

- What is observational learning?

- What factors determine the extent to which we acquire new information through observational learning?

- In what forms of behaviour does observational learning play a role?

- In what ways can observational learning be used to solve some problems of everyday life?

Making Psychology Part of Your Life

What about Punishment?

The use of punishment seems universal. Parents scold children; teachers give detentions; professors deduct marks; referees charge penalties; police distribute tickets; courts sentence criminals to jail. In one study of college-educated mothers with three-year-old children, two and one-half spankings a week was the average (Holden et al., 1995).

That is not new. Here is psychologist B.F. Skinner on this topic fifty years ago: "The commonest technique of control in modern life is punishment. The pattern is familiar: if a man does not behave as you wish, knock him down; if a child misbehaves, spank him; if the people of a country misbehave, bomb them. Legal and police systems are based on such punishments as fines, flogging,

incarceration and hard labor. Religious control is exerted through penances, threats of excommunication and consignment to hell-fire…. In everyday personal contact, we control through censure, snubbing, disapproval, or banishment…. All of this is done with the intention of reducing tendencies to behave in certain ways" (1953, pp. 182–183). Skinner went on to be very critical of the use of punishment in these ways.

Nevertheless, sometime in our lives we will use punishment to control the behaviour of other people, and when we do, we will want our punitive action to be effective in suppressing behaviour; otherwise there is not much point! Research tells us that these are the steps to take for effective punishment.

■ *Administer the punishment as soon after the undesirable behaviour as possible.* Saying "Wait until your Mom/Dad gets home" is never a good idea. Since there must be a clear and unambiguous connection established between the undesirable behaviour and the consequence, the shorter the delay in delivering the aversive consequence, the more probable it is that the behaviour will change. That is the classic finding of animal studies (Azrin, 1968) and human studies as well.

Sometimes the connection between response and consequence is faulty. For example, the parent who says "Come here or I'll give you what for" is misleading the child since the parent is really saying "Come here *and* I'll give you what for." Furthermore, the child may think approaching the parent is the behaviour that is being punished. The resulting avoidance of the parent is not healthy for either party to this difficult situation.

■ *Punish consistently.* A child who is punished for bad language on one day and not on another, or by one parent and not another, in one context and not another, does learn something, but it is not about swearing, it is about how unreliably and how unpredictably the world responds to their behaviour. The result is not only that the misbehaviour continues (Walters & Grusec, 1977), but also that the child develops into a person who cannot predict the consequences of his or her actions—one who is uncertain and confused.

■ *Punish the behaviour, not the person.* Be certain to differentiate between the two and ensure that the difference is clearly understood. The withdrawal of love is not advisable, nor is it an effective punishment. The effects on self-esteem and feelings of self-worth may be serious consequences that last a lifetime. The effects upon the relationship between parent and child may outlast either one's recall of the particular incident.

■ *Begin with moderate severity.* How severe should punishment be in order to produce changes in behaviour? The results of fifty years of research indicate that, to be effective, moderate punishment on the first occasion is preferable to low-intensity pun-ishment that escalates each time (Azrin 1950). Too lenient a punishment is a waste of time and energy; too severe a punishment is abuse. This is true not only for several animal species, but also human adults and children (Parke & Walters, 1967).

■ *Provide a rationale for the punishment and explain response alternatives.* Punishment influences responses according to the way in which the child interprets what has happened. Beliefs about what will happen in the future and knowledge about what was wrong with the punished behaviour and what to do instead are critical. Studies of young children show that the largest decrease in misbehaviour follows frequent reasoning that is backed up by punishment. Note that punishment in these circumstances does *not* include the infliction of physical pain. Frequent reasoning that is not backed up is not effective and may even produce an increase in disruptive behaviours (Larzelere et al., 1998).

Since it is the child's interpretation that determines how the punishment will affect future behaviour (Parke, 1969, 1972), that interpretation needs to be as correct as possible. For example, threats like "I'd better not catch you doing that again" are mixed messages and subject to different interpretations. Saying "Come here" before punishing may result in the child refusing to approach the authority figure. In other words, according the University of Guelph researchers, emphasizing what the child *should* do instead of what he or she should *not* do is beneficial to the development of socially skilled youngsters (Kuczynski & Kochanska, 1995).

What can a parent or a camp counsellor or a day care worker or a work supervisor use to change behaviour instead of punishment? There are other ways of eliminating unwanted behaviour (Holtz & Asrin, 1963). It may take longer and require more effort, but in the long run it is better to value long-term goals (Kuczynski, 1984) and develop alternatives. Remove the child from the situation and impose "time out" from reinforcement or withdrawal of privileges. Use negative reinforcement to reinforce the termination of the undesirable behaviour. Whenever the opportunity arises, model, praise and otherwise reward appropriate behaviour (Zahn-Waxler & Robinson, 1995).

Summary and Review

Key Questions

Classical Conditioning

What is learning? Learning is any relatively permanent change in behaviour (or behaviour potential) produced by experience.

What is classical conditioning? Classical conditioning is a form of learning in which neutral stimuli (stimuli initially unable to elicit a particular response) come to elicit that response through their association with stimuli naturally able to do so.

Upon what factors does acquisition of a classically conditioned response depend? Acquisition is dependent upon temporal arrangement of the CS–UCS pairings, intensity of the CS and UCS relative to other background stimuli, and familiarity of potentially conditioned stimuli present.

What is extinction? Extinction is the process through which a conditioned stimulus gradually ceases to elicit a conditioned response when it is no longer paired with an unconditioned stimulus. However, this ability can be quickly regained through reconditioning.

What is the difference between stimulus generalization and stimulus discrimination? Stimulus generalization allows us to apply our learning to other situations; stimulus discrimination allows us to differentiate among similar but different stimuli.

Where in the brain does classical conditioning take place? Research shows that the cerebellum, a structure in the brain involved in balance and coordination, plays a key role in the formation of simple forms of classically conditioned responses.

Is classical conditioning equally easy to establish with all stimuli for all organisms? Because of biological constraints that exist among different species, types of conditioning readily accomplished by some species are only slowly acquired—or not acquired at all—by others.

How do we acquire conditioned taste aversions? Conditioned taste aversions are usually established when a food or beverage (CS) is paired with a stimulus that naturally leads to feelings of illness (UCS). Conditioned taste aversions can be established after a single CS–UCS pairing.

How do modern ideas of classical conditioning differ from earlier perspectives? Modern views of classical conditioning emphasize the important role of cognitive processes. A large body of research suggests that conditioning is a complex process in which organisms form representations of the relationships among a variety of factors—including many aspects of the physical setting or context in which the conditioned and unconditioned stimuli are presented.

What is blocking? In blocking, conditioning to one stimulus is prevented by previous conditioning to another stimulus.

What is flooding? Systematic desensitization? Flooding and systematic desensitization are procedures used to extinguish fears established through classical conditioning. In flooding, a person is forced to come into contact with fear-eliciting stimuli without an avenue of escape. Cases in which fearful thoughts are too painful to deal with directly are treated by systematic desensitization—a progressive technique designed to replace anxiety with a relaxation response.

How can classical conditioning principles solve problems of everyday life? Basic principles of classical conditioning have been used to solve a variety of everyday problems, including phobias (learned fears) and unexplained instances of drug overdose. The principles may also play a role in suppressing or increasing aspects of the immune system.

Operant Conditioning

What is operant conditioning? In operant conditioning, organisms learn the relationships between certain behaviours and the consequences they produce.

What are examples of primary reinforcement? Of conditioned reinforcement? Primary reinforcers include food, water, and sexual pleasure; conditioned reinforcers include money, status, and praise.

Which operant techniques strengthen behaviour? Weaken behaviour? Both positive and negative reinforcement strengthen or increase behaviour. In contrast, positive and negative punishment are procedures that suppress or weaken behaviour.

How do negative reinforcement and punishment differ? Both negative reinforcement and punishment involve aversive events. They differ, however, in terms of their effects on behaviour: Negative reinforcement is a procedure in which behaviours that allow an organism to escape from an aversive event, or to avoid it altogether, are strengthened. Punishment is a procedure in which an aversive event weakens the behaviour it follows.

What are shaping and chaining? Shaping is useful for establishing new responses by initially reinforcing behaviours that resemble the desired behaviour, termed successful approximations. Chaining is a procedure used to establish a complex sequence or chain of behaviours. The final response in the chain is trained first; then, working backwards, earlier responses in the chain are reinforced by the opportunity to perform the last response in the chain, which leads to a reward.

■ **How does reward delay affect operant conditioning?** When asked to choose between a smaller-but-sooner and a larger-but-later reward—and both options are relatively distant events—people often choose the latter option. As access to the smaller reward draws near, however, their impulsive tendencies tend to overpower their earlier decision to hold out for the better reward. Getting people to make a commitment ahead of time may help reduce this tendency. People exhibit a similar tendency when faced with a choice between performing a smaller, less effortful task now, or a larger, more effortful task later on: they procrastinate, choosing the more delayed alternative, even when it leads to more work.

■ **What are schedules of reinforcement?** Schedules of reinforcement are rules that determine the occasion on which a response will be reinforced. Schedules of reinforcement can be time-based or event-based, fixed or variable. Each schedule of reinforcement produces a characteristic pattern of responding.

■ **When is the use of continuous reinforcement desirable?** A continuous reinforcement schedule is desirable for establishing new behaviours; partial or intermittent schedules of reinforcement are more powerful in maintaining behaviour.

■ **What are concurrent schedules of reinforcement and the matching law?** In a concurrent schedule, an organism's behaviour is free to alternate between two or more responses, each of which has its own schedule of reinforcement. The matching law suggests that an organism distributes its behaviour between response alternatives such that it maximizes the reinforcement it receives from each alternative.

■ **What is a discriminative stimulus?** Discriminative stimuli signal the availability of specific consequences if a certain response is made. When a behaviour occurs consistently in the presence of a discriminative stimulus, it is said to be under stimulus control.

■ **What evidence supports the involvement of cognitive factors in operant conditioning?** Studies of learned helplessness, contrast effects, and memory of reward events support the coclusion that cognitive factors play an important role in operant conditioning.

■ **Why is knowledge of operant conditioning important?** Procedures based on operant conditioning principles can be applied to address many problems of everyday life; for example, improving classroom instructional technology; developing interventions to solve community-based problems, such as crime, health-care, and safety; and improving employee performance in the workplace.

Observational Learning

■ **What is observational learning?** Observational learning is the acquisition of new information, concepts, or forms of behaviour through exposure to others and the consequences that happen to them.

■ **What factors determine the extent to which we acquire new information through observational learning?** In order for observational learning to be effective, we must pay attention to those modelling the behaviour, remember the modelled speech or action, possess the ability to act upon this memory, and have the motivation to do so.

■ **In what forms of behaviour does observational learning play a role?** Observational learning plays an important role in many types of behaviour, including aggression.

■ **In what ways can observational learning be used to solve problems of everyday life?** Observational learning can play an important role in work settings; for example in training workers to interact more effectively with people from different cultural backgrounds.

Key Terms

Acquisition (p. 183)
Applied Behaviour Analysis (p. 212)
Backward Conditioning (p. 184)
Biological Constraints on Learning (p. 188)
Chaining (p. 200)
Concurrent Schedule of Reinforcement (p. 207)
Conditioned Response (p. 182)
Conditioned Stimulus (p. 182)
Continuous Reinforcement Schedule (p. 203)
Delayed Conditioning (p. 184)
Discriminative Stimulus (p. 207)
Extinction (p. 185)
Fixed-Interval Schedule (p. 203)

Fixed-Ratio Schedule (p. 204)
Flooding (p. 191)
Learned Helplessness (p. 208)
Learning (p. 180)
Negative Punisher (p. 197)
Negative Reinforcers (p. 195)
Observational Learning (p. 214)
Operant Conditioning (p. 194)
Phobias (p. 191)
Positive Punisher (p. 196)
Positive Reinforcers (p. 195)
Premack Principle (p. 195)
Punishment (p. 196)
Reconditioning (p. 186)

Reinforcement (p. 195)
Schedules of Reinforcement (p. 203)
Shaping (p. 200)
Simultaneous Conditioning (p. 184)
Spontaneous Recovery (p. 186)
Stimuli (p. 181)
Stimulus Control (p. 207)
Stimulus Discrimination (p. 186)
Stimulus Generalization (p. 186)
Trace Conditioning (p. 184)
Unconditioned Response (p. 182)
Unconditioned Stimulus (p. 182)
Variable-Interval Schedule (p. 204)
Variable-Ratio Schedule (p. 204)

Critical Thinking Questions

Appraisal

At the present time, many psychologists are moving increasingly toward a cognitive view of the learning process. Do you think this movement is appropriate, or is there still a role for the views of operant psychologists?

Controversy

List three ways in which the consequences of criminal behaviour delivered by the Canadian courts violate the laws of learning. Suggest improvements that might be made.

Making Psychology Part of Your Life

Knowing something about important principles of learning is very useful to people in applying punishment. This is only one way in which knowledge of learning can be applied. For example, how would you use learning to design a fitness program?

Weblinks

Check out our Companion Website at www.pearsoned.ca/baron for additional Websites, activities, and more.

Operant Conditioning

www.biozentrum.uni-wuerzburg.de:80/genetics/behavior/learning/operant.html

Operant conditioning is defined at this site, which includes links to other sites on such topics as classical conditioning, the Skinner box, and a general model of operant conditioning.

How to Toilet Train Your Cat

www.rainfrog.com/mishacat/toilet.shtml

Although not presented as such, this site is an example of applied behaviour analysis. The photographs illustrate steps in the procedure.

Positive Reinforcement: A Self-Instructional Exercise

server.bmod.athabascau.ca/html/prtut/reinpair.htm

This Athabaska University tutorial should require one to two hours to complete. In the first part of the exercise, the examples define and illustrate the concept of positive reinforcement. In the second part, the reader may classify fourteen examples and receive feedback on his or her choices.

The Electrical Stimulation of Brain Pleasure Centers

www.epub.org.br/cm/n08/doencas/drugs/videorat_i.htm

At this address you will find video clips of Olds' original self-stimulation experiments done in the 1960's.

Conditioned Taste Aversion in Male Rats

web.cs.mun.ca/~david12/papers/psyc2250/cc.html

This is an interesting report of an experiment on conditioned taste aversion done by a student at the Memorial University of Newfoundland—an example of the kind of research experience of undergraduates who study learning. Read about why he did the study and what he found.

Conditioned Emotional Reactions

www.ipfw.edu/nf1/abbott/web/Watson-Rayner.htm

Here you will find the original report about conditioned fear by Watson and Rayner published in 1917. The report is very readable and most remarkable. You will find the methodology that was used and many details of observations of Little Albert that were made over a number of weeks and months later.

Chapter 6

Memory

Of Things Remembered
... and Forgotten

CHAPTER OUTLINE

Personal Past Experience: Better Not to Leave Home without It

An interview in the *London Free Press* featured an expert on memory for personal past experience—episodic memory. The researcher commented on the power of this kind of memory—a truly remarkable advance in evolution. Normally, all humans are equipped at birth with the potential for laying down memory traces throughout life. As far as we can tell, only human beings have an awareness of time and can do "mental time travel" back into their past history and forward into the future.

Damage to memory for personal past experience may occur because of a blow to the head (as a result of an automobile or a sports collision), a disease (such as Alzheimer's), or a chronic use of designer drugs. Some patients are then unable to recall anything of their personal past history.

What is memory? What are the different kinds of remembering? Is memory accurate? Where are memories located? Why can't we remember more? Why do some people lose their memory? As you work your way through Chapter 6, Memory, you will discover the results of many fascinating studies designed to answer those questions and many more about how we remember and why we forget.

Source: Habib, M. (2000, March 24). Memories of past vital to your future. *London Free Press*, p. C10.

> **While memory is clearly far from perfect, it is also very impressive in several respects.**

Memory, people often say, is a very funny thing, and our life experience tends to confirm this. Have you ever forgotten a phone number you looked up in the directory before you could manage to dial it? Have you ever taken a wrong turn while driving because your memory told you that your destination was off in one direction, when, as you learned later, you should have gone the opposite way? Have you ever had your mind go blank when you were about to introduce two people to each other, or during an exam? Nearly everyone has had such experiences. In these situations we come face to face with the imperfect nature of our own memory—our cognitive system for storing and retrieving information.

We often retain vivid—and accurate—memories of events and scenes from months, years, or even decades in the past. Your high school days are still recent memories. As time passes and you begin your career, your high school days will become experiences of the distant past. If you come upon your high school graduation picture thirty years from now, will you recognize your friends' pictures? Without question! Bahrick, Bahrick, and Wittlinger (1975) found that even after thirty-four years, memory for faces of high school friends remained unimpaired. It is equally likely that you will still be able to ride a bicycle thirty years from now, even if you never go near one in the intervening years. In these and other respects, memory truly *is* impressive.

Because it is clearly a crucial aspect of cognition, memory has long occupied a central place in psychological research. In fact, memory was the focus of some of the earliest systematic work in the field—studies conducted more than one hundred years ago, in 1885, by Hermann Ebbinghaus. Using himself as a subject, Ebbinghaus memorized and then recalled hundreds of nonsense syllables—meaningless combinations of letters, such as TEG or XOT. Some of his findings about the nature of forgetting are valid even today. For example, he found that a good deal of the material we learn is forgotten very rapidly, and what remains is lost more slowly.

While Ebbinghaus's studies were ingenious in many respects, modern research on memory has gone far beyond these simple beginnings. It is probably safe to say that psychologists now know more about memory than about any other basic aspect of cognition. To provide you with an overview of this diverse and intriguing body of knowledge, we'll proceed in the following manner. First, we'll consider a basic model of human memory—one that is currently accepted by many psychologists. This model suggests that we actually possess three distinct memory storage systems. After describing the model, we'll examine these systems, indicating how each carries out the basic tasks of memory: (1) entering information into storage, (2) retaining such input for varying periods of time, and (3) retrieving it when it is needed. Next, we'll explore the operation of memory in natural contexts—how memory operates in daily life, outside the confines of the experimental laboratory. We will consider

> **Memory:** The capacity to retain and later retrieve information.

Calvin and Hobbes

by Bill Watterson

WHY IS IT THAT I CAN RECALL A CIGARETTE AD JINGLE FROM 25 YEARS AGO, BUT I CAN'T REMEMBER WHAT I JUST GOT UP TO DO?

© 1994 Watterson/Dist. by Universal Press Syndicate

When Memory Fails—or Does It?

As shown here, we sometimes forget what we are about to do just as we are about to do it, but can remember events that happened many years ago with vivid clarity.

Source: Universal Press Syndicate, 1994.

such issues as *autobiographical memory,* or memory of events and experiences in our own lives; *distortion* and *construction* in memory; and *eyewitness testimony.* We'll conclude by examining several memory disorders and what these disorders (and other research) tell us about the biological nature of memory.

Human Memory

Have you ever operated a personal computer? If so, you already know that computers, like people, have memories. Most have two different types of memory: a temporary working memory (known as random access memory), and a larger and more permanent memory (a hard drive). Do computers' memories operate like those of human beings? There are many differences. Unless you correctly specify the precise nature and location of information you want to find, computers are unable to recover it. They merely flash an error message such as NOT FOUND. In contrast, you can often find information in your own memory even on the basis of a partial description. Similarly, information that is lost from a computer is often permanently gone. In contrast, you can fail to remember a fact or information at one time but remember it readily at another. And you can often remember part of the information you want, even if you can't remember all of it. Clearly, human memory and computer memory are not identical.

Even so, many researchers have concluded that there is sufficient similarity between computer memory and human memory for the former to serve as a rough working model for the latter. Both types of memory, after all, must accomplish the same basic tasks: (1) **encoding**—converting information into a form that can be entered into memory; (2) **storage**—retaining information over varying periods of time; and (3) **retrieval**—locating and accessing specific information when it is needed later. Please don't misunderstand: The fact that computers and human memory deal with the same basic tasks in no way implies that they operate in an identical manner. They certainly do not. Thus, you should view this information-processing approach, with its emphasis on encoding, storage, and retrieval, mainly as a useful and convenient way of discussing memory—not as a claim that human memory and computer memory operate in exactly the same way.

A Basic Model of Human Memory

What kind of model of human memory does this general approach yield? One like that portrayed in Figure 6.1, which is based on an influential model of memory proposed by Atkinson & Shiffrin (1968) and is often referred to as the *modal model* of memory. Perhaps the most surprising aspect of this model is that it suggests that, in fact, we possess not one but *three* distinct systems for holding information. One of these, known as *sensory memory*, provides temporary storage of information brought by our senses. If you've ever watched someone wave a flashlight in a dark room and perceived what seem to be trails of light behind it, you are familiar with the operation of sensory memory.

A second type of memory described in the Atkinson and Shiffrin model is *short-term memory*. It is now more commonly referred to as *working memory*. This change in phrasing is a result of a very detailed elaboration of the character of short-term memory furnished by Baddeley (1992), which we will describe shortly. For now it is enough to know that short-term working memory allows us to retain, and give conscious attention to, small amounts of information for brief periods of time. It is this memory system that permits you to hold a just-looked-up telephone number long enough to dial it without looking back at the source.

Encoding: The process through which information is converted into a form that can be entered into memory.

Storage: The process through which information is retained in memory.

Retrieval: The process through which information stored in memory is located.

Figure 6.1
Human Memory: How Psychologists See It

Most psychologists accept a model of human memory like the one shown here. This model involves three memory holding systems plus mechanisms that move information from one system to another.

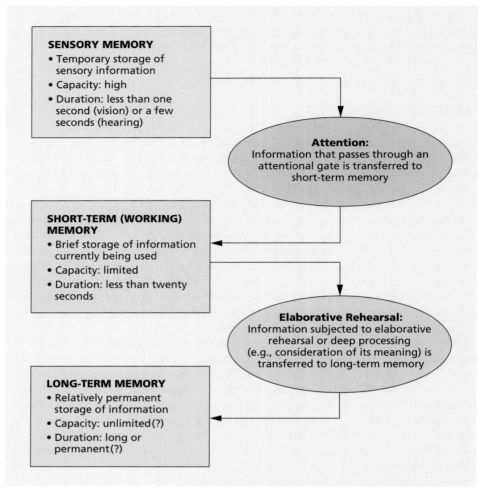

SENSORY MEMORY
• Temporary storage of sensory information
• Capacity: high
• Duration: less than one second (vision) or a few seconds (hearing)

Attention:
Information that passes through an attentional gate is transferred to short-term memory

SHORT-TERM (WORKING) MEMORY
• Brief storage of information currently being used
• Capacity: limited
• Duration: less than twenty seconds

Elaborative Rehearsal:
Information subjected to elaborative rehearsal or deep processing (e.g., consideration of its meaning) is transferred to long-term memory

LONG-TERM MEMORY
• Relatively permanent storage of information
• Capacity: unlimited(?)
• Duration: long or permanent(?)

Our third memory system, *long-term memory*, allows us to retain vast amounts of information for very long periods of time. It is this type of memory system that permits you to remember events that happened a few hours ago, yesterday, last month—or many years in the past. And it is long-term memory that allows you to remember the capital of your province or the nation, the name of the prime minister, and the information in this book, and to bring it into consciousness when it is needed—for example, during an examination.

How does information move from one memory system to another? Atkinson and Shiffrin proposed that this involves the operation of active control processes that act as filters, determining which information will be retained. Information in sensory memory enters short-term working memory when it becomes the focus of our attention; sensory impressions that do not engage attention fade and quickly disappear. Thus **selective attention**—our ability to pay attention to only some aspects of the world around us while largely ignoring others—plays a crucial role in memory (Johnston, McCann, & Remington, 1995; Posner & Peterson, 1990).

Selective attention is also influential in determining what is transferred from short-term working memory to long-term memory. Simply repeating information silently to ourselves, a process known as *maintenance rehearsal*, will hold information in working memory. However, it will not move the information into long-term memory. Material moves from working information to long-term memory if we

Selective Attention: Our ability to pay attention to only some aspects of the world around us while largely ignoring others.

engage in a control process known as *elaborative rehearsal*—when we think about something's meaning and relate it to other information already in long-term memory. Unless we engage in such cognitive effort, information in short-term memory fades quickly away and is lost

Types of Information in Memory

What types of information are stored in long-term memory? After careful study, psychologists have concluded that most, if not all, information in memory can be placed in one of three distinct categories.

Semantic Memory in Action
People who are highly successful on television quiz shows like *Jeopardy* have stored a tremendous amount of general knowledge in semantic memory.

The first kind of information can be described as involving an individual's general abstract knowledge about the world, and it is described by the term **semantic memory**. What is the population of Canada? Is Alberta larger or smaller than New Brunswick? Are clams crustaceans or mollusks? And, whatever their place in the animal kingdom, how long does it take to cook them? The answers to these and countless other questions are contained in semantic memory. Semantic memory allows us to represent and mentally operate on objects or situations that are not present to our senses. As one expert on memory puts it (Tulving, 1993, p. 687), "The owner of a semantic memory system can think about things that are not here now."

A second type of information we retain relates to specific events that we have experienced personally. This is **episodic memory** (sometimes known as autobiographical memory), which allows us, in a sense, to travel back in time and retrieve personal experiences we have had. It is your episodic memory that allows you to answer questions such as: When was the last time you went to a movie? How did you feel on the day of your most recent graduation? What was it like to drive a car for the first time? In essence, your episodic memory contains a record of the things you've seen, done, and heard, along with information about when they happened.

Endel Tulving
Rotman Research Institute

Finally, we retain information relating to the performance of various tasks. Do you know how to ice skate? Tie a necktie? Ride a bicycle? If you do, then you are well aware of the operation of our third type of memory, known as **procedural memory**—a memory system that holds information that is *implicit* and cannot be put into words, but nevertheless underlies our ability to perform skilled tasks.

As you can readily guess, we often require—and use—information of all three types at once. Consider what happens when you take an examination. First, you draw on facts stored in semantic memory. Second, you use complex motor skills such as writing, which are represented in procedural memory. Third, as you take the exam you may recover from your episodic memory system experiences you have had on other exams. For instance, you may remember that on your last exam, you changed many of your answers at the last minute and your score was lower than usual. This may cause you to refrain from changing answers on this test. In many situations, then, we use all three types of memory at once.

How do we know that these different forms of memory exist? One reason is that studies using brain imaging techniques, such as the PET scan described in Chapter 2, indicate different brain regions are active when individuals attempt to recall general information (semantic memory) as opposed to information they acquired in a specific context (episodic memory) (e.g., Kounious, 1996). Another source of information is provided by memory disabilities that emerge after brain injury. The **Canadian Focus** feature provides a description of an individual who lost his episodic memory as a result of brain injury.

Semantic Memory: The content of our general, abstract knowledge about the world.

Episodic Memory: Memories of events that we have experienced personally (sometimes termed autobiographical memory).

Procedural Memory: A memory system that retains information we cannot readily express verbally—for example, information necessary to perform skilled motor activities such as riding a bicycle.

Canadian Focus

The Story of a Man without Episodic Memory

For more than ten years, researchers in the Unit for Memory Disorders at the University of Toronto have been studying a man with a quite remarkable memory deficit. In October 1981, K.C., as he is known in the psychological literature, ran off the road on his motorcycle on his way home from work and received a severe head injury. He was unconscious for seventy-two hours and in intensive care for a month. As a consequence of the accident, he suffered very extensive memory impairment. In this discussion we are going to focus on only one aspect of the memory problems of K.C.—his loss of episodic memory (Tulving, 1989; Tulving, Schacter, McLachlan, & Moscovitch, 1988).

If you were to meet K.C., you would find him to be cooperative and responsive. He has normal intelligence. His speech and reading abilities are largely unimpaired. He has a reasonable knowledge of the world and of events that occurred prior to his injury. He also has memories about experiences that he had before the accident. His memory tends to be better for events that are remoter from the time of his accident. There is, however, a peculiar character to his descriptions of these experiences: They are strangely detached and factual, as if he were describing his past from the point of view of an observer rather than a participant. He knows that his family owns a cottage in Ontario and that he has spent substantial time there, but he can recall nothing about any experiences he had at the cottage. He knows that he has owned a car and two motorcycles, and can even provide physical descriptions of these vehicles, but he is quite unable to provide information about any specific trips or experiences that he had with these vehicles. He knows that he can play chess and change a tire, but he has no recollection of any particular chess game or any tire-changing episode. In short, he has a reasonable knowledge of what he can and cannot do, and of things he has done and places he has gone, but he has no recollection of the subjective experience associated with the learning or doing of any of these things.

The case of K.C. provides compelling support for the claims of Tulving and his associates that episodic memory can be distinguished from semantic and procedural memory. K.C. has retained substantial factual material about the nonpersonal aspects of events that took place prior to the accident—his semantic memory is relatively intact. He has lost, however, all information about the personal experiences he had as an individual in living through this period of his life—his episodic memory has vanished.

KEY QUESTIONS

- What tasks are involved in encoding, storage, and retrieval?
- What are sensory memory, working memory, and long-term memory?
- What are semantic memory, episodic memory, and procedural memory?

Our Basic Memory Systems:
Sensory Memory, Working Memory, and Long-Term Memory

You should now have a basic idea of how psychologists think about—and study—human memory. We will now take a closer look at the three kinds of memory described briefly above—sensory memory, short-term working memory, and long-term memory. We will examine how each system carries out the basic tasks of memory—encoding information (that is, entering it into storage), retaining such information, and retrieving it when it is needed.

Sensory Memory

We have to make sense of the information that is continuously bombarding our senses. **Sensory memory** is the memory system responsible for holding representations of information from our senses very briefly—just long enough to determine that some aspect of this input is worthy of further attention. How much can sensory memory hold? And how long does such information last? Existing evidence suggests that the capacity of sensory memory is quite large—indeed, it may hold fleeting representations of virtually everything we see, hear, taste, smell, or feel (Reeves & Sperling, 1986). Visual sensory memory seems to last for less than a second, while acoustic sensory memory lasts for no more than a few seconds (Cowan, 1984). What is important is that sensory memory endures long enough for us to transfer that which engages our attention into a second memory system—short-term working memory.

Visual Sensory Memory

Visual sensory memory holds an image, such as a flash of lightning, for only a fraction of a second—just long enough for us to determine if it is worthy of further attention.

K E Y   *QUESTIONS*

- What kind of information does sensory memory hold?
- How long does such information last in sensory memory?

Working Memory

Our second memory system is referred to by Atkinson and Shiffrin as *short-term memory*. As we mentioned previously, this stage of memory is now usually described as **working memory**—a term introduced by Baddeley to more appropriately reflect its structure and function. Working memory holds a limited amount of information for a very limited period of time. Despite its limitations, working memory, like sensory memory, is very important. In a sense, it is the "workbench" of consciousness—the "place" where information we are using right now is held and processed. It is this memory system that allows us to hold the name given by a stranger, phoning for an absent roommate, long enough to write it down, or to retain the call number of a book as we search for its location in a library.

THE STRUCTURE OF WORKING MEMORY   According to Baddely (1992), working memory is a dynamic, interactive memory system that allows us to hold visual and auditory information while we carry out other behaviours. It allows us the opportunity to ponder the importance of the information and decide whether the information is significant enough to be committed to long-term memory. The working memory system consists of two storage components and a controller: (1) a *phonological loop* that processes information relating to the sounds of words, (2) a *visuospatial sketchpad* that processes visual and spatial information (i.e., information about the visual appearance of objects such as colour and shape and where they are located in space), and (3) a *central executive mechanism* that supervises and coordinates the operation of the two storage components.

The **visuospatial sketchpad** allows salient information about the visual and spatial aspects of our immediate surroundings to be briefly retained—that we put our coffee cup on the hall table when we bent down to collect the newly arrived mail, or that the bread knife remains on the counter as we search the refrigerator for the butter. We also use this store to perform imagery-type tasks such as naming the letter of the alphabet that would be produced by mentally rotating the letter *d* 180 degrees.

Sensory Memory: A memory system that retains representations of sensory input for extremely brief periods of time.

Working Memory: A memory system that holds limited amounts of information for relatively short periods of time.

Visuospatial Sketchpad: A component of working memory that allows us to hold important information about visual and spatial memory for a short period of time.

The **phonological store** allows us to hold salient speech or speech-like information, for about two seconds—enough time to consciously interpret or relate the material being held to preceding speech sounds. Information in the phonological store has to be continuously refreshed to be held. If you have ever tried to keep a phone number or someone's name in mind by saying it to yourself over and over again, you are familiar with this facility. Only by rehearsing the items—saying them to yourself—can you hold them in the phonological store for more than a second or two.

The **central executive mechanism** (what Atkinson and Shiffrin would refer to as a control process) determines what material will be directed into the visuospatial sketchpad. It also regulates the flow of information into the phonological loop, and determines whether it is to be refreshed and held in the loop, or discarded.

How do we know there are separate and distinct visual and phonological subsystems in working memory? Experiments in which participants perform a task that requires use of the visuospatial sketchpad, such as memorizing a difficult chess configuration, reveal that performance does not suffer if at the same time participants are required to attend to speech-like sounds. If, however, subjects attend to visual stimuli—even if they are told they can ignore what is being presented—performance is severely impaired. The exact opposite interference pattern is evident if participants have to hold information in the phonological store and attend to visual and speech-like sounds (Baddeley, 1990, 1992). Two tasks can often be managed if they engage separate working-memory systems, but if responsibilities for both tasks fall on the same single system, there is memory failure. These findings point to the existence of two separate and independent subsystems in working memory. Additional compelling evidence is provided by studies using *neuroimaging* techniques that scan people's brains while they work on various tasks. These studies indicate that spatial and phonological information are processed in different areas of the brain (e.g., Awh et al., 1996; Jonides, 1995).

We will comment further on the role of the visuospatial sketchpad when we discuss mental imagery in Chapter 7. In the remainder of this section we will focus on some experimental evidence that illustrates the nature of the short-term phonological store and its relationship to long-term memory. Studies of the serial position curve and word-length and word-similarity effects are particularly informative in this respect.

THE SERIAL POSITION CURVE Suppose that someone read you a list of about twenty unrelated words and asked you to recall as many as possible in any order you wished. Which words would you be most likely to remember? Research findings indicate that you would be more likely to remember words at the beginning and at the end of the list than words in the middle (see Figure 6.2). Why does this effect, known as the **serial position curve**, occur? The answer is that two memory systems interact to generate a curve of this shape (Postman & Phillips, 1965). You remember the last words you heard quite well—a *recency* effect—because they are still in the phonological store of working memory when you are asked to recall them. You remember words at the start of the list better because you are able to engage in a measure of elaborative rehearsal at the start of processing, and get them into long-term memory, before the flood of incoming words becomes overwhelming. There is very little opportunity to encode words in the middle of the list, and they have vanished from working memory. The result? You remember few of them until the list has been presented many times. The serial position curve, then, provides support for the existence of two distinct memory systems, one of which retains information only for short periods of time.

Phonological Store: A component of working memory that permits us to hold speech or speech-like material for about two seconds.

Central Executive Mechanism: A control process that regulates the operations of the phonological loop and the visuospatial sketchpad.

Serial Position Curve: The greater accuracy of recall of words or other information early and late in a list, than words or information in the middle of the list.

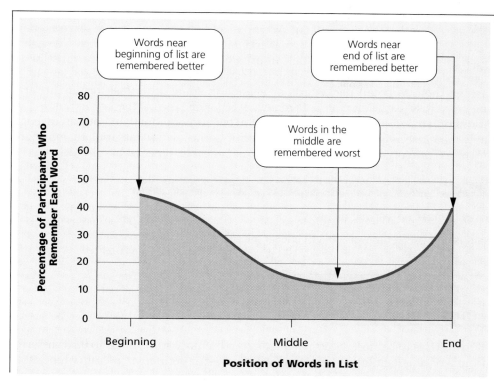

Figure 6.2
The Serial Position Curve

When people try to recall a list of unrelated words, they usually remember more words from the beginning and end of the list than from the middle. This serial position curve provides evidence for the existence of two distinct memory systems: a short-term working memory and a more durable long-term memory.

WORD-LENGTH AND WORD-SIMILARITY EFFECTS Direct evidence of a unique phonological component in working memory is provided by experimentation on the word-length and word-similarity effects. The *word-similarity effect* refers to the repeated finding that it is more difficult to hold words that sound alike in working memory than words that have distinctively different sounds. Why does this occur? The answer is that the phonological store component of working memory is speech-based. Similar sounding items get confused and the resulting interference impairs retention. The *word-length effect* refers to the fact that memory span for immediate recall is greater for lists of short words than for lists of longer words (e.g., Longoni, Richardson, & Aiello, 1993). The phonological-store component of working memory can only retain speech-based material for a second or two unless these materials are refreshed by silent rehearsal. Long words take more time to pronounce and this limits the number that can be rehearsed.

BOUNDARIES OF WORKING MEMORY We have noted that unless information in the phonological store is rehearsed, it is lost in a second or two. What we have not said anything about is the number of items that can held in working memory. Research shows that on average about seven, plus or minus two, separate pieces of information can be held in short-term working memory—and as we have noted, this nicely encompasses the average seven-digit telephone number. Can this limit be exceeded? It can be if steps are taken to compact the excess material in a clever fashion. Consider the following list of letters: RNCATAFNPDNVTCPMCR. After hearing or reading it once, would you remember it? Probably not. You would most likely recall seven plus or minus two letters. But suppose the letters were reorganized in the following fashion: CNR, NAFTA, NDP, CTV, RCMP. Could you remember them now? The chances are much better that you would. The many separate individual letters have been compacted into a smaller number of meaningful unitary **chunks**—in this case, well-known initials and acronyms. These are only five in number, well within the span of working memory. This process of chunking permits us to extend the overall grasp of working memory without violating the seven plus or minus two limit imposed by the system (Miller, 1956).

Chunk: Stimuli perceived as a single unit or a meaningful grouping. Most people can retain seven to nine chunks of information in short-term memory at a given time.

What can be said in the way of summary about short-term working memory? It seems clear that the visuospatial sketchpad and phonological store serve as short-term repositories for incoming visual and verbal information to which we wish to give attention. It is also clear that information in working memory must be rehearsed or it will be lost. Preventing individuals from rehearsing, for example, by asking them to count backwards or engage in some other task results in rapid memory loss (e.g., Peterson & Peterson, 1959). Rehearsal is the key to holding information in working memory—and if you encounter more than you can manageably rehearse, you have to either commit some of the material to long-term memory, or reorganize the material into manageable, rehearsable chunks.

KEY QUESTIONS

- What three components make up working memory?

- What are the serial position curve, the word-length effect, and the word-similarity effect?

Long-Term Memory

Long-Term Memory: A memory system for the retention of large amounts of information over long periods of time.

If material is to be stored permanently in our memory store, it has to be transferred from working memory to **long-term memory**—our permanent memory repository. Before we go on to describe how information is entered into long-term memory, it would be useful to have a look at the various methods psychologists use to gather information about memory. Please see the **Research Process** section below.

The Research Process:
Methods Used to Study Memory

We noted earlier that when Ebbinghaus began the systematic study of memory more than one hundred years ago, he used himself as a subject and studied his ability to retain meaningless nonsense syllables. Since those early days, psychologists have developed many additional techniques for studying memory. Why many? Because, as we've already noted, there appear to be several kinds of memory, and a method useful for studying one type may not be ideal for studying another. We will now provide you with an overview of some of the major methods used in research on memory, explaining which methods are used to study which type of memory.

Free recall and recognition   These methods are used to study memory for *explicit factual information* (episodic memory). When you are planning a Friday night party, a decision is made about requirements: chips, beer, bottled water, dip, vegetables, napkins, and so on. If you do not write down a list of your needs, you will be faced with a *free recall* situation when you get to the shopping area. You have to try and remember each of the individual things you were supposed to pick up. Tasks of this type are used commonly in research studies on memory for factual material. In such studies, participants are presented with a list of words and later asked to recall them in any order. The more they get right, the higher their performance. In *recognition* tests of memory, participants are not asked to generate material. They are exposed to previously presented words or other stimuli in the company of other words or stimuli that are new. They are required to differentiate between the items originally presented and new items. The more original items they identify correctly, the better their memory score.

What Was That I Needed?

If you do not take a list when you go shopping, you will be forced to use free recall to remember each of the individual items you need.

Sentence verification The time required to verify sentences is commonly used to study *semantic memory*. We all have a vast store of information that we cannot remember acquiring at a specific time or place. For instance, when did you learn that canaries are yellow birds that sing, or that British Columbia is west of Ontario? In all probability you cannot recall when it was. Such information is a part of a general store of knowledge we possess. Psychologists use *sentence verification tasks* to try and map out the structure of semantic memory. For example, it has been found that it takes less time to verify that a canary is yellow or that it sings than to verify it is an animal. Why? Because memory of immediate physical attributes appears to be stored in closer proximity to our representation of a canary in semantic memory than memory of the general properties it shares with other organisms. Sentence-verification tasks can provide important insights into the way in which semantic information is structured in memory.

Priming: Measuring memory for information we cannot report verbally Information is stored in memory that cannot be readily described in words—for instance, information necessary for skilled actions (e.g., riding a bicycle, playing the piano). There are also other types of information in memory of which we are quite unaware; it's there, but we don't know we possess it. Such memory is sometimes described as *implicit* memory, because it is present, but cannot be articulated. What measures can be used to demonstrate implicit memory effects? One technique involves *priming*. In this procedure, research participants are first exposed to some stimuli (e.g., a long list of words, such as *hotel, river, stadium*). After a passage of time during which participants are required to complete an unrelated task, they are shown parts of some of the words with which they were originally presented (e.g., *hot, riv, stad*), along with other parts of words they have not seen, and asked to complete the words as rapidly as possible. The missing words are filled in more quickly if they have been seen previously. Yet, if asked, participants are typically unaware that they saw these words earlier. They believe they simply guessed to form the completed word. Thus priming is one way of demonstrating that memory holds information we can't readily articulate.

Neuroimaging: Techniques for studying the biological basis of memory Neuroimaging techniques involve forming images (scans) of peoples' brains as they work on various tasks, and have been described in Chapter 2. For example, one commonly used procedure involves PET imaging. A harmless amount of a radioactive substance is injected into the bloodstream, and research participants are asked to perform various memory tasks. Because the areas of the brain that are active require more blood, we can track the radioactive materials and learn what areas of the brain are actively involved in performing memory operations.

These are not the only methods used by psychologists to study memory—far from it. But they are among the most basic, and play a role in much of the information we will present throughout this chapter.

LONG-TERM MEMORY: ITS BASIC OPERATION How does information enter long-term memory from working memory? The answer involves a process we have already discussed: rehearsal. In this case, though, the rehearsal does not consist simply of repeating what we wish to remember, as in restating a phone number over and over again. Rather, for information to enter long-term memory, **elaborative rehearsal** seems to be required. This is rehearsal requiring significant cognitive effort, such as thinking about the meaning of the new information and attempting to relate it to information already in memory (see Figure 6.3). For example, if you wish to enter into long-term memory the facts and findings presented in a section of this chapter, it is not sufficient merely to rehearse them over and over again. Instead, you should think about what they mean and how they relate to things you already know.

If elaborative rehearsal is required for information to enter long-term memory, then anything that interferes with such rehearsal should also interfere with long-term memory. Many factors produce such effects. For example, drugs such as alcohol can impair long-term memory when consumed in sufficient quantity (Birnbaum & Parker, 1977). It is also the case that an individual's mood state can prevent the necessary degree of elaborative rehearsal required to ensure effective long-term retention of material, especially if the mood state is one of depression and there is an attendant loss of energy, motivation, and concentration difficulties (e.g., Burt, Zembar, & Niederehe, 1995). We will have more to say about the effect of mood on memory in later sections of this chapter.

LEVELS OF PROCESSING: COGNITIVE EFFORT AND LONG-TERM MEMORY We have been emphasizing the importance of elaborative rehearsal in committing information to long-term memory. Now let's have a more systematic look at the evi-

The Role of Rehearsal

In order to pass from short-term to long-term memory, information must be rehearsed repeatedly.

Elaborative Rehearsal: Rehearsal in which the meaning of information is considered and the information is related to other knowledge already present in memory.

Figure 6.3
Entering Information into Long-Term Memory

In order for information to move from working memory to long-term memory, *elaborative rehearsal* is required. Such rehearsal involves thinking about the meaning of new information and attempting to relate it to information already in memory. If this cognitive effort is not expended, the new information may fail to enter long-term memory and be rapidly forgotten.

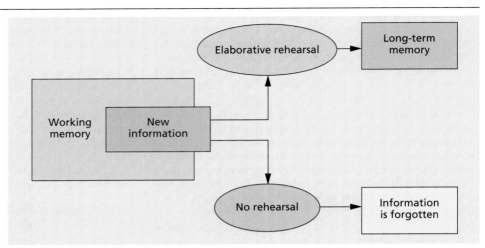

Levels of Processing View: A view of memory suggesting that the greater the effort expended in processing information, the more readily it will be recalled at later times.

dence to justify the claim that what we do with information determines how well it will be remembered by considering the **levels of processing view**. Like many influential models of memory processes, it emerged from research carried out at the University of Toronto. Craik and Lockhart (1972), who were the proponents of this approach, suggested that rather than concentrating on the *structure* of memory and the different systems it involves, it might be more useful to concentrate on the *processes* that contribute to remembering. They noted that information can be processed in several different ways, ranging from relatively superficial *shallow processing* to more effortful and lasting *deep processing*. Shallow processing might consist of merely repeating a word or making a simple sensory judgment about it—for example, do two words or letters look alike? A deeper level of processing might involve more complex comparisons—for example, do two words rhyme? A much deeper level of processing would include attention to meaning—for example, do two words have the same meaning? Does a word make sense when used in a specific sentence?

Considerable evidence suggests that the deeper the level of processing that takes place when we encounter new materials, the more likely the materials are to enter long-term memory. In one well-known study, Craik and Tulving (1975) presented unrelated words and asked participants one of three kinds of questions about each word: Was the word written in capital or lower-case letters? Did the word rhyme with another word? Did the word fit within a given sentence? After answering a large number of such questions, participants were given a recognition test for the words that had been presented. They were asked to pick out the words seen previously from a set of words that included both old and new words. The results offered clear support for the levels of processing view. The deeper the level of processing performed by subjects, the more accurately their recognition of previously encountered words (see Figure 6.4).

Why does deeper and more effortful processing of information lead to better long-term memory? One possibility is that such cognitive effort leads us to encode more features of the items in question. This, in turn, makes it easier to locate the information later.

Although research findings strongly support the levels of processing model, there are some difficulties with the model that cannot be overlooked. For example, it is difficult to specify in advance just what constitutes a deep rather than a shallow level of processing. It is also not clear that someone can read a word over and over again and not be aware of, or think about, its meaning. In fact, several forms of processing (such as acoustic and semantic) may occur at once. So it is difficult to speak about discrete levels of processing.

Despite such problems, there can be little doubt that the levels of processing view has added to our understanding of long-term memory, and especially to our knowledge of how information is entered into this system.

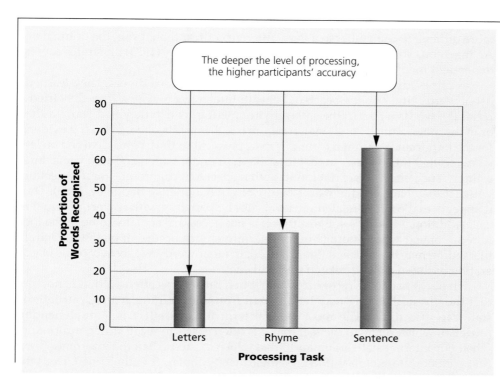

The deeper the level of processing, the higher participants' accuracy

Figure 6.4
Levels of Processing and Memory

Individuals were asked one of three kinds of questions with respect to unrelated words. These questions required varying levels of processing. The deeper the level of processing required, the more accurately the participants could later identify the words.

Source: Based on data from Craik and Tulving, 1975.

RETRIEVAL As noted earlier, the limitations of working memory are all too obvious: it has limited capacity, and information is quickly lost unless it is continually rehearsed. Long-term memory, of course, does not have these problems. It has a seemingly limitless capacity and can retain information for very long periods, perhaps indefinitely. Is it, then, a perfect system? Unfortunately, no. All too often we are unable to remember information we need just when we need it. Only later—maddeningly!—does it sometimes appear effortlessly in our mind (Payne, 1987). What is the cause of this? The answer involves the process of *retrieval*—our ability to locate information that has previously been stored in memory.

Where long-term memory is concerned, it is difficult to separate retrieval from the issue of storage—the way information is initially placed in long-term memory. Storage plays an important role in determining how readily information can later be retrieved. In general, the better organized materials are, the easier they are to retrieve (Bower et al., 1969). One key to the effective retrieval of information from long-term memory, then, is organization. Organizing information requires extra effort, but it appears that the benefits in terms of later ease of retrieval make this effort well worthwhile.

Retrieval cues: Stimuli that help us remember Imagine that after an absence of several years, you return to a place where you used to live. On your arrival, memories of days gone by come flooding back, with no apparent effort on your part to bring them to mind. You remember incidents you had totally forgotten, conversations with people you haven't seen in years, even the weather during your last visit. Have you ever had this kind of experience? If so, you are already familiar with the effects of what psychologists term **retrieval cues**. These are stimuli that are associated with information stored in memory and so can help bring it to mind at times when it cannot be recalled spontaneously. Such cues can be aspects of the external environment—a place, sights or sounds, even smells. Indeed, some evidence suggests that odours are particularly effective in evoking memories of events in our lives (Richardson & Zucco, 1989).

Many studies point to the strong impact that retrieval cues have on long-term memory. Perhaps the most intriguing research on this topic involves the concept of

Retrieval Cues: Stimuli associated with information stored in memory that can aid in its retrieval.

context-dependent memory: the fact that material learned in one environment is more difficult to remember in a very different context than it is in the original one. An ingenious study performed by Godden and Baddeley (1975) illustrates context-dependent memory.

In this study, the participants were practised deep-sea divers. They learned a list of words either on the beach or beneath fifteen feet of water; then they tried to recall the words either in the same environment in which they had learned them or in the other setting. As shown in Figure 6.5, the results offered striking evidence for the importance of context—in this case, physical setting. Words learned on land were recalled much better in that location than under water, and vice versa. Interestingly, such effects were not found with respect to recognition—merely deciding whether they had seen the words before or not (Godden & Baddeley, 1980). Thus, it appears that context-related retrieval cues help mainly with respect to actual recall. Additional findings suggest that it is not necessary actually to be in the location or context where storage in long-term memory occurred; merely imagining this setting may be sufficient (Smith, 1979). In other words, we seem capable of generating our own context-related retrieval cues.

Finally, it has to be recognized that when retrieval is attempted, it is not only that the physical setting may be different from the learning setting, our internal state can also differ. The most general term for this effect is **state-dependent retrieval**, which refers to the fact that it is often easier to recall stored information when our internal state is similar to that which existed when the information was first entered into memory (Eich, Weingartner, Stillman, & Gillin, 1975). Does this mean that if you consume very large amounts of coffee while studying for an exam you should also drink enough coffee to ensure that the effects of caffeine are present during the time you are writing the exam? According to state-dependent retrieval theory, the answer is *yes*, but you should bear in mind that, as with context-related memory, state-dependent retrieval seems to apply only to free recall; recognition is not necessarily enhanced.

Context-Dependent Memory: The fact that information entered into memory in one context or setting is easier to recall in that context than in others.

State-Dependent Retrieval: Information tends to be easier to recall when our internal state is similar to that which existed when the information was first entered into memory.

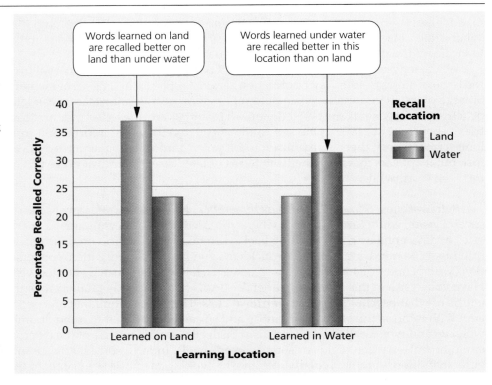

Figure 6.5
Context-Dependent Memory

Participants learned a list of words either on the beach or when under water. Later, they recalled the words more successfully in the same physical setting (context) where the learning took place.

Source: Based on data from Godden and Baddeley, 1975.

The most compelling evidence that variations in internal states can significantly influence retention comes from what are known as **mood-dependent memory** studies. As you would expect, these studies are based on the assumption that recovery of information in a given mood state will be influenced by the degree to which you were in a similar mood state during the time when the material was originally acquired (Eich, Macauley, & Lam, 1997). Mood-dependent memory effects are well established, but research findings suggest that the most distinctive effects occur if we are in a particularly pronounced mood state when we self-generate the items being entered into memory—rather than having them presented to us (Eich,1995; Eich, Macaulay, & Ryan, 1994).

The concept of mood-dependent memory effects has important implications. It helps explain why depressed persons have difficulty in remembering times when they felt better (Schacter & Kihlstrom, 1989). Their existing very negative mood favours recovery of information they entered into memory when in the same mood—and this information is associated with states of depression. This is unfortunate because being able to remember what it felt like to not be depressed can play an important part in successful treatment of this problem.

KEY QUESTIONS

- How does information move from short-term working memory to long-term memory?
- What role do levels of processing and organization play in long-term memory?
- What are retrieval cues and what role do they play in long-term memory?
- How are state-dependent retrieval and mood-dependent memory related to context-dependent memory?

Critical Thinking

With the right retrieval cues and reinstatement of the appropriate context, memories of seemingly forgotten experiences sometimes inundate the mind. Does this mean that nothing is ever forgotten and that with the appropriate retrieval cues any memory can be recovered?

Forgetting from Long-Term Memory

When are we most aware of memory? Typically, when it fails—when we are unable to remember information that we need at a particular moment. Often, it seems to let us down just when we need it most—for instance, during an exam! Why does this occur? Why is information entered into long-term memory sometimes lost, at least in part, with the passage of time? Many explanations have been offered. Here we'll focus on the two that have received the most attention. Then we'll examine a far different view of forgetting—repression—and its bearing on the tragedy of childhood sexual abuse (Loftus, 1993).

The Trace-Decay Hypothesis

Perhaps the simplest view of forgetting is that information entered into long-term memory fades or decays with the passage of time. Although the **trace-decay hypothesis** seems to fit with our subjective experience, many studies indicate that the amount of forgetting is not simply a function of how much time has elapsed; rather,

Mood-Dependent Memory: The finding that what we remember while in a given mood may be determined, in part, by what we learned when previously in that same mood.

Trace-Decay Hypothesis: A theory of forgetting that assumes information in long-term memory fades or decays with the passage of time.

what happens during that period of time is crucial (e.g., Jenkins & Dallenbach, 1924). For instance, in one unusual study, Minami and Dallenbach (1946) taught cockroaches to avoid a dark compartment by giving them an electric shock whenever they entered it. After the subjects had mastered this simple task, they were either restrained in a paper cone or permitted to wander around a darkened cage at will. Results indicated that the insects permitted to move about showed more forgetting over a given period of time than did those who were restrained. Thus, what the roaches did in between learning and testing for memory was more important than the mere passage of time. Perhaps even more surprising, other studies indicated that recall sometimes improves over time (e.g., Erdelyi & Kleinbad, 1978). So, early on, psychologists rejected the notion that forgetting stems from passive decay of memories over time and turned, instead, to the views we'll consider next.

Forgetting as a Result of Interference

If forgetting is not a function of the passage of time and the weakening of materials stored in memory, then what is its source? The answer currently accepted by most psychologists focuses on *interference* between items of information stored in memory. Such interference can take two different forms. In **retroactive interference**, information being learned now interferes with information already present in memory. If learning the rules of a new board game causes you to forget the rules of a similar game you learned to play last year, you are the victim of retroactive interference. In contrast, **proactive interference** occurs when previously learned information interferes with information you are acquiring at present. If information you acquired about operating an old VCR interferes with your ability to operate a new one that has very different controls, you are experiencing proactive interference (see Figure 6.6).

A large body of evidence offers support for the view that interference plays a key role in forgetting from long-term memory (e.g., Tulving & Psotka, 1971). For example, in many laboratory studies, the more similar the words or nonsense syllables learned on different lists, the more interference among them, and the poorer participants' ability to remember these materials (Gruneberg, Morris, & Sykes, 1988). What remains unclear, however, is precisely how interference causes forgetting. Does it actively push information out of memory? Or does it merely impede our ability to retrieve information? A final answer to such questions must await the completion of additional research.

Retroactive Interference: Interference with retention of information already present in memory by new information being entered into memory.

Proactive Interference: Interference with the learning or storage of current information by information previously entered into memory.

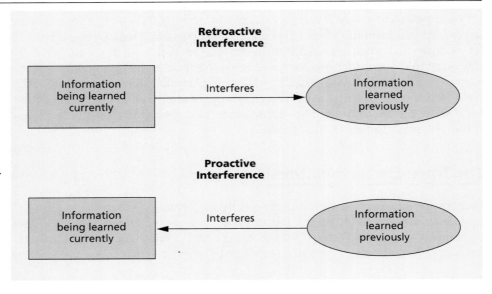

Figure 6.6
Retroactive and Proactive Interference: Important Factors in Forgetting

In retroactive interference, information currently being learned interferes with retention of previously acquired information. In proactive interference, information learned previously interferes with retention of new information.

Repression

In 1991, George Franklin Sr. was convicted of sexually attacking and then murdering an eight-year-old girl who was a friend of his daughter. The crime had occurred in 1969—more than twenty years earlier. How had he escaped prosecution for all these years, and why was he finally placed on trial so long after this tragic crime? The answer is that in 1990 his daughter Eileen came forward and accused her father of being the murderer. Further—and this is directly related to our discussion of forgetting—she claimed that she had not come forward sooner because she had not remembered these events until shortly before she made her accusations. How could she "forget" such a traumatic event for so long a period?

Repression and Memory

In the trial of George Franklin, his daughter testified that she witnessed the murder, which had taken place more than twenty years earlier. She claimed that she had repressed the memory in the years since the traumatic event.

One answer is provided by a third theory of forgetting from long-term memory—the theory of **repression**. According to this theory, which plays a key role in Freud's views of personality and mental illness (see Chapters 12 and 14), traumatic events such as the one described here are so shocking that all memory of them is forced from consciousness—*repressed*—into hidden recesses of the unconsciousness. There, the memories lie hidden until they are brought back into consciousness by some specific event—for example, by the probings of a therapist. In short, the theory of repression suggests that we forget some information and experiences because we find them too frightening or threatening to bear.

The existence of repression is accepted by a good many psychologists and psychiatrists, as well as by society at large (Loftus & Herzog, 1991). Thus, Eileen Franklin's charges carried great weight with the jury who tried her father—so much weight, in fact, that he was convicted primarily on this evidence. Although his conviction was to be subsequently overturned, the Franklin case stands as a good example of many recent dramatic trials focusing on charges of *early childhood sexual abuse*. In these trials, repression has been put forward to explain the fact that the victims failed to remember their terrible experiences until many years after they occurred. The suggestion is that only when these individuals were exposed to careful questioning by trained therapists did memories of their abuse during early childhood come flooding back into consciousness. Such trials, and the accounts of the people involved, certainly make for dramatic reading. Indeed, in recent years, many public figures—including entertainers and famous athletes—have reported the sudden emergence of traumatic memories of childhood abuse.

The growing frequency of these reports raises a question: Are the frightening "memories" always—or even usually—accurate? Did the people reporting them actually experience the devastating events? This is a complex question, because often the alleged events occurred so long ago that concrete, objective evidence of them is difficult to obtain. In addition, as noted recently by Loftus (1993), a leading expert on memory, there are reasons for viewing at least some of these claims with a healthy degree of skepticism.

First, and most important, there is little scientific evidence for the principle of repression. Most support for the theory of repression derives from case studies. While these are often quite impressive, they do not, as we saw in Chapter 1, generally provide conclusive evidence on the issues they address. Indeed, so weak is present evidence for the existence of repression that one researcher (Holmes, 1990, p. 97) has suggested that use of the concept of repression in psychological reports should be preceded by the following statement: "Warning: The concept of repression has not been validated with experimental research and its use may be hazardous to the accurate interpretation of behaviour."

Second, the fact that many therapists believe strongly in the existence of repression and its role in psychological disorders indicates that, in at least some instances, therapists may act in ways that lead clients to report repressed memories even if they don't really have them. For example, a therapist who believes in the

Repression: A theory of forgetting that suggests that memories of experiences or events we find threatening are sometimes pushed out of consciousness so that they can no longer be recalled.

powerful impact of repressed memories might say something like this: "You know, in my experience a lot of people who are struggling with the same kind of problems as you had painful experiences as kids—they were beaten or even molested. I wonder if anything like that ever happened to you." Faced with such questions and their corresponding demand characteristics (see Chapter 1), clients may begin to search their memories for traces of traumatic early events. This search, in turn, may sometimes lead them to generate memories that aren't there, or to distort ones that do exist. As we'll see later in this chapter, there is growing evidence to suggest that memories can be generated or altered in precisely this fashion (e.g., Haugaard, et al., 1991; Loftus, Coan, & Pickrell, 1996).

Is there any way to distinguish false memories from real ones? Recent findings suggest that PET scans may provide one key to this puzzle. In several studies (e.g., Hilts, 1996; Schacter, 1996), different patterns of brain activation have been observed when individuals remember stimuli that were actually presented during the study as opposed to stimuli they erroneously "misremembered" as having been presented. Such methods are only in their infancy, so they must be viewed with considerable caution. The debate over these complex issues is certain to continue for some time to come. What is already clear, though, is this: We must be careful to avoid assuming that all reports of "repressed memories" of childhood abuse are accurate. If we do, we run the risk of falsely accusing at least some innocent persons of crimes they never committed (Loftus, 1993; Roediger & McDermott, 1996).

We are not denying the possibility that repressed memories exist or that they can't be accurate. Nor are we denying that childhood sexual abuse is disturbingly common (Kutchinsky, 1992). However, when one considers the uncertainty of our information about the nature and the occurrence of repression, and available evidence indicating that memories of traumatic events can be unintentionally fabricated, there appear to be good grounds for caution. This is certainly the position adopted by Bowers and Farvolden (1996) of Waterloo University in a very thorough review of the issues surrounding repression and psychotherapy. They contend that therapists should recognize that repression of extremely traumatic experiences is uncommon—such events are simply too disturbing, and generate too many intrusive thoughts, to be entirely pushed from memory. They also point out that, from Freud onward, clinicians have all too often not been sufficiently sensitive to the degree to which they can influence clients through suggestion. Bowers and Farvolden maintain that therapists should develop a greater understanding of memory processes and the way in which they can influence suggestion. Finally, they suggest that therapists should try and avoid automatically seizing upon a single principle such as repression to explain a client's problems—alternative possibilities should be always considered.

KEY QUESTIONS

- Why does forgetting from long-term memory occur?
- What is retroactive interference? Proactive interference?
- What is repression, and why is there such controversy surrounding reports of repressed memory of traumatic events?

Memory in Natural Contexts

Much of the research mentioned so far has involved the performance of relatively artificial tasks: memorizing nonsense syllables, lists of words, or lists of numbers. While we do have to remember some such items in real life, this kind of research seems fairly remote from many situations in our daily experience. In this section, we'll turn to the operation of memory in natural contexts and see how it operates in our daily lives.

Autobiographical Memory

How do we remember information about our own lives? **Autobiographical memory**, also known as *episodic memory*, has long been of interest to psychologists, and has been studied in several different ways. For example, Baddeley and his colleagues (Kopelman, Wilson, & Baddeley, cited in Baddeley, 1990) have developed an *autobiographical memory schedule*, in which individuals are systematically questioned about different periods of their lives. They are asked about their childhood, the names of their teachers, friends, and the addresses at which they lived, and to describe incidents in their early lives. Additional questions are asked about other periods in their lives. The information obtained is then checked for accuracy against objective records. In this way, the accuracy of autobiographical memory can be assessed.

> **Autobiographical Memory:**
> Memory for information about events in our own lives.

DIARY STUDIES: RECALLING THE DAILY EVENTS OF OUR LIVES Another technique for studying autobiographical memory involves efforts by individuals to keep detailed diaries of events in their own lives (Linton, 1975). In one such study, the Dutch psychologist Willem Wagenaar (1986) kept a diary for six years. On each day he recorded one or two incidents, carefully indicating *who* was involved, *what* happened, *where* it happened, and *when* it took place. He rated each incident in terms of whether it was something that happened frequently or rarely, and he also indicated the amount of emotional involvement he experienced.

During the course of the study, he recorded a total of 2400 incidents. Then he tested his own memory for each, over a period of twelve months. To do so, he took each incident and, after cueing himself with one piece of information, tried to recall the rest. Thus, he might provide the *who* and then try to recapture the *what, where,* and *when.* Needless to add, he randomly selected the cue; for some incidents it involved *what,* for others *where,* and so on.

Autobiographical Memories

One technique for studying autobiographical memory involves efforts by individuals to keep detailed diaries of their own lives.

As expected, Wagenaar found that the more cues he provided himself, the more successful he was in answering correctly. Thus, if he knew *who, what,* and *when,* he was more successful in supplying the *where* than if he knew only *who* or *what* alone. He also found—again, far from surprisingly—that incidents that were unusual, emotionally involving, or pleasant were easier to recall than ones that were unpleasant. This is not to say that he was always successful in recovering recorded events. There was substantial loss for distant diary entries. Even when all available cues were provided, he was able to recover only about 40 percent of the diary events that had been recorded five years earlier. The memory loss may seem substantial, but one should not lose sight of the fact that the events recorded were, for the most part, relatively insignificant everyday events.

Keep in mind that there was only one subject in Wagenaar's (1986) study, and that the study was essentially observational in nature. As noted in Chapter 1, while such research is often informative, it cannot establish causal relationships or test hypotheses with the same degree of precision as experimentation. This said, Wagenaar's project, and the results of similar studies, indicate that autobiographical memory is affected by many of the same variables—such as retrieval cues and emotional states—that have been found to affect memory for abstract information presented under controlled laboratory conditions. This is valuable information in itself, and it suggests that further efforts to investigate autobiographical memory may indeed prove fruitful.

INFANTILE AMNESIA   What is your earliest memory? If you are like most people, it probably dates from your third or fourth year of life, although some people seem capable of recalling events that occurred when they were as young as two (Usher & Neisser, 1993). This inability to recall events that happened to us during the first two or three years of life is known as **infantile amnesia.** (Moscovitch, 1985)

It is obvious that we do retain information we acquired during the first years of life, for it is then that we learned to walk and to speak. Why, then, is *autobiographical memory* absent for this period? Until recently, two explanations were widely accepted. According to the first, autobiographical memory is absent early in life because the brain structures necessary for such memories are not sufficiently developed at this time. A second possibility has to do with the absence of language skills (Baddely, 1990).

More recent findings, however, suggest that neither of these explanations is entirely accurate. Contrary to widespread belief, infants appear to possess relatively well-developed memory abilities. For example, infants can imitate actions shown by an adult even after a twenty-four-hour delay (Meltzoff, 1990). It has been shown also that children as young as two can recount events that happened as long as six months earlier (Fivush, Gray, & Fromhoff, 1987). It seems unlikely, therefore, that underdeveloped brain structures, or limited linguistic resources, are responsible for infantile amnesia.

Howe and Courage (1993) of Memorial University contend that infants cannot store autobiographical memories until they have developed a clear *self-concept*. Without a self-concept, they lack the necessary personal frame of reference needed for autobiographical memory. In other words, we cannot remember events that happened to us until we have a clear sense of ourselves as individuals—a stage we do not reach until we are about two years of age. Perhaps we should refer to this gap in our autobiographical memory not as a period of amnesia, but rather as a period of infantile non-self.

FLASHBULB MEMORIES   Think back over your life. Select a surprising event to which you had an emotional reaction when you were informed about it. Can you remember where you were, and what you were doing, when you first learned about this event? If you can, you have a personal, first-hand example of what Brown and Kulik (1977) term **flashbulb memories**—vivid memories of what you were doing at the time of an emotion-provoking event.

Flashbulb memories tend to be very vivid and realistic. But are they accurate? Psychologists have begun to scrutinize them, and it turns out that they are often inaccurate (Neisser, 1991). In one study, students were asked, the day after the space shuttle *Challenger* exploded, how they had first heard this news. Three years later, the same individuals were asked to recall this information again. Most were sure that they could remember; but in fact, about one-third of their accounts were completely wrong. Flashbulb memories are a unique type of autobiographical memory. They may be vivid and real, but one should be cautious about assuming that they provide a precise and accurate account of a particular personal experience.

See the **Key Concept** on the opposite page for an overview of the kinds of memory we possess. ▶

Infantile Amnesia: Inability to remember events from the first two or three years of life.

Flashbulb Memories: Vivid memories of what we were doing at the time of an emotion-provoking event.

KEY *QUESTIONS*

▪ What is autobiographical memory?

▪ What is infantile amnesia?

▪ What are flashbulb memories?

Key Concept

Different Kinds of Memory: An Overview

Primary Memory Systems

Sensory Memory

Holds information from our senses for brief periods of time.

An image of a flash of lightning is held in visual sensory memory for just a fraction of a second.

Working Memory

Allows us to hold and selectively change a limited amount of information. If attention shifts, the information is lost.

Working memory allows us to remember a phone number we have just looked up long enough to dial it.

Long-Term Memory

Holds seemingly unlimited amounts of information for long periods of time—perhaps indefinitely.

The wide range of questions asked on quiz shows severely tests long-term memory skills.

Forms of Information in Long-Term Memory

Explicit Forms of Memory

Episodic Memory: Our autobiographical memory of personal experiences.

Semantic Memory: Our repository of factual information about the world.

Implicit Forms of Memory

Procedural Memory: Our memory for various different skills we possess, such as riding a bicycle, which we cannot put into words.

Priming studies reveal that under some circumstances, previous experience that we cannot explicitly remember can influence the subsequent choices we make.

▶ Memory Distortion and Construction

Moments before taking a mid-term exam, students at Concordia University were asked by Michael Conway to fill in a questionnaire requesting details about the amount of time they had spent in preparing for the exam, the grade they anticipated receiving, and the degree of satisfaction they would likely experience on knowing the outcome of the exam.

Some two weeks later, they were surprised by a request that they recall as precisely as possible the answers that they had previously provided about preparation time, and the level of satisfaction they would experience with respect to the exam.

What Conway (1990) found was that the recall of students expecting a grade higher than they received indicated that they had spent significantly less time on preparation and had lower expectancies than initially reported. Students expecting a grade lower than they received recalled spending more time on preparation and having higher expectancies than initially reported.

Students knew that Conway had their original estimates and that accuracy was important, and they must have assumed he would be comparing the two sets of estimates. In spite of this, they systematically erred in their recollection. To what are the distortions to be attributed? It seems likely that they fell prey to one of two basic types of error that affect memory for events. These are *distortion*—alterations in what is remembered and reported—and *construction*—the addition of information that was not actually provided, or, in some cases, the creation of "memories" of events or experiences that never actually took place.

Students who received poorer marks had a distorted recollection of their original estimations of study time and expectations, believing them to be lower than in fact they were. Students who received a higher mark than anticipated added to their memory, constructing a more expansive account of study activities and expectations than had actually taken place.

Distortion and the Influence of Schemas

Many factors contribute to memory distortion. One factor that plays an influential role is our tendency to keep our memory record consistent with our self-concept and current motives. This is reflected in the memory record. Just as we sometimes alter our memories to make them consistent with our self-concept, we sometimes also distort our memories to bring them "in line" with our current motives. For example, if we are disposed to like someone, we will be likely to remember positive information about him or her. Conversely, if we dislike someone, we will more likely remember negative information about this person.

Effects of this kind have recently been observed in a series of studies conducted by McDonald and Hirt (1997). These researchers had participants watch an interview between two students. The likability of the participants was varied by having one of the students act in a polite, a rude, or a neutral manner. When later asked to recall information about the actor's grades (information that was provided previously during the interview), those who were induced to like the actor distorted their memories of the assigned grades so as to place him or her in a more favourable light, while those induced to dislike the actor showed the opposite pattern.

Memory distortion can also be introduced through the use of cognitive structures that we use to guide and direct our behaviour in specific situations, called **schemas**. The easiest way to understand the idea of a schema is to think of an established experience or event: a day at work, eating a meal at restaurant, attending a party, or giving a party. As a result of our experiences in these situations, we inevitably develop, for each situation, a framework of expectancies—a schema—that provides us with the information needed to deal efficiently and effectively with

Schemas: Cognitive frameworks representing our knowledge about aspects of the world.

that situation in the future. If we enter a restaurant, we expect to be shown to a table, to be handed a menu, and to inform a waiter about our selections. If we are invited to a party, we have one set of expectancies, if we are giving a party, another set of expectancies. We have schemas for almost all of life's experiences. Such schemas make life much easier for us—they provide the organizational frameworks for regulating our interactions with the world.

How do schemas affect or distort memory? The answer is that the schema we apply to a situation influences what we attend to, store, and subsequently recall about it. A convincing demonstration of the influence of schemas is provided in a study by Anderson and Prichert (1978). Participants in their study read an account of a description of a boy's visit to another boy's house from the point of view of a potential burglar or a potential home buyer. The description included information about the layout and contents of the expensive house as well as a good deal of information about its many desirable and undesirable features. They were then asked to recall as much as they could about the story. The results were exactly as would be expected from a schema perspective. Those that applied a burglar schema to the reading paid attention to, and remembered, information about the various valuables and how they could be accessed. Those that applied a house-buying schema focused on, and remembered, the desirable and undesirable features of the house. Participants were then presented with an unexpected request to attempt a second recall using a different schema. Those who read the story from the perspective of a burglar were asked to recall details about the house from the point of view of a house buyer, and those who had read the story from the point of view of a house buyer were asked to base their recall on the point of view of a burglar. Using a different schema resulted in additional detail being recovered that had not been included in their original descriptions. What this study shows is that schemas strongly influence both what information is stored in memory, and what information can be recovered from memory.

We do well to keep in mind that we are more likely to notice and remember information that is consonant with our beliefs and the schemas we employ to direct us in everyday encounters—than contrary and incompatible information—and that information we recover from memory is influenced in a similar selective fashion by beliefs and schemes.

MEMORY CONSTRUCTION   As we have seen, schemas can powerfully influence what information we select to retain and the information we can recover from memory. Another powerful influence on memory is our disposition to make what are called *construction errors:* our tendency to fill in the details when recalling natural events, sometimes causing us even to remember experiences we never actually had. As one expert on memory has put it, "Memory is not so much like reading a book as it is like writing one from fragmentary notes" (Kihlstrom, 1994, p. 341). In other words, we all too often flesh out skeletal recollections of events, experiences, and reports with detail that we do not directly remember. Even experts are not immune. Vincente and Brewer (1993) report on a construction error that is commonly made in textbook descriptions of the well-known studies of the memory of chess experts by de Groot. These studies were quite important, but could have been much more so if a particular control condition had been included. What Vincente and Brewer found is that many descriptions of the chess expert articles in the scientific literature mistakenly include the missing control condition as part of the original study. It is as if scientists, who are normally compulsively accurate in reporting details, are led into error by the importance of the study and infer that the required control condition was present.

It is now known that the addition of the missing control does not alter the conclusions drawn about the memory abilities of chess experts, and memory construction in this case had no enduring consequences. There are times however, when memory reconstruction can have devastating consequences. For example, in a widely publicized court case, two young women accused their father, Paul Ingram of Olympia, Washington, of having sexually abused them for many years when they were children. Very little confirming evidence was available for the women's stories, and Ingram at first denied the charges. Under repeated questioning by police and lawyers, however, he began to report "recovered memories" for these crimes. Were these memories accurate? Or did Ingram construct them in response to the repeated suggestion that he had committed the crimes? To find out, a psychologist, Richard Ofshe, made up a completely false story in which Ingram forced his son and daughter to have sex (Ofshe, 1992; Loftus, 1993). Ofshe then presented this story to Ingram, urging him to try to remember these events. At first Ingram denied any knowledge of them, but later he reported that he could remember them—indeed, he gradually developed detailed "memories" for events that were entirely fabricated!

This situation dramatically illustrates that, under the power of suggestion, people may often construct memories of events that never took place. Challenged by this example, a number of researchers have demonstrated that suggestion can be used to implant a false memory for an early childhood event (e.g., Loftus & Pickrell, 1995). A recent study indicates that it is even possible to implant in adults false childhood memories of highly stressful and emotional events such as a serious medical procedure or a serious animal attack (Porter, Yuille, & Lehman, 1999). Porter et al. report that 26 percent of the participants in their study developed a "complete" memory for the false event. The effect of suggestion is strong, and we know that memory is imperfect. Does it follow that researchers could willy-nilly insert any sort of memory they wished in a substantial number of individuals participating in their studies? The answer is no. Events or situations have to be plausible, and consonant with the character of individuals' experiences, or they will be rejected (Pezdek, Finger, & Hodge, 1997).

Very young children seem to be especially susceptible to suggestions, readily constructing detailed memories of events that never took place when prompted by repeated questions from adults (Bruck, 1999; Goleman, 1993). A compelling demonstration of the alteration of young children's memory is provided in a series of studies reported by Ceci (1995). Ceci was interested in knowing whether young children sometimes have difficulty discriminating between actual events they experience and events that they imagine (or think about happening to them) and treat imagined events as actual memories.

In his study, Ceci had preschoolers meet with a researcher over a ten-week period. In each weekly session, the child was asked to report whether a series of events had ever been experienced. The child was asked to think about each event and try to visualize it. Some of the events described were those the child certainly would have experienced. Others, for example, getting a finger caught in a mousetrap and having to go to a hospital to get it removed, were not.

At the end of the ten-week period, in a videotaped interview conducted by a different person, the children were asked whether the various events had taken place. If the child reported the event had occurred, additional probing questions were asked about the event. Children very frequently reported that the imagined events had occurred, and provided surprisingly detailed accounts about how they happened. As many as 58 percent of the children falsely maintained that at least one of the thought-about and imagined events occurred, and 25 percent claimed that a majority of imagined events had taken place.

Ceci's study has important implications with respect to court cases in which very young children are asked to provide evidence or testimony about sexual misconduct

Evidence for the Occurrence of False Memories

When young children were shown drawings of fictitious events and asked whether they had experienced them, a majority reported that they had. Moreover, they provided detailed descriptions of these imaginary events. Even worse, trained psychologists who saw videotapes of the children describing both real and fictitious events could not accurately distinguish between the false memories and real ones. These findings suggest the need for considerable caution in interpreting supposedly repressed memories of early childhood abuse.

Source: Photos courtesy Dr. S.J. Ceci.

or child abuse. Repeated questioning under conditions in which leading questions are asked, accompanied by requests to try to imagine themselves in a particular situation or circumstance, can lead to the construction of very erroneous memories. Obviously, very great care has to be exercised in the questioning of young children.

Why do the children in Ceci's study accept imagined events as real? One possible answer involves processes at work during encoding. When we enter information into memory, we may store the information itself, but omit details about the source—how and when the information was obtained. This is referred to as **inadequate source monitoring.** In Ceci's study, the children did not differentiate between events that were real and those that they only imagined happening. In a similar vein, as young children we are often told at family gatherings about experiences and encounters that caused the family great amusement or distress. Even though we may not personally remember an event at the time of first telling, exposure to repeated tellings will contribute to the construction of a memory of it. If we do not encode the source of our knowledge about the event—family gatherings—we will tend to believe that we experienced the original event.

Eyewitness Testimony

Evidence given by persons who have witnessed a crime—**eyewitness testimony**—plays an important role in many trials. At first glance, this makes a great deal of sense: What better source of information about the events of a crime than the persons who actually saw them. But is such testimony accurate? To provide a balanced assessment of this issue we have to consider information from both laboratory and field studies.

We will start by considering two principal difficulties associated with assessing eyewitness testimony. One difficulty concerns deficiencies that are often present in the line-up and photo identification procedures used by law enforcement officials. For example, officials may instill bias in witnesses by emphasizing that an offender is in the line-up, or by failing to inform them that a "not present" response is acceptable (Wells, 1993). The other difficulty stems from possible changes that may take place in the memory record over time, especially from exposure to misleading information. We have seen how vulnerable memory can be to distortion and construction errors, and how *leading questions* and inadequate *source monitoring* can alter recollection of events. These factors certainly are capable of influencing eyewitness testimony. Indeed, researchers such as Loftus (1980) have found that, in the laboratory, eyewitness testimony is readily altered by misleading information, and suggest caution has to be exercised in accepting the claims of eyewitnesses (Christianson, Goodman, & Loftus, 1992).

Although Loftus and others have marshalled substantial evidence in support of the view that eyewitness testimony is vulnerable to error, recent field studies suggest that the memory of real-life eyewitnesses may be better than we might expect on the basis of laboratory studies. Yuille and his associates at the University of British Columbia make the important point that in life, witnesses to crime are often not passive, detached observers. Studies show that real-life witnesses are likely to have a much greater degree of personal involvement in events witnessed than do laboratory subjects. For example, an examination of RCMP records by Yuille and his associates found that in the vast majority of offenses involving robbery or sexual or nonsexual assault, the victim was the only witness—a very direct form of involvement. When witnesses other than the victim were present, they tended to be acquaintances of either the victim or the assailant, if not both. Even in cases of robbery, where the witness knew neither the assailant nor the victim, a sense of personal involvement may well have arisen through the feelings of threat and intimidation produced by the experience (Yuille & Tollestrup, 1992).

Eyewitnesses: Do They Remember What They See?

Growing evidence suggests that eyewitnesses are not nearly as accurate in remembering events they have seen as was once believed. Many factors (e.g., source confusion, suggestibility) can distort their memories and lead them to describe events inaccurately—or even report seeing events that never took place.

Inadequate Source Monitoring: The ability to remember factual information, but not the source whereby this information was acquired.

Eyewitness Testimony: Information provided by witnesses to crimes or accidents.

John C. Yuille
University of British Columbia

Field study assessments by Yuille, Tollestrup, and others (e.g., Fisher, Geiselman, & Amador, 1989) of the memories of witnesses to actual crimes support the view that such personal involvement does lead to the formation of memories that are qualitatively different from those created in a laboratory with uninvolved bystanders. The memories of witnesses to actual crimes are found by Yuille and Tollestrup to be accurate and detailed. Further, those memories appear to be highly durable, thus the reliability of eyewitness testimony for situations where witnesses are directly involved appears to be better than laboratory studies alone would lead us to conclude.

Although field studies may provide us with some comfort about the accuracy of eyewitness reports in circumstances where there is a high degree of personal involvement, it has to be acknowledged that eyewitnesses can be called to testify about events in which they have little sense of direct personal involvement. Under such circumstances, the memory record remains vulnerable to distortion. Can remedies be applied to enhance the accuracy of their testimony under such circumstances? Fortunately, the answer is yes.

One promising approach to increasing the accuracy of eyewitness testimony focuses on improving the procedures used to question witnesses (Geiselman et al., 1985). The results of this research indicate that a witness's accuracy improves substantially when procedures based on current scientific knowledge of memory are employed. Techniques that appear to be useful include asking witnesses to report everything—even partial information—and asking them to describe events from several different perspectives and in several different orders, not just the one in which the events actually occurred. Research on memory suggests that these techniques should enhance recall, and indeed, when they are used, witnesses' accuracy increases by almost 50 percent in some cases (Fisher & Geiselman, 1988). A related procedure involves asking eyewitnesses to imagine themselves back at the scene and then to reconstruct as many details as possible (Malpass & Devine, 1981). This process seems to provide witnesses with additional retrieval cues, thereby enhancing their memory. What seems not to help is the practice of asking eyewitnesses to recall what they saw over and over again (Turtle & Yuille, 1994). Surveys indicate that there is growing awareness among law enforcement officials that special precautions have to be taken in assessing eyewitness testimony, but the complaint is that, all too often, they are not allowed the time to carry out adequate eyewitness interviews (Kebbell & Milne, 1998).

Perspectives on Diversity

Culture and Memory

MEMORY IS A VERY BASIC ASPECT OF COGNITION, and people all around the world seem to have the same basic memory abilities. The differences one finds from culture to culture is in the use to which memory is put (Mistry & Rogoff, 1994).

In many industrialized societies, students learn, as part of their education, to remember lists of unrelated terms or definitions, and they also practise entering abstract information such as mathematical and chemical equations in their memories. In non-industrialized, traditional societies, individuals have little or any practise with such tasks. They, too, commit large amounts of information to memory, but most of it is directly linked to their daily lives. For instance, they do not learn the names of plants and animals they may never see, but they *do* memorize the names of large numbers of plants and animals that *are* a part of everyday life.

Formal educational systems in industrialized societies require children to become very practised in special kinds of interactions with adults—interactions in which the adult (as teacher or examiner) asks them specific questions about information they have committed to memory. In traditional societies, children typically do not interact with adults in this manner. For instance, in the Mayan culture of Central America, it is viewed as very rude for children to answer questions from adults in a direct manner (Rogoff & Mistry, 1985). Rather, they must say, "So I have been told…" to avoid appearing to know more than the adult—which would be the height of bad manners in that culture!

In short, what—and how—we remember material is influenced by the culture in which we live, and children raised in traditional cultures often encounter difficulty in coping with standard memory tasks used in research in industrialized countries. Thus memory, like every like every other aspect of human behaviour, occurs against a cultural backdrop. If we ignore cultural factors and influences, we run the risk of confusing culture-produced differences with ones relating to memory abilities themselves—and that would be inappropriate indeed.

K E Y QUESTIONS

- What are schemas and what role do they play in memory distortion?

- What are memory construction errors ? Does suggestion contribute to the production of construction errors?

- What factors do we have to take into consideration in assessing the accuracy of eyewitness testimony?

Critical Thinking
If eyewitnesses' testimony can be inaccurate, why does the legal system continue to place so much emphasis on their testimony?

The Biological Bases of Memory

Let's begin with a simple but compelling assumption: When you commit information to memory, something must happen in your brain. Given that memories can persist for decades, it seems reasonable to suggest that this "something" involves relatively permanent changes within the brain. Where, precisely, are these changes located? And what kind of alterations do they involve? Questions such as these have fascinated—and frustrated—psychologists and other scientists for decades. Only recently have even partial answers begun to emerge.

Amnesia and Other Memory Disorders

The study of **amnesia**, or loss of memory, has added greatly to our understanding of the biological bases of memory. Amnesia is far from rare. Among human beings, it can stem from accidents that damage the brain, from drug abuse, or from operations performed to treat various medical disorders. Two major types exist. In **retrograde amnesia**, memory of events *prior* to the amnesia-inducing event is impaired. Individuals suffering from such amnesia may be unable to remember events from specific periods in their lives, such as events they experienced between the ages of eighteen and twenty-two. In **anterograde amnesia**, individuals cannot remember events that occur *after* the amnesia-inducing event. For example, if they meet someone for the first time after the onset of amnesia, they cannot remember this person the next day, or even a few minutes after being introduced.

ANTEROGRADE AMNESIA AND THE ROLE OF THE MEDIAL TEMPORAL LOBES
We will start by considering a mystery. Two patients were admitted to the Montreal Neurological Institute in the early 1950s because they were experiencing epileptic seizures that resisted conventional drug treatment. In an effort to control these seizures, an operation previously shown to be effective with other patients was

Amnesia: Loss of memory stemming from illness, accident, drug abuse, or other causes.

Retrograde Amnesia: The inability to store in long-term memory information that occurred before an amnesia-inducing event.

Anterograde Amnesia: The inability to store in long-term memory information that occurs after an amnesia-inducing event.

Brenda A. L. Milner
McGill University

performed by Dr. Wilder Penfield, a celebrated Canadian neurosurgeon. This procedure involved removal of part of the medial temporal lobe on one side of the patient's brain. Penfield was distressed to find that both patients developed a profound anterograde amnesia—they were quite unable to retain information about new experiences (Penfield & Milner, 1958). What went wrong?

The answer came when Penfield and Milner examined reports by an American surgeon, W.B. Scoville, indicating that two of his patients who had undergone a similar surgical procedure on both sides of the brain were unable to remember new information. Scoville's report, and other hints from the scientific literature about the relationship between the temporal lobes and memory, caused Penfield and Milner to wonder if the two Montreal patients had unsuspected damage in temporal lobe areas on the side of their brain untouched by surgery. This was found to be the case.

It seems obvious from these reports that the temporal lobes are significantly involved in the **consolidation of memory**. Without at least one functioning temporal lobe, information cannot be shifted from short-term to longer-term storage. More recent investigations have strengthened this conclusion and identified one structure in the temporal lobes—the hippocampus—as crucial for memory consolidation.

What is life like for an individual who has experienced destruction of the hippocampus in both temporal lobes? The most direct way to answer this question is to look at H.M.—one of the original two patients operated on by Scoville. The operation helped control H.M.'s seizures but had a devastating affect on his memory. This became obvious once he had recovered from surgery. He would meet and have a conversation with someone new, and moments after the meeting be quite unaware that either the meeting or the conversation had taken place. He would read the same magazine or do the same crossword puzzle repeatedly. He seemed to have no recollection of having ever seen the magazine or puzzle once he turned away to attend to something else. Formal memory assessment tests confirmed that his short-term working memory was intact, and he could hold information in short-term memory long enough to understand and answer questions. What he could not do was transfer information from short-term working memory to long-term memory, where it could be preserved and accessed on demand. He became effectively suspended in time on that day when the surgical procedures rendered him unable to store new information about his own experiences or to record new happenings in the world at large.

ANTEROGRADE AMNESIA AND THE DISTINCTION BETWEEN EXPLICIT AND IMPLICIT MEMORY Psychologists find the memory impairments of H.M. and other anterograde amnesics particularly important because their memory difficulties provide a compelling demonstration of the distinction between **explicit** and **implicit memory.**

Explicit memory reflects our ability to be consciously aware of information that we have in memory about our personal experiences (*episodic memory*) and information about the world we live in (*semantic memory*), and to be able to draw on that information when required. It is the explicit memory system that is impaired in H.M. and other individuals with anterograde amnesia. They are incapable of forming new episodic memories about their personal experiences or semantic memories about events in the world about them.

What is fascinating is that although amnesics such as H.M. have lost their capacity to form new explicit memories, their implicit memory functions, which rely on what we described earlier in the chapter as *procedural memory*, appear to be largely unimpaired. In short, amnesics can acquire and retain a variety of different procedural skills (Parkin, 1993). For example, if H.M is required to trace the outline of a geometric form under conditions in which he can only see a mirror image reflection of his hand and the form to be traced, he initially performs poorly. This is to be expected, since the mirror reverses the direction of some of his hand movements. If testing is continued over several days, H.M. becomes increasingly adept at tracing

Consolidation of Memory: The process of shifting new information from short-term to long-term storage.

Explicit Memory: A memory system that permits us to express the information it contains verbally; sometimes termed *declarative memory*. It includes both semantic and episodic memory.

Implicit Memory: A memory system that stores information that we cannot express verbally; sometimes termed *procedural memory*.

the form reflected in the mirror. This means that he is retaining information about the procedures required to perform mirror-image tracing. Repeated testing on certain types of puzzle tasks similarly results in steady improvement. It has been shown also that H.M. becomes increasingly rapid at identifying a fragmented picture of a face presented over several days. Finally, H.M., and other amnesic patients like him, show what are termed normal implicit memory priming effects, such as those described in the Research Process section on page 233. If such patients are asked to read a short list of words and after a short delay are presented with the first few letters or initial stem of the words and told to use these cues to reproduce the words that were read to them, they cannot do so. If, however, they are provided with the first few letters or initial stem, and are asked to guess at how the word should be completed they produce a surprising number of the words that were read to them (Graf, Squire, & Mandler, 1984). At some implicit level in memory these words have been primed and are readily activated when cues are provided, but for some reason they cannot be explicitly tied to the memory test setting, just as the memory tracing and puzzle task skills that amnesics can learn are never explicitly remembered. Even though they improve with repeated exposure to these tasks, they deny on every exposure they have ever previously performed the task.

In summary, patients with anterograde amnesia present an interesting paradox. They can acquire a variety of different skills, but because their explicit memory functions are impaired they are not aware that they have such skills or the circumstances under which they were acquired.

BRAIN MECHANISMS UNDERLYING THE IMPLICIT/EXPLICIT MEMORY DISTINCTION What can be said about brain structures that underlie implicit and explicit memory? An influential study by Knowlton, Mangel, and Squire (1996) tells us much about brain structures that are crucial to the formation of explicit and implicit memories. In their study, they compared the performance of two different types of intellectually intact but memory-impaired patients on explicit and implicit memory tasks. They compared amnesic patients who had bilateral injuries to hippocampal or diencephalic midline structures with Parkinson's patients who had injuries to basal ganglia structures (caudate nucleus and putamen, which form the neostriatum). The implicit memory task required patients to predict outcomes associated with changing cues that were repeatedly presented on a computer screen. The explicit memory task required patients to answer specific questions about the training episode and the layout of items on the computer screen at the end of a session. Amnesic patients were able to master the implicit task, but not the explicit memory task. The reverse was true for the Parkinson's patients: they could answer explicit questions about experimental procedures and computer screen layout, but they could not learn the implicit memory task. The study provides persuasive evidence that hippocampal and diencephalic structures are crucial for the formation of explicit memories and that basal ganglia structures are crucial for the formation of implicit memories.

AMNESIA AS A RESULT OF KORSAKOFF'S SYNDROME Individuals who consume large amounts of alcohol for many years sometimes develop **Korsakoff's syndrome.** The many symptoms of Korsakoff's syndrome include sensory and motor problems as well as heart, liver, and gastrointestinal disorders. In addition, the syndrome is often accompanied by both anterograde amnesia and severe retrograde amnesia: Patients cannot remember events that took place even many years before the onset of their illness. Careful examination of these individuals' brains after death indicates that they have experienced extensive damage to portions of the diencephalon, especially to the thalamus and hypothalamus. This suggests that these portions of the brain play a key role in long-term memory.

THE AMNESIA OF ALZHEIMER'S DISEASE One of the most tragic illnesses to strike human beings in the closing decades of life is **Alzheimer's disease.** This

Korsakoff's Syndrome: An illness caused by long-term abuse of alcohol that often involves profound retrograde amnesia.

Alzheimer's Disease: An illness primarily afflicting individuals over the age of sixty-five and involving severe mental deterioration, including retrograde amnesia.

Memory Failure: Alzheimer's Disease

Damage to specific neurons in the brain is implicated in Alzheimer's disease, one of the most tragic illnesses to affect older people.

illness occurs among 5 percent of all people over age sixty-five. It begins with mild problems, such as increased difficulty in remembering names, phone numbers, or appointments. Gradually, though, patients' conditions worsens until they become totally confused, are unable to perform even simple tasks like dressing or grooming themselves, and experience an almost total loss of memory. In the later stages, patients may fail to recognize their spouse or children. The magnitude of memory loss such individuals experience far exceeds that normally associated with advanced age.

Careful study of the brains of deceased Alzheimer's patients has revealed that in most cases they are dotted with concentrations of what are termed amyloid plaques. These plaques are composed of *amyloid beta protein*, a substance not found in similar concentrations in normal brains. The tangle of degenerating axons and dendrites surrounding amyloid plaques lends credibility to the view that amyloid plaque deposits are responsible for damage to neurons—primarily those that project from nuclei in the basal forebrain to the hippocampus and cerebral cortex (Coyle, 1987; Yankner et al., 1990). Essentially there is a selective assault on neurons that transmit information primarily by means of the neurotransmitter acetylcholine. Studies show that the brains of Alzheimer's patients contain lower than normal amounts of acetylcholine. Further support is provided by animal studies in which destruction of the acetylcholine-transmitting neurons has been shown to produce major memory problems (Fibiger, Murray, & Phillips, 1983). Until recently there has been little that could be done to control the growth of amyloid plaque deposits that seem to precipitate neural damage. This may be changing. A vaccine that prevents the build-up of amyloid deposits in mice that have been genetically engineered to acquire Alzheimer's-like deficiencies has been developed (St. George-Hyslop & Westaway, 1999). The vaccine not only prevented the development of amyloid deposits; there were indications that it was able to reduce concentrations of amyloid plaque in mice with significant plaque deposits. The full import of the vaccine must await human research trials, but this may well prove to be an important new tool in the struggle to control Alzheimer's disease.

In sum, evidence obtained from the study of memory disorders indicates that specific regions and systems within the brain play central roles in our ability to transfer information from short-term to long-term storage and to retain it in long-term memory for prolonged periods of time.

Memory and the Brain: A Modern View

Where does all this evidence leave us? A number of conclusions can be drawn. It is evident that memory functions do show some degree of localization within the brain: hippocampal and diencephalic structures are crucial for the formation of explicit memories and basal ganglia structures are crucial for the formation of implicit memories. Damage to these areas disrupts these key functions, but may leave other aspects of memory intact.

Why does damage to various brain structures produce amnesia and other memory deficits? A number of possibilities exist, and there is evidence consistent with each, so it is too early to choose between them. One possibility is that damage to these areas prevents consolidation of the memory trace: these are formed, but cannot be converted to a lasting state (e.g., Squire, 1995). Another is that when information is stored in memory, not only the information itself but its context, too—when and how it was acquired—is stored. Amnesia may result from an inability to enter this additional information into memory (Mayes, 1996).

What about the memory trace itself—where is it located and what is it? Over the years, the pendulum of scientific opinion concerning this issue has swung back and forth between the view that memories are highly localized within the brain—

they exist in specific places—to the view that they are represented by the pattern of neural activity in many different brain regions. At present, most experts on memory believe that both views are correct, at least to a degree. Some aspects of memory do appear to be represented in specific portions of the brain, and even, perhaps, in specific cells. For instance, cells in the cortex of monkeys that respond to faces of other monkeys and humans, but not other stimuli, have been identified (Desimone & Ungerleider, 1989). So there do appear to be "local specialists" within the brain. At the same time, however, networks of brain regions seem to be involved in many memory functions—the *distributed* or *equipotential view*. So, in answer to the question, "Where are memories located?" the best available answer is—there is no single answer. Depending on the type of information or type of memory we are considering, memories may be represented in individual neurons, the connections between them, complex networks of structures throughout the brain, or all of the above. Given the complexity of the functions memory involves, this is not surprising; after all, no one ever said that the task of understanding anything as complicated and wonderful as human memory would be easy!

Finally, what is the memory trace—what happens within the brain when we enter information into memory? Again, we are still far from a final, complete answer, although we are definitely getting there. The picture provided by current research goes something like this: The formation of long-term memories involves alterations in the rate of production or release of specific neurotransmitters (especially acetylcholine). Such changes increase the ease with which neural information can move within the brain and may produce *localized neural circuits*. Evidence for the existence of such circuits, or *neural networks*, is provided by research in which previously learned conditioned responses are eliminated when microscopic areas of the brain are destroyed—areas that, presumably, contain the neural circuits formed during conditioning (Thompson, 1989).

Long-term memory may also involve changes in the actual structure of neurons—changes that strengthen communication across specific synapses (Teyler & DeScenna, 1984). For instance, after learning experiences, the shape of dendrites in specific neurons may be altered, and these changes may increase the neurons' responsiveness to certain neurotransmitters. Some of these changes may occur very quickly, while others may require considerable amounts of time. This, perhaps, is one reason why newly formed memories are subject to disruption for some period after they are formed (Squire & Spanis, 1984).

In sum, it appears that we are now in an exciting period of rapid progress; sophisticated research techniques (e.g., PET scans) have armed psychologists and other scientists with important tools for unravelling the biological bases of memory. When they do, the potential benefits for persons suffering from amnesia and other memory disorders will probably be immense.

K E Y   QUESTIONS

- What are retrograde amnesia and anterograde amnesia?

- What are explicit and implicit memory? Are they related to different parts of the brain?

- What are Korsakoff's syndrome and Alzheimer's disease? What do they tell us about the biological bases of memory?

Critical Thinking

Suppose that someday we are able to identify all the changes that occur when memories are formed. What benefits would this offer? What potential dangers (e.g., threats to human freedom) might stem from such knowledge?

making **Psychology** Part of Your Life

Improving Your Memory: Some Useful Steps

*H*ow good is your memory? If you are like most people, your answer is probably "Not good enough!" At one time or another, most of us have wished that we could improve our ability to retain facts and information. Fortunately, with a little work, almost anyone can improve her or his memory. Here are some tips for reaching this goal:

1. *Think about what you want to remember.* If you wish to enter information into long-term memory, it is important to think about it. Ask questions about it, consider its meaning, and examine its relationship to information you already know. In other words, engage in elaboration or "deep processing." Doing so will help make the new information part of your existing knowledge frameworks—and increase your chances of remembering it at a later time.

2. *Pay attention to what you want to remember.* Quick: Does the Queen's head face to the right or to the left on a loonie? On a quarter? All Canadians have seen these images many, many times, yet the odds favour your misremembering. When students at Bishop's University in Quebec were asked this question, 71 percent picked the wrong direction (McKelvie & Aikins, 1993). What this shows is that you can see something hundreds of times, but unless you attend to it, there is little chance of it really getting into long-term memory. Pay careful attention to information you want to remember. This involves a bit of hard work, but in the long run, it will save you time and effort.

3. *Use visual imagery and other mnemonics.* Imagery plays a central role in several well-known *mnemonics*—that is, strategies for improving memory (Paivio, 1986). One of these, the *method of loci,* involves the following steps. Suppose you want to remember a series of points for a speech or a quiz. First, imagine walking along a street that is familiar to you. At each corner or distinctive landmark, use an image to tie the to-be-remembered item to the landmark. For example, say you wanted to remember the three stages of memory: sensory store, working memory, and long-term memory. You might start at a corner restaurant making an image of yourself standing in the doorway "sensing" the wonderful odour of fresh food; you might then imagine "workers" fixing up a very evident break in the sidewalk further along the street; and finally you might imagine yourself taking

a "long-term" loan from a bank still further along the street. To recover this information, all you have to do is again imagine yourself walking down that street. When you arrive at these locations in your imagined walk, the image and the sought-after item will immediately come to mind.

4. *Use all available retrieval cues.* As we hope you remember, a key problem with long-term memory involves retrieving stored information. You can help yourself in this area through the use of retrieval cues. One type of cue is the context in which the information was first acquired. In other words, pause for a moment and try to remember the situations or surroundings in which you first entered the information into memory. Often, remembering the context will help you retrieve the information you seek. For example, suppose you are trying to recall the name of a movie you saw. Try as you may, you can't bring the name to mind. If you pause and think about where you saw the movie, who was with you, and some of the leading characters, the name may quickly follow.

5. *Develop your own shorthand codes.* For example, a traditional way of remembering the nine planets employs what is known as the first-letter technique. The first letter of each word in a phrase stands for an item to be remembered. The standard phrase has been "Mary's Violet Eyes Make John Stay Up Nights Pondering" (for Mercury, Venus, Earth, Mars, Jupiter, Saturn, Uranus, Neptune, and Pluto). This technique can be adapted to cover any list of items.

6. *Engage in distributed learning/practice.* Do not try to cram all the information you want to memorize into long-term storage at once. Rather, if at all possible, space your studying over several sessions—preferably, several days. This is especially true if you want to retain the information for long periods of time rather than just until the next exam!

7. *Finally, organize your material.* One basic finding of research on memory is that organized information is much easier to remember than unorganized material. If you wish to retain a large array of facts, dates, or terms, it is very helpful to organize them in some manner. Organization provides a framework to which new information can be attached—a kind of mental scaffold that facilitates both storage and subsequent recovery of material.

There are additional techniques for enhancing your memory, but most would be related to the points already described. Whichever techniques you choose, you will learn that making them work does require effort. In memory training, as in any other kind of self-improvement, it appears, "No pain, no gain" holds true.

Summary and Review

Key Questions

Human Memory

■ **What tasks are involved in encoding, storage, and retrieval?** Encoding involves converting information into a form that can be entered into memory. Storage involves retaining information over time. Retrieval involves locating information when it is needed.

■ **What are sensory memory, working memory, and long-term memory?** Sensory memory holds fleeting representations of our sensory experiences. Working memory holds a limited amount of information for short periods of time. Long-term memory holds large amounts of information for long periods of time.

■ **What are semantic memory, episodic memory, and procedural memory?** Semantic memory holds general information about the world. Episodic memory holds information about experiences that we have had in our own lives. Procedural memory holds nonverbal information that allows us to perform various motor tasks, such as riding a bicycle or playing the piano.

Our Basic Memory Systems: Sensory Memory, Working Memory, and Long-Term Memory

■ **What kind of information does sensory memory hold?** Sensory memory holds representations of information brought to us by our senses.

■ **How long does such information last in sensory memory?** This information generally lasts for less than a second.

■ **What are the serial position curve, the word-length effect, and the word-similarity effect?** The serial position curve refers to the finding that items near the beginning and end of a list are remembered more accurately than items near the middle. The word-length effect refers to the fact that memory span for immediate recall is greater for lists of short words than lists of longer words. The word-similarity effect refers to the finding that memory span for immediate recall is greater for words that do not sound alike than for words that do sound alike.

■ **What are the basic components of short-term working memory?** There is a visuospatial store to hold information about visual and spatial events, a phonological store to hold speech or speech-like material, and an executive controller that supervises and coordinates the operation of the two storage components.

■ **How does information move from short-term working memory to long-term memory?** Information moves from short-term working memory into long-term permanent memory through the process of elaborative rehearsal.

■ **What role do levels of processing and organization play in long-term memory?** Research findings indicate that the deeper the level of processing, the better information is recalled from long-term memory.

■ **What are retrieval cues and what role do they play in long-term memory?** Retrieval cues are stimuli associated with information stored in long-term memory; they help us bring such information to mind.

■ **How are state-dependent retrieval and mood-dependent memory related to context-dependent memory?** Context-dependent memory refers to the fact that material learned in one environment is more difficult to remember in a very different context than it is in the original one. State-dependent retrieval reflects the fact that it is often easier to recall stored information when our internal state is similar to that which existed when the information was first entered into memory, and mood-dependent memory reflects the fact that memory recovery can be influenced by whether you are in a mood state similar to the time at which material was entered into memory.

Forgetting from Long-Term Memory

■ **Why does forgetting from long-term memory occur?** Forgetting from long-term memory results mainly from interference.

■ **What is retroactive interference? Proactive interference?** Retroactive interference occurs when information being learned currently interferes with information already present in memory. Proactive interference occurs when information already present in memory interferes with the retention of new information.

- **What is repression, and why is there such controversy surrounding reports of repressed memory of traumatic events?** Repression is the active elimination from consciousness of memories or experiences we find threatening. There is concern that the role of repression is being overemphasized and that in at least some cases these memories may be induced by suggestions conveyed by therapists and the media.

Memory in Natural Contexts

- **What is autobiographical memory?** Autobiographical memory contains information about our own lives.
- **What is infantile amnesia?** Infantile amnesia refers to our inability to recall events from the first two to three years of life.
- **What are flashbulb memories?** Flashbulb memories are memories connected to dramatic events in our lives.

Memory Distortion and Construction

- **What are schemas and what role do they play in memory distortion?** Schemas are cognitive structures representing individuals' knowledge and assumptions about some aspect of the world. Once formed, they influence the ways in which we process new information—what we notice, what we store in memory, and what we remember. This can lead to memory distortion.
- **What are memory construction errors? Does suggestion contribute to the production of construction errors?** Memory construction errors occur as a result of our disposition to fill in the details when recalling events, sometimes even causing us to remember experiences we never actually had. Suggestion may induce others, especially young children, to remember events that did not happen.

- **What factors do we have to take into consideration in assessing the accuracy of eyewitness testimony?** Research shows the importance of the way in which individuals are asked questions: inappropriate questioning can result in biases. The degree of personal involvement in the event witnessed is also an important factor.

The Biological Bases of Memory

- **What are retrograde amnesia and anterograde amnesia?** Retrograde amnesia involves loss of memory of events prior to the amnesia-inducing event. Anterograde amnesia is loss of memory for events that occur after the amnesia-inducing event.
- **What are explicit and implicit memory? Are they related to different parts of the brain?** Explicit memory is the memory system that permits us to remember information that has been stored in memory, which we can bring to mind and describe verbally. Implicit memory is a memory system that allows us to use stored information and engage in skilled procedures without necessarily being able to put this information into words; it often operates in very subtle ways, below the level of conscious awareness. Different brain structures appear to be responsible for regulation of the two different memory systems.
- **What are Korsakoff's syndrome and Alzheimer's disease? What do they tell us about the biological bases of memory?** Individuals with Korsakoff's syndrome have both anterograde and retrograde amnesia. Such individuals display injury to the diencephalon, especially the thalamus and hypothalamus, suggesting that these play and important role in memory. Alzheimer's disease occurs in older people, and terminates in total memory loss. The amnesia seems to result from damage to neurons that transmit information by means of the neurotransmitter acetylcholine.

Key Terms

Alzheimer's Disease (p. 251)
Amnesia (p. 249)
Anterograde Amnesia (p. 249)
Autobiographical Memory (p. 241)
Central Executive Mechanism (p. 230)
Chunk (p. 231)
Consolidation of Memory (p. 250)
Context-Dependent Memory (p. 236)
Elaborative Rehearsal (p. 233)
Encoding (p. 225)
Episodic Memory (p. 227)
Explicit Memory (p. 250)
Eyewitness Testimony (p. 247)
Flashbulb Memories (p. 242)

Implicit Memory (p. 250)
Inadequate Source Monitoring (p. 247)
Infantile Amnesia (p. 242)
Korsakoff's Syndrome (p. 251)
Levels of Processing View (p. 234)
Long-Term Memory (p. 232)
Memory (p. 224)
Mood-Dependent Memory (p. 237)
Phonological Store (p. 230)
Proactive Interference (p. 238)
Procedural Memory (p. 227)
Repression (p. 239)
Retrieval (p. 225)

Retrieval Cues (p. 235)
Retroactive Interference (p. 238)
Retrograde Amnesia (p. 249)
Schemas (p. 244)
Selective Attention (p. 226)
Semantic Memory (p. 227)
Sensory Memory (p. 229)
Serial Position Curve (p. 230)
State-Dependent Retrieval (p. 236)
Storage (p. 225)
Trace-Decay Hypothesis (p. 237)
Visuospatial Sketchpad (p. 229)
Working Memory (p. 229)

Critical Thinking Questions

Appraisal

We have looked at how memory is studied in the behavioural laboratory, at how memory is studied in real-world natural contexts, and how memory can be investigated by directly studying the brain and brain injuries. Which of these approaches to the study of memory do you think is likely to make the largest contribution to our understanding in the future? Why?

Controversy

Public concern about childhood sexual abuse has increased greatly in recent years, as many people have come forward with claims that they were subjected to such treatment. Growing evidence indicates, however, that some charges of this type are false—they are based on false memories suggested by therapists, lawyers, and others. What steps, if any, do you think should be taken to protect innocent persons against such charges, while also protecting the rights of persons who may have actually suffered sexual abuse?

Making Psychology Part of Your Life

Now that you know how fallible and prone to errors memory can be, can you think of ways in which you can put this knowledge to use? In other words, can you think of situations in your own life in which you may be less willing to rely on memory in making judgments or decisions than was true in the past? And if so, what steps would you take in those situations to improve the accuracy of your judgments or decisions?

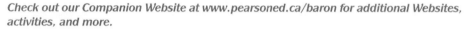

Weblinks

Check out our Companion Website at www.pearsoned.ca/baron for additional Websites, activities, and more.

Short-Term Memory

www.as.ua.edu/psychology/cognitive/stm.htm

The article at this site provides information about short-term (working) memory, including its capacity and mental code, the role of rehearsal in transferring information from short- to long-term memory, forgetting, Baddeley's working memory model, a diagram of the Atkinson-Shriffrin model of memory, hippocampal lesion evidence, an experiment illustrating decay theory, and various other related topics.

Disease Information Center: Amnesia

www.diseases.nu/amnesia.htm

This Website provides links to various sources of information about different kinds of amnesia.

Human Memory: What It Is and How to Improve It

www.epub.org.br/cm/n01/memo/memory.htm

This is a page from *Brain and Mind* edited at the University of Campinas in Brazil. If you follow the links, you will find some very clear explanations of different memory systems and the basis in the brain for recording past experience. You will get a good review of the fundamentals in Chapter 6.

NASA Cognition Lab

olias.arc.nasa.gov/cognition/tutorials/index.html

This page was created by psychologists at NASA to illustrate the ways in which human memory works. You will review your knowledge and have fun at this site.

Cognition
Thinking, Deciding,
Communicating

Solving Anagrams

 A new game called "Saskatchemimes" is featured in the Regina *Leader Post*. By running the word *Saskatchewan* through a computer, the author found a set of comical expressions that could be made out of those twelve letters. Then he created a cue for each expression. If you want to try it out, he suggests using refrigerator magnets or scrabble tiles to play.

Here are the basic rules of this game:

1. Read the cue.
2. Guess the anagram.
3. Earn two points.

Here is an example:

Cue: "Why Aunt Gert threw out the mixed nuts…"

Answer: "A cashew stank."
Cue: "Drove along south shore of Wascana Creek."
Answer: "Saw neat shack."

How is it that people are able to rearrange these letters to make a meaningful expression? What does psychological science tell us about how we think when we solve these and other puzzles? How do we make choices and take decisions? What is language and how do we use it to communicate with other people? Those are some of the intriguing topics you will encounter as you work your way through Chapter 7 on cognition.

Source: Petrie, R. (2000). Some Anagram fun with Saskatchewan. Regina *Leader Post*, February 28.

> Have you ever agonized over an
> important decision, carefully
> weighing the advantages and
> disadvantages of potential
> alternatives?

Have you ever wondered how we think? Why some people are more adept at solving problems than others? What factors should be considered in making decisions? These and related questions have to do with **cognition**—a general term used to describe various aspects of our higher mental processes. But *thinking, decision making,* and *problem solving* are only some of the issues focused on by cognitive psychologists. Other issues of concern are whether other animals can think; whether computers can be developed to reason like humans; and whether humans are the only species on planet Earth that have a language. It is on these and related topics that we'll focus in the present chapter.

We'll begin our discussion by examining the nature of *thinking,* an activity that involves the manipulation of mental representations of various features of the external world. Thinking includes *reasoning*—mental activity through which we transform available information in order to reach conclusions. We will try and unravel the mechanisms and operations employed in thinking and reasoning. Next, we'll turn to *decision making,* the process of choosing between two or more alternatives on the basis of information about them. Here we'll explore different factors that influence the decision-making process. After that, we'll examine several aspects of *problem solving,* which typically involves processing information in various ways in order to move toward desired goals. Finally, we'll examine an aspect of cognition that provides the basis for much of the activity occurring in each of the processes listed so far: *language.* It is through language that we can share the results of our own cognition with others and receive similar input from them. We'll also consider new evidence suggesting that other species may also possess several basic elements of language.

One additional point: As you'll soon see, our abilities to think, reason, make decisions, and use language are impressive in many respects. But they are far from perfect. As is true for memory, cognitive activities are subject to many forms of error: When we think, reason, make decisions, solve problems, and use language, we do not always do so in ways that would appear completely rational to an outside observer (Hawkins & Hastie, 1990; Johnson-Laird, Byrne, & Tabossi, 1989). As we examine each aspect of cognition, we will draw attention to these potential sources of distortion, because understanding the nature of such errors can shed important light on the nature of the cognitive processes they affect (Smith & Kida, 1991).

Thinking

Cognition: The activities involved in thinking, reasoning, decision making, memory, problem solving, and all other forms of higher mental processes.

What are you thinking about right now? If you've answered the question, then it's safe to say that at least to some extent you are thinking about the words on this page. But perhaps you are also thinking about a snack, the movie you saw last night, the argument you had with a friend this morning—the list could be endless. At any given moment, consciousness contains a rapidly shifting pattern of diverse thoughts, impressions, and feelings. In order to try to understand this complex and ever-changing pattern, psychologists have often adopted two main strategies. First, they have focused on the basic elements of *thought*—on how, precisely, aspects of the external world are represented in our thinking. Second, they have sought to determine the manner in which we *reason*—how we attempt to process available information cognitively in order to reach specific conclusions.

Basic Elements of Thought

What, precisely, does thinking involve? In other words, what are the basic elements of thought? While no conclusive answer currently exists, it appears that our thoughts consist largely of three basic components: *concepts, propositions,* and *images*.

CONCEPTS: CATEGORIES FOR UNDERSTANDING EXPERIENCE   What do apples, oranges, and cherries have in common? You probably have no difficulty in replying that they are all fruits. Now, how about a Nissan Pathfinder, an Air Canada jet, and an elevator? Perhaps it takes you a bit longer to answer, but soon you realize that they are all vehicles. Within each of these groups, the items look different from one another, yet in a sense you perceive them, and think about them, as similar at least in certain respects. The reason you find the task of answering these questions relatively simple is that you already possess well-developed **concepts** for both groups of items. Concepts are mental categories for objects, events, experiences, or ideas that are similar to one another in one or more respects. They allow us to compress a great deal of information about diverse objects, events, or ideas in a highly efficient manner.

LOGICAL AND NATURAL CONCEPTS   Psychologists often distinguish between logical and natural concepts. **Logical concepts** are ones that can be clearly defined by a set of rules or properties. Thus, an object's membership in a category is unambiguous: Any object or event either is, or is not, a member in a given concept category by virtue of whether it has the defining feature or features (Jahnke & Nowaczyk, 1998). For example, in geometry, a figure can be considered to be a triangle only if it has three sides whose angles add to 180 degrees, and can be a square only if all four sides are of equal length and all four angles are ninety degrees. In contrast, **natural concepts** are ones that are fuzzy around the edges; they have no fixed or readily specified set of defining features. Yet they more accurately reflect the state of the natural world, which rarely offers us the luxury of hard-and-fast, clearly defined concepts. Natural concepts are often based on **prototypes**—the best or clearest examples (Rosch, 1975). Prototypes emerge from our experience with the external world, and new items that might potentially fit within their category are then compared with them. The more attributes new items share with an existing prototype, the more likely they are to be included within the concept. For example, consider the following natural concepts: fruit and art. For fruit, most people think of apples, peaches, or pears. They are far less likely to mention avocados, pomegranates, or olives. Similarly, for art, most people think of paintings, drawings, and sculptures. Fewer think of artwork of the type shown in the photo on the right on page 262.

CONCEPTS: HOW THEY ARE REPRESENTED   That concepts exist is obvious. But how are they represented in consciousness? No firm answer to this question exists, but several possibilities have been suggested. First, concepts may be represented in terms of their features or attributes. As natural concepts are formed, the attributes associated with them may be stored in memory. Then, when a new item is encountered, its attributes are compared with the ones already present. The closer the match, the more likely is the item to be included within the concept.

A second possibility is that natural concepts are represented, at least in part, through images. Paivio (1990) at the University of Western Ontario has long argued

Concepts: Mental categories for objects or events that are similar to one another in certain respects.

Logical Concepts: Concepts that can be clearly defined by a set of rules or properties.

Natural Concepts: Concepts that are not based on a precise set of attributes or properties, do not have clear-cut boundaries, and are often defined by prototypes.

Prototypes: Representations in memory of various objects or stimuli in the physical world; the best or clearest examples of various objects or stimuli in the physical world.

Prototypes and Natural Concepts

Prototypes are the best or clearest examples of concepts. For the concept *art*, which of the examples shown here is more prototypical?

that knowledge of the world is conveyed to us through the various senses, and that our representations of the world retain the character or properties of the sensory systems in which they first come to us. To put it more simply, we have visual-like images in consciousness of objects and events we have experienced by sight; we have auditory images of voices, sounds, and music we have heard; and we have haptic images of feelings that derive from the touching and manipulating of objects and materials. Although we have a variety of different non-verbal ways of conceptually representing objects and experiences, it is generally held that **visual images** play the most significant role in the representation of natural concepts. For example, concrete nouns—nouns representing things that can be readily visualized—are much more easily remembered than abstract nouns representing things that cannot be visualized (Paivio, Walsh, & Bons, 1994). We will have more to say about the role of images—especially visual ones—later in this discussion.

Finally, it is important to note that concepts are closely related to *schemas*, cognitive frameworks that represent our knowledge of and assumptions about the world (see Chapter 6). Like schemas, natural concepts are acquired through experience and represent information about the world in an efficient summary form. However, schemas appear to be more complex than concepts, and to contain a broader range of information; also, they may include a number of distinct concepts. For example, each of us possesses a *self-schema*, a mental framework holding a wealth of information about our own traits, characteristics, and expectations. This framework, in turn, may contain many different concepts, such as intelligence, attractiveness, health, and so on. Some of these are natural concepts, so the possibility exists that natural concepts are represented, at least in part, through their links to schemas and other broad cognitive frameworks. To summarize, concepts may be represented in the mind in several ways and they play an important role in thinking and in our efforts to make sense out of a complex and ever-changing external world.

Visual Images: Mental pictures or representations of objects or events.

PROPOSITIONS: RELATIONS BETWEEN CONCEPTS Thinking is not a passive process. Instead it involves active manipulation of internal representations of the external world. As we have already noted, the representations that are mentally manipulated are often concepts. Frequently, thinking involves relating one concept to another, or one feature of a concept to the entire concept. Because we possess highly developed language skills, these cognitive actions take the form of **propositions**—sentences that relate one concept to another and can stand as separate assertions. Propositions such as "Bob kissed Sandra" describe a relationship between two concepts—in this case, an affection between two people. Others, such as "polar bears have white fur," describe the relationship between a concept and its properties. Research evidence indicates that much of our thinking involves the formulation and consideration of such propositions. Thus, propositions can be considered one of the basic elements of thought. Clusters of propositions are often represented as **mental models**, knowledge structures that guide our interactions with objects and events in the world around us (Johnson-Laird et al., 1992). For example, the various activities involved in preparing a meal could be readily encapsulated in a propositional format: Set the table. Remove the food from the refrigerator. Turn on the stove....

IMAGES: MENTAL PICTURES OF THE WORLD Look at the drawing in Figure 7.1. Now cover it up with a piece of paper and answer the following questions: (1) Was there a flag? If so, in what direction was if fluttering? (2) Was there a handle attached to the rudder? (3) Was there a porthole, and if so, on which side of the boat? You probably answered all of these questions quite easily. But how? If you are like most people, you formed a visual image of the boat. Then, when asked about the flag, you focused on that part of your image. Next, you were asked to think about the rudder at the opposite end of the boat. Did you simply jump to that end of the boat or scan the entire image? Research findings indicate that you probably scanned the entire image: After being asked about some feature near the front of the boat, most people take longer to answer a question about a feature near the back than to respond concerning a feature somewhere in the middle (Kosslyn, 1980). Such findings suggest that once we form a mental image, we think about it by scanning it visually just as we would if it actually existed. How do we hold the image to carry out these operations? The most likely answer is that the visuospatial sketchpad component of working memory that we described in Chapter 6 serves as a workbench for such imaginal operations.

Images can be manipulated in much the same way as visual objects in the real world. This is nicely illustrated in an example provided by Paivio (1983). He tells how he once asked his young daughter to form a pictorial image of a capital *N*. She readily did so. He then asked her to tip it over onto its right side and tell him what it looked like. She immediately reported that it looked like a *Z*. Could his daughter have provided the answer in any way other than by mentally rotating her image of the *N*? Paivio thinks not, and there is an enormous amount of literature on the rotation of mental images that supports his conclusion (e.g., Shepard & Metzler, 1971).

Not everyone supports the role of imagery in thought processes as enthusiastically as Kosslyn and Paivio. For example, a colleague of Paivio's at the University of Western Ontario, Zenon Pylyshyn, has been especially critical of the notion that having an image is akin to having a picture in the head (Pylyshyn, 1973, 1981). Indeed, there are studies indicating that our use of visual images in thinking does not correspond precisely to actual vision. In one such study, participants were asked to imagine carrying either a cannonball or a balloon along a familiar route (Intons-Peterson & Roskos-Ewoldsen, 1988). As is usual in such studies, the time required for the subjects to complete their imaginary journey was carefully measured. The outcome expected was that the longer the imagined distance to be traversed, the more time would be required to complete the journey. However, it was found that even when the distance over which the two objects were carried was the same, it took the participants longer to complete their imaginary journey when carrying the heavy object. Such findings suggest that we don't simply "read" the visual images we generate; if we did, the participants in this study should have been able to

Figure 7.1
Mental Scanning of Visual Images

When shown a drawing such as this one and then asked questions about it, most people take longer to estimate the distance between the flag and the rudder than between the flag and the porthole.

Source: Based on an illustration used by Kosslyn, 1980.

Propositions: Sentences that relate one concept to another and can stand as separate assertions.

Mental Models: Knowledge structures that guide our interactions with objects and events in the world around us.

move through the imagined route equally quickly in both conditions. The fact that they could not indicates that visual images are actually embedded in our knowledge about the world, and are interpreted in light of such knowledge rather than simply scanned.

Our tendency to develop and interpret imagery within the context of a real-world framework explains why imagery techniques are used so commonly in Canadian sports training programs. Having players imagine, as realistically as possible, various aspects of the training program, with as much attendant kinesthetic feeling as they can generate, seems to facilitate skill development and can even be used to improve game strategies. In fact, there is evidence that elite athletes make more use of imagery than their less successful teammates (Barr & Hall, 1992; Mckenzie & Howe, 1997; Salmon, Hall, & Haslam, 1994). Mental images are used also for other purposes. People report using them to understand verbal instructions by converting the words into mental pictures of actions, to increase motivation, and to enhance mood states by visualizing positive events or scenes (Kosslyn et al., 1991). Clearly, then, visual images constitute a basic element of the thinking process.

For more information on how psychologists study various aspects of thinking, please see the **Research Process** section below.

> **Reaction Time:** The time that elapses between the presentation of a stimulus and a person's reaction to it.

The Research Process:
How Psychologists Study Cognitive Processes

People think—that's obvious. But since it is difficult to measure cognition directly, how do psychologists measure these processes? One of the earliest techniques used by psychologists to study cognitive processes involves reaction time: the time that elapses between the presentation of a stimulus and a person's reaction to it. Why measure reaction time? If thinking involves distinct processes, then each of them must take some time to complete. Researchers have used the information derived from **reaction time** experiments as the basis for drawing conclusions about underlying cognitive processes.

In a typical reaction time experiment, participants are asked to respond verbally or press a button as quickly as possible following the presentation of a cue, say a light, a tone, or a word on a computer screen. What can reaction time tell us about cognitive processes? Reaction time can be used to measure how long it takes for a person to complete various types of perceptual tasks; for example, the time required to react to the presentation of a visual stimulus, name letters presented on a computer screen, or decide whether a letter is a vowel or a consonant. Analysis of the various reaction times can be used to make inferences about the speed of various components involved in a mental operation, such as the time required to detect a stimulus, reach a decision, or make a manual response to the stimulus.

Through the use of reaction time measures, psychologists have gained tremendous insight into the timing of mental events. This said, it has to be recognized that reaction time provides, at best, a relatively coarse-grained measure of a mental process. It represents the final outcome of what is often a complicated series of mental cognitive events, and it takes a very clever experimenter to

tease out the role played by various components in the mental operation under investigation. It is not surprising that researchers often resort to other types of measurement to supplement reaction time studies and expose details that might be otherwise overlooked. To illustrate this point, let's consider oft-noted changes in cognitive processing associated with aging.

Among the most commonly observed cognitive changes associated with old age are declines in memory and attention and in mental processing speed. These changes—usually gauged by measures of accuracy and reaction time—have led researchers to conclude that

Event-Related Brain Potentials: A Tool to Measure Cognitive Processes

Event-related brain potentials, or ERPS, are one of several high-tech tools used to measure aspects of cognitive processing.

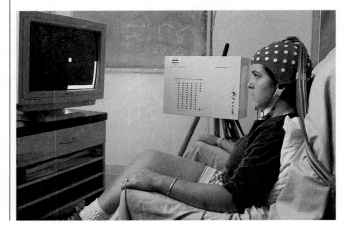

age-related declines in cognitive ability stem from an overall decline in mental processing, which is magnified as the complexity of the task increases (Cerella et al., 1980). Recent research findings employing event-related brain potentials (ERPs) suggest the story is more complicated.

As noted in Chapter 2, ERPs reflect the momentary changes in electrical activity of the brain that occur as a person performs a cognitive task (Ashcraft, 1998). To measure ERPs, electrodes are placed at standard locations on the scalp and a computer analyzes the underlying neural patterns. An ERP actually consists of a series of changes in brain electrical activity that reflect different aspects of cognitive activity, such as detecting and identifying a visual stimulus, or selecting and executing the appropriate response to the stimulus. These changes are called *components* of the ERP and are named on the basis of the charge of the current flow (P for positive and N for negative) and the time at which they achieve their maximum amplitude following presentation of a stimulus. For example, the P300 component is a positive charge that achieves its maximum amplitude about 300 milliseconds after a stimulus is presented.

Event-related potential studies have proven very useful in providing a fuller picture of age-related cognitive decline (Bashore et al., 1997). It appears that age-related cognitive declines are not evident during the initial processing of a visual stimulus, and older subjects actually process information faster than their younger counterparts until about 200 milliseconds after the initial presentation of a stimulus. The major decline in performance among older subjects seems to occur at about 260 milliseconds, suggesting that the decline in cognitive performance typically observed in reaction time studies may be primarily based on executive functions associated with selection and execution of an appropriate response.

What this section should serve to make clear is that a single measurement technique seldom provides us with a full understanding of the nature of a cognitive process. Understanding is best achieved through the use of a variety of measures: reaction time, event-related potentials, and other brain imaging techniques (refer to Chapter 2 for additional information on brain imaging tools). We will now turn now to a discussion of another important aspect of cognition: reasoning.

K E Y *QUESTIONS*

- What are concepts?
- What is the difference between artificial and natural concepts?
- What are the basic elements of thought?
- What are ERPs and what can they tell us about cognition?

Critical Thinking

Research shows a decline in speed of cognitive processing in older persons as they select and execute the appropriate response to a stimulus, but not in the initial stages of processing. Could scientists use this information to home in on the reason for such declines, and find ways of diminishing their effect?

Reasoning

One task we often face in everyday life is **reasoning**: drawing conclusions from available information. More formally, in reasoning we make cognitive transformations of appropriate information in order to reach specific conclusions (Galotti, 1989). How do we perform this task? To what extent are we successful at it, and how likely are the conclusions we reach to be accurate or valid?

First, it's important to draw a distinction between *formal reasoning* and what might be described as *everyday reasoning*. In formal reasoning, all the required information is supplied, the problem to be solved is straightforward, there is typically only one correct answer, and the reasoning we apply follows a specific method. In contrast, everyday reasoning involves the kind of thinking we do in our daily lives: planning, making commitments, evaluating arguments. In such reasoning, important information may be missing or left unstated; the problems involved often have several possible answers, which may vary in quality or effectiveness; and the problems themselves are not self-contained—they relate to other issues and questions of daily life (Hilton, 1995). Everyday reasoning, then, is far more complex and far less definite than formal reasoning. Since it is the kind we usually perform, however, it is worthy of careful attention.

Reasoning: Cognitive activity that transforms information in order to reach specific conclusions.

REASONING: SOME BASIC SOURCES OF ERROR How good are we at reasoning? Unfortunately, not as good as you might guess. Several factors, working together, seem to reduce our ability to reason effectively.

The Role of Mood States. You may not be surprised to learn that the way we feel—our current moods or emotions—can dramatically reduce our ability to reason effectively (Forgas, 1995). Most of us have experienced situations in which we've lost our cool—and unfortunately, our ability to reason effectively, as well. You may be surprised to learn, however, that *positive* moods can also reduce our ability to reason effectively. In one recent study, Oaksford et al. (1996) used brief film clips to induce either a positive, negative, or neutral mood in the study participants. Following the mood induction, all participants in the study attempted to solve a difficult analytical task. Interestingly, the participants in the positive mood condition required significantly *more* trials to solve the problem than participants in the other groups. How do we account for these results? Apparently, inducing positive mood states makes more diffuse memories available to us—definitely an asset if the task at hand requires a creative solution. Solving analytic tasks like the one used in this study, however, relies less on long-term memory retrieval and more on the ability to work through the discrete steps necessary to solve the problem. In short, a positive mood state does not guarantee that our ability to reason effectively will be enhanced.

The Role of Beliefs. Reasoning is often influenced by emotion-laden beliefs. For example, imagine that a person with deeply held convictions against the death penalty listens to a speech favouring capital punishment. Suppose that the arguments presented by the speaker contain logical arguments the listener can't readily refute that point to the conclusion that the death penalty is justified for the purpose of preventing further social evil. Yet the listener totally rejects this conclusion. Why? Because of his or her passionate beliefs and convictions against the death penalty, the listener may alter the meaning of the speaker's arguments or "remember" things the speaker never really said. This, of course, serves to weaken the speaker's conclusion. Such effects can arise in many ways. Whatever your views on this particular issue, the general principle remains the same: when powerful beliefs come face to face with logical arguments, it is often the latter that gives way. We'll consider the powerful effects of emotion again in Chapter 10.

The Confirmation Bias. Imagine that over the course of several weeks, a person with deeply held convictions against the death penalty encounters numerous magazine articles; some report evidence confirming the usefulness of the death penalty, while others report evidence indicating that it is ineffective in terms of deterring crime. As you can readily guess, the individual will probably remember more of the information that supports the anti-death penalty view. In fact, there is a good chance that he or she will read only these articles, or will read them more carefully than ones arguing in favour of capital punishment. To the extent that this happens, it demonstrates the **confirmation bias**—our strong tendency to test conclusions or hypotheses by examining only, or primarily, evidence that confirms our initial views (Baron, 1988; Nickerson, 1998). (Please refer to Chapter 1 for additional information on the confirmation bias.) Because of the confirmation bias, individuals often become firmly locked into flawed conclusions; after all, when this bias operates, it prevents people from even considering information that might call their premises, and thus their conclusions, into question (see Figure 7.2).

Hindsight: The "I Knew It All Along" Effect. Have you ever heard the old saying "Hindsight is better than foresight"? What it means is that after specific events occur, we often have the impression that we could have predicted or actually did predict them. This is known in psychology as the **hindsight effect** (Hawkins & Hastie,

Confirmation Bias: The tendency to pay attention primarily to information that confirms existing views or beliefs.

Hindsight Effect: The tendency to assume that we would have been better at predicting actual events than is really true.

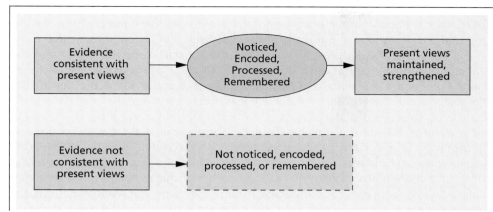

Figure 7. 2
The Confirmation Bias

The confirmation bias leads individuals to test conclusions or hypotheses by examining primarily—or only—evidence consistent with their initial views. As a result, those views may be maintained regardless of the weight of opposing evidence.

1990). In many studies, conducted in widely different contexts, learning that an event occurred causes individuals to assume that they could have predicted it more accurately than is actually the case (Christensen-Szalanski & Willham, 1991; Dawson et al., 1988; Hawkins & Hastie, 1990).

Interestingly, most research on the hindsight effect has involved soliciting the opinions of observers to an event or decision outcome—not those of the participants or decision makers themselves. More recent research on this topic has examined whether decision makers themselves show hindsight bias (Mark & Mellor, 1991). Of particular interest to researchers is how individuals show the bias when their decisions reflect upon their ability or skill. Some evidence seems to indicate that hindsight may be influenced by whether outcomes reflect positively or negatively upon the decision maker (Dunning et al., 1995). In the process of taking credit for outcomes that reflect well on them, people may show significant hindsight effects, as in "I knew the outcome would be favourable because I made a wise decision." Similarly, if people deny responsibility for unsuccessful outcomes, hindsight effects may be reduced or eliminated altogether, as in "The outcome was not foreseeable, and therefore, it was not my fault." This suggests that because of our tendency to act in ways that are self-serving, the effects of hindsight may be most evident for events for which we receive favourable feedback for our actions.

To test this possibility, Louie (1999) asked participants to read a case study of a company about to embark on a new venture. On the basis of their assessment of the company's chance of succeeding, participants were asked to decide whether they believed it would be advantageous to buy shares of the company's stock. After making their decision, participants received either no outcome information about the subsequent performance of the stock, information that the stock price had increased, or information that the stock price had dropped. They were then asked to rate what they thought would have happened to the stock price before they were informed. Results showed that the degree to which participants exhibited the hindsight bias depended on the favourableness of the match between their stock purchase decisions and corresponding outcome information. Only participants who received favourable decision outcome information exhibited hindsight bias. These findings seem to point to the following conclusion: In decision-making settings, individuals want to appear as if they "knew all along" what would occur—especially when it supports their self-serving tendencies.

Related to the hindsight bias is the **illusory-knowledge effect** described by Begg and his associates (1996) at McMaster University. In their studies, Begg et al. required participants to provide answers to trivia-type questions. Participants were able to answer some of the questions on the basis of general knowledge, but other questions could be answered only because they were required to take part in a special study session prior to testing. It was found that participants overestimated by 20 percent the number of questions they were able to answer correctly from

Illusory-Knowledge Effect: Our tendency to assume we always knew information that we have only recently acquired.

general knowledge. Just as we often tend to think we knew all along that something was going to happen after we hear about it, we have a penchant for assuming that we always knew information that has been only recently presented to us.

Can anything be done to counteract the hindsight effect and illusory-knowledge effect? The hindsight effect can be reduced if individuals are asked to provide the reported outcome along with *other* possible outcomes that did *not* occur: they are better able to recall their actual views before learning of the event, and this reduces the hindsight effect (Davies, 1987; Slovic & Fischoff, 1977). However, the illusory-knowledge effect is difficult to overcome. Begg et al. found that even though participants in the study were capable of accurately specifying the factual material learned during the pretest study session, they ignored the advantage this information afforded them and consistently overestimated the number of questions they felt they were able to answer from general knowledge. In sum, it appears that we have a strong tendency to assume we are better at predicting events than we actually are, and that we are also inclined to assume that we always knew information with which we have just been acquainted. Countering these biases requires careful, conscious monitoring of experience—a practice that we all too commonly choose to skirt.

K E Y QUESTIONS

▪ What is the process of reasoning?

▪ How does formal reasoning differ from everyday reasoning?

▪ What forms of error and bias can lead to faulty reasoning?

Making Decisions

Reasoning is hard work; in fact, it's an activity many people try to avoid. In some respects, though, reasoning is less difficult than another cognitive task you perform many times each day: **decision making**. Throughout our waking hours, life presents a continuous series of choices: what to wear, what to eat, whether to attend a class meeting, and so on—the list of everyday decisions is endless.

If you were a perfectly rational decision maker, you would make each of these choices in a cool, almost mathematical way, taking into consideration (1) the utility or value to you of the outcomes each alternative might yield, and (2) the probability that such results would actually occur. Having taken these two factors into account, you would then make your decision on the basis of **expected utility**—the product of the value and the probability of each possible outcome. As you might expect, people don't usually reason in such a systematic manner. Instead, decisions are made informally, on the basis of hunches, intuition, the information stored in our memories, and on the opinions of others (Christenfeld, 1995; Dougherty et al., 1999). We will consider next several factors that influence the decision-making process, making it less rational or effective than might otherwise be the case.

Heuristics

Where cognition is concerned, human beings often follow the path of least resistance. Since making decisions is hard work, it is only reasonable to expect people to take shortcuts in performing this activity. One group of cognitive shortcuts is known as **heuristics**—rules of thumb that reduce the effort required to make decisions, though they may not necessarily enhance the quality or accuracy of the decisions reached (Kahneman & Tversky, 1982). Heuristics are extracted from past experience and serve as simple guidelines for making reasonably good choices quickly and efficiently. We'll focus on the three heuristics that tend to be used most frequently.

Decision Making: The process of choosing among various courses of action or alternatives.

Expected Utility: The product of the subjective value of an event and its predicted probability of occurrence.

Heuristics: Mental rules of thumb that permit us to make decisions and judgments in a rapid and efficient manner.

CALVIN AND HOBBES   By Bill Watterson

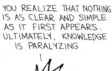

Heuristics: Quick but Fallible Decision Tools

Calvin recognizes that decision making is hard work. Like many people, Calvin may resort to heuristics—rules of thumb that reduce the amount of effort required—to help him make quicker, but not necessarily better, decisions.

Source: Universal Press Syndicate, 1993.

AVAILABILITY: WHAT COMES TO MIND FIRST? Let's start with the **availability heuristic**: the tendency to make judgments about the frequency or likelihood of events in terms of how readily examples of them can be brought to mind. This shortcut tends to work fairly well, because the more readily we can bring events to mind, the more frequent they generally are; but it can lead us into error as well.

A good example of the availability heuristic in operation is provided by a study conducted by Tversky and Kahneman (1974). They presented participants with lists of names like the one in Table 7.1 and then asked them whether the lists contained more men's or women's names. Although the numbers of male and female names were equal, nearly 80 percent of the participants reported that women's names appeared more frequently. Why? Because the women named in the lists were more famous, so their names were more readily remembered and brought to mind.

The availability heuristic also influences many people to overestimate their chances of being a victim of a violent crime, being involved in an airplane crash, or winning the lottery. Because such events are given extensive coverage in the mass media, people can readily bring vivid examples of them to mind. They conclude that such outcomes are much more frequent than they actually are (Tyler & Cook, 1984).

TABLE 7.1

The Availability Heuristic in Operation

Does this list contain more men's or women's names? The answer may surprise you: The number of male and female names is equal. Because of the *availability heuristic*, however, most people tend to guess that female names are more numerous. Since the women listed are more famous than the men, it is easier to bring their names to mind, and this leads to overestimates of their frequency in the list.

Margaret Atwood	Bruce Holliday	Peter Mitchell
Anne Murray	Arthur Hutchinson	Mary Walsh
Shania Twain	Sarah McLachlan	Cliff Newman
Céline Dion	Margaret Laurence	Edward Palmer
Michael Drayton	Edward Lytton	Robert Porter
Larry Schneider	Jack Lindsay	Sheila Copps
Pamela Anderson	Elizabeth Manley	Henry Vaughan
Charles Fisher	Roberta Bondar	Pamela Wallin
Ron Fisher	Alannah Myles	

Availability Heuristic: A cognitive rule of thumb in which the importance or probability of various events is judged on the basis of how readily they come to mind.

REPRESENTATIVENESS: ASSUMING THAT WHAT'S TYPICAL IS ALSO LIKELY

Imagine that you've just met your next-door neighbour for the first time. On the basis of a brief conversation, you determine that he is neat in his appearance, has a good vocabulary, seems very well read, is somewhat shy, and dresses conservatively. Later, you realize that he never mentioned what he does for a living. Is he more likely to be a business executive, a dentist, a librarian, or a waiter? One quick way of making a guess is to compare him with your idea of typical members of each of these occupations. If you proceeded in this fashion, you might conclude that he is a librarian, because his traits seem to resemble those of your image of the proto-typical librarian more closely than the traits of waiters, dentists, or executives. If you reasoned in this manner you would be using the **representativeness heuristic**. In other words, you would be making your decision on the basis of a relatively simple rule: The more closely an item—or event, or object, or person—resembles the most typical examples of some concept or category, the more likely it is to belong to that concept or category.

Unfortunately, the use of this heuristic sometimes causes us to ignore forms of information that could potentially prove very helpful. The most important of these is information relating to *base rates*—the relative frequency of various items or events in the external world. Returning to your new neighbour, there are many more businessmen than male librarians. Thus, of the choices given, the most rational guess might be that your neighbour is a business executive. Yet because of the representativeness heuristic, you might falsely conclude that he is a librarian (Tversky & Kahneman, 1974).

ANCHORING-AND-ADJUSTMENT: REFERENCE POINTS THAT MAY LEAD US ASTRAY

Once we gain something in the way of a steady income, most of us start to look around for our first car. We scan the newspaper ads zealously, and inevitably meet up with the ideal solution to our transportation problems. The question then becomes, "How much will it cost?" A totally rational person obtains this information from a guide book that lists the average prices paid for various used cars in recent months. Do most of us proceed in this fashion? Absolutely *not*. Given our strong tendency to follow the path of least resistance (and the fact that such guide books are not readily available everywhere), we use the simpler approach of asking the seller the price of the car, and bargaining from there. At first glance, this may seem like a reasonable strategy, but it is not. If you adopt this tactic, you allow the seller to set a *reference point*—a figure from which your negotiations will proceed. If this price is close to the true average price, all well and good. If it is much higher, though, you may end up paying more for the car than it is really worth—as many of us often do.

In such cases, decisions are influenced by what is known as the **anchoring-and-adjustment heuristic**, a mental rule of thumb for reaching decisions by making adjustments in information that is already available. The basic problem with the anchoring-and-adjustment heuristic is that the adjustments are often insufficient in magnitude to offset the impact of the original reference point. In this case, the reference point was the original asking price. In other contexts, it might be a performance rating assigned to an employee, a grade given to a term paper, or a suggested asking price for a new home (Northcraft & Neale, 1987).

See the **Key Concept** on page 271 for an overview of the heuristics we have discussed. Although the influence of heuristics appears to be quite strong, growing evidence indicates that it is often reduced in the case of experts working on tasks with which they are very familiar (Frederick & Libby, 1986; Smith & Kida, 1991). So, while the impact of such potential sources of error is strong, it is not irresistible; it can be reduced by expertise and experience.

Representativeness Heuristic: A mental rule of thumb suggesting that the more closely an event or object resembles typical examples of some concept or category, the more likely it is to belong to that concept or category.

Anchoring-and-Adjustment Heuristic: A cognitive rule of thumb for decision making in which existing information is accepted as a reference point but then adjusted in light of various factors.

Key Concept

Factors That Influence the Decision-Making Process

Heuristics

Rules of thumb extracted from past experience that serve as guidelines for making decisions quickly and efficiently—but not necessarily infallibly.

Because lotto winners are given extensive media coverage, people can readily bring examples of them to mind. They falsely conclude that such outcomes are much more frequent than they really are.

Availability Heuristic
The tendency to make judgments about the frequency or likelihood of events in terms of how readily examples of them can be brought to mind.

Representativeness Heuristic
A rule of thumb suggesting that the more closely an event or object resembles typical examples of some concept or category, the more likely it is to belong to that concept or category.

Gang members typically dress in the same fashion. These young people have similar dresses and hairstyles. The representativeness heuristic might lead you to the conclusion that they are gang members.

Anchoring-and-Adjustment Heuristic
A rule of thumb in which existing information (such as the seller's asking price for a house) is accepted as an anchor, and then adjusted—usually insufficiently—through negotiation.

Using the seller's asking price as the anchor point to start negotiations puts the buyer at a disadvantage. It imposes a downward limit on the price that can be negotiated.

▶ ## Framing and Decision Strategy

Imagine that a new, virulent strain of flu is on its way toward Canada and is expected to kill 600 people. Two plans for combating the disease exist. If plan A is adopted, 200 people will be saved. If plan B is adopted, the chances are one in three that all 600 will be saved, but two in three that no one will be saved. Which plan would you choose?

Now consider the same situation with the following changes. Again, there are two plans. If plan C is chosen, 400 people will definitely die; if plan D is chosen, the chances are one in three that no one will die, but two in three that all 600 will die. Which would you choose now?

If you are like most respondents to these scenarios, you probably chose plan A in the first example but plan D in the second example (Tversky & Kahneman, 1981). Why? Plan D is just another way of stating the outcomes of plan B, and plan C is just another way of stating the outcomes of plan A. Why, then, do you prefer plan A in the first example but plan D in the second? Because in the first example the emphasis is on *lives saved*, while in the second the emphasis is on *lives lost*. In other words, the two examples differ in what psychologists term **framing**—presentation of information about potential outcomes in terms of gains or in terms of losses. When the emphasis is on potential gains (lives saved), research indicates that most people are *risk averse*. They prefer avoiding unnecessary risks. Thus, most choose plan A. In contrast, when the emphasis is on potential losses (deaths), most people are *risk prone*; they prefer taking risks to accepting probable losses. As a result, most choose plan D.

Framing effects have been found to be quite general in scope. For example, negotiators tend to evaluate offers from their opponents more favourably, and to make more actual concessions, if they are urged to think about potential gains than if they are urged to think about potential losses that may result from such concessions (Neale & Bazerman, 1985).

Research indicates that the framing effect may stem partly from the scenarios that are used to introduce decison-making problems (Jou, Shanteau, & Harris, 1996; Wang, 1996). The disease example just described is arbitrary in the sense that it does not provide a rationale for the relationship between the potential gains and losses. People usually have a general understanding about how events are related based on *schemas,* a term we discussed in Chapter 6. When events we encounter cannot be fit into a schema—as in the disease scenario above—the relationship between the events may not be apparent. In one study, Jou and his colleagues (1996) asked participants to read either the original disease examples or the same ones revised to include a rationale that explained why a choice must be made. The rationale indicated that saving some proportion of lives would require sacrificing other lives because of limited resources. The researchers reasoned that including this rationale would clarify the relationship between lives saved and lives lost, which in turn might reduce the effects of framing. As shown in Figure 7.3, the researchers' predictions were confirmed: framing effects were apparent for participants who read the original disease examples, but not for participants who read the revised examples. These results suggest that the effects of framing, though powerful, are not immutable; they are affected by people's attitudes and they can be offset when people are given a more complete picture of the choices to be made (Rothman & Salovey, 1997).

Framing: Presentation of information concerning potential outcomes in terms of gains or losses.

Escalation of Commitment

Have you ever heard the phrase "throwing good money after bad"? It refers to the fact that in many situations, persons who have made a bad decision tend to stick to it even as the evidence for its failure mounts. They may even commit additional

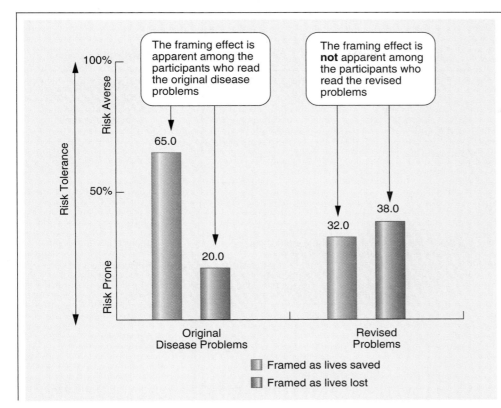

The framing effect is apparent among the participants who read the original disease problems

The framing effect is **not** apparent among the participants who read the revised problems

Figure 7.3
Understanding the Effects of Framing

The effects of framing are evident among participants who read the original disease problem: these participants were risk averse when it was framed positively (lives saved), but risk seeking when the same problem was framed negatively. The effects of framing disappeared, however, when participants were given a rationale that helped them to understand the relationship between lives saved and lives lost

Source: Based on data from Jou et al., 1996.

time, effort, and resources to a failing course of action in order to turn the situation around. This tendency to become trapped in bad decisions, known as **escalation of commitment**, helps explain why many investors hold on to what are clearly bad investments and why people remain in troubled marriages or relationships (Brockner & Rubin, 1985). In these and many other situations, people seem to become trapped in bad decisions with no simple or easy means of getting out.

WHY DOES ESCALATION OF COMMITMENT OCCUR?   Escalation of commitment is both real and widespread. But why, precisely, does it occur? Research suggests that escalation of commitment probably stems from several different factors (Staw & Ross, 1989). Early in the escalation process, initial decisions are based primarily on rational factors. People choose particular courses of action because they believe that these will yield favourable outcomes. When things go wrong and negative results occur, it is at first quite reasonable to continue. After all, temporary setbacks are common and there may also be considerable costs associated with changing an initial decision before it has had a chance to succeed (Staw & Ross, 1987).

As negative outcomes continue to mount, however, psychological factors come into play. Persons responsible for the initial decision may realize that if they back away from or reverse it, they will be admitting that they made a mistake. Indeed, as negative results increase, these individuals may experience a growing need for self-justification—a tendency to justify both their previous judgments and the losses already endured (Bobocel & Meyer, 1994).

In later phases of the process, external pressures stemming from other persons or groups affected by the bad decision may come into play. For example, individuals who did not originally make the decision but have gone along with it may now block efforts to reverse it because they too have become committed to actions it implies. Figure 7.4 summarizes the escalation process and several factors that play a role in its occurrence and persistence.

Escalation of Commitment: The tendency to become increasingly committed to bad decisions even as losses associated with them increase.

Figure 7.4
Escalation of Commitment: An Overview

Early in the escalation-of-commitment process, there may be a rational expectation of a positive outcome. As losses occur, however, people are reluctant to admit their errors. Later, external factors may strengthen tendencies to stick to the initial bad decision. However, other conditions may reduce the likelihood of escalation of commitment.

Sources: Based on suggestions by Staw and Ross, 1989; and Garland and Newport, 1991.

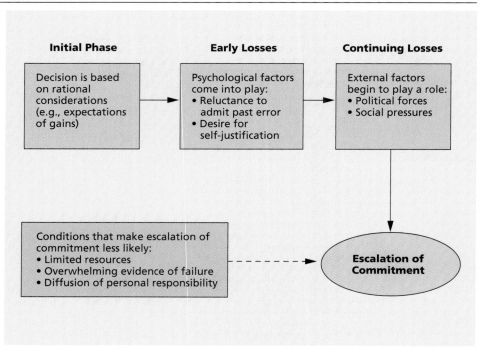

Can anything be done to counter these effects? Researchers have found that under several conditions, people are less likely to escalate their commitment to a failed course of action (please refer to Figure 7.4). First, people are likely to refrain from escalating commitment when available resources to commit to further action are limited and the evidence of failure is overwhelmingly obvious (Garland & Newport, 1991). Thus, an individual or a group can decide in advance that if losses reach certain limits, no further resources will be squandered. Second, escalation of commitment is unlikely to occur when people can *diffuse their responsibility* for being part of a poor decision (Whyte, 1991). In other words, the less we feel personally responsible for making a bad decision, the less we may be motivated to justify our mistake by investing additional time or money. Thus, a helpful strategy is to assign the tasks of making decisions and implementing them to different individuals. This allows the people who carry out decisions to be psychologically aloof from them. Together, these steps can help both individuals and groups to avoid getting trapped in costly spirals that magnify the harmful effects of poor decisions. (See Chapter 16 for more information on the effects of diffusion of responsibility.)

Naturalistic Decision Making

Naturalistic Decision Making: A movement toward studying decision making as it occurs in naturalistic settings.

Much of what is known about decision making is based on controlled laboratory studies in which study participants read a brief story and then make a decision based on its contents. The stories are often very contrived and without context—and therefore have little real meaning to the participants who read them. Concerns have been raised about whether studies of this type adequately assess the decision-making processes that we face in everyday life (Fischhoff, 1996). Researchers are increasingly turning their attention to focus on the study of decision making as it occurs in the real world. This emphasis on what is termed **naturalistic decision making** deepens our understanding of decision making in several ways (Cannon-Bowers, Salas, & Pruitt, 1996). First, it focuses attention on how decision makers bring their experience to bear in making a decision. Second, it broadens the focus of decision making to include the decision-making context. Finally, it emphasizes the dynamic nature of decision making and takes into account the complexity of modern decision environments—including the enormous costs of making bad decisions, both in terms of money and loss of life. The overall goal is to provide a fuller, and perhaps more accurate, description of the decision-making process as it unfolds in environments in which the accuracy of decisions is paramount. To this end, studies have been carried out in military, healthcare, and courtroom settings, and in one case on an oil-drilling platform in the North Sea (Flin, Slaven, & Stewart, 1996; Kaempf, 1996; Pennington & Hastie, 1993; Pierce, 1996).

The shift toward studying decision making in naturalistic settings has had another, unexpected effect as well. It has forced researchers to acknowledge that sometimes research findings derived from laboratory studies may not accurately depict decision making in the natural environment. A widely reported finding that has recently been called into question pertains to a tendency referred to as the *base-rate problem:* people's tendency to ignore the relative frequency of various events when making decisions and, instead, opting for simpler heuristics. As we saw earlier, when someone is given a general description of a person and then asked to judge whether that person is a businessman or a librarian, many people tend to rely on the representativeness heuristic. They make their judgment that he is a librarian rather than a businessman largely on the basis of how closely the description matches the central features of each occupation, ignoring the fact that there are many more businessmen than librarians.

Recent evidence seems to indicate that we've been oversold on the base-rate problem and that people in natural situations do consider base rates in their decisions (e.g., Koehler, 1996). It has been argued also that as people gain real-world experience in making specific types of judgments, they do tend to take base-rate biases into consideration. Current interest in naturalistic decision making promises to enhance our understanding of how decisions are made in real-world settings. For information about how to apply what we know about problem solving to your own personal decision-making experience, see the Making Psychology Part of Your Life section on page 294.

K E Y *QUESTIONS*

- What are heuristics?
- What are the availability, representativeness, and anchoring-and-adjustment heuristics and what role do they play in reasoning?
- What is framing and how does it relate to decision making?
- How does escalation of commitment affect decision making?
- What is naturalistic decision making?

Problem Solving: Finding Paths to Desired Goals

Imagine that you are a parent whose son is attending university in another province. You've asked him to keep in touch, but long periods go by without a word—by either phone or mail. You phone him repeatedly, but all you get is his answering machine. What do you do? Several possibilities exist. You could call his friends and ask them to urge him to get in touch with you. You could leave a message that, you hope, will cause him to phone. Or—and here's the interesting one—you could try something like this: You write a letter to your son in which you mention that you've enclosed a cheque—but you don't enclose one. Is the problem solved? In all probability, yes. Your son will no doubt call to find out what happened to the cheque.

The Card Players by Paul Cézanne

How are problem-solving skills used during card games? The winner is the person who has successfully solved the problem set by the rules of the game. (Of course, luck may also play a role!)

Problem Solving: Efforts to develop or choose among various responses in order to attain desired goals.

While you may not have any children, there is little doubt that you have encountered situations that resemble this one in basic structure: You would like to reach some goal, but there is no simple or direct way of doing so. Such situations involve **problem solving**—efforts to develop responses that permit us to attain desired goals. In this section we'll examine the nature of problem solving, techniques for enhancing its effectiveness, and factors that interfere with its successful execution. (Please note that we'll consider *creativity*—the ability to produce new and unusual solutions to various problems—in Chapter 11).

Problem Solving: An Overview

What does problem solving involve? Psychologists are not totally in agreement on this basic issue (e.g., Lipshitz & Bar-Ilan, 1996), but many believe that four major steps are central, as summarized in Figure 7.5.

The first step is *problem identification:* we must recognize that a problem exists and then figure out just what issues, obstacles, and goals are involved. In the example above, the immediate problem boils down to this: You want to find some way of inducing your son to contact you. But understanding the nature of the problems we face is not always so simple. For example, suppose your car won't start. Why? Is it a bad battery? Bad ignition? Lack of fuel? Until you identify the problem and understand the issues involved, it is difficult to move ahead with its solution.

Figure 7.5
Problem Solving: An Overview

Effective problem solving involves four stages. First, the problem must be identified and understood. Next, potential solutions must be generated. Third, these must be examined and evaluated. Finally, solutions must be tried and then evaluated in terms of their successes.

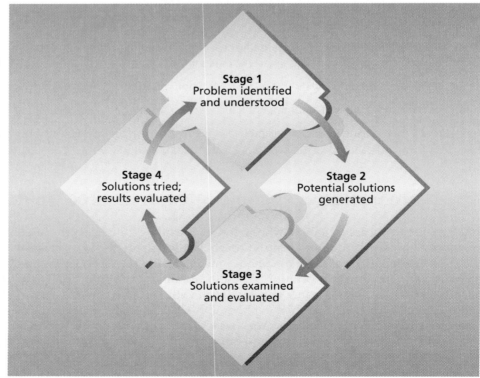

Stage 1
Problem identified
and understood

Stage 2
Potential solutions
generated

Stage 3
Solutions examined
and evaluated

Stage 4
Solutions tried;
results evaluated

Second, we must *formulate potential solutions.* While this too might seem fairly simple, it is actually very complex (Treffinger, 1995). Solutions do not arise out of a cognitive vacuum; they require thinking critically about a problem, and they depend heavily on the information at our disposal—information stored in long-term memory that can be retrieved (see Chapter 6). The more information available, the greater the number and the wider the scope of potential solutions we can generate. Formulating a wide range of possible solutions is an extremely important step in effective problem solving (and in creativity—see Chapter 11).

Third, we must *evaluate* each alternative and the outcomes it will produce. Will a given solution work—bring us closer to the goal we want? Are there any serious obstacles to its use? Are there hidden costs that will make a potential solution less useful than it seems at first? These are important considerations that must be taken into account.

Finally, we must *try* potential solutions and evaluate them on the basis of the effects they produce. All too often, a potential solution is only partially effective: It brings us closer to where we want to be but doesn't solve the problem completely or finally. The letter-without-a-cheque strategy described above illustrates this point. Yes, it may induce a response from the erring child on this occasion. But it does not guarantee that he will write or phone more frequently in the future, so it constitutes only a partial solution to the problem. In this case it is easy to recognize that the solution will be only a partial one. In many other situations, though, it is difficult to know how effective a potential solution will be until it is implemented. Thus, careful assessment of the effects of various solutions is another key step in the problem-solving process.

Methods for Solving Problems: From Trial and Error to Heuristics

Suppose that you are working on your friend's computer, trying to complete a term paper that is due tomorrow. The pressure is mounting. You decide to take a break and then realize—with panic—that you don't remember how to save what you've written with this word processor. You think for a moment, then try hitting one of the keys, but nothing happens. You try another key—again, no result. You hit a third one, and the message "Find What?" appears on the screen. Now you decide to try a combination of keys. You are still trying, and still in a panic, when your friend arrives and rescues you.

This incident illustrates a problem-solving technique you have certainly used yourself—**trial and error**. Trial and error involves trying different responses until, perhaps, one works. Sometimes this is all you can do: You do not have enough information to adopt a more systematic approach. But this approach is not very efficient and offers no guarantee that you'll actually find a useful solution. A manageable trial and error problem is shown in Figure 7.6. The trick is to work out how to transform the word "pint" to the word "lass" by changing a single letter in each of three successive intervening words. The only way to go about this is to try and specify the correct words by trial and error.

A second general approach to solving problems involves the use of **algorithms.** These are rules for a particular kind of problem that will, if followed, yield a solution. For example, imagine that you are supposed to meet a friend at a Chinese restaurant. Try as you may, you can't remember the name of the place. What can you do? One approach is to get out the Yellow Pages and see if this refreshes your memory. If it doesn't, you can try calling all the restaurants listed to ask if your friend made a reservation (which you know she was planning to do). Following this algorithm—"Call every restaurant in the book"—will eventually work; but it is time-consuming and inefficient. A much more effective way to solve many problems is by using an appropriate *heuristic.*

**Figure 7.6
Trial and Error Problem Solving**

To solve this word puzzle, start with the word at the top and change one letter to generate the next word. Continue to change a single letter in each of the next two words to produce the word at the bottom. Generating successive words to get to the final word demonstrates trial-and-error problem solving.

Source: Adapted from Stickels (1998).

PINT

_____

_____

_____

LASS

Solution: pint, pant, past, last, lass.

Trial and Error: A method of solving problems in which possible solutions are tried until one succeeds.

Algorithm: A rule that guarantees a solution to a specific type of problem.

Heuristics, as you'll recall, are rules of thumb we often use to guide our cognition. With respect to problem solving, heuristics involve strategies suggested by prior experience—ones we have found useful in the past. These may or may not work in the present case, so a solution is not guaranteed. But what heuristics lack in terms of certainty they gain in efficiency: They often provide useful shortcuts. In the case of the Chinese restaurant search, you might begin by assuming that your friend probably chose a restaurant close to where she lives. This simple rule could eliminate many of the most distant restaurants and considerably simplify your task.

Finally, we sometimes attempt to solve problems through the use of **analogy**— by applying techniques that worked in similar situations in the past. For example, imagine that while driving through an unfamiliar town, you are suddenly seized by an uncontrollable desire for a cup of Tim Hortons coffee. You don't know your way around this town, but you know from past experience that many Tim Hortons shops are located near busy entry and exit ramps to the Trans-Canada Highway. Applying this knowledge, you follow signs showing the way to the nearest link to the Trans-Canada. If you are then rewarded with a cup of coffee (with a bag of Timbits), you have solved the problem through analogy. Emerging new evidence on this topic seems to suggest that people frequently solve problems through the use of analogy—although they may remain unaware that they've done so (Burns, 1996; Schunn & Dunbar, 1996). To summarize, selecting an appropriate strategy is critical to effective problem solving.

KEY QUESTIONS

- How do psychologists define problem solving?
- Through what two mechanisms are problems usually solved?
- What role do heuristics play in problem solving?

Metacognitive Processing and Lateral Thinking

Sometimes simply concentrating on a problem gets us nowhere. What we need to find is a technique or process that will serve to solve the problem. Two approaches that are often useful in helping us find appropriate problem-solving techniques are *metacognitive processing* and *lateral thinking*.

Metacognitive processing encourages us to think about our own thought processes—to focus on the way in which we are thinking about a problem. One way to do this is to think aloud about the problem confronting us. It seems that talking through a problem helps divert attention away from the problem's content, and toward the process—what we are *doing* to solve the problem. In other words, talking through the problem may facilitate our ability to solve problems by expanding our level of awareness of the particular steps that we are taking to solve the problem—and to determine whether they seem to be leading to a meaningful solution. A direct assessment of metacognitive processing on problem solving by Berardi-Coletta, Buyer, Dominouski, and Rellinger (1996) suggests it can improve problem-solving performance.

Although their study was complex, it can be summarized as follows. Participants had to solve a problem requiring them to order a set of playing cards so that when the cards were dealt they appeared in a prescribed order (ace, one, two, three, etc.). Prior to the test, participants practised the task as members of one of three groups: a group in which metacognitive processing was encouraged by asking participants process-oriented questions as they practised ("How are you deciding on a way to work out the order for the cards?"); a group in which participants were asked problem-focused questions (What is the goal of the problem?"); or a control group

Analogy: A strategy for solving problems based on applying solutions that were previously successful to other problems similar in underlying structure.

Metacognitive Processing: An expanded level of awareness that can be achieved by having a person monitor the steps that he or she is taking in attempting to solve a problem.

in which participants merely worked on the problem with no additional instructions or discussion. The metacognitive group performed best, and the problem-focused group worst. These results indicate that talking through a problem can be useful if it causes us to focus on the problem-solving *process*, but if we dwell solely on the problem per se, it can have detrimental effects.

Lateral thinking is another approach that can often help us find an appropriate problem-solving technique. All too often, we tend to engage in what De Bono (1990, 1991) terms *vertical thinking*. We look at a problem from a single perspective. This prevents us from seeing alternative solutions that may be readily available. What we should do, according to De Bono, is to engage in lateral thinking in the early stages of problem solving. Engaging in lateral thinking means that we seek alternative ways of conceptualizing and dealing with a problem. To illustrate lateral thinking, consider the nine-dot problem in Figure 7.7. The task seems simple. All you have to do is a draw straight lines through all the dots without lifting your pencil from the surface of the page. What makes it challenging is the requirement that you must not use more than four straight lines to join the dots. See if you can find a way to do this before reading the next sentence. If you are like most people who try to solve this problem, you did not allow the lines you drew to stray outside of the boundaries of the nine dots. This is an example of constrained vertical thinking. If you engage in lateral thinking, and consider alternative ways of drawing the lines, you will realize that the constraint requiring you to stay within the lines is self-imposed, and that if you allow the lines you draw to extend far enough beyond the boundaries of the outer dots the problem is easily solved. Both metacognitive processing and lateral thinking can be very helpful in coping with a variety of factors that are well known to interfere with effective problem solving. We will consider these in the next section.

Figure 7.7
Using Lateral Thinking

Draw straight lines through all the dots without lifting your pencil from the surface of the page. You cannot use more than four straight lines to join the dots. The solution is on page 280.

Source: Adapted from Guenther, 1998.

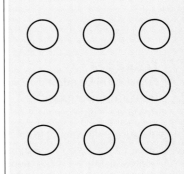

Factors That Interfere with Effective Problem Solving

Sometimes, despite our best efforts, we are unable to solve problems. In many cases our failure has obvious causes, such as lack of necessary information or experience. Similarly, as we'll soon see, we may lack internal frameworks that allow us to represent the problem situation fully and effectively. As a result, we don't know which variables or factors are most important, and we spend lots of time "wandering about," using an informal type of trial and error approach (Johnson, 1985). In other cases, though, difficulties in solving problems seem to stem from more subtle factors. Let's consider some of these now.

FUNCTIONAL FIXEDNESS: PRIOR USE VERSUS PRESENT SOLUTIONS Suppose you want to use the objects shown in Figure 7.8 to attach the candle to a wall so that it can stand upright and burn properly. What solution (or solutions) do you come up with? If you are like most people, you may mention using the tacks to nail the candle to the wall, or attaching it with melted wax (Duncker, 1945). While these techniques may work, they overlook a much more elegant solution: emptying the box of matches, attaching the box to the wall, and placing the candle on it (see Figure 7.9). Described this way, the solution probably sounds obvious. Then why don't most people think of it? The answer involves **functional fixedness**—a strong tendency to think of using objects only in ways they have been used before. Since most of us have never used an empty box as a candle holder, we don't think of its use in these terms and so fail to hit upon this solution. Interestingly, if the matchbox is shown empty, people are much more likely to use it as a candle holder (Weisberg & Suls, 1973); it doesn't take much to overcome such mental blind spots. But unless we can avoid functional fixedness, our ability to solve many problems can be seriously impaired.

Lateral Thinking: A problem-solving approach that encourages early consideration of alternative ways of conceptualizing a problem.

Functional Fixedness: The tendency to think of using objects only as they have been used in the past.

Figure 7.8
Solving Complex Problems

How can you attach the candle to a wall so that it stands upright and burns normally, using only the objects shown here?

Figure 7.9
Functional Fixedness: How It Interferes with Problem Solving

Because of functional fixedness, surprisingly few people think of using the tacks to attach the box to the wall as a candle holder.

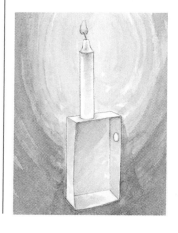

MENTAL SET: STICKING TO THE TRIED-AND-TRUE   Another factor that often gets in the way of effective problem solving is **mental set.** This is the tendency to stick with a familiar method of solving particular types of problems—one that has worked before. Since past solutions have in fact succeeded, this is certainly reasonable—at least up to a point. Difficulties arise, however, when this tendency causes us to overlook other, more efficient approaches. The powerful impact of mental set was first demonstrated by Luchins (1942) in what is now a classic study. Luchins presented study participants with the problems shown in Table 7.2, which involve using three jars of different sizes to measure amounts of water. If you work through the first two or three items, you will soon discover that you can solve them all by following this simple formula: Fill jar B, and from it fill jar A once and jar C twice. The amount of water then remaining is the desired amount.

Because this formula works for all items, subjects in Luchins's study tended to stick with it for all seven problems. But look at item 6, which can be solved in a simpler way: Just fill jar A, then from it fill jar C. The amount remaining in jar A is precisely what's required (20 units). A simple solution also exists for item 7; see if you can figure it out. Do you think many of the subjects in Luchin's experiment noticed these simpler solutions? Absolutely not. When they reached item 6, almost all continued to use their old tried-and-true formula and overlooked the more efficient one.

Similar effects occur in many other contexts. For example, commuters often continue to take the same crowded roads to work each day because they have always done so; they don't even consider alternative routes that might seem less direct but are actually easier to travel. In these and many other situations, sliding into mental ruts can indeed prove costly.

Solution to Figure 7.7

Mental Set: The impact of past experience on present problem solving; specifically, the tendency to retain methods that were successful in the past even if better alternatives now exist.

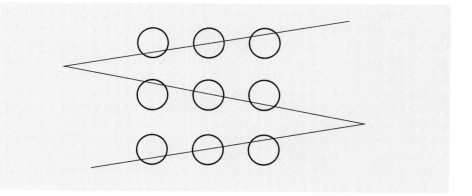

TABLE 7.2

Mental Set: Another Potential Deterrent to Problem Solving

How can you use three jars, A, B, and C, each capable of holding the amounts of liquid shown, to end up with one jar holding the exact amount listed in the right-hand column? See the text for two possible solutions.

	Amount Held by Each Jar			
Problem	Jar A	Jar B	Jar C	Goal (amount of water desired)
1	24	130	3	100
2	9	44	7	21
3	21	58	4	29
4	12	160	25	98
5	19	75	5	46
6	23	49	3	20
7	18	48	4	22

Artificial Intelligence

Newspapers, magazines, television, and movies have defined the future of technology for us. We know that at some point—probably in the not-too-distant future—we will be able to talk to computers and receive an intelligent and intelligible answer back. Those of us who have survived generations of *Star Trek* spin-offs know that computers will ultimately have mental capacities on par with those that humans possess. We are at present somewhat short of this goal: Witness the difficulties computer companies have had in getting notepad computers to perform the relatively simple task of deciphering an owner's handwriting. Nevertheless, progress is being made, and every year we move closer to the goal of producing an intelligent computer. This goal is pursued by those who work in **artificial intelligence**—an interdisciplinary branch of research in which psychologists and other scientists study the capacity of computers to perform in a way that, in humans, would be described as intelligent. (We will examine the nature of intelligence in more detail in Chapter 11.)

How much intelligence do computers actually show? Actually, quite a lot. Modern computers perform at blinding speeds, often at a rate of millions of computations per second—a capability far beyond that of mere mortals. It is therefore not surprising that computers are more proficient than people at doing repetitive tasks requiring speed and accuracy.

But is it possible to construct robots capable of interacting with humans in more meaningful ways? Ongoing research at the Massachusetts Institute of Technology (MIT), termed Cog Project, suggests the answer may be yes. One example of this work is Kismet, an autonomous robot designed to engage in social interactions with humans (Breazeal & Scassellati, 2000). The development of Kismet was inspired by the way infants learn to communicate with adults. According to researcher Cynthia Breazeal, basic motivational factors play an important role in establishing meaningful social interactions between human infants and their caretakers. In an attempt to understand how these interactions develop, Kismet has been endowed with a motivational system that mirrors our own. This system

Artificial Intelligence: A branch of science that studies the capacity of computers to demonstrate performance that, if it were produced by human beings, would be described as showing intelligence.

Social Interactions between Robots and Humans

Kismet, a robot developed by researchers affiliated with the Cog process at MIT, is capable of a wide range of facial expressions that can be interpreted by an untrained human observer.

Source: Photos courtesy of Sam Ogden Photography.

Neural Networks: Computer systems modelled after the brain and made up of highly interconnected elementary computational units that work together in parallel.

works to maintain homeostasis and motivates the robot to learn behaviours that satisfy its needs. As shown in the photo, Kismet is capable of a wide range of facial expressions that tell potential caregivers which of its needs must be tended to, and allows them to act accordingly. An all-too-human feature built into Kismet is the capacity to become overwhelmed by too much stimulation. When this occurs, Kismet is designed to terminate the interaction so it can restore homeostatic balance. To do so, Kismet shuts its eyes and goes to sleep. When balance is achieved, Kismet wakes up ready to resume interaction. Through a series of such interactions the robot learns how its actions influence the behaviour of the caretaker, which ultimately serves to satisfy Kismet's own needs.

Although computers seem capable of simulating some aspects of human activities, other aspects have proven frustratingly difficult—especially those associated with human language. Some large corporations have developed voice recognition systems that can be used to handle certain business transactions and bookings, but understanding the subtleties of everyday conversation is something that exceeds the capacity of even the most powerful of today's computers. Difficulties in making advances in speech recognition and in reasoning and problem solving have led some researchers to try and design computers that imitate the way in which the brain—perhaps the most powerful computer in the universe—operates. As we noted in Chapters 2 and 6, computers process information in a sequential fashion, one step at a time; in contrast, the brain processes the input from all of our senses simultaneously through a complex network of highly interconnected neurons. The new computer systems, called **neural networks,** are structures consisting of highly interconnected elementary computational units that work together in parallel (Denning, 1992; Levine, 1991). The primary advantage of neural networks comes not from the individual units themselves but from the overall pattern resulting from millions of these units working together. In addition, neural networks have the capacity to learn from experience by adjusting the strength of the output from individual units based on new information.

Such networks can readily learn to make discriminations. The high degree of interconnection among the units can be weakened or strengthened by special built-in algorithms that nudge the network toward a desired discriminative output (Rumelhart, Hinton, & Williams, 1986). Although research on neural networks is still in its infancy, this technology shows enormous promise in its ability to produce intelligent behaviour in machines and to provide insight into brain function. Neural network analysis has been applied to a wide variety of problems in human perception, such as figure–ground differentiation, shape perception, and stereopsis (e.g., Hinton & Parsons, 1988; Kienker, Sejinowski, Hinton, & Schumacher, 1986). More recently, research on neural network modelling has extended to include clinical problems such as schizophrenia and Alzheimer's disease (Spitzer, 1999).

Where does all this leave us with respect to artificial intelligence? Most psychologists who specialize in this field would readily admit that early predictions about the capacities of computers to show such characteristics as intention, understanding, and consciousness were greatly overstated (Levine, 1991; Searle, 1980). However, these specialists note that computers are indeed exceptionally useful in the study of human cognition and can, in some contexts, demonstrate performance that closely resembles that of intelligent human beings.

K E Y *QUESTIONS*

- What is metacognitive processing?
- What factors can interfere with effective problem solving?
- What is artificial intelligence?

Critical Thinking

Research conducted with Kismet, the autonomous robot, seems to indicate that it is able to engage in rudimentary forms of social communication with its caretakers. Do you think that robots can ever achieve true meaningful social interaction with humans? Why or why not?

Animal Cognition

We have considered the degree to which computers can simulate various kinds of human cognitive operations. It seems only fair to give some consideration to the cognitive capacities of the other animals with whom we share this planet. Our discussions in this chapter have implied so far that cognitive processes are mainly a human attribute—a view that was prevalent for many years in research laboratories. Several developments have led researchers to reconsider this assessment of animal intelligence. One reason, which was noted in Chapter 5, is that behavioural researchers throughout this century have encountered many instances of animal learning that cannot be explained solely through conditioning processes (e.g., Capaldi, 1996; Tolman & Honzik, 1930). Another reason is that there is growing evidence to suggest that animals do form complex mental representations of their environment—a cognitive activity that helps them adapt to changing conditions they often face in nature (Cook, 1993).

ASSESSING ANIMAL COGNITION Traditionally, research efforts designed to assess animal cognition have focused on the degree to which they can perform tasks analogous in some respect to those that characterize human cognitive activity. Consider categorization: Humans learn to categorize objects at a very early age. We learn that lions, tigers, and bears are animals, whereas football, soccer, and hockey are sports. Can animals categorize objects? Since animals do not speak, one cannot obviously expect them to provide category names for objects. There are, however, ways to assess animals' categorizing abilities,

One technique Bhatt and his colleagues (1988) devised was a "name game" for pigeons that did not require the use of language. Pigeons were asked to "name" examples of four distinct categories—cats, flowers, cars, and chairs—by pecking coloured keys that corresponded to each of the four categories. The subjects viewed slides depicting examples of each of the four categories and received food reinforcement for their correct responses. The pigeons quickly learned to categorize these stimuli correctly—and subsequent testing with novel slides showed that they were able to extend their categorization abilities beyond the slides used during training. These results suggest that pigeons, like people, have the ability to behave conceptually.

Although some critics argue that these results may be the product of simple conditioning, additional research has shown that learning occurs faster and accuracy is higher when pigeons are asked to sort pictures into "human" categories than when they are asked to sort stimuli into arbitrary "pseudocategories" (Wasserman, Kiedinger, & Bhatt, 1988). In other words, pigeons, like their human counterparts, can categorize stimuli on the basis of physical similarity (Astley & Wasserman, 1992; Wasserman et al., 1988). But can pigeons and other animals categorize stimuli that differ in ways other than physical similarity? Many researchers are actively exploring this and other possibilities (e.g., Church, 1993; Terrace, 1993; Tomasello & Call, 1997).

Sara J. Shettleworth
University of Toronto

These studies suggest that when appropriate methods are used, other animal species demonstrate cognitive abilities that are similar in many respects to those of humans. The question that has to be asked is whether the cognitive processes of animals should be measured by singling out cognitive abilities that play an important role in the everyday life of humans and attempting to determine whether animals can display these skills. Some scientists think not. Sara Shettleworth, of the University of Toronto, thinks that a different, *ecological approach* is required. Shettleworth (1993) suggests that animal cognition studies should not be about how closely a non-human animal can emulate peculiarly human cognitive skills; rather, they should focus on the cognitive skills that allow these animals to deal effectively with the day-to-day problems of survival in their natural habitat. Animals certainly do possess distinctive cognitive abilities that allow them to cope effectively with environmental demands. Some display remarkable foraging strategies; some demonstrate extraordinary navigation skills; some are remarkably adept at hoarding and recovering food; and all are capable of discriminating their direct kin from the offspring of other members of their group. Advocates of the ecological approach take the position that cognitive operations underlying these sorts of tasks are much more worth studying than seeing whether animals can perform human-like cognitive tasks (Shettleworth, 1993, 1998).

K E Y   *QUESTIONS*

▪ What is the ecological approach to understanding animal cognition?

Language

At present, most scientists agree that what truly sets us apart from other species is our use of **language**—our ability to use an extremely rich set of symbols, as well as rules for combining them, to communicate information. While the members of all species do communicate with one another in some manner, and while some may use certain features of language, the human ability to do so far exceeds that of any other organism on earth. In this final section we'll examine the nature of language and its relationship to other aspects of cognition.

Language: Its Basic Nature

Language uses symbols for communicating information. In order for a set of symbols to be viewed as a language, however, several additional criteria must be met.

First, information must be transmitted by the symbols: The words and sentences must carry *meaning*. Second, although the number of separate sounds or words in a language may be limited, it must be possible to combine these elements into an essentially infinite number of sentences. Finally, the meanings of these combinations must be independent of the settings in which they are used. In other words, sentences must be able to convey information about other places and other times. Only if all three of these criteria are met can the term *language* be applied to a system of communication. In actual use, language involves two major components: the *production* of speech, and its *comprehension*.

THE PRODUCTION OF SPEECH All spoken language consists of **phonemes**, a set of basic sounds; **morphemes**, the smallest units of speech that convey meaning; and **syntax**, rules about how these units can be combined into sentences.

Language: A system of symbols, plus rules for combining them, used to communicate information.

Phonemes: A set of sounds basic to a given language.

Morphemes: The smallest units of speech that convey meaning.

Syntax: Rules about how units of speech can be combined into sentences in a given language.

English has forty-six separate phonemes: the vowels, *a, e, i, o,* and *u*; consonants, such as *p, m, k,* and *d*; and blends of the two. Other languages have more or fewer basic sounds. Further, different languages often employ different groups of phonemes; sounds used in one may be absent in another.

English has about 100 000 morphemes. Some of these are words; others, such as the plural *s* or prefixes such as *un* or *sub*, are not. The number of English words is greater still—about 500 000. And the number of combinations of these words, or sentences, is for all practical purposes infinite.

Language: Symbols for Communicating Information

The symbols used in language transmit information: the words and sentences carry meaning, are able to be combined into an infinite number of sentences, and are independent of the settings in which they are used.

SPEECH COMPREHENSION Have you ever listened to a conversation between two people speaking a foreign language you don't know? If so, you may recall that it seemed very confusing. In part, this confusion results from the fact that when you listen to a language you don't speak, you can't recognize the boundaries between words.

Even in our own language, not all speech is equally easy to interpret. For example, sentences containing *negatives* (not, no) are more difficult to understand than sentences without them (Clark & Chase, 1972). Also, ambiguous sentences—those with two or more possible meanings—are harder to understand than unambiguous sentences (Mistler-Lachman, 1975). Compare "Last night I saw a wolf in my pyjamas" with "Last night I saw a wolf, while wearing my pyjamas." Clearly, the first is harder to understand than the second. Incidentally, such ambiguity is far from rare; newspaper headlines often show this characteristic. Does "HOMELESS APPEAL TO MAYOR" mean that homeless people are making an appeal to the mayor for help, or that the mayor finds homeless people personally attractive? The first possibility is much more likely, but from the structure of the sentence, it's really not possible to be completely certain.

SURFACE STRUCTURE AND DEEP STRUCTURE Suppose you run into one of your cousins on the street and he introduces you to his companion with the following statement: "Meet Stuart; he's my oldest friend." Does that mean that he is the oldest person your cousin has as a friend, or that your cousin has been friends with him longer than with anyone else? In all probability, you can tell from the context. If Stuart is about your cousin's age, you would conclude that your cousin has been friends with Stuart longer than anyone else. If, however, Stuart is much older than your cousin, you would conclude that the first meaning applies: He's the oldest person your cousin calls "friend."

This simple example illustrates one aspect of the difference between what linguists such as Noam Chomsky (1968) describe as the **surface structure** and **deep structure** of language. Surface structure refers to the actual words people use and what's readily apparent about them, whereas deep structure refers to the information that underlies a sentence and gives it meaning. Another way of seeing this distinction is by considering sentences that are grammatically correct but totally devoid of meaning. For example, consider the sentence, "Dark purple ideas eat angrily." It is perfectly correct in terms of grammar but has no meaning whatsoever. In view of such facts, Chomsky and others have argued that we can never understand the true nature of spoken language by focusing only on words and grammatical rules. Rather, we must search for underlying meaning and for the ways in which people translate, or transform, this into overt speech. While some psychologists question the validity of the distinction between surface and deep structure, most agree that it is useful to look beyond verbal behaviour and rules of grammar and to examine the cognitive representations on which speech is based. In this sense, the distinction Chomsky proposed has been extremely useful.

Surface Structure: The actual words of which sentences consist.

Deep Structure: Information that underlies the form of a sentence and is crucial to its meaning.

The Development of Language

Throughout the first weeks of life, infants have only one major means of verbal communication: crying. Within a few short years, however, children progress rapidly to speaking whole sentences and acquire a vocabulary of hundreds or even thousands of words. Some of the milestones along this remarkable journey are summarized in Table 7.3. Although we'll consider other developmental issues in more detail in Chapter 8, this section will focus on two questions relating to the development of language: What mechanisms play a role in this process? And how, and at what ages, do children acquire various aspects of language skills?

THEORIES OF LANGUAGE DEVELOPMENT The *social learning view* suggests one mechanism for the rapid acquisition of language. This view proposes that speech is acquired through a combination of operant conditioning and imitation. Presumably, children are praised or otherwise rewarded by their parents for making sounds approximating those of their native language. In addition, parents often model sounds, words, or sentences for them. This view contends that, together, these basic forms of learning contribute to the rapid acquisition of language.

A sharply different view has been proposed by linguist Noam Chomsky (1968): the *innate mechanism view*. According to Chomsky, language acquisition is at least partly innate. Human beings, he contends, have a language acquisition device—a built-in neural system that provides them with an intuitive grasp of grammar. In other words, humans are prepared to acquire language and do so rapidly for this reason.

A First Step Toward Language Development

Most children say their first spoken words by their first birthday. After this milestone their vocabulary grows rapidly.

TABLE 7.3

Language Development: Some Milestones

Children develop language skills at an amazing pace. Please note: These approximate ages are only *averages;* individual children will often depart from them to a considerable degree.

Average Age	Language Behaviour Demonstrated by Child
12 weeks	Smiles when talked to; makes cooing sounds
16 weeks	Turns head in response to human voice
20 weeks	Makes vowel and consonant sounds while cooing
6 months	Progresses from cooing to babbling that contains all sounds of human speech.
8 months	Repeats certain syllables (e.g., "ma-ma")
12 months	Understands some words; may say a few
18 months	Can produce up to fifty words
24 months	Has vocabulary of more than fifty words; uses some two-word phrases
30 months	Has vocabulary of several hundred words; uses phrases of three to five words
36 months	Has vocabulary of about a thousand words
48 months	Has mastered most basic elements of language

Finally, a *cognitive theory* offered by Slobin (1979) recognizes the importance of both innate mechanisms and learning. This theory suggests that children possess certain information-processing abilities or strategies that they use in acquiring language. These are termed *operating principles* and seem to be present, or to develop, very early in life. One such operating principle seems to be, "Pay attention to the ends of words"—children pay more attention to the ends than to the beginnings or middles of words. This makes sense, since in many languages suffixes carry important meanings. Another principle is, "Pay attention to the order of words." And indeed, word order in children's speech tends to reflect that of their parents. Since word order differs greatly from one language to another, this, too, is an important principle.

Which of these theories is correct? At present, all are supported by some evidence, but none seems sufficient by itself to account for all aspects of language development. For example, the social learning view is supported by research showing that parents provide differentiating feedback to their children; praising or rewarding them for correct grammar and syntax and correcting them when they make mistakes (Bohannon & Stanowicz, 1988). And, in every culture, children's speech resembles that of their parents in many important ways, so learning does seem to play an important role. Critics maintain, however, that parental feedback may be too infrequent to account fully for the observed rapidity of language acquisition (Gordon, 1990; Pinker, 1989, 1994).

Turning to the possibility of an innate language acquisition device, some findings suggest that there may be a *critical period* during which neural mechanisms appear to be primed for language development (Elliott, 1981). If for some reason children are not exposed to normal speech at this time, mastery of language becomes increasingly difficult (De Villiers & De Villiers, 1978). Further, certain kinds of linguistic deficits provide very strong evidence for the role of genetic determinants. This said, it has be admitted that details regarding the neural structure and precise function of an innate "language acquisition device" remain somewhat vague.

Although there is strong support for the role of innate processes in language acquisition, this does not mean that conditioning, learning, and social reinforcement do not play an important role. Infants have to be exposed to an appropriate linguistic milieu. Also, interaction between children and caregivers is crucial in narrowing, or tuning, the phonetic distinctions made by young children, thus ensuring that their language development proceeds smoothly and uneventfully. In fact, the linguistic interaction between caregivers and child probably begins before birth. As Werker and Tees (1999) point out, the fetus experiences regular exposure to caregivers' voices through air and bone conduction. This sensitizes the fetus to sounds of human language, which likely plays an important role in the early listening preferences very young infants show for their native language (Moon, Cooper, & Fifer, 1993) Genetically determined innate processes are important, but they are in no sense wholly responsible for language acquisition.

PHONOLOGICAL DEVELOPMENT: INITIAL UTTERANCES At some point between three and six months, babies begin **babbling**. They begin doing this at about the same age in all parts of the world, and the babble sounds are much the same. It is a rich auditory blend, full of intonation variations and complex sound patterns. After about ten months, the worldwide similarity in the sounds of babbling begins to diminish. What is happening is that the babies are beginning to articulate linguistic variations that are peculiar to the language group of their caregivers. Because all languages of the world do not use the same set of phonemes, or speech sounds, the babbling of infants in different language groups becomes increasingly different.

The process whereby infants acquire the set of speech sounds they need to function within their linguistic community has been clarified in a series of studies by Werker at the University of British Columbia (e.g., Werker, 1989; Werker & Tees, 1999). Werker's studies suggest that at first, infants have **universal phonetic sensitivity**—that is, they seem to be able to discriminate the contrasts between

Babbling: An early stage of speech development in which infants emit virtually all known sounds of human speech.

Universal Phonetic Sensitivity: The ability of infants at birth to discriminate contrasts between speech sounds that occur in any human language.

speech sounds that are necessary for learning any human language. Although equipped with the ability to register speech sounds in any language, infants will capture and retain only speech sounds that are associated with the natural language (or languages) they are exposed to through caregivers. This period of plasticity is quite short. Studies in **phonological development** typically show a loss in universal phonetic sensitivity by the end of the first year. One such study, carried out by Werker, showed that children of exclusively English-speaking parents could easily discriminate phonetic contrasts required in both Hindi and English when first tested at six to eight months. Four months later, they had retained this adeptness in contrast discrimination in English, but had lost it for Hindi. Although universal phonetic sensitivity is lost rapidly, once a phonetic contrast has been established, it may well be locked in forever. Werker reports that two English-speaking adults who were exposed to Hindi for only their first two years, and who acquired no more than a few words of the language, were later in life as capable as native Hindi speakers in discriminating phonetic contrasts in that language.

The period of universal phonetic sensitivity is an important adaptive device. It provides the newborn child with a way of adjusting rapidly to its linguistic community (of which there is a huge variety). The rather rapid decline in sensitivity to speech sounds of foreign languages does not mean that we cannot learn them; it does mean, as most of us can testify, that the learning process is much more difficult.

VOCABULARY DEVELOPMENT   Once the child has locked on to the appropriate phonetic contrasts for his or her linguistic group, vocabulary growth flourishes. By the time they are eighteen months old, many toddlers have a vocabulary of fifty words or more. What are these first words? Generally, they include the names of familiar objects important in the children's own lives—for instance foods (juice, cookie), animals (cat, dog), toys (block, ball), body parts (ear, eye), clothing (sock, hat, shoe) and people (momma, dadda). Children make the most of these words, often using them as *holophrases*—single word utterances that communicate much meaning, especially when combined with pointing and other gestures. A child wanting some chocolate milk may point to the shelf on which chocolate syrup is kept while saying "milk," thus indicating that she wants some milk with syrup in it. Often the child's pronunciation leaves much to be desired, with many of their words taking a simple form, consisting of a consonant and a vowel, so that the child described above might say "mih" instead of "milk." They frequently have difficulty with consonant clusters, two or more consonants, saying "tairs" for example, instead of "stairs," or "banky" instead of "blanket."

As for verbs—words describing action—when do children acquire these? Until recently, it was widely assumed that acquisition of such words follows the acquisition of simple nouns—words referring to specific objects (e.g., Gentner, 1982). However, recent evidence suggests that in some cultures, this order may be reversed. For instance, Tardif (1996) found that in their naturalistic speech, twenty-two-month-old Chinese children had *more* verbs than nouns in their everyday speech. Thus, the order in which children acquire nouns and verbs may vary somewhat from culture to culture, and further research is needed to determine precisely why this is so.

SEMANTIC DEVELOPMENT: ACQUISITION OF MEANING   As we have noted, vocabulary development is very rapid. By the time children are six, most have a vocabulary of several thousand words. It is important to realize, however, that by this time, their vocabulary consists of more than nouns and verbs. They will have learned new forms of expression that enormously enrich their communication skills, and allow them to convey an extremely complex and varied range of thoughts and ideas. For example, they acquire an understanding of *negatives* such as "no" and how to use these in sentences. Similarly, they acquire many adjectives and prepositions—words that allow them to be more specific in describing their

Phonological Development: Development of the ability to produce recognizable speech.

own thoughts and the world around them. They start with simple adjectives such as "little," "good," and "bad," but soon move on to ones with more specific meaning such as "high," "low," "narrow," "wide," "in front of," and "behind." Children also learn to use question words—words that allow them to ask for information from others in efficient and specific ways: why? when? who? where? These are key words children acquire between the ages of two and three.

Although children acquire words very rapidly, their performance is not errorless, and the errors they make demonstrate interesting aspects of the process whereby word meanings become narrowed and refined. One such error involves *overextension*—a tendency to extend the meaning of a word beyond its actual usage. This is illustrated by an often observed tendency for those around eighteen months of age to use a single word to refer to many totally different things, for example, using the word "raisin" to refer to all small objects—flies and pebbles—as well as raisins themselves. Similarly, the word "meow" might be used as a shorthand word for all small furry animals—dogs as well as cats. With experience, the meaning of the word becomes more specific, and ultimately is restricted to the particular object or entity it represents. Children also often display the error of *underextension*—limiting the meaning of a word more than is appropriate. For example, they may think that the word "cat" applies to the family's pet cat and to no others.

DEVELOPMENT OF GRAMMAR: SENTENCE STRUCTURE Every language has **grammar,** a set of rules dictating how words can be combined into sentences. Children must learn to follow these rules, as well as to utter sounds that others can recognize as words. At first, grammar poses little problem, since, as noted above, children's earliest speech uses single words, often accompanied by pointing and other gestures. By the time most children are two, two-word sentences make their appearance—a pattern sometimes known as *telegraphic* speech. A child who wants a book may say "Give book," and then—if this doesn't produce the desired action—switch to another two-word utterance: "Daddy give." Youngsters can pack quite a bit of meaning into these simple phrases by changing the inflection: "Go swim" to indicate that they are going for a swim, or "Go swim?" in order to ask permission for taking a swim.

Children's grasp of grammar continues to increase as they move to longer sentences of three words or more (generally between the ages of two and three). They add *inflections* to their words—endings that carry meaning, such as the letter "s" to indicate more than one object (plurals) and endings that change the tense of a verb (e.g., "ed" to indicate that something happened in the past, as in "He picked up the ball" rather than "He pick up the ball").

From this, children move on to an increasing grasp of their language's grammar and to the production of ever more complex sentences. They begin to link two or more ideas in a single utterance (e.g., Clark & Clark, 1977), and gradually learn to understand, and use, sentences in which important ideas are implied or understood rather than directly stated. For instance, what does the following sentence mean to you? "Stacy promised Jason to bring the book." As an adult, you understand that Stacy will bring the book; she has promised to do so. Three-year-olds, however, may misinterpret it as meaning that Jason will bring the book because they don't fully understand that the word "promised" refers to Stacy. As they grow older, they learn to unravel this and many other mysteries of grammar.

In sum, language development is definitely a continuing feature of cognitive development throughout childhood. Given the complexity it involves and its central role in many aspects of cognition, this is far from surprising.

Language learning is a very protracted process. What happens when an individual is required to master not one but two languages simultaneously? Are there costs in cognitive development? Some understanding of some of these issues can be provided by looking at studies of bilingualism (see the **Canadian Focus** feature).

Grammar: Rules within a given language indicating how words can be combined into meaningful sentences.

Canadian Focus

Benefits of Bilingualism

Both English and French are official languages of Canada, but only about 16 percent of the population is bilingual. Thus, cereal boxes and it seems just about anything else in Canada must come with French on one side and English on the other so that the rest of us more or less monolinguals can read about the contents and/or instructions in the language of our choice.

Are there advantages to bilingualism that extend beyond being able to move freely from one language group to another, and not having to turn packages over to find instructions in the right language? There are indeed, but it is only in recent years that these advantages have been detailed with any measure of certainty. Prior to the early 1960s, it was believed that the imposition of a second language imposed a drain on finite cognitive resources, and resulted in diminished overall competence. Research at that time suggested that bilinguals, compared to monolinguals, "were handicapped in terms of measured intelligence, school performance, and even social and personal adjustment" (Lambert, 1992, p. 535).

This view of bilingualism changed with the publication of an important study by Peal and Lambert (1962) of McGill University that addressed design deficiencies in earlier studies. They found that when monolinguals and bilinguals were suitably matched for economic status and background, bilinguals scored higher on intelligence tests and tended to have better school performance records. The findings of Peal and Lambert have been largely confirmed in other world language communities, and it seems clear that there are advantages that accrue to bilingualism over and beyond those associated with free movement between different linguistic groups. These findings rekindled interest in bilingualism and raised all sorts of questions about the best way to acquire bilingual skill.

The most common Canadian approach to the acquisition of bilingualism is through the French immersion programs that have become a familiar part of the educational landscape. This approach grew out of concerns expressed by a group of parents in St. Lambert, Quebec, that their children were not be-

ing provided with adequate opportunity to develop bilingual skills. They proposed what was, at that time, the very radical notion of immersing English-speaking students into a monolingual French instructional milieu from kindergarten to grade three. They sought help from Lambert and others at McGill University in developing and monitoring such a program and managed to convince reluctant school boards to go along with the program. Doubts were raised about whether young children would be able to cope simultaneously with one language in the home and another in the school. The children laid to rest such doubts and the program flourished.

Many assessments of the immersion program have been carried out. What is found is that students completing the program achieve a high level of proficiency in French and show no impairment in acquisition of curriculum content or diminished skills in English. In fact, immersion students show, from about the third grade onward, enhanced skills in English (presumably through some interlinguistic facilitation) when measured against comparable monolingual groups. There is even some evidence of superior performance in other areas (Lambert, 1991, 1992), and the improvements do not appear solely attributable to a selective process whereby better students are enrolled into the immersion process. In addition, immersion students display more positive attitudes toward French cultural values.

In spite of what may seem to be an overwhelming amount of evidence favouring bilingualism, societal attitudes toward bilingualism tend to be closely linked to membership in minority and majority language groups (Lambert, 1991). Members of majority language groups see the bilingual process as positive. They see bilingualism as an opportunity to acquire fluency in a second language, and exposure to second-language cultural values, at no cost to first-language skills and prevailing social and cultural values. Members of minority language groups often tend to see bilingualism from a different perspective. They are concerned that the total embrace of a more dominant majority language at an early age will result in a loss of interest in first language skills and an erosion of cultural traditions.

Language in Other Species

Members of non-human species communicate with one another in many ways. Bees do a complex dance to indicate the distance to and direction of a food source; birds sing songs when seeking to attract a mate; seagoing mammals in the wild, such as whales, communicate with one another through complex patterns of sounds. But what about language? Are we the only species capable of using this sophisticated means of communication? Until the 1970s, there seemed little question about this. Early efforts to teach chimpanzees to speak failed miserably. For example, during the 1940s, Keith and Cathy Hayes raised a chimp named Vicki from infancy in their home and provided her with intensive speech training, but she was able to utter only a few simple words such as "mama," "papa," and "cup."

These disappointing results were due in part to the fact that non-human primates (and other animals) lack the vocal control necessary for spoken language. But the ability to speak is not essential for the use of language. There are other alternatives, the foremost of which is sign language—a route a number of investigators have followed.

Beatrice and Allen Gardner succeeded in teaching Washoe, a female chimp, to use and understand almost 200 words in American Sign Language (ASL), which is used by many deaf people (Gardner & Gardner, 1975). After several years of practise, Washoe learned to respond to simple questions and to request actions such as tickling and objects such as food. Patterson (1978) has also reported some success teaching a gorilla named Koko a vocabulary of several hundred signs, and reportedly Koko even created her own signs for new objects (for example, she termed zebras "white tigers").

In what may be the most surprising evidence of all, Irene Pepperberg has trained an African grey parrot named Alex to use speech in what appears to be a highly complex way (Stipp, 1990). Alex can name more than eighty objects and events, frequently requests things he wants ("I want shower"), and has been known to give directions to his human trainers. But does Alex really understand the words he uses? Professor Pepperberg believes that he does. On one occasion, Alex was given an apple for the first time. He immediately labelled it "banerry," and he stuck with this word despite her best efforts to teach him "apple." Her explanation: Apples taste somewhat like bananas and look something like cherries, so Alex had chosen a word that from his perspective was quite appropriate.

Alex: The African Grey Parrot

Irene Pepperberg has trained an African grey parrot to use speech in apparently complex ways. But does Alex really understand the words he uses?

ARE WE THE ONLY SPECIES CAPABLE OF USING LANGUAGE? Based on the evidence presented thus far, you may now be ready to conclude that members of other species can indeed use language. Note, however, that many psychologists have carefully examined the data reported in the studies described and take the position that the animals in these studies, while exhibiting impressive learning, are not really demonstrating the use of language (e.g., Davidson & Hopson, 1988; Terrace, 1985; Wallman, 1992). For instance, close examination of the procedures used to train and test the animals suggests that their trainers may often unintentionally provide subtle cues that help the animals respond correctly to questions. It also appears that in some cases, trainers may have wildly overinterpreted the animals' responses, reading complex meanings and intentions into relatively simple signs. Finally, it is still very unclear whether animals are capable of mastering several basic features of human language—for example, *syntax* (the rules by which words are arranged to form meaningful sentences) and *generativity* (the ability to combine a relatively limited number of words into unique combinations that convey a broad range of meaning).

Recent studies involving other species of animals, including bonobos (a rare type of chimpanzee) and dolphins, have begun to address these and related issues. For example, consider the language abilities demonstrated by a twelve-year-old bonobo named Kanzi (Linden, 1993). Psychologist Sue Savage-Rumbaugh first began studying bonobos in the 1980s. While attempting to teach Kanzi's mother to use an artificial language made up of abstract visual symbols, she noticed that Kanzi (then an infant) had learned several symbol-words just by watching. Intrigued by the possibilities this raised, Savage-Rumbaugh and her colleagues continued to train Kanzi in this informal way—speaking to him throughout the day, while simultaneously pointing to the corresponding word symbols on portable language boards they carried with them. Kanzi quickly learned to combine the

Language in Other Species: Kanzi

Researcher Sue Savage-Rumbaugh has taught Kanzi, a chimp, to communicate using symbols on a special keyboard. Kanzi is unusual because he can also respond to spoken commands like "Please bring me the flashlight."

"Sorry, ma'am, but your neighbors have reported not seeing your husband in weeks. We just have a few questions, and then you can get back to your canning."

Talking to the Animals

Although non-human species have not yet demonstrated the ability to carry on conversations like this one, growing evidence suggests that some species of animals, including dolphins, comprehend several basic aspects of language.

Source: Universal Press Syndicate, Inc., 1993.

symbol-words to request tasty snacks and preferred activities, such as watching Tarzan movies.

Since then, Kanzi has demonstrated a grasp of grammatical concepts, and he now comprehends several hundred spoken words. In one experiment, Savage-Rumbaugh and her colleagues compared Kanzi and a two-year-old girl in terms of their ability to respond to commands expressed in spoken sentences (Savage-Rumbaugh et al., 1992). The sentences consisted of familiar words that were combined to produce commands that Kanzi and the little girl had never heard before. Surprisingly, Kanzi's progress in comprehending the novel commands paralleled the little girl's throughout most of the experiment, although her language abilities eventually surpassed Kanzi's (his ability topped out at the level of an average two-year-old child). More important, though, the use of strict control procedures ruled out the possibility that Kanzi was responding to subtle cues from his trainers—a criticism levelled against many early demonstrations of animal language. For instance, a one-way mirror prevented Kanzi from seeing who gave him the commands, and the people recording his responses wore headphones to prevent them from hearing the requests. Psychologists are now more willing to accept that Kanzi was responding solely to the requests.

But what about more complex features of language? Are animals capable of grasping these concepts, too? Psychologist Louis Herman believes they are. Herman and his colleagues taught a female dolphin named Akeakamai—or Ake for short—an artificial language in which sweeping hand gestures are the words (Herman, Richards, Wolz, et al., 1984). Each gesture symbolizes either an *object* such as "Frisbee," an *action* such as "fetch," or a *description of position* such as "over" or "left." Ake has learned more than fifty of these gesture-words. Next, to test whether Ake was capable of comprehending complex features of language, the researchers established a set of rules governing word order and the grammatical function of each type of gesture. Herman and his colleagues have discovered that Ake comprehends word order and syntax in word sequences up to five gestures. For example, RIGHT BASKET LEFT FRISBEE instructs Ake to take the Frisbee on her left to the basket on her right. More impressively, though, when familiar gestures are rearranged to form novel commands—ones Ake has never seen before—she continues to respond correctly.

Herman has continued to probe Ake's language comprehension through the use of *anomalous sentences*—sentences that are grammatically incorrect, use nonsense words, or make impossible requests, such as asking her to fetch an immovable object. These procedures are often used to test children's comprehension of language. In one instance, Herman and his colleagues issued a series of commands to Ake that consisted of either grammatically correct sequences or anomalous sequences (Herman, Kuczaj, & Holders, 1993). Interestingly, Ake was highly accurate in responding to requests that were grammatically correct and rarely refused to carry them out. In contrast, she refused nearly all of the anomalous requests, making no attempt to respond to them. It appeared as if Ake recognized that the requests were "silly," a response often observed in children who are presented with anomalous sentences. Although dolphins may be a long way from achieving the level of language proficiency illustrated in the cartoon on this page, it is clear that they are capable of comprehending features of language that go beyond the forms of behaviour observed in the earlier studies of animal language.

Research with highly intelligent animals such as primates and dolphins is proceeding. To some, the findings to date suggest that language may not be a uniquely human possession. A recent review of animal language studies by Kako (1999) concludes that a few other species may be capable of acquiring some core properties of syntax. Others remain unconvinced (Gisiner & Schusterman, 1992; Pinker, 1994; Wallman, 1992). The field of study is a fascinating one. Further studies will undoubtedly shed additional light on the scope of animal abilities in this domain. It does seem unlikely, however, that we'll "talk with the animals" any time soon.

Evolution, Language, and Thought

At some point in the very distant past, humans branched off from the evolutionary path of gorillas and chimpanzees and moved much further down the linguistic road. What can be said about the road they travelled? How did human language evolve?

Standard accounts of the evolution of language begin with the notion that gesture and mimicry were first used to convey information about events and to re-enact experiences. Selective adaptation of speech and brain structures followed and finally spoken language emerged (e.g., Donald, 1991). This seems to be logical and believable. The problem is that we have no way of knowing whether this account is correct. Why are we so uncertain? There are two reasons. First, there is nothing in the fossil record that can provide us with information about the role played by gesture and mimicry, or any other forms of communicative interaction that might have served to trigger the linguistic evolution. Second, there is nowhere to look in the human or animal kingdom of today for information about the evolution of language. Language is for the most part a peculiarly human accomplishment. And no matter how obscure or isolated the human linguistic community investigated, the language found is no less rich or complex than that used by the researchers. The absence of a partially developed or incomplete language in the present-day human or animal kingdom is troublesome. If one looks at the evolution of other complex structures such as the visual system, there are abundant examples in other species of different stages of evolutionary development of the eye, but not so with language (Pinker, 1994). This has led some theoreticians to argue that language did not evolve in a piecemeal fashion, but rather "piggy-backed" on other adaptations associated with the development of increasingly complex brain structure and articulatory capacities, and emerged effectively full-blown when a certain stage of cortical specialization had been reached. This is currently the subject of extensive debate (Botha, 1998; Pinker & Bloom, 1990).

Although the evolutionary footprints of language development cannot be clearly discerned in the sands of our distant past, it is clear that the emergence of language must have profoundly expanded human cognitive capacities. The ability to learn about events through conversations with others confers an enormous advantage. Language allows elders to inform young members of a group about dangers that threaten them without having to wait until a dangerous situation arises. Language allows the location of good hunting areas to be reported, and instruction in tool use and production to be given. Animal migration paths can be described, and history of the group can be preserved through storytelling. In short, the availability of language provides immediate access to information held by others, and facilitates immensely the rapidity with which information about the world can be acquired (Donald, 1991; Pinker & Bloom, 1991). A clear indication of just how much difference language makes can be seen in case reports of (thankfully few) deaf children who have been raised in environments that prevented the formation of any meaningful communicative linkage with caregivers or peers. As would be expected, the cognitive development of these children is enormously impaired when compared to deaf children raised in environments in which the development of communicated capacities is actively promoted (Sacks, 1989).

Given how influential language is in facilitating acquisition of information about the world in which we live, it is reasonable to ask whether the language we acquire and use also influences the character of our thought processes. A well-known advocate of this view is Whorf (1959). His **linguistic relativity hypothesis** takes the position that the language we speak does shape the way in which we think. He argues that people who speak different languages may actually perceive the world in different ways because their thinking is determined, at least in part, by the words available to them. In addition, he contends that different languages cut up and categorize events and experiences in different ways. Whorf's approach is interesting, but existing evidence seems to argue against it (Miura & Okamoto, 1989). If Whorf is correct, it follows that people who speak a language that has few words to describe colours should have greater difficulty in perceiving various colours than people who speak a language rich in colour words. Research designed to test such possibilities has generally failed to support them. In one experiment, Rosch (1973) studied natives of New Guinea. Their language, Dani, has only two colour names: *mola*, for bright, warm colours, and *mili*, for dark, cool ones. Rosch found that despite this fact, Dani speakers perceived colours in much the same manner as English speakers, whose language contains many colour words.

In sum, available evidence suggests that language enormously facilitates our capacity to acquire information about the world. Language does not seem to influence the character of our thought processes. It may indeed be easier to express a particular idea or concept in one language than another, but this does not mean that our thoughts or perceptions are strongly shaped by language. On the contrary, basic aspects of human perception and thought seem to be very much the same around the world, regardless of spoken language.

Linguistic Relativity Hypothesis: The view that language shapes thought.

K E Y QUESTIONS

- What abilities are involved in the production of language and how is language acquired in humans?
- What factors are involved in language acquisition?
- Do animals possess language?
- What is the linguistic relativity hypothesis?

---

making **Psychology** Part of Your Life

Making Better Decisions

*H*ave you ever made a bad decision—one that you later wished you could change? Unless you have led a charmed life, you probably have. Given the vast complexity of the world and the diversity of options we often face, it is unlikely that anyone can provide you with a perfect system for making correct decisions. Nevertheless, here are some guidelines, based on principles covered in the chapter, that may increase the chances that your decisions will be good ones—or at least as free from sources of error and bias as possible.

1. *Do not make hasty decisions.* Hasty decisions usually reflect a reliance on the availability heuristic (Kahneman & Tversky, 1982). Your decision is likely to be based on recent and oft-repeated information about a situation that is fresh in memory. For example, in making a quick decision about how to travel to a distant destination, your immediate recollection of extensive media coverage of a recent air disaster may tempt you to see air travel as more dangerous than car travel—which it is not. Another problem with

We make decisions every day, some relatively trivial (such as which brand to buy in the supermarket), some relatively important (such as which job offer to accept). How can you improve your decision-making skills?

hasty decisions results from our noted tendency to store information in memory about individuals, groups, schools, and even sport teams selectively in accordance with our likes, dislikes, and beliefs. A snap judgment, without an extensive search of memory or research, is likely to be biased in terms of your general likes, dislikes, and beliefs rather than being objectively balanced—and may well be ultimately regretted.

2. *Examine how problems and proposals are framed.* One thing that should have been clear in our consideration of problem solving is that the way a problem is framed can influence the decision we make. A common tactic is to present only favourable information about a proposal or proposition. For example, recruiters for various kinds of summer employment—especially if the job involves sales— often frame presentations to students in terms how much money can be made, without revealing how much the average job-holder makes, or how many of those who are recruited drop out. If applicants do not recognize the effect this kind of framing can have on decision making and request additional information required to make an informed deci-

sion, they may be in for an unhappy and unrewarding summer.

3. *Live with decisions , but admit mistakes.* If you take the time to make a decision carefully, you should be able to live with it. If setbacks occur, evaluate them carefully. Be objective and try to avoid the escalation of commitment dilemma. Do not remain so committed to a decision that you escalate your commitment beyond the point where you should cut your losses and move in another direction.

4. *Take care in bargaining.* There will be times when you are going have to negotiate to resolve an issue. The issue may be the price to pay for an expensive article, or perhaps the amount of time and energy you will commit to a project. Carefully examine what is proposed in the way of an initial commitment. Research on the anchoring-and-adjustment heuristic suggests that if you automatically accept as a starting point the price or time commitment in a proposal, you may commit to giving more than you sensibly should and severely limit the degree to which you can negotiate adjustments (Northcraft & Neale, 1987). It is often advantageous to insist on starting at a lower initial level of commitment of money or time to try and increase the negotiating range.

5. *Finally, react positively to frustration.* Problem solving is difficult. Every problem may have a solution, but finding that solution often involves a tedious and tiresome struggle. If you meet with a problem that seems to resist solution, do not continue to hammer away at it from the same perspective. Engage in lateral thinking and see if you can find alternative ways of conceptualizing and dealing with the problem.

Summary and Review

Key Questions

Thinking

- **What are concepts?** Concepts are mental categories for objects, events, or experiences that are similar to one another in one or more respects.

- **What is the difference between logical and natural concepts?** Logical concepts can be clearly defined by a set of rules or properties. Natural concepts cannot; they are usually defined in terms of prototypes—the most typical category members.

- **What are the basic elements of thought?** The basic elements of thought are concepts, propositions, and images. Propositions are sentences that can stand as separate assertions and are useful for relating one concept to another (or one feature of a concept to the entire concept), and images are mental pictures of the world.

- **What are ERPs and what can they tell us about cognition?** ERPs, or event-related brain potentials, reflect the momentary changes in electrical activity of the brain that occur as a person performs a cognitive task.

- **What is the process of reasoning? How does formal reasoning differ from everyday reasoning?** Reasoning involves transforming available information in order to reach specific conclusions. Formal reasoning derives conclusions from specific premises. In contrast, everyday reasoning is more complex and less clear-cut.

- **What forms of error and bias can lead to faulty reasoning?** Reasoning is subject to several forms of error and bias. It can be distorted by emotion and belief; by the tendency to focus primarily on evidence that confirms our beliefs, or confirmation bias; and by the tendency to assume that we could have predicted actual events more successfully than is really the case, or the hindsight effect.

Making Decisions

- **What are heuristics?** We do not make all decisions on the basis of expected utility—the product of the probability and the subjective value of each possible outcome. Instead, we often use heuristics, or mental rules of thumb.

- **What are the availability, representativeness, and anchoring-and-adjustment heuristics and what role do they play in reasoning?** The availability heuristic is our tendency to make judgments about the frequency or likelihood of various events in terms of how readily they can be brought to mind. The representativeness heuristic is the tendency to assume that the more closely an item resembles the most typical examples of some concept, the more likely it is to belong to that concept. The anchoring-and-adjustment heuristic is the tendency to reach decisions by making adjustments to reference points or existing information.

- **What is framing and how does it relate to decision making?** Decisions can be strongly affected by framing, the presentation of information about possible outcomes in terms of gains or losses.

- **How does escalation of commitment affect decision making?** People often become trapped in bad decisions through escalation of commitment, an effect that derives from reluctance to admit past mistakes and a desire to justify past losses.

- **What is naturalistic decision making?** Naturalistic decision making refers to studying decision making in the natural environment. Proponents argue that this approach has several advantages over laboratory research: it focuses attention on how decision makers use past experience in making a decision, it broadens the focus from a single decision "event" to a focus on the decision context, and it emphasizes the dynamic nature of decision making and takes into account the complexity of modern decision environments.

Problem Solving

- **How do psychologists define problem solving?** Problem solving involves efforts to develop or choose among various responses in order to attain desired goals.

- **What are two general approaches to problem solving?** One common problem-solving technique is trial and error. Another is the use of algorithms rules that will, if followed, yield solutions in certain situations.

- **What role do heuristics play in problem solving?** Heuristics are rules of thumb suggested by our experience that we often use to solve problems.

- **What is metacognitive processing, and how does it contribute to more effective problem solving?** Metacognition involves expanding our level of awareness—in a sense, observing ourselves engaged in the problem-solving process. Metacogntive processing activates processes that lead to more effective problem solutions, such as monitoring, planning, and critically evaluating whether particular strategies are working.

- **What is lateral thinking?** Engaging in lateral thinking means that one seeks alternative ways of conceptualizing and dealing with a problem

- **What factors can interfere with effective problem solving?** Both functional fixedness (the tendency to think of using objects only as they have been used before) and mental sets (tendencies to stick with familiar methods) can interfere with effective problem solving.

- **What is artificial intelligence?** Artificial intelligence is an interdisciplinary field concerned with the capacity of computers to demonstrate intelligent performance.

- **What is the ecological approach?** The ecological approach focuses on how animals solve cognitive problems that are important to their survival.

Language

- **What abilities are involved in the production of language and how is language acquired in humans?** Language involves the ability to use a rich set of symbols, plus rules for combining these, to communicate information. It includes the abilities to produce and to comprehend speech. Language seems to involve more than mere spoken words and rules of grammar, or surface structure. The underlying meaning, or deep structure, is important too. Contrasting theories of language development suggest that language is acquired by children through (1) social learning, (2) innate mechanisms, and (3) cognitive mechanisms.

- **What basic components are involved in language acquisition?** Language acquisition involves phonological development—learning to produce the sounds of words; semantic development—learning to understand the meaning of words; and the acquisition of grammar—rules through which words can be combined into sentences in a given language.

- **What is the linguistic relativity hypothesis?** According to the linguistic relativity hypothesis, language shapes or determines thought. Existing evidence does not offer strong support for this hypothesis.

- **Do animals possess language?** Growing evidence suggests that some species of animals, including bonobo chimpanzees and dolphins, are capable of grasping some basic aspects of language including word order and grammar.

■ **How did language evolve?**   Most accounts of the evolution of language begin with the notion that gesture and mimicry are used to convey information about events and to re-enact experiences. Selective adaptation of speech and brain structures follows. However, the absence of a partially developed or incomplete language has led some theoreticians to argue that language did not evolve in a piecemeal fashion, but rather emerged full-blown and complete.

Key Terms

Algorithms (p. 277)
Analogy (p. 278)
Anchoring-and-Adjustment Heuristic (p. 270)
Artificial Intelligence (p. 281)
Availability Heuristic (p. 269)
Babbling (p. 287)
Cognition (p. 260)
Concepts (p. 261)
Confirmation Bias (p. 266)
Decision Making (p. 268)
Deep Structure (p. 285)
Escalation of Commitment (p. 273)
Expected Utility (p. 268)
Framing (p. 272)

Functional Fixedness (p. 279)
Grammar (p. 289)
Heuristics (p. 268)
Hindsight Effect (p. 266)
Illusory-Knowledge Effect (p. 267)
Language (p. 284)
Lateral Thinking (p. 279)
Linguistic Relativity Hypothesis (p. 294)
Logical Concepts (p. 261)
Mental Set (p. 280)
Mental Models (p. 263)
Metacognitive Processing (p. 278)
Morphemes (p. 284)
Natural Concepts (p. 261)
Naturalistic Decision Making (p. 274)

Neural Networks (p. 282)
Phonemes (p. 284)
Phonological Development (p. 288)
Problem Solving (p. 276)
Propositions (p. 263)
Prototypes (p. 261)
Reasoning (p. 265)
Reaction Time (p. 264)
Representativeness Heuristic (p. 270)
Surface Structure (p. 285)
Syntax (p. 284)
Trial and Error (p. 277)
Universal Phonetic Sensitivity (p. 287)
Visual Images (p. 262)

Critical Thinking Questions

Appraisal

Throughout this chapter, we've seen that human thought processes are less than optimal in several important respects. For instance, relying on heuristics frequently leads to flawed decision making. And we often fall prey to biases that lead us astray in our ability to think and reason effectively. How can psychology help people reduce or eliminate the effects of these errors?

Controversy

The results of many studies demonstrate that animals are capable of grasping important aspects of language that many believed were beyond their capabilities. Do you think it is possible that in the coming years scientists will discover ways to "talk with the animals"? If so, why? If not, why not?

Making Psychology Part of Your Life

Now that you understand the basic nature of cognitive processes and the many factors that affect them, can you think of ways in which you can use this knowledge to improve your problem-solving abilities? Name several specific steps you could take to become more proficient at in this regard.

Weblinks

Check out our Companion Website at www.pearsoned.ca/baron for additional Websites, activities, and more.

Natural Language Laboratory at Simon Fraser University

fas.sfu.ca/cs/research/groups/NLL/toc.html

The natural language laboratory at Simon Fraser University is one of the larger North American labs working on natural language processing (NLP). This site includes an outline of natural language and of the laboratory's theoretical and applied work in NLP.

Cognitive Psychology

www.academicpress.com/www/journal/cgnojs.htm

Cognitive Psychology is available online at this site.

The University of Alberta's Cognitive Science Dictionary

web.psych.ualberta.ca/%7emike/Pearl_Street/Dictionary/entries.html#top

This useful site contains a dictionary of terms relevant to cognitive science.

Scientists Interested in Animal Cognition and Behaviour

www.pigeon.psy.tufts.edu/people.htm

This is a list providing links to many researchers interested in animal cognition and behaviour at universities around the world, including researchers working in Canada. Follow the links and find out what these scientists are doing currently.

Cardboard Cognition

edweb.sdsu.edu/courses/edtec670/Cardboard/cardboardcognition.html

This Website is your link to hundreds of card games and board games that will require you to exercise your cognitive processes.

Mind Games

www.q-net.net.au/~gihan/mindgames/

Here you will find a number of exercises, lessons and games which were designed to foster creativity. There is an excellent Help feature which will give you a kick-start for a particular game.

Dyslexia and Language Brain Areas

www.sfn.org/briefings/dyslexia.html

This page gives you a brief introduction to new advances in the study of dyslexia, having to do with reading difficulties.

Chapter 8

Human Development I
The Childhood Years

CHAPTER OUTLINE

One Drink

In a report on the effects of alcohol upon brain cell development, the *Whitehorse Star* told about a brain-growth spurt in rats that starts two weeks after birth. Beginning then and going on for a considerable length of time, brain cells develop the connections that will permit remembering, learning, and thinking in later life. Researchers discovered that, in these young animals, "one round of intoxication lasting about four hours" causes massive nerve cell "suicide." Alcohol disrupts the balance between two types of neurotransmitters, and as a result, millions of brain cells die.

This research has implications for pregnant women and the well-being of the fetus they carry. In humans, the brain-growth spurt begins months before birth. Drinking alcohol during that time may have serious repercussions for the unborn child—possibly lifelong learning disabilities.

How does normal prenatal development proceed? What is the usual plan for growth and maturation? How does the thinking of children change with age? How do children learn the difference between right and wrong? These are some of the topics you will find as you continue your introduction to psychology through Chapter 8, Human Development I.

Source: One drinking binge may result in fetal brain damage. (2000). The *Whitehorse Star,* February 11, p. 26.

> **Change is basic to human development: We are all in a continuous state of flux as we journey through life.**

Human Development: A Long—and Interesting—Journey

Can you remember when you had to bend your head back to look up at adults? What it's like *not* to be able to read? If so, you realize how much you've changed in the intervening years.

Change, it is often said, is the only constant. And where human beings are concerned, that is certainly true. Some changes are obvious—growth in size and sexual maturity. Others are less apparent—the acquisition of knowledge, ways of thinking that are more complex and sophisticated, formation of a personal code of ethics, and development of a much deeper understanding of human relationships. Not all the changes we experience as we grow older are positive, of course, but in a very real sense, change is basic to human development.

The field of **developmental psychology** focuses on *physical growth and development, cognitive development,* and *social and emotional development.* In this chapter, we will consider these as they occur during childhood—the years between birth and adolescence. In the next chapter we will examine changes occurring during adolescence and in the adult years.

An additional topic we will examine is the development of *gender identity,* the process by which children learn that they belong to one of the two sexes and acquire knowledge of the behaviours and attitudes their culture associates with being male or female.

To what extent does development represent an unfolding of "biological scripts," largely determined by our genes, and to what extent does experience in external world matter? Developmental psychologists often grapple with these complex issues of nature versus nurture (e.g., Collaer & Hines, 1995), so you will encounter them again and again in this chapter.

Physical Growth and Development

When does human life begin? That may be a philosophical or a religious issue, outside the realm of science. However, from a biological standpoint, you began when one of the millions of sperm released by your father during sexual intercourse fertilized an ovum deep within your mother's body. The product of this union was less than half a millimetre in diameter—smaller than the period at the end of this sentence. Yet packed within this tiny speck were the genetic blueprints (twenty-three chromosomes from each parent) that directed your subsequent physical growth. One of these pairs determines biological sex, with females possessing two X chromosomes (XX) and males possessing one X and one Y (XY).

Developmental Psychology: The branch of psychology that studies all types of changes that occur throughout the lifespan.

The Prenatal Period

After fertilization, the *prenatal period*—the period prior before birth—begins. The ovum moves through the female reproductive tract until it reaches the womb, or uterus. That trip takes several days, and meanwhile, the ovum divides frequently. Ten to fourteen days after fertilization, the ovum becomes implanted in the wall of the uterus. For the next six weeks it is known as the **embryo** and develops very rapidly. By the third week, a primitive heart has formed and begun to beat and the basics of the central nervous system have formed. By the fourth week the embryo is about half a centimetre long and the region of the head is visible. Rapid growth continues, so that by the end of the eighth week the embryo is about 2.5 centimetres long and a face, arms, and legs are present. By that time, all major internal organs have also begun to form. Some of these, such as the sex glands, are already active. Also, the nervous system develops rapidly; simple reflexes begin to appear during the eighth or ninth week after fertilization.

During the next seven months, the developing child—now known as the **fetus**—takes on an increasingly human form. Different parts of the body grow at different rates. The external genitals take shape, so that the sex of the baby is recognizable externally by the twelfth week. Fingernails and toenails form, hair follicles appear, and eyelids develop that can already open and close. Physical growth is also impressive. By the end of the twelfth week the fetus is 7.6 centimetres long and weighs about 21 grams. By the twentieth week it is almost 25 centimetres long and weighs between 227 and 255 grams. By the twenty-fourth week, all the neurons that will be present in the brain have been produced. The eyes are formed and are sensitive to light by the end of the twenty-sixth week.

During the last three months of pregnancy, the fetus gains about 250 grams each week and grows rapidly. By the seventh and eighth months, he or she appears to be virtually fully formed. However, if born at this time, there may still be difficulties in breathing, because the *alveoli*—the tiny air sacs within the lungs—are not yet fully formed. At birth, babies weigh more than 3.17 kilograms on average and are about 50.8 centimetres long.

Cognitive abilities also take shape during the prenatal period. In an ingenious series of studies, DeCasper and his colleagues (e.g., DeCasper & Spence, 1986) arranged for mothers-to-be to read *The Cat in the Hat* to their unborn children twice each day during the last six weeks of pregnancy. At the end of that period, the familiar story produced a slight decrease in fetal heart rate, while an unfamiliar one produced a slight increase. Because a decrease in heart rate is taken as a sign of increased attention, these findings suggest that the fetuses could indeed distinguish between familiar and unfamiliar stories—or at least react differently to the two.

Embryo: The developing child during the second through the eighth weeks of prenatal development.

Fetus: The developing child during the last seven months of prenatal development.

Prenatal Influences on Development

Under ideal conditions, development during the prenatal period occurs in an orderly fashion and the newborn child is well equipped at birth to survive outside its mother's

The Stages of Prenatal Development

This series of photos illustrates prenatal development, from fertilization to the embryo at seven weeks and the fetus at twenty-two weeks.

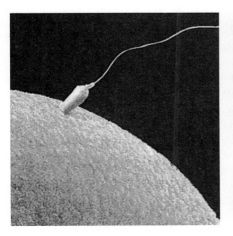
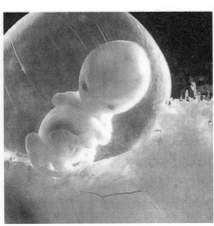
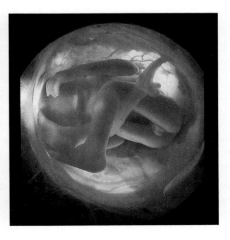

body. Unfortunately, however, conditions are not always ideal. Studies show that physical trauma, fear, or psychological stress may disrupt pregnancy, both in humans and in animals. In the case of stress, this disruption may result from an increase in the release of estrogens (de Catanzaro & MacNiven, 1992). Many other environmental factors can cause damage and interfere with normal patterns of growth. Such factors are known as **teratogens**; their impact can be significant (e.g., Bookstein et al., 1996).

DISEASE DURING PREGNANCY The blood supply of the fetus and that of its mother come into close proximity in the **placenta**, the structure within the uterus that holds, protects, and nourishes the growing child. As a result, disease-producing organisms present in the mother's blood can sometimes infect the developing child. Tragically, diseases that exert only relatively minor effects on mothers can be very serious for the fetus. For example, rubella, or German measles, can cause blindness, deafness, or heart disease in the fetus if the mother contracts this illness during the first four weeks of pregnancy. Other diseases that can be transmitted to the fetus and inflict serious damage include chicken pox, mumps, tuberculosis, malaria, syphilis, and herpes (Samson, 1988).

Since the early 1980s, two other illnesses, genital herpes and AIDS (acquired immune deficiency syndrome) have been added to this list. Genital herpes is usually transmitted during birth, when the newborn comes into contact with lesions present in the mother's genitals. When newborns contract this disease, they may suffer many harmful effects, ranging from paralysis and brain damage through deafness and blindness; the disease is fatal for many babies (Rosenblith, 1992). AIDS, in contrast, can be transmitted to the fetus prior to birth, as well as during the birth process (Kuhn et al., 1994; Matheson et al., 1997). Tragically, few babies born with AIDS survive until their first birthday.

PRESCRIPTION AND OVER-THE-COUNTER DRUGS The use of drugs by the mother can also exert important effects on the developing fetus. Excessive use of aspirin, a drug most people take without hesitation, can result in harm to the circulatory system (Kelsey, 1969). Some evidence suggests that caffeine can slow fetal growth and contribute to premature birth. Children born to mothers who consume large amounts of caffeine show increased irritability and a higher than normal incidence of vomiting (Aaronson & MacNee, 1989).

ILLEGAL DRUGS The abuse of heroin, cocaine, crack, and other illegal drugs is a major problem of our time. The use of such drugs by prospective mothers can be disastrous. Infants born to heroin-addicted mothers suffer from numerous problems, including physical malformations, respiratory disease, and premature birth. Thousands of babies addicted to cocaine or its derivatives are born each year, and these infants suffer from a wide range of physical problems, including low birth weight, breathing difficulties, brain lesions, impaired sensory functioning, increased irritability, heart deformities, and other physical defects (e.g., Chasnoff et al., 1998; Richardson et al.; 1995; Volpe, 1992). Given that they are usually born to mothers who are also poor and malnourished, the outlook for these infants is bleak.

ALCOHOL Although consumption of alcohol is legal in most countries, the harm it produces can be devastating. Children born to mothers who use this drug heavily may have *fetal alcohol syndrome*, or FAS (e.g., Janzen et al., 1995). Full-blown FAS includes severely retarded growth, heart defects, and limb and joint abnormalities. There are distortions in the normal shape of the face, including widely spaced eyes, short eyelid openings, a small, upturned nose, and a thin upper lip. There is damage to the brain and the rest of the nervous system. Some infants suffer from attention deficits and mental retardation (Nanson & Hiscock, 1990). Currently, fetal alcohol syndrome is the third-highest cause of childhood retardation. As youngsters with FAS grow older, they have increasing difficulty interacting with other children and they may develop serious behaviour problems (e.g., Becker et al., 1994).

Teratogens: Factors in the environment that can harm the developing fetus.

Placenta: A structure that surrounds, protects, and nourishes the developing fetus.

How much alcohol is too much during pregnancy? The best answer is this: A mother who abstains from drinking alcohol during this period will not bear an infant with FAS. The prevalence of FAS in some areas of the Northwest Territories (one in every three infants born) has led some legislators there to propose laws that would impose penalties upon pregnant women who drink alcohol. Others argue strongly that prevention through public education is more likely to reduce the prevalence of FAS.

SMOKING The proportion of adults who smoke is increasing in many parts of the world. Moreover, the proportion of those who smoke who are women is rising as well. From the standpoint of fetal development this is indeed unfortunate, for smoking by future mothers may have consequences for both the fetus and the newborn child—greater risk of miscarriage and stillbirth, as well as small size (Wen et al., 1990). Maternal smoking may also slow cognitive development in early childhood, perhaps because of elevated levels of carbon monoxide in the blood (Cunningham et al., 1994; Sexton et al., 1990). Even if a pregnant woman does not smoke but spends time in a smoky environment, the infant may be harmed (Dreher, 1995).

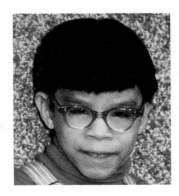

Fetal Alcohol Syndrome

As shown here, children suffering from the fetal alcohol syndrome often have a distinctive appearance. Sadly, this can be viewed as the least of the many problems they suffer.

Physical and Perceptual Development: Early Years

Physical growth is rapid during infancy. Assuming good nutrition, infants almost triple in weight (to 9 kilograms) and increase in body length by about one-third (to 71–74 centimetres) during the first year alone.

Newborns possess a number of simple reflexes at birth. They can follow a moving light with their eyes, suck on fingers or a nipple placed in their mouth, and turn their head in the direction of a touch on the cheek. In addition, they can grasp a finger placed in their palm and make stepping motions if held so that their feet barely touch a flat surface. Table 8.1 lists a number of other reflexes present in the newborn.

Initially, of course, infant ability to move about and reach out for objects is quite limited, but this changes quickly. Within a few months, infants can sit and then crawl. And as proud parents quickly learn, most infants are quite mobile by the time they are fifteen months old. Figure 8.1 summarizes several milestones of motor development. It is important to keep in mind that the approximate ages indicated are merely average values. Even large departures may be of little importance.

TABLE 8.1

Reflexes in the Newborn

Newborns show all the reflexes described here at birth or very shortly thereafter.

Reflex	Description
Blinking	Baby closes eyes in response to light
Rooting	When cheek is touched or stroked, baby turns toward touch; moves lips and tongue to suck
Sucking	When nipple or other object is placed in mouth, baby sucks
Tonic neck	When baby is placed on back with head turned to one side, baby stretches out arm and leg on side baby is facing
Moro	Baby throws out arms and fans fingers, extends neck, and cries in response to loud noise or sudden drop of head
Babinski	When baby's foot is stroked from heel to toe, toes fan out
Grasping	When palms of hands are stroked, baby closes fingers around the object in a strong grasp
Stepping/ Dancing	Baby makes stepping motions if held upright so feet just touch a surface

Figure 8.1
Milestones of Motor Development

Here are some highlights of motor development. Note that the approximate ages shown here are only averages. Most children will depart from them to some extent; departures are of little importance unless they are extreme.

Source: Frankenberg and Dobbs, 1992.

After the initial spurt of the first year, the rate of physical growth slows considerably; both boys and girls gain about five to ten centimetres and two to four kilograms per year. The rate accelerates during adolescence, when both sexes experience a growth spurt lasting about two years. The brain expands rapidly through the first eighteen months of life, and reaches more than half of the adult brain weight by the end of this period. There is a rapid growth of dendrites and axons within the brain during this period, and glial cells rapidly increase in number.

LEARNING ABILITIES OF NEWBORNS What can newborn infants learn? Classical conditioning studies have found that newborn infants (only two hours old) readily learn to associate gentle stroking on the forehead with the taste of a sweet solution. After these two stimuli have been paired repeatedly, they suck when their foreheads are stroked (Rosensztein & Oster, 1988). However, until they are at least eight months old, human infants do not readily acquire conditioned fears. Remember Little Albert, discussed in Chapter 5, who acquired fear of a white rabbit (CS) after it was paired with a loud sound (UCS)? He was already eleven months old at the time the study was conducted. Why do infants not acquire conditioned fears earlier? Perhaps it is because doing so has little survival value for them: They lack the motor skills needed to escape from unpleasant events, so acquiring such fears would do them little good (Berk, 1993). In addition, newborns show stimulus generalization and habituation.

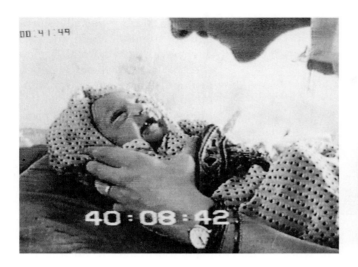 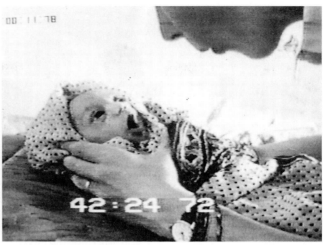

Turning to operant conditioning, there is considerable evidence that newborns learn new behaviours because of their consequences. For example, they readily learn to suck faster in order to see visual designs, or to hear music or human voices (Sansavini et al., 1997). And by the time they are two months old, they will move their heads against a pressure-sensitive pillow in order to produce movements of a mobile hung above their cribs (Pomerleau et al., 1992).

Infants are able, at birth, to express pain through their cries and their facial expressions. These behaviours develop further over the early months (Craig et al., 1988; Johnson, 1993). Also, newborns are capable of imitation. In a series of well-known studies, Meltzoff and his colleagues (e.g., Meltzoff & Moore, 1989, 1999) found that infants between twelve and twenty days of age could imitate facial gestures shown by an adult—for example, sticking out their tongue or opening their mouth. Indeed, infants tested only a few minutes after birth imitated two facial expressions: widened lips and pursed lips (Reissland, 1988).

PERCEPTUAL DEVELOPMENT: METHODS How do infants perceive the world around them? Do they recognize shapes, see colour, perceive depth? Of course infants cannot talk, thus they cannot tell us directly what it is they perceive. Nevertheless, they can tell us in other ways—by changes in heart rate, sucking rate, and duration of gaze. They can show us that they perceive a stimulus by turning their head or eyes toward it or looking at it longer. They show us their preferences by turning toward one stimulus and not another and by looking at it longer They show us they are less interested in a stimulus by turning toward it less often, after it has been presented a number of times. These are some of the observable behaviours that tell researchers about the perceptual world of the not-yet-verbal infant, and this is how we know that newborns can distinguish between odours (Balogh & Porter, 1986; Porter & Winberg, 1999), tastes (Granchrow et al., 1983), sounds (Morrongiello & Clifton, 1984), and different colours, but that early colour vision is very limited (Adams et al., 1994).

Do very young infants remember what they see? By using looking time as the measure of memory, researchers found that three-month-old infants recognized visual events they had seen before—even over intervals as long as three months (Courage & Howe, 1998).

INFANT AUDITION: SOUND, LANGUAGE, MUSIC The auditory systems of infants are functional before birth. Researchers at Queen's University (Kisilevsky, 1992; Kisilevsky et al., 1999) have shown that the fetus perceives in-utero vibration and sound. After birth, infants as young as three days old can detect sounds and turn toward them with their eyes and head.

Newborns Imitating Adult Facial Expressions

Research by Dr. Nadja Reissland-Burghart has shown that newborns only a few minutes old can imitate facial expressions. Widened lips were modelled for the infant on the left, and pursed lips were modelled for the infant on the right.

Research in Developmental Psychology

Janet Werker at the University of British Columbia studies the development of language in infants and young children.

Infants are especially sensitive to sounds within the frequency range of normal human speech. Indeed, they can even distinguish between similar stimuli such as the sounds *ba* and *ga* (Eimas & Tarter, 1979). Very early in life, infants can discriminate among many more speech sounds than those in their native language (Werker, 1999).

When can infants distinguish their own name from similar sounds? Apparently, that happens by the time they are only a few months old. In one study, researchers played the sounds of names to infants who were between four and five months of age (Mandel et al., 1995). On each trial, they heard their own name, a name with the same stress pattern as their own name, or a name with the opposite stress pattern. For instance, for a child named Christine, *Michelle* has the same stress pattern and *Corey* has the opposite. The amount of time spent looking in the direction of the speaker was recorded, and as you can see from Figure 8.2, the infants spent significantly more time looking in the direction of their own names than in the direction of names with the same stress pattern as theirs, and even less time looking in the direction of names with the opposite pattern. These findings indicate that by four or five months of age, infants can recognize their own names and respond differentially to them.

One of the most recent findings is that newborns can tell the difference between the sound of their own cry and that of another newborn infant (Dondi et al., 1999). Awake or asleep, infants only one to three days old were more responsive to the sound of another infant crying than to the sound of their own crying.

Figure 8.2
Evidence That Infants Can Recognize Their Own Names

As shown here, infants only a few months old spent more time looking in the direction of their own spoken names than in the direction of other spoken names.

Source: Based on data from Mandel, Jusczyk, and Pisoni, 1995.

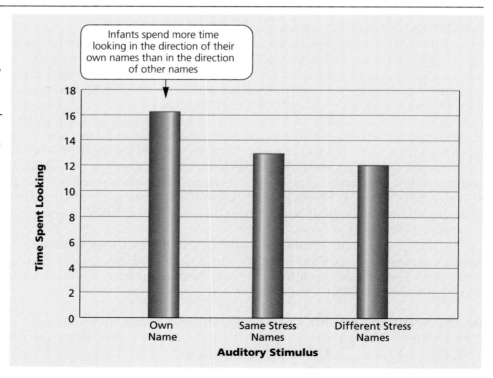

Infants spend more time looking in the direction of their own names than in the direction of other names

What do young infants know about music? Infants perceive and prefer special kinds of songs we call *lullabies*. You probably have a favourite of your own. What makes a lullaby special to a child? Researchers have found that there is a distinctive way people in many cultures sing to infants. A song sounds different when a mother is singing to her infant from when she is singing the same song—but her infant is absent (Bergeson and Trehub, 1999; Trehub et al., 1993). Moreover, this distinctive way of singing to infants is recognizable even after the songs have been recorded and electronically filtered so that the words are removed. According to these researchers, there may be something in the tone of the singing—perhaps a kind of "musical prosody" that is analogous to the prosody of language—that makes the difference (Trehub et al., 1994).

What do infants know about *musical structure*? In one study (Cohen et al., 1987), infants aged seven to eleven months showed by their head-turning responses that they could distinguish that a note was in the wrong key. This supports a general conclusion that "infants possess the prerequisite skills for analyzing complex auditory input, and that [those skills] may be musical universals available early in life" (Schellenberg & Trehub, 1996; see also Trehub et al., 1999).

Sandra Trehub
University of Toronto

INFANT VISION: FORM AND DEPTH PERCEPTION Infants have impressive abilities in visual perception—particularly in form or pattern perception. Although they cannot see very clearly at birth, they do have distinct preferences for particular kinds of visual stimuli. In early studies of infant perception, researchers found that infants as young as six months prefer patterned as opposed to plain targets (Fantz, 1961), symmetrical rather than asymmetrical stimuli (Humphrey & Humphrey, 1989), and human faces over all other stimuli tested. Subsequent research found evidence of even earlier face perception. By two months of age, infants prefer faces with features in the normal locations. By three months they can distinguish between their mother's face and that of a stranger, and distinguish one stranger's face from another (Maurer & Young, 1983). Even infants two days old can distinguish their mother's face from the face of a female stranger (Field et al., 1984; Walton et al., 1992).

The ability to perceive depth also develops rapidly in the months immediately after birth. Early studies on depth perception used an apparatus known as the *visual cliff* (Gibson & Walk, 1960). As you can see from the photo, the patterned floor drops away on the deep side of the cliff. A transparent surface actually continues across this chasm, so that there is no actual drop, and no real danger. Yet human infants six or seven months old refuse to crawl across the deep side, thus indicating that they perceive depth by this time. Does this perceptual ability appear prior to this age? Since younger infants cannot crawl across the cliff even if they want to, it is necessary to use other measures to find that out. Such research indicates depth perception in infants as young as three months old (Fox et al., 1979; Yonas et al., 1987).

Of course, these competencies in sensation and perception develop normally when environmental stimulation is provided, as experiments with animals have often shown. A great deal of what we know about the fundamentals of perceptual development has come from comparisons with animals (e.g., Mitchell, 1989; Timney, 1990).

In summary, shortly after birth, infants have sophisticated abilities to interpret complex sensory input. How do they then combine this information into a frameworks for understanding the world? That is the question we will turn to next. First, however, let us consider the basic research methods used by psychologists to understand human development, which are described in the **Research Process.**

The Visual Cliff: Studying Infant Depth Perception

Infants six or seven months old refuse to crawl out over the deep side of the visual cliff. This indicates that they can perceive depth.

The Research Process:
Human Development: Basic Methods

That people change with the passage of time is obvious. But how can we map the course of development and identify the factors that affect it? Developmental psychologists use several different methods for reaching this goal.

Longitudinal Research

Longitudinal research studies use the same individuals repeatedly over long intervals of time (see Figure 8.3). For example, researchers might identify two groups of children, one being cared for by their own mothers and the other in daycare centres, and study them for several years to determine whether the groups differ in cognitive development—for example, in their language skills or their ability to solve problems.

Longitudinal research offers important advantages. First, since the same individuals are tested or observed repeatedly, individual variations in the course of development can be observed. Second, because the same individuals are studied over relatively long periods of time, it may be possible to draw conclusions about how specific events influence the course of development.

Longitudinal research has several potential disadvantages, however. First, some participants may be lost over the course of the project. In the case of daycare, families may move, break up, or lose interest, the result being that their children are lost to the study. As well, the children who remain in the study may be different in important respects to those who withdrew. To the extent this is the case, any differences between the mother's care and daycare groups may be a result of factors that do not involve being raised at home or in a daycare centre. Also, there may be practice effects. People who are tested or observed repeatedly may become familiar with the kinds of tasks used in the research. To the extent that these effects occur, the results obtained may be invalid.

Cross-Sectional Research

Now, consider another way of studying the mother/daycare question. Instead of following the development of two groups of children for several years, we might instead compare children who are different ages right now. For example, we might study three-, four-, and five-year-olds who have been cared for by their mothers and compare them with three-, four-, and five-year-olds in daycare centres, to determine (for each age) whether the two groups differ with respect to cognitive development. This is an example of **cross-sectional research**, in which people of different ages are studied at the same point in time (refer to Figure 8.3).

Cross-sectional research also offers several advantages. It can be conducted much more quickly than longitudinal research—in the time it takes to collect the data. And since participants are tested only once, practice effects are minimal.

Unfortunately, cross-sectional research also has several disadvantages. Perhaps the most important one has to do with **cohort effects**. These are differences between groups of individuals of different ages that derive not only from differences in age but also from the fact that the subjects were born at different times and so may have had different life experiences. As an illustration, assume that people who are sixty-five engage in a narrower range of sexual practices than those who are twenty-five. Is this finding a result of age differences? Perhaps. But it may also be a result of the fact that the older individuals grew up at a time when society showed much less tolerance for many forms of sexual behaviour. Thus, cohort effects sometimes make it difficult to interpret the findings of cross-sectional research.

Summing Up and an Alternative Approach

Faced with the mixed advantages and disadvantages outlined above, developmental psychologists have devised an approach to research that maximizes the advantages of longitudinal and cross-sectional research while minimizing the disadvantages. In this third method, known as **longitudinal–sequential design**, several different ages are studied repeatedly over a period of years. In effect, the longitudinal and cross-sectional methods are combined. Since each sample of participants is studied over time, changes within each group can be attributed to development. But since several ages are studied, researchers can also assess the impact of cohort effects and cultural changes, by comparing, at the same age, people born in different years. This type of design permits both longitudinal and cross-sectional comparisons. If the results of both are the same, we can be quite confident about the validity of the findings. While the longitudinal–sequential design is still vulnerable to participant attrition, practice effects, and the like, it does offer a means of untangling the influences of cultural change and individual development.

Longitudinal Research: Research in which the same individuals are studied over long intervals, such as years.

Cross-Sectional Research: Research comparing groups of individuals of different ages in order to determine how some aspect of behaviour or cognition changes with age.

Cohort Effects: Differences between individuals of different ages stemming from the contrasting social or cultural conditions of the periods in which they grew up.

Longitudinal–Sequential Design: A research approach in which several groups of individuals of different ages are studied across time.

▶ **Figure 8.3**
Basic Methods of Studying Human Development

In the longitudinal method, the same individuals are studied across a long period of time. In the cross-sectional method, people of different ages are studied at one time.

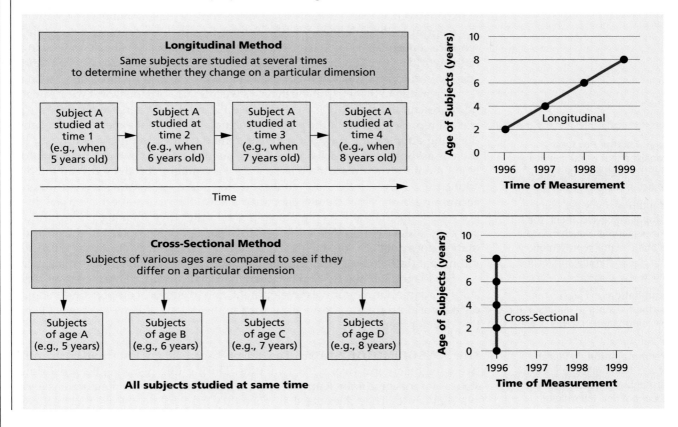

K E Y   QUESTIONS

▨ Which environmental factors can adversely affect the development of a fetus?

▨ Which perceptual abilities are shown by infants?

▨ What are the three basic methods used by psychologists to study human development?

Cognitive Development

Do children think, reason, and remember like adults? Until well into the twentieth century, it was believed that they did. This assumption was challenged by the Swiss psychologist Jean Piaget. On the basis of careful observation of his own and many other children, Piaget concluded that, in several important ways, children do not think or reason like adults.

Piaget's theory of cognitive development contains many valuable insights (Case, 1993) and has generated much important research. In recent years, Piaget's theory has been challenged by several newer approaches (e.g., Gopnik, 1996), and we will review Piaget's and those newer theories also.

An Overview of Piaget's Theory

Piaget's theory of cognitive development is a **stage theory**. It proposes that, in the development of our thinking, we move through an orderly and predictable series of steps (see Table 8.2). Stage theories have been applied to many other aspects of human behaviour as well—notably to the development of personality (see Chapter 12).

Central to Piaget's theory is the assumption that children are active thinkers who are constantly trying to construct a more accurate or advanced understanding of the world around them (e.g., Siegler & Ellis, 1996). In other words, from this perspective, children construct their knowledge of the world by interacting with it.

According to Piaget, from birth on, as we interact with the world we create mental representations of it (Olson, 1993) (see Figure 8.4). When we change our past mental representations of the world to include our current experience, we are undergoing **adaptation.** This kind of change may happen in one of two ways. First, there is **assimilation,** which occurs when we incorporate new information into existing mental structures known as *schemas.* Assimilation occurs when an infant encounters a new rattle and shakes it to make a sound. Second, there is **accommodation.** When infants encounter a new kind of toy—perhaps a jack-in-the-box—they try to treat it as they have treated other toys, shaking it like a rattle or banging it like a drum. When these old strategies do not work and the new information does not fit the old mental representation, a new way of dealing with the environment (in this case, turning a handle) must be found. That is accommodation.

For Piaget, it is the tension between assimilation and accommodation that results in adaptation, cognitive development, and ever more complex understanding of the world around us. Now let us turn to the details of Piaget's stages of cognitive development.

THE SENSORIMOTOR STAGE The first of Piaget's stages lasts from birth until between eighteen and twenty-four months. During this period—the **sensorimotor stage**—infants gradually learn there is a relationship between their actions and the external world. They discover that when they manipulate objects, there are consequences. For example, they learn to perform movements that affect the physical world: pulling, striking, swinging, and rubbing. They learn to reach for objects while looking at them, and they begin to experiment with various actions to see what effects they produce. In short, they acquire a basic idea about cause and effect.

Stage Theory: Any theory proposing that all human beings move through an orderly and predictable series of changes.

Adaptation: In Piaget's theory of cognitive development, the process through which individuals build mental representations of the world through interaction with it.

Assimilation: In Piaget's theory, the tendency to understand new information in terms of existing mental frameworks.

Accommodation: In Piaget's theory, the modification of existing mental frameworks to take account of new information.

Sensorimotor Stage: In Piaget's theory, the earliest stage of cognitive development.

TABLE 8.2

Major Stages in Piaget's Theory

According to Piaget, we move through the stages of cognitive development described here.

Stage	Age	Major Accomplishments
Sensorimotor	0–2 years	The child develops basic ideas of cause and effect and object permanence
Preoperational	2–6 or 7 years	The child begins to represent the world symbolically
Concrete Operations	7–11 or 12 years	The child gains understanding of principles such as conservation; logical thought emerges
Formal Operations	12–adult	The adolescent becomes capable of several forms of logical thought

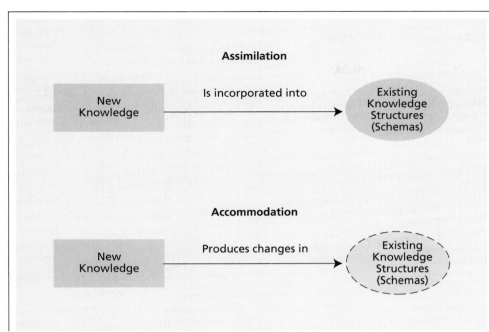

Assimilation

New Knowledge → Is incorporated into → Existing Knowledge Structures (Schemas)

Accommodation

New Knowledge → Produces changes in → Existing Knowledge Structures (Schemas)

Figure 8.4
Assimilation and Accommodation

According to Piaget, children build increasing knowledge of the world through two processes: *assimilation*, in which new information is incorporated into existing schemas, and *accommodation*, in which existing schemas are modified in response to new information and experiences.

Throughout the sensorimotor period, infants know the world through motor activities (Bebko et al., 1992) and sensory impressions (Reid, 1989). They have not yet learned how to *use* mental representations or images when real objects are absent. This results in some interesting contradictions. For example, if an object is hidden from view, four-month-old babies will not attempt to search for it. Generally for these infants, it is "out of sight, out of mind." By eight or nine months of age, however, the situation changes. Infants of this age will search for the hidden object. They have developed **object permanence**—the understanding that objects continue to exist even after they are no longer seen. In contrast, object permanence in kittens appears much more rapidly (Dumas & Dore, 1989).

THE PREOPERATIONAL STAGE Some time between the ages of eighteen and twenty-four months, Piaget contends, children develop the ability to *use* mental representations of objects and events. At the same time, language develops, as does the beginning of thinking in words. These developments mark the end of the sensorimotor period and the start of the **preoperational stage.**

During this stage, which lasts until about age seven, children gradually begin to act upon objects—for instance, they begin to feed their dolls or dress them. Furthermore, they demonstrate **symbolic play,** in which they pretend that one object is another—for instance, that a pencil is a rocket or a dinner roll is a frog. One variant of this is *make-believe play*, in which youngsters pretend to perform various activities they have seen adults perform, such as reading, working with tools, cutting the lawn, and so on.

Object Permanence: An understanding of the fact that objects continue to exist when they are out of sight.

Preoperational Stage: In Piaget's theory, a stage of cognitive development during which children become capable of mental representations of the external world.

Symbolic Play: Play in which children pretend that one object is another object.

Make-Believe Play

When they engage in make-believe play, children demonstrate that they can represent everyday activities mentally. According to Piaget, they become capable of such behaviour during the preoperational stage.

Figure 8.5
Lack of Understanding of Conservation during the Preoperational Stage

A four-year-old is shown two identical lumps of clay (left). Then one lump is flattened into a large pancake (right). Asked whether the two lumps still contain the same amount of clay, the child may answer "no." Such behaviour indicates that the child lacks understanding of the concept of conservation.

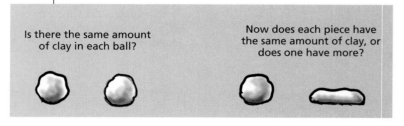

Is there the same amount of clay in each ball?

Now does each piece have the same amount of clay, or does one have more?

Children at this stage of cognitive development are still quite immature in several important respects. First, they are limited by **egocentrism**; that is, they have difficulty understanding that other people may perceive the world differently (Piaget, 1975). Consider the following demonstration (Flavell, 1973): Two-year-olds are shown that a card has a picture of a dog on one side and a cat on the other. The card is then placed between the child and the experimenter so that each can see only one side. Now the experimenter asks the child two questions: What do you see? and What do I see? Because of egocentric thought, many children say that the experimenter sees the same picture as they do.

Children in the preoperational stage lack understanding of relational terms, such as *darker*, *larger*, and *harder*. Further, they lack *seriation*—the ability to arrange objects in order from large to small, for example. Finally, and perhaps most important, they lack an understanding of **conservation**—the principle that the physical attributes of an object remain the same even though its appearance has changed. For example, a four-year-old is shown two identical lumps of clay. One lump is then flattened into a large pancake as the child watches. Asked whether the two lumps still contain the same amount of clay, the child may answer *no* (see Figure 8.5).

THE STAGE OF CONCRETE OPERATIONS By the time they are six or seven, most children have gained an understanding of conservation. According to Piaget, this marks the beginning of the third major stage of cognitive development—the stage of **concrete operations.**

During this stage, which lasts until about the age of eleven, many important cognitive skills emerge. Children gain an understanding of relational terms and seriation. They come to understand reversibility—the fact that many physical changes can be undone by reversing the original action. They also begin to make greater use of categories in describing and thinking about the physical world. Thus, if asked to sort various objects, four-year-olds will often do so in terms of colour or size. Older children place objects in more complex categories that take account of several features at once. For example, they will categorize bananas, oranges, apples, and pineapples as fruits, despite major variations in colour, shape, and size.

Finally, when children reach the stage of concrete operations, they begin to engage in logical thought. If asked, "Why did you and your mother go to the store?" they will reply, "Because my mother needed some milk." Younger children, in contrast, might say, "Because afterwards, we came home."

THE STAGE OF FORMAL OPERATIONS At about the age of twelve, Piaget suggests, most children enter the final stage of cognitive development—the stage of **formal operations**. During this time, major features of adult thought appear. This may have to do with changes in frontal lobe function by this age (Segalowitz et al., 1992).

While children in the stage of concrete operations can think logically, they do so about concrete events and objects. In contrast, at the stage of formal operations, they can think abstractly. That is, they can deal not only with the real, or concrete, but also with possibilities—with potential events or relationships that do not exist but can be imagined. As a result, they become able to experience doubt, as studies by Boyes and Chandler at the University of Calgary have shown (1992).

Egocentrism: The inability of young children to distinguish their own perspective from that of others.

Conservation: Principle that states that certain physical attributes of an object remain unchanged even though its outward appearance changes.

Concrete Operations: In Piaget's theory, a stage of cognitive development occurring roughly between the ages of seven and eleven. It is at this stage that children grasp such principles as conservation, and that the capacity for logical thought emerges.

Formal Operations: In Piaget's theory, the final stage of cognitive development, during which individuals may acquire the capacity for deductive or propositional reasoning.

During this final stage of cognitive development, children become capable of what Piaget termed **hypothetico-deductive reasoning**. This involves the ability to formulate hypotheses about some aspect of the external world, and to think logically about abstractions, such as symbols and propositions.

Thus, older children, and especially adolescents, often use their new reasoning abilities to construct broad theories about human relationships, what makes a given behaviour right or wrong, and political systems. The reasoning behind these views may be logical in the sense of meeting the formal requirements of logic, but the theories themselves are often flawed because the young persons who construct them do not know enough about these complex matters to do a thorough job.

One final point: While people who have reached the stage of formal operations are *capable* of engaging in hypothetico-deductive reasoning, propositional thought, and other advanced forms of thinking, there is no guarantee that they will actually do so. On the contrary, even adults slip back (Kuhn, 1989). Having the capacity for logical thought, then, does not ensure that it will actually occur.

A Contemporary Assessment of Piaget's Theory

All theories in psychology are subject to rigorous scientific scrutiny. However, many psychologists currently question the ideas that (1) all human beings move through set stages; (2) they do so at certain ages; and (3) the order of this progress is unchanging (Flavell, 1985).

Piaget's ideas have been the focus of a large number of investigations (Flavell, 1982). The results suggest revisions to the theory with respect to these three issues: (1) the ages at which infants and preschoolers reach the milestones of cognitive development; (2) how distinct the stages of cognitive development are; and (3) the importance of language and social interaction with caregivers to cognitive growth.

THE CASE OF THE COMPETENT PRESCHOOLER   There is reason to believe that Piaget seriously underestimated the cognitive abilities of infants and young children (Siegel & Peterson, 1996). For example, a recent study at the University of Waterloo used an ingenious method to demonstrate that two-year-old toddlers know about what other people know and do not know (O'Neill, 1996). Toddlers were introduced to a new toy and then it was placed on a high shelf. For some children, the parent was a witness to these events; for some children, the parent was out of the room. The ways in which the children asked their originally present or originally absent parents for help in gaining access to the toy indicated that they had some knowledge of how much *the parents* knew or did not know—based upon whether the parent had witnessed what had happened or not. Moreover, under the right conditions, children can take the perspective of another person—as young as age three or four (Newcombe & Huttenlochber, 1992). Indeed, even infants fourteen to eighteen months old show some awareness of the fact that other people may not see exactly what they do (Schikedanz et al., 1999).

Piaget also underestimated young children's understanding of the nature of the physical world (Baillargeon, 1999), conservation of number, what it means to be alive (Bullock, 1985), and their ability to classify objects (e.g., Mandler et al., 1991). Piaget made a major contribution to our understanding of cognitive development; however, the tasks Piaget used led him to underestimate the abilities of young children—in several important ways.

DISCRETE STAGES IN COGNITIVE DEVELOPMENT   Piaget proposed that cognitive development happens in discrete steps and that these are discontinuous: children must complete one before entering the next. Most current research findings, however, indicate that cognitive changes occur in a gradual manner.

Hypothetico-Deductive Reasoning: In Piaget's theory, a type of reasoning first shown during the stage of formal operations. It involves formulating a general theory and deducing specific hypotheses from it.

The Social Context of Cognitive Development

According to Vygotsky (1987), children often learn in situations in which parents present them with cognitive tasks that are slightly too difficult for them to perform alone. The social interaction and dialogue that occur in such situations help children master new skills.

THE SOCIAL CONTEXT OF COGNITIVE DEVELOPMENT While Piaget certainly recognized the importance of social interactions in cognitive development, they were not central to his theory. A growing body of evidence suggests, however, that social interactions between children and adults may play a key role in at least some kinds of cognitive growth (e.g., Rogoff, 1990). First, when an adult calls a child's attention to particular aspects of the environment, that increases the likelihood of the child acquiring certain kinds of knowledge and certain ways of looking at the world. As noted recently by Gopnik (1996), a child who plays with mixing bowls may not have the same sorts of experiences as a child who plays with toy arrows or spears.

Second, adults may engage children in *reciprocal teaching*—teacher and child taking turns performing an activity and verbal interactions between parents and children can play an important role in cognitive development (Vygotsky, 1987). This allows the adult (or other tutor) to serve as a model for the child. During their interactions with children, adults provide *mental scaffolding*—supports that children use as they proceed to master new tasks and new ways of thinking. When adults provide scaffolding in a new learning task they do part of the job for the child, so that what the child has to do is only a small step further than what he or she can do already. These social interactions between children and older tutors that Vygotsky emphasized do indeed enhance cognitive development, helping children to acquire specific skills such as reading, and new insights and advances in inferential thinking (e.g., Azmitia, 1988).

Social learning includes children learning from each other—classmates, for example (Astington, 1995). And being socially skilled (being able to get along well with peers and others) seems to be an important "plus" in this process: the more socially skilled children are, the more advanced they are in their understanding of how other people think—an important aspect of cognitive development we'll soon consider (Watson et al., 1999).

Perhaps the main point here is that cognitive development is not an automatic unfolding of one stage after another, but rather a more flexible process, in which progress can be—and often is—affected by social experiences (e.g., Behrend, Rosengren, & Perlmutter, 1992).

LANGUAGE AND COGNITIVE DEVELOPMENT Young children often talk to themselves as they go about their daily activities, giving themselves instructions about what to do next. Piaget called this *egocentric speech* and suggested that it was a sign of cognitive immaturity—an inability to take account of the perspective of others. Vygotsky objected strongly, contending that private speech is not egocentric (Lloyd et al., 1999). Rather, it occurs when young children encounter obstacles and difficulties, and that it represents their efforts at self-guidance. Vygotsky felt that this early use of language helps young children reflect on their own behaviour, and that it plays a key role in cognitive development. The results of many studies have confirmed his views (e.g., Bivens & Berk, 1990).

In summary, Piaget's theory profoundly altered our ideas about how children think and reason, and it has served as a framework for much research on cognitive development (Brainerd, 1996). His work has made a lasting contribution to psychology and provided a framework for much research. Nevertheless, current findings continue to point to ways in which Piaget's theory may need revision.

■ What are the major stages in Piaget's theory, and what cognitive abilities do infants, children, and adolescents acquire as they move through these stages?

■ In which three respects does Piaget's theory appear to be inaccurate?

Beyond Piaget: Information Processing and Theory of Mind

While Piaget's theory remains influential even today, several other approaches to the study of cognitive development have emerged in recent years (e.g., Gopnik, 1996). Let's turn now to the second contemporary approach to cognitive development.

INFORMATION-PROCESSING APPROACH: PROGRESS IN PERCEPTION Earlier in this chapter you learned that newborns perceive many events in the world around them. From early infancy on, however, that ability improves rapidly. Over the years, children become more and more proficient in perceiving subtle features of the external world. They progress from being able to discriminate between a human face and a jumbled pattern, to being able to tell the difference between individual faces that are quite similar. This growth requires the development of sophisticated mental structures (frameworks or schemas)—for interpreting new experiences. The *information-processing approach* seeks to understand the place in human development of encoding, storage, and later retrieval of information from memory.

INFORMATION PROCESSING: ATTENTION If you have ever observed very young children you know that they are easily distracted. As children grow older, however, they acquire an increasing ability to concentrate. By the time they are about seven years old, they can tune out interference such as music or other background noises (e.g., Higgins & Turnure, 1984). The increasing ability to focus on the most important aspects of a given situation, to the exclusion of others, offers important advantages. However, some children are unable to concentrate for more than a few minutes. They have attention-deficit/hyperactivity disorder and you will read more about them in Chapter 14.

INFORMATION PROCESSING: MEMORY Short-term memory improves as children mature (e.g., Cohen & Griffiths, 1987). Not only do they remember more items and for longer intervals of time, but also children (as young as age three) recognize the fragility of their short-term memories. When children of this age are given familiar toys and asked to remember as many as possible, they spend less time playing with the toys and spend more time naming them than children not asked to remember (Baker-Ward et al., 1984). As they grow older, children make use of other techniques for retaining information in working (short-term) memory, such as organization (e.g., Bjorklund & Muir, 1988).

With development, infants increasingly use various strategies for retaining information in short-term working memory. Rehearsal is perhaps the most important of these. As you might expect, five- and six-year-olds are much less likely than adults to repeat information to themselves as they try to memorize it. By the time children are eight years old, however, they can do this much more effectively. Interestingly, even very young children use strategies—although not necessarily rehearsal—to improve their memories. For instance, when trying to remember information, they point at it, stare at it, or name it; they will engage in such activities as long as they can understand why they are being asked to remember something (e.g., Wellman et al., 1975).

Figure 8.6
Drawing as an Aid to Memory for Young Children

Children five to six years old who drew pictures of events they experienced were later able to recall more of these events than children who were simply asked to describe them verbally. Similar effects did not occur for children three to four years old, however. These findings suggest that drawing is an aid to memory, but only for children five years old or older.

Source: Based on data from Butler, Gross, and Hayne, 1995.

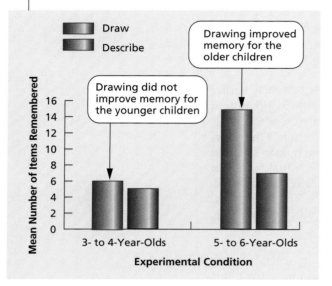

With respect to long-term memory, it is clear that as children mature, the amount of information they have entered into memory grows considerably. Moreover, such information becomes better organized, primarily into various schemas—cognitive frameworks that help individuals organize existing information and both interpret and store new information. The overall result is that new information is processed more efficiently, and memory improves in several respects. Such effects are illustrated by an intriguing study conducted by Butler, Gross, and Hayne (1995).

These researchers took children in two age groups—three to four years old and five to six years old—on an exciting visit to a fire station. One day later, half the children in each age group were asked either to tell a researcher or to draw pictures of what happened during the visit. Then, a month later, all the children were asked to describe verbally what happened during their visit. As shown in Figure 8.6, the five- to six-year-olds who drew the events remembered more than those who simply described them orally—but not the three- to four-year-olds. However, as is true for adults (see Chapter 6), sometimes there are distortions and errors in what children recall. For example, Marche and Howe (1995) found that preschoolers reported misleading information to which they had been exposed after an initial memory test. Furthermore, when five- and six-year-olds heard that a visitor to their classroom had engaged in various activities—such as tearing a book—children reported having witnessed those events even though they never occurred (Leichtman & Ceci, 1995).

The development of memory for source—where an original experience occurred—proceeds as well (Butler, 1997). In one study, Gopnik and Graf (1988) examined the ability of three- to six-year-olds to remember how they had learned about the contents of a drawer—whether they had seen the item in the drawer, heard about it, or figured it out from a clue that they were given. With increasing age, their memory for the source of the information improved considerably, particularly if a delay was imposed between learning about the contents of the drawer and being asked to remember how they had learned that information.

INFORMATION PROCESSING: COGNITION As childhood proceeds, the mental representations produced by children—of the physical world, the social world, and the personal world—change. How do children mentally represent a cube, a close relationship, pain, early injuries, and illness as they grow more and more mature?

At Scarborough College of the University of Toronto, Nicholls and Kennedy (1992) had their subjects (about 1700 volunteers at the Ontario Science Centre) handle a small cube and then draw it on a blank piece of paper. The various results are shown in Figure 8.7. Until age five, children are satisfied that their single square (example 2) is the best representation of the cube. After age fourteen, the most common representation is the square with parallel oblique lines (example 6) to show depth. Between these two ages, various other kinds of drawings are made. According to Nicholls and Kennedy, these data say that, between ages five and fourteen, children may take different routes to the mature representation that is most commonly found later on.

Children represent the social world around them as well. At the University of Winnipeg, Baldwin (1995) has studied how children develop mental structures for close social relationships. As these cognitive structures develop, children can handle more complex social relationships because they have better mental representations of social information. Involved also are developmental changes in memory, emotional control, and self-knowledge. You will find much more information about this topic in Chapter 16.

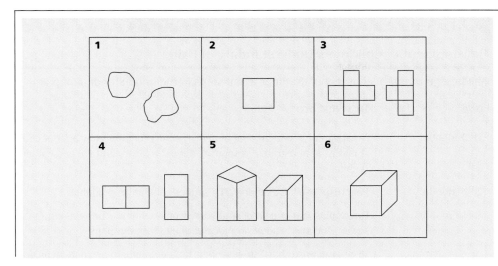

TABLE 8.3	

Development of Children's Understanding of Pain

Children go through a number of developmental steps in the understanding of pain.

Age	Description
0–3 months	No apparent understanding of pain; memory for pain likely but not conclusively demonstrated; responses appear reflexive and are perceptually dominated
3–6 months	Pain response supplemented by sadness and anger response
6–18 months	Developing fear of painful situations; words common for pain, e.g., "owie," "ouchie," "boo-boo"; localization of pain develops
18–24 months	Use of the word "hurt" to describe pain; beginning to use noncognitive coping strategies
36–60 months	Can give a gross indication of the intensity of the pain, and beginning to use more descriptive adjectives and attach emotional terms such as "sad" or "mad" to the pain
5–7 years	Can more clearly differentiate levels of pain intensity; beginning to use cognitive coping strategies
7–11 years	Can explain the value of pain

What do children understand about illness and how does that understanding develop? That is another real-life question that has been investigated (Crisp et al., 1996). In two studies, children between age four and age fourteen were asked questions about illness: for example, "How do you get a cold?" The responses were assigned to Piaget's stages: preoperational (e.g., "You get it from the sun I think"); concrete operational (e.g., "The germs go in your mouth"); and formal operational ("When you're all stressed out and that makes your body not work properly"). The children were either "experts" on illness, in the sense that they had been hospitalized repeatedly for a major chronic illness—cancer or cystic fibrosis—or "novices" who had been hospitalized also, but for other kinds of illnesses, such as measles.

As expected, children's level of understanding of illness increased as they got older. However, their experience with illness also determined their level of understanding. Thus, experience and cognitive development are related. The information provided by this kind of research has important practical applications because what we tell children about their illnesses—how we advise them or explain their condition to them—is best delivered at their own level of understanding.

INFORMATION PROCESSING: METACOGNITION   Another important aspect of cognitive development that fits very well with the information-processing approach is **metacognition**: what we know about our own cognitive processes, or, in other words, what we think about thinking, know about knowing. We use the term *metamemory* to refer to what we believe we know about remembering (O'Sullivan & Howe, 1995, 1998)! Such knowledge is very helpful, for it tells us

Metacognition: Awareness and understanding of our own cognitive processes.

what would be most useful to know in a given situation. For instance, as a result of our understanding of our own cognitive processes, we can generate such thoughts as these: "I'd better read this paragraph again; I didn't understand it the first time," or "I'd better make a note of that information—it seems important." Clearly, young children lack such insights in comparison to older children and adults. Yet they are not totally lacking where metacognition is concerned. For example, three-year-olds understand that thinking about other things can affect how well they do. At the age of four or five, most children realize that their own memories are limited and that how much effort they put forth affects how much they will remember (O'Sullivan, 1996).

O'Sullivan and Joy (1994) studied metacognition about reading problems. Students in grades one, three, five, and seven read about the reading problems of four imaginary children. They were given information about the ability of each child and how much effort he or she put into reading. The subjects then suggested the cause of each child's reading problem and recommended what could be done about it. Children at all these grade levels gave complex causal explanations for reading problems, but they were less able to suggest remedies that would clear up the difficulty.

Gradually, as they develop increasing understanding of how their own minds work, children acquire new and more sophisticated schemes for maximizing their efficiency. They combine various strategies for enhancing attention and memory, monitor their own progress toward chosen goals, and examine their own understanding of information and feedback as it is received. In short, they become increasingly capable of self-regulation of their own cognitive processes, as well as of other aspects of their behaviour.

CHILDREN'S THEORY OF MIND Development occurs also in children's ability to understand what other people are doing, thinking, and believing. As human adults, we possess a highly evolved, sophisticated understanding of thinking—not only our own, but also that of other people (e.g., Moore, 1996). We realize that our own thoughts may change over time and that we may have false beliefs or reach false conclusions. Furthermore, we realize that given the same information, other people may come to conclusions that differ from ours. Similarly, we realize that other people may have goals or desires that differ from our own and that they may sometimes try to conceal them from us.

But what about children? How does their thinking about thinking—their **theory of mind**—develop? When—and how—do they acquire such understanding? This has been a major focus of recent research on cognitive development, and it has yielded some surprising findings. For example, most four-year-olds—and even some three-year-olds—understand the difference between making a mistake and telling a lie (Siegal & Peterson, 1996).

Do children recognize that other people can hold beliefs different from their own? That does not happen until they are about four or five years old (e.g., Harris, 1991; Naito et al., 1994). For an illustration of this finding, see Figure 8.8. These and related results suggest that, as development proceeds, children acquire a more and more sophisticated understanding of their own cognitive processes and those of others.

The information-processing perspective suggests that cognitive development can best be understood as improvement in basic aspects of information-processing—in the ways in which we perceive, attend, memorize, retrieve, and manipulate information. This is a very different view of cognitive development from Piaget's. See the **Key Concept** on page 323 for a comparison of these two important perspectives on cognitive development.

Theory of Mind: Refers to children's growing understanding of their own mental states and those of others.

K E Y *QUESTIONS*

■ According to the information-processing perspective, what does cognitive development involve?

■ Which changes occur in children's ability to focus their attention and to enhance their own memory as they grow older?

■ What is metacognition?

Critical Thinking

Do you think that young children's inability to understand adult thinking explains why they are so vulnerable to child molesters?

Figure 8.8
Children's Theory of Mind: Their Understanding That Others Can Hold Different Beliefs Than They Do

If young children (e.g., three-year-olds) are told the story depicted here, they predict that the character in the story will look for the candy where his mother left it: they don't understand that what *they* know can be different from what the story character knows, or that he can hold false beliefs. Four-year-olds, however, predict that the character will look where *he* left the candy, thus demonstrating their growing understanding of how others, and they, think.

Source: Schikedanz et al., 1998, p. 335.

Key Concept
Two Views of Cognitive Development

Piaget's Theory

- There is tension between these drives: assimilation and accommodation.
- Cognitive development is an invariant movement through a fixed order of stages.
- New cognitive abilities appear at each stage:

Sensorimotor stage
0–2: The child begins to interact with the environment; the idea of permanence develops.

Concrete operational stage
7–11 or 12: The child learns to appreciate such principles as conservation; logical thought emerges.

Preoperational stage
2–6 or 7: The child begins to represent the world symbolically.

Formal operational stage
12–adulthood: The adolescent becomes capable of logical thought.

Information-Processing Approach

- Children's capacities to process information increase with age.
- Neither the rate nor the order of these changes is invariant.
- Improvements occur with respect to each capacity:

Attention
Children's ability to focus attention and make plans increases with age.

Memory
Children acquire increasing capacity and more sophisticated techniques for enhancing memory.

Sensory processing
The child gains in ability to notice subtle features of the external world.

Metacognition
As children grow, their capacity to regulate their own cognitive processes increases.

▶ ## Moral Development

Is it ever right to cheat on an exam? Is it right to lie to another person—to say that you like their new haircut when you really hate it? These are questions about what is right and what is wrong in a given situation. As adults, we realize that such matters are complex. Whether a given action is right or wrong may depend on many factors, including the specific circumstances involved, legal considerations, cultural factors (Lee Kang et al., 1997), and our own personal code of ethics.

But how do children learn the difference between right and wrong? Grusec and Goodnow (1994) have studied how children acquire morals—that is, how they "internalize" values. We will look at their ideas and then at Kohlberg's views about **moral development** and how moral reasoning changes from early childhood on.

Joan E. Grusec
University of Toronto

Moral Development: Changes that occur with age in the capacity to reason about the rightness or wrongness of various actions.

LEARNING THE DIFFERENCE BETWEEN RIGHT AND WRONG   Researchers Joan Grusec and Jacqueline Goodnow have some novel ideas about how society's values become incorporated, or *internalized,* into children's thinking. They begin with the assumption that parents discipline their children for these reasons: to pass on ideas of right and wrong and to enable their children to form their own moral codes as new situations arise. In order for moral values to be acquired by children, two conditions—having to do with communication between parent and child—must be met (see Figure 8.9). First, the child must listen to what the parent means to say and perceive how important it is. Second, and equally necessary, the child must accept what is being said. Acceptance means: "The child must perceive the message as appropriate, the child must be motivated to comply ... and the child must feel that the message ... has been self-generated." So not only is accurate perception *by the child* necessary for communicating right and wrong, but the child's acceptance of the parent's moral message is also essential (Grusec & Goodnow, 1994).

Figure 8.9
Features of Parental Discipline

For moral values to be acquired by children, they must listen accurately and accept what is being said.

Source: After Grusec and Goodnow, 1994. Copyright © 1994 by the American Psychological Association. Reprinted with permission.

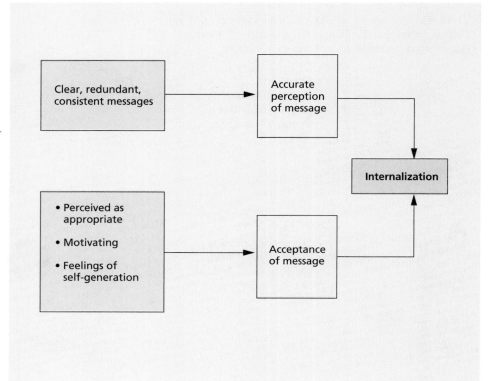

Successful internalization also relies on the child seeing the message as appropriate and on the child's self-esteem remaining intact. At the same time, differences between parent and child should be tolerated when they promote the development of the child's own set of values.

There is another side to accurate perception, of course, and that is the accuracy of the perception of the children's cognitions *by their parents*. Hastings and Grusec (1997) found that disagreements between parents and children (adolescent subjects) occurred less often and were more satisfactorily resolved when fathers and mothers more correctly perceived their children's thoughts and feelings.

A different line of research on moral development has been this: How do we change the way we draw conclusions about right and wrong as we grow older and more experienced? The most influential view on this has been that of Lawrence Kohlberg (1984).

KOHLBERG'S STAGES OF MORAL REASONING   Building on earlier views proposed by Piaget (1932/1965), Kohlberg studied boys and men and suggested that human beings move through three distinct levels of moral reasoning, each divided in two separate phases. In order to determine the stage of moral development people had reached, Kohlberg asked them to consider imaginary situations that raised moral dilemmas. Participants then indicated the course of action they would choose, and explained why.

One such dilemma is this: A man's wife is ill with a special type of cancer. There is a drug that may save her, but it is very expensive. The pharmacist who discovered this medicine will sell it for $2000, but the man has only $1000. He asks the pharmacist to let him pay part of the cost now and the rest later, but the pharmacist refuses. Being desperate, the man steals the drug. Should he have done so? Why?

Note that according to Kohlberg, it is not the judgment of whether he should have stolen the drug or not—but rather the explanation given—that reveals the individual's stage of moral development. An overview of these levels (or stages) is provided in Table 8.4.

The Preconventional Level   At the first level of moral development, children judge morality largely in terms of consequences. Actions that lead to rewards are perceived as good or right; those that lead to punishments are seen as bad or unacceptable. Within the **preconventional level,** Kohlberg describes two distinct stages. In the first stage, children have a punishment-and-obedience orientation. For example, a child at this stage might state, "The man should steal the drug because if he lets his wife die, he'll get in trouble." Later, in stage 2, children are aware of the fact that people can have different points of view about a moral issue, but they judge morality in terms of what satisfies their own needs or what satisfies the needs of others. A child at stage 2 might say, "The man shouldn't steal the drug unless he's so crazy about his wife that he can't live without her."

The Conventional Level   As their cognitive abilities increase, children enter the **conventional level** of moral development. Now they judge morality in terms of the laws and rules of their society. In stage 3, people judge morality in terms of social rules or norms (but only with respect to people they know personally). Thus, a child at this stage might state, "It's OK to steal the drug because your friends will not think you are bad if you do." In stage 4, judgments of morality include the perspective of third persons in general, not just of themselves or people they know. For example, a child at stage 4 who argues for stealing the drug might state, "The man should steal the drug since that's what you do after you take a marriage vow to stand by your wife."

Preconventional Level (of morality): According to Kohlberg, the earliest stage of moral development, in which individuals judge morality in terms of the effects produced by various actions.

Conventional Level (of morality): According to Kohlberg, a stage of moral development during which individuals judge morality largely in terms of existing social norms or rules.

Cultural Influences on Moral Development

Children raised in an Amish community learn to judge morality in terms of the laws and rules of their society.

> ### TABLE 8.4
>
> ### Kohlberg's Theory of Moral Development: A Summary
>
> According to Kohlberg, we move through three distinct levels of moral development.
>
> | Level/Stage | Description |
> |---|---|
> | **Preconventional Level** | |
> | *Stage 1:* Punishment-and-obedience orientation | Morality judged in terms of consequences |
> | *Stage 2:* Naïve hedonistic orientation | Morality judged in terms of what satisfies own needs or those of others |
> | **Conventional Level** | |
> | *Stage 3:* Good boy-good girl orientation | Morality judged in terms of adherence to social rules or norms with respect to personal acquaintances |
> | *Stage 4:* Social-order-maintaining orientation | Morality judged in terms of social rules or laws applied universally, not just to acquaintances |
> | **Postconventional Level** | |
> | *Stage 5:* Legalistic orientation | Morality judged in terms of human rights, which may transcend laws |
> | *Stage 6:* Universal ethical principle orientation | Morality judged in terms of self-chosen ethical principles |

The Postconventional Level In adolescence or early adulthood, many (though by no means all) individuals enter the **postconventional level**, or principled level. At this stage, people judge morality in terms of abstract principles and values, rather than in terms of existing laws or rules of society. At stage 5, people realize that laws can sometimes be inconsistent with the rights of individuals or the interests of the majority, and that such laws should be changed. They might reason as follows: "Although it is against the law to steal, stealing the drug is justified. In this case, that is because life is more important than property."

Finally, in stage 6, individuals judge the morality of actions in terms of self-chosen ethical principles. Individuals who attain this highest level of moral development believe that certain obligations and values may transcend the laws of society—in certain very specific situations. The rules they follow are based on inner conscience rather than external sources of authority. Individuals at stage 6 might argue for stealing the drug as follows: "If the man doesn't steal the drug, he is putting property above human life; that makes no sense. People could live together without private property, but not without respect for human life."

EVIDENCE CONCERNING KOHLBERG'S THEORY Do we really pass through the series of stages described by Kohlberg and become increasingly sophisticated in our judgments of morality as we gain more experience? As suggested by Kohlberg, individuals do generally seem to progress through the stages of moral reasoning he described, moving from less sophisticated to increasingly sophisticated modes of thought (e.g., Walker, 1989). Also, people in many different cultures move through the six levels of moral reasoning.

However, moral reasoning is strongly affected by environmental factors, such as level of formal education (Rest & Thoma, 1985) and parents' child-rearing practices (Boyes & Allen, 1993; Walker & Taylor, 1991). There are cultural effects upon moral development as well (Fuchs et al., 1986).

Postconventional Level (of morality): According to Kohlberg, the final stage of moral development, in which individuals judge morality in terms of abstract principles.

CONSISTENCY OF MORAL JUDGMENTS Kohlberg's theory, like other stage theories, suggests that as people grow older, they move through a successive series of discrete stages. If that is true, then it could be predicted that individuals' moral reasoning across a wide range of moral dilemmas should be consistent—it should reflect the stage they have reached. Do people show such consistency? The answer appears to be no. For example, in one revealing study on this issue, Wark and Krebs (1996) asked college students to respond to the moral dilemmas developed by Kohlberg, and also to describe real-life dilemmas they had experienced or witnessed—both dilemmas that affected them personally and dilemmas they knew about, which had not affected them personally. For these real-life dilemmas, they also described their moral reasoning—their thoughts about them, what they felt was the right course of action, and so on. Results indicated that contrary to Kohlberg's theory, participants showed little consistency across the various types of moral dilemmas. In fact, only 24 percent obtained the same stage score (e.g., stage 3, stage 4) across all three types of dilemmas, while a large majority—fully 85 percent—made judgments that ranged across three different stages. So, contrary to what Kohlberg's theory suggests, people do not show a high degree of consistency reflecting a specific stage of moral reasoning.

GENDER DIFFERENCES IN MORAL DEVELOPMENT Although early studies did suggest that females score somewhat lower on Kohlberg's moral stages (e.g., Holstein, 1976), his tests of moral judgment were declared biased against women (Gilligan, 1982), and later studies failed to report such differences or found that females scored higher than males (Wark & Krebs, 1996). Overall, then, there is no clear reason to conclude that males and females differ with respect to level of moral development or moral reasoning. However, Ozier and Morris (1987) identified a different methodological problem in Kohlberg's research—the main figure in each dilemma had a male name. In their study, male and female students were presented with the same dilemmas, but there were two versions of each—Kohlberg's original with a male name for the main figure, and one with a female name for the main figure. The results were surprising. They showed that both males and females set higher moral standards for the behaviour of members of their own sex and lower moral standards for members of the opposite sex.

> **K E Y** *QUESTIONS*
>
> - What are the major stages of moral development described by Kohlberg's theory?
> - What do research findings indicate with respect to gender differences in moral reasoning?
> - Do cultural factors have any impact on moral development?

Social and Emotional Development

Cognitive development is a crucial aspect of human growth. Yet it does not occur in a social vacuum. As Chris Moore (1996) at Dalhousie University explained, some social understanding has developed by the end of the first year of life and there are many theories as to how that happens. All agree that, at the same time that infants and children are acquiring the capacities to think, reason, and use language, they are also gaining the basic experiences, skills, and emotions that permit them to interact socially. According to Moore, a developmental theory of social understanding will require three kinds of information. First, we need to know what infants know about the actions of other people; second, we need to know how infants make sense of their own selves and how they affect the social world; third, we need to know what infants understand about the interaction between themselves and other people. Here is an example of research about the development of early social interaction.

One of the interactive social behaviours that develops early in the first year of life is **gaze following**. To understand that concept, imagine that you have made eye contact with a friend, who then turns her head as if to look at something over to the side. Or maybe she just turns her eyes that way. What do you do? Most normal adults will turn their head and/or their eyes in the same direction to focus on the same target. Your eyes have followed the other person's and you end up looking together—or jointly attending—to the same visual stimulus. Gaze following or joint attention is just about the earliest way in which children can start to learn about the world in the company of other people. That ability is essential, and it stays with us for the rest of our lives.

According to researchers at Queen's University, infants of five months are already very sensitive to small shifts in gaze (Symons et al., 1999). When the experimenter broke eye contact and shifted her gaze to the infant's ear, smiling decreased. Reliable gaze following in infants does not normally occur, however, until about the age of ten months (Corkum & Moore, 1998). Before that time, children do not naturally follow an experimenter's gaze, but they do improve with practice if gaze following is rewarded with the sight of a moving toy. Figure 8.10 shows you the results of this experiment as development proceeds within the first year. Note the dramatic increase in gaze following over the course of the five months. Is that change a matter of maturity or experience, or a combination of both? The answer remains to be determined.

Here is another example of social development. In the second year of life, children as young as eighteen months of age appear to recognize that an adult is imitating their behaviour, and will "test" the adult to see if she or he will continue doing so (Asendorpf et al., 1996).

Let's now turn to the emotional developments that occur in early life.

> **Gaze Following:** Moving the eyes to where someone else is looking.

Figure 8.10
Origins of Joint Attention

One way we use other people to tell us about the world is gaze following. That is when we move our eyes to where someone else is looking. Up to six months, looking to the side occurs for a variety of reasons that do not seem to be associated with gaze following. From about six months on, infants can be taught to gaze follow by rewarding the side-looking response. You can see that development just beginning in the first bar of the figure. At eight or nine months, some infants begin spontaneously—without reward—to gaze follow. The number of infants who do so increases dramatically from ten months on.

Source: Based on data from Corkum and Moore, 1998. Copyright © 1998 by the American Psychological Association. Reprinted with permission.

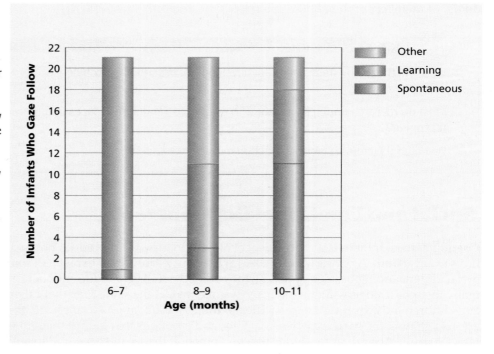

Emotional Development and Temperament

Do you know someone who is usually happy, active, and upbeat? And do you know someone who is just the opposite—a person who is usually gloomy, quiet, and reserved? Psychologists refer to such stable individual differences in characteristic mood, activity level, and emotional reactivity as **temperament** (e.g., Stifter & Fox, 1990). Growing evidence suggests that these differences are present very early in life— perhaps at birth (e.g., Kagan & Snidman, 1991; Seifer et al., 1994). There is increasing evidence that individual differences in temperament are at least partially inherited (e.g., Lytton 1990). However, different aspects of temperament may be influenced by genetic and environmental factors to varying degrees (e.g., Magai & McFadden, 1995).

How stable are such differences in temperament? Research findings present a mixed picture (e.g., Lemery et al., 1999). On the one hand, some studies indicate that certain dimensions of temperament—attentiveness, activity level, and irritability—are quite stable (e.g., Rothbart & Ahadi, 1994). Children who test high on these dimensions at four months of age tend to be high on them months or even years later, while those who test low on these dimensions at four months remain relatively low as they grow older. Figure 8.11 illustrates the stability of reactivity in four-month-old infants who are tested again after a year had passed. On the other hand, additional studies indicate that, although temperament may be quite stable for some people, it can be altered by experience for others (e.g., Saarni, 1993).

Whatever the relative contributions of genetic and environmental factors to temperament, individual differences in emotional style have important implications for social development. For example, a much higher proportion of difficult than easy children experience behavioural problems later in life (Chess & Thomas, 1984). They find it more difficult to adjust to school, to form friendships, and to get along with others. In addition, many highly reactive children demonstrate shyness as they grow older and enter an increasingly broad range of social situations. Finally, temperament can influence the kinds of bonds infants form with their caregivers—and hence important aspects of their personality and even their abilities to form close relationships with other persons when they are adults (Shaver & Brennan, 1992; Shaver & Hazan, 1994). Given the importance of the bonds between infants and caregivers, the earliest social ties, let's turn to this topic now.

Temperament: Stable individual differences in the quality and intensity of emotional reactions.

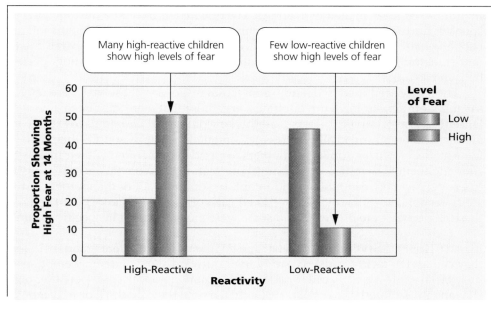

Figure 8.11
The Stability of Temperament

Four-month-olds who showed fretting, crying, and a high level of motor activity when exposed to unfamiliar events (high-reactive infants) were much more likely than infants who did not fret or cry (low-reactive infants) to show a high level of fear when tested again in unfamiliar situations at fourteen months. These findings suggest that some aspects of temperament are quite stable over time.

Source: Based on data from Kagan, Snidman, and Arcus, 1992.

Emotional Development and Maternal Responsiveness

The moment of childbirth represents an enormous change for both the fetus and the woman who has just given birth. There are biological and psychological factors that increase the mother's responsiveness to her newborn child, not only in humans but also in animals (Fleming & Corter, 1988). The first changes—hormonal levels—take place in the early postpartum period. Specific changes follow that relate to caregiving. For example, new mothers are faced immediately after birth with a number of new odours: the infant's body, urine, and stool. An investigation of mothers' attraction to their newborns' odours by Fleming et al. (1993) found that new mothers were more positive about their infant's body odours than were other females—and fortunately so. All of these factors contribute to *maternal responsiveness* to infants during periods of distress and nondistress. This is important not only for the emotional well-being of the child, but also for the mental development of attention span, symbolic play, and language comprehension (Bornstein & Tamis-Lemonda, 1997).

Sometimes, however, mothers have negative reactions. Most women have only informal training for motherhood. For some, low self-esteem and self-doubt about their ability to parent successfully may influence their mood. *Postpartum depression* may be the result. The mother's depressed mood may influence her ability to cope with even the minor stresses of everyday life, and alter her perceptions of her children and her emotional responses to their behaviour (Krech & Johnston, 1992), although that may not reflect the quality of her marital relations (Whiffen & Gotlib, 1993).

For a look at maternal responsiveness in different cultures, see **Perspectives on Diversity**.

Perspectives on Diversity

Maternal Responsiveness and Diversity

IN A 1992 STUDY CONDUCTED IN New York City, Paris, and Tokyo, Bornstein and colleagues observed mothers as they responded to the needs of their five-month-old children in their own homes. The researchers observed the following responses: nurturing (feeding and comforting, for example), imitating (of the infant's babbling by the mother), extradyadic (occasions when the mother showed the infant something), and dyadic (affectionate interactions—kissing, tickling, peek-a-boo, and so on).

The study identified two kinds of maternal responses: those that were universal and were similar in all three settings, and those that were specific to a particular setting. For example, in all cases mothers encouraged their infants to explore the area around them, and in all cultures they imitated the happy sounds their own infants made. However, American mothers responded more often to their infants by showing them how things work, and Japanese mothers were the most responsive to eye contact between mother and infant. In summary, all of the mothers in this study responded to their children—in all categories of responding—but some of these responses were universal and some were more apparent in specific cultures.

INFANT RESPONSIVENESS At what age do infants feel different emotions? Since they cannot tell us in words, we study their outward signs of distinct emotions—their facial expressions. Facial expressions of emotion appear very soon after birth (Kavanagh, Zimmerberg, & Fein, 1996). By the time they are three or four months old, babies laugh. Other emotional expressions, such as anger, sadness, and surprise, also appear very early and are easily recognized by adults. Not only do young infants produce recognizable facial expressions of emotion spontaneously, they also imitate the facial expressions of other people. Open your mouth or stick out your tongue and the young infant will do the same. This kind of social interaction between child and caregivers contributes much to normal social development. Smile at an infant as young as two months and you will find the infant smiling in return. Note, however, that this social smiling does not occur in response to objects (Ellsworth et al., 1993).

Can you have a social conversation with young infants? Not in words, but infants do imitate the sounds that other people make. Thus an exchange of sounds is certainly possible. This kind of social interaction is also important to normal social development.

What do infants know about the sounds we make? At York University, Legerstee (1990) had infants watch an adult mouth vowel sounds. The adults were actually silent; the sounds came from a tape recorder. Sometimes the sounds matched the vowel that was being mouthed, and sometimes there was a mismatch between the visual and the auditory information. At about four months, infants imitated only when the auditory and visual information indicated the *same* vowel sound— that is, when the person was perceived to be making the sound. Not only do young infants imitate sounds, they seem to recognize when we speak to them. Recent studies show that young infants have a preference for infant-directed speech (i.e., baby talk, or talk that is directed to infants) over adult-directed speech. This is true in many cultures and languages, including those of Britain, France, Germany, Italy, Japan, Mandarin China, and the United States (Pegg et al., 1992). Why this should be the case is not clear, but baby talk may be effective because it grabs the attention of the infant or because it communicates positive emotion (McLeod, 1993).

SOCIAL REFERENCING As babies grow older, they also become increasingly able to comprehend the emotional expressions of others (Strayer, 1985). Face-to-face interactions provide cues to infants that tell them what other people desire (Moore, 1999) and regulate their social behaviour (Muir & Hains, 1999). For example, at three months, they become upset when their mother's face remains immobile. This happens even when the mother's expression is neutral. However, touching the infant (while keeping the face still) seems to reduce the distress (Stack & Muir, 1992). By eight or ten months, infants actively seek out information about other people's feelings and begin **social referencing**—that is, using the reactions of others to evaluate uncertain situations. Thus, after a fall, a one-year-old will look at the caregivers and, depending on their reactions, will cry or merely continue whatever he or she was doing (Walden & Ogan, 1988). Also, the pain that infants experience, for example when getting a needle, is much influenced by the behaviour of the mother at the time (Sweet et al., 1999).

Social understanding on the basis of facial expression becomes more complex as infancy proceeds. For example, in a recent study (Repacholi & Gopnik, 1997), researchers asked when children begin to reason about other people's desires from their facial expressions. They had fourteen- and eighteen-month-olds observe an experimenter expressing happiness when she tasted one kind of food and disgust when she tasted another kind. Then children were asked to predict which food the experimenter would want afterwards. The results showed that by eighteen months, but not by fourteen months, children indicated that the experimenter would want food that made her happy—and they could do that whether the food that made her happy was to their taste or not. The experimenters concluded that by age eighteen months, infants understood how desires are related to emotions—in other people.

Finally, children also grow in the ability to regulate their own emotional reactions, and to express these to others. Infants have very little capacity to do this, but within a few years, they begin to make active efforts to understand and regulate their own feelings. If you have ever seen a four-year-old cover his or her eyes while watching a frightening television show or film, you have witnessed such efforts

Social Referencing in Action

In uncertain situations, children look to adults for information about what to do.

Social Referencing: Using others' reactions to appraise an uncertain situation or experience.

directly: the children involved are trying to regulate their own feelings by preventing exposure to something they do not like! Children's abilities to regulate their emotions increase through the grade-school years, as does the range of strategies available to them for expressing these feelings—for communicating them to others (e.g., Saarni, 1993). By the time they are ten, therefore, most children are quite adept at these tasks. For instance, they have learned to express sadness, both verbally and nonverbally, in order to gain sympathy and support, and to withhold or disguise anger in order to avoid adult disapproval for such reactions (e.g., Zeman & Shipman, 1996).

By the same age, children have also learned how to regulate the emotions of others. Children between ages four and nine (volunteers at the Ontario Science Centre) were able to identify ways they could behave that would reduce the emotions of the parents—for example, the anger that occurs during an argument. Their choices were: "give ... a hug, play games…, be very good, make ... a card or picture, smile ..." (Covell & Miles, 1992). Moreover, parents rated these as effective ways of doing just what the children intended.

The Beginnings of Empathy—and Prosocial Behaviour

By the time they are eighteen months old, toddlers will try to comfort another child who is crying; and by the time they are two, they may offer this person a toy or go to seek help from an adult. Such actions mark the beginnings of empathy and prosocial behaviour.

Children's emotional development includes increasingly general self-awareness. They grow more and more accurately aware of their own personal tastes and the fact that others may have personal tastes that differ. They grow in their understanding that other people may have different beliefs and those beliefs may be correct or incorrect (Carpendale & Chandler, 1996; Chandler & Carpendale, 1998).

How does **empathy**—our ability to know how somebody else is feeling, to recognize the emotions of others and to experience them ourselves—develop? Many psychologists believe that empathy begins during the first two years of life as we continue to distinguish ourselves clearly from other people and to form a concept of *self*. The developing theory of mind permits us to realize that other people have feelings too and that those may differ from our own.

Newborns already show more distress in response to the sound of another infant crying than to the sound of their own cries—even when they are asleep (Dondi et al., 1999). Infants as young as eighteen months old attempt to do something when another person is upset—for instance, touching or patting that person. By the time they are two, children may offer the distressed person comfort—a toy—or go and find help (e.g., Zahn-Waxler et al., 1992). At age four, most children can understand why other people are upset, and have ideas about the kinds of situations that can cause emotional distress.

Ultimately, empathy develops to the point where we feel guilty about causing another person to be upset, and that serves as one important source of *prosocial behaviour*—actions designed to help another in some way that do not necessarily benefit the persons who perform them. Clearly, then, empathy represents an important advance in emotional and social development (Roberts, 1998; Strayer & Roberts, 1997). Thus, as they grow older, children gain increasing ability to express emotions, regulate them, and recognize and even regulate the emotions of others. These are important changes and, as they develop, they lead to more and more complex social interactions during the early years of life.

Empathy: Our ability to recognize the emotions of others, to understand these reactions, and to experience them ourselves, at least to a degree.

Attachment: A strong affectional bond between infants and their caregivers.

Attachment

Do infants love their parents? They cannot say so directly, but by the time they are six or seven months old infants recognize their mothers, fathers, and other caregivers, smile at them more than at other people, seek them out, and protest when separated from them (Ainsworth, 1973; Lamb, 1977). This bond between infants and their caregivers is known as **attachment**; in an important sense, it is first love.

What are the origins of this early form of love? The ethological theory (Bowlby, 1969) maintains that infants are born with a set of behaviours that elicit parental care and thus increase the child's chances of survival. These behaviours include sucking, clinging, crying, smiling, gazing at the caregiver's face, and (later) crawling after the caregiver. In these ways, infants elicit attention and caring from adults. This lays the foundation for reciprocal bonds of attachment. Another theory of attachment emphasizes the role of *learning*. Both operant conditioning and classical conditioning may play a role in the formation of attachment. For example, caregivers provide for infants' needs, so caregivers are associated with many forms of reward.

Either way, most often, if the infant's needs are attended to reliably, and if the infant can count on a response to distress, there is a basis for trust. If the child is mistreated and hurt—by rejection, neglect, abuse, or a combination of these—bonding goes bad, and the basis is laid for attachment problems (e.g., Marshall & Mazzucco, 1995), which may lead to loneliness and psychological distress as young adults (Lambert et al., 1995). Most seriously, the "unattached child" is self-destructive, deceitful and cruel to others, without friends, and unable to offer or accept affection. In adult life, this individual's psychopathic behaviour may be a serious threat to the safety of others (Magid & McKelvey, 1993).

MEASURING ATTACHMENT How can the strength of attachment be measured? Mary Ainsworth and her colleagues (e.g., Ainsworth et al., 1978) studied babies in social situations where fear and distress sometimes occur. In assessing attachment, researchers place mother and baby in an unfamiliar room; then a stranger enters. The mother departs and then returns. As each change takes place, the babies' reactions are carefully noted. Do they appear confident in her presence, despite the stranger? Do they cry when the mother leaves? How do they react to her when she returns? These are the kinds of questions considered in this **strange situation test**. See Table 8.5 for an outline of the major steps involved.

TABLE 8.5

Sequence of Events in the Strange Situation Test

The strange situation test is used to study infants' attachment to their caregivers (typically, their mothers). Researchers carefully study the infant's reactions to each of the events described here.

Episode	Persons Present	Duration	Events/Procedures
1	Caregiver and baby	30 seconds	Experimenter brings caregiver and baby to the room; leaves
2	Caregiver and baby	3 minutes	Baby plays; caregiver seated
3	Caregiver, baby, and stranger	3 minutes	Stranger enters; talks to caregiver
4	Stranger and baby	3 minutes (or less)	Caregiver leaves room; stranger remains, offers comfort to baby
5	Caregiver and baby	3 minutes (or more)	Caregiver returns, greets baby, offers comfort
6	Baby alone	3 minutes (or less)	Caregiver leaves room
7	Stranger and baby	3 minutes (or less)	Stranger enters room, offers comfort
8	Caregiver and baby	3 minutes	Caregiver returns, offers comfort

Source: Adapted from Ainsworth, 1978.

Strange Situation Test: A procedure for studying attachment in which mothers leave their children alone with a stranger for several minutes and then return.

This strange situation test has been used to study attachment in young children. The results reveal four different patterns of attachment between child and caregiver—usually the mother. About 67 percent of middle-class babies show **secure attachment.** They may or may not cry on separation from their mother, but they take no comfort from the presence of a stranger, and when the mother returns, they actively seek contact with her and crying stops. About 20 percent show **avoidant attachment.** They don't cry when their mother leaves, and they react to the stranger in much the same way as to their mother. When the mother returns, they typically avoid her or are slow to greet her (Trabulsy et al., 1996). About 10 percent of middle-class babies show a different pattern known as **resistant attachment.** Before separation, these infants seek contact with their mother. After she returns, however, they seem angry and they push her away. Many continue to cry, even after she picks up and attempts to comfort them. Finally, about 5 percent of middle-class infants show **disorganized** or **disoriented attachment.** When reunited with their mothers, these babies make disorganized or even contradictory responses. They look away from the mother while being held by her, or approach her with a lack of emotion. They show a dazed facial expression and often adopt odd, frozen postures after being comforted.

Which factors determine the pattern of attachment shown by a child? There are several. For example, children who experience maternal deprivation—for example, separation from their mother as a consequence of being placed for adoption—may not form secure attachments with any caregiver, and may later experience a wide range of behavioural problems, ranging from depression to an excessive desire for adult attention (e.g., Hodges & Tizard, 1989). These infants who "fail to thrive" may also develop a relationship disorder with their caregivers (Benoit et al., 1989). Animal studies have shown that maternal deprivation may predispose rats to increased alcohol consumption and susceptibility to stress as adults (Rockman et al., 1987).

Quality of caregiving also plays a role. *Maternal sensitivity* is important to secure attachment of normal children and of children whose development occurs later than usual (Moran et al., 1992; Pederson et al., 1990). When caregivers are alert to the needs and signals of children and respond appropriately, infants are much more likely to form secure attachments (Isabella & Belsky, 1991). In contrast, avoidant infants tend to have mothers who are either intrusive or overstimulating—that is, who act without waiting for signals from their infants. There is some recent evidence that other factors, such as infant temperament, may actually be important as well (e.g., Rosen & Rothbaum, 1993).

For instance, in research conducted by Seifer and his colleagues (e.g., Seifer et al., 1996), infants' attachment to their mothers was studied when the infants were six months, nine months, and twelve months old. Observations of attachment were made both in the laboratory by means of the strange situation test, and in the infants' homes, through careful study of their behaviour. Certain aspects of infants' temperament were strongly related to attachment. Specifically, infants who were difficult and those who were often unhappy were less likely to show secure attachment. Whatever the reason for this difference, one fact seems clear: several factors—ranging from parents' responsiveness to their children's needs, to parents' memories of their own childhood attachment experiences (e.g., Ijzendoorn, 1995), to the temperament of the child—probably influence attachment.

THE LONG-TERM EFFECTS OF ATTACHMENT
Do differences in pattern of attachment have effects that persist beyond infancy? A growing

Secure Attachment: A pattern of attachment in which infants actively seek contact with their mother and take comfort from her presence when they are reunited with her during the strange situation test.

Avoidant Attachment: A pattern of attachment in which infants don't cry when their mother leaves them alone during the strange situation test, and are slow to greet their mother when she returns.

Resistant Attachment: A pattern of attachment in which infants reject their mother and refuse to be comforted by her after she leaves them alone during the strange situation test.

Disorganized (or Disoriented) Attachment: A pattern of attachment in which infants show contradictory reactions to their mother after being reunited with her during the strange situation test.

body of research indicates that they do. During childhood, youngsters who are securely attached to their caregivers are more sociable, better at solving certain kinds of problems, more tolerant of frustration, and more flexible and persistent in many situations than children who are avoidantly or insecurely attached (e.g., Beksly & Cassidy, 1994). Further, securely attached children seem to experience fewer behavioural problems during later childhood (Fagot & Kavanaugh, 1990).

Infant attachment may also affect adult relationships (e.g., Baldwin et al., 1996; Fehr, 1996). Those who do not trust their caregivers as infants often distrust their spouses or lovers as adults. Similarly, people who had resistant or ambivalent attachment perceive their adult partner as distant and unloving. In contrast, people who are securely attached as infants seek closeness in their adult relationships, and are comfortable with having to depend on their partners (Shaver & Hazan, 1994). In a sense, then, it seems that the pattern of our relationships with others is set—at least to a degree—by the nature of the very first relationship we form, attachment to our caregivers.

How can that be? Bowlby (1969, 1988) proposed that securely attached and insecurely attached infants learn to filter information differently, and then they act in ways that confirm their filtered information. Specifically, those who are securely attached see themselves as lovable, others as caring, and the world as basically benevolent. In contrast, those who are insecurely attached view themselves as unlovable, other persons as uncaring, and the world as a dangerous and threatening place. Indeed, one study found that three-year-olds who were securely attached remembered positive events in puppet shows they had seen, while insecurely attached children of the same age remembered negative events (Belsky et al., 1996). Once again, therefore, we see the complex interaction between nature (e.g., temperament) and nurture (parents' behaviour toward their children and the course of adult relationships), which is a basic theme of human development.

Here is a contemporary question: What do we know about attachment and infants in daycare? Does placing children in daycare centres interfere with their forming secure attachments to their parents? For information on this issue, see the **Canadian Focus** feature.

Canadian Focus

Daycare: A Threat to Attachment?

In these times, in most Canadian families with preschoolers, parents go to work and that work is usually full-time. A study conducted at the University of Guelph (Lero, 1992) found that, in Canada, at least one in every two very young children requires childcare while the single or both parents are at work. Where are the children when their parents are at work? Many senior citizens in Canada provide some kind of childcare for relatives—some of it being full-time daycare. Sometimes, neighbours or other relatives become caregivers. Also, many infants and toddlers spend their days in full-time daycare centres. When those options are not available, the choice boils down to work or welfare. The issue of how the children in these families fare has become a matter of government concern and public policy debate and research (e.g., Symonds & McLeod, 1994).

Daycare does leave lasting impressions upon those who attend. Adolescents were interviewed ten years after they had attended preschool daycare centers in Victoria, British Columbia (Markowsky & Pence, 1997). Almost 90 percent of them remembered early experiences—relationships, environment, activities, and emotions. What was the most often recalled activity? Naptime!

How do children in daycare centres compare with those raised at home? More specifically, does being separated from parents affect the child's ability to form secure attachments?

Research confirms that more than two-thirds of infants of working mothers are securely attached (Thompson, 1988). This compares favourably with the general proportion in the population. Moreover, comparisons of young adolescents who took care of themselves after school with those who spent their after-school hours in the care of adults (Galambos & Maggs, 1991) found "that self-care adolescents who stayed in the home were not different on any variable studied from those adolescents in adult care." The variables these researchers looked at included coping ability, emotional tone, and impulse control—all of these taken to be measures of adolescent self-image—and several measures of interactions with peers.

The fact that most infants cared for in daycare centres form secure attachments despite the absence of their parents—on most days—suggests that daycare, in and of itself, does not interfere with attachment. Indeed, in some cases of problem attachment, daycare can be a positive influence on parents and children (Petrie & Davidson, 1995). Where insecure attachment does occur, it may be because the parents of such children may be stressed from full-time work and may not interact with their children as often or as well. Finally, much hinges on the quality of the daycare infants receive. In a daycare centre with a large number of children and few adults, any one child may be ignored. Attachment and other aspects of development may indeed suffer as a result. But in centres where children receive high levels of social stimulation and attention from adults, those negative effects may not occur. In fact, under these conditions, children benefit much from the special care they receive—not only in social adjustment, but also in cognitive development, such as comprehension of words (Schliecker et al., 1991).

In sum, existing evidence indicates that daycare, in and of itself, is neither a definite plus nor a clear-cut minus where social development is concerned. What is more important is that the care children receive both at home and in the daycare centre be the best that it can be (Hausfather et al., 1997).

Daycare Centre
Studies suggest that most infants cared for in daycare centres form secure attachments.

CONTACT COMFORT AND ATTACHMENT An additional factor that plays an important role in attachment is *contact comfort:* the hugs, cuddles, and caresses babies receive from adults. The classic research that first established this fact was conducted by Harry Harlow and his colleagues. Harlow is best known for his research on emotional development. His studies with baby rhesus monkeys and wire surrogate "mothers" showed that early social deprivation is correlated with later socially deviant behaviour.

Originally, Harlow was interested in the effects of brain damage on learning. Since he could not perform such tests with humans, he worked with rhesus monkeys. In order to prevent baby monkeys from catching various diseases, Harlow raised them in isolation, away from their mothers and each other. This precaution led to a surprising observation. Many of the infants became quite attached to small scraps of cloth in their cages. They would hold tightly to these "security blankets" and protest strongly when they were removed for cleaning.

In order to find out more, Harlow built two artificial mothers. One consisted of bare wire while the other had a soft terry-cloth cover. The infants had access to both mothers, although they could get milk only from the wire mother. According to the conditioning explanation of attachment, they should soon have developed a strong bond to this cold, wire mother, which was the source of all their nourishment. In fact, this was not what happened. Instead, the infants spent almost all of their time clinging tightly to the soft, cloth-covered mother. Only when driven by pangs of hunger did they leave to obtain milk from the wire mother.

Additional and even more dramatic evidence that the infants formed strong bonds with the cloth mothers was obtained in further research (Harlow & Harlow, 1966) in which young monkeys were exposed to various forms of rejection by their artificial mothers. Some of the mothers blew them away with strong jets of air; others contained metal spikes that suddenly appeared from inside the

Harlow's Studies of Attachment
Although the wire "mothers" used in Harlow's research provided monkey babies with nourishment, the babies preferred the soft, cloth-covered mothers that provided contact comfort.

cloth covering and pushed the infants away. However, none of these actions had any lasting effects on the infants' attachment. They waited until these periods of rejection were over and then clung to the cloth mother as tightly as before.

On the basis of these and related findings, Harlow concluded that a young monkey's attachment to its mother rests, at least in part, on her ability to satisfy its need for contact comfort. The satisfaction of other physical needs, such as for food, is not enough.

Human infants also need contact comfort for secure attachment (Stack & Muir, 1992). Moreover, two- and three-year-old blanket-attached children placed in a strange room play for longer periods of time (almost as long as when their mother is there) without becoming distressed—if their security blanket is present (Passman & Weisberg, 1975). Thus the data from monkey and human studies are consistent in this area.

FATHERS AND ATTACHMENT Infants form strong attachments to their fathers, even though they often spend less time together. Fathers are important to infants, but perhaps in different ways. While mothers spend more time providing physical care to their children, fathers spend more time in playing with them (Roopnarine et al., 1990). Mothers provide toys, talk to infants, and initiate games such as peekaboo; fathers engage in more physical play, such as lifting, swinging, and bouncing their infants. Even when fathers are the primary caregivers, they still interact with their children in a more vigorously physical manner (Yogman, 1981). Also, fathers discipline their children in accordance with established and specific rules, while mothers discipline them on a moment-by-moment basis. And while mothers worry more about the infant's welfare, fathers worry more about future success (Gibbs, 1993).

School and Friendships

Children spend more of their time at school, and in school-related activities (homework, sports, social events), than in any other way. In school, children acquire and practise many social skills. They learn to share, to cooperate, to work together in groups to solve problems, and perhaps most important of all, they acquire growing experience in forming and maintaining **friendships**—relationships with strong emotional ties.

How do friendships differ from other relationships children have with their peers? A recent review of many studies dealing with this topic (Newcomb & Bagwell, 1995) indicates that children's friendships are marked by the following characteristics:

Friendships: Relationships involving strong mutual affective (emotional) ties between two persons.

- Friends have stronger affective ties to each other than they have to other peers.

- Friends cooperate with and help each other more than they do with other peers.

- Friends have conflict with each other, but are more concerned with resolving such disputes than is true with respect to other peers.

- Friends see themselves as equals and engage in less intense competition and fewer attempts at domination than is true for other peers.

- Friends are more similar to one another, and also express more mutual liking, closeness, and loyalty.

Friendships contribute in important ways to social and emotional development, and to cognitive growth as well. First, friendships give children an opportunity to learn and practise social skills needed for effective interpersonal relationships. Second, friendships give children opportunities to experience intense emotional bonds, closeness, and loyalty and the opportunity to express these feelings in their behaviour. Third, cognitive functioning is enhanced by children's friendships because friends are more likely to exchange ideas and to share reactions. In support of that idea are the data from one recent study (Teasley, 1995) in which pairs of fourth-graders who were instructed to talk with their partners—as they worked on the task of discovering how a "mystery key" on a computer worked—solved the problem more quickly than children who were told to work quietly, without talking. Findings such as these offer support for the conclusion that friendship can teach children skills useful in solving many problems, such as a candid exchange of views and the mutual testing of ideas.

Of course early interpersonal experiences may have negative effects as well. When you were in school, did you ever encounter a *bully*—someone who liked to push other children around either physically or verbally? For the victims of such children, there can be devastating effects. In fact, research findings indicate that being victimized by bullies produces anxiety, depression, loneliness, and low self-esteem in children (e.g., Boivin & Hymel, 1997; Eagan & Perry, 1998).

Nevertheless, even in these circumstances, friendship can have a positive effect. Recent findings indicate that children who have close friends are less likely to be victimized by bullies. Even for children who are worried and fearful, work alone, and appear sad or close to tears—behaviours that attract bullies—friends make a difference. Apparently, close friends play a protective role—telling the teacher when bullies swing into action, or even fighting back to protect their friends (Hodges et al., 1999).

In sum, through a wide range of experiences in school—and especially through the formation of friendships—children expand their social and emotional skills and acquire the skills needed for forming close and lasting relationships with others. Indeed, one psychologist (Harris, 1998) has suggested that friends play an even more important role in the social development of children than do parents!

KEY QUESTIONS

- At what age do infants first show recognizable facial expressions?
- How do children's abilities to regulate their own emotions develop?
- What is temperament and what role does it play in later development?
- What is attachment, and how is it measured?
- Which factors affect attachment between infants and their caregivers?
- How does attachment influence later social development?

Gender

How do children develop ideas about **gender**—their society's beliefs about males and females? Recently, Ruble and her colleagues (e.g., Ruble & Martin 1998; Szkrybalo & Ruble, 1999) have listed three components of our understanding of gender: *gender identity* (boy or girl), *gender stability* (the idea that gender remains constant through life), and *gender consistency* (the idea that gender identity remains the same even if the person dresses or behaves like the opposite sex). In this theory, all three components contribute to **sex category constancy**, emphasizing the link between gender and biological sex.

Our thinking about males and females and the differences between them is influenced also by **gender stereotypes**—sets of beliefs and expectations about the ways in which members of the two genders *should* behave and the gender roles they are expected to play (e.g., Deaux, 1993; Eagly & Wood, 1999; Unger & Crawford, 1993).

In the next sections, you will find more about the development of all of these components of gender.

Some Contrasting Views of Gender Identity

By the time they are two, many children have learned to label themselves appropriately as a girl or a boy. Certainty that they will always be a boy or a girl—gender stability—is usually in place by the time they are four. At this age, they can answer correctly such questions as "When you grow up, will you be a mother or a father?" and "Could you change into a girl/boy from what you are now?" It is not until they are about six or even seven, however, that children acquire gender consistency and understand that even if they adopted the clothing, hairstyles, and behaviours of the other sex they would still retain their current sexual identity. Moreover, these ideas about gender become embedded in their own self-concept and their own self-esteem (Absi-Semaan, 1993; Bem, 1981; Spence, 1993).

How do children acquire gender-stereotyped beliefs and behaviours? According to the *social-learning theory*, these developments rely upon observational learning and operant conditioning that treat boys and girls differently. First, various role models—family, teachers, and peers—all confirm that boys and girls differ in important ways and that certain activities are *appropriate* for boys and others for girls (e.g., Weisner & Wilson-Mitchell, 1990). Recent findings indicate that when children are exposed to environments in which adults label and refer to gender frequently, they quickly acquire gender stereotypes of traits and occupations (e.g., Bigler, 1995; McLean & Kalin, 1994). According to Bem (1984, 1989), children think along gender lines in part because adults call attention to gender differences in subtle ways—even in situations where it is irrelevant—as in "Good morning, boys and girls!"

In research conducted at the University of Quebec at Montreal, Pomerleau and her associates (1990) found that: "Boys were provided with more sports equipment, tools and large and small vehicles. Girls had more dolls, fictional characters, child's furniture, and other toys for manipulation. They wore pink and multicoloured clothes more often, had more pink pacifiers and jewellery. Boys wore more blue, red, and white clothing and had more blue pacifiers." And they concluded, "It thus seems that very early in their development, girls and boys already experience environments that are dissimilar, which may affect the later development of specific abilities and preferred activities." Through observational learning, children gradually match their behaviours to those of same-sex individuals, especially those of their parents (e.g., Bandura, 1986; Baron, 1970). Moreover, children are praised for same-sex behaviours and reprimanded for acting like members of the opposite sex.

Researchers at the University of Calgary (Lytton & Romney, 1991) have a different opinion about the origins of gender stereotypes. They challenged the widely

Gender: An individual's membership in one of the two sexes; all the attributes, behaviours, and expectancies associated with each sex in a given society.

Sex Category Constancy: Understanding of one's sexual identity, centring around a biologically based categorical distinction between males and females.

Gender Stereotypes: Cultural beliefs about differences between women and men.

Gender Roles and Stereotypes

Every culture has *gender roles*—expectations concerning the roles people of each gender should play—and *gender stereotypes*—beliefs about the traits of each gender. As you can see, not all persons behave in ways predicted by these beliefs.

held assumption that parents treat boys and girls differently. Their analysis of the results of 172 studies led them to conclude that, in North America at least, there are few confirmed differences in how parents treat their male and female children. How, then, do such differences arise? Here is their novel analysis. Lytton and Romney maintain that similar treatment of boys and girls by their parents produces different results because boys and girls respond differently—as a result of biological differences (genetic, or hormonal, or both). For example, it may be that parents treat boys and girls with similar warmth, but boys and girls respond differently to that warmth. This is an intriguing idea, but further research is needed to test its validity.

A second view—*cognitive-development theory*—suggests that children's increasing understanding of gender is a consequence of steady cognitive growth. Below the age of two, children lack a clear concept of self, and therefore they do not identify themselves consistently as a boy or a girl. Once they acquire a concept of self, they begin to show gender identity and then gender stability. Later, as they acquire the understanding that objects belong permanently to specific categories, they begin to form an idea of gender consistency. As a consequence, children understand that even if they adopted the clothing, hairstyles, and behaviours of the other sex, they would still retain their own gender identity. This understanding leads them to adopt behaviours they view as consistent with being a boy or a girl, a man or a woman.

As you can see, social-learning theory and cognitive-development theory make different predictions. The first suggests that children imitate the behaviour of same-sex models, and then they develop sexual identity. The second suggests that children develop their gender identity, and then they adopt behaviours consistent with it. Which of these ideas is correct? It seems likely that both social learning and cognitive processes contribute to the formation of gender identity. Together, these views provide a more complete picture of this process.

Whatever the correct explanation, observation of children confirms that boys and girls play differently from a very early age (e.g., Pomerleau et al., 1992). Groups of boys engage in much more rough-and-tumble play. Also, for boys, maintaining status within the group seems to be much more important than for girls. Girls behave more politely, waiting for a turn to speak, and they often try to influence by polite requests rather than through demands—unlike boys, who assert themselves in order to maintain high status. Because children prefer playmates whose behaviour matches their own, they gradually come to spend more and more time interacting with peers of their own sex. In the elementary school years, children play with same-sex peers almost exclusively (Maccoby & Jacklin, 1987). These differences are in part the result of cognitive and social learning and natural differences between the two genders. Let's turn our attention to some of those now.

Gender Differences

The focus on social learning is not to say that gender differences are entirely acquired by experience. That is of course not the case. Besides the obvious differences in hormonal levels, internal and external sex organs, and reproductive equipment, males and females differ in various brain structures—as you learned in Chapter 2. On the one hand, an area of the human hypothalamus has twice as many cells in men. That difference develops from birth to puberty; thus gender differentiation of the brain continues through childhood—as development proceeds (Swaab et al., 1995). On the other hand, some parts of the corpus callosum are larger in women. The way functions are distributed between the two hemispheres in males and females—in language, for example—differs as well. Why do those differences occur? There is good reason to believe that male and female hormones are important here. In other words, *gonadal hormones*—those produced by the ovaries and testes—influence brain development (e.g., Kolb & Stewart, 1995).

There is evidence that hormonal imbalances at birth influence future behaviour. For instance, some females are born with a condition known as *congenital adrenal hyperplasia*, in which their own pituitary glands secrete abnormally high levels of androgen—a male sex hormone. Careful studies of these females show that, as children, they engage in the kind of rough, active outdoor play and their spatial skills resemble those of boys (e.g., Hampson et al., 1994). They have less interest in makeup, feminine clothing, doll play, child care, and in having children than most girls (e.g., Dittman et al., 1990). In short, it is almost as if their early exposure to high doses of male hormones has "masculinized" their behaviour to some extent.

A very different pattern is shown by males who have *low androgen levels* because they have fewer of the enzymes required for androgen synthesis. These boys are often born with female-appearing genitalia, and typically they are raised as girls. At puberty, however, they undergo changes associated with being male, such as deepening of the voice and masculinization of their genitals. What happens then? They reverse their previous sexual identity and show a shift in interest to typical male patterns of preferences and behaviours (e.g., Herdt & Davidson, 1988). While there are many complexities in interpreting these cases, they do suggest that hormonal factors play some role in gender-related behaviour differences.

Some differences are clearly more a result of social and cultural influences. A Carleton University study found that even when they are just as competent and well prepared, female students avoid major subjects requiring even modest amounts of mathematical skill (LeFevre et al., 1992). Researchers at Lakehead University suggest that, although both women and men students experience math anxiety, women are much more aware and concerned about such feelings, and more self-critical of their own performance (Flessati & Jamieson, 1991). As a consequence, they are much less likely to enter mathematics courses or math-related subjects. Of course, this can restrict their career goals in important ways.

K E Y *QUESTIONS*

- How do children acquire gender identity—the understanding that they are male or female?

- Which gender differences in behaviour have been reported in systematic research?

- What are the relative roles of social and cultural factors on the one hand and biological factors on the other, with respect to gender differences?

Making **Psychology** Part of Your Life

Being an Effective Parent

*T*hese days, people may change their careers, their spouses, and virtually every aspect of their lives. But once you are a parent, you are a parent for life. Given the huge investment of time, love, and other resources required, you will want to know as much as possible about how parents influence children.

Over the past century, there have been varying theories about parenting (Muzi, 2000). Recently, one psychologist has attributed adult personality, values, and aptitudes to genetic blueprints and he has questioned the degree to which parents have any influence whatsoever on the behaviour of their children (Cohen, 1999). On the other hand, a vast number of research studies have shown that parenting is a most important influence in emotional adjustment and adult well-being in general (Gottman, 1986). These studies conclude that if you change the behaviour of the parents, you can change the behaviour of the child.

The controversy surrounding the relative contributions of heredity and early experience is ongoing and may never really be settled. Here are some basic principles that research supports—if parenthood is your choice.

■ *Keep your expectations realistic.* Many first-time parents anticipate that *their* child will walk, talk, and do just about everything else ahead of what the charts suggest. Such unrealistic expectations can mean unnecessary and added stress for both you and your child. Remember that, most often, earlier development has little bearing on anything else.

■ *Be consistent.* Children need to learn that their behaviours have predictable consequences. If you set a rule for your children, enforce it consistently. One of the surest ways to confuse your child is to enforce rules on some occasions but not on others. If, however, you do want to bend a rule occasionally, be sure to make it clear how this is a special situation, and that at other times the standard rule will apply. Make certain that rules are agreed on by all caregivers. Children have enough trouble following clear, consistent rules—with-

out having to figure out whether the adult presently in the room agrees with a particular rule or not.

■ *Understand that children do not and cannot reason like adults.* Parents are often tempted to talk to their children as though the youngsters are mini-adults. Then parents are mystified when that approach does not work. In fact, young children cannot think and reason like adults. Trying to reason about abstract concepts like fairness and consideration too early is probably worse than useless, although that is not the case later on. Therefore, be ready to turn difficult situations into joint problem-solving projects. For example, "How can we fix this together?" is a question young children can understand.

■ *Use discipline sensibly, moderately, and with love.* Avoid common mistakes like overreacting with anger, irritation, and harsh punishment. Do not talk too much or offer lengthy explanations—not only because children may not understand your abstract principles, but also because they may be in an emotional state that makes it impossible for them to listen effectively.

■ *Remember that young children are highly observant.* They acquire a tremendous amount of information—and many behaviours—by observing adults. They are alert and adept at watching intently from the sidelines as important events take place, but they do not yet have the cognitive capacity to decide what is appropriate and what is not. Many parents are shocked when—at the most embarrassing moment—their children repeat things in public that they have overheard at home. There are also far-reaching effects of observations children make at home, including how they reward and punish their own children—twenty or more years later (Covell et al., 1995).

All things considered, parenting can be a most wondrous experience. These suggestions based upon the results of psychological research will help you make it as pleasurable as it can be—for your children as well as for yourself.

Summary and Review

Key Questions

Physical Growth and Development

■ **Which environmental factors can adversely affect the development of a fetus?** Diseases, drugs, alcohol, and smoking by prospective mothers are all teratogens that can harm the developing fetus.

■ **Which perceptual abilities are shown by infants?** Infants can distinguish among different colours, sounds, and tastes, and they prefer certain patterns, such as the features of the human face.

■ **What are the three basic methods used by psychologists to study human development?** In longitudinal research, the same individuals are studied for extended periods of time. In cross-sectional research, persons of different ages are studied at the same time. In longitudinal–sequential research, persons of different ages are studied over extended periods of time.

Cognitive Development

■ **What are the major stages in Piaget's theory, and what cognitive abilities do infants, children, and adolescents acquire as they move through these stages?** During the sensorimotor stage, infants acquire basic understanding of the links between their own behaviour and the effects it produces. During the preoperational stage, infants can form mental representations of the external world, but show egocentrism in their thinking. During the stage of concrete operations, children are capable of logical thought and show understanding of conservation. During the stage of formal operations, children and adolescents can think logically.

■ **In which three respects does Piaget's theory appear to need revision?** Piaget's theory needs revision in that it underestimates the cognitive abilities of young children, overstates the importance of discrete stages, and underestimates the importance of language and social interactions.

■ **According to the information-processing perspective, what does cognitive development involve?** According to this approach, cognitive development involves the increasing ability to process, store, retrieve, and manipulate information.

■ **What changes occur in children's ability to focus their attention and to enhance their own memory, as they grow older?** Children become better able to ignore distractions and to focus their attention on tasks they are currently performing. They acquire increased capacity to rehearse information they want to memorize, and greatly expand their domain-specific knowledge. Finally, they acquire increasingly sophisticated schemas and scripts.

■ **What is metacognition?** Metacognition is awareness and understanding of our own cognitive processes.

■ **What are the major stages of moral development described by Kohlberg's theory?** At the first, or preconventional level, morality is judged largely in terms of its consequences. At the conventional level, morality is judged in terms of laws and rules of society. At the third, or postconventional level, morality is judged in terms of abstract principles and values.

■ **What do research findings indicate with respect to gender differences in moral reasoning?** Contrary to suggestions by Gilligan, there is no evidence that males and females differ in moral reasoning or attain different levels of moral development.

■ **Do cultural factors have any impact on moral development?** Cultural factors do appear to influence moral development. Depending on the society in which they live, individuals learn to make moral judgments on the basis of different criteria.

Social and Emotional Development

■ **At what age do infants first show recognizable facial expressions?** Infants show discrete facial expressions as early as two months of age.

■ **How do children's abilities to regulate their own emotions develop?** As they grow older, children acquire increasing abilities to avoid disturbing stimuli and to adjust their expectations.

■ **What is temperament and what role does it play in later development?** Temperament refers to stable individual differences in the quality or intensity of emotional reactions. It plays a role in characteristics such as shyness and in the later occurrence of several kinds of behavioural problems, and may even influence the nature of adult romantic relationships.

■ **What is attachment, and how is it measured?** Attachment refers to infants' strong emotional bonds with their caregivers. It is measured by the *strange situation test*, in which infants' reactions to being separated from their caregivers are studied, and through careful observations of infants' behaviour in their own homes.

■ **Which factors affect attachment between infants and their caregivers?** Attachment is influenced by infants' temperament and several other factors including parents' responsiveness to children's needs, and contact comfort.

■ **How does attachment influence later social development?** Children who are securely attached to their caregivers are more sociable, better at solving some problems, more tolerant of frustration, and more flexible and persistent in many situations than children who are avoidantly or insecurely attached. In addition, persons who were securely attached to their caregivers as infants seem more capable of forming close, lasting relationships than persons who were avoidantly or insecurely attached.

■ **What role do children's friendships play in their social and emotional development?** Children's friendships, which are often formed in school, provide them with opportunities to acquire and practise essential social skills, such as sharing, cooperation, and closeness, and also provide them with the opportunity to experience and express intense emotions.

Gender

■ **What is gender identity? Gender stability? Gender consistency?** Gender identity refers to children's ability to label their own sex and that of others accurately. Gender stability is children's understanding that sex identity is stable over time. Gender consistency is children's understanding that sex identity won't change even if they adopt the clothing, hairstyles, and activities of the other sex.

■ **What is sex-category constancy?** Sex-category constancy refers to children's understanding that sex identity is a biologically based categorical distinction.

■ **How do social-learning theory, cognitive-development theory, and gender-schema theory explain gender development?** Social-learning theory emphasizes the role of operant conditions and modelling. Cognitive-development theory emphasizes the role of children's growing cognitive abilities. Gender-schema theory emphasizes the role of gender schemas.

Key Terms

Accommodation (p. 312)

Adaptation (p. 312)

Assimilation (p. 312)

Attachment (p. 332)

Avoidant Attachment (p. 334)

Cohort Effects (p. 310)

Concrete Operations (p. 314)

Conservation (p. 314)

Conventional Level of Morality (p. 325)

Cross-Sectional Research (p. 310)

Developmental Psychology (p. 302)

Disorganized (or Disoriented) Attachment (p. 334)

Egocentrism (p. 314)

Embryo (p. 303)

Empathy (p. 332)

Fetus (p. 303)

Formal Operations (p. 314)

Friendships (p. 337)

Gaze Following (p. 328)

Gender (p. 339)

Gender Stereotypes (p. 339)

Hypothetico-Deductive Reasoning (p. 315)

Longitudinal Research (p. 310)

Longitudinal-Sequential Design (p. 310)

Metacognition (p. 320)

Moral Development (p. 324)

Object Permanence (p. 313)

Placenta (p. 304)

Postconventional Level of Morality (p. 326)

Preconventional Level of Morality (p. 325)

Preoperational Stage (p. 313)

Resistant Attachment (p. 334)

Secure Attachment (p. 334)

Sensorimotor Stage (p. 312)

Sex Category Constancy (p. 339)

Social Referencing (p. 331)

Stage Theory (p. 312)

Strange Situation Test (p. 333)

Symbolic Play (p. 313)

Temperament (p. 329)

Teratogens (p. 304)

Theory of Mind (p. 321)

Critical Thinking Questions

Appraisal

Physical, cognitive, and emotional/social development obviously occur together, in a simultaneous manner. Given this fact, why study each one separately?

Controversy

Growing evidence suggests that genetic factors, such as differences in hormonal levels, may play a role in the development of at least some differences in the behaviour of boys and girls. These differences, in turn, may influence several aspects of their development. Do you think that these findings mean that efforts to ensure equal opportunities for women in all walks of life will run into obstacles that can't be overcome? If so, why? If not, why?

Making Psychology Part of Your Life

Many parents worry about the impact of television, movies, and other forms of the mass media on their children. Do you think that such concerns are justified? And if so, how can you—when you are a parent—reduce these potential harmful effects on your own children? What role should society play in regulating the content of television programs and movies?

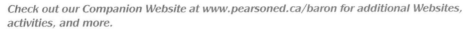

Weblinks

Check out our Companion Website at www.pearsoned.ca/baron for additional Websites, activities, and more.

Developmental Psychology

www.apa.org/journals/dev.html

Abstracts of articles from *Developmental Psychology* are available online here.

Kohlberg Tutorial

snycorva.cortland.edu/~ANDERSMD/KOHL/CONTENT.HTML

This tutorial contains information about Lawrence Kohlberg's concept of moral reasoning and its roots in Jean Piaget's ideas of moral realism and morality of cooperation. Some criticism of Kohlberg's theory is included.

Helping to Form a Secure Attachment

www.nncc.org/Child.Dev/dc25_secure.attach.html

How highly skilled caregivers can help the infant form a trusting and secure attachment is the topic of this paper from the (U.S.) National Network for Child Care.

Prenatal Development

www.zerotothree.org/brainworks/care_prenatal.html

The links from this page will give you much information about how brain and behaviour develop from age zero to three. There are also answers to some very interesting questions.

Invariance Problems

plato.acadiau.ca/courses/educ/piper/invarian.html

This page will lead you to some ways of assessing whether a child is in the Preoperational or Concrete Operational stage in Jean Piaget's theory of congitive development.

Psychology: Attachment Web Page

www.le.ac.uk/education/resources/SocSci/attach.html

This page gives a brief review of various attachment theories.

Chapter 9

Human Development II
Adolescence, Adulthood, and Aging

CHAPTER OUTLINE

Brains Take a Long Time

According to this report in *The Globe and Mail,* there is brand new evidence about the development of human brains. When scientists used magnetic resonance imaging to measure the ways in which brains change from ages three to fifteen, the results were surprising.

While prior studies had shown that remarkable advances take place during the first three years of life, the new studies revealed that after age three, and for at least the next twelve years, the brain continues to organize connections, streamline them, and discard extra nerve cells. Thus, over time, some parts of the brain grow larger and some shrink. Also, the connections between the right and left hemispheres increase. Therefore, not only is the behaviour of teens different from that of adults, but so are their brains.

Of course, the brain does not cease to change at age fifteen! Other evidence indicates that there are waves of development at least until age twenty-two, and the frontal lobes keep developing until age thirty. Future research will tell us what happens after that.

What are the physical, emotional, cognitive, and social developments that result as we grow older? How do the experiences of childhood, such as attachment, affect adult behaviour? In Chapter 9, you will discover the findings of psychological science with respect to those questions as you continue through Human Development II.

Source: Foss, K. (2000, March 10). Brains develop into puberty, study says. *The Globe and Mail.*

347

⌈ **Development during adulthood**
⌈ **derives primarily from the effects**
⌊ **of varied life experience.**

Imagine that you are transported, by time machine, twenty-five years into the future, where you encounter … yourself! What will you be like? Will you have the same personality traits, attitudes, beliefs, and feelings? How much will this future self resemble … you? These are absorbing questions, and they relate to one of psychology's grand themes—*stability versus change*. Some of our central traits remain stable for years or even decades (Stein et al., 1991). Yet others change in many different ways through the adult years—although we cannot be quite sure what the outcome will be.

Physical Change

As these photos of a man at ages four, seventeen, and fifty show, we all change tremendously in appearance over the course of our lives.

One important reason for the uncertainty in predicting change during our adult years is this: While development during childhood is determined to an important extent by *maturation*—physical growth and change—development during the decades after childhood is tied more closely to social and environmental factors. Since these factors are unique for each individual, the course of development is also highly variable. While we change in many ways as we proceed along life's journey, the physical alterations that are most obvious are a very small part of a much larger set (e.g., Duncan & Agronick, 1995; Friedman et al., 1996). In this chapter you will learn about some of the changes individuals encounter during *adolescence*—the years between *puberty* (sexual maturity) and entry into adult status; and during *adulthood*—the remaining decades, which constitute the longest portion of our lives. As in Chapter 8, we'll consider changes during each of these periods under three headings: *physical, cognitive,* and *social and emotional*. And as *aging* and *death* are inevitable facts of life, those topics will also be part of our discussion.

Adolescence

When does childhood end and adulthood begin? Since development is a continuous process, there is no hard-and-fast answer to this question. Rather, every culture draws its own dividing line. In some primitive cultures, there are "rites of passage." Young adolescents must successfully overcome challenges, which may involve instruction, isolation, pain, and other tests of endurance. In this tradition, "to become fulfilled members of their society, adolescents must understand when childhood ends, adulthood begins, and what their culture expects of them" (Cohen, 1991). Many cultures mark this transition with special ceremonies.

In contrast, in many Western countries, the transition from child to adult takes place gradually, during a period known as **adolescence**, which lasts for several years. Here the informal rites of passage may include a driving test, a liquor ID, or a grad ball—hardly events that count as earning passage to adulthood. Some

psychologists argue that this is why adolescents in our culture go to such lengths to do adult things—they are trying to prove themselves worthy of that status. Thus, the definition of adolescence is largely a social one, determined by culture. Moreover, ideas concerning this phase of life can change greatly *within* a given culture over time.

Development: A Continuous Process

As this cartoon suggests, we continue to change throughout our lives.

Source: The New Yorker.

Physical Development during Adolescence

Adolescence begins with a sudden increase in the rate of physical growth. While this *growth spurt* occurs for both sexes, it starts earlier for girls (at about age ten or eleven) than for boys (about age twelve or thirteen). Prior to this spurt, boys and girls are similar in average height; in early adolescent phases, girls are frequently taller than boys. Eventually, however, men are several inches taller (on average) than women.

This growth spurt is just one event that takes place at **puberty,** the period of rapid change during which individuals of both genders reach sexual maturity. During puberty, the *gonads*, or sex glands, produce increased levels of sex hormones, and the external sex organs assume their adult form. Girls begin to *menstruate* and boys start to produce sperm. These are *primary sexual characteristics.* In addition, both sexes undergo many other changes in sexual maturity. Boys develop facial and chest hair, and their voices deepen; girls experience breast enlargement and a widening of their hips. Both sexes develop pubic hair.

There is great variability in the onset of sexual maturity. Most girls have begun to menstruate by the time they are thirteen; but for some this process does not start until fifteen or sixteen, and for others it may commence as early as seven or eight. Most boys begin to produce sperm by the time they are fourteen or fifteen, but for some the process may begin considerably earlier or later.

Facial features, too, change during puberty. Characteristics associated with childhood, such as large eyes, a high forehead, round cheeks, and a small chin, give way to a more adult appearance. Recent studies indicate that individuals who retain childlike facial features—a *baby face*—are perceived as being weaker, more naïve, and more submissive. Interestingly, however, baby-faced people are also perceived as being more honest, warm, and sincere, and baby-faced females (though not males) are perceived as attractive (Berry & Zebrowitz-McArthur, 1988).

There are sex differences in the consequences of early sexual maturation. Early-maturing boys seem to have a definite edge over those who mature somewhat later. They are stronger and more athletic than their later-maturing counterparts, and so they often excel in competitive sports. Partly as a result of these advantages, they tend to be more self-assured and popular and are often chosen for leadership roles (Blyth et al., 1981; Blyth et al., 1998). In contrast, early sexual maturation seems to confer fewer benefits on girls. Early-maturing girls are taller than their classmates—frequently taller than boys of their age—and their increased sexual attractiveness may invite envy from classmates and unwanted sexual advances from older people (Peterson, 1987). In short, the timing of puberty can play an important role in adolescents' developing self-identities and in their later social development.

See the **Canadian Focus** feature for more about adolescent identity.

Puberty and the Spurt of Growth

Girls tend to mature somewhat earlier than boys; they experience a growth spurt one or two years sooner.

Adolescence: A period beginning with the onset of puberty and ending when individuals assume adult roles and responsibilities.

Puberty: The period of rapid change during which individuals reach sexual maturity and become capable of reproduction.

Canadian Focus

Puberty, Subjective Age, and Pseudomaturity

The age at which puberty occurs influences adolescents' developing self-identity and the way they are seen and treated by others—and thus, their later social development. Other factors matter too, including parents' and teachers' attitudes, media messages, and examples set within the family. As important, however, may be *subjective age*—the age adolescents perceive themselves to be.

Nancy L. Galambos
University of Victoria

At the University of Victoria, Nancy Galambos and her colleagues (1990) have studied subjective age in young adolescents between the ages of eleven and thirteen. In their research, they have investigated adolescent *gender intensification*—the "behavioural, attitudinal, and psychological differences between adolescent boys and girls" as they increase in age. The purpose of one study was to determine how differences in gender intensified across grades six, seven, and eight.

Two hundred adolescents completed a gender role identity questionnaire. On a scale from one (almost never true) to seven (almost always true), they rated themselves on ten adjectives commonly associated with masculinity (e.g., "self-reliant") and on ten others most often associated with femininity (e.g., "affectionate"). For each group, then, both an average masculinity rating and an average femininity rating were calculated.

The results indicated that, over the years, the ratings of feminine characteristics increased in intensity in a similar way for male and female adolescents. Both groups saw themselves as more and more affectionate, sympathetic, or cheerful, for example, as they progressed in age. However, in their ratings of masculinity, the two sexes saw themselves differently. The ratings of male adolescents for how assertive, competitive, and ambitious they saw themselves to be intensified at a much faster rate than those of female adolescents. The researchers interpreted that result as reflecting the general social value placed upon masculine characteristics, and the severe social pressure on young male teens to conform to a gender identity—one that is particularly masculine.

Surprisingly, gender intensification increased whether puberty had passed or not. Galambos concluded that what mattered to adolescents is how old they perceive themselves to be—their *subjective age*—rather than their chronological age or when they passed puberty (Galambos et al., 1995).

Does perceiving oneself as older mean behaving more maturely also? That is not necessarily so, concludes research that used subjective age to study a special group of adolescents—youngsters who seem to grow up too quickly. These teens perceive themselves to be older and more mature than they really are. There is a mismatch between their subjective age and their behaviour (Galambos & Tilton-Weaver, 2000). The term that has been used to identify these adolescents is *adultoid*. According to Greenberger and Steinberg (1986), an adultoid "simply mimics adult activity without being accompanied by the underlying perceptions, beliefs or understanding that a person who is psychologically adult would bring to a similar situation" (p. 174).

When psychosocial maturity—autonomy with social responsibility—is missing, the adolescent copies the behaviour of a more mature person—plays the role of being older. This *pseudomaturity* may lead to problem behaviours—conflict with parents and teachers, truancy, dropping out of school, association with deviant peers, sexual relations, smoking, and alcohol and drug use. Too-early entrance into the workforce without the maturity or the experience to deal with the responsibility may also occur (Greenberger & Steinberg, 1986).

In order to find out about pseudomaturity, the UVic researchers studied the subjective age, psychosocial maturity, and problem behaviours of a large group of young adolescents (Galambos & Tilton-Weaver, 2000). Their studies confirmed that adultoid adolescents—whose subjective age was older and psychosocial maturity lower—do exist. Moreover, they found that in adultoid adolescents, problem behaviours were much more common.

Future studies of how adolescents become adultoid may be very useful in the design of programs to help these teens adjust their behaviours to fit their ages and in our general efforts to understand why it is that adolescents feel, think, and behave the way they do (Turner et al., 1999).

Let's return to those adolescents now.

Cognitive Development during Adolescence

Do most adolescents think and reason like adults? In some ways that is generally not the case. For example, adolescents are *egocentric*, and they assume that everyone else thinks the way they do. Since adolescents' thoughts are focused upon themselves, it follows that the attention of other people must be as well. As a result, adolescents act as though they have an imaginary audience. They try out different acts (grunge, punk, prep) and are painfully self-conscious—embarrassed by any apparent defect, such as parents, bad hair, zits, and so on.

On occasions, adolescents assume that their feelings and thoughts are totally unique—that no one else on the planet has ever had experiences like theirs. Elkind (1967) described this as the *personal fable,* and he believes that it is responsible for the difficulties many parents and teachers experience when trying to communicate with teenagers. It seems that no matter what the parents say, adolescents assume that it doesn't apply to them because they are different and unique!

Piaget contended that adolescent thinking still differs from that of adults in several important respects. Adolescents use their newly found cognitive skills to construct sweeping theories about various aspects of life, although their theories often seem naïve and reflect a lack of experience. During this period, adolescents' *theory of mind*—their understanding of how they and others think—continues to change and develop. Younger children take what has been described as a *realist approach* to knowledge; they believe that knowledge is a property of the real world and that there are definite "facts" or "truths" that can be acquired. In contrast, older children become aware that even experts disagree; this leads them to develop a *relativist approach,* which recognizes that different people may interpret the same information in contrasting ways.

Preadolescents go a bit further, adopting a *defended realism approach,* which recognizes the difference between facts and opinions. Still later, adolescents come to realize that there is no secure basis for knowledge or making decisions; at this point, they adopt an approach described as *dogmatism-skepticism,* in which they alternate between blind faith in some authority and doubting everything. Finally, some adolescents, at least, realize that while there are no absolute truths, there are better or worse reasons for holding certain views—an approach described as *postskeptical-rationalism.* This, of course, is the kind of thinking democratic societies wish to encourage among their citizens, because only people capable of thinking in this way can make the kind of informed judgments necessary for free elections.

In sum, cognitive development continues throughout adolescence and results, ultimately, in more mature modes of thought (Klaczyinski, 1997). Perhaps the most remarkable research findings in this area are that adolescents and adults think about *risk* in different ways.

ADOLESCENT INVULNERABILITY Why is it that adolescents engage in lots of high-risk behaviours—unprotected sex; drug, alcohol, and substance abuse; reckless driving; academic failure; delinquency; violence and crime (Lerner & Galambos, 1998)? One explanation (Baron & Brown, 1991) is that young people suffer from **adolescent invulnerability**—the belief that they are immune from the potential harm of high-risk behaviours. Is that explanation correct? Surprisingly, several studies indicate that adolescents are no more likely than adults to view themselves as invulnerable to the negative outcomes of risky behaviour (e.g., Beyth-Marom et al., 1997; Davis et al., 1993; Rucker & Greene, 1995).

A very clear illustration of this point is provided by a study conducted by Quadrel, Fischoff, and Davis (1993). Individuals in three groups—teenagers living in group homes for troubled teens, teenagers living at home with their parents, and the parents of those living at home—were asked to rate the probability that negative events would happen to them: auto accident injury, alcohol dependency, unplanned pregnancy, mugging, sickness from air pollution, injury in an explosion, sickness from pesticides, and sickness from radiation. The results were clear: Adolescents and adults did not seem to differ greatly in the way they thought about vulnerability. The teenagers did *not* rate themselves as more invulnerable than the adults. In fact, the teens living at home with their parents had less confidence in their own invulnerability than did their parents!

Adolescent Invulnerability: Adolescents' belief that they are immune from the potential harm of high-risk behaviours.

Adolescents: A Propensity for High-Risk Behaviours

Adolescents often engage in high-risk behaviours. Is this because they feel invulnerable to the potential risks of such actions? Recent evidence casts doubt on this widely held belief.

Nevertheless, adolescents do engage in high-risk behaviours, some of which are very likely to cause them problems. They are more likely to drink and drive, although they understand the dangers to themselves and to others. One recent study examined the behaviour at "bush parties" of Ontario high school students (Stoduto et al., 1998). The impetus for the study were associated car crashes that had taken the lives of several young people and in which drinking and driving was involved. The most prone to drink and drive after bush parties were male smokers who drank not only at bush parties but also in a larger number of other places and used other drugs.

How do psychological scientists find out about risk-taking behaviours? One novel method was used by Shapiro et al. (1998) in their study of female college students. They gave each student a structured diary to keep for one week. Each day, the subjects filled out a "risk behaviour daily monitoring card" and on each card, the participants were asked to record their five most risky behaviours that day, rate how risky they considered each behaviour was on a nine-point scale, give reasons for the reported behaviours, tell if they would do that again, and say whether they would recommend that behaviour to their best friend. The advantage of this methodology was that the students told the researchers which behaviours they themselves considered risky and why they acted the way they did—in their natural environment.

These subjects reported over one hundred different risky behaviours, including doing drugs, drinking and driving, speeding, driving without insurance, leaving the coffee pot on the stove, and not going to church. Three results stood out as surprising. First, these students reported just as many risky behaviours during the week as on weekends—a result quite different from that found with adult subjects, who risk more often on weekends. Second, these female college students took similar kinds of risks, and in similar numbers, as male students in other studies. Third, subjects were able to report reasons for their risky behaviours. In very few instances did they not know why they took risks. Finally, two of the kinds of reasons they gave were emotional (to feel good) or social (to spend time with friends). These results suggest also that there may be positive consequences for those who engage in some risk taking during adolescence.

Even so, these behaviours may well be illegal and dangerous, and hazardous to health. Moreover, they put future opportunities at risk and there are serious costs for relationships with parents and teachers. Why, then, do teenagers engage in so many risky behaviours? According to one psychologist who has studied this issue in detail (Arnett, 1995), several factors play a role.

First, adolescents are high in a characteristic known as **sensation seeking**—the desire to seek out novel and intense experiences (e.g., Zuckerman, 1990). Many high-risk behaviours—driving very fast, experimenting with drugs (DeWit et al., 1995), "living dangerously" where sex is concerned—yield such experiences. Second, adolescents do indeed engage in egocentric thinking that leads them to the conclusion that they are somehow "special." They tend to believe that what happens to other people probably will not happen to them. For instance, when asked to estimate the likelihood of becoming pregnant, adolescent girls who have engaged in sex without contraception show a strong tendency to underestimate this figure (e.g., Arnett, 1992). Finally, adolescent males tend to be aggressive in comparison to adults; and their aggression often shows up in dangerous driving and criminal behaviour—two activities that are certainly reckless and put them at considerable risk.

At home, sometimes adolescents disregard rules by deliberately staying out very late at night; they disregard rules at school by skipping class; they disregard rules of society by drinking when they are not of age and by shoplifting items of little value; and they show a willingness to engage in unprotected sex, even when they understand the risk of AIDS and other sexually transmitted diseases (e.g., Fisher & Misovich, 1989; Netting, 1982).

Sensation Seeking: A characteristic of individuals who seek and enjoy high levels of stimulation.

Maggs and others (1995) maintain that these problem behaviours are not entirely negative. On the positive side, adolescents enjoy the risks involved and see them as a source of good feelings and good times. Also, "forbidden" behaviours are a way to make friends, blow off steam, and establish independence. Through them, adolescents gain experience in making choices and in evaluating potential gains and losses. It may be that some risk taking in adolescence is a natural and normal part of growing up. Other researchers argue that adolescents' behaviour results from millions of years of evolution, and is genetically determined. It is not consistent with the demands of society, and that is where the difficulty arises (Csikszentmihalyi & Schmidt, 1998).

Naturalistic Observation: A research method in which various aspects of behaviour are carefully observed in the settings where such behaviour naturally occurs.

KEY QUESTIONS

- What physical changes occur during puberty?
- Why do adolescents often engage in reckless behaviour?

Social and Emotional Development during Adolescence

It would be surprising if the major physical and cognitive changes that occur during adolescence were not accompanied by equally extensive changes in social and emotional development. How do psychologists study these complex changes? The **Research Process** section will explain two methods that have been used.

The Research Process:
Studying Development in Natural Settings

In their efforts to study cognitive development, psychologists focus on the abilities and achievements of single individuals: How much can they remember? How do they reason about moral dilemmas? What factors influence their decisions? Researchers can investigate various aspects of cognitive development under controlled laboratory conditions by asking study participants to work on tasks designed to test memory, reasoning, and so on. Although such tasks are not exactly like the ones people perform in their everyday lives, most psychologists believe that they do tap basic aspects of cognition; thus, results obtained with them can be generalized outside the confines of the research laboratory.

Social behaviour, on the other hand, presents a very different situation. Such behaviour, by definition, involves interactions between two or more persons (see Chapter 16). And it is sometimes difficult to observe certain aspects of it in laboratory settings. How do friendships form (e.g., Berndt, 1992)? What makes specific individuals popular (Jarvinen & Nicholls, 1996)? Questions such as these can sometimes only be answered through **naturalistic observation** of behaviour in the settings where it normally occurs.

In the past, research on such behaviour involved careful observation—watching youngsters—as they interact with one another, then recording their actions on

special data-collection forms or checklists. However, there are other ways of studying behaviour in more naturalistic settings.

For example, in one study, researchers collected observations of the social behaviours of 145 boys—in their classrooms—when they were in grades three to six and then four years later when the same children were in grades seven through ten (Pope & Bierman, 1999). They obtained *peer ratings*—ratings by other children in their classes—of these boys with respect to various behaviours, including aggression, disruptive-hyperactivity behaviours (fidgets, excitable, thinks before acting), and withdrawn behaviours (shy, bashful, seems sad, unhappy, puts self down). The results indicated that aggression and withdrawn behaviour in the early grades were linked to rejection and victimization by peers in the later grades, as were antisocial activities—vandalism and alcohol abuse—by the boys themselves. As you can see, certain characteristics on the part of pre-teenagers and adolescents contribute to poor adjustment later on.

Developmental psychologists have also adopted a more high-tech approach, using small, light video cameras and wireless microphones. It is now possible to equip children with wireless microphones—for example, in school playgrounds, on streets, or in parks—and to record what they say and videotape what they do as they play in natural settings. For instance, using such measures, Pepler and Craig (1995) found that aggression between children and adolescents is even more common than was previously believed. While they are at play, and even among children rated as *nonaggressive* by their teachers and peers, verbal aggression occurs once very five minutes and physical aggression once very eleven minutes—on average. Among highly aggressive youngsters, rates are even higher (once every three and eight minutes). Other research is beginning to discover the particular factors that result in aggressive reactions and how teachers, parents,

and other adults can work to reduce this kind of behaviour (e.g., Coie & Jacobs, 1993).

Of course, there are ethical issues here. Is it appropriate to listen in on children's conversations—even if they give consent themselves? What is the responsibility of the researcher who observes one child doing harm to another? These are questions with which researchers in developmental psychology must struggle as technology becomes more and more capable of observing the way people behave in everyday life.

A Special Time of Change
Adolescence is a time of great social and emotional change, though most teenagers report feeling happy and self-confident.

EMOTIONAL CHANGES: THE UPS AND DOWNS OF YOUTH Common folklore suggests that adolescents are unpredictable creatures, prone to wide swings in mood and wild outbursts of emotion. Are these assertions true? To some degree, they are. In several studies, large numbers of teenagers wore beepers and were signalled at random times throughout an entire week. When signalled, they entered their thoughts and feelings in a diary. The results indicated frequent and large swings in mood—from the heights to the depths (Csikszentmihalyi & Larson, 1984). Moreover, these swings occurred very quickly, sometimes within only a few minutes. Older people also show shifts in mood, but theirs tend to be less frequent, slower, and smaller in magnitude. Some evidence, then, supports the view that adolescents (at least in Western nations) are more emotionally volatile than adults.

Other widely accepted ideas about adolescent emotionality, however, do not appear to be correct. For example, it is often assumed that adolescence is a period of great stress and unhappiness. To the contrary, most teenagers report feeling quite happy and self-confident, *not* unhappy or distressed (Diener & Diener, 1996). Moreover, and again contrary to a prevailing stereotype about adolescence, most teenagers report that they enjoy relatively good relations with their parents. They *agree* with their parents' basic values; on future plans, such as whether they should continue in school; and on many other issues as well (Bachman, 1987).

There are, of course, points of friction: Teenagers often *disagree* with their parents about how they should spend their leisure time; how much money they should have or spend; and to some extent about sexual behaviour, though this seems to be decreasing (Kelley & Byrne, 1992). Other variables are also important in determining adolescent–parent conflict. For example, within families in which both parents are overloaded at work, adolescent–parent conflict is highest. In this situation, there is the greatest potential for disagreement and disharmony. Also important, however, is the quality of the relationship that has been established between adolescents and their parents (Galambos et al., 1995). By and large, however, the so-called *generation gap* is much narrower than many people have assumed (Galambos, 1992).

Parental Demandingness: The extent to which parents are strict or controlling, and confront their children (often angrily) when they do not meet the parents' expectations.

Parental Responsiveness: The extent to which parents are involved in and supportive of their children's activities.

PARENTING STYLES AND THEIR EFFECTS ON ADOLESCENTS Parenting styles differ in two ways. One is **parental demandingness**—the extent to which parents are strict or controlling. Parents high on this dimension seek to control their children through status and power, and confront them when they do not meet their expectations. The other is **parental responsiveness**—the extent to which parents are supportive of their children. Parents high on this dimension listen actively to their children, respond to their requests, show warmth, and focus on their children's concerns and interests during conversations with them (Beaumont, 1996). Together, these two dimensions yield the parenting styles shown in Figure 9.1. Authoritarian parents are high in demandingness (controlling) and low in responsiveness. They establish strict rules for their children and don't give them much say in decisions. Authoritative parents, in contrast, are high in both demandingness and responsiveness: they establish rules for their children, but show great interest in and responsiveness to them. Permissive parents are high in responsiveness but low in demandingness: they are warm and responsive, but set no rules or standards for their children and don't hold them accountable for their actions. Finally, rejecting/neglecting parents are low in both responsiveness and demandingness—they just don't seem to care what children do or what they become.

		Parental Demandingness	
		Low	High
	Low	*Rejecting/Neglecting*	*Authoritarian*
Parental Responsiveness			
	High	*Permissive*	*Authoritative*

Figure 9.1
Styles of Parenting

Two key dimensions seem to underlie differences in parenting styles: parental demandingness and parental responsiveness. Together, these yield the four distinct patterns of parenting shown here and described in the text.

Not surprisingly, these contrasting styles have strong and lasting effects. In fact, growing evidence (e.g., Baumrind, 1991) suggests that an authoritative style may yield the most beneficial effects. Adolescents whose parents adopt this approach are competent both socially and cognitively. They are confident, yet friendly and cooperative, and tend to do well in school. In contrast, adolescents whose parents show a rejecting/neglecting style tend to do least well in social and cognitive competence. Moreover, they often show unsettled patterns of behaviour, rejecting their parents and engaging in various forms of antisocial behaviour that can get them into serious trouble.

FRIENDSHIPS, THE QUEST FOR IDENTITY, AND SEXUALITY While most adolescents report mainly positive relations with their parents, such family-based relationships are only part of their social development. *Friendships*, not only with members of one's own sex but also with members of the other sex, become increasingly important to personal adjustment (Claes, 1992). In fact, most adolescents are part of extensive social networks, consisting of many friends and acquaintances. Girls tend to have somewhat larger networks than boys, and these networks tend to become smaller and more exclusive as adolescents grow older (Urberg et al., 1995), but for most, forming friendships and learning about trust and intimacy within them are important aspects of social development.

While adolescents' growing and deepening friendships confer important benefits, the potential costs of such relationships should not be ignored. Many studies indicate that adolescents experience intense conflicts with friends—conflicts that can leave serious psychological scars. Adolescents may acquire undesirable attitudes and self-destructive patterns of behaviour from friends (Shantz & Hartup,

1993). For example, they may be influenced to smoke (Van Roosmalen & McDaniel, 1992), consume alcohol or other drugs (Hundleby & Mercer, 1987), or engage in multiple sexual relationships just because members of their gang do so. As Berndt (1992) notes, however, influence among adolescent friends flows in both directions, so the potential negative effects of having "wild" or risk-taking friends should not be overemphasized.

Since having lots of friends and being popular are important to adolescents, it is not surprising that they soon acquire clear social goals—ends they want to achieve in their social relationships. Further, they also form beliefs about how they can attain these goals (e.g., Berndt & Savin-Williams 1993). What are these goals and strategies like? A study performed recently by Jarvinen and Nicholls (1996) provides some revealing answers.

These researchers asked several hundred high school students (about fourteen years old) to describe their social goals by indicating the extent to which they agreed or disagreed with statements that began with the phrase "When I'm with people my own age, I like it when …" or "… I dislike it when …." Careful analysis of the students' replies indicated that they sought five major goals in their social relations. For each, an example of the kind of statements reflecting this goal is provided:

- *Dominance:* "I like it when they are afraid of me."
- *Intimacy:* "I like it when I can tell them my private thoughts."
- *Nurturance:* "I like it when I can make their lives easier."
- *Leadership:* "I like it when I'm in charge."
- *Popularity:* "I like it when everyone wants me for a friend."

Sound familiar? They probably do, because these are very much like the kinds of social goals we continue to seek throughout life. Interestingly, some small gender differences emerged here (see Figure 9.2).

How did the adolescents plan to reach these goals? Another part of the study asked them to respond to statements about strategies for getting along well with others. The major strategies identified were:

- Be sincere (e.g., never pretend to be something you aren't).
- Aim for high status (e.g., be really good-looking or good at sports, have lots of money).
- Be responsible (e.g., do your homework, work hard).
- Pretend to care (e.g., pretend to like everyone; tell people what they want to hear).
- Entertain (e.g., be good at small talk, tell good jokes).
- Be tough (e.g., push people around; be the toughest).

FRIENDSHIPS AND GENDER When do you seek the company of your close friends—to do something together, to share inner feelings and thoughts, or to ask for help or emotional support? While people of both sexes seek contact with their friends for all these reasons, there appear to be some gender differences. Males more often hang out with friends in order to participate in shared activities, while females more frequently spend time with friends to discuss feelings and thoughts and to obtain social support (Barth & Kinder, 1988).

Figure 9.2
Gender Differences in Adolescent Goals

As shown here, male adolescents express stronger interest in attaining such goals as dominance and leadership, while female adolescents express more interest in attaining the goals of intimacy and nurturance.

Source: Based on data from Jarvinen and Nicholls, 1996.

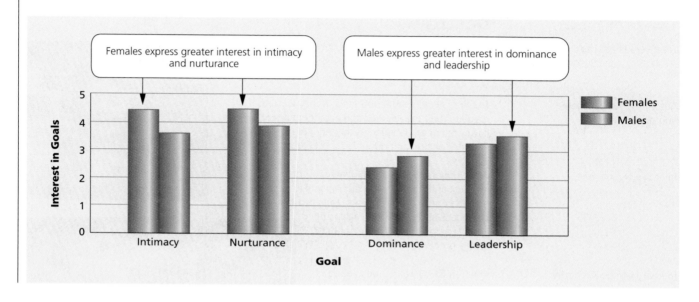

Although both have about the same number of close friends, females report greater satisfaction with these friendships (Reis et al., 1985). Also, females feel more strongly attached to their friends, view their friendships as more intimate, and expect more from a friendship than males (Claes, 1992). Moreover, close friendships seem to be more beneficial for females, at least with respect to reducing unhappiness and raising self-esteem.

Friendships and social success also play an important role in another key aspect of social development during adolescence—the quest for a personal identity. This process is the key element in adolescent psychosocial development proposed by Erik Erikson (1950, 1987).

ERIKSON'S EIGHT STAGES OF LIFE Erikson's theory deals with development across the entire lifespan. Like Piaget's theory, Erikson's is a stage theory: It suggests that all human beings pass through specific stages or phases of development in a certain order. In contrast to Piaget's theory, however, Erikson is concerned primarily with social development. Erikson believed that each stage of life is marked by a specific crisis, struggle, or conflict. Only if individuals negotiate each of these hurdles successfully will they continue to develop normally.

The stages in Erikson's theory are summarized in the **Key Concept** feature on page 358. The first four occur during childhood; one takes place during adolescence; and the final three occur during our adult years. The first stage, which occurs during the first year of life, centres on the struggle between *trust* and *mistrust*. Infants trust others to satisfy their needs. If those needs are not met, they fail to develop trust in others and may remain suspicious and wary throughout life.

Key Concept

Erikson's Eight Stages of Psychosocial Development

Crisis/Phase	Description
Trust versus mistrust	Infants learn either to trust the environment (if their needs are met) or to mistrust it (if their needs are not consistently met).
Autonomy versus shame and doubt	Toddlers acquire self-confidence if they learn to regulate their own bodies and act independently. If they fail or are labelled as inadequate, they experience shame and doubt.
Initiative versus guilt	Preschoolers (3–5 years old) acquire many new physical and mental skills but must also learn how to control their impulses. Unless a good balance is struck between skills and impulses, they may become either unruly or too inhibited.
Industry versus inferiority	Children (6–11 years old) acquire many skills and competencies. If they take justified pride in these, they acquire high self-esteem. If, in contrast, they compare themselves unfavourably with others, they may develop low self-esteem.
Identity versus role confusion	Adolescents must integrate various roles into a consistent self-identity. If they fail to do so, they may experience confusion over who they really are.
Intimacy versus isolation	Young adults must develop the ability to form deep, intimate relationships with others. If they do not, they may become socially or emotionally isolated.
Generativity versus self-absorption	During adulthood, individuals must take an active interest in helping and guiding younger people. If they do not, they may become preoccupied with selfish needs and desires.
Integrity versus despair	In the closing decades of life, individuals ask whether their lives have had any meaning. If they can answer yes, they attain a sense of integrity. If they answer no, they may experience deep despair.

▶   The second crisis occurs during the second year of life and involves *autonomy versus shame and doubt*. During this time, toddlers are learning to regulate their own bodies and to act in independent ways. If they succeed in these tasks, they develop a sense of autonomy. If they fail, or if they are labelled inadequate by their caregivers, they may experience shame, and doubt their ability to interact effectively with the external world.

The third stage takes place during the preschool years, between the ages of three and five. The conflict then involves *initiative versus guilt*. At this time, children acquire many new physical and mental skills. Simultaneously, however, they must develop the capacity to control their impulses, some of which can lead to unacceptable behaviour. If they strike the right balance between initiative and guilt, all is well. If initiative overwhelms guilt, children may become too unruly for their own good; if guilt overwhelms initiative, they may become too inhibited.

The fourth and final stage of childhood occurs during the elementary school years, when children are between six and eleven or twelve years of age. This stage involves the struggle between *industry* and *inferiority*. During these years, children learn to make things and use tools, and acquire many of the skills necessary for adult life. Children who successfully acquire these skills develop their own sense of competence; those who do not may compare themselves unfavourably with others and suffer from low self-esteem.

Now we come to the adolescent years in Erikson's theory, and the crisis of *identity versus role confusion*. At this time of life, individuals ask themselves, "Who am I?" "What am I *really* like?" "What do I want to become?" In other words, they seek to establish a clear *self-identity*—an understanding of their own unique traits and what really matters to them. These questions, of course, are asked at many points in life. According to Erikson, though, during adolescence it is crucial that these questions be answered effectively. If they aren't, individuals may drift along uncertain of who they are or what they wish to accomplish.

Adolescents adopt many different strategies to help themselves resolve their own personal identity crises (Kroger, 2000). They try out many different roles—the good girl/boy, the rebel, the dutiful daughter/son, the athlete—and join many different social groups. They consider many possible *social selves*—different kinds of people they might potentially become (Markus & Nurius, 1986). Out of these experiences, they gradually piece together a cognitive framework for understanding themselves—a *self-schema*. Once formed, this framework remains fairly constant and serves as a guide to behaviour in many different contexts.

The remaining three stages in Erikson's theory relate to crises we face as adults, and we will discuss them later on. However, they are included in the Key Concept page on page 358.

Perspectives on Diversity

Living in Two Worlds: Bicultural Adolescents

DO ADOLESCENTS WHOSE PARENTS COME from two different ethnic or cultural groups experience special problems in forming a clear identity? Growing research on this issue suggests that they do (Phinney & Devich-Navarro, 1997). After all, such children must understand not one culture and their place in it, but two cultures, which differ in many respects. How do they cope with this situation? One possibility is that they achieve separate identities in both cultures, and then alternate between these depending on the social situation; this is known as *alternation*. For instance, children with one European and one Asian parent may act differently depending on whether they are interacting with relatives or friends from each group.

Another pattern is known as **identity fusion**. Here, the children combine the two cultural identities into one. This has been found in the United States, where the number of biracial (or multiracial) children is increased rapidly. Such adolescents describe themselves as belonging to neither group, but as "biracial" or "mixed race." A third pattern is for such adolescents to reject one of their cultural heritages and to identify entirely with the other. This is especially likely for children who recognize that adopting a social identity in one of the two cultures may be a disadvantage (Lafrombiose et al., 1995).

Bicultural Adolescents: Fusing Two Cultures

In Canada and many other countries, the number of adolescents with a biracial or multiracial background is increasing rapidly. These young people often fuse their two cultures into a new identity and do not view themselves and belonging wholly to either group.

KEY *QUESTIONS*

◼ According to Erikson, what is the most important crisis faced by adolescents?

◼ How do psychologists study adolescents' social behaviour?

◼ How do bicultural adolescents cope with belonging to two cultural groups?

Adolescence in the New Millennium: A Generation at Risk?

During many periods of world history, adolescents have been at great risk of psychological and physical harm. War, revolution, plague, invasion, and conquest by foreign powers—such events have torn the social fabric and crushed families in all corners of the world. In view of this, it is difficult to contend that today's adolescents face a more dangerous and threatening world than preceding generations. Yet in the first years of the twenty-first century, they *do* seem to face uniquely disturbing challenges.

DIVORCED, PARENT-ABSENT, AND BLENDED FAMILIES At present more than half of all marriages in Canada and other countries end in divorce, although towards the end of the 1990s that number for Canada declined some. Furthermore, marriages ending in divorce last longer than they did in the early 1990s—about thirteen years rather than twelve. Nevertheless, many children and adolescents will spend at least part of their life in a different kind of family arrangement (Anderson & Greene, 1999) and face special problems in adjustment. Like all adolescents, teens of divorced parents continue to need love, limits, emotional space, and access to adults. Adolescents react to divorce with fear, anxiety, and feelings of insecurity about their future. Divorce can cause stress and psychological vulnerability, as well as hostility toward parents or siblings, or both (Kurtz & Derevensky, 1993). Further, many adolescents blame one or the other of the parents for the divorce. Some turn these feelings inward and feel guilty—as though *they* were responsible for the separation of their parents.

How divorce affects adolescent emotional well-being depends on many different factors, including the quality of the care they received before the divorce and the nature of the divorce—that is, whether it was amicable or filled with anger and resentment. Findings at the University of Quebec in Montreal (Tousignant et al., 1993) indicate that poor care by the father is the best predictor of adolescent suicidal behaviour after divorce. Needless to say, the more negatively the parents act toward each other, the more likely that emotional harm will be done. In addition, adolescents described as *academic underachievers*—those whose academic performance is below what their intelligence would predict—are more likely to come from divorced than two-parent homes (McCall, 1994).

Identity Fusion: A pattern in which bicultural children combine their two cultural identities into one.

Adolescents living in *parent-absent* families face different problems. Many children are born to single mothers, and some of these children may not know their fathers at all. As in other families, there are some special risks associated with growing up in a parent-absent (typically *father-absent*) family. Research findings suggest that they may include the following: increased risk for delinquent behaviours, reduced school performance (Bisnaire et al., 1990), and difficulties in forming meaningful relationships—including stable romantic ones—with members of the opposite sex (Eberhardt & Schill, 1984).

Is the happiest outcome for adolescents from single-parent families the remarriage of the remaining parent? When their divorced or single parents marry, adolescents find themselves facing other problems. The resulting **blended families** of one biological parent, one step-parent, and perhaps siblings and step-siblings, creates new complications. Favouritism by parents toward biological children, rivalries with step-siblings, and friction with step-parents generate painful conflicts. These conflicts are intensified by the fact that most step-parents, having had experience with being a parent to their own children, expect the role of step-parent to be one they already know how to play. Imagine the shock—and anger—when their step-children make such comments as, "You're not my real parent; I don't have to listen to you!" Clearly, then, shifting patterns of birth, marriage, divorce, and remarriage create serious challenges for today's adolescents. Many children adjust well to their altered circumstances, and progress normally (Galambos & Ehrenberg, 1997). Others suffer.

"Father Knows Best": A 1950s View of Family

During the 1950s, American television shows painted a glowing picture of the joys of family life. Even then, few families could live up to this unrealistic image.

DYSFUNCTIONAL FAMILIES: THE INTIMATE ENEMY

During the 1950s, television painted a glowing picture of ideal family life. A caring, loving mother, a kind and wise father, considerate siblings—that was the image portrayed on the screen. Today, many teenagers find themselves in **dysfunctional families**—families that do not meet children's needs and that may do them serious harm. From experience, Priest (1985) concluded that "most of such children suffer disabling emotional effects [of fear, anger, and grief] that they will carry over to adulthood and that adversely affect at least one more generation."

CHILD VICTIMS: ABUSE WITHIN FAMILIES Some dysfunctional families are neglectful or engage in mistreatment of adolescents. Violence, family instability, poverty, and psychiatric disorders among members of the family are some of the factors involved (Ledingham & Crombie, 1988). Some adolescents deal with parents who have serious psychological problems—problems that may cause them to act in ways that are unpredictable, physically threatening, or abusive (e.g., Ge et al., 1995). These young people can only guess what normal parental behaviour is like, since they see very little of it at home. Their parents cannot provide the kind of guidance, consistent control, and support needed for successful development, and recent findings indicate that when these factors are lacking, children and adolescents are at increased risk for a wide range of problems, such as drug abuse, stealing, disobedience at home and at school, and overt aggression (Stice & Barrera, 1996).

For some teenagers, family life includes **sexual abuse**. Unfortunately, this type of abuse is far from rare (Kendall-Tackett et al., 1993); indeed, every year, large numbers of children and adolescents are betrayed by adults they know. Common among adolescent victims of sexual abuse are depression, withdrawal, anxiety, psychiatric disorders, substance abuse, and physical complaints (Morrow & Sorrell, 1989). These harmful effects increase with the frequency and duration of the abuse; when the perpetrator is a close family member such as father, mother, or sibling; and when overt force is involved (Kendall-Tackett, 1991).

Blended Families: Families resulting from remarriage, consisting of biological parents, step-parents, and biological children of one or both spouses.

Dysfunctional Families: Families that do not meet the needs of children and in fact do them serious harm.

Sexual Abuse: Sexual contact or activities forced on children or adolescents by other persons, usually adults.

Has the incidence of sexual abuse increased in recent years? Or does the rise in complaints reflect greater attention to this problem on the part of society and greater willingness of victims to come forward? This is a difficult question to answer, but many experts feel that because of other changes in society, children and adolescents may be at greater risk for such abuse than was the case in the past. Whatever the ultimate conclusion, it is clear that mistreatment in general, and sexual abuse in particular, have serious consequences.

CHILD PARENTS: THE "ATLAS PERSONALITY" In some dysfunctional families, the responsibilities older children assume go far beyond reasonable limits. Two researchers at St. Michael's Hospital in Toronto (Vogel & Savva, 1993) focus on children who find themselves in troubled and chaotic family settings, where one or both parents are incapable of caring for their family or themselves. Often under these circumstances, one of the children gradually assumes more and more responsibility for managing both the household and the parents. This child tends to develop an "Atlas personality." This term refers to the Greek god Atlas, who in Greek mythology was sentenced to support the weight of the heavens on his back. In a similar manner, the child is sentenced to support the entire family.

Typically, the parents are incapable of providing direction, control, or support. The child has to learn to anticipate and deal with recurrent destructive encounters and with the often erratic emotional excesses and demands made by the parents. Often the child is forced to learn how to mediate disputes between the parents, and between parents and other family members, while trying to conceal the disorder of the household from the community. Instead of being sheltered and protected and nourished, these children have to provide shelter, protection, and nourishment for others.

Children in such an environment learn to focus their concern on the welfare of others and to ignore or deny their own personal needs. When these children become adults, they continue to display the same excessive sensitivity to the needs and welfare of others. What they do not learn is how to recognize and address their own needs. In later life, they tend to be chronically depressed and continually anxious for reasons that are not clear to them. Their focus on the needs of others is so extreme that even in therapy, they display an extraordinary concern for the well-being of the therapist. In group therapy settings, Vogel and Savva report, they often intrude to protect and defend individuals they think are not being given fair treatment. These people provide a sad example of what can happen when children are assigned responsibilities beyond those that are reasonable for their age. They also illustrate clearly how coping and life management practices learned within the family setting can permanently shape one's personality.

ADOLESCENT SEXUALITY Some surveys have shown that adolescents and college and university students are actually becoming more conservative about several aspects of sexual behaviour. The shift toward greater restraint among adolescents may reflect the growing—and justified—concern with *sexually transmitted diseases*. Many people in North America are now infected with illnesses such as *chlamydia*, *gonorrhea*, and *herpes*. And many others are carrying HIV, the virus that causes AIDS (Blinn-Pike, 1999).

At Okanagan College, Netting (1992) conducted a study of the sexual behaviour of students and the sexual choices they make. She compared their responses with those of other students she had tested ten years earlier. Netting made a deliberate effort to sample widely and to include night students who were somewhat older. She found that students today make one of three choices with respect to sexual lifestyle: celibacy, monogamy, or free. There was a dramatic *decrease* in the free lifestyle between 1980 and 1990—but not necessarily because students believed that the disease was relevant to them. In fact, one of them said, "I don't worry [about AIDS] because I live in Kelowna." Results were similar in a study done 5000 kilometres to the east, in Montreal, by Maticka-Tyndale (1991).

Studies of another aspect of adolescent sexuality found that rates of single motherhood have increased substantially in recent decades. More and more of these mothers are teenagers, some only thirteen or fourteen years old. Given the pressures placed on these young mothers, such statistics indicate a serious social issue. Prevention is of key importance here (Jaccard, 1992). Particularly critical is that the example of sexual responsibility be set early by members of the immediate family (Hornick et al., 1986).

What are the effects of being a teenage mother? That depends, to an important extent, on the degree to which the pregnant teen is ready, emotionally and cognitively, for the burdens of motherhood. That was the finding of a recent study by Miller and her colleagues (1996). These researchers assessed the readiness of pregnant girls to be parents by testing their knowledge about children and their attitudes on various aspects of parenting: attention, discipline, and so on. Then, three years later, the researchers returned and administered standard measures of cognitive development and language development to the children who were now three years old. Results were clear: Children of the mothers who were less ready to parent showed poorer cognitive and language development and higher levels of depression and anxiety.

The fact that large numbers of adolescents are at risk for psychological or even physical harm is obvious. Yet despite the adverse conditions when they are raised, many of these young people grow up to lead normal lives. How is this possible? This question is being investigated in much ongoing research.

OVERCOMING THE ODDS: ADOLESCENTS IN HIGH-RISK ENVIRONMENTS Perhaps you grew up in an extremely impoverished environment. If not, imagine what it must be like. These are some of the things you would have to face every day: severe economic hardship; schools where the teachers spend their time maintaining order and re-

Protecting Adolescents at Risk
These residents of Iqaluit, Northwest Territories, are protesting the sale of drugs to adolescents in their community. By combating this problem, they hope to make their neighbourhoods safer for teenagers.

sponding to violent behaviour; and adolescents engaged in drug dealing, prostitution, theft, and so on. There seems every reason to predict that you would choose a way of behaving or a lifestyle similar to that you saw around you.

This does often happen. For example, child molesters often have a history of child abuse (Hilton, 1993), as do patients with some personality disorders (Links & Van Reekum, 1993). According to studies at the University of Victoria and the Addiction Research Foundation in Toronto, some children from disadvantaged backgrounds join the ranks of the homeless (McCarthy & Hagan, 1991, 1992; Smart & Walsh, 1993), roaming the streets, malls, arcades, and other public places, panhandling for a living, and becoming involved in theft, burglary, prostitution, and the drug trade. Nevertheless, millions of other young people, despite their serious early disadvantages, grow into productive and well-adapted adults. They do legitimate and honourable work and are responsible spouses and parents.

What determines which outcome will occur? Those who grow up well adjusted in spite of the harsh environment are said to show **resilience in development.** Several protective factors buffer them against conditions around them (e.g., Werner, 1995). First, these young people have an "easy" temperament. This allows them to recruit the help of competent caregivers who contribute, willingly, to their development. In addition, such youngsters are often highly intelligent and have good communication and problem-solving skills. As a result, they get along well with others and form friendships easily. These factors, in turn, help contribute to their resilience.

Resilience in Development: Refers to the capacity of some adolescents raised in harmful environments to somehow rise above these disadvantages and achieve healthy development.

Second, they also benefit from a close bond with at least one competent and emotionally stable person. What is crucial is not the biological relationship between the adolescents and adults in question, but rather the fact that these adults serve as models for the teens and provide them with encouragement for autonomy and initiative.

Finally, resilient youngsters are protected by their schools (Anson et al., 1991) and their community. Favourite teachers are often positive role models for them. Caring neighbours, youth workers, clergy, and others can all give adolescents the boost they need to rise above the poverty, shattered homes, and parental instability that mark their early lives (see Figure 9.3 for a summary of these factors).

Figure 9.3
Factors Contributing to Adolescent Resilience

The factors summarized here have been found to contribute to resilience in development—the ability to develop normally even in potentially harmful environments.

Source: Based on suggestions by Werner, 1995.

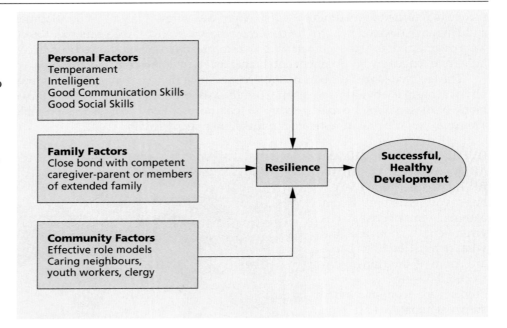

When children and adolescents benefit from such protective factors, they can beat the odds and develop into competent, confident, responsible, and caring adults—good parents and role models for their own children. Clearly, then, providing as many of these protective factors as possible would seem to be a high-priority task for any society that wishes to nurture its children—and so assure its own future stability.

KEY *QUESTIONS*

- What are some of the major threats to the well-being of adolescents at the present time?

- What factors contribute to adolescent resilience—the ability to rise above conditions that threaten healthy development?

Critical Thinking

What factors do you think contribute to rising violence in high schools in Canada? What can be done to reduce such violence?

Adulthood and Aging

If you live for an average number of years, you will spend more than 70 percent of your life as an adult. How will you change during that period? This section will focus on key aspects of physical, cognitive, and social development during adulthood. Before we turn to specific changes, however, here are two different general views.

Contrasting Views of Adult Development

What causes the changes that occur over the adult years? One idea is this: it may be that we change primarily as a function of the passage of time. Small adjustments in response to the everyday events of life may, over time, accumulate. While that idea seems reasonable, there are other perspectives on adult development as well. These are called the *crisis* or *stage approach*, the *life-event* (or *timing of life events*) approach, and the *developmental regulation* approach.

THE CRISIS APPROACH: ERIKSON'S THEORY REVISITED   You have already met the crisis-oriented theory of adult development, proposed by Erikson (1950, 1987). He taught that as people grow older, they confront new combinations of biological drives and societal demands. The biological drives reflect individual growth and physical change, while the societal demands reflect the expectations and requirements that society places on people at different ages. During adulthood, Erikson suggested, we encounter three major crises.

Kim Bartholomew
Simon Fraser University

The first of these is the crisis of *intimacy versus isolation*. During late adolescence and early adulthood, individuals develop the ability to form deep, intimate relationships with others. This does not refer only to sexual intimacy; rather, it is the more general ability to form intense interpersonal attachments (Ratenberg et al., 1993). According to Erikson, people who fail to form such attachments live their lives in isolation—unable to form truly intimate, lasting relationships with others. The development of commitment at this stage determines how we contribute in later life to career, family, and society at large.

In Chapter 8 you learned that some infants develop secure attachments and others do not—depending upon how the world responds to their needs. When those infants become adults, the quality of their early attachments continues to make a difference—in this case to their adult relationships (Hazan & Shaver, 1987; Scharfe & Bartholomew, 1998). Thus, attachment in adulthood has become a contemporary focus of research in lifespan development (Simpson & Rholes, 1998).

What kinds of adult attachments are there? Kim Bartholomew at Simon Fraser University and others have identified four kinds of attachment in young adults depending upon the subjects' attitudes towards themselves (positive or negative), and towards others (positive or negative). As you can see from Figure 9.4 (Bartholomew & Shaver, 1998), the result is secure attachment (positive/positive), and three kinds of insecure attachment (preoccupied, fearful, and dismissive). Those whose adult attachment is *secure* have a positive sense of self-worth and are comfortable with intimacy. Those with *preoccupied*

Figure 9.4
Adult Attachment

The type of attachment adults form depends on their attitudes towards themselves and towards others.

Source: After Bartholomew and Shaver, 1998. Measures of attachment: Do they converge? In J.A. Simpson & W.S. Rholes (Eds.), Attachment theory and close relationships, pp. 25–45. New York: Guilford Press. Reprinted by permission of Guilford Publications.

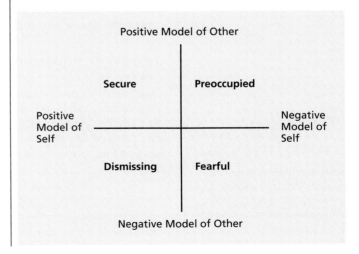

366 **CHAPTER 9** Human Development II: Adolescence, Adulthood, and Aging

attachment think negatively of themselves and positively of others. The *dismissing* kind of attachment is characteristic of those who think positively of themselves but negatively about other people. Those with *fearful* attachment think negatively of themselves and other people. Those who are in the dismissing and the fearful categories avoid intimacy—they are dismissing in order to maintain their own self-esteem, and fearful in order to avoid the pain of anticipated rejection. Bartholomew finds that a positive attitude towards other people is what is essential in establishing mutual-trust relationships with friends and romantic partners.

Are these kinds of attachments characteristic of other cultures? There is confirmation from at least one study, in which the subjects were second-year student teachers at the Hong Kong Institute of Education (Man & Hamid, 1997). These students showed the same four types of attachment and in the same proportions as the Canadian study. Adding to our understanding of adult attachment styles, the Hong Kong subjects provided data about self-esteem and loneliness: secure attachment predicted higher self-esteem and less loneliness, while insecure attachment may be linked to social withdrawal in adults. There are obviously differences between early infancy, during which the child is dependent upon the caregiver, and adult life, during which attachments are more equal; nevertheless, the attachment patterns established in early infancy continue to affect the way in which people think about themselves and the quality of their lives—very likely throughout the lifespan.

Erikson calls the second crisis of adult life the crisis of *generativity versus self-absorption:* the need for individuals to overcome selfish, self-centred concerns and to take an active interest in the next generation. For parents, such activities are focused on their children. After the children have grown, however, and for those who are not parents, the tendency toward generativity may involve being a *mentor* or guide for members of the younger generation, providing help and guidance to many young people—students, younger co-workers, nieces, nephews, and so on. Individuals who successfully resolve this crisis discover new meaning in life. People who do not resolve this crisis become absorbed in their own lives and deprive themselves of important growth and satisfaction.

Erikson called the last crisis of adult development *integrity versus despair.* As people reach the last decades of life, it is natural for them to look back and ask, "Did my being here really matter?" This is the "human quest for meaning," according to Wong (1998). If they feel that they have reached many of their goals and have made positive contributions to others and to society, they attain a sense of *integrity.* Otherwise, they may experience intense feelings of *despair.* Successful resolution of this final crisis can have important effects on how individuals come to terms with their own mortality and with the inevitable fact of death.

In sum, according to Erikson and to others who view adult development in terms of discrete phases or stages, lifespan development is a series of crises (or struggles) we face as we mature and grow older. It is the way we deal with each of these that determines the course of our lives from that point on (Quirouette & Pushkar, 1999).

LIFE-EVENT MODELS: THE SOCIAL CLOCK A different perspective on adult development is offered by the *life-events* or *timing-of-life-events* model. This approach suggests that people change and develop in response to specific life events, which may or may not be crises. During childhood and even adolescence, such theories acknowledge, development occurs in accordance with a built-in *biological clock* that sets the pace of development. During our adult years, however, change occurs in response to important life events—one of which of course is graduation. Development then becomes tied much more closely to a *social clock* than to a biological one.

All societies have what Neugarten (1987) describes as **social age clocks**—internalized calendars telling us when certain events should occur in our lives and what we should be doing at certain ages. The points on the social clock include a number of other transitions: marriage, parenthood, retirement, and so on. Most people expect certain life events to occur at specific times. For example, in Canada,

Social Age Clocks: Internalized calendars that tell us when certain events should occur in our lives and what we should be doing at certain ages.

graduation from university and leaving home are both expected to happen when people are in their twenties; the death of one's parents (Gee, 1991) is expected to come much later, as is grandparenthood.

Research results support both of these ideas. On the one hand, some researchers find that the timing of life events is very important to development (Neugarten, 1987). Several life-events models divide the marks on the social clock into two categories: events that occur at the "right time" and so are expected, or *normative*, and those that are unexpected or *nonnormative* (Neugarten, 1979, 1987). Normative events include graduation from school, marriage, parenthood during the early adult years, and retirement in later life. Nonnormative events include divorce, traumatic accidents, the sudden death of loved ones, and the unexpected loss of a long-term job or position. Normative events, although of crucial importance, are generally less stressful and less disruptive. If events occur when they are unexpected—for example, the death of a spouse when a couple is quite young—the stress associated with such life events can be greatly magnified.

On the other hand, some developmental psychologists maintain that the social clock is really a number of different clocks (Schroots & Birren, 1990), which can vary greatly depending on our occupation, socioeconomic status, and when and where we live. For instance, Olympic gymnasts are considered "old" at sixteen or seventeen; professional baseball players aren't viewed as "old" until they are over thirty or even thirty-five. People nowadays often enter the labour force at a later age. University graduates tend to get married and have children several years later than others (Lemme, 1999). Thus, the social context in which we live determines when various events are supposed to occur in our lives; these do not take place solely on the basis of our chronological age or in response to the orderly unfolding of specific stages.

Interestingly, most people seem to feel younger as they grow older. For example, when asked to indicate how old they feel, both men and women above the age of twenty-five report feeling younger they actually are. And this gap widens with the passing years (Montepare & Lachman, 1989), as Figure 9.5 illustrates. In a sense, then, in many societies chronological age matters less and less. As a consequence, adult development is more a function of social definitions, perceptions, and beliefs than it is of specific, age-linked stages.

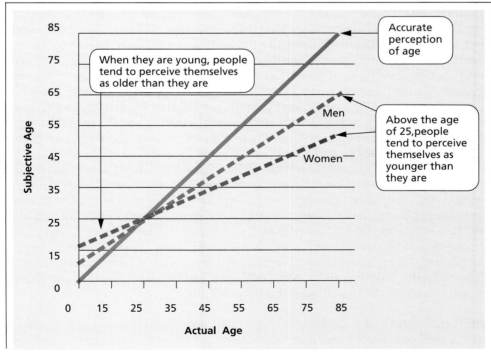

Figure 9.5
Subjective Age: Feeling Younger Than We Are

Until they are about twenty-five, most people report perceiving themselves as older than they are. Above this age, however, most report that they perceive themselves as feeling *younger* than they actually are.

Source: Based on data from Montepart and Lachtman, 1989.

DEVELOPMENTAL REGULATION: ADJUSTING OUR GOALS AS WE AGE
A third approach to adult development, proposed very recently (Heckhousen, 1997, 1999), focuses on the ways in which individuals regulate their own lives, strive for developmental growth, and avoid a developmental decline during the adult years. Here is the basic idea. As they grow older, people find that some goals are no longer attainable. As a result, they adjust, matching their goals to the changing realities of adult life. For example, as they grow older, individuals often recognize that certain career objectives are less and less likely to be met, so they tend to give those up as unrealistic. Similarly, as they age, many people shift from focusing on gains in some areas of life—for example, work and family—to minimizing losses in these areas. Research results emphasize the importance of each individuals' active efforts to regulate their own development and come to terms with the changing realities of life in the later decades of their lives (Heckhausen, 1997).

In sum, contrasting perspectives about development during our adult years hold, respectively, that such change occurs (1) in response to a series of internal conflicts or crises, (2) in response to specific life events and timing of these events, or (3) as a result of active efforts to regulate one's own development. While all these views provide insights into the nature of adult development, many psychologists question the idea that all human beings pass through a discrete series of stages. For this reason, many prefer or emphasize either a life-event approach or an approach emphasizing developmental regulation. However, we do seem to be concerned with different challenges at different points in our lives; so Erikson's approach, too, offers insights into change during our adult years.

Physical Change during Our Adult Years

Looking through a family photo album—one that spans several decades—can be a very revealing experience. There, with youthful faces that you may not recognize immediately, are your grandparents, parents, aunts, and uncles. When you compare their appearance in the photos with their appearance today, you can easily see the physical changes that happen during the adult years.

PHYSICAL CHANGE DURING EARLY ADULTHOOD   Physical growth is usually complete by the time people leave their teens; however, for some parts of the body, the aging process actually begins long before that time. For example, the lenses in our eyes begin to lose their flexibility by the time we are only twelve or thirteen years old; and for some people, the tissues supporting the teeth may begin to recede even before they have attained full physical maturity. So physical aging, like growth, is a continuous process that starts early. Changes in the brain as a result of aging also occur. As we get older, the brain gets slightly smaller, and so do some brain structures. For example, between the ages of twenty and seventy, the corpus callosum (the bridge between the two hemispheres) shrinks slightly in size, particularly in men (Witelson, 1991).

Muscular strength, reaction time, sensory acuity, and heart action and output are all at or near their peak through the mid-twenties. They then decline slowly—usually imperceptibly—through the mid-thirties. Many members of both sexes gain weight during early adulthood, and some men undergo significant hair loss. Balding is now thought to be associated with a gene that is passed on from parents to children. When the particular gene is identified, it may be possible for scientists to develop a drug that blocks its action—for those men who do not understand how attractive balding can be. Note, however, that by and large, physical change is both slow and minimal during this period of life.

PHYSICAL CHANGES DURING MID-LIFE   By their forties, most people are aware that age-related changes are occurring within their bodies. *Cardiac output*, the amount of blood pumped by the heart, decreases noticeably, and the walls of the large arteries lose some flexibility. As a result, less oxygen can be delivered to working muscles within a given period of time. Those who exercise regularly become aware of some decline in this respect—they cannot do quite as much as they once could. The performance of other major organ systems also declines—for example, there are difficulties with the digestion of food. Other changes are readily visible when middle-aged people look in the mirror: thinning and greying hair, bulges and wrinkles in place of the sleek torso and smooth skin of youth. There are huge individual differences in the rate at which such changes occur, however. Thus, while some forty- and fifty-year-olds closely match common stereotypes concerning middle age, most retain much of their youthful appearance and vigour during this period of life.

Among the most dramatic changes occurring during middle adulthood is the **climacteric**—a period of several years during which the functioning of the reproductive system changes greatly, along with various aspects of sexual maturity. For men, the climacteric involves reduced secretion of testosterone and reduced functioning of the *prostate gland,* which may become enlarged and cause interference in sexual functions and urination. Men may experience reduced sexual drive at this time of life, but although sperm production decreases, many are still capable of fathering children.

For women, there is **menopause**—the cessation of the menstrual cycle—in their late forties or early fifties. During menopause the ovaries stop producing the hormone estrogen, and many changes in the reproductive system occur: thinning of the vaginal walls, reduced secretion of the fluids that lubricate the vagina, and so on. Since females no longer release ova, natural pregnancy no longer occurs.

The rate of aging is strongly influenced by individual lifestyle (Avis, 1999). Physical exercise, personal nutrition, and effective management of stress may be better predictors of physical vigour and health than biological age (Roskie, 1987). In other words, a fifty-year-old who exercises regularly, eats a balanced diet, avoids excessive stress, and doesn't smoke may show higher performance on a wide range of tests of physical fitness than a twenty-five-year-old who gets no exercise, lives on fast food, smokes heavily, and burns the candle at both ends.

That is because we are not naturally couch potatoes. The human body evolved to be used, to move us around—so that we could search for food and safety. Our cells, bones, and muscles rely for their health on the biological processes that occur when we are active. Although most Canadians know that exercise is good for them (studies confirm this to be the case up to the age of ninety-six), most do not act on that knowledge. However, inactivity does increase the likelihood of health problems at all ages, and "participaction" reduces it. Moreover, elderly people who engage in cognitively demanding activities not only do better on tests of cognitive ability, but also report better physical health (Hultsch et al., 1993). Clearly, the best advice for maintaining body and brain function over the whole lifespan continues to be "Use it or lose it."

For that reason, a number of Canadian studies have looked for ways to improve exercise participation rates among elderly adults (e.g., Cousins-Obrien, 1996). The key may be to learn which type of motivation—social reinforcement, for example, or maintenance of self-esteem—will work best (Pelletier et al., 1995).

PHYSICAL CHANGES IN LATER LIFE Average lifespan in many countries is increasing (see Figure 9.6). In Canada, for example, the proportion of the population sixty-five or older was 4 or 5 percent in 1900; it is now about 12 or 13 percent, and it will rise to almost 20 percent when the "baby boom" generation born during the 1950s and 1960s turns sixty-five. This trend gives sharp focus to the question of physical changes during the closing decades of life, for the nature and magnitude of these changes have important implications for Canada's health care system and, therefore, for the national economy as well.

Climacteric: A period during which the functioning of the reproductive system, and various aspects of sexual activity, change greatly.

Menopause: Cessation of the menstrual cycle.

Figure 9.6
The Greying of the World's Population

As shown here, the proportion of the population over age sixty-five will increase considerably in many countries in the coming decades.

Source: Based on data from the U.S. Senate Special Committee on Aging, 1991.

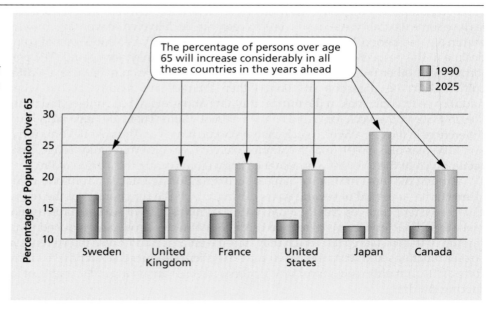

The percentage of persons over age 65 will increase considerably in all these countries in the years ahead

- 1990
- 2025

What do we know from systematic research about physical changes in later life? First, the idea that in later life people are generally frail, in poor health, and unable to take care of themselves is *false*. People in their sixties, seventies, and even eighties report excellent or good health and are not much more likely than middle-aged people to suffer from *chronic illnesses*—ones that are long-term, progressive, and incurable. Further, even in their seventies and eighties, many elderly people do not receive hospital care during any given year (Thomas, 1992). There are indeed declines in physical functions and health as people age, but these are not nearly as prevalent or pronounced as our stereotypes of old age would suggest.

One additional—and important—point: While many physical changes do occur with increasing age, it is crucial to distinguish between **primary aging**—changes caused by the passage of time and, perhaps, inherited biological factors—and **secondary aging**—changes due to disease and disuse or abuse of our bodies with substances like alcohol (Adlaf & Smart, 1995). Bearing this in mind, let's briefly examine some of the physical changes that are a result of primary aging.

There are several kinds of decrements in *sensory abilities*. As people age, and more so beyond mid-life, they gradually decline with respect to vision, hearing, smell, taste, and other senses. *Visual acuity*, as measured by the ability to read letters on a standard eye examination chart, drops off sharply after age seventy; many people experience these changes as slower *dark adaptation* and reduced ability to notice moving targets, such as cars on a highway (Long & Crambert, 1990). Cooper and colleagues (1993) tested adults aged twenty to eighty-nine for discrimination of colour (saturation, hue, and brightness). They found changes after age sixty, and suggested that this information be used when designing environments for senior citizens. Moreover, training in sensory discrimination may be helpful (Trudeau et al., 1990).

Similarly, *auditory sensitivity* decreases with age, especially among people who have worked in noisy environments (Corso, 1977). Declines also occur in ability to identify specific tastes and aromas, although this does not become noticeable until after seventy-five (Spence, 1989).

There is also a gradual slowing of responses in general. For example, *reaction time* increases with age (Spirduso & Macrae, 1990). Changes in reaction time have important practical implications, especially with respect to driving, for which good vision and normal reaction times are essential. Kline and colleagues (1992) tested drivers of various ages on five kinds of visual problems: unexpected vehicles, speed of vehicles, reading of signs, dim displays, and windshield difficulties. In

Primary Aging: Aging due to the passage of time and, to some extent, inherited biological factors.

Secondary Aging: Aging due to the effects of disease, disuse, or abuse of the body.

each case, age was a factor in performance. However, there were wide individual differences. A particular seventy-year-old may still respond more quickly than a particular thirty-year-old.

The perceptions younger and older drivers have of each other was the focus of a study by Nelson and colleagues (1992). They had younger drivers (about nineteen years old) and older drivers (about sixty-six years old) rate each other on driving attitudes, driving courtesy and discourtesy, and safe and unsafe driving. The two age groups were consistent in their views of the younger drivers, and differed in their evaluations of older ones. Younger drivers were rated as overly aggressive, unsafe, and discourteous by both age groups. Older people rated drivers in their own age group as courteous, cautious, and aware of their limitations. However, younger drivers rated older ones as too cautious, too slow, and likely to cause accidents.

The bottom line here is that some people in their seventies and eighties are a menace on the roads, but many are safe and competent drivers. For example, in his research, Harrell (1992) has found that drivers over the age of sixty-five are just as likely to stop for a pedestrian at a city crosswalk as younger ones. Perhaps, then, for drivers above age seventy or seventy-five who wish to renew their licenses, there might be a test of visual acuity, hearing, reaction time, and the ability to detect motion to identify those who are fully capable of safe driving. Then, if advisable, older drivers might be certified only for daytime driving. In that way, a balance would be struck between the rights of older drivers and the interests of safety.

K E Y QUESTIONS

- How do stage theories such as Erikson's and life-event theories explain the changes we experience during our adult years?

- At what age are we most influenced by the events occurring in our society?

- What physical changes do men and women experience during early and middle adulthood?

- What physical changes occur in later life?

Cognitive Change during Adulthood

What about *cognition*? Do adults change in this respect as well? And if so, how? Do more experience, more practice, and a richer knowledge base lead to enhanced or reduced or different cognitive performance as we age? These are the findings that begin to answer those questions.

AGING AND MEMORY   The variety of ways of investigating aging and memory is remarkable. Data are provided by *clinical cases* in which elderly patients show memory loss as a symptom; and, of course, there are numerous *experimental approaches* to the study of human memory (Webster & Cappeliez, 1993). Many *animal studies* look into the brain structures involved in different kinds of memory (e.g., Winocur, 1992); others even examine the effects of radiation in outer space on the aging of the brain and on memory (Joseph, 1992).

First, let's consider the impact of aging on different memory systems (e.g., Hay & Jacoby, 1999). Research on *working memory* indicates that older people are able to retain just as much information in this limited-capacity system as younger people (Poon & Fozard, 1980). However, when they must perform several working-memory tasks in a row, older people do not perform as well as younger ones (e.g., Shimamura & Jurica, 1994). That may be because, as we grow older, our ability to deal with proactive interference declines.

Turning to *long-term memory*, in one set of studies (Shimamura et al., 1996), researchers compared the memories of university professors in three age groups (age group averages were 38.4 years, 52.2 years, and 64.7 years) with undergraduate students and a group of "standard" older persons (average age 66.5 years)—on several memory tasks. When they had to remember meaningful information even if they had heard it only once, there were no differences among the three groups of professors—young, middle-aged, and older. In contrast, for the standard groups, older participants did not perform as well as young ones did. One interpretation of these data might be that memory will remain good for individuals who continue to exercise their cognitive processes in their later years.

A very recent study reported the word and story recall of young-old (fifty-five to seventy) and old-old (seventy-one to eighty-six) participants in the Victoria Longitudinal Study. The study concluded that the overall qualitative performance—the way in which long-term recall was organized, for example—was maintained into later life (Brent et al., 1999).

What about memory for yet more meaningful information—memory in everyday life? Here, older people often perform as well as younger ones (May et al., 1993). For example, in one revealing study, Sinnott (1986) asked individuals to recall information in *intentional memory*—that is, information that was meaningful to them and that they *wanted* to remember. This included the date of their next appointment, the hours during which the hospital cafeteria served dinner, and so on. In addition, participants were asked to recall information in *incidental memory*—that is, information that was less meaningful to them and that they had not intended to remember, such as the objects that had been on the table while they worked on various tasks. In recalling information that was meaningful to them and that they intended to remember, older people did just as well as younger ones.

What do we know about age and memory for locations? In one of two experiments, Uttl and Graf (1993) used Science World in Vancouver for an experiment on *spatial memory*. In their second experiment, these researchers set up an office environment for the same purpose. Twenty-two objects were placed at various typical locations in the office: for example, a plant, a stapler, and a telephone book. Subjects performed a series of secretarial-type tasks in the office and then their memory for the objects was tested in two ways. In one test, they viewed a series of photos of the objects and labelled their location on a map of the office. In another test, the subjects actually put the object back where it had been in the office where they had worked. The subjects were men and women aged from twenty-one to eighty-five years.

What was found in these studies? Until the sixth decade of life, subjects of different ages were equally able to recall location. After that, the data showed an age-related decline in spatial memory. Uttl and Graf (p. 272) interpreted these changes after age sixty to be processing strategy—that is, change in brain "software," rather than damage to the brain structure or "hardware" required to recall spatial location.

Possibly influential on memory performance are the beliefs we hold about how memory changes with age (Hultsch et al., 1987; Ryan, 1992; Ryan & See, 1993). Both younger and older adults have more positive opinions about memory in young people than about memory in older people. How these beliefs interact with performance is an important question, because it is possible that memory performance could change as a consequence of altered *beliefs about memory*.

For several biological reasons, as people get older, they shift more and more toward being most alert and active early in the day. In one study of circadian rhythms and memory for two age groups by May, Hasher, and Stoltzfus (1993), older adults (ages sixty-six to seventy-eight) and young adults (ages eighteen to twenty) performed a recognition task. Testing occurred early in the day at eight or nine a.m., or later in the day, at four or five p.m. As you can see in Figure 9.7, young adults performed significantly better than older ones during the afternoon, but not in the morning. These findings indicate that research designed to investigate memory should take age and circadian rhythms into account.

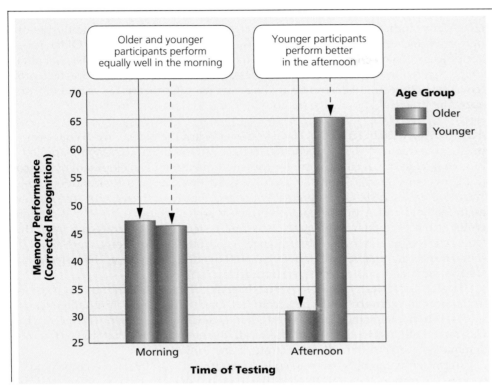

Figure 9.7
Circadian Rhythms and the Effects of Age on Memory

When tested in the morning—a time when they are operating at peak efficiency—people in their sixties and seventies performed as well as much younger people. However, when tested in the afternoon, older people were outperformed by younger ones. These findings demonstrate the importance of taking circadian rhythms into account when investigating the impact of aging on memory.

Source: Based on data from May et al., 1993.

There are other changes in the brain. As we age, total brain weight decreases—5 percent by age seventy, 10 percent by age eighty, and 20 percent by age ninety (Wisniewski & Terry, 1976). Further, the frontal lobes, a region with a key role in working memory, has a greater loss of neurons (Parkin & Walter, 1992; Parkin et al., 1999), as does the hippocampus. There are gender-related differences also. Women seem to experience smaller changes than males in brain structure (e.g., Gur et al., 1991). This may mean that female hormones slow down age-related changes in women's brains as they age.

AGING AND VERBOSITY You may have noticed that some older individuals make long verbal speeches that seem not quite to the point. *Verbosity* is the term Arbuckle and Gold gave to the off-target stream of speech one sometimes finds in elderly people. For example, one longitudinal study (Gold & Arbuckle, 1995) tested 175 subjects, sixty-five years and older. Verbosity was evaluated at the beginning and the end of a fifteen-month period, and results showed that there are age-related increases. Why does this occur? Perhaps there is an age-related decline in the ability to ignore thoughts that interfere with the meaningful flow of speech (Arbuckle & Gold, 1993). In another study, researchers found that older adults produced more off-topic speech when they were talking about their past experiences, but not when they were describing pictures (James et al., 1998). These results were taken to mean that conciseness is not a goal for older adults when they are telling a personal story.

AGING AND MIND WANDERING Another feature of cognitive behaviour that we sometimes attribute to aging is mind wandering. Are older folks more likely to let irrelevant information interfere with their current cognitive tasks? In their study of aging and mind wandering, Einstein and McDaniel (1997) presented lists of words to twenty-four younger and twenty-four older individuals. Occasionally, at unpredictable intervals, the presentation stopped, and subjects were asked to report the last item they saw. Comparing these two age groups, these researchers found that there was more mind wandering in general after longer intervals, but that there was no evidence of age differences in mind wandering.

Tannis Y. Arbuckle-Maag
Concordia University

Delores (Gold) Pushkar
Concordia University

AGING AND PROBLEM SOLVING Does the ability to solve problems change with age? Many studies indicate that, in general, people in their twenties and thirties out-perform middle-aged and older people (Reese & Rodeheaver, 1985). Older people adopt less efficient problem-solving strategies—in *some* cases (Denney & Palmer, 1981). Again, these differences in strategies do *not* hold true for more practical problems that people might encounter in their own lives (Cornelius & Caspi, 1987) or in applying practical knowledge (Labouvie-Vief & Hakim-Larson, 1989).

AGING AND INTELLIGENCE Have you ever heard the old saying "What goes up must come down"? Many psychologists once assumed that this saying applied to human *intelligence*. At the Centre for Research in Human Development at Concordia University, Tannis Arbuckle, Dolores Gold Pushkar, and their students (e.g., Arbuckle et al., 1998; Gold et al., 1995) tested that hypothesis with this research method: Gold and Arbuckle contacted men who had been World War II army recruits at the time their intelligence was first tested. About forty years later, they were retested, in either English or French. Their intelligence scores were about the same, indicating that verbal, non-verbal, and overall intelligence—as tested in this study—remained stable over those decades.

In another series of studies (Arbuckle et al., 1992), it was found that most age differences in memory could be accounted for by differences in intelligence test scores. When intelligence scores were equated statistically, the only difference that was directly linked to age was in free recall, the memory task that makes the most demands on the individual's own strategy and initiative.

In earlier research, Schaie and colleagues (1986, 1990, 1993) tested thousands of people, ranging in age from twenty-five to eighty-one, at seven-year intervals. As shown in Figure 9.8, various components of intelligence (as measured by the Primary Mental Abilities Test, a standard test of intelligence) remain stable through-

Figure 9.8
Evidence for the Relative Stability of Intelligence across the Lifespan

Longitudinal research indicates that intelligence is stable across virtually the entire lifespan. Significant declines in components of intelligence measured by standardized tests of intelligence do not occur for most people until they are well into their seventies. (Scores for inductive reasoning, one important component of intelligence, are shown here.)

Source: Based on data from Schaie, 1993.

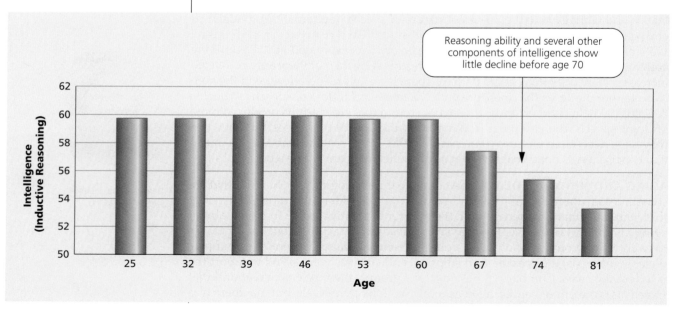

Reasoning ability and several other components of intelligence show little decline before age 70

out adult life. A reliable average decline appears only when people are in their seventies. Further, even at age eighty-one, fewer than half of the people show any
changes over the preceding seven years. Only on speed of reasoning does there appear to be a consistent decline in performance. Since that may reflect increased reaction time, there is little if any indication of a general decrease in intelligence with age.

Such longitudinal findings may not show the whole story because standardized intelligence tests may not capture all different components of adult intelligence. The distinction between crystallized intelligence and fluid intelligence is
especially relevant here. As you will find in Chapter 11, *crystallized intelligence* refers
to the aspects of intelligence that draw on previously learned information to make
decisions or solve problems. Classroom tests, vocabulary tests, and many social situations require crystallized intelligence. In contrast, *fluid intelligence* includes the
abilities to form concepts, to reason, and to identify similarities. Research shows
that fluid intelligence increases into the early twenties and then gradually declines.
In contrast, crystallized intelligence increases across the lifespan (Lerner, 1990;
Willis & Nesselroade, 1990).

AGING AND WISDOM   Many cultures assume that as people grow older, they
gain in *wisdom*—in insight and judgment about practical matters and life problems.
Several studies have used the following method to study the development of wisdom. Researchers present young and older adults with complex problems and ask
them to solve these *out loud*. Participants' reasoning is then assessed for wisdom
(Thomas, 1992) by external judges. From this cross-sectional research, it appears
that older people offer wiser solutions—when the problems involve complex or unusual situations (Smith & Baltes, 1990).

AGING AND CREATIVITY   Finally, does *creativity* change with age? To answer this
question, some researchers focus on the age at which scientists, authors, poets,
painters, and architects make their most creative contributions (e.g., Abra, 1989;
Dudek & Hall, 1991; Lehman, 1953; Simonton, 1990): mathematicians and physi-
cists—in their twenties or thirties; historians, philosophers, and psychologists—in
their forties and fifties (Horner et al., 1986). Thus far, however, the conclusion as to
whether creativity changes with age depends upon the definition and the kind of
measurement applied.

Where does all this leave us? An overall pattern of evidence from both longitudinal and cross-sectional studies suggests that, in general, few intellectual abilities decline sharply with age. Some do decrease—especially those that rely on
speed of responding—but some aspects of intelligence may actually increase with
age as individuals gain experience (e.g., Sternberg et al., 1995). Others remain quite
stable over many years; for example, there may be no decline in practical intelligence—the ability to solve everyday problems.

KEY *QUESTIONS*

▨ What changes in memory occur as we age?

▨ How do intelligence and creativity change over the lifespan?

Critical Thinking

Does the fact that crystallized intelligence increases throughout life mean
we should trust important decisions to
older, more experienced people or not?
Explain your thinking on this question.

Social Changes in Adult Life

Next we will look at some *major events* of adult life, and how we are affected by them.

Friends for Life: The Convoy Model

One model of friendship during the adult years suggests that beyond mid-life, we reduce the size of our social networks to about ten people with whom we are especially close. We then maintain social contacts with these people throughout the remainder of our lives—like a convoy of ships crossing the ocean together.

FRIENDSHIPS: THE CONVOY MODEL The reasons we form friendships and maintain them are clear: Humans have a strong need to *affiliate*—to interact in positive ways with others. We gain much help, information, and social support from such relationships, and that continues throughout the lifespan. Early in our adult years, we interact with a large number of people and have many casual friends. As we enter our middle years, we reduce the size of our social networks—to about ten people on average. Then we tend to maintain these close ties, moving together through the years. This is the **convoy model** of adult social networks (Kahn & Antonucci, 1980).

Why do we gradually reduce the number of friends we have? At this time of life, there is a growing realization that time is limited and that we should, therefore, invest most of our effort in a relatively small number of social partners. Recent findings indicate that the more time is perceived as limited, the greater the preference of all persons—young and old—for limiting interactions to close friends or relatives (e.g., Carstensen et al., 1999; Fung et al., 2000).

EMOTIONAL EXPERIENCES Do we feel emotions less intensely as we age? Growing evidence suggests that this is not the case. Older adults report emotional experiences as rich and intense as younger ones, and they show facial expressions and patterns of physiological reactions when experiencing specific emotions that are virtually identical to those of younger adults (e.g., Levenson et al., 1991). Here is a difference, however. While older individuals report positive emotions such as happiness and joy just as frequently as younger people, they report negative emotional experiences such as anger or sorrow less frequently (Carstensen et al., 1998). Further, older persons report greater control over their emotions and greater stability of mood than younger persons.

DIVORCE Clearly, divorce is a major life event—and one that is very common. Divorce rates are at historically high levels. Between one-third and one-half of all first marriages end in divorce. Among the feelings most often experienced by divorced people are these: *anger*—relating to the conflict, the bitterness leading up to and surrounding the divorce, and the feelings of unfair treatment afterwards; *depression*—from the loss of contact with children and other family members, from the financial consequences of divorce, and from the loneliness that often follows; and *disequilibrium*— feelings of being lost, aimless, and adrift, resulting from physical relocation, severe disruption of established routines, and the many other changes that take place. Additional emotional experiences are insecurity, disillusionment, and helplessness (Forest, 1992). It is also true that some divorced people experience feelings of *relief* because the intense conflict is behind them and they perceive an opportunity to begin a new, perhaps better, life (Tschann et al., 1989).

A new suggestion is that *genetic factors* may play a role in divorce (e.g., Jocklin et al., 1996). Researchers compared the divorce rates of hundreds of monozygotic (identical) and dizygotic (nonidentical) twins whose parents were or were not divorced. If monozygotic twins were more likely to both divorce than dizygotic twins, that would be evidence for a genetic contribution to divorce. As shown in Figure 9.9, that is precisely what was found. Moreover, divorce was more likely if either the twins' own parents or their spouses' parents had been divorced.

Convoy Model: A model of social networks suggesting that from mid-life on, we tend to maintain close relationships with only a small number of people.

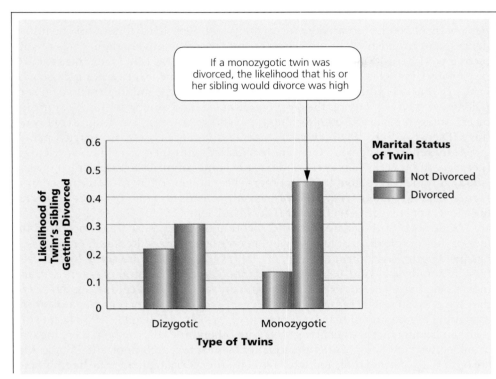

Figure 9.9
Evidence for the Role of Genetic Factors in Divorce

If a monozygotic twin was divorced, the likelihood that his or her twin would also be divorced was higher than if a dizygotic twin was divorced. These and other findings offer support for the view that genetic factors play some role in divorce, presumably through their influence on various aspects of personality.

Source: Based on findings from McGue and Lykken, 1992.

Is risk for divorce inherited? How could genetic factors influence divorce? McGue and Lykken (1992) suggest that people whose parents are divorced may inherit *biologically based personality characteristics* that make it difficult for them to maintain long-term relationships. These specific characteristics remain to be identified.

UNEMPLOYMENT Work is central to our lives. When asked, "Who are you?" a large proportion of employed adults reply in terms of their job or occupation (Greenberg & Baron, 1993). Thus, it is not surprising that losing a job—or even the prospect of losing a job—is considered a crisis in adult life (Konovsky & Brockner, 1993). In Canada, many of the new unemployed are men in their forties and fifties, and because being employed is so central to their self-concept, and their self-esteem, they are crushed when their employment is terminated. In particular, they feel they no longer "matter" (Amundson, 1993) and they may become more susceptible to disease as the stress affects their immune systems.

As you may know from personal experience, there are equally negative effects on young adults who find themselves unemployed or underemployed (Empsom-Warner & Krahn, 1992). Indeed, full-time employment is the usual exit from adolescence and entrance to full adult status (Hagan & Wheaton, 1993). Perhaps the negative effects of being unemployed are most vividly illustrated by longitudinal research conducted in Australia. Hundreds of students between fifteen and seventeen were followed for eight years after graduation (Winefield & Tiggemann, 1991). During this time, the participants completed questionnaires designed to measure their self-esteem, feelings of depression, negative affect, and general health. They also reported on whether they were employed and recorded their level of satisfaction with their current work. The results were clear: Unemployed youths reported lower self-esteem, greater depression, more negative affect, and poorer personal health than those who were employed; this was especially true when unemployed participants were compared with employed people who were satisfied with the work they had found.

See **Making Psychology Part of Your Life** on page 384 for a look at how you can prepare for the job market you will face after graduation.

SUBJECTIVE WELL-BEING In recent studies (e.g., Diener et al., 1999) about 80 percent of all people reported being satisfied with their lives: their work, health, finances, and friendships. In other words, they report relatively high levels of **subjective well-being** (Kahneman, Diener & Schwarz, 1999). Moreover, this seems to be true over the world, across age groups, across income levels, among those who have just the necessities of life, among relatively attractive and unattractive persons (Diener et al., 1995), among the severely disabled, and among various historically disadvantaged racial and ethnic groups, and shows no decline with age in many nations (Diener & Suh, 1998). Of course, some differences do exist: married people generally report being somewhat more satisfied with their lives than single ones (Lee, Seccombe, & Shehan,1991), and those in some countries report being more satisfied with their lives than those in others (Veenhoven, 1993). As you can see from Figure 9.10, no matter what kind of measure was used, large majorities reported high levels of subjective well-being (Diener & Diener, 1996).

While such findings are certainly encouraging, they raise this concern: In the face of the complexities of life, why are people so satisfied? Research on this issue has just begun, so no firm answers are yet available. Here are some hypotheses. First, generally speaking, being in a good mood is adaptive, promotes survival, and makes negative events or experiences stand out; and these, of course, are the events that we need to notice to protect ourselves. Second, for some people, a pleasant, easygoing temperament may be genetic (e.g., Lykken & Tellegen, 1996). Because of their temperament, they get along well with others, and this can help pave the way to subjective well-being. Other personality factors, too, are important. People who are optimistic, extraverted, and who avoid undue worrying tend to be happier than those who are pessimistic, introverted, and prone to worry excessively (e.g., DeNeve & Cooper, 1998). Third, feeling happy may be motivating. When people are in a relatively positive state, they approach and explore new situations and stimuli, and seek out new contacts with others. No doubt you know yourself that, on days when you are feeling "down," everything seems to be more of an effort.

A fourth factor involves having goals, and the resources—personal, economic, and otherwise—needed to reach them. Many studies indicate that people who have concrete goals, especially goals that they have a realistic chance of reaching, and who feel (realistically or otherwise) that they are making progress toward these, are happier than persons lacking in such goals (Cantor & Sanderson, in press). Finally, external conditions over which individuals have varying degrees of influence also play a role in personal happiness. In general, married people tend to

Subjective Well-Being: Personal happiness.

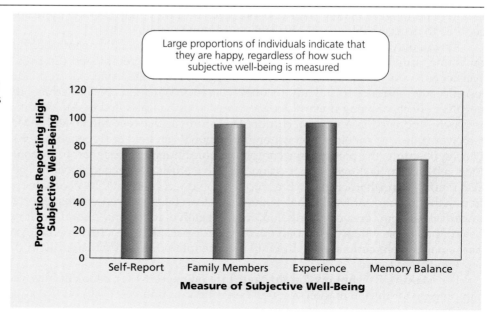

Figure 9.10
Who Is Happy? Most People, It Appears

No matter what kind of measure is used, most people report fairly high levels of personal happiness or subjective well-being.

Source: Based on data from Diener and Diener, 1996.

Large proportions of individuals indicate that they are happy, regardless of how such subjective well-being is measured be happier than single people—although this varies with how their particular culture views marriage (Diener, Gohm, Suh, & Oishi, 1998), and people who are satisfied with their jobs and careers tend to be happier than those who are not (e.g., Weiss & Cropanzano, 1996).

Perhaps much more surprising are some negative findings. For instance, contrary to widespread beliefs, wealthy people are not significantly happier than those who are less wealthy (e.g., Clark & Oswald, 1994). Similarly, as you can see in Figure 9.11, personal happiness does not decline with age, despite the fact that income and the proportion who are married drop as people grow older.

Figure 9.11
Subjective Well-Being and Age

Contrary to what you might expect, subjective well-being does *not* decline with age, despite the fact that income and other resources do tend to decline beyond mid-life.

Source: Based on data from Diener and Suh, 1998.

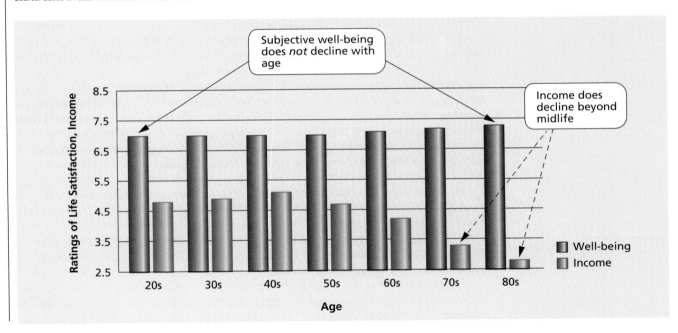

Finally, there appear to be no substantial sex differences in terms of personal happiness (e.g., White, 1992). This is true despite the fact that women seem to experience wider swings in mood than men (e.g., Nolen-Hoeksema & Rusting, 2000). Apparently, their "lows" are lower than those experienced by men but their "highs" are also higher, and, overall, the two sexes do not differ significantly in subjective well-being (Diener et al., 1999).

In summary, although a number of factors influence personal happiness, most adults report relatively high levels of subjective well-being and are quite satisfied with their lives. Despite the many negative events that occur during our adult years, therefore, we tend to retain a degree of optimism and a positive outlook on life. So the poet Theodosia Garrison was correct about most of us when she wrote: "The hardest habit of all to break is the terrible habit of happiness."

K E Y *QUESTIONS*

■ What are the effects of unemployment on the psychological and physical health of persons who experience this crisis?

Aging, Death, and Bereavement

Since ancient times, human beings have searched for the "Fountain of Youth"—some means of staying young and living indefinitely. But alas, while life and health may be prolonged through proper diet, exercise, and control of stress, there appears to be no way to live forever. The upper limit may be in the range of 120 years. Therefore, the challenge for elderly Canadians is "successful aging" (Butt & Beiser, 1987). In this section, we'll consider three questions about the conclusion of life: (1) What, specifically, are the causes of aging and death? (2) How do terminally ill people react to their own impending death? (3) How do people cope with the loss of their loved ones?

Theories of Aging

Many different views about the causes of aging have been proposed, but most fall into two categroies: *stochastic* or *wear-and-tear theories* and *genetic theories.*

STOCHASTIC THEORIES **Stochastic theories of aging** (also known as wear-and-tear theories) suggest that we grow old because various organs of our bodies, or the cells of which they are composed, wear out. One such theory emphasizes the role of *free radicals*—atoms that are unstable because they have lost electrons. The thinking here is that these highly unstable particles are continuously produced by metabolism; and once formed, they react with other molecules in cells, producing damage. When this damage affects DNA, free radicals may interfere with cell maintenance and repair. The free-radicals theory proposes that this damage accumulates over time and results in an age-related decline in biological function associated with aging. Other wear-and-tear theories focus on different mechanisms, but the outcome—cumulative damage to cells and organs—is similar.

In one theory, the changes that brain cells undergo over time are likened to a kind of biological "rust" (Janzen et al., 1991). Another stochastic theory stresses the effects of damage to our DNA—damage produced either because cell division somehow "goes wrong," or by external causes such as viruses or various toxins in the environment. As the number of cells damaged in this way increases, we age and our internal systems gradually decline.

Indirect evidence for wear-and-tear theories of aging is provided by individuals who repeatedly expose their bodies to harmful conditions and substances—for example, large doses of alcohol, various drugs, or harsh environments. Such individuals often show premature signs of aging, presumably because they have overburdened their capacity for internal repair.

GENETIC PROGRAMMING A second group of theories attributes physical aging primarily to **genetic theories of aging.** The idea here is that every living organism contains a built-in biological clock (located in all cells or in special groups of cells within the brain) that regulates the aging process by limiting the number of times various cells can reproduce. Involved are *teleomeres*—strips of DNA that cap the ends of our chromosomes (Gladwell, 1996). Each time a cell divides, the teleomere becomes shorter; when it reaches some critical length, the cell can no longer divide. For instance, when the teleomeres of the skin cells are shortened to a critical length, they can no longer divide, and normal repair processes for keeping skin healthy and young-looking break down.

There is some support for genetic program theories. First, maximum lifespan is a characteristic of each species, even under ideal conditions of nutrition and health. Second, longevity appears to be an inherited trait. One rough indicator of

Stochastic Theories of Aging (also known as **wear-and-tear theories of aging**): Theories suggesting that we grow old because of cumulative damage to our bodies from both external and internal sources.

Genetic Theories of Aging: Theories that attribute physical aging primarily to genetic factors.

how long you will live is the lifespan of your grandparents and parents. Finally, certain cells do indeed divide only a set number of times before dying. Moreover, no environmental conditions seem capable of altering this number.

Which of these theories is most accurate? At present the best scientific guess is that aging is the result of several different biological processes and a complex interaction between environmental and genetic factors.

Meeting Death

What does death mean? The answer to that question is most complex. To begin, there are several kinds of death. *Physiological death* occurs when all physical processes that sustain life cease. *Brain death* is defined as a total absence of brain activity for at least ten minutes. *Cerebral death* means cessation of activity in the cerebral cortex. And *social death* refers to a process through which other people relinquish their relationships with the deceased (Thomas, 1992).

There are complex ethical issues connected with death, as became clear in the Supreme Court of Canada ruling in the case of Sue Rodriguez, who suffered from a terminal illness and was denied the legal right to end her own life. Should individuals have the right to die when they choose, perhaps by asking their doctor to "pull the plug" on life-sustaining medical apparatus? Out of every ten Canadians, about eight believe that individuals should have the right to die when and how they choose (Singer et al., 1993). Since physicians are not likely to take on the responsibility, a person may, in a living will, state in advance who *may* decide (i.e., which family members or friends) when life support should be terminated. The legality of living wills varies from province to province.

People confronted with their own death are faced with several serious challenges—for example, lack of control over their residence (home or hospital), poor memory, and loss of physical mobility (Chipperfield, 1993). What people think about death and about dying has been studied (e.g., de Vries et al., 1993), but perhaps the best known investigation was by Elizabeth Kübler-Ross (1969), who studied the reactions of patients who learned that they were terminally ill. On the basis of detailed interviews, she concluded that they pass through a series of five distinct stages.

The first stage is *denial*. In this phase, patients refuse to believe that the end is in sight. "No, it can't be true," they say. "I won't believe it." This stage is soon replaced by a second—*anger*. "Why me?" dying people ask. "It isn't fair." In the third stage, patients do what Kübler-Ross calls *bargaining*: They offer good behaviour, prayer, or other changes in their lifestyle in exchange for the postponement of death. When it becomes apparent that their best offers have not been accepted, many dying people enter a stage of *depression*. This may also occur because they are growing weaker, or because medical efforts to help them, such as surgery, have failed.

According to Kübler-Ross, however, this is not the final stage in the process. Rather, many terminally ill people move from depression to *acceptance*. At this stage, dying individuals are no longer angry or depressed. Instead, they seem to accept their oncoming death with dignity, and they concentrate on putting their affairs in final order and taking leave of important people in their lives.

"Look, I'm dying. Gotta go."

An Unusual Attitude Toward Death!

Few persons could face their own deaths with the composure shown by the person in this cartoon. Yet many persons do believe that they should have the right to end their lives with dignity and without being a burden to others

Source: The New Yorker.

As in all research, some different findings have been reported. Aronoff and Spilka (1984–85) examined facial expressions for evidence of the five stages described by Kübler-Ross. They found no evidence that these dying individuals became calmer or happier as death approached. However, other researchers have found expressions of hope throughout a terminal illness (Metzger, 1980) or of personal meaning in life (Cohen & Mount, 1992).

CAREGIVING AND CAREGIVERS Terminal illness takes a profound toll upon those who care for those who are dying. These caregivers must make important decisions with respect to the extent of their responsibilities to the family member or friend who is now dying (e.g., Wolfson et al., 1993). They must make adjustments and accommodate demands; at the same time, they must not forget their own needs (Rosenthal et al., 1993). Patients develop "emotional silence" in order to survive and caregivers suffer in silence to hide their pain (de Montigny, 1993). Nevertheless, as studies of caregiving partners of individuals with AIDS have shown, there are also positive events that occur throughout caregiving and bereavement to those who are able to apply positive meaning to everyday experiences (Folkman, 1997).

Bereavement

People grieve when they experience a loss: a friendship over, a relationship ended, or an opportunity missed. However, the loss most intensely felt is **bereavement**— loss by death. As William Worden has put it: "When you lose your parent, you lose your past. When you lose your spouse, you lose your present. When you lose your child, you lose your future. When you lose your friend, you lose yourself." Freud taught that the outcome of loss is depression, but the emotional response is complex, as you will find below.

When mourning a loved one, most people experience the following reactions (Norris & Murrell, 1990): *shock,* a feeling of numbness and unreality that lasts hours or even days; *protest and yearning,* as the bereaved person objects to the loss and yearns for the deceased person; *disorganization and despair,* which may last a year or more, during which the person in mourning may become apathetic and depressed (Hearty, 1989), and life does not seem worth living without the deceased; and *detachment, reorganization, and recovery,* as the individual establishes new roles, regains a sense of purpose in life, and psychologically picks up the pieces. Even during this stage, however, painful bouts of grieving recur on birthdays, anniversaries, and other occasions that remind the bereaved person of their loss. (Figure 9.12 summarizes the major stages of bereavement.)

Bereavement requires adjustments (Arbuckle & de Vries, 1995; Lehman et al., 1993; Tudiver et al., 1992). Adolescents who experience the death of a schoolmate as a result of violence, drug overdose, or suicide are in particular need of immediate attention. At this time they may appear normal, yet they are experiencing silent suffering. For adults, the loss of a child has short-term and long-term consequences for husband and wives, such as guilt, meaninglessness, and yearning, and these may be more intense for men than for women (Lang et al., 1996). In the case of loss of a parent, marital conflict may occur if the grieving partner withdraws and becomes angry without reason (Guttman, 1991); in these cases, therapy may be helpful (e.g., Piper & McCallum, 1991).

Recent research on bereavement has focused on the reactions to death of people who care for individuals dying from AIDS. Those reactions include grief and burnout; in some cases there is a disorder similar to post-traumatic stress (see Chapter 10). In one set of studies, Folkman and her colleagues (1996) interviewed the male caregivers of male AIDS patients—on several occasions before and after the partner's death. Results indicated that grief declined during the course of the

Bereavement: The process of grieving for the people we love who die.

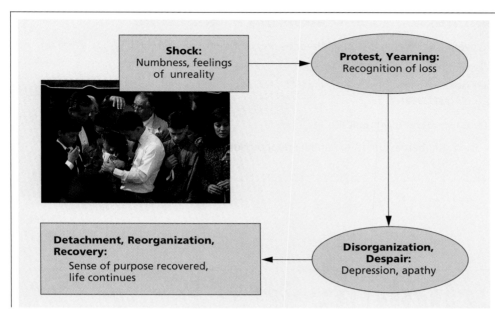

Figure 9.12
Major Stages of Bereavement

People undergoing *bereavement* seem to pass through the stages of mourning shown here.

study, as caregivers came to terms with the loss of someone they loved. Finding positive meaning in the process of caregiving led to faster recovery from grief. In contrast, being HIV-positive themselves, having been in a long-term relationship with the partner, and taking the blame for events during caregiving led to slower recovery from grief and depression. The participants in this particular study were homosexual males, but the findings are very similar to those in studies of bereavement for heterosexual spouses, parents, or children (e.g., Wortman et al., 1994). The AIDS Bereavement Project of Ontario provides support in the area of grief due to losses as a result of AIDS (Perreault, 1995).

Some researchers suggest that grief and mourning promote recovery because of the physiological events that occur during this process; these include changes in levels of a number of different neurohormones and neurotransmitters (Olders, 1989). Bereavement is a painful and relatively long process, but, after a period of mourning of about a year, most people do recover and go on with their lives.

Research by psychologists suggests that engaging in *condolence behaviours*—actions designed to help comfort grieving persons—can be very helpful. Here are some recommendations based on the research results. First, be present. Often, the best thing you can do for a grieving person is to be there physically, while remaining silent. Second, listen to their expression of grief. Expressing grief to someone who hears, understands, and cares is consoling. Continue your contacts with the grieving person—even though they may refuse invitations and visits. Do not say things like, "Wait, it will get easier." While this is true, research findings indicate that a grieving person will resent such statements—because they indicate that you do not really appreciate their loss (e.g., Rigdon, 1986).

Bereavement is a time for grieving but also for celebrating a life lived. However, at any age and at every stage, different life crises seem the most serious and the most stressful. Below are some findings to help you meet one of the most challenging of the positive sources of stress—planning for employment after graduation.

Funerals: Definitely for the Living

Almost all societies have funerals—formal rituals in which grieving persons take final leave of their deceased loved ones. Funerals permit grieving persons to express their sorrow and also keep these persons occupied at a time when they are experiencing intense emotions.

K E Y *QUESTIONS*

■ How do stochastic (wear-and-tear) and genetic theories account for aging and death?

■ According to Kübler-Ross, what stages do terminally ill persons pass through when confronting their own death?

■ What are the major stages of bereavement?

■ What do we know about the bereavement of caregivers of persons who die from AIDS?

Making **Psychology** *Part of Your Life*

Preparing for Tomorrow's Job Market Today

*I*n this chapter you have learned about the milestones that are characteristic of the adult years. For many university students the major challenge following graduation has to do with finding *employment* (Kennett & Miller, 1995; Krahn & Lowe, 1999). Faced with the uncertainties of that decision and the importance of that choice, are there any steps you can take to increase your chances of finding the right job after graduation? While they do not guarantee that you will get the job you want, these suggestions may give you an edge in a competitive economic climate.

■ *Choose a field with a future.* Consider a career in a sector of the economy that promises to grow rapidly in the years ahead. What are these sectors? Like everything in life, the job market changes constantly. Each month, Statistics Canada publishes the Help-Wanted Index, a survey of the help-wanted ads in twenty Canadian metropolitan areas, to show the current job situation. This index measures the degree of change in the job market in various regions of the country. You can also use the Internet to find useful information about different careers. Web pages (such as the one for Job Futures shown in Figure 9.13) can be an excellent resource.

By the way, information supplied by a federal database indicated that in 1993, there were 15 397 jobs in psychology across Canada. By 1999, there were expected to be 18 351 or more: a growth of over 19 percent. The Human Resources Development

Canada 1997–98 projections for the year 2001 predicted that current and future job prospects for psychologists would continue to be "good."

■ *Take the time to make a thoughtful choice.* Find out what the work is really like in various fields that look good to you. Visit someone who is in that line of work and shadow them for a day or so. Take advantage of the workshops and seminars offered at your school's career centre.

■ *Practise the skills that you will need.* Employers are looking for a number of strengths in the people they interview. Among them are initiative, creativity, leadership potential, and communication skills. Take the opportunity to develop your speaking and your writing proficiency. Be prepared to document your strengths and your experience in those areas.

■ *Consider large and small.* In the past, many graduates sought jobs with prestige companies—those with big reputations and lots of glamour. In today's job market, in several fields, those corporations are recruiting again. However, those are precisely the companies that make the biggest cutbacks—"right-size"—when the going gets tougher—governments as well. Seriously consider small and medium-sized companies. Bigger is not always better—in the long run.

■ *Check it out first.* Before you accept employment, however, check out the corporate climate and the possibilities for advancement. Find out which kinds

Figure 9.13
Using the Internet for Information about Careers

Web pages, such as this one for Job Futures, can be of great help to students seeking information about future career prospects.

Source: This information is reproduced from Job Futures 2000, a product of the Applied Research Branch, Human Resources Development Canada. Reproduced with the permission of the Minister of Public Works and Government Services Canada, 2000.

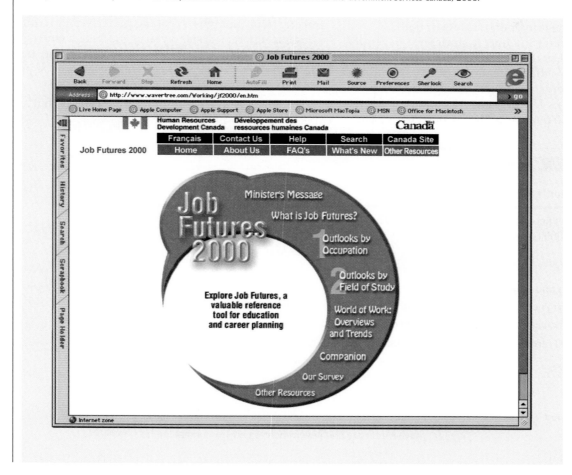

of students have been successful in that work environment. If possible, go to see the place and the people to check whether you fit into that workplace.

■ *Be prepared to travel to a new location.* Job opportunities vary from place to place, and from time to time, in our country. For various reasons (the relative cost of office space being one of them), companies move from province to province, and jobs move from the downtown core of some big cities to smaller centres.

■ *Be ready to work for a multinational company.* Multinational corporations that are expanding their operations are often the ones with the jobs. Working for a foreign company may mean that you must learn a new set of rules, because such companies of-

ten follow the home country's customary practices with respect to employees and to work. Given the continued movement toward a global economy, this is good experience and may create new opportunities for you.

■ *Consider part-time or contract work as a way to get started.* Full-time jobs with large corporations may not be the right place to begin, partly because many large companies hire outsiders to do many jobs. Consider starting in this way because often people who are hired on a part-time or contract basis gain an important advantage. They get as much varied experience, in many kinds of job settings and they may get the first shot at the permanent full-time work they want—when it becomes available.

■ *Look forward to studying longer.* Understand that knowledge is changing so fast that you will spend a lifetime learning new facts and new skills. After earning your first degree, you may need to take post-graduate classes in a specialty of one kind or another, or in a technical field, or in management training. That may be in-house at your place of work, or it may be within the university setting, or both.

Notwithstanding the horror stories we have all heard about Ph.D.s driving taxis and graduates on welfare, the fact is that education is the best predictor, by far, of whether or not you will get a good job. Human Resources Development Canada reported that more than 50 percent of the jobs created in this country during the 1990s required more than high school education. Statistics Canada found that—when total employment is falling—the proportion of university graduates who find work increases steadily; and this is true in every province.

The skills you gain in post-secondary education, in learning new material, in listening carefully, in organizing your thoughts, speaking publicly, and writing original reports will stand you in good stead wherever your career path leads. While you are doing that, perfect your people skills. Those will turn out to be just as important for success in today's workplace!

See Table 9.1 for a list of some of the careers that are expected to grow in the future.

TABLE 9.1

Careers with a Future

The careers listed here are among those expected to grow in the years ahead, but there are also many other possibilities for today's graduate.

Job/Career	Description
Education and Training	
Employee trainers	Help people develop new skills needed to perform rapidly changing jobs
Diversity managers	Help diverse groups of employees work together
Fitness and recreation	Program design for fifty-plus age group
Teaching	All levels, including special education and preschool, English as a second language, and adult literacy
Writers	Create technical manuals
Environment	
Consultant	Advise industry and government on environmental impact
Health Care	
Nurse practitioners	Deal with a wide range of health problems
Physical therapists	Specialize in rehabilitation of patients
Occupational therapists	Specialize in retraining of patients for new jobs
Speech pathologists	Treat patients with speech and language disorders
Applied Psychology	Many applications of psychological principles
Information Technology	
Computer programmers	Develop new computer programs
Systems analysts	Create computer applications for specific needs
Telecommunications	Specialize in the transfer of information through telephones, modems, fax machines, voice mail
Entertainment	Game design and computer animation
Management	
Fifty-plus marketing specialists	Promote and sell products designed for people over fifty
Employee leasing agents	Help companies "lease" employees for specific projects
Tourism, travel, and hospitality	Hotel management

Summary and Review

Key Questions

Adolescence

■ **What physical changes occur during puberty?** Puberty, the most important stage of physical development during adolescence, is a period of rapid change and growth during which individuals attain sexual maturity.

■ **Why do adolescents often engage in reckless behaviour?** Recent findings indicate that such behaviour does not necessarily stem from feelings of invulnerability on the part of adolescents. Instead, it seems to stem from their tendencies toward sensation seeking, egocentric thinking, and aggressiveness.

■ **What goals do adolescents often seek in their friendships?** They seek dominance, intimacy, nurturance, leadership, and popularity. They believe that these goals can be reached through specific strategies, which differ somewhat between the two genders.

■ **According to Erikson, what is the most important crisis faced by adolescents?** Erikson suggests that this is a crisis involving identity versus role confusion, which concerns establishment of a clear self-identity.

■ **How do psychologists study adolescents' social behaviour?** In recent studies, psychologists have employed video cameras and wireless microphones to study adolescent social behaviour in the settings where it normally occurs.

■ **What are parental demandingness and parental supportiveness? What styles of parenting do they yield?** Demandingness refers to parents' tendency to set firm rules for their children. Supportiveness refers to parents' tendency to be supportive of and interested in their children's activities. Differences on these dimensions yield the following parenting styles: authoritarian, authoritative, permissive, and rejecting/neglecting.

■ **How do bicultural adolescents cope with belonging to two cultural groups?** They do this either by obtaining separate identities in each culture and alternating between these, or by fusing their two cultural identities into one.

■ **What are some of the major threats to the well-being of adolescents at the present time?** These threats include the effects of growing up in families where their parents are divorced, where one or more parents is absent, or in dysfunctional families, where they are exposed to various forms of abuse.

■ **What factors contribute to adolescent resilience—the ability to rise above conditions that threaten their healthy development?** Factors contributing to resilience include personal characteristics that make adolescents easy to get along with; family-based factors, including a close bond with one or more competent, emotionally stable caregivers; and community-based factors such as supportive teachers, neighbours, or clergy.

Adulthood and Aging

■ **How do stage theories such Erikson's and life-event theories explain the changes we experience during our adult years?** Stage theories propose that we move through distinct stages during our adult years. In contrast, life-event theories view adult development as tied to important events occurring in our lives.

■ **At what age are we most influenced by the events occurring in our society?** Recent findings indicate that we are most influenced by events occurring when we are adolescents or young adults. For example, women who were in these age groups when the women's movement started report being most influenced by this important social event.

■ **What physical changes do men and women experience during early and middle adulthood?** Reduced physical functioning and decreased vigour plus changes in appearance occur during middle adulthood. In addition, both women and men experience changes in their reproductive systems during mid-life.

■ **What physical changes occur in later life?** Among the many physical changes occurring in later life are declines in sensory abilities and a slowing of reflexes.

■ **What changes in memory occur as we age?** Working memory does not decline with age, but it becomes more subject to proactive interference. Recall of information from long-term memory does decline somewhat, but such effects are greater for meaningless information than for meaningful information. Recent findings indicate that individuals who engage in mental "exercise" experience smaller declines in memory functioning as they age.

■ **How do intelligence and creativity change over the lifespan?** There may be some declines in some aspects of intelligence with age, but these are smaller and more limited in scope than was once widely believed. Further, there appears to be little or no decline in creativity with age.

■ **What are the effects of unemployment on the psychological and physical health of persons who experience this crisis?** Being unemployed can undermine self-esteem and can also put people at risk for various physical illnesses.

■ **To what extent are people satisfied with their lives, and does such happiness vary greatly across different groups?** A large majority of individuals report that they are satisfied with their lives—they experience high levels of subjective well-being. This is true across many different groups—people of different ages, living in different countries, and with different income levels.

■ **What factors may explain the prevalence of high levels of subjective well-being?** Being in a positive mood may be a dominant tendency for most persons. Further, being in a positive mood may be necessary for many forms of motivated behaviour.

Death and Bereavement

■ **How do stochastic and genetic theories account for aging and death?** Stochastic or wear-and-tear theories suggest that aging results from the fact that cells and organs in our bodies wear out with continued use. In contrast, genetic theories suggest that we possess biological clocks that limit longevity.

■ **According to Kübler-Ross, what stages do terminally ill persons pass through when confronting their own death?** Kübler-Ross reported five stages: denial, anger, bargaining, depression, and acceptance.

■ **What are the major stages of bereavement?** These stages include shock, protest and yearning, disorganization and despair, and detachment and recovery.

■ **What do we know about the bereavement of caregivers of persons who die from AIDS?** Caregivers of AIDS patients recover from their grief more quickly if they start out with very high levels of grief and depression, and if they perceive positive value in their caregiving. Their recovery from such grief is slowed if they had a long-term relationship with the AIDS victim, if they blame themselves for events during this period, and if they themselves are HIV-positive.

Key Terms

Adolescence (p. 349)
Adolescent Invulnerability (p. 351)
Bereavement (p. 382)
Blended Families (p. 361)
Climacteric (p. 369)
Convoy Model (p. 376)
Dysfunctional Families (p. 361)
Genetic Theories of Aging (p. 380)

Identity Fusion (p. 360)
Menopause (p. 369)
Naturalistic Observation (p. 353)
Parental Demandingness (p. 354)
Parental Responsiveness (p. 354)
Primary Aging (p. 370)
Puberty (p. 349)

Resilience in Development (p. 363)
Secondary Aging (p. 370)
Sensation Seeking (p. 352)
Sexual Abuse (p. 361)
Social Age Clocks (p. 366)
Stochastic Theories of Aging (p. 380)
Subjective Well-Being (p. 378)

Critical Thinking Questions

Appraisal

The changes we experience during childhood are truly huge. How do the changes we experience during our adult years compare?

Controversy

Some psychologists believe that today's adolescents face a unique set of risks and dangers. Do you agree or not? Give your reasons for taking either position.

Making Psychology Part of Your Life

On the basis of what you have learned from this chapter, what steps could you take to increase your own longevity? How could you increase the likelihood that your adult life will be happy, productive, and healthy?

Weblinks

Check out our Companion Website at www.pearsoned.ca/baron for additional Websites, activities, and more.

Journal of Adolescence

www.idealibrary.com/cgi-bin/links/toc/ad

The Journal of Adolescence is available online at this site.

Physical Development in Adolescence

oldwww.ballarat.edu.au/bssh/psych/hp602/60205.htm

Review the physical changes that occur at puberty.

Beyond "Peer Pressure"

www.hc-sc.gc.ca/hppb/socialmarketing/smq-abstracts/abstract3.htm

This is a page from the Health Canada Website that will help you understand adolescent risk behaviour better. In particular, the effects of different kinds of peer pressure are discussed in detail.

Aging Brain Compensates for Loss in Function

www.slam.ca/Health9910/24_brain.html

This is a brief description of a recent study about brain function in older adults, conducted by scientists at the University of Toronto and the Rotman Institute. There are many links to other topics relevant to this chapter.

Is Well-Being Subject to an Adaptive Process in Old Age?

www.unige.ch/CIG/gsa/gsa99dsnv.htm

The results of a Swiss study on subjective well-being and aging give us an idea as to why that personality characteristic increases with age.

Alzheimer Society of Canada

www.alzheimer.ca/alz/content/mainmenu1-eng.htm

It is predicted that Alzheimer disease will be the "plague" of the 21st century. This award-winning Website of the Alzheimer Society of Canada will tell you about current research, new medications and recent news on this brain disorder. Information about caregiving is also provided.

Chapter 10

Motivation and Emotion

CHAPTER OUTLINE

Climbing Blind

An unusual event took place in Kluane National Park in the Yukon. There, in May 2000, four out of an expedition of six climbers viewed first-hand the summit of Mount Logan, Canada's tallest peak. According to the report in the *Winnipeg Free Press*, even as they reached for the top, they saw a vicious storm ahead and they wondered if, in the end, they would be blown off the mountain. Nevertheless they prevailed!

What was most unusual about this particular group was the fact that one of its members had been blind for almost forty years. He managed the climb by feeling the tracks that the others left as they proceeded, listening to the sound of their axes and boots, and following the direction of the rope.

Why do human beings strive like this? Why do they persist in the face of insurmountable odds? Why did these climbers endure danger and hardship, cold and wind, day after day after day—in order to reach the top of a mountain? What was the reason for their behaviour? How did their success make them feel? These are some of the questions you will ponder as you work your way through Chapter 10, Motivation and Emotion.

Sources: Kenny, E. (2000, May 1). Blind climber taking on Canada's highest peak. *Winnipeg Free Press*. Necheff. J. (2000, May 27). Stormy weather cuts victory celebration short. *Winnipeg Free Press*.

> **This chapter is about the "feeling" side of life—what James Brown means when he sings "I feel good!"**

Why do some of us seek success, while others are satisfied with whatever life happens to send their way? Why do we continue to eat when we are no longer hungry? What makes some movies sexually arousing? How do we tell when someone is lying? Why do some of us continue to work long hours, well after we have plenty of money in the bank? What do our expectations have to do with our likes and dislikes? How does mood affect our judgment? Why does the world seem beautiful when we are up, but bleak when we are having a down day? Do grey skies really clear up if we put on a happy face? These questions are about the "feeling" side of life—about, as psychologists would put it, the topics of motivation and emotion.

The term *motivation* refers to internal processes that activate, guide, and maintain our behaviour. Motivation has to do with the goals we choose and the ways we achieve them. Understanding motivation often helps us to answer the question *why*—that is, to give reasons for our behaviour and that of others. Clearly, motivation is relevant to several of the questions just raised—the differences between workaholics and "shirkaholics," the regulation of body weight, and the nature of sexual arousal are examples (Silver et al., 1997).

Emotion, in contrast, is about how we feel: happy or sad, afraid or angry, proud or ashamed. In psychology, emotion refers to physiological responses such as changes in blood pressure and heart rate; subjective cognitive judgments—the labels we apply to feelings, for example, joy, anger, sorrow, sexual arousal, disgust, and so on; and expressions of these internal states—such as facial expression or body posture. Emotions play a crucial role in all aspects of behaviour. Moreover, emotions influence our perceptions—when we are in a good mood, we tend to see the world through rose-coloured glasses (e.g., Forgas, 1991; Smith & Shafer, 1991).

This chapter will provide an overview of current knowledge about these two topics. First, we will consider contrasting theories about the basic nature of motivation. Then we will examine several important forms of motivation: hunger, sexual motivation, aggression, and motivation as it relates to achievement and power. After that we will turn to emotion. Again, we will begin by examining several theories; then we will turn to the physiological bases of emotion, and consider the expression and communication of emotion and how emotional reactions are reflected in external behaviour. Finally, we will look at the complex relationship between emotion and cognition—how feelings shape thoughts and how thoughts shape feelings. Remember that motivation is what we ask about in the question, "Why did I do that?" And emotion is what we ask about in the question, "How did I feel?"

As with other aspects of our behaviour, motivational and emotional states are biologically based—in the central and peripheral nervous systems. When those systems become damaged in some way, changes occur. It is when the prefrontal lobes of the cerebral cortex are damaged that there are motivational and emotional consequences that may change the individual's personality and alter the "stable response patterns that define the individual as a unique self" (Stuss et al., 1992). The psychological disorders you will read about in Chapter 14 tell more.

Motivation

Consider the following events:

- A group of young people hurl themselves out of a plane. Then, as they fall toward earth, they join hands and form a circle. After that, they divide into pairs and swing round and round each other in a kind of dance. Only at the last minute do they open their parachutes and glide safely to the ground.

- Employees of a large bank remain on strike for month after month, even though any settlement they ultimately obtain will never compensate them for the lost wages and benefits.

On the face of it, these actions are somewhat puzzling. Why would people risk life and limb, even though there is no practical benefit of doing so? Why would people continue to strike even if there was nothing to be gained? One answer is this: Such actions occur because the individuals involved are *motivated* to perform them. In other words, they are responding to internal states that cannot be directly observed but that activate, guide, and maintain overt behaviours. While there is general agreement on this basic point, there has been considerable disagreement, over the years, about the basic nature of **motivation**. Let us consider some of these contrasting perspectives.

Motivation: A Useful Concept for Understanding Behaviour

Why do people engage in risky behaviours? One answer involves motivation—an internal process that cannot be directly observed but that activates, guides, and maintains overt behaviour.

Theories of Motivation

Over the years, many different theories of motivation have been proposed. The views described below are the ones that have received the most attention.

DRIVE THEORY: MOTIVATION AND HOMEOSTASIS What do feelings like hunger, thirst, chill, and burning have in common? That is right ... they are all unpleasant and we try to eliminate them. This is the basis for the first major approach to motivation: **drive theory.** According to drive theory, biological needs arising within our bodies create unpleasant states such as hunger, thirst, fatigue, and so on. In order to eliminate these feelings and restore a balanced physiological state (known as **homeostasis**) we engage in certain directed behaviours (Winn, 1995). Behaviours that reduce the appropriate drive are strengthened and tend to be repeated. Those behaviours that fail to produce such effects are weakened and are less likely to be repeated when the drive is present again (see Figure 10.1).

In its original form, drive theory focused primarily on biological needs and the aroused states they produce. Soon, though, psychologists extended this model to forms of behaviour not so clearly tied to basic needs: drives for stimulation, for status, for wealth and power, and for stable social relationships (e.g., Baumeister & Leary, 1995).

Drive theory persisted in psychology for several decades; it has not been totally discarded even today. However, there is widespread agreement that this approach has several major drawbacks: Contrary to what drive suggests, human beings often engage in actions that *increase* rather than reduce various drives. For example, people sometimes skip snacks and let their appetites increase in order to maximize their enjoyment of a special dinner. Similarly, some people watch or read erotic materials in order to increase their sexual excitement, even when they do not anticipate immediate gratification (Kelley & Byrne, 1992). In view of such evidence, most psychologists now believe that drive theory, by itself, does not provide a full understanding of human motivation.

Motivation: An inferred internal process that activates, guides, and maintains behaviour over time.

Drive Theory: A theory of motivation suggesting that behaviour is "pushed" from within by drives stemming from basic biological needs.

Homeostasis: A state of physiological balance within the body.

Figure 10.1
Drive Theory: An Overview

According to drive theory, biological needs lead to the arousal of appropriate drives that activate specific forms of behaviour. Actions that satisfy (reduce) these drives are strengthened and tend to be repeated when the drive is again present. Behaviours that fail to satisfy the drives are weakened.

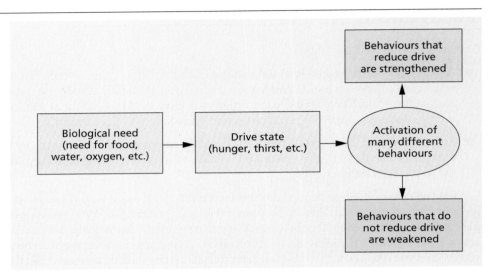

AROUSAL THEORY: SEEKING OPTIMUM ACTIVATION When it became clear that people sometimes seek to increase rather than to decrease existing drives, an alternative theory of motivation known as **arousal theory** was formulated (Geen, Beatty, & Arkin, 1984). This theory focuses on *arousal*, our general level of activation. Measures of arousal include heart rate, blood pressure, muscle tension, and brain activity (Brehm & Self, 1989). Arousal varies throughout the day, from low levels during sleep to much higher ones when we are performing strenuous tasks or ones we find exciting. Arousal theory suggests that what we seek is *optimal arousal*—the level of arousal that is best suited to our own personal characteristics and whatever activity we are currently performing. So, for example, if you are listening to soothing music, a relatively low level of arousal will be optimal. If you are competing in a sports event, a much higher level will be best.

Many studies offer indirect support for arousal theory. For example, there is often a close link between arousal and performance (see Figure 10.2; Weiner, 1989). However, large individual differences exist with respect to preferred levels of arousal. At one extreme are individuals who prefer and seek high levels and therefore seek out situations that are exciting and/or risky (Coren & Mah, 1993). At the other extreme are those who prefer much lower levels (Zuckerman, 1990). Furthermore, it is often difficult to determine in advance the optimal level of arousal for a given task or situation. Thus, while the theory does provide useful insights into the nature of motivation, it also has important limitations.

EXPECTANCY THEORY: A COGNITIVE APPROACH Why are you reading this book? It is probably not to reduce some biologically based drive. The chances are good that you are reading it because you expect that doing so will help you reach important goals: to gain useful and interesting knowledge, to get a higher grade on the next exam, to graduate from college or university. In short, your behaviour is determined by your *expectancies*—that is, by your belief that your present actions will yield various outcomes in the future. This point provides the foundation for a third major theory of motivation, **expectancy theory**.

This theory suggests that motivation is not primarily a matter of being pushed by various urges; rather, it is more a question of being pulled by expectations of attaining desired outcomes. Such outcomes, known as **incentives**, can be almost anything we have learned to value—money, status, power, and the admiration of others, to name just a few. Why do people engage in complex, effortful, or even painful behaviours such as working long hours at the office, performing aerobic exercises, or studying long into the night? Expectancy theory answers this way: Because they believe that doing so will yield outcomes they wish to attain.

Arousal Theory: A theory of motivation suggesting that human beings seek an optimal level of arousal, not minimal levels of arousal.

Expectancy Theory: A theory of motivation suggesting that behaviour is elicited by expectations of desirable outcomes.

Incentives: Rewards individuals seek to attain.

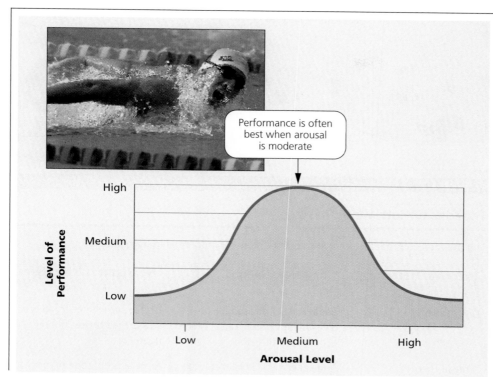

Figure 10.2
Arousal and Performance

Across a wide range of tasks, performance increases as arousal rises to moderate levels. Beyond some point, however, optimal levels of arousal are exceeded, and performance begins to decline.

Expectancy theory has been applied to many aspects of human motivation. For example, at the University of Windsor, Rodgers and Brawley (1991) studied the expectancies of undergraduates as related to their motivation for participating in an exercise program. However, it is work motivation—the energy and effort we put out on the job—that has been found most central to our lives (Locke & Latham, 1990). Research in organizational/industrial psychology is dedicated to understanding people at work. Studies indicate that people will work hard at their jobs when they believe that doing so will yield outcomes they desire: improved performance (greater competence), recognition (praise), rewards (raises in pay), or increased status (promotion).

In short, expectancy theory suggests that our motivation to engage in various activities will be high when we expect that performing them will somehow pay off—that is, yield outcomes or results we desire.

GOAL-SETTING THEORY   Actually, goal-setting theory began as an interesting finding that was simple but impressive: On a wide variety of tasks, people performed better when they were given specific goals than when they were told simply to "do your best" (e.g., Wood & Locke, 1990). This finding was central to the development of **goal-setting theory** (e.g., Lock & Latham, 1990), which suggests that motivation can be strongly influenced by generating step-by-step performance targets. For example, suppose that you are studying for a big exam. Do you ever tell yourself, in advance, that you won't stop until you have read a certain number of pages, memorized some specific number of definitions, or solved a fixed number of problems? Then you are using goal setting to increase your performance level.

Goal setting works best when the goals set are highly *specific*—people know just what they are trying to accomplish, the goals are *challenging*—meeting them requires considerable effort, but they are perceived as *attainable*—people believe they can actually reach them. Finally, goal setting is most successful when there is personal commitment and feedback with respect to progress. When the conditions are met, goal setting is a highly effective way of increasing motivation and performance (e.g., Mento et al., 1992; Wright et al., 1994). You will find an overview of these four theories of motivation in Table 10.1 on the next page.

Goal-Setting Theory: A theory that explains why setting specific, challenging goals for a given task often leads to improvements in performance.

Goal Setting: How *Not* to Do It

As shown here, goals setting can actually backfire and *reduce* motivation if the persons involved are not committed to reaching them.

Source: King Features Syndicate, 1988.

TABLE 10.1

Theories of Motivation: An Overview

The theories summarized here are among the most influential in psychology.

Theory of Motivation	Key Assumptions	Strengths/Weaknesses
Drive Theory	Biological needs produce unpleasant states of arousal which people seek to reduce	People sometimes try to *increase* their drives, not reduce them
Arousal Theory	Arousal (general level of activation) varies throughout the day and can motivate many forms of behaviour; people seek *optimal* arousal, not low arousal	Arousal is only one of many factors that influence motivated behaviour
Expectancy Theory	Behaviour is "pulled" by expectations of desired outcomes rather than "pushed" from within by biologically based drives	Focus on cognitive processes in motivation is consistent with modern psychology; widely used to explain *work motivation*
Goal-Setting Theory	Setting specific, challenging, but attainable goals can boost motivation and performance, especially when individuals are committed to reaching the goals and receive feedback on their progress	Highly effective in increasing performance, but mechanisms that explain these effects are still somewhat uncertain

---

MASLOW'S NEEDS HIERARCHY: RELATIONSHIPS AMONG MOTIVES Suppose that you were very hungry and very cold; could you study effectively under these conditions? Probably not. Therefore, Maslow (1970) proposed that different motives—or needs, as he called them—form a hierarchy. He also stipulated that the needs at the bottom of the hierarchy must be at least partly satisfied before those higher up can influence behaviour. At the base of Maslow's **hierarchy of needs** are *physiological needs,* such as for food, water, oxygen, and sleep. One step above these are the *safety needs,* for feeling safe and secure in one's life. Above the safety needs are *social needs,* which include the need to have friends, to be loved and appreciated, and to belong—to fit into a network of social relationships (e.g., Baumeister & Leary, 1995).

Maslow describes physiological, safety, and social needs as *deficiency needs:* They are the basics and must be satisfied before higher levels of motivation, or *growth needs,* can emerge. Above the social needs in the hierarchy are *esteem needs,* which include the needs for self-respect, for the approval of others, and for success. Ambition

Hierarchy of Needs: In Maslow's theory of motivation, an arrangement of needs from the most basic to those at the highest levels.

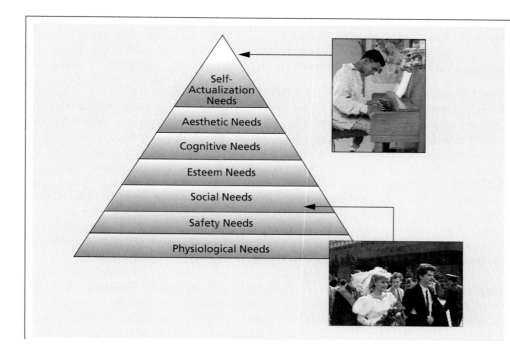

Figure 10.3
Maslow's Needs Hierarchy

According to Maslow (1970), needs exist in a hierarchy. Only when lower-order needs are satisfied will higher-order needs be activated.

and the need for achievement, to which we will return in a later section, are also closely linked to esteem needs. On the next level are *cognitive needs,* which include the need to know, to understand, and to satisfy our curiosity. Higher yet Maslow placed *aesthetic needs*—our need for beauty and order. Finally, at the pinnacle of this hierarchy are *self-actualization needs,* which include the need for self-fulfillment—the desire to become all one is capable of being. Self-actualization needs include concerns not only with one's selfish interests but also with issues that affect the well-being of others. Figure 10.3 provides an overview of Maslow's theory.

Maslow's theory is intuitively appealing, but is it accurate? Do needs exist in a hierarchy, and must lower-level needs be met before higher-level ones can have a motivating effect? Research findings on these issues are mixed. Some results suggest that growth needs do come after lower-level deficiency needs (Betz, 1982). But other findings indicate that people sometimes seek to satisfy higher-order needs even when those lower in the hierarchy have not been met (Williams & Page, 1989). For these reasons, Maslow's needs hierarchy is best viewed as an interesting but largely unverified framework for organizing our thoughts about motivation.

KEY *QUESTIONS*

▪ According to drive theory, what is the basis for various motives?

▪ Why is expectancy theory described as a cognitive theory of motivation?

▪ What are the basic ideas behind Maslow's need hierarchy theory?

Hunger and Eating

A Greek proverb states, "You cannot reason with a hungry belly; it has no ears." This statement suggests—eloquently!—that **hunger motivation,** the urge to obtain and consume food, is a powerful one. When people are hungry, hunger motivation takes precedence over all others. You likely know from personal experience what a powerful source of motivation those strong and insistent feelings of hunger can be.

Hunger Motivation: The motivation to obtain and consume food.

But where do such feelings come from? And how do we manage to regulate the amount of food we consume so that, for most people, body weight remains fairly stable even over long periods of time? These are some of the questions psychologists have addressed in their efforts to understand the nature of hunger motivation.

THE REGULATION OF EATING: A COMPLEX PROCESS Consider the following: If you consume just twenty calories more than you need each day (less than the amount of a single small carrot), you will gain about a kilogram a year—10 kilograms in a decade. How do people keep caloric input and output closely balanced and so avoid such outcomes? How do we maintain a stable body weight? The answer involves a complex system of regulatory mechanisms located in the hypothalamus, liver, and elsewhere. These systems contain special *detectors*, cells that respond to variations in the concentration of several nutrients in the blood. One type of detector responds to the amount of *glucose*, or blood sugar. Other detectors respond to levels of *protein*, and especially to certain amino acids. Finally, other detectors respond to *lipids*, or fats. Even if glucose levels are low, when the amount of protein or lipid circulating in the blood is high, we do not feel hungry.

Complex as all this seems, it is still only part of the story. Eating and hunger are also strongly affected by the smell and taste of food and by feedback produced by chewing and swallowing. The impact of these factors is well documented. For example, in one series of studies, volunteers wore special equipment fitted to their teeth that permitted the researchers to obtain records of their actual chewing (Stellar, 1985). Participants also reported on their feelings of hunger and on the tastiness of the foods they ate. At first, when they were very hungry, the volunteers chewed less and swallowed more often. As they satisfied their hunger, they reported that the foods were less and less tasty and they chewed more and swallowed less often; their rate of intake dropped. Tasty food is more satiating than bland (but nutritionally identical) versions of the same meal (Warwick et al., 1993).

The sight of food is also important. Foods that are attractive in appearance are hard to resist; many people eat more when food is presented attractively. Cultural factors also play a major role in determining what, when, and how much we eat. Would you happily munch on fried grasshoppers? Octopus cooked in its own ink? How about snails or snake? Or does the thought of such items induce nausea? Depending on the culture in which you have been raised, the thoughts of such items may induce hunger pangs—or feelings of disgust (Rozin, 1996).

Cognitive factors, too, play a role. Recent findings reported by Rozin and his colleagues (Rozin et al., 1998) indicate that memories about when we last ate can influence whether we decide to eat and how much we consume at any given time, quite apart from what internal cues from our bodies may be telling us. In this research, Rozin et al. (1998) offered several meals in a row to individuals who had suffered extensive bilateral damage to the hippocampus and amygdala—structures that play a role in memory. Both individuals were offered a meal at lunch time. A few minutes after eating it, they were offered a second meal, and then, a few minutes after eating that one, were offered yet a third meal. Results indicated that both persons consumed the second meal, and that one of them ate part of the third meal as well. Yet,

Visual Cues Play an Important Role in Hunger

Even though you cannot smell or taste the foods shown here, you would probably choose the one on the right as the more appetizing dish.

both rated their hunger as lower after consuming the first meal than before it. Why, then, did they eat again? Apparently because they could not remember that they had just eaten! Findings such as these underscore the main point we wish to make: many mechanisms operating together influence hunger motivation and eating.

FACTORS IN OBESITY: THE LONG-TERM REGULATION OF BODY WEIGHT People who weigh 28 kilograms (60 pounds) or more above what they should for their height and body build have a condition known as **obesity**. In the year 2000, in Canada, about four in ten men, three in ten women, and two in ten children (six to eleven years old) were obese. There is now convincing medical evidence that obesity is a health hazard. This level of excess weight has been linked to serious disorders such as high blood pressure, diabetes, and arthritis. Also, employees who are significantly overweight miss more days of work than those who are not (Goode, 1990).

Why do some people weigh so much more than they should? There are a number of different reasons. First, genetic factors may be involved—that is, some obese individuals may have inherited their condition. Over millions of years, and in all animals, body weight has come to be carefully maintained at a stable level by powerful internal control systems. That is why some people find it hard to lose weight—those control systems continue to increase weight back to its original level. That level is maintained so that the body is able to cope with future energy demands (Assanand et al., 1998a, 1998b), but not all bodies are the same. There are individual differences that are genetically determined.

How is that possible? Consider the situation faced by our ancient ancestors: periods of plenty alternated with periods of famine. Under these conditions people who were efficient at storing excess calories as fat during times of plenty gained an important advantage: they were more likely to survive during famine and to reproduce. Today, we still inherit that tendency and, as a result, all of us living today have some tendency to gain weight when we overeat.

Evidence for that conclusion comes from study of the Pima—a Native American group living in the state of Arizona. Because the Pima live in a harsh, desert environment, they apparently possess a powerful genetically inherited tendency to gain weight readily. In recent decades, they have shifted from their traditional diet consisting mainly of vegetables and grain to the "normal" American diet, one that is high in fat—and fast foods. As a result, the Pima are currently suffering an epidemic of obesity (Gladwell, 1998). Those who changed their diet weigh over 200 kg, but those who maintained the classic diet remain slim.

The Pima: A Culture in the Grip of an Obesity Epidemic

Because the Pima (a Native American group that lives in Arizona) once faced harsh environmental conditions, only those who could gain weight readily in times of plenty survived. As a result, the Pima, who now eat a normal American diet, are experiencing a virtual epidemic of obesity that seriously threatens their health.

How do genetics influence weight gain? First, it may be because individuals differ in their basal metabolic rate, which is a measure of the number of calories the human body burns when at rest. Individuals of the same age and weight performing the same activities differ greatly in this measure of metabolism; as a result, one person may be able to consume twice as many calories as another and still maintain a stable weight. Second, it may be the relation between appetite and obesity that is the genetic factor. Mutant mice are now being used to reveal the influences of genetics on behaviour (Wahlsten, 1999) and there are now mutant mice bred for obesity and eating disorders. Some of these experimental animals may allow us to determine the relation between appetite and obesity and inheritance.

Third, one study has found a gene that was implicated in several different addictions (alcohol, nicotine, and cocaine), including the craving for sweets (Morris et al., 1993; Noble et al., 1994). Reportedly, the sugar rush that occurs when we consume sugar is linked to the neurotransmitter dopamine, which is important to feelings of happiness and satisfaction. Because of their genetic inheritance, obese people may have fewer dopamine receptors than normal. For them, it takes more dopamine to produce the same positive effects.

Obesity: The state of being significantly overweight.

However, many people are seriously overweight for other reasons. Learning plays an important role in the regulation of eating behaviour. First, the desire to eat can be classically conditioned. Cues associated with eating when we are hungry can acquire the capacity to prompt eating even when we are not hungry. Further, we learn to associate eating with particular contexts and situations—for example, a strong urge to snack in front of the television set or movie screen. Second, many children are rewarded with high-calorie foods and they acquire that preference by operant conditioning. Third, we also learn to eat by observational learning. Goldman (et al., 1991) demonstrated this in an experiment with female undergraduate non-dieters at the University of Toronto. In this study, the amount of food consumed was compared when subjects ate in the presence of another person who ate either a little or a lot. The subjects' eating behaviour followed the example set by their companion—and for some the *reduction* in consumption of food lasted as long as twenty-four hours (Pliner & Chaiken, 1990).

A fourth factor that plays an important role in the regulation of weight is stress. How do *you* react to stress—for example, to a big exam, a quarrel with a friend, or a traffic ticket? If you are like most people, that unpleasant feeling in the pit of your stomach makes eating unattractive, at least temporarily. Overweight people, however, often have a different reaction—they tend to eat more during periods of stress.

Yet a fifth factor seems to contribute to unwanted weight gain. Overweight people respond more strongly to external cues relating to food (Rodin & Slochower, 1976). They report feeling hungrier in the presence of food-related cues—the sight or smell of foods—than others do; also, they find it harder to resist eating when tasty foods are available, even if they are not hungry (Rodin, 1984).

Taking all these reasons together, it is not surprising that many people experience difficulties in regulating their own weight. There are simply too many variables that, together or separately, can overwhelm the exquisitely balanced—and extraordinarily complex—biological mechanisms that normally keep body weight stable. The remedy for most may be a lifestyle that balances eating and exercise, a topic to which we will return in Chapter 13. In the meantime, please note that in children and adolescents who have juvenile obesity, for which there may be a genetic link, low physical activity is one characteristic found commonly as well (Bar-Or et al., 1998).

SERIOUS EATING DISORDERS: ANOREXIA NERVOSA AND BULIMIA In Canada, one percent of adolescent and young females suffer from **anorexia nervosa**. These young women literally starve themselves, often losing dangerous amounts of weight—reducing to less than 85 percent of the normal minimum for their height and age (Thompson, 1992). Such losses can be tragically serious. In the 1980s, anorexia was fatal for singer Karen Carpenter. In 1999, Anne Murray performed a benefit concert for Sheena's Place, a support centre for persons with eating disorders in Toronto. Sheena's Place was founded by Sheena's mother after her daughter died of anorexia. Anne Murray and her daughter, Dawn, revealed that Dawn had been treated for anorexia, bringing national attention to this eating disorder. While over 90 percent of individuals suffering from eating disorders are female, the number of males is rising, notably among athletes (Stoutjesdyk & Jevene, 1993) and compulsive exercisers.

Reports indicate that 1.5 percent of young women in their late teens or twenties suffer from **bulimia** (Garfinkel et al., 1995; Hinz & Williamson, 1987). Bulimics are individuals who engage in excessive or binge eating. Then they purge themselves by means of self-induced vomiting, laxative abuse, fasting, and/or excessive exercise. The late Princess Diana was a bulimic who made her eating disorder public. Bulimics are more preoccupied with their physical appearance than other people (e.g., Casper, 1990), less satisfied with their own bodies (Striegel-Moore, Silberstein, & Rodin, 1993), and lower in social self-confidence and higher in social anxiety (e.g., Tobin et al., 1991).

Anorexia Nervosa: An eating disorder in which individuals starve themselves and often lose a dangerous amount of weight.

Bulimia: An eating disorder in which periods of binge eating alternate with periods of self-induced purging.

Anorexia nervosa and bulimia are somewhat different, although they may coexist in the same person. They affect different age groups and different numbers of individuals. Their biological reactions are distinct to some neurohormones (Vaccarino et al., 1993) or neurotransmitters (Goldbloom & Garfinkel, 1990).

Female competitive athletes in sports where appearance counts are especially at risk for these eating disorders (Davis, 1994). This is true not only for elite gymnasts, but also for ballet dancers, figure skaters, and others. Indeed, strenuous physical activity contributes to the eating disorder of undernourished individuals (Davis et al., 1997). However, anorexics are *less* likely to commit suicide, concluded University of British Columbia researchers who examined the death records of five million women (Coren & Hewitt, 1998).

Why do so many young women deny themselves food in these ways? Perhaps most fundamental is the dissatisfaction many young women feel about their own bodies (Allgood-Merton & Lewinsohn, 1990). In response to the relentless "thin is in" message put out by the mass media, many young women conclude that their bodies are much rounder than the ideal female form of fashion models or the centrefolds in some magazines (Boaert et al., 1993). Therefore, they see themselves as imperfect (Hewitt et al., 1995). Their self-esteem becomes dependent upon what the scale says, and their self-image becomes more and more distorted. Distorted body image is characteristic of both anorexia and bulimia (e.g., Thompson, 1992). For example, in one investigation (Williamson et al., 1993), both anorexics and bulimics viewed themselves further from their ideal than those who were not suffering from any eating disorder (see Figure 10.4). Even at weights well below normal, they saw themselves as heavy. Thus, attractiveness and appearance are not necessarily about weight, but rather about self-esteem and how one feels regarding one's own appearance (Mendelson et al, 1996).

One result of anorexia in particular may be "reproductive suppression" (Anderson & Crawford, 1992). By denying their bodies food, some young adolescent girls stop the development of secondary sex characteristics, including the onset of menstruation, which, for some, relieves them of the stresses of puberty.

According to research in the United States, distorted thinking about their bodies is most characteristic of white female adolescents. For example, Nicher and Parker (1994) found that 90 percent of the white teens—but only 30 percent of African American teens—were unhappy with their weight. Nevertheless, increasing numbers of eating disorders are reported among Black women in North America. In Canada, researchers at the University of Windsor studied body-image perception among women of African Canadian/American descent and Blacks living in the Caribbean and Africa. They concluded that "there is a general preference for a fuller and shapelier figure within the [Black] ...community." Nevertheless, many Blacks exist not only in the Black world—but also in the white world—where attractiveness is dictated by the white standard of ideal body image (Ofosu et al., 1998). Another study compared body image in Canadian and Filipino women who were born in the Philippines and living in B.C. Researchers found that Filipinos valued "fatness," and that was related to their ideas about resisting disease (Farrales & Chapman, 1999).

Does Thinness Equal Sex Appeal?

Many men do not find excessive thinness in women to be attractive. Yet many women believe that unless they are extremely thin, they will not be physically appealing.

Figure 10.4
Dissatisfaction with One's Own Body: An Important Factor in Eating Disorders

As shown here, when actual body size was statistically controlled, both anorexics and bulimics viewed their current body size as larger than did controls, and both rated their ideal body size as smaller than did controls. However, many men do not find extreme thinness in women attractive; on average, they prefer a woman whose body size is somewhat larger than the one selected by women as ideal (Fallon & Rozin, 1985).

Source: Based on data from Williamson, Cubic, and Gleaves, 1993.

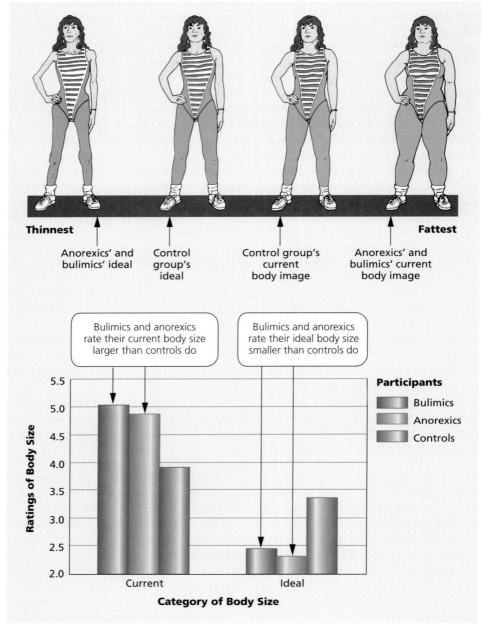

Eating disorders continue to trap young women in a vicious cycle from which they may not escape—without professional help (Thompson, 1992). At eating disorder clinics across Canada, including those at the Douglas Hospital in Montreal, the Toronto Hospital, and St. Paul's Hospital in Vancouver, various forms of treatment are used: nutrition programs, pharmacological intervention, and expressive therapies (Porter & Waisberg, 1992). In some cases, bulimic patients who show the same moods and appetite swings as those with seasonal affective disorder may benefit from light therapy (Lam & Goldner, 1998). All of these treatments may be helpful to some degree.

Although eating disorders are far more prevalent in women, men and women have similar concerns about their attractiveness and appearance (Garcia, 1998), and appearance anxiety among young men is increasing (Davis et al., 1993). One difference between men and women is the hypermasculine stereotype of the ideal male body (Gillett & White, 1992), which includes exaggerated muscular development. For many young men, the purpose of bodybuilding is to increase feelings of self-worth. That may lead to the unhealthy practice of using anabolic steroids, particularly among bodybuilders with lower self-esteem (Blouin & Goldfield, 1995)

K E Y QUESTIONS

■ What factors play a role in the regulation of eating?

■ What factors override this regulatory system, so that many people do not maintain a stable weight?

Critical Thinking

Do you think that the percentage of people who weigh more than they need to will continue to rise in the future? Explain your answer. What could reverse this trend?

Sexual Motivation

Suppose that visitors from another planet arrived on earth and visited one of our cities. What would they see? That's right—it would be countless signs, billboards, and advertisements focused on two topics: food and sex. The space aliens might quickly conclude that human beings are obsessed with these two topics—particularly with images of women (Lanis & Covell, 1995). Since we have already considered human behaviour with respect to food in some detail, we will now turn to **sexual motivation**, or the motivation to engage in sexual activity.

HORMONES AND SEXUAL BEHAVIOUR: ACTIVATION AND DIFFERENTIATION

As we saw in Chapter 9, at the onset of puberty there are rapid increases in the activity of the sex glands, or **gonads.** The hormones produced by the gonads influence sexual motivation. Sex hormones have *activation effects*. In most animals, females are receptive to males only at times when the concentrations of certain hormones are high. At other times, sexual behaviour takes place with very low frequency or does not occur at all. Furthermore, in many animals removal of the ovaries totally eliminates female sexual receptivity to males. Removal of the testes in males produces similar (though somewhat less clear-cut) results. In many species then, hormones produced by the gonads play a key role in sexual motivation (Rissman, 1995).

Human beings, however, are somewhat exceptional. Most women do not report large changes in sexual desire over the course of their monthly cycle, despite major shifts in the concentration of various sex hormones in their blood (Kelley & Byrne, 1992). Further, many women continue to engage in and enjoy sexual relations after menopause, when the hormonal output of their ovaries drops sharply. And in men there is little evidence of a clear link between blood levels of sex hormones (such as testosterone) and sexual responsiveness (Byrne, 1982). In general, the link between sex hormones and sexual motivation appears to be far less clear-cut and less compelling for human beings than for many other species.

Other chemical substances in the body, however, may play a more direct and dramatic role. Recent findings suggest that when people are sexually attracted to another person, the brain produces increased amounts of several substances that are related to *amphetamines*. These are stimulants; thus the increased production of amphetamine-like substances in the body may account for the feelings of falling in love. As one researcher puts it, "love is a natural high" (Walsh, 1993), one that confirms the words of the old song, "I get a kick out of you."

Sexual Motivation: Motivation to engage in various forms of sexual activity.

Gonads: The primary sex glands.

In sum, sex hormone levels do not seem to be as clearly linked to sexual motivation in humans as in other species; at the same time, there is some scientific evidence that other substances produced by our bodies do play an important role in sexual motivation, and even in romantic love. Does this mean that we will someday be able to produce pills that cause us to fall in (or out of) love? Probably not, because, as we will now see, where human beings are concerned, cognitive factors—our own thoughts, fantasies, and memories—play a very powerful role in sexual motivation. There does, however, seem to be a biochemistry of love, and biochemical effects, too, deserve careful attention as we try to understand the nature of human sexual motivation.

HUMAN SEXUAL BEHAVIOUR: SOME BASIC FACTS   Before the 1960s, the only scientific information about human sexual motivation was provided by surveys, for example the Kinsey Reports, published in the 1940s and 1950s (Kinsey, Pomeroy, & Martin, 1984; Kinsey et al., 1953). These were based on interviews with more than 10 000 women and men and they concluded that, where sexual behaviour is concerned, individual differences are enormous. Some people reported little or no interest in sex and indicated that they had been celibate for years, while others reported engaging in sexual relations with a large number of partners and having three or more orgasms every day.

In the 1960s, however, direct and systematic observation of actual sexual activities began. The first and still the most famous was the project conducted by Masters and Johnson (1966). These researchers observed, filmed, and monitored the reactions of several hundred volunteers of both sexes as they engaged in sexual intercourse or masturbation. More than 10 000 cycles of arousal and satisfaction were studied. The results yielded important insights into the nature of human sexuality. Perhaps the clearest finding was that both men and women move through four distinct phases during sexual behaviour.

First, there is the *excitement phase*. During this time, many physiological changes indicative of growing sexual excitement occur. The penis and clitoris become enlarged, vaginal lubrication increases, and nipples may become erect in both sexes. If sexual stimulation persists, both women and men enter the *plateau phase*. The size of the penis increases still further, and the outer third of the vagina becomes engorged with blood, reducing its diameter. Muscle tension, respiration, heart rate, and blood pressure all rise to high levels.

After a variable period of direct stimulation, both men and women approach the *orgasmic phase*. This consists of several contractions of the muscles surrounding the genitals, along with intense sensations of pleasure. The pattern of contractions, including their timing and length, is virtually identical in women and men.

The most striking difference between the two sexes occurs during the final *resolution phase*. For men, orgasm is followed by a reduction in sexual and physiological arousal. At that point, men enter a *refractory period* during which they cannot be sexually aroused or experience another orgasm. Among women, in contrast, two distinct patterns are possible. They, too, may experience a reduction in sexual and physiological arousal. Alternatively, if stimulation continues, they may experience additional orgasms.

The basic pattern just described seems to apply to all human beings. However, practically everything else seems to vary from one culture to another. Different cultures have widely different standards about such matters as the age at which sexual behaviour should begin, the frequency with which it should occur, physical characteristics considered sexually attractive, the particular positions and practices that are acceptable, the proper time and setting for sexual relations, the people who are appropriate partners, and the number of partners individuals should have at one time or in succession. So, to repeat: Where human sexuality is concerned, *variability* is definitely the central theme.

HUMAN SEXUAL BEHAVIOUR: WHAT IS AROUSING AND WHY? Clearly, sexual motivation plays an important role in human behaviour. But what, precisely, stimulates arousal? In certain respects, the same events or stimuli that produce such arousal in other species. First, direct physical contact—various forms of touching and foreplay—generates arousal. Second, human beings, like other organisms, can be sexually aroused by certain naturally occurring odours. For example, one study found that approximately 20 percent of men appear to be sexually stimulated by the scents of *copulins*, chemicals found in vaginal secretions (Hassett, 1978). More recently, some scientists have reported that odourless natural substances known as *pheromones* can produce attraction and arousal in both men and women (Bishop, 1996; Blakeslee, 1993). On the basis of these findings, large perfume companies have added synthetic human pheromones to their products. Will wearing such perfumes make you more attractive to the opposite sex, as advertised? That is yet to be determined, and you probably should not count on it (Cain, 1988; Ehrlichman & Bastone, 1990; Galef, 1993).

One potential source of sexual motivation, however, does seem to set human beings apart from their species: real or imagined erotic stimuli and images. Unlike other species, human beings possess the capacity to generate their own sexual arousal on the basis of erotic fantasies or daydreams (Leitenberg & Henning, 1995). And many people respond strongly to erotic materials containing either visual images or verbal descriptions of sexual behaviour. As one famous researcher put it: "The mind is the only true erogenous zone" (Byrne, 1992).

If the only effects produced by erotic materials were increases in sexual motivation and perhaps sexual behaviour, there would be little reason to discuss them further. However, growing evidence suggests that exposure to such materials produces other effects as well. First, repeated exposure to explicit erotica has been found to increase viewers' estimates of the frequency of several unusual sexual practices, including *sadomasochism* (sexual practices in which participants physically hurt one another), human–animal contact, and sex between adults and children (Zillmann & Bryant, 1984). Second, exposure to explicit erotic materials may reduce viewers' satisfaction with their own sex life and with their current sexual partner (e.g., Zillmann & Bryant, 1988). The link between explicit pornography and sexual dissatisfaction was one point made by the film called *Not a Love Story*, produced by the National Film Board of Canada. The reality of the situation is that most women (and most men) do not measure up to the standards of eroticism set by pornographic videos, and that exposure may result in sexual dysfunction—in some men in particular.

GENDER DIFFERENCES: EVOLUTION AND SEXUAL JEALOUSY Some non-human species are monogamous—some seabirds, for example, mate for life (Jones & Hunter, 1993). Do these animals experience jealousy if they discover their mate with another member of the opposite sex? At present, we do not know. But we *do* know that **sexual jealousy**—aroused by a perceived threat to a valued sexual relationship—is very common among our own species (Salovey, 1991; White & Mullen, 1990). Indeed, in a *Maclean's*/CTV poll, seven out of every ten Canadians agreed that extramarital sex is unacceptable. Furthermore, there is a definite connection between jealousy and domestic abuse (Wilson & Daly, 1996).

As you undoubtedly know, both women and men experience sexual jealousy. Recent findings suggest, however, that the two sexes may differ in this regard. Specifically, it appears that men may experience more intense jealousy in response to *sexual* infidelity on the part of their partners, while women may experience more intense jealousy in response to *emotional* infidelity. Why should this be so? The field of sociobiology (or evolutionary psychology, as it is sometimes known; Buss, 1990) provides one potential answer.

Sexual Jealousy: A negative state aroused by a perceived threat to one's sexual relationship with another person.

Here are the findings of several studies conducted by Buss and his colleagues (Buss et al., 1992). Male and female students were asked to indicate which would upset them more—learning that their romantic partner was forming a deep emotional attachment to another person, or that their partner was enjoying passionate sexual intercourse with that person. Results were clear: A large majority of the men (60 percent) reported greater distress over sexual infidelity, while a large majority of the women (83 percent) reported greater distress over emotional infidelity.

In a follow-up study, male and female participants were asked to imagine that their partner was either having sexual intercourse with another person or falling in love with another person. While the participants were imagining these scenes, the researchers recorded their physiological reactions: activity in a facial muscle involved in frowning, pulse rate, and electrodermal activity (electrical conductivity of the skin). Again, the results were clear. Males showed greater arousal and more signs of frowning when imagining sexual infidelity. Females showed greater arousal and more frowning when imagining emotional infidelity.

Taken together, these findings and those of other studies (Buss, 1999) indicate that males and females differ with respect to the kinds of events that make them jealous. Men seem to find sexual infidelity more disturbing than emotional infidelity, and it seems that male sperm do something about it. There is some recent evidence of special male sperm that block the sperm of other males which might also be present (Baker & Bellis, 1995). These differences in responses to infidelity may indicate ways in which the two genders evolved differently over millions of years—in order to maximize the probability of passing on their own genes.

SEXUAL ORIENTATION Estimates vary, but about 6 percent of all adults are exclusively **homosexual**: they engage in sexual relations only with members of their own sex (Kelley & Byrne, 1992). Some others are **bisexual**: they seek out and enjoy sexual contact with members of both sexes. The remainder of the population is **heterosexual** and engages in sexual relations only with members of the opposite sex. Why are some people exclusively homosexual, while most others are exclusively heterosexual? We have already examined some of the research relating to this issue in Chapter 2. Many factors probably play a role—genetic factors (Bailey & Pillard, 1991, 1993; Gladue, 1994; Turner, 1995), behaviours and feelings during childhood (Johnson & Bell, 1995), and individual differences in temperament that predispose children to prefer activities associated with one gender or the other (Bem, 1996).

With respect to the nervous system, recall from Chapter 2 that there are subtle differences between the brains of heterosexual and homosexual individuals. Twin studies, too, point to the role of genetic and biological factors in homosexuality. Finally, homosexuals differ in some cognitive abilities from heterosexual men and women in their performance on tests of visual/spatial ability (Witelson, 1991).

But how, precisely, do genetic and biological factors shape sexual orientation? Psychologist Daryl Bem proposes that biology and experience interact to determine sexual orientation in his "exotic leads to erotic" theory. According to Bem (1996), biological variables, such as genes, do not determine sexual orientation directly, but instead shape childhood temperaments that predispose some children to prefer male-typical activities, such as rough-and-tumble play, and others to prefer female-typical activities. Over time, gender-conforming children—those who prefer sex-typical activities—begin to feel different from their opposite-sex peers. In support of that idea, Bem cites the reports of many homosexuals that they knew they were different from early childhood. In contrast, gender-nonconforming children—those who prefer sex-atypical activities—begin to feel different from their same-sex peers, perceiving them as dissimilar and perhaps exotic.

Bem claims that every child—conforming or nonconforming—experiences heightened nonspecific arousal in the presence of peers from whom he or she feels different. Later on, that arousal may be transformed into romantic attraction. Although at this point Bem's theory is just that, a theory, it appears consistent with

Homosexual (sexual orientation): A sexual orientation in which individuals prefer sexual relations with members of their own sex.

Bisexual (sexual orientation): A sexual orientation in which individuals seek sexual relations with members of both their own and the other sex.

Heterosexual (sexual orientation): A sexual orientation in which individuals engage in sexual relations only with members of the other sex.

available evidence about nature and nurture. Still, given the complexity of sexual orientation, only time—and additional systematic research—will determine the theory's accuracy.

KEY QUESTIONS

- What is the role of hormones in human sexual motivation?

- What are the major phases of sexual activity?

- What is a key difference between human beings and other species with respect to sexual arousal?

- Is there any scientific evidence for the role of pheromones in human sexual behaviour?

- What factors appear to play a role in determining sexual orientation?

Aggressive Motivation

Atrocities in Europe, Asia, and Africa; mass murder in high schools; alarming rates of child abuse; a rising tide of workplace violence and road rage—these facts suggest that **aggressive motivation**—the desire to inflict harm others—plays an all-too-common role in human affairs (Baron & Richardson, 1994) and that includes Canada (Pihl, 1995).

THE ROOTS OF AGGRESSION: INNATE OR LEARNED?
After witnessing World War I, Sigmund Freud concluded, pessimistically, that human beings possess a powerful built-in tendency to harm others. Was Freud correct? Today, there is good reason to believe that **aggression** does have biological and/or genetic roots (e.g., Buss & Schackelford, 1997). For example, men convicted of impulsive crimes of violence, such as murdering strangers, have lower than normal levels of serotonin in their brains (Pihl, et al., 1995); in contrast, those convicted of cold-blooded and premeditated aggressive crimes show normal levels of serotonin (Toufexis, 1993). It may be that deficits in serotonin somehow interfere with the neural mechanisms that normally inhibit the expression of rage. Thus, there is some evidence to indicate that these factors play a role in violent crime (Gladue, 1991).

Aggressive Motivation: Often, the Results Are Tragic

What makes some people want to harm others? Students at W.R. Meyers high school in Taber, Alberta, where Jason Lang was murdered by another teenager, have seen the effects of aggressive motivation first hand.

In addition, recent findings suggest that hormones, especially the male hormone testosterone, may play a role in aggression. First, drugs that reduce testosterone levels in violent human males seem to reduce their aggression. Second, among prisoners, testosterone levels tend to be higher for those who have committed unprovoked violent crimes than among those who have committed nonviolent crimes (Dabbs, 1992; Dabbs et al., 1995). These findings certainly do not suggest that high testosterone levels, in and of themselves, stimulate overt aggression. However, they do point to the conclusion that individual differences with respect to these and perhaps other biochemical processes, can play some role in aggressive behaviour.

Aggressive Motivation: The desire to inflict harm on others.

Aggression: Behaviour directed toward the goal of harming another living being who wishes to avoid such treatment.

SOCIAL FACTORS IN AGGRESSION
On the other hand, many psychologists (Anderson et al., 1996; Berkowitz, 1993) note that there are significant cultural differences in aggression (Kuchinsky, 1993; Ostermann et al., 1994). For example, murder rates are more than one hundred times higher in some countries than in others

(Scott, 1992). Also, rates of aggression vary in the same country at different times in its history. The current crime statistics in some newly democratic countries illustrate this point. Those findings lead to the conclusion that human aggression is influenced by more than biology.

Aggression often stems from other social causes, including (to name a few) direct provocation, unexpected annoyances (Ahmed, 1992), observing other people behaving in an aggressive manner, the presence of weapons or other stimuli associated with aggression, sexually violent pornography, anti-woman attitudes (Demare et al., 1993), and the consumption of alcohol (Baron & Richardson, 1994; Seto & Barbaree, 1995).

An important social cause of aggressive motivation is **frustration**—the thwarting or blocking of goal-directed behaviour (Dollard et al., 1939). When individuals feel not only that their interests have been thwarted, but also that this has been arbitrarily done and without good cause, frustration can indeed be a powerful cause of aggression. In fact, feelings of injustice have recently been found to play an important role in instances of *workplace violence*—violent outbursts in which employees attack and even kill people with whom they work (e.g., Baron et al., 1999). However, frustration is only one of many factors that elicit aggression and seems to produce such effects only when it is unexpected (Ahmed & Mapletoft, 1989), unfair, or illegitimate (Berkowitz, 1989).

As you learned in Chapter 4, violence in the media—television, movies, and so on—is very common and increases aggression on the part of viewers (e.g., Huesmann, 1994). That is one of the most consistent findings in research on aggression—the result of hundreds of studies. In the past, it has been assumed by sponsors that "violence sells." Is that idea correct? Recent studies (Bushman, 1998) suggest that people who watch violent programs are *less* likely to remember the content of commercials shown during these programs. Apparently, violent images distract attention from the advertisements. These findings suggest that sponsoring violent television programs may not only be harmful to viewers, but, also, it may not make economic sense.

GENDER DIFFERENCES AND AGGRESSION Statistics Canada confirms that, in this country, males are much more likely than females to be arrested and convicted for violent acts. What do those data mean?

On the one hand, males do seem to be more likely both to instigate aggression and to be its target. Why is that so? In research at Bishop's University, researchers reported that sexually aggressive male students also tended to be "physically aggressive, masculine, traditional in sex role beliefs, accepting of interpersonal violence, and members of fraternities" (Lackie & de Man, 1997). Similarly, a study of bullies and their victims in elementary schools in one school district in British Columbia showed that bullies endorsed positive beliefs about aggression, whereas victims and other peers did not (Bentley & Li, 1995).

On the other hand, research reveals a qualitative difference between males and females in this regard. The tendency for males to engage in aggressive actions is greater for *physical* forms of aggression (hitting, kicking, use of weapons) than for other forms of aggression (yelling, swearing, and treating people in a condescending manner; Harris, 1992). In fact, recent findings indicate that females are *more* likely to engage in various *indirect* forms of aggression, such as malicious gossip, sulking, or withdrawal. (Bjorkqvist et al., 1992; Lagerspetz et al., 1988).

There is evidence that when females are made to feel *de-individuated*—anonymous and unaccountable for their actions—they are just as aggressive as males (Lightdale & Prentice, 1994). Thus, when the social prohibitions about appropriate feminine behaviour were weak, differences in aggressive behaviour between males and females disappeared. That may be a good part of the explanation for the radical changes in youth gang activity by girls—beatings, assault, and armed robberies—that have been reported recently in Toronto and other cities across Canada (Mathews, 1996).

A method of studying aggression in humans—with a long history— is the topic of the **Research Process** feature below.

Frustration: The blocking of on-going goal-directed behaviour.

The Research Process:
How Psychologists Study Aggression

Acts of aggression seem to be all around us. At one time or another, most people get so angry that thoughts of inflicting harm—on somebody else—come to mind. It is not surprising, then, that psychologists have studied aggression for many years. However, researchers in this area face a serious dilemma: The behaviour they wish to study is potentially dangerous and they cannot allow actual harm to be inflicted on real people. How can this predicament be resolved? One answer—which remains controversial even today—emerged in experiments conducted during the 1960s (e.g., Buss, 1961). In these experiments, participants believed that they were inflicting harm upon somebody else when, in reality, no harm actually occurred.

Research participants were told that they were in a study of the effects of punishment on learning—with a partner. The participants were told that they would serve as a *teacher*, and their partner as the *learner*. When the learner made a correct response, the teacher would provide a reward—a flashing light would indicate "Correct." When the learner made an error, however, the teacher would deliver an electric shock as punishment for this mistake. The electric shocks would be delivered by means of a device like the one shown in Figure 10.5, which came to be known as the **aggression machine.** Teacher-participants were told that the higher the number button they

pushed, the stronger the shock, and the longer they held it down, the longer the pulse would last. Then the teacher-participant received a sample Level 3 shock in order to experience what the punishment was like.

In reality, however, the learner was an *assistant to the researcher,* and received no shocks at all. Of course that was not known to the teacher-participant. During the course of the experiment, the learner-assistant made many pre-arranged errors. On each of these occasions, then, participants faced a choice: they could choose the mildest shock button on the aggression machine or they could choose higher numbered buttons that, presumably, delivered very intense shocks. On each occasion when the learner made an error, the choice was theirs: they could inflict harm or not, as they wished.

What did the teacher-participants do? As you can guess, this depended very much on other conditions in the study. For instance, if the learner- assistant acted in a rude or condescending manner, the participants tended to choose higher numbered shocks than if the assistant had behaved in a courteous and pleasant manner. Similarly, if the study took place where the room temperature was uncomfortably hot, participants tended to choose higher numbered buttons. In summary, the aggression machine seemed to be a tool that could be used to investigate the potential effects of many different variables on aggression.

Did these procedures really measure human aggression? This question has never been totally resolved, but several lines of evidence did suggest that Buss's procedures—or similar ones—did measure human aggression. Many studies found that people with a prior history of actual aggressive behaviour—criminals, for instance—chose stronger shocks than persons without such a history of aggression (e.g., Wolfe & Baron, 1971), and university students with a history of violent behaviour do too (Gully & Dengerink, 1983). More recent research has confirmed that the same variables influence aggression in real-life settings as in laboratory studies—for instance, direct provocation, exposure to media violence, high temperatures, and the consumption of alcohol (e.g., Anderson & Bushman, 1997).

Other procedures have been developed as well (e.g., Cherek et al., 1996) and used to reveal variables that had previously been ignored—for example, the link between aggression and exposure to erotic materials (e.g., Baron & Richardson, 1994) and the connection between violent film content and aggressive behaviour (e.g., Doob & Clime, 1972).

Figure 10.5
The Aggression Machine

The device shown here has been used to study aggression under safe laboratory conditions. Participants are told that they can deliver shocks (or other unpleasant stimuli such as heat) to another person by pushing buttons on the machine. The higher the number of the button being pushed, the stronger the shock. In fact, however, there is no "victim" and no shocks (or heat) are ever delivered.

Aggression Machine: A device used in the laboratory study of human aggression.

You will read more in Chapter 16 about the controversial experiments on obedience that used the aggression machine. In retrospect, however, the early experiments using the aggression machine have raised serious concerns. Notwithstanding the fact that Buss's procedures provided psychologists with a method of studying aggression and stimulated a great deal of research, as pointed out by researchers at the University of Calgary, the early experiments violated contemporary ethical research guidelines—for example, the requirement for informed consent (Stam, Lubek, & Radtke, 1998).

ENVIRONMENTAL FACTORS AND AGGRESSION While social factors seem to be among the most important causes of aggression, there are other causes as well. Especially important here are any conditions in the physical environment that cause individuals to experience discomfort—for instance, uncomfortably high temperatures (e.g., Bell, 1992) or unpleasant, irritating noises (e.g., Baron, 1994). The negative feelings produced by such conditions can increase aggressive motivation in several ways. First, they may trigger aggression directly: when we feel bad—whatever the cause—we tend to lash out against others (e.g., Berkowitz, 1993). Alternatively, such unpleasant feelings may trigger negative thoughts and memories, or lead us to perceive hostility and defend ourselves aggressively, even when that is not the case. In other words, unpleasant feelings may lead us to think in ways that produce aggressive behaviours.

Sports events seem often to include aggression as part of the game. Why do athletes fight fiercely in team sports like football or even floor hockey, for example (Palmer, 1993)? Researchers at the University of Lethbridge (Arms & Russell, 1997; Russell & Arms, 1995, 1998) studied the aggressive behaviour of men at an ice hockey game. These subjects filled out questionnaires about anger, how much they liked to watch fighting, and how likely they were to join into a fight in a crowd. On the one hand, the men who liked watching players fight and being in fights scored higher on the anger scales, were more impulsive, and were more likely to escalate a disturbance themselves. Similar results were found for male ice hockey spectators in Finland (Mustonen et al., 1996). On the other hand, which factors predict whether a fan will intervene to try to stop fighting at a sports riot? The factor that best identified a potential "peacemaker" was a positive attitude toward law and order (Russell et al., 1999).

In another study (Russell et al., 1995) a national sample of Canadian high school students was asked to what extent viewing and engaging in aggression produces relief (or catharsis) and a subsequent reduction in aggression. The males in this sample believed strongly that a link exists. Whatever the precise mechanism or emotions involved, research findings do offer strong support for the view that environmental stimuli sometimes increase our aggressive behaviours—something to keep firmly in mind the next time you are caught in traffic on a hot and sweltering day and feel your temper beginning to fray around the edges—the first sign of road rage. In Figure 10.6, you can compare the reasons that hockey fans in Canada and Finland attend games. Note the difference between the two countries with respect to watching fights (Mustanen et al., 1996).

ALCOHOL AND AGGRESSION Much research tells us that alcohol consumption is a common factor in cases of marital abuse and in violent crime. Studies at McGill University, the Alcohol Research Foundation in Toronto, and the Alberta Children's Hospital confirm the link between alcohol consumption and aggression. That co-occurrence does not tell us, however, how drinking alcohol leads to violence.

There are several different ideas about how this might happen. First, alcohol may disrupt the inhibition that controls aggressive behaviour. Here is what McGill University researchers Pihl and Peterson (1995, p. 141) had to say about this possi-

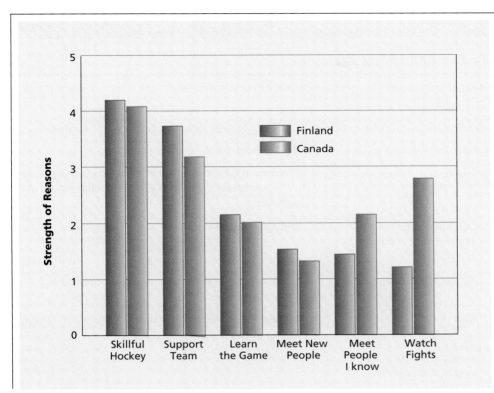

Figure 10.6
Reasons for Attendance at Hockey Games in Canada and Finland

Hockey fans in the two countries were similar except for how much they like to watch fights.

Source: Reprinted from Personality and Individual Differences, Vol. 21, No. 4, Mustonen, Anu, Arms, Robert L., and Russell, Gordon W. "Predictors of sports spectators' proclivity for riotous behaviour in Finland and Canada," pp. 519–526, © 1996, with permission from Elsevier Science.

bility: "During the course of socialization, most individuals develop anxiety [as a response to situational] cues to become aggressive; when drugs and alcohol inhibit this anxiety, the individual is more likely to engage in dangerous activities."

Second, alcohol may increase our sensitivity to pain, leading us to aggressive acts in our own defense. Third, it may reduce fear of injury during aggressive acts. Fourth, it may narrow our attention, reduce our ability to plan, and limit the control that our past experience exerts on our present behaviour. These are all functions of the pre-frontal cortex, the most highly evolved part of the brain, and the hypothesis that this is the area that is involved in aggressive behaviour and alcohol consumption has been put forward (Hoaken et al., 1998). Fifth, people with low brain serotonin levels may be particularly likely to act violently when drinking alcohol (Pihl & Lemarquand, 1998).

R. O. Pihl
McGill University

A very new finding should be added here, however. Pihl and his co-workers (Hoaken et al., 1998) conducted an experiment in which half of the subjects were sober and half were highly intoxicated. Both groups were asked to deliver electric shocks to "opponents" who did not really exist. Half of the members of each group were offered money for choosing lower shocks. To their surprise, the experimenters found that the intoxicated subjects (who were quite impaired in their thinking) had no difficulty inhibiting their aggression in order to obtain a monetary reward. What that implies for control of aggression in persons under the influence of alcohol remains to be seen.

An overview of the many social, environmental, and personal factors that increase the likelihood of aggression is presented in Table 10.2. This table suggests that reducing the level of aggression in any given society is a complex and challenging task.

For information about one of the most tragic examples of aggression in recent history, see the **Canadian Focus** feature.

<table>
<tr><td colspan="2">**TABLE 10.2**</td></tr>
</table>

Factors Influencing Aggression

Reducing the level of aggression in any society is a difficult task. Even so, ways must be found.

Factor	Effect on Aggression
High temperatures	Increase aggression
Audience	Increases aggression when this is a strong (dominant) tendency; decreases aggression if audience disapproves of this behaviour
Exposure to aggressive models (others behaving aggressively)	Increases aggression
Heightened arousal	Increases aggression when arousal is interpreted as provocation or frustration
Alcohol	Increases aggression in large doses; reduces aggression in very small doses
Apologies, explanations for provocative actions	Reduce aggression if accepted as sincere
Humorous materials	Reduce aggression if they induce feelings of amusement
Signs of pain on part of victim	Increase aggression if aggressor is very angry; reduce aggression if anger is low
Type A behaviour pattern	Increases aggression in many situations
Presence of weapons (not used in assault)	Increases aggression because of previous association with such behaviour.

Canadian Focus

The Montreal Massacre: Gender Hatred

In December 1989, Marc Lepine roamed the halls of L'École Polytechnique in Montreal looking for victims. Not just any victims—female victims. He entered a classroom brandishing a semi-automatic weapon and separated the women from the men. He told the men to leave. He then lined up the ten remaining women along the wall and gunned them down, shouting, "You're all a bunch of feminists, and I hate feminists!" He then went in pursuit of other female students. He killed a total of fourteen women before he killed himself (Came et al., 1989).

How are we to understand such an act? According to psychologists at Mount St. Vincent University (Kafer et al., 1993), the media focused on two explanations. One explanation assumes that we live in a profoundly sexist society, and that acts of people like Marc Lepine are an expression of the violent antagonism men harbour against women. The other explanation is this: In any society, there are misfits and mad people who commit unpredictable acts of extreme violence. In other words, the women Lepine killed just happened to be the target of this misfit's violence.

Single-factor explanations are appealing in that they are both simple and straightforward, but the behaviour they are called upon to explain in this case is not simple or straightforward. As Boyanowski (1991) points out, Lepine attributed all his failures in life to a single cause—women—and it is a mistake for us to follow this same logic and attempt to account for his behaviour in terms of a single cause.

Kafer and his colleagues sampled the opinion of students at Dalhousie, Mount Saint Vincent, and the Technical University of Nova Scotia. Most of the students they asked agreed with Boyanowski in that they saw many interacting factors as responsible for Lepine's murderous aggression. For most, neither the sexism explanation nor the unpredictable-violence explanation was seen as tenable on its own. Rather, they were seen as valid *in combination with* many other factors, such as violence on television, the portrayal of women as victims in horror movies, a prevailing high tolerance for violence, and the fact that the victims were entering a "male" profession.

There is merit in avoiding simplistic interpretations of complicated activities, and it seems likely that a host of interacting factors molded Lepine into the killer he became. Even so, none of the explanations are really satisfactory. Somehow, seeing Lepine's behaviour as rising from many factors diminishes the horror of what he did. It dilutes his responsibility as an individual for his behaviour, and this is a mistake. Perhaps the best way to try to understand the Montreal massacre is to ask a general question: Why do men aggress against women?

This is the approach taken by Brickman (1992) in her consideration of the Montreal massacre. The conclusions she draws are disturbing. She maintains that men aggress against women because it is rewarding (Russell et al., 1996). It can relieve sexual urges, release tension, and reduce anger. Normally, she holds, much of this aggression is carried out in private, unseen and unreported. It is, as she says, "socially invisible," and because it is invisible, men as a group escape censure. She makes the discomfiting but defensible argument that even when the violence becomes visible, as in the Montreal massacre, a man can benefit. At the expense of his female victims, Lepine gained attention and enduring notoriety that he would have otherwise never had.

KEY QUESTIONS

- Why do psychologists generally reject the view that aggression stems from innate factors?

- What are some important social factors that facilitate aggression?

- What are some important environmental causes of aggression?

Critical Thinking

What is your opinion of studies of aggression that take place in the research laboratory? Would it be better to study such behaviour only in natural environments? How would you defend the position you take on this issue?

Achievement: A Complex Human Motive

Hunger, sex, and aggression: These are motives we share with many other forms of life. There are some motives that appear to be unique to our own species. One of those—**achievement motivation**—is the desire to meet standards of excellence, to outperform others and accomplish difficult tasks (McClelland, 1961). Achievement motivation does not derive directly from basic biological factors, as do hunger, thirst, and, to some extent, sexuality. Yet it does influence behaviour in many different circumstances.

ACHIEVEMENT MOTIVATION: THE QUEST FOR EXCELLENCE For some people, accomplishing difficult tasks and meeting high standards of excellence are extremely important. For others, just getting by is quite enough. How can differences in this motive be measured? What are the effects of these differences? Achievement motivation is measured by the **Thematic Apperception Test** (or TAT)—a series of ambiguous pictures, such as an individual staring thoughtfully into space. Subjects are shown these pictures, one at a time, and asked to make up a story about each.

Achievement Motivation: The desire to accomplish difficult tasks and meet standards of excellence.

Thematic Apperception Test: A psychological test used to assess individual differences in several motives, such as achievement motivation and power motivation.

Measuring Achievement Motivation

One measure of achievement motivation is the TAT (Thematic Apperception Test). Persons taking the test make up stories about ambiguous scenes; the amount of achievement-related imagery in these stories is then scored.

These stories are then evaluated for achievement context according to carefully developed scoring manuals (e.g., Smith, 1992). The result is a score for achievement motivation, and scores may be calculated for several other motives as well. Two of these are *power motivation*—the desire to exert influence over others and *affiliation motivation*—the desire for close friendly relations with other people. While the TAT continues to be used in its original form, Winter (1983) has also developed a technique for scoring these motives directly from any type of verbal material—books and speeches, for example. This permits psychologists to study the achievement motivation of political and military leaders and to compare achievement motivation across cultures.

Recent findings indicate that achievement motivation contributes to similar success in various ethnic and cultural groups (Rowe et al., 1995). In other words, *within* different cultures, success depends on the same factors, regardless of ethnic and cultural background. However, average levels of achievement motivation vary sharply *between* different cultures. For example, in classic research on this topic, McClelland (1985) analyzed the degree to which children's stories in twenty-two different cultures showed themes of achievement motivation. He then related these levels of achievement motivation to measures of economic development— average income per person, for example. The results were clear. The greater the emphasis placed on achievement in the stories told to children, the more rapid the economic growth in these nations as the children grew up. Moreover, a massive study (over 12 000 participants in 41 different countries) found a significant relationship between achievement-related attitudes and economic growth (Furnham, Kirkcaldy, and Lynn, 1994).

These findings, and those reported in many other studies, support McClelland's original suggestion that a nation's economic success is related, at least in part, to the level of achievement motivation of its population. Of course, such research is correlational in nature, so we *cannot be certain* that differences in achievement motivation across various cultures cause differences in economic growth—perhaps that relationship is causal and perhaps not. That is a matter for further research.

EFFECTS OF ACHIEVEMENT MOTIVATION Do individual differences in achievement motivation really matter? As you might expect, individuals high in achievement motivation tend to get higher grades in school, earn more rapid promotions, and attain greater success in running their own businesses than people who are low in such motivation (Andrews, 1967; Raynor, 1970). However, people who are high in achievement motivation prefer situations involving moderate levels of risk or difficulty to ones that are very low or very high on these dimensions (Sorrentino et al., 1992). That may be because in situations involving moderate risk or difficulty, there is a good chance of success, but there is also a sense of challenge. In contrast, in situations that are very high in risk or difficulty, failure is likely—and high-achievement individuals dislike failure intensely. Moreover, situations that are very low in risk or difficulty fail to provide the challenge that people high in achievement motivation relish.

People who are high in achievement motivation have a stronger-than-average desire for feedback. They want to know how well they are doing so they can set goals that are challenging—but not impossible. Because of this desire for feedback, they prefer jobs in which rewards are given for individual performance—merit-based pay systems. They generally do not like working in situations where everyone receives the same across-the-board raise, regardless of their performance (e.g., Turban & Keon, 1993). Finally, as you might expect, people high in achievement motivation tend to excel in situations in which they are challenged to do their best or are confronted with difficult goals (e.g., McClelland, 1995).

POWER MOTIVATION   People who obtain high TAT scores on power motivation are more likely to be aggressive and to seek public recognition. They are more likely also to make career choices that will provide them with prestige and opportunities to dominate other people. Are there gender differences in power motivation? Contrary to what is popularly believed, women express as strong a power motive as do men (Winter, 1988). McClelland identified two types of power motivation, which are quite different. The first type is a need to have social influence that is for the benefit of other people. Some individuals do achieve power by doing good works. A high need for this kind of power is the result of rewards in childhood, not only for being assertive, but also for taking responsibility for oneself and for others (Winter & Stewart, 1978).

The second type of power motivation is summarized by the phrase "power for power's sake." This is the motivation of individuals who see their success in life in terms of winning at the expense of others. As adults, these individuals are competitive, aggressive, manipulative, and responsive to advertisements for powerful automobiles.

In a very interesting study (McLelland & Franz, 1992), researchers studied the achievement and power motivation of CEOs of some of the largest companies in the United States. There was a difference between the CEOs who scored high in power motivation and those who scored high in achievement motivation. The power-motivated CEOs' companies showed better increases in profit; the achievement-motivated CEOs' companies showed better growth in sales. How those differences came about remains to be determined by future research.

AFFILIATION MOTIVATION   Those who are high on the affiliation motive seek out the company of other people—to interact, associate, and relate to them. In a well-known classic experiment, subjects were told that they would be receiving painful electric shocks or mild electric shocks and given the option of waiting for the experiment alone or with other people. Twice the number of subjects who were told about painful shock chose to be with other people (Schachter, 1959). Why did that result occur? Here are some reasons confirmed by psychological science (Hill, 1991). First, other people provide us with a means of social comparison. They help us deal with uncertainties and evaluate and understand our own anxieties. Second, other people provide us with emotional support. They encourage and calm us. Third, they are a source of attention and appreciation. Finally, the company of other people can be a source of pleasure.

Some psychologists suggest that the affiliation motive is an adaptive, basic biological need that has evolved over millions of years for the benefit of our species. Not only the biological basis for this motive has evolved, but also the capacity to learn, on the basis of early rewards, to affiliate with other people.

K E Y *QUESTIONS*

- What is achievement motivation and how is it measured?
- What are the effects of achievement on individual behaviour and on the economic fortunes of countries?
- What is the need for cognition? What are its effects?

Intrinsic Motivation: Turning Play into Work

People perform many activities simply because they find them enjoyable. Everything from bungee jumping to gourmet cooking fits within this category. Such activities derive from **intrinsic motivation**; that is, we perform them primarily

Intrinsic Motivation: The desire to perform activities because they are rewarding in and of themselves.

because of the pleasure they yield, not particularly because they lead to external rewards. If people are given external rewards for performing such activities—money for pursuing their favourite hobby, for example—it may surprise you to learn that they become less motivated. They shift from explaining their behaviour in terms of intrinsic motivation ("I did it because I enjoy it") to explaining it in terms of external rewards ("I did it because I was paid").

Many studies support this explanation (e.g., Cialdini et al., 1998). In such research, some participants are provided with extrinsic rewards for doing something they enjoy, while others are not. When subsequently given an opportunity to perform the task again, those who receive the external rewards are less motivated to do so (Deci, 1975; Lepper & Green, 1978). These results have important implications for anyone seeking to motivate others by means of rewards—parents, teachers, and managers, for example. The research suggests that if people already enjoy various activities, offering them rewards may lower their intrinsic motivation and, ultimately, produce the paradoxical effect of reducing rather than enhancing performance!

At the University of Quebec in Montreal, Vallerand and his associates have developed, in both French and English, an *Academic Motivation Scale* that assesses an individual's intrinsic and extrinsic motivation. These researchers have shown how academic motivation and school performance are related (Fortier et al., 1995; Pelletier et al., 1995). When college students who persisted to the end of a compulsory course were compared with those who dropped out, Vallerand and Bissonnette (1992) found that those who completed the course were more intrinsically motivated.

Fortunately, intrinsic and extrinsic motivation are not necessarily incompatible (Rigby et al., 1992). In fact, Deci and his colleagues (e.g., Deci & Ryan, 1985) argue that what is important is that people perceive their behaviours to be self-determined—that is, intrinsically motivated. If individuals find their actions to be consistent with their self-image, their preferences, and their values, they may view them as self-determined even though they yield extrinsic rewards.

If people perceive that they have a choice as to which external rewards will be received (Feehan & Enzle, 1991), if external rewards are identified as recognition rather than as bribes (Rosenfield, Folger, & Adelman, 1980), and if the rewards provided are large and satisfying (Fiske & Taylor, 1991), intrinsic motivation may be enhanced (Ryan, 1982). In view of these facts, we can conclude that paying people for doing things they enjoy can sometimes reduce their intrinsic motivation—turn

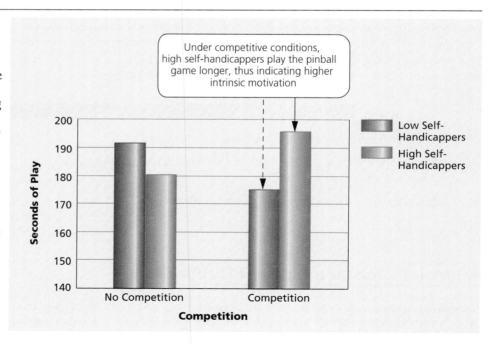

Figure 10.7
Self-Handicapping and Intrinsic Motivation

Under conditions where they were competing with another person, persons high in self-handicapping spent more time playing with a pinball machine than persons low in self-handicapping when they were free to choose any activity they wished. These findings suggest that self-handicapping can protect individuals from reductions in intrinsic motivation resulting from poor performance on a task.

Source: Based on data from Deppe and Harakiewicz, 1996.

play into work. But that is not always the case. When external rewards are delivered with care and in accordance with the principles just described, they can enhance rather than reduce motivation and performance.

PROTECTING INTRINSIC MOTIVATION If you have ever said, before beginning some activity, "I really did not sleep well last night," or "I am really not feeling too great today," you have used *self-handicapping*. The goal is to be able to explain away poor performance, in advance or afterwards, by pointing to various external factors that could, potentially, be the cause (e.g., Szmajke, 1998). Using self-handicapping, we "buffer" ourselves against reductions in intrinsic motivation (Deppe & Harackiewicz, 1996). By being able to "explain away" poor performance, we maintain intrinsic motivation. That is more likely to be the case in individuals with less self-esteem, but self-handicaps are also used by elite athletes (Hausenblas & Carron, 1996; Prapavesses & Grove, 1998).

To test this reasoning, persons who had been identified as high or low self-handicappers (based on results of a prior assessment) played an enjoyable, intrinsically motivating pinball game. Before playing, all of these subjects were given an opportunity to practise. As expected, high self-handicappers practised less, thus giving themselves a ready explanation for poor performance on the pinball task. Afterwards, when they were free to play or not, some high self-handicappers played the pinball game longer than low self-handicappers.

These results, shown in Figure 10.7, indicate that if individuals want to protect their intrinsic motivation from possible reductions, they can readily do so. Moreover, since most of us become experts at self-handicapping early in life, it appears that we have effective techniques for doing so readily at our disposal. In short, we can prevent the conversion of "play" into "work" in at least some situations.

K E Y QUESTIONS

- What is intrinsic motivation?

- Why is intrinsic motivation sometimes reduced when individuals receive external rewards for performing activities they enjoy?

- What is self-handicapping and how can it protect against reductions in intrinsic motivation?

Emotions

Can you imagine life without **emotions**—without joy, anger, sorrow, or fear—the world of Mr. Spock of *Star Trek*, who prided himself on being totally lacking in emotion? Probably you cannot, for emotions are essential to our personal existence. They are the flavour of life. Without them, we would not really be ourselves.

But what are emotions? The closer we look, the more complex these reactions seem to be. Among scientists there is general agreement that emotions are physiological changes within our bodies—shifts in heart rate, blood pressure, and so on; expressive behaviours—outward signs of these internal reactions; and subjective cognitive states—the personal experiences we label as emotions (e.g., Prkachin et al., 1999). In the discussion that follows, we will first look at several contrasting theories of emotion and the biological basis of emotional states. Then we will consider how emotions are expressed. Finally, we will examine the complex interplay between emotions and cognition—how the way we feel influences the way we think, and vice versa.

Mr. Spock: A Person without Emotions?

Mr. Spock, science officer of the USS Enterprise in the *Star Trek* series, claimed to have no emotions. However, in many episodes, he seemed to suffer greatly from this lack—thus indicating that he did have emotions, after all!

Emotions: Reactions consisting of physiological reactions, subjective cognitive states, and expressive behaviours.

The Nature of Emotions

Among the many theories of emotion that have been proposed, three have been most influential. These are known (after the scientists who proposed them) as the *Cannon-Bard*, *James-Lange*, and *Schachter-Singer* theories. A fourth theory—the *opponent-process* theory—adds additional insights into the nature of emotion.

THE CANNON-BARD AND JAMES-LANGE THEORIES: WHAT COMES FIRST, ACTION OR FEELING? Imagine that in one of your courses, you are required to make a class presentation. As you walk to the front of the room, your pulse begins to race, your mouth feels dry, and beads of perspiration form on your forehead. What is the basis for this reaction? Sharply contrasting answers are offered by the Cannon-Bard and James-Lange theories of emotion.

Let us begin with the **Cannon-Bard theory**, because it is consistent with our own informal observations of our emotions. This theory suggests that various events induce *simultaneously* the subjective experiences we label as emotions and the physiological reactions that accompany them. Thus, the sight of the audience and of your professor (pen poised to evaluate your performance) causes you to experience a racing heart, a dry mouth, and other signs of physiological arousal, and, at the same time, to experience subjective feelings you label as fear. In other words, this situation stimulates various portions of your nervous system to produce both arousal, mediated by your autonomic nervous system (see Chapter 2), and subjective feelings, mediated by other parts of your brain.

In contrast, the **James-Lange theory** offers a more surprising view of emotion. It suggests that subjective emotional experiences are actually *the result of* physiological changes within our bodies. In other words, you feel frightened when making your speech *because* you notice your heart is racing, your mouth is dry, and so on. As James himself put it in 1890, "We feel sorry because we cry, angry because we strike, and afraid because we tremble."

Which of these theories is correct? Until recently, most evidence seemed to favour the Cannon-Bard approach: emotion-provoking events produce both physiological arousal and the subjective experiences we label as emotions. Now, however, the pendulum of scientific opinion has moved toward greater acceptance of the James-Lange approach—the view that we experience emotions because of our awareness of physiological reactions to various stimuli or situations. Several lines of evidence point to this conclusion. First, recent studies conducted with sensitive technology indicate that different emotions are indeed associated with different patterns of physiological activity (Levenson, 1992). Not only do various emotions *feel* different, it appears, they also result in somewhat different patterns of bodily changes, including contrasting patterns of brain and muscle activity (Ekman, Davidson, & Friesen, 1990; Izard, 1992).

Second, support for the James-Lange theory is provided by research on the **facial feedback hypothesis** (Laird, 1984; McIntosh, 1996) that changes in our facial expressions may produce shifts in our emotional experiences rather than merely reflecting them. Similarly, other research indicates that changing our body posture (e.g., Flack, Laird, & Cavallaro, 1999) or even the tone of our voices (e.g, Siegman & Boyle, 1993) may influence how we feel.

In view of such findings, the facial feedback hypothesis has been re-named the *peripheral feedback effect*, to suggest that emotions can be influenced by more than facial expressions. Several studies offer support for this hypothesis (e.g., Ekman et al., 1990) and therefore for the James-Lange theory. Subjective emotional experiences do often arise directly in response to specific external stimuli, as the Cannon-Bard view suggests. However, they can also be generated by changes in awareness of the look and feel of our own bodies (Ekman, 1992).

"I don't sing because I am happy. I am happy because I sing."

The James-Lange Theory in Operation

The James-Lange theory suggests that the bird is correct: The subjective experiences we label as emotions are the result of changes within our body or our overt behaviour.

Source: Drawing by Frascino: © 1991 The New Yorker Magazine, Inc.

Cannon-Bard Theory: A theory of emotion suggesting that various emotion-provoking events simultaneously produce subjective reactions labelled as emotions and physiological arousal.

James-Lange Theory: A theory of emotion suggesting that emotion-provoking events produce various physiological reactions and that recognition of these is responsible for subjective emotional experiences.

Facial Feedback Hypothesis: A hypothesis indicating that facial expressions can influence as well as reflect emotional states.

SCHACHTER AND SINGER'S TWO-FACTOR THEORY   Strong emotions are a common part of daily life, but how do we tell them apart? How do we know that we are angry rather than frightened, sad rather than surprised? One potential answer is provided by a third theory of emotion. According to this view, known as the **Schachter-Singer theory** or the *two-factor theory,* emotion-provoking events produce increased arousal (Schachter & Singer, 1962). In response to feelings of arousal, we search the external environment in order to identify the causes of such feelings. The causes we then select play a key role in determining the label we place on our arousal, and so in determining the emotion we experience. If we feel aroused after a near-miss in traffic, we will probably label our emotion as "fear" or perhaps "anger." If, instead, we feel aroused in the presence of an attractive person, we may label our arousal as "attraction" or "love." In short, we perceive the emotion that external cues suggest we should be feeling. The theory is described as a two-factor view because it considers both the arousal and the cognitive appraisal we perform in our efforts to identify the causes of the arousal.

Many studies provide support for the Schachter-Singer theory. A classic one was done in 1974, by Dutton and Aron (of the University of British Columbia) on a suspension bridge over the deep Capilano Gorge in North Vancouver. The Capilano Bridge is very high and narrow, and it sways; it is said to be a "very scary" crossing. Male hikers met an attractive female research assistant either while crossing high above the rocky gorge or while on solid ground. Later, the men were asked to rate their attraction to the assistant. As the Schachter-Singer theory predicts, those who met her on the swaying bridge, when arousal was high, found her more attractive and they were more likely to actually call her for a date! Apparently, the male hikers interpreted their feelings of arousal on the bridge as attraction. In her absence they might well have labelled it fear. Findings such as these suggest that the Schachter-Singer theory provides important insights into the way in which we label our own emotions.

OPPONENT-PROCESS THEORY: ACTION AND REACTION TO EMOTION   Have you ever noticed that when you experience a strong emotional reaction, it is soon followed by the opposite reaction? Thus, elation is followed by a letdown, and anger is followed by calm or even by regret over one's previous outbursts. This relationship is an important focus of the **opponent-process theory of emotion** (Solomon, 1982). The theory has two central assumptions: emotional reactions to a stimulus are followed automatically by an opposite reaction, and repeated exposure to a stimulus causes the initial reaction to weaken and the opponent process, or opposite reaction, to strengthen. So, for example, a politician who initially enjoys making speeches in public may experience a severe letdown after each speech is finished. With repeated experiences in delivering speeches, the pleasure she feels at addressing large crowds may weaken, while the letdown intensifies or occurs sooner after the speech is over. The result: She may gradually cut down on her public-speaking engagements.

Opponent-process theory provides important insights into drug addiction. For example, heroin users initially experience intense pleasure, followed by unpleasant sensations of withdrawal. With repeated use of the drug, the pleasure becomes less intense and unpleasant withdrawal reactions strengthen (Marlatt et al., 1988). In response, addicts begin to use the drug not for the pleasure it provides but to avoid the negative feelings that occur when they do not use it. In summary, according to opponent-process theory, emotional reactions often occur in action–reaction cycles, and many aspects of behaviour can be interpreted within this framework. An overview of the theories of emotion discussed in this section is provided in the **Key Concept** on page 420.

Schachter-Singer Theory (two-factor theory): A theory of emotion suggesting that our subjective emotional states are determined, at least in part, by the cognitive labels we attach to feelings of arousal.

Opponent -Process Theory of Emotion: A theory suggesting that an emotional reaction to a stimulus is followed automatically by an opposite reaction.

Key Concept

Four Major Theories of Emotion

Cannon-Bard Theory

- Emotion-provoking events or stimuli (e.g., watching or participating in an exciting sports event) stimulate the nervous system.
- The stimulation results in physiological reactions (e.g., faster pulse and higher blood pressure).
- Simultaneously, this stimulation also produces the subjective cognitive states we label emotions (e.g., anxiety, joy, anger).

James-Lange Theory

- Emotion-provoking events (e.g., watching or participating in an exciting sports event) produce physiological reactions (e.g., faster pulse, higher blood pressure, increased perspiration).
- Our awareness of these reactions results in the subjective cognitive states we label emotions (e.g., anger, joy, fear). That is, we feel frightened because we notice that our heart is racing, our mouth is dry, the palms of our hands are wet, and so on.

Schachter-Singer Two-Factor Theory

- Emotion-provoking events (e.g., watching or participating in an exciting sports event) produce increased arousal.
- In response to this state of increased arousal, we search the external environment to identify possible causes for it (especially in situations where several potential causes exist).
- The emotions we experience depend on the causes we choose.

Opponent-Process Theory

- Emotional reactions to a stimulus are followed automatically by an opposite reaction.
- Repeated exposure to a stimulus causes the initial reaction to weaken and the opponent process (opposite reaction) to strengthen.

Event

Exposure to emotion-provoking events is the starting point for all major theories of emotion.

Emotions

Athletes in an emotion-provoking situation such as a close, hard-fought game have little doubt about the causes of the arousal they experience. In other situations, however, the causes of arousal will be far less obvious.

K E Y QUESTIONS

■ How do the Cannon-Bard and James-Lange theories differ?

■ What is the Schachter-Singer theory of emotion?

■ What is the opponent-process theory of emotion?

The Biological Basis of Emotion

Emotions are complex reactions involving subjective feelings. However, not only do we feel our emotions, we also have the capability of communicating how we feel to other people, and comprehending their emotional state as well. Research on the neural basis of emotion finds that different structures in the brain are responsible for each of these functions—although they all work together, of course.

As you may recall from Chapter 2, the internal reactions that accompany emotions are regulated by the two parts of the autonomic nervous system. That is, activation of the *sympathetic nervous system* readies the body for vigorous activity, producing such reactions as increases in heart rate, blood pressure, and respiration. In contrast, activation of the *parasympathetic nervous system* influences activity related to restoration of the body's resources. For example, blood is diverted away from large muscles and to the digestive organs, and digestion itself is facilitated. As we saw earlier, different emotions are associated with somewhat different patterns of physiological reactions; so the fact that emotions such as anger, joy, and disgust feel very different subjectively does appear to be mirrored, to some degree, in different biological reactions. In addition, different emotions are related to specific patterns of activation in the cerebral cortex (Davidson, 1992).

As you learned in Chapter 2, the right cerebral hemisphere plays an especially important role in the expression and comprehension of emotions. Healthy individuals with intact brains are better at identifying the emotions of other people when such information is presented to their right hemisphere rather than to their left hemisphere (e.g., Ladavas, Umilta, & Ricci-Bitti, 1980). Individuals with damage to the right hemisphere have difficulty understanding the emotional tone of another person's voice or in correctly describing emotional scenes (Heller, 1997). Furthermore, communication of emotion also takes place in the tone of voice—prosody—which is controlled by the right hemisphere (Lalande et al., 1992), and patients with damage to the right hemisphere are less successful at expressing their own emotions through the tone of their voice (Borod, 1993).

However, the left hemisphere is also involved—although not in quite the same way. There appear to be important differences between the left and right hemispheres of the brain in the *valence* of emotion—the extent to which an emotion is pleasant or unpleasant, and the *arousal level*—its intensity. Activation of the left hemisphere (as revealed by brain imaging) is linked to positive emotions, approach, and response to reward, while activation of the right hemisphere is linked to negative emotions, avoidance, and withdrawal from aversive stimuli (Heller et al., 1998). That confirms what medical reports have indicated for years—people who experience damage to the left hemisphere often develop deep depression, while those with damage to the right hemisphere show euphoria (Robinson et al., 1984).

These cases suggest that positive feelings result from activity in the left hemisphere, while negative ones arise in the right hemisphere. When watching films designed to elicit happiness or amusement, participants generally show greater activation in the left than in the right cortex. In contrast, when watching films designed to elicit disgust, they show greater activation in the right cortex (Davidson, 1992; Tomarken, Davidson, & Henriques, 1990). It may be that we recruit those centres when we are listening to pleasant and unpleasant musical pieces (Blood et al., 1999). Similar findings have been obtained with infants less than three days old: They show greater right-side activation in response to unpleasant tastes, and greater left-side activation in response to pleasant ones (Davidson & Fox, 1988). Thus, the cerebral hemispheres show early specialization with respect to emotions.

Depressed people have reduced brain activity in the right posterior region, while persons suffering from anxiety have increased brain activity in that same place (Heller et al, 1995). Those data are illustrated in Figure 10.8. Insight into the neural mechanisms that underlie such disordered emotions can be an important first step toward developing effective treatments, so our growing knowledge of the neural bases of emotions has important practical as well as scientific implications.

Structures deep within the brain play an important role in emotions. In particular, the amygdala is the key to emotional information relating to threat or danger—for instance, signs of fear or anger in other people (Adolphs, 2000; Adolphs & Tranel, 1999). From an evolutionary perspective, the existence of systems within the brain that focus on such stimuli makes considerable sense: being able to respond to such stimuli very quickly can mean the difference between survival and death.

Figure 10.8
Role of the Cerebral Hemispheres in Emotion—and in Psychological Disorders

Growing evidence indicates that activation of the left cerebral hemisphere is associated with positive affect while activation of the right hemisphere is associated with negative affect. Further, activation of anterior portions of both hemispheres is associated with the valence of emotions, while activation of the posterior portions of the hemispheres is associated with arousal—the intensity of emotions.

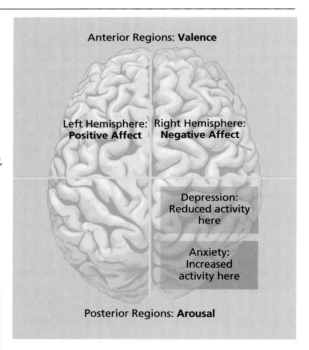

Anterior Regions: **Valence**

Left Hemisphere: **Positive Affect**   Right Hemisphere: **Negative Affect**

Depression: Reduced activity here

Anxiety: Increased activity here

Posterior Regions: **Arousal**

K E Y   QUESTIONS

■ Are different emotions associated with contrasting patterns of physiological reactions?

■ Are different emotions related to different patterns of brain activity?

Critical Thinking

Suppose that, in the future, we learn enough about the brain to produce specific emotions by stimulating certain portions of it. Would these emotions be "real" or not? Explain your answer.

The External Expression of Emotion

Emotions are private. No one can truly share our subjective experiences. Yet we are able to recognize the presence of various emotions in others, and we are able to communicate our own feelings to them in words (Storm & Storm, 1987). But how well do we understand what other people are telling us about their emotions? A study by Bortolotti and others (1993) at Laurentian University examined how well children (in grades two and five) and university students understand statements about emotions of children. In general, verbal statements about happiness and comfort were understood best, while those about anger and guilt were most poorly understood.

We also communicate emotion without words. **Non-verbal cues** are outward signs of internal emotional states shown in facial expression, body posture, and other behaviours. In deaf-parented families, "visual language" messages have a special part to play (Mallory et al., 1992). Some non-verbal messages involve objects. Reportedly, Queen Elizabeth always carries a purse, which she uses to send as many as twenty different signals to her guards when she needs assistance of some kind. The most revealing of non-verbal communications, however, involve non-verbal cues.

Non-verbal Cues: Outward signs of others' emotional states. Such cues involve facial expressions, eye contact, and body language.

NON-VERBAL CUES: THE BASIC CHANNELS The communication of emotion occurs over several basic channels or paths simultaneously. The most revealing of these are *facial expressions, eye contact, body movements and posture,* and *touching.* Much research on the transmission and interpretation of non-verbal cues (facial expressions, eye contact, body posture or movements) suggests that there are gender differences here. Females seem to be not only better at communicating their own feelings through non-verbal messages, but also better at understanding the non-verbal messages sent by others (e.g., DePaulo, 1992). Since non-verbal cues are often very revealing, females' superior skills are very beneficial in many different social contexts (e.g., Hall & Veccia, 1990). Indeed, this may be an explanation for so-called "feminine intuition"—the ability to tell in advance how other people will feel or behave.

Non-verbal Cues: External Guides to Internal Reactions

People often reveal their emotions through *non-verbal cues*—facial expressions, body movements or postures, and other observable actions.

UNMASKING THE FACE: FACIAL EXPRESSIONS AS GUIDES TO OTHERS' EMOTIONS More than 2000 years ago, the Roman orator Cicero stated, "The face is the image of the soul." By this he meant that feelings and emotions are often reflected in the face and can be read there from specific expressions. Modern research suggests that Cicero was correct in this belief: It is possible to learn much about others' current moods and feelings from their facial expressions. In fact, it appears that six different basic emotions are represented clearly, and from an early age, on the human face: anger, fear, sadness, disgust, happiness, and surprise (Ekman, 1992). Recent findings suggest that another emotion—contempt—may also  be a fundamental human facial expression (e.g., Rosenberg & Ekman, 1995).

It is the thinking of Kenneth Prkachin at the University of Northern British Columbia (e.g., 1997; 1999) that the expression of pain is universal as well. This researcher suggests that four facial actions are used to express pain: lowering the eyebrows, tightening up the eyes, closing the eyelids, and wrinkling the nose—thus raising the upper lip. Try doing those all together and see whether you agree. We use our faces to broadcast to the world that we are in pain for a number of reasons—for example, to ask for help or to give other people a warning of danger (Prkachin & Craig, 1995). Of course we humans are also able to pretend we are in pain, and that is of practical concern. How well do we distinguish genuine from deceptive pain? Our ability to tell facial expressions of genuine pain from suppressed

Kenneth Prkachin
*University of Northern
British Columbia*

or fake pain has been the focus of research at Simon Fraser University and at the University of Waterloo, where undergraduates were able to tell "to a modest degree" deliberate from fake pain in facial expressions (e.g., Poole & Craig, 1992; Prkachin, 1992b).

A test developed especially for infant pain has been used to show that facial *expression* of pain is similar in infancy, even in infants who are born prematurely (e.g., Craig & Grunau, 1993; Craig et al., 1993). This evidence is taken as support for the idea that human faces express pain similarly throughout the lifespan. During development, however, changes do occur in the *comprehension* of emotions in general (Staver, 1993), and of facial expressions in particular. At the University of Lethbridge, these changes were studied by Kolb (et al., 1992) in children from age six to fifteen and in adults up to age thirty. The findings indicated two ages at which important increases in correct understanding of facial expressions occurred—six to eight years, and thirteen to fourteen years. Kolb and his associates linked this to changes occurring in the development of the frontal lobes, which may take place until age fourteen.

Of course, we are capable of showing many more than six different facial expressions. Emotions occur in many combinations—for example, anger along with fear, surprise combined with happiness. Further, each emotion can vary greatly in intensity: fear from apprehension to terror; anger from annoyance to rage. Thus, while there is a small number of basic themes in facial expression of emotions, the number of variations on those themes is large.

Until recently, it was widely assumed that basic facial expressions (such as those for happiness, anger, or disgust) are universal—that they indicate specific emotions to people all over the world (e.g., Ekman & Friesen, 1975). As in all scientific endeavour, the opinion with respect to the universality of basic emotions is not unanimous. In particular, the part that cultural factors play is a point of debate. Moreover, a recent review of the evidence on this issue suggests that the interpretation of facial expressions may also be influenced by situational factors. That is because while facial expressions may indeed reveal much about emotions, judgments about the emotion being presented are also affected by context. For instance, if people are read a story about an angry person but are shown a face showing fear, many describe the face as showing the emotion in the context and not the emotion on the face. Thus, facial expressions do not always provide clear signals about underlying emotions. In short, it appears that we must be cautious about assuming that a smile, for example, will be seen as a sign of happiness by all people and in all situations (Carroll & Russell, 1996; Russell, 1994).

GAZES AND STARES: THE LANGUAGE OF THE EYES   Have you ever had a conversation with someone wearing dark glasses? If you have, you know that this can be an uncomfortable situation. When you cannot see the other person's eyes, you cannot tell how he or she is reacting. Ancient poets often described the eyes as "windows to the soul," and in one important sense they were right. We do often learn much about others' feelings from their eyes. For example, we interpret direct eye contact as a sign of liking or friendliness (Kleinke, 1986). In contrast, if others avoid eye contact with us, we may conclude that they are unfriendly, do not like us, or are shy (Zimbardo, 1977).

There is one important exception to this general rule. If another person gazes at us continuously and maintains this contact regardless of any actions we perform, he or she can be said to be *staring*. Most people attempt to minimize exposure to this particular kind of non-verbal cue if possible (Ellsworth & Carlsmith, 1973). Stares are often interpreted as a sign of anger or hostility, and may cause a great deal of anxiety and discomfort. Indeed, in one case it was clearly deemed sexual harassment; at one Canadian university, a professor was sanctioned for repeatedly leering at a female student.

BODY LANGUAGE: GESTURES, POSTURE, AND MOVEMENTS Try this simple demonstration: Recall an incident that made you angry—the angrier the better. Think about it for a minute. Now bring another incident to mind—one that made you feel sad—again, the sadder the better. Did you change your posture or move your hands, arms, or legs as your thoughts shifted from the first incident to the second? The chances are good that you did, for our current mood or emotion is often reflected in the posture, position, and movement of our body. Such non-verbal behaviours are termed **body language** or, more technically, *kinesics*, and they can provide several useful kinds of information about others' emotions.

First, frequent body movements—especially ones in which a particular part of the body does something to another, such as touching, scratching, or rubbing—suggest emotional arousal. The greater the frequency of such behaviour, the higher a person's level of arousal or nervousness seems to be (Harrigan et al., 1991). The specific movements made, too, can be revealing. Consider the statements "He adopted a *threatening posture*" and "She greeted him with *open arms*." Different body postures are suggestive of particular emotional states (Rossberg & Poole, 1993).

Direct evidence is provided by research conducted by Aronoff, Woike, and Hyman (1992). These researchers first identified characters in classical ballet who played dangerous or threatening roles (the Angel of Death, Macbeth) or warm, appealing roles (Juliet, Romeo). Then they carefully examined samples of dancing by these characters in actual ballets to see the postures they used. Aronoff and his colleagues found that the threatening characters used diagonal poses three times as often as the friendly characters, and that the friendly characters adopted rounded poses almost four times as often as the threatening characters. These and related findings suggest that large-scale body movements or postures are an important source of information about emotions.

Finally, more specific information about others' feelings is often provided by **gestures** or *emblems*, body movements that have highly specific meaning in a given culture. For example, in several countries, holding the thumb up is a sign of approval. Similarly, holding the nose between the thumb and index finger is a sign of displeasure or disgust. Emblems vary greatly from culture to culture, but all human societies have signals of this type for greetings, departures, insults, and descriptions of various physical states—"I am full," "I am tired," and so on. Do you recognize the gestures shown in the photos? In Canada and several other countries, these movements have clear and definite meanings. However, in other cultures, they might have no meaning or a different meaning. For this reason, it is wise to be careful about using gestures while travelling in cultures different from your own: you may offend the people around you without intending to do so!

Gestures: Body Language That Communicates

Can you guess what the person shown is trying to communicate? Probably you can, because within a given culture, *gestures* often carry highly specific meanings.

TOUCHING: THE MOST INTIMATE NON-VERBAL CUE Suppose that while you were talking with another person, he or she touched you briefly. What would you think? The answer is, "It depends." Touch can suggest affection, sexual interest, dominance, caring, or even aggression. Important factors include these: who does the touching (i.e., a friend or a stranger); which gender (e.g., Roese, et al., 1992; Stoppard & Gruchy, 1992); the nature of the touching (i.e., brief or prolonged, gentle or rough); and the context in which it takes place (i.e., a business or social setting, a doctor's office).

Body Language: Non-verbal cues involving body posture or movement of body parts.

Gestures: Body movements that may have highly specific meaning in a given culture.

Despite these complexities, touching in a nonthreatening and appropriate manner can have positive effects. Consider, for example, the results of an ingenious study by Crusco and Wetzel (1984). These investigators enlisted the aid of waitresses, who agreed to treat customers in one of three different ways when giving them their change. Either they touched the customer briefly on the hand (about half a second), or they touched them on the shoulder for a longer period of time (one to one-and-a-half seconds), or they did not touch them at all. The researcher tallied up the tips the customers left. The results were clear: Both a brief touch on the hand and a longer touch on the shoulder resulted in significantly more money. Thus, touching in a nonthreatening and appropriate manner can have positive effects. More recent research indicates that other gestures that convey friendliness to customers, such as drawing a smiling face on the back of a bill or writing "thank you" (Rind & Bordia, 1996; 1995) are like touching in this way.

There are some differences in the non-verbal communication between women and men. For example, when women become hostile, they cease speaking and draw their bodies away, while men show hostility by raising their voices and leaning forward (Davidson, 1994).

Would You Trust This Man?

Many people expect a used car salesperson to be dishonest.

DETECTING LIES FROM NON-VERBAL CUES In everyday life we are often tempted to tell lies, and recent research findings indicate that, all too often, we yield to these temptations. One recent study of lying found that college students typically tell about two lies per day. Most of those lies are designed to enhance social "image" or advance personal interests (DePaulo et al., 1996). How successful are people at reading non-verbal cues for what is true and what is false (Guerrero et al., 1999)?

The general finding is that our abilities are moderately good, if we see only the person's face, and even better if we see the whole body (Ekman, 1985)—although we are more confident about our abilities than we really should be. This makes us prone to making mistakes and easy to mislead. The following *external* cues are often present when someone is lying.

■ Fleeting facial expressions, known as *microexpressions,* can appear on the face very quickly after an emotion-provoking event, and they are difficult to suppress (Ekman, 1985). As a result they can be quite revealing of a person's true emotions.

■ *Discrepancies* may occur. For example, a liar may succeed in managing facial expressions, but body language may reveal a different story.

■ Lack of verbal fluency, inappropriate tone of voice, even a rise in pitch (e.g., Zuckerman, DePaulo, & Rosenthal, 1981) can be indicative of lying. In addition, when people lie, they engage in more sentence repairs; they start a sentence, interrupt it, and then start again (Stiff et al., 1989).

■ Maintaining an unusually low level of eye contact or, surprisingly, an unusually high level (Kleinke, 1986), which is often done in attempts to deceive.

■ Exaggerated facial expressions may indicate that someone is trying to mislead.

Under some circumstances, we use *lie detectors* (polygraph equipment) to record the physiological arousal that occurs during questioning and we rely upon a professional examiner (who is trained in this work) to tell—from the pattern of physiological responses— whether the individual's answers are truthful or not.

A major shortcoming of this kind of lie detection is that the emotional arousal may actually result from nervousness, embarrassment, or other legitimate reasons.

Moreover, people can and do intentionally influence their own physiological reactions—by tensing their muscles or changing their breathing (Iacono & Lykken, 1997; Lykken, 1998; Zajonc & McIntosh, 1992). Also, some people—such as accomplished con artists—may only show little or no emotional response even while they are telling huge lies. Hence, attributing the changes indicated by the polygraph to lying, or interpreting no change in the polygraph record as honesty, can be quite a mistake. Recognizing that the reliability of polygraph results is a matter of dispute, in 1987 the Supreme Court of Canada decided that the outcome of polygraph testing is not admissible as evidence under Canadian law.

Meanwhile, psychologists are working on an improved kind of interrogation that allows judgments of true and false to be based on questions that are answered truthfully (Bradley & Black, 1998), and testing the polygraph in other situations. For example, Bradley and Cullen (1993) had students at the University of New Brunswick record embarrassing incidents that had happened to them. These embarrassing incidents proved to be a useful alternative to mock crimes for studying the reliability of the polygraph.

Lie Detectors: A Reliable Measure of the Truth?

Lie detectors measure changes in physiological reactions during questioning. The pattern of such changes reveals the truthfulness of the person's answers. However, growing evidence indicates that lie detectors are not reliable in determining truth.

K E Y *QUESTIONS*

- What emotions are shown by clear facial expressions? What do research findings indicate about the universality of such expressions?

- What information about others' emotions is conveyed by body language? By touching?

- Do "lie detectors" provide a valid means of determining whether individuals are lying?

Emotion and Cognition

Being in a happy mood often causes us to think happy thoughts, while feeling sad tends to bring negative memories and images to mind. In short, there appear to be important links between *emotion* and *cognition*—between the way we feel and the way we think. Let us take a brief look at some of the scientific evidence for this link and its importance (e.g., Forgas & Fiedler, 1996).

HOW MOOD INFLUENCES COGNITION   Does our current mood, or **affect,** influence the way we think? The findings of many different studies indicate that it does. For example, affect influences the way we understand ambiguous stimuli (Isen, 1987). In general, we perceive and evaluate ambiguous stimuli more favourably when we are in a good mood than when we are in a bad one. When asked to interview applicants whose qualifications for a job are ambiguous, subjects assign higher ratings when in a positive mood (such as when they have just received favourable feedback or won a small prize) than when they have just received negative feedback and are in a negative mood (Baron, 1987, 1993). Mood can influence cooperation as well. For instance, recent findings reported by Forgas (1998b) suggest that negotiators who are in a good mood adopt more cooperative strategies and expect better outcomes than ones who are in a bad mood.

Another way in which affect influences cognition is through its impact on the *style of information processing* we adopt. A growing body of research findings indicates that a positive affect encourages us to adopt a flexible, fluid style of thinking. That idea is consistent with research findings at the University of Alberta, where students were less accurate in judging statistical relationships—from graphs they examined—when they were in a happy mood (Sinclair & Mark, 1995). Negative

Affect: A person's current mood/state.

affect leads us to engage in more systematic and careful processing (e.g., Stroessner & Mackie, 1992). Why might that be? Perhaps we interpret negative affect as a kind of danger signal, indicating that the current situation requires our full attention (e.g., Edwards & Bryan, 1997).

Positive and negative moods influence memory as well. In general, information consistent with our current mood is easier to retrieve from memory (Forgas, 1991). That means when we are feeling happy, we tend to retrieve positive ideas and experiences from memory and to think happy thoughts, and when we are sad, we tend to retrieve negative information from memory and to think unhappy thoughts (Seta et al., 1994).

Moods often influence the decisions we make. In a sad mood, we make decisions more slowly. Would you be more likely to take risks in a good mood or in a bad mood? Research findings indicate that the answer is complicated. People experiencing positive affect are indeed more likely to make risky decisions, but only when the potential losses involved are minor or unlikely (Arkes et al., 1988). They are actually less willing to take risks when potential losses are important or likely to occur—perhaps because they do not want to lose their current positive feelings.

Finally, people in a good mood are more creative than those in a bad mood. They are more successful in creative problem solving—thinking up novel uses for everyday objects, for example (e.g., Sinclair & Mark, 1995). Why might that be? Perhaps, being in a positive mood activates a wider range of ideas or associations from which to create new ideas (Estrada, Isen, & Young, 1995).

HOW COGNITION INFLUENCES AFFECT Most research on the relationship between affect and cognition has focused on how feelings influence thought. However, there is also compelling evidence for the reverse—that cognition influences affect. For example, when the reasons for our internal reactions are ambiguous, we look outward—for clues about what we are feeling. In such cases, the emotions or feelings we experience are strongly determined by the *cognitive labels* we select (Schachter & Singer, 1962).

Also, cognition can influence emotions through the activation of *schemas* containing a strong affective component. Activation of strong racial, ethnic, or religious schema or stereotypes may exert powerful effects on our current feelings or moods.

Furthermore, our thoughts can often influence our reactions to emotion-provoking events by determining how we *interpret* or *appraise* those events. For example, imagine that you are standing in line outside a theatre and a man bumps into you. How will you interpret his action? If you decide that he is trying to shove you, the chances are high that you will become angry. If, instead, you conclude that he merely tripped on the sidewalk, you may be sympathetic.

Finally, *expectancies* have an impact on our emotional reactions. When individuals have expectations about how they will react to a new event or stimulus, these expectations shape their perceptions and feelings. Thus, if you expect to dislike a new food, you probably will. If you expect to enjoy a film or a joke, the chances are good that you will. Moreover, expectations shape our later *memories* of how we felt about events (Wilson & Klaaren, 1992). In a real sense, then, expectations may sometimes override actual experience; indeed, expectations may become our reality! In such cases, cognition is a more important determinant of our emotions and our behaviours than reality itself.

KEY *QUESTIONS*

- In what ways do our affective states influence cognition?

- In what ways does cognition influence our affective states?

Making Psychology Part of Your Life

Getting Motivated: Some Practical Techniques

*A*t one time or another, almost all of us feel that getting motivated is difficult, if not impossible. Are there any techniques you can use to help overcome this kind of *behavioural inertia*? This question has been asked in the context of **work motivation**—the motivation to perform various tasks. The results suggest that one technique is especially helpful: goal setting, or establishing specific levels of performance or achievement that people then work towards (Locke & Latham, 1990). You probably already use goal setting informally, but here are several guidelines that will help you maximize its benefits.

1. *Set specific goals.* This means indicating precisely what will be defined as adequate performance. For example, if you are preparing for an exam, do not set yourself the general goal of "reading all the material twice." Instead, decide how many pages you must read each day in order to be ready for the test. Then be sure to stick to this specific goal.

2. *Set challenging goals.* Do not fall into the trap of setting your goals so low that meeting them is trivial. People seem to be motivated to a much greater extent by goals that are challenging than by ones that are too easy to attain. So set your goals high enough that they stretch your ability to reach them.

3. *Set attainable goals.* But do not fall into the opposite trap—setting your goals so high that you cannot possibly reach them. When this happens, it is easy to get discouraged and give up. The trick is to choose goals that are difficult enough to present a challenge but not so difficult that failure is guaranteed. Remember the discussion of achievement motivation? High achievers tend to prefer goals of moderate but not excessive difficulty; you should too.

4. *Reward yourself for reaching each goal.* Often, people forget to reward themselves for reaching each goal:

As soon as one goal is attained, they rush full steam ahead to the next one. This is a mistake! When choosing your goals, also identify rewards you will give yourself for reaching them. For example, in studying for a test, plan to give yourself a break—popcorn, or some other treat—after you finish each chapter. Doing so can be a big help in terms of keeping your momentum going.

5. *Become committed to your goals.* Once you establish your goals, it is important that you accept them as goals—ones you are really committed to reaching. If you do not have such a commitment, it is too easy to change the goals, to ignore them, or just to give up altogether. So be sure to adopt your goals as ones you are committed to reaching, as real standards for your behaviour.

6. *Build feedback into the process.* A final question you should ask yourself before you begin is this: "How will I know when I have reached each goal?" This sounds simple, but in some instances it's more complicated than it seems. For example, in writing a term paper, you can set a specific goal, such as, "I will do five pages each night." In this case the feedback is obvious: You know you have reached the goal when you have a pile of five completed pages in front of you.

For other tasks you may have to turn to other people for feedback. For example, suppose that you have decided to work on getting along better with your roommate. How will you know when you have made real progress? One way is to set very specific goals, such as, "I will not get into arguments over the groceries or over cleaning the apartment." But it may also be necessary to ask the roommate directly whether she or he perceives any changes in your behaviour. The main point is that feedback is essential for goal setting to work, so be sure to build this kind of information into the process.

Work Motivation: Motivation to perform and complete various tasks.

Summary and Review

Key Questions

Motivation

■ **According to drive theory, what is the basis for various motives?** Drive theory suggests that motivation is a process in which various biological needs push (drive) us to actions designed to satisfy them.

■ **Why is expectancy theory described as a cognitive theory of motivation?** Expectancy theory is a cognitive theory because is suggests that behaviour is motivated by beliefs about the outcomes that will result from specific actions.

■ **What are the basic ideas behind Maslow's needs hierarchy theory?** Maslow's theory suggests that needs exist in a hierarchy and that higher-level needs cannot be activated until lower-level ones are satisfied.

■ **What factors play a role in the regulation of eating?** Eating is regulated by complex biochemical systems within the body involving detector cells in the hypothalamus and elsewhere, and is also affected by the sight of food, feedback from chewing and swallowing, and cultural factors.

■ **Which factors override this regulatory system, so that many people do not maintain a stable weight?** Many factors tend to override this system, including the impact of learning (e.g., associating eating with specific contexts), responses to food-related cues, genetic factors (a predisposition to gain weight), and contrasting reactions to stress.

■ **What role do hormones play in human sexual motivation?** Sex hormones seem to play only a subtle and relatively minor role in human sexual motivation. However, other chemicals produced within the body may play a more important role.

■ **What are the major phases of sexual activity?** During sexual activity both males and females move through a series of distinct phases: excitement, plateau, orgasm, and resolution.

■ **What is a key difference between human beings and other species with respect to sexual arousal?** In contrast to other species, human beings can be sexually aroused by self-generated fantasies and by exposure to erotic stimuli.

■ **Is there any scientific evidence for the role of pheromones in human sexual behaviour?** At present, there is little if any scientific evidence for such effects.

■ **What factors appear to play a role in determining sexual orientation?** At present, it appears that many factors, including genetic factors, early experiences, and differences in temperament may all play a role.

■ **Why do psychologists generally reject the view that aggression stems from innate factors?** Psychologists reject this view because of huge variations in the incidence of aggression across different cultures. Such variations suggest that social and cultural factors play a key role in aggression.

■ **What are some important social factors that facilitate aggression?** Aggression is increased by some forms of frustration, direct provocation, and exposure to media violence.

■ **What are some important environmental causes of aggression?** Environmental factors that influence aggression include uncomfortably high temperatures, irritating noise, crowding, and any factors that tend to induce negative moods or feelings among the persons exposed to them.

■ **What is achievement motivation and how is it measured?** Achievement motivation is the desire to meet standards of excellence or outperform others. It is measured by the Thematic Apperception Test (TAT) and by the content of verbal materials.

■ **What are the effects of achievement on individual behaviour and on the economic fortunes of countries?** Individuals high in achievement motivation tend to excel in school and in running their own business. Some research findings indicate that the higher the level of achievement motivation in a given society, the greater its economic success.

■ **What is the need for cognition? What are its effects?** Need for cognition refers to motivation to engage in and enjoy complex cognitive activities. Persons high on this motive tend to receive higher grades in school, to think more, and to pay closer attention to the quality of arguments in persuasive appeals than persons low on this motive.

■ **What is intrinsic motivation?** Intrinsic motivation involves motivation to engage in some activity simply because it is enjoyable.

■ **Why is intrinsic motivation sometimes reduced when individuals receive external rewards for performing activities they enjoy?** When individuals receive rewards for performing activities they enjoy, they reach the conclusion that they perform these activities not only because they like them, but also because of the external rewards for doing so.

■ **What is self-handicapping and how can it protect against reductions in intrinsic motivation?** Self-handicapping is a strategy in which individuals provide themselves—in advance—with good excuses for poor performance. Individuals who use self-handicapping protect themselves against reductions in intrinsic motivation that may follow from poor performance on some task.

Emotions

▨ **How do the Cannon-Bard and James-Lange theories differ?** The Cannon-Bard theory suggests that emotion-provoking stimuli simultaneously elicit physiological arousal and the subjective cognitive states we label as emotions. The James-Lange theory suggests that emotion-provoking stimuli induce physiological reactions and that these form the basis for the subjective cognitive states we label as emotions.

▨ **What is the Schachter-Singer theory of emotion?** The Schachter-Singer theory suggests that when we are aroused by emotion-provoking stimuli, we search the external environment for the causes of our feelings of arousal. The causes we select then determine our emotions.

▨ **What is the opponent-process theory of emotion?** The opponent-process theory suggests that strong emotional reactions are followed by opposite emotional reactions, and that our reactions to emotion-provoking stimuli tend to decrease over time.

▨ **Are different emotions associated with contrasting patterns of physiological reactions?** Recent findings indicate that different emotions are indeed associated with contrasting patterns of physiological reactions.

▨ **Are different emotions related to different patterns of brain activity?** Recent findings indicate that positive emotional reactions are associated with greater activity in the left cerebral hemisphere, while negative emotional reactions are associated with greater activity in the right cerebral hemisphere.

▨ **What emotions are shown by clear facial expressions? What do research findings indicate about the universality of such expressions?** Research findings indicate that clear facial expressions exist for anger, fear, sadness, disgust, happiness, and surprise. Recent findings indicate that such expressions, while informative, may not be as universal in meaning as was previously assumed.

▨ **What information about others' emotions is conveyed by body language? By touching?** Body language provides information about others' overall level of arousal, their reactions to us, and about specific reactions they may be having. Touching can convey a wide range of information, including affection, sexual interest, dominance, caring, or even aggression.

▨ **Do "lie detectors" provide a valid means of determining whether individuals are lying?** Some findings suggest that when used with special refined methods, lie detectors can yield valid information about lying. However, because the reactions measured by such devices are subject to "faking," most psychologists remain skeptical about the benefits of lie detectors.

▨ **In what ways do our affective states influence cognition?** Our affective states can influence our perception of ambiguous stimuli, our memory, decisions and judgments we make, and our creativity.

▨ **In what ways does cognition influence our affective states?** Cognition can influence our affective states by activating schemas containing strong affective components, by shaping our interpretation of emotion-provoking events, and through the impact of expectancies, which can shape our affective reactions to new stimuli or experiences.

Key Terms

Achievement Motivation (p. 413)
Affect (p. 427)
Aggression (p. 407)
Aggression Machine (p. 409)
Aggressive Motivation (p. 407)
Anorexia Nervosa (p. 400)
Arousal Theory (p. 394)
Bisexual (p. 406)
Body Language (p. 425)
Bulimia (p. 400)
Cannon-Bard Theory (p. 418)
Drive Theory (p. 393)
Emotions (p. 417)

Expectancy Theory (p. 394)
Facial Feedback Hypothesis (p. 418)
Frustration (p. 408)
Gestures (p. 425)
Goal-Setting Theory (p. 395)
Gonads (p. 403)
Heterosexual (p. 406)
Hierarchy of Needs (p. 396)
Homeostasis (p. 393)
Homosexual (p. 406)
Hunger Motivation (p. 397)
Incentives (p. 394)

Intrinsic Motivation (p. 415)
James-Lange Theory (p. 418)
Motivation (p. 393)
Non-verbal Cues (p. 423)
Obesity (p. 399)
Opponent-Process Theory of Emotion (p. 419)
Schachter-Singer Theory (p. 419)
Sexual Jealousy (p. 405)
Sexual Motivation (p. 403)
Thematic Apperception Test (p. 413)
Work Motivation (p. 429)

Critical Thinking Questions

Appraisal

Motivation is, by definition, a hidden, internal process: we can measure its effects, but we can't "see" it directly. Given this fact, in what ways is the concept of motivation useful to our scientific understanding of human behaviour?

Controversy

Research findings suggest that exposure to violence in the media contributes to increased aggression in the real world. In view of this fact, how would you respond to a proposal that the government pass laws designed to control the amount of violence included in films and television shows? Explain your thinking.

Making Psychology Part of Your Life

Now that you understand the basic nature of hunger motivation and the many factors that affect it, can you think of ways in which you can use this knowledge to regulate your own weight better? Describe at least three concrete steps you can take, based on the research findings discussed in this chapter, to help ensure that your own weight stays at desirable levels in the decades of life that lie ahead of you.

Weblinks

Check out our Companion Website at www.pearsoned.ca/baron for additional Websites, activities, and more.

Something Fishy's Eating Disorder Site

www.something-fishy.org

Something Fishy has information about a range of eating disorders. Included are sections on anorexia nervosa and its history; bulimia; compulsive overeating; the signs, dangers, and prevention of such disorders; and links to online information and resources.

Motivation: Hierarchy of Needs Theory

choo.fis.utoronto.ca/FIS/Courses/LIS1230/LIS1230sharma/motive1.htm

The page presents the different theories of motivation and provides a reading list for each.

Theories on the Role of Brain Structure in the Formation of Emotions

www.epub.org.br/cm/n05/mente/teorias_i.htm

Review the classic theories of emotion here.

The Main Areas Involved with Emotions

www.epub.org.br/cm/n05/mente/struct_i.htm

This page introduces several brain structures involved in emotion and explains the contribution of each. The clear illustrations are a great help.

Definitions and Humanistic Background

www.britannica.com/bcom/eb/article/5/0,5716,108515+2+106029,00.html

This site from the *Encyclopaedia Britannica* contains a long list of links to clear explanations of the expression, comprehension and function of emotion.

How Psychology Conceives Emotions

www.britannica.com/bcom/eb/article/5/0,5716,108515+7,00.html

This site from the *Encyclopedia Britannica* describes briefly Charles Darwin's ideas about human emotions.

Motivating Humans: Psychology Group Web-Site

chat.carleton.ca/~jlalonde/Group/socialanxiety.htm#Goals

This innovative page tells about achievement motivation, perfectionism, and procrastination.

Chapter 11

Intelligence
Cognitive and Emotional

CHAPTER OUTLINE

Calculation Error

When a grade five student enrolled in a new school, reported the *Edmonton Journal*, he was given a set of psychological tests— a "psycho-educational assessment"—in order to determine the right class placement for him. Apparently he achieved an IQ score of 76 and was placed in a limited-enrollment, special program for the "educable mentally handicapped."

However, this class was known in the schoolyard as "the dummy class." The other children called the new boy "stupid" and a "retard." After more than two years of this kind of humiliation, the boy's parents hired two psychologists to review his case. Remarkably, his latest IQ score was 113—high average!

A law suit has been filed against the school division alleg-

ing that the original calculation was wrong and that the resulting placement has affected not only the student's educational opportunities but also his self-esteem— what he believed about himself and his potential.

What is intelligence? What are the various meanings of the word? How do we measure such mental abilities and what determines our scores? What uses do we make of the test results? How can we guard against outcomes such as those described above? These are some of the important topics you will consider as you proceed to study the materials in Chapter 11, Intelligence.

Source: Dustin is a 'dummy' no longer. (2000, February 17). *Edmonton Journal*, p. 1.

Intelligence is more easily recognized than defined.

What precisely is intelligence? How can it be measured? Is there only one kind or many? And to what extent is intelligence influenced by genetic factors and by environmental factors such as our unique life experience? These are the kinds of questions psychologists have sought to answer in their research on human intelligence, and we'll address all of them in this chapter. Our discussion of human intelligence will proceed as follows: First, we'll examine several different perspectives on the nature of intelligence—contrasting views about what it is and how it operates. Next, we'll consider some of the ways in which intelligence is measured—psychological tests, measures of basic cognitive processes, and even measures of neural functioning. As part of this discussion, we'll examine three basic requirements of any psychological test—reliability, validity, and standardization. After that, we'll focus on a very basic question concerning intelligence: To what extent do individual differences in intelligence stem from genetic factors and from environmental factors? This same question also applies to *group differences* in intelligence, so we'll examine that highly controversial topic, too. Then we'll briefly examine *emotional intelligence*—our abilities to deal effectively with the emotional side of life (Mayer & Salovey, in press). Finally, we'll focus on *creativity*—a characteristic that is related to, but not identical with, intelligence (e.g., Sternberg & Lubart, 1996).

Contrasting Views of the Nature of Intelligence

Intelligence is another one of those concepts that, like love, is easier to recognize than to define. We often refer to others' intelligence, describing them as *bright, sharp,* or *quick* on the one hand, or *slow, dull,* or even *stupid* on the other. And slurs on one's intelligence are often "fighting words" where children—and even adults—are concerned. So what, precisely, is **intelligence**? Psychologists don't entirely agree, but as a working definition, we can adopt one offered recently by a distinguished panel of experts (Neisser et al., 1966): Intelligence refers to individuals' abilities *to understand complex ideas, to adapt effectively to the environment, to learn from experience, to engage in various forms of reasoning, and to overcome obstacles by careful thought.*

Why do we place so much importance on evaluating others' (and our own) intelligence? Partly because we believe that intelligence is related to many important aspects of behaviour: how quickly individuals can master new tasks and adapt to new situations, how successful they will be in school and in various kinds of jobs, and even how well they can get along with others (e.g., Goleman, 1998). To some extent, our common-sense ideas in this respect are correct. Various measures of intelligence are related to important life outcomes, such as success in school, job performance, social status, and income (Neisser et al., 1996). However, such relationships between intelligence and life outcomes are far from perfect—because many other factors also play a role. Let's now take a look at some of the contrasting views of intelligence.

Intelligence: The ability to think abstractly and to learn readily from experience.

Intelligence: Unified or Multifaceted?

Is intelligence a single characteristic, or does it consist of several distinct parts? In the past, psychologists often disagreed sharply on this issue. In one camp were scientists who viewed intelligence as a general, unified capacity—as a single characteristic or dimension along which people vary. An early supporter of this view was Spearman (1927), who believed that performance on any cognitive task depends on a primary general factor, which he named g, and on one or more much less significant specific factors relating to the particular task on which an individual is assessed. Spearman based this view on the following finding: Although tests of intelligence often contain different kinds of tasks designed to measure different aspects of intelligence, scores on these tasks often correlate highly with one another. This suggested to him that all expressions of intelligence were primarily determined by a single general factor.

In contrast, other experts believed that intelligence is actually composed of many separate mental abilities that operate more or less independently (Gardner, 1993; Guilford, 1967, 1985; Thurstone, 1938). Thurstone's position was that intelligence is a composite of seven primary mental abilities. Gardner prefers to talk in terms of domains of intelligence. He initially held that there were seven distinct domains of intelligence: linguistic, musical, logical-mathematical, spatial, bodily-kinesthetic, interpersonal knowledge of others, and personal knowledge of self. He subsequently added an eighth domain: *naturalist intelligence*, which deals with the ability to discern and understand regularities in the world of nature (Gardner, 1997). His most recent book explores the possibility of even further subdividing intelligence (Gardner, 1999).

On what basis can it be claimed that a particular domain of intelligence exists as a unique entity? Gardner requires that three conditions be met. First, there has to be psychometric and experimental evidence available that makes it possible to define or specify the distinct nature of a particular domain of intelligence. Second, there has to be evidence that the various operations associated with that particular domain of intelligence can function normally in the presence of widespread impairment in other areas of intellectual function. Third, it has to be shown that there can be selective impairment in that particular domain of intelligence in the absence of intellectual disabilities in other domains.

To illustrate this approach, consider musical and spatial intelligence. There is certainly psychometric and experimental evidence to specify the nature of these particular intellectual domains. It is also the case that studies of brain-injured patients show that an individual can be impaired in musical or spatial-imaginal abilities and be otherwise unimpaired intellectually. Finally, the reverse is also true. As you will see in the **Canadian Focus** feature, musical and spatial-imaginal abilities can be preserved even though intellectual function in other domains is severely impaired.

Not all views of intelligence divide sharply on the unified/multifaceted issue, however. One influential perspective, proposed by Cattell (1963; 1987), adopts a more integrated approach. According to Cattell, intelligence consists of two major components: *fluid intelligence* and *crystallized intelligence*. **Crystallized intelligence** includes those aspects of intelligence that involve drawing on previously learned information to make decisions or solve problems. Classroom tests, vocabulary tests, and many social situations involve crystallized intelligence. In contrast, **fluid intelligence** involves the abilities to form concepts, reason, and identify similarities. In short, fluid intelligence is more intuitive, and it is active in forming new mental structures rather than in making use of existing ones. Research focusing on these two types of intelligence suggests that fluid intelligence may peak in early adulthood, while crystallized intelligence increases across the life span (Lerner, 1990; Willis & Nesselroade, 1990).

Where does the pendulum of scientific opinion rest today? Somewhere in the middle. Today most psychologists believe that intelligence involves both a *general* ability to handle a wide range of cognitive tasks and problems and a number of more *specific* abilities.

Of late, attention has shifted from the unitary-versus-multifaceted issue. Currently, much effort is being made to understand the different kinds of thinking and reasoning operations that characterize what we consider to be intelligent behaviour. A good example of this more recent approach is Sternberg's triarchic theory.

Skilled Athletic Performance: Another Kind of Intelligence

Gardner's theory of multiple intelligences views athletic achievement such as that shown here as evidence for a high level of bodily–kinesthetic intelligence.

Crystallized Intelligence: Aspects of intelligence that draw on previously learned information to make decisions or solve problems.

Fluid Intelligence: Aspects of intelligence that involve forming concepts, reasoning, and identifying similarities.

Canadian Focus

Studies of the Savant Syndrome

The **savant syndrome** supports the notion of independent domains of intelligence. Individuals afflicted with this disorder typically display intellectual impairment in all but one particular domain of function, and different individuals show different domains of expertise. Most often, the level of ability displayed in the spared domain is remarkable only in the degree to which it contrasts with the deficiencies evident in other intellectual domains. In some cases, however, evidence of clearly superior abilities in a specific intellectual domain can be seen.

The savant syndrome is most commonly observed among those afflicted with early infantile autism. Slightly over 9 percent of individuals with autistic disabilities show some evidence of superior ability in a specific intellectual domain (Treffert, 1989).

To illustrate the high level of accomplishment that can be achieved by individuals with the savant syndrome, let's have a look at two cases reported by Canadian researchers.

The case of J.L., described by Charness, Clifton, and Mac-Donald (1988) of the University of Waterloo, is particularly interesting. J.L. is profoundly impaired. He has been institutionalized since the age of fifteen. He is blind and has experienced epileptic seizures since early childhood. He has very limited linguistic abilities. Communicating with him is extremely difficult. He often displays echolalia—a tendency to simply repeat the words that are addressed to him. His cognitive abilities are so impaired that normal intelligence tests cannot be used to assess him. His ability to care for himself is very limited. He is unable to shave, comb his hair, or discriminate simple forms by touch. He can convey food to his mouth but is reportedly unable to understand when the plate from which he is eating is empty.

Amid this intellectual wreckage, one single ability has been preserved and developed to a superior level. He has extraordinary musical skills. He is able to make absolute-pitch judgments. Although blind and capable of using only one hand, he can perform skillfully on the piano, organ, melodica, and harmonica. His musical repertoire is wide: he can engage in jazz improvisation, and he is very adept at reproducing musical pieces by ear. His melody and chord spans are held by Charness and colleagues to be comparable with those of a competent musician. In sum, J.L. has above-normal musical abilities yet is profoundly impaired in virtually every other intellectual domain.

A second case of savant skills has been reported by Mottron and Belleville (1988) of the University of Montreal. The

individual on whom they report, E.C., is not nearly as impaired as J.L. He is autistic and has many speech irregularities. Communication with him can be readily established, however, and he has reasonable social skills. Although unable to count, he can read in a slow and deliberate manner. He can also write, though only in an idiosyncratic, sound-based, expressive fashion. He tends to interpret words very literally, and this makes it difficult for him to understand any form of humorous wordplay that involves variations in the meanings of words. Although he is in his mid-thirties, academic performance tests involving reading and classification operations suggest that, in these domains, he functions at the level of a six-year-old.

Like J.L., E.C. has a single, remarkable skill, which lies in the domain of spatial–imaginal intelligence. He can produce highly detailed drawings of objects and landscapes, from imagination or from a model. He is quite accomplished. The objects he draws are very accurately detailed and appropriately placed. Perspective is precisely rendered. In fact, E.C.'s drawing of a three-dimensional object proved to be more accurate than comparison drawings provided by a group of professional draughtspeople (Mottron & Belleville, 1995). His drawing technique is unusual: Instead of starting with an overall sketch, he begins at a peripheral location and adds detail until the drawing is complete. His drawings are painstakingly executed and completed without error or correction. Interestingly, he can draw physical objects effortlessly but has problems drawing human and animal faces.

In E.C. and J.L. we see two individuals who have broad general intellectual impairment. What is unique about them is that, in spite of their general impairment, both have a domain of expertise in which they demonstrate abilities well above those of the average person. Advocates of the view that there are multiple, relatively independent intellectual domains—such as Gardner—take this as strong evidence that there are multiple intelligences. Their argument is that if there were only a single unitary intellectual process, all intellectual capacities should be impaired to a comparable degree, and there should be no isolated islands of ability. This argument is compelling, but it has to be admitted that it is not embraced by all workers in the field. For example, Charness and colleagues are more comfortable with the view that the abilities displayed by savants result from a massive amount of attention being focused on a single pursuit by individuals who lack the resources to be distracted by other concerns.

Figure 11.1
Sternberg's Triarchic Theory of Intelligence

According to Sternberg's triarchic theory, there are three distinct types of intelligence: analytical, creative, and practical.

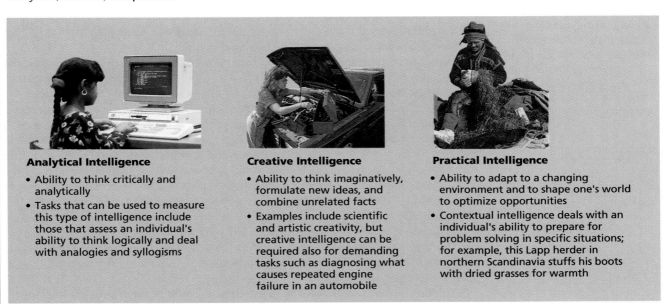

Analytical Intelligence
- Ability to think critically and analytically
- Tasks that can be used to measure this type of intelligence include those that assess an individual's ability to think logically and deal with analogies and syllogisms

Creative Intelligence
- Ability to think imaginatively, formulate new ideas, and combine unrelated facts
- Examples include scientific and artistic creativity, but creative intelligence can be required also for demanding tasks such as diagnosing what causes repeated engine failure in an automobile

Practical Intelligence
- Ability to adapt to a changing environment and to shape one's world to optimize opportunities
- Contextual intelligence deals with an individual's ability to prepare for problem solving in specific situations; for example, this Lapp herder in northern Scandinavia stuffs his boots with dried grasses for warmth

Sternberg's Triarchic Theory

An important modern theory of intelligence is one proposed by Robert Sternberg (Sternberg, 1985; Sternberg & et al., 1995; Sternberg & Kaufman, 1998). According to this **triarchic theory**, there are actually three basic types of human intelligence (see Figure 11.1). The first, known as *analytical intelligence,* involves the abilities to think critically and analytically. Persons high on this dimension usually excel on standard tests of academic potential and make excellent students. It's a good bet that your professors are high on this aspect of intelligence.

The second type of intelligence, known as *creative intelligence,* emphasizes insight and the ability to formulate new ideas. Persons who rate high on this dimension excel at zeroing in on what information is crucial in a given situation, and at combining seemingly unrelated facts. This is the kind of intelligence shown by many scientific geniuses and inventors, such as Einstein, Newton, and—some would say—Freud. For example, Johannes Gutenberg, inventor of the printing press, combined the mechanisms for producing playing cards, pressing grapes, and minting coins into his invention (see Figure 11.2); thus, he showed a high level of *creative* intelligence.

Sternberg terms the third type of intelligence **practical intelligence**, and in some ways, it is the most interesting of all. Persons high on this dimension are intelligent in a practical, adaptive sense—they have what many would term "street smarts." They are adept at solving the problems of everyday life. For example, consider the following example, cited by Sternberg and his colleagues as an example of high practical intelligence.

In Tallahassee, Florida, all residents were provided with trash containers. The practice followed was for garbage collectors to retrieve each full container from backyards, bring it to the truck, empty it, and then return it to its original location.

Savant Syndrome: A condition in which an individual has general cognitive impairment but nevertheless demonstrates normal or above-normal skills in one or more intellectual domains.

Triarchic Theory: A theory suggesting that there are actually three distinct kinds of intelligence.

Practical Intelligence: Intelligence useful in solving everyday problems.

Figure 11.2
Creative Intelligence in Operation

When Gutenberg combined existing technology used in making playing cards, pressing grapes, and minting coins to invent the printing press with movable type, he was showing what Sternberg would term *creative intelligence*.

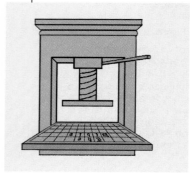

One day, a newly hired employee considered this situation and realized that the amount of work involved could be cut almost in half through one simple, but ingenious, change. Can you guess the solution he devised? Here it is: after emptying each trash can, it would be brought to the next yard instead of being returned to its original location. There, it would replace the full container that would then be brought to the truck. Since all trash cans were identical, it made no difference to each resident which trash can they received back, but this simple step saved one entire trip to each backyard for the trash collectors.

According to Sternberg, solving practical problems requires a different kind of intelligence from that required for success in school or other intellectual pursuits. Specifically, he notes that solving problems related to academic tasks requires that individuals work on problems formulated by others, that are of little interest to them, and that are disconnected from the problem-solver's ordinary experience. In contrast, solving problems of everyday life—the kind requiring high practical intelligence—involves working on problems that are unformulated or in need of reformulation, are of personal interest to the problem-solver, and are directly related to everyday experience. As a final example of practical intelligence, consider a report by Moon (1997) on the difficulties experienced by a group of Canadian soldiers while training in an area near Hudson Bay in temperatures of –45°C to –65°C. Sleeping in tents on the frozen ground often led to frostbite. Helpful local Cree rangers provided a simple, practical way to reduce the likelihood of frostbite. They showed the soldiers how to cover the area under the tents with fresh spruce boughs, thus insulating their bodies from the frozen ground.

In sum, growing evidence suggests that there is indeed more to intelligence than the verbal, mathematical, and reasoning abilities that are often associated with academic success. Practical intelligence is also important and contributes to success in many areas of life. As a final demonstration of the fact that there are, indeed, many kinds of intelligence, construct a list of prominent figures (e.g., Conrad Black, David Suzuki, Don Cherry, Margaret Atwood, Alanis Morissette, and Jean Chrétien), and for each, ask yourself, "What kinds of intelligence do they show?" You'll probably come up with very different patterns for each.

K E Y QUESTIONS

- What is intelligence?
- What is Gardner's theory of multiple intelligences?
- What is Sternberg's triarchic theory of intelligence?
- What is practical intelligence?

Measuring Human Intelligence

Alfred Binet
1857–1911

In 1904, when psychology was just emerging as an independent field, members of the Paris school board approached Alfred Binet with an interesting request: Could he develop an objective method for identifying the children who were mentally retarded, so that they could be removed from the regular classroom and given special education? Binet was already at work on related topics, so he agreed, enlisting the aid of his colleague, Theodore Simon.

In designing this test, Binet and Simon were guided by the belief that the items used should be ones children could answer without special training or study. They felt that this was important because the test should measure the ability to handle intellectual tasks—*not* specific knowledge acquired in school. To attain this goal, Binet and Simon decided to use items of two basic types: ones so new or unusual that none of the children would have prior exposure to them, and ones so familiar that almost all youngsters would have encountered them in the past. For example, children were asked to perform the following tasks:

- Follow simple commands or imitate simple gestures.

- Name objects shown in pictures.

- Repeat a sentence of fifteen words.

- Tell how two common objects are different.

- Complete sentences begun by the examiner.

The first version of Binet and Simon's test was published in 1905 and contained thirty items. Much to the two authors' satisfaction, it was quite effective: With its aid, schools could readily identify children in need of special help. Encouraged by this success, Binet and Simon broadened the scope of their test to measure variations in intelligence among all children. This revised version, published in 1908, grouped items by age, with six items at each level between three and thirteen years. Items were placed at a particular age level if about 75 percent of children of that age could pass them correctly.

Binet's tests were soon revised and adapted for use in many countries. In the United States, Lewis Terman, a psychologist at Stanford University developed the **Stanford-Binet test**—a test that was soon put to use in many different settings. Over the years, the Stanford-Binet has been revised several times (see Figure 11.3). One of the features of the Stanford-Binet that contributed to its popularity was the fact that it yielded a single score assumed to reflect an individual's level of intelligence—the now famous IQ.

The Stanford-Binet Test

Materials used in the current Stanford-Binet intelligence test.

Lewis Madison Terman
1877–1956

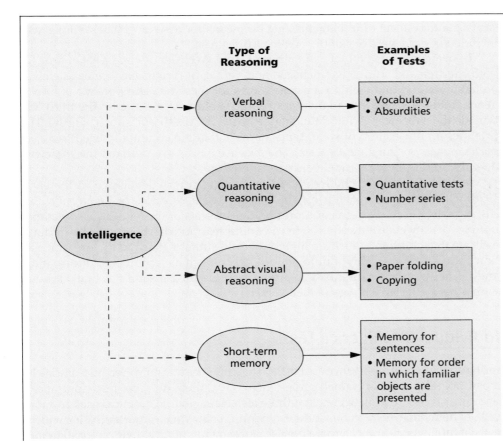

Figure 11.3
The Stanford-Binet Test

A recent version of the Stanford-Binet test measures intelligence with a composite score made up of four scores for broad types of mental activity: verbal reasoning, quantitative reasoning, abstract visual reasoning, and short-term memory. Each of the scores is obtained through a series of subtests that measure specific mental abilities.

Stanford-Binet Test: A popular test for measuring individual intelligence.

IQ: Its Meaning Then and Now

Originally, the letters **IQ** stood for *intelligence quotient*, and a "quotient" is precisely what scores represent. To obtain an IQ score, an examiner divides a student's mental age by his or her chronological age, and then multiplies this number by 100. For this computation, mental age is based on the number of items a person passes correctly on the test: test-takers receive two months credit of "mental age" for each item passed. If an individual's mental and chronological ages are equal, an IQ of 100 is obtained; this is considered to be an average score. IQs above this figure indicate that a person's intellectual age is greater than his or her chronological age—in other words, the individual is more intelligent than typical students of this age. In contrast, numbers below 100 indicate that the individual is less intelligent than his or her peers.

Perhaps you can already see one obvious problem with this type of IQ score: At some point, mental growth levels off or stops, while chronological age continues to rise. As a result, IQ scores begin to decline after the early teen years! Partly because of this problem, IQ scores now have a different meaning. They simply reflect an individual's performance relative to that of persons of the same age who have taken the same test. Thus, an IQ above 100 indicates that the person has scored higher than the average person in his or her age group, while a score below 100 indicates that the person has scored lower than the average.

> **IQ:** A numerical value that reflects the extent to which an individual's score on an intelligence test departs from the average for other people of the same age.

The Wechsler Scales

As noted above, the tests developed by Binet and later adapted by Terman and others remained popular for many years. They do, however, suffer from one major drawback: all are mainly verbal in content. As a result, they pay little attention to the fact that intelligence can be revealed in non-verbal activities as well. For example, an architect who visualizes a majestic design for a new building is demonstrating a high level of intelligence, yet no means for assessing such abilities was included in early versions of the Stanford-Binet test.

To overcome this problem and others, David Wechsler devised a set of tests for both children and adults that included non-verbal, or *performance*, items as well as verbal ones, and that yielded separate scores for these two components of intelligence. Table 11.1 presents an overview of the subtests that make up the third edition of the Wechsler Adult Intelligence Scale (WAIS-III for short). Figure 11.4 provides an illustration of some types of tasks that are commonly used to assess performance on intelligence tests. The Wechsler tests are perhaps the most frequently used individual intelligence tests today.

A Wechsler test for children aged six to sixteen was developed in the early 1970s. The 1991 revision of the test, the *Wechsler Intelligence Scale for Children* (WISC-III), is widely used. Patterns of scores on the subtests of the WISC are sometimes used to identify children suffering from various learning disabilities. Some findings indicate that children who score high on certain subtests (such as Picture Completion and Object Assembly) but lower on others (such as Arithmetic, Information, and Vocabulary) are more likely to suffer from learning disabilities than children with other patterns of scores (Aiken, 1991).

The WISC–III

Developed by David Wechsler, the WISC–III (a third revision of the WISC) is one of the most widely used intelligence tests for children.

Individual Intelligence Tests

Individual tests of intelligence are costly: They must be administered one-on-one by a psychologist or other trained professional. Why, then, do these tests continue in widespread use? The answer is that these tests have several practical uses and provide benefits that help to offset their obvious costs. Most importantly, individual tests of intelligence afford a more precise assessment of individuals at the extremes

TABLE 11.1

Subtests of the Wechsler Intelligence Scale

This widely used test of adult intelligence includes the subtests described here.

Verbal Tests	Description
Information	Examinees are asked to answer general information questions, increasing in difficulty.
Digit span	Examinees are asked to repeat series of digits read out loud by the examiner.
Vocabulary	Examinees are asked to define thirty-five words.
Arithmetic	Examinees are asked to solve arithmetic problems.
Comprehension	Examinees are asked to answer questions requiring detailed answers; answers indicate their comprehension of the questions.
Similarities	Examinees indicate in what way two items are alike.

Performance Tests	Description
Picture completion	Examinees indicate what part of each picture is missing.
Picture arrangement	Examinees arrange pictures to make a sensible story.
Block design	Examinees attempt to duplicate designs based on red and white blocks.
Object assembly	Examinees attempt to solve picture puzzles.
Digit symbol	Examinees fill in small boxes with coded symbols corresponding to a number above each box.

Mental Retardation: Considerably below-average intellectual functioning combined with varying degrees of difficulty in meeting the demands of everyday life.

Down's Syndrome: A disorder caused by an extra chromosome and characterized by varying degrees of cognitive impairment and physical disorders.

with respect to intelligence—those who suffer from some degree of *mental retardation* and those who are *intellectually gifted*—than do various group tests of intelligence which we will consider shortly. It is also true that, in the case of children, individual test patterns can be useful in developing remedial programs (Das, 1992).

Mental retardation refers to considerably below-average intellectual functioning, combined with varying degrees of difficulty in meeting the demands of everyday life (Aiken, 1991; Wielkiewicz & Calvert, 1989). As shown in Figure 11.5, persons with mental retardation are typically described according to four broad categories of retardation: mild, moderate, severe, and profound. Individuals' level of retardation is determined by at least two factors: their test scores *and* their success in carrying out activities of daily living expected of persons their age. As you can guess, persons whose retardation is in the "mild" category can usually learn to function quite well.

What causes mental retardation? In some cases, it can be traced to genetic abnormalities such as **Down's syndrome,** which is caused by the presence of an extra chromosome; persons with Down's syndrome usually have IQs below 50. Mental retardation can also result from environmental factors, such as inadequate nutrition or use of drugs or alcohol by mothers during pregnancy, infections, toxic agents, and traumas resulting from a lack of oxygen during birth. Most cases of mental retardation, however, cannot readily be traced to specific causes.

Intelligence tests have also been used to identify the intellectually gifted—those whose intelligence is far above average (Goleman, 1980; Terman, 1954). The

Down's Syndrome: A Genetic Cause of Mental Disability

One cause of intellectual impairment is Down's syndrome, a genetic defect that occurs when the cells in the body have an extra copy (or trisomy) of chromosome 21.

Figure 11.4
Performance Tasks Used in Assessment of Intelligence

Examples of some types of tasks that are commonly used to measure performance on intelligence tests. Note that verbal skills are not required to complete these tasks.

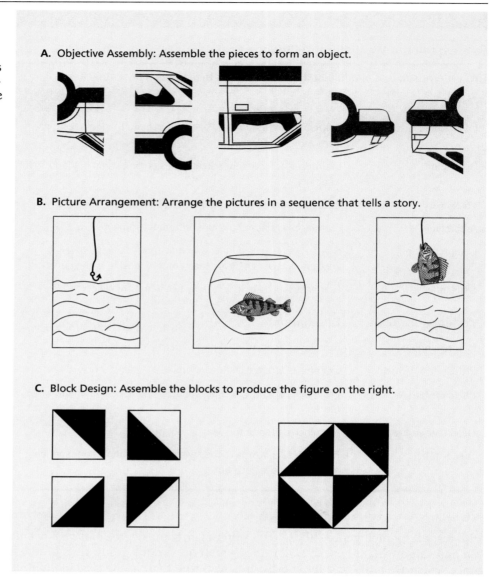

A. Objective Assembly: Assemble the pieces to form an object.

B. Picture Arrangement: Arrange the pictures in a sequence that tells a story.

C. Block Design: Assemble the blocks to produce the figure on the right.

most comprehensive study of people with high IQs was begun by Lewis Terman in 1925. He followed the lives of 1500 children with IQs of 130 or above to determine the relationship between high intelligence on the one hand, and occupational success and social adjustment on the other. As a group, the gifted children in Terman's study were tremendously successful: They earned more academic degrees, attained higher occupational status and salaries, experienced better personal and social adjustment, and were healthier than the average adult. You might be interested to learn that a recent comparison of the hundred most successful and the hundred least successful subjects in Terman's study by Pyryt (1993) of the University of Calgary found that the major discriminating factor separating the two groups was educational achievement. It would seem that attaining an advanced degree can pay off even if you are gifted.

Although intelligence tests are most commonly used to "sort" individuals on the basis of intellectual abilities, there is reason to expect this may change in the future. The American Association on Mental Retardation has proposed a definition

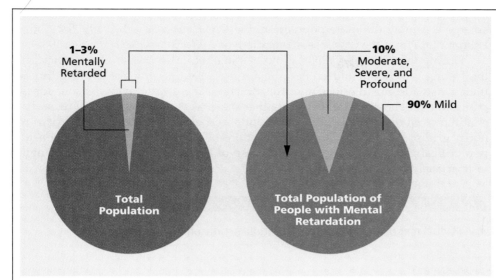

Degrees of Intellectual Impairment

Degree of intellectual impairment is often identified according to IQ scores on standard tests of intelligence. In general, an IQ score that falls below 70 suggests some level of intellectual impairment. IQ scores are not the only consideration, however; the individual's capacity to function adequately in everyday life is also important.

Classification	Stanford-Binet IQ Score	Wechsler IQ Score	Percentage of Mentally Handicapped	Education Level Possible
Mild	52–68	55–69	90	Sixth grade
Moderate	36–51	40–54	6	Second to fourth grade
Severe	20–35	25–39	3	Limited speech
Profound	Below 20	Below 25	1	Unresponsive to training

of mental retardation that focuses less on IQ and more on the functional capacities of the individual. This position has long been advocated by Das and his associates at the University of Alberta. They maintain that intelligence tests should not be designed to rank individuals in terms of general ability, but rather to provide information about the basic cognitive mechanisms that underlie intelligent behaviour. He and his colleagues see intelligent behaviour as involving three interdependent components: attention, processing, and planning, and they have developed a number of assessment devices to examine the role these factors play in intelligent behaviour (Das, Naglieri, & Kirby, 1994; Jarman & Das, 1996). Sternberg and Kaufman (1998) have similarly attempted to move away from the notion that there is a fixed IQ. They advocate employing a dynamic assessment procedure that provides a more fluid and adaptive appraisal of intelligence. Whether the approaches proposed by Das and his colleagues or by Sternberg and Kaufman will win widespread endorsement remains to be determined.

Group Tests of Intelligence

Both the Stanford-Binet and the Wechsler Scales are *individual* tests of intelligence: They are designed for use with one person at a time. This is very time consuming. Obviously, it would be advantageous to have tests that could be administered to large numbers of people at a time, even if there is some associated loss of precision with respect to the accuracy of positioning individuals—especially at extreme ends of the intelligence continuum. To meet this need, group tests were developed. Initially they were used as a screening device for new recruits at the start of World War I. Over the intervening years, a large number of additional group tests of intelligence have emerged. Among the more popular are the *Otis-Lennon School Ability Test* (Otis & Lennon, 1967) and the *Cognitive Abilities Test*, or CAT (Thorndike & Hagen, 1982).

During the 1940s and 1950s, group testing became increasingly common, and the testing of school children became almost a routine practice. During the '60s there was widespread criticism of this practice. There were many reasons for this criticism—the most prominent being that these were unfair in several respects to children from disadvantaged backgrounds—especially children from certain minority groups. We'll return to these objections below. Now, however, let's consider two critical issues associated with the use of these, or any other, psychological tests: *reliability* and *validity*.

KEY QUESTIONS

- What was the first individual test of intelligence, and what did scores on it mean?
- What are the Wechsler scales?
- What is the main practical reason for administering individual tests of intelligence?

Reliability and Validity of Tests

Suppose that in preparation for a summer at the beach, you decide to go on a diet in order to lose 5 kilograms. Your current weight is 60 kilos, and for two weeks you skip desserts and engage in vigorous exercise. Then you step on your bathroom scale to see how much progress you've made. To your shock, the needle reads 63; you've actually *gained* 3 kilos! How can this be? Perhaps you made a mistake. So you step back on the scale. Now it reads 61. You get off and step on again; now it reads 62. At this point you realize the truth: Your scale (thank goodness!) is *unreliable*—the numbers it shows change even though your weight, obviously, can't change from one second to the next.

This is a simple illustration of a very basic point. In order to be of any use, measuring devices must have high **reliability**—that is, they must yield the same result each time they are applied to the same quantity. If they don't, they are essentially useless. The same principle applies to psychological tests, whether they are designed to measure intelligence or any other characteristics. But how do we know whether and to what extent a test is reliable? In fact, several different methods exist for assessing a test's reliability.

INTERNAL CONSISTENCY If we wish to develop a test that measures a single psychological characteristic, such as intelligence, then it is important to establish that all the items actually measure this characteristic—that the test has what psychologists call *internal consistency*. One measure of the internal consistency of a test is known as **split-half reliability**. Checking for split-half reliability involves dividing the test into two equivalent parts, such as the first and second halves or odd- and even-numbered items, and then comparing people's scores on each. If the test really measures intelligence, the correlation between the scores on each half should be positive and high. If it is not, some of the items may be measuring different things, and the test may be unreliable. There are several statistical formulas for measuring internal consistency. The most widely used formula, *coefficient alpha*, simultaneously considers all of the possible ways of splitting the items on a test into halves. Since this is done by computer, the process is very efficient, and coefficient alpha has become a standard measure of tests' internal consistency.

Reliability: The extent to which any measuring device (including psychological tests) yields the same result each time it is applied to identical quantities.

Split-Half Reliability: The extent to which an individual attains equivalent scores on two halves of a psychological test.

TEST–RETEST RELIABILITY   A test that yields very different scores when taken by the same individual at different times is of little value if the characteristics it supposedly measures are ones that are stable over time, such as intelligence. Thus, another type of reliability, **test–retest reliability**, is also important. Test evaluators can measure this by giving the test to the same group of people on more than one occasion and comparing the scores. The more similar these are, the higher the test's reliability.

One obvious problem with the test–retest method is that people's scores on the retest may increase simply because they have taken the test again—that is, because of *practice effects*. To reduce this problem, psychologists often use alternate forms of the same test—two different forms that cover the same material at the same level of difficulty. Figure 11.6 provides an overview of assessment procedures for both split-half and test–retest reliability.

Test–Retest Reliability: The extent to which a psychological test yields similar scores when taken by the same person on different occasions.

Figure 11.6
Reliability: A Basic Requirement of Psychological Tests

In order to be useful, psychological tests must be reliable. Two ways of assessing reliability are shown here: (A) split-half reliability, which assesses the internal consistency of a test (Do individual test items all measure the same thing?); and (B) test–retest reliability (Does the test give the same score when individuals are tested on a second occasion?). If split-half and test–retest correlations are high, a test can be considered reliable.

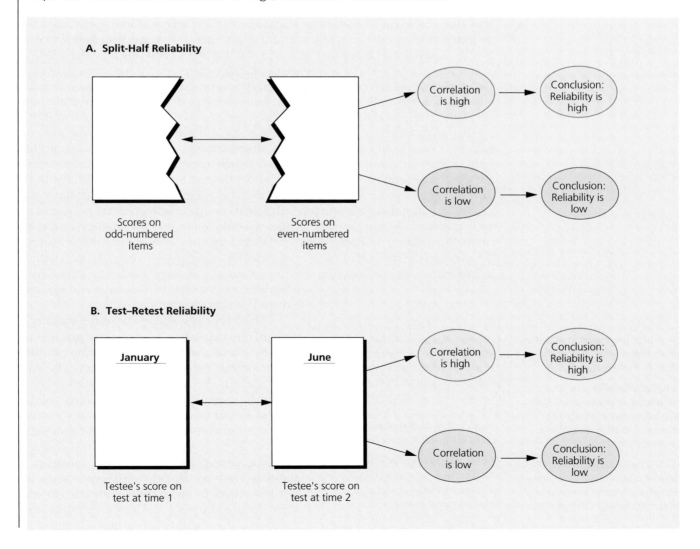

VALIDITY On a recent visit to one of your local malls, you may have noticed a new type of machine outside one of the stores. A sign on the machine reads "Test Your Sex Appeal" and goes on to explain that after inserting a quarter and pushing some buttons, users will receive a score indicating their appeal to members of the opposite sex. Do you think a machine like this is really capable of measuring sex appeal? The answer is obvious: It measures nothing at all except, perhaps, the user's willingness to believe silly claims. Psychologists say that such machines are low in **validity**, which is a device's ability to measure what it is supposed to measure.

The same principle applies to psychological tests: They too are useful only to the extent that they really measure the characteristics they claim to assess. How do we determine whether a test is valid? There are three criteria that we can use to examine the validity of a test.

The first and simplest way to examine the validity of a test to look at the questions that make up the test, and determine whether the questions realistically assess the trait or attribute the test is designed to measure. For example, suppose we were presented with a test that was designed to measure a person's aptitude for general office work. If we examined the test and found that the test items probed the test-taker's understanding of word processing packages, spreadsheets, filing, and accounting practices, we could reasonably assume that the test has **content validity**. The test is composed of questions about office-work procedures—and the test is intended to assess the capacity of individuals to perform office work.

A second criterion that we can use to examine the validity of a test is to ask whether it has **predictive validity**. Does the test provide us with information that will allow us to predict the future behaviour of test-takers? More specifically, will an individual's score on an office-aptitude test, such as the one described above, allow us to predict whether that individual will make a good office worker? Will an individual's score on an intelligence test allow us to predict whether an individual will perform well in a post-graduate educational program? The only way we can answer such questions is to correlate test scores with performance on a relevant independent **criterion measure** that we are confident will serve to demonstrate the predictive power of the test. In the case of an aptitude test, the criterion measure might be successful completion of an office-training program. If it turns out that high scorers on our aptitude test almost always complete such programs successfully and low scorers do not, then we know the test has predictive validity. In the case of an intelligence test, the criterion measure might be high school or university grades. Finding that high-scoring individuals on the intelligence test perform very well academically and low scorers do not would tell us that the intelligence test has predictive validity. In sum, content validity does not guarantee predictive validity. To ascertain the predictive validity of a test, test scores have to be correlated with an appropriate criterion measure. (See **Key Concept** on page 449 for an overview of what it means for tests to have high and low content and predictive validity.)

A third type of validity, **construct validity**, is brought into play when it is necessary to assess the validity of tests that purport to measure complex, psychological concepts or constructs. In such cases, there is often no single criterion measure that can be used to establish the predictive validity of a test. Under these circumstances, all we can do is make judgments about the kind of behavioural evidence that we would view as being consistent with our conceptualization of the construct in question. The next step is to see if scores on the test sort test-takers in accordance with our expectations. As an example, consider the problem of establishing the validity of a test designed to

Validity: The extent to which tests actually measure what they claim to measure.

Content Validity: The extent to which the items on a test sample the skills or knowledge needed for achievement in a given field or task.

Predictive Validity: The extent to which scores on a test serve to predict future performance in a particular realm of behavioiur.

Criterion Measure: An independent index of performance that can serve to demonstrate the predictive validity of a test. For example, high school grades are an index of performance that should be highly correlated with scores on an intelligence test.

Construct Validity: The extent to which a test measures a complex variable or concept described by a psychological theory.

Key Concept
The Highs and Lows of Test Validity

Measuring Validity

No psychological test is useful unless it actually measures what it claims to measure—that is, unless it has high validity. Here are some basic ways to assess this important requirement.

Content Validity: The extent to which items on a test are related in a straightforward way to the characteristic the test supposedly measures.

High Content Validity
The flight simulator here provides a valid test of the abilities needed to pilot a plane, because the behaviours it requires are closely related to those needed by pilots during actual flight. Thus, it has a high level of content validity.

Low Content Validity
In the past, employers used various kinds of "aptitude tests" to select candidates for various jobs. Often, the content of these tests had little or nothing to do with what people actually did in these jobs. As a result, such tests were low in content validity.

Predictive Validity: The extent to which scores on a test serve to predict future performance in a particular domain of behaviour.

High Predictive Validity
Scores on several standard tests of academic intelligence are correlated with success in school. It would be expected that persons who make high scores on intelligence tests will do well in academic programs, and those who make low scores will not. Such tests have relatively high predictive validity.

Low Predictive Validity
At one time it was believed that intelligence could be estimated from measurements of people's skulls. In fact, the correlation between such measurements and various criteria indicative of intelligence, such as success in school or job performance, is negligible. Thus, such tests have very low (or non-existent) predictive validity.

▶ measure the tendency of individuals to take risks. Risk-taking is a complicated psychological construct. There are so many ways in which individuals can take risks it is impossible to single out a specific type of risk-taking behaviour and claim that it will serve a criterion measure for risk-taking in general. The best we can do is see if the test does differentiate between those individuals whose behaviour fits our construct of risk-taking, and those individuals whose behaviour does not. Thus we would expect individuals who score high on the test to have more traffic accidents and be more likely to belong to skydiving or mountaineering clubs than those who score low on the test. By determining whether the test does discriminate between those who indulge in behaviours that fit our construct of risk-taking, and those who do not, we can accumulate *convergent evidence* that the test has construct validity, and determine that it does provide a measure of something akin to risk-taking tendencies.

In sum, any psychological test is useful only to the extent that it is both reliable and valid—to the extent that the test yields consistent scores and that independent evidence confirms that it really does measure what it purports to measure. How do intelligence tests stack up in this respect? In terms of reliability, the answer is "quite well." Widely used tests of intelligence do yield consistent scores and do possess internal consistency. The question of validity is much more complicated, especially where group tests of intelligence are concerned. The issue of validity leads us back to an issue raised earlier: Are intelligence tests suitable for use with individuals from all minority groups?

Are Intelligence Tests Fair?

Objections to the widespread use of group tests of intelligence have touched on many different points. Perhaps the most important of these is the possibility that such tests are biased against certain groups. The basis for such concerns is obvious: In North America and elsewhere, people belonging to several minorities score lower than other people on group tests of intelligence (Weinberg, 1989). For example, Native people, and members of other minority groups, often score lower on intelligence tests than do North Americans of European ancestry (Aiken, 1991; Cohen et al., 1988; Darou, 1992). Further, it appears that these tests may be less *valid* when used with such groups; for example, these groups' scores on the tests are less successful in predicting future performance in school (Aiken, 1991; Darou, 1992). What factors are responsible for such differences? Many critics of group intelligence tests contend that the differences stem mainly from a strong **cultural bias** that is built into these tests. In other words, because the tests were developed by and for people belonging to a particular culture, individuals from other backgrounds may be at a disadvantage when taking them.

Are such concerns valid? Careful examination of the items used on intelligence tests suggests that they are. Many items assume that all children have had the opportunity to acquire certain kinds of information. Unfortunately, this is not always true for children from disadvantaged or minority backgrounds, who may never have had the chance to acquire the knowledge being tested. Thus, they cannot answer correctly, no matter how high their intelligence.

An example of this problem is provided by Darou in his description of his experiences with intelligence testing in northern Canada. His initial assumption was that a question such as, "Saw is to whine as snake is to ___," which is used on a well-known test, would be culture-free on the grounds that it dealt with tools and animals. He rapidly discovered that Native Canadians in the Far North are unfamiliar with the hissing of snakes and have experience only with saws that do not whine. Other test items were found to be biased in the opposite direction. On certain tests requiring patterns to be discerned and reproduced, individuals with extensive hunting and navigational experience are so adept they are off-scale. On the basis of these and other experiences, Darou (p. 98) maintains that "virtually all intelligence tests lack validity with Native subjects."

Cultural Bias: The tendency of items on a test of intelligence to require specific cultural experience or knowledge.

A further issue, raised by Helms (1992), is that widely used intelligence tests may suffer from other forms of cultural bias that, while somewhat more subtle, are just as damaging for minority children. Such tests, Helms contends, incorporate unstated values that derive primarily from a *Eurocentric perspective*—that is, they implicitly accept European values as the standards against which everything is to be judged (Helms, 1989). For example, Helms contends, European cultures accept a *dualist* view—that is, the idea that answers are either right or wrong and that only logical thinking is to be valued. Children from European cultural backgrounds accept this value, so when they take intelligence tests, they look for the one correct answer on each item. According to Helms, children from other backgrounds may hold views or maintain perspectives that place them at a disadvantage. For example, they may be uncomfortable with the notion that each question has a single correct answer and spend much time reasoning about the extent to which each of the various possible answers is correct, or they may be disposed to consider questions from an intuitive, subjective viewpoint rather than from a stance that relies on formal logical reasoning. In short, Helms suggests that subtle cultural factors may influence the tactics children use when taking intelligence tests, and these, in turn, may influence their scores.

In an effort to eliminate cultural bias from intelligence tests, some psychologists have attempted to design *culture-fair* tests. Such tests attempt to include only items to which all groups, regardless of background, have been exposed. Because many minority children are exposed to languages other than standard English, these tests tend to be non-verbal in nature. One of these—the **Raven Progressive Matrices Test** (Raven, 1977)—is quite widely used. It consists of sixty matrices of varying difficulty, each containing a logical pattern or design with a missing part. Evidence indicates that the Raven test is a valid measure of general intelligence (Paul, 1985); however, it is not clear that it or any other supposedly culture-fair test fully addresses the sources of cultural bias described by Helms (1992) and others. Items from another such test, the *Culture-Fair Intelligence Test*, are shown in Figure 11.7. As you can see, it requires test takers to work with abstract figures or with relationships between various objects. Presumably, such items are less subject to cultural bias than verbal items; but again, this has not been clearly established.

It is the position of some that the problem of designing completely culture-fair tests of intelligence may be resolved by the development of reliable *physiological measures*—ones that assess the speed and efficiency with which the human brain processes information (e.g., Matarazzo, 1992).

Raven Progressive Matrices Test: One popular test of intelligence that was designed to be relatively free of cultural bias.

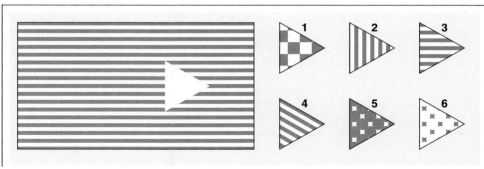

Figure 11.7
An Example of a Test Item on a Culture-Fair Test

This culture-fair test does not penalize test takers whose language or cultural experiences differ from those of the urban middle or upper classes. Subjects are to select, from the six samples on the right, the patch that would complete the pattern. Patch number 3 is the correct answer.

Source: Adapted from the Raven Standard Progressive Matrices Test.

KEY *QUESTIONS*

- What is reliability and how do psychologists attempt to measure it?
- What is validity, and how do psychologists attempt to measure it?
- What is cultural bias and how may it affect scores on standard intelligence tests?

Measuring Intelligence through Processing Speed

Processing Speed: The speed with which individuals can process information.

Inspection Time: The minimum amount of time a particular stimulus must be exposed for individuals to make a judgment about it that meets some pre-established criterion of accuracy.

"Quick study," "quick witted," "fast learner." Phrases such as these are often used to describe people who are high in intelligence—both academic and practical. They suggest that being intelligent involves being able to process information quickly. Is there any scientific evidence for this view? In fact, there is.

Over the past few years, an increasing number of researchers have examined the relationship between **processing speed**—the speed with which individuals can process information—and intelligence. There is now a substantial body of evidence indicating that the speed with which individuals perform simple perceptual and cognitive tasks are positively correlated with scores on intelligence tests (e.g., Neisser et al., 1996; Vernon, 1991). An example of how these studies are carried out is provided in the **Research Process** section.

The Research Process:
How Reaction Time and Inspection Time are Related to Intelligence

Psychologists are interested in the relationship between speed of information processing and intelligence for a number of reasons. One reason is the widespread assumption that perceiving new information and making decisions about this information are basic to all higher mental operations (e.g., Deary, 1995; Deary & Stough, 1996). A second reason relates to the problem of developing a culture-free way of assessing intelligence alluded to above. If a reasonable indication of intelligence can be obtained by measuring the speed with which elementary perceptual or cognitive processing operations are carried out, this might well provide a foundation for developing a relatively culture-free test of intelligence.

Two different approaches are commonly employed in assessing the speed at which elementary perceptual or cognitive tasks can be performed. The most common procedure involves the measurement of reaction time. In a typical reaction-time study, a participant sits before a display board on which there is a central button and six or more additional buttons arranged in a semicircle—all being equidistant from the central button. The participant is required to depress the central button with his or her index finger and wait until one of the buttons in the semicircle is illuminated. At that time the participant releases the central button and depresses the illuminated button as rapidly as possible. The average time required to move the index finger from the central button to the various different surrounding buttons serves as the measurement of reaction time.

At first glance, measures of reaction time seem to offer a useful means for estimating processing speed. Recently, however, concerns have been voiced about this approach. While reaction time measures are indeed correlated with scores on intelligence tests, these correlations are not as strong as might be expected (e.g., Deary & Stough, 1996). Further, it has proven more difficult to relate reaction time measures to basic aspects of cognitive activity than was initially assumed (Brody, 1992). Finally, because the procedure involves the regulation of relatively complex motor control operations (holding one button down, moving the finger, and depressing another button), reaction time measures may be affected by factors other than the mental response time assumed to be related to intelligence.

Because of these problems, many researchers have turned, instead, to a different measure of the speed of mental operations—a measure known as **inspection time.** This measure reflects the minimum amount of time a particular stimulus must be exposed for individuals to make a judgment about it that meets some pre-established criterion of accuracy. The shorter the duration time necessary for individuals to attain a given level of accuracy, presumably, the faster the speed of important aspects of their cognitive (mental) operations. To measure inspection time, psychologists often use procedures in which individuals are shown simple target drawings like the one in Figure 11.8, and are asked to indicate whether the longer side occurs on the left or right. Immediately after the target drawing is presented it is totally occluded by a second masking figure. The length of time the target drawing is shown is increased until the effect of the mask is overcome and participants can make the required decision at some pre-specified level of accuracy. Participants are *not* instructed to respond as quickly as possible (as would be the case in a reaction-time study). Rather, they are instructed to take their time and try to be accurate. Inspection time is defined as the duration of time the target drawing has

Figure 11.8
Inspection Time: How It's Measured

To measure inspection time, psychologists ask research participants to indicate whether the longer side is on the left or the right. Immediately after seeing each stimulus, it is masked by another one in which both sides are long (right-hand drawing, labelled *mask*). Participants are not told to respond as quickly as possible; rather, they are instructed to take their time and to be accurate. Inspection time is measured in terms of the time they take to make such decisions at some pre-determined level of accuracy.

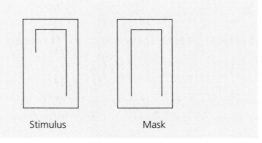

Stimulus   Mask

to be shown in order for decisions to be made at whatever pre-specified level of accuracy has been selected—for example, 85 percent.

Growing evidence indicates that inspection time is indeed closely related to intelligence, as measured by standard tests. In fact, inspection time scores and scores on standard tests correlate—at .50 or more (e.g., Kranzler & Jensen, 1989). Additional support for the value of this measure is provided by the findings that improvements in inspection time measures may be one cause of increases in IQ with age (Deary, 1995).

In sum, inspection time appears to be a very promising measure for examining some of the operations that may underlie basic intelligence. It does not, however, constitute the only alternative approach to measuring intelligence by the standard IQ test. Another approach that has captured the interest of many investigators is the notion that intelligence can be assessed in terms of the efficiency with which our neural systems function.

The Neurological Basis of Intelligence

Everything we do, think, or feel rests, in an ultimate sense, on neurochemical events occurring in our brains. If that is indeed true—and virtually all psychologists believe that it is—then an interesting possibility arises: Can some of the variation among individuals in intelligence be related to differences in efficiency of neural functioning? A number of researchers think so. In Canada, P.A. Vernon and his associates at the University of Western Ontario have been particularly active in pursuing this possibility (e.g., Vernon, 1991, 1994; Vernon & Mori, 1992; Wickett & Vernon, 1994).

P.A. Vernon
University of Western Ontario

A number of different techniques are currently being used to measure the neural efficiency of the physiological processes assumed to underlie intellectual operations. One technique involves recording, through electrodes attached to the surface of the skull, evoked potentials produced by neural activity in reaction to stimuli. In one recent study using this technique, researchers recorded evoked potentials (electrical responses to visual stimuli) in the brains of 147 male volunteers. The average latency (delay) with which these potentials followed presentation of the visual stimuli was obtained for each volunteer; then this number was divided by the length of the volunteer's head to obtain a measure of the speed with which nerve impulses were conducted in the visual system. This measure, known as *nerve conduction velocity*, was then correlated with scores on one standard test of intelligence (the Raven Progressive Matrices considered earlier in the chapter). As shown in Figure 11.9, results were encouraging: the higher this measure of neural speed was, the higher was the participant's measured intelligence. Although encouraging, the generality of the relationship between the nerve conduction velocity and intelligence remains to be fully determined. Attempts to relate nerve conduction velocity measured at more peripheral locations, such as the arm, to intelligence have produced, at best, mixed results (e.g., Vernon & Mori, 1992; Wickett & Vernon, 1994).

Figure 11.9
Neural Efficiency and Intelligence

The faster their nerve impulses in response to visual stimuli were, the higher research participants scored on one test of intelligence. These findings, and many others, suggest that intelligence may rest in part on the efficiency with which individuals' brains process information.

Source: Based on data from Reed and Jensen, 1993.

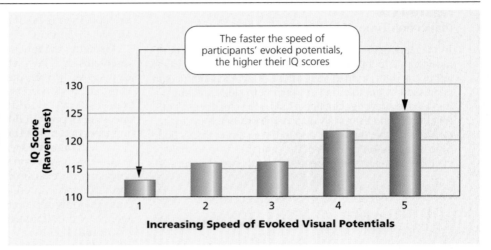

A second technique involves examining metabolic activity in the brain during cognitive tasks (e.g., Haier et al., 1996). The assumption underlying this technique is that if intelligence is related to efficient brain functioning, then the more intelligent people are, the less energy their brains should expend on various tasks. There is a measure of support for this position: The brains of individuals scoring highest on written measures of intellectual ability *do* expend less energy when they perform complex cognitive tasks. The data in these studies have been gathered using the PET technique of brain imaging described in Chapter 2.

Given that neural efficiency seems to be correlated with intelligence, it will come as no surprise that there is a link between brain structure and intelligence (Andreasen et al., 1993). Specifically, scores on standard measures of intelligence such as the *Wechsler Adult Intelligence Scale* are related to the size of certain portions of the brain, including the left and right temporal lobe and the right and left hippocampus. Moreover, this is true even when corrections are made for individuals' overall physical size.

In sum, advanced techniques are beginning to make it possible for researchers to try and determine the degree to which variations in neural efficiency contribute to individual differences in intelligence, and to start mapping areas of the brain that may play an active role in some types of intelligent behaviour. It would be a mistake, however, to assume that differences in neural efficiency can account for more than a small part of the variation we see from person to person in intelligence. To think otherwise would be akin to assuming that variations in intelligence are wholly attributable to biologically determined differences in brain function, and that experience and education play no role. As we will see in the next section, this is simply not the case.

K E Y *QUESTIONS*

- What is inspection time and what does it measure?
- What findings suggest that intelligence is related to neural functioning or brain structure?

Critical Thinking

Will we ever be able to develop a single measure of intelligence that will capture all aspects of intellectual behaviour, or is the best we can hope for a variety of tests, each of which predicts the likelihood of intelligence in a different domain of human endeavour?

The Roles of Heredity and the Environment in Intelligence

That people differ in intelligence is obvious. Indeed, we rarely need test scores to remind us of this fact. The causes behind these differences, though, are less obvious. Are they largely a matter of heredity—differences in the genetic materials and codes we inherit from our parents? Or are they primarily the result of environmental factors—conditions favourable or unfavourable to intellectual growth? You probably know the answer: Both types of factors are involved. Human intelligence appears to be the product of an extremely complex interplay between genetic factors and environmental conditions (Plomin, 1989; Weinberg, 1989). Let's now review some of the evidence pointing to this conclusion.

Evidence for the Influence of Heredity

The strongest early advocate of the view that intelligence is determined by one's ancestors and not by one's environment was Galton (1869). In his book *Hereditary Genius,* he provided an extensive account of the family trees of celebrated Victorian writers, intellectuals, jurists, and scientists. Galton concluded that the incidence of high intelligence and genius in such families was far too common to be accidental. Influenced by Darwin, he took the position that intelligence had to be an inherited trait. It followed, therefore, that because members of eminent families tended to marry members of other eminent families, greatness and giftedness would tend to be concentrated over generations in such families. What Galton *failed to consider* was that the prominent Victorian families he studied had wealth, resources, and privileges that afforded the members of such families advantages that less distinguished families lacked. He ignored entirely the contribution of such environmental factors.

Although extreme views such as those of Galton are most certainly wrong, several lines of research offer support for the view that heredity plays a significant role in human intelligence (see Figure 11.10). First, consider findings with respect to family relationship and measured IQ. If intelligence is indeed determined by heredity, we would expect that the more closely two individuals are related, the more similar their IQs will be. This prediction has generally been confirmed (Bouchard & McGue, 1981; Erlenmeyer-Kimling & Jarvik, 1963). For example, the correlation of IQs of identical twins raised together is almost +0.90; for brothers and sisters, it is about +0.50; and for cousins, the correlation is about +0.15. (Remember: Higher correlations indicate stronger relationships between variables.)

Additional support for the impact of heredity upon intelligence is provided by studies involving adopted children. If intelligence is strongly affected by genetic factors, the IQs of adopted children should resemble those of their biological parents more closely than those of their adoptive parents. In short, the children should be more similar in IQ to the people from whom they received their genes than to the people who raised them. This prediction, too, has been confirmed. While the IQs of adopted children correlate about +0.40 to +0.50 with those of their biological parents, they correlate only about +0.10 to +0.20 with those of their adoptive parents (Jencks, 1972; Munsinger, 1978). Be aware, though, that not all studies have yielded such results. Further, in some investigations, the IQs of adopted children have been observed to become increasingly similar to those of their adoptive parents over time (Scarr & Weinberg, 1976). These findings indicate that environmental factors, too, play an important role.

Some of the most interesting evidence for the role of genetic factors in intelligence has been provided by the Minnesota Study of Twins Reared Apart undertaken by Bouchard and his colleagues (Bouchard, Lykken, McGue, Segal, & Tellegren, 1990; Bouchard, 1997). They tracked more than several dozen pairs of

Figure 11.10
Correlations between IQ Scores of Individuals in Varying Relationships

The closer the biological relationship of two individuals, the more similar their IQ scores—strong support for a genetic component to intelligence.

Source: Based on data from Bouchard and McGue, 1981; and Erlenmeyer-Kipling and Jarvis, 1963.

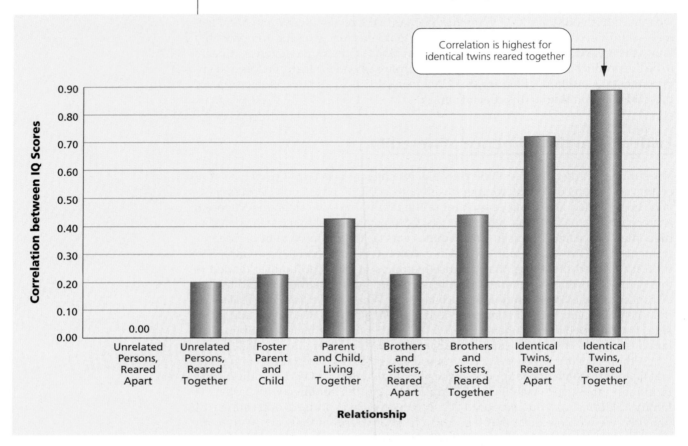

identical twins who were separated early in life and raised in different homes. Since these people had been apart on average thirty years and were exposed to different environmental conditions—in some cases, sharply contrasting ones—a high correlation between their IQs would suggest that heredity plays a key role in human intelligence. Expectations were confirmed. The IQs of identical twins reared apart (in many cases, from the time they were only a few days old) correlate almost as highly as those of identical twins reared together. Moreover, such people are also amazingly similar in many other characteristics, such as physical appearance, preferences in dress, mannerisms, and even personality. Clearly, such findings suggest that heredity plays an important role in intelligence and in many other aspects of psychological functioning.

On the basis of these and other findings, some researchers have estimated that the **heritability** of intelligence—the proportion of the variance in intelligence within a given population that is attributable to genetic factors—ranges from about 35 percent in childhood to as much as 75 percent in adulthood (McGue et al., 1993), and may be about 50 percent overall (Plomin et al., 1997). Why does the contribution of genetic factors to intelligence increase with age? Perhaps because as individuals grow older, their interactions with their environment are shaped less and less by restraints imposed on them by their families or by their social origins, and are shaped more and more by the characteristics they bring with them to these

Heritability: The proportion of the variance in any trait within a given population that is attributable to genetic factors.

environments. In other words, as they grow older, individuals are increasingly able to choose or change their environments so that these permit expression of their genetically-determined tendencies and preferences (Neisser et al., 1996).

Whatever the precise origin of the increasing heritability of intelligence with age, there is little doubt that genetic factors do play an important role in intelligence throughout life. Indeed, some researchers are now actively trying to identify specific genes that influence intelligence (e.g., Rutter & Plomin, 1997; Sherman et al., 1997). In one such study, Chorney and his colleagues (1998) compared the genetic structure of individuals with extremely high intelligence and those of normal intelligence. A difference was found in the form of one particular gene, but the estimated overall effect of this gene on intelligence was extremely small. It seems likely that many genes work together to determine high or low levels of intelligence. Unravelling these many interactions is going to be an extremely difficult task. Nevertheless, the work continues, and we can expect to read about advances in this quarter in the not-too-distant future. Let's now consider the role of environmental factors on intelligence.

Evidence for the Influence of Environmental Factors

Genetic factors are definitely not the total picture where human intelligence is concerned, however. Other findings point to the conclusion that environmental variables are also of great importance. One such finding is that, in recent decades, there has been a gradual increase in IQ scores at all age levels in Canada, as well as other industrialized countries in the world. This is sometimes known as the *Flynn effect*, after the psychologist who first reported it (Flynn, 1987). On average, increases have been about three IQ points per decade, but in some countries they have been even larger. For instance, in the Netherlands, the average IQ of nineteen-year-olds increased more than eight points between 1972 and 1982. What accounts for this increase? Since it seems unlikely that massive shifts in human heredity have occurred during this time period, a more reasonable explanation seems to lie in changing environmental conditions. Urbanization has increased all over the world, with the result that growing numbers of people are being exposed, through television and other media, to an increasing amount of information. Similarly, there have been improvements in nutrition and educational opportunities in many countries (e.g., Lynn, 1990). To the extent that these variables are responsible for the increase in IQ, of course, this provides strong support for the role of environmental factors in human intelligence.

Additional evidence for the role of environmental factors in intelligence is provided by the findings of studies of *environmental deprivation* and *environmental enrichment*. With respect to deprivation, it has been found that intelligence can be reduced by the absence of certain forms of environmental stimulation early in life (Gottfried, 1984). In terms of enrichment, removing children from sterile, restricted environments and placing them in more favourable settings seems to enhance their intellectual growth. For example, in one of the first demonstrations of the beneficial impact of an enriched environment on IQ, Skeels (1938, 1966) removed thirteen children, all aged about two, from the impoverished orphanage in which they lived and placed them in the care of a group of cognitively impaired women living in an institution. After a few years, Skeels noted that the children's IQs had risen dramatically—29 points on average. Interestingly, Skeels also obtained IQ measures of children who had remained in the orphanage and found that the average IQ for this group had actually *decreased* by 26 points—presumably as a result of the impoverished environment at the orphanage. Twenty-five years later, the thirteen children who had experienced the more favourable environment were all doing well; most had graduated from high school, found work, and married. In contrast, those in the original control group either remained institutionalized or were functioning poorly in society.

While more recent—and more carefully controlled—efforts to increase intelligence through environmental interventions have not yielded gains as dramatic as those reported by Skeels (1966), some of these programs *have* produced beneficial results. For example, in one such study, known as the *Venezuelan Intelligence Project,* hundreds of seventh-grade children from disadvantaged backgrounds were exposed to special school programs designed to improve their thinking skills. This intervention produced significant gains in the children's scores on many tests (Herrnstein et al., 1986). In another program, the *Carolina Abecedarian Project* (Campbell & Ramey, 1994), children were provided with enriched environments from early infancy through preschool. The test scores of these youngsters were higher than those of children who did not benefit from this intervention, and remained higher even at age twelve, seven years after the end of the program. Together, findings such as these suggest that improving the environment in which children live can indeed affect their IQs.

A fourth source of evidence for the impact on intelligence of environmental factors is provided by the finding, in many studies, that the longer students remain in school, the higher their IQ scores tend to be (e.g., Ceci, 1991). While this finding could also be interpreted as suggesting that it is the more intelligent people who choose to remain in school, several facts point to the conclusion that staying in school may actually benefit intelligence. For example, it has been found that people who attend school regularly score higher on intelligence tests than persons who attend irregularly. Similarly, when children of nearly identical age but who are one grade apart in school are compared, those who have attended school longer have higher average IQs. (This occurs because all school systems have a "cut-off" date for birthdays. Only children born before that date can start school in a given year.)

Finally, support for the role of environmental factors in intelligence is provided by the finding that many factors can influence basic biological functions and impair intellectual development. Prolonged malnutrition can certainly adversely affect IQ (e.g., Sigman, 1995), as can exposure of the developing fetus to such factors as alcohol and drugs (e.g., Neisser et al., 1996). It seems clear, therefore, that many forms of evidence support the view that intelligence is determined, at least in part, by environmental factors.

Summation of Environment, Heredity, and Intelligence

In sum, there is considerable evidence that both environmental and genetic factors play a role in intelligence. This is the view accepted by almost all psychologists, and there is little controversy about it. Greater controversy continues to exist, however, concerning the relative contribution of each of these factors. Do environmental or genetic factors play a stronger role in shaping intelligence? As noted earlier, existing evidence seems to favour the view that genetic factors may account for more of the variance in IQ scores within a given population than environmental factors (e.g., McGue et al., 1993; Neisser et al., 1996). Many persons—including psychologists—are made somewhat uneasy by this conclusion, in part because they assume that characteristics that are heritable—ones that are strongly influenced by genetic factors—cannot readily be changed. It's important to recognize that this assumption is false! For instance, consider height: this is a characteristic that is highly heritable—one that is influenced by genetic factors to a greater extent than intelligence. Yet, despite this fact, average heights have increased in many countries as nutrition has improved. So height provides an example of a trait that is strongly determined by genetic factors, yet is still responsive to shifts in environmental conditions.

The same thing is almost certainly true for intelligence. Even if it is influenced by genetic factors, it can still be affected by environmental conditions. For this reason, programs designed to enrich the intellectual environments of children from disadvantaged backgrounds may still produce beneficial results. Whether they actually do so or not is an empirical question open to scientific study; however, there is no reason to assume, in advance, that such programs cannot succeed because intelligence is influenced by genetic factors. Heredity, in short, should not be viewed as a set of biological shackles, nor as an excuse for giving up on children who are at risk because of poverty, prejudice, or neglect.

K E Y *QUESTIONS*

- What evidence suggests that intelligence is influenced by genetic factors?
- What evidence suggests that intelligence is influenced by environmental factors?
- Can characteristics that are highly heritable be influenced by environmental factors?

Critical Thinking

Suppose several genes that influence intelligence are identified. Would it be ethical to alter these genes so as to produce higher levels of intelligence in many persons? What might be the effects on society of doing so?

Group Differences in Intelligence Test Scores

Earlier, it was noted that there are sizable differences in the average IQ scores of various ethnic groups. In North America and elsewhere, members of various minority groups score lower, on average, than members of the majority group. Why do such differences occur? We've already looked at one possibility: standard IQ tests suffer from cultural bias. Here, we'll expand upon this earlier discussion by examining several other potential causes for such group differences in intelligence test scores. In addition, we'll briefly examine the possibility that gender differences also exist.

Possible Causes of Group Differences in IQ Scores

While many different factors may contribute to group differences in IQ scores, three, in addition to test bias, have received the greatest amount of attention: *socioeconomic factors*, *cultural factors*, and *genetic factors*.

SOCIOECONOMIC FACTORS In North America and many other countries, members of minority groups have much lower incomes than persons belonging to the majority group. Further, much larger proportions of several ethnic minorities live below the poverty line (Neisser et al., 1996). Since poverty is associated with many factors that can exert adverse effects on intelligence—for instance, poorer nutrition, inadequate prenatal care, substandard schools—it seems possible that economic disadvantage may be one important cause of lower IQ scores among ethnic minorities.

While there seems little doubt that economic disadvantage plays some role in this respect, research findings indicate that it is only part of the total story. When persons in the majority group and in various ethnic minorities who are closely matched in terms of socioeconomic status are compared, those in the majority group still score somewhat higher (e.g., Loehlin et al., 1975). The difference is small, but it is still present. This suggests that while socioeconomic factors contribute to group differences in IQ scores, other factors also play a role.

CULTURAL DIFFERENCES Another possibility is that certain aspects of various minority cultures interfere, in subtle ways, with test performance. For example, according to Boykin (1994), several features of African American culture conflict with features of the majority culture in the United States, and therefore with several practices in U.S. schools. For instance, while the majority culture insists that children work alone and sit still and quietly in class, African American culture emphasizes sharing work and high levels of expressiveness and movement. The result, Boykin (1994) contends, is that African Americans can find school an unpleasant, constraining, and oppressive environment and quickly become alienated from the educational process, which in turn leads to reduced test scores. Similar views are expressed in an extensive analysis by Collier (1994) of the way in which social factors influence and determine the expression of intelligence.

Another factor that may adversely affect the test scores of minorities involves what psychologists describe as the effects of belonging to *caste-like minorities* (e.g., Ogbu, 1994). The nature of such minorities is best captured, perhaps, by the Indian term "untouchables." It implies that persons are assigned to the caste-like minority in an involuntary manner, that their membership in this minority is permanent, and that they will experience sharply restricted opportunities. Ogbu (1994) argues that in the United States, many African Americans feel that they have been assigned to such a caste-like minority, and that they can never escape from it. The result: they grow up convinced that no matter what they do, they will never share in "the American dream." In terms of expectancy theory (see Chapter 10), they grow up with low expectancies, believing that effort on their part will not result in better outcomes. This leads them to reject academic achievement and other forms of behaviour described as "acting white," and these reactions, in turn, tend to lower their test scores.

The third potential cause of group differences in IQ scores listed above—genetic factors—is so important and so controversial that we'll examine it in the **Perspectives on Diversity** section below.

Perspectives on Diversity

Genetic Factors and Group Differences in IQ Scores

IN 1994, A HIGHLY CONTROVERSIAL book entitled *The Bell Curve* was published. Because the book was written by two well-known American psychologists (Richard Herrnstein and Charles Murray), it received a great deal of media attention in both the United States and Canada (Whalsten, 1995). The book focused on human intelligence and covered many aspects of this topic. The most controversial portions, however, dealt with what is known as the **genetic hypothesis**—the view that group differences in intelligence are due, at least in part, to genetic factors.

In *The Bell Curve*, Herrnstein and Murray (1994) voiced strong support for this view, noting, for instance, that there are several converging sources of evidence for "a genetic factor in cognitive ethnic differences" (p. 270) between African Americans and white Americans and between other ethnic groups as well. Proceeding from this conclusion, they suggested that intelligence may not be readily modifiable through changes in environmental conditions, and proposed, therefore, that efforts to raise the IQ scores of disadvantaged minorities through special programs were probably a waste of effort. In their own words: "Taken together, the story of attempts to raise intelligence is one of high hopes, flamboyant claim, and disappointing results. For the foreseeable future, the problems of low cognitive ability are not going to be solved by outside interventions to make children smarter" (p. 389).

As you can guess, these suggestions were challenged vigorously by many psychologists (e.g., Sternberg, 1995; Kirby, 1995; Wahlsten, 1995). These critics argued that much of the reasoning in *The Bell Curve* was flawed and that the book overlooked many important findings. Perhaps the harshest criticism of this book centred on its contention that because individual differences in intelligence are

Genetic Hypothesis: The view that group differences in intelligence are due, at least in part, to genetic factors.

strongly influenced by genetic factors, group differences are also influenced. Several researchers took strong exception to this reasoning (e.g., Schultze, Kane, & Dickens, 1996; Sternberg, 1995). They argued that this argument could be advanced only if the environments of the various groups being compared were essentially identical. Under those conditions, it could be argued that differences between the groups stemmed, at least in part, from genetic factors. However, in reality, the environments in which the members of various ethnic groups exist are far from identical. As a result, it is false to assume that differences between them with respect to IQ scores stem from genetic factors, even if we know that individual differences in such scores are strongly influenced by these factors. Perhaps this point is best illustrated by a simple analogy.

Imagine that a farmer plants two fields with seeds that are known to be genetically identical. In one field, the farmer fertilizes, waters, and cultivates the crop very carefully. In the other, the farmer does none of these things, and also removes key nutrients needed for growth. Several months later, there are large differences between the plants growing in the two fields, *despite the fact that their genetic make-up is identical*. In a similar manner, it is entirely possible that differences in the IQ scores of various groups occur primarily because of contrasting life environments, and that genetic factors play little if any role in such differences.

If you think this analogy is far-fetched, consider the children removed from an impoverished orphanage environment we referred to earlier and more recent French adoption studies, cited by Wahlsten (1995) in his criticism of *The Bell Curve*. These studies found a twelve- to sixteen-point increase in the IQ scores of children who were moved (or, to continue the above analogy, transplanted) from homes of low socioeconomic status to homes of high socioeconomic status.

So where does all this leave us? With the conclusion that although we know fairly certainly that individual differences in IQ scores are influenced by genetic factors, we have no meaningful way of concluding that this is true with respect to group differences.

Gender Differences in Intelligence

Do males and females differ in intelligence? Overall, they score virtually identically on standard tests of this characteristic (e.g., Lynn, 1994). There are, however, small but reliable differences in the dexterity with which males and females can carry out certain kinds of cognitive-processing operations. Females tend generally to be more adept than males at verbal tasks, such as naming synonyms and generating words that start with a given letter, and on tasks requiring rapid visual scanning. Females also score higher than males on college achievement tests in literature, spelling, and writing (e.g., Stanley, 1993). Such differences are relatively small, and there are those who claim they seem to be decreasing (Feingold, 1992), but they have been repeatedly and reliably observed (Kimura & Hampson, 1993).

Males, on the other hand, tend to score somewhat higher than females on visual-spatial tasks, such as capturing visually distant objects, and precise specification of vertical and horizontal orientations (Kimura & Hampson, 1993). They tend also to be more adept at mentally rotating or tracking a moving object through space (Law et al., 1993).

You may be able to demonstrate such differences for yourself by following the instructions in Figure 11.11. Ask several male and female friends to try their hand at the task it involves. You may find that the males find the visuospatial task slightly easier than the females, and that the females are more adept at completing the verbal synonym task. However, gender differences in performing visual-spatial and verbal tasks, like almost all gender differences, are far smaller than gender stereotypes suggest, so if you do observe any difference, it is likely to be a small one.

Figure 11.11
Gender Differences in Visual-Spatial and Verbal Abilities

There are small gender differences in some tests of cognitive skills. Two types of task are illustrated here: (A) a visuospatial task on which males usually tend to perform slightly better than females, and (B) a synonym generation task on which females tend to perform slightly better than males.

Source: Adapted from Azar, 1996.

Which figure on the right is identical to pattern 1 on the left?

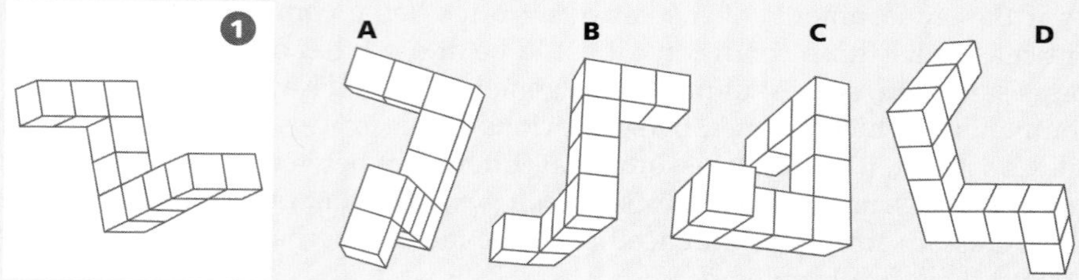

All of the words below have more than four synonyms. How many can you generate for each word? Try the test before looking at possible appropriate responses listed in small print below.

Famous _____ _____ _____

Part _____ _____ _____

Secret _____ _____ _____

Conquer _____ _____ _____

Possible answers: Famous (celebrated, distinguished, eminent, illustrious, noted); Part (division, member, piece, portion, section, segment); Secret (covert, clandestine, furtive, stealthy, underhanded); Conquer (beat, defeat, lick, overcome, overthrow, subdue, vanquish)

To what are these small, but persistent, differences in the facility with which males and females perform certain spatial and verbal tasks attributable? The currently favoured notion is that these differences are attributable to subtle differences in the way the brain is organized in males and females. For example, there is evidence to suggest that spatial processing operations are more asymmetrically organized (concentrated in one hemisphere of the brain) in males than in females, and this may allow males to perform such tasks with greater efficiency than females. Other structural differences of a very different kind are assumed responsible for the more efficient processing of verbal operations by females. The interesting question, of course, is why there should be any form of organizational variation or disparity in the brains of males and females.

The answer, according to a number of researchers, may well lie in our evolutionary history. Kimura and Hampson (1993), of the University of Western Ontario, point out that prior to civilization—which began only some ten thousand years ago—our species lived by hunting and gathering: men hunted and women foraged for edible plants. It is quite understandable under such circumstances that evolutionary pressures might encourage the refinement of certain types of spatial skills, such as targeting distant objects and throwing skills, in males. It seems equally reasonable that if females were responsible for foraging, evolutionary pressures might encourage the development of skills in discernment and registration of the locations of objects. An experiment by Eals and Silverman (1994) at York University offers evidence to support this position. The researchers performed a series of studies in which male and female participants performed several tasks in a small office. In one condition, participants were told to try to remember the location of various objects in the room, while in another condition, no mention was made of this additional task. When later tested for naming the objects and indicating their locations, women outperformed men in both conditions. The difference was much larger in the condition in which participants were not told to try to remember this information. This suggests that women may be much more automatically disposed to register location information about objects in their environment than men.

We are far from understanding all the subtle gender differences displayed by males and females in performing various different cognitive operations. Nevertheless, it is an interesting thought that some of the small performance differences now discernable may have be been determined, at least in part, by different domains of responsibility in our very distant past.

KEY QUESTIONS

- What role do socioeconomic and cultural factors play in group differences in IQ scores?

- In *The Bell Curve*, the authors argue that because individual differences in IQ are highly heritable, group differences in IQ must also be highly heritable. How do most psychologists view this argument?

- Do any gender differences exist with respect to intelligence? If so, what is the possible origin of such differences?

Emotional Intelligence

Up to this point, we have focused on intelligence primarily from a thinking, reasoning, and problem-solving perspective. In this section we will consider another kind of intelligence, quite distinct from that measured by IQ tests. This kind of intelligence has been described as **emotional intelligence** in a recent book by Daniel Goleman (1995). Basically, such intelligence can be defined as a cluster of traits or abilities relating to the emotional side of life—abilities such as recognizing and managing one's own emotions, being able to motivate oneself and restrain impulses, recognizing and managing others' emotions, and handling interpersonal relationships in an effective manner (Goleman, 1995). Growing evidence suggests that such skills are important for personal success and for having a happy, productive life. In other words, as we've already noted at several points in this chapter, it is not enough to be bright in an academic sense (that is, to have a high IQ); in addition, other aspects of intelligence are also crucial. Let's take a closer look at the major components of emotional intelligence and how they influence important forms of behaviour.

Major Components of Emotional Intelligence

Goleman (1995) suggests that emotional intelligence consists of five major components: (1) knowing our own emotions, (2) managing our emotions, (3) motivating ourselves, (4) recognizing the emotions of others, and (5) handling relationships. Each of these, he contends, plays an important role in shaping our life outcomes.

KNOWING OUR OWN EMOTIONS   Emotions are often powerful reactions, so it would seem, at first glance, that all of us would be able to recognize our own feelings. However, this is not the case. Some persons are very aware of their own emotions and their thoughts about them, while others seem to be almost totally oblivious to their feelings. What are the implications of such differences? First, to the extent individuals are not aware of their own feelings, they cannot make intelligent choices. How do they decide with whom they should seek friendship, what

Emotional Intelligence: A cluster of traits or abilities relating to the emotional side of life—abilities such as recognizing and managing one's own emotions, being able to motivate oneself and restrain impulses, recognizing and managing others' emotions, and handling interpersonal relationships in an effective manner.

academic program to study, or what recreational activities to pursue? Second, because such persons aren't aware of their own emotions, they are often low in expressiveness—they don't show their feelings clearly in their facial expressions, body language, and other cues most of us use to recognize others' feelings (Malandro et al., 1994), and this can profoundly affect interpersonal relationships.

MANAGING OUR OWN EMOTIONS We have all betrayed our emotions at some time to someone, or some group, and spent hours, and sometimes weeks, regretting the experience. Management of emotions is important, but emotional intelligence requires more than merely controlling the expression of emotions. The real intellectual challenge is to develop the necessary skills to change the nature of the emotions we experience—to move from a mood state that causes discomfort to another that does not. This need is most commonly felt when we are overcome by feelings of melancholy or depression. Persons who are high in emotional intelligence develop effective tactics to deal with dark times of disappointment or defeat (e.g., Tice & Baumeiseter, 1993). They know enough about themselves to be able to engage in precisely the right type of activity—phoning a friend, seeing a movie, going out to a favourite hang-out—to lift their spirits. Persons low in this aspect of emotional intelligence, in contrast, have fewer tactics for countering depression or other negative moods. As a result, they often ruminate about the experience, thus lengthening and deepening their despair.

MOTIVATING OURSELVES Thomas Edison, the famous inventor, once remarked: "Success is two percent inspiration and ninety-eight percent perspiration." Edison may have underestimated to some degree the importance of inspiration or creativity (see the next section of the chapter), but he is certainly correct in claiming that successfully completing a project or life-long goal requires "perspiration." But the perspiration that is produced has to be generated by work on the project or goal and not some peripheral but pleasurable target. A crucial part of emotional intelligence is being able to motivate oneself to remain focused on the end goal and being able to delay gratification—to put off receiving small rewards now in order to get larger ones later on (e.g., Shoda et al., 1990).

Emotional Intelligence in Action

An important aspect of emotional intelligence is being able to recognize the emotions of others. Particularly important is the ability to read *non-verbal cues*, since it is primarily through such cues that people generally communicate their feelings.

RECOGNIZING OTHERS' EMOTIONS We all know people who appear to be absolutely insensitive to reactions of others. They ignore obvious signs of discomfort in others and continue to engage in a line of conversation or other kinds of behaviour that those with them would prefer to see ended. An important aspect of emotional intelligence is being able to recognize the emotions of others. Particularly important is the ability to read *non-verbal cues*, since it is primarily through such cues that people generally communicate their feelings (e.g., Carroll & Russell, 1996). Those skilled in being able to rapidly and accurately read the reactions of others can readily turn interactions to their advantage. For example, good politicians can sense how others are reacting to their words or actions, and adjust these accordingly. Such individuals don't merely recognize others' reactions—they also manage them. They know exactly what it takes to induce the kind of reactions in others they want—a positive attitude towards them and their office.

HANDLING RELATIONSHIPS It takes more than being able to recognize others' reactions and to try and manage them to produce a relationship. A relationship involves give and take. It entails an understanding of the goals, ambitions, and peculiarities of another individual and a willingness to tailor your needs and plans to fit those of another person in a fashion that benefits both. According to Goleman (1995), those with genuine skills in this domain of emotional intelligence not only have the ability to mesh their plans, ambitions, and needs with another person, but are able to direct and coordinate the efforts of several people in working toward a goal. Such individuals are very adept at resolving various complex interpersonal problems typically encountered in managing group projects. Again, it is worth noting that such skills are clearly distinct from the more "selfish" skills needed for getting good grades or scoring high on tests of intelligence, but in circumstances requiring some form of coordinated group action or leadership, they can be crucially important.

An Assessment of Emotional Intelligence

The concept of an emotional intelligence is appealing, but it must be admitted that some experts in the field of intelligence have difficulty in accepting the idea that anything "emotional" can be intelligent. They claim that for a process to be "intelligent," there have to be specifiable abilities and talents. They also argue that, in the case of emotional intelligence, these abilities are either absent or, at best, take the form of vague expressions of enhanced sensitivity to one's own personal feelings and the feelings of the other person. Scarr (1989), for example, argues that social competence and social perceptiveness may be correlated with intelligence, but holds that it is a mistake to see these qualities, in and of themselves, as intelligent.

Can the notion of emotional intelligence be defended? In an editorial in the journal *Intelligence*, Mayer and Salovey (1993) provide an affirmative answer. In defense of emotional intelligence, they point out that thoughts always accompany emotions, and those capable of fluent manipulation of their emotions have an ability to consider a much wider variety of thoughtful alternatives for action in various circumstances than those lacking in such capabilities. They argue also that those who clearly understand their feelings, and are capable of altering emotional states, can respond both more rapidly and more effectively to difficult and troubling experiences. They agree with Goleman (1995) that individuals with high emotional intelligence can manage their emotions and cope more efficiently in times of emotional distress. Such individuals do not allow themselves to become so overwhelmed with feelings of concern about the adverse aspects of a situation that they close their minds to what is going on around them. Instead, they continue in an open and analytical manner to monitor the situation, seeking to discern ways to turn it to their advantage.

In short, just as classic problem-solving intelligence offers an adaptive advantage to those who possess it—so too does emotional intelligence. In fact, it is arguable that in the world of business, high emotional intelligence may be a better predictor of career success than high academic intelligence (e.g., Sternberg et al., 1995). Further, as we'll see in Chapter 13, emotional intelligence may also play an important role in personal health and in the effectiveness of the health care system: Physicians high in emotional intelligence may be more successful in treating their patients than physicians who are low in such intelligence. The common-sense notion that there is more to intelligence than "book smarts" seems correct, and one of the very important "other" aspects of intelligence is emotional intelligence.

KEY *QUESTIONS*

- What is emotional intelligence?
- Can the notion of an "emotional" intelligence be defended?
- What role does emotional intelligence play in success and personal happiness?

Creativity

Suppose you were asked to name people high in creativity—who would be on your list? When faced with this question, many people name such famous figures as Albert Einstein, Leonardo da Vinci, Thomas Edison, Marie Curie, and Sigmund Freud. What do these diverse individuals have in common? All were responsible for producing something—a theory, inventions—that were viewed as unexpected and new. More formally, psychologists generally define **creativity** as involving the ability to produce work that is both novel (original, unexpected) and appropriate (it works—it is useful or meets task constraints; e.g., Lubart, 1994).

Clearly, creativity is important. In a sense, it is responsible for all of the advances made by our species since its emergence on the planet. It is somewhat surprising to learn, therefore, that until recently, it was not the subject of extensive study by psychologists. Why was this so? One important reason was that although several methods for measuring creativity existed—for instance, asking individuals to come up with as many uses for everyday objects as possible (known as the Unusual Uses Test; Guilford, 1950), or to formulate as many ways of improving a product as possible (Torrance, 1974)—none of these seemed to be completely satisfactory. They did not seem to capture all aspects of creativity as it occurs in real-life situations (Sternberg & Lubart, 1996). Another problem was the fact that the concept of creativity was associated, in many people's minds, with forces outside the realm of science—for instance, with vague notions of "the creative spirit." This made psychologists somewhat reluctant to address this topic.

During the past two decades, however, this situation has changed, and rapid advances have been made in our understanding of creativity. Because creativity is clearly related to certain aspects of intelligence, and because it is an important topic in its own right, we'll now look at what psychologists have discovered about this fascinating topic.

Contrasting Views of Creativity

A basic question about creativity is "What factors underlie its occurrence?" Until recently, different branches of psychology offered contrasting answers. Cognitive psychologists, for example, tended to focus on the basic processes that underlie creative thought. Research findings indicate that such processes as retrieval of information from memory, association, synthesis, transformation, and categorical reduction (mentally assigning objects to basic categories) may all play a role in creativity. In contrast, social psychologists generally focused on the personality traits that make people creative and the environmental conditions that either encourage or discourage creativity (e.g., Simonton, 1994).

While these approaches have certainly added to our understanding of creativity, most researchers now believe that even more can be learned through what is termed a **confluence approach**—one that assumes that for creativity to occur, multiple components must converge (Amabile, 1983). For example, according to an influential confluence model of creativity proposed by Lubart (e.g., Lubart, 1994), creativity requires a confluence of six distinct resources:

- *Intellectual abilities:* The ability to see problems in new ways, the ability to recognize which of one's ideas are worth pursuing, and persuasive skills (being able to convince others of these new ideas).

- *Knowledge:* Enough knowledge about a field to move it forward.

- *Certain styles of thinking:* A preference for thinking in novel ways, and an ability to "see the big picture" (to think globally as well as locally).

Creativity: Cognitive activity resulting in new or novel ways of viewing or solving problems.

Confluence Approach: An approach suggesting that for creativity to occur, multiple components must converge.

■ *Personality attributes:* Such traits as willingness to take risks and tolerance for ambiguity.

■ *Intrinsic, task-focused motivation:* Creative people usually love what they are doing and find intrinsic rewards in their work;

■ *An environment that is supportive of creative ideas.*

Only when all of these conditions are present, Sternberg and his colleagues (e.g.,Sternberg & Lubart, 1996) argue, can a high level of creativity emerge (see Figure 11.12).

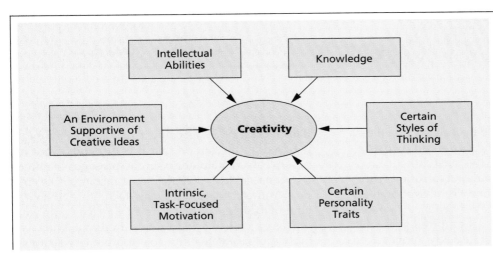

Figure 11.12
Creativity: A Confluence Approach

According to modern confluence theories, creativity can emerge only when a number of different conditions are present or converge.

Source: Based on suggestions by Sternberg and Lubart, 1996.

Recent Research on Creativity

Is there any support in scientific research for the confluence view of creativity described above? Absolutely. For example, consider one recent study by Lubart and Sternberg (1995). In this study, forty-eight adults ranging in age from eighteen to sixty-five were asked to produce creative products in each of four domains: writing, art, advertising, and science. For example, in the art category, they were asked to produce drawings showing "hope" and "rage," and "the earth from an insect's point of view." With respect to advertising, they were asked to design television ads for "bow ties" and "the Internal Revenue Service." All the products participants created were rated for overall creativity, novelty, and perceived effort. Participants also completed a measure of fluid intelligence, a measure of thinking style, and two personality measures.

Results indicated, first, that there was considerable agreement among raters: they agreed on what was creative and what was not creative. This is an important finding, because it indicates that creativity can be studied scientifically. Second, it was found that creativity in one domain (art, writing, and so on) was only moderately related to creativity in other domains. Thus, as common sense suggests, people can be creative in one area but not in another. Third, intellectual ability, thinking style, and personality were all significantly related to creativity. Additional research (e.g., Sternberg et al., in press) indicated that willingness to take intellectual risks was also related to creativity.

Taken together, these findings, and those of other recent studies, offer support for the confluence approach. Creativity, it appears, requires the convergence of many factors for its emergence. None of these are unusual in and of themselves, but together, they produce outcomes and results that are, in some cases, extraordinary.

KEY *QUESTIONS*

- What is creativity?
- What are confluence theories, and what factors do they view as essential to creativity?
- What evidence offers support for the confluence approach?

Making **Psychology** *Part of Your Life*

Managing Anger

*I*n discussing emotional intelligence, we noted that one key aspect of such intelligence is the ability to manage our own emotions. Perhaps the most difficult emotion of all to manage is anger, which all too often erupts into open rage. You probably know from your own experience that once it starts, anger tends to be self-perpetuating—and sometimes, self-amplifying as well. What begins as mild irritation quickly moves into strong anger, and then, if we don't take active steps to stop it, a virtual emotional explosion. What can you do to avoid such outcomes—to manage your own anger more effectively? Here are some useful steps.

- *Stop the process early.* Because anger is self-amplifying, it is easier to break the annoyance–anger–rage cycle early on. So, if you feel yourself getting angry and feel that this emotion is inappropriate or might get out of hand, take one of the actions described below as soon as possible. Delay can be quite costly in terms of your ability to break this cycle.

- *Try a cooling-off period.* If possible, leave the scene, change the subject, or at least stop interacting with the other person. Doing so can give your emotional arousal a chance to dissipate, as long as you don't use this time to mull over the causes of your anger.

- *Do something to get yourself off the anger track.* As we just noted, if you think angry thoughts, you will remain angry—and perhaps become even angrier. So, it's important to do something to get your mind off the causes of your anger. Here's where a technique known as the incompatible response approach (e.g.,

Baron, 1983, 1993) can come in handy. This technique is based on the notion that it is difficult, if not impossible, to remain angry in the presence of stimuli that cause us to experience some incompatible emotion. You can readily use this technique to control your own anger if you can find a way to expose yourself, as quickly as possible, to stimuli you know will induce pleasant feelings, or find some way to see some humour in the situation. Your anger should quickly vanish.

- *Seek positive explanations for the things others say or do that make you angry.* When others make us angry, we usually attribute their actions to insensitivity, selfishness—or worse! If, instead, you try to come up with other explanations for the words or actions that have made you angry, this may greatly reduce your annoyance. Did the other person mean to say something that hurt your feelings? Perhaps that person didn't realize the implications of what he or she said. If you concentrate on interpretations like this, your anger may quickly dissipate.

- *Whatever you do, don't rely on "catharsis"—on getting it out of your system.* A large body of research findings indicates that giving vent to anger does not usually reduce it. On the contrary, as noted above, such actions tend to fan the flames of anger—not drown them. So, whatever else you do, don't follow your impulse to give the other person a dirty look, to shout, or to pound your fist. Doing so will only make the situation worse—so a little restraint is definitely in order.

Summary and Review

Key Questions

Contrasting Views of the Nature of Intelligence

■ **What is intelligence?** Intelligence refers to individuals' abilities to understand complex ideas, to adapt effectively to the environment, to learn from experience, to engage in various forms of reasoning, and to overcome obstacles by careful thought.

■ **What is Gardner's theory of multiple intelligences?** This is a view suggesting that there are eight different kinds of intelligence, such as verbal, mathematical, musical, and bodily-kinesthetic intelligence.

■ **What is Sternberg's triarchic theory of intelligence?** Sternberg's theory suggests that there are three basic kinds of intelligence: analytical, creative, and practical.

■ **What is practical intelligence?** Practical intelligence is intelligence useful in solving everyday problems.

Measuring Human Intelligence

■ **What was the first individual test of intelligence, and what did scores on it mean?** The first individual test of intelligence was devised by Binet and Simon. It yielded an IQ (intelligence quotient) score obtained by dividing a child's mental age by chronological age and multiplying by 100.

■ **What are the Wechsler scales?** The Wechsler scales are individual tests of intelligence (for children and adults) that seek to measure several aspects of intelligence—performance components of intelligence as well as verbal components of intelligence.

■ **What is the main practical reason for administering individual tests of intelligence?** The most important reason for using these tests is to accurately identify individuals at the extremes of intelligence—those who suffer from some degree of mental retardation, and those who are intellectually gifted.

■ **What is reliability and how do psychologists attempt to measure it?** Reliability refers to the extent to which a test yields the same scores when applied more than once to the same quantity. Measures of reliability include *internal consistency* and *test–retest reliability.*

■ **What is validity, and how do psychologists attempt to measure it?** Validity refers to the extent to which a test measures what it purports to measure. Measures of validity include *content validity, predictive validity,* and *construct validity.*

■ **What is cultural bias and how may it affect scores on standard intelligence tests?** Cultural bias refers to the extent to which intelligence tests place members of various minority groups at a disadvantage because the tests were developed for use with members of the majority group. Such bias may adversely affect the scores of persons from various minorities.

■ **What is inspection time and what does it measure?** Inspection time is the minimum amount of time a particular stimulus must be exposed for individuals to make a judgment about it that meets some pre-established criterion of accuracy.

■ **What findings suggest that intelligence is related to neural functioning or brain structure?** Research findings indicate that scores on standard tests of intelligence are correlated with nerve conduction velocity and also with efficiency in brain functioning.

The Roles of Heredity and Environment in Intelligence

■ **What evidence suggests that intelligence is influenced by genetic factors?** Evidence for the role of genetic factors is provided by the findings that the more closely related persons are, the higher the correlation in their IQ scores, by research on adopted children, and by research on identical twins separated early in life and raised in different homes.

■ **What evidence suggests that intelligence is influenced by environmental factors?** Evidence for the role of environmental factors is provided by the world-wide rise in IQ scores in recent decades (the Flynn effect), studies of environmental deprivation and enrichment, the beneficial effects of special environmental interventions, and the fact that the longer children remain in school, the higher their IQs are.

■ **Can characteristics that are highly heritable be influenced by environmental factors?** Traits that are highly heritable can be strongly influenced by environmental factors. For example, height is highly heritable, yet average height has increased in many countries as a result of improved nutrition.

Group Differences in Intelligence Test Scores

■ **What role do socioeconomic and cultural factors play in group differences in IQ scores?** Socioeconomic factors, such as poverty, appear to exert adverse effects on IQ scores. Cultural factors, such as being assigned to a caste-like minority and holding values that are in conflict with those of the majority group, can cause minority group children to feel alienated from the educational process, and so can reduce their IQ scores.

- ■ **In *The Bell Curve*, the authors argue that because individual differences in IQ are highly heritable, group differences in IQ must also be highly heritable. How do most psychologists view this argument?** Most psychologists reject this view because they realize that it would be valid only if the environmental conditions experienced by various groups were identical in all respects.

- ■ **Do any gender differences with respect to intelligence exist? If so, what is the possible origin of such differences?** Males and females do not differ on IQ scores. Small gender differences are evident on certain types of tasks. Females tend to score higher than males with respect to verbal abilities, while males tend to score higher in visual-spatial abilities (e.g., mental rotation of objects). Some theoreticians explain such differences in evolutionary terms.

Emotional Intelligence

- ■ **What is emotional intelligence?** Emotional intelligence is a cluster of traits or abilities relating to the emotional side of life—abilities such as recognizing and managing one's own emotions, being able to motivate oneself and restrain impulses, recognizing and managing others' emotions, and handling interpersonal relationships in an effective manner.

- ■ **Can the notion of an "emotional" intelligence be defended?** Yes! Emotional intelligence offers, as does IQ intelligence, a number of adaptive advantages to those who possess it, and emotional intelligence may be a better predictor of career success than high academic intelligence.

- ■ **What role does emotional intelligence play in success and personal happiness?** People with high emotional intelligence understand their feelings and are adept at altering their emotional states. This allows them to respond rapidly and effectively to difficult and troubling experiences. There is reason to believe that such individuals are more likely to have better personal health and more successful careers than those who have low emotional intelligence.

Creativity

- ■ **What is creativity?** Creativity involves the ability to produce work that is both novel (original, unexpected) and appropriate (it works—it is useful or meets task constraints).

- ■ **What are confluence theories, and what factors do they view as essential to creativity?** Confluence theories suggest that for creativity to occur, multiple components must converge. Among the factors such theories view as crucial for creativity are certain intellectual abilities (e.g., the ability to see problems in new ways), knowledge of a given field, certain styles of thinking (e.g., a preference for thinking in novel ways), certain personality traits (e.g., a willingness to take risks), intrinsic motivation, and an environment supportive of creative ideas.

- ■ **What evidence offers support for the confluence approach?** Recent findings indicate that all of the factors mentioned by confluence theories are significant predictors of creativity across many different domains (e.g., writing, art, science).

Key Terms

Confluence Approach (p. 466)

Construct Validity (p. 448)

Content Validity (448)

Creativity (p. 466)

Criterion Measure (p. 448)

Crystallized Intelligence (p. 437)

Cultural Bias (p. 450)

Down's Syndrome (p. 443)

Emotional Intelligence (p. 463)

Fluid Intelligence (p. 437)

Genetic Hypothesis (p. 460)

Heritability (p. 456)

Inspection Time (p. 452)

Intelligence (p. 436)

IQ (p. 442)

Mental Retardation (p. 443)

Practical Intelligence (p. 439)

Predictive Validity (p. 448)

Processing Speed (p. 452)

Raven Progressive Matrices Test (p. 451)

Reliability (p. 446)

Savant Syndrome (p. 439)

Split-Half Reliability (p. 446)

Stanford-Binet Test (p. 441)

Test–Retest Reliability (p. 447)

Triarchic Theory (p. 439)

Validity (p. 448)

Critical Thinking Questions

Appraisal

Psychologists have long assumed that intelligence is a crucial dimension along which people differ. Do you think this assumption is justified? Or do you think that other characteristics of behaviour are even more important?

Controversy

Growing evidence indicates that practical intelligence and emotional intelligence may be just as important as academic intelligence in determining success and happiness. Yet, school systems throughout the world tend to focus on increasing academic intelligence. Do you think this should be changed so that more attention is devoted to helping children develop practical and emotional intelligence? If so, why?

Making Psychology Part of Your Life

Now that you understand some of the basic requirements of all psychological tests, do you think you will be more skeptical of the kinds of questionnaires that are published in many magazines that claim to measure various traits? We hope so! Why should you view these "tests" with caution? Under what conditions could you view them as useful or informative?

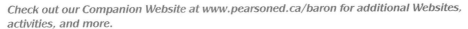

Weblinks

Check out our Companion Website at www.pearsoned.ca/baron for additional Websites, activities, and more.

Multiple Intelligences

www.gwu.edu/~tip/gardner.html

This site contains an overview of Howard Gardner's multiple intelligences theory.

Interview with Robert Sternberg on *The Bell Curve*

www.skeptic.com/03.3.fm-sternberg-interview.html

This interview with Robert Sternberg about Hernnstein and Murray's *The Bell Curve* is from *Skeptic* magazine.

Is Intelligence Inherited?

www.yorku.ca/bethune/bc1850/intellig.htm

York University maintains this extensive collection of resources on intelligence.

Classics in the History of Psychology

www.yorku.ca/dept/psych/classics/Terman/intro.htm

This interesting page tells about Louis Terman, his life, and his 1916 revision that created the "Stanford-Binet" intelligence test.

Tests, Tests, Tests ...

www.queendom.com/tests.html

This Website has lots of different kinds of "original" tests of unknown reliability and validity, but creative, challenging, and lots of fun nevertheless.

Can computers possess emotional intelligence?

www.psych.utoronto.ca/~reingold/courses/ai/emotional.html

Can computers possess emotional intelligence? That is the question posed on this Website.

Chapter 12

PERSONALITY

Uniqueness and
Consistency in the
Behaviour of
Individuals

CHAPTER OUTLINE

About Clones

This editorial in the *Moncton Times and Transcript* illustrates the widespread lack of understanding of genetic duplication, particularly the duplication of animals and dogs. The editor told of a new company that was prepared to save an animal's DNA—so that the owners could have an identical pet after the original had passed away!

What is wrong with that promise? The answer is this: Animals that are genetic copies are not necessarily the same in all respects. Clones do have the same DNA, and may appear the same, but the environment in which each animal is raised is different. The animals become more and more individual as they grow older; they develop differences in personality and in behaviour. Cloned animals may even be different in appearance and in size, since they develop in different mothers' wombs.

Why are there individual differences—even among animals that are genetically identical? How does variation in personality and behaviour come about? What are the ways we measure these differences and what do they mean? In Chapter 12, you will find the answers to these questions and many more as you consider the findings of psychological research into personality.

Source: Cunningham, N. (2000, February 29). Clones and other science need not be feared. *Moncton Times and Transcript.*

We expect others to demonstrate consistency in their behaviour across different situations and over long periods of time.

Interest in **personality** is as old as civilization: ancient philosophers and poets often speculated about why individuals were unique, and why they differed from each other in so many ways. It was not until the emergence of a scientific field of psychology, however, that personality became the focus of systematic research and revealing answers to these ancient questions were offered. What have psychologists learned about personality, and how can you use this information to gain insight into your own personality and the personalities of others? These are the central themes of this chapter.

To acquaint you with psychology's knowledge about personality, our discussion will proceed as follows. First, we'll consider what is, perhaps, the most basic question we can ask about personality: Is it real? In other words, do people really show consistency in their behaviour over time and across situations, or is our belief that they do merely another kind of cognitive or perceptual error. After addressing this question, we'll describe several major *theories of personality*—grand and sweeping frameworks for understanding personality offered by some of the true "giants" in the history of psychology. A word of caution: While these theories make for fascinating reading, few of them are currently accepted as accurate by psychologists. As a group, though, they do call our attention to important issues worthy of careful thought. For each theory, we'll first describe it, then present some research evidence relating to it, and finally offer an evaluation of its current status. After examining these theories, we'll turn to another basic question: How personality is measured. Finally we'll provide you with the flavour of modern research on personality by examining some recent research trends—ones viewed by psychologists as having particularly important effects on behaviour (e.g., Kilduff & Day, 1994; Zuckerman, 1995).

Is Personality Real?

In our everyday life, we behave as though personality is a fact: We expect others—and ourselves—to demonstrate consistency in behaviour across different situations and over long periods of time. In other words, once we conclude that a specific person possesses certain traits—that, for instance, he or she is *friendly*, *neat*, *impulsive*, and *good-natured*—we expect that person to behave in ways consistent with these traits in many situations and over long periods of time.

This idea raises an important question: Does such consistency really exist? Some psychologists have argued that it does not—that behaviour is largely determined by external situational factors rather than by stable traits or dispositions (Mischel, 1977, 1985). According to these critics of the concept of personality, individuals actually behave very differently in different situations; our perception that they act consistently is largely an error stemming from our desire to simplify the task of trying to predict their actions (Kunda & Nisbett, 1986; Reeder, Fletcher, & Furman, 1989).

Personality: Individuals' unique and relatively stable patterns of behaviour, thoughts, and feelings.

While these arguments are interesting ones, the weight of existing evidence seems to be against them: Personality, defined in terms of stable behaviour tendencies, is indeed real. Many studies indicate that people *do* show at least a moderate degree of consistency with respect to many aspects of behaviour (e.g., Pulkinen, 1996; Woodall & Matthews, 1993). Indeed, some of these research projects have continued for more than fifty years, studying the same people from early childhood to old age, and in general, they have reported an impressive amount of consistency in at least some traits (e.g., Heatherton & Weinberger, 1994). In other words, the traits individuals show today are also likely to be present tomorrow—even if "tomorrow" occurs years or even decades in the future.

Having said that, we should quickly note that such consistency over long periods of time does *not* exist for all traits or for all persons (Tice, 1989). In fact, the extent to which people show such consistency across time and situations may itself be an important aspect of personality (Koestner, Bernieri, & Zuckerman, 1992). Some people are more consistent than others! Also, the existence of stable traits in no way implies that situational factors are *not* important. On the contrary, most psychologists agree that *both* traits and situations shape behaviour. Overall, the pattern is something like this: Individuals do have traits that predispose them to behave in certain ways—for instance to be friendly, neat, and good-natured. Whether these tendencies actually appear in their overt behaviour, however, depends on many situational factors. If situations permit the expression of traits and dispositions, then they may well be reflected in overt behaviour. If situations make it very costly or difficult for these traits and dispositions to appear, they may not. For instance, even people with wild tempers tend to behave politely when stopped for speeding by a police officer. We conclude, therefore, that personality is indeed real and does influence behaviour—providing that external factors permit such influence to occur.

"I'm sorry, dear, but you knew I was a bureaucrat when you married me."

Personality: Consistency in the Behaviour of Individuals

In our everyday life, we expect others—and ourselves—to demonstrate consistency in behaviour across different situations and over long periods of time.

Source: The New Yorker.

KEY QUESTIONS

- What is personality, and does it really exist?
- What role do personality traits and situational factors play in influencing human behaviour?

Critical Thinking

Can you formulate a list of the characteristics that make you a unique person? If so, how do you know what belongs on this list, and what does not?

The Psychoanalytic Approach

Before you took this course, who would you have named as the most famous psychologist in history? If you are like most students, your answer would probably be *Freud*. He is, by far, the most famous figure in the history of psychology. Why is this so? The answer lies in several provocative and influential theories he proposed—theories that focus on personality and the origins of psychological disorders. Before turning to his theories, however, it seems appropriate to spend a moment or two on Freud the individual—*his* personality, if you will.

Sigmund Freud

Freud is clearly a major figure in the history of psychology. His theories of personality had a profound effect on intellectual thought for many decades.

Sigmund Freud

Sigmund Freud was born in what is now part of the Czech Republic. When he was four years old, his family moved to Vienna, and he spent almost his entire life in that city. As a young man, Freud was highly ambitious, and he decided to make a name for himself as a medical researcher. He became discouraged with his prospects, however, and soon after receiving his medical degree, he entered private practice. It was at this time that he formulated his theories of human personality and psychological disorders.

Freud's mother was his father's second wife, and she was much younger than her husband. In fact, she was only twenty-one when Freud was born. Although she had other children, Sigmund was always his mother's favourite. Among the Freud children, only Sigmund had his own room, and when his sister's piano practice disturbed his studies, her lessons were stopped and the piano sold. Freud's relationship with his father, in contrast, was cold and distant. Indeed, he even arrived late at his father's funeral and missed most of the service.

At the age of twenty-six, Freud married Martha Bernays. The marriage was a happy one and produced six children. Freud had a powerful personality, and as he developed his controversial theories, he attracted many followers. In many cases, these people began as ardent supporters but came to question some aspects of his work. Freud was intolerant of such criticism, and this often led to angry breaks with once-cherished students. One disciple, however, never broke with his views: his daughter Anna, who became a famous psychoanalyst in her own right.

Freud loved antiques and collected them throughout his life. His collection filled the walls and shelves of his office and even the top of his desk. Each morning, the first thing he did was reach over and affectionately pat one or more of his stone sculptures. Freud recognized that there was a connection between his hobby and his work; he told many of his patients that his search for hidden memories in their unconscious minds was similar to the excavation of a buried ancient city.

Freud smoked heavily (he was often photographed with a large cigar in his hand). He eventually contracted oral cancer, which caused him great pain, and starting in 1923 he underwent many operations for this disease. These interfered with his speech and finally ended his career as a public speaker.

Like many people of Jewish descent, Freud found it necessary to flee the Nazis, and in 1938 he left Vienna for England. He died there of throat cancer the following year. Many biographies of Freud have been written, and several draw connections between his theories and his personal experiences—for example, his close relationship with his mother and distant relationship with his father. Whether such links actually exist remains open to debate. What is certain, however, is that this complex, brilliant, and domineering man exerted a powerful impact upon many of our ideas about personality and psychological disorders.

Freud's Theory of Personality

As noted earlier, Freud entered private practice soon after obtaining his medical degree. A turning point in his early career came when he won a research grant to travel to Paris in order to observe the work of Jean-Martin Charcot, who was then using hypnosis to treat several types of mental disorders. When Freud returned to Vienna, he worked with Joseph Breuer, a colleague who was using hypnosis in the treatment of *hysteria,* a condition in which individuals experience physical symptoms—such as blindness, deafness, or paralysis of arms or legs—for which there seems to be no underlying physical cause. Out of these experiences, and out of his growing clinical practice, Freud gradually developed his theories of human personality and mental illness. His theoretical writings were rich and complex and touched on every aspect of personality. Interestingly, he believed that his psychological theories were interim formulations that would ultimately be replaced by knowledge of underlying biological and neural processes (Sulloway, 1992; Zuckerman, 1995). With respect to personality, four aspects of his work are central: levels of consciousness, the structure of personality, anxiety and defence mechanisms, and psychosexual stages of development.

LEVELS OF CONSCIOUSNESS: BENEATH THE ICEBERG'S TIP   Freud saw himself as a scientist, and he was well aware of research on thresholds for sensory experience (see Chapter 3). He applied some of these ideas to the task of understanding the human mind and reached the remarkable conclusion that most of the mind lies below the surface—in other words, below the threshold of conscious experience. Above this threshold is the realm of the *conscious,* which includes our current thoughts—that is, whatever we are thinking about or experiencing at a given moment. Beneath the conscious realm is the much larger *preconscious,* which contains memories that are not part of current thoughts but can readily be brought to mind if the need arises. Finally, beneath the preconscious, and forming the bulk of the human mind, is the *unconscious*—those thoughts, desires, and impulses of which we remain largely unaware (see Figure 12.1). Although some of this material has always been unconscious, Freud believed that much of it was once conscious, but has been actively *repressed*—driven from consciousness because it was too anxiety-provoking. For example, Freud contended that shameful experiences or unacceptable sexual or aggressive urges are often driven deep within the unconscious. The fact that we are not aware of them, however, in no way prevents them from affecting our behaviour. Indeed, Freud believed that many of the symptoms experienced by his patients were disguised and indirect reflections of repressed thoughts and desires. This is why one major goal of **psychoanalysis**—the method of treating psychological disorders devised by Freud—is to bring repressed material back into consciousness. Presumably, once such material is made conscious, it can be dealt with more effectively, and important determinants of mental distress can be removed.

THE STRUCTURE OF PERSONALITY: ID, EGO, AND SUPEREGO   Do you know the story of Dr. Jekyll and Mr. Hyde? If so, you already have a basic idea of some of the key structures of personality described by Freud. He suggested that personality consists largely of three parts: the *id,* the *ego,* and the *superego* (refer to Figure 12.1). As we'll soon see, these correspond, roughly, to *desire, reason,* and *conscience.*

The **id,** or desire, consists of all our primitive, innate urges. These include various bodily needs, sexual desire, and aggressive impulses. In this scheme of things, the id is totally unconscious and operates in accordance with what Freud termed the **pleasure principle:** It wants immediate, total gratification and is not capable of considering the potential costs of seeking this goal. In short, the id is the Mr. Hyde of our personality—although, in contrast to this literary character, it is not necessarily evil.

The world offers few opportunities for instant pleasure, and attempting to gratify many of our innate urges would soon get us into serious trouble. It is for these reasons that the second structure of personality, the **ego,** develops. The ego's task is to hold the id in check until conditions exist that are appropriate for satisfying its impulses. Thus, the ego operates in accordance with the **reality principle:** It considers the external consequences of actions and directs behaviour so as to maximize pleasure *and* minimize pain. The ego is partly but not entirely conscious; thus, some of its actions—for example, its eternal struggle with the id—are outside our conscious knowledge or understanding.

Psychoanalysis: A method of therapy based on Freud's theory of personality, in which the therapist attempts to bring repressed unconscious material into consciousness.

Id: In Freud's theory, the portion of personality concerned with immediate gratification of primitive needs.

Pleasure Principle: The principle on which the id operates—immediate pleasure with no attention to possible consequences.

Ego: In Freud's theory, the part of personality that takes rational account of external reality in the expression of instinctive sexual and aggressive urges.

Reality Principle: The principle on which the ego operates, according to which the external consequences of behaviour are considered in the regulation of expression of impulses from the id.

Figure 12.1
Freud's Views about Levels of Consciousness and Structures of Personality

An iceberg metaphor is often used to illustrate levels of consciousness and other components of personality in Freud's theory. The *conscious* level of experience refers to the present contents of consciousness— matters of which we are immediately aware. Our rather limited conscious awareness is represented by the small tip of the iceberg that lies above the water surface. Just below the surface of the water lies *preconscious* material that can be brought up to the level of consciousness. Below these two components, and constituting the largest mass of the iceberg, lies the *unconscious*. Three other important structures, which interact to determine behaviour, are the *id*, the *ego*, and the *superego*.

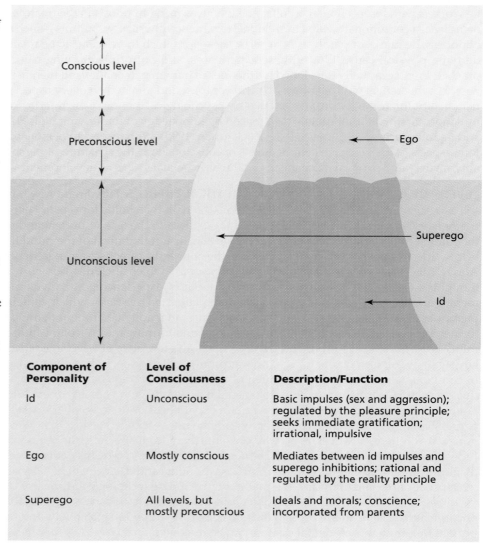

Component of Personality	Level of Consciousness	Description/Function
Id	Unconscious	Basic impulses (sex and aggression); regulated by the pleasure principle; seeks immediate gratification; irrational, impulsive
Ego	Mostly conscious	Mediates between id impulses and superego inhibitions; rational and regulated by the reality principle
Superego	All levels, but mostly preconscious	Ideals and morals; conscience; incorporated from parents

Superego: According to Freud, the portion of human personality representing the conscience.

The final aspect of personality described by Freud is the **superego.** It too seeks to control satisfaction of the id's impulses, permitting their gratification only under certain conditions. In contrast to the ego, however, the superego is concerned with morality: It can tell right from wrong according to the principles of a given society. The superego permits gratification of id impulses only when it is morally correct to gratify them—not simply when it is safe or feasible, as required by the ego. In this scheme, it is the superego, not the ego, that prevents a stockbroker from defrauding clients even when this could be done without risk.

The superego is acquired from our parents and through experience and represents our internalization of the moral teachings and norms of our society. Unfortunately, such teachings are often quite inflexible and leave little room for gratifying our basic desires. They require us to be good at all times, like Dr. Jekyll. Because of this problem, the ego faces another difficult task: It must mediate between the id and superego, striking a balance between our primitive urges and our learned moral constraints. Freud felt that this constant struggle among id, ego, and superego plays a key role in the development of personality and in many psychological disorders.

ANXIETY AND DEFENCE MECHANISMS: SELF-PROTECTION BY THE EGO In its constant struggle to prevent the outbreak of unbridled impulses from the id, the ego faces a difficult task. Yet for most people, most of the time, the ego is capable of performing this crucial function. Sometimes, though, id impulses grow so strong that they threaten to get out of control. For example, consider the case of a middle-aged widow who finds herself strongly attracted to her daughter's boyfriend. She hasn't had a romantic attachment in years, so her sexual desire quickly rises to powerful levels. What happens next? According to Freud, when her ego senses that unacceptable impulses are about to get out of hand, it experiences **anxiety**—unpleasant feelings of nervousness, tension, or worry. These feelings arise because the unacceptable impulses are getting closer and closer to consciousness, as well as closer and closer to the limits of the ego for holding them in check.

At this point, Freud contended, the ego may resort to one of several different **defence mechanisms.** These are all designed to keep unacceptable impulses from the id out of consciousness and to prevent their open expression. Defence mechanisms take many different forms. For example, in **sublimation,** the unacceptable impulse is channelled into some socially acceptable action. Instead of trying to seduce the young man, as Freud would say the widow's id wants to do, she might "adopt" him as a son and provide financial support to further his education. Other defence mechanisms are described in Table 12.1. While they differ in form, all serve the function of reducing anxiety by keeping unacceptable urges and impulses from breaking into consciousness.

> **Anxiety:** In Freudian theory, unpleasant feelings of tension or worry experienced by individuals in reaction to unacceptable wishes or impulses; increased arousal accompanied by generalized feelings of fear or apprehension.
>
> **Defence Mechanisms:** Techniques used by the ego to keep threatening and unacceptable material out of consciousness, and so to reduce anxiety.
>
> **Sublimation:** A defense mechanism in which threatening unconscious impulses are channelled into socially acceptable forms of behaviour.

TABLE 12.1

Defence Mechanisms: Reactions to Anxiety

According to Freud, when the ego feels that it may be unable to control impulses from the id, it experiences anxiety. To reduce such feelings, the ego employs various defence mechanisms, such as the ones described here.

Defence Mechanism	Its Basic Nature	Example
Repression	"Forgetting"—or pushing from consciousness into unconsciousness—unacceptable thoughts and impulses	A woman fails to recognize her attraction to her handsome new son-in-law.
Rationalization	Conjuring up socially acceptable reasons for thoughts or actions based on unacceptable motives	A young woman explains that she ate an entire chocolate cake so that it wouldn't spoil in the summer heat.
Displacement	Redirection of an emotional response from a dangerous object to a safe one	Anger is redirected from one's boss to one's child.
Projection	Transfer to others of unacceptable motives or impulses	A man sexually attracted to a neighbour perceives the neighbour as being sexually attracted to him.
Regression	Responding to a threatening situation in a way appropriate to an earlier age or level of development	A student asks a professor to raise his grade; when she refuses, the student throws a temper tantrum.

PSYCHOSEXUAL STAGES OF DEVELOPMENT   Now we come to what is perhaps the most controversial aspect of Freud's theory of personality: his ideas about its formation or development. Freud's views in this respect can be grouped under the heading **psychosexual stages of development:** innately determined stages of sexual development through which, presumably, we all pass and which strongly shape the nature of our personality. Before turning to the stages themselves, however, we must first consider two important concepts relating to these stages: libido and fixation.

Libido refers to the instinctual life force that energizes the id. Release of libido is closely related to pleasure, but the focus of such pleasure—and the expression of libido—changes as we develop. In each stage of development, we obtain different kinds of pleasure and leave behind a small amount of our libido—this is the normal course of events. If an excessive amount of libido energy is tied to a particular stage, however, **fixation** results. This can stem from either too little or too much gratification during this stage, and in either case, the result is harmful. Since the individual has left too much "psychic energy" behind, less is available for full adult development. The outcome may be an adult personality reflecting the stage or stages at which the fixation has occurred. To put it another way, if too much energy is drained away by fixation at earlier stages of development, the amount remaining may be insufficient to power movement to full adult development. Then, an individual may show an immature personality and several psychological disorders.

Now let us look at the actual stages themselves. According to Freud, as we grow and develop, different parts of the body serve as the focus of our quest for pleasure. In the initial **oral stage,** lasting until we are about eighteen months old, we seek pleasure mainly through the mouth. If too much or too little gratification occurs during this stage, an individual may become *fixated* at it. Too little gratification results in a personality that is overly dependent on others; too much, especially after the child has developed some teeth, results in a personality that is excessively hostile, especially through verbal sarcasm and "biting" forms of humour.

The next stage occurs in response to efforts by parents to toilet train their children. During the **anal stage,** the process of elimination becomes the primary focus of pleasure. Fixation at this stage, stemming from overly harsh toilet-training experiences, may result in individuals who are excessively orderly or *compulsive*—they can't leave any job unfinished, and strive for perfection in everything they do. In contrast, fixation

Psychosexual Stages of Development: According to Freud, an innate sequence of stages through which all human beings pass. At each stage, pleasure is focused on a different region of the body.

Libido: According to Freud, the psychic energy that powers all mental activity.

Fixation: Excessive investment of psychic energy in a particular stage of psychosexual development, which results in various types of psychological disorders.

Oral Stage: In Freud's theory, a stage of psychosexual development during which pleasure is centred in the region of the mouth.

Anal Stage: In Freud's theory, a psychosexual stage of development in which pleasure is focused primarily on the anal zone.

Freud's Anal Stage of Development

The anal stage occurs when children are being toilet trained. Freud believed that fixation during this stage, resulting from traumatic toilet-training experiences, could lead to an excessive need for order and a stubborn personality in adults.

stemming from very relaxed toilet training may result in people who are undisciplined, impulsive, and excessively generous. Freud himself might well be described as compulsive; even when he was seriously ill, he personally answered dozens of letters every day—even letters from total strangers asking his advice (Benjamin & Dixon, 1996).

At about age four, the genitals become the primary source of pleasure, and children enter the **phallic stage.** Freud speculated that at this time we fantasize about sex with our opposite-sex parent—a phenomenon he termed the **Oedipus complex** (after Oedipus, a character in ancient Greek literature who unknowingly killed his father and then married his mother). Fear of punishment for such desires then enters the picture. Among boys, the feared punishment is castration—leading to *castration anxiety.* Among girls, the feared punishment is loss of love. In both cases, these fears bring about resolution of the Oedipus complex and identification with the same-sex parent. In other words, little boys give up sexual desires for their mothers and come to see their fathers as models rather than as rivals, while little girls give up their sexual desires for their fathers and come to see their mothers as models.

Perhaps one of Freud's most controversial suggestions is the idea that little girls experience *penis envy,* stemming from their own lack of a male organ. Freud suggested that because of such envy, girls experience strong feelings of inferiority and jealousy—feelings they carry with them in disguised form even in adult life. As you can readily guess, these ideas are strongly rejected by virtually all psychologists.

After resolution of the Oedipus conflict, children enter the **latency stage,** during which sexual urges are, according to Freud, at a minimum. During puberty, they enter the final **genital stage.** During this stage, pleasure is again focused on the genitals. Now, however, lust is blended with affection and the person becomes capable of adult love. Remember that, according to Freud, progression to this final stage is possible only if serious fixation has *not* occurred at the earlier stages. If such fixation exists, development is blocked and various disorders result. The major stages in Freud's theory are summarized in Figure 12.2.

Phallic Stage: In Freud's theory, a psychosexual stage of development during which pleasure is centred in the genital region. It is during this stage that the Oedipus complex develops.

Oedipus Complex: In Freud's theory, a crisis of psychosexual development in which children must give up their sexual attraction to their opposite-sex parent.

Latency Stage: In Freud's theory, the psychosexual stage of development that follows resolution of the Oedipus complex. During this stage, sexual desires are relatively weak.

Genital Stage: In Freud's theory, the final psychosexual stage of development—one in which individuals acquire the adult capacity to combine lust with affection.

Figure 12.2
Psychosexual Stages of Development: Freud's View

According to Freud, all human beings pass through a series of discrete psychosexual stages of development. At each stage, pleasure is fixated on a particular part of the body. Too much or too little gratification at any stage can result in fixation and lead to psychological disorders.

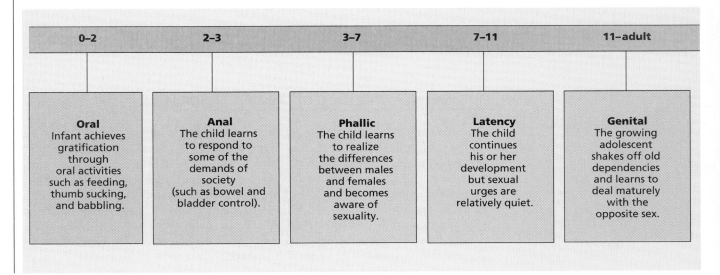

0–2	2–3	3–7	7–11	11–adult
Oral Infant achieves gratification through oral activities such as feeding, thumb sucking, and babbling.	**Anal** The child learns to respond to some of the demands of society (such as bowel and bladder control).	**Phallic** The child learns to realize the differences between males and females and becomes aware of sexuality.	**Latency** The child continues his or her development but sexual urges are relatively quiet.	**Genital** The growing adolescent shakes off old dependencies and learns to deal maturely with the opposite sex.

Research Related to Freud's Theory

Freud's theories contain many fascinating notions, and as you probably already know, several of these have entered into the mainstream of our culture. People commonly discuss unconscious motives and repressed impulses. Has research afforded support to his theory? Numerous efforts have been made to investigate those aspects of Freudian theory that *can* be studied through scientific means. The results of such studies have been, all too often, disappointing. For example, Freud's use of dream analysis as a mechanism for gaining insight into the unconscious has not fared well under study. There is virtually no scientific evidence for his belief that dreams carry messages from the unconscious (Macmillan, 1992).

Some aspects of Freud's ideas about the unconscious, however, have fared somewhat better, including his contention that our feelings and behaviour can be influenced by information we can't bring to mind and can't describe verbally. Research in a variety of areas suggests that, at least to some extent, this is true (e.g., Bornstein, 1992, 1993). Consider, for example, the study by Greenwald et al. (1996) we described in Chapter 3, which found that pleasant or unpleasant subliminal visual primes—*stimuli presented too briefly to be consciously registered*—could influence how research participants assessed a closely following stimulus. Similarly designed studies have shown that stimuli presented too briefly to be consciously interpreted can influence our reaction to other people.

A very interesting demonstration of how subliminal stimuli can influence our attitude toward others has been provided by Krosnick and his colleagues (Krosnick et al., 1992; Krosnick, 1993). Participants in these studies were presented with photos of strangers engaged in routine daily activities—walking into an apartment, shopping in a grocery store, sitting in a restaurant. They were required to indicate their attitudes toward the person shown in the photos and to rate that person on a variety of trait dimensions (unfriendly/friendly, cruel/kind, considerate/thoughtless). To determine whether subliminal presentations could influence the way in which photos of strangers were assessed, a *subliminal* presentation of another photograph preceded each presentation of a stranger's photograph. As you may have guessed, *the too brief to be consciously registered* subliminal presentations were composed of photographs that were capable of generating negative feelings (e.g, a bloody shark) or positive feelings (e.g., a happy bridal couple). The results were as expected. Participants who saw photos that were capable of inducing positive feelings rated the stranger more favourably than those who saw photos that induced negative feelings. While these findings certainly do not address Freud's ideas about repressed impulses, they do, when combined with other findings (e.g., Bornstein, 1993), support the view that our behaviour is sometimes influenced by thoughts, ideas, or feelings we can't bring to mind—by information that Freud would have argued is in the unconscious.

An Overall Evaluation of Freud's Theory

As noted earlier, Freud's place in history is assured: His ideas and writing have exerted a profound impact on society. What about his theory of personality? Is it currently accepted by most psychologists? As you can probably guess from earlier comments, the answer is *definitely not*. The reasons for this rejection are also clear. First, many critics have noted that Freud's theory is not really a scientific theory at all. True, as we just saw, some of his ideas, or hypotheses derived from them, can be tested. But many concepts in his theory cannot be measured or studied systematically. How, for instance, can one go about observing an *id*, a *fixation*, or the psychic energy contained in the *libido*? As noted in Chapter 1, a theory using concepts and principles that cannot be tested is of dubious value to science.

Second, as we have already seen, several of Freud's proposals are not consistent with the findings of modern research—for instance, his ideas about the meaning of dreams. Third, in constructing his theory, Freud relied heavily on a small number of case studies—no more than a dozen at most. Almost all of these persons came from wealthy backgrounds and lived in a large and sophisticated city within a single culture. Thus, they were not representative of human beings generally. Moreover, Freud indicated that he accepted for study and treatment only persons he viewed as particularly good candidates for successful therapy, and he himself recorded and later analyzed all of the information about these cases. According to Freud's critics, all sorts of error of reporting and interpretation could, and did, occur under these circumstances (Crews, 1998; Esterson, 1993).

Finally, and perhaps most important of all, Freud's theories contain so many different concepts that they can explain virtually any pattern of behaviour in an after-the-fact manner. If a theory can't be disconfirmed—shown to be false—then, once again, it is of dubious value.

For these and other reasons, Freud's theory of personality is not currently accepted by most psychologists. Even so it is clear that in many ways, Freud has had a major and lasting impact on psychology and on society (Stafford-Clark, 1997). For this reason, his views deserve the close attention we've given them here.

K E Y QUESTIONS

- According to Freud, what are the three levels of consciousness?

- In Freud's theory, what are the three basic parts of personality?

- According to Freud, what are the psychosexual stages of development?

- Do research findings support Freud's views about the unconscious?

Other Psychoanalytic Views

Whatever else Freud was, he was certainly an intellectual magnet. Over the course of several decades, he attracted as students or colleagues many brilliant people. Most of them began by accepting Freud's views. Later, however, they often disagreed with some of his major assumptions. Let's see why these **neo-Freudians** broke with Freud, and what they had to say about the nature of personality.

JUNG: THE COLLECTIVE UNCONSCIOUS Perhaps the most bitter of all the defections Freud experienced was that of Carl Jung—the follower Freud viewed as his heir apparent. Jung shared Freud's views concerning the importance of the unconscious, but contended that there is another part to this aspect of personality that Freud overlooked: the **collective unconscious**. According to Jung, the collective unconscious holds experiences shared by all human beings—experiences that are, in a sense, part of our biological heritage. The contents of the collective unconscious, in short, reflect the experiences our species has had since it originated on earth. The collective unconscious finds expression in our minds in several ways, but among these, **archetypes** are the most central to Jung's theory. These are manifestations of the collective unconscious that express themselves when our conscious mind is distracted or inactive, for example, during sleep or in dreams or fantasies (e.g., Neher, 1996). The specific expression of archetypes depends, in part, on our unique experience as individuals, but in all cases such images are representations of key aspects of the human experience—images representing *mother, father, wise old man, the sun, the moon, God, death,* and *the hero*. It is because of these shared innate images, Jung contended, that the folklore of many different cultures contains similar figures and themes.

Carl Jung
(1875–1961)

Neo-Freudians: Personality theorists who accepted basic portions of Freud's theory but rejected or modified other portions.

Collective Unconscious: In Jung's theory, a portion of the unconscious shared by all human beings.

Archetypes: According to Jung, inherited images in the collective unconscious that shape our perceptions of the external world.

The Young Hero: An Archetype

According to Jung, all human beings possess a *collective unconscious*. Information stored there is often expressed in terms of *archetypes*— representations of key aspects of human experience, such as the hero (shown here), mother, father, and so on.

Two especially important archetypes in Jung's theory are known as the *animus* and the *anima*. The **animus** is the masculine side of females, while the **anima** is the feminine side of males. Jung believed that in looking for a mate, we search for the person onto whom we can best project these hidden sides of ourselves. When there is a good match between such projections and another person, attraction occurs.

Another aspect of Jung's theory was his suggestion that we are all born with innate tendencies to be concerned primarily either with ourselves or with the outside world. Jung labelled persons in the first category **introverts** and described them as being hesitant and cautious; they do not make friends easily and prefer to observe the world rather than become involved in it. He labelled persons in the second category **extroverts.** Such persons are open and confident, make friends readily, and enjoy high levels of stimulation and a wide range of activities. While many aspects of Jung's theory have been rejected by psychologists—especially the idea of the collective unconscious—the dimension of introversion–extroversion appears to be a basic one of major importance, and it is included in several *trait theories* we'll consider in a later section (although in these modern theories the term is spelled extr*a*version).

Karen D. Horney
(1885–1952)

Alfred Adler
(1870–1937)

KAREN HORNEY AND ALFRED ADLER Two other important neo-Freudians are Karen Horney and Alfred Adler. Horney was one of the few females in the early psychoanalytic movement, and she disagreed with Freud strongly over his view that differences between men and women stemmed largely from innate factors— for example, anatomical differences resulting in *penis envy* among females. Horney contended that each sex has attributes admired by the other, and that neither should be viewed as superior *or* inferior. In addition, she emphasized the point that psychological disorders did not stem from fixation of psychic energy, as Freud contended, but rather from disturbed interpersonal relationships during childhood. In a sense, therefore, she emphasized the importance of social factors in shaping personality—a view echoed by modern psychology.

Alfred Adler also disagreed with Freud very strongly, but over somewhat different issues. In particular, he emphasized the importance of feelings of inferiority, which he believed we experience as children because of our small size and physical weakness. He viewed personality development as stemming primarily from our efforts to overcome such feelings, through what he termed **striving for superiority.** Like Horney and other neo-Freudians, Adler also emphasized the importance of social factors in personality; for instance, he called attention to the importance of birth order. Only children, he suggested, are spoiled by too much parental attention, while first-borns are "dethroned" by a second child. Second-borns, in contrast, are competitive, because they have to struggle to catch up with an older sibling.

By now the main point should be clear: Neo-Freudians, while accepting many of Freud's basic ideas, rejected his emphasis on innate patterns of development. On the contrary, they perceived personality as stemming from a complex interplay between social factors and the experience we have during childhood, primarily in our own families. While the theories proposed by neo-Freudians are not widely accepted by psychologists, they did serve as a kind of bridge between the provocative views offered by Freud and more modern conceptions of personality. In this respect, at least, they made a lasting contribution.

Animus: According to Jung, the archetype representing the masculine side of females.

Anima: According to Jung, the archetype representing the feminine side of males.

Introverts: Individuals who are quiet, cautious, and reclusive, and who generally inhibit expression of their impulses and feelings.

Extroverts: Individuals who are talkative and sociable, and who often give free rein to their impulses and feelings.

Striving for Superiority: Attempting to overcome feelings of inferiority. According to Adler, this is the primary motive for human behaviour.

KEY QUESTIONS

▪ According to Jung, what is the collective unconscious?

▪ To what aspects of Freud's theory did Horney object?

▪ According to Adler, what is the role of feelings of inferiority in personality?

Humanistic Theories

Id versus ego, Jekyll versus Hyde—on the whole, psychoanalytic theories of personality take a dim view of human nature, contending that we must struggle constantly to control our bestial impulses if we are to function as healthy, rational adults. Is this view accurate? Many psychologists doubt that it is. They believe that human strivings for growth, dignity, and self-determination are just as important, if not more important, in the development of personality, than the primitive motives Freud emphasized. Because of their more optimistic views concerning human nature, such views are known as **humanistic theories** (Maslow, 1970; Rogers, 1977, 1982). These theories differ widely in the concepts on which they focus, but share the following characteristics.

First, they emphasize *personal responsibility.* Each of us, these theories contend, is largely responsible for what happens to us. Our fate is mostly in our own hands; we are *not* mere ciphers driven here and there by dark forces within our personalities. Second, while these theories don't deny the importance of past experience, they generally focus on the present. True, we may be influenced by traumatic events early in life. Yet these do *not* have to shape our entire adult lives. Our capacity to overcome such experiences and move forward is both real and powerful. Third, humanistic theories stress the importance of *personal growth.* People are not, such theories argue, content with merely meeting their current needs. They wish to progress toward "bigger" goals, such as becoming the best they can be. Only when obstacles interfere with such growth is the process interrupted. A key goal of therapy, therefore, should be to remove obstacles that prevent natural growth processes from proceeding. As examples of humanistic theories, we'll now consider the views proposed by Carl Rogers and Abraham Maslow.

Rogers's Self Theory

Carl Rogers planned to become a minister, but after exposure to several courses in psychology, he changed his mind. He decided, instead, to focus on efforts to understand the nature of human personality—and why it sometimes goes off the track. The theory Rogers formulated played an important role in the emergence of humanistic psychology and remains influential today.

One central assumption of Rogers's theory was this: Left to their own devices, human beings show many positive characteristics and move, over the course of their lives, toward becoming **fully functioning persons.** What are such individuals like? Rogers suggests that they are people who strive to experience life to the fullest, who live in the here and now, and who trust their own feelings. They are sensitive to the needs and rights of others, but they do not allow society's standards to shape their feelings or actions to an excessive degree. "If it feels like the right thing to do," such people reason, "then I should do it." Fully functioning people aren't saints; they can—and do—lose their tempers and act in ways they later regret. But throughout life, their actions become increasingly dominated by constructive impulses. They are in close touch with their own values and feelings and experience life more deeply than most other people.

Humanistic Theories: Theories of personality emphasizing personal responsibility and innate tendencies towards personal growth.

Fully Functioning Persons: In Rogers's theory, psychologically healthy people who enjoy life to the fullest.

If all human beings possess the capacity to become fully functioning individuals, why don't they all succeed? Why, in short, aren't we surrounded by models of health and happy adjustment? The answer, Rogers contends, lies in the anxiety generated when life experiences are inconsistent with our ideas about ourselves—in short, when a gap develops between our **self-concept** (our beliefs and knowledge about ourselves) and reality, or our perceptions of it. For example, imagine an individual who believes that she is very likable and that she makes friends easily. One day she happens to overhear a conversation between two other people who describe her as moody, difficult to get along with, and definitely not very likable. She is crushed; here is information that is highly inconsistent with her self-concept. As a result of this experience, anxiety occurs, and she adopts one or more psychological defences to reduce it. The most common of these is *distortion*—for example, the woman convinces herself that the people discussing her do not really know her very well or that they have misinterpreted her behaviour. Another defence process is *denial*. Here, the woman may refuse to admit to herself that she heard the conversation or that she understood what the other people were saying.

In the short run, such manoeuvres are successful: They help reduce anxiety. Ultimately, however, they produce sizable gaps between an individual's self-concept and reality. The larger such gaps, Rogers contends, the greater the individual's maladjustment and personal unhappiness (see Figure 12.3).

Rogers suggests that the major reason that most people experience difficulties in psychological adjustment is that they grow up in an atmosphere of *conditional positive regard*. They learn that others, such as their parents, will approve of them only when they behave in certain ways and express certain feelings. As a result, they are forced to deny the existence of various natural impulses and feelings. The all-too-common result is a badly distorted self-concept.

How can such distorted self-concepts be repaired so that healthy development can continue? Rogers suggests that therapists can help accomplish this goal by placing individuals in an atmosphere of **unconditional positive regard**—a setting in which they will be accepted by the therapist *no matter what they say or do*. Such conditions are provided by *client-centred therapy*, a form of therapy we'll consider in detail in Chapter 15. Here, we will simply make the point that such therapy is closely linked to Rogers's theory of personality and seeks to remove obstacles interfering with healthy development. Remove these, Rogers contends, and individuals will move, once again, toward the goal they naturally seek: becoming fully functioning persons.

Self-Concept: All the information and beliefs individuals have about their own characteristics and themselves.

Unconditional Positive Regard: In Rogers's theory, communicating to others that they will be respected or loved regardless of what they say or do.

Figure 12.3
Rogers's View of Adjustment

According to Rogers, the larger the gap between an individual's self-concept and reality, the poorer this person's psychological adjustment.

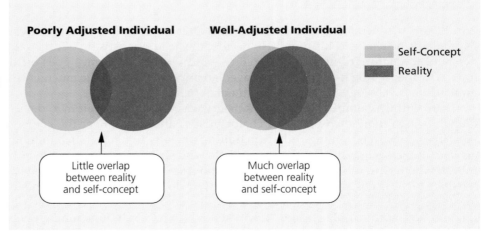

Maslow and the Study of Self-Actualizing People

Another influential humanistic theory of personality was proposed by Abraham Maslow (1970). We have already described a portion of Maslow's theory, his concept of a *needs hierarchy,* in Chapter 10. As you may recall, this concept suggests that human needs exist in a hierarchy ranging from *physiological needs* on the bottom through *self-actualization needs* at the top. According to Maslow, lower-order needs must be satisfied before we can turn to more complex, higher-order needs (Neher, 1991).

The needs hierarchy, however, is only part of Maslow's theory of personality. Maslow has also devoted much attention to the study of people who, in his terms, are *psychologically healthy.* These are individuals who have attained high levels of **self-actualization**—a state in which they have reached their fullest true potential. What are such people like? In essence, they are much like the fully functioning persons described by Rogers. Self-actualized people accept themselves for what they are; they recognize their shortcomings as well as their strengths. Being in touch with their own personalities, they are less inhibited and less likely to conform than most of us. Self-actualized people are well aware of the rules imposed by society, but feel greater freedom to ignore them than most persons. Unlike most of us, they seem to retain their childhood wonder and amazement with the world. For them, life continues to be an exciting adventure rather than a boring routine. Finally, self-actualized persons sometimes have what Maslow describes as **peak experiences**— instances in which they have powerful feelings of unity with the universe and feel tremendous waves of power and wonder. Such experiences appear to be linked to personal growth, for after them, individuals report feeling more spontaneous, more appreciative of life, and less concerned with the problems of everyday life.

Research Related to Humanistic Theories

At first glance, it might seem that humanistic theories, like psychoanalytic ones, are not readily open to scientific test. In fact, however, the opposite is true. Humanistic theories were proposed by psychologists, and a commitment to empirical research is one of the true hallmarks of modern psychology. For this reason, several concepts that play a key role in humanistic theories have been studied quite extensively. Among these, the one that has probably received most attention is the concept of the *self-concept,* which is so central to Rogers's theory.

Research on the self-concept has addressed many different issues—for instance, how our self-concept is formed (e.g., Sedikides & Skowronski 1997), how it influences the way we think (e.g., Kendzierski & Whitaker, 1997), and what information it contains (e.g., Rentsch & Heffner, 1994). In an effort to detail the informational structure of the self, Rentsch and Heffner (1994) asked several hundred college students to give twenty different answers to the question "Who am I?" Careful analysis of these data indicated that while the contents of each person's self-concept is unique, the basic structure remains much the same. All of us seem to include information on the categories shown in Figure 12.4—information about our traits, our beliefs, what makes us unique, and so on.

An Evaluation of Humanistic Theories

Humanistic theories have had a lasting impact on psychology. Several of the ideas first proposed by Rogers, Maslow, and other humanistic theorists have entered into the mainstream of psychology. As noted earlier, interest in the self or self-concept

Rick Hansen: An Example of Self-Actualization

Rick Hansen covered over 40 000 km on his Man in Motion World Tour between 1985 and 1987. He raised millions of dollars for medical research and demonstrated to the world how a person with a disability could overcome impediments to self-actualization. According to Maslow, only a few people become fully self-actualized. Rick Hansen could be one example—can you think of any others?

Self-Actualization: A stage of personal development in which individuals reach their maximum potential.

Peak Experiences: In Maslow's theory, intense emotional experiences during which individuals feel at one with the universe.

Figure 12.4
Contents of the Self-Concept: Shared Categories

Research findings indicate that while each person's self-concept is unique, almost everyone's self-concept contains information relating to the categories shown here.

Source: Based on findings reported by Rentsch and Heffner, 1994.

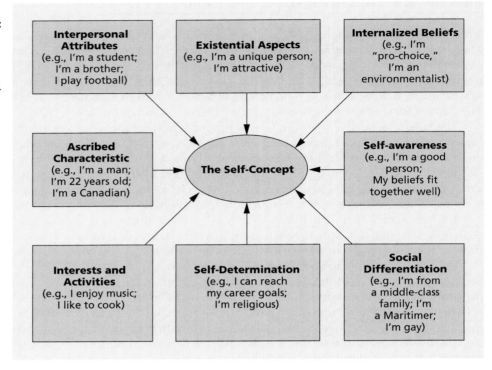

has remained a major focus of research (e.g., Baumeister, 1993). Similarly, the view that behaviour stems more from positive forces, such as tendencies toward personal growth, than from primitive sexual and aggressive urges has done much to restore a sense of balance to current views of personality.

Humanistic theories have also been subject to strong criticism, in part because they propose that individuals are wholly responsible for their own actions and can change these if they wish to do so. To an extent, this is certainly true, but circumstance, inherent abilities, and genetic dispositions can impose constraints on the amount and character of possible change.

Another concern is that many key concepts of humanistic theories are loosely defined. What, precisely, is self-actualization? A peak experience? A fully functioning person? Until such terms are clearly defined, it is difficult to conduct systematic research on them. Despite such criticisms, the impact of humanistic theories has persisted, and they do indeed constitute a lasting contribution to our understanding of human personality.

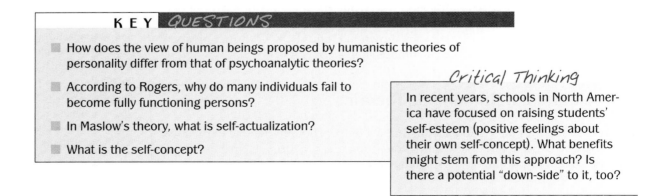

KEY *QUESTIONS*

■ How does the view of human beings proposed by humanistic theories of personality differ from that of psychoanalytic theories?

■ According to Rogers, why do many individuals fail to become fully functioning persons?

■ In Maslow's theory, what is self-actualization?

■ What is the self-concept?

Critical Thinking

In recent years, schools in North America have focused on raising students' self-esteem (positive feelings about their own self-concept). What benefits might stem from this approach? Is there a potential "down-side" to it, too?

Trait Theories

When we describe other persons, we often do so in terms of specific **personality traits**—stable dimensions of personality along which people vary, from very low to very high. This strong tendency to think about others in terms of specific characteristics is reflected in **trait theories** of personality. Such theories focus on identifying key dimensions of personality—the most important ways in which people differ.

Unfortunately, this task sounds easier than it actually is. Human beings differ in an almost countless number of ways. Allport and Odbert (1936) first revealed the magnitude of the problem. They identified 17 953 dictionary terms that reflected traits. Even when words with similar meanings were combined, 171 distinct traits remained. How can we hope to deal with this multitude of traits? One solution is to try to *classify or categorize traits in terms of their significance.* We'll now take a brief look at two theories that adopted this approach. Then we'll turn to evidence suggesting that in the final analysis, the number of key traits or dimensions of personality is actually quite small—perhaps no more than five

Allport's Central, Secondary, and Cardinal Traits

Allport concluded that personality traits can be divided into several major categories. Most important are **central traits:** the five to ten traits that together best account for the uniqueness of an individual's personality. Of less importance are **secondary traits,** which exert relatively weak effects on behaviour. Finally, Allport noted that a few people are dominated by a single all-important **cardinal trait.** A few examples of such individuals and the cardinal traits that seem to have driven their personalities are Alexander the Great (ambition), Machiavelli (lust for power), and Don Juan (just plain lust).

Gordon W. Allport
(1887–1967)

Cattell's Surface and Source Traits

Another well-known advocate of the trait approach is Raymond Cattell. He and his colleagues have focused firmly on the task described earlier: identifying the basic dimensions of personality. Instead of beginning with hunches or insights, however, Cattell has followed a very different approach. In the course of his extensive research, literally thousands of individuals have been measured for individual differences on hundreds of traits. These responses have then been subjected to a statistical procedure known as *factor analysis.* This technique has revealed patterns in the extent to which various traits are correlated. In doing so, it has helped identify important clusters of traits. As such clusters are identified, Cattell reasoned, the number of key traits in human personality will be reduced until we are left with those that are truly central.

Using this approach, Cattell and his associates (e.g., Cattell & Dreger, 1977) have identified sixteen basic **source traits**—ones he believes underlie differences in many other, less important *surface* traits. A few of the source traits identified by Cattell are cool versus warm, easily upset versus calm, stable, not assertive versus dominant, trusting versus suspicious, and undisciplined versus self-disciplined. The list is lengthy, but it is certainly more manageable in length than previous ones.

Personality Traits: Specific dimensions along which individuals' personalities differ in consistent, stable ways.

Trait Theories: Theories of personality that focus on identifying the key dimensions along which people differ.

Central Traits: According to Allport, the five or ten traits that best describe an individual's personality.

Secondary Traits: According to Allport, traits that exert relatively specific and weak effects upon behaviour.

Cardinal Trait: According to Allport, a single trait that dominates an individual's entire personality.

Source Traits: According to Cattell, key dimensions of personality that underlie many other traits.

The "Big Five" Factors

In a recent major review of advances in personality theory, Wiggins and Pincus (1992) of the University of British Columbia noted that there has been a resurgence of interest in trait theory. A major reason for this new-found interest in trait theory is that a consensus is beginning to emerge that there may be only five key or central dimensions of personality (e.g., Costa & McCrae, 1994; Zuckerman, 1994). These are sometimes labelled "The Big Five," and they can be described as follows:

1. **Extraversion:** A dimension ranging from sociable, talkative, fun-loving, affectionate, and adventurous at one end to retiring, sober, reserved, silent, and cautious at the other.

2. **Agreeableness:** A dimension ranging from good-natured, gentle, cooperative, trusting, and helpful at one end to irritable, ruthless, suspicious, uncooperative, and headstrong at the other.

3. **Conscientiousness:** A dimension ranging from well-organized, careful, self-disciplined, responsible, and precise at one end to disorganized, careless, weak-willed, and neglectful at the other.

4. **Emotional stability:** A dimension ranging from poised, calm, composed, and not hypochondriacal at one end to nervous, anxious, excitable, and hypochondriacal at the other.

5. **Openness to experience:** A dimension ranging from imaginative, sensitive, intellectual, and curious at one end, to down-to-earth, insensitive, tradition-bound, and simple at the other.

How basic and therefore important are the "big five" dimensions? Although there is far from complete agreement on this point (e.g., Zuckerman, 1995), many researchers indicate that these dimensions are indeed very basic ones. This is indicated, in part, by the fact that these dimensions are ones to which most people in many different cultures refer in describing themselves (Funder & Colvin, 1991), and by the fact that we can often tell where individuals stand along at least some of these dimensions from an initial meeting with them that lasts only a few minutes. We know this from several studies in which strangers met and interacted briefly with one another, and then rated each other on measures of the "big five" dimensions. When these ratings by strangers were then compared with ratings by other people who knew the participants in the study very well (e.g., their parents or best friends), a substantial amount of agreement was obtained for at least some of the "big five" dimensions (e.g., Funder & Sneed, 1993; Watson, 1989). For instance, strangers who met each other for a few minutes were quite accurate in rating one another with respect to the dimensions of extraversion and conscientiousness. While this may seem surprising, it actually fits quite well with our informal experience. Think about it: If someone met *you* for the first time, could they tell right away whether you are friendly and outgoing or shy and reserved? Whether you are neat and orderly or impulsive and disorganized? The answer offered by research findings is clear: they probably could!

Extraversion: One of the "big five" dimensions of personality; ranges from sociable, talkative, fun-loving at one end to sober, reserved, cautious at the other.

Agreeableness: One of the "big five" dimensions of personality; ranges from good-natured, cooperative, trusting at one end to irritable, suspicious, uncooperative at the other.

Conscientiousness: One of the "big five" dimensions of personality; this dimension ranges from well-organized, careful, responsible at one end to disorganized, careless, unscrupulous at the other.

Emotional Stability: One of the "big five" dimensions of personality; ranges from poised, calm, composed at one end to nervous, anxious, excitable at the other.

Openness to Experience: One of the "big five" dimensions of personality; ranges from imaginative, sensitive, intellectual at one end to down-to-earth, insensitive, crude at the other.

Research on Trait Theories

If the "big five" dimensions of personality are really so basic, then it is reasonable to expect that they will be related to important forms of behaviour. In fact, many studies indicate that this is the case. As noted recently by Hogan et al. (1996), individuals' standing on the "big five" dimensions is closely linked to success in performing many jobs. For example, in one large-scale study, Barrick and Mount (1993) examined the results of over 200 separate studies in which at least one of these dimensions was related to job performance. *Conscientiousness* was found to be a good predictor of performance for all types of jobs. *Extraversion* was highly related to job success in managerial and sales positions. *Agreeableness* and *emotional stability* are good predictors of success in customer service jobs—ones like working in a complaint department (McDaniel & Frei, 1994).

In sum, existing evidence indicates that the "big five" dimensions are indeed basic and important ones where human personality is concerned. No, they are not all there is to personality, but *yes*, they are dimensions we notice, and they are related to important life outcomes

An Evaluation of Trait Theories

At present, most research on personality by psychologists occurs within the context of the trait approach. Instead of seeking to propose and test grand theories such as the ones offered by Freud, Jung, and Rogers, most psychologists currently direct their efforts to the task of understanding specific traits (e.g., Friedman et al., 1993; Kring, Smith, & Neale, 1994). This is due both to the success of the trait approach and to the obvious shortcomings of the theories described in earlier sections of this chapter.

We are not implying that the trait approach is perfect, however. On the contrary, it can be criticized in several respects. First, the trait approach is largely *descriptive* in nature. It seeks to describe the key dimensions of personality but does not attempt to determine how various traits develop or how they influence behaviour. Fully developed theories of personality must, of course, address such issues. Second, despite several decades of careful research, there is still no final agreement concerning the traits that are most important or most basic. Although the "big five" dimensions are widely accepted, it has to be admitted that they are certainly not universally accepted, and some psychologists feel that the "big five" trait approach is far from definitive (e.g., Block, 1995; Goldberg & Saucier, 1995).

As you can readily see, these criticisms relate primarily to what the trait approach has not yet accomplished rather than to its findings or proposals. All in all, we can conclude that the trait approach provides a very useful way to look at personality, and that it is very broadly applicable. A recent cross-cultural study by McCrae and Costa (1997) found that the "big five" trait patterns obtained in six very disparate groups— German, Portuguese, Israeli, Chinese, Korean, and Japanese— were remarkably similar to those obtained in North America—suggesting the universality of trait structures in humankind.

Trait theory not only provides a basis for understanding how humans differ from one another; it can also be applied to other species. An example of the application of trait theory to animal behaviour is furnished by Jennifer Mather of the University of Lethbridge and her colleague Roland Anderson of the Seattle Aquarium. Mather and Anderson (1993) undertook a trait analysis of octopus behaviour. Three major dimensions of temperament, or personality, on which individual octopuses differed—activity, reactivity, and avoidance—were found to account for a substantial portion of octopus behaviour. *Activity* refers to the degree to which an octopus is alert and interactively responsive to stimulation. *Reactivity* refers to whether it is anxious or calm in various situations. *Avoidance* refers to whether it

Kurt Browning: An Example of Extraversion

According to the five-factor theory of personality, there are only five key dimensions that make up personality, and extraversion is one of them. How would you describe yourself on each trait?

tends to withdraw or display boldness in its interactions with the world. Other applications of trait theory to animals have looked at fish (Huntingford, 1976) and monkeys (Stevenson-Hinde et al., 1980).

There is much to be said in favour of an interpretive framework that can span species differences the way trait theory can. The approach provides us with a very useful technique to study the uniqueness and consistency of key aspects of both human and animal behaviour.

K E Y QUESTIONS

▪ What are central traits? Source traits?

▪ What are the "big five" dimensions of personality?

▪ What do research findings indicate about the effects of the "big five" dimensions?

Biological Approaches to Personality

We have looked at a host of different mechanisms that have been held to serve as an impetus to personality development. We have considered such things as unconscious motives, a striving for superiority, self-development, and self-actualization. What we have not considered is the degree to which *inherent biological factors* determine and regulate the expression of personality. Why should we look to biological mechanisms to try to explain what makes us unique and distinctive as persons? One reason is that *abnormalities* in brain function can profoundly alter personality. As we will see in Chapter 15, depression or schizophrenia appear to be linked to changes in the level of neurotransmitters in the brain (chemicals that play an important function in regulating neural transmission). *Brain injury* can also profoundly influence personality. The fact that brain injury, and changes in brain chemistry, can so readily change personality has led many investigators to look to *variations in brain function and structure* to account for personality differences. Eysenck (1967), whose work we will consider shortly, attempted to relate variations in personality trait expression to differences in the arousal level of brain systems. Other advocates of the biological approach take the position that our personalities are shaped to a surprising degree by the genes we receive from our parents, and the various personality types that populate the human landscape are just as much a product of evolutionary pressures as our physical appearance.

Hans Eysenck
(1916–1997)

Personality and the Biology of Arousal

The first modern attempt to provide a biological explanation for a significant dimension of personality was made by Eysenck (1967). His studies focused on *extraversion* and *introversion,* which he saw as one of the key dimensions of personality. As you will remember from our earlier discussion of trait theories, extroversion reflects the degree to which one is adventurous, outgoing, gregarious, and actively seeking new experiences, whereas introversion reflects the degree to which one is quiet, shy, and withdrawn.

Eysenck sought to explain the extraversion and introversion dimension of personality in terms of an **arousal process**—a general activation or energization of brain and body systems. The key brain structures assumed to be involved in arousal of major brain and body systems were the cerebral cortex, the thalamus, and the ascending reticular activating system. Because of the many ascending and descending connections within these components of the brain, arousal can occur through

Arousal Process: *A general activation or energization of brain and body systems.*

activation of the ascending reticular activating system when an individual experiences an exciting external event, or through self-stimulation of the cerebral cortex by thinking about an interesting and exciting event.

The critical notion in Eysenck's theory is that there is an *optimal level of arousal* with which individuals are comfortable. What differentiates extraverts and introverts is the resting level of the arousal system. Introverts are held to have a near optimal level of arousal. Because of this, they tend to *avoid* situations or circumstances that might further increase their arousal level. Extraverts, on the other hand have an arousal level well below the optimal level. Because of this, they are *drawn to* situations, experiences, and interactions that will increase their level of arousal.

If Eysenck's analysis is correct, then it should be possible to detect differences in the *general level of arousal* of introverts and extraverts. A wide variety of techniques have been used, such as attaching recording electrodes on the surface of the skull, measuring skin conductance (which tends to increase as a consequence of arousal), and observing reactions to drugs that are known to stimulate the nervous system (e.g., Green, 1984; Matthews & Amelang, 1993; Smith, Wilson, & Davidson, 1984). The results of these studies have provided only a *marginal* level of support for Eysenck's theory (Green, 1997). The basic problem appears to be that many different brain and body response systems contribute to arousal, but just how their interactions are synchronized to produce a general state of arousal is far from clear. The pursuit of a single overall measure of general arousal no longer seems as reasonable as it once did. Research now appears to be focused on providing a detailed analysis of the various subsystems that are know to be involved when we become aroused. A good example of this approach is the work of Zuckerman (1995) on the catecholamine system and sensation seeking.

Sensation seeking is an impulsive urge to seek out new and exciting experiences. Zuckerman (1995) maintains that high sensation seekers have a higher optimal level of activity in what is known as the catecholamine system, a system within the brain that plays a role in mood, performance, and social behaviour. In a sense, the "thermostat" for activity in this neurotransmitter system is set higher in such persons than in most others, and they feel better when they are receiving the external stimulation that plays a role in activating this system.

How do these individuals behave? High sensation seekers show a stronger orienting response to the initial presentation of an unfamiliar auditory or visual stimulus (Zuckerman et al., 1988). In other words, they seem to pay more attention to such stimuli than other people do. They are very good at zeroing in on new stimuli and giving them their full attention (Ball & Zuckerman, 1992; Martin, 1986). Research indicates that high sensation seekers drive faster (Arnett, 1998; Zuckerman & Neeb, 1980); are more likely to engage in substance abuse (Teichman et al., 1989); are more likely to seek out more sexual partners (Bogeart & Fisher, 1995); and are more likely to engage in high-risk sports such as hang-gliding, and skydiving. Franken et al. (1992) of the University of Calgary found that individuals scoring high and low on sensation seeking scales assessed risk taking and danger differently. High sensation seekers were less anxious about, and less threatened by, risky and dangerous activities.

High-Risk Sports: A Favourite Pastime of Sensation Seekers

People who rate high in sensation seeking are attracted to activities like white-water kayaking.

Genetics and Personality

An integral part of any biologically based approach to personality is an assessment of the role played by *genetics* in influencing the development of personality. How does one go about studying how genes influence personality? Galton (1883)

Sensation Seeking: The desire to seek out novel and intense experiences.

speculated that the study of identical twins would provide significant information about the heritability of traits. His observation was apt. The most compelling evidence about the role of genetic factors in personality development comes from comparisons of identical and fraternal twins. This may be seen in Figure 12.5, which shows the similarity of pairs of identical and fraternal twins on each of the "big five" personality traits that we discussed in the preceding section of this chapter. The correlations on each of the big five personality traits are much higher between individual pairs of *identical twins* (who have an identical genetic structure) than between individual pairs of *fraternal twins* (who have only half their genes in common). The much greater similarity in shared traits evident in identical twins provides clear evidence that personality is affected by genetic factors.

Is it possible to move beyond the direct comparison of identical and fraternal twins and provide a more general estimate of the overall heritability of personality traits that holds for the population at large? Such estimates can be obtained by making use of complicated mathematical modelling procedures (Loehlin, 1992). These procedures generate *heritability estimates.* The heritability estimate for a given trait is expressed in terms of a ratio that can range from 0 to 1. A value close to 0 implies that genetic factors have very little influence on the expression of a trait. A value close to 1 implies that the expression of a trait is largely determined by genetic factors. What do we find when these modelling procedures are employed? Figure 12.6 is based on the genetic modelling data of Loehlin (1992). It shows heritability estimates for each of the big five personality traits, which range from .38 for conscientiousness to .49 for extraversion, with a mean overall heritability estimate of .42. These estimates fit reasonably well with those obtained in other studies. For example, Bouchard (1994), using data from the Minnesota Twins studies, arrived at a mean overall heritability estimate for the big five traits of .46. What these data mean in percentage terms is that 42 to 46 percent of the total variance in expression of the big five personality traits is attributable to *genetic* factors. A precise measure of how much of the total variation in trait expression is attributable to environmental factors is difficult to calculate because of esoteric issues associated with measurement error. Nevertheless, the influence of the environment is obviously substantial. Scarr (1997) estimates that at least 50 percent of the overall variation in trait expression is likely determined by *environmental* factors.

Figure 12.5
Correlation of Personality Traits of Identical and Fraternal Twins

These data show the degree to which the scores of identical and fraternal twins are correlated on each of the "big five" personality traits. The correlations for identical twins are more than double those of fraternal twins on each trait. This indicates that genes we receive from our parents do influence personality structure.

Source: Adapted from Bouchard (1997).

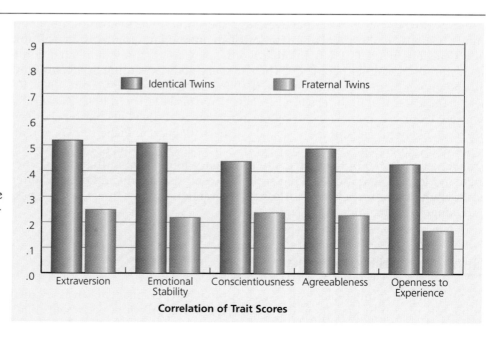

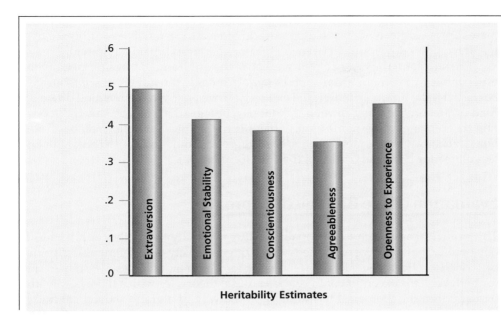

Figure 12.6
Estimates of the Heritability of the "Big Five" Personality Traits

Heritability estimates reflect the proportion of variance in a trait that can be attributed to genetic factors. Heritability estimates range from 0 to 1. An estimate of 0 would mean that genetic factors do not influence the expression of a trait, and an estimate of 1 would mean that trait expression is totally determined by genetic factors.

Source: Adapted from Loehlin, 1992, p. 67. Reprinted by permission of Sage Publications, Inc.

Research Related to Biological Approaches to Personality

Researchers have long struggled to account for personality in terms of biological mechanisms. Attempts such as that of Eysenck to relate very broad-based personality traits, such as extraversion, to equally broad-based arousal processes have been supplanted by approaches with a narrower and sharper focus. Much attention is now being directed to working out the role of biological processes that underlie anomalies and aberrations in personality. The work of Zuckerman (1995) on sensation seeking is representative of this approach. It has achieved a substantial measure of success, and we are gaining an increasingly detailed understanding of the neurotransmitters and neurotransmitter regulatory mechanisms that underlie sensation-seeking behaviour. Researchers are also beginning to look at the role of genetic factors in sensation seeking (Zuckerman, 1996).

Research on the degree to which genetic factors influence personality has provoked much discussion and has encouraged a reconsideration of many traditional assumptions—even those about the degree to which the home environment influences personality development. Parents tend to worry about whether they are providing the best possible home environment for their children. A recent poll sponsored by *The Globe and Mail* reports that approximately 80 percent of Canadian parents worry about whether they are raising their children properly (Mitchell, 1999). Many of those polled were sufficiently troubled about this issue to admit to experiencing sleep disturbances and feelings of depression. The primary concern of the parents polled was that their children might not realize their full potential because of some deficiency in the home environment. However, genetic modelling data suggest the home environment may not be as important as many parents think.

Estimates of how much the family setting has upon personality traits can be obtained in a variety of different ways. The simplest procedure is to compare adopted children of different parents—raised in the same home—on various different personality traits. Any similarity in personality trait expression, over that which would be observed by comparing any two children chosen at random, has to be attributable to the effect of the *shared home environment*. The interesting finding is that the trait variance attributable to the shared environment tends to be relatively small. The home environment appears to account for no more than 7 to 11 percent of the total variation in expression of a trait (Bouchard, 1994; Rowe, 1997). If these estimates are accurate, it means that parents do indeed have much less influence over the personality development of their children than traditionally assumed.

The substantial influence that we know the environment has on personality must come, in the main, from sources largely outside the home—the *unshared environment*—the uniquely individual experiences we have while travelling down the road of life. One leading developmental psychologist has, in fact, taken the position that as long as the home environment is not atypical or abnormal, basic adequacy needs are being met. Parents, she suggests, should take both less credit and less blame for how their children turn out (Scarr, 1997).

Evaluation of the Biological Approach

The biological approach to personality differs markedly from other approaches to personality that we have examined, which offer a variety of different global principles or theoretical mechanisms to account for how personalities are shaped and formed. With the exception of Eysenck's arousal theory, for which there is only limited support, the biological has nothing in the way of a grand theoretical framework. It is not so much a theory as an approach or perspective on personality. This does not mean it is lacking in significance or importance.

By far the most important contribution made by the biological approach to our understanding of personality is the information it has provided about the heritability of traits. The heritability of the "big five" personality traits has been studied repeatedly, and pronounced evidence of heritability has been consistently observed. What this means, according to theoreticians such as Buss (1997), is that the big five personality traits *must* have been shaped by evolutionary pressures.

What evolutionary pressures might have favoured selection of the big five personality traits? One possibility is the *complexity of human social interactions.* Dealing with others is always difficult, and as human populations grew, and the likelihood of increasingly frequent interactions with strangers increased, there would have been an increasing need to rapidly understand and reliably predict the behaviour of others. To interact effectively with others, we need to be able to make rapid judgments about their personality characteristics. We need to know whether they are extraverted, introverted, emotionally stable, or conscientiousness and whether they are open to new experiences. Individuals who possessed such dispositions would have had a survival advantage, and these traits would have entered the gene pool. According to Buss (1997, p. 334), the reason the "big five" personality traits—extraversion, agreeableness, conscientiousness, emotional stability, and openness to experience—have been subject to evolutionary selection is because they "summarize the most important features of the social landscape."

Before we end our consideration of the biological approach, we must point out that it focuses on only *one side* of the nature–nurture issue, and if we are not careful, it can lead us to ignore, or underestimate, the very large effect the *environment* has upon personality. As we emphasized in Chapter 1, all behaviour reflects a complex interaction between environment and heredity. It has to be acknowledged also that there are researchers who question the adequacy of heritability estimates and argue that they *overestimate* the significance of genetic factors (e.g., Baumrind, 1993).

K E Y *QUESTIONS*

▢ How does Eysenck account for the difference in behaviour of extraverts and introverts?

▢ What is sensation seeking and how does it influence behaviour?

▢ What do genetic studies tell us about personality?

Learning-Theory Approaches to Personality

All personality theories must ultimately come to grips with two basic questions: What accounts for the *uniqueness* of human behaviour? And what underlies its *consistency*? Classic theories of personality such as Freud's dealt with these questions by positing instinctive urges and elaborate systems of regulatory controls. A much simpler approach is to see personality as largely determined by *learning and experience*. A learning-theory approach sees our uniqueness as reflecting the fact that we have all experienced distinctively different learning experiences. Consistency in behaviour over time and across situations is explained simply by noting that responses, associations, and habits acquired through learning tend to persist. Also, since people often find themselves in situations very similar to the ones in which they acquired these tendencies, their behaviour, too, tends to remain quite stable.

Early learning-oriented views of personality took what now seems to be a somewhat extreme position: they denied the importance of *any* internal causes of behaviour—such as motives, traits, intentions, or goals (Skinner, 1974). The only things that matter, these early theorists suggested, are external conditions determining patterns of reinforcement (recall the discussion of *schedules of reinforcement* in Chapter 5). At present, few psychologists agree with this position. Most now believe that internal factors—especially many aspects of *cognition*—play a crucial role in behaviour. A prime example of this modern approach is provided by Bandura's *social cognitive theory* (e.g., Bandura, 1986, 1997).

Social Cognitive Theory

In his **social cognitive theory,** Bandura places great emphasis on what he terms the **self-system**—the cognitive processes by which a person perceives, evaluates, and regulates his or her own behaviour so that is appropriate in a given situation. Reflecting the emphasis on cognition in modern psychology, Bandura calls attention to the fact that people don't simply respond to reinforcements; rather, they think about the consequences of their actions, anticipate future events, and establish goals and plans. In addition, they engage in **self-reinforcement,** patting themselves on the back when they attain their goals. For example, consider the hundreds of amateur runners who participate in major marathons. Few believe that they have any chance of winning and obtaining the external rewards offered—status, fame, cash prizes. Why, then, do they run? Because, Bandura would contend, they have *self-set goals,* such as finishing the race, or merely going as far as they can. Meeting these goals allows them to engage in self-reinforcement, and this is sufficient to initiate what is obviously very effortful behaviour.

Another important feature of Bandura's theory is its emphasis on *observational learning* (which we described in Chapter 5), a form of learning in which individuals acquire both information and new forms of behaviour through observing others (Bandura, 1977). Such learning plays a role in a very wide range of human activities—everything from learning how to dress and groom in the style of one's own society through learning how to perform new and difficult tasks. In essence, any time that human beings observe others, they can learn from this experience, and such learning can then play an important part in their own behaviour. Such *models* don't have to be present "in the flesh" for observational learning to occur. Human beings can also acquire new information and new ways of behaving from exposure to models who are presented symbolically, in films, on television, and in literature.

Perhaps the aspect of Bandura's theory that has received most attention in recent research is his concept of **self-efficacy**—an individual's belief that he or she can perform some behaviour or task successfully. If you sit down to take an exam in your psychology class and expect to do well, your self-efficacy is high; if you have doubts about your performance, then your self-efficacy is lower. Self-efficacy has been found to play a role in success on many tasks (e.g., Maurer & Pierce, 1998),

Social Cognitive Theory: A theory of behaviour suggesting that human behaviour is influenced by many cognitive factors as well as by reinforcement contingencies, and that human beings have an impressive capacity to regulate their own actions.

Self-System: In Bandura's social cognitive learning theory, the set of cognitive processes by which a person perceives, evaluates, and regulates his or her own behaviour.

Self-Reinforcement: A process in which individuals reward themselves for reaching their own goals.

Self-Efficacy: Individuals' expectations concerning their ability to perform various tasks.

TV and Violence

According to Bandura, children learn that aggression is acceptable—and sometimes even admirable—through watching violent role models on television.

and can influence our health—people who expect to handle stress effectively or to get better actually do (Bandura, 1992), as well as our personal happiness and life satisfaction (Judge et al., 1998). Such generalized beliefs about task-related capabilities are stable over time, and these can be viewed as an important aspect of personality.

It should be noted that other learning-oriented approaches to personality have much in common with Bandura's views. For example, the social-learning theory proposed by Julian Rotter (1954, 1982) suggests that the likelihood that a given behaviour will occur in a specific situation depends on an individual's expectancies concerning the outcomes different possible behaviours will produce, and the value they attach to these different outcomes. According to Rotter, individuals tend to develop a generalized expectancy about the extent to which they can shape their destiny and the degree to which their actions determine outcomes that they experience in life. Persons who strongly believe that the outcomes they experience are the consequences of their own actions, and who feel they are able to shape and control their own destinies, are said to have an **internal locus of control.** Those who believe their behaviour is largely determined by factors outside their control are said to have an **external locus of control.** Certainly, such suggestions contrast very sharply with the view, stated in early learning approaches to personality, that only external reinforcement contingencies should be taken into account.

Research on the Learning Perspective

Because they are based on well-established principles of psychology, learning theories of personality have been the subject of a great deal of research attention (e.g., Wallace, 1993). In fact, efforts to test these theories have led to the development of several new and highly effective techniques for treating psychological disorders. To illustrate the type of research carried out within the learning perspective, let's briefly consider efforts to investigate the effects of *self-efficacy* (e.g., Burger & Palmer, 1992).

Recall that self-efficacy refers to our beliefs concerning our ability to perform a specific task or reach a specific goal (Bandura, 1987). Can anything be done to increase individuals' self-efficacy in various situations? Research on this topic offers an encouraging answer: Self-efficacy *can* be increased through relatively straightforward procedures (e.g., Riskind & Maddux, 1993). For instance, in a study on finding another job after becoming unemployed, efforts were made to increase the self-efficacy of participants (Eden & Aviram, 1993). The researchers felt this would be useful because after losing their jobs, many people experience reductions in self-efficacy—they begin to wonder how good they are at what they do for a living and whether they will ever get another position. To counter such feelings, Eden and Aviram (1993) had newly unemployed persons participate in workshops designed to enhance their self-efficacy. The workshops sought to accomplish this goal by showing them films in which good job-seeking skills were demonstrated. After watching these films, the participants practised these skills themselves and received feedback and encouragement. Results indicated that these procedures did increase participants' self-efficacy. Did they also help them to get another job? Again, findings were encouraging: six months later, fully 67 percent of those who took part in the workshops were re-employed. In contrast, only 23 percent of those in a carefully matched control group had found a new job. Findings such as these suggest that self-efficacy is an important aspect of personality but—like many other traits or characteristics—it can indeed be changed.

Evaluation of the Learning Approach

Do all human beings confront an Oedipus conflict? Are peak experiences real, and do they in fact constitute a sign of growing self-actualization? Considerable

Internal Locus of Control: Individuals are held to have internal locus of control if they believe their actions largely determine the outcomes that they experience in life.

External Locus of Control: Individuals are held to have an external locus of control if they believe that factors outside of their control largely determine the outcomes that they experience in life.

controversy exists with respect to these and many other aspects of psychoanalytic and humanistic theories of personality. In contrast, virtually all psychologists agree that behaviours are acquired and modified through basic processes of learning. Moreover, there is general agreement about the importance of cognitive factors in human behaviour. Thus, a key strength of the learning approach is obvious: It is based on widely accepted and well-documented principles of psychology. Another positive feature of this framework involves the fact that it has been put to practical use in efforts to modify maladaptive forms of behaviour. We will return in such efforts in detail in Chapter 15.

Turning to criticisms, most of these have focused on older approaches rather than on the more sophisticated theories proposed by Bandura (1986, 1997) and others. Those early behaviourist theorists generally ignored the role of cognitive factors in human behaviour, but this is certainly *not* true of the modern theories. A related criticism centres around the fact that learning theories generally ignore inner conflicts, and the influence of unconscious thoughts and impulses, on behaviour. However, while such issues are not explicitly addressed by theories such as Bandura's, their existence and possible impact is not in any way denied by these theories. Rather, modern learning theories would simply insist that such effects be interpreted within the context of modern psychology.

As you can readily see, these are not major criticisms. Thus, it seems fair to state that at present, these social cognitive theories of personality are more in tune with the eclectic, sophisticated approach of modern psychology than earlier theories. As such, they are certain to play an important role, along with the trait approach and the biological approach, in continuing efforts to understand the uniqueness and consistency of human behaviour.

See the **Key Concept** on page 500 for an overview of several major theories of personality discussed in this chapter.

K E Y *QUESTIONS*

- According to learning theories of personality, what accounts for the uniqueness and consistency of human behaviour?
- What is Bandura's social cognitive theory?
- What is Rotter's social learning theory?
- What is self-efficacy and what effects does it have on behaviour?

Critical Thinking

In your own everyday life, do you think that your behaviour is more strongly influenced by external events, such as reinforcements or punishments, or by your own plans, expectations, and goals?

Measuring Personality

To study personality scientifically, we must first be able to measure it—or at least, to measure some of its many aspects. Thus, a key task facing psychologists who want to investigate personality in their research is this basic issue of *measurement*. We have already considered some aspects of this question in Chapter 11, where we discussed several issues relating to the measurement of intelligence. Here, we'll focus on how psychologists deal with the issue of measurement with respect to personality. Although many different procedures exist, most fall into two major categories often described by the terms *objective* and *projective*.

Key Concept

Major Theories of Personality

Theory/Major Advocate	Major Focus	Key Concepts
Psychoanalytic  Freud	Levels of consciousness States of psychosexual development Anxiety and defence mechanisms	Conscious, preconscious, unconscious Oral, anal, phallic, latency, genital Repression, rationalization, displacement, projection, regression 
Humanistic Theories  Rogers	Personal growth, personal responsibility, the present rather than the past	Self-concept, self-actualization  Maslow
Trait Theories  Allport	Stable dimensions of personality along which people vary Recent focus on the "big five" personality traits	Cardinal traits, central traits, surface and source traits
Biological Approach  Eysenck	Brain mechanisms underlying various personality characteristics, genetic influences, and evolutionary pressure for trait selection	Arousal, sensation seeking, heritability estimates, shared and unshared environmental effects
Learning Approaches  Bandura	Role of basic learning processes in uniqueness and stability of individual behaviour Self-regulation of behaviour	Operant conditioning, observational learning Self-efficacy Internal versus external locus of control

▶ Objective Tests of Personality

Objective tests of personality consist of questions or statements to which individuals respond in various ways. For example, commonly employed self-report inventories or questionnaires ask respondents to indicate the extent to which each of a set of statements is true or false about themselves, the extent of their agreement with the content of various sentences, or to indicate which of a pair of activities they prefer. For instance, here are a few items that are similar to those appearing on one widely used measure of the "big five" dimensions of personality. Test-takers would be asked to designate the degree to which they agree or disagree with each item (1 = strongly disagree, 2 = disagree, 3 = neutral, 4 = agree, and 5 = strongly agree).

> I am very careful and methodical.
>
> I generally get along well with others.
>
> I cry easily.
>
> Sometimes I feel totally worthless.
>
> I have a lot of trust in other people.

Answers to the questions on such objective tests are scored by means of special keys. The score obtained by a specific person is then compared with those obtained by hundreds or even thousands of other people who have taken the test previously. In this way, an individual's relative standing on the trait being measured can be determined.

In the case of a test composed of items such as those listed above, it is quite apparent that the test items are related to the "big five" dimensions of personality. For instance, the first item seems to be related to the *conscientiousness* dimension, the second is related to the *agreeableness* dimension, the third to *emotional stability,* and so on. On some tests, the connection between the individual test items and the personality traits or characteristics being measured is not so obvious. This usually means that a procedure known as *empirical keying* has been used in constructing the test. The items are given to hundreds of persons belonging to groups known to differ from one another—for instance, psychiatric patients with a specific form of mental illness and normal persons—and the answers given by the two groups are compared. Items answered differently by these groups are included in the test, *regardless of whether they seem to be related to the traits being measured*. The reasoning is as follows: As long as a test item differentiates between the groups in question, the specific content of the item itself is unimportant.

One widely used test designed to measure various types of psychological disorders, the **MMPI** (short for *Minnesota Multiphasic Personality Inventory*), uses precisely this method. The MMPI was developed during the 1930s, but it underwent a major revision in the 1980s. The current version, the MMPI-2, contains ten *clinical scales* and several *validity scales*. The clinical scales, which are summarized in Table 12.2, relate to various forms of psychological disorder. Items included in each of these scales are ones that are answered differently by persons who have been diagnosed as having this particular disorder and a comparison group who do *not* have the disorder. The validity scales are designed to determine whether, and to what extent, people are trying to "fake" their answers—for instance, whether they are trying deliberately to seem bizarre or, conversely, to give the impression that they are extremely "normal" and well-adjusted. If persons taking the test score high on these validity scales, their responses to the clinical scales must be interpreted with special caution.

Another widely used objective measure of personality is the *Millon Clinical Multiaxial Inventory* (MCMI; Millon, 1987). Items on this test correspond more closely than those on the MMPI to the categories of psychological disorders currently used by psychologists. This makes the test especially useful to clinical psychologists, who must first identify individuals' problems before recommending specific forms of therapy for them.

MMPI: A widely used objective test of personality based on empirical keying.

TABLE 12.2

Clinical Scales of the MMPI-2

The MMPI is designed to measure many aspects of personality related to psychological disorders.

Clinical Scale	Description
Hypochondriasis	Excessive concern with bodily functions
Depression	Pessimism; hopelessness; slowing of action and thought
Hysteria	Development of physical disorders such as blindness, paralysis, and vomiting as an escape from emotional problems
Psychopathic deviance	Disregard for social customs; shallow emotions
Masculinity–femininity	Differences between men and women
Paranoia	Suspiciousness; delusions of grandeur or persecution
Pschasthenia	Obsession; compulsions; fears; guilt; indecisiveness
Schizophrenia	Bizarre, unusual thoughts or behaviour; withdrawal; hallucinations; delusions
Hypomania	Emotional excitement; flight of ideas; overactivity
Social introversion	Shyness; lack of interest in others; insecurity

A third objective test, the *NEO Personality Inventory* (NEO-PI; Costa & McCrae, 1989), is used to measure aspects of personality that are *not* directly linked to psychological disorders. Specifically, it measures the "big five" dimensions of personality described earlier in this chapter. These dimensions appear to represent basic aspects of personality. Because of this, the NEO Personality Inventory is commonly used as a research tool in the study of personality.

Objective tests of personality are generally used to identify and measure specific aspects of personality—specific traits. How are such measurements used in research? Often in the following manner: A psychologist interested in studying a specific aspect of personality gives a test that measures this trait in a large number of persons. Then groups of individuals scoring very low and very high (and perhaps those in between) on this trait are chosen to participate in the study and compared with respect to a particular kind of behaviour or, perhaps, to how they react in a particular situation (see Figure 12.7). If the behaviour of these groups does indeed differ, this constitutes evidence that the trait tested for is related to the behaviour or the situational circumstances examined.

Projective Tests of Personality

In contrast to objective tests, *projective tests* of personality adopt a very different approach. They present individuals with ambiguous stimuli—stimuli that can be interpreted in many different ways. For instance, these can be inkblots such as the one shown in Figure 12.8, or ambiguous scenes of the type described in Chapter 10 in our discussion of achievement motivation. Persons taking the test are then asked to indicate what they see, to make up a story about this stimulus, and so on. Since the stimuli themselves are ambiguous, it is assumed that the answers given by respondents will reflect significant aspects of their personality. In other words, different persons see different things in these stimuli because these persons differ from one another with respect to various aspects of personality.

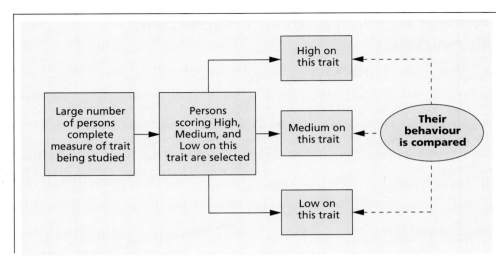

Figure 12.7

Studying the Effects of Personality: One Basic Approach

In order to study the effects of a specific personality trait, a large number of persons complete a measure of this trait. Then, persons scoring high, medium, and low on this trait are selected for further study. Their behaviour is then compared. If it differs, evidence that this trait is related to the form of behaviour being studied is obtained.

Do such tests really work—do they meet the criteria of reliability and validity discussed in Chapter 11? For some projective tests, such as the Thematic Apperception Test (TAT), which is used to measure achievement motivation and other social motives, the answer appears to be *yes:* such tests do yield reliable scores, and do seem to measure what they are intended to measure. For others, such as the famous **Rorschach test**, which uses inkblots like the one in Figure 12.8, the answer is more doubtful. Responses to this test are scored in many different ways. For instance, one measure involves responses that mention *pairs* of objects or a *reflection* (e.g., the inkblot is interpreted as showing two people, or one person looking into a mirror). Such responses are taken as a sign of self-focus—being overly concerned with oneself. Other scoring involves the number of times individuals mention movement, colour, or shading in the inkblots. The more responses of this type they make, the more sources of stress they supposedly have in their lives.

Are such interpretations accurate? Psychologists disagree about this point. The Rorschach test, like other projective tests, has a standard scoring manual (Exner, 1993), which tells psychologists precisely how to score various kinds of responses. Presumably, this manual is based on careful research designed to determine just what the test measures. Recent findings, however, suggest that the scoring advice provided by the manual may be flawed in several respects and does not rest on the firm scientific foundation psychologists prefer (Wood, Nezworski, & Stejskal, 1996). Such findings indicate the need for caution in the use of projective tests. Projective tests vary widely with respect to validity, and unless they rank relatively high in this respect, it is not likely that they will provide useful information about personality.

In sum, while many objective and projective tests for measuring personality (and carrying out systematic research on it) exist, these must be chosen and used with care. Only to the extent that these tests meet the criteria of reliability and validity applied to all psychological tests can they assist us in the task of adding to our knowledge of personality.

Figure 12.8

The Rorschach Test: One Projective Measure of Personality

Persons taking the Rorschach Test describe what they see in a series of inkblots. Supposedly, their responses reveal much about their personality. However, recent findings cast doubt on the validity of this test.

Rorschach Test: A widely used projective test of personality in which individuals are asked to describe what they see in a series of inkblots.

K E Y *QUESTIONS*

- What are objective tests of personality?
- What are projective tests of personality?

Recent Research on Key Aspects of Personality

In recent decades, efforts to understand personality have undergone a major shift. Rather than attempting to construct grand theories, psychologists have focused on efforts to identify and study key aspects of personality. Many different theorists—Rogers is perhaps the prime example—believe that our self-concept plays a crucial role in our total personality (Bentsch & Page, 1989). Reflecting this view, much current research on personality is concerned with various aspects of the self. Here, we'll focus on three aspects of the self that have been the focus of a great deal of attention: *self-perception*, *self-esteem*, and *self-monitoring*.

Aspects of the Self

SELF-PERCEPTION: KNOWING YOUR OWN PERSONALITY   Is there something special about self-perception that sets it apart from the perception of others? The fact is that we do seem to accord ourselves a special status. A series of experiments undertaken by Sande, Goethals, and Radkiff (1988), at the University of Manitoba, required undergraduates to make judgments about the personality traits they possessed and about the personality traits they would attribute to others of the same age and sex. Participants consistently judged themselves to have a wider variety of traits and to be more complex and less predictable than casual acquaintances. Why should this be so? Sande and colleagues suggest a major reason is that as individuals, we have a long history of personal experience to draw upon when it comes to assessing our own behaviour. Because we are aware how wide and varied our behaviour has been in different situations, we are inclined to conclude that our personality is more complex and multifaceted than that of people whose behaviour we have observed in only a limited number of situations. Sande's research suggests it is probably wise to resist our tendencies to underestimate personality complexities of casual acquaintances.

SELF-ESTEEM: EFFECTS OF HOW WE FEEL ABOUT OURSELVES   How do you feel about yourself? Generally good? Generally bad? Most people tend to hold a relatively favourable view of themselves; they realize that they are not perfect, but, in general, they conclude that their good points outweigh their bad ones. Large individual differences exist with respect to such self-evaluation, however, so one important aspect of the self is **self-esteem:** the extent to which our self-evaluations are favourable or not (e.g., Marsh, 1993).

Research findings indicate that self-esteem is extremely important to our well-being. In fact, self-esteem may actually be beneficial to our physical as well as our emotional health. Persons high in self-esteem appear to be more resistant to disease than persons low in self-esteem. That is, their immune systems seem to operate more effectively. Why? Some recent findings indicate that self-esteem may be linked to biochemical changes within the body; for instance, high self-esteem is associated with increased levels of *serotonin* in the blood, and this neurotransmitter may play a role in effective functioning of the immune system (e.g., Wright, 1995). Whatever the specific mechanisms involved, having high self-esteem does seem to be beneficial in many different ways.

As you will discover in the **Canadian Focus** feature, self-esteem is a very influential factor in determining the ease with which adjustment can be made to life in a different culture.

Self-Esteem: The extent to which individuals have positive or negative feelings about themselves and their own worth.

Canadian Focus

Self-Esteem and Adjusting to Life in a New Culture

Moving to a new country as a student to undertake a program of study, or as an immigrant to take up permanent residence, can be stressful. For example, Asian students, who have a very different cultural background, often find university in Canada to be very stressful. Evidence of this has been provided by Chataway and Berry (1989). Similar findings were reported in an extensive study by Kathryn Mickel of York University (Bowen, 1986), involving a variety of Canadian universities. The stress experienced by newcomers reflects not only difficulties in adjusting to a new country, but also the effects of the prejudice and discrimination often encountered. The resulting pressure can affect both the mental and the physical health of newcomers (Chataway & Berry, 1989; Dion & Giordano, 1990).

Karen K. Dion
University of Toronto

Kenneth L. Dion
University of Toronto

In an effort to understand what personality characteristics would serve to cushion newcomers against the effects of acculturation and discrimination, Dion, Dion, and Pak (1992) studied a large number of volunteers from Toronto's Chinese community. These people filled out an extensive questionnaire that probed for information about personality characteristics and health-related problems of a psychological nature (e.g., sleep difficulties, headaches, worries, and mood disturbances). Information was also requested about the amount of readjustment participants had to undergo in coping with a wide variety of life events and the degree of satisfaction they felt regarding these readjustments.

As expected, health-related problems of a psychological nature were found to increase with adjustment difficulties and with perceived (and experienced) discrimination. Interestingly, the degree to which health problems were experienced depended on personality factors, two of which were found to be important: self-esteem, which, as we have pointed out, influences stress tolerance and health; and the individual's perceived sense of personal control. A high level of self-esteem together with a strong sense of personal control was found to be effective in cushioning participants from physical and psychological problems associated with stress.

This does not mean that an exaggerated sense of confidence and an unrealistic conviction of personal control will facilitate coping with a new culture. Dion et al. emphasize that there must be a genuine basis for both high self-esteem and feelings of personal control. The individuals in their study who reported these did have higher educational levels, better English, and greater professional experience.

What conclusions can be drawn? It seems clear that individuals entering a different culture with a substantial measure of self-esteem and a strong sense of personal control will be more able to cope with the stress produced by acculturation and discrimination than those who are lacking in these attributes. This is especially true in the case of children. In a recent review of mental health problems facing immigrant and refugee children, Beiser and colleagues (1995) place particular emphasis on the importance of self-esteem and the degree to which it seems to be a determinant of successful adjustment and achievement.

SELF-MONITORING: INNER CONVICTIONS VERSUS PUBLIC IMAGE At the start of this chapter, we noted that the extent to which individuals show consistent behaviour across situations and over time may itself be an important aspect of personality. Some people remain much the same in all contexts, while others show a marked disposition to change their behaviour patterns from situation to situation. According to many investigators, these differences in the consistency of behavioural expression are attributable to differences in what is termed **self-monitoring**. Self-monitoring refers to the degree to which individuals regulate their behaviour on the basis of situational factors such as the reactions they expect their behaviour will have on others who may be present, as opposed to internal factors such as their own beliefs and attitudes (Snyder, 1974, 1987).

Self-Monitoring: A personality trait involving sensitivity to social situations and an ability to adapt one's behaviour to the demands of those situations in order to make favourable impressions on others.

People high in self-monitoring are social chameleons—they can skillfully alter their behaviour to match the current situation. If high self-monitors find themselves among beer-drinking construction workers, they roll up their sleeves and swig some beer. If, instead, they find themselves among wine connoisseurs, they roll down their sleeves and sip with the best of them. In short, they adjust what they say and what they do to the current situation in order to make a positive impression on others (Snyder, 1987; Snyder & Gangestad, 1986). In contrast, low self-monitors tend to show a higher degree of consistency. They act much the same across a wide range of situations on the basis of their particular beliefs and attitudes (Koestner et al., 1992).

Given the character of high self-monitors and their ability to adapt readily to different situations, it will probably not surprise you that they often become leaders in group situations. Researchers at Wilfrid Laurier University and the University of Guelph found this to be especially true if the task or responsibilities of a situation require group effort and consensus (Crownshaw & Ellis, 1991; Ellis, 1988). Because of their better overall ability to read others' emotional reactions and manage their own non-verbal cues, high self-monitors tend to be more successful in their careers than low self-monitors (Kilduff Day, 1994). Studies by Kirchmeyer (1990), of the University of Lethbridge, suggest that in the business world, the domain of office politics tends to be dominated by highly self-monitoring men and women.

High and low self-monitors also differ in terms of the kind of relationships they form with others—and the reasons behind these relationships. Low self-monitors tend to choose their friends on the basis of shared attitudes and values—factors that are very important to them. In contrast, high self-monitors tend to choose friends with whom they can share specific activities—people who enjoy doing the same things they enjoy (Jamiesen et al., 1987).

One potential downside to high self-monitoring is that, because they are so changeable, high self-monitors may be viewed by others as inconsistent, lacking in sincerity, or even manipulative (Turban & Dougherty, 1994). This was shown in a study made by Jiujias and Horvarth (1991) at Acadia University. An individual engaged in a social interaction was less well-liked when she was deemed to be engaging in a high level of self-monitoring than when she was deemed to be engaging in a low level of self-monitoring. In short, as is true of virtually every aspect of personality, there is no single point on this dimension that is always best.

To find out whether you are high or low in self-monitoring, see **Making Psychology Part of Your Life** on page 508.

Before concluding, we should address one final question about personality: Do cultural factors play a role in personality traits or in the measurement of them? For some information on this issue, see the **Perspectives on Diversity** section below.

Perspectives on Diversity

Cultural Differences in the Concept of Self

DOES CULTURE SHAPE PERSONALITY? Cross-cultural studies tell us that culture does influence some aspects of personality. Studies carried out by Markus and Kitayama (1991) are particularly useful in illustrating how cultural factors influence the formation of our *self-concept*, which, as we have seen, plays a pivotal role in personality.

Markus and Kitayama found that persons in Western nations tend to have an *individualistic* self-concept. In such societies, individual self-achievement, self-satisfaction, and self-fulfillment are highly prized goals. Efforts are made on the part of the individual to develop skills, abilities, or interests that set the individual apart, or make him or her distinctively different to others in the society. The goals of the individual are perceived as quite separable from the family and/or the social group to whom the individual is bound.

Persons in other cultures, especially those in Asia, Africa, and Latin America, tend to have a more *interdependent* self-concept. One's self is defined in terms of relationships one has with others. In such societies, the emphasis is on a network of dependent relationships binding each individual to his or her family or social group. Self-esteem does not come from developing skills or abilities that distinguish oneself from others; it comes from developing skills or abilities that add to and benefit the social group with whom one is tightly linked. Commitment to group interests does not go unrewarded. The family and social groups play an important role in supporting and promoting the advancement of the individual.

Markus and Kitayama maintain that individuals with independent and interdependent selves are driven by different motives and deal with situations in different ways. One clear illustration of this difference is the way in which they approach love and marriage (Dion & Dion, 1993).

Dion and Dion (1993) point out that members of interdependent and individualistic societies think differently about love and marriage. In individualistic societies, romantic notions of love flourish because romantic love is essentially "selfish" in the dictionary sense of "seeking or concentrating on one's own welfare or advantage." Each individual has an idealized notion of a relationship with another that will bring him or her great personal satisfaction. In a collectivist society, on the other hand, the individual is interactively dependent on his or her family and reference group. In such societies, the individual must consider carefully the degree to which a prospective partner will fit into this relationship. In short, the self-concept that characterizes collectivist societies does not allow love and marriage to be considered exclusively in terms of the narrow needs of the individual.

Although romantic love and intimacy flourish in individualistic societies, excessive individualism can have a disturbing influence on the character of the romantic experience. Love relationships can become simply competitive games in which the object is to gain the most and give the least. Should the game cease to be sufficiently rewarding, it is abandoned. Dion and Dion (1991) claim that such considerations may play an important role in the high divorce rate in North America.

In summary, culture influences our concept of self, and our concept of self in turn influences the nature of interactions we tend to pursue.

K E Y *QUESTIONS*

■ How do persons high in self-esteem differ from those low in self-esteem?

■ What are the characteristics of low self-monitors and high self-monitors?

■ What is sensation seeking and how does it influence behaviour?

■ What cultural differences in the concept of self exist, and how can they influence behaviour?

Making **Psychology** *Part of Your Life*

Are You a High or Low Self-Monitor?

*S*elf-monitoring appears to be one important aspect of personality—it is related to many forms of behaviour, from making good impressions on others to success in one's career. For this reason, you may find it interesting—and useful—to know just where you stand on this dimension. To find out, follow the instructions below.

Indicate whether each of the statements below is true (or mostly true) or false (or mostly false) about yourself. If a statement is true (or mostly true) write the letter T in the blank space. If it is false (or mostly false), enter the letter F.

_F_ 1. It is difficult for me to imitate the actions of other people.

_F_ 2. My behaviour usually reflects my true feelings, attitudes, or beliefs.

_T_ 3. At parties, I always try to say and do things others will like.

_T_ 4. I can give a speech on almost any topic.

_F_ 5. I would probably make a very poor actor.

_T_ 6. Sometimes I put on a show to impress or entertain people.

_F_ 7. I find it difficult to argue for ideas in which I don't believe.

_T_ 8. In different situations, and with different people, I often act in very different ways.

_F_ 9. I would not change my attitudes or my actions in order to please others.

_T_ 10. Sometimes other people think I am experiencing stronger emotions than I really am.

_F_ 11. I am not very good at making other people like me.

_T_ 12. If I have a strong reason for doing so, I can look others in the eye and lie with a straight face.

_F_ 13. I make up my own mind about movies, books, or music; I don't rely on others' opinions in this respect.

_T or F_ 14. At a party, I usually let others keep the jokes going.

_T_ 15. I'm not always the person I seem to be.

To obtain your score, use the following key:

1. F, 2. F, 3. T, 4. T, 5. F, 6. T, 7. F, 8. T, 9. F, 10. T, 11. F, 12. T, 13. F, 14. F, 15. T

Give your self one point for each of your answers that agrees with this key.

If you scored eight or higher, you are probably a high self-monitor. If you scored four or lower, you are probably a low self-monitor. (But remember: scores on self-tests like this are highly subject to error, so please take them with a large grain of salt!) Now that you have some idea of where you stand on this dimension, can you think of situations in your own life where being a low or high self-monitor can be helpful to you? How about situations in which it might be harmful?

Summary and Review

Is Personality Real?

▧ **What is personality, and does it really exist?** Personality consists of the unique and stable patterns of behaviour, thoughts, and emotions shown by individuals. Existing evidence suggests that people do show a high degree of consistency in their behaviour, so personality does appear to exist.

▧ **What role do personality traits and situational factors play in influencing human behaviour?** Behaviour is influenced by both situational factors and personal dispositions. Personality traits influence overt behaviour only when situational conditions permit such expression.

The Psychoanalytic Approach

▧ **According to Freud, what are the three levels of consciousness?** According to Freud, three levels of consciousness exist: conscious, preconscious, and unconscious.

▧ **In Freud's theory, what are the three basic parts of personality?** The three basic parts of personality are the id, ego, and superego, which correspond roughly to desire, reason, and conscience.

▧ **According to Freud, what are the psychosexual stages of development?** Freud believed that all human beings move through a series of psychosexual stages during which the id's search for pleasure is focused on different regions of the body: the oral stage, anal stage, phallic stage, latency stage, and finally the genital stage.

▧ **Do research findings support Freud's views about the unconscious?** Research findings indicate that our behaviour can sometimes be influenced by stimuli or information we can't express verbally. Thus, in this limited sense, there does appear to be some support for Freud's suggestions.

▧ **According to Jung, what is the collective unconscious?** Jung believed that all human beings share memories of our collective experience as a species. These are expressed when our conscious mind is distracted or inactive, often through archetypes.

▧ **To what aspects of Freud's theory did Horney object?** Horney rejected Freud's suggestion that females experience penis envy and that psychological disorders stem only from fixation.

▧ **According to Adler, what is the role of feelings of inferiority in personality?** Adler believed that human beings experience strong feelings of inferiority during early life and must struggle to overcome these through compensation.

Humanistic Theories

▧ **How does the view of human beings proposed by humanistic theories of personality differ from that of psychoanalytic theories?** Humanistic theories of personality suggest that human beings strive for personal development and growth; in contrast, psychoanalytic theory views human beings as constantly struggling to control the sexual and aggressive impulses of the id.

▧ **According to Rogers, why do many individuals fail to become fully functioning persons?** Rogers believed that many individuals fail to become fully functioning persons because distorted self-concepts interfere with personal growth.

▧ **In Maslow's theory, what is self-actualization?** Self-actualization is a stage at which an individual has reached his or her maximum potential and becomes the best human being he or she can be.

▧ **What is the self-concept?** The self-concept consists of all of our beliefs and knowledge about ourselves.

Trait Theories

▧ **What are central traits? Source traits?** Allport suggested that human beings possess a small number of central traits that account for much of their uniqueness as individuals. According to Cattell, there are sixteen source traits that underlie differences between individuals on many specific dimensions.

▧ **What are the "big five" dimensions of personality?** Research findings point to the conclusion that there are only five basic dimensions of personality: extraversion, agreeableness, conscientiousness, emotional stability, and openness to experience.

▧ **What do research findings indicate about the effects of the "big five" dimensions?** Research indicates that where individuals stand on several of the "big five" dimensions is readily apparent even during a brief first meeting. In addition, the "big five" dimensions are related to important aspects of behaviour, ranging from personal adjustment to career success.

Biological Approaches to Personality

▧ **How does Eysenck account for the difference in behaviour of extroverts and introverts?** Extroverts have an arousal level below the optimal level, and seek out experiences that will increase their level of arousal. Introverts have a near optimal level of arousal, and tend to avoid situations or circumstances that will increase further their arousal level.

■ **What is sensation seeking and how does it influence behaviour?**   Sensation seeking involves individual differences in the tendency to seek out intense and novel experiences. High sensation seekers engage in more high-risk behaviours than low sensation seekers.

■ **What do genetic studies tell us about personality?**   Twin studies indicated that personality traits of identical twins are much more similar than those of fraternal twins. Genetic modelling studies indicate that genetic factors do account for a significant portion of the variability, or *variance*, that we see in personality traits.

■ **What evolutionary pressures might have led to the selection of the "big five" personality traits?**   The big five personality traits may have been selected because they facilitate social interaction. Rapid assessment of these traits allow us, and others, to anticipate the probable nature of a social encounter.

Learning Approaches to Personality

■ **According to learning theories of personality, what accounts for the uniqueness and consistency of human behaviour?**   Learning theories of personality suggest that uniqueness derives from the unique pattern of learning experiences each individual has experienced. Such approaches explain consistency by noting that patterns of behaviour, once acquired, tend to persist.

■ **What is Bandura's social cognitive theory?**   Bandura's social cognitive theory assumes that behaviour is influenced by cognitive factors and personal dispositions, as well as by reinforcement contingencies and the social and physical environment.

■ **What is Rotter's social learning theory?**   Rotter's social learning theory stresses the importance of generalized expectancies concerning the internal or external control of outcomes.

■ **What is self-efficacy and what effects does it have on behaviour?**   Self-efficacy is belief in one's ability to perform a specific task. Self-efficacy influences actual performance across many tasks, and it may affect individuals' self-concept and self-esteem.

Measuring Personality

■ **What are objective tests of personality?**   Objective tests of personality consist of questions or statements to which individuals respond in various ways. Examples are the MMPI and MCMI (Millon Clinical Multiaxial Inventory).

■ **What are projective tests of personality?**   Projective tests present individuals with ambiguous stimuli—stimuli that can be interpreted many different ways. Subjects' responses to these stimuli are assumed to reflect various aspects of their personalities.

Recent Research on Key Aspects of Personality

■ **How do persons high in self-esteem differ from those low in self-esteem?**   Persons high in self-esteem perform better on many tasks, are healthier, and are more confident in social situations.

■ **What are the characteristics of low self-monitors and high self-monitors?**   Low self-monitors tend to regulate their behaviour on the basis of internal factors such as attitudes and values; they are highly consistent across situations. In contrast, high self-monitors tend to regulate their behaviour to match the requirements of each new situation; as a result, they tend to show lower consistency.

■ **What cultural differences in the concept of self exist, and can they influence behaviour?**   Persons living in individualistic societies have a self-concept that prizes individual achievement and satisfaction, whereas persons living in a interdependent culture have an extended sense of self that includes family and social group. Differences in self-concept are influential in the formation of marital and other relationships.

Key Terms

Agreeableness (p. 490)

Anal Stage (p. 480)

Anima (p. 484)

Animus (p. 484)

Arousal Process (p. 492)

Anxiety (p. 479)

Archetypes (p. 483)

Cardinal Trait (p. 489)

Central Traits (p. 489)

Collective Unconscious (p. 483)

Conscientiousness (p. 490)

Defence Mechanisms (p. 479)

Ego (p. 477)

Emotional Stability (p. 490)

External Locus of Control (p. 498)

Extroverts (p. 484)

Extraversion (p. 490)

Fixation (p. 480)

Fully Functioning Persons (p. 485)

Genital Stage (p. 481)

Humanistic Theories (p. 485)

Id (p. 477)

Internal Locus of Control (p. 498)

Introverts (p. 484)

Latency Stage (p. 481)

Libido (p. 480)

MMPI (p. 501)

Neo-Freudians (p. 483)

Oedipus Complex (p. 481)

Openness to Experience (p. 490)

Oral Stage (p. 480)

Peak Experiences (p. 487)

Personality (p. 474)

Personality Traits (p. 489)

Phallic Stage (p. 481)

Pleasure Principle (p. 477)

Critical Thinking Questions

Appraisal

Although many people tend to show consistency in their behaviour, some do not. Does this mean that the concept of personality is applicable only to people who show consistency in their behaviour over time and across situations?

Controversy

Growing evidence indicates that some aspects of personality are influenced by genetic factors. Does this mean that personality can't be changed? Or, even if genetic factors do play a role, do you think that personality remains open to change throughout life?

Making Psychology Part of Your life

Different jobs or careers seem to require different traits for success. Taking your own personality into account, can you think of careers for which you are, or are not, personally suited? How do your current career plans fit with these conclusions?

Weblinks

Check out our companion website at www.pearsoned.ca/baron for additional websites, activities, and more.

FreudNet: The A.A. Brill Library

plaza.interport.net/nypsan/freudarc.html

This site provides links to an overview of the Abraham A. Brill Library and its services, electronic resources at Brill, Internet resources about Sigmund Freud, news in psychoanalysis, the New York Psycholanalytic Institute and Society, the American Psychoanalytic Association, and other related sites.

C.G. Jung, Analytical Psychology, and Culture

www.cgjung.com/cgjung/linkx.html#Jungian

Dozens of resources related to Jungian psychology, analytical psychology, and culture are provided here. Included are links to related Jungian themes, Jungian societies and organizations, dreams, mythology, personality tests, electronic publishers, multilingual sites, references, graduate programs, and other topics.

Personality Tests

www.2h.com/Tests/personality.phtml

At this site, the interested reader can take many tests that measure personality type and lifestyle, social anxiety, stress, self-esteem, assertiveness, right- and left-brain thinking, and various other factors.

Chapter 13

Health Psychology
Health, Stress, and Coping

CHAPTER OUTLINE

Stress Busting

 According to the feature in the *Victoria Times Colonist*, men and women in mid-life are being called the "sandwich generation." Because they are in the middle, they care for their children as well as their aging parents.

Furthermore, the expectations that these "boomers" had about what their life would be like at this time are not being met and they are having to make huge adjustments. Specific sources of stress include corporate reorganization, job loss, early retirement, divorce, remarriage, blended families, mid-life pregnancy, and growing older.

Those may be sources of stress for those in mid-life at the beginning of the twenty-first century, but here is one we all face together: *With the brain we evolved many thousands of years ago, we are all trying to process twice the amount of information every year!*

What is stress? How does it affect our bodies, our brains, our health, our thinking, and our behaviour? How can we apply psychological findings to cope with stress, and what happens when we're overcome—and suffer burnout? Those are some of the questions you will encounter as you work your way through Chapter 13, Stress, Health and Coping.

Source: Senick, D. (2000, February 29). Chilling out the boomers. *Victoria Times Colonist*, p. B1.

> Many Canadian residents are becoming increasingly aware of the importance of good health and the value of taking active steps to ensure it.

Stress

Health Psychology considers the nature of stress, how it influences health, and how it affects performance.

Imagine that you've been granted three wishes. How would you use them? Fame and power? Immense wealth? Irresistible charm or beauty? And what about good health—would that be among your choices?

Fortunately, over the past several decades, we have become increasingly aware of the value of good health and the importance of taking active steps to ensure it. Thus, we eat healthier foods, refrain from smoking, drink alcohol only in moderation, and engage in regular physical exercise. Psychologists, too, have become increasingly interested in the links between our thoughts, beliefs, emotions, and behaviours and the health of our bodies. To emphasize those links, one researcher has advocated an "Annual Psychological Checkup" for all Canadians (Evans, 1997).

In this chapter we'll begin with a relatively new branch of psychology known as **health psychology.** The goal of research in health psychology is to determine how health is related to psychological variables (Gatchel, Baum, & Krantz, 1989; Matarazzo, 1980). Then we'll turn to the nature of *stress,* a major health-related problem. We'll focus on the causes of stress, how it influences health and how it affects performance. Next, we'll consider *environmental stressors,* which may be natural or caused by human error. After that, we'll consider how *beliefs and attitudes* influence the way we think about our own health and our willingness to seek necessary medical assistance. We'll also examine behaviours that can directly affect our risk of contracting certain lifestyle-related illnesses, such as cancer, heart disease, and AIDS. Finally, we'll look at some psychologists at work promoting personal health by encouraging healthy lifestyles.

Health Psychology: An Overview

Health psychology is the branch of psychology that studies the relationship between psychological variables and health. Health psychologists assume that beliefs, attitudes, and behaviours contribute significantly to the prevention, onset, and course of illness.

Research in health psychology covers a wide range of *general* health problems (such as coronary heart disease), as well as *specific* health problems, such as low back pain (e.g., Chenard et al., 1991), dental anxiety (Liddell & Gosse, 1998), and maternal stress (Krech & Johnston, 1992). Canada is one of the few countries that have specific training programs in this special field of psychology. A closely related area, *behavioural medicine,* combines biomedical with behavioural science to learn how disease can be treated, and how it can be prevented.

In 1900, many of the leading causes of death could be traced to infectious diseases such as influenza, pneumonia, tuberculosis, and diphtheria. As shown in Figure 13.1, these days the leading causes of death are more attributable to **lifestyle**—that is, to the choices we make that determine health and quality of life (Lalonde, 1974). Currently, more than half of all premature deaths (i.e., those that

Health Psychology: The study of the relation between psychological variables and health; reflects the view that both mind and body are important determinants of health and illness.

Lifestyle: In the context of health psychology, the overall pattern of decisions and behaviours that determine health and quality of life.

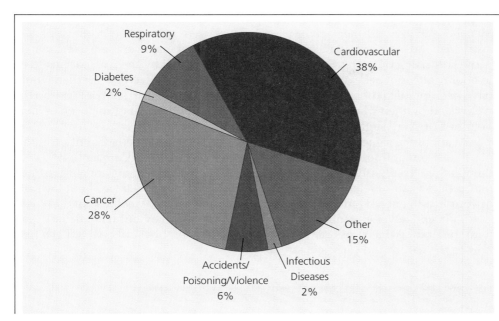

Figure 13.1
Leading Causes of Death in Canada

Here are the top causes of death in Canada for 1994.

Source: Laboratory Centre for Disease Control, 1996, using Statistics Canada data. From Leading Causes of Death: Percentage by Subgroup Canada, Health Canada, 1994. *© Minister of Public Works and Government Services Canada, 2000.*

occur before age sixty-five) result from unwise lifestyle choices (Burton, 1990). Thus, many people would live longer if they ate healthier foods, reduced their alcohol consumption, practised safe sex, quit smoking, and exercised regularly. Now, more than ever, health psychologists must strive to learn how people can eliminate behaviours that lead to illness, and adopt behaviours that keep them well.

How Psychologists Study Health-Related Behaviour

How do we learn about the ways in which knowledge, beliefs, and actions contribute to good health? Much of our basic understanding has emerged from **epidemiological studies**—large-scale efforts to identify the risk factors that predict the development of certain diseases (Winett, 1995). Why are epidemiological studies important? First, they are often huge in size and scope. In many epidemiological studies, researchers study thousands of people over long periods of time. These data help explain why certain groups are more at risk for acquiring some diseases than others. For example, epidemiological studies first alerted scientists that the groups most likely to become HIV-positive are those who engage in unprotected sex and intravenous drug use.

Second, epidemiological studies help us sort out the multiple causes of many illnesses. For example, the World Health Report confirmed that heart disease—the leading cause of death in many countries around the world—results from a combination of biological, behavioural, and environmental factors. Epidemiological studies can help identify these contributing conditions for us. Also, Statistics Canada data showing that twice as many men as women (between the ages of twenty and forty-four) take their own lives has forced us to do epidemiological studies into the causes of male suicide, with the goal of developing programs that will promote good health. Finally, and perhaps most importantly for students of psychology, the results of epidemiological studies have highlighted correlations between our attitudes and beliefs, and health-related behaviours.

Here are two examples to illustrate this point. In the 1970s, 3500 Manitoba seniors were involved in a seven-year study of the relation between health and many other variables (Mossey & Shapiro, 1982). Measures of their actual health included physicians' reports, hospitalizations, and so on. Measures of their beliefs about their own health were also taken. For example, they were asked to rate the state of

Epidemiological Studies:
Large-scale efforts to identify the risk factors that predict the development of certain diseases.

their own health as excellent, good, fair, poor, or bad. After seven years, it was clear that those who rated themselves as unhealthy were more likely to have passed away than those who rated themselves as healthy. That may seem sensible, but here is the surprising outcome. Some people who were rated by their physicians to be in poor health, but believed that they were in good health, lived longer than would have been predicted by the ratings of their physicians. Also, some of those who were rated by their physicians as in good health, but thought of themselves as in poor health, were slightly more likely to die.

At about the same time, a classic research project in Alameda County, California, had a similar finding (Kaplan & Camancho, 1983; Wiley & Camacho, 1980). Although these results are based on correlation and are therefore not conclusive, they may reflect a causal relationship between beliefs (what you believe about the state of your health), behaviours (how healthy your lifestyle is), and lifespan.

The rapid development of health psychology and behavioural medicine began with the finding that stress can have adverse effects on physical health. Let's turn now to the nature and causes of stress.

K E Y *QUESTIONS*

■ What is health psychology?

■ To what can we attribute today's leading causes of premature death?

■ What are epidemiological studies?

Stress: Its Causes, Effects, and Control

Have you ever felt that you were on the verge of being overwhelmed by events in your life or felt so overwhelmed that you just gave up? If so, you are already familiar with **stress**. Stress is natural and a fact of human life. It is a response to events that disrupt, or threaten to disrupt, our physical or psychological functioning (Lazarus & Folkman, 1984; Taylor, 1999). Indeed, in 1973, the University of Montreal's Hans Selye, a major contributor to our understanding of stress, argued that "complete freedom from stress is … incompatible with … life." Because it affects physical health and psychological well-being, stress has become an important topic of research in psychology.

Stress: Its Basic Nature

Stress is a physical and psychological response to life experiences that challenge or threaten us. These experiences (or **stressors**) vary widely—a raging forest fire is a stressor, and so is a vicious snowstorm; but so, also, is the death of a grandparent or separation from a friend. Stressful events need not be as catastrophic as these. Stress may occur when playing hockey or chess, when the telephone bill is beyond belief, when the line-up at the registrar's office is taking "just too long," when you transfer to a new university, or change your major subject. Stress also occurs when something you expected fails to happen (Wheaton, 1999). Of course there are some occupations in which stress goes with the territory—for example, police work and fire fighting (Corneil et al., 1999; Violanti & Paton, 1999).

Note also that the same stressor may affect the same person differently at different times. Moreover, there are individual differences in how people react to stress. Some will interpret a particular situation as stressful; others will simply take it in

Stress: The process that occurs in response to events that disrupt, or threaten to disrupt, our physical or psychological functioning.

Stressors: Events or situations in our environment that cause stress.

their stride. Stress may vary also with the pace of life in different countries. Faster pace of life, in Western Europe and Japan, for example, is linked to higher rate of death from heart disease and higher smoking rates (Levine & Norenayan, 1999).

STRESSORS: THE ACTIVATORS OF STRESS   Events that can produce stress share several characteristics: (1) they are so intense in some respect that they put us into a state of overload—we can no longer adapt to them; (2) they evoke incompatible tendencies in us, such as tendencies both to approach and to avoid some object or activity; and (3) they are uncontrollable—that is, beyond our limits of control. There is much evidence that when people can predict, control, or terminate an aversive event or situation, they perceive it to be less stressful than when they feel less in control (e.g., Rodin & Salovey, 1989). Although we normally think of stress as stemming from negative events in our lives, positive events such as graduating or receiving a job promotion can also produce stress (Brown & McGill, 1989).

PHYSIOLOGICAL RESPONSES TO STRESSORS   If you've ever been caught off-guard by a car that appears out of nowhere, you are probably familiar with some common physical reactions to stress. Initially, your blood pressure soars, your pulse races, and you may even begin to sweat. As you saw in Chapter 2, it is the sympathetic nervous system that prepares our bodies for "fight or flight"—for immediate action. Usually these responses are brief, and we soon return to normal levels. When we are exposed to stress chronically, however, there follows a longer sequence of responses caused by our efforts to adjust.

This sequence, which Selye called the **general adaptation syndrome,** has three stages. As shown in Figure 13.2, the earliest is the *alarm* stage, in which the body prepares itself for immediate action: arousal of the sympathetic nervous system releases hormones that help prepare our body to meet threats or dangers (Selye, 1976). If stress is prolonged, the *resistance* stage begins. During this second stage, arousal is lower, but our bodies continue to draw on internal resources at an above-normal rate in order to cope effectively. Continued exposure to the same stressor, or the appearance of additional stressors, drains the body of its resources and leads to the third stage, *exhaustion*. During this stage our capacity to resist is depleted, and our susceptibility to illness increases. In severe cases of prolonged physical stress, the result may be death.

> **General Adaptation Syndrome:** A three-phase model of how organisms respond to stress: (1) alarm or mobilization, (2) resistance, and (3) exhaustion.

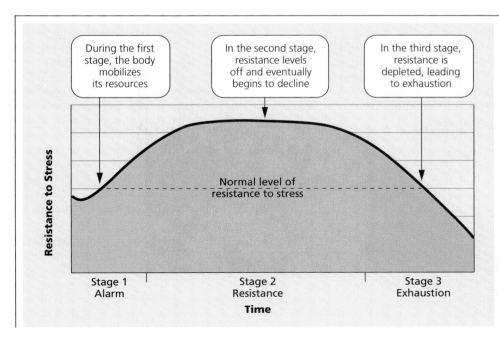

Figure 13.2
Selye's General Adaptation Syndrome

Stress is the body's physical and emotional response to painful events in the environment. Selye proposed that the body's reaction to prolonged stress progresses through three stages: alarm, resistance, and, finally, exhaustion.

During the first stage, the body mobilizes its resources

In the second stage, resistance levels off and eventually begins to decline

In the third stage, resistance is depleted, leading to exhaustion

Normal level of resistance to stress

Resistance to Stress

Stage 1
Alarm

Stage 2
Resistance

Stage 3
Exhaustion

Time

Hans Selye
(1907–1982)
University of Montreal

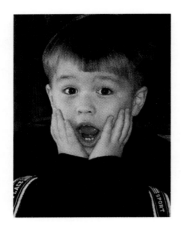

Physiological Reactions to Stressors

When we encounter stressors that frighten or surprise us, we experience a wave of physiological reactions, as illustrated in the photo above. These are part of a general pattern of reactions referred to as the fight-or-flight syndrome, a process controlled through the sympathetic nervous system.

The body's response to stress is widespread and complex. It involves structures in the central and the autonomic nervous systems, plus the endocrine and the immune systems. When faced with an emergency, for example, it is the sympathetic branch of the autonomic system—under the control of the hypothalamus—that quickly readies the body for action. There are increases in pupil size, heart rate, blood pressure, and in the blood supply directed to the muscles that move the limbs. To maintain the stress response and to provide energy to the body, the pituitary gland—under the direction of the hypothalamus—readies the various glands of the endocrine system. The two parts of the adrenal gland pump hormones (adrenalin and cortisol, for example) into the blood stream. The cerebral cortex provides our understanding of the environmental stimuli that produce stress and modulates our emotional response so that control is maintained in the face of threat or danger.

The immune system is the body's natural defense against disease caused by bacteria and viruses. Normally, the immune system is hugely powerful, producing B-cells, T-cells and natural killer cells that destroy foreign substances invading the body. Stress, however, reduces the ability of the immune system to function at its best. As a consequence, our resistance to infectious diseases decreases. Many different infectious diseases, such as herpes, AIDS, cancer, flu, and the common cold, worsen under stress. This may occur also as a result of academic stress—before exams, for example (Guidi et al., 1999).

COGNITIVE APPRAISAL OF OUR STRESSORS Selye's general adaptation syndrome provides a framework for understanding our physiological responses to stressful events and suggests at least one reasonable explanation for the relationship between stress and illness (Gottlieb, 1997). However, Selye's model did not originally recognize the impact of cognitive processes—the importance of which is made clear by this fact: When confronted with the same potentially stressful situation, some people experience stress, while others do not. That is because their cognitive appraisals differ (see Figure 13.3). In simple terms, stress occurs only to the extent that the individuals involved perceive the situation as threatening to them—*primary appraisal*—and believe they will be unable to cope with its dangers or demands—*secondary appraisal* (e.g., Chang, 1998; Lazarus & Folkman, 1984).

Figure 13.3
Stress: The Role of Cognitive Appraisals

The amount of stress you experience depends in part on your cognitive appraisal—the extent to which you perceive a situation as threatening and believe that you will be unable to cope.

Source: Based on data from Hingson et al., 1990.

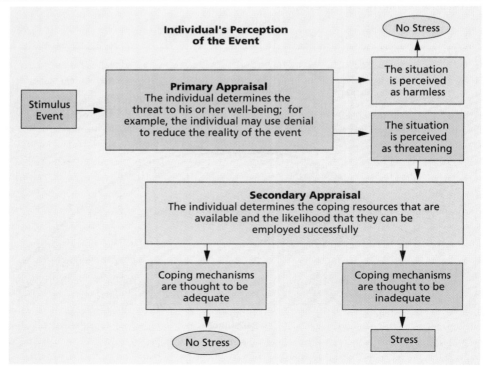

Here is an example to illustrate this point. Participants in one study were initially told that the researchers were interested in measuring their physiological responses (heart rate, pulse) while they performed a mental task: counting backward from the number 2737 by sevens (that is, 2730, 2723, 2716, and so on). Just before they began, the researchers assessed primary appraisals by asking, "How threatening do you expect the upcoming task to be?" They assessed secondary appraisals by asking, "How able are you to cope with this task?" The results were these: Although those who felt they could succeed actually had greater physiological arousal, they *reported less stress* and they scored higher (Tomaka et al., 1993).

The **Key Concept** illustration on page 520 provides an overview of both the physical and cognitive aspects of stress.

K E Y *QUESTIONS*

- What is stress?

- What is the General Adaptation Syndrome model?

- What determines whether an event will be interpreted as stressful or as a challenge?

Some Major Causes of Stress

Among the most common causes of stress are major life events (such as the death of a loved one or a painful divorce), hassles of everyday life, conditions and events relating to one's job or career, and certain aspects of the environment.

STRESSFUL LIFE EVENTS The death of a parent or a spouse, an injury to a child, war, failure in school or at work, an unplanned pregnancy, a provincial referendum in Quebec (Flett et al., 1999)—unless we lead truly charmed lives, most of us experience traumatic changes at some time or other. What are their effects on us? This question was first investigated by Holmes and Rahe (1967), who asked a large number of people to assign arbitrary points (between one and one hundred) to various life events according to how much readjustment each had required. They reasoned that the greater the number of points assigned to a given event, the more stressful it was for those experiencing it.

As you can see from Table 13.1, participants in this study assigned the greatest number of points to such serious events as the death of a spouse, divorce, or marital separation. In contrast, they assigned much smaller values to such events as a change in residence, a vacation, or a minor violation of the law (such as a parking ticket).

Holmes and Rahe then related the total number of points accumulated by individuals during a single year to changes in their personal health. The results were dramatic and did much to stir psychologists' interest in the effects of stress. The greater the number of "stress points" people accumulated, the greater was their likelihood of becoming seriously ill.

The picture is complicated by large differences in the ability to withstand the impact of stress. Some people suffer ill effects after exposure to a few mildly stressful events; others remain healthy even after prolonged exposure to high levels of stress. They are described as being stress-resistant or hardy, and they are better able to control any negative thoughts that may occur (Locker et al., 1999). In general, however, the greater the number of stressful life events experienced by an individual, the greater the likelihood that the person's subsequent health will be adversely affected (Rowlison & Felner, 1988).

▶

Key Concept   *Two Sides of Stress*

The Physical Side of Stress

Selye's *general adaptation syndrome* provides a model for understanding how stress affects us physically.

Stage One
During the *alarm stage,* the body prepares itself for immediate action (increased heart rate, blood pressure, and energy consumption).

Stage Two
During the *resistance stage,* the body draws on resources at an above-normal rate to cope with a prolonged stressor.

Stage Three
During the *exhaustion stage,* the body's capacity to cope with stress is depleted and susceptibility to illness increases dramatically.

After finishing a race, long-distance runners may find themselves in the exhaustion stage of Seyle's model: They have totally drained their body's capacity to cope with stress.

The Cognitive Side of Stress

The *cognitive-appraisal model* illustrates how our interpretations of potentially stressful events—such as the one depicted in the photo to the right—greatly affect our reactions to them.

Primary appraisal addresses the following question: How threatening is a potentially stressful event?

Event not perceived as threatening—no stress.

Event perceived as threatening—leads to a secondary appraisal of the situation.

Secondary appraisal addresses the following question: Given that an event is viewed as a threat, do we have the resources to cope with it effectively?

If the answer is yes, stress will not be experienced.

If the answer is no, stress will be experienced.

If we interpret an event, such as news conveyed in a letter, as threatening, it will tend to be more stressful than if we interpret the same event as non-threatening.

TABLE 13.1

Life Events, Stress, and Personal Health

When individuals experience stressful life events, such as those near the top of this list, their health often suffers. The greater the number of points for each event, the more stressful it is perceived as being.

Life Event	Life Change Unit Value	Life Event	Life Change Unit Value
Death of spouse	100	Taking out mortgage for a major purchase (e.g., a home)	31
Divorce	73	Change in responsibilities at work	29
Marital separation	65	Son or daughter leaving home	29
Jail term	63	Trouble with in-laws	29
Death of close family member	63	Outstanding personal achievement	28
Personal injury or illness	53	Spouse beginning or stopping work	26
Marriage	50	Beginning or ending school	26
Getting fired at work	47	Change in living conditions	25
Marital reconciliation	45	Revision of personal habits	24
Retirement	45	Trouble with boss	23
Change in health of family member	44	Change in work hours or conditions	20
Pregnancy	40	Change in residence	20
Sex difficulties	39	Change in schools	20
Gain of new family member	39	Taking out a loan for a lesser purchase	17
Business readjustment	39	Change in sleeping habits	15
Change in financial state	38	Vacation	13
Death of close friend	37	Minor violation of the law	11
Change to different line of work	36		
Change in number of arguments with spouse	35		

Source: Based on data from Holmes and Masuda, 1974.

▶ This picture is complicated yet further, however, by the finding that while some positive changes in life—such as graduation and retirement—cause anxiety and stress, some negative changes—like death or divorce—may actually bring *relief from stress*, if the stress that preceded the crisis was high (Wheaton, 1990).

THE HASSLES OF DAILY LIFE Certain catastrophic events are clearly stressful but—fortunately—occur fairly infrequently. Does this mean that people's lives are generally calm? Hardly. As you know, daily life is filled with countless minor sources of stress that seem to make up for their relatively low intensity by their much higher frequency. That is true for every age group, including young adolescents (Dumont & Provost, 1999) and elderly adults (Bodenstein, 1998).

Daily Hassles as a Source of Stress

Many everyday hassles are stressful. Would you experience stress in the situation shown here?

A Hassles Scale has been developed to measure the extent to which people have been "hassled" by common events during the past month (e.g., Kanner et al., 1981; Lazarus et al., 1985). The individual items on this scale deal with a wide range of everyday events, such as having too many things to do at once, dealing with delays, and owing money. Not on this list, but relevant to many new immigrants to Canada, are daily hassles that produce stress for newcomers to this country (e.g., Lay & Nguyen, 1998).

A special paper-and-pencil scale, the Inventory of College Students' Recent Life Experiences, has been developed and tested by Kohn and colleagues at York University (Kohn & Macdonald, 1992). "Hassles" may seem relatively minor when compared with the major life experiences listed in Table 13.1, and they may not be as profoundly depressing (Clark & Oates, 1995), but they are very significant sources of stress. For example, daily stress predicts later health problems—including headaches, backaches, sore throats, and flu as well as negative moods for some patients (DeLongis et al., 1988). Findings like this suggest that the more minor hassles of everyday life (perhaps because of their frequent, repetitive nature) may be as problematic as the major ones.

A special Computer Hassles Scale has been used to study the stress of people interacting with computers. Remarkably, research using this scale has found that subjects with college degrees suffer more computer user's stress than those without degrees. As you might expect, however, there is a decrease in the severity of the anxiety and stress that computer users suffer as their knowledge about computers increases. Students who reported high computer-stress need to cope not only with the challenges of the computer but their own emotional responses as well (Hudiburg et al.,1995, 1996).

As students are well aware, money can also be a daily hassle and an important source of stress. When you ask people what causes them to worry, financial considerations are high on the list. However, worries about money and stress are not related, in any simple manner, to the amount of money you have or earn. Rich folks are not more immune to stress than poor ones. For example, a Canadian survey showed that people with annual incomes over $100 000 were most likely (almost seven out of ten) to report frequent stress. This is probably the opposite of what most of us would expect.

Are major life stresses and daily hassles linked? That was the question asked in a recent study (Pillow, Zautra, & Sandler, 1996). These researchers selected people who had recently experienced a major life event (such as the death of a spouse, a divorce, or a serious health problem with a child). They interviewed each participant to determine the number and type of minor stressors they had experienced after the traumatic event.

Here is one of their findings. Each type of life event was associated with a consistent pattern of hassles—for example, divorced participants seemed to experience stress over finances, transportation, personal relationships, and work. In contrast, participants who had recently lost their spouse were more likely to report stress-related health problems. However, at York University, Flett and his coworkers (Flett et al., 1995) discovered that students who had suffered major life stresses were more likely to seek emotional and practical support from others when they were faced with daily hassles.

ENVIRONMENTAL SOURCES OF STRESS In Canada, as in countries all around the world, there have been large-scale *natural disasters*. Perhaps you have lived through a killer blizzard like the one that hit Southern Ontario in January of 1999, which required the Canadian Forces to assist in cases of emergency and in cleaning the streets of Toronto. Perhaps you experienced the terrifying ice storms of winter 1998, or summer storms like those in July 1996 in Lac-St-Jean Saguenay, Winnipeg, and Calgary, which cost human lives and hundreds of millions of dollars in damage. These events cause people stress (Dohrenwend, 1998).

Also in Canada, we also have had our own *human-produced disasters*, the worst of which was the Halifax Explosion of 1917, which took 1600 lives. More recently, there were the 229 deaths that occurred when Swissair 111 disappeared into the North Atlantic in September 1998. We have also produced some large-scale financial disasters—including the closures of the Eaton's stores, and the alleged Bre-X mining scam. In some respects, the psychological trauma that results from human-produced disasters can be more dramatic and longer lasting than those associated with natural disasters (Baum & Fleming, 1993). Why is that so?

One important reason is *perceived loss of control*. If a natural disaster strikes—a hurricane, earthquake, or tornado—we do not expect to have control, although there are obviously precautions that we can take, and sometimes do not (Lehman & Taylor, 1987). However, when a disaster occurs as a result of human actions—for example, in cases of violence against our person (e.g., sexual assault) (Moscarello, 1991), when we breathe in office fumes (Schmidt & Gifford, 1989) or machinery exhaust (Schell et al., 1992), or when our assumptions about our personal safety are violated—we have the impression that our lives are out of control. The Y2K near-miss was one of those circumstances.

Commonly reported psychological problems that result from natural and human-produced stress include nightmares and flashbacks, distress when reminded of the event, irritability, and a general unresponsiveness (Lindy, Green, & Grace, 1987). When severe, these symptoms are often referred to as **post-traumatic stress disorder.** Those suffering from this disorder experience the trauma they have survived over and over again, in their thoughts and in their dreams. They avoid people or places connected with the traumatic event, and they have a variety of chronic difficulties, such as difficulty concentrating and falling asleep.

Post-traumatic stress disorder can stem from a wide range of traumatic events—natural disasters, accidents, assaults such as rape, or the horrors of war. In one study (Beal, 1995), Canadian veterans of World War II who were prisoners of war were compared with veterans who had the same combat exposure but did not become prisoners of war. Post-traumatic stress disorder was more prevalent and more serious for the prisoners of war, and that difference was still evident fifty years later. In some cases, the onset may be delayed for thirty years afterwards (Herrmand & Eryavec, 1994).

Canadian peacekeepers also serve in stressful situations. For example, in the former Yugoslavia, they experienced events such as a mock execution by drunken soldiers and witnessed the explosion of a mortar round among children (Carbonneau, 1994). You will learn more about this topic in the **Canadian Focus** section.

Post-Traumatic Stress Disorder: Psychological disorder resulting from a very stressful experience; includes nightmares and flashbacks, distress at exposure to reminders of the event, irritability, difficulty concentrating, and a general unresponsiveness.

Canadian Focus

Peacekeeping Post-Traumatic Stress Disorder

In 1956, Lester Pearson (the prime minister of Canada from 1963 to 1968) suggested that the United Nations send international forces to the Middle East, under the UN flag. His idea was to place neutral military personnel between warring parties in order to ensure that an agreement to "cease fire" continued uninterrupted. There was to be the minimum use of force. The peacekeepers deployed to the "hot spots" of the world were intended to be UN "observers." Pearson's work was a major contribution to the maintenance of world peace, and he was awarded the Nobel Peace Prize in 1957. Since then, Canadians have participated in every UN peacekeeping initiative—in at least thirty-five different countries. In recognition of their work, the Canadian Forces were awarded the Nobel Peace Prize in 1992. It seems as if this approach to conflict has become the Canadian way, and even the political attitudes of Canadian preteens emphasize peacekeeping (Covell, 1996).

From the observer role that was originally proposed, however, UN peacekeepers have graduated to more and more active involvement (Langholtz, 1998). The responsibilities now

Source: The Lester B. Pearson Canadian International Peacekeeping Training Centre (PPC). The Centre, established by the Government of Canada in 1994, is funded, in part, by the Department of Foreign Affairs and International Trade, and by the Department of National Defence.

are to settle disputes by peaceful means, manage conflict, promote cooperation, and reconstruct destroyed societies. More specific duties include distributing relief supplies, ensuring human rights, returning refugees to their homes, disarming warring parties, and organizing elections. Peacekeeping in the twenty-first century is more formalized—an international army, composed of contingents from many countries, with multinational leadership (Gurstein, 1999).

Peacekeeping has been called "the most severe and disabling variation of occupational stress known" (Everly & Mitchell, 1992). Some of the sources of peacekeeping stress were identified by Cheryl Lamerson and Kevin Kelloway (1996) of the University of Guelph. First, there are the stressors associated with *combat* itself: the real threat of attack, injury, and death; the deaths of others; and the task of handling dead bodies. Second, there are the stressors associated with the nature of the *work*—the need to be able to do many different things under the pressure of very little time. Third, there are the contradictions and ambiguities of the *role* played by peacekeepers: the need to defend the rights of people who are against you and the need to provide assistance in dangerous circumstances where there is also the need to preserve your own life (Britt, 1998). Fourth, there are *personal stresses*: separation from family, inability to deal with family matters from long distance, and difficulty managing family finances from away. Finally, there is *"UN role stress,"* which arises when peacekeepers find themselves disagreeing with the policy of neutrality and personally judging one side of the conflict to be in the right. These causes have been summarized as "isolation, ambiguity, powerlessness, boredom, and danger/threat" (Barton et al., 1998).

What are the symptoms of peacekeeping post-traumatic stress disorder? Common difficulties are headaches , sleep disturbances, negative mood, and depression. Peacekeepers may be hostile and have difficulty managing anger. Their anxiety and arousal levels are elevated and they are overly vigilant—on guard. They may medicate themselves to excess with nicotine, alcohol, and other drugs. Peacekeepers may feel that they are not in control of their lives. They may have marital and parenting difficulties and job dissatisfaction. Their performance on the job may worsen, particularly with respect to making good decisions. A very troubling symptom is *intrusion,* which refers to the reliving of the traumatic events—terrible memories that intrude into awareness repeatedly during waking hours and in dreams. They may suffer from a special survivor guilt that is experienced by those who live through a traumatic event that has taken the lives of others, or guilt, for example, about being unable to save the Somali children who were starving (Erlick et al., 1997).

Studies have been conducted of Swedish personnel in Lebanon and Cyprus (Lundin, 1992) and U.S., Australian, and New Zealand peacekeepers in Somalia (Ward, 1997; Orsillo et al., 1998). Figure 13.4 shows the psychological impact on New Zealand Defense Force Peacekeepers in Somalia (MacDonald et al., 1998). Each bar represents a different psychological measure: well-being, distress, anxiety, and depression across the stages of deployment.

What can be done? Here are some of Lamerson and Kelloway's suggestions for preventing peacekeeping post-traumatic stress disorder. First, there are *selection* criteria. These should limit participation in peacekeeping as much as possible to those who do not have serious pre-existing stressors in their family or financial circumstances. Second, there are suggestions that focus on the kind of *preparation* required prior to taking up the mission. These include clear understanding of the peacekeeping mission and the objectives and responsibilities. Preparation includes "stress-inoculation"— instruction about how to recognize anticipated stressors in advance and how to handle the pressure associated with them (Rosebush, 1998). Third, management should provide direct and clear *communication* at all times and debriefings after crises have occurred.

Other investigators suggest that research should be designed to identify the characteristics of combat-trained soldiers who are particularly at risk for peacekeeper stress (Litz et al., 1997). Others emphasize the importance of military pride and unit cohesion (Bartone & Adler, 1999) and that continued psychological research on peacekeeping stress, particularly its *prevention*, is essential and urgent (Allodi, 1994). In the twenty-first century, Canada's contribution to this research will continue—at international peacekeeping training centres for the study of theory and practice in peacekeeping— like the one already established in Cornwallis, Nova Scotia.

Figure 13.4
The Psychological Impact of Peacekeeping

These results illustrate stress among New Zealand peacekeepers serving in Somalia.

Source: From "Mental Health, Physical Health, and Stressors Reported by New Zealand Defence Force Peacekeepers: A Longitudinal Study," by C. MacDonald et al., 1998, Military Medicine: International Journal of AMSUS, 163, p. 479. *Reprinted with permission.*

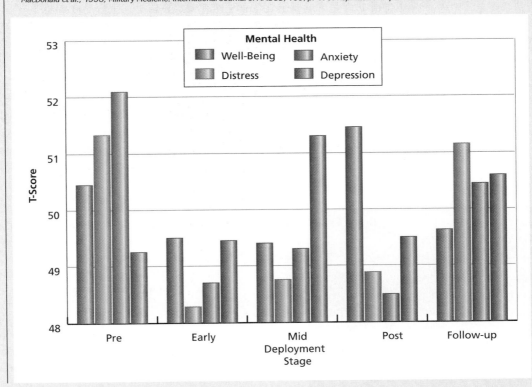

Figure 13.5
Sources of Work-Related Stress

Many factors contribute to stress at work. Several of the most important are summarized here.

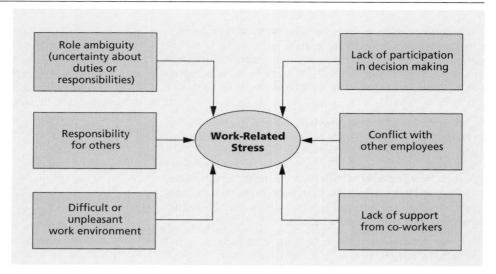

WORK-RELATED STRESS Most adults spend more time at work than almost anywhere else. Some work-related stress factors are obvious—for example, discrimination, harassment, or overload. Too much to do in too short a time is stressful, but so is too little. Work underload produces intense feelings of boredom, which can be very stressful. Role conflict for those in management positions arises when people face conflicting demands or expectations from different groups. Subordinates often expect improved work assignments, pay, and conditions, while supervisors expect the opposite—that employees will work harder for fewer rewards. These and additional factors are summarized in Figure 13.5. Examine them carefully, for you are certain to encounter several in your own career and recognizing sources of stress is a giant step toward dealing with stress successfully. Take note, however, that stress at work and stress at home do not come in separate packages, but stress "spills over" from one domain to another (Leiter & Durup, 1996).

Figure 13.6
On-Screen Instructions for User-Hostile Condition

ATM users find this kind of screen unfriendly.

Source: Reprinted from Muter, Furedy, Vincent, and Pelcowitz (1993). User hostile systems and patterns of psychological activity. Computers in Human Behaviour, *9, 105–111. Reprinted with permission.*

YOUR CHEQUING ACCOUNT IS NUMBER 1. YOUR SAVINGS ACCOUNT IS NUMBER 2, AND YOUR CREDIT CARD ACCOUNT IS NUMBER 3. THE KEYWORD FOR WITHDRAW IS 'With'. (CASE IS IMPORTANT.) THE KEYWORD FOR DEPOSIT IS 'Dpos'. THE KEYWORD FOR TRANSFER IS 'Trfr'. THE KEYWORD FOR ACCOUNT BALANCE IS 'Bala'. TO ERASE, SIMULTANEOUSLY PRESS THE CLOVER-LEAF KEY AND 'H'. TO MAKE A TRANSACTION, ENTER TRANSACTION TYPE, FOLLOWED BY ACCOUNT TYPE, FOLLOWED BY AMOUNT OF MONEY (IF RELEVANT), INCLUDING DECIMAL POINT AND CENTS. TO TRANSFER, SPECIFY TWO ACCOUNTS, FIRST THE FROM ACCOUNT AND THEN THE TO ACCOUNT. THUS THERE ARE 2,3, OR 4 FIELDS. TO DENOTE THE END OF A FIELD, TYPE A COLON. IMPORTANT: IT MAY BE NECESSARY TO UNPACK BYTES.

Stress is a problem in almost any workplace where computers are used heavily. To study stress and user-friendliness, University of Toronto researchers gathered twenty-five volunteers from an introductory psychology class (Muter et al., 1993). All of the students had used a personal computer: a PC or a Macintosh. These students were given four tasks to perform for six minutes each. Two of the tasks involved recalling series of numbers that were easy or difficult to remember.

For the other two assignments, participants used a computer, as if it were a bank machine, to type in a set of transactions. In this case, the "user-friendly" computer program worked like an ATM machine but even more simply. The "user-hostile" program presented a screen that looked the one in Figure 13.6. The instructions were difficult to read, there was no menu to follow, and time limits were imposed. There was no positive feedback when the student performed correctly, but when an error was made, the computer buzzed loudly and flashed "Fatal Error" or "Too Slow."

The investigators took readings of the heart rate and the spontaneous conductance of the skin in order to measure the psychophysiological responses of the subjects' bodies during these tasks. You can see the results in Figure 13.7. These results were taken to mean that user-hostile systems "... produce the increased sympathetic excitation that typically accompanies human fight-or-flight responses." The interactions between humans and computers may affect the most fundamental biopsychology of the computer user, and information provided by psychological research can contribute much to our general well-being at work.

For still more information about computers and stress, see **Making Psychology Part of Your Life** on page 551.

The cost of ignoring stress in the workplace is staggering—for example, in the United Kingdom, estimates are that 30 million working days a year are lost to stress. Can anything be done to reduce the effects of stress in the workplace? The answer appears to be yes. Workplace stress can be minimized by hiring workers with characteristics that closely match the demands of the job, thus achieving a **person–environment (P–E) fit**. When there is a "misfit" between the strengths of the employee and the demands of the job, negative outcomes may follow, including psychological disturbances, job dissatisfaction, and increases in stress and stress-related illnesses (Harrison, 1985).

When it is not practical or possible to arrange a perfect fit for all employees, *social support,* both on and off the job, can serve as a buffer against stressful events that occur (Frese, 1999; Uchino et al., 1996). Also, companies may monitor the work environment and change unhealthy practices, as well as introduce programs that improve their employees' ability to cope with workplace stress (Maturi, 1992). For example, for over twenty years, the University of Ottawa has been assessing the fitness of over 5000 federal public servants. This program involves taking resting and exercise heart rate, blood pressure, upper body strength and muscular endurance, body function, and blood tests. The results of the tests are reported to each participant, and during those sessions, efforts are made to raise awareness of stress and to influence attitudes and identify healthier behaviours.

Person–Environment (P–E) Fit: The appropriateness of the match between a person and his or her work environment; a poor P–E fit may produce stress.

Figure 13.7
Stress and Computers

Clearly, in the study, the user-hostile computer program had the greatest effect on skin conductance. Memory tasks had less effect on heart rate than either computer task.

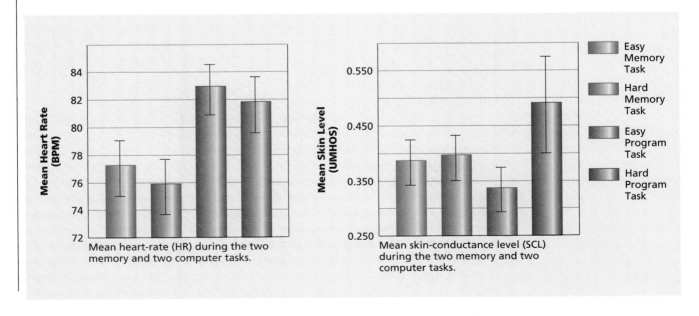

Mean heart-rate (HR) during the two memory and two computer tasks.

Mean skin-conductance level (SCL) during the two memory and two computer tasks.

Do these programs work? In a study by Gregg (1990), 7800 employees in four large manufacturing plants were assessed for health risks—high blood pressure, obesity, and smoking. Then they were each assigned to one of three groups, each of which had different amounts of follow-up contact with wellness counsellors over the next three years. Then their health risks were re-assessed. The more follow-up the workers received, the greater the reduction in their risk for serious health problems. As psychologists continue to refine their techniques, they will no doubt discover additional ways to help workers cope more effectively with the stressors they encounter at work.

K E Y *QUESTIONS*

- What are stressors?
- What are some sources of work-related stress?
- What is the person–environment fit and why is it important?

Some Major Effects of Stress

By now you understand that stress stems from many different sources and exerts profound effects on those who experience it. What is sometimes difficult to grasp, however, is just how far-reaching these effects can be.

STRESS AND HEALTH: THE SILENT KILLER   According to medical experts, the link between stress and personal health is very strong indeed (Kiecolt-Glaser & Glaser, 1992). In fact, some authorities estimate that stress plays some role in 50 to 70 percent of all physical illness (Frese, 1985). Included in these percentages are some of the most serious and life-threatening ailments known to medical science: heart disease, high blood pressure, hardening of the arteries, ulcers, and even diabetes.

How does stress produce such effects? The general idea is that by draining our resources and keeping us off balance physiologically, stress upsets the complex internal chemistry of our bodies. In particular, stress interferes with the efficient operation of the immune system—the elaborate internal mechanism through which our bodies recognize and destroy intruders, such as bacteria, viruses, cancerous cells, and other potentially harmful substances (Maier & Watkins, 1999).

When functioning normally, the immune system is nothing short of amazing: Each day it removes or destroys many potential threats to our health and well-being. However, prolonged exposure to stress disrupts this system. A variety of stressors, including disruptions in interpersonal relations, family discord, loneliness, academic pressure, daily hassles, and the lack of social support, can interfere with our immune systems (Cohen et al., 1992; Miller et al., 1999).

Here is more about how that happens. Foreign substances that enter our bodies are known as *antigens*. When they enter, some white blood cells, known as *lymphocytes,* begin to multiply. They then attack the antigens, often destroying them by engulfing them. Other white blood cells produce *antibodies,* chemical substances that combine with antigens and neutralize them. How does stress interact with these events in the immune system of the body? In their research, Cohen and his colleagues (1992) investigated the immune systems of monkeys. First, the animals were randomly assigned to stable or unstable social conditions for a twenty-six-month period. Some monkeys remained with the same group for the entire study period; others were frequently reassigned to different social circles. The researchers observed and assessed the amount of time each monkey spent in various forms of social interaction, including affiliative behaviours such as grooming and passive physical contact. The results showed that the stable social support in the first group was a stress buffer for the immune system of those animals.

That conclusion is relevant to people as well. The immune systems of divorced or recently separated individuals were compared with those of happily married couples. This study found that poorer immune function was associated with marriage disruption (Kiecolt-Glaser et al., 1987, 1988). Also, people who lack effective ways of dealing with stress management may be more at risk. Optimism, regular exercise, and feelings of control are all beneficial in this regard (Taylor, 1999). These findings are both unsettling and encouraging. They suggest that a complex, high-stress lifestyle has a serious cost in that it undermines the ability to resist many serious illnesses, but they also show that reductions in stress may be of major benefit to a person's overall health (Ollf, 1999).

STRESS AND TASK PERFORMANCE Psychologists once believed that some stress actually improved performance on a wide range of tasks. They theorized that as stress increased, performance improved, presumably because it aroused and energized the individual, until the level of stress reached the point where it was distracting, and performance actually deteriorated. That *was* the theory, but not any more. We now know that even low or moderate levels of stress may interfere with performance (Motowidlo, Packard, & Manning, 1986; Steers, 1984).

There are several ways in which that might happen. First, people experiencing stress may focus on their unpleasant feelings and emotions rather than on the task at hand. Second, prolonged or repeated stress may harm health, and this may interfere with effective performance. Finally, how well we do under stress depends greatly on the complexity of the task: the more complex it is, the more stress interferes with performance (Berlyne, 1967). Therefore, in today's exceedingly complex workplace, even relatively low levels of stress may interfere with performance (Mitchell & Larson, 1987).

However, people sometimes turn in extraordinary performances at times when stress is most intense. Perhaps the most reasonable conclusion, then, is that while stress can interfere with task performance in many situations, its precise effects depend on many different factors, such as the complexity of the task being performed and personal characteristics of the individuals involved, about which you will read below. As a result, generalizations about the impact of stress on work effectiveness should be made with considerable caution.

INDIVIDUAL DIFFERENCES IN COPING WITH STRESS: OPTIMISM AND PESSIMISM While some people suffer ill effects from even mild levels of stress, others are resilient and continue to thrive and to function effectively even in the face of intense, ongoing stress. They are called *self-healers* (Friedman et al., 1994). How are these people different?

One answer involves the dimension of optimism–pessimism. Optimists are people who see the glass as half full; pessimists are those who see it as half empty. Some evidence indicates that optimists—people who have general expectancies for good outcomes (Scheier & Carver, 1988)—are much more stress-resistant than pessimists—people who have general expectancies for poor outcomes. For example, optimists are much less likely to report physical illnesses and symptoms during highly stressful periods, such as final exams.

This resistance may be linked to their immune systems. For example, in one recent study, researchers examined the effects of optimism on mood and immune system responses among law students in their first semester of study (Segerstrom et al., 1998). The results showed that optimism was associated with better mood, higher numbers of helper T-cells—involved in immune reactions to infections, and higher natural killer cell activity—important in fighting viral infection and some types of cancers.

Additional evidence helps explain why this might be the case. Briefly, optimists and pessimists adopt different tactics for coping with stress (Scheier & Carver, 1992). Optimists use problem-focused coping: making and carrying out specific plans for dealing with sources of stress. They also remain flexible and seek out social support—the advice and help of others. In contrast, pessimists adopt different strategies, such as giving up the goal or denying the stress (Carver et al., 1993). Table 13.2 presents a summary of the different strategies adopted by optimists and pessimists.

TABLE 13.2	

Optimists and Pessimists: Contrasting Strategies for Coping with Stress

Optimists and pessimists employ different strategies in coping with stress. The strategies used by optimists seem to be more effective than those used by pessimists.

Strategies Preferred by Optimists	Description
Problem-focused coping	Making specific plans for dealing with the source of stress; implementing such plans
Suppressing competing activities	Refraining from other activities until the problem is solved and stress is reduced
Seeking social support	Obtaining the advice of others; talking the problem over with others

Strategies Preferred by Pessimists	Description
Denial/distancing	Ignoring the problem or source of stress; refusing to believe that it exists or is important
Disengagement from the goal	Giving up on reaching the goal that is being blocked by stress
Focusing on the expression of feelings	Letting off steam instead of working on the problem directly

However, some kinds of optimism decrease healthy behaviour. Davidson and Prkachin (1997) found that students who were both hopeful (optimistic) and denied the risk of later health problems (unrealistic) were less likely to exercise and less knowledgeable about coronary heart disease after they attended a session on the prevention of heart trouble. This finding may help explain why not all optimists are stress resistant. How they differ is a matter for future research.

Note also that there are individual differences in sense of humour—the better sense of humour, the less the stress (Lefcourt et al., 1997; Kuiper et al., 1998a). This has been found in a variety of groups of people—students taking examinations, for example, and even patients with clinical depression (Kuiper et al., 1998b). Thus, individual differences in the way we think is an important determinant of the response we make to the stressors in our environment.

INDIVIDUAL DIFFERENCES IN COPING WITH STRESS: GENDER, CULTURE, AND ATTACHMENT Some evidence indicates that men and women, too, differ in their choices of coping strategies. Studies have reported that men engage in more problem-focused coping and that females tend more to seek social support from friends or to engage in emotion-focused strategies. These findings have been attributed to the different ways men and women are taught to cope with stress. A recent study by Porter and Stone (1995), however, seems to cast doubt on these conclusions. Their results indicate instead that men and women differ very little in the amount of stress they report or in the strategies they use to cope with the stress. They do differ, however, in the content of their respective problems—men are more likely to report work-related problems, whereas women tend to report problems relevant to themselves, parenting, and interactions with others.

People from different cultures may also differ in the ways they handle stress. In one recent study, Chang (1996) examined whether Asian students and students of European descent differed in terms of optimism, pessimism, and their preferences for coping strategies. The results indicated that the Asian students were more pessimistic and tended to use more problem avoidance and social withdrawal as coping strategies.

Adult attachment style influences the way in which individuals cope with stress as well. That was the finding of research by DiTomasso (1998), who studied coping with chronic loneliness of female partners of members of the Canadian Forces base in Gagetown, New Brunswick. The results showed that those women who had a more secure attachment style had a more positive view of themselves and intimacy, and were trusting and confident about other people. They used more active coping by trying to solve their problems and seeking help from other people. Other women spent their time over-sleeping, over-eating, drinking, and denying the situation—leading to higher stress from chronic loneliness.

These and other findings indicate that individuals differ greatly in terms of their ability to deal with stress. Understanding the reasons for such differences can be of considerable practical value in promoting a healthy lifestyle.

BURNOUT: WHEN STRESS CONSUMES Most work involves at least some stress. Yet somehow the people performing them manage to cope and they continue to function despite their daily encounters with various stressors. Some individuals, however, are not so lucky. Over time, they are ground down by repeated encounters with stress and they burn out. Burnout occurs in many fields of endeavour, including athletes and coaches (e.g., Kallus & Kellmann, 2000), teachers (Greenglass et al., 1998), and nurses (Leiter et al., 1998)

What are the signs of this effect of repeated stress? First, victims of burnout often suffer from exhaustion, both physical and emotional. They have low energy and feel tired all the time. In addition, they report frequent headaches, nausea, poor sleep, and changes in eating habits. Emotional exhaustion, depression, feelings of hopelessness, and feelings of being trapped in one's job are all part of this, and the result is an inability to maintain relationships with other people. Second, burnout victims become depersonalized. They are cynical and negative and care nothing about the people with whom (and for whom) they work. Third, burnout victims denigrate themselves. They lose all sense of accomplishment (Maslach & Jackson, 1984)—they are convinced that they have not been able to accomplish much in the past and probably will fail in the future, too.

Burnout is by no means limited to high-powered executives in the express lane. For example, several hundred employees of a telecommunications corporation in Atlantic Canada were studied by researchers at St. Mary's University. Each subject completed a burnout inventory and provided several other kinds of information. The men in this study were more likely to experience emotional exhaustion if they were managers, while the women who were most prone to this were non-managers. With respect to the psychological environment at work, women placed more importance on their relationships with others, while control was more important to men (Pretty, McCarthy, & Catano, 1992).

What are the causes of burnout? The first is prolonged exposure to stress, but other factors play a role too, as shown in Figure 13.8. The perception that our efforts are useless, ineffective, or unappreciated contributes much to burnout. Obstacles to promotion, inflexible rules, and feelings of lesser personal accomplishment lead individuals to feel that they are trapped in an unfair system. As a result, they may develop a negative view of their work. Perfectionism is also a factor that has been identified as a cause of burnout (e.g., Flett et al., 1998; Fry, 1995). Personal factors can also play a role: People with satisfying lives outside the work setting—for example, those who have stable relationships—are less likely to experience burnout. A sense of humour also helps.

Figure 13.8
Burnout: An Overview

Individuals exposed to high levels of work-related stress over long periods of time may suffer from *burnout*. This state involves *physical, emotional,* and *mental* (or *attitudinal*) exhaustion, as well as low estimates of personal accomplishment.

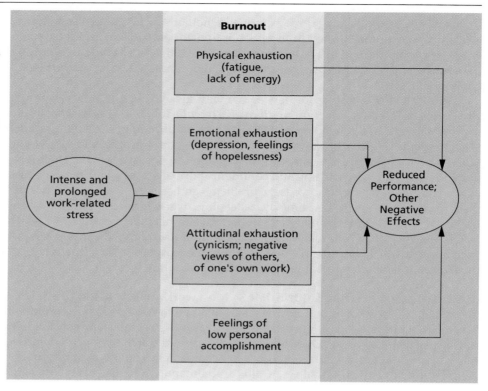

Whatever its precise causes, once burnout develops, many victims change jobs or withdraw psychologically, marking time until retirement. Fortunately, recovery from the physical and psychological exhaustion of burnout is possible. If ongoing stress is reduced, if individuals gain added social support from friends and co-workers (Greenglass et al., 1997, 1996), and if they cultivate hobbies and other outside interests, some regain positive attitudes and return to their original high levels of productivity.

KEY *QUESTIONS*

■ Does stress play a role in physical illness?

■ What are the effects of exposure to low levels of stress? High levels?

■ What is burnout? What are the causes?

■ Why are some people better able to cope with the effects of stress?

Critical Thinking
Research indicates that access to strong sources of social support can be beneficial. Why do you think this factor reduces the effects of stress?

Understanding Our Health Needs

There is no doubt that modern medicine has provided us with the means to alleviate many diseases and illnesses that were considered incurable until this century. Yet that does not ensure that we will seek proper treatment when we need it, or that we possess the knowledge necessary to realize when help is required. Moreover, because of the beliefs and attitudes we often hold, health professionals fail to convince us to comply with good, healthy advice. Consider the following example.

In an Australian study, people were asked to identify the lifestyle or behaviour patterns responsible for health problems in their country (Hetzel & McMichael, 1987). The most frequently cited examples were alcohol and drug abuse, poor diet, lack of exercise, and smoking—a clear indication that respondents were aware of the health risks associated with these behaviours. Similarly, when asked to name the changes that would most likely improve their own future health, the respondents cited better diet, more exercise, stopping or reducing smoking, reducing alcohol consumption, and coping better with their worries—again proof that they knew what they were supposed to do to improve their health. Yet when they were asked why they did not behave in ways that would be better for their own health, their answers included "laziness," "lack of time," "not worthwhile," "too difficult or expensive," or "lack of social support." An important and difficult challenge for health psychologists, then, is to discover ways to promote healthier lifestyles to people who do not practise what they know to be best for them.

Health Beliefs

Early recognition of symptoms is very important to the potential for recovery. For example, the first hour after symptoms of heart attack begin is crucial in this respect, yet most people wait from two to six and a half hours before they seek help (Dracup et al., 1995). How do we decide that a symptom is severe enough to require medical attention? When do we actually go to a doctor, clinic, or emergency room? Surprisingly, some people do not seek help even when they know that something is seriously wrong (Pennebaker, 2000). In general, that is particularly true for some men. Why is that so? One study identified three reasons: Men get health support from their partners, they use denial to reduce fear, and they believe that seeking help is not macho (Tudiver & Talbot, 1999).

The **health-belief model** was initially developed to explain specifically why people do not use medical screening services. As shown in Figure 13.9, our willingness to seek medical help depends on two factors: the extent to which we perceive a threat to our health and the extent to which we believe a particular action will effectively reduce that threat (Rosenstock, 1974; Strecher et al., 1997).

The health-belief model helps explain why people who have never experienced a serious illness or injury often fail to engage in actions that would prevent illness or injury, such as stopping smoking (Ayanian & Cleary, 1999), using sunscreen outdoors, or using a condom during sexual intercourse (Hollar & Snizek, 1996), and why some people have motorcycle accidents that could have been prevented (Rutter et al., 1995), fail to exercise in order to prevent their bones from softening (Taggart & Connor, 1995), or fail to take the steps necessary to keep their contact lenses sterile (Trick, 1993). In part, they fail to engage in such preventive actions because they believe that the likelihood of illness (or injury) to themselves is low—so why bother?

For example, we may decide to stop smoking if we value our health, if we feel that our smoking might lead to fatal lung cancer, and if we do not like what we hear about death from lung cancer. However, whether a smoker concerned about developing cancer will actually quit depends on two beliefs: that giving up smoking will reduce the risk of cancer and that the benefits in doing so will outweigh the immediate pleasures of smoking. Similarly, whether a person concerned about contracting AIDS will actually practise safe sex depends on two beliefs: that the use of condoms will reduce the risk of exposure to HIV and that the benefits of doing so will outweigh the pleasures of high-risk, or unprotected, sex (Kelly & Kalichman, 1998).

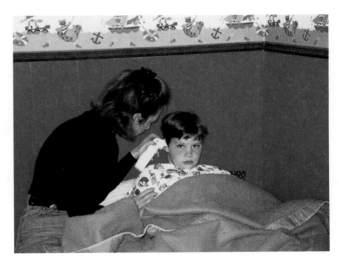

When Do People Seek Out Medical Treatment?

According to the health-belief model, our willingness to seek medical help depends on the extent to which we perceive a threat to our health and believe that a particular behaviour will effectively reduce that threat.

Health-Belief Model: A model predicting that whether a person practises a particular health behaviour depends on the degree to which the person believes in a personal health threat and believes that the behaviour will reduce that threat to their health.

Figure 13.9
The Health-Belief Model

The health-belief model suggests that whether a person practises a particular health behaviour depends on the degree to which he or she believes in a personal health threat—and believes that practising the behaviour will reduce that threat. Each of these beliefs is influenced by additional variables. Here, the health-belief model is applied to smoking.

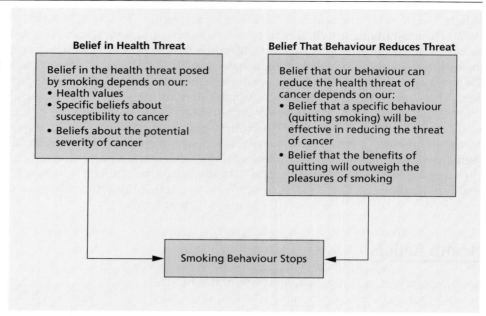

Belief in Health Threat

Belief in the health threat posed by smoking depends on our:
• Health values
• Specific beliefs about susceptibility to cancer
• Beliefs about the potential severity of cancer

Belief That Behaviour Reduces Threat

Belief that our behaviour can reduce the health threat of cancer depends on our:
• Belief that a specific behaviour (quitting smoking) will be effective in reducing the threat of cancer
• Belief that the benefits of quitting will outweigh the pleasures of smoking

Smoking Behaviour Stops

The health-belief model also suggests that if people believe that their actions will be ineffective in changing their health status, they will be less likely to seek help or engage in healthy behaviours. For example, suppose you are overweight and have a family history of high blood pressure. Because you do not believe that anything can be done to lessen your genetic predisposition for heart attacks, you may refuse to adhere to a recommended diet and exercise program, even when you begin to experience symptoms.

Doctor–Patient Interactions

Imagine the following situation: You feel ill and you go to the Student Health Centre. After a rapid succession of questions, pokes, and prods, the doctor scribbles a prescription onto a piece of paper and says, "Take two of these four times a day, and call my office in a week if you have further problems."

Such ineffective doctor–patient interactions cause vast frustration. In that connection, researchers have systematically examined the doctor–patient communication process (Engel, 1997). Here is why that matters. There is growing evidence that the quality of information communicated by a physician to a patient and the rapport between them are critical factors in successful treatment of both the disease and the individual (Roter & Ewart, 1992; Whaley, 1999). Patient satisfaction, recall of important medical information, and compliance with instructions were linked to the amount of information given by the doctor during the medical encounter. Greater patient satisfaction is important because it is associated with additional beneficial outcomes, including better emotional health and fewer hospitalizations (Hall et al., 1999). Physicians can influence the degree to which their patients comply with instructions by discussing beliefs about compliance during office visits (Clark et al., 1995).

- What is the health-belief model?
- Which factors determine our willingness to make lifestyle changes or seek medical help?
- Why is it important for psychologists to study aspects of doctor–patient interactions?

Critical Thinking

Do you think it is wise for people to use medical information they find on the Web to self-diagnose their health problems? Give reasons for your opinion.

Cognition and Health

Consider this surprising chain of events. During the 1950s, a terminally ill cancer patient learned of an experimental anticancer drug. Though the odds were slim, he took the drug, hoping it would result in a cure. Amazingly, the patient's cancer went into remission and he was able to leave the hospital and even to return to work. Then a curious thing happened: Researchers found that the anticancer drug he had taken was ineffective as a cancer treatment. When the patient learned this, his cancer returned (Levy, 1990).

Although one should be skeptical of any miraculous cure for **cancer**—a group of illnesses in which abnormal cells proliferate till they overwhelm normal ones—there are important ways in which psychological variables interact with physical conditions to determine how a cancer progresses (McGuire, 1999). In other words, our personality, perceptions, and behaviours do contribute to the disease process. Of course, there are inherited factors as well. For example, individuals from families with high cancer rates have less efficient natural killer cells—those cells that are designed specifically for the surveillance and destruction of cancerous tumour cells (Kiecolt-Glaser & Glaser, 1992).

In most cases, however, whether we actually develop cancer or another disease depends on **risk factors**—aspects of our lifestyle that affect our chances of developing or contracting a particular disease, within the limits established by our genes (Canadian Cancer Society, 1994). Risk factors are tobacco and the smoke it produces, some chemicals in the food that we eat and in the air that we breathe, alcohol in the beverages we drink, and radiation from overexposure to the sun. Here is what we know about some of those risk factors.

Risky for You and Everyone around You

Cigarette smoking is addictive and it is dangerous to your health. Indeed, active smoking is the leading *preventable* cause of death. Smoking causes 90 percent of all cases of lung cancer in Canada, and it is the leading cause of several other types of cancers, including cancer of the larynx, the bladder, and the cervix. It also causes diseases of the heart and the blood vessels (**cardiovascular disease**). According to Health and Welfare Canada, tobacco kills 35 000 Canadians every year. The health risk is widely known, even to most children by seven years of age (Bhatia et al., 1993). For a summary of some of the benefits of ceasing to smoke, see Figure 13.10.

Cancer: A group of illnesses in which abnormal cells are formed that are able to proliferate, invade, and overwhelm normal tissues, and to spread to distant sites in the body.

Risk Factors: Aspects of our environment or behaviour that influence our chances of developing or contracting a disease, within the limits set by our genetic structure.

Cardiovascular Disease: All diseases of the heart and blood vessels.

Figure 13.10
When Smokers Quit

Within twenty minutes of smoking that last cigarette, the body begins a series of changes that continue for years. All benefits are lost by smoking just one cigarette a day, according to the Cancer Societies of the United States and Canada.

Source: American Cancer Society, Washington Division, Inc. Reprinted with permission.

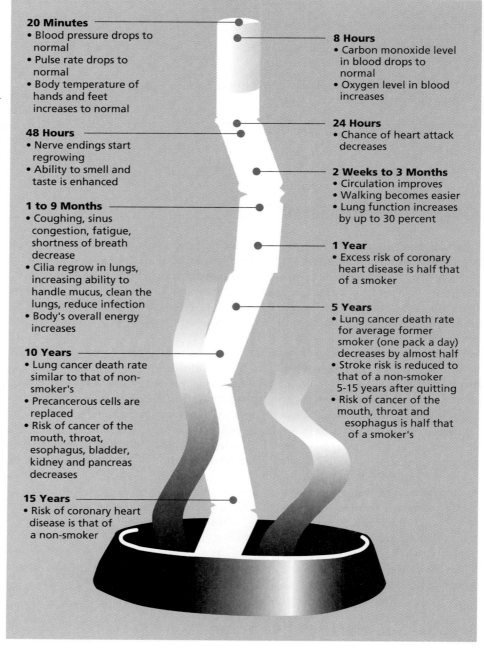

20 Minutes
• Blood pressure drops to normal
• Pulse rate drops to normal
• Body temperature of hands and feet increases to normal

48 Hours
• Nerve endings start regrowing
• Ability to smell and taste is enhanced

1 to 9 Months
• Coughing, sinus congestion, fatigue, shortness of breath decrease
• Cilia regrow in lungs, increasing ability to handle mucus, clean the lungs, reduce infection
• Body's overall energy increases

10 Years
• Lung cancer death rate similar to that of non-smoker's
• Precancerous cells are replaced
• Risk of cancer of the mouth, throat, esophagus, bladder, kidney and pancreas decreases

15 Years
• Risk of coronary heart disease is that of a non-smoker

8 Hours
• Carbon monoxide level in blood drops to normal
• Oxygen level in blood increases

24 Hours
• Chance of heart attack decreases

2 Weeks to 3 Months
• Circulation improves
• Walking becomes easier
• Lung function increases by up to 30 percent

1 Year
• Excess risk of coronary heart disease is half that of a smoker

5 Years
• Lung cancer death rate for average former smoker (one pack a day) decreases by almost half
• Stroke risk is reduced to that of a non-smoker 5-15 years after quitting
• Risk of cancer of the mouth, throat and esophagus is half that of a smoker's

Smoking is also dangerous to the health of other people. Indeed, cigarette smoke consists of about 4000 chemicals, of which forty-three have been linked to cancer. Inhaling second-hand smoke—that is, **passive smoking**—can increase the incidence of respiratory disease and cardiovascular disease for smokers' family members and co-workers. An English survey reported that in various European countries (including Germany, France, and Poland), tobacco-smoke pollution kills almost 140 000 people every year through cancer and heart disease.

Passive smoking also adversely affects children. It causes more frequent and more severe attacks of asthma and may even produce brain tumours (Chilmonczyk et al., 1993; Gold et al., 1993). Children who smoke passively are at risk for numerous diseases, as shown in studies from around the world: A U.S. investigation has linked second-hand smoke to ear and lung infections and worsened asthma; an

Passive Smoking: Inhaling other people's cigarette smoke.

Irish study has confirmed the increase of sudden infant death syndrome (crib death) among babies of smokers; and a British report has confirmed that passive smoking can increase the risk of meningitis and cystic fibrosis in children.

Yet despite the health risk, the almost universal disapproval, the real inconvenience, and the significant cost, about one in every four Canadian adults continues to smoke cigarettes. Among members of the Canadian Navy between the ages of seventeen and nineteen, the figure is one in two, and the beginning age has been steadily declining (Dewit & Beneteau, 1999).

Why do people smoke? Genetic, psychosocial, and cognitive factors all play a role. Individual differences in the reaction to **nicotine** are taken as evidence that our genes play a role in determining which people will become smokers (Pomerleau & Kardia, 1999), as is evidence from studies of identical twins (Kendler et al., 1999). That may be because, for some people more than others, nicotine enhances the availability of certain neurotransmitter substances, such as acetylcholine, norepinephrine, dopamine, and endogenous opioids. As you may recall from Chapter 2, these substances influence memory, attention, performance, pleasure, tension, anxiety, appetite, and pain, and can be pleasurable for some people. Perhaps the most specific evidence for a genetic link with cigarette smoking comes from recent studies of the genes involved in dopamine transmission (Lerman, et al., 1999; Sabol et al., 1999). The results show that certain individuals with a particular inherited genetic characteristic are less likely to be smokers or more likely to have quit smoking successfully.

Psychosocial factors also play a role in establishing smoking behaviour, especially among young people. Adolescents may be more likely to smoke if their parents or other role models smoke, or if they experience peer pressure to do so (Aloise-Young et al., 1994; Millar & Hunter, 1990), or if their brothers or sisters do (Santi et al., 1990–91). When asked to give reasons why they smoke, students in Australia cited "image" and "friends" (Stanton et al., 1993). The irony is that, at least among university students, quite the opposite is the case. Dermer and Jacobsen (1986) studied the effects of cigarette smoking on first impressions made by average-looking other students. They found that nonsmokers made a better impression, even upon students who were smokers themselves. (Of course, you cannot tell smokers from nonsmokers by examining faces. In this experiment, the impression that a person smoked was given by including a cigarette package on the desk in the photo.)

Finally, there are cognitive factors. Smokers believe that smoking allows them to stay alert and handle stress, even though there is no clear evidence in support of those ideas. For many smokers who recognize that smoking is harmful to their health, their beliefs and their actions are out of synch. For that reason, they think that they, personally, are exempt from the harmful consequences of smoking. Chapman and colleagues (1993) found that smokers also believed that "most people smoke," and that "medical evidence that smoking causes cancer is not convincing." As shown in Figure 13.11, smokers were more likely to agree with these beliefs than ex-smokers.

These results suggest that helping smokers quit ought to involve consciously correcting their erroneous beliefs (Sadava & Weithe, 1985). Although many smokers try, nicotine addiction is really difficult to overcome. For example, in the study of Ontario high school students, out of every two smokers who tried to stop, only one was able to stop for more than one week.

Why is it so hard to quit smoking? First, as we've seen earlier in our discussions of smoking, is that some people may be biologically predisposed to smoking, making quitting especially difficult for them. Second, there are reminders—cues in the environment to light up now: having a cup of coffee or meeting with smoker friends. Third, there are the difficulties of withdrawal: physiological cravings, headache, and sleeplessness. There is also weight gain and emotional distress. Next, there is the ordinary stress of everyday life. Smokers

Nicotine: The addictive substance in tobacco.

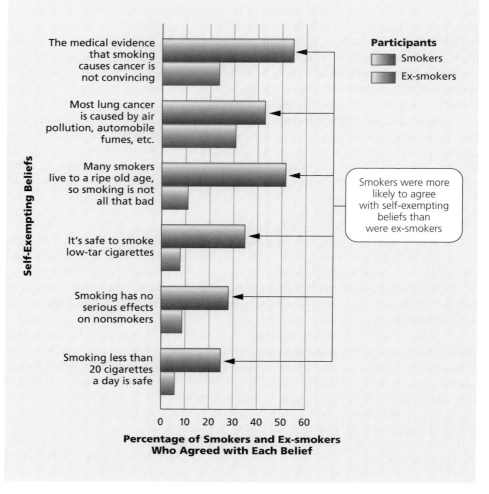

Figure 13.11
The Role of Self-Exempting Beliefs in Smoking

As predicted, smokers were more likely to agree with *self-exempting beliefs* than ex-smokers. These data help explain why smokers continue to smoke, even when they are aware of the danger of doing so. These results also illustrate the important role of cognitive processes in determining health-related behaviours, including smoking.

Source: Based on data from Chapman et al., 1993.

Treatment Programs for Addiction to Nicotine

Recent research has shown that smoking treatment programs using trained health-care providers tend to be more effective than self-help programs (e.g., videotapes, audio tapes, pamphlets), and that the more time the health-care providers spend with the smokers, the more effective the treatment is.

often relapse after encountering difficulties unrelated to smoking. Motivation and social support are both necessary. Finally, there are other factors as well. For example, at the Clarke Institute of Psychiatry in Toronto, Devins (1992) found that what was important in abstaining from cigarettes was whether the smoker had confidence in his or her ability to quit, and whether he or she expected success or failure.

What makes a treatment program effective? A recent review of smoking cessation programs revealed that certain key characteristics are associated with better treatment outcomes (Wetter et al., 1998). First, trained health-care providers tend to be more effective than self-help programs (e.g., videotapes, audio tapes, pamphlets). Second, time and attention are important. The more time the health-care provider spends with the smoker the more effective the treatment. Third, aversive smoking procedures, designed to associate smoking stimuli with feeling ill (by rapid smoking, for example) seem to be most effective, but they must be followed by instruction in how to cope with events that increase the likelihood of smoking. Fourth, nicotine replacement therapies (e.g., patch, gum), are helpful—especially when combined with person-to-person contact tailored to the needs of individual smokers (Silagy et al., 1994; Tang et al., 1994).

Diet and Nutrition

We are the foods we eat. When we make wise choices—for example, foods rich in vitamin A (carrots, spinach, cantaloupe)—proper cell division is supported and the destruction of healthy cells by *carcinogens* is inhibited (Willet & MacMahon, 1984). Broccoli and cauliflower may reduce the risk of cancer by discouraging tumour growth. When we make poor choices, we put ourselves at risk for diseases of the heart and circulatory system. The research findings implicate dietary fat and cholesterol in this. One major cause of heart disease is *arteriosclerosis* (also known as hardening of the arteries), caused by a buildup of cholesterol and other substances on arterial walls, which in turn narrows the blood vessels.

But why do we prefer foods that are not healthy? Learning plays a role in the way the brain and body work. Apparently, through learning, we acquire associations between the sensory properties of foods—tastes, textures, and smells—and their nutritional effects on the body (Warwick & Schiffman, 1992). High-fat foods are energy dense—they contain more calories than foods high in carbohydrate or protein—and they tend to elevate natural opiate levels in the body. As we discussed in Chapter 2, natural opiates have pain-killing properties that can be extremely pleasurable for some people. Thus, it is not surprising that people learn to prefer eating high-fat foods. Interestingly, when people are given a drug that blocks the effects of opiates, and allowed to choose between different foods, they tend to reduce their intake of fat (Schiffman et al., 1998).

For psychologists, the challenge here is to discover how to help high-risk individuals make long-term changes in their eating habits. Although the link between diet and good health is clear, it is difficult to get people to adhere to a healthy diet (Brownell & Cohen, 1995). In addition, many of us simply eat too much. Although most interventions designed to help people lose weight work initially, the weight loss achieved through these programs does not typically last (Garner & Wooley, 1991).

Why is maintaining weight loss a continuous struggle for some people? Actually, there are various reasons, including genetic, behavioural, and environmental factors (Grilo & Pogue-Geile, 1991). However, recent evidence on this topic indicates that the type of motivation behind the decision to begin dieting may also be important in maintaining weight loss over time (Williams et al., 1996).

According to **self-determination theory** (Deci & Ryan, 1985), long-term maintenance of weight loss depends on whether the motivation for doing so is perceived by the dieter as autonomous or controlled. Overweight persons frequently begin dieting on the advice of their doctor or at the insistence of concerned family members. Others begin a weight-loss program because they want to do it for themselves, and they may experience the same activity (dieting) quite differently. In a recent study, Williams and his colleagues (1996) found that participants who reported entering a weight-loss program for themselves attended the program more regularly, lost more weight during the program, and were more likely to maintain the weight loss nearly two years later, than those who reported joining the program because of other people's wishes. These results indicate that the type of motivation underlying a decision to lose weight may be an important predictor of successful weight loss and, more importantly, successful maintenance of weight loss over time.

Self-Determination Theory: Theory suggesting that motivation for health-promoting behaviours is highest when it is autonomous and lowest when it is prompted by others.

K E Y *QUESTIONS*

■ What is cancer?

■ What determines who will become addicted to smoking?

■ What are the potential consequences of smoking and exposure to second-hand smoke?

■ What are the effects of poor dietary practices?

■ What is self-determination theory?

Alcohol Consumption

While current "wisdom" has it that a daily glass of red wine may have health benefits, more alcohol than that can be harmful and may lead to a variety of diseases and disorders. The consequences of drinking can include stomach disease, cirrhosis of the liver, cancer, impaired sexual functioning, and cognitive impairment. Also (as we saw in Chapter 8), fetal alcohol syndrome can occur in children of mothers who drink heavily during pregnancy, resulting in developmental handicaps and physical abnormalities. Alcohol interacts with smoke to increase cancer risk (Grobe & Campbell, 1990; Sobel et al., 1990), and drinkers of alcohol who smoke heavily have twenty-two times the risk of developing cancer of individuals who neither smoke nor drink (Rothman et al., 1980). Furthermore, heavy drinking has also been identified as a risk factor for suicide and suicide attempts (Borges & Rosovsky, 1996).

Chronic excessive alcohol consumption can lead to deficits in many different cognitive abilities, including learning and memory, perceptual-motor skills, visual-spatial processing, and problem solving (e.g., Evert & Oscar-Berman, 1995; Oscar-Berman et al., 1997). Newer research also suggests that the effects of chronic alcohol exposure may be more diffuse, perhaps leading to an overall reduction in the efficiency of our cognitive functions (Nixon, 1999). One manifestation of this general decline is an inability to tune out irrelevant information in order to focus on the critical aspects of a task. For example, in studies in which participants are asked to focus their attention on only one aspect of a task, say speed or accuracy, alcoholics have a difficult time ignoring the irrelevant part of the task, whereas non-alcoholics do not (Nixon, Paul, & Phillips, 1998).

Moreover, several psychosocial factors, including stress, environmental cues, and social pressure from peers, also influence drinking behaviour. There is evidence also that biological and genetic factors contribute to alcoholism and problem drinking (Reid & Carpenter, 1990). Some of the most direct evidence comes from adoption studies investigating rates of alcoholism among adopted children raised apart from their natural parents. Such studies show, for example, that the sons of male alcoholics raised in adoptive homes have higher rates of alcoholism than the sons of non-alcoholics who grow up under similar circumstances (McGue, 1999). That is not only the case for identical twins—but also for male children in general. Ironically, the strongest evidence for the role of environmental factors in drinking also comes from studies of adoption. Biologically unrelated siblings who are raised together eventually exhibit similar drinking practices (McGue et al., 1996).

Given the many negative health effects associated with excessive alcohol consumption, why do people continue to drink? Here is one recent clue. New findings from animal studies show that genetically engineered "knockout" mice, so named because they lack the gene responsible for production of brain chemical called neuropeptide Y, drink more alcohol than normal mice and appear to have a greater tolerance for its effects (Koob et al., 1998). Because neuropeptide Y also appears to calm anxiety, at least in animals, these findings suggest that some alcoholics may drink excessively to relieve stress and help explain the high rates of alcoholism among people with anxiety disorder.

Mood and Health

Type D Personality Type: A term used to describe a general tendency to cope with stress by keeping negative emotions to oneself. People who exhibit this behaviour pattern are more likely to experience suppressed immune systems and health-related problems.

Have you ever had to hold your temper or swallow your tears when the need to express yourself was very strong? Or are you the kind of person who just lets it all out? Individuals who routinely cope with stress by keeping their negative emotions to themselves are likely to experience a suppression of their immune systems. This in turn creates a biological vulnerability, which may lead to the aggravation of disease (such as cancer) when the individual is exposed to environmental stress (Levy et al., 1985). These individuals have been identified recently as the **Type D**—or distressed— **personality type** (Denollet, 1999).

Open expression of negative feelings and a willingness to fight illness have been connected to heightened immune function, decreased recurrence rates, and increased survival time—even among patients at advanced stages of cancer. For example, combative individuals (those who express anger about getting cancer and hostility toward their doctors and family members) often live longer than patients who passively accept their fate and quietly undergo treatment (Levy, 1990).

Emotion plays a role in cardiovascular disease, which is Canada's top killer and is a factor in about 40 percent of all deaths. Several factors put people at risk for heart disease (and stroke), including smoking, obesity, high blood pressure, high **serum cholesterol** levels, and the use of oral contraceptives. Here is one example: Prolonged **hypertension** (also referred to as *high blood pressure*) may result in extensive damage to the entire circulatory system. In fact, about 30 percent of deaths from cardiovascular disease each year are attributable to hypertension. In order to see the connection here, you must understand that blood vessels are not simply hollow tubes through which blood circulates. Rather, their walls are made of regulated and responsive tissue and have many functions—for example, they dilate or constrict as appropriate. Very recently, renegade cells have been found in the blood vessel walls of patients with heart disease. These cells may actually cause the heart disease, and cause it to return after surgery.

Heightened emotion affects blood pressure (Krakoff et al., 1985). For example, anxiety and hostility can increase general arousal and facilitate the release of catecholamines—a class of neurotransmitters that plays an important role in the sympathetic nervous system. Not surprisingly, the strongest relationships between emotions and blood pressure have been found for unexpressed anger and hostility. Although the effects of emotional stressors are usually brief, anxiety, hostility, and anger may indicate a predisposition to hypertension (Rosenman, 1988).

Why do some young adults who are nonsmokers and who seem to be doing everything right, as far as exercise and diet are concerned, suffer heart disease even before they are forty years of age? Scientists in Western Australia have recently isolated a gene that may predict this pattern. That heredity may play a role here is confirmed also by the fact that many children of hypertensive parents are also hypertensive. However, the relationship here is complex. For example, Miller (1992) found that some sons of hypertensive parents respond to stress (e.g., from the pain of electric shock while playing a video game) *less* emotionally than others.

PERSONALITY AND HEALTH: TYPE A BEHAVIOUR Think about the people you know. Can you name one person who always seems to be in a hurry, is extremely competitive, and is often hostile and irritable? Now, can you name another person who is relaxed, relatively noncompetitive, and easygoing? If you can, you now have in mind two people who show Type A and Type B behaviour patterns, respectively.

Interest in the **Type A behaviour pattern** was first stimulated by medical research. Several physicians (Jenkins et al., 1979) noticed that many patients who had suffered heart attacks shared certain personality traits (see Chapter 12). These individuals are competitive, aggressive, hostile, and impatient. They are likely to be hard workers and often seek out the most challenging and stressful work conditions. Some researchers now believe that certain aspects of the Type A pattern are related to increased risk of heart disease, and that those Type A individuals who fail to express their emotions (especially anger, cynicism, and hostility) and who ignore early symptoms of cardiovascular disease, are most at risk (Matthews, 1988).

How does a Type A profile promote heart disease? First, the emotional reactions among Type A individuals may result in the constriction of peripheral blood flow, higher blood pressure, and increased pulse rate (Lyness, 1993). All of these changes lead to cardiovascular disease (Contrada, 1989). Next, the emotional responses of Type A individuals reflect increased hormone levels in the bloodstream—in particular, increased levels of adrenaline and noradrenaline, which are both catecholamines. Here they act as hormones and these increased hormone levels may lead to greater fatty deposits on the walls of blood vessels, and ultimately

Type D Personality and Stress
Individuals with the Type D (distressed) personality who routinely keep their negative emotions to themselves may suppress their immune systems, making them vulnerable to disease.

Serum Cholesterol: The amount of cholesterol in one's blood.

Hypertension: High blood pressure, a condition in which the pressure within the blood vessels is abnormally high.

Type A Behaviour Pattern: A cluster of traits (including competitiveness, aggressiveness, urgency, and hostility) related to important aspects of health, social behaviour, and task performance.

Cynical Hostility: A Learned Behaviour?

Cynical hostility, the "toxic" component of Type A behaviour pattern, is characterized by suspiciousness, resentment, anger, antagonism, and distrust of others.

to heart disease (Dembrowski & Williams, 1989). Also, Type A individuals appear to evaluate themselves negatively, and this may be an important factor in explaining their maladaptive behaviour patterns (Yuen & Kuiper, 1992).

Other differences between these two types of personalities have been found. At York University, Esther Greenglass has described the coping strategies of Type A and Type B women and men. In one study (Greenglass, 1990), her subjects were front-line supervisors at government social service offices. These supervisors completed a psychological inventory that covered four ways of dealing with stress: focusing on the problem, handling emotions, resolving potential problems, and dealing with general conditions of life. One difference she found was that Type B supervisors were more likely to cope with job stress by using social support, while the Type A supervisors were more likely to focus on problems. Can Type A individuals be treated before they develop cardiovascular disease? That question was asked by Roskies (1988), who found that stress management training was the most effective of the programs she studied.

A particular type of hostility—cynical hostility, which is characterized by suspiciousness, resentment, anger, antagonism, and distrust of others—may be especially detrimental. The discovery that cynical hostility—and not Type A behaviour pattern—leads to heart disease provided researchers with an important clue to aid them in the design of treatment. For example, in one program, persons high in cynical hostility monitored their hostility daily and received instruction in the use of specific coping skills. They learned to use relaxation exercises and practised alternative ways to vent their angry feelings. The participants in the treatment group made significant improvements as shown by their post-treatment measures of cynical hostility (Gidron & Davidson, 1996).

HIV/AIDS

Acquired immune deficiency syndrome (AIDS) is a contagious disease caused by the human immunodeficiency virus (HIV). As a result of the HIV infection, immune cells are disabled and destroyed, and this results in a diminished ability to fight infection. Over time, this gradual decline leaves people susceptible to the serious infections that are the actual cause of death for people with the end stage of HIV, which is AIDS (Weiss, 1993).

It was not until 1984 that the HIV virus that causes AIDS was isolated and a test developed to detect its presence. Since then, researchers have uncovered a number of basic facts about this disease. According to the Canadian Public Health Association, there are five key factors in HIV transmission. First, there must be a source of HIV—that is, an HIV-infected individual. Second, there must be a means of transmission—most commonly, certain kinds of sexual activity. Third, the host individual must be susceptible to infection (which almost all human beings are). Fourth, there must be an point of entry to the blood stream of the host, such as a break in the skin. Finally, there must be a sufficient concentration of HIV in the body fluids that are exchanged.

Like the song says, this is a dangerous time for lovers—because HIV is sexually transmitted, most often during sexual intercourse, in the semen or vaginal fluids of HIV carriers. Also, one of every four pregnant women infected with HIV transmits the virus to her fetus. HIV can be spread through transfusion of contaminated blood and through use of contaminated syringes. HIV is a "slow" virus—the incubation period from HIV to AIDS may be as long as ten years (Bachetti, 1990). Thus, the disease can be spread without either partner being aware. This is one reason why the incidence of HIV/AIDS has increased so rapidly. Another is the reluctance of many individuals who know they are at risk for HIV/AIDS to volunteer to be tested (Houston et al., 1998).

The HIV virus has now been traced as far back as the 1940s and is thought to have crossed from chimpanzees to human beings in west central Africa—perhaps from bites or blood—as the animals were killed for meat (Gao et al., 1999). The migration from rural to urban communities, the appearance of the passenger jet in the 1960s, and the global use of blood products are all responsible for the rapid spread of the disease—to over 190 countries. To the end of 1999, UNAIDS estimates that almost 34 million people worldwide are living with HIV, and about 16 million people have died from AIDS (UNAIDS, December 1999). Because chimps and humans share more than 98 percent of their genes, it seems remarkable that chimpanzees with HIV do not develop AIDS. Do the chimps have genetic protection from this fatal disease? That is a question for future research.

One source of important information about HIV/AIDS comes from the tiny number of individuals who engage in sexual activities with HIV-infected partners—without seeming to contract HIV. These few cases have been of great interest to scientists such as Frank Plummer of the University of Manitoba. He and his research team identified a group of about thirty female prostitutes in a poor slum in Pumwani, Kenya. These women have had unprotected sex with hundreds (perhaps thousands) of HIV-positive men and, amazingly, they show no trace of HIV infection (Purvis, 1993). Plummer and his co-workers believe that the immune systems of these women mount an extraordinary defence against the virus. For that reason, they are a source of important information for scientists seeking an effective vaccine against HIV. There is some evidence that another special population—one percent of the Caucasian race—is resistant to HIV. This may be due a genetic anomaly that confers immunity to this virus upon some people.

Although there is no cure for AIDS and at this time a cure is nowhere in sight, there are now medicines—drug cocktails—which, when used in combination, significantly reduce levels of HIV detectable in the blood. The drugs slow the progression of the disease and prolong the lives of those who are infected with HIV. For the most part, the management of this infection is a drug regimen—several times a day—for life. Recently, intermittent drug therapy has been successful in a few test cases. However, even when the virus is reduced to undetectable levels, there is evidence that there are viral reservoirs in the body where the virus remains and continues to reproduce.

Because there is no vaccine against HIV, the virus continues to spread. In 1999, worldwide, 7500 individuals aged fifteen to twenty-four became infected with HIV every day. There remains, therefore, an urgent need to understand how to influence people to change their behaviours in order to gain control over the spread of HIV.

It is clear, however, that just knowing about AIDS and the risks involved is not enough to stop risky behaviours—for example, unsafe sex or the sharing of needles. In his 1992 study of students at ten colleges and universities across Canada, Charles Hobart found this paradox: Those "who knew the most AIDS victims and so were most aware of the spread of the disease and rated the seriousness of the AIDS threat most highly … rated sex with briefly known partners as least risky and … were least inclined to use condoms with passing acquaintances." Indeed, in an investigation in nine dating bars in Ontario (Herold & Mewhinney, 1993), many of the participating men and women were concerned about AIDS, but they had not used a condom during their last sexual encounter.

Why do people who know the risks fail to practise safe sex? Social norms—the unspoken rules that influence us to act in certain ways in social situations—are important determinants of whether or not people will take the preventative measures necessary (Herold et al., 1998). If a social network does not support the use of condoms to prevent the spread of HIV, the individual is not likely to use condoms (Fisher & Misovich, 1989). Gender role differences between men and women may also play a role. For example, some women yield to pressure to engage in unprotected sex because they see themselves in a traditional female role (Amaro, 1995). A related problem is the communication skills required to persuade her partner to use a condom—or not have sex with him if he refuses (Ploem & Byers, 1997). Here the ability to be appropriately assertive about the use of condoms is crucial (e.g., Elkins et al., 1998; Fisher & Fisher, 1992). Fear may also be an important factor, especially among women in abusive relationships. Under conditions like these, in which the potential for personal injury is high, it is understandable that women are reluctant to negotiate safe sex with their partners, let alone refuse to have sex with them (Gomez & Marin, 1993; Hobfall, 1994).

Can anything be done about the risk of women for contracting HIV and AIDS? One idea that seems to be having some success is the Information-Motivation-Behavioural (IMB) model. According to this model, people are more likely to perform HIV-preventive behaviours to the extent that they know how HIV is acquired and the specific actions they must take to avoid it; that they are motivated to perform HIV-preventive behaviours and omit risky ones; and that they possess the skills necessary to perform relevant HIV-preventive behaviours—to use condoms correctly.

In one test of this approach, participants (inner-city women) were given either general health training or training in preventing HIV specifically (Hobfoll et al., 1994). The HIV-prevention training program was designed to increase the women's knowledge of HIV transmission and prevention, motivate them to perform HIV-preventive behaviours by highlighting their specific risks of acquiring HIV, and provide them with behavioural skills necessary to convince their sexual partners to adopt HIV-preventive behaviours, such as condom use. This program produced consistent increases in knowledge and in safe sex practices that remained present six months afterwards.

In a most innovative study, Ploem and Byers (1997) gave two groups of college women information about AIDS. In this study, however, an attempt was made to change the *attitudes* of women towards condoms—suggesting that they could be erotic stimuli and normal in sexual intercourse. Their results showed that this group of women did acquire more positive attitudes towards condoms and were more likely to use them.

For more about special research strategies, see the **Research Process** section below.

The Research Process:
Changing Risky Behaviours

Why are psychologists relevant to the AIDS epidemic? The primary reason is that HIV spreads as a result of particular *behaviours*. An individual can be infected only if the virus is introduced into the bloodstream, and that can only happen as a result of unprotected sexual intercourse, or the "swapping" of infected blood, blood products, or needles. At present, the only effective means we have of preventing AIDS are programs that focus on changing the behaviours that place people most at risk for acquiring HIV— injecting drugs with previously used needles, engaging in unprotected sex, and having sex with multiple partners (Reinecke et al., 1996). Although efforts to develop an effective vaccine or a cure for HIV are ongoing, at present, the only effective means to combat the spread of HIV/AIDS is to convince people not to engage in high-risk behaviours.

To change these risky behaviours, we need to understand what influences people to practise safe sex—or not. Intoxication may be one factor. One series of studies found that people who were intoxicated were less likely to use condoms than people who were sober (MacDonald et al.,

1996). Given that people who engage in casual sex frequently meet potential partners in bars or at parties, these findings are alarming indeed.

A series of studies by Tara MacDonald, Mark Zanna, and Geoffrey Fong illustrates a set of procedures designed to investigate how intoxicated individuals think about safe sex. The variables in these studies were level of intoxication, sexual arousal, and intention to engage in sex without a condom (MacDonald et al., in press a). In this research, about 350 male students selected from introductory psychology classes were the participants. Female students were not invited because of the potential negative effects of alcohol consumption on any participant who might be pregnant.

Tara MacDonald
Queen's University

The students were assigned randomly to one of three conditions: sober, placebo (given a non-alcoholic beverage that smelled of alcohol), or intoxicated (three alcoholic beverages over the course of an hour). All were shown a video in which a couple warm up to sex and then discover that neither has a condom, nor could one be obtained easily. In the last frame of the video, they ask each other "What do you want to do?"

The participants were then asked rate their own sexual arousal at that point in time and to fill in a questionnaire that asked them questions about what they would do if they found themselves in the situation of the couple in the video. They were asked a number of other questions (to provide justification for their intentions, for example) and then they took a breathalyzer test. Figure 13.12, Panel A, shows the results for those subjects who reported high or low sexual arousal as a result of watching the video.

Figure 13.12
Alcohol Intoxication and Intentions to Practise Safe Sex

Here are the results of three studies comparing intoxicated and sober subjects and their intentions to practise safe sex—under different sets of conditions.

Sources: The data from Panel A are from T.K. MacDonald, G. MacDonald, M.P. Zanna, and G.T. Fong, "Alcohol, sexual arousal, and intentions to use condoms: Applying alcohol myopia to risky sexual behavior," Healthy Psychology, in press. The data from Panels B and C are from T.K. MacDonald, G.T. Fong, M.P. Zanna, and A.M. Martineau, "Alcohol myopia and condom use: Can alcohol intoxication be associated with more prudent behavior?" Journal of Personality and Social Psychology, in press.

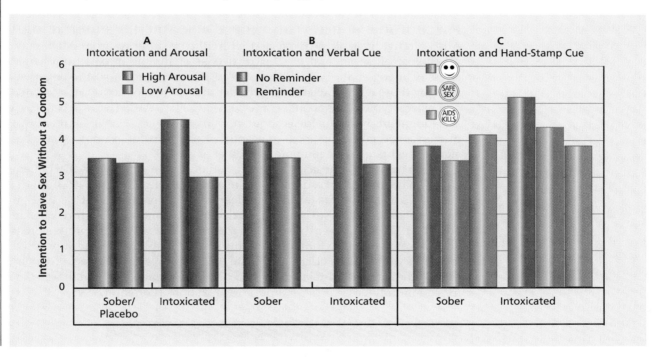

The data for the sober and placebo groups have been combined because they were not different. Notice that subjects in the intoxicated group who were highly aroused reported that they were more likely to proceed without a condom than any of the other groups. The overall results were taken as support for the idea that alcohol myopia—restricted cognitive capacity—occurs when people are under the influence of alcohol (Steele & Josephs, 1990). In this case, intoxicated subjects restricted their thinking to a single internal state—sexual arousal.

In a second set of studies, these investigators collected data not only in the laboratory, but also in four different bars in Calgary and Lethbridge (Macdonald et al., in press b). In these studies, both male and female bar patrons participated. All patrons were invited to volunteer to fill out a questionnaire and take a breathalyzer test. In return for their cooperation, their names were entered into a draw for $500. The questionnaire began with a short vignette, the story line of which was similar to the video described above. Then the subjects were asked a number of questions, including whether they would proceed to have sex under those conditions. Half the subjects were asked about their intentions to proceed with this question: "If I were in this situation, I would have sex." The other subjects were given a reminder—that is, they were asked to express their intentions with this question: "If I were in this situation, I would have sex **without a condom.**" Participants marked a nine-point scale from 1 (strongly disagree) to 0 (strongly agree).

The results are shown in Panel B of Figure 13.12. Sober subjects are those patrons whose breathalyzer scores were below 0.08 and intoxicated subjects are those whose scores were above 0.08 (the Alberta level). Here you see that the reminder "without a condom" in bold letters—which drew subjects' attention to the risk involved—influenced the intoxicated students' reported intentions dramatically.

In another study, using the same methods as above, bar patrons received one of three small stamps on the hand at the door—a smiley face, the words SAFE SEX, or the words AIDS KILLS. Otherwise, the stamps were the same—two concentric circles intended to represent the outline of a condom. The results are shown in Figure 13.12, Panel C. Here you see that the intoxicated subjects were more likely than others to proceed to have unprotected sex if their hand stamp had a smiley face, but less likely to do so if their hand stamp reminded them that AIDS KILLS.

Taken together, these methods provide valuable information about the thinking of people under the influence of alcohol. The research has shown that alcohol intoxication—and the restricted cognitive capacity or alcohol myopia that results—leads people to focus on the most obvious cues in the environment. If cues that would lead a person to have unprotected sex are obvious (e.g., high sexual arousal), then intoxicated people will be more likely than sober ones to report intentions to engage in risky behaviours.

However, if cues that would prevent a person from having unprotected sex are obvious (e.g., reminders of AIDS), then intoxicated people will be less likely to report intentions to have sex without a condom. These results show also how cues in the immediate environment can alert intoxicated individuals to the risky business of sex without a condom—and produce different intentions about unsafe sex. Furthermore, the methodology shows us how to study this very complex behaviour not only in the laboratory, but also in a realistic setting.

PSYCHOLOGICAL HELP FOR PEOPLE WHO ARE HIV-POSITIVE OR HAVE AIDS Individuals already infected with HIV or suffering from AIDS may have psychological, social, and psychiatric needs—stemming in part from heightened stress (Chuang et al., 1992). People with AIDS are often subject to negative treatment by those whose beliefs and attitudes include homophobia (Fish & Rye, 1991), other stereotypic views about people who have HIV/AIDS (Esses & Beaufoy, 1994), and judgments based on ideas about morality (Bush et al., 1993; Clarke, 1992). Programs for special populations—gay and bisexual men, for example—have been designed, evaluated, and compared (Tudiver et al., 1992).

With respect to physicians, nurses, and others dealing with AIDS patients, occupational stress may result in AIDS-related burnout (Garside, 1993; Taerk et al., 1993). In some cases this results from fear of contagion (Gallop et al., 1992), in others from homophobia, sexism, and a lack of understanding of high-risk behaviours (Whyte, 1992). Whatever the source of their stress, however, the professionals who are dedicated to caring for these patients require preventative and supportive programs as well (Gallop et al., 1992). The AIDS Bereavement Project of Ontario addresses the occupation-related grief needs of AIDS caregivers and those who work for community-based AIDS support organizations (Perreault, 1995).

KEY *QUESTIONS*

- What are the consequences of heavy consumption of alcohol?

- How is the way in which we express our emotions related to our health?

- What are the characteristics of Type A persons? What diseases have been linked to Type A persons?

- What is AIDS? How is AIDS transmitted?

Promoting Wellness

Have you ever wondered why some people live to be more than one hundred? Several factors may play a role in this. One of these is diet: Long-lived individuals often eat more grains, leafy green and root vegetables, fresh milk, and fresh fruits, and eat low to moderate amounts of meat and animal fat. In addition, they maintain a low to moderate daily caloric intake (1200 to 3000 calories) and consume only moderate amounts of alcohol (Pelletier, 1986). Regular physical activity throughout life—working outdoors and walking often—is perhaps the most important factor contributing to longevity and good health. Additional factors that may contribute to an extended life span are continued sexual activity and continued involvement in family and community affairs. So, while genetic factors definitely play a role in determining lifespan, we also know that people may be able to extend their lives significantly by choosing a healthy lifestyle and maintaining it throughout life.

On the basis of these and similar findings, a growing number of health psychologists are focusing on prevention strategies—techniques designed to reduce the occurrence of illness and other physical and psychological problems. *Primary prevention* is considered the optimal approach. Its goal is to reduce or eliminate altogether the incidence of preventable illness and injury. It usually involves one or more of the following components: educating people about the relationship between their behaviours and their health, providing skills and motivation to practise healthy behaviours, and directly modifying poor health practices through intervention. *Secondary prevention* focuses on early detection of illness. This involves individuals learning about their health status through medical tests that screen for the presence of disease. Screening for certain diseases is traditionally carried out by health professionals and often requires sophisticated medical tests; however, there are some methods of self-examination, especially for early detection of breast and testicular cancer.

Decreasing the Risks of Illness and Injury

In most cases, our initial attempts to change unhealthy behaviours are unsuccessful. Whether we smoke, eat unhealthy foods, or fail to exercise, bad habits can be difficult to overcome. For example, because smoking is part of a smoker's identity, encouragement to stop smoking may be taken as a threat and elicit defensive reactions (Falomir et al., 2000).

Typically, we become aware of the need to change our behaviours; we initiate change; we experience a series of failed attempts to change these behaviours; and sometimes—if we're persistent enough—we succeed. The nature of this process indicates that we need help—a variety of intervention programs to meet our varied needs and purposes.

HEALTH PROMOTION We often receive health warnings and information about disease. Canada's Tobacco Products Control Act requires strongly worded health warnings on cigarette packages. In addition, numerous health organizations use television commercials, newspaper articles, magazine and radio ads—and now the Internet—to warn us about smoking (and about other unhealthy behaviours, such as unprotected sex and alcohol and drug abuse, and their associated risks, which include cancer, heart disease, and AIDS).

Can mass-media campaigns alone produce widespread changes in behaviour? On the one hand, there has been some success. For example, Blashko and Paterson (1990) did the following study. First, on five consecutive occasions, an open-line radio station featured experts on heart disease. Then, after six months, they interviewed listeners who had filled out a questionnaire. The researchers learned that, overall, half of the listeners had changed to a more healthy way of living. Moreover, 66 percent had been checked for high blood pressure and 25 percent for diabetes.

On the other hand, many messages on TV are contradictory. Health messages are used to promote less-than-ideal fast foods, and unhealthy habits are often depicted as cool. This directly counters attempts to promote healthier practices (Winett, 1995). Moreover, television provides information overload, and that is not helpful. The use of fat-free, low-fat, sugar-free, and "lite" as offered on television commercials illustrates this point.

Furthermore, those who produce material for the mass media sometimes misunderstand their target audience(Azer, 1999; Velicer & Prochaska, 1999). The Break Free anti-smoking campaign conducted by our federal government is a case in point. Ottawa spent $8 million to produce ads intended to influence teens against smoking. However, the campaign had no effect on smoking habits. Why not? Some teens called the commercials annoying, stupid, ineffective, irritating, and unreal. Others felt that they had been depicted as "gullible, ill-informed and naïve." The person in charge of the campaign defended it by maintaining that "advertising does not change behaviour"—which is exactly the point being made here.

Finally, the effectiveness of health prevention depends on the messages being properly framed (Rothman & Salovey, 1997). Some health prevention messages work best when they emphasize the *benefits* of a certain healthy habit —condom or sunscreen use, for example, whereas health detection messages work best when they emphasize the *costs*—for example, of breast or prostrate cancer (Detweiler et al., 1999).

It seems, however, that where there is a will to succeed and the know-how and the financial resources, something can be done. In combination with community programs, higher taxes on tobacco products, and school-based programs, in 1990, anti-smoking advertising began in some states of the United States. In California, between 1990 and 1998, more than two billion fewer packages of cigarettes were sold than would otherwise have been the case. In Figure 13.13 you will see the data collected by Goldman and Glantz (1998).

These researchers conducted extensive evaluations of the anti-smoking programs in California. Their goal was to find out why the anti-smoking advertising worked and with whom. In that effort, they identified eight different kinds of messages that had been used. For example, some ads focused upon the long-term gains in health, and others centred on the addictive properties of nicotine. The most influential message was one about the way in which the tobacco companies' advertisements manipulate people by making smoking glamorous—for their own profit motive.

Why was this particular message so effective in changing behaviour? In a word, it changed the way people thought about themselves—differently for adults and youth. Adults who felt guilty and were angry at themselves became angry and resentful against the tobacco industry instead. Adolescents learned how they had been deliberately influenced to smoke—in order that they become addicted—so the companies continue to make pots of money. They discovered that the choice to smoke was not what they had thought—a gesture of indepen-

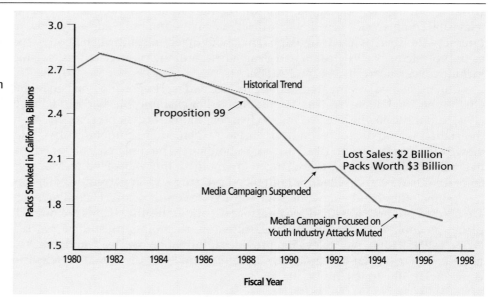

Figure 13.13
The Long-Term Pattern of Decline in Tobacco Consumption in California

Tobacco consumption declined in California during the 1990s.

Source: Goldman and Glantz, 1998.

dence from their parents. As a result, parents and their children had a common enemy—the tobacco industry.

Another powerful message was the one about second-hand smoke. It seemed as though smokers were less influenced by the deleterious effects on their own health and more influenced by the idea that their smoking endangers other people—portraying the way in which children are helpless victims of those who smoke in their presence. The researchers concluded that the media do have the power to shape public attitudes toward tobacco and the tobacco industry.

Here is another example. You probably know that lying in the sun is bad for your health, unless you use proper sunscreen. In North America each year there are about 400 000 cases of skin cancer, and about 6000 people die of melanoma (the deadliest form of it). The latest public health figures show that it is Australia that has the highest rate of skin cancer in the world. Indeed, an estimated two out of every three people there are expected to develop skin cancer during their lifetime. Yet, Australians tan without taking precautions, know little about skin cancer, have friends who admire a dark tan, are more relaxed than others, and tend to take more risks (Keesling & Friedman, 1987).

What can be done to convince people to take the proper precautions? As you now know, knowledge does not always translate into action. In Australia, for instance, mass-media campaigns to increase public awareness of the danger of unprotected sunning have had mixed results. On the one hand, many children and most adults have become generally knowledgeable about the risks of over-exposure to sunlight. On the other hand, though, many of those who know about the risks still do not wear proper protective clothing or use sun screens or avoid getting too much sun. Why would that be?

First, many people believe a tan makes them look better and therefore they feel better about their appearance and themselves when they have a tan. More important to many, they believe that a tan makes them more attractive to other people. For adolescents and young adults, this belief is a powerful source of motivation, and thus, a difficult one to combat. Second, most people have an *optimistic bias* concerning themselves (Moore & Rosenthal, 1992). That means that they believe negative outcomes are more likely to happen to other people. This may be another reason they disregard the risks of excessive sun exposure. For example, in one study, Miller (et al., 1990) asked a group of participants with varying levels of suntan (light, medium, dark) to rate their chances of developing skin cancer. The results showed that they all had an optimistic bias with regard to their own chances of developing skin cancer. There is a third reason for people to ignore these warnings and that has to do with a different belief—that skin cancer is a disease of older people. Adolescents and young adults frequently interpret this to mean that they cannot get skin cancer for at least another twenty or thirty years. Therefore, why worry? A study of four age groups in Israel confirmed that the youngest age group was the least likely to change beliefs about suntanning or exposure to the sun (Carmel et al., 1994).

Is the reasoning of younger people correct? Definitely not! Experts on skin cancers claim that over-exposure to the sun during youth is one of several important factors that predict skin or other forms of cancer later in life. They add that the consistent use of sunscreens during the first eighteen years of a child's life can potentially reduce the lifetime incidence of some forms of skin cancers by nearly 80 percent. Of course, other factors, including heredity and other lifestyle factors, also determine whether we will develop skin cancer.

What can psychological research contribute to the reversal of worldwide increases in skin cancers? Health psychologists are using the available data to increase awareness of skin cancers by dealing with erroneous beliefs, to design programs that motivate people to perform self-examinations early, and to take the simple precautions necessary to prevent this disease. Using the IMB model and health-belief model described earlier in this chapter, many health psychologists are currently hard at work getting us to "lighten up."

Motivating the Couch Potato

Evidence suggests that regular and vigorous exercise reduces the risk of coronary disease.

THE WORK OF STAYING HEALTHY It is now widely accepted that exercise has an important impact on physical and mental health (e.g., Long & Flood, 1993). An active lifestyle reduces the risk of many illnesses that lead to premature death. Exercise also contributes much to the rehabilitation of those who have been ill or injured. Exercise can reduce the likelihood of coronary heart disease, even in the presence of other health risk factors, including smoking, obesity, high blood pressure, and high blood cholesterol (Dishman, 1988).

Despite the great benefit and the low cost, only one in five of us does enough physical activity to reduce the risk of chronic disease and premature death (Dubbert, 1992). This is surprising, because research also indicates that exercise can have a significant impact on our psychological well-being. For example, it may improve our self-concept, alleviate feelings of depression, and reduce anxiety (Dubbert, 1992). These effects are particularly apparent just after a workout, but there may also be some benefits long afterwards. There are changes in mood following exercise, which may result from socializing and being involved with others (Plante & Rodin, 1990). Mood may also improve because exercise affects our confidence in our ability to execute a particular behaviour (that is, our self-efficacy)—for example, to run a mile or complete an aerobics workout (Rodin & Plante, 1989).

Why then do we not do what we know is good for us? Again, psychological research suggests we are held back by our beliefs about our ability to succeed, our attitudes toward trying, and our feelings of threat or challenge regarding the physical activity (Crocker, 1993, 1989).

So how do we get off the couch? First, it is important to identify effective cues that will become a signal to exercise. Working out in the same location, doing a consistent warm-up, and recording and posting the results are all helpful in this regard. Second, arrange a regular time that minimizes the likelihood of competing demands—a time at which you would probably not be doing much of anything. For example, if you tend to work best late in the day, arrange to exercise in the morning. Third, to maintain your new activities, provide yourself with pleasurable consequences. Reward yourself, and avoid potential sources of punishment, such as sore muscles, fatigue, and injury.

Fourth, choose an exercise that you enjoy. As in life generally, there is no such thing as the only correct choice. There are lots of options here—an exercise for almost every letter of the alphabet, from aerobics to walking. According to Wankel (1993), the more you enjoy a physical activity, the more useful it is for countering stress. Fifth, let your motives for engaging in physical activity centre upon fitness and health rather than appearance. Gauvin (1990) studied autonomous exercisers, sedentary people, fitness program dropouts, and fitness program enrollees. She found that autonomous exercisers gave fitness and health as their primary motivation. Finally, find some social encouragement (not competition); the other people in your life are an important resource in maintaining an exercise program.

Early Detection of Disease and Illness

When is the last time you had your blood pressure taken? If you are like most people, procedures for early detection of the "silent killers"—high blood pressure, high blood cholesterol, and several types of cancer—are furthest from your mind. Yet identifying these conditions at an early stage can make an enormous difference—in some cases the difference between life and death. It is estimated that widespread use of available screening procedures could significantly reduce the number of deaths from cervical, colon, and prostate cancer. For that reason, psychological strategies are being developed to motivate people to take part in early detection programs.

Many companies, universities, community groups, and hospitals have screening programs to test for high blood pressure and serum cholesterol. Unfortunately, many people either do not take advantage of screening programs at all, or they fail to get screened regularly. Reminders from physicians and local ad campaigns do increase the frequency of screening visits (Mitchell, 1988).

DETECTING THE EARLY SIGNS OF ILLNESS Whether we take preventative measures depends, generally, on the perceived severity of the possible illness, our perceived vulnerability to disease, and our beliefs about what those people close to us think about screening (Henna & Knolls, 1990).

As is understood widely, self-examination is imperative for the early detection of breast cancer and skin cancer. In women over fifty, for breast cancers that are detected early through secondary prevention programs (such as self-examination, clinical breast examination, and mammography), there is an 85 to 90 percent chance of full recovery. However, testicular cancer—which, although quite rare, is the most common cancer found in males between fifteen and thirty-five—is less well known. Early detection is important and self-examination once a month, for a hard bit right at the surface, is recommended. (Goldenring & Putrell, 1984; Steffen, 1990). One study (Katz et al., 1995) investigated cancer awareness and self-examination practices in college students. Researchers had men students complete the Testicular Cancer Awareness Survey and women students complete the Breast Cancer Awareness Survey. Those who were most aware, most afraid of developing cancer, and most confident that they knew how do self-examination, were the ones who were most likely to do the self-examination.

K E Y QUESTIONS

- What role do the mass media play in our health?
- What are the effects of regular exercise on our health?
- What is primary prevention? Secondary prevention?

Making Psychology Part of Your Life

Computers and Repetitive Strain Injury

When human muscles are used over and over again in precisely the same way for long periods of time, they become overreactive, and instead of relaxing, they remain tense. The result is a variety of symptoms, such as tingling in the fingers and hands; pain in the arms, the back, and the neck; swelling; tenderness; weakness; and reduced function (Sheon, 1997a). *Repetitive strain injury* (RSI) is the general term for this disorder (Tyrer, 1999). RSI is of interest to psychologists because it is stress-related and because changes in behaviour are required to prevent or remedy this condition.

RSI is found among musicians (drummers), factory workers (on assembly lines), athletes (tennis players) and house painters (Sheon, 1997b). One recent case involved an amateur cyclist who had numbness and tingling in a small area of the upper right buttock (Green et al., 1999).

In their study of 800 sewing-machine operators in Quebec, Brisson, Vezina, and Vinet (1992) found a population of women under psychological and ergonomic stress. The psychological stress related to their having to perform a complex task under serious time pressure. The ergonomic stress was related to their having to sit with their heads forward for a long time while continuously repeating the same upper-limb movements. The researchers found that "the psychological tension associated with the time pressure may play a direct role in the development of musculoskeletal disorders … in that muscle tension … increases with psychological tension." They pointed out also the significant cost to the health care system of work-related health problems.

The incidence of RSI in its various forms is increasing rapidly among those who use computers at work

(Greening & Lynn, 1999) —for example, in the news-room, at the office, and even in the offices of authors of psychology textbooks. Researchers Kamienska-Zyla and Prync-Scotniczny (1996) studied 600 computer systems operators in Poland. In addition to eye strain, there was a high incidence of back problems, and these researchers recommended special attention to the ergonomic design of computer workstations.

The symptoms of RSI include annoying to severe pains in the neck and back, and tingling and weakness of the hands and arms. Warning signs include tingling or burning sensations that persist, and sensitivity to touch. Three stages have been identified and, as time goes on, the likelihood that the injury can be reversed decreases (Quilter et al., 1998). Eventually the individual can no longer use the arms or the hands, even to hold a book or use cutlery or a hair dryer. In part, the stress of this disorder occurs because it is not commonly understood and does not show up on X-rays. It can have a very serious effect on the individual, not only because of lost employment income but also because of the resulting inability to do even their usual household chores (Levenstein, 1999).

Researchers and therapists believe that the difficulty begins with the muscles of the back and neck, particularly the trapezius muscles, which are responsible for holding the arms in a steady position at the keyboard (Pascarelli & Quilter, 1994). Little by little, the trauma those muscles experience from their inability to relax accumulates, and the electrical messages between muscle and brain begin to falter. "With a repetitive strain injury," wrote Taylor in 1993, "… these [electrical] messages get mixed up. The muscles will contract, or they contract out of sequence. Or they may contract and then be unable to relax." If this continues, scar tissue and permanent damage may result. Other research has attempted to determine whether there is a link between RSI and changes in the cerebral cortex. In one experiment, monkeys who developed RSI in their hands were found to have marked changes in the hand area of the cerebral cortex (Byl et al., 1997).

The diagnosis of RSI has been made simpler by electromyography (EMG), a procedure in which a surface electrode is used to identify which muscles are not working properly. There are now treatment centres in several cities in Canada. The general idea is to start the muscles working again, to re-establish the flow of electrical information between the muscles and the brain. Various professionals, including medical researchers, neuropsychologists, and occupational and physical therapists, are now doing research on RSI. A very

recent report has suggested use of the other hand may be beneficial; with some practice, the non-dominant hand may become almost as fast (Peters & Ivanoff, 1999).

What can you do to prevent RSI? What can you do if you have noticed what you think may be mild symptoms of RSI? Here are five ways of applying current knowledge to your situation:

1. *Check out the ergonomics of your computer station.* The top drawing in the figure below shows you the general idea: monitor at eye level, keyboard at the proper height. Recent evidence suggests that the ideal distance from the screen differs among individuals (Jaschinski et al., 1999). Try out a number of different ones to see which one is most comfortable for you.

2. *Consider the way you use your body:* how you hold the telephone receiver, how you pound the keys. Hold your head up naturally, your wrists at neutral rather than bent or twisted to the right or the left, your arms and legs at right angles. Notice that over time your shoulders will rise up; lower them often.

3. *Examine the chair you use.* Do you need a wrist rest, a copy holder, a specially designed back support?

Choosing the Right Angles to Prevent Keyboard Injury

Posture
Arms relaxed and loose at sides; forearms and hands parallel to floor.
Thighs at right angle to torso.
Knees at right angle to thighs.
Arm and hand supports can take the load off back muscles, but ergonomists cannot agree

Limbering Up: Exercises for the Hands, Wrists, and Fingers

Massage inside and outside of hand with thumb and

Grasp fingers and gently bend back wrist. Hold for five

Gently pull thumb down and back until you feel the stretch. Hold

Clench fist tightly, then release, fanning out

By sitting with the correct posture at a well-designed workstation, you can avoid RSI.

Sources: John Kella, Ph.D., Miller Health Care Institute for the Performing Arts; Joyce Institute; New York Times.

Or a specially designed pillow that may provide relief to the muscles of your head, neck, and back while you sleep?

4. *Take regular breaks,* during which you can relax and move your body in different ways and with different muscles.

5. *Practise the exercises that are recommended for RSI.* Some of these are presented in the illustration. They are designed to stretch the taut muscles and to encourage them to continue functioning normally. They will make you feel better whether you have RSI or not, and they will contribute to prevention of RSI if you are at risk.

The prevention and treatment of RSI requires people to change their behaviour at work and at play. Undoubtedly, making that happen will require future research and the application of the principles to which you have been introduced in this introduction to psychology.

Summary and Review

Key Questions

Health Psychology: An Overview

■ **What is health psychology?** Health psychology is the study of the relation between psychological variables and health.

■ **To what can we attribute today's leading causes of premature death?** Many of today's leading causes of premature death can be attributed to unhealthy lifestyles.

■ **What are epidemiological studies?** Epidemiological studies are large-scale research efforts that focus on identifying the risk factors that predict development of certain diseases, such as heart disease and cancer.

Stress: Its Causes, Effects, and Control

■ **What is stress?** Stress is the process that occurs in response to situations or events (stressors) that disrupt, or threaten to disrupt, our physical or psychological functioning.

■ **What is the General Adaptation Syndrome model?** The general adaptation syndrome, first reported by Hans Selye, describes how our bodies react to the effects of stress. It includes three distinct stages: alarm, resistance, and finally, exhaustion.

■ **What determines whether an event will be interpreted as stressful or as a challenge?** Cognitive appraisals play an important role in determining whether we interpret potentially stressful events as stressful or as a challenge.

■ **What are stressors?** Stressors can be major life events (such as the death of a spouse) or daily hassles of everyday life (such as receiving a minor traffic ticket or having to wait in a line at the grocery store).

■ **What are some sources of work-related stress?** Sources of work-related stress include work overload and underload, role conflict, and performance appraisals.

■ **What is the person–environment fit and why is it important?** The person–environment fit refers to the match between characteristics of workers and characteristics of their jobs or work environments. Mismatches between these characteristics can lead to increases in stress-related illnesses.

■ **Does stress play a role in physical illness?** Stress may play a role in 50 to 70 percent of all physical illness, primarily through its effect on the immune system.

■ **What are the effects of exposure to low levels of stress? High levels?** Even relatively low levels of stress may interfere with task performance. Prolonged exposure to high levels of stress may cause burnout.

■ **What is burnout? What are its causes?** Burnout is the physical and psychological exhaustion that some people experience after prolonged exposure to stress. Burnout occurs when valued resources are lost or are inadequate to meet demands or do not yield the expected returns. Job conditions implying that one's efforts are useless, ineffective, or unappreciated also contribute to the feelings of low personal accomplishment that are an important part of burnout.

■ **Why are some people better able to cope with the effects of stress?** Individual differences in *optimism* help explain why some people cope with stress better than others. Optimists generally focus on problem-focused ways of coping with stress and actively seek out social support.

Understanding Our Health Needs

■ **Why are symptoms and sensations important?** Symptoms and sensations, such as irregularities in heartbeat, are useful because they may help alert us to underlying health problems.

■ **What is the health-belief model?** The health-belief model was initially developed to help explain why people do not use medical screening services. It suggests that willingness to seek medical help depends on the extent to which we perceive a threat to our health and the extent to which we believe that a particular behaviour will effectively reduce that threat.

■ **What factors determine our willingness to make lifestyle changes or seek medical help?** According to the health-belief model, our willingness to make lifestyle changes or seek medical help depends on our beliefs concerning our susceptibility to an illness, the severity of the illness, and the effectiveness of steps taken to deal with the illness.

■ **Why is it important for psychologists to study aspects of doctor–patient interactions?** Physicians are often more effective in dealing with the technical aspects of medicine than the psychosocial aspects. Because of this fact, psychologists have begun to develop interventions aimed at improving the nature of doctor–patient interactions, which in turn, can have a beneficial impact on important medical outcomes.

Cognition and Health

■ **What is cancer?** Cancer is actually a group of diseases characterized by a loss of some cells' ability to function normally. Cancerous cells multiply rapidly, generating tumours.

■ **What determines who will become addicted to smoking?** Individual differences in people's reaction to nicotine, the addictive substance in tobacco, helps determine who will become a smoker.

■ **What are the potential consequences of smoking and exposure to second-hand smoke?** Both smoking and exposure to second-hand smoke have been implicated in many types of cancer, in cardiovascular disease, and in a host of pathologies in children.

■ **What are the effects of poor dietary practices?** Poor dietary practices can increase the risks of colon and rectal cancer, breast cancer, and cardiovascular disease.

■ **What is self-determination theory?** Self-determination theory predicts that autonomously motivated health-preserving behaviour is more likely to be maintained over

time, whereas maintenance of such behaviour achieved at the urging of others is less likely.

■ **What are the consequences of heavy consumption of alcohol?** Heavy drinking can cause a variety of health problems including stomach, liver, and intestinal cancer. It can also impair mental and sexual functioning, and it can result in fetal alcohol syndrome.

■ **How is the way in which we express our emotions related to our health?** Failure to express our emotions can adversely affect the progression of a cancer. Emotions can also lead to an increase in a person's blood pressure.

■ **What are the characteristics of Type A persons? What diseases have been linked to Type A persons?** Type A persons tend to be competitive, aggressive, hostile, and impatient. Persons who fail to express or vent their emotions and ignore early signs of cardiovascular disease are at the highest risk for experiencing a heart attack.

■ **What is AIDS? How is AIDS transmitted?** Acquired Immune Deficiency Syndrome (AIDS) is a reduction in the immune system's ability to defend the body against invaders and is caused by the HIV virus. AIDS is transmitted primarily through unprotected sex and infected blood.

Developing A Healthier Lifestyle

■ **What role can the mass media play in health promotion?** The mass media, when combined with other health promotion programs, can have a beneficial impact on health behaviours.

■ **What are the effects of regular exercise on our health?** Regular, moderately vigorous exercise promotes both physical and psychological health. Starting and maintaining an exercise habit requires that people arrange their environment in a way that supports the desired exercise behaviours and weakens competing behaviours.

■ **What is primary prevention? Secondary prevention?** Primary prevention emphasizes disease prevention by educating people about the relation between their behaviour and their health, promoting healthy behaviour, and directly modifying poor health practices. Secondary prevention emphasizes early detection of disease to decrease the severity of illness that is already present.

Key Terms

Critical Thinking Questions

Appraisal

Throughout this chapter we've seen that lifestyle factors—what we choose to eat, drink, or smoke, and whether we choose to exercise regularly—greatly influence our health. If one can achieve good health simply by changing one's own behaviours, then why aren't more people doing so?

Controversy

The number of people infected with HIV throughout the world is increasing. Since it is clear that many infections result from unprotected sex with an infected person, behav-ioural researchers have developed interventions that effectively promote the use of condoms—particularly among high-risk populations. Others argue, however, that these interventions simply promote promiscuity and thereby worsen the problem. What are your views on this issue?

Making Psychology Part of Your Life

Now that you know something about the many practices that can improve your physical and psychological health, how will you follow these practices yourself?

Weblinks

Check out our Companion Website at www.pearsoned.ca/baron for additional Websites, activities, and more.

Coping with Stress Index

www3.sympatico.ca/cmha.toronto/sindex.htm

The Canadian Mental Health Association Metro Toronto Branch provides this site as a resource on stress. It examines the stages of stress, the effects of stress on health, and coping strategies, among other topics.

Stress Busters

www.stressrelease.com/strssbus.html

Stress Busters is about the dangers of stress, stress-building beliefs, helpful techniques to reduce stress, and stress builders and stress busters.

Healthwise

www.cc.columbia.edu/cu/healthwise

Healthwise is the Health Education and Wellness program of the Columbia University Health Service. Included at this site are an interactive health question and answer service, "Go Ask Alice!" and the Healthwise Highlights newsletter.

The Unseen Scars: Post-Traumatic Stress Disorder

www.tv.cbc.ca/national/pgminfo/ptsd/wounds.html

This CBC report is entitled *Peacekeeping: The Invisible Wounds.*

Harvard RSI Action Home Page

www.rsi.deas.harvard.edu/

This site is maintained by students at Harvard University and contains lots of information about repetitive strain injury as well as many links to other relevant pages.

Chapter 14

Psychological Disorders

Their Nature
and Causes

CHAPTER OUTLINE

Charming Liars

Psychopaths are charming pathological liars who think a lot of themselves. They have no regard for the consequences of their behaviour on other people. They do not share society's moral code, they appear to have no conscience to guide their behaviour, and they feel no remorse for the pain they cause those around them.

The *Halifax Chronicle Herald* told of a psychopath who had sexually assaulted three women, broken into homes, trafficked in drugs, and robbed banks. The report went on to explain that not all psychopaths are violent criminals: "Some rise to positions of power in fields like business or politics." Estimates put the number of individuals with this parti-cular psychological disorder at one percent of the population at large.

How do we distinguish between normal and abnormal behaviour? What causes some people to behave so differently from the rest? What are some other psychological disorders? What kinds of people are likely to develop abnormal behaviour? Why do some people become profoundly depressed, fearful of open spaces, or subject to hallucinations? These are some of the difficult questions that you will consider in Chapter 14, Psychological Disorders, Their Nature and Causes.

Source: Schneidereit, P. (2000, February 20). No known causes. *Halifax Chronicle Herald*, p. C5.

> There appear to be no simple ways
> of distinguishing abnormal
> behaviour from normal behaviour.
> The two lie on a continuum.

Think of all the people you have ever known. Can you remember ones who experienced any of the following problems?

■ Deep feelings of depression that did not seem to be related to any events in their lives.

■ Unusual preoccupation with illness, health, and a large array of symptoms— some of which, at least, were of doubtful reality.

■ An indifference to rules and conventions along with a tendency to impulsively engage in behaviours that endanger both themselves and others.

■ Heavy dependence on alcohol, cigarettes, or various drugs, coupled with an inability to stop using these substances.

Psychological Disorders: Atypical and Maladaptive

Is the man shown here suffering from a psychological disorder? We can't be sure without careful diagnosis, but his behaviour certainly meets some of the key criteria defining such disorders.

Psychological Disorders: Behaviours or thoughts that are unusual in a given society, that are maladaptive, and that cause the persons who experience them considerable distress.

If you *haven't* known people who have experienced one or more of these problems, then you have certainly led a charmed life, for disorders like these are experienced by many millions of people in every corner of the earth every year. It is on these and other **psychological disorders**—maladaptive patterns of behaviour and thought that cause the people who experience them considerable distress—that we will focus in this chapter.

But, what, precisely, are such disorders? Most psychologists agree that psychological disorders include the following features. First, they involve patterns of behaviour or thought that are judged to be unusual or *atypical* in their society. People with these disorders do not behave or think like most others, and these differences are often apparent to the people around them. Second, such disorders usually generate *distress*—negative feelings and reactions—in the persons who experience them. Third, they are *maladaptive*—they interfere with individuals' ability to function normally and meet the demands of daily life. Combining these points, we can define psychological disorders as *disturbances of an individual's behavioural or psychological functioning that are not culturally accepted and that lead to psychological distress, behavioural disability, or impaired overall functioning* (Nietzel et al., 1998).

In this chapter, we'll examine a number of different mental disorders and some of the factors that lead to their occurrence; in the next chapter, we'll turn to procedures for treating or alleviating such disorders. Before undertaking our consideration of mental disorders, we will focus on two preliminary tasks. First, we'll review contrasting perspectives on the nature of psychological disorders and indicate how views concerning them have changed over the centuries. Second, we'll examine a widely used system for diagnosing various psychological disorders—the DSM-IV. After that, we will turn to the disorders themselves and consider both the symptoms they produce and potential reasons why they occur.

Changing Conceptions of Psychological Disorders

The pendulum of history swings, and like other pendulums, it does not move in only one direction. Over the course of the centuries and in different societies, abnormal behaviour has been attributed to natural factors or forces (e.g., imbalances within our bodies) or, alternatively, to supernatural ones (such as possession by demons or gods). Let's take a look at a few of these perspectives and at the modern view of abnormal behaviour.

The Ancient World: Of Demons and Humours

The earliest view of abnormal behaviour emphasized supernatural forces. In societies from China to ancient Babylon, unusual or bizarre behaviour was generally attributed to possession by evil spirits or other forces outside our everyday experience. Ancient Greece, however, provided an exception to this picture. Several centuries before the start of the contemporary era, Hippocrates, a famous Greek physician, suggested that all forms of disease, including mental illness, had natural causes. He attributed psychological disorders to such factors as brain damage, heredity, and imbalance of the body's *humours*—four essential fluids that, he believed, influenced our health and shaped our behaviour. He even suggested treatments for these disorders that sound impressively modern: rest, solitude, and good food and drink. The Romans generally accepted this view of psychological disorders, and since they spread their beliefs all around what was then the known world, the idea that psychological disorders resulted from natural rather than supernatural causes had widespread acceptance.

The Middle Ages and the Renaissance: The Pendulum Swings

After the fall of Rome, and the advent of the *dark* and *middle* ages, religion came to dominate Western societies in a way it had not done in ancient times. The result was that abnormal behaviour, once again, was attributed largely to supernatural forces. There were exceptions—some physicians suggested that strange behaviour might stem from natural causes—but they were ignored, or worse. The result of this shift in perspective was that persons with serious psychological disorders were increasingly likely to be perceived as having become victim to some form of demonic possession. In an effort to rid them of their demons, they were commonly subjected to painful *exorcisms,* and often beaten, starved, and exposed to other mistreatments to make their body an uncomfortable and undesirable abode for demonic occupants.

With the Renaissance, however, which began in Europe in the 1400s, the pendulum began to swing again. For instance, the Swiss physician Paracelsus (1493–1541) suggested that abnormal behaviour might stem, at least in part, from the influence of natural forces such as the moon (hence, the term *lunatic* to describe someone with bizarre behaviour). As the Renaissance continued and knowledge of anatomy and biology increased, the view that abnormal behaviour was a disease— a kind of illness—began to take place, and the common practice was to house mentally ill persons in *asylums*. These asylums or "madhouses" were designed as much to keep the mentally ill out of society as to protect or treat them. Conditions in these institutions were brutal. Patients were shackled to walls in dark, damp cells, were never permitted outside, and were often punished and abused by their guards. Indeed, tickets were sold to the public to view them and their strange antics, just as individuals would pay to visit zoos.

Humane Treatment of People with Psychological Disorders

Until the eighteenth century, people suffering from psychological disorders were subject to harsh conditions. Philippe Pinel introduced more humane procedures in a large Paris hospital, with very positive results.

Change, however, was in the wind again. During the 1700s, a series of reformers—for instance, Jean-Baptiste Pussin and Phillippe Pinel, physicians in charge of a large mental hospital in Paris—reached the conclusion that patients there were suffering from a kind of illness, and that they would do much better if freed from their chains, moved to bright, sunny rooms, and permitted to go outside for exercise. These changes did produce beneficial effects, so these ideas soon spread and did much to reduce the suffering of patients in such "hospitals." The result, ultimately, was development of the **medical perspective** of abnormal behaviour—the view that psychological disorders are a form of illness, produced, like other illnesses, by natural causes. This perspective is the basis for the field of **psychiatry,** a branch of modern medicine specializing in the treatment of psychological disorders.

Within psychology, there is currently less emphasis on abnormal behaviour as a disease and more on its potential *biological* or *biochemical* roots (e.g., Heinrichs, 1993). Current evidence suggests that changes in the structure or functioning of the brain may play an important role in several forms of abnormal behaviour (Raz, 1993). It also appears that genetic factors, too, may play a role in some psychological disorders (e.g., Gottesman, 1993; McGue, 1993). Although psychologists prefer to avoid describing psychological disorders in strictly medical terms, they do accept the view that such disorders often involve biological causes.

The Psychodynamic Perspective

A very different perspective on abnormal behaviour was offered by Freud and several other important figures in the history of psychology. According to this *psychodynamic perspective,* discussed in detail in Chapter 12, many mental disorders can be traced to unconscious urges or impulses and to the struggle over their expression that takes place in the hidden depths of human personality. Remember that in Freud's theory, the *id* (repository of our primitive desires) demands instant gratification, while the *superego* (conscience) denies it. The *ego* (consciousness) must strive to maintain a balance between these forces. According to Freud, mental disorders arise when the ego, sensing that it may soon be overwhelmed by the id, experiences anxiety. To cope with this *anxiety*, the ego employs different *defence mechanisms*, as described in Chapter 12. These serve to disguise the nature of the unacceptable impulses and so reduce the anxiety experienced by the ego; but they may also generate maladaptive behaviour.

While few psychologists currently accept Freud's theory about the origins of psychological disorders, his suggestion that unconscious thoughts or impulses can play a role in abnormal behaviour remains influential. In this respect, the psychodynamic perspective has contributed to our modern understanding of abnormal behaviour.

Medical Perspective: The view that psychological disorders have a biological basis and should be viewed as treatable diseases.

Psychiatry: A branch of medicine that focuses on the diagnosis and treatment of psychological disorders.

The Modern Psychological Approach

The term "mental illness" makes some psychologists uneasy. Why? Because it implies acceptance of the medical view described above. To call an individual "mentally ill" implies that his or her problems constitute a disease that can be cured through appropriate medical treatment. In one respect, this view makes sense. As has been already noted, many psychological problems do seem to have an important biological component. In another sense, though, the medical perspective is somewhat misleading. Decades of research suggest that full understanding of many psychological disorders requires careful attention to *psychological* processes such as learning, perception, and cognition, as well as recognition of the complex interplay between the environment and heredity that seems to affect all forms of behaviour.

Cultural Factors and Abnormal Behaviour

Normal behaviour in one culture may be considered quite abnormal in another. The Ashura ritual, practised in the Middle East, involves self-flagellation, a behaviour that many cultures would consider abnormal.

For example, consider what is perhaps the most common form of psychological disorder, *depression,* which involves intense sadness, lack of energy, and feelings of hopelessness and despair. What are the roots of this complex problem? Existing evidence suggests that biochemical and genetic factors probably play an important role (Henriques & Davidson, 1990). But so do cognitive factors, such as what people think about and how they interpret various events in their lives (e.g., Watkins et al., 1996), and social factors, such as how much support and encouragement they receive from important people in their lives (e.g., Terry et al., 1996). In order to understand fully the nature of depression as well as its origins, we must take careful account of such factors.

Finally, most psychologists also attach considerable importance to *cultural factors* in their efforts to understand abnormal behaviour. Some disorders—especially those that are quite severe—appear to be universal, occurring in all or at least most cultures (Al-Issa, 1982). Other disorders, however, vary greatly across cultures in terms of their frequency, severity, and precise form. For example, depression appears to be more common in Western nations than in Asian ones (Kleinman, 1986). Serious *eating disorders* such as anorexia nervosa and bulimia, which can result in individuals starving themselves until they become very thin, have tended also to occur primarily in Western cultures—but as Western "pop culture" spreads throughout the world, such problems are now appearing in other cultures too, everywhere that Western magazines, films, and television programs reach (Chun et al., 1992; Mumford et al., 1992). Findings such as these suggest that some psychological disorders can have important roots in cultural beliefs and practices, and that these should not be overlooked.

In sum, the modern psychological perspective on abnormal behaviour suggests that such behaviour can best be understood in terms of complex and often subtle interactions between biological, psychological, and sociocultural factors. This perspective is certainly more complex than one that views such disorders as exclusively biological in origin. As we'll discover later in this chapter, it is also likely to be considerably more accurate. See the **Key Concept** on page 562 for an overview of contrasting viewpoints on abnormal behaviour.

K E Y *QUESTIONS*

▨ What are psychological disorders?

▨ To what factors were such disorders attributed in the past?

▨ What is the modern psychological view of such disorders?

▶

Key Concept

Contrasting Viewpoints on Abnormal Behaviour

Supernatural View

Abnormal behaviour stems from supernatural causes—possession by demons, evil spirits, goddesses or gods.

Some evidence indicates that persons burned at the stake in the Middle Ages because they were thought to be witches were actually suffering from psychological disorders.

Psychodynamic View

Abnormal behaviour stems from hidden inner forces—that is, conflict between unconscious impulses and aspects of personality that restrain them.

Medical View

Abnormal behaviour is a treatable disease and, like other diseases, has biological causes.

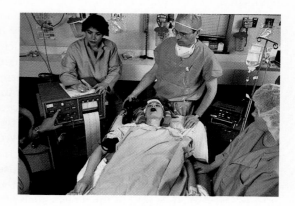

Electroconvulsive therapy, which involves the delivery of electric shocks to the patient's head, reflects the view that psychological disorders stem primarily from biological causes.

Modern Psychological View

Abnormal behaviour has multiple causes. Careful account must be taken of biological, psychological, and sociocultural factors.

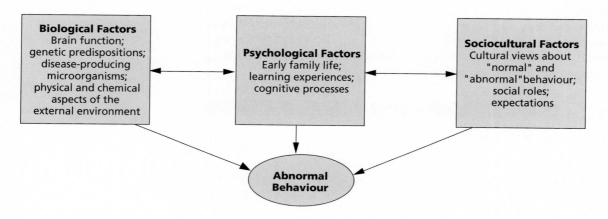

Biological Factors Brain function; genetic predispositions; disease-producing microorganisms; physical and chemical aspects of the external environment

Psychological Factors Early family life; learning experiences; cognitive processes

Sociocultural Factors Cultural views about "normal" and "abnormal" behaviour; social roles; expectations

Abnormal Behaviour

▶ Identifying Psychological Disorders

No competent physician would attempt to treat a common cold through surgery, or internal injuries with a Band-Aid. The first and often most crucial step in medical practice is *diagnosis*—identifying the nature of the problem that brought the patient to the doctor in the first place. Even if we do not view psychological disorders as medical illnesses, the need to identify these problems in a clear and reliable manner remains. Without an agreed-upon system of *classification*, different psychologists or psychiatrists might refer to the same disorder with different terms, or use the same term to describe very different problems (Millon, 1991).

The need for an agreed-upon system for diagnosing such disorders is addressed by the **Diagnostic and Statistical Manual of Mental Disorders-IV** (or DSM-IV for short; American Psychiatric Association, 1994). Although this manual is published by the American Psychiatric Association, psychologists have long contributed to its development—increasingly so in recent years. Thus, it is designed to help all mental health practitioners to recognize and correctly identify specific disorders.

The major distinguishing feature of DSM-IV is that it classifies disorders along five axes. Table 14.1 details the character of each of the different axes. Along Axis I are the *major diagnostic categories* of DSM-IV. Only a selective sampling of the more common major disorders are included in Table 14.1. The full manual describes

Diagnostic and Statistical Manual of Mental Disorders-IV (DSM-IV): The latest version of a manual widely used for diagnosing various psychological disorders.

TABLE 14.1

The Basic Layout of the DSM-IV Diagnostic System

DSM-IV is the standard system used to classify psychological disorders in North America. As may be seen, clinical material relevant to five different axes must be considered in making a diagnosis.

Major Diagnostic Categories of the DSM-IV

Axis I: The Various Different Clinical Syndromes

Disorders Usually First Diagnosed in Infancy, Childhood, or Adolescence
These encompass problems in learning, attention, communication, and social interactions. Examples include attention-deficit hyperactivity, and conduct disorder.

Mood Disorders
Emotional state imbalances characterize this disorder. Variations in emotional state can range from euphoria to total despair. Examples include major depression, and the bipolar mood disorder.

Anxiety Disorders
A specific, or broad-based sense of apprehension and foreboding, underlie anxiety disorders. Examples of anxiety disorders are panic attacks, phobias, and the obsessive-compulsive disorder.

Dissociative Disorders
Dissociative disorders involve an inability to remember significant details about one's personal self. Examples of this disorder are the fugue state and the dissociative identity disorder.

Eating Disorders
Eating disorders are concerned with a dissatisfaction about one's body weight and various unhealthy compensating activities that may be employed to deal with this dissatisfaction. Examples include anorexia nervosa and bulimia nervosa.

Somatoform Disorders
Somatoform disorders are characterized by a disposition to report experiences of physical pain, distress, or disease for which there is no organic cause. Examples include the somatization and conversion disorders as well as hypochondriasis.

Sexual and Gender Identity Disorders
These disorders embrace a variety of different sexual dysfunctions. Deficiencies in desire, arousal, and in the ability to achieve orgasm fall within this classification, as do pedophilia, fetishism, and gender identity conflicts.

Schizophrenia and Other Psychotic Disorders
A set of very severe afflictions that adversely affect virtually all aspects of psychological functioning. Delusional and hallucinatory experiences characterize this set of disorders. Examples include paranoid, catatonic, and residual types of schizophrenia.

Substance-Related Disorders
These disorders involve maladaptive abuse of and/or a dependency on drugs or other substances. Examples include amphetamine-, cocaine-, and opioid-related disorders.

continued

TABLE 14.1 *continued*

Axis II: Personality Disorders and Mental Retardation

Axis II of the DSM IV is used to detail the presence of personality disorders as well as mental retardation. Extreme and inflexible behaviour and insensitivity to the consequences of one's own behaviour on others are trademark characteristics of personality disorders. There may be accompanying discordant emotional reactions and problems with impulse control. Examples of personality disorders include the antisocial, dependent, borderline, and paranoid personality types.

Axis III: General Medical Conditions

Axis III is used to describe any present medical condition that might contribute to, or complicate, treatment of disorders detailed on Axis I. For example, a disease of the central nervous system could contribute to the production of symptoms of mental dysfunction and would require consideration in any treatment program.

Axis IV: Psychosocial and Environmental Problems

Axis IV details the source and severity of any environmental or social stressors that may influence the course or character of a clinical disorder. Social stressors refer to social interactions with others that are a source of discomfort or distress. Included would be such experiences as the end of a romantic relationship, family problems, and the illness or death of a family member or friend. Environmental stressors refer to any non-social events or experiences that currently impact in a negative way on an individual such as, work-related problems, unemployment, or entanglement in court proceedings.

Axis V: Global Assessment of Function

Code		Code	Symptoms
100	Superior functioning in a wide range of activities	50	Serious symptoms, or substantial impairment in functioning in social, home, occupational, or school settings
90	Absent or minimal symptoms, generally good functioning in all areas	40	Some impairment in reality assessment, or serious impairments in judgment, mood, thinking, and social interactions
80	Transient symptoms, or minor problems in social, occupational, school, or home settings	30	Evidence of thought processes being influenced by delusions or hallucinations. Major problems in almost all areas of functioning
70	Mild symptoms, or difficulties in functioning in some areas of social, home, occupational, or school settings	20	Some danger that injury will be inflicted on self or others. Lapses in standard of normal hygiene. Impaired capacity to communicate with others
60	Moderate symptoms, or moderate difficulty in functioning in some areas of social, home, occupational, or school settings	10	Persistent danger of severe injury to self or others, and inability to maintain minimal standards of personal hygiene.

Source: Adapted, with permission, from the *Diagnostic and Statistical Manual of Mental Disorders, 4th ed.* © American Psychiatric Association, 1994.

hundreds of disorders—far more than we will have time to consider. The descriptions provided on Axis I focus on observable diagnostic features—*symptoms* that must be present before an individual is diagnosed as suffering from a particular problem.

Axis II details what are known as *personality disorders.* These are maladaptive aspects of personality (including mental retardation) that have a powerful influence on the character of an individual's behaviour and that can complicate the course and treatment of a clinical disorder. Axis III focuses on any concurrent *medical conditions* that might similarly influence the course and treatment of a clinical disorder. Axis IV considers psychosocial and environmental *sources of stress* that may serve to exacerbate a disorder. Finally, Axis V provides a way of assessing the overall *level of functioning* of an individual in his or her day-to-day life. The five-axis classification system used in DSM-IV provides a much richer and detailed appraisal of an individual's current psychological condition than did earlier diagnostic procedures. To illustrate the overall comprehensiveness of a DSM-IV evaluation, a multiaxial assessment of a male government employee suffering from both generalized anxiety and panic attacks is shown in Table 14.2.

TABLE 14.2

A DSM-IV Multiaxial Assessment

The following appraisal of a twenty-eight-year-old male government employee illustrates assessment using the DSM-IV axes.

Axis I	Generalized Anxiety Disorder accompanied by panic attacks
Axis II	Dependent personality
Axis III	Arrhythmia
Axis IV	Psychosocial stressors: Unable to maintain employment because of reluctance to leave security of home. Lives with parents and lacks friends outside his family.
Axis V	Current global level of functioning: 45
	Highest global level of functioning in past year: 50

DSM-IV differs from earlier diagnostic manuals in several important respects. Perhaps most important, it is the first version to which psychologists have had major input (Barlow, 1991). Partly as a result of this occurrence, and partly as a result of changes within psychiatry, strenuous efforts were made to base the DSM-IV more firmly than ever on empirical evidence concerning the nature and prevalence of psychological disorders. The task force of psychiatrists, psychologists, and other professionals who worked on this new version relied heavily on published studies and the re-analysis of existing data when refining descriptions of each disorder. The task force also conducted special field trials in which they compared new descriptions and categories with existing ones to determine if the proposed changes would indeed improve the reliability of diagnosis—that is, the consistency with which specific disorders could be identified (e.g., Widiger et al., 1996).

Additional changes in the DSM-IV reflect efforts to take fuller account of the potential role of cultural factors in psychological disorders. For example, in the DSM-IV, the description of each disorder contains a new section that focuses on *culturally related features*—aspects of each disorder that are related to, and may be affected by, culture. Symptoms specific to a given culture and unique ways of describing distress in various cultures are included whenever available. This information is designed to help professionals recognize the many ways in which an individual's culture can influence the form of psychological disorders.

In these and other ways, the DSM-IV does seem to represent an improvement over earlier versions. However, it's important to note that it is still largely *descriptive* in nature: it describes psychological disorders, but it makes no attempt to explain them. This is deliberate; the DSM-IV was specifically designed to assist in diagnosis. It remains neutral with respect to various theories about the origins of psychological disorders. Since psychology as a science seeks *explanation*, not simply description, however, many psychologists view this aspect of the DSM-IV as a shortcoming that limits its value. (For more information on other tools used by psychologists to assess individuals' functioning and the extent to which they are experiencing psychological disorders, see the **Research Process** section below).

Culture and the Diagnosis of Psychological Disorders

Clinical judgments about psychological disorders can be influenced by cultural factors, including differences in ethnic background between therapists and clients. Such factors are given increased attention in the DSM-IV.

The Research Process:

How Psychologists Study Psychological Disorders

As noted earlier, an agreed-upon system for identifying psychological disorders is a necessary first step for effective treatment of them. This is not the only reason why accurate diagnosis is necessary. One must be able to accurately specify disorders in order to carry out systematic research on them and answer such questions as, "Why do they occur?" "What effects do they have on the persons experiencing them?" "How can they best be alleviated?" It is these kinds of questions that *clinical psychologists* address in their research (e.g., Chosen et al., 1996; Vernberg et al., 1996). Although the DSM-IV is an important guide in identifying various psychological disorders, it is important to recognize that it is not the only tool used by psychologists. Here are some of the other approaches psychologists use to specify and understand psychological disorders.

Assessment Interviews

As experts in human behaviour, psychologists realize that much can be learned from direct interactions with individuals who seek their help. Thus, they often conduct **assessment interviews** in which they seek information about individuals' past and present behaviours, current problems, interpersonal relations, and personality. Such interviews can be *structured*, in which case psychologists follow a detailed set of questions prepared in advance and known to get at the information they want, or *semistructured*, in which they follow an outline of major topics, but do not have a list of specific questions. Through such procedures, much can be learned about specific persons, and interesting hypotheses concerning the origins of their problems can be formulated.

Personality Measures

Since personality is closely related to certain forms of psychological disorder, psychologists often use various measures of personality as a means of studying such disorders. Both *projective* tests, such as the Rorschach and TAT, and *objective* tests, such as the MMPI, are examined in Chapter 12.

Biological Measures

Revealing information is often provided by various *neuroimaging techniques* discussed in Chapter 2—computerized axial tomography (CAT scans), magnetic resonance imaging, and positron emission tomography. These tools are often used by psychologists to study the biological basis of various psychological disorders. In addition, various *biological markers*—biological changes associated with specific mental disorders—have also been identified. Such markers include changes in liver enzymes—a useful marker for alcoholism (e.g., Allen & Litten, 1993), and elevations in heart rate, blood pressure, and muscle tension, which are often a sign of anxiety disorders.

Observations of Behaviour

Another source of assessment information used by psychologists is observation of individuals' behaviour—especially behaviour relevant to problems suggested by other assessment tools. Psychologists often observe individuals in specific situations, ones in which the target behaviours—those causing them distress—occur. Another observational technique involves *self-monitoring* by patients themselves, who keep records of the frequency, duration, and quality of their own behaviours and moods (e.g., Nietzel, Bernstein, & Milich, 1998).

In sum, psychologists use many different tools—not simply the DSM-IV—as a basis for identifying psychological disorders and planning systematic research focused on them. We'll encounter many examples of these methods as we discuss various psychological disorders and efforts by psychologists to uncover the factors that lead to their occurrence.

Assessment Interviews: Interviews conducted by psychologists in which they seek information about individuals' past and present behaviours, current problems, interpersonal relations, and personality.

DESCRIBING PSYCHOLOGICAL DISORDERS: AN EXPLANATORY NOTE We will now consider individual psychological disorders. As mentioned earlier, the DSM-IV lists and describes literally hundreds of different disorders. All of these are important, but space limitations make it impossible to cover all of them here. Instead, therefore, we'll focus on those disorders which are most common and which, for that reason, have received the most attention from psychologists. For an indication of the frequency with which various different psychological disorders occur, see the **Canadian Focus** feature.

Canadian Focus

Assessing the Prevalence of Psychological Disorders in Canada

How common are psychological disorders? For some insight into this question, consider the Stirling County study from the late 1950s (Leighton, 1959). The objective of this pioneering study was to examine the impact of social and cultural factors on the mental health of 20 000 inhabitants of a 2500-square-kilometre, largely rural area of Nova Scotia.

The initial approach involved a procedure termed *total case finding*. The investigators assumed that psychological disorders would be limited in number and that it would be possible to obtain information about virtually every individual in the community suffering from some form of psychological disorder. Sensibly enough, they began with an examination of mental and general hospital records, county homes, and poorhouses. Information from these sources was then supplemented, as in traditional anthropology, with information from informants such as teachers, community leaders, and general practitioners.

The deficiencies of the approach rapidly became clear. Institutional records were often lacking in necessary detail. Much more problematical was the incorrect assumption that only a relatively modest number of psychological disorders would be encountered. In fact, many more cases than anticipated were encountered; further, the investigators suspected that many more individuals in the community might be experiencing difficulties and not seeking assistance. These individuals would have no medical records and might well escape the attention of the various mental health informants. To try to find these people, health assessment questionnaires were developed and administered to a representative sample of the population.

In the end, researchers had to base their conclusions on information from a variety of interlaced sources, including mental and general hospital records, questionnaire assessments, and the treatment records of local physicians, which were examined by psychiatrists who then made diagnostic assignments. What was concluded? That approximately 20 percent of the population experience some form of psychological disability meriting attention (Murphy, 1980).

More recent efforts to assess the prevalence of psychological disorders rely exclusively on questionnaires and other surveys, and the data from these can be analyzed and classified by computer. Good examples of this approach are a study by Bland, Newman, and Orn (1988), who looked into the prevalence of psychological disorders in the city of Edmonton, and a broader-based Ontario study by Offord and his colleagues (1996). Both studies used similar methodologies.

Trained interviewers administered a special diagnostic interview questionnaire to individual family members in a very large number of different households. In the Edmonton study, individuals in slightly more than three thousand households were interviewed, and in the Ontario study, individuals in almost ten thousand households were interviewed.

In spite of differences in time, location, and procedure, the results of the Edmonton and Ontario studies indicate an overall prevalence rate for psychological disorders close to the 20 percent reported in the Stirling County study. Bland and his colleagues found that about 17 percent of Edmontonians had experienced some form of psychological disorder over the preceding six months, and Offord and his colleagues found that just under 19 percent of Ontarians had experienced some form of psychological disorder over the previous year.

Are some disorders more common than others? Very much so. A graphic representation of the study by Bland and his colleagues is shown in Figure 14.2. (Note that a number of the individual disorders reported have been clustered to form more general categories.) As can be seen, the most common general categories of disorders are anxiety disorders (phobias, panic reaction, obsessive-compulsive disorders), mood disorders (manic episodes, major depressions), and substance abuse disorders (drug and alcohol abuse). Clearly, there are significant male/female differences. Substance abuse disorders are much more common among males, as are symptoms indicating antisocial disorders. Anxiety disorders and mood disorders, however, are much more common among females.

What else should be said about the prevalence of psychological disorders? Several things. First, it should be noted that the overall prevalence rate is not the same for all age groups. For example, in the Ontario study the overall prevalence rate was close to 25 percent for those fifteen to twenty-four years of age, but only about 12 percent for those in the forty-five to sixty-four year old range. Second, it should be emphasized that in our discussion we have focused upon what are termed *period prevalence rates*. These rates reflect the prevalence of disorders over a previous six-month or full-year period. If *lifetime prevalence rates* are examined—that is, the occurrence of a disorder during any period of life up to the date of the study—the rates rise markedly. Further analysis of the Edmonton study data indicated that almost 34 percent of the population sampled had personal experience with at least one type of psychological disorder at some point in their lives (Bland et al., 1988). Finally, it is important to recognize that comorbidity is common—individuals very often have symptoms indicating the presence of *more than one disorder*. This explains why, as some of you may have noticed, the individual percentages for the various disorders shown on our graph of the Edmonton study add up to over 40 percent. Only 17 percent of individuals in the population specifically experi-

enced problems, but many had symptoms indicating the presence of more than one disorder.

What this brief consideration of the prevalence of disorders shows is that psychological disorders are not rare curiosities; rather, they occur in the general population far more often than most people realize.

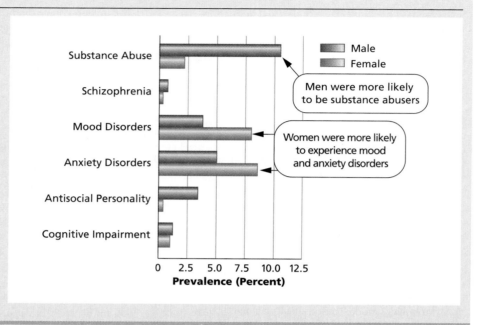

Figure 14.2
Prevalence of Psychological Disorders in a Large Canadian Urban Centre

Disorders involving mood, anxiety, and substance abuse are the most common in this Canadian city. As may be seen, there are pronounced gender differences in the incidence of these disorders.

Source: Based on a survey of Edmonton, Alberta, reported by Bland et al., 1988.

KEY QUESTIONS

- What is the DSM-IV?
- In what ways is it an improvement over earlier versions?
- What other methods do psychologists use to identify psychological disorders?
- How common are psychological disorders?

Critical Thinking

We have moved from DSM-1 to DSM-IV. The list of mental disorders has grown longer with each revision. Have we become more accurate in discerning disorders, or have we have become less and less discriminating about what we classify as a mental disorder?

Disorders of Childhood and Adolescence

We tend to think that psychological disorders are afflictions of adulthood. This is not so. There are some disorders that become apparent between birth and adolescence. There is good reason to expect that everyone who reads this book has, in his or her passage through the school system, shared classes with children experiencing some of problems that fall within this diagnostic domain—children who had problems in learning, reading, communication, maintaining social interactions, and in conduct.

Disruptive Behaviour Disorders

Disruptive behaviours are the most common single reason why children are referred to psychologists for diagnosis and treatment. In fact, such problems are quite common: as many as 10 percent of children may show such problems at some time or other. Disruptive behaviors are divided by the DSM-IV into two major categories: *oppositional defiant disorder* and *conduct disorder*.

Oppositional defiant disorder involves a pattern of behaviour in which children have poor control of their emotions or have repeated conflicts with parents and teachers. Consider this description of Nick, a nine-year old boy brought by his mother to a mental health centre:

> Within the past month, Nick has been sent to the principal's office three times for swearing at his teacher in front of other children. At home ... he is argumentative and spiteful. He has to be told again and again to do the smallest chore, and complains about all the work expected of him.... His mother says she is fed up with Nick, claiming, "It's just one battle after the next with him...."

Children showing this pattern have problems getting along with others, and may develop more serious difficulties such as *conduct disorder*. An oppositional defiant disorder usually starts when children are quite young (ages three to seven). Conduct disorder begins somewhat later, often when children enter puberty. Conduct disorder involves more serious antisocial behaviours that go beyond throwing tantrums or disobeying rules; it involves actions that are potentially harmful to the child, to others, or to property.

What are the causes of these disruptive patterns of behaviour? Biological factors appear to play a role. Boys show such problems much more often than do girls, thus suggesting that sex hormones play a role. Some findings suggest that children who develop conduct disorder have unusually low levels of general arousal—and seem to crave the excitement that accompanies their disruptive behaviours (e.g., Rain, Venebles, & Williams, 1990). Psychological factors also play a role. Children with conduct disorder often show insecure attachment to their parents, and often live in negative environments involving poverty, large family size, and being placed in foster care (Biederman et al., 1990). In addition, their parents often use coercive child-rearing practices, which may actually encourage disruptive behaviour (e.g., Campbell et al., 1986). Whatever the cause, it is clear that conduct disorder is a serious problem that can well pave the way to additional problems during adulthood.

Attention-Deficit/Hyperactivity Disorder

If you have ever observed very young children, you know that they are easily distracted. As children grow older, however, they acquire an increasing ability to concentrate; by the time they are about seven years old, they can tune out interference such as music or other background noise (e.g., Higgins & Turnure). This is not the case for all children. Some children suffer from **attention-deficit/hyperactivity disorder**. Such children display an inability to sustain attention and a lack of impulse control. They talk during quiet periods, ignore social rules, leave their seats, and create disturbances in the classroom. They have normal intelligence, but the difficulty they experience in focusing attention prevents them from dealing constructively with assigned tasks. Their restless energy and inability to concentrate provide a constant challenge to the patience of both parents and teachers (Johnston, 1996). Unfortunately, attention-deficit/hyperactivity disorder is *not* a problem that fades with the passage of time: 70 percent of children diagnosed with this disorder in elementary school still show signs of it when they are sixteen (Barkley et al., 1990). Moreover, by this time, it is often accompanied by conduct disorder.

Disruptive Behaviours: Childhood mental disorders involving poor control of impulses, conflict with other children and adults, and, in some cases, more serious forms of antisocial behaviour.

Attention-Deficit/Hyperactivity Disorder: A psychological disorder in which children are unable to concentrate their attention on any task for more than a few minutes.

Attention-Deficit/Hyperactivity Disorder

Children with this disorder cannot focus their attention on any task for more than a few minutes. As a result, they quickly become bored and often disrupt classroom activities.

What are the causes of this disorder? Genetic factors do play a role; children whose parents or siblings have attention-deficit/hyperactivity disorder are more likely to develop the disorder (Biederman et al., 1992). Environmental factors such as exposure to lead (Needleman et al., 1990) and smoke (Millberger et al., 1998) may also enhance susceptibility. As far as psychological factors are concerned, a dysfunctional home situation will almost certainly aggravate the severity of the symptoms displayed, but there does not seem to any evidence that the disorder can arise solely from adverse home conditions. Current thinking is that it is triggered by a genetically based biological predisposition that influences brain function in an as-yet-to-be-fully understood fashion (Firestone, 1999).

In treating the disorder, the drug Ritalin is commonly used to help manage symptoms of the disorder. Family therapy and training programs can help diminish the stress this disorder imposes on the home. There are also some *behaviour* therapies available that can provide some assistance in focusing attention and controlling impulsive inclinations (Blakemore et al., 1993; Mash & Johnston, 1990).

Autism: A Pervasive Developmental Disorder

There is one remaining class of childhood disorders that we will briefly consider: **pervasive development disorders.** Such disorders involve lifelong impairment in mental or physical functioning. Perhaps the most prominent of these disorders is *autism.* Children with this disorder seem to live in an almost totally private world. They typically have deficient language skills and do not make appropriate use of nonverbal behaviours such as eye contact in interacting with others. In fact, they show little interest in social interactions, and do not develop peer relationships. When they do notice others, they often seem to treat them as objects rather than people.

The causes of autism are not fully understood. Genetic factors appear to play a role. Twin studies, for instance, show a higher *concordance rate* (the likelihood that if one twin displays the disorder, the other will be similarly affected) for identical than for fraternal twins (e.g., Rutter et al., 1990). From a psychological perspective, the most interesting hypothesis is that autistic children appear to have deficits in their *theory of mind*, a concept we discussed in Chapter 8. As you may recall, this term refers to children's understanding of their own and others' mental states. Advocates of this view argue that autistic children are unable to realize that other individuals have a mind. They seem to be unaware that other people may have access to different sources of information about situations than they do, and that they may view things differently. In short, they are unable to make inferences about the beliefs of others and anticipate their reactions—a deficiency that prevents them from engaging in meaningful social interactions. Autism is an enduring and troubling disorder for which there appears to be no cure.

Pervasive Development Disorders: Disorders that involve lifelong impairment in mental or physical functioning.

Mood Disorders: Psychological disorders involving intense and prolonged mood shifts.

Mood Disorders

Everyone experiences swings in mood or emotional state—these are a normal part of life. Some people experience disturbances in mood that are both extreme and prolonged. Their highs are higher, their lows are lower, and the periods they spend at these emotional heights and depths are lengthy. Such people are described as suffering from **mood disorders,** which the DSM-IV describes under two major categories: *depressive disorders* and *bipolar disorders.*

Depressive Disorders

None of us leads a perfect life; we all experience some events that make us feel sad or disappointed. An unexpectedly poor grade, breaking up with one's lover or spouse, failure to get a promotion or a raise—these and countless other events tip our emotional balance toward sadness. When do such reactions constitute depression? Most psychologists agree that several criteria are useful for making this decision.

First, people suffering from **depression** experience truly profound unhappiness, and they experience it much of the time. Second, people experiencing depression report that they have lost interest in all the usual pleasures of life. Eating, sex, sports, hobbies—all fail to provide the enjoyment and satisfaction people expect and, usually, derive from them. Third, people suffering from depression experience a major loss of energy. Everything becomes an effort, and feelings of exhaustion are common. Additional symptoms of depression include loss of appetite, disturbances of sleep, difficulties in thinking (depressed people are indecisive and find that they cannot think, concentrate, or remember), recurrent thoughts of death, feelings of worthlessness or excessive guilt, and frequent feelings of agitation.

When individuals experience five or more of these symptoms at once, they are classified by the DSM-IV as showing a *major depressive episode*. Depression is all too common in our society. The most recent Statistics Canada figures show that 6.6 percent of males and 10.8 percent of females eighteen to twenty-four years of age (the age group of individuals most likely to be reading this book) experienced depression. Other studies estimate that, over the lifespan, depression will be experienced by 21.3 percent of women and 12.7 percent of men (Kessler et al., 1994).

Why is the rate higher for women than men? According to Strickland (1992), there are a number of reasons, including the fact that females have had traditionally lower status, power, and income; must worry more than males about their personal safety; and are much more often than males the victims of sexual harassment and assaults. In addition, recent findings indicate that such differences in rates of depression may also stem, at least to a degree, from the fact that females are more willing to admit to such feelings than males, or from the fact that women are more likely than men to remember such episodes (Wilhelm & Parker, 1994).

Depression: The Emotional Dark Side of Life

Many people suffering from severe depression seek a drastic solution to their problems—suicide.

Bipolar Disorders

If depression is the emotional black hole of life, then bipolar disorder is its emotional roller coaster. People suffering from **bipolar disorder** experience wide swings in mood. They move, over varying periods of time, between deep depression and an emotional state known as *mania,* in which they are extremely excited, elated, and energetic. During manic periods, these people speak rapidly, show a sharply decreased need for sleep, jump from one idea or activity to another, and show excessive involvement in pleasurable activities that have a high potential for painful consequences; for example, they may engage in uncontrolled buying sprees or make extremely risky investments. Bipolar disorders are very disruptive not only to the individuals who experience them but also to other people in their lives.

The Causes of Depression

BIOLOGICAL FACTORS The most direct evidence that biological factors play a significant role in depression is provided by genetic studies, which show that mood disorders tend to run in families (Egeland et al., 1987). Comparisons of identical and

Depression: A psychological disorder involving intense feelings of sadness, lack of energy, and feelings of hopelessness and despair.

Bipolar Disorder: A mood disorder involving swings between depression and mania.

fraternal twins reveal that the *concordance rate* for major depressive episodes is much higher for identical twins (40 percent) than for fraternal twins (20 percent). For bipolar depression, the genetic link is even stronger. The concordance rate is about 70 percent for identical twins, and 15 to 20 percent for fraternal twins (Allen, 1976; Bertelson, Harvald, & Hauge, 1977). Clearly, heritable dispositions increase susceptibility to the disorder.

Other findings suggest that mood disorders may involve abnormalities in brain biochemistry. For example, it has been found that levels of two neurotransmitters, *norepinephrine* and *serotonin,* are lower in the brains of depressed persons than in those of nondepressed persons. Similarly, levels of such substances are higher in the brains of persons showing mania. Further, when persons who have recovered from depression undergo procedures that reduce the levels of serotonin in their brains, their depressive symptoms return within twenty-four hours (Delgado et al., 1990).

Unfortunately, this relatively neat picture is complicated by the following facts: Not all people suffering from depression show reduced levels of norepinephrine or serotonin; and not all those who demonstrate mania have increased levels of these neurotransmitters. In addition, there is reason to believe that the drugs used to treat both types of disorders have effects other than simply changing the level or activity of these specific neurotransmitters. So, while it is clear at this time that biological factors play a role in depression, the precise nature of these factors remains to be determined.

PSYCHOLOGICAL FACTORS Although biochemical factors clearly play an important role in depression, psychological mechanisms are also important. One of these is **learned helplessness** (Seligman, 1975)—beliefs on the part of individuals that they have no control over their own outcomes. Such beliefs often develop after exposure to situations in which such lack of control is present, but then generalize to other situations where individuals' fate is at least partly in their hands. As you can readily guess, one outcome resulting from feelings of learned helplessness is depression (e.g., Seligman et al., 1988).

Depressed persons are prone also to several types of faulty or distorted thinking (e.g., Persad & Polivy, 1993; Tripp, Catano, & Sullivan, 1997). Since they often experience negative moods, *mood-dependent memory* processes (which we described in Chapter 6) tend to operate against them. They tend to bring unhappy thoughts and memories to mind and to dwell on them. They tend to notice, store, and remember information consistent with their negative moods (e.g., Mason & Graf, 1993; Roediger & McDermott, 1992). Especially important in this respect is the fact that depressed individuals characteristically possess negative *self-schemas*—negative conceptions of their own traits, abilities, and behaviour (Beck, 1976; Beck et al., 1979). They also tend to be especially sensitive to any additional negative information about themselves, such as criticism from others (Joiner et al., 1993). Since they tend to notice and retain this information, their feelings of worthlessness strengthen—and so does their depression. In short, these processes set up a self-perpetuating cycle in which the possibility of escape from depressing thoughts—or depression itself—decreases over time.

An interesting illustration of such effects is provided by research conducted recently by Watkins and his colleagues (1996). These researchers wondered whether the tendency of depressed persons to think negative thoughts is so strong that it occurs automatically (i.e., without any willful intention on their part). To test this possibility, Watkins and his colleagues exposed individuals who were depressed and persons who were not depressed to lists of positive words (e.g., admired, optimistic, talented), neutral words (e.g., dresser, flannel, propane, turtles), or negative

Learned Helplessness: Feelings of helplessness that develop after exposure to situations in which no effort succeeds in changing outcomes. Learned helplessness appears to play a role in the occurrence of depression.

words (e.g., punished, hopeless, failure, rejected). As each word was shown on a screen, participants in the study were told to think about these words by imagining themselves in a scene involving the word. After studying the words in this fashion and completing a number of intervening requirements, they were then presented with cue words that were related to the words they had previously studied, and they were asked to generate as many associations to these cues as possible within a thirty-second period. There was no hint or suggestion that the participants provide those words that they had previously seen and thought about as responses to cue words. In fact, every effort was made to convey to participants the idea that the two tasks were separate and independent. Nevertheless, many of the words thought about and imagined in the initial part of the experiment were generated as free associates to cue words. The investigators assumed that if depressed individuals unconsciously dwell on negative information, they would more likely generate negative words from the earlier list as associates to cue words than would nondepressed individuals. As you can see from Figure 14.3, this is precisely what was found. Moreover, and also as expected, the opposite was true with respect to positive words: nondepressed persons provided more of these words than did depressed persons.

As indicated by the Watkins study (1996, p. 39), these findings have important implications for understanding the cognitive roots of depression. Since depressed persons seem to bring negative information to mind without trying to do so, their tendency to perceive the world through "dark grey glasses" is intensified, and they have little opportunity to engage in activities that might boost their mood—after all, they don't even think of such activities! There can be little doubt that cognitive factors play an important role in depression. Fortunately, as we'll see in Chapter 15, effective procedures for countering these factors have been developed, and they offer considerable hope for persons who experience depression (e.g., Zuroff et al., 1999).

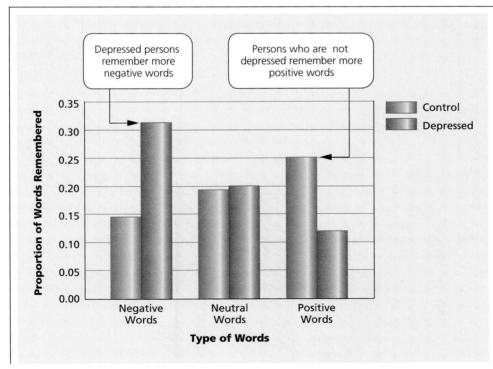

Figure 14.3
Unconscious Memory Bias among Depressed Persons

When exposed to cue words related to words they had previously studied, depressed individuals remembered more negative words than persons who were not depressed. In contrast, persons who were not depressed remembered more positive words. These findings suggest that depressed persons tend to remember negative information even when not actively attempting to do so.

Source: Based on data from Watkins et al., 1996.

Suicide

Hopelessness, despair, negative views about oneself and others—these are some of the hallmarks of depression. Given such symptoms, it is not surprising that many people suffering from this disorder seek a drastic solution to their problems—suicide. Suicide rates have been increasing since the middle of the century. Strachan, Johansen, Nair, and Nargundkar (1990) report that several million people in the world attempt suicide every year, and that more than a thousand a day succeed at it. Canada has not escaped this trend.

In Figure 14.4, Canadian suicide rates are shown separately for males and females over a fifty-year period. When we examine this figure, it is clear that the increase in the suicide rate that has occurred since 1947 is almost exclusively attributable to growth in suicide among males. The female suicide rate has remained roughly stable. The shift in the male suicide rate is mainly attributable to a large increase in frequency with which teenage to young adult males elect to commit suicide (Segal & Ferguson,1999). Leenaars and Lester (1990) report that teenage boys have a suicide rate five times that of teenage girls. In fact, for males in the fifteen to twenty-four age group, suicide is now the second-leading cause of death (Thibault, 1992). Besseghini (1997) reports that two-thirds of adolescents who do commit suicide have made at least one previous attempt, and have contemplated the act over a long period of time. A common pattern seen in many teenage suicides is a gradual withdrawal from family and friends—a process that leaves them with no one to turn to in a time of crisis. Especially vulnerable are adolescents who turn to alcohol and drugs for support or opt for a life in the streets. Without question, distressingly large numbers of young people do consider suicide. In a large Ontario study, it was found that 5 to 10 percent of boys and 10 to 20 percent of girls between twelve and sixteen had either thought about or attempted suicide over the six-month period assessed by the study (Joffe et al., 1988).

You may be puzzled by the fact that the Ontario findings indicate that more girls than boys seem to contemplate or attempt suicide. Why, then, should the suicide rate for males be so much higher, if females contemplate or attempt suicide more often? The answer is that women are much more likely to think about and attempt suicide than men, but for men an attempt is much more likely to end in death. Men use more lethal devices: They resort to guns or hanging, whereas women tend to use less certain methods, such as a sleeping pill overdose or cutting their wrists.

Figure 14.4
Canadian Suicide Rates by Sex, 1947–1997

The overall suicide rate increased during this fifty-year period. The increase is almost entirely attributable to an increase in the suicide rate of young males. The female suicide rate was relatively unchanged.

Source: Statistics Canada.

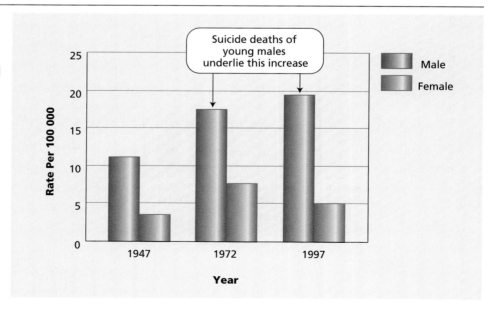

Factors Leading to Suicide

Many factors influence the likelihood of suicide. Psychological disorders play a role: depression and substance abuse (especially alcohol abuse) are commonly linked with suicide. A study of suicides in Edmonton by Dyck, Bland, Newman, and Orn (1988) found that about half of those who had attempted suicide had previously suffered from a major depression or alcohol dependency. A more recent study of youth suicide in Manitoba by Sigurdson and colleagues (1994) found that alcohol was a factor in about 50 percent of reported suicides, and that in 90 percent of the cases there was evidence of a mood disorder. What can be said about the psychological states that characterize an individual contemplating suicide? Baumeister (1990) suggests that suicide is the result of efforts by individuals to escape themselves—or, more accurately, to escape from awareness of their own faults and shortcomings. Various environmental conditions and stresses such as unemployment and exposure to ongoing family violence can contribute to suicide. (See the **Perspectives on Diversity** section, which provides information about the high suicide rates that prevail in some isolated Canadian Communities).

Perspectives on Diversity

Suicide in Isolated Communities

LOCATION CAN HAVE A SIGNIFICANT influence on suicide. Suicide rates are higher in the North and in other isolated areas of Canada (Aldridge & Kimberly, 1991). Some Native communities have intolerably high suicide rates. The suicide rate among Native people in British Columbia is estimated to be one and one-half times that found among non-Native people (Cooper et al., 1992). Aldridge and Kimberly report a suicide rate in Labrador that is about three and one-half times the Newfoundland average, and the newly created Arctic territory of Nunavut has a suicide rate at least six times the overall Canadian average (Lankan & Vincent, 1999). Davis Inlet has been described as having the highest suicide rate in the world in news media (e.g, Demont, 1999). In assessing these numbers, it is important not to lose sight of one important fact: High suicide rates are not observed in all Native communities; rather, rates depend on conditions within the specific community. For example, the high suicide rates in Labrador are confined to that one-quarter of the community living in isolated settlements on the north shore, such as Davis Inlet. During the ten-year period assessed in the study by Aldridge and Kimberly, no suicides were reported among the three-quarters of the Native people living in the remaining area of Labrador. Similarly, studies in British Columbia indicate that high suicide rates are evident only in certain communities.

What is it about some communities that contributes to a high suicide rate? In some cases, one does not have to look far to understand the high suicide rates. In Davis Inlet, for example, conditions within the community have been described as appalling. The traditional lifestyle has been destroyed; no meaningful alternative lifestyle has been established; there is almost no possibility of employment; the proportion of young people in the community is extremely large (40 percent are under fifteen years of age); and there is widespread substance abuse. In those areas of British Columbia associated with high suicide rates, factors typically found include crowding, few elders, many single-parent and low-income families, and large households with many children living at home (Cooper et al., 1992).

Can anything be done to address these problems? A recent health survey undertaken by First Nation and Innuit people indicated a need for a broadening of health care services and endorsed a return to a more traditional lifestyle as a valuable way to promote community health (Ayed, 1998). Whether steps will be taken to deal with the many concerns addressed in this survey remains to be seen.

Are there any preventative steps that can be taken to reduce suicide levels? Attempts have been made to develop high school education programs to provide students with information about the incidence of teenage suicide, characteristic warning signs, and the various avenues whereby help can be sought. Concern has been expressed that these programs have not proven effective, and that by focusing attention on suicide they may encourage consideration of the act by adolescents confronted with seemingly insoluble problems (Segal & Ferguson, 1999; Shaffer et al., 1988). Possibly the most effective preventative agent is the presence of caring friends or family who are sensitive to the signs that suicide is being considered—and who are prepared to provide support and assistance in obtaining professional help. See **Making Psychology Part of Your Life** on page 593 for some basic steps that you should take if you suspect someone you know is suicidal.

K E Y QUESTIONS

▓ What are the major symptoms of depression? Of bipolar disorder?

▓ What factors play a role in the occurrence of mood disorders?

▓ What are the major factors contributing to suicide?

▓ What factors contribute to gender differences in suicide rates?

Anxiety Disorders

At one time or another, we all experience **anxiety**—increased arousal accompanied by generalized feelings of fear or apprehension. If these feelings become very intense and persist for long periods of time, they can produce harmful effects. Such **anxiety disorders** take several different forms.

Generalized Anxiety Disorder

The broadest form of anxiety disorder is *generalized anxiety disorder*. It is characterized by a sense of uneasiness, discomfort, and distress that is not restricted to any specific identifiable circumstance or situation. It is a pervasive, "free-floating" disposition to worry simultaneously, and to a needless degree, about a wide variety of situations and events such as family, work, finances, and social interactions. It tends to be continuous and is often accompanied by excessive irritability, problems in concentration, and sleep disturbances.

Panic Attack Disorder

Everyone has experienced *panic*—very high levels of physical arousal coupled with an intense fear of losing control. For most of us, this is a relatively rare event. But people who suffer from a psychological condition known as **panic attack disorder** experience such reactions often, and sometimes without any specific triggering event. As defined by the DSM-IV, such attacks involve a discrete period of fear or discomfort in which at least four of the following symptoms occur suddenly and rise to a peak within ten minutes: palpitations, pounding heart, sweating, trembling or shaking, sensations of shortness of breath, feeling of choking, chest pain or discomfort, nausea, feeling dizzy or lightheaded, feelings of unreality, fear of losing control, fear of dying, numbness or tingling sensation, or chills or hot flashes. Consider the following case history:

Anxiety: Increased arousal accompanied by generalized feelings of fear or apprehension.

Anxiety Disorders: Psychological disorders that centre on the occurrence of anxiety and include generalized anxiety, phobias, and obsessive-compulsive disorders.

Panic Attack Disorder: An anxiety disorder characterized by relatively brief periods during which individuals experience unbearably intense anxiety.

Sally experienced her first panic attack out of the blue.... She had just finished a job interview and was meeting some friends for dinner. In the restaurant, she began to feel dizzy. Within a few seconds, her heart was pounding and she was feeling breathless—as though she might pass out. Sally experienced a similar episode a week later while at a movie.... Before long, she was having several attacks each week. In addition, she constantly worried about having attacks.... She avoided driving, shopping in large stores, and eating in all restaurants. Some weeks she avoided leaving the house completely. Sally stopped looking for work, fearing that she would be unable to stay at her job in the event of a panic attack.... [Barlow, 1992, p. 79]

For some people, like Sally, panic attacks occur out of the blue, without any apparent cause. For others, they are linked with specific situations. In that case, panic disorder is associated with **agoraphobia**—intense fear of specific situations in which individuals suspect that help will not be available should they experience an incapacitating panic attack. Common patterns for agoraphobia include fear of being in a crowd; of standing in a line; of being on a bridge; of travelling in a bus, train, or car; or of merely leaving home.

What causes panic attacks? Existing evidence indicates that both biological factors and psychological factors play a role. With respect to biological factors, it has been found that there is a genetic component in this disorder: About 50 percent of people with panic disorder have relatives with this disorder (Barlow, 1988). In addition, PET scans of the brains of persons who suffer from panic attacks suggest that even in the nonpanic state, their brains may be functioning differently, in subtle ways, from those of other persons (e.g., Reiman et al., 1989).

With respect to psychological factors, one possibility currently being explored is that individuals who experience panic attacks are excessively sensitive to changes in bodily sensations and tend to exaggerate their importance, or even engage in **catastrophic thinking** about their significance—causing an outpouring of anxiety that leads to panic. A further compounding factor is the worry that the panic attack will be repeated—a worrisome prospect that leads to further anxiety (e.g., Barlow, 1988; Clark & Ehlers, 1993). The result: A vicious circle is established—panic ... anxiety ... panic ... anxiety ... A recent University of Windsor study shows that women are more prone to panic attacks than men, and that many people who experience them resort to drugs, especially alcohol, in an attempt to self-medicate their problem—a practice that can lead to drug dependency (Malan et al., 1993).

Phobias

People often tend to be fearful of snakes, heights, violent storms, and buzzing insects, such as bees or wasps. Since all of these can pose real threats to our safety, such reactions are adaptive, up to a point. Some people, though, experience intense anxiety when in the presence of these objects or even when they merely think about them. These **phobias** can be so strong that they interfere with everyday activities. Those who suffer from animal phobias may avoid visiting friends who own dogs, or may cross the street to avoid passing a person taking a pet for a walk. Similarly, those with social phobias may avoid a wide range of social situations in which they fear they will be exposed to and scrutinized by unfamiliar people.

What accounts for the development of phobias? Once again, both biological and psychological factors play a role. One often-cited biologically based account we mentioned in Chapter 1 starts with the assumption that our evolutionary development stretched over an enormously long time period. The position taken is that during that time, repeated adverse experience with certain objects and situations may have induced a biological disposition for us to rapidly acquire an aversive avoidance reaction to these objects and events. This is why phobias directed toward pencils, rabbits, or palm trees are virtually nonexistent, while those toward snakes or spiders (which, at some point in our evolutionary history, may well have constituted a significant threat to our well-being) are much more common (Seligman, 1971).

Munch's *The Scream*
This famous painting seems to evoke the feelings associated with panic attack disorder.

Agoraphobia: Fear of losing control and experiencing a panic attack in specific situations, such as in open places, in a crowd, or on an airplane.

Catastrophic Thinking: Thoughts about impending disaster that may result in a full-blown panic attack.

Phobias: Intense, irrational fears of objects or events.

Psychological accounts of phobias are most commonly based on *classical conditioning* theory. Through classical conditioning, stimuli that do not initially elicit strong emotional reactions often come to do so. The account of "Little Albert" described in Chapter 5 is an excellent example of an acquired phobic reaction. Exposed to an inoffensive white laboratory rat, Albert reached out to touch it. Just before he managed to reach the animal, Watson and Raynor (1920) caused a very loud noise to occur—which much distressed Albert. These pairings were repeated several times. After this experience, Albert cried and crawled away whenever he was shown the rat. Through the pairing of a strong emotional response with an initially neutral stimulus (white rat), Albert developed a classically conditioned phobic reaction to the white rat, which reportedly extended to other furry white objects, such as a white stuffed rabbit.

Among the phobias, *social phobias* are, perhaps, the most devastating. Persons with such phobias are afraid of a wide range of social settings and interactions—parties, eating in public, giving speeches, using public washrooms. Their intense fear of such situations often dooms them to a restricted social life, and sometimes to painful loneliness. What are the causes of such phobias? Existing evidence indicates that several factors may play a role: childhood shyness, certain aspects of personality (e.g., being low in extraversion), and an early traumatic experience—a social situation in which the individual felt uncomfortable, and something negative happened (e.g., being laughed at, making a mistake). In one recent study, individuals who had a history of childhood shyness and a traumatic early experience were much more likely to experience social phobias than individuals for whom neither of these factors was present (Stemberger et al., 1995).

Obsessive-Compulsive Disorder

Most of us have had the experience of leaving our home, getting halfway down the street, and then suddenly having the thought that we had not turned the stove off or perhaps locked the door, and having to return home to check. These things occasionally happen; it is part of life. For individuals afflicted with an **obsessive-compulsive disorder,** this happens not just occasionally, but repeatedly, and they may have to return not once, but many times to still their anxiety over some imagined negligence. Individuals with this disorder have recurrent modes of thoughts called *obsessions*. These obsessional thoughts are coupled with intensifying *anxiety*, and compel them to engage in various types of repetitive behaviours known in the clinical literature as *compulsions*. Engaging in the compulsive behaviour reduces their anxiety, but *only* temporarily. Consider the following account of a person suffering from an obsessive-compulsive disorder (Rachman & Hodgson, 1980):

> When George wakes in the morning … he feels that his hands are contaminated so he cannot touch his clothing…. He won't wash in the bathroom because he feels that the carpet is contaminated…. I have to dress him…. He holds his hands above his head … to make sure that he doesn't contaminate the outside of his clothing. Any error or mishap and he will have to have clean clothes…. George then goes downstairs, washes his hands in the kitchen and thereafter spends about twenty minutes in the toilet…. Basically he has to be completely sure that there is no contamination around because if he is not then he will start to worry about it later on (pp. 66–67).

Obsessive-Compulsive Disorder: Anxiety disorder in which an individual is unable to stop thinking the same thoughts or performing the same ritualistic behaviours.

What is the cause of such reactions? One admittedly speculative biologically based explanation takes the position that anomalies in the functioning of particular brain structures—the caudate nucleus and basal ganglia—may be responsible for compulsive behaviours (Rappoport, 1989). It is held that this anomalous functioning unlocks, or releases, primitive behaviour patterns that may have been important at one time in the evolutionary past, but have been subsequently inhibited or overwritten. For example, the compulsive door checking that often afflicts those with obsessive-compulsive disorder has similarities to highly ritualized boundary checking that can be seen in many mammalian species, and may once have been part of our early behavioural repertoire. There is also a suggestive similarity between the compulsive washing behaviour engaged in by many of those with obsessive-compulsive disorder and the highly ritualized washing behaviour that can be observed in some mammalian species—especially under conditions of fear and anxiety.

Psychological explanations of the disorder tend to focus on anxiety and the reinforcing character of anxiety reduction. Even the most well-adjusted people often experience difficulty in dismissing a disturbing experience from their minds. Generally, however, if we engage in some form of distracting activity, or even sleep, intrusive thoughts about the experience diminish in intensity and ultimately vanish. Those with an obsessive-compulsive disorder cannot do so. They can find relief from the attendant anxiety only by performing some form of compulsive ritualistic behaviour. The anxiety reduction that follows the performance of the compulsive behaviour is reinforcing, and the frequency with which they engage in the compulsive behaviour increases, and can—in some cases—fill much of the day. Unless they receive effective outside help, people suffering from obsessive-compulsive disorders have little chance of escaping from their anxiety-ridden prisons.

K E Y QUESTIONS

- What are anxiety disorders?
- What are panic attacks?
- What are phobias?
- What is an obsessive-compulsive disorder?

Somatoform Disorders

Several of Freud's early cases, ones that played an important role in his developing theory of personality, involved the following puzzling situation. An individual would show some physical symptom (such as deafness or paralysis of some part of the body); yet careful examination would reveal no underlying physical causes for the problem. Such disorders are known as **somatoform disorders**—disorders in which individuals have physical symptoms without identifiable physical causes for these symptoms.

One such disorder is **somatization disorder,** a condition in which an individual has a history of many physical complaints beginning before age thirty that occur over a period of years. Treatment is sought because of an inability to engage in social, occupational, or other activities as a consequence of experienced physical afflictions. Symptoms may include pain in various parts of the body (head, back, abdomen), gastrointestinal problems (e.g., nausea, vomiting, bloating), sexual symptoms (e.g., sexual indifference, excessive menstrual bleeding), and a neurological symptom not related to pain (e.g., impaired coordination or balance, paralysis, blindness).

Another somatoform disorder is **hypochondriasis**—preoccupation with fears of disease. Such persons do not actually have the diseases they fear, but they persist in worrying about them, despite repeated reassurance by their doctors that they are healthy. Many hypochondriacs are not simply faking; they feel the pain and discomfort they report and are truly afraid that they are sick or will soon become sick.

The final somatoform disorder we will consider is known as **conversion disorder.** Persons with this disorder actually experience physical problems such as *motor deficits* (poor balance or coordination, paralysis or weakness of arms or legs) or *sensory deficits* (loss of sensation to touch or pain, double vision, blindness,

Somatoform Disorders: Category of disorders in which psychological conflicts or other problems take on a physical form.

Somatization Disorder: A psychological condition in which individuals report physical complaints and symptoms, including aches and pains, problems with their digestive systems, and sexual problems such as sexual indifference or irregular menstruation.

Hypochondriasis: A psychological disorder in which individuals convert anxiety into chronic preoccupations with their health and bodily functions.

Conversion Disorder: Psychological disorder in which individuals experience real motor or sensory symptoms for which there is no known organic cause.

deafness). While these disabilities are quite real to the persons involved, there is no medical condition present that would produce them.

What causes somatoform disorders? Freud suggested that persons experiencing unacceptable impulses or conflicts converted these into various symptoms. By doing so, they reduced the anxiety generated by the impulses and at the same time gained much sympathy and attention. While psychologists generally reject this view, it does seem accurate in one respect: People suffering from somatoform disorders do often seem to benefit from these disorders in terms of attaining much sympathy from important people in their lives, such as spouses, parents, or children. In addition, research by one team of psychologists (Lecci et al., 1996) suggests that persons suffering from hypochondria often tend to have health-related goals such as trying to maintain or lose weight, managing stress, and coping with chronic illnesses. Thus, they tend to focus much of their thinking on health-related issues, and this preoccupation feeds directly into their hypochondria.

KEY *QUESTION*

▪ What are somatoform disorders?

Dissociative Disorders

Have you ever awakened during the night and, just for a moment, been uncertain about where you were? Such temporary disruptions in our normal cognitive functioning are far from rare; many people experience them from time to time as a result of fatigue, illness, or the use of alcohol or other drugs. Some individuals, however, undergo much more profound and lengthy losses of identity or memory. These are known as **dissociative disorders**, which, like several other psychological disorders, can take several different forms.

In **dissociative amnesia,** individuals experience a loss of memory that does not stem from medical conditions or other mental disorders. Such losses can be localized, involving only specific periods time, or generalized, involving memory for the person's entire life. For example, in the case of a **dissociative fugue,** an individual's entire identity can be lost. Such individuals wander off, adopt a new identity, and are unable to recall their own past.

As dramatic as these disorders are, they pale in comparison with the most controversial of the dissociative disorders—the **dissociative identity disorder.** This was known as *multiple personality disorder* in the past, and it involves a cleaving of personal identity into at least two—and often more—separate but coexisting personalities, each possessing different traits, behaviours, memories, and emotions. Usually, there is one *host personality*—the primary identity that is present most of the time, and one or more *alters*—alternative personalities that appear from time to time. *Switching*, the process of changing from one personality to another, often seems to occur in response to anxiety brought on by thoughts or memories of previous traumatic experiences.

To illustrate the disorder, let's consider the case of Jenny Z. reported by Ross (1994). Jenny sought help from Ross because she was experiencing blank periods. She had returned from a three-day trip to Vancouver and could remember nothing that had transpired during those three days. There were other problems. For example, a joint bank account that she held with her boyfriend had been emptied, and some of the money had been spent on goods that she had no recollection of purchasing. This puzzling sequence of events was explained during the course of treatment when it became apparent that Jenny had a second personality named Sally, who would assume control of her life for periods of time, and would leave Jenny with no recollection of these experiences. It was Sally who admitted removing and spending the money in the joint account. The two personalities were very different.

Dissociative Disorders: Psychological disorders in which individuals experience profound and lengthy losses of identity or memory.

Dissociative Amnesia: Amnesia for which there is no organic cause.

Dissociative Fugue: Form of dissociative amnesia in which individuals forget their identity and virtually all of their past life.

Dissociative Identity Disorder: A dissociative disorder in which a single individual seems to possess more than one personality.

Jenny was quiet and lacking in self-confidence. Sally was confident and prone to impulsive behaviour. Sally was quite aware of Jenny's activities and disdainful of her many deficiencies. Jenny, on the other hand, was initially unaware of Sally's existence and amnesic for the periods during which she was in control. As therapy progressed, five other personalities surfaced. Eventually Ross was able to integrate the personalities into a single unified self. At last report, Jenny was much improved.

How does such a disorder develop? A widely held psychodynamic explanation takes the position that it grows out of a background of early and sustained physical and sexual abuse. Ross and colleagues (1991) examined the background of over 100 people diagnosed as having dissociative identity disorder in both Canada and the United States. They found that 95 percent experienced either sexual or physical abuse, or both, during childhood. It is assumed that, under such circumstances, some children develop the habit of dissociating themselves from the experienced abuse by assuming the guise of another personality or self. This allows them to stand apart from the situation—-the abuse is held to be experienced by another separate self, who is walled off by amnesia from other selves within the system. It is suggested that this process of dissociation may provide a way of coping with sustained abuse, but it can lead to a progressive fragmentation of the self into multiple personalities—each personality being specialized to function in a different type of situation. For example, a protector personality becomes dominant in times of threat, and often a child personality, experienced in absorbing pain, dominates when pain and suffering are experienced. Most often, the host personality is amnesic with respect to the experiences of the other personalities.

Although individual case histories that support the psychodynamic interpretation appear compelling, some, such as the late Nick Spanos (1994, 1996) of Carleton University, deny that the dissociative identity disorder constitutes a clinical syndrome. Spanos's position is that one should look to sociocognitive factors to explain the behaviour. He assumes that widespread media coverage of what he sees as an "alleged" disorder has encouraged its acceptance as a legitimate affliction, and that "enactment" of the disorder by those in deep distress is now culturally countenanced. Why would anyone undertake such an enactment? One reason, according to Spanos, is that it provides a dramatic way to draw attention to one's problems. Another reason is that it provides a convenient way to escape responsibility for unacceptable behaviour. Responsibility can be shifted to the action of other "selves" of which one is "unaware." Spanos contends that clinicians often unintentionally encourage patients to enter into a multiple identity enactment by using hypnosis and asking them leading questions about whether they feel they are always in control of their behaviour, and whether they sometimes have trouble remembering things they have done or places they have been. Those opposed to Spanos's views contend that simulation of the type described by Spanos is no more common in the case of dissociative identity disorder than in other clinical syndromes. They contend also that present-day clinicians are very aware of the possibility of unwittingly encouraging simulation though the use of leading questions and hypnosis (eg., Gleaves, 1996).

Resolution of conflicting perspectives is important because they favour very different treatment practices. Those who are convinced of the clinical reality of the dissociative identity disorder see the uncovering and subsequent integration, or unification, of the diverse resident personalities as the appropriate treatment (Ellason & Ross, 1997; Ross 1997). Spanos, on the other hand, would argue that one should focus directly on the problems the patient is having coping with his or her life and do nothing to encourage the belief that multiple selves are present.

K E Y QUESTIONS

- What are dissociative disorders such as dissociative amnesia?
- What is dissociative identity disorder?

Critical Thinking

What is it about the dissociative identity disorder that makes it so difficult for researchers to determine whether is a valid clinical disorder or, as Spanos would have it, an enactment?

Sexual and Gender Identity Disorders

As we saw in Chapter 12, Freud believed that many psychological disorders can be traced to disturbances in psychosexual development—our progression through a series of stages in which our quest for pleasure is centred on different parts of the body and different activities. While this theory is not currently accepted by most psychologists, there is little doubt that problems relating to sexuality and gender identity constitute an important group of psychological disorders. Several of these are considered below.

Sexual Dysfunctions

Sexual Desire Disorders: Psychological disorders involving a lack of interest in sex or active aversion to sexual activities.

Sexual Arousal Disorders: Psychological disorders involving inability to attain an erection (males) or absence of vaginal swelling and lubrication (females).

Sexual dysfunctions include disturbances in sexual desire, sexual arousal, disturbances in the ability to attain orgasms, and disorders involving pain during sexual relations. **Sexual desire disorders** involve a lack of interest in sex or active aversion to sexual activity. Persons experiencing these disorders report that they rarely have the sexual fantasies most persons generate, that they avoid all, or almost all, sexual activity, and that these reactions cause them considerable distress.

In contrast, **sexual arousal disorders** involve the inability to attain or maintain an erection (men) or the absence of vaginal swelling and lubrication (women). *Orgasm disorders* involve the delay or absence of orgasm in both sexes, and may also include *premature ejaculation* (reaching orgasm too quickly) in men. Needless to say, these problems can cause considerable distress to the persons who experience them (e.g., Rowland, Cooper, & Slob, 1996).

Paraphilias

What is sexually arousing? For most people, the answer involves the sight or touch of another human being. But many people find other stimuli arousing, too. The large volume of business done by Victoria's Secret and other companies specializing in alluring lingerie for women stems, at least in part, from the fact that many men find such garments mildly sexually arousing. Other persons find either inflicting or receiving some slight pain during love-making increases their arousal and sexual pleasure. Do such reactions constitute sexual disorders? According to most psychologists, and the DSM-IV, they do not. Only when unusual or bizarre imagery or acts are *necessary* for sexual arousal (that is, it cannot occur without them), do such preferences qualify as a disorder. Such disorders are termed **paraphilias,** and take many different forms.

Individuals with *fetishes* become aroused exclusively by inanimate objects. Often these are articles of clothing, but in more unusual cases, they can involve animals, dead bodies, or even human waste. *Frotteurism,* another paraphilia, involves fantasies and urges focused on touching or rubbing against a nonconsenting person. The touching, not the coercive nature of the act, is what persons with this disorder find sexually arousing. Perhaps more disturbing is *pedophilia*, in which individuals experience sexual urges and fantasies involving children, generally ones younger than thirteen. When such urges are translated into overt actions, the effects on the young victims can, as we noted in Chapter 9, be devastating (e.g., Ambuel, 1995). Two other paraphilias are *sexual sadism* and *sexual masochism*. In the former, individuals become sexually aroused only by inflicting pain or humiliation on others. In the latter, they are aroused by receiving such treatment.

Gender Identity Disorders

Have you ever read about a man who altered his gender to become a woman, or vice versa? Such individuals feel, often from an early age, that they were born with the wrong sexual identity. They identify strongly with the other sex, often showing preferences for cross-dressing (wearing clothing associated with the other gender) and for stereotypical games and pastimes of the other gender. They are displeased with their own bodies and request—again often from an early age—that they receive medical treatment to alter their primary and secondary sex characteristics. In the past, there was little that medicine could do satisfy these desires on the part of persons suffering from **gender identity disorder.** Advances in surgical techniques, however, have now made it possible for such persons to undergo *sex-change operations* in which their sexual organs are actually altered to approximate those of the other gender. Several thousand individuals have undergone such operations, and existing evidence indicates that most report being satisfied with the results and happier than they were before (Green & Fleming, 1990). However, follow-up studies suggest that some persons who undergo such operations experience regrets and continued unhappiness, sometimes to the point that they commit suicide (Abramowitz, 1986). So, it appears that such operations have a serious potential downside that should be carefully considered.

Paraphilias: Sexual disorders involving choices of inappropriate sexual objects, such as young children, or the inability to experience arousal except in the presence of specific objects or fantasies.

Gender Identity Disorder: A disorder in which individuals believe that they were born with the wrong sexual identity.

K E Y *QUESTIONS*

■ What are sexual dysfunctions and paraphilias?

■ What is gender identify disorder?

Critical Thinking

Can gender-altering surgical procedures and drug therapies designed to alter the character of dominant hormonal functions succeed in making a member of one sex think and feel in precisely the same fashion as a member of the opposite sex?

Changing Ideals of Feminine Beauty: One Factor in the Growing Incidence of Eating Disorders

Until the 1960s, well-rounded female figures (e.g., Marilyn Monroe) were considered to be the most attractive. After that time, however, a trend toward being thin developed and grew stronger (e.g., today's "supermodels"). Research findings suggest that this shift is one factor that has contributed, along with many others, to the rising incidence of eating disorders in recent decades.

Eating Disorders

In our discussion of motivation (Chapter 10), we considered at some length two serious **eating disorders:** *anorexia nervosa* and *bulimia*. Given that these clinical disorders are very common and adversely affect the health and well-being of millions of young people, we will briefly review the main characteristics of these disorders.

Anorexia nervosa is a disorder in which individuals, intensely fearful of being or becoming "fat," literally starve themselves, failing to maintain a normal body weight. Bulimia involves episodes of binge eating followed by various forms of compensatory behaviour designed to avoid weight gain—for example, self-induced vomiting or overuse of laxatives. Both of these eating disorders are much more common among young women than among young men (Hinsz & Williamson, 1987). Both disorders seem to stem at least in part from dissatisfaction with personal appearance and efforts to match the "thin is in" model that is held up by the mass media (Thompson, 1992; Williamson et al., 1993).

KEY *QUESTIONS*

■ What are anorexia nervosa and bulimia?

■ What factors play a role in the occurrence of these eating disorders?

Personality Disorders

Eating Disorders: Serious disturbances in eating habits or patterns that pose a threat to individuals' physical health and well-being.

Personality Disorders: Extreme and inflexible personality traits that impair an individual's ability to enter into and maintain social relationships with others.

Have you ever known someone who was highly suspicious and mistrustful of others in virtually all situations? Someone who had no close friends and was a true loner in all respects? Someone who showed a strong need to be taken care of by others, coupled with a dependent, clinging approach to relationships? If so, these may well be people with specific **personality disorders.** These are defined by the DSM-IV as extreme and inflexible personality traits that are distressing to the persons who have them or cause such individuals to have problems in school, work, or interpersonal relations. The emphasis should probably be on "cause them to have problems" rather than "distress" because many people with this kind of disorder are *not* disturbed by it: they view their behaviour, strange as it may seem to others, as perfectly normal and acceptable, at least to them!

The DSM-IV divides personality disorders into three distinct clusters, so let's take a look at some of the traits that fit under these categories. The first is described as involving odd, eccentric behaviour or traits, and includes three personality disorders: *paranoid, schizoid,* and *schizotypal.*

Persons suffering from the *paranoid personality disorders* believe that everyone is out to get them, deceive them, or take advantage of them in some way. Persons suffering from the *schizoid personality disorder* display a quite different behaviour pattern. They show little or no sign of emotion, and tend to lack basic social skills. As a result, they form few, if any, social relationships and often live an almost totally solitary life. Individuals with the third type of personality disorder, *schizotypal personality disorder,* tend to be anxious and uncomfortable in interpersonal relationships, and display irregular eccentric behaviour. They frequently show evidence of distorted thinking and perception—sometimes believing that mysterious forces that can't be seen are affecting their behaviour.

The second major cluster of personality disorders described by the DSM-IV includes disorders involving dramatic, emotional, and erratic forms of behaviour. One of these, the *borderline personality disorder,* includes people who show tremendous instability—in their interpersonal relationships, self-image, and moods. Did you ever see the movie *Fatal Attraction*? It depicts a very unstable woman who has a brief affair with a married man. When he indicates that he does not want to continue the relationship, she responds by engaging in impulsive, erratic, and very dangerous behaviour. That is the kind of pattern shown by persons with this personality disorder. For these persons, mood swings are huge, love often quickly changes to hate, and best friends become enemies overnight.

In sharp contrast is the *histrionic personality disorder,* which characterizes people who show a consistent and enormous need for attention from others. They want to be the centre of attention and will do almost anything to attain this goal—even if it means dressing and behaving in unusual and dramatic fashions.

Also included in this cluster of personality disorders is the one that is, in some ways, the most important and most disturbing—the **antisocial personality disorder.** Individuals with this disorder show an almost total disregard for the rights and well-being of others. In addition, they demonstrate several characteristics that make them dangerous to others. Rules and regulations are not for them, so they often have a history of antisocial behaviour: delinquency, theft, vandalism, drug abuse, and the like. They lie readily, if they perceive this to be advantageous. They are unpredictable, and their behaviour seems to be without direction or goal. If they injure others, they typically show no remorse. To illustrate the disorder, consider the following statement made by Gary Gillmore, a convicted multiple murderer.

> I pulled up near a gas station.... I told the service station guy to give me all his money. I then took him to the bathroom and told him to kneel down and then I shot him in the head twice. The guy didn't give me any trouble but I just felt like I had to do it.

Gillmore was totally indifferent to his victim. Because of their almost total lack of feelings of responsibility or concern for others, persons with the antisocial personality disorder are often truly dangerous. When these traits are coupled with intelligence, good looks, or a charming manner, they can be devastating. Confidence artists and serial killers who lure numerous victims to their doom—such persons are true predators, and many have been diagnosed as showing the antisocial personality disorder.

What are the origins of this disorder? Many factors seem to play a role. The impulsivity and aggression it involves may be linked to deficits in the ability to delay gratification—a skill most people acquire during childhood (e.g., Sher & Trull, 1994). Biological factors, too, may play a role. Some findings suggest that persons with this disorder show disturbances in brain function, including abnormalities in the neurotransmitter serotonin (Lahey et al., 1993). Additional evidence indicates

Antisocial Personality Disorder: A personality disorder involving a lack of conscience and sense of responsibility, impulsive behaviour, irritability, and aggressiveness.

that such persons show reduced reactions to negative stimuli—for instance, ones that are related to unpleasant experiences such as punishment (Patrick, Bradley, & Lang, 1993). In several studies, individuals with the antisocial personality disorder showed poorer performance than normal controls in learning to inhibit punished responses (e.g., Newman et al., 1985).

Of course, the interesting question is *why* those with an antisocial personality disorder appear to have difficulty inhibiting responses that have negative consequences. One possibility, proposed by Hare and his associates at the University of British Columbia (Harpur & Hare, 1990), is that those with the disorder allocate attention in a very different way from those who are not so afflicted. Essentially, the argument is that individuals with an antisocial personality disorder engage in what is termed "overfocusing" of attention. It is argued that when these individuals focus attention on a desired course of behaviour, or objective, they do so in a way that "blocks off" or excludes from consideration any negative or opposing information or argument. This process would explain why they have such difficulty in learning to avoid punishing responses: The disposition to overfocus attention blocks off or masks consideration of potential punishing responses.

Overall, these studies tend to confirm that people with an antisocial personality disorder differ from others in a number of ways. They appear to be less emotionally reactive. They also appear to have difficulty in inhibiting responses that lead to punishment, ignoring signals that would serve as a warning to most people to withdraw or "back off." Whatever the origins of this disorder, one point is clear: Persons with the antisocial personality disorder often pose a serious threat to themselves and to others.

A third cluster of personality disorders described by the DSM-IV includes disorders involving anxious fearful behaviour. The disorders in this group, plus a number of other personality disorders, are described in Table 14.3.

TABLE 14.3

Personality Disorders

The DSM-IV divides personality disorders into three major clusters. Personality disorders in each cluster are described here.

Odd and Eccentric Personality Disorders

Paranoid personality disorder	Pervasive distrust and suspiciousness of others
Schizoid personality disorder	Pervasive pattern of detachment from social relationships and restricted range of emotions
Schizotypal personality disorder	Intense discomfort in interpersonal relationships, cognitive or perceptual distortions and eccentric behaviour

Dramatic, Emotional, and Erratic Personality Disorders

Antisocial personality disorder	Deceitfulness, impulsivity, irritability, reckless disregard for safety and welfare of others, lack of remorse
Borderline personality disorder	Pervasive pattern of instability in interpersonal relationships, self-image, moods
Histrionic personality disorder	Pervasive pattern of excessive emotionality and attention seeking
Narcissistic personality disorder	Pervasive pattern of grandiosity in fantasy or behaviour, plus lack of empathy

continued

TABLE 14.3 *continued*

Anxious and Fearful Personality Disorders

Avoidant personality disorder	Pervasive pattern of social inhibition, feelings of inadequacy, hypersensitivity to negative evaluation
Obsessive-compulsive personality disorder	Preoccupation with orderliness, perfectionism, and mental and interpersonal control
Dependent personality disorder	Pervasive and excessive need to be taken care of

K E Y *QUESTIONS*

▪ What are personality disorders?

▪ What characteristics are shown by persons who have the antisocial personality disorder?

Substance-Related Disorders

Do you know a heavy smoker who has tried, over and over again, to quit this habit? And do you know anyone who can't get through the day without several beers? If so, you already have first-hand experience with another major category in the DSM-IV: **substance-related disorders**. These are disorders involving the maladaptive use of various substances or drugs, leading to significant impairment or distress. Such disorders are generally divided into **substance abuse** and **substance dependence,** depending on the kind of problems involved. *Substance abuse* is diagnosed when individuals show one or more of the following problems: recurrent substance use resulting in a failure to fulfill major role obligations at work, school, or home; recurrent substance use in situations where it is physically hazardous to do so; and repeated legal problems stemming from the use of substances. In contrast, *substance dependence* is diagnosed when individuals require increasing amounts of the substance to achieve the desired effect, experience withdrawal symptoms when they do not take the substance in question, are unable to cut down or control use of the substance, and spend a great deal of time in activities necessary to obtain the substance.

Substance abuse and substance dependence are far from rare. In the extensive survey of mental disturbances in Ontario by Offord and colleagues (1996) that we referred to earlier in the chapter, it was found that 5.2 percent of the population sampled indicated substance abuse or substance dependence problems. Substance abuse was also found to be four times more common among males than females.

The harmful effects of substance-related disorders, coupled with the very large numbers of persons involved, suggest that these are among the most damaging psychological disorders. Moreover, because they stem from many different factors (biological, social, and personal), they are often very difficult to treat. However, several forms of therapy do seem at least moderately effective in treating such problems.

Returning briefly to the question of substance abuse among young people, recent findings suggest that a combination of factors may place this age group at serious risk for such disorders. These factors include high levels of stress in their lives; a tendency to cope with problems in maladaptive ways (e.g., by avoiding them or using substances to feel better); exposure to peers who smoke, drink, or use drugs; and a low degree of support from their parents (Wills et al., 1996). University stu-

Substance-Related Disorders: Disorders involving maladaptive patterns of substance use leading to clinically significant impairment.

Substance Abuse: Substance-related disorders involving one or more of the following: recurrent use resulting in a failure to fulfill major role obligations at work, school, or home, recurrent substance use in situations in which it is physically hazardous to do so, recurrent substance-related legal problems.

Substance Dependence: Substance-related disorders involving one or more of the following: the need for increasing amounts of the substance to achieve the desired effect, withdrawal symptoms when the substance isn't taken, an inability to cut down or control use of the substance, and spending a great deal of time in activities necessary to obtain the substance.

dents can take some measure of comfort from a recent study of Stewart, Zeitlin, and Samoluk (1996) of Dalhousie University, which examined the drinking motives of students. It is reassuring to find that students more commonly consume alcohol for social motives than for coping or self-enhancement reasons, but, as might be expected given that males more commonly engage in substance abuse than women, male students were more likely to consume alcohol for enhancement motives than female students. It is important that such studies be pursued. Understanding the factors that place young people at risk may prove very helpful in designing programs to help them avoid the profound risks of substance-related disorders.

K E Y *QUESTIONS*

▪ What are substance-related disorders?

▪ What factors place teenagers at risk for developing these disorders?

Schizophrenia

All of the disorders we've considered cause distress for the people who experience them. Yet, for the most part, these people *can* continue with their lives. Like people loaded down with lead weights, they toil and suffer but generally can struggle on somehow. Individuals afflicted with **schizophrenia,** a complex disorder characterized by hallucinations (e.g., hearing voices), delusions (beliefs with no basis in reality), disturbances in speech, and several other symptoms, face a different situation. They are so disturbed that they usually cannot live ordinary lives. Indeed, in many cases, they must be removed from society, at least temporarily, for their own protection as well as to undergo treatment. What is the nature of this disorder? What are its major causes? These are the questions on which psychologists who study schizophrenia have focused.

The Basic Nature of Schizophrenia

Schizophrenia involves severe disruptions in virtually all aspects of psychological functioning. As noted by Heinrichs (1993, p. 221), schizophrenia depletes the mind's resources, just as severe brain damage depletes these resources. But while persons suffering from brain damage experience a world that is stripped of its meaning in many respects, those suffering from schizophrenia experience a world that has become bizarrely distorted. Let's look more closely at the major symptoms of this serious disorder. But first, one important point: Although we'll discuss schizophrenia as though it is a single disorder, many experts believe that it may actually involve several different—and distinct—disturbances (Bellak, 1994). Please keep this point in mind when we examine the potential causes of schizophrenia.

DISTURBANCES OF THOUGHT AND LANGUAGE First, and perhaps foremost, schizophrenics do not think or speak like others. Their words jump about in a fragmented and disorganized manner. There is a loosening of associations so that one idea does not follow logically from another; indeed, ideas often seem totally unconnected. In addition, schizophrenics often create words of their own—neologisms such as "littlehood" for childhood, or "crimery" for bad actions. Their sentences often begin with one thought and then shift, abruptly, to another, and they include *incompetent references*—it's impossible to tell to what their words refer (e.g., Barch & Berenbaum, 1996). In extreme cases, their words seem to be totally jumbled into what is sometimes termed a *word salad.*

Schizophrenia: A group of serious psychological disorders characterized by severe distortions in thought and language, perceptions, and emotion.

These problems, and several others, seem to stem from a breakdown in the capacity for *selective attention*. Normally we can focus our attention on certain stimuli while largely ignoring others. This is not true for schizophrenics, who are easily distracted by anything and everything. Even the sound of their own words may disrupt their train of thought and send them wandering off into a mysterious world of their own creation.

Schizophrenics also frequently suffer from **delusions**—firmly held beliefs that have no basis in reality. Such delusions can take many different forms. One common type is *delusions of persecution*—the belief that one is being plotted against, spied upon, threatened, or otherwise mistreated. For example, Leopold Bellak (1994), who has studied schizophrenia for more than fifty years, describes a female patient who would shout "Here comes Bellak, the Russian spy!" from her window every morning as he approached the hospital building. Another common type is *delusions of grandeur*—the belief that one is extremely famous, important, or powerful. People suffering from such delusions may claim that they are the prime minister, a famous rock star, or even Jesus, Mohammed, or Buddha. Finally, schizophrenics also sometimes suffer from *delusions of control*—the belief that other people, evil forces, or perhaps even beings from another planet are controlling their thoughts, actions, or feelings, often by means of electronic devices implanted in or aimed at their brain. As you can see, schizophrenics' ties to reality are tenuous at best and may seem almost nonexistent in some cases.

DISTURBANCES OF PERCEPTION Schizophrenics also show many signs of disturbed perceptions. Simply put, they do not perceive the world in the same way as other people do. Many experience **hallucinations**—vivid sensory experiences that have no basis in physical reality. The most common type of hallucinations are auditory. Schizophrenics "hear" voices, music, or other sounds that aren't present. Visual hallucinations are also quite frequent; and again, these experiences can be quite intense. Hallucinations of smells and tastes are sometimes also reported.

DISTURBANCES OF EMOTION OR MOOD A third key symptom of schizophrenia involves inappropriate or unusual emotional reactions. Some schizophrenics show almost no emotion at all: They remain impassive in the face of events that evoke strong reactions from others. Others do show emotion, but their reactions are inappropriate. They may giggle when describing a painful childhood experience or when receiving tragic news. In sum, schizophrenics' disturbed patterns of thought, perception, and emotion weaken their grip on reality and virtually ensure that they will live in a private world largely of their own creation.

DISTURBANCES OF BEHAVIOUR A fourth symptom of schizophrenia involves unusual actions. These can take an incredible range of forms, as the following description (Hagen, 1993) of a hospital ward for schizophrenics suggests:

> Lou stands hour after hour … just rubbing the palm of his hand around the top of his head. Jerry spends his days rubbing his hand against his stomach and running around a post.… Helen paces back and forth … mumbling about enemies who are coming to get her, while Vic grimaces and giggles over in the corner.… Nick tears up magazines, puts bits of paper in his mouth, and then spits them out.… Bill sits immobile for hours, staring at the floor.…

DISTURBANCES IN SOCIAL FUNCTIONS Given the difficulties outlined above, it is far from surprising that schizophrenics also frequently show seriously impaired social functioning. Their relationships with others deteriorate and they experience increasing social isolation and withdrawal (Bellack et al., 1990). Further, they show severe deficits in basic social skills, such as solving problems through conversation, compromising with others, and negotiating (Bellack et al.,1994).

Delusions: Irrational but firmly held beliefs about the world that have no basis in reality.

Hallucinations: Vivid sensory experiences that occur in the absence of external stimuli yet have the full force of impact of real events or stimuli.

Catatonic Schizophrenia

People who suffer from catatonic schizophrenia may remain totally immobile, frozen in a single posture, for long periods of time.

POSITIVE AND NEGATIVE SYMPTOMS   As you can readily see, schizophrenia is a complex disorder. Are there any underlying dimensions to it that can help us make sense of the vast range of diverse symptoms? One approach that has proved useful, and that has provided insights into the nature of this disorder, divides symptoms into two types. *Positive symptoms* involve the presence of something that is normally absent, such as hallucinations and delusions. *Negative symptoms* involve the absence of something that is normally present and include withdrawal, apathy, absence of emotion, and so on. (These two groups of symptoms are sometimes referred to as *Type I* and *Type II* schizophrenia, respectively.) Patients with negative symptoms generally have a poorer prognosis: They remain hospitalized longer and are less likely to recover than patients with positive symptoms (Fenton & McGlashan, 1991). In addition, patients with positive and negative symptoms appear to experience different kinds of cognitive deficits. Those with negative symptoms do worse on tests that measure visual and spatial skills; for example, they have more difficulty in recognizing visual stimuli. In contrast, patients with positive symptoms do worse on tests of short-term memory (Braff, 1989).

Types and Phases of Schizophrenia

Schizophrenia is a *chronic* disorder, as defined by the DSM-IV: it lasts at least six months. For most people, however, the disease lasts far longer, and symptoms come and go. They have periods when they appear almost normal, and long periods when their symptoms are readily apparent.

Some experts describe schizophrenia as involving three phases: the *prodromal phase,* when the functioning of persons with this disorder begins to deteriorate and they withdraw more and more from others; the *active* or *acute phase*, when they exhibit many positive symptoms; and the *residual phase*, during which they again show fewer symptoms but withdraw and continue to have bizarre thoughts.

Schizophrenia is also divided into five distinct types. The most dramatic of these is the **catatonic type,** in which individuals show marked disturbances in motor behaviour. Many alternative between total immobility—they sit for days or even weeks frozen in a single posture—and wild, excited behaviour in which they rush madly about. Other types are described in Table 14.4.

Catatonic Type of Schizophrenia: A dramatic type of schizophrenia in which individuals show marked disturbances in motor behaviour. Many alternate between total immobility and wild, excited behaviour in which they rush madly about.

TABLE 14.4

Types of Schizophrenia

Schizophrenia is often divided into the types shown here, each marked by a different pattern of symptoms.

Type	Description
Catatonic	Unusual patterns of motor activity, such as rigid posture or excited movements; also speech disturbances, such as repetitive chatter
Disorganized	Delusions are present but disconnected (i.e., a common theme or structure is not evident, and verbal expressions tend to be incoherent)
Paranoid	Preoccupation with one or more sets of delusions, often centring around the belief that others are "out to get them" in some way
Undifferentiated	Many symptoms, including delusions, hallucinations, and incoherence
Residual	Schizophrenia that occurs after prominent delusions and hallucinations are no longer present, but involving withdrawal, minimal affect, and no motivation

The Causes of Schizophrenia

Schizophrenia is certainly one the most bizarre and troubling psychological disorders. It is not a common disorder, being found in less than one percent of the Canadian population (Bland et al., 1988). It does not strike all age groups equally, however. On the contrary, it usually doesn't appear until between the ages of sixteen and twenty-five, and it occurs much less frequently after age thirty-five (Mueser & Gingerich, 1994). What are the causes of the disorder? Research findings point to the role of many factors.

BIOLOGICAL FACTORS The most direct overall evidence that biological factors play an important factor in schizophrenia is provided by genetic studies. Schizophrenia, like several other psychological disorders, tends to run in families (Nicole & Gottesman, 1983). Concordance rates are much higher for pairs of individuals who are closely related genetically. This is made very apparent in Figure 14.5. Identical twin pairs are more than three times more likely to both experience the disorder than fraternal twin pairs, and forty-six times more likely to both have the disorder than a randomly selected pair of unrelated individuals (e.g., Gottesman, 1993). Schizophrenia does not appear to be traceable to a single gene, however; on the contrary, research findings suggest that many genes and many environmental factors operate together to produce a tendency toward this disorder (e.g., Fowles, 1994). For example, one model of the origins of schizophrenia, the **diathesis–stress model,** suggests that genetic factors may predispose individuals to develop schizophrenia if they are exposed to certain kinds of stressful environmental conditions. If these environmental conditions are absent, however, schizophrenia is much less likely to occur.

Diathesis–Stress Model: A model of schizophrenia suggesting that individuals with inherited dispositions to develop this disorder do so only when subjected to stressful environmental conditions.

Figure 14.5
Family Relationship and Schizophrenia

The more closely two individuals are related, the greater the likelihood that if one develops schizophrenia, the other will too. This finding suggests that genetic factors play a role in the occurrence of schizophrenia.

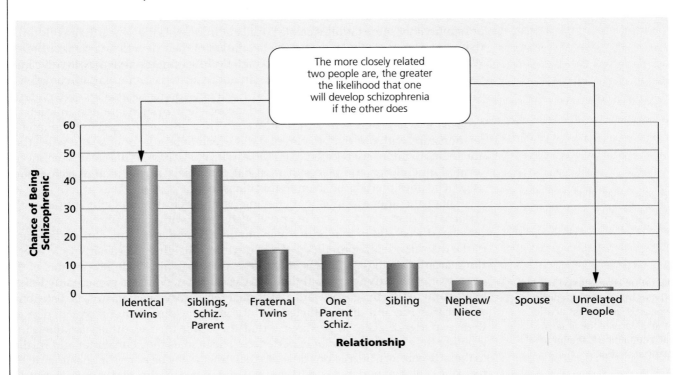

Additional evidence for the role of biological factors is provided by studies linking several types of brain dysfunction to schizophrenia. For instance, some findings indicate that some ventricles (fluid-filled spaces within the brain) are larger for schizophrenics than normal persons, and this increased size may produce abnormalities in the cerebral cortex (e.g., Weinberger, 1994). In fact, in studies using magnetic resonance imaging techniques, it has been found that enlarged ventricles are related to increased hallucinations and reduced emotion among schizophrenics (e.g., Gur & Pearlson, 1993; Klausner et al., 1992). Schizophrenics also show reduced activity in the frontal lobes, relative to normal persons, during tasks involving memory or abstract thought (Gur & Pearlson, 1993). Together, all these findings suggest that schizophrenia is related to cognitive deficits and several types of abnormalities in brain functioning.

Further support for the role of biological factors is provided by *biochemical* studies. Several findings point to the possibility that disturbances in the functioning of certain neurotransmitters may play a role in schizophrenia. It has been found that drugs that increase dopamine activity in the brain tend to intensify schizophrenic symptoms (e.g., Lieberman & Koreen, 1993); and that drugs that block the action of dopamine in the brain are effective in reducing many positive symptoms of schizophrenia (Syvalahti, 1994). These and other findings suggest that excessive activity in the dopamine system may lead to positive symptoms of schizophrenia, while deficits in dopamine activity may lead to negative symptoms (e.g., Julien, 1995). Although this **dopamine hypothesis** is intriguing, findings have been reported that are not consistent with this hypothesis. For example, direct comparisons of dopamine levels in schizophrenic patients and other persons do not always reveal the expected differences (Lieberman & Koreen, 1993). The prevailing view appears to be that dopamine is not *the* crucial biochemical factor in schizophrenia. Growing evidence suggests that many neurotransmitters, and perhaps other chemicals in the brain as well (e.g., glutamate), play a role in its occurrence. This is why the newest drugs used in the treatment of schizophrenia target not one neurotransmitter or chemical, but many (Tanouye, 1999b).

PSYCHOLOGICAL FACTORS The fact that schizophrenia seems to run in families provides evidence for the role of genetic factors in this disorder. It also raises the possibility that some families create social environments that place their children at risk—environments that increase the likelihood of their developing schizophrenia. What are such environments like? Research findings suggest that they involve high levels of conflict between parents, or situations in which one parent completely dominates the family (e.g., Arieti, 1974). Such environments also involve patterns of communication that are confusing and inconsistent. In such families, children are exposed to what is known as the *double bind:* They are encouraged to form intense relationships with one or both parents, and urged to be affectionate, but when they are, their advances are rejected (e.g., Miklowitz et al., 1989). This creates emotional turmoil for children and places them at risk for schizophrenia if other factors such as genetic ones predispose them to this illness.

There are other grounds for believing psychological factors may influence the onset of the disorder. As we noted previously, those with schizophrenia tend to display a reduced ability to ignore irrelevant or distracting stimuli. During the onset of the disorder, schizophrenics seem to develop a heightened sensitivity to everything around them (e.g., Elkins et al., 1992; Grillon et al., 1990). Proponents of the cognitive perspective point out that this dysfunction, which is presumably linked to a neural deficit in sensory and attentional regulatory mechanisms, is disturbing and distressful, and those afflicted seek to provide some form of explanation for their experience. The suggestion is that they first turn to others to determine whether they too have similar experiences. The denials they encounter add further to their discomfort. Suspicions develop that others may be lying, or questioning the reality of their experience, and they become increasingly distrustful. They turn

Dopamine Hypothesis: The hypothesis that schizophrenia is associated with excess activity in those parts of the brain in which dopamine is the primary neurotransmitter.

inward and concentrate more and more on developing their own independent explanation for the experiences they are undergoing. Very often this leads to the development of delusional belief structures— assumptions that an external agency or force is trying to contact and convey information to them, or that others around and about them are deliberately trying to persecute them by tampering with their mind. As time progresses, delusional structures can become more and more elaborate and more firmly entrenched, ultimately resulting in a paranoid state wherein individuals become totally out of touch with reality (Firth, 1979; Maher, 1974).

Cognitive-type accounts of the disorder's development such as the one offered above are interesting, but remain largely conjectural. It is very difficult to find conclusive evidence that the developmental sequence unfolds precisely as described. As Comer (1992) notes, the cognitive account, with its amalgamation of biological dysfunction and psychological causes, does capture accurately at least one aspect of the prevailing view of schizophrenia—the notion that there are multiple determinants. Genetic factors, certain types of home environments, brain dysfunction, biochemical factors, and psychological factors all seem to play a role in schizophrenia. It remains for future research to determine the precise manner in which such factors combine to place specific persons at risk for this very serious disorder.

KEY QUESTIONS

- What is schizophrenia?
- What are positive and negative symptoms of schizophrenia?
- What are the major types of schizophrenia?
- What factors play a role in the occurrence of schizophrenia?

Making Psychology Part of Your Life

Preventing Suicide: Some Basic Steps

When terminally ill persons choose to end their lives rather than endure continued pain, their actions seem understandable, even if we disapprove of them on moral or religious grounds. But when young persons whose lives have just begun follow this route, nearly everyone would agree that their death is tragic. And, as we noted in our coverage of suicide on page 574, the increase in the suicide rate over the past fifty years is largely attributable to the frequency with which teenage-to-adult males elect to commit suicide. Can you do anything to help prevent suicides among people you know? Research findings suggest that you can—if you pay careful attention to several warning signs:

- *Take suicide threats seriously.* One common myth about all suicide is that people who threaten to kill themselves rarely do—only those who tell no one about their plans commit suicide. This is untrue! Approximately 70 percent of all suicides tell others about their intentions. So, when someone talks about suicide, take it seriously.

- *If someone mentions suicide, don't be afraid to discuss it.* Another common myth about suicide is that this topic should never be discussed with another person—it will only make matters worse. This, too is false. Encouraging people to talk about suicidal thoughts gets their problems out into the open and can be helpful. So don't ignore it if someone you know mentions suicide; talking about it is usually better.

- *Recognize the danger signs.* These include (a) statements by someone that he or she has no strong reasons for living, (b) agitation or excitement followed by a period of calm resignation, (c) sudden efforts to give valued possessions away to others, (d) direct statements such as "I don't want to be a burden any more" or "I don't really want to go on living," and (e) revival from a deeply depressed state, coupled with apparent leave-taking. If you observe these changes in others, they may well be danger signs worth considering carefully.

■ *Discourage others from blaming themselves for failure to reach unrealistic goals.* Many people who attempt suicide do so because they feel they have failed to measure up to their own standards—even if these are unrealistically high. If you know someone who is prone to this pattern, try to get them to focus on their good points and to realize that their standards are unrealistic—ones no one could hope to attain.

■ *If a friend or family member shows the danger signs described above, don't leave this person alone.* With rare exceptions, suicide is a solitary act. So if you are concerned that someone might attempt suicide, stay with the person. If for some reason you can't stay, try to get this person to go along with you, or get others to lend assistance by staying with the person.

■ *Most important of all: Get help!* Perhaps the most important point to keep in mind is that determining whether someone is at risk for suicide is a complex judgment—one that is difficult even for trained experts. Thus, you should definitely not try to make this judgment for yourself. Rather, if you have even the slightest concern that someone you know is seriously thinking of suicide, seek professional help. Call a local suicide hot line; or discuss your concerns with a physician, psychologist, counsellor, or member of the clergy. And, if possible, try to get the person to seek help from one or more of these sources. Don't be afraid of overreacting. In signal-detection theory terms, this is one of those cases where a miss (failing to notice suicidal tendencies when they are present) is much worse than a false alarm (concluding that suicidal tendencies are present when in fact they are not).

Summary and Review

Key Questions

Changing Conceptions of Psychological Disorders

■ **What are psychological disorders?** These are patterns of behaviour and thought that are atypical, viewed as undesirable or unacceptable in a given culture, maladaptive, and that usually (although not always) cause the persons who experience them considerable distress.

■ **To what factors were such disorders attributed in the past?** At different times in the past, psychological disorders were attributed to supernatural causes (e.g., evil spirits) or natural causes (e.g., injuries to the brain).

■ **What is the modern psychological view of such disorders?** The modern psychological view suggests that psychological disorders involve biological, psychological, social, and cultural factors.

Identifying Psychological Disorders

■ **What is the DSM-IV?** The DSM-IV—Diagnostic and Statistical Manual of Mental Disorders—is a widely used guide to various psychological disorders. It provides descriptions of the symptoms that are associated with the various disorders and employs a five-axis classification system.

■ **In what ways is it an improvement over earlier versions?** The DSM-IV rests on a firmer basis of published research than did earlier versions, and it directs increased attention to the role of cultural factors.

■ **What other methods do psychologists use to identify psychological disorders?** Psychologists also use assessment interviews, psychological tests, observations of behaviour, and biological measures.

■ **How common are psychological disorders?** Approximately 20 percent of the population experience some form of psychological disorder over a six- to twelve-month period. Close to a third of the population will experience some form of psychological disorder over the course of their life span.

Disorders of Childhood and Adolescence

■ **What is oppositional defiant disorder? Conduct disorder?** Oppositional defiant disorder involves behaviour in which children have poor control of their emotions or have repeated conflicts with parents and other adults (e.g., teachers). Conduct disorder involves more serious antisocial behaviours that are potentially harmful to the child, to others, or to property.

■ **What is attention-deficit/hyperactivity disorder?** A childhood disorder in which one in which children show inattention, hyperactivity, and impulsivity, or a combination of these behaviours.

■ **What is autism?** A disorder in which children show marked impairments in establishing social interactions with others, have nonexistent or poor language skills, and show stereotyped, repetitive patterns of behaviour or interests.

Mood Disorders

■ **What are the major symptoms of depression? Of bipolar disorder?** Major symptoms of depression include negative mood, reduced energy, feelings of hopelessness or despair, loss of interest in previously satisfying activities, and difficulties in sleeping. Bipolar disorders involve wide swings in mood between deep depression and mania.

■ **What factors play a role in the occurrence of mood disorders?** Mood disorders are influenced by genetic factors and by disturbances in brain activity. Psychological factors that play a role in such disorders include learned helplessness, negative perceptions of oneself, and tendencies to bring negative thoughts and memories to mind.

■ **What are the major factors contributing to suicide?** Many factors influence the likelihood of suicide. Particularly important are depression and substance abuse, as well as the presence of environmental stressors such as unemployment and family violence.

■ **What factors contribute to gender differences in suicide rates?** Women are much more likely than men to think about and attempt suicide, but men's suicide attempts are much more likely to end in death because they use more lethal devices.

Anxiety Disorders

■ **What are anxiety disorders?** These are disorders involving increased arousal accompanied by intense, persistent, generalized feelings of fear or apprehension.

■ **What are panic attacks?** Panic attacks involve symptoms of arousal coupled with intense fear—often of losing control in some specific situation.

■ **What are phobias?** Phobias are excessive fears focused on specific objects or situations.

■ **What is an obsessive-compulsive disorder?** This is an anxiety-based disorder in which individuals have repetitious thoughts and engage in repetitious behaviours they can't seem to control.

Somatoform Disorders

■ **What are somatoform disorders?** These are disorders in which individuals have symptoms typically associated with physical diseases or conditions, but in which no known organic or physiological basis for the symptoms can be found.

Dissociative Disorders

■ **What are dissociative disorders such as dissociative amnesia?** Dissociative disorders involve a significant loss of personal memory or identity. In dissociative amnesia, individuals are unable to remember various events, especially ones they found traumatic or disturbing.

■ **What is dissociative identity disorder?** In dissociative disorder (formerly known as multiple personality disorder), individuals seem to possess several distinct personalities that alternate in controlling their behaviour.

Sexual and Gender Identity Disorders

■ **What are sexual dysfunctions and paraphilias?** Sexual dysfunctions involve disturbances in sexual desire, sexual arousal, or the ability to attain orgasm. In paraphilias, unusual imagery or acts are necessary for sexual arousal.

■ **What is gender identify disorder?** Gender identity disorder involves feelings on the part of individuals that they were born with the wrong sexual identity, coupled with strong desires to change this identity through medical treatment or other means.

Eating Disorders

■ **What are anorexia nervosa and bulimia?** In anorexia nervosa, individuals literally starve themselves until their body weight falls to dangerously low levels. In bulimia, individuals maintain normal weight, but they engage in repeated cycles of binge eating and purging.

■ **What factors play a role in the occurrence of these eating disorders?** Eating disorders seem to stem, to an important degree, from the "thin is beautiful" image promoted heavily by the mass media. This image makes many people—especially young women—unhappy with their body shape, leading them to try extreme methods of weight control.

Personality Disorders

■ **What are personality disorders?** Personality disorders are extreme and inflexible personality traits that are distressing to the persons who have them or cause them problems in school, work, or interpersonal relations.

■ **What characteristics are shown by persons who have the antisocial personality disorder?** Persons who have the antisocial personality disorder show such characteristics as deceitfulness, impulsivity, irritability and aggressiveness, reckless disregard for their own safety and that of others, lack of remorse, failure to conform to social norms, and little or no concern for the rights of others.

Substance-Related Disorders

■ **What are substance-related disorders?** Substance-related disorders involve maladaptive patterns of substance use, leading to significant impairment or distress.

■ **What factors place teenagers at risk for developing these disorders?** These factors include high levels of life stress and maladaptive ways of coping with it, exposure to substance use by peers, and low parental support.

Schizophrenia

■ **What is schizophrenia?** Schizophrenia is a very serious psychological disorder characterized by hallucinations (e.g., hearing voices), delusions (beliefs with no basis in reality), and disturbances in speech, behaviour, and emotion.

■ **What are positive and negative symptoms of schizophrenia?** Positive symptoms involve the presence of something that is normally absent, such as hallucinations and delusions. Negative symptoms involve the absence of something that is normally present and include withdrawal, apathy, and absence of emotion.

■ **What are the major types of schizophrenia?** Major types of schizophrenia include catatonic, paranoid, disorganized, undifferentiated, and residual.

■ **What factors play a role in the occurrence of schizophrenia?** Schizophrenia has complex origins involving genetic factors, certain aspects of family environment, cognitive deficits, brain dysfunction, and biochemical factors.

Key Terms

Agoraphobia (p. 577)

Antisocial Personality Disorder (p. 585)

Anxiety (p. 576)

Anxiety Disorders (p. 576)

Assessment Interviews (p. 566)

Attention-Deficit/Hyperactivity Disorder (p. 569)

Bipolar Disorder (p. 571)

Catastrophic Thinking (p. 577)

Catatonic Type of Schizophrenia (p. 590)

Conversion Disorder (p. 579)

Delusions (p. 589)

Depression (p. 571)

Diagnostic and Statistical Manual of Mental Disorders-IV (DSM-IV) (p. 563)

Diathesis–Stress Model (p. 591)

Disruptive Behaviours (p. 569)

Dissociative Amnesia (p. 580)

Dissociative Fugue (p. 580)

Dissociative Identity Disorder (p. 580)

Dissociative Disorders (p. 580)

Dopamine Hypothesis (p. 592)

Eating Disorders (p. 584)

Gender Identity Disorder (p. 583)

Hallucinations (p. 589)

Hypochondriasis (p. 579)

Learned Helplessness (p. 572)

Medical Perspective (p. 560)

Mood Disorders (p. 570)

Obsessive-Compulsive Disorder (p. 578)

Panic Attack Disorder (p. 576)

Paraphilias (p. 583)

Personality Disorders (p. 584)

Pervasive Development Disorders (p. 570)

Phobias (p. 577)

Psychiatry (p. 560)

Psychological Disorders (p. 558)

Schizophrenia (p. 588)

Sexual Arousal Disorders (p. 582)

Sexual Desire Disorders (p. 582)

Somatization Disorder (p. 579)

Somatoform Disorders (p. 579)

Substance-Related Disorders (p. 587)

Substance Abuse (p. 587)

Substance Dependence (p. 587)

Critical Thinking Questions

Appraisal

Suppose that in a given society, cannibalism is viewed as fully acceptable, is practised by most members of the culture, and causes persons who engage in it no distress. Would it still constitute a mental disorder?

Controversy

Research on stereotypes suggests that when people are labelled in some way (e.g., intolerant, elitist, greedy, etc.), strong stereotypes may be activated. Such stereotypes may then exert a powerful influence on the way in which we think about and interact with these people. Do you think the practice of using DSM-IV to label people as "schizophrenic," "autistic,"

or "depressed" has similar effects? Consider this issue from both the perspective of how those labelled may come to think about themselves as a consequence of labelling, and how it may affect how others think and act toward them.

Making Psychology Part of Your Life

Now that you know about the major kinds of mental disorders, and their causes, do you think this will help you to recognize these problems in yourself and other persons? Do you think this knowledge has increased the likelihood that you would seek professional help yourself, or recommend to others that they seek such assistance, if you discerned such problems?

Weblinks

Check out our Companion Website at www.pearsoned.ca/baron for additional Websites, activities, and more.

Internet Mental Health

www.mentalhealth.com/p.html

Internet Mental Health is a free encyclopedia of mental health information. The creators of Internet Mental Health hope that it will promote improved understanding, diagnosis, and treatment of mental illness throughout the world. The encyclopedia includes information on mental disorders and medications, online diagnosis, a magazine, and many links to other mental health sites.

Anxiety-Panic Internet Resource

www.algy.com/anxiety/index.shtml

This page of anxiety-panic disorder resources includes articles and stories, information on medications, bibliographies, Internet and local resources, coping skills and relaxation exercises, a bulletin board, news, information about depression, advice, a chat group, and other related links.

The Clarke Institute of Psychiatry

www.camh.net/CLARKEPages/research/

Learn about the research programs at the Clarke Institute in Toronto where there are studies into the biochemical, cultural, genetic and behavioural components of psychological disorders, as well as explanations of the neuroimaging techniques being used to illuminate brain abnormalities in patients.

The Psychopath's Brain

www.epub.org.br/cm/n07/doencas/index.html

This Website discusses the psychopathic personality.

Schizophrenia Society of Canada

www.schizophrenia.ca/

The home page of the Schizophrenia Society of Canada has links to all of the provincial and territorial branches as well as lots of additional information.

Welcome All Abnormal Psychology Students

www.yorku.ca/faculty/academic/rmuller/

This Website for students of abnormal psychology has links to DSM-IV diagnoses and an alphabetical index to search for more specific details.

Famous People Who Have Experienced Depression

www.frii.com/~parrot/living.html

On this page you will find a list of famous people who suffer from depression or manic-depression as well as links to many of their personal stories. There is also a link to a long list of sources for information on these psychological disorders.

Chapter 15

Therapy

Diminishing the Pain
of Psychological Disorders

CHAPTER OUTLINE

Therapies

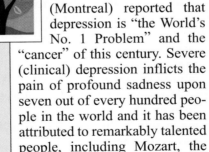

This article in *The Gazette* (Montreal) reported that depression is "the World's No. 1 Problem" and the "cancer" of this century. Severe (clinical) depression inflicts the pain of profound sadness upon seven out of every hundred people in the world and it has been attributed to remarkably talented people, including Mozart, the composer, and Van Gogh, the artist. Depressed people commonly turn to alcohol, illegal drugs, and some even to suicide to relieve their suffering.

Researchers have investigated genetics in their search for an explanation for depression and have found that several genes are involved. These are not recently developed genes, and for that reason researchers have concluded that this disorder has afflicted humans from ancient times. The finding that there is a chemical imbalance in the brains of depressed individuals has led to the discovery of prescription drugs—antidepressants—that often provide relief, along with psychotherapy.

What are the kinds of therapies that psychologists offer to patients who suffer from the many psychological disorders that plague humankind? What is psychotherapy? How do the drug therapies work? These are the kinds of compelling topics you will encounter as you proceed with Chapter 15.

Source: Francis, D. (2000, February 13). Opinion. *The Gazette* (Montreal).

There is a lot of pain in life—more than enough psychological discomfort to go around.

"I beg your pardon, I never promised you a rose garden." So starts a popular old song. Life is good, the lyrics suggest, but it's definitely no Eden free of problems. A few statistics from the Canadian Mental Health Association (2000) will help to drive this point home:

- About 20 percent of Canadians will be affected by mental illness during the course of their life.

- About 12 percent of Canadians will experience a mental illness troubling enough to cause them to seek professional help.

- About one in ten Canadians suffer from mood disorders and depression.

- About one in ten Canadians experience anxiety disorders.

- About one out of every twenty-five Canadians will attempt suicide at some point in his or her life.

Yes, there is a lot of pain in life—more than enough to go around. But there are also many effective techniques for alleviating such discomfort. Many procedures for treating various psychological disorders exist. To acquaint you with the most important of these, this chapter will proceed as follows.

We'll begin with **psychotherapies**—procedures in which a trained person establishes a professional relationship with the patient in order to remove or modify existing symptoms, change disturbed patterns of behaviour, and promote personal growth and development (Wolberg, 1977). You will find that many forms of psychotherapy exist, ranging from *psychoanalysis* (the famous procedures devised by Freud) to modern procedures founded on basic principles of learning and cognition. Following this, we'll explore several forms of therapy that involve several people rather than a single individual—*group therapies*. After that, we'll consider therapies focused on interpersonal relations—*marital* and *family therapy*. We'll then turn to some basic questions about all of these approaches: Are they successful in alleviating psychological disorders? And if they are, are some more helpful than others? We'll examine also several *biologically based therapies*—efforts to deal with psychological disorders through biological means. Finally, we'll look at the various settings in which different kinds of therapy are provided and how these have changed in the past few decades.

Psychotherapies

Psychotherapies: Procedures designed to eliminate or modify psychological disorders through the establishment of a special relationship between a client and a trained therapist.

Say the word *psychotherapy* and many people quickly conjure up the following image: A "patient" lies on a couch in a dimly lit room while a therapist sits in the background. The therapist urges the patient to reveal the deepest secrets of his or her mind—hidden urges, frustrated desires, traumatic early experiences. As these painful revelations are brought to the surface, the patient, suffering much emotional turmoil, moves toward psychological health. This popular image, however, has little to do with many modern forms of psychotherapy. In fact, it applies primarily to only one type, an approach developed by Freud that is now rarely used by psychologists (although it is still used by some psychiatrists). Psychotherapy, as it is currently practised by psychologists and other professionals, actually takes place in many dif-

ferent settings, employs a tremendously varied range of procedures, and can be carried out with groups as well as with individuals. Let's take a closer look at several important forms of psychotherapy—including the early methods used by Freud.

Psychodynamic Therapies

Psychodynamic therapies are based on the assumption that abnormal behaviour stems primarily from the kind of hidden inner conflicts first described by Freud—for instance, conflicts between our primitive sexual and aggressive urges (id impulses) and our conscience (superego), which cautions about the consequences of surrender to these urges (see Chapter 12). More specifically, psychodynamic therapies assume that psychological disorders occur because at some time something has seriously disturbed the balance among these inner forces. While several forms of therapy are based in these assumptions, the most famous is certainly *psychoanalysis*, the approach developed by Freud.

PSYCHOANALYSIS It is unlikely that Freud would have viewed favourably the many movies, television shows, and even cartoons that are loosely based on his method of psychotherapy. He regarded himself as a serious scientist and would probably have found popular representations of his work objectionable. Let's attempt to have a dispassionate look at his method of therapy. The best way to begin our examination is with a brief review of the reasoning on which Freud's methods are based.

As you may recall from Chapter 12, Freud believed that personality consists of three major parts—the *id, ego,* and *superego,* which correspond roughly to desire, reason, and conscience. Freud suggested that psychological disorders stem from the fact that many impulses of the id—whether acted upon or merely contemplated— are unacceptable to the ego or superego and are therefore repressed—driven into the depths of the unconscious. There they persist, and individuals must devote a considerable portion of their psychic energy to keeping them in check and out of conscious experience—and to various *defence mechanisms* that protect the ego from feelings of anxiety. In short, Freud believed that hidden conflicts among the basic components of personality, if left unresolved, interfere with normal psychosexual development and so cause psychological disorders.

How can such problems be relieved? Freud felt that the crucial task is for people to overcome repression and come face to face with their hidden feelings and impulses. Having gained such insight into their inner conflicts, they experience a release of emotion known as *abreaction*. Their energies having been at last freed from the task of repression, patients can direct these into healthy growth. Figure 15.1 summarizes these suggestions.

Freud's Famous Couch

This scene of Freud's London office, which he opened after fleeing Nazi persecution in Vienna, shows the famous couch.

Psychodynamic Therapies: Therapies based on the assumption that psychological disorders stem primarily from hidden inner conflicts with repressed urges and impulses.

Figure 15.1
Psychoanalysis: An Overview

Psychoanalysis, the kind of therapy developed by Freud, is primarily designed to provide individuals with insight into their hidden inner conflicts and repressed wishes. Freud assumed that once this insight overcomes the defence mechanisms used by patients to keep their hidden conflicts unconscious, and they move into consciousness, psychological disorders will fade away. In fact, there is little support for these views.

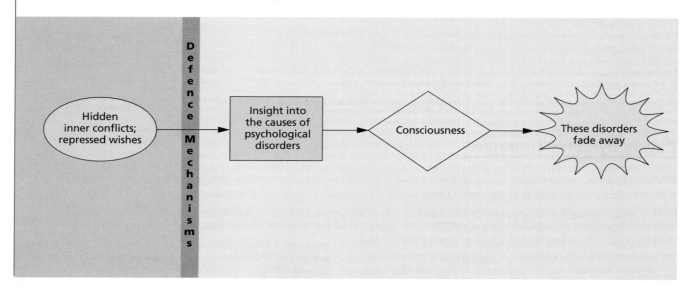

These ideas concerning the causes and cure of mental illness are reflected in the specific procedures used in psychoanalysis. As popular images suggest, the patient undergoing psychoanalysis lies on a couch in a partly darkened room and engages in **free association.** This involves reporting everything that passes through his or her mind, no matter how trivial it may appear to be. Freud believed that the repressed impulses and inner conflicts present in the unconscious would ultimately be revealed by these mental wanderings, at least to the trained ear of the analyst. He felt that dreams were especially useful in this respect, since they often represented inner conflicts and hidden impulses in disguised form. As psychoanalysis progresses and the analyst gains an understanding of the patient's problems, he or she asks questions and offers suggestions designed to enhance the patient's awareness of inner conflicts. It is through this process of *interpretation* that the patient finally gains increased insight.

During the course of psychoanalysis, Freud reported, several intriguing phenomena often occur. The first of these is **resistance**—the patient's refusal to report certain thoughts, motives, and experiences, or overt rejection of the analyst's interpretations (Strean, 1985). Presumably, resistance occurs because of the patient's desire to avoid the anxiety produced as threatening or painful thoughts come closer and closer to consciousness.

Another aspect of psychoanalysis is **transference**—intense emotional feelings of love or hate toward the analyst on the part of the patient. Typically, patients develop a state of emotional dependency on their analyst akin to the relationship they once had as children with their parents. Freud believed that the transference relationship is an essential part of the therapeutic process—an indispensable supportive crutch to help patients work through their conflicts. As a patient's insight increases, and self-confidence grows, the transference relationship diminishes and ultimately fades away.

Free Association: A key procedure in psychoanalysis in which individuals spontaneously report all thoughts to the therapist.

Resistance: Efforts by individuals undergoing psychoanalysis to prevent repressed impulses or conflicts from entering consciousness.

Transference: Strong positive or negative feelings toward the therapist on the part of individuals undergoing psychoanalysis.

AN EVALUATION OF PSYCHOANALYSIS Psychoanalysis is probably the best-known form of psychotherapy. Early efforts by psychologists to ignore it and later to discredit it largely failed: Psychoanalysis gained great popularity and refused to vanish, no matter how fervently psychologists pointed out that it was not based on scientific findings (Hornstein, 1992). What accounts for its fame? Certainly not its proven effectiveness. It is fair to say that its reputation far exceeds its success in alleviating mental disorders. In the form proposed by Freud, it has a variety of major deficiencies. First, psychoanalysis is a costly and time-consuming process. Several years and large amounts of money are usually required for its completion—assuming it ever ends! Second, it is based largely on Freud's theories of personality and psychosexual development. As noted in Chapter 12, these theories are provocative but difficult to test scientifically, so psychoanalysis rests on shaky scientific ground. Third, Freud designed psychoanalysis for use with highly educated persons with impressive verbal skills—ones who could describe their inner thoughts and feelings with ease. Fourth, psychoanalysis has often adopted the posture of a closed logical system. A failure to accept psychoanalysis is a clear sign of resistance and reflects the fact that one is suffering from a serious mental disorder that *prevents* the truth from being seen.

Finally, the major assumption of psychoanalysis—that once insight is acquired, mental health will follow automatically—is contradicted by research findings. Over and over again, psychologists have found that insight into one's thoughts and feelings does *not* necessarily change them or prevent them from influencing behaviour (e.g., Rozin, 1996). In fact, as we'll see in a later discussion of cognitive therapies, changing distorted or maladaptive modes of thought often requires great effort—and persistence.

BEYOND PSYCHOANALYSIS: PSYCHODYNAMIC THERAPY TODAY Because of such problems, classical psychoanalysis is a relatively rare type of therapy today. However, modified versions introduced by Freud's students and disciples, including the neo-Freudians we discussed in Chapter 12, are in more common use. These modified forms of psychodynamic therapy share these features: (1) they focus more on patients' present life and personal relationships than on the past, (2) they require less time, usually a few months rather than years, and (3) the therapist plays a more active and directive role in advising and counselling patients. Despite these differences, however, the basic goal remains the same: helping patients to gain insight into their hidden motives and inner conflicts.

K E Y *QUESTIONS*

- What is psychoanalysis and what are its major assumptions?
- What is the role of free association in psychoanalysis?
- How are psychodynamic therapies practised today?

Humanistic Therapies

Freud was something of a pessimist about basic human nature. He felt that we must constantly struggle with primitive impulses from the id. As we saw in Chapter 12, many psychologists reject this view. They contend that people are basically good and that our strivings for growth, dignity, and self-control are just as strong as—if not stronger than—the powerful aggressive and sexual urges Freud described. According to these *humanistic* psychologists, psychological disorders do not stem from unresolved inner conflicts. Rather, they arise because the environment somehow interferes with personal growth and fulfillment.

These views, of course, lead to forms of psychotherapy that are very different, both in purpose and procedure, from those developed by Freud. **Humanistic therapies** focus on the task of helping *clients* (note that humanistic therapists dislike the term "patient") to become more truly themselves—to find meaning in their lives and to live in ways consistent with their own inner values and traits. Unlike psychoanalysts, humanistic therapists believe that the client, not the therapist, must take essential responsibility for the success of therapy. The therapist is primarily a guide and facilitator, *not* the one who runs the show. Let's take a closer look at several major types of humanistic therapy.

CLIENT-CENTRED THERAPY: THE BENEFITS OF BEING ACCEPTED Perhaps the most influential humanistic approach is the **client-centred therapy** developed by Carl Rogers (1970, 1980). Rogers strongly rejected Freud's view that psychological disorders stem from conflicts over the expression of primitive, instinctive urges. On the contrary, he argued that such problems arise primarily out of a distorted *self-concept*. According to Rogers, individuals often acquire unrealistic **conditions of worth** early in life. That is, they learn that they must be something other than what they really are in order to be loved and accepted. For example, they come to believe that they will be rejected by their parents if they harbour hostility toward their siblings. In response to such beliefs, people refuse to acknowledge or accept large portions of their experience and emotions—any portions that violate their implicitly accepted conditions of worth. This in turn interferes with normal development of the self and results in various forms of maladjustment.

Client-centred therapy, as explained in Chapter 12, focuses on eliminating these unrealistic conditions of worth by creating a psychological climate in which clients feel valued as individuals. Client-centred therapists offer *unconditional acceptance,* or *unconditional positive regard,* of the client and his or her feelings; a high level of *empathetic understanding;* and accurate reflection of the client's feelings and perceptions. In the context of this warm, caring relationship, and freed from the threat of rejection, individuals can come to understand their own feelings and accept even previously unwanted aspects of their own personalities. As a result, they come to see themselves as unique human beings with many desirable characteristics. To the extent that such changes occur, Rogers suggests, many psychological disorders disappear and individuals can resume their normal progress toward self-fulfillment (see Figure 15.2).

GESTALT THERAPY: BECOMING WHOLE The theme of incomplete self-awareness —especially of gaps in clients' awareness of their genuine feelings—is echoed in a second humanistic approach, **Gestalt therapy.** According to Fritz Perls, originator of this type of therapy, many people have difficulties in directly experiencing and expressing emotions such as anger or the need for love. As a result, they

Humanistic Therapies: Forms of psychotherapy based on the assumption that psychological disorders stem from environmental conditions that block normal growth and development.

Client-Centred Therapy: A form of psychotherapy that concentrates on eliminating irrational conditions of worth— conditions people believe they must meet in order to be loved or accepted.

Conditions of Worth: In Rogers's theory, individuals' beliefs that they must meet certain unrealistic conditions in order to be loved or accepted.

Gestalt Therapy: A form of humanistic psychotherapy designed to increase individuals' awareness and understanding of their own feelings.

Figure 15.2
The Nature of Client-Centred Therapy

The high degree of empathetic understanding extended by client-centred therapists provides a setting in which clients can re-assess the way they feel about themselves and move in directions that are more self-fulfilling.

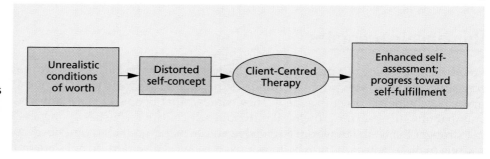

engage in manipulative social games, or pretense, in their interactions with others. These games and pretenses, in turn, lead the players to believe that they are not responsible for their own behaviour; they blame others and come to feel powerless. The goals of Gestalt therapy, therefore, are to help clients become aware of the feelings and needs they have disowned, and to recognize that these are a genuine part of themselves.

How can these goals be reached? Only by re-experiencing old hurts, jealousies, fears, and resentments. To do this, Gestalt therapists often use the *empty chair* technique. The client imagines an important person from his or her past—a parent, child, spouse—is sitting in the chair and then, perhaps for the first time, expresses his or her true feelings to this person (feelings about the person or about events or conflicts in which this person played a part). As a result, clients gain insight into their true feelings. This may actually help to reduce the emotional turmoil that brought clients to therapy in the first place—an important benefit in itself (Greenberg et al., 1994).

AN OVERVIEW OF HUMANISTIC PSYCHOTHERAPY Humanistic therapies certainly have a much more optimistic flavour than psychoanalysis; they don't assume that human beings must constantly struggle to control the dark forces and instincts within them. In this sense, certainly, they cast bright sunshine into the shadowy world envisioned by traditional psychoanalysis. In addition, several techniques devised by humanistic therapists are now widely used, even by psychologists who do not share this perspective. For instance, Carl Rogers was one of the first therapists to tape record therapy sessions so that they could be studied at a later time by therapists. This not only helps therapists to assist their clients; it also provides information about which techniques are most effective during therapy. Finally, some of the assumptions underlying humanistic therapies have been subjected to scientific test, and found to be valid. For instance, research findings tend to confirm Rogers's view that the gap between an individual's self-image and his or her "ideal self" plays a crucial role in maladjustment (e.g., Bootzin, Acocella, & Alloy, 1993). In these ways, then, humanistic therapies have made lasting contributions to the practice of psychotherapy.

On the other side of the coin, such therapies have been criticized for their lack of a unified theoretical base and for being vague about precisely what is supposed to happen between clients and therapists. So although they are certainly more widely used at present than psychoanalysis, they do not stand on the firm scientific ground that most psychologists strongly prefer.

The Empty Chair Technique Used in Gestalt Therapy

In the *empty chair* technique, clients are asked to imagine that an important person from their past—a parent, child, spouse—is sitting in the chair. Then clients hold a conversation with this person. As a result, they presumably gain increased insight into their true inner feelings.

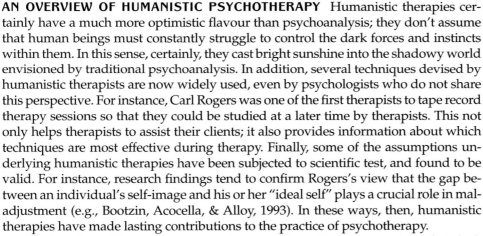

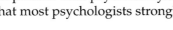

K E Y QUESTIONS

◼ According to humanistic therapies, what is the cause of psychological disorders?

◼ What is the major goal of Rogers's client-centred therapy?

◼ What is the major goal of Gestalt therapy?

Critical Thinking

Since clients come to therapy seeking help from an "expert," can the goal of equality between client and therapist, sought by humanistic therapists, actually be attained?

Behaviour Therapies

Behaviour Therapies: Forms of psychotherapy that focus on changing maladaptive patterns of behaviour through the use of basic principles of learning.

Systematic Desensitization: A form of behaviour therapy in which individuals imagine scenes or events that are increasingly anxiety-provoking and at the same time engage in procedures that induce feelings of relaxation.

Although psychodynamic and humanistic therapies differ in many ways, they both place importance on early events in clients' lives as a key source of current disturbances. In contrast, another major group of therapies, known collectively as **behaviour therapies**, focus primarily on individuals' current behaviour. These therapies are based on the belief that many mental disorders stem from faulty learning. Either the persons involved have failed to acquire the skills and behaviours they need for coping with the problems of daily life, or they have acquired *maladaptive* habits and reactions—that cause them considerable distress. Within this context, the key task for therapy is to change current behaviour, not to correct faulty self-concepts or resolve hidden, inner conflicts.

What kinds of learning play a role in behaviour therapy? As we saw in Chapter 5, there are several basic kinds. Reflecting this fact, behaviour therapies, too, employ techniques based on major kinds of learning.

Stanley J. Rachman
University of British Columbia

THERAPIES BASED ON CLASSICAL CONDITIONING As you may recall, *classical conditioning* is a process in which organisms learn that the occurrence of one stimulus will soon be followed by the occurrence of another. As a result, reactions that are at first elicited only by the second stimulus gradually come to be evoked by the first as well. (One example: your salivation to the beep of a microwave oven into which you've placed a container of popcorn.)

What does classical conditioning have to do with psychological disorders? According to behaviour therapists, quite a lot. Experts in behaviour therapy, such as Rachman at the University of British Columbia, suggest that some *phobias* can be acquired through conditioning (Rachman, 1991). That is, stimuli that become associated with real dangers may acquire the capacity to evoke the intense fear reactions that initially were elicited only by the actual dangers. However phobias are acquired, individuals with phobias experience intense fears of objects and situations that really pose no threat to their well-being, and they avoid exposure to these objects or situations. In order to reduce such fears, behaviour therapists sometimes employ a technique known as *flooding*. This involves prolonged exposure to the feared stimulus, or to a mental representation of it, under conditions in which the person suffering from the phobia can't avoid the stimulus. Under these conditions, *extinction* of fear can occur, so that the phobia fades away (Levis, 1985).

Another technique based at least in part on principles of classical conditioning is known as **systematic desensitization**. In systematic desensitization, which is also used to treat various phobias, individuals first learn to how to induce a relaxed state in their own body—often by learning how to relax their muscles. Then, while

**Systematic Desensitization:
A Behavioural Technique for
Eliminating Phobias**

In systematic desensitization, individuals first learn how to induce a relaxed state in their own bodies—often by learning how to relax their muscles. Then, while in this relaxed state, they are exposed to stimuli that elicit fear. Since relaxation is incompatible with fear, the conditioned link between these stimuli and fear is weakened and the phobia is reduced.

in a relaxed state, they are exposed to the stimuli that elicit anxiety. Since they are now experiencing relaxation, which is incompatible with fear, the conditioned link between these stimuli and anxiety is weakened, and extinction of anxiety reactions can occur.

THERAPIES BASED ON OPERANT CONDITIONING Behaviour is often shaped by the consequences it produces; actions are repeated if they yield positive outcomes or if they permit individuals to avoid or escape from negative ones. In contrast, actions that lead to negative results are suppressed. These basic principles are applied in several forms of therapy based on *operant conditioning*. These therapies differ considerably in specific procedures, but all incorporate the following basic steps: (1) clear identification of undesirable or maladaptive behaviours currently shown by individuals; (2) identification of events that reinforce and so maintain such responses; and (3) efforts to change the environment so that these maladaptive behaviours no longer receive reinforcement.

Operant principles have sometimes been used in hospital settings, where a large degree of control over patients' reinforcements is possible (Kazdin, 1982). Several projects have involved the establishment of **token economies**—systems under which patients earn tokens they can exchange for various rewards, such as television-watching privileges, candy, or trips to town. These tokens are awarded for various forms of adaptive behaviour, such as keeping one's room neat, participating in group meetings or therapy sessions, coming to meals on time, and eating neatly. The results have often been impressive. When individuals learn that they can acquire various rewards by behaving in adaptive ways, they often do so, with important benefits to them as well as to hospital staff (e.g., Paul, 1982; Paul & Lentz, 1977).

Token Economies: Forms of behaviour therapy based on operant conditioning, in which hospitalized patients earn tokens they can exchange for valued rewards when they behave in ways the hospital staff consider to be desirable.

MODELLING: BENEFITING FROM EXPOSURE TO OTHERS Suppose that an individual came to a psychologist seeking help for an all-too-common problem: lack of *assertion*. In other words, this individual is one who can't stand up for his or her own rights, is often "pushed around" by others, and can't say "no" in many situations. How can the psychologist help? One answer involves the use of *modelling*—techniques based on *observational learning*. As we saw in Chapter 5, human beings have a tremendous capacity to learn from observing others (e.g., Bandura, 1986). This fact is put to use by behaviour therapists in treating a wide range of personal problems.

For instance, persons like the one described above are often given *assertion training* in which they are taught the basic social skills they are lacking. How is this accomplished? Often by exposing to them others who demonstrate (model) appropriate ways of standing up for one's rights. This can involve watching live demonstrations or videotapes in which the actors show, very clearly, how one can respond adaptively to such situations as having another push ahead of you while you are in line or sending back food you didn't order in a restaurant. Such demonstrations focus on adaptive reactions to these situations: responding firmly, but without excess anger or aggression. After watching such displays, individuals practise certain behaviours themselves and so, quite quickly, acquire new and more effective ways of behaving in many situations (Wilson et al., 1996).

Modelling techniques have also been used, with impressive success, in the treatment of phobias. Many carefully conducted studies indicate that individuals who experience intense fear of relatively harmless objects can be helped to overcome these fears through exposure to appropriate social models who demonstrate lack of fear in their presence, and show that no harm occurs as a result of contact with these objects (e.g., Bandura & Maddux, 1977). Such procedures have been found to be effective in reducing a wide range of phobias, such as fears of dogs, snakes, and spiders, to mention just a few (Bandura, 1986, 1995). In sum, behavioural therapies based on basic principles of learning are useful in alleviating many types of mental disorders.

Modelling: Changing Behaviour Through Observing Others

Seeing other people act in various ways can strongly influence our behaviour.

- According to behaviour therapies, what is the primary cause of psychological disorders?

- On what basic principles of learning are behaviour therapies based?

- What is modelling, and how can it be used in treating psychological disorders?

Critical Thinking

It has sometimes been argued that behaviour therapies treat symptoms of mental disorders without changing their underlying causes. Do you think that is a fair criticism? If so, why? If not, why?

Cognitive Therapies

A central theme in modern psychology—and one has been emphasized throughout this book—is this: Cognitive processes exert powerful effects on emotions and behaviour. In other words, what we *think* strongly influences how we *feel* and what we *do*. This principle forms the basis for another major approach to psychotherapy, **cognitive therapies.** The basic idea behind all cognitive therapies is this: Many mental disorders stem from faulty or distorted modes of thought. Change these, and the disorders, too, can be alleviated. Let's examine several forms of therapy based on this reasoning.

RATIONAL–EMOTIVE THERAPY: OVERCOMING IRRATIONAL BELIEFS Examine the list of beliefs or assumptions below:

- Everyone who meets me should like me.

- I should be perfect (or very near perfect) at everything I do.

- Because something once affected my life, it will always affect it.

- It is unbearable and horrible when things are not the way I would like them to be.

- It is impossible to control my emotions, and I can't help feeling the way I do about certain things.

Do such views ever influence *your* thinking? While you may strongly protest that they do not, one psychologist—Albert Ellis (1987)—believes that they probably *do* influence your thinking. Moreover, he contends that such *irrational thoughts* play a key role in many psychological disorders. Why do we have such thoughts? Not, Ellis contends, because we consciously choose to do so. Rather, they, are often automatic reactions stemming from our strong desires for love, success, and a safe, comfortable existence. We *want* these things to be true—we want to be liked by everyone, to be perfect, and so on—so we let these powerful desires colour our perceptions and our thinking..

Whatever their origins, irrational beliefs generally serve to escalate reasonable desires into "musts," as in "I *must* be loved by everyone," or "I *must* experience continuous success to be happy." Closely linked to such ideas are tendencies Ellis describes as *awfulizing* or *catastrophizing*—beliefs that if a certain event occurs or fails to occur, it will be a disaster of unbearable proportions from which one can never hope to recover. Here are two examples: "If I don't get that promotion, *my career will be completely over,*" and "If I don't get an A in that course after working so hard, *I just won't be able to stand it!*"

Ellis maintains that because they hold these irrational beliefs, people are often their own worst enemies. They cause their own problems by worrying about their inability to reach impossible goals and by convincing themselves that they simply cannot tolerate the normal frustrations and disappointments of everyday life. To make matters worse, once such thoughts take hold, negative feelings and maladaptive behaviours soon follow (see Figure 15.3).

Cognitive Therapies: Psychotherapies that concentrates on altering faulty or distorted modes of thought so as to alleviate psychological disorders.

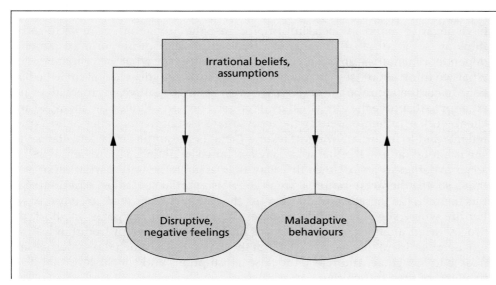

Figure 15.3
Rational–Emotive Therapy

According to Ellis, many psychological disorders stem from irrational thoughts. These create disruptive feelings and maladaptive behaviours, which in turn sometimes trap people in a vicious circle. Rational–emotive therapy seeks to break this cycle.

How can this self-defeating cycle be broken? Ellis suggests that the answer involves forcing disturbed individuals to recognize the irrationality of their thoughts.

Rational–emotive therapy (RET) is designed to accomplish this task. During this form of therapy, the therapist first attempts to identify irrational thoughts and then tries to persuade clients to recognize them for what they are. For example, imagine that a therapist practising RET is confronted with a client who says, "My girlfriend just dumped me for another guy; *I'll never find anyone else who will love me like she once did!*" The therapist might reply, "So your girlfriend dumped you; why does that mean that no one else will ever love you? Is she really the only woman in the world with whom you could have a relationship?" By challenging the irrationality of their clients' beliefs, therapists practising RET get them to see how ridiculous and unrealistic some of their ideas are, and in this way, help them to stop being their own worst enemy.

BECK'S COGNITIVE BEHAVIOUR THERAPY FOR DEPRESSION The discussion of depression in Chapter 14 noted that this common and serious psychological disorder has an important cognitive component: It stems, at least in part, from distorted and often self-defeating modes of thought. Recognizing this important fact, Beck and his colleagues (Beck, 1985) have devised a therapy (known as **Beck's cognitive behaviour therapy**) for alleviating this problem. Like Ellis, Beck assumes that depressed individuals' problems result from illogical thinking about themselves, the external world, and the future. Moreover, he contends, these illogical ideas and tendencies are often maintained in the face of evidence that contradicts them. In an important sense, then, they are both self-defeating and self-fulfilling. What are the cognitive tendencies that foster depression? Among the most important are these:

■ A tendency to overgeneralize on the basis of limited information—for example, to see oneself as totally worthless because of one or a few setbacks.

■ A tendency to explain away any positive occurrences by interpreting them as exceptions to the general rule of failure and incompetence.

■ A tendency toward selective perception—especially, to perceive the world as a dangerous, threatening place.

■ A tendency to magnify the importance of undesirable events—to perceive them as the end of the world, and unchangeable.

■ A tendency to engage in absolutistic, all-or-none thinking—for example, to interpret a mild rejection as final proof of one's undesirability.

Rational–Emotive Therapy: A cognitive therapy that focuses on changing irrational beliefs.

Beck's Cognitive Behaviour Therapy: A form of cognitive therapy that focuses on changing illogical patterns of thought that underlie depression.

Central to Beck's therapy is the idea that such thinking leads individuals to have negative moods, which, in turn, increase the probability of more negative thinking (see Figure 15.4). In other words, he emphasizes the importance of mood-dependent memory—how our current moods influence what we remember and what we think about (see Chapters 6 and 14). How can this vicious circle be broken? In contrast to rational–emotive therapy, Beck's cognitive approach does not attempt to disprove the ideas held by depressed persons. Rather, the therapist and client work together to identify the individual's assumptions, beliefs, and expectations, and to formulate ways of testing them. For example, if a client states that she is a total failure, the therapist may ask how she defines failure, and whether some experiences she defines this way may actually be only partial failures. If that's so, the therapist inquires, aren't they also partial successes? Continuing in this manner, the therapist might then ask the client whether there are *any* areas of her life where she *did* experience success and did reach her goals. In short, the process used to alter distorted patterns of thought is different from (and somewhat gentler than) that used in RET, but the major goal is much the same: helping people to recognize, and reject, the false assumptions and conclusions that lie at the heart of their difficulties.

**Donald H.
Meichenbaum**
University of Waterloo

Stress Inoculation Training: A form of behaviour therapy dealing with anxiety problems.

MEICHENBAUM'S STRESS INOCULATION TRAINING PROGRAM FOR ANXIETY   In introducing the cognitive therapies, it was noted that cognitive processes influence not only our behaviour but also our emotional reactions to situations. Our consideration of cognitive therapies will conclude with a consideration of troubling relationships that can develop between thoughts and emotions and how they can be managed.

We often become anxious when we think about how we are going to deal with difficult tasks that lie before us. A little anxiety is often useful. It encourages that extra bit of preparation for such important events as final examinations and job interviews, but too much anxiety can be crippling. Are there ways to deal with excessive amounts of anxiety? One widely used cognitive approach is that developed by Donald Meichenbaum of the University of Waterloo.

Meichenbaum's **stress inoculation training** has proven extremely useful in dealing with a host of problems that are often encountered in academic and other settings—test anxiety, social anxiety, panic and generalized anxiety disorders, and even anger (e.g., Meichenbaum & Deffenbacher, 1988). There are *three stages* to the program.

**Figure 15.4
Beck's Cognitive Behaviour Therapy: An Overview**

Beck's cognitive therapy is designed to change cognitive tendencies that contribute to depression. Such patterns of thought often produce negative affect, which increases the likelihood of further negative thoughts. Beck's cognitive behaviour therapy attempts to break the cycle and, thus, reduce depression.

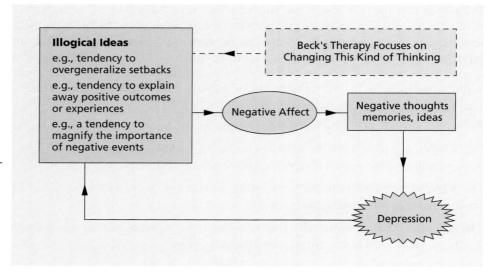

In the *first* stage, the primary objective is for clients to acquire an understanding of the nature of anxiety and how it is generated. They learn that anxiety involves an exaggerated emotional reaction, in conjunction with troublesome thoughts and expectations. The client and therapist work together to define, as accurately as possible, the situations and circumstances that generate anxiety, as well as the accompanying thoughts and expectations. Commonly, the therapist assigns self-monitoring exercises so that the client can gain the fullest possible understanding of these matters. As a result of this assessment, clients see their problems more objectively and begin to understand that anxiety management requires development of control over their emotions and thoughts and the expectations that accompany them.

In the *second* stage, clients develop skills that will allow them to gain control over their emotional reactions—and over the inappropriate thoughts and expectations that attend those reactions. They learn emotion-management skills, such as relaxation procedures and breathing exercises, that help regulate physiological arousal. At the same time, the therapist leads the client through cognitive restructuring exercises. The purpose of these exercises is to increase the client's self-awareness of negative (and inappropriate) thoughts and expectations. The emphasis here is on changing self-concepts of inadequacy or incompetence. Together, the therapist and client systematically develop ways of dealing with problem situations and experiences. Exercises and role-playing techniques are used to increase the client's confidence. The overall goal is to change the ways individuals think about anxiety-provoking situations, so that they stop seeing themselves as the *victims* of events, and start seeing themselves as *controlling* and *effectively managing* their interactions with the world.

The *third* stage involves the application of coping responses to specific problem areas. Clients are encouraged to *imagine,* as vividly as possible, particular situations that provoke anxiety and to employ the relaxation and cognitive coping skills they have acquired to alleviate that anxiety. Next, the application of coping skills to *real-world situations* is gradually introduced. To ensure that the client practises coping skills, the therapist assigns *homework* involving application of these skills in daily real-world situations. The results of the homework exercises are discussed and evaluated, and modifications are suggested and applied. Most important of all, the client's progress is carefully *monitored* on an ongoing basis to ensure that any setbacks are not viewed as defeats, but as challenges that can be readily overcome.

Stress inoculation training is a flexible and widely applicable technique for dealing with a host of difficulties that generate unmanageable anxiety. It is important to realize that most practising psychotherapists do not spend all of their time dealing with major incapacitating disorders requiring extensive or total reconstruction of the person. They are consulted most frequently by individuals who are having problems coping with particular situations, tasks, and experiences that occur in everyday life. It is necessary that therapists have techniques available that can be readily applied to these various situations and circumstances. Stress inoculation training is one such technique.

AN EVALUATION OF COGNITIVE THERAPIES An essential question about any form of therapy is "Does it work?" Cognitive therapies pass this test with flying colours: Growing evidence indicates that they can be highly effective in treating several mental disorders. Many studies indicate that changing or eliminating irrational beliefs, such as the unstated desire to be perfect, can be very effective in countering depression and other personal difficulties (e.g., Blatt et al., 1996; Dobson & Craig, 1996). Similarly, the procedures outlined by Beck have been found to be highly effective in treating depression (e.g., Bruder et al., 1997). Perhaps even more important, the effects they produce tend be longer lasting than those produced by other forms of therapy for depression, for example, antidepressant drugs, which we will examine in a later section (e.g., Segal et al., 1999).

KEY *QUESTIONS*

▓ According to cognitive therapies, what is the primary cause of psychological disorders?

▓ What is the major goal of rational–emotive therapy?

▓ What is the major goal of Beck's cognitive therapy for depression?

▓ What is stress inoculation training?

Group Therapies

Group Therapy: It Can Be Effective

In group therapy, people with similar problems work together under the direction of a trained therapist to reduce these problems. For several reasons—people learn that their problems are not unique, group members share information and insights, and the group provides a supportive environment for practising social skills—such therapy can often be beneficial.

All of the therapies we have considered so far are conducted on a one-on-one basis—that is, one therapist works with one client. However, this is not the only approach to helping individuals deal with psychological problems. In recent decades, **group therapies,** in which treatment takes place in groups, have grown tremendously in popularity. We'll now examine several important types of group therapy, beginning with those that are closely linked to the individual therapies we considered earlier.

Psychodynamic Group Therapies

The techniques Freud developed for individual therapy have been modified for use in group settings. Perhaps the most popular form of psychodynamic group therapy is **psychodrama,** in which group members act out their problems in front of other group members, often on an actual stage. Psychodrama also involves such techniques as *role reversal,* in which group members switch parts, and *mirroring,* in which they portray one another on the stage. In each case, the goal is to show clients how they actually behave and to help them understand *why* they behave that way—what hidden inner conflicts lie behind their overt actions (Olsson, 1989). While psychodrama is highly appealing to many people, it is subject to the same criticisms as all psychodynamic therapies, and its potential benefits may be somewhat overstated by its often ardent supporters.

Behavioural Group Therapies

Although there is very limited support for psychodrama as a therapeutic procedure, there is very compelling evidence that various *behavioural group therapies*—group approaches in which basic principles of learning are applied to solve specific behavioural problems—are effective. Such therapies have been especially successful in teaching individuals basic *social skills* and in helping them learn how to stand up for their own rights without being aggressive (the kind of *assertion training* described earlier). Behavioural group therapies have also proven helpful in teaching individuals *self-control*—the capacity to regulate their own behaviour. Many persons experience serious problems in life because they lack this basic skill. They can't force themselves to get up in the morning so they can get to work on time; they can't stop themselves from buying things they can't afford; they can't hold their tempers in check when annoyed (e.g., Bandura, 1986). Group therapy based on behavioural principles can be highly effective in teaching individuals these skills.

In such sessions, each person describes how he or she is currently behaving in situations requiring self-control. Then each receives suggestions from other group members about how to do a better job in this respect. Since different members of the group have different problems with respect to self-control, they can serve as models of more effective behaviour for each other and also as sources of positive reinforcement by praising one another when progress is made toward appropriate goals.

Group Therapies: Therapies conducted with groups of clients.

Psychodrama: A form of psychodynamic group therapy in which people act out their problems in front of fellow group members.

Humanistic Group Therapies

Psychologists who practise humanistic therapies have been by far the most enthusiastic about adapting their techniques to group settings. In fact, interest in group therapy first originated among humanistic therapists, who developed two forms of such therapy—**encounter groups** and **sensitivity-training groups**. Both of these techniques focus on the goals of personal growth, increased understanding of one's own behaviour, and increased honesty and openness in personal relations. In both, members are encouraged to talk about the problems they encounter in their lives. The reactions they receive from other group members are crucial in helping them understand their own responses to these problems. The major difference between encounter groups and sensitivity training groups lies in the fact that encounter groups carry the goal of open exchange of views to a greater extreme: Members in these groups are encouraged to yell, cry, touch each other, and generally to act in a completely uninhibited manner. Sensitivity-training groups, in contrast, are somewhat more subdued.

Humanistic group therapies use several ingenious warm-up exercises to start the open exchange of views. In one warm-up, for example, participants are blindfolded and wander around the room communicating only by touch. These procedures are designed to help members realize that normal restraints and rules don't operate in the group setting: that they are free to say and do almost anything—and so to come face to face with their own distorted self-concepts and perceptions.

Do such groups really produce beneficial changes? Many people who have participated in them attest that they do, but most research on this issue has been informal in nature, so it is difficult to reach firm conclusions (Kaplan, 1982).

Self-Help Groups

When we are anxious, upset, or otherwise troubled, we often seek comfort and support from others. Long before there were psychologists or psychiatrists, people sought informal help with their personal difficulties from family, friends, or clergy. This natural tendency has taken a new form in **self-help groups** (Christensen & Jacobson, 1994). These are groups of individuals experiencing the same kinds of problems, who meet to help each other in their efforts to cope with their difficulties. Self-help groups are a very common fact of life at the turn of the millennium. What kinds of problems do these groups address? Almost everything you can imagine—and then some. Self-help groups have been formed to help their members cope with alcoholism (Alcoholics Anonymous is perhaps the most famous of all self-help groups), the death of a spouse, rape, AIDS, childhood sexual abuse, being a single parent, divorce, stuttering, abusive spouses, breast cancer … the list is almost endless.

A guiding principle behind these groups is that people who share a problem have a unique understanding of it and can offer one another a level of empathy that no one else can provide. Do self-help groups succeed? Few scientific studies of the impact of such groups have yet been conducted, but there is some indication that they can yield important benefits (Christensen & Jacobson, 1994). In any case, these groups do provide their members with emotional support and help them to make new friends. These outcomes alone may justify their existence.

The **Key Concept** on page 614 provides an overview of the major forms of psychotherapy discussed so far in this chapter.

Encounter Groups: A form of group therapy in which people are urged to tell other group members exactly how they feel; designed to foster personal growth through increased understanding of one's own behaviour and increased honesty and openness in personal relations.

Sensitivity-Training Groups: A form of group therapy designed to foster personal growth through increased understanding of one's own behaviour and increased honesty and openness in personal relations.

Self-Help Groups: Groups of individuals experiencing the same kinds of difficulties that meet to discuss their shared problem and find solutions to it.

K E Y QUESTIONS

- What is the major focus of psychodynamic group therapies, such as psychodrama?
- What is the major focus of behavioural group therapies?
- What is the major focus of humanistic group therapies?
- What are self-help groups, and what do they provide?

Key Concept *Major Forms of Individual Psychotherapy*

Therapy	Major Focus	Key Procedures
Psychoanalysis (Freudian)	Bringing repressed feelings and impulses into consciousness	Free association Dream interpretation Analysis of resistance

Humanistic therapies (Client-centred therapy)	Eliminating unrealistic conditions of worth Correcting distortions in self-concept	Therapist's expression of unconditional positive regard for the client Therapist's empathy toward client and reflection of client's feelings and reactions

Behaviour therapies	Changing maladaptive patterns of behaviour Overcoming/changing past faulty learning	Systematic desensitization Shaping of adaptive behaviour through reinforcement Modelling 
Cognitive therapy	Changing faulty or distorted modes of thought Changing irrational beliefs and assumptions	Clarification of the irrational nature of client's beliefs Evaluation of self-defeating ideas and assumptions to demonstrate that they are false
Group therapies	Inducing beneficial individual change or change in important interpersonal relations (e.g., family, couple) in context of a group setting	Group activities, mutual empathy, and guidance to increase individuals' self-insight and help them learn new social skills

▶ Therapies Focused on Interpersonal Relations

The therapies we have considered so far differ greatly in many respects, yet in one sense they are all related: They search for the roots of psychological disorders in processes operating within individuals. Another group of therapies adopts a sharply different perspective. According to practitioners of this *interpersonal* approach, disturbed or maladaptive interpersonal relationships lie at the heart of many psychological disorders (Gurman et al., 1986). In other words, individuals experience personal difficulties because their relationships with others are ineffective or unsatisfying—or worse. Several forms of therapy based on this idea are described below.

Marital Therapy

In Canada, more than 50 percent of all marriages now end in divorce; moreover, since many people remarry—and hope seems to spring eternal—growing numbers of persons have been married three or more times (Brody et al., 1988). Keeping people in joyless marriages where each spouse is destructive to the other's psychological health is definitely *not* a goal of therapy. However, it appears that many marriages that fail could be saved and converted into loving, supporting relationships—if the persons involved sought help before the downward spiral went too far (Hendrick, 1989). Further, marital problems appear to be closely linked to several psychological disorders, such as depression and drug dependency (Gotlib & McCabe, 1990). For these reasons, **marital therapy** (sometimes known as *couple therapy*)—therapy designed to help couples improve the quality of their relationship—can often be highly valuable.

Before turning to the goals and procedures of such therapy, let's first consider a very basic question: What is the number-one reason why couples seek professional help in the first place? If you guessed "sexual problems," guess again; such difficulties are a distant second in the list (see Figure 15.5). *Communication* problems loom as the foremost difficulty faced by couples. Couples entering marital therapy often state that their spouse "never talks to them" or "never tells them what she/he is thinking." Or they say that the only kind of communicating their spouse ever does is *complaining.* "He/She never tells me that he/she loves me," they remark, "All he/she does is tell me about my faults and what I'm doing wrong." Given that couples begin their relationships with frequent statements of mutual esteem and love, the pain of such faulty communication patterns is doubled: each partner wonders what went wrong—and then generally blames the other!

Marital Therapy: Psychotherapy that attempts to improve relations and understanding in couples.

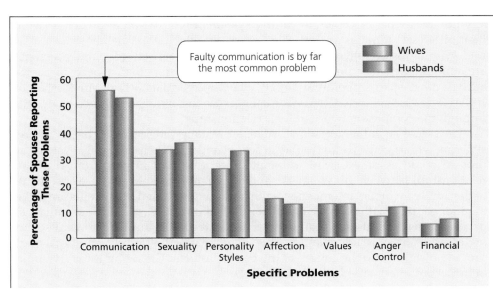

Figure 15.5
Why Couples Seek Marital Therapy

As shown here, the number-one reason why couples seek help with their relationships from a trained therapist involves faulty communication. Other problems are important too, but these are mentioned less frequently by couples.

Source: Based on data from O'Leary et al., 1992.

A key goal of marital therapy, then, is to improve communication between spouses or partners. Therapists work to foster such improvements in many different ways, including having each partner play the role of the other person in order to see their relationship as the other does. Other techniques involve having couples watch videotapes of their own interactions. This procedure is often truly an eye-opener: "Wow, I never realized that's how I come across!" is a common reaction to seeing themselves interacting with their spouse. As communication between members of a couple improves, many other beneficial changes occur. They stop criticizing each other in destructive ways (e.g., Baron, 1993), express positive sentiments toward each other more frequently, and stop attributing actions by their spouse or partner to internal causes or stable traits. In other words, they stop assuming that anything their partner does that annoys them is done on purpose, or that such actions can't be changed because they stem from their partner's traits (e.g., Kubany et al., 1995). Once communication is re-established, couples may also find it easier to resolve other sources of friction in their relationships: conflicts over sexuality, money, attitudes, and values. The result may then be a happier and more stable relationship, and one that increases, rather than reduces, the psychological well-being of both partners.

Family Therapy

Family Therapy

Family therapy is based on the view that many psychological disorders stem from disturbed interpersonal relations among family members.

Families involve more than just couples, and family settings can have a powerful influence on the well-being of individual family members. Let's begin with a disturbing fact: When individuals who have been hospitalized for the treatment of serious psychological disorders and who have shown marked improvement return home, they often experience a relapse. All the gains they have made through individual therapy seem to vanish quickly (Carson et al., 1988). This fact points to an important conclusion: The problems experienced by such people can be traced, at least in part, to their families—or more specifically, to disturbed patterns of interaction among family members (Hazelrigg et al., 1987). To the extent that this situation exists, attempting to help one member of a family is not sufficient: unless changes are also made in their family environment, any benefits they have experienced may disappear once they return home.

Recognition of this important fact spurred the development of several types of **family therapy**—therapy designed to change the relationships among family members in constructive ways. Perhaps the most common approach to such therapy involves what is known as **family systems therapy**—an approach in which therapists view families as dynamic systems in which each member has a major role. Within this framework, it is assumed that relations between family members are more important in producing psychological disorders than aspects of personality or other factors operating largely *within* individuals (Minuchin & Fishman, 1981). It is also assumed that all members of the family influence each other through the complex network of their relationships.

How does such therapy work? Take, for instance, the case of a highly aggressive son, who is getting into trouble in school and elsewhere. A family systems approach would assume that his difficulties stem, at least in part, from disturbed relationships between this youngster and other family members. Close observation of the family members interacting together might reveal that the parents are locked in bitter conflict, with each trying to recruit the boy to their side. The result: he experiences tremendous stress and anger, and directs this outward toward schoolmates and others. Understanding the dynamics of his family, in short, could provide insights into the causes of the boy's problem. Changing these dynamics, in turn, could help to reduce his difficulties.

Family Therapy: A form of psychotherapy that focuses on changing interactions or relations among family members.

Family Systems Therapy: Therapy designed to change the relationships among family members in constructive ways.

A second major approach is known as **problem-solving therapy** (e.g., Robin & Foster, 1988). This approach focuses not so much on the complex dynamics within families—although it views these as important—but on instituting specific, well-defined changes within a family. In essence, the problem-solving approach involves four distinct phases:

1. *Defining the problem.* Different family members may have contrasting views about just what problem the family faces, so it is important for the therapist to step in and help them see the underlying pattern, not just their own views.

2. *Generating alternative solutions to the problem.* Again, different family members may have contrasting perspectives, and it is important for all of these to be represented in the discussion.

3. *Evaluating the alternative solutions.* Each solution is examined by the family, and a consensus is reached on which is the best or which to try first.

4. *Implementing the solution.* Plans for putting the solution to work are made and used.

For example, consider a family in which the teenage daughter is threatening to run away from home. The parents might view the problem as their daughter's rebelliousness and her boyfriend's bad influence on her. She, in turn, might view this friction as stemming from unrealistic restrictions placed on her by her parents: "You treat me like a child!" The therapist might then step in and define the basic problem as one of faulty communication in which the parents and their daughter exchange primarily angry criticisms rather than discussing important issues clearly. Possible solutions are that the daughter would agree to do her homework or to come home by a specified hour if her parents treat her more as an adult or are pleasant to her boyfriend. The family would then select one or more of these steps and try them out, reporting to the therapist on the results. Through this kind of process—which involves open discussion and a healthy chunk of trial-and-error, they would move toward solving their basic problems—and a happier family relationship (see Figure 15.6).

Does family therapy work? Research findings indicate that in many cases it is quite successful. After undergoing such therapy, family members are rated by therapists, teachers, and other observers as showing more adaptive behaviour and better relations with each other than was true before the therapy (Hazelrigg et al., 1987). Family therapy does seem to help reduce problems experienced by individual members. For example, consider a study of juvenile offenders conducted by Henggeler, Melton, and Smith (1992). The youths involved had an average of three and one-half previous arrests and seemed headed for a life of serious crime. Instead of the usual "treatment"—monthly meetings with the probation officer—a problem-focused family therapy approach was used. Sessions were conducted in the

Problem-Solving Therapy: A form of family therapy that focuses on instituting specific, well-defined changes within a family in order to eliminate specific problems.

Figure 15.6
Problem-Solving Family Therapy

Problem-solving family therapy focuses on instituting specific changes within a family that will help family members to cope with specific problems. It involves the four steps shown here.

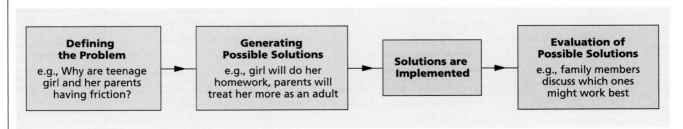

teenagers' homes, over a period of about four months, and involved all available family members. Many serious problems within these families were uncovered in these meetings, and therapists worked hard at resolving them. Results were encouraging: Youngsters who received family therapy experienced fewer arrests and reported engaging in fewer crimes than those who received the typical "visits-to-the-probation-officer" approach. Findings like these suggest that family therapy may well be a useful approach to dealing with at least some psychological disorders.

One possible exception to this otherwise optimistic assessment of marital and family therapy has to do with interactions involving violence. Avis (1992) claims that journals concerned with family and marital therapy neglect or minimize the significance of the problem. There is little question that family violence is both pervasive and corrosive. Avis cites statistics indicating that as many as one in every ten Canadian women suffers some form of abuse from the man with whom she lives. Avis also points out that a very high percentage of men who observe domestic abuse as children become abusers as adults (p. 227). The major challenge facing marital and family therapists may well be to develop ways to counter and control violence and abuse within the home.

K E Y QUESTIONS

▩ What is the major focus of marital or couple therapy?

▩ What is family systems therapy?

▩ What is problem-solving family therapy?

Some Current Issues in Psychotherapy

We have examined a wide variety of therapies involving individuals, groups, and family members. We have also considered the types of problems that different therapeutic approaches target and the strengths of these various therapies. What we have not done is discuss, in any systematic fashion, the overall effectiveness of psychotherapy as a treatment for psychological disorders.

Your first assumption may be that it is unnecessary to raise this issue, and that it is quite apparent that psychotherapy has a beneficial effect on those experiencing psychological problems. After all, you might argue, there are large numbers of practising psychotherapists and an enormous number of people under treatment at any given time. Given the general acceptance of psychotherapy and the extent to which it is practised, you could conclude that the only question that can be sensibly asked is whether some types of psychotherapy are more effective than others—not whether psychotherapy itself is helpful. Unfortunately, the issue is not this simple. The effectiveness of psychotherapy as a treatment practice has to be raised. It has to be raised because of our resilience and adaptiveness, as individuals, in the face of adversity. The fact is that many individuals with psychological problems get better even if they do not receive treatment. What has to be shown is that recovery is more likely with psychotherapy than without.

The first serious effort to assess the effectiveness of psychotherapy was a controversial study undertaken by Eysenck in 1952. What he found was that about 67 percent of patients with a wide range of psychological disorders improved after therapy but, surprisingly, he found that about the same proportion of people receiving *no treatment* also improved. Fortunately for both practitioners of psychotherapy and patients receiving psychotherapy, Eysenck was in error. Subsequent investigation has indicated that he *over*estimated the proportion of persons who recover without any therapy and *under*estimated the proportion who improve after receiving therapy. Although Eysenck's conclusions were incorrect, he did force psychologists and others to think carefully about the procedures that should be employed in assessing the effectiveness of psychotherapy.

Determining exactly how to assess the effectiveness of psychotherapy remains a much-debated issue to this day. What is it that makes assessment so difficult? First, patients experiencing a particular disorder vary widely in the character of the symptoms they display and in the intensity of their affliction. Second, it is often the case that individuals experience difficulty in more than one area of functioning. For example, in addition to a depression, an individual may also suffer from some degree of substance abuse or substance dependency. This variability in the way disorders are expressed makes it difficult to establish closely matched groups of patients that will allow meaningful comparisons of the effectiveness of the various therapies, or a more basic comparison of a group of subjects receiving psychotherapy with a control group of subjects not receiving treatment. There are also differences in effectiveness among individual therapists that can cloud any comparison process. Finally, consider the question of time. How much time should we allow in order to be sure that there has been ample opportunity for a form of psychotherapy to have a meaningful effect on clients? Should this vary for different disorders?

Determining the Worth of Psychotherapy: Efficacy versus Effectiveness Studies

Assessing the worth of psychotherapy is a difficult task. Martin Seligman, a prominent clinical psychologist, argues that to assess psychotherapy, we have to consider evidence provided by two very different types of studies: efficacy studies and effectiveness studies (Seligman, 1995). *Efficacy* studies are carefully designed and controlled laboratory studies. *Effectiveness* studies are studies that attempt to provide information about the adequacy of psychotherapy as it is actually practised in real-life situations. Let's first consider efficacy studies. In the **Research Process** section below, you will find a description of the procedures that should be followed to provide an experimental assessment of the efficacy of different therapies. This will be followed by a description of the results of such studies.

Efficacy Study: Carefully controlled laboratory studies designed to determine whether a particular form of psychotherapy benefits those receiving it more than a comparable control group that does not receive psychotherapy.

The Research Process:
How Psychologists Assess Various Forms of Psychotherapy

What research strategies should be pursued to determine whether a given form of therapy is beneficial? Several different approaches exist, but most psychologists would agree that by far the most powerful, from a scientific view, is one known as the **efficacy study** (e.g., Seligman, 1995).

What is an efficacy study? One that applies the basic methods of scientific experimentation to find out whether a specific form of therapy really works; that is, whether the therapy produces beneficial outcomes for the persons who undergo it. Efficacy studies involve the following basic requirements—which, as you'll see, are very similar to the ones outlined in Chapter 1 as criteria for valid experimentation on virtually *any* topic in psychology:

- Inclusion in the study of at least one experimental group (persons with a given psychological disorder who are exposed to the therapy) and at least one control group (persons with the same disorder who are *not* exposed to the therapy).

- Random assignment of participants to these two conditions: All participants must have an equal chance of being assigned to the control (no therapy) or experimental (therapy) condition.

- Rigorous controls: Individuals receiving therapy may seem to improve not because of the therapy but because they are receiving attention from the therapist, expect to get better, and have a friendly relationship with the therapist; so these potential confounding factors must be eliminated by additional control groups. These are groups in which such factors are present, but the key aspects of the therapy under examination are *not* present.

- Standardization of the experimental treatment: Persons delivering the therapy must be thoroughly trained in it and must know precisely what to do; sessions should be videotaped to ensure that the therapists are doing exactly what the training manuals for the therapy require—*and nothing else* that might influence participants' behaviour.

- A fixed number of sessions: Participants in the control and experimental conditions must receive the same number of sessions.

- Clear definition of the dependent measures: How will changes in behaviour be measured? This must be specified in advance.

- Participants must have only one psychological disorder—the one for which the therapy is designed. If they have several disorders, changes in one may influence changes in others, thus making it impossible to clearly assess effectiveness of the therapy.

- Well-trained "blind" raters: If the dependent variables involve ratings of participants' behaviour, the raters must be thoroughly trained and must *not* know whether participants were assigned to the experimental or the control condition.

Under these circumstances, if participants who receive therapy show greater improvement than those who do not, we can have high confidence in the conclusion that "this form of therapy works—it is significantly better than no treatment." Efficacy studies are a powerful tool of research. They allow psychologists to go far beyond the informal methods, such as personal testimonials from satisfied patients or impassioned praise from true believers, that are sometimes offered as "evidence" for the value of psychotherapy.

Laboratory Research on the Efficacy of Psychotherapy

Many independent experimental analyses of psychotherapy have confirmed its efficacy (e.g., Bergin & Lambert, 1978; Clum & Bowers, 1990). Extensive reviews employing meta-analysis, a statistical procedure that allows an overall comparison of the results of many different independent studies, have been carried out (see Chapter 1 to review information about this procedure). Some of these studies provide a statistical comparison of the results of more than four hundred separate experiments (e.g., Andrews & Harvey, 1981; Smith, Glass, & Miller, 1980). These studies show that the condition of 75 to 80 percent of those under treatment is better than individuals in an untreated control condition. The more treatment people receive, the more they improve, the fewer symptoms they show, and the less distress they report (Howard et al., 1986; Orlinsky & Howard, 1987). Such effects are not restricted to adults; they have also been found with children and adolescents (e.g., Kazdin, 1993; Weisz et al., 1992). As is the case with adults, children and teenagers who receive therapy show greater improvements than those who do not. It seems clear that there is abundant evidence from experimental studies that psychotherapy works. The question that remains to be answered is whether psychotherapy is efficacious outside, as well as inside, the experimental laboratory.

The Effectiveness of Psychotherapy in Actual Practice

Efficacy studies have been generally viewed as the most adequate assessment of psychotherapy. As we have noted, they provide confirming evidence for the value of psychotherapy. Nevertheless, efficacy studies have some inherent limitations. The most important of these have to do with the fact that in most laboratory studies, psychotherapy is not practised as it is in real life. Thus, it is difficult to know whether various forms of therapy found to be efficacious in laboratory studies are efficacious in actual practice. What are the differences in the way psychotherapy is carried out in laboratory studies and the way it is normally practised? Here are some of the most important differences:

- In research studies of the efficacy of psychotherapy, treatment continues for a fixed number of sessions; in actual practice, this is rarely the case—therapy continues until people improve.

- In research studies, only one type of therapy is used; in natural conditions, therapists switch between techniques until they find one that works.

- In research studies, participants are assigned to a type of therapy they have not necessarily sought; in actual practice, individuals actively shop for and choose therapists.

- In research studies, participants have a single psychological disorder; in field settings, patients often have several disorders.

- In research studies, the focus is on improvements with respect to specific symptoms or disorders; in actual practice, psychotherapy is directed toward producing more general improvements in functioning.

Because of these differences, Seligman concludes, laboratory studies cannot provide us with all the information needed to assess that adequacy of psychotherapy. What are required are **effectiveness studies**—studies that are designed to assess the degree to which psychotherapy is effective when practised in actual clinical settings. In short, it would be helpful to have some form of consumer assessment of the therapeutic experience—direct information about whether psychotherapy has been helpful to the thousand of individuals who have actually undergone therapy. No wholly satisfactory assessment of this type has been carried out. The closest approximation, which Seligman views very favourably, is an extremely large-scale questionnaire assessment provided by *Consumer Reports* magazine that polled its 180 000 subscribers about their experience with mental health professionals in 1994.

The survey asked individuals whether they had ever sought help with an emotional problem during the past three years and, if so, who had helped them— friends, clergy, family doctors, self-help groups, or a wide range of mental health professionals (psychiatrists, psychologists, social workers, marriage counsellors, and so on). The survey asked questions about the duration and frequency of therapy respondents had received, and—perhaps most important of all—how much help they gained from the therapy.

More than seven thousand subscribers completed the questionnaire, and their responses corroborate more objective experimental studies. Most respondents to the survey indicated that the help they did receive made them feel better and assisted in the elimination of problems and symptoms, especially if therapy continued for six months or more. It was found that such improvements were greatest when respondents received therapy from psychologists, psychiatrists, and social workers; improvements were somewhat less evident when they received therapy from physicians and marriage counsellors. There was also evidence that the longer therapy continued, the greater the improvement. See Figure 15.7 for an overview of the results.

Effectiveness Studies: Studies designed to assess the degree to which psychotherapy is beneficial as it is practised in actual clinical settings.

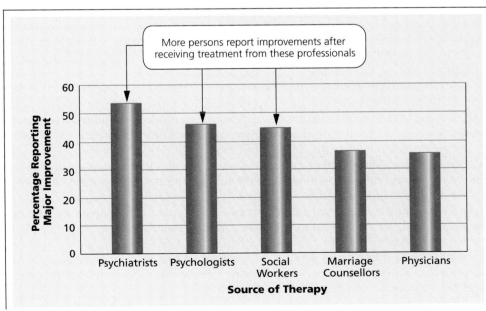

More persons report improvements after receiving treatment from these professionals

**Figure 15.7
Evidence for the Effectiveness of Psychotherapy**

As shown here, large proportions of people who received psychotherapy from professionals (psychiatrists, psychologists, and social workers) reported feeling much better as a result of such treatment. Somewhat smaller proportions reported improvements after visiting marriage counsellors or physicians.

Source: Based on data reported by Seligman, 1995.

It has to be emphasized that caution is necessary in interpreting the results of this type of questionnaire study. The information obtained is based entirely on self-report—what those participants who returned the forms *said* happened purely as a result of therapy. Changes in surrounding circumstances associated with the difficulties experienced may well have played an important role in relieving distress. We have no way of knowing whether this is the case. Also, there is always a concern about the representativeness of the sample in such studies—the concern being whether those who returned the questionnaire differed in some significant way from those who did not. Lastly, there is the question of whether those who may have invested a great deal of time, effort, and money in psychotherapy would be prepared to admit to a less than positive outcome when filling out the questionnaire.

Despite these important flaws, however, Seligman (1995) points out that this study *does* tell us much about the experience of several thousand people with therapy as it is actually delivered and, moreover, this is the only large-scale study of this type available. He believes that it provides evidence that complements—and helps complete—the picture provided by experimental studies. Psychotherapy does help.

Are Some Forms of Psychotherapy More Successful Than Others?

The procedures used in various forms of psychotherapy differ sharply. It seems only reasonable, then, to expect that some types of therapy will be more effective than others. It is surprising that comparisons among therapies have generally yielded inconclusive results. Despite their contrasting procedures, all therapies seem to yield roughly equivalent benefits (Hollon et al., 1987; Hollon et al., 1991). How can therapies employing sharply different procedures yield similar results? There are two possible answers.

One answer is that various forms of therapy share common features. All major forms of psychotherapy provide troubled individuals with a special type of setting—one in which they interact closely, usually one-on-one, with a highly trained, empathetic professional. Under such circumstances a *therapeutic alliance* develops—a partnership in which powerful emotional bonds are forged between the person seeking help and the therapist. The therapeutic process also demystifies disorders by providing an explanatory rationale and a recommended course of action. Finally, all therapies involve a personal commitment to the therapeutic process. This is a decisive action that provides a heightened sense of *hope* and *personal control* and it encourages a sense of optimism about the future (Garfield, 1995, 1998). In sum, a core set of characteristics, such as those we have described, are common to all therapies, and may be the reason why research studies find no difference among therapies.

A very different answer is that differences *do* exist, but we have not as yet discerned them. There is some merit to this position. Rachman and Wilson (1980) point out that the idea that one can choose any therapy at random for all problems is inherently absurd. Others question whether large statistical meta-analyses of treatment are sufficiently sensitive to pick out individual differences in the efficacy of various different kinds of therapy, and take the position that a finer-grain analysis might well reveal differences among the therapies (see Stiles, Shapiro, & Elliot, 1980).

A definitive determination of whether a common set of core characteristics are responsible for the failure to find differences among various therapies, or whether detection of differences must await more carefully detailed research, is not likely to be obtained anytime soon. To a large degree, practical problems associated with the delivery of therapeutic services at the turn of the century have shouldered aside traditional concerns, and forced many psychologists to look at psychotherapy from a new perspective.

The Quest for Empirically Validated Therapies

Consumers of therapy, health care insurers, and government agencies have become increasingly troubled about escalating treatment costs. As a consequence, there has been growing pressure for demonstrable evidence that treatment programs are *efficacious* and can be completed within a *reasonable* time period. Professional organizations such as the American Psychiatric Association, and the American Psychological Association have responded to these pressures by creating task forces to consider commonly encountered problems and disorders and provide guidelines indicating treatment programs that are demonstrably efficacious for these problems and disorders.

The ultimate objective is to provide, for each problem or disorder, a list of **empirically validated therapies**—therapies that have been *scientifically* demonstrated to be efficacious for that particular problem or disorder. In the case of the American Psychological Association, empirical validation of a treatment practice for a problem or disorder requires a minimum of two well-designed experimental assessments. These studies have to confirm that the treatment is *more effective* than a placebo condition (a condition designed to control for the expectancy for change and attention that are normally associated with all forms of therapy).

Lists of *empirically validated* therapies for specific problems and disorders appear regularly in clinical journals published by the American Psychological Association and are available on its website. The research literature is monitored regularly and the list of empirically validated therapies is updated at regular intervals.

Some examples of empirically supported therapies for a number of common problems and disorders may be seen in Table 15.1. Fuller listings may be found on the Division 12 (Clinical Psychology) section of the American Psychological Association website (**www.apa.org/divisions/div12/est/est.html**). As you might assume from examining Table 15.1, behaviour therapy and cognitive therapy appear prominently as efficacious treatments for a wide variety of disorders.

Empirically Validated Therapies: Therapies that have been scientifically demonstrated to be efficacious in treating particular problems or disorders.

TABLE 15.1

Some Examples of Empirically Validated Therapies

Listed below are some examples of therapies that have been empirically validated as treatments for a variety of specific psychological problems and disorders.

Therapy

Behavioural marital therapy

Behavioural therapy for enuresis

Beck's cognitive therapy for depression

Cognitive therapy for bulimia

Cognitive therapy for generalized anxiety disorder

Cognitive therapy for panic disorders

Exposure and response prevention for obsessive compulsive disorders

Interpersonal therapy for depression

Stress inoculation training for coping

Systematic desensitization for phobia

Source: Adapted from Chambless et al., 1997.

The practice of listing empirically validated therapies for specific problems and disorders has won much praise and some criticism (Nathan, 1998). There is certainly widespread support for publicly identifying therapeutic practices that are known to be effective, and it appears that this policy is beginning to influence clinical training programs. One concern, which we discussed previously, centres on the degree to which laboratory-based efficacy testing generalizes to real-life practise situations. The *Consumer Report* study described earlier provides reason for a measure of optimism in this respect, but it is not definitive. Another significant concern is that the empirical validation process underestimates the degree to which the outcome of therapy is influenced by individual differences in the personal characteristics of patients, and variations in the skill of individual therapists (Garfield, 1998).

Advocates of empirical validation of therapies, such as Dianne Chambless, who directed the American Psychological Association Task Force, recognize there are problems with current formulations. Their view is that current efforts constitute only the *first step* in the refinement of procedures that will lead ultimately to the scientific demonstration of *effectiveness* of therapies in general clinical settings (Chambless & Hollon, 1998).

One remaining issue about the practice of psychotherapy requires mention. Special care and concern has to be taken when psychotherapy is being administered to members of minority groups. This issue is discussed in the **Perspectives on Diversity** section below.

Perspectives on Diversity

The Necessity for Culturally Sensitive Psychotherapy

DESPITE CHANGES TO MAKE DIAGNOSTIC devices such as DSM-IV more sensitive to cultural differences, available evidence indicates that race, sex, ethnic background, and social class can influence the process of diagnosis. An illustration of such influence is provided by Snowden and Cheung (1990), who found that people of African descent are more likely to be diagnosed as schizophrenic and less likely to be diagnosed as showing affective (mood) disorders than people of European descent.

If racial and ethnic factors can influence diagnosis, it will not surprise you to learn that these factors can also influence the course of psychotherapy. One obvious difficulty is that therapists and clients from different cultures may find it difficulty to communicate effectively with one another and the necessary level of empathy, acceptance, and understanding required in the psychotherapeutic setting may not be achieved.

It is fair to say that therapists have become increasingly sensitive to the way in which cultural factors can influence therapeutic practices. It is currently recognized that good therapeutic practice requires taking careful account of the values and traditions of members of minority groups, and that failure to do so can lead therapists to engage in treatment practices that are quite inappropriate. A single example will serve to illustrate this point. Therapists working with clients from Asia or the Middle East have to be cognizant of the different self-concept that is dominant in these cultures. As we noted in Chapter 12, individuals in these cultures typically have an interdependent or collectivist sense of self that binds them tightly to their family and social group. Engaging in therapy that encourages development of an independent North American sense of self that focuses on self-actualization and self-fulfillment can place a client in conflict with his or her family and culture (Dwairy & Van Sickle, 1996).

In summary, therapists have to take very careful consideration of the cultural, economic, and educational background of their clients to ensure that the therapy accomplishes its major goal: helping to lessen the pain of psychological disorders (e.g., Hammond & Yung, 1993).

KEY QUESTIONS

- What are efficacy studies of psychotherapy?

- Why are effectiveness studies of psychotherapy required?

- Does available evidence indicate that psychotherapy is effective?

- Are some types of psychotherapy more effective than others?

- What are empirically validated therapies?

Biologically Based Therapies

Mind and body are intimately linked. Everything we think, remember, feel, or do is manifested through some form of activity in the central nervous system. This basic fact has led some researchers to take the position that psychological disorders are rooted in aberrations in the functioning of neural mechanisms. In this section, we'll consider a variety of **biologically based therapies** that reflect this approach.

Early Forms of Biological Therapy

Efforts to address psychological disorders by altering the function of the nervous system have a long history. Early expressions of this approach were dismayingly direct and disturbingly crude. Skulls from early civilizations often show neatly drilled holes, suggesting that some individuals may have experienced a primitive form of surgery on their brains as a means of attempting to deal with psychological disorders. Even as recently as the nineteenth century, many physicians kept devices like the one shown in the accompanying photo in their offices. The physician would apply the electrodes to different portions of a patient's anatomy in an effort to counter various kinds of "nervous disorders." Although these early efforts were misdirected and ineffectual, more sophisticated variants of both psychosurgery and electric shock would come to play a significant role in the treatment of mental disorders in the twentieth century.

Electroconvulsive Therapy

For at least the last half century, the application of electric shock to the brain has been used to treat certain types of mental disorders. What would prompt anyone to think that application of an electric current to the brain could possibly be therapeutic? To answer the question, we have to go back to the 1930s. At that time many physicians believed that schizophrenics rarely had epileptic seizures. Although this assumption was in error, it led a Hungarian psychiatrist, Von Meduna, to suggest that inducing such seizures artificially might be an effective means of treating this serious disorder. At first, psychiatrists produced convulsions by the injection of drugs such as camphor; and at least a momentary clearing of symptoms was often observed. After witnessing the use of shock to render animals unconscious in slaughterhouses, two Italian physicians, Cerletti and Bini, proposed and tested the notion of using powerful electric shocks instead of drugs (Bini, 1938). This procedure, known as **electroconvulsive therapy (ECT),** became quite common; even today, it is widely used in North America. It involves placing electrodes on the patient's temples and delivering shocks of 70 to 130 volts for brief intervals (less than one second). These are continued until the patient has a seizure, involving muscle contractions lasting at least thirty seconds. In order to prevent broken bones and other injuries, a muscle relaxant and a mild anesthetic are administered before the start of the shocks. Patients typically receive three treatments a week for several weeks.

Early Biological Therapy

Electrical devices such as this one were widely used by physicians in the late nineteenth century to "treat" many psychological disorders.

Biologically Based Therapies: Forms of therapy that attempt to reduce psychological disorders through biological means such as drug therapy or surgery.

Electroconvulsive Therapy (ECT): A treatment for depression that entails passing brief pulses of mild electric shock through the brain until a seizure ensues.

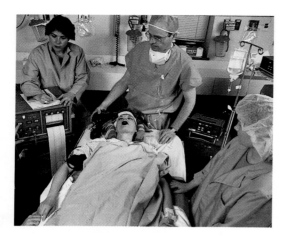

Electroconvulsive Therapy Today

In electroconvulsive therapy, a mild electric current passes through the brain for less than a second, causing a brief seizure.

ECT is most commonly used as a treatment for severe depression. It is customarily employed when drug treatments prove ineffective or cannot be utilized. Because it works more rapidly than drugs, it may be the treatment of first choice if the depression is severe and the patient has a suicidal disposition (Endler & Persad, 1988).

Although ECT is widely employed, its use remains controversial. Many are convinced that applying sufficient electric current to induce a seizure must be injurious to the brain. For example, Breggin (1979) is certain it does cause harm and has called for its elimination as a form of therapy. Others are just as strongly convinced of its value and safety. The latest position paper of the Canadian Psychiatric Association on ECT concludes that, if properly used, ECT is a "safe and effective treatment" and recommends its continued use as a therapeutic procedure (Enns & Reiss, 1992). Also supportive is a review of the history and use of ECT by Endler and Persad (1988). Endler, a prominent Canadian professor of psychology at York University, provides an interesting personal account of own his experience with depression in his book *Holiday of Darkness,* which is well worth reading. Although he had a strong initial bias against the use of ECT, he credits the procedure with lifting his depression.

It is safe to conclude that the controversy over the use of ECT is likely to continue. Given the character of the procedure and the absence of any real understanding as to why it works, a degree of caution is necessary. The advantages and disadvantages of ECT—and of alternative drug therapies—should be weighed carefully before consent is given for use.

Psychosurgery

In 1935, a Portuguese psychiatrist, Egas Moniz, attempted to reduce aggressive behaviour in psychotic patients by severing neural connections between the prefrontal lobes and the remainder of the brain. The operation, known as *prefrontal lobotomy,* seemed to be successful—aggressive behaviour by unmanageable patients did decrease. Moniz received the 1949 Nobel Prize in medicine for his work—but, in one of those strange twists of history, he was later shot by one of his lobotomized patients!

Encouraged by Moniz's findings, psychiatrists all over the world rushed to treat a wide range of disorders through various forms of **psychosurgery**—brain operations designed to change abnormal behaviour. Tens of thousands of patients were subjected to prefrontal lobotomies and related operations. Unfortunately, it soon became apparent that results were not always positive. While some forms of objectionable or dangerous behaviour did decrease, serious side effects sometimes occurred. Some patients became highly excitable and impulsive; others slipped into profound apathy and a total absence of emotion. A few became living vegetables, requiring permanent care after the operation.

In view of these harmful outcomes, most physicians stopped performing prefrontal lobotomies. Prefrontal lobotomies had all but faded from the scene worldwide by the 1960s. In part, this dramatic decline reflected the development of drugs for treating psychoses—substances we'll consider in detail below. Today, psychosurgery, when it is performed, takes a much more limited form than prefrontal lobotomy. Instead of cutting connections between whole areas of the brain, modern-day brain surgery focuses on destroying tiny areas or on interrupting specific neural circuits. For instance, in one modern procedure, connections between a very small area of the brain and the limbic system are severed. Results indicate that this limited kind of psychosurgery may be effective with individuals suffering from obsessive-compulsive disorder who have not responded to any other type of treatment (e.g., Jenike, 1991).

Psychosurgery: Efforts to alleviate psychological disorders by performing surgery on the brain.

One final point has to be made about psychosurgical procedures. Even if such operations are successful, are they ethically justifiable? Is it right to destroy healthy tissue in a person's brain in the hope that this will relieve symptoms of psychological disorders? These and related issues have led most mental health practitioners to conclude that psychosurgery should be viewed as a very drastic form of treatment—something to be tried only when everything else has failed. For these reasons, only a small number of such operations are now performed in North America each year, and psychosurgery is no longer an important form of treatment for psychological disorders.

Drug Therapy

In the 1950s and early 1960s, a remarkable change began to occur in the mental health field. The number of full-time resident patients in psychiatric hospitals in Canada and the United States began to fall; within twenty years, it had declined by more than two-thirds. Were North Americans achieving mental health at a dizzying pace? Absolutely not. What happened in those years was something many describe as a *pharmacological revolution*: A great number of *psychotropic drugs* effective in treating many serious psychological disorders were developed and put to use. So successful was **drug therapy** in reducing major symptoms that hundreds of thousands of individuals who had previously been hospitalized for their own safety (and that of others) could now be treated as outpatients. What are these wonder drugs, and how do they produce their positive effects? It is to these questions that we turn next.

The Pharmacological Revolution

Drugs effective in treating a wide range of psychological disorders were developed during the 1950s and 1960s. As a result, the number of full-time patients in psychiatric hospitals decreased dramatically.

ANTIPSYCHOTIC DRUGS If you had visited the wards of a psychiatric hospital for seriously disturbed people before about 1955, you would have had some very unsettling experiences. You would have observed some distressed patients confined in rooms with padded walls and floors, and at some point in your visit you would likely have heard a patient rattling the protective mesh on his or her window and screaming. You would have visited locked wards where personnel would instruct you on entering that it was advisable that you always keep your back close to a wall. If you had returned a few years later, however, you would have observed a dramatic change: peace, relative tranquillity, and many patients now capable of direct, sensible communication. What accounted for this startling change? The answer involves the development of *antipsychotic drugs*, sometimes known as *major tranquilizers*.

The most important group of antipsychotic drugs—*phenothiazines*—were discovered by accident. In the early 1950s, a French surgeon, Henri Laborit, used a drug in this chemical family, *Thorazine* (chlorpromazine), to reduce blood pressure in patients before surgery. He found that their blood pressure didn't drop, but they become much less anxious. French psychiatrists tried the drug with their patients and found that it worked: it reduced anxiety and—even more important—it also reduced hallucinations and delusions among schizophrenic patients. Chemists quickly analyzed chlorpromazine and developed many other drugs related to it, but which are even more effective in reducing psychotic symptoms (e.g., clozapine, haloperidol).

Antipsychotic drugs relieve a wide range of symptoms, including hallucinations, thought disorders, anxiety, and extreme hostility. The overall result is nothing short of amazing. Patients who are almost totally out of touch with reality and must be given custodial care can, after receiving the drugs, re-establish contact with reality and interactions with others. Perhaps even more important, they can improve to the point where they become candidates for various forms of psychotherapy. The scope of the changes produced is perhaps best summarized by the following statistic: In the mid-1950s, 70 percent of all individuals diagnosed as suffering from schizophrenia spent most of their lives in mental hospitals. The present figure is less than 5 percent. How do the antipsychotics produce such effects? Apparently by blocking *dopamine* receptors in the brain. As noted in Chapter 14, the presence of an excess of this neurotransmitter, or increased sensitivity to it, seems to play a role in schizophrenia.

Drug Therapy: Efforts to treat psychological disorders through administration of appropriate drugs.

The use of these drugs, however, is not without drawbacks. They often produce fatigue and apathy as well as calming effects. And after receiving antipsychotic drugs for prolonged periods of time, many patients develop a side effect called **tardive dyskinesia**: loss of motor control, especially in the face. As a result, they show involuntary muscle movements of the tongue, lips, and jaw. These movements often decrease when patients stop taking the drug, but they continue unchanged in at least some individuals (Yudofsky et al., 1991). In order to avoid such side effects, many psychiatrists no longer place patients on maintenance doses of the drug. Rather, they employ *target dosing*—that is, they administer drugs only when serious symptoms appear and discontinue them when the symptoms are eliminated. One relatively new antipsychotic drug, Clozaril (clozapine) appears to be effective without producing tardive dyskinesia, but it can have other side effects.

While the antipsychotic drugs are of great value, they do not provide a total answer to schizophrenia and other serious psychological disorders. True, the most bizarre symptoms of schizophrenia decrease under medication. However, this does not usually result in an individual who can return to normal life. People on antipsychotic drug therapy often remain somewhat withdrawn and show relatively slow reactions and reduced levels of affect. And more serious symptoms often reappear if the drug therapy is stopped. In short, antipsychotic drugs seem to relieve the major symptoms of schizophrenia but don't deal with the precipitating causes. For these reasons, it is imperative that people receiving drug therapy also receive other forms of psychotherapy, counselling, and community support—otherwise, the probability of relapse is high.

ANTIDEPRESSANT DRUGS Shortly after the development of chlorpromazine, drugs effective in reducing depression made their appearance. There are three basic types of antidepressants: *tricyclics, selective serotonin re-uptake inhibitors (SSRIs),* and *MAO inhibitors.* All three seem to exert their antidepressant effects by influencing neurotransmitters, especially *serotonin.* In fact, it has been suggested that SSRIs affect only the re-uptake of serotonin, while tricyclics may affect both norepinephrine and serotonin. Both serotonin and norepinephrine levels are low in depressed individuals, so it seems possible that these drugs make neurotransmitters more available by reducing their re-uptake or re-absorption (Julien, 1995).

Among the SSRIs, *Prozac* (fluoxetine) is by far the most famous—and also the most commonly prescribed. Depressed persons taking this drug often report that they feel better than they have in their entire lives. There are some side effects. A small number of patients taking the drug report suicidal thoughts (Teicher et al., 1990), and some others report loss of sexual desire, but overall the proportion of persons who experience such side effects seems small (Walker et al., 1993). In contrast, side effects associated with other antidepressants are much more extreme. The MAO inhibitors can produce severe headaches, heart palpitations, stroke, or even death. These are most likely to occur when individuals consume certain foods, such as chocolate, beer, or wine. For this reason, these drugs are used less often than the other two types of antidepressants. The tricyclics also produce side effects, such as disturbances in sleep and appetite, but these tend to decrease within a few weeks. Widely prescribed tricyclics include Elavil (amitriptyline) and Tofranil (imipramine).

LITHIUM An entirely different kind of mood-stabilizing drug is *lithium* (usually administered as *lithium carbonate*). About 60 to 70 percent of those with a manic-depressive disorder respond well to treatment with lithium (Julien, 1995). It is effective in diminishing the excesses associated with both the manic and depressive phases of the disorder. Since those experiencing this disorder are often quite agitated and even psychotic in the manic phase, lithium is often administered in combination with other antipsychotic and/or other antidepressant drugs.

Tardive Dyskinesia: A side effect of prolonged exposure to antipsychotic drugs in which individuals experience involuntary muscular movements, especially of the face.

Unfortunately, lithium has serious side effects—excessive doses can cause convulsions, delirium, and even death. Thus, it has a very small "therapeutic window" or dose level that is effective without being dangerous. Exactly how lithium exerts its effects is not known; one possibility is that it alters brain levels of serotonin. Whatever its mechanism, it is one of the few drugs effective in treating manic-depressive disorders, so its continued use seems likely.

ANTIANXIETY DRUGS Alcohol, a substance used by many people to combat anxiety, has been available for thousands of years. Needless to say, however, it has important negative side effects. Synthetic drugs with antianxiety effects—sometimes known as *minor tranquilizers*—have been manufactured for several decades. The most widely prescribed at present are the *benzodiazepines*. This group includes drugs whose names you may already know: Valium, Ativan, Xanax, and Librium.

The most common use for antianxiety drugs, at least ostensibly, is as a sleep aid. They are safer for this purpose than barbiturates since they are less addicting. However, substances derived from the benzodiazepines remain in the body for longer periods of time than those from *barbiturates*, and can cumulate until they reach toxic levels. Thus, long-term use of these drugs can be quite dangerous. In addition, when they are taken with alcohol, their effects may be magnified; this is definitely a combination to avoid. Finally, they do tend to produce dependency; individuals experience withdrawal symptoms when they are abruptly stopped. It is better, therefore, to withdraw from them gradually (Yudofsky et al., 1991). Antianxiety drugs seem to inhibit the central nervous system by acting on specific receptor sites in the brain (Hayward et al., 1989).

One additional antianxiety drug is not related to the benzodiazepines: BuSpar (buspirone). It seems to be effective, and does not appear to produce the dependence often produced by the benzodiazepines (Long & Rybacki, 1994). It does produce other side effects in some persons, however, including dizziness, faintness, and mild drowsiness. Also, there is a lag of between one and three weeks before BuSpar produces its antianxiety effects. However, it does seem to be a useful alternative to the benzodiazepines.

Sizing Up Drug Therapy and Psychotherapy

Drug therapies have had an enormous positive impact on treatment of those suffering from various types of psychological disorders. As we have noted, before the advent of drug therapy, many individuals suffering chronic severe depression, or experiencing psychotic disorders, would have been sentenced to a lifetime of hospitalization. Drug therapies now allow the management of these disorders outside of hospital settings. Given the remarkable ability of pharmacological agents to regulate the symptoms associated with so many different disorders, it is tempting to see them as almost magical curative agents that are able to correct chemical imbalances and restore brain and body function to their original rightful state. However, person-to-person interactions with patients undergoing various drug treatments have convinced many mental health workers that the drug therapies currently available fall well short of this state of perfection (Fischer & Greenberg, 1997).

There are almost always side effects associated with drug therapies. In the case of antipsychotic drugs, these drugs can effectively control the symptoms of the disorder, but not always the underlying psychosis. In addition, some patients find the blunting of emotional and attention reactivity so subjectively distasteful that they are reluctant to continue taking the medication (Cohen, 1997). Many find interpersonal interactions and participation in social events difficult. What has to be kept in mind is that these drugs cannot compensate for deficiencies in interpersonal social skills, and life skills, that may be absent and may have contributed to the onset and the persistence of a disorder. Drug dependency—especially in the case of antianxiety drugs—remains an enduring problem.

Drugs have had, and will no doubt continue to have, a profound influence on the treatment of mental disorders. In some cases, such as those involving severe psychosis and severe depression, they provide the most obvious treatment choice. For other problems, psychotherapies are available, and in many instances they can provide insight, understanding, and coping skills that are not typically an inherent part of a drug treatment regimen. There are a wide variety of such therapies—especially for anxiety-based disorders and depression—and there is some evidence that remission is *less* likely with these therapies than drug therapies (Fischer & Greenberg, 1997; Segal, Gemar, & Williams, 1999).

In some sense, it is possible to look at drug therapies and psychotherapies as convergent approaches that may lead to the same goal at the level of brain function. Recent studies using brain imaging techniques have shown that the changes in brain function induced by behaviour therapy for at least one anxiety-based disorder are similar to those that are produced by drug treatment (Schartz, Stoesel, Baxter, Martin, & Phelps, 1996).

KEY *QUESTIONS*

- What is electroconvulsive therapy?
- What is psychosurgery?
- What drugs are used in the treatment of psychological disorders?

Canadian Treatment Centres for Major Therapy

Therapeutic treatments for the less serious mental disorders are available in a host of different settings. In the case of major, incapacitating disorders, this has not always been the case. We will now look at where treatment is carried out and give some consideration to significant changes that have occurred over the years.

In 1714, the first small abode to house a dozen mentally ill patients was established in Quebec. In 1758, Nova Scotia set up a similar "dwelling" for the mentally ill (Sussman, 1998). The first specialized treatment facilities for those with serious mental disorders emerged in the 1840s. Gradually, during the remaining 1800s, large mental hospitals dedicated exclusively to the treatment of mental illness were built in various provinces. These hospitals continued as primary treatment centres until well into the middle of the twentieth century. The prevailing practice was to treat mental disorders as if they were akin to physical diseases requiring hospital care and treatment. Unfortunately, few effective treatment programs were available for those with serious disorders. Before the 1950s, the only therapies for the truly disturbed were electroconvulsive shock therapy, insulin therapy (inducing a comatose state by lowering blood sugar levels), and psychosurgery. As a result, these institutions were largely custodial in character—often no more than places to hide the disturbed from the public eye—and were often overcrowded and understaffed.

As already mentioned, in the 1950s and early 1960s the winds of change swept through the field of mental health. The development of effective drug therapies allowed, for the first time, a large measure of control over the troubling symptoms exhibited by the seriously disturbed. Many patients no longer required long-term custodial care. Those who made mental health policy saw this as the end of the need for large mental hospitals and began a process of **deinstitutionalization.**

The process of deinstitutionalization was accelerated by federal-provincial funding arrangements associated with the introduction of universal health coverage in Canada. The federal government agreed to match provincial health expenditures to ensure universal coverage, but it would not enter into a cost-sharing arrangement for provincial mental hospitals (Rochefort, 1992). Provinces dealt with this problem by adding psychiatric units, and in many cases a variety of community service functions,

Deinstitutionalization: Ending the practice of committing patients with many serious disorders to mental hospitals for long periods of time, made possible by new drug therapies introduced in the 1950s and 1960s that allowed control over the symptoms of these disorders.

to general hospitals for which joint funding was available. As would be expected, the number of resident patients in provincial mental hospitals dropped drastically. There were 57 000 patients in Canadian mental hospitals in the early 1960s. By the early 1970s, the patient population had fallen to 13 000 (Rochefort & Portz, 1993).

Has this change been beneficial? Yes, in the sense that it has ended the separation of those with mental disorders from those with other disorders. There have been costs, however, the heaviest of which have been borne by those with enduring serious mental disabilities. For many of these individuals, life follows a pattern of admissions to, and releases from, treatment centres. When their symptoms become pronounced, the seriously disabled are admitted to the psychiatric wards of general hospitals, where they are placed on a drug regimen. When the drugs have made their influence felt and the symptoms have abated, these people are released back into the community. On release, all too often, they have no place to go and no likelihood of employment. The result is that they join the ranks of the homeless. In these circumstances, the symptoms almost inevitably return. Once more, they are readmitted to a treatment centre, and the cycle begins again. A substantial portion of the homeless street people who can be seen in any large Canadian city have had experience with the mental health system. A survey of the homeless carried out in Toronto in 1986 revealed that 43 percent had been hospitalized because of a psychiatric disorder within the previous three years (Wasylenki et al., 1993). The situation has not changed over the years. A more recent Toronto study reported in the *Journal of Addiction and Mental Health* (1998) found that 38 percent of those sampled had been assigned a mood disorder diagnosis at some point in time in their life. It was reported also that 30 percent of those surveyed were concurrently experiencing some form of mental illness and having difficulty with substance abuse. Is there any way to break the **revolving door** pattern of hospitalization, admission, and release? One way is to provide a system of community support services.

Institutions for Treating Psychological Disorders

Large provincial institutions for treating psychological disorders were placed far from urban areas and operated on limited budgets. As a result, they were often able to provide only custodial care to patients.

Community Mental Health Services

Patients who have been hospitalized because of a severe mental disorder need support on their release from a hospital setting. They need help in finding accommodation, as well as continuing case management to ensure that their prescribed drug programs are followed and continue to be effective. They need counselling and assistance in obtaining financial support and, if feasible, employment. Unfortunately, few urban centres have adequate community support systems. In an examination of the Canadian mental health care system, Rochefort observes that a "prime deficiency lies in therapeutic and community support services for chronic mentally ill persons, as one report after another from across Canada has documented" (Rochefort, 1992, p. 1087). A much-hospitalized, self-described "psychiatric survivor" of Canada's mental health system stated the problem clearly to a newspaper reporter: "We need income. We need housing. We need the dignity that goes with work." The same person pointed out that satisfaction of these needs "doesn't come from medication and it doesn't come from an institution" (Mittelstaetd, 1993).

A good example of what can be provided in the way of services can be seen in the work of the Greater Vancouver Mental Health Service Society. This is a decentralized, community-based organization that employs multidisciplinary teams to work with both the patients and their families. It provides continuing treatment for clients and counselling services for family members. It offers housing assistance, money management advice, and employment services, and can respond to emergencies (Sladen-Dew et al., 1993). Other Canadian locations are also adopting a more activist intervention role. In Edmonton, for example, there is now a team of mental health workers that will respond with direct visits to homes of recently discharged patients who are experiencing problems (Swift, 1998). Service agencies such as these serve to substantially reduce the institutional readmission rate.

Revolving Door: An ineffective cycle of psychological treatment consisting of hospitalization, admission to treatment centres, and release.

In most of Canada, diagnosis and treatment for psychological problems is available on demand. What about in Canada's Far North? Northern communities are a long way from Canada's urban centres, where most psychological services are located. Also, these communities are small and far apart. How are psychological services provided under these circumstances? In the **Canadian Focus** feature, you will find a description of one interesting approach to the problem.

Canadian Focus

Addressing Mental Health Problems in Canada's North

The Clarke Institute in Toronto provides a consulting service for the Baffin Regional Health Board in the Northwest Territories (Abbey et al., 1993; Young et al., 1993). Looking at this program can provide some understanding of the mental health problems facing Canada's northern people—and how they can be addressed.

Health workers from the Clarke Institute visit the Baffin Island area of the Eastern Arctic on average eight times a year. The area consists of thirteen scattered communities with a total population of about 10 000. Consultants interview and provide diagnostic and treatment recommendations for those who are referred to them by health workers in the community or who seek assistance independently. Because four-fifths of the population are Inuit, Inuktitut-speaking interpreters are available to help bridge any cultural gaps.

Are psychological disturbances common in the North? Young and colleagues report that between 1986 and 1989, about 6 percent of the population either sought an interview or were referred for one. Any effort to compare this 6 percent figure with the actual prevalence of disorders (see Chapter 14) would be doomed. There is no way of estimating how many individuals are experiencing difficulties but were passed over or refused to participate in the consultative process. All that can be said is that referral rates for mental disorders in the North seem to be modest relative to other Canadian areas.

A few types of disorders dominate the referrals. Personality disorders, schizophrenia, and affective disorders are common. Also common are stress-induced disorders resulting from family and relationship conflicts, socio-cultural conflicts, and traumatic experiences. Finally, there are disorders associated with substance abuse. The first two categories are about equal in size and account for the largest number of consultations. Substance abuse is pervasive, not so much as an isolated problem, but as a compounding factor in at least one-quarter of all the cases considered; it is, therefore, a major source of concern. The most common reason for consultation was depression, followed by attempted suicide or suicidal thoughts.

Does the North differ from the rest of Canada in the way in which these disorders express themselves? There are some similarities. As in southern areas, women are more likely to seek help without referral, and depression is twice as common

in women. One major difference, however, is the infrequency of anxiety-based disorders. These are among the most common in the South, but not in the North. Another difference is in the high rates of suicide and suicidal thoughts—in some locations in the North these are three to six times those found in the South. Unlike in the South, where women tend to use less lethal methods in suicide attempts, women in the North tend to use methods that are every bit as lethal as those employed by men.

Treatment in the North is generally carried out at the community level. Hospitalization is not common unless there is clear evidence of an acute psychosis or affective disorder that involves a high suicide risk. Drug therapy is monitored by local health workers. Wherever possible, non-drug treatment is used. Because the number of trained professional therapists is obviously limited, there is a heavy reliance on community resources for counselling and support. Elders and other local volunteers have been pressed into service, and it is claimed that these "generic" therapies are very effective (Young et al., 1993). The Clarke Institute team recognizes the contrast between traditional Inuit lifestyle and the growing influence of Western ways, and endeavours to respect the wishes of those who seek assistance from more traditional healers (Shu, 1995).

Therapy in Diverse Cultural and Geographical Contexts
Local community organizations are becoming an effective means of dealing with mental health problems in Canada's Far North.

It seems clear that local community organizations are going to become even more prominent in helping residents cope with stress in the rapidly changing North. Other community initiatives besides peer counselling are beginning to appear. For example, a theatre production has been used to focus awareness on spousal abuse, and the first safe house for battered women—Nataraq's Place—has opened in the Eastern Arctic (Abbey et al., 1993).

The approach used by the Clarke Institute illustrates the fact that all forms of psychotherapy, as well as other intervention techniques, should be conducted against a backdrop of awareness of cultural differences. If important ethnic and cultural differences are overlooked, much effort may be wasted, and even dedicated, talented therapists may fail to accomplish their goals.

K E Y QUESTIONS

▪ What is deinstitutionalization?

▪ What are community mental health services and why are they needed?

Prevention

Therapies, whatever their nature, are designed to correct or repair damage that has already occurred: They swing into action after individuals have begun to experience psychological disorders. A different approach to psychological problems is *prevention.* When psychologists use this term, they are referring to one of three goals: *primary prevention,* or preventing disorders from developing; *secondary prevention,* or early detection and treatment so that minor disorders do not become major; and *tertiary prevention,* or efforts to minimize the harm done to the individual and to society. In an important sense, prevention is where a considerable part of the action promises to be in the mental health field in the years ahead. Unfortunately, there seems to be a marked reluctance on the part of governments to provide the necessary funding. A survey of prevention programs in Canada carried out by Nelson (1996) found that less than 1 percent of public health funding is dedicated to prevention programs. He reports that a number of promising programs have been introduced, but they are all too often short-lived research grant projects. He takes the position that a collaborative effort must be mounted at both the federal and provincial level to develop and sustain early detection and prevention programs.

K E Y QUESTIONS

▪ What are primary, secondary, and tertiary prevention?

Critical Thinking

Given the high cost of dealing with mental disorders and an increasing population, will we ever be able to deal effectively with mental disorders on a one-on-one basis? Have you any suggestions about how we could make this problem more manageable?

Making **Psychology** Part of Your Life

How to Choose a Therapist: A Consumer's Guide

*T*he odds are quite high that at some point during your life, you or someone very close to you will experience a psychological disorder. Depression, phobias, and anxiety are all very common. If there's one point this chapter should have made clear by now, it is that effective help is available. When psychological problems occur, don't hesitate to seek assistance. But how should you go about obtaining such help—that is, choosing a therapist? Here are some basic pointers.

Where to Go First The first question—how to start the process—is perhaps the trickiest. While you are a student, this task is fairly simple. Virtually every college and university has a department of psychology and a student health centre, and in these locations you are almost certain to find someone who can direct you to valuable sources of help—clinics, individual practitioners, referral services, and so on. Don't be shy—the people there want to help, but they can't approach you—you have to take the first step.

But what if you are no longer a student and have no contact with a university campus? There are other routes you can follow. First, you can ask your physician or a member of the clergy to direct you to the help you need. Both will almost certainly know someone you can contact in this regard. If you have no local physician and don't know any clergy, you can contact your local Mental Health Services Department. This organization will be listed in the phone book and will be able to direct you to the help you need. In short, there are several ways to proceed. Not knowing where to begin is definitely not a good excuse for delay.

How would you seek help for psychological problems if you needed to?

Choosing a Therapist Let's assume that by following one of the routes outlined above, you have obtained the names of several different therapists. How can you choose among them? Several guidelines are useful.

First, always check for credentials. Therapists should generally be trained professionals. Before you consult one, be sure that this person has a Ph.D. in psychology, an M.D. with a residency in psychiatry, or other equivalent training. While such credentials don't guarantee that the therapist can help you, they are an important step in this direction.

Second, try to find out something about the kinds of disorders in which each therapist specializes. Most will readily give you this information. What you are looking for is a good match between your needs and the therapist's special competence. Additional assistance may be provided by consulting the American Psychological Association website mentioned earlier in the chapter and determining whether any particular type of therapy has been demonstrated to be efficacious in treating the difficulty being experienced.

Signs of Progress: How Long Should Therapy Take? If therapy is going well, both you and the therapist will know it. You'll be able to see the beneficial changes in your behaviour, your thoughts, and your feelings. But what if it is not going well? When and how should you decide to go elsewhere? This is a difficult decision, but a rough rule of thumb is that if you have been visiting a therapist regularly (once a week or more) for three months and see no change, it may be time to ask the therapist whether he or she is satisfied with your progress. Most forms of therapy practised by psychologists at present are relatively short term: They are designed to produce results relatively quickly. If several months have passed and your distress has not decreased, it is probably time to raise this issue with your therapist. It is, in fact, a good idea to ask about the anticipated length of treatment when therapy begins.

Danger: When to Quit Therapy is designed to help; unfortunately, though, there are instances in which it can hurt. How can you tell that you are in danger of such outcomes? Several basic points can help.

First, if you or the people around you notice that you are actually becoming more distressed—more depressed, more anxious, more nervous—you should ask yourself whether you are satisfied with what is happening. At the very least, discuss these feelings with your therapist.

Second, never, in any circumstances, should you agree to perform activities during therapy that run counter to your own moral or ethical principles. A very large majority of therapists adopt extremely high standards and would never dream of making such requests. Sad to say, however, there are a few who will take advantage of the therapeutic relationship to exploit their patients. The most common forms of this exploitation are sexual in nature. Unprincipled therapists may suggest that their clients engage in sexual relations with them as part of their "treatment." This is never appropriate and is strongly censured by all professional associations. So if your therapist makes such suggestions, it's time to leave.

Third, beware of exaggerated claims. If a therapist guarantees to remake your life, convert you into a powerhouse of human energy, or ensure your total happiness, be cautious. This is probably a sign that you are dealing with an unprincipled—and probably poorly trained—individual. Again, make a hasty retreat.

All of these suggestions are merely guidelines you can follow in order to be a sophisticated consumer of psychological services. There may be cases, for example, in which therapy requires considerably longer than the several months noted above; in which the therapist has valid reasons for being reluctant to discuss the procedures he or she will use; or in which someone without full credentials can be exceptionally helpful. These guidelines, however, should help you avoid some of the pitfalls that exist with respect to finding a competent, caring therapist. Remember: Effective help is definitely out there if you take the trouble to look for it.

Summary and Review

Key Questions

Psychotherapies

What is psychoanalysis and what are its major assumptions? Psychoanalysis is the form of therapy developed by Freud. It assumes that psychological disorders stem from hidden, internal conflicts and that making these conflicts and hidden wishes conscious is crucial.

What is the role of free association in psychoanalysis? Free association is a technique that is supposed to lead patients to bring hidden urges and conflicts into consciousness.

How are psychodynamic therapies practised today? At present, psychodynamic therapies are shorter in length and focus more on the patient's current life than events in his or her distant past.

According to humanistic therapies, what is the cause of psychological disorders? Humanistic therapies assume that psychological disorders stem from factors in the environment that block or interfere with personal growth.

What is the major goal of Rogers's client-centred therapy? Client-centred therapy focuses on eliminating unrealistic conditions of worth in a therapeutic environment of unconditional positive regard.

What is the major goal of Gestalt therapy? Gestalt psychology holds that difficulties are experienced because individuals do not recognize and accept key aspects of their emotions and feelings. Therapy is designed to get clients to acknowledge and accept these emotions and feelings.

According to behaviour therapies, what is the primary cause of psychological disorders? Behaviour therapies are based on the view that psychological disorders stem from faulty learning.

On what basic principles of learning are behaviour therapies based? Behaviour therapies are based on principles of classical conditioning, operant conditioning, and observational learning.

What is modelling, and how can it be used in treating psychological disorders? Modelling is a process through which individuals acquire new information or learn new behaviours by observing the actions of others. Modelling is effective in treating several disorders, including phobias and sexual dysfunctions.

According to cognitive therapies, what is the primary cause of psychological disorders? Cognitive therapies assume that the major cause of psychological disorders is distorted patterns of thought.

■ **What is the major goal of rational–emotive therapy?** The major goal of rational–emotive therapy is persuading individuals to recognize and reject irrational beliefs and assumptions in their thinking.

■ **What is the major goal of Beck's cognitive therapy for depression?** The major goal of Beck's cognitive therapy is persuading individuals to recognize and change irrational patterns of thought that induce negative affect and so contribute to their depression.

■ **What is stress inoculation training?** Stress inoculation training is a technique for managing anxiety. The objectives of the training are to make clients understand that, to deal with anxiety, they have to develop control over emotions and attendant thoughts, imaginings, and expectations; and to aid them in developing the coping skills to achieve this goal.

Group Therapies

■ **What is the major focus of psychodynamic group therapies, such as psychodrama?** Psychodynamic group therapies are designed to help individuals bring inner conflicts into consciousness.

■ **What is the major focus of behavioural group therapies?** Behavioural group therapies focus on changing specific aspects of behaviour, such as social skills or assertiveness.

■ **What is the major focus of humanistic group therapies?** Humanistic group therapies focus on enhancing personal growth and improving self-knowledge.

■ **What are self-help groups and what do they provide?** Self-help groups consist of persons who share a problem and who provide each other with social and emotional support in coping with this problem.

Therapies Focused on Interpersonal Relations

■ **What is the major focus of marital or couple therapy?** Marital or couple therapy focuses on improving the relationship between members of a couple, often by enhancing their communication skills.

■ **What is family systems therapy?** Family systems therapy is an approach in which therapists view families as dynamic systems in which each member has a major role.

■ **What is family problem-solving therapy?** Family problem-solving therapy focuses on instituting specific changes within a family that will help it to solve specific problems.

Some Current Issues in Psychotherapy

■ **What are efficacy studies of psychotherapy?** Efficacy studies are carefully designed and rigorously controlled laboratory studies that are carried out to determine whether a form of therapy is efficacious in treating a disorder.

■ **Why are effectiveness studies of psychotherapy required?** There are many differences in the ways in which therapy is assessed in laboratory studies and how it is administered in actual practice. Assessments of the results of therapy—as it is actually practised—are required to confirm that it is effective under normal circumstances.

■ **Does available evidence indicate that psychotherapy is effective?** Existing evidence suggests that psychotherapy is indeed effective: most people who undergo it are helped by it.

■ **Are some types of psychotherapy more effective than others?** Research findings indicate all types of therapy are roughly equal in their effectiveness. This may be because they all share certain inherent features, or because available research techniques are not sufficiently sensitive to discern differences.

■ **What are empirically validated therapies?** These are therapeutic treatment practices that have been scientifically confirmed as being efficacious for the treatment of a particular disorder. Updated lists of empirically validated therapies regularly appear in clinical publications of the American Psychological Association.

Biologically Based Therapies

■ **What is electroconvulsive therapy?** Electroconvulsive therapy is a treatment for depression that entails passing brief pulses of mild electric current through the brain until a seizure occurs.

■ **What is psychosurgery?** Psychosurgery involves surgery performed on the brain in order to reduce or eliminate psychological disorders.

■ **What drugs are used in the treatment of psychological disorders?** Drugs are used to treat many psychological disorders. Antipsychotic drugs reduce many symptoms such as hallucinations and delusions. Antidepressant drugs counter depression. Antianxiety drugs reduce anxiety.

Canadian Treatment Centres for Major Therapy

■ **What is deinstitutionalization?** Patients with severe mental disturbances used to be housed for long periods of time in mental hospitals. New drug therapies introduced during the 1950s and 1960s allowed control over the troubling symptoms of serious disorders, and long-term commitment practices ended.

■ **What are community mental health services and why are they needed?** The drug revolution ended the need for long-term commitment of those with serious mental disorders. After a short period of hospitalization and drug treatment to bring symptoms under control, these individuals are released into the community. Often they have nowhere to go and no likelihood of employment. Community health services are needed to provide support, accommodation, and counselling for such patients so that they can cope effectively with the transition from hospital to community.

Prevention

■ **What are primary, secondary, and tertiary prevention?** Primary prevention involves efforts to prevent the occurrence of psychological disorders. Secondary prevention involves efforts to detect psychological problems early, before they have escalated in intensity. Tertiary prevention involves efforts to reduce the long-term harm stemming from psychological disorders.

Key Terms

Beck's Cognitive Behaviour Therapy (p. 609)

Behaviour Therapies (p. 606)

Biologically Based Therapies (p. 625)

Client-Centred Therapy (p. 604)

Cognitive Therapies (p. 608)

Conditions of Worth (p. 604)

Deinstitutionalization (p. 630)

Drug Therapy (p. 627)

Effectiveness Studies (p. 621)

Efficacy Study (p. 619)

Electroconvulsive Therapy (ECT) (p. 625)

Empirically Validated Therapies (p. 623)

Encounter Groups (p. 613)

Family Systems Therapy (p. 616)

Family Therapy (p. 616)

Free Association (p. 602)

Gestalt Therapy (p. 604)

Group Therapies (p. 612)

Humanistic Therapies (p. 604)

Marital Therapy (p. 615)

Problem-Solving Therapy (p. 617)

Psychodrama (p. 612)

Psychodynamic Therapies (p. 601)

Psychosurgery (p. 626)

Psychotherapies (p. 600)

Rational–Emotive Therapy (RET) (p. 609)

Resistance (p. 602)

Revolving Door (p. 631)

Self-Help Groups (p. 613)

Sensitivity-Training Groups (p. 613)

Stress Inoculation Training (p. 610)

Systematic Desensitization (p. 606)

Tardive Dyskinesia (p. 628)

Token Economies (p. 607)

Transference (p. 602)

Critical Thinking Questions

Appraisal

If various forms of therapy are as effective as suggested in this chapter, then why are psychological disorders so common? Why, in short, don't more people seek out appropriate treatment for their psychological problems?

Controversy

Electroconvulsive therapy continues to be widely used in North America to treat depression. Supporters of its use argue that it is both effective and safe. Those opposed to its use maintain that there is no suitable explanation for its effec-

tiveness, and that repeated application of an electric current sufficiently strong to induce convulsions must have negative consequences. What kind of evidence would you see as being crucial to resolving this issue?

Making Psychology Part of Your Life

Now that you know something about how various forms of therapy work, do you think you are more likely to seek out the help of a trained psychologist or other professional if you experience psychological distress? If not, what factors would deter you from doing so?

Weblinks

Check out our Companion Website at www.pearsoned.ca/baron for additional Websites, activities, and more.

The Albert Ellis Institute

www.irebt.org

The Albert Ellis Institute site includes information about the institute and its services, has a file of frequently asked questions and their answers, and features a rational–emotive therapy essay of the month. Visitors to the site can submit questions directly to Dr. Ellis (only one submission is answered each month).

What Is Therapy?

www.helping.apa.org/brochure/broch2.html

This Website has the American Psychological Association's answers to questions about psychotherapy. How does therapy work? How can I evaluate whether therapy is working well? Follow the links for some informative material on these intriguing issues.

Psychosurgery: Then and Now

www.epub.org.br/cm/n02/historia/psicocirg_i.htm

Here you will find an illustrated history of psychosurgery including a link to information about psychosurgery today. The explanations are easy to understand, and extensive illustrations are provided.

Chapter **16**

Social Thought and Social Behaviour

Thoughtful Thief

This story about an unusual thief appeared in *The Guardian*. (Prince Edward Island). Here's what happened.

One mid-afternoon, a man walked into a Tim Hortons coffee shop and ordered a cup of coffee. When the coffee arrived, he refused to pay. He instructed the server to open the cash register and when she did, he took the money—and the coffee—and made for the door. Before leaving, however, he turned around and came back. Did he want a donut too?

At the counter, he returned that portion of the cash that he realized was servers' tips, because, he said, he knew they "did not make a lot of money." Then he left with the rest of the money and his coffee.

This thoughtful thief was able to divide the world into two kinds of people—those from whom he would steal and those from whom he would not!

How is it that humans divide people into these kinds of categories? More generally, how do we perceive and understand the social world that surrounds us? How do other people influence our behaviour? How do we act in groups? You will find the latest findings of psychological science as you work your way through Chapter 16, Social Psychology.

Source: Tim Hortons thief leaves workers' tips (2000, February 28). *The Guardian*, p. B8.

> We not only interact with other
> people; we also spend lots of time
> thinking about them.

The Social Side of Life

Interacting with others and thinking about them occupy much of our time every day.

There is no doubt that other people are central to our lives. They are the source of our most valued forms of reward—praise, approval, sympathy, affection—and of our most devastating forms of punishment—criticism, rejection, disapproval. They are the focus of our most important emotions: love, anger, envy, jealousy. Life without other people is, in a very real sense, painful to imagine. Nevertheless, sometimes we do find ourselves feeling alone, even though we are surrounded by other people. That is a kind of social loneliness—for a community into which you fit (Cameron & Barry, 1999; DiTommaso & Spinner, 1997). You may have had that reaction when you first arrived at college or university, when you entered a large class, when you stood looking for a place to put your tray in the new-to-you dining hall (Weiss, 1987).

As important as they are, even so, other people remain a mystery to us. They say and do things we do not expect; they have motives we do not understand; and they often see the world differently. Therefore, we do not merely interact with other people, we also spend lots of time thinking about them. These two topics—social thought and social interaction—are central to **social psychology,** the branch of psychology that investigates how other people affect our behaviour.

Social psychology is a very diverse field. It covers love and hate, and everything in between. First, on the following pages, you will find information about social thought—how and what we think about other people. Included here will be three important topics: *attribution*—how we explain to ourselves why other people behave the way they do; social cognition—how we *perceive and process* social information; and *attitudes*—the opinions we have about various features of the social world.

Then we'll turn to important aspects of social interaction: *prejudice*—negative attitudes toward the members of various social groups; *social influence*—the many ways in which individuals attempt to change each other's behaviour; *prosocial behaviour*—the actions we perform that benefit others; and *attraction, love, and close relationships*—why we like or dislike other people, why we fall in (and out of) love, and how we form close interpersonal bonds.

In the last part of this chapter, we'll apply social psychological principles to how groups act in real-world settings—how groups take decisions and how leadership works.

Social Thought: Thinking about Other People

Do you ever try to figure out why people act the way they do? Do you ever try to change somebody else's opinions? Do you make judgments about people—for example, about their suitability as a roommate or as a romantic mate? When you do, you are engaging in *social thought.* Here we will focus on three topics that have been identified by social psychologists as among the most important areas in social thought: attribution, social cognition, and attitudes.

Attribution: Understanding the Causes of Behaviour

Social Psychology: The branch of psychology that studies all aspects of social behaviour and social thought.

Imagine the following situation. You're standing at a ticket counter waiting your turn when suddenly another student walks up in front of you and hands the clerk money for a ticket. How do you react? Did he do it on purpose? If so, you probably would get angry. But perhaps he just didn't see you. In that case, you might clear your throat or otherwise indicate your presence to see what would happen next. So it's not just what he did that matters; your understanding of *why* he did it matters too.

This question of *why* others act as they do is one we face every day in many different contexts. The process through which we attempt to answer this question—to determine the causes behind the behaviour of other people—is known as **attribution.** In general, attribution is a fairly orderly process. We look for clues as to the causes of what people say and do, and then reach our decision.

What kind of information do we consider here? According to Kelley (1972), the first question we ask is this: Did the actions stem from *internal* causes (their own traits, intentions, or motives) or from *external* causes (luck or other factors beyond their control). To answer this question, we consider three factors: **consensus**—do other people behave in the same way; **consistency**—does this person behave in the same way in the same place repeatedly; and **distinctiveness**—does this person behave in the same way in different situations (Kelley, 1972). Figure 16.1 illustrates how this works.

If very few people act the same way (consensus is low), the person behaves in the same way repeatedly (consistency is high), and the person behaves in much the same manner in many situations (distinctiveness is low), we conclude that the behaviour stemmed from internal causes: This is the kind of person he or she is, and will probably remain. In contrast, if all three of these factors (consensus, consistency, and distinctiveness) are high, we are more likely to conclude that the causes were external—something about the current situation; for instance, there may have been no choice.

Attribution: The processes through which we seek to determine the causes behind others' behaviour.

Consensus: The extent to which behaviour by one person is shown by others as well.

Consistency: The extent to which a given person responds in the same way to a given stimulus on separate occasions under the same circumstances.

Distinctiveness: Information regarding the extent to which a given person reacts in the same way to different stimuli or in different circumstances.

Figure 16.1
Causal Attribution

Research findings suggest that when consensus and distinctiveness are low but consistency is high, we tend to attribute others' behaviour to internal causes (upper diagram). When consensus, distinctiveness, and consistency are all high, in contrast, we attribute their behaviour to external causes (lower diagram).

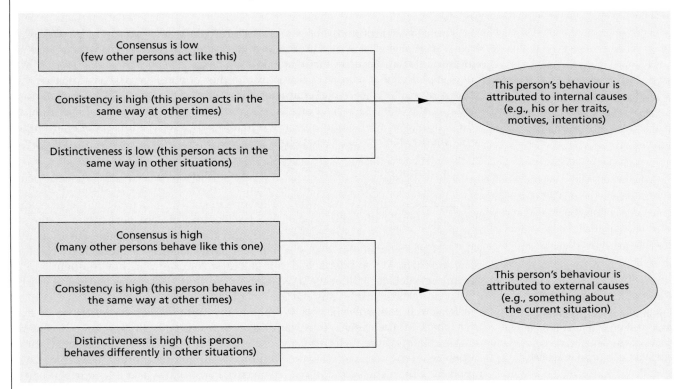

Attribution

As Charlie Brown finds out here, we can't always predict why people do what they do.

Do we really think about others and the causes behind their actions this way? Because performing the kind of analysis described by Kelley requires a lot of effort, in situations where we feel that a lot of cognitive effort is justified, we do use the kind of information emphasized by Kelley. Those are primarily situations where it's important to understand why other people behaved the way they did, or when we cannot readily explain their actions based on what we already know. In many other cases, however, we do not bother because, quite simply, it requires too much effort (e.g., Hansen, 1980; Lupfer et al., 1990).

SOME BASIC SOURCES OF BIAS   While attribution often involves the logical kind of reasoning described above, that is not always the case. In fact, attribution is subject to several kinds of errors—mistakes that result in false conclusions about other people. Let's consider some of these here.

The Fundamental Attribution Error: Overestimating Dispositional Causes   Suppose you witness the following scene. A man arrives at a meeting thirty minutes late. On entering, he drops his notes, falls over, and breaks his glasses. How would you explain these events? It is likely that you would conclude this man is a disorganized and clumsy person—attributing his behaviour to internal (dispositional) causes. Would you be correct? Perhaps. However, you might be wrong. It could be these behaviours were the result of external (situational) causes—circumstances beyond his control—a major traffic jam and new shoes on a newly polished floor.

Thus, in attributing his behaviour to internal causes, you might be making an error. That error is so common and happens so often that it is called the **fundamental attribution error,** also known as *correspondence bias* (Gilbert & Malone, 1995). In short, when we think about other people, we first assume that their actions reveal their personal characteristics (Gifford & Hine, 1997). Then, as an afterthought, we try to correct our thinking for any possible effects of the situation. Often, however, we do not make enough allowance for the impact of external factors when reaching our conclusions (Leyens et al., 1996). That is a fundamental error in the way we think and it happens very often.

The fundamental attribution error has important social implications (Guimond & Dube, 1989). For example, even when we are aware of situational causes that adversely affect disadvantaged groups in society—factors such as poor diet, disrupted family life, and exposure to lawless and violent peer models—we still think people in such groups are weak and therefore responsible for their own plight. This is particularly true when we blame victims of crime for what happened to them. When people hear about a rape, for example, they frequently make comments such as, "She must have led him on" and "What was she doing in a bar at that hour of the night, anyway?"

Research confirms that we lay blame on these victims as much as, or even more than, on the rapists. For example, in one study researchers asked male and female college students to read one of two descriptions of a rape (Bell et al., 1994). In one case, the woman was attacked by a stranger. In another, the woman was raped by a man she was dating. Then participants were asked to rate how much the victim was to blame for the crime. As you can see from Figure 16.2, both males

Fundamental Attribution Error: The tendency to attribute behaviour to internal causes to a greater extent than is actually justified.

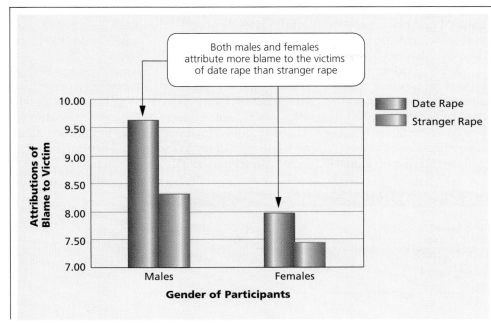

Figure 16.2
Attributing Blame to Rape Victims

Both males and females assigned considerable blame to the victim of a rape. In addition, they tended to blame her more when she knew the rapist than when this person was a stranger.

Source: Based on data from Bell et al., 1994.

and females attributed considerable blame to the victim; males blamed the victim more than females; and both males and females blamed the victim more when she knew the rapist than when he was a stranger (Cowan & Curtis, 1994). These findings, and those of related studies, help explain why so many victims of date rape—an alarmingly common event (Koss & Harvey, 1991)—are reluctant to report this crime: they realize that they are likely to be blamed.

Thus, there are disturbing social implications of our tendency to overlook external or situational factors in explaining other people's behaviour. Hopefully, by being aware of this bias in our thinking, we will be less likely to blame other people for their own misfortune.

The Self-Serving Bias Suppose that you write a term paper for one of your classes. After reading it, your professor gives you an A. To what will you attribute your success? If you are like most people, the chances are good that you will explain it in terms of internal causes—your own talent or hard work. Now, in contrast, imagine that your professor gives you a D. How will you explain *this* outcome? Here, there is a real possibility that you will focus mainly on external causes—lack of time, unrealistic high standards, and so on. In situations like this one, you are making another attribution error known as the **self-serving bias.** The self-serving bias is our tendency to take credit for our own *positive* outcomes by attributing them to internal causes, but to blame *negative* ones on external causes, especially on factors beyond our control (Brown & Rogers, 1991; Miller & Ross, 1975).

The self-serving bias is common; it has been observed, for instance, in many different cultures (e.g., Al-Zahrani & Kaplowitz, 1993). Even when we interact with computers and we feel in control, we tend to give ourselves the credit for a successful outcome (Moon & Nass, 1998). In the case of negative outcomes, however, we blame the computer! As you can see, the self-serving bias is quite the opposite pattern to the fundamental attribution error we make about other people—when negative events are blamed on internal causes and positive events are credited to external causes.

Why does this self-serving "slant" in our attributions occur? The most important factors are our need to enhance our own self-esteem and our desire to look good to other people (e.g., Greenberg et al., 1982). Attributing our successes to internal causes while attributing failures to external causes permits us to accomplish these ego-protective goals.

Self-Serving Bias: The tendency to attribute positive outcomes to our own traits or characteristics but negative outcomes to factors beyond our control.

The self-serving bias also has a number of important implications for social thought and behaviour. For example, it leads people to see their own negative actions—for example, a temper tantrum—as justified and excusable, and identical actions by others as irrational and unjustified (Sande et al., 1989).

Recent evidence suggests that the self-serving bias occurs in sports as well. In an ingenious study, researchers examined hundreds of newspaper statements by athletes to see whether they used the self-serving bias in their explanations for why they, or their teams, had won or lost. In general, athletes did tend to attribute wins to internal factors—their own skill or abilities. However, athletes performing alone, such as golfers or tennis players, were more likely to use the self-serving bias than athletes playing on teams (Rosech & Amirkhan, 1997).

KEY QUESTIONS

- What is the fundamental attribution error?
- What role does attribution play in perceptions of rape victims?
- What is the self-serving bias?

Social Cognition: How We Process Social Information

Identifying the causes of others' behaviour is an important part of social thought, but it is far from the whole picture. In this section, therefore, we will focus on other ways we make sense out of the social world in which we live. We use the term **social cognition** to refer to how we notice, interpret, remember, and then use social information.

Just how *accurate* are we at social cognition? The answer provided by research is somewhat mixed. On the one hand, we seem to be quite good at sorting, combining, and remembering a wealth of social information (Fiske & Taylor, 1991). On the other hand, social cognition is subject to a number of different kinds of errors. Most of these are the result of *heuristics*—mental shortcuts we use to make judgments quickly—with the least amount of mental effort (see Chapter 7). Errors in social cognition may be quite useful from an adaptive point of view. They help us to focus on the kinds of information that are usually most useful, and they reduce the effort required to understand the social world.

THE FALSE CONSENSUS EFFECT: ASSUMING THAT OTHERS THINK AS WE DO Imagine that you have signed up to participate in a psychology experiment. When you arrive, you are told that you may choose the experiment you will do. In one experiment, you will watch gruesome films. In the other, you will panhandle in a shopping mall. Which experiment would you choose? Which experiment do you think most of your classmates would choose? When these questions were posed to students at Simon Fraser University, regardless of the experiment they chose themselves, they overestimated the number of classmates who would choose the same one (McFarland & Miller, 1990).

This tendency to overestimate the number of other people who think the way we do is called the **false consensus effect,** and it occurs in many different ways. For example, college students overestimate the proportion of other students who agree with their own ideas about drugs, abortion, seatbelt use, university policies, politics, colour preference, and even Ritz crackers or Oreo cookies (e.g., Gilovich, 1990).

Why does the false consensus effect occur? Several factors seem to play a role, but the most important involves the *availability heuristic*—the mental rule of thumb that suggests the easier it is to bring information to mind, the more important we judge it to be. For most people, it is easier to remember when other people have agreed with them than when others have disagreed. The result: They overestimate the extent to which others share their views.

Social Cognition: The processes through which we notice, interpret, remember, and later use social information.

False Consensus Effect: The tendency to believe that other people share our attitudes to a greater extent than is true.

While the false consensus effect is common, it's also important to note that it does not occur in all situations. Sometimes people like to see themselves as different—better—than they actually are (Suls & Wan, 1987). As a result, we tend to perceive ourselves as happier, more intelligent, more ethical, and less prejudiced than the people around us (Miller & McFarland, 1987).

DEALING WITH WHAT "DOESN'T FIT" Consider the following scenario. It is Sunday afternoon and you are listening to *Cross-Country Checkup* on CBC radio. The guest is the leader of a political party. You only half listen as he makes his usual comments about tax reform, balanced budgets, and gun control. Suppose then, in a quiet voice, he says this: His years in Ottawa have shown him that Western Canada is not nearly as disadvantaged as he had thought. Therefore, he has decided to retire and move to Quebec. You perk up your ears. Did he really say *that*?

This fictitious example illustrates another characteristic of social cognition. In general, we pay much more attention to information that is somehow *inconsistent* with our expectations. Because inconsistent information is unexpected and surprising, we have to work harder to understand it (e.g., Srull & Wyer, 1989). Furthermore, the more attention we pay, the better chance information has of entering into long-term memory and influencing later social judgments (Bardach & Park, 1996; Fiske & Neuberg, 1990). Thus, this tendency has important consequences.

Although we readily *notice* information that is inconsistent with our expectations, sometimes we discount or downplay it because it's simply too unexpected to accept. For example, you probably cannot help noticing the weird headlines on the tabloid newspapers ("Teen marries monster from outer space"). But the chances of their influencing your thinking in any serious way are slight because they are beyond belief!

AUTOMATIC VIGILANCE: NOTICING THE NEGATIVE In general, we seem to pay much more attention to negative information than to positive information about other people. In fact, it is fair to say that we are ultrasensitive to negative social information. If another person smiles at us twenty times during a conversation but frowns once, it is the frown we tend to notice and remember. This strong tendency to pay attention to negative information is called **automatic vigilance**—the tendency to pay special attention to negative information or events (e.g., Shiffrin, 1988).

In an important sense, this tendency is a very reasonable consequence of human evolution. After all, automatic vigilance alerts us to negative information that may signal potential danger when it is critical that we recognize a problem and respond as quickly as possible (Pratto & John, 1991). However, when we direct attention to negative events, we run the risk of overlooking other valuable information. Thus, automatic vigilance may cause us to overestimate the negative, and discount the positive, in our interpersonal interactions.

One final point: The automatic vigilance effect helps explain why it is so important to make a good first impression. Since people are highly sensitive to negative information, anything we say or do during a first meeting that triggers negative reactions is likely to make a strong impression. In this and many other ways, automatic vigilance can have important consequences for us and requires us to think carefully about the impression that we are making—*impression formation*— and how we can manage the impressions that other people get—*impression management*.

COUNTERFACTUAL THINKING: CONSIDERING "WHAT MIGHT HAVE BEEN"
Contrast the following events:

- Mr. Caution never picks up hitchhikers. Yesterday, however, he broke his rule and gave a stranger a lift. The stranger repaid his kindness by robbing him.

- Mr. Risk frequently picks up hitchhikers. Yesterday, he gave yet another stranger a ride. The stranger repaid his kindness by robbing him.

Automatic Vigilance: The strong tendency to pay attention to negative social information.

Counterfactual Thinking

Suppose the people in this photo had purchased home insurance every year since they bought the house, except this year. One day, they arrive home to discover that an explosion has levelled the house. They might be tempted to think, "If only we hadn't changed our pattern, this wouldn't have happened to our home." That would be counterfactual thinking.

Counterfactual Thinking: The tendency to evaluate events by thinking about alternatives to them—"what might have been."

Which of these two people will experience greater regret? Rationally, there should be no difference. Both individuals have suffered precisely the same negative outcome: They have been robbed. However, when students at the University of British Columbia were asked this question, an overwhelming majority predicted Mr. Caution would experience greater regret than Mr. Risk (Kahneman & Miller, 1986; Kahneman & Tversky, 1982), and that is likely what you think too.

Why, then, do we perceive Mr. Caution as experiencing greater regret? Research results suggest that our reactions depend not only on the events themselves, but also on what the events bring to mind. In other words, when we think about an experience, we engage in **counterfactual thinking**—bringing to mind alternative outcomes. In this particular instance, we think, "If only Mr. Caution had not broken his rule against picking up hitchhikers, he'd be okay." Alternatively, we may imagine that "If Mr. Risk read the papers and thought about what he was doing, he would probably act differently."

But why does such counterfactual thinking lead us to believe that Mr. Caution will experience more regret? That is because it is easier think of alternatives to *unusual* behaviour. So, we conclude that Mr. Caution experienced more regret because it is easier to imagine him acting in a different way—sticking to his standard rule— than it is to imagine Mr. Risk acting differently. It also allows us to believe we are in control of our own lives (Nasco et al., 1999).

Counterfactual thinking influences our behaviour, too (Roese & Olson, 1993; Roese & Olson, 1995). In one study, two groups of students read different versions of an incident in which a young woman got food poisoning after eating in a restaurant (Macrae, 1992). In one condition, the restaurant was one she visited regularly. In the other condition, it was her first visit to that restaurant. Participants were then asked to indicate how much compensation the victim should receive and how large a fine the restaurant should pay for its negligence. As shown in Figure 16.3, both amounts were larger in the "unusual behaviour" condition than in the "usual behaviour" condition.

Figure 16.3
Counterfactual Thinking in Operation

Research participants indicated that a restaurant that had served tainted food should pay a larger fine to the victim when she had never eaten there. That is because, when the customer's behaviour was unusual, it was easier for participants to imagine a different outcome—one in which she did not experience food poisoning.

Source: Based on data from Macrae, 1992.

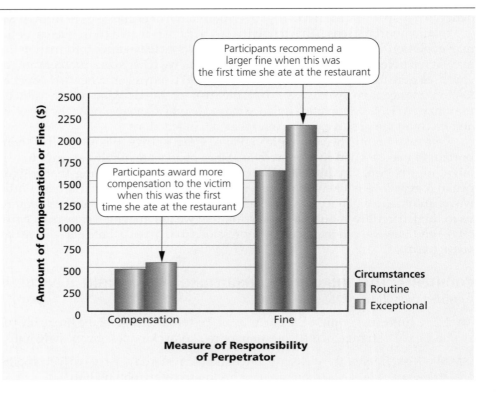

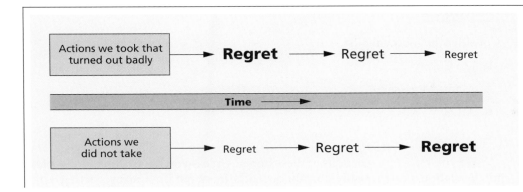

Figure 16.4
Regrets: Why They Change
with the Passage of Time

Actions we took that turned
out badly can be reversed;
even if they are not, we tend
to think of many good reasons
why we *had* to act this way. As
a result, regret over such actions decreases over time. In
contrast, regrets over actions
we *didn't take* may increase
with time because we con-
tinue to wonder what the effects of such actions would
have been, and because the
factors that prevented us from
acting (fear, lack of confidence) tend to seem less disturbing with the passage of
time.

*Source: Based on suggestions by Gilovich
and Medvec, 1994.*

There is also evidence that the closer in time the imagined alternative, the greater the regret (Kahneman & Miller, 1986). For example, missing an airplane by five minutes causes greater regret than missing an airplane by half an hour. Also, distance affects the sympathy we feel for others in such situations. Students read two scenarios in which a man attempted to walk to safety after his plane crashed in a remote northern area. If the man died half a kilometre from the nearest town, the students awarded greater compensation to his wife and children than if he died 120 kilometres from the nearest town (Miller & McFarland, 1987).

Engaging in counterfactual thinking can alter our moods. On the one hand, for example, Olympic athletes who are disappointed to win a bronze medal feel bet-ter when they imagine what it would be like to win no medal (Gleicher et al., 1995). On the other hand, imagining better outcomes may produce strong feelings of re-gret, dissatisfaction, or envy (Sanna, 1997). In short, imagining what might have been can have different results—ranging from despair and intense regret on the one hand, through hopefulness and increased determination to do better in the future on the other (Roese, 1997).

Does counterfactual thinking, with its emotional consequences, happen in real life? Regret does change over time—about real-life actions we took that turned out badly (parked in a no-parking zone) and actions we did not take (did not fasten the seat belt). For an illustration, see Figure 16.4. In studies of counterfactual thinking by victims of traumatic events—losing a spouse or child in a car accident or the death of an infant due to sudden infant death syndrome, the results showed that thoughts such as "If only I had done something differently, my child/spouse would still be alive" were very common. For half of the participants, these thoughts per-sisted for four to seven years after the event. Furthermore, the more participants en-gaged in counterfactual thinking, the greater the distress they experienced. Similarly, in a study of spinal cord injury victims, the more time the patients spent thinking about how the accident could have been avoided, the greater their feelings of self-blame (Davis et al., 1995, 1996). Thus, counterfactual thinking occurs in real life as well as in the laboratory, and it can have long-lasting emotional consequences.

K E Y *QUESTIONS*

- What is the false consensus effect?
- How do we deal with social information that is inconsis-tent with our expectations?
- What is counterfactual thinking? How does it change over time?

Critical Thinking

Some people seem to engage more in automatic vigilance than others. Why do you think this is so?

Attitudes

Consider the following list:

- Jim Carrey
- Alanis Morissette
- AIDS
- NHL salaries

Do you have any reactions to these items? Unless you have been living a life of total isolation, you probably do. You may admire or not Jim Carrey's acting, enjoy or not Alanis Morissette's music, worry or not about AIDS, and believe that hockey players' salaries are deserved or outrageous. Such reactions, which social psychologists describe as attitudes, generally involve a an emotional or affective component (e.g., liking or disliking), a cognitive component (a set of beliefs), and a behavioural component (a set of tendencies to act toward these items in various predetermined ways). More simply, **attitudes** are lasting evaluations of various aspects of the physical and social world. These are schemas of things, people, or ideas that are stored in memory (Fazio & Roskos-Ewoldsen, 1994; Judd et al., 1991).

Attitudes are formed through the basic processes of learning we considered in Chapter 5. For example, they often stem from *operant conditioning,* because we are frequently rewarded by our parents, teachers, or friends for expressing the "correct views"—the ones they hold. Similarly, attitudes derive from *observational learning.* Throughout life we tend to adopt the views and preferences expressed by people we like or respect, because we are exposed to those views and want to be like those persons. Even *classical conditioning* plays a role; in fact, it may be especially influential in acquiring the emotional or affective aspect of attitudes (e.g., Betz & Krosnick, 1993; Cacioppo, Priester, & Berntson, 1993).

The Politics of Persuasion

At present, we encounter many attempts to change our attitudes. These students chose to demonstrate publicly in order to influence the provincial government's attitude towards their education.

Perhaps most surprising of all are the recent findings that genetic factors may play a role in shaping attitudes (e.g., Arvey et al., 1989; Keller et al., 1992). The attitudes of identical twins, who share all of the same genes, have been found to be more similar than those of nonidentical twins, and this is so even if the twins were separated early in life and raised in sharply contrasting environments from then on (Hershberger et al., 1994)

The study of attitudes has long been a central area of research in social psychology. In this discussion, we'll focus on *persuasion*—how we change the attitudes of other people, and on *cognitive dissonance*—one way we change our own attitudes.

PERSUASION: THE PROCESS OF CHANGING ATTITUDES

As the twenty-first century begins, television commercials, magazine ads, Internet promotions, giant billboards, political campaigns, public service announcements, warnings on products, and even documentary films (Linton, 1992) all have the ultimate goal of changing people's attitudes and their behaviour. What determines whether persuasion will succeed? Here are some of the findings of social psychologists.

- Experts are more persuasive than nonexperts (Hovland & Weiss, 1951). We give more weight to arguments delivered by someone who is an authority—who should know what they are talking about.

- Messages that do not appear to be intended to change our attitudes are often more successful than ones that seem intended to manipulate us (Walster & Festinger, 1962). We do not trust information that we believe was meant to be persuasive.

Attitudes: Mental representations and evaluations of features of the social or physical world.

- Popular and attractive sources are more effective in changing attitudes than unpopular or unattractive ones (Kiesler & Kiesler, 1969). Personal appeal is important, particularly in politics, as many of our politicians have found out.

- Some personal characteristics are important. For example, individuals who are relatively low in self-esteem are often easier to persuade (Janis, 1954). These people are more susceptible to persuasion from high-status or attractive sources.

- When an audience holds attitudes contrary to those of a would-be persuader, it is often more effective to adopt a *two-sided approach,* in which both sides of an issue are presented. Acknowledging that the competition has a few points in its favour builds credibility and disarms the audience, making it harder to resist the main arguments. In this connection, arguments that come from an unexpected source, for example, a member of Parliament speaking against the party's official position, are particularly persuasive (e.g., Pancer et al., 1992).

- People who speak rapidly are generally more persuasive than ones who speak slowly (Miller et al., 1976), partly because they seem more competent, confident, and expert.

One word of caution: Changing attitudes is a complex and tricky business. Many different factors play a role. The findings reported above have generally withstood the test of time and additional research, and therefore they are useful basic principles.

COGNITION AND PERSUASION The traditional approach to understanding persuasion has certainly been useful; it provided a wealth of information about the "who" and "how" of persuasion. It did not, however, address the *why* of persuasion. Why do people change their attitudes in response to persuasive messages?

The Cognitive Approach to Persuasion: Heuristic versus Systematic Processing

What happens when you are exposed to a persuasive message—for instance, when you watch a television commercial or listen to a political speech? Your first answer might be: "I think about what is being said." But how much real thinking do we actually do in those circumstances? In other words, how do we process—absorb, interpret, and evaluate—the information contained in such persuasive messages?

Current research focuses on the cognitive processes that occur when individuals are persuaded. This approach seeks to understand what people think about when they are exposed to persuasive messages, and how these thoughts determine whether attitudes change (Petty et al., 1991; Petty et al., 1994). Let's examine the basic ideas of a cognitive theory of persuasion—the *elaboration likelihood model.*

According to the **elaboration likelihood model** of persuasion (Eagly & Chaiken, 1998; Petty & Cacioppo,1986; Petty & Wegener, 1999), it is the thinking that the persuasive message produces—not the persuasive message itself—that results in attitude change or resistance to attitude change. Furthermore, there are two routes to persuasion (e.g., Petty et al., 1999), When persuasive messages deal with issues that are important or have personal significance—when information-processing capacity and motivation are high—people are likely to give careful consideration to a message and to the arguments it makes. In such cases, persuasion occurs through effortful *systematic processing,* or the **central route** to persuasion (Zuwerink & Devine, 1996).

When there is systematic processing, attitude change occurs to the extent that the arguments are judged strong and the facts are thought to be convincing. A simple message with strong arguments handled by the central route receives serious scrutiny, and any changed attitudes endure (e.g., Hafer et al., 1996). Here is one finding about central processing that may surprise you. People who are low in prejudice use the central—more effortful—route when evaluating messages from sources that are not like them—a different race or different sexual orientation. This finding suggests that the low-prejudice people take greater care in evaluating messages from these sources in order to guard against reacting unfairly (Petty et al., 1999).

Elaboration Likelihood Model (of persuasion): A theory suggesting that there are two distinct routes to persuasion involving different amounts of cognitive elaboration in response to a persuasive message.

Central Route (to persuasion): Attitude change resulting from systematic processing of information contained in persuasive messages.

The other path to persuasion is *heuristic processing,* or the **peripheral route.** Here, little cognitive work is performed, there's not much thinking, and attitude change is a seemingly automatic response. This kind of processing occurs when messages deal with issues that are relatively unimportant, not personally relevant or interesting. Attitude change is more likely to occur through the peripheral route when people are distracted and therefore do not take the time to do a careful analysis of the message itself (see Figure 16.5).

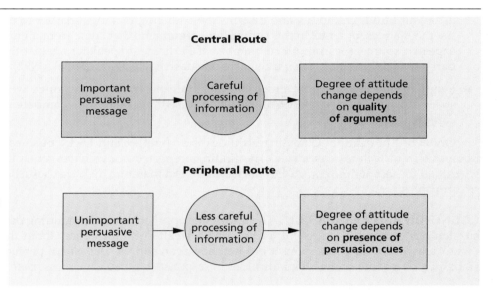

Figure 16.5
The Elaboration Likelihood Model: An Overview

According to the elaboration likelihood model, persuasion can occur through two different processes. If the messages are important or personally relevant, we pay careful attention to the arguments and persuasion occurs through the central route. If we find the messages unimportant or irrelevant, however, persuasion proceeds through the peripheral route, largely in response to persuasion cues.

Source: Based on suggestions by Petty and Cacioppo, 1986.

When does heuristic processing change attitudes? Perhaps the message induces positive feelings by way of a very attractive model, or a scene of breathtaking natural beauty. Perhaps the source of the message is very high in status, prestige, or credibility. Under these conditions, attitude change may occur in the absence of a critical analysis of the contents of the message.

Persuasion is often less successful when strong and weak arguments are presented together. That is because, particularly for important issues, individuals use systematic processing and scrutinize messages very carefully. Such careful processing leads to unfavourable thoughts about weak arguments and persuasion is less effective (e.g., Friedrich et al., 1996). In brief, then, the cognitive approach has added much to our understanding of how attitude change takes place.

COGNITIVE DISSONANCE: HOW WE CHANGE OUR OWN ATTITUDES   There are many occasions in everyday life when we feel compelled to say or do things that are not consistent with our true attitudes. Social psychologists refer to such actions as **forced compliance,** or *attitude-discrepant* behaviour. Here are two examples: Your friend shows you a new sweater and asks how you like it. You think that the colour is gross, but you say, "Cool . . . really cool." Your boss describes a new idea for increasing sales. You think that it is idiotic, but you respond, "Hmmm… Sounds very interesting."

When we act in ways that are contrary to our beliefs, we feel uncomfortable. The term **cognitive dissonance** refers to the discomfort we experience when there is a gap between two attitudes we hold, or between our attitudes and our actions—for example, between what we think and what we say (Brehms, 1998; Festinger, 1957). Cognitive dissonance is unpleasant, and when we experience it, we try to reduce it (e.g., Elliot & Devine, 1994; McGregor et al., 1999).

Peripheral Route (to persuasion): Attitude change resulting from peripheral persuasion cues—information concerning the expertise, status, or attractiveness of would-be persuaders.

Forced Compliance: A situation in which we feel compelled to say or do things inconsistent with our true attitudes.

Cognitive Dissonance: The state experienced by individuals when they discover inconsistency between two attitudes they hold or between their attitudes and their behaviour.

Reduced cognitive dissonance may be accomplished in three different ways. First, we can change our attitudes or behaviour so that they are more consistent with each other. For instance, we might decide that the colour of the sweater is particularly becoming or very fashionable. Second, we can acquire new information that supports our attitude or our behaviour. For example, we can seek out information that indicates the boss's plan makes sense. Third, we can engage in *trivialization*—concluding that the attitudes or behaviours in question are not important (e.g., Simon et al., 1995). In short, after praising your friend's sweater or your boss's idea, you may actually persuade yourself that these things were better than you thought they were—because that reduces the discomfort of cognitive dissonance. Thus, when individuals express "politically correct" attitudes that are contrary to their own views, their own thinking may actually change in the direction of the politically correct statements they made (Maio & Olson, 1998).

Here is a practical application of these findings. In one study (Weltzl-Fairchild et al., 1997), researchers identified the kinds of dissonance experienced by visitors to the Montreal Museum of Fine Art. The purpose of the study was to develop ways in which the museum could help gallery goers enjoy their visits more. By gathering information about the points at which discomfort (dissonance) occurred during their visit to the museum, they could plan changes to the way in which the museum displays were organized.

Of course the negative feelings generated by dissonance may be reduced without a change in attitude (Steele, 1988). For instance, if you experienced dissonance as a result of telling the boss that the plan was good but you did not want to change your opinion that it was silly, you could think about what is positive about you as a person, focusing on your own good works when you volunteered for a local charity, helped a friend move, and so on. These reminders reduce the discomfort of the dissonance and make you feel better—without changing your attitude (Tessor et al., 1996).

Which of these tactics do we choose? As you might guess, we often do whatever requires the least effort, and it is most often easiest—especially in forced-compliance situations—to change our attitudes so that they match what we have actually said or done.

Dissonance and the Less-Leads-to-More Effect When people act in ways that are contrary to their views, there is another variable to be considered: How strong are their reasons for doing so? If their reasons are very good—for example, if telling your friend or your boss the truth will be costly in terms of your relationship—then little or no dissonance will be generated if you tell them what they want to hear. In short, the better the original reasons for saying what you do not believe, the less dissonance you will experience, and the weaker the pressure to change your own views. When we have only weak reasons for engaging in attitude-discrepant behaviour, however, dissonance is stronger, and so is the pressure to change our attitudes (see Figure 16.6).

Social psychologists refer to this unexpected state of affairs as the **less-leads-to-more effect.** The stronger the reasons for engaging in attitude-discrepant behaviour, the weaker the pressures toward changing the underlying attitudes. Surprising as it may seem, this effect has been confirmed in many different studies (e.g., Riess & Schlenker, 1977). In all of these, people provided with a small reward for stating attitudes contrary to their own views changed these attitudes so that they became closer to the opinions they had expressed.

This phenomenon was initially demonstrated in Festinger and Carlsmith's (1959) classic study. In their experiment, participants first performed an extremely boring task (turning pegs in a board for 20 minutes). After the task, they were offered either $20 (a lot of money in 1959) or $1 (not much then either) to tell the next participant that the experiment was interesting and enjoyable. Those who were paid $20 for lying did not have to reduce dissonance because they had strong reasons for doing so—the money was well worth it. However, those who were paid

Less-Leads-to-More Effect: The fact that rewards just barely sufficient to induce individuals to state positions contrary to their own views often generate more attitude change than larger rewards.

Figure 16.6
Why, Where Attitude Is Concerned, "Less" Sometimes Leads to "More"

When individuals have strong reasons for engaging in attitude-discrepant behaviour (e.g., they receive large rewards for doing so), they experience little or no dissonance and show little attitude change. When they have weak reasons for engaging in attitude-discrepant behaviour (e.g., they receive only small rewards for doing so), dissonance is much greater, and attitude change is also increased. In such cases, "less" does indeed lead to "more."

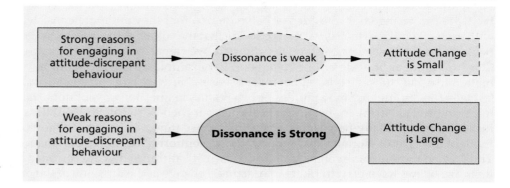

only $1 had a more difficult time justifying why they would lie. To reduce the dissonance this created, these participants later rated the experiment as having been more interesting than those who were paid $20.

The less-leads-to-more effect does not happen in all cases, however. In order for it to occur, first people must feel that they had a choice as to whether they would perform the attitude-discrepant behaviour, and second, they must believe that they were personally responsible both for the chosen course of action and any negative effects it produced (Cooper & Scher, 1990). Third, people must view the payment as well-deserved and for services rendered—not as a bribe. When these conditions exist—and they often do—then the less-leads-to-more effect occurs, and small rewards will produce greater attitude change than larger rewards.

Dissonance and the Misattribution of Arousal If you are like most students, the idea of taking classes at 6:30 a.m. is not particularly appealing. Imagine, however, that you are asked to write an essay in favour of 6:30 a.m. classes and that your essay might affect whether or not your university actually implements such a policy. As you are writing the essay, you begin to experience an uneasy feeling that you recognize as cognitive dissonance. You really do not like the idea of 6:30 a.m. classes, but here you are arguing for them. As you now know, one way to alleviate these uneasy feelings is to change your attitudes—to decide that early morning classes are not such a bad idea, after all. This is the situation in which female students participating in a study at the University of Alberta found themselves, and most of them did just that—changed their attitudes so that they would now be consistent with their behaviour (Wright et al., 1992).

In this study, there was an additional "twist." Before writing the essay, some of the students were given a drug—supposedly to improve memory. Half of the participants were told that the drug had no side effects and half of them were told that the drug would make them feel tense. The researchers reasoned that participants who were led to expect to feel tense would attribute their uneasy feelings while writing their essays to the drug. As a result, they would not feel a need to change their attitudes. And that is indeed what happened. Thus, if we mistakenly attribute the discomfort of dissonance to some other cause, such as a drug, we are less likely to change our attitudes to be consistent with our behaviour.

Misattribution of arousal has consequences in other situations also. For example, as students get closer and closer to exams, their arousal increases. That increasing anxiety is attributed to lack of confidence in their preparedness for the test. To the extent that confidence influences performance, such attributions may influence performance. Thus, attributing pre-test jitters to another external source may improve test results (Savitsky et al., 1998).

ATTITUDE–BEHAVIOUR INCONSISTENCY: SAFE SEX People who won't wear seat belts are more likely to sustain serious injuries if they are in a car accident.

People who smoke are more likely to suffer from lung cancer and heart disease. People who engage in unprotected sex are more likely to contract sexually transmitted diseases, including AIDS. Most individuals know these statements are true (e.g., Carey et al., 1997), so their attitudes are generally favourable towards seat belts, nonsmoking, and safe sex. However, these attitudes are often not translated into action, even though these inconsistencies between attitudes and behaviour may actually have life-and-death consequences.

Understanding attitude–behaviour inconsistency with regard to safe sex was the goal of researchers at McGill University. They presented women with excerpts from the diary of a fictitious woman named Anne-Marie. In the diary, she described a sexual encounter with her partner, Eric. Participants assumed that Eric would feel more negatively about Anne-Marie if she provided a condom than if he did or if they had unprotected intercourse (Rosenthal et al., 1998). Thus, women may be reluctant to provide condoms because they fear that their partner will think negatively about them for doing so (Hynie & Lydon, 1995; Hynie et al., 1998). As Figure 16.7 illustrates, there are various reasons why people find it difficult to act in accordance with their attitudes.

Changing attitude–behaviour inconsistency with respect to condoms was the goal of a most innovative study at the University of New Brunswick (Ploem & Byers, 1997). These researchers began with the assumption that the typical response towards condoms is negative. They tested the idea that negative beliefs about condoms—for example, that they reduce intimacy and pleasure—could be changed to positive ones, thereby increasing the likelihood of safe sex. In this study, two groups of university women received information about AIDS. In one of the groups, an attempt was made also to change the beliefs of women by eroticizing and normalizing condoms. This was done by playing an erotic, sexually stimulating tape in which the heterosexual partners engaging in sex were positive about the condom, conveyed the impression that condom use was widespread and normal, and modelled successful communication skills. Their results showed that this group of women did acquire more positive beliefs about condoms and were more likely to engage in safe sex.

Figure 16.7
Attitude–Behaviour Inconsistency and Safe Sex

Even though both men and women express favourable attitudes towards condom use, they are often reluctant to use them because they believe that they will be perceived negatively by their sexual partner.

Source: Used with permission of the Committee on Unplanned Pregnancy of Winnipeg, Manitoba.

DISSONANCE AND HYPOCRISY Are there ways to increase attitude–behaviour consistency in sexually active students by using what social psychologists have learned about cognitive dissonance? In one study, researchers assigned sexually active college students to one of four experimental conditions (Stone et al., 1994), Participants in the *commitment* condition were asked to prepare a videotape urging others to use condoms if they were sexually active. Those in the *mindfulness* condition were asked to recall situations in which they had failed to use condoms. Those in the *hypocrisy* condition received both of the commitment and the mindfulness treatments: they made the public commitment to engage in safe sex *and* recalled occasions when they had not done so. A control group—the *information-only* condition—made no commitment about safe sex and was not asked to recall times when it failed to follow such practices.

Participants were then given an opportunity to purchase condoms at a reduced price—with the money they were paid for taking part in the study. Results indicated that a much higher proportion of participants in the hypocrisy condition actually bought condoms. These findings and those of several related studies (e.g., Aronson, 1992) indicate that inducing individuals to experience hypocrisy—and the strong dissonance this produces—can be an effective way of promoting consistency in attitudes and behaviour. In short, it appears we can sometimes change our own attitudes by saying or doing things we do believe, as well as by saying or doing things we do not believe.

K E Y *QUESTIONS*

- What are attitudes?
- What factors were found to influence persuasion in early research?
- What is the elaboration likelihood model, and how does it explain persuasion?
- What is the less-leads-to-more effect?
- What is cognitive dissonance, and how can it be reduced?
- How can hypocrisy be used to change behaviour?

Critical Thinking
Given the powerful effects of cognitive dissonance, how do people reduce the dissonance that occurs when they smoke or engage in unsafe sex?

Social Behaviour: Interacting with Others

Social thinking is an important aspect of our social existence, but as you know from your own life, we also *interact* with other people in many ways. In this section, we'll consider three aspects of social interaction: prejudice and how it works; social influence and what it does; and interpersonal attraction and when it happens.

Prejudice: Distorted Views of the World

Ethnic cleansing in Kosovo, mass murder in East Timor, Pakistan versus India—every day brings us more evidence of the tragic consequences of racial, ethnic, or religious hatred. Such actions arise out of **prejudice**—negative attitudes toward the members of specific social groups that are based solely on their membership in that group (Dovidio & Gaertner, 1986). When we practice **discrimination,** we treat other people differently—solely because they belong to a particular group. Research at the University of Manitoba (Altemeyer, 1988) and at Wilfrid Laurier University (Hunsberger, 1995) has shown, for example, that people who are high in right-wing authoritarianism and who have a fundamentalist orientation to religion are especially likely to hold prejudiced views. However, all of us are guilty of holding prejudiced attitudes to some extent. Where do such attitudes come from? And what can be done to reduce such behaviours? These are the questions we will now consider.

THE ORIGINS OF PREJUDICE Many different explanations for the origins of prejudice have been proposed. Here are four that have been especially influential.

Direct Intergroup Conflict: Competition as a Source of Bias It is sad but true that many of the things we value most—a good job, a nice home, high status—are often in short supply. That is the basis for the first explanation of prejudice: **realistic conflict theory** (Bobo, 1983; Esses, et al., 1998). According to this theory, prejudice stems from competition between social groups over valued commodities or desired opportunities. The theory further suggests that as such competition persists, the members of the groups involved come to view each other in increasingly negative

Prejudice: Negative attitudes toward the members of some social group based on their membership in this group.

Discrimination: Negative actions toward the targets of prejudice.

Realistic Conflict Theory: A theory proposing that prejudice stems, at least in part, from economic competition between social groups.

ways (White, 1977). They label competitors "enemies," they view their own group as superior, and they draw the boundaries between themselves and their opponents ever more firmly. A study by researchers at Concordia University (Hilton et al., 1989) found evidence of these ways of thinking by French-Canadian landlords in Montreal about some ethnic groups (e.g., Asians, Haitians, and Italians).

Please do not misunderstand: The fact that competition between groups can be a source of prejudice does not mean that it always is that way. Indeed, one researcher at the University of Calgary (Abra,1993) takes the position that interpersonal competition may be both enjoyable and productive, and that competition provides much of the motivation for creative work. Nevertheless, it is often the case that groups in competition perceive each other in increasingly negative ways. The realistic conflict theory sees this as where prejudice begins.

Social Categorization

In general, we divide the social world into two categories: "us" and "them". The crowd shown here clearly has this division in mind as they cheer for their team.

The Us-versus-Them Effect: Social Categorization as a Basis for Prejudice

A second opinion about the origins of prejudice begins with this basic fact: Just as our perception of the physical world follows orderly rules (e.g., Earhard, 1990), so too does our perception of other people. For example, we concentrate on the eyes and mouth when we inspect the face of another person, because that is where the useful information is located. In the same way, our perception of the social world uses categories—for example, young or old, male or female (Bourhis et al., 1992). That is, "We all belong to many more categories than we probably even realize, categories based not only on gender, nationality, colour, and occupation, but also on religion, age group, ethnic group, geographical origin, or marital status" (Alcott et al., 1994). We call the process of assigning individuals to these kinds of distinct social groups **social categorization**.

Warm and *cold* are categories we give much meaning. At the University of Waterloo, students learned that the lecture would be given by a visiting professor. Half of the students were led to expect a warm person and half were led to expect a cold person (Widmeyer & Loy, 1988). The students perceived the "warm" professor as a better teacher, more sociable, more humorous, more humane, less unpleasant, less irritable, less ruthless, and less formal than the "cold professor," even though all of the students took the same lecture at the same time! Thus the social classifications like warm and cold are really mini-theories about people and their behaviour.

People generally divide the social world into those belonging to their own social group (*in-group)*, or not (*out-groups)*. Such distinctions are made on the basis of many dimensions, including race, religion, sex, age, ethnic background, occupation, and even the town or 'hood where people live. The basis of social categorization may be trivial, those who prefer chocolate over vanilla, or it may be serious. For example, in many different cultures, the word used for other groups translates as "non-human."

If social categorization stopped there, it would have little connection to prejudice. Unfortunately, it does not. First, people in the "us" category or in-group are viewed in favourable terms, while those in the "them" category or out-group are perceived negatively. For instance, men expect better service from men in restaurants, whereas women expect better service from women (Fischer et al., 1997). Second, out-group members are assumed to be "all alike." They are thought to possess more undesirable traits and they are often disliked (e.g., Lambert, 1995; Linville & Fisher, 1993). That was the case for fans at home games of the McGill University hockey team, who judged opposing teams most negatively on behaviours like aggressiveness and arrogance and whose negative judgments intensified as a game progressed (Lalonde et al.,1987). Third, the in-group/out-group distinction affects the attributions we make. We attribute desirable behaviours of our in-group to stable, internal causes such as admirable personal traits, and those of out-groups to

Social Categorization: Our tendency to divide the social world into two distinct categories: "us" and "them."

temporary or external factors, such as luck (e.g., Hewstone et al., 1983). This tendency is sometimes called the *ultimate attribution error*—because of the potentially devastating results.

Why do we engage in this kind of social categorization? That question has been a focus of much research in social psychology. Here are two reasons. First, social categorization provides us with an important component of our social identity and a way of protecting it. By perceiving members of out-groups as alike and with more negative traits, we can boost the importance of our own group and ourselves and feel more positive about being a member of the in-group (Gagnon & Bourhis, 1996).

These findings suggest that if an individual's social identity is threatened, he or she might be especially likely to denigrate an out-group. That prediction was tested in a series of studies conducted at the University of Saskatchewan (Grant, 1992, 1993). Participants were students who were selected on the basis of caring about either a "female" issue (women should be encouraged to apply for high-status jobs) or a "male" issue (roles for men have become confusing and unclear). As expected, participants whose social identity was threatened rated the other group more negatively than those whose identity was not threatened.

Second, social identity enhances self-esteem. In one study (Lemyre & Smith, 1985), students were told that they were part of either the "red" or the "blue" group. No other information was provided. Some participants were then given an opportunity to discriminate against the out-group (by giving them fewer points), whereas others were not. The participants who were given an opportunity to discriminate showed increased self-esteem. Thus it seems there are social identity and self-esteem benefits for organizing the world into "us" and "them."

The Role of Social Learning as a Basis for Prejudice A third perspective on the origins of prejudice begins with the obvious fact that infants are not born that way. Rather, prejudice is learned when children observe their parents, friends, teachers, and others expressing prejudiced views, or because they are directly rewarded for expressing the "right" opinions—those held by the adults. For example, instead of learning what is positive about the real differences between the sexes, children acquire the sex-role stereotypes used in their own social world (Bowen, 1973).

In a study of young children, Aboud (1988) found that there are three stages in the development of basic social categorization. First, children base their reactions to other people upon their own needs and emotional state, then on perceptions of differences in appearance and behaviour, and third (by age eight) on ideas about characteristics shared by members of a group. This researcher provided evidence that some awareness of ethnic groups is present by age four or five.

While people with whom children interact play a key role in this process, the mass media are also important (Currie, 1997). For example, researchers studied the way in which movie summaries on the Internet described stepfathers and stepmothers. None of the plot summaries were positive about these characters (Claxton-Oldfield & Butler, 1998). They also studied the stereotypes held by Newfoundland students of the small group of Native Canadian Innu who live in Davis Inlet, Labrador (Claxton-Oldfield & Keith, 1999) and the image of this group portrayed in daily newspapers. They found that "the students' stereotypes of the Innu (Study 1) map fairly closely onto the kinds of information reported about the Innu in the daily press (Study 2)." To the extent that television, films, and other media present members of various social groups in an unflattering light, they contribute directly to the development of prejudice.

Social Learning

Children acquire their ideas about social groups as they proceed through the preschool years.

Cognitive Sources of Prejudice: Stereotypes Perhaps most fundamental is the finding that prejudice originates in the way in which human brains handle social information. Most important, we often think in **stereotypes**. A stereotype is a cognitive schema or a set of beliefs about a specific social group—that all members of the group have certain characteristics in common (e.g., Haddock & Zanna, 1998; Kunda & Oleson, 1995). While most research has been conducted on racial stereotypes, there are many other kinds of stereotypes as well—stereotypes about ethnic groups, gays and straights, overweight and underweight people (Miller, 1998), sexual coersion, (Morrison et al., 1997), women and men, and so on. For example, we have stereotypes for attractive people, whom we expect to have better personalities than unattractive ones (Dion & Dion, 1987). We apply our gender stereotypes not only to people, but also to computers, depending on whether the computer's voice is male or female (Nass et al., 1997).

Even the labels that are used to describe individuals or groups can evoke different stereotypes and, as a result, different attitudes. We think in stereotypes about women who use "Ms." (rather than "Miss" or "Mrs.")—who are perceived as more masculine and less likeable than those who use other titles (Dion & Schuller, 1991). Stereotypes go with labels—for example ""Aboriginal Peoples," "Native Indians," or "Native Peoples" get more positive ratings than "Native Canadians" and "First Nations People" (Donakowski & Esses, 1996). However, the results of a study at Lakehead University revealed that those are not the labels used by students with Native ancestry. Rather, when they think about themselves, they use their tribal designation (e.g., Cree, Ojibway) rather than any of the terms commonly used by others (Bowd & Brady, 1998).

Like other cognitive schemas, stereotypes influence the ways in which we process social information. For instance, information related to a stereotype is processed more quickly. In one study, researchers asked students to rate the characteristics of various groups (Gardner et al., 1995). When rating "males," for example, participants responded more quickly to stereotypical characteristics (e.g., rugged, impatient, and talkative) than to characteristics that are not usually found in the male stereotype (e.g., irreligious, artistic, and impolite). Stereotypes also lead us to pay attention to specific types of information and stereotypes determine what we remember best—information that is consistent with the beliefs we already hold (Seta & Hayes, 1994).

What happens when we encounter someone who does not fit a stereotype? Does exposure to an exception change our thinking? In their studies, Kunda and Olson (1995, 1997) gave participants descriptions of individuals who challenged their stereotypes of lawyers, homosexuals, and public relations agents. Participants handled this new information by leaving their original stereotypes intact and creating a new subcategory—for atypical group members (O'Sullivan & Durso, 1984).

Together, these results tell us that stereotypes are self-confirming. Once we engage in stereotypic thinking about a social group, we notice the details that fit and we remember as "facts" only those particulars that are consistent. As a result, the stereotype becomes invulnerable to new information and more and more inflexible over time. Indeed, some researchers describe stereotypes as *inferential prisons*—mental frameworks for which it is difficult to escape (Dunning & Sherman, 1997).

Given that stereotypes often lead us to serious errors in our social thinking, why do we continue to think in this way? First, stereotypes require minimal effort (Macrae et al., 1994). In other words, stereotypes allow us to make quick and easy judgments without engaging in complex, effortful thought (e.g., Forgas & Fiedler, 1996). Second, attributing negative qualities to other groups can make positive contributions to our own social identity and self-esteem.

For a further look at how victims of prejudice and discrimination think about themselves, see the **Perspectives on Diversity** section.

Stereotypes: Cognitive frameworks in which that all members of specific social groups share certain characteristics.

<u>Perspectives on Diversity</u>

When Victims Blame Themselves

MOST RESEARCH ABOUT PREJUDICE HAS focused on prejudiced people and discriminatory behaviour. In contrast, the experience of the victims of prejudice and discrimination has received very little attention. Recently there has been progress in our understanding of the victims' perspective (Ruggiero & Taylor, 1995). Researchers invited female students from various faculties at McGill University to take a test that would predict how successful they would be in their future careers. After taking the test, the women were informed that the test would be graded by a group of male judges who had a record of discrimination against women of 100 percent, 75 percent, 50 percent, 25 percent, or zero percent. Then each participant was told that she had received an F on the test and asked to answer questions about why she thought she had failed. Perhaps not surprisingly, those who believed there was a 100 percent chance of discrimination attributed their poor mark to discrimination on the part of the male judge. The other women attributed their failure to themselves—to their poor answers, for example (see Figure 16.8).

In another study (Ruggiero & Taylor, 1997), the participants were East Asian and Black (of West Indian heritage) students. Participants again took the career success test. They were informed that white judges would be evaluating their test and that there was a 100 percent, 75 percent, 50 percent, 25 percent, or zero percent chance that the judge would discriminate against their ethnic group. Again, failure was attributed to discrimination only if it was 100 percent certain that discrimination had occurred. Otherwise they blamed themselves.

These findings help explain why members of disadvantaged groups often report that their group is discriminated against, but that they, themselves, have not been the target of discrimination (e.g., Dion & Kawakami, 1996; Taylor et al., 1996). They minimize the discrimination they experience by blaming themselves instead. The societal implications of these findings are disturbing indeed. Ruggiero and Taylor (1997) comment that, "If minority group members do not perceive themselves to be discriminated against … they may not be oriented toward removing discriminatory barriers to their own personal advancement." Furthermore, they noted: "The tendency of minority group members to attribute negative outcomes internally may provide majority group members with justification for ongoing discrimination."

Figure 16.8
Self-Blame and Discrimination

When told that there was a 100 percent chance of discrimination, female students were very likely to attribute a poor test grade to discrimination. If, however, there was any ambiguity about the chance of discrimination, the students were much more likely to attribute poor grades to the poor quality of their answers.

Source: Ruggiero and Taylor, 1995.

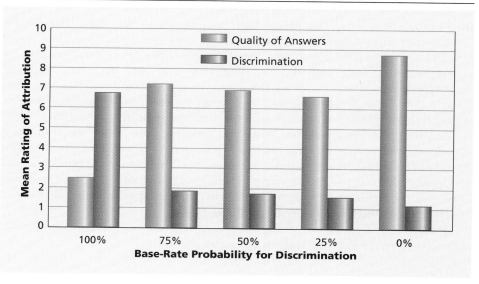

These research findings suggest also that intervention in the form of increasing self-esteem and control for members of disadvantaged groups may enable them to acknowledge the discrimination that confronts them.

STEREOTYPES AND JURY DUTY One basic principle of our legal system is this: defendants must be judged according to the evidence rather than their background or personal characteristics. At the same time, jurors, lawyers, and judges cannot help but notice—and perhaps be affected by—a defendant's physical appearance, gender, age, and race (Roesch et al., 1999). Thus stereotypes impact the thoughts, feelings, and behaviours of jurors when they are engaged in coming to a verdict in a court case.

Clearly, many factors enter into jurors' deliberations as to the guilt or innocence of a defendant. First, with respect to the defendant personally, juries are usually more sympathetic to attractive defendants (McKelvie & Coley, 1993a, 1993b), viewing them as less dangerous and less likely to engage in future criminal acts (Esses & Webster, 1988). Some studies show that attractive defendants are acquitted more often and receive lighter sentences (Stewart, 1980). Second, the gender of the defendant often plays a role as well. While you might predict that juries would show more leniency toward female defendants, the situation is more complicated than that. Often, females do seem to have an edge in terms of sympathy from juries (Michelini & Snodgrass, 1980). However, that is not the case when females are charged with crimes that are inconsistent with traditional sex-role stereotypes—murder, for instance (Cruse & Leigh, 1987).

Third, as you might guess, the defendant's ethnic background may influence the process. For example, defendants of northern European background are less likely to be convicted and less likely to receive a prison sentence (Stewart, 1980). This may stem from prejudice (Stephan & Stephan, 1986), or it may reflect also that for economic reasons, defendants from some minority groups are less able to obtain high-quality legal assistance (Welch et al., 1984). It is clear, however, that minority stereotypes do influence social judgments on the part of jurors, and this plays at least some role in the greater conviction rates for members of visible minorities (Bodenhausen, 1990).

In sum, the human tendency to engage in cognitive shortcuts such as stereotyping can have particularly damaging real-world consequences. Despite attempts to be objective, not all defendants will receive just treatment under the law. Social psychological research on stereotyping and its effects deserves further careful attention as psychologists attempt to apply their knowledge to improving the fairness of legal proceedings.

CHALLENGING PREJUDICE What steps can be taken to reduce the negative and brutal influence of prejudice on human affairs? The following techniques have been found effective by careful research in social psychology.

Breaking the Cycle of Prejudice: Learning Not to Hate Bigots are made, not born. All of us have the potential to acquire prejudices, but we acquire particular ones as a result of experience—social learning, for example. How can we encourage prejudiced parents, teachers, and other adults to change the messages they deliver to their own children? The first step is to raise caregivers' awareness of their own biased beliefs and their own discriminatory behaviours. Most people realize that we live in a world of increasing diversity and that attitudes of tolerance are, in the long run, much more adaptive. Thus, campaigns designed to enhance awareness of prejudice and its harmful effects may yield desirable results (Aronson, 1990).

A second way to combat prejudice is to increase awareness that prejudice harms those who hold such views (Dovidio & Gaertner, 1993). There is growing evidence that the personal world of prejudiced people is filled with needless fears, anxieties, and anger. As a result, they experience unnecessary emotional turmoil that can adversely affect their own health and that of their children (Jussim, 1991). Being aware of these potential costs, adults may choose to promote tolerance because that produces emotional well-being.

Children may also teach one another not to be prejudiced. Aboud and Doyle (1996) conducted a study with white students in grades three and four attending various schools in Quebec. First, their attitudes toward whites, Blacks, and Chinese Canadians were assessed. Then the researchers matched pairs of high- and low-prejudiced children and asked them to discuss their perceptions of different races. These discussions had the effect of reducing prejudice among high-prejudiced children. Fortunately, the converse was not true—high-prejudiced children did not create more prejudice in low-prejudiced children. These findings are encouraging and suggest that children themselves may play an important role in altering prejudiced views.

Direct Intergroup Contact: The Potential Benefits Prejudice builds social walls between people—for example, between Westerners and Ontarians, between Newfoundlanders and Quebecers, between Cape Bretoners and other Nova Scotians. Restricted contact between members of different ethnic, racial, or religious groups makes it easier for stereotypes to persist. How can we break out of this vicious cycle?

The **contact hypothesis** suggests that intergroup exposure is the key requirement (Schwarzwald et al., 1992; Stephan, 1987). According to this hypothesis, increased contact between members of various groups reduces prejudice discrimination—provided that contact occurs under the following conditions:

1. The groups that interact are roughly equal in social, economic, or task-related status.

2. The contact situation requires cooperation and interdependence so that the groups work toward shared goals.

3. Contact between the groups is informal, so they can get to know one another on a one-to-one basis.

4. Contact occurs in a setting where existing norms favour group equality.

5. The participants view one another as typical members of their respective groups.

When contact between initially hostile groups occurs under these conditions, prejudice does seem to decrease for a number of reasons. First, increased contact leads to appreciation of similarities, which increases interpersonal attraction. Second, stereotypes meet sufficient "exceptions" to induce change (Kunda & Oleson, 1995). Third, increased contact alters the idea that all members of the other group are the same.

Furthermore, the outcome of increased contact is more general, so that increased tolerance toward one group extends to other groups as well (Pettigrew, 1997). Remarkably, direct contact may not even be necessary. Rather, simply knowing that people in one's own group have developed cross-group friendships can reduce prejudice—by making interaction acceptable and by reducing anxiety (Pettigrew, 1997; Wright et al., 1997).

Recategorization: Resetting the Boundary between "Us" and "Them" Suppose that a team from your university played against a team from a rival university: Which would be "us" and which would be "them"? The answer is obvious: Your own school's team would constitute your in-group, while the other school's

Contact Hypothesis: The suggestion that increased contact between members of different social groups will reduce prejudice between them.

Recategorization: Shifting the boundary between "us" and "them" so that persons previously seen as belonging to outgroups are now seen as belonging to the in-group.

team would be the out-group. But now imagine that the team from the other school had won many games, and was chosen to represent your province in a national tournament. When it played against a team from another province, would you now perceive the team as "us" or "them"? Now, this former "enemy" team may be your in-group.

Note then that the boundary between "us" and "them" is flexible. It can change to include—or exclude—various groups of people. When we shift the boundary between "us" and them," **recategorization** occurs. According to current research, the result is a reduction in prejudice. In one example, researchers investigated the attitudes of students at a multicultural high school in the United States from many different backgrounds—African American, Chinese, Hispanic, Japanese, Korean, Vietnamese, and Caucasian (Gaertner et al., 1993). The more individual students felt that they belonged to a single group—all students attending the same high school—the more positive were their feelings toward people from backgrounds other than their own. These findings suggest that recategorization may be a very useful technique for reducing prejudiced thinking.

In the **Canadian Focus** section, you will find more information about changing attitudes and ethnic groups in Canada.

Recategorization: Moving the Boundary between "Us" and "Them"

Recategorization, or moving the boundary between "us" and "them," has been identified by researchers in social psychology as an effective way of reducing prejudice.

Canadian Focus

Living Side by Side: Canadian Multiculturalism

In Canada, we encourage diversity. Multiculturalism: that is the Canadian way. We encourage different cultures to maintain their identities, while individuals work together within shared institutions—for the common good. Thus, within our vast borders live together groups of people with different languages, ethnic origins, racial backgrounds, and cultural customs. Among us there are different beliefs—ranging from religion, to health and illness (Armstrong & Swartzman, 1999), deviant behaviour (Kirkmeyer et al., 1997) and sexuality (Moston et al., 1998). How individuals behave in a society such as ours—that is the subject matter of the studies in social psychology that are described in this Canadian Focus.

Berry (1999) has listed two research traditions in social psychology relating to how we manage to live together. One is the study of how people such as immigrants or refugees change when they migrate into another culture (e.g., Aycan & Kanungo, 1998). Some immigrants become assimilated and take on the beliefs perceived to be those of the majority, some attempt to maintain the culture of their society of origin, and some keep the "best of both worlds." Psychological *acculturation*—the changes in an individual as a result of contact with other cultures—generates acculturation stress, which varies with other factors, such as the nature of the larger society and

the psychological characteristics of the individual (Berry, 1995).

The other research tradition focuses on *perceptions and behaviours* that occur within and between groups that live together within one country. Let's look at a sample of the newest findings in four areas: intergroup comfort levels, stereotypes and academic performance, prejudice and mood, and ambivalence and attitude change.

Intergroup Comfort Levels How comfortable with each other are the different groups who live in Canada? Kalin and Berry (1996) studied a representative sample of over three thousand members of the Canadian population. The participants (from twelve ethnic groups) gave information about their *comfort levels* with members of fourteen different ethnic groups. Here are two of the results. First, individuals in all of the groups were most comfortable with people of their own ethnic origin. Second, regardless of the ethnic origin of those surveyed, their rankings of comfort—and discomfort—with the various other ethnic groups were similar. Data such as these are helpful in identifying the ethnic groups with which most of us experience discomfort—the first step in dealing with these negative reactions.

Narrowing the Gap between Groups How accurate are our stereotypes about ethnic groups and *academic performance*? That was a question asked in one study about nine ethnic groups in Canada. The results showed that people do estimate average academic performance—grades—of students quite accurately according to the ethnic group to which they belong (Ashton & Esses, 1999). This accurate stereotype may be useful in determining why some groups perform better or worse academically (on average) and may lead to a better understanding of the challenges facing particular ethnic groups. It may also inform us about how to narrow the gap between groups, and decrease secondary school drop-out rates—of Native youngsters, for example (Brady, 1996).

Feeling Better about Our Neighbours Prejudice may be one of the main obstacles to harmony in our diverse society. Prejudice arises not just from our thoughts about different groups but also from our feelings. To explore the role of feelings in prejudice, participants in a study were asked what *emotions* they felt when thinking about or interacting with a member of a different ethnic group (Haddock et al., 1994). The clearest finding was this: the more negative the *emotions* participants felt, the greater the prejudice they expressed.

That response led the researchers to ask, Can we change attitudes by changing the emotional state of an individual (Esses & Zanna, 1995)? In four experiments, participants were put into a positive, neutral, or negative mood. These moods were created in a variety of ways—by having participants read positive, neutral, or negative statements into a tape recorder, by describing events in their lives that made them extremely happy, unhappy, or neutral, or by listening to music that was intended to create these different moods.

Victoria Esses
University of Western Ontario

Here is one of the findings. The participants in a bad mood described various ethnic groups more negatively than those in a neutral or positive mood. These effects were most evident in descriptions of Native, Pakistani, and Arabic people. For example, some of the participants originally described Native people as "proud" and viewed this as a positive characteristic. Later, those who were put in a bad mood perceived this as a more negative characteristic. Here is evidence that the very same characteristic is evaluated differently depending on a person's mood!

Telling funny jokes is another way of putting people in a good mood. Funny people—stand-up comics, talk show hosts, and others—use stereotypes in their jokes. Often, the target of a joke will be a group of people. What is the effect of listening to that kind of humour? What is the effect of telling that kind of joke?

Researchers at the University of Western Ontario asked those questions in two sets of studies. The targets of the jokes were men, lawyers, or Newfoundlanders (Maio et al., 1997; Olson et al., 1999). The results indicated that listening to such humour had no demonstrable effect on stereotypes of the listeners—perhaps because they were in a good mood. However, telling disparaging jokes made the jokers' stereotypes more negative. That finding is consistent with what we know about social cognition. The more you repeat an idea about another group of people, even in jest, the more likely it is that the message of the joke will become integrated into your own thinking. Thus, it is the thinking of the *joker* that is at risk here.

These studies inform us about how our emotions affect the way we think about other groups of people and how to use that information to combat prejudice.

Ambivalence and Changing Attitudes Thus far we have discussed attitudes as though they were either positive or negative. But the truth is that many of our attitudes are mixed. They contain both positive and negative elements—at the same time. For example, in 1999, when boatloads of illegal immigrants came to the shores of British Columbia from China, the polls reported that the respondents were both favourable and unfavourable towards these new arrivals. Thus there are separate positive and negative dimensions to some attitudes, and these are in conflict. When people are aware that their positive and negative attitudes are not consistent, they experience the discomfort of cognitive dissonance (McGregor et al., 1999).

Attitudes that are both positive and negative have been termed *ambivalent* (Olson & Zanna, 1993). To measure attitude ambivalence, researchers assessed the attitudes of students towards Asian immigrants, French Canadians, Natives, and other Canadians (Bell et al., 1996). The questions asked about three different dimensions of attitudes: traits, beliefs, and feelings. For example, the participants were asked to list the beliefs of a typical member of the target group and then to rate each of the items in their list as positive or negative. From these data, a measure of attitude ambivalence was developed.

M.P. Zanna
University of Waterloo

What is the relevance of ambivalence to attitudes about minority groups? To answer that question, these researchers assessed the ambivalence of a large number of participants on an attitude "thermometer." They identified two groups—those who were highly ambivalent and those who were not at all ambivalent. These two groups then read a message that advocated increased immigration to Canada from Hong Kong. The results showed that ambivalence increased the systematic processing of the persuasive messages. In other words, the details in the persuasive messages had an impact on individuals who were ambivalent and who therefore were more careful to evaluate new information. That result highlights the importance of ambivalent attitudes because they are flexible and therefore subject to change. How to change fixed ideas into ambivalent ones—how to create cognitive dissonance in order to increase the likelihood of attitude change towards other groups in our country—is a matter for further investigation.

Social Influence: Efforts by one or more individuals to change the attitudes or behaviour of one or more others.

Social Norms: Rules in a given group or society indicating how individuals ought to behave in specific situations.

Conformity: A type of social influence in which individuals experience pressure to adhere to existing social norms.

Social Influence

How many times each day do other people try to change your behaviour in some way? And how often do *you* try to do that to other people? If you stop and count, you will probably come up with a surprisingly large number. Efforts at **social influence**—pressure to change the attitudes or behaviour of other people—is very common and takes many different forms. We've already considered persuasion in our discussion of attitudes. Here, we will briefly examine three other important forms of social influence: *conformity, compliance,* and *obedience*.

CONFORMITY   In many situations, there are spoken or unspoken rules indicating how we *should* behave. These rules are known as **social norms.** Some norms are detailed and precise—for example, written constitutions, sports rules, and traffic signs. Other norms—"Do not make eye contact in the elevator," "Do not show up an hour early for the party"—are implicit, but still exert powerful effects on our behaviour. In these circumstances, we encounter powerful pressures toward **conformity**—pressures to act or think like those around us (Cialdini, 1988). Why do we conform to social norms? There are at least three reasons: We conform to be liked by other people, to gain their approval, and to avoid rejection.

Other people affect our behaviour in many social systems. For instance, there are social rules about how to behave when we wait in line—at the supermarket, at the movie theatre, or at the registrar's office. In one study (Milgram, 1986), a paid employee of the experimenter intruded into 129 actual lineups waiting at railway ticket counters and so on in New York City. The intruder entered between the third and the fourth person in line and said, "Excuse me, I'd like to get in here." The researchers noted a number of characteristics about the defensive reactions of those in line. First, they found that the defensive reactions were "local," in that most often the response was from the person who was fifth in line—that is, right after the place where the intrusion had occurred (see Figure 16.9). The defensive reactions in this study were of different kinds: verbal reactions ("Get to the end!"), non-verbal objections (hostile gestures and stares); and physical responses (tugging and pushing). Second, if the people immediately behind the intruder were quiet, there was not much of a response anywhere else (Milgram et al., 1986). The researchers concluded that, in lineups of strangers, each person is a segment and there is a social understanding that people are expected to defend the space just ahead of themselves.

In Milgram's study of people in lines, the pressures on the intruder to conform were direct. However, pressures to conform can be very subtle and people can fail to detect the changes that occur in

Figure 16.9
Social Rules and Lineups

The percentage of people objecting to intrusion into lineups is highest immediately after the intrusion point.

Source: Milgram, 1986, Journal of Personality and Social Psychology, 51 (4), 683–689.

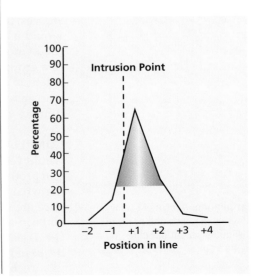

Figure 16.10
Asch's Line-Judging Task: An Example

In one of the problems used by Asch in his famous research on conformity, the participants' task was to indicate which of the comparison lines (A, B, or C) best matched the standard line in terms of length.

Standard Line

A   B   C

Compliance: A form of social influence in which one or more individuals accept direct requests from one or more others.

their own behaviour (Vorauer & Miller, 1997). This was first revealed by Asch (1951) in an experiment that has become a classic in social psychology. To investigate conformity, Asch asked male students to make simple perceptual judgments—to indicate which of three comparison lines matched a standard line in length (see Figure 16.10).

Six to eight other people were also present, but all of them were accomplices of the experimenter. These "subjects" gave their answer before the participant gave his, and in twelve out of eighteen trials, their answer was clearly wrong. In those trials, however, fully 76 percent of the participants when along with the wrong answers at least once. These findings demonstrate that pressures to conform may be so strong that, faced with a group of strangers who unanimously voice one opinion, most people will agree, even when doing so requires them to contradict what their own eyes are telling them!

FACTORS AFFECTING DEGREE OF CONFORMITY Several variables influence whether conformity occurs and to what extent. Up to a point, the more people around us who agree with each other, the greater the pressure is to think and do as they do. However, after the number reaches three or four, the pressure to go along with the group increases very little. The reason is this: Beyond three or four, we begin to suspect that, rather than giving independent judgments, the other people are working together to influence us (Wilder, 1977).

Participants in Asch's classic study faced a unanimous (albeit wrong) opinion about the size of the standard line. But what would have happened if some of the others had given the correct answer instead of the wrong one? In Asch's studies, if even one of the accomplices gave the correct instead of the incorrect response, participants were much less likely to conform to the rest of the group. This finding has been obtained in subsequent research and it leads to the conclusion that, in order to resist group pressure to conform, people need at least one supporter who agrees with their view.

Thus social pressure to conform is a fact of human life. Is conformity necessarily bad? To the contrary, if most people did not follow social rules on most occasions, shoppers waiting to pay for their purchases would not form lines, motorists would drive on whichever side the road they preferred, and people would come to work or meetings whenever they felt like it. It seems as though conformity to social norms is necessary—if we are to survive in the social world in which we live.

Of course conformity is not the only effect of the presence of other people. In some instances, we work harder when others are present—for example, when we jog with a person who runs faster. That is called *social facilitation*. In other circumstances, the presence of other person may cause us to work somewhat less than we would when we are alone. An example of this *social loafing* occurs when people applaud more softly as part of an audience rather than alone. Often when we are part of a group we do things that we would not do alone; a food fight in the residence cafeteria or a brawl at a soccer game are two examples. Under these group circumstances, we become less aware of ourselves—more anonymous—and we abandon our normal standards of behaviour. That result is called *deindividuation*.

COMPLIANCE Suppose that you wanted somebody to do something for you. How would you go about seeing to it that it happened? If you are like most other people, you probably have quite a few tricks up your sleeve for getting agreement—for gaining what social psychologists call **compliance**. Those talented in achieving compliance are often salespeople, advertisers, political lobbyists, fundraisers, politicians, and con-artists. To study these *compliance professionals* and their techniques, Cialdini (1994) concealed his identity and took temporary jobs in several of these fields. On the basis of this research, he concluded that there are many tactics for achieving compliance, but the basic principles are those shown in Table 16.1 and discussed below.

TABLE 16.1

Basic Principles behind Compliance

Research findings indicate that most techniques for gaining compliance rest, to some extent, on the principles shown here.

Principle	Description
Friendship/Liking	In general, we are more willing to comply with requests from friends or from people we like than with requests from strangers or people we don't like.
Commitment/Consistency	Once we have committed ourselves to a position or action, we are more willing to comply with requests for behaviours that are consistent with this position.
Reciprocity	We are generally more willing to comply with a request from someone who has previously provided a favour or concession to us than one from someone who has not.
Scarcity	We value (and try to secure) opportunities, people, or objects that are scarce or decreasing. As a result, we are more likely to comply with requests that focus on the scarcity of such items than ones that do not.
Authority	We value authority, so we are usually more willing to comply with requests from someone who is (or seems to be) a legitimate authority than someone who is not.

Source: Based on suggestions by Cialdini, 1994.

Ingratiation: A technique of social influence based on inducing increased liking in the target person before influence is attempted.

Foot-in-the-Door Technique: A technique for gaining compliance in which a small request is followed by a larger one.

Tactics based on liking: Ingratiation People are most likely to comply with a request—for a raise in pay, a review of a grade, a donation at the door—from somebody they like. The goal of **ingratiation** is to increase liking before a request is made (e.g., Liden & Mitchell, 1988). How is that goal achieved? First, we use praise or flattery and positive non-verbal cues (eye contact and smiling). Second, we highlight points of similarity by sharing common views. Third, we increase our own personal appeal or power, perhaps by mentioning connections with important people—dropping the names of important clients, for example. These tactics work because they increase liking and therefore produce greater compliance (Baron et al., 1990; Wayne & Liden, 1995). Note, however, that if obvious or overdone, ingratiation may fail or even backfire, causing dislike instead.

Tactics Based on Consistency or Commitment Recently, some introductory psychology students were asked if they would stay for five or ten minutes after their experiment and help the experimenter by rating some materials for her next study. Once they had agreed, she made another request—would they volunteer extra time (one to three hours) so that graduate students could complete their research (Gorassini & Olson, 1995)? This is an example of the **foot-in-the-door technique**—starting with a small request and then, after it has been granted, moving on to a larger one. Why does this

Getting Others to Say "Yes": One Unusual Technique

How do *you* get other people to say "yes" to your requests—to show compliance? Your favourite tactics are probably different from the one shown here, but may be highly effective, too!

Source: Scott Adams, 1998.

technique work? Research findings indicate that people think they need to appear consistent (e.g., Beaman et al., 1983). Thus, once they have said yes to the first small request, they feel it is inconsistent to say no to the second one, and so there is pressure to comply with the much larger favour.

Another tactic in this category is the **lowball procedure.** In this case, an agreement is reached and then the deal is changed. In negotiating the sale of a truck, for example, the salesperson may claim that the sales manager would not agree to the original terms. Instead of walking away, often people increase their offer. They feel they have made a commitment to buy—which they now find it socially awkward to retract. In one study (Cialdini et al., 1978), introductory psychology students were asked to participate in an experiment. In the lowball condition, students were told that the experiment was scheduled for 7:00 a.m. *after* they agreed to participate. Yet when asked to confirm that they would participate, 56 percent who had agreed said yes, and nearly all of them showed up!

Tactics Based on Reciprocity Reciprocity is a basic rule of social life: we tend to treat other people as they have treated us. Several tactics for gaining compliance are based on this fact. One of these is the **door-in-the-face** technique. This tactic starts with a very large request. After it is refused, a much smaller request is made—the one that was planned all along. The target feels pressure to reciprocate by saying yes to the smaller request, because it seems like the other person made a concession by scaling down their large one. The success of this tactic seems to rest largely on the principle of reciprocity (Cialdini, 1994).

A related procedure for gaining compliance, known as the **that's-not-all technique,** uses the following approach. An initial request is followed immediately by something that sweetens the deal—a little "extra"—free floormats in a truck sale, for example. The free option is usually of little value—in comparison to the total value of the truck— but it works. Customers feel compelled to reciprocate by saying yes to the purchase.

Reciprocity has been used to explain the increase in tips received by restaurant servers when they write "Thanks" or draw a happy face on the bill (Rind & Bordia, 1996). In one study (Rind & Strohmetz, 1999), servers wrote a helpful message about an upcoming dinner special. The customers responded to that "tip" by leaving a bigger tip for the server!

Tactics Based on Scarcity In general, the more rare or scarce an item, the more desirable it is. The **playing hard to get** tactic creates the illusion of high popularity and much demand. This puts pressure to comply on would-be romantic partners or would-be employers. The requests can range from "Let's get engaged" to "Pay me a high salary" (e.g., Williams et al., 1993).

A related tactic is the **fast-approaching-deadline technique**. Here, a deadline is established after which, presumably, it will be impossible to obtain something—an item for sale, a romantic partner, or a prospective employee. Although this deadline is probably not as firm as it sounds, there is pressure to comply.

Tactics Based on Complaining Griping, complaining, whining—expressing discontent or dissatisfaction—are effective ways to achieve compliance in some situations. In one study, students reported that in 25 percent of the cases, complaining succeeded (Alicke et al., 1992). While both sexes use complaints for social influence, there are some differences in precisely how

Lowball Procedure: A tactic for gaining compliance in which, after a deal or arrangement is made, it is changed by the person using this tactic.

Door-in-the-Face Technique: A technique for gaining compliance in which a large request is followed by a smaller one.

That's-Not-All Technique: A technique for gaining compliance in which a small extra incentive is offered before the target person has agreed to or rejected a request.

Playing Hard to Get: A tactic for gaining compliance in which individuals try to create the image that they are very popular or very much in demand.

Fast-Approaching-Deadline Technique: A technique for gaining compliance in which a deadline is established after which it will be impossible to obtain something desired by the target person.

they use the technique for gaining compliance (Klotz & Alicke, 1993). Women complain more about themselves, their appearance, or their feelings, whereas men complain more about other people. Women react more to complaints: they offer more suggestions and more emotional support. Men are more likely to ignore complaints or to reject them, saying—for example—"Do I care about that?"

There are other means for gaining compliance, but by now the main point should be clear: Many of these procedures rest on basic principles long studied and well-understood by psychologists. The success of salespeople, fundraisers, and others in getting people to say yes is no mystery: these people are simply good applied social psychologists, whether they realize it or not!

OBEDIENCE: SOCIAL INFLUENCE BY DEMAND The most direct way to influence another person is to give direct orders—simply tell them what you want them to do. This approach occurs in many situations where one person has clear authority over another—in the military, in sports, and in business, for example. **Obedience** to authority is not surprising; officers, coaches, and executives have the power to enforce their commands. More surprising, though, is the fact that even persons *lacking in such authority* can sometimes induce high levels of obedience by giving orders. Unsettling evidence for such effects was first reported in a series of famous—and controversial—experiments (Milgram, 1963, 1974). You will recognize the methodology and the ethical concerns (e.g., Korn, 1997) from studying Chapter 10.

Destructive Obedience: Basic Findings In order to find out about obedience, Milgram used the following procedure. Participants (male students) were told that they were taking part in an experiment about the effects of punishment on learning. Their role was that of the "teacher" and they were to deliver electric shocks to the "learner"—who was really an assistant of the experimenter—each time the learner made a mistake in a simple learning task. The teacher and learner were separated by a wall, and the shocks were delivered by means of switches on a special device (see Figure 16.11). Participants were told to deliver the next higher level of shock each time the learner made an error. The first switch delivered a shock of 15 volts, the second was a shock of 30 volts, and so on up to the last switch, which supposedly delivered a shock of 450 volts. In reality, of course, there was no real shock except for brief pulse used to convince participants that the equipment was real at the beginning of the experiment.

During the session, the learner seemed to make many errors, so participants soon faced a dilemma: Should they continue delivering increasingly strong shocks to this person or not? The choice was not easy, because when the teachers hesitated, the experimenter pressured them to continue. Since participants were volunteers and were paid in advance, you might predict that most would quickly refuse such orders. In reality, though, *65 percent were fully obedient,* continuing through the entire series to the final 450-volt shock level (refer again to Figure 16.11).

Many of the participants protested and expressed concern over the learner's welfare. Nevertheless, when ordered to proceed, most yielded to the experimenter's social influence and continued to obey. In fact, they did so even when the victim pounded on the wall as if in protest against the shocks he was receiving. Similar findings have been obtained in studies conducted around the world (Jordan, Germany, Australia) and with children as well as adults; so the tendency to obey commands from even a powerless source of authority appears to be frighteningly general in scope (e.g., Kilham & Mann, 1974; Shanab & Yahya, 1977).

Milgram's results were disturbing. The parallels between the behaviour of participants in his studies and atrocities during times of war are clear. Why does destructive obedience occur? Several factors play a role. First, in Milgram's study the experimenter deliberately and expressly relieved participants of all personal responsibility for what was happening in the experiment. He indicated that he, not they, had responsibility for the learner's welfare. Thus, these participants could say,

Obedience: A form of social influence in which one individual issues orders to another to behave in a specific way.

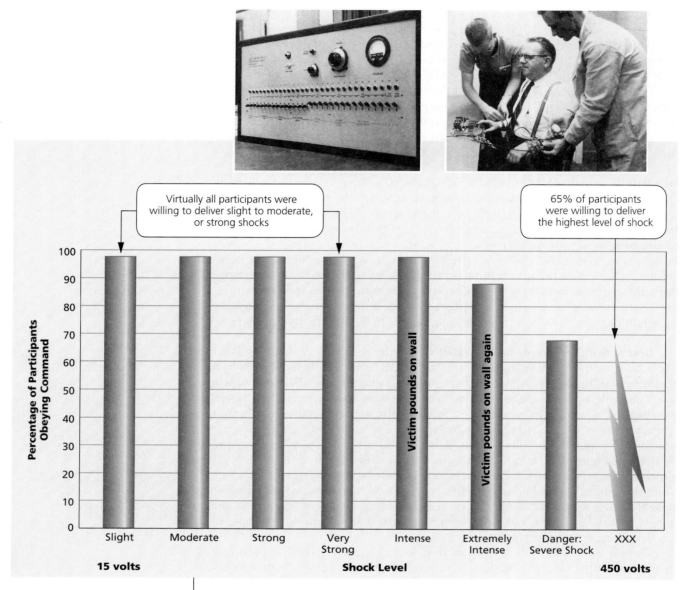

Figure 16.11
Milgram's Research on Obedience

The photo on the left shows the apparatus that was used by Milgram in his famous studies of obedience. The photo on the right shows the experimenter (Milgram, in a white coat) and a participant (rear) attaching the electrodes to the learner's (accomplice's) wrists. Results of the research, shown in the graph, indicated that 65 percent of participants were fully obedient to the experimenter's commands—they advanced to the highest shock level.

Source: Photos from the film Obedience, *Copyright 1965 by Stanley Milgram; Data based on Milgram, 1963.*

"I was just following orders." An analysis of real-life situations in which people obey commands that violate moral or ethical standards suggests that this diffusion of personal responsibility, or its absence, plays a major role. Indeed, these have been called "crimes of obedience"(Hans, 1992; Kelman & Hamilton, 1989).

Second, the Milgram experimenter presented clear and visible signs of authority, and in most societies, we learn very early that people in authority must be obeyed. In one experiment (Bushman, 1988), an older man ask adult pedestrians to give him money for a parking meter. The older man dressed either as a "business executive, or a bum or a fire-fighter." Power dressing made a difference to whether people gave money and why they did so, and that was the case also for a woman in uniform. Dress makes a difference whether it signals authority directly, as in the case of a uniform, or indirectly, as in the case of business clothes.

Third, and equally important, in Milgram's studies the experimenter's commands escalated gradually. That is, he did not request that participants administer the 450-volt shock immediately. Rather he proceeded one increment at a time. This gradual approach is important to achieving obedience. In short, several factors contributed to the high levels of obedience observed in Milgram's research and related studies.

Moreover, these factors merge together into a powerful force that most people find difficult to disobey. This does not deny however, that the commands of authority figures can be resisted (Zimbardo, 1995). Rather, history is filled with cases in which brave people opposed entrenched dictators and triumphed. Events in South Africa, some countries in Asia, and throughout Eastern Europe clearly illustrate that even powerful regimes can be resisted. What factors contribute to such dramatic events? Careful research on the nature of obedience indicates that *disobedient models*—people who are willing to oppose by taking the first, dangerous steps—make a difference.

For an overview of various tactics of social influence, see the **Key Concept** feature on page 670.

K E Y *QUESTIONS*

- What is conformity and what role do social norms play in it?
- What are some of the basic principles on which many different tactics of compliance are based?
- What is obedience, and how can it be resisted?

Critical Thinking

Think about situations in which people do annoying things—for example, carry on audible conversations in class or in movies. What is the social expectation as to whose responsibility it is to deal with those situations?

Prosocial Behaviour

Each day we help each other in various ways. Most often, we do so without expectation of direct or immediate repayment. **Prosocial behaviour** is actions we perform for the benefit of other people—without any direct advantage to ourselves; that is, *altruism*. However, sometimes people do not respond when help is needed and they may even ignore direct pleas for assistance (Steinfels, 1992). Let's consider the findings of psychological science in this area.

WHY DOES PROSOCIAL BEHAVIOUR OCCUR? Helping others is a common aspect of everyday life. Yet it is also a puzzling form of behaviour. Why, after all, should we help when we expect little or nothing in return? Research findings have identified three possible motives as the ones most likely to play a role.

The first of these is the **empathy–altruism hypothesis.** It suggests that when we encounter people who need help, we experience empathy—we somehow share their feelings or needs—and so are motivated to help them to make them feel better (e.g., Batson, 1991).

A second, and sharply contrasting, possibility is known as the **negative-state relief hypothesis** (e.g., Fultz et al., 1988). According to this view, when we see another person in need of help, this induces negative feelings in us. To relieve these, we help the person. Notice that although the result is the same, according to this idea, helping someone else makes *us* feel better.

Prosocial Behaviour: Actions that benefit others without necessarily providing any direct benefit to the persons who perform them.

Empathy–Altruism Hypothesis: A view suggesting that when we encounter someone who needs help, we experience empathy, and as a result, are motivated to help them in an unselfish manner.

Negative-State Relief Hypothesis: A view suggesting that we sometimes help others in order to relieve the negative feelings that their plight arouses in us.

Key Concept

Major Forms of Social Influence

Conformity

Individuals experience pressure to "stay in line"—to adhere to widely accepted social norms.

Obedience

One person issues direct orders to another.

Destructive Obedience
Sometimes individuals, such as those in Milgram's experiments, will obey a destructive request from an authority.

Compliance

Ingratiation
An individual (such as the salesperson below) tries to get a target person to like him or her and then uses this liking as a basis for exerting influence (e.g., making requests or selling a product).

Foot-in-the-Door Technique
The requester makes an initial small request, one with which the target person is almost certain to comply. This is followed by a larger request—the one the requester really wants.

Door-in-the-Face Technique
The requester makes a large initial request, one that the target person is almost certain to reject. This is followed by a smaller request—the one the requester really wants.

That's-Not-All Approach
An initial request or offer is made, and then, before the target person can respond, a small "extra" is added.

Playing Hard to Get
Individuals try to create the impression that they are very much in demand, so when they make a request, the target person fears losing a valuable friend or employee and, therefore, feels compelled to comply.

Fast-Approaching-Deadline Technique
A deadline is established to make the target person feel that it will be impossible to obtain something, such as an item for sale, after the deadline.

Finally, a third view emphasizes the role of genetic factors. According to the **genetic determinism hypothesis,** we help others because doing so increases the likelihood that our genes—or ones similar to them—will be passed on to the next generation (e.g., Browne, 1992; Burnstein et al., 1994). According to this view, then, we will offer help only to others who are somehow similar to ourselves and therefore likely to share some of our genes. Thus, we are especially likely to offer help to people who are related to us rather than to total strangers.

Figure 16.12 provides an overview of these three explanations for helping. Which of these views is most accurate? In many cases, we provide assistance because we empathize and our motivation to help is unselfish (e.g., Batson & Weeks, 1996; Shaw et al.,1994). However, helping may sometimes stem from more selfish motives as well (e.g., Burnstein et al., 1994; Cialdini et al., 1987).

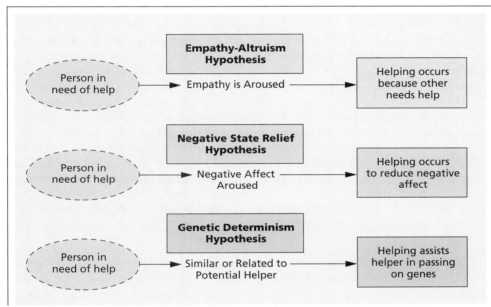

Figure 16.12
Three Possible Motives for Prosocial Behaviour

As shown here, prosocial behaviour may potentially stem from very different motives.

FACTORS THAT CHANGE THE TENDENCY TO HELP Now that we've examined some of the potential motives for prosocial behaviour, let's consider some of the situational factors that have been found to increase or reduce the likelihood that it will occur.

The Bystander Effect: There Is Not Always Safety in Numbers. The attention of the world was captured by a dramatic incident that occurred in New York City in the mid-1960s. A young woman named Catherine (Kitty) Genovese was attacked by a man with a knife as she was returning home from work. She screamed and screamed for help, and lights came on in many windows in nearby buildings. Not a single person came to her assistance, no one called the police, and the attack continued—until she died. The case of Kitty Genovese is not unique. In 1978, Ross used a hidden camera to show that, in Toronto, when an actor collapsed on Yonge Street or snatched a woman's purse in front of the City Hall, many saw what had happened, but no one helped (cited in Alcock et al., 1994).

What were the invisible barriers that prevented all of the witnesses from doing something about what was happening? Social psychologists Darley and Latane (1968) suggested that no one had come to Genovese's assistance because there were many potential helpers and everybody assumed that someone else would come to her assistance; they called this the **bystander effect.** In other words, these researchers suggested that, where helping is concerned, there may be danger—not safety—in numbers.

Genetic Determinism Hypothesis: The view that we help other persons who are similar or related to us because this increases the likelihood of our genes, or related genes, being passed on to the next generation.

Bystander Effect: A reduced tendency of witnesses to an emergency to help when they believe that there are other potential helpers present.

Many different studies have used staged emergencies—fires, the collapse of another participant, an accident of some sort—to study this hypothesis (e.g., Cramer et al., 1988; Darley & Latané, 1968). In every case, the more bystanders present, the less likely they were to offer to help. Moreover, the higher the population density in various cities, the lower the incidence of spontaneous helping behaviour (Levine et al., 1994). Why is that so? It appears that *diffusion of responsibility*—sharing responsibility among all potential helpers—plays a key role in such situations. Of course, diffusion of responsibility happens in other situations as well. For example, how likely people are to look both ways before they cross the street depends on whether there are other people crossing too—at least that is the case at traffic lights in Edmonton (Harrell, 1991).

Mood and Prosocial Behaviour Are you more likely to help when you are in a good mood or a bad mood? The answer to that question turns out to be more complicated than you might think. People in a good mood *are* often more willing to help (e.g., Baron, 1997; Isen, 1987; Wilson, 1981). But there are some complications in this seemingly straightforward picture. When helping might spoil a good mood, people in a good mood are less likely to help than those in a neutral or negative mood (Shaffer & Graziano, 1983).

Finally, what do we know about helping in a bad mood? Again the answer is not simple. When potential helpers focus on their own needs or misfortunes, they are indeed less likely to help. But when helping has the potential for making the helper feel good—for countering their current negative mood (for example, boosting their self-esteem), then the opposite may be true: people in a bad mood may actually be more helpful (e.g., Cunningham et al., 1990). In sum, prosocial behaviour is often influenced by our current moods. However, helping may be more or less likely in both good and bad moods—depending upon other factors present in the situation.

Costs of Helping Some forms of helping can cause embarrassment. Is the man on the park bench sleeping or is he in a coma? Are the children playing or are they fighting? Whether help is required is often an ambiguous question. If you are wrong, the result may be embarrassing. In a Canadian shopping centre, McDonald and McKelvie (1992) had a male accomplice drop either a mitten or a box of condoms. Nearly half (43 percent) of the bystanders helped retrieve the mitten, whereas only 17 percent returned the condoms. One man "helped" by kicking the condoms along the floor until they "caught up" with the accomplice! Thus, we are more reluctant to help if it is embarrassing to do so (Edwards, 1975).

People also are less likely to help if doing so will make them late for an appointment (Darley & Batson, 1973). This is particularly true when the appointment is perceived as important (Batson et al., 1978). Thus if you are already late for a final exam, you will be more likely to pass by someone who is in need of help.

Help is not always welcome. Why is that the case? First, there is a strong emphasis, in many Western cultures, on being independent. Needing help runs counter to that value and makes many people uneasy (Baron & Byrne, 1997). Second, when we need help, that implies that we cannot cope with the current situation ourselves or that someone else is somehow smarter, stronger, or more knowledgeable than we are (Nadler, 1987; Yates, 1992). Third, help often comes with strings attached. Accepting help obligates us to return the favour, and sometimes that is the motivation behind the offer of assistance. Fourth, sometimes help comes from even worse motives—to make us look less competent than we really are and undermine our self-esteem. This is called **overhelping,** and it is sometimes used to make another person "look bad" (Gilbert & Silvera, 1996). For all these reasons, many people may be reluctant to ask for help and may react negatively when help is offered.

Overhelping: Help given to others when they really don't need it, in order to make them appear less competent than they really are.

Attraction and Love

According to the lyrics of one old song, "Love makes the world go round." And most people agree: love—an intense emotional state involving attraction, sexual desire, and deep concern for another person—exerts a profound influence on our lives (Hecht et al., 1994; Hendrick & Hendrick, 1993). In this section, we'll examine what psychologists have discovered about love.

INTERPERSONAL ATTRACTION: WHY WE LIKE OR DISLIKE OTHERS Why do you like some people, but dislike others? The answers are provided by research on the nature and causes of liking and disliking, or **interpersonal attraction.**

Propinquity: Nearness Makes the Heart Grow Fonder In general, the closer to one another people live, work, or even sit in a large university classroom, the more likely they are to grow to like one another. Indeed, many friendships and romances start when individuals find themselves sitting near each another—often by chance (Festinger et al., 1950). *Propinquity* refers to physical proximity to other people, and it is an important factor in interpersonal attraction. Although recent developments in computer-mediated communication (for example, electronic mail) are creating new kinds of distance relationships (Lea & Spears, 1995), nevertheless, most friendships are still formed through face-to-face contact.

However, propinquity does more than simply bringing people into contact with one another. For example, the more often we are with other people, the more familiar they become, the more comfortable we feel, and the more we tend to like them (e.g., Moreland & Beach, 1992). That finding is known as the **repeated exposure effect,** and it operates with not only with people, but also with other features of our physical and psychological world (Bornstein, 1989; Jacoby et al., 1989; Zajonc, 1968).

Propinquity and Interpersonal Attraction

Most friendships and romances begin when people are brought into contact with one another—often by chance.

Similarity: Liking Others Who Are Like Ourselves You've probably heard both of the following proverbs: "Birds of a feather flock together" and "Opposites attract." Which is true? Existing evidence leaves little room for doubt: similarity wins hands down (e.g., Alicke & Largo, 1995; Byrne, 1971; Fehr, 1996). Similarity between individuals may relate to attitudes and beliefs, personality traits, personal habits such as drinking and smoking, sexual preferences, views about gender roles, or even to whether they are morning or evening persons (see Chapter 4; Joiner, 1994; Pilkington & Lydon, 1997). Even children and adolescents select their friends on the basis of similarity in sex, race, age, and preferences for certain activities (Aboud & Mendelson, 1998). It seems predictable then that we are more comfortable with computers that we perceive to have "personalities" that are similar to our own (Moon & Nass, 1996; Nass et al., 1995).

Interpersonal Attraction: The extent to which we like or dislike other persons.

Repeated Exposure Effect: The fact that the more frequently we are exposed to various stimuli (at least up to a point), the more we tend to like them.

Similarity: One Basis for Attraction

As this cartoon suggests, we often like persons who are similar to ourselves in some respect.

Source: Scott Adams, 1996.

Similarity works for attraction between groups as well. When groups believe their views are similar, they profess more liking for each other, even under circumstances where they never actually met. According to Grant (1993), "emphasizing intergroup similarities can improve intergroup relations provided that the members of both groups do not feel that their social identity is threatened." That seems like good advice. In Canada, we are really talented at celebrating our intergroup differences, but we seem to take for granted the values and beliefs we hold in common—to the point that sometimes we wonder if there *are* any, aside from the CBC.

Why do we like others who are similar to ourselves? The most plausible explanation is that they provide validation for our views or our personal characteristics (Goethals, 1986). That makes us feel good, and as a consequence, liking increases. Whatever the precise mechanisms involved, similarity is certainly one powerful determinant of attraction.

Reciprocity: Liking Others Who Like Us It may seem passing strange, but one important determinant of how attracted we are to another person is what we think they think of us. In general, the more other people like us, the more we like them (Condon & Crano, 1988; Curtis & Miller, 1986). Why is that the case? Largely, it is because we find positive evaluations rewarding and negative ones unpleasant. Remarkably, that happens even when we believe that others' assessments of us are not accurate (Swann et al., 1987) or that they are making an obvious attempt to use flattery (Drachman, DeCarufel, & Insko, 1978)!

Reciprocity goes beyond reciprocal liking. Social bonds require that confidences between friends be exchanged. Those confidences are called self-disclosures, and, between friends, self-disclosures are expected to be reciprocal. If not, liking decreases. For example, anxious people are less liked because they do not make disclosures about themselves when others do—presumably in order to protect themselves (Meleshko & Alden, 1993). The development of reciprocity in self-disclosure was studied by researchers at Lakehead University (Rotenberg & Chase,1992). They showed videotapes of children making self-disclosures to boys and girls in kindergarten and in grades two, four, and six, who sent a message back to the child in the videotape. The results showed that reciprocity develops sometime between ages seven and nine.

Mood and Attraction Suppose that you meet a stranger just after receiving some really good news: you got an A on an examination when you expected only a C. Would that make a difference to how you felt about the stranger? Positive feelings or moods—whatever their source—cause us to like people better (e.g., Byrne & Smeaton, 1998)—even if the positive feelings have nothing to do with the stranger. This is most likely to occur when we are neutral about the stranger to start with, and when we know little about him or her (Ottati & Isbell, 1996).

Physical Attractiveness Perhaps the most obvious factor affecting interpersonal attraction is *physical beauty*. Research findings indicate that humans are indeed suckers for a pretty or handsome face (e.g., Collins & Zebrowitz, 1995; Sprecher & Duck, 1994). This is true for both women and men, but the effects seem to be somewhat stronger for men (Feingold, 1990; Pierce, 1992). Looks influence attraction not only to potential romantic partners, but also to potential friends (e.g., Fehr, 1996). Moreover, research at the University of Saskatchewan has shown that we are quite aware of how much physical attractiveness matters to us even though we may be reluctant to admit it (Hadjistavropoulos & Genest, 1994). But what, precisely, makes other persons physically attractive? Clearly, concepts of beauty vary from culture to culture—but, surprisingly, less than you might guess. People tend to agree on what is or is not attractive even when judging other persons who differ from themselves in terms of race or ethnic background (Cunningham et al., 1995; Johnston & Franklin, 1993).

Judgments of attractiveness are also influenced by other aspects of appearance—eye glasses for example, although faces with glasses are perceived as more intelligent also (McKelvie, 1997). *Physique* is another important determinant of attraction, especially among young people. People whose physique matches the popular model—currently, slim but muscular—tend to receive higher evaluations than persons who depart from this model (e.g., Ryckman et al., 1995). In one ingenious study, researchers used a computer to vary the apparent physique (as shown in photos) of the very same male and female individuals. When these persons were made to appear overweight, they were rated as less attractive than when they were shown to be of normal weight or as very slim (Gardner & Tockerman, 1994).

Why is physical appearance so important? One reason is our assumption that physically attractive people also have attractive personalities, a phenomenon known as the *"what is beautiful is good"* stereotype (Dion et al., 1972). In one study (Dion & Dion, 1987), visitors to the Ontario Science Centre were asked to rate the personality traits and expected life outcome of attractive or unattractive individuals shown in photographs. Attractive people were rated as having more socially desirable personalities (e.g., warm, kind, exciting) than unattractive people. Moreover, they were expected to have more positive life outcomes (e.g., greater success, happiness, good relationships). Interestingly, people from collectivist cultures—cultures that place more emphasis on the group and less emphasis on the individual—are less likely to show these effects (Dion et al., 1990). Evolutionary psychology (e.g., Buss, 1997) suggests that we associate attractiveness with good health and good reproductive capacity. Choosing good-looking mates, therefore, increases the chances of contributing our genes to the next generation.

Whatever the causes, we do tend to like physically attractive persons more than physically unattractive ones. Moreover, such effects occur across the entire lifespan (Singh, 1993). Indeed, even one-year-old infants show a preference for attractive rather than unattractive strangers (Langlois, Roggman, & Riser-Danner, 1990), and people in their seventies and eighties still report a preference for those who are high in physical attractiveness (Pittenger, Mark, & Johnson, 1989).

LOVE: THE MOST INTENSE FORM OF ATTRACTION How do we know when we are in love? What *is* love? These questions have been pondered by countless poets, philosophers, and ordinary human beings for thousands of years (Hendrick & Hendrick, 1993), and also by social psychologists (e.g., Sternberg, 1998). Let's take a look at the answers that have emerged from psychological science on this fascinating topic.

Beverley Fehr
University of Winnipeg

Companionate and Passionate Love Social psychologists tend to distinguish between two major forms of love—*companionate* and *passionate* (Hatfield & Walster, 1978). **Companionate love** is defined by trust, respect, caring, and commitment. It is a stable, low-key emotion. In contrast, **passionate love** is an intense state in which the person experiences powerful feelings of attraction, sexual desire, and emotional highs and lows.

Which of these meanings—companionate or passionate—do people have in mind when they use the word "love"? To answer this question, researchers asked students to define *love* (Fehr, 1988; Fehr & Russell, 1991). The features that were listed were both companionate (e.g., caring, friendship, respect) *and* passionate (e.g., sexual attraction, butterflies in your stomach, thinking about the other person all the time). However, companionate love was seen as capturing the true meaning of love—the "essence" of love. These results have been replicated in other regions of Canada and in the United States, in both marital and dating couples (Fehr, 1993; Grote & Frieze, 1994) and with people ages seven to seventy years (Fehr, 1995). When people speak of "falling in love," however, typically they have in mind passionate love.

Companionate Love: A form of love involving a high degree of commitment and deep concern for the well-being of the beloved.

Passionate Love: A form of love in which feelings of strong attraction and sexual desire toward another person are dominant.

Companionate Love

Despite the excitement of passionate romantic love, research shows that companionate love is more highly correlated with satisfaction in dating and marital relationships.

Falling in Love Most experts agree that several conditions must be present for people to fall in love. First, the idea of romantic love must exist in their culture. In some cultures that is not the case (Lee, 1998). Second, there is intense emotional arousal. Third, there is a desire to be loved in return and fear that the relationship might end.

Romantic love sometimes develops quite suddenly. Many people fall in love as if they had been struck by emotional lightening (Murray & Holmes, 1993). Why does that happen? One explanation is based in evolutionary theory (Buss, 1999). According to this view, the reproductive success of our species depended on two factors—the desire to engage in sexual intercourse and the investment of time and energy to feed and protect offspring. Love leads to a lasting bond between males and females that is necessary for prolonged childcare. Lust is not enough. According to this theory, then, we are genetically prepared to fall in love. Another explanation suggests that early infant attachment to caregivers, which is essential to the survival of the infant, is the forerunner of love (Hatfield & Rapson, 1993).

Attachment and Love Which of the following best describes your feelings?

A. I find it relatively easy to get close to others and am comfortable depending on them and having them depend on me.

B. I find that others are reluctant to get as close as I would like. I often worry that my partner does not really love me or would not want to stay with me.

C. I am somewhat uncomfortable being close to others; I find it difficult to trust them completely and difficult to allow myself to depend on them.

These are descriptions of different attachment styles: (A) secure, (B) anxious/ambivalent and (C) avoidant. As you found in Chapter 8, people who experience a loving, responsive caregiver are likely to develop a *secure* attachment style not only as infants but also in their later relationships, which are loving, stable, and caring (Shaver et al., 1996). Infants whose primary caregiver was inconsistent— sometimes unavailable, other times intrusive—are said to develop an *anxious/ambivalent* style and as adults they frequently fall in and out of love. They are clingy, extremely jealous, and obsessive in their relationships. Finally, infants with a cold, unresponsive caregiver become *avoidant*. They remain relatively detached in romantic relationships, break up more, and experience less distress after breakups. Thus, people with different attachment styles appear to have different experiences in romantic relationships.

Does attachment style remain fixed for life in infancy? Not necessarily so. Attachment styles can, and do, change (Baldwin & Fehr, 1995). For example, people become more secure during the first year of marriage (Senchak & Leonard, 1972) and become avoidant when relating to a clingy, anxious partner. Conversely, many of us have also felt that someone we want to be close to is pulling away. Despite our past experience, we find ourselves needy and dependent.

Before continuing, please read the attachment style descriptions again. For each description, try to think of a relationship (e.g., with a romantic partner, friend, parent) in which you felt that way. When students at the University of Winnipeg were asked to do this, most of them were able to think of relationships that matched all three styles (Baldwin et al., 1996). Thus most people may have a range of attachment experiences and their self-reported attachment "style" may represent their typical pattern of relating.

Love: Why It Sometimes Dies Some romantic relationships do blossom into lifelong commitment. For many couples, however, the glow of love fades and leaves behind empty relationships from which one or both partners soon seek escape. For couples marrying today, it is far from certain that they will remain together permanently.

What makes the difference? Studies by social psychologists find that the reasons relationships end are complicated; many factors are at work here. Moreover, reasons vary with the type of relationship (Sprecher & Fehr, 1998). For example, marriages frequently end due to stressors such as financial difficulties, unemployment, and alcoholism, as well as sexual infidelity. Not all of these factors would necessarily be as relevant to dating couples. Nevertheless, there also are some common difficulties across relationships.

First, note that similarity is important not only in attraction, but also in the maintenance of a lifelong relationship. When partners discover that they are *dissimilar*—in important ways—love weakens and may die. For a person who is neat in his or her personal habits, a lover's relative sloppiness may have seemed charming—a breath of fresh air—when the relationship was new. According to Felmlee (1995), qualities that initially attracted us to a partner are sometimes the very qualities that later are seen as responsible for the breakup. For example, one participant in this research reported that he was initially attracted to her "refreshing innocence." When asked about qualities that contributed to the demise of the relationship, he mentioned her "lack of maturity." Another participant was initially attracted to her former partner because he was "funny and fun"; later she despised his "constant silliness." Such "fatal attractions" are most likely to occur for qualities on which the partners are dissimilar. Dissimilarities that were not present initially may also emerge with the passage of time as the two partners change—and perhaps diverge.

A second, potentially serious problem is simple boredom. Over time, unchanging routines of living together may lead partners to look for excitement—and perhaps new romantic partners—elsewhere (Fincham & Bradbury, 1993). Indeed, there is considerable evidence that people are more likely to end a relationship if they perceive that an attractive alternative partner is available to them (Sprecher & Fehr, 1998).

Third, sexual jealousy can undermine a loving relationship. While both sexes experience jealousy, they differ in some ways. For women, intense jealousy is their response when their partner is unfaithful emotionally. The issue here is the transfer of emotional commitment and the loss that results. For men, the most intense jealousy is triggered by apprehension that the partner has been unfaithful sexually (Bunk et al., 1995).

Fourth, as relationships continue, *self-defeating* patterns of behaviour may develop. Dating couples and newlyweds frequently express positive evaluations and feelings to one another. As time passes, however, partners may be more likely to fall into a pattern of making critical, hurtful comments. One interaction pattern that is particularly damaging to relationships is known as the **demand-withdraw pattern** (e.g., Christensen & Heavey, 1990). This is a vicious circle in which one person, typically the woman, puts pressure on her partner by making requests, criticizing, or complaining. He reacts by retreating and becoming unresponsive, causing her to intensify the demands. This in turn, precipitates further withdrawal from him. Unless couples can find a way to overcome such defeating patterns, their relationship is unlikely to survive.

Fifth, attributions may change as well, particularly if one or both partners are experiencing dissatisfaction with the relationship. Unhappy couples tend to attribute their partner's negative behaviours to internal factors ("she snapped at me because she is a nasty person") and positive behaviours to external factors ("he took out the garbage because his mother happens to be visiting"; e.g., Bradbury & Fincham, 1991). Happy couples show the reverse pattern ("she snapped at me because her boss has been very demanding lately"; "he took out the garbage because he is a thoughtful person"). Once partners begin to make internal attributions for one another's behaviour, it is difficult for a relationship to survive. A summary of the reasons why relationships end is shown in Figure 16.13.

Demand-Withdraw Pattern: An interaction pattern in which one partner criticizes or blames, and the other partner responds by retreating and becoming silent.

Figure 16.13
Factors That Cause Love to Fade

When several of these factors are present in a romantic relationship, they may undermine the love that brought the couple together in the first place, and ultimately destroy the relationship.

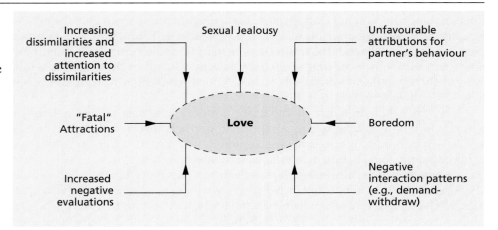

Keeping Love Alive Fortunately, many relationships continue to be satisfying and fulfilling for both partners. Recently, researchers have begun to examine ways in which intimate relationships are maintained. When people are asked, they list strategies such as "direct discussions and listening to one another" and "communicating that the relationship is important." Being supportive to one another, spending time together, and trying to make interactions pleasant are also regarded as important (e.g., Canary et al., 1993). According to research on the maintenance of marriage relationships, other important strategies include prosocial strategies (e.g., being pleasant, refraining from criticism), ceremonial strategies (e.g., celebrating special events, reminiscing), open communication, and spending time together. Granted, these strategies require effort; but given the rewards of maintaining a long-term intimate relationship, it would appear to be well worthwhile—even contributing to long life (Trovato, 1998).

In addition to these conscious maintenance strategies, fascinating new research suggests that we also may keep love alive in ways we are not aware of, as discussed in the **Research Process** section below.

the research process: *The Research Process:*
Maintaining Love: Does Illusion Help?

Typically, partners in a romantic relationship are less than perfect, and the same can be said for their relationships (Murray, 1999). Conflicts arise over how much time to spend together, whose friends to spend time with, what activities to do, and so on. During these times, people may begin to have doubts about their choice of mate. Recent research raises the intriguing possibility that people preserve happiness by living in a fantasy world in which their partner has only virtues and no faults. This process of *idealization* has been studied (e.g., Murray & Holmes, 1993, 1997) and here are the results.

In their first study, the researchers used the *experimental method* to investigate whether people in successful relationships deal with doubt by creating *illusions*—by reinterpreting their partner's shortcomings as strengths. In order to test this hypothesis, the researchers needed to design an experiment in which one group (the experimental group) would be made to have doubts about their partner, whereas another group (the control group) would not.

Here the researchers faced a distinct challenge—how does one get people in relationships to have doubts about their partner? To meet that challenge, they devised an ingenious procedure. Students in dating relationships were asked whether their partner tended to initiate conflict. As expected, most participants rated their partner as low in conflict initiation. Those in the experimental group then read a fake *Psychology Today* article in which it was argued that engaging in conflict is healthy for relationships. Presumably, this information threatened the participants' view of their partners. As predicted, those who read the fake article later described their partner as much more willing to initiate conflicts. By taking this kind of poetic licence, these participants were able to retain a positive view of their partner and relationship.

Similar findings were obtained in a follow-up study in which another group of participants was asked to list similarities between themselves and their dating partner. Most participants generated many similarities, but few differences. Those in the experimental group then read a bogus *Psychology Today* article suggesting that partners' awareness of differences promotes relationship intimacy. Later, when given an opportunity to add to their original responses, participants who were made to experience doubts about their relationship altered their previous responses. They now emphasized their differences and de-emphasized their similarities. The adjustments these participants made suggest that people changed their thinking to preserve positive perceptions of their partner and their relationship. If they were led to believe that there was a flaw, they constructed a new, more flattering image of reality. These data led Murray and Holmes to predict that people who are satisfied in relationships would see their partner in idealized ways.

This reasoning was tested in a *correlational study* by Murray, Holmes, and Griffin (1996a). Again, the researchers faced a methodology challenge: How could they assess whether participants' views of their partners were realistic or idealistic? Here is the procedure they adopted: married and dating couples were asked to rate themselves, their partner, and their ideal partner on a variety of attributes. The results indicated that participants tended to see their partners in a more positive light than their partners saw themselves. In addition, there was a close correspondence between individuals' ratings of their partner and their ratings of an ideal partner. Moreover, these idealized constructions were correlated with satisfaction—people were happier in their relationships when they idealized their partners and their partners idealized them (McGregor & Holmes, 1999).

While the results of this study are fascinating, the use of correlational methods does not permit conclusions about causality. Thus, we do not know whether idealization produced satisfaction or vice versa. That is, did satisfaction cause the participants to see their partners in glowing terms? Or did idealization produce satisfaction? There are other possibilities. For example, idealization could cause satisfaction, which, in turn, could cause partners to idealize one another even more.

In a third study, these researchers (Murray et al., 1996b) assessed idealization and satisfaction in dating couples three times over a one-year period. This was *longitudinal* research in which satisfaction and idealization are measured at various times. The researchers found that, over the year, partners who idealized each other more at the beginning experienced greater increases in satisfaction and greater decreases in conflicts and doubts. In fact, relationships were most likely to endure when individuals idealized their partners the most. The most amazing finding was that over time, individuals began think of themselves in accordance with their partner's idealized image. Thus, couples who idealized each other ultimately created the partners and the relationships they imagined!

K E Y *QUESTIONS*

- What factors influence interpersonal attraction?
- What are the two major forms of love studied by social psychologists?
- Under what conditions do people conclude that they are in love?
- What factors cause love to fade and perhaps disappear?
- What are the conscious strategies that people use to maintain relationships?
- What role does idealization play in the maintenance of intimate relationships?

Applying Social Psychology

Now that you are familiar with some basic concepts and principles of social psychology, we will discuss the application of this knowledge in real-world settings. Specifically, we will focus on the qualities of leadership and on how groups make decisions.

Leadership

Some people in groups have more influence than others. Psychologists define **leadership** as the process through which one member of a group (its leader) influences other group members toward the attainment of specific group goals (Yukl, 1994).

> **Leadership:** The process through which one member of a group (its leader) exerts influence over other group members with respect to the attainment of shared group goals.

Aung San Suu Kyi: An Example of Charismatic Leadership

This charismatic advocate of human rights in Burma/Myanmar was awarded the Nobel Peace Prize in 1991.

Who is most likely to become a leader? What are the different styles of leadership? What is charismatic leadership? Those are the questions we will ask here.

Recent research suggests that those who become leaders do, indeed, differ from others in a group (Kirkpatrick & Locke, 1991). They possess characteristics such as *drive* (the desire for achievement coupled with high energy and resolution), *self-confidence, creativity,* and *leadership motivation* (the desire to be in charge and exercise authority over others). Perhaps the most important single characteristic of leaders, however, is a high level of *flexibility*—the ability to recognize what actions or approach are required in a given situation, and then to act accordingly (Zaccaro et al., 1991).

Even though leaders may possess many similar characteristics, they differ from each other in their approach to leadership (e.g., George, 1995). These differences in leadership style are basic: they have been observed among thousands of different leaders in many different contexts (e.g., business groups, military groups, and sports teams), and in several different countries (Bass, 1990).

First, leaders differ in the extent to which they permit their followers to have any say in decision making. *Autocratic* leaders make decisions unilaterally, while *democratic* leaders invite input and participation in decision making from their followers. Second is the extent to which leaders are *directive*—dictate how followers should carry out their assigned tasks—versus *permissive*—give them the freedom to work in any way they wish (Muczyk & Reimann, 1987). Third, leaders' styles differ in emphasis. *Task-orientated* leaders focus on getting the task done—whatever it happens to be. *Person-oriented* leaders put a high priority on maintaining good, friendly relations with their followers.

Some leaders exert powerful effects on millions of people, and by doing so, change their society. Examples are Winston Churchill, Nelson Mandela, and Aung San Suu Kyi. These special people are examples of **charismatic leaders.**

Charismatic leaders develop a special kind of relationship with their followers, one in which the leader can "make ordinary people do extraordinary things" (Conger, 1991). Followers are devoted and loyal. They subscribe to the leader's ideas and sacrifice their own best interests. They achieve levels of performance that are beyond expectations. But what, precisely, do charismatic leaders do to generate this kind of relationship with followers?

Studies designed to answer this question point to the following conclusion: First, and most important, charismatic leaders propose a vision (Howell & Frost, 1989)—a vivid, emotion-provoking image of what their followers can—and should—become. Second, they offer a way of reaching this goal, because a goal that seems perpetually out of reach is unlikely to motivate people. Third, charismatic leaders engage in *framing* (Conger, 1991). They define the goal in a way that gives meaning and purpose to followers. Consider this example of two stonecutters working on a cathedral in the Middle Ages. When asked what they were doing, one replied, "Why, cutting this stone, of course." The other answered, "Building the world's most beautiful temple to the glory of God." Which one would you follow? The answer seems obvious. See Figure 16.14 for more about charismatic leaders.

Many charismatic leaders use their skills in the best interests of their group or society. But others use this leadership style for selfish, immoral, and illegal purposes (Howell & Avolio, 1993). A recent example is the cult leader Luc Jouret, who ultimately led fifty-three people in Quebec and Switzerland to their deaths in October 1994. In short, charismatic leadership is definitely a two-edged sword. It can be used to promote beneficial social change consistent with the highest principles and ethical standards; or it can be used for evil purposes. The difference lies in the personal conscience and moral code of the person who wields it.

Charismatic Leaders: Leaders who exert profound effects on their followers and establish special types of relationships with them.

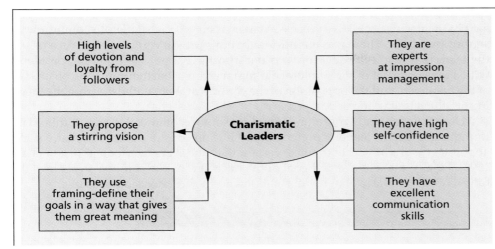

Figure 16.14
Charismatic Leaders: How They Operate

Research findings indicate that transformational leaders exert their profound effects on others because of the factors shown here.

Making Decisions in Groups

Groups of people make decisions often. These may vary from which movie to go to Saturday night, to which play to make in a football game. More serious, perhaps, are the group decisions made in industry about taking over another company, or in government retaliating with force in response to threat, in the RCMP about how to handle a crowd of people, or in child protection agencies about which children to take into custody (Kelly & Milner, 1996).

Sometimes groups of people make bad decisions; it is to the findings of social psychologists as to why that happens and what we can do to prevent bad decision making that we will now turn.

MAKING BAD DECISIONS: GROUPTHINK In 1986, a decision was taken to launch the spaceship Challenger into space. The consequence was the loss of every person on board as well as the spaceship itself. An investigation was held into how the decision to proceed with the launch was taken (Report of the [U.S.] Presidential Commission, 1986). The finding was that there was "a serious flaw in the decision making process leading up to the launch of the flight." That process showed symptoms of **groupthink** (Janis, 1967, 1997; Peterson et al., 1998; Whyte, 1998).

The Result of Groupthink at NASA

The tragedy of the space shuttle *Challenger*, which exploded just after take-off, can be attributed to *groupthink*, a process in which faulty decisions are made by groups because of the pressure to conform.

Groupthink is the result of a number of conditions that occur frequently when groups try to take decisions. These conditions amount to pressure towards conformity. First, the group has a directive leader who is known to favour a particular decision. The group discussion is therefore limited to one solution. Second, because only one solution is discussed, there is an illusion that the group members are unanimous in their opinions. If someone tries to raise another alternative, self-appointed mind-guards discount what is said and discredit the speaker. Thus there is direct pressure on members with different views to keep quiet. As a result, the discussion is biased, it fails to consider all of the alternatives, and it fails to consider the risks of the favoured solution. Third, the members of the group feel that they are invulnerable—that failure is not a possibility. The outcome of groupthink is a bad decision, and the research effort to understand how that happens is ongoing (Esser, 1998).

> **Groupthink:** A set of conditions in a group that leads to bad decisions.

After the Challenger was lost, it was discovered that these factors had been present in the decision-making process. Management officials failed to communicate serious problems. There was an illusion that this project could not fail. As a result, the team that made the decision was not informed about the potential problems with a particular set of seals in too-cold temperatures. Furthermore, the objections of the engineers and the opposition of the contractor were withheld from the meeting at which it was decided to proceed.

How can we avoid groupthink? Here are some recommendations: Withhold information about the leader's preference; invite and consider every alternative; and appoint a devil's advocate to make certain that no risk is overlooked (Chen et al., 1996). Finally, make the stated goal of the decision-making process to achieve the fullest review of the available information and the best decision possible.

KEY QUESTIONS

- How do charismatic leaders influence their followers so strongly?
- What factors predict that a group may make a bad decision?
- How can we avoid groupthink?

Making Psychology Part of Your Life

Enhancing the Accuracy of Your Social Judgments

*D*uring the course of daily life, you make many judgments about others. *Will two people hit it off if I arrange for them to meet? Should I recommend a friend for a job?* In making such judgments it is important to be as accurate as possible. Yet, as we have seen, social cognition is subject to many potential sources of error and bias. Keep the following points in mind, and the chances are good that the accuracy of your judgments about others will be markedly improved.

1. *Be aware—and beware—of the impact of heuristics.* Try to avoid the path of least resistance associated with the use of heuristics. In evaluating another's performance on a job, on the playing field, or elsewhere, it is tempting to follow the availability heuristic and weigh information that comes readily to mind more heavily than information that is harder to recall. This can be a serious mistake. In making such judgments, try to remember as much information about people as possible *before* forming conclusions. This requires extra work, but increased accuracy may well justify the effort.

2. *Avoid errors of attribution.* It is often tempting to assume that other people act as they do because they are "that kind of person"—that their overt actions stem from internal traits. Frequently this is not the case. Yet because of the fundamental attribution error, we tend to assume that we know more about others than we do. Try to consider the context of others' behaviour and the impact of potential external causes. Consider also your mood, because you are more likely to make the fundamental attribution error when you are in a good mood (Forgas, 1998). Doing so may help you avoid jumping to false conclusions.

3. *Remember that not everyone shares your views.* Because of the false consensus effect, it is tempting to assume that others are more similar to us than they really are. Try to remind yourself from time to time that it is dangerous to assume that other people share your views, your preferences, and your perspective. The chances are better than fifty-fifty that they are less similar to you in these respects than you think.

4. *Recognize the self-serving bias.* In almost any situation where we interact with others, it is tempting to view ourselves as the major cause of positive outcomes while blaming others—even computers (Moon & Nass, 1998)—for negative results. In fact, this tendency—the *self-serving bias*—is so powerful and pervasive that we are often totally unaware of its presence. Do not overlook it! It can lead you to undervalue the contributions of others while inflating

your own. Try to remember that in their eyes, it is probably you who are to blame for negative outcomes while they are responsible for positive ones.

5. *Remember that no one—not even you—is totally immune to prejudice.* Growing evidence indicates that prejudice has deep roots in basic social cognition and cannot be easily avoided by anyone (Anderson et al., 1990). Stereotypes, and the tendency to divide the social world into "us" and "them," are matters of fact in social thought. Recognize the toll on your own emotions that prejudice takes (Jussim, 1991) and at telling jokes that diminish minority groups has an effect upon your own thought processes (Maio et al., 1997). Ask yourself, "Am I assuming certain traits because people belong to some group?" and "Am I judging them on the basis of their background?" If you keep asking these questions and answer them honestly, you will learn to recognize prejudice and lessen its impact on your thoughts and judgments.

Summary and Review

Key Questions

Social Thought

■ **What is the fundamental attribution error?** The fundamental attribution error (also known as *overattribution*) is our tendency to overestimate the importance of internal (dispositional) causes of others' behaviour.

■ **What role does attribution play in perceptions of rape victims?** Rape victims are often blamed by other people for this crime against them.

■ **What is the self-serving bias?** The self-serving bias is our tendency to attribute our own positive outcomes to internal causes and our own negative outcomes to external factors, including other people.

■ **What is the false consensus effect?** The false consensus effect refers to our tendency to assume that others share our views to a greater extent than is really true.

■ **How do we deal with social information that is inconsistent with our expectations?** In general, we tend to pay greater attention to such information than to information that is consistent with our expectations, but we also tend to reject it as useless.

■ **What is counterfactual thinking? How does it change over time?** Counterfactual thinking involves imagining events and outcomes that didn't occur. Over time, we shift from focusing on things we did that didn't turn out well, to focusing on things we didn't do but should have done.

■ **What are attitudes?** Attitudes are lasting evaluations of various aspects of the social world—evaluations that are stored in memory.

■ **What is the less-leads-to-more effect?** The less-leads-to-more effect refers to the fact that the weaker the reasons we have for engaging in attitude-discrepant behaviour, the more likely we are to change these attitudes.

■ **What is cognitive dissonance, and how can it be reduced?** Cognitive dissonance is an unpleasant state we experience when we notice that two attitudes we hold, or our attitudes and our behaviour, are somehow inconsistent. Dissonance can be reduced by changing our attitudes or behaviour so that they are consistent.

■ **How can hypocrisy be used to change behaviour?** Hypocrisy can lead individuals to change their behaviour by causing them to recognize gaps between their attitudes and their behaviour, thereby generating high levels of cognitive dissonance.

■ **What factors were found to influence persuasion in early research?** Early research on persuasion found that the success of persuasion was strongly affected by characteristics of the sources (e.g., their expertise), characteristics of the persuasive messages sent (e.g., whether they were one-sided or two-sided), and characteristics of the audience.

■ **What is the elaboration likelihood model, and how does it explain persuasion?** The elaboration likelihood model is a cognitive model of persuasion that focuses on the thoughts people have about a persuasive communication. Persuasion occurs via the *central route* when people are able to think carefully about the arguments presented, and via the *peripheral route* when people are not motivated to think carefully about these arguments.

Social Behaviour

■ **What are some of the major causes of prejudice?** Prejudice stems from direct competition between social groups, social categorization, social learning, cognitive factors such as stereotypes, and our emotions and moods.

■ **What do research findings indicate about the effects of mood on prejudice?** People are more likely to express prejudiced views when they are in a bad mood. They are less likely to show prejudice when they are in a good mood.

- **What attributions do members of disadvantaged groups make for a failure experience? Why?** Members of disadvantaged groups tend to minimize the discrimination they experience and instead blame themselves for failure. This allows them to preserve social self-esteem and maintain the perception of control.

- **How can prejudice be reduced?** Prejudice can be reduced by socializing children to be tolerant of others, through increased intergroup contact, and through recategorization—shifting the boundary between "us" and "them" so as to include previously excluded groups.

- **What is conformity and what role do social norms play in it?** Conformity refers to the tendency to behave like others and to act in accordance with existing social norms.

- **What are some of the basic principles on which many different tactics of compliance are based?** Tactics of compliance are based on the principles of liking or friendship (e.g., ingratiation), commitment or consistency (e.g., the foot-in-the-door technique), reciprocity (e.g., the door-in-the-face technique), and scarcity (e.g., playing hard to get).

- **What is obedience, and how can it be reduced?** Obedience is a form of social influence in which individuals obey the commands of persons in authority. It can be reduced by convincing the persons involved that authorities are pursuing selfish goals, by exposure to disobedient models, and by increased personal responsibility.

- **How do the empathy–altruism, negative-state relief, and genetic determinism hypotheses explain prosocial behaviour?** The empathy–altruism hypothesis proposes that we help others out of the unselfish desire to assist them. The negative-state relief hypothesis suggests that we help them because this makes us feel better. The genetic determinism hypothesis suggests that we help others who are similar to ourselves in order to get our genes (or, at least, similar genes) into the next generation.

- **What is the bystander effect and why does it occur?** The bystander effect refers to the fact that the more persons present at the scene of an accident, the less likely the victim is to receive aid. It occurs because of diffusion of responsibility among all bystanders.

- **How does mood affect helping?** Being in a good mood can enhance helping unless the costs of helping are high and will interfere with this mood. Being in a bad mood can enhance helping by making the persons who help feel better.

- **How do people react to being helped by others?** People sometimes react to being helped with feelings of gratitude, but they may also fear the strings attached to such help, and may realize that unnecessary helping (overhelping) can harm their public image.

- **What factors influence interpersonal attraction?** Interpersonal attraction is influenced by propinquity, similarity, and physical attractiveness, plus many other factors as well.

- **What are the two major forms of love studied by social psychologists? How are they defined?** Companionate love is a steady, stable, low-key emotion characterized by trust, respect, caring, and so on. Passionate love is an intense state involving emotional highs and lows, sexual desire, and powerful feelings of attraction.

- **Under what conditions do people conclude that they are in love?** Individuals conclude that they are in love when their culture has the concept of romantic love and when they experience strong emotional arousal in the presence of a person defined as appropriate for love by their culture.

- **What factors cause love to fade and perhaps disappear?** Love can be weakened by such factors as sexual jealousy, increased dissimilarity or increased recognition of existing dissimilarity, "fatal attractions," boredom, and patterns in which negative statements and attributions replace positive ones.

- **What role does idealization play in the maintenance of intimate relationships?** The more individuals idealize their partner, the greater their satisfaction in the relationship will be. In part, this occurs because eventually partners begin to live up to these ideals.

- **What are the conscious strategies that people use to maintain their relationships?** Direct discussions, open communication, spending time together, refraining from criticism, and celebrating special events are among the ways that people maintain their relationships.

Applying Social Psychology

- **How do charismatic leaders influence their followers so strongly?** Charismatic leaders are able to propose an attractive vision or dream, along with a route for reaching this vision. Such leaders also are self-confident, charismatic, and able to make a good impression on others.

- **What factors predict that a group may make a bad decision?** Bad decisions are the result of a directive leader with a stated opinion—with which group members feel they must agree. The result is pressure towards conformity and biased discussion, which produce an illusion of unanimity. Also present is a sense of invulnerability—that the group cannot fail—which leads the group to ignore potential risks.

- **How can we avoid groupthink?** To avoid groupthink, make each member of the group responsible for seeing to it that there is the fullest possible consideration of the available information, including all potential risks, and the best decision possible.

Key Terms

Attitudes (p. 648)

Attribution (p. 641)

Automatic Vigilance (p. 645)

Bystander Effect (p. 671)

Central Route to Persuasion (p. 649)

Charismatic Leaders (p. 680)

Cognitive Dissonance (p. 650)

Compliance (p. 664)

Companionate Love (p. 675)

Conformity (p. 663)

Consensus (p. 641)

Consistency (p. 641)

Contact Hypothesis (p. 660)

Counterfactual Thinking (p. 646)

Demand-Withdraw Pattern (p. 677)

Discrimination (p. 654)

Distinctiveness (p. 641)

Door-in-the-Face Technique (p. 666)

Elaboration Likelihood Model (p. 649)

Empathy–Altruism Hypothesis (p. 669)

False Consensus Effect (p. 644)

Fast-Approaching-Deadline Technique (p. 666)

Foot-in-the-Door Technique (p. 665)

Forced Compliance (p. 650)

Fundamental Attribution Error (p. 642)

Genetic Determinism Hypothesis (p. 671)

Groupthink (p. 681)

Ingratiation (p. 665)

Interpersonal Attraction (p. 673)

Leadership (p. 679)

Less-Leads-to-More Effect (p. 651)

Lowball Procedure (p. 666)

Negative-State Relief Hypothesis (p. 669)

Obedience (p. 667)

Overhelping (p. 672)

Passionate Love (p. 675)

Peripheral Route to Persuasion (p. 650)

Playing Hard to Get (p. 666)

Prejudice (p. 654)

Prosocial Behaviour (p. 669)

Realistic Conflict Theory (p. 654)

Recategorization (p. 660)

Repeated Exposure Effect (p. 673)

Self-Serving Bias (p. 643)

Social Categorization (p. 655)

Social Cognition (p. 644)

Social Influence (p. 663)

Social Norms (p. 663

Social Psychology (p. 640)

Stereotypes (p. 657)

That's-Not-All Technique (p. 666)

Critical Thinking Questions

Appraisal

Social thought and social interaction occur together in everyday life. Do you think that studying them separately makes sense? Or should they be studied together, as they occur in most situations? Explain your opinion.

Controversy

Do you think that racial, ethnic, and religious prejudices can ever be completely eliminated? If not, how does our tendency to divide the social world into "us" and "them" assure that we will always have such attitudes?

Making Psychology Part of Your Life

Now that you know more about the many techniques people use to influence each other, how do you think that you can use this information to (1) be more effective in exerting influence over others, and (2) resist such influence yourself? What techniques do you think might be most useful to you in your own life? Which do you feel might be hardest to resist when used by other people?

Weblinks

Check out our Companion Website at www.pearsoned.ca/baron for additional Websites, activities, and more.

False Consensus Effects for the 1992 Canadian Referendum

www.cpa.ca/cjbsnew/1995/july/koestner.html

The authors of this study used an important Canadian political event to examine the extent to which cognitive and motivational factors influence consensus estimates. A significant false consensus bias was observed in estimates of how Canadians would vote in the 1992 constitutional referendum.

Online Social Psychology Studies

www.socialpsychology/expts.htm

This site contains links to social psychology studies that are being conducted currently on the Internet. Areas of study include interpersonal relations, social perception, and other aspects of social psychology. To participate in a study, simply click on the underlined hypertext.

Can you guess?

www.zzyx.ucsc.edu/~archer/

On this page you will find a number of sample nonverbal social communications that vary in different cultures. See if you can guess the answers, then check and see if you were correct.

Should have...Could have

www.psych.nwu.edu/psych/people/faculty/roese/research/cf/cfnews.htm

Interested in knowing more about counterfactual thinking? Log on here and follow the links to news and online articles.

Challenger Report

www.ksc.nasa.gov/shuttle/missions/51-l/docs/rogers-commission/table-of-contents.html

This is the report on the space shuttle *Challenger* accident. Key in this address and click on "the contributing cause of the accident" to read about the contribution of groupthink to this disastrous decision.

Ethnic Issues

www.cpa.ca/cjbsnew/1996/ful_edito.html

This is an article by Esses and Gardner entitled "Multiculturalism in Canada." It appeared in a special issue of the *Canadian Journal of Behavioral Science,* dedicated to research findings on ethnic relations in Canada.

APPENDIX

Statistics
Uses and Potential
Abuses

At many points in this text, it has been noted that one benefit you should gain from your first course in psychology is the ability to think about human behaviour in a new way. This appendix will expand on that theme by offering a basic introduction to one essential aspect of psychological thinking: **statistics**.

What does this special form of mathematics have to do with psychology or with thinking like a psychologist? The answer involves the fact that all fields of science require two major types of tools. First, scientists need various kinds of equipment to gather the data they seek. Obviously, this equipment differs from field to field; for example, biologists use microscopes, astronomers employ telescopes, and geologists wield hammers (or even dynamite) in their work.

Second, all scientists need some means for interpreting the findings of their research—for determining the meaning of the information they have acquired and its relationship to important theories in their field. Again, this varies from one science to another. In most cases, though, some type of mathematics is involved. Psychology is no exception to this general rule: To understand the findings of their research (and, hence, important aspects of human behaviour), psychologists perform statistical analyses of the data they collect.

As you'll soon see, statistics are a flexible tool and can be used for many different purposes. In psychology, however, they are usually employed to accomplish one or more of the following tasks: (1) summarizing or describing large amounts of data; (2) comparing individuals or groups of individuals in various ways; (3) determining whether certain aspects of behaviour are related (whether they vary together in a systematic manner); and (4) predicting future behaviour from current information. In the pages that follow we'll consider each of these major uses of statistics by psychologists. After doing so, we'll explore several ways in which statistics can be abused—how they can be employed to disguise or conceal important facts rather than to clarify them.

Statistics: Mathematical procedures used to describe data and draw inferences from them.

Descriptive Statistics

Suppose that a psychologist conducts an experiment concerned with the effects of staring at others in public places. The procedures of the study are simple. He stares at people in stores, airports, and a variety of other locations, and he records the number of seconds until they look away—or until they approach to make him stop! After carrying out these procedures twenty times, he obtains the data shown in Table A.1. Presented in this form, the scores seem meaningless. If they are grouped together in the manner shown in Figure A.1, however, a much clearer picture emerges. Now we can see at a glance that the most frequent score is about four seconds; that fewer people look away after three or five seconds; and that even fewer look away very quickly (after two seconds) or after a longer delay (six seconds). This graph presents a **frequency distribution:** It indicates the number of times each score occurs within an entire set of scores. Here, the frequency distribution indicates how many times scores of one, two, three, four, five, or six seconds were recorded in the study of staring.

Frequency Distribution: The frequency with which each score occurs within an entire distribution of scores.

TABLE A.1

Raw Data from a Simple Experiment

When a psychologist stares at strangers in a public place, these people either look away or approach him in the number of seconds shown. Note that more people look away or approach after four seconds than at any other value.

	Number of Seconds until Person Either Looks Away or Approaches
Person 1	4
Person 2	4
Person 3	1
Person 4	4
Person 5	3
Person 6	2
Person 7	5
Person 8	3
Person 9	6
Person 10	5
Person 11	4
Person 12	4
Person 13	3
Person 14	3
Person 15	5
Person 16	4
Person 17	4
Person 18	2
Person 19	6
Person 20	5

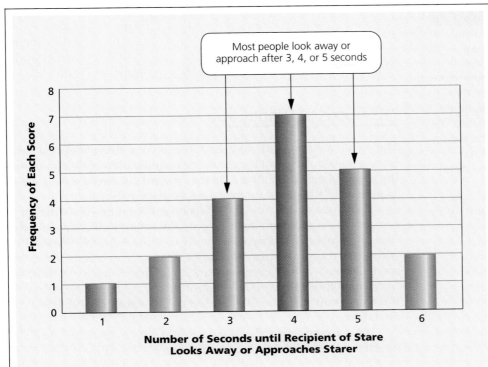

Figure A.1
A Frequency Distribution

In a frequency distribution, scores are grouped together according to the number of times each occurs. This one suggests that most people react to being stared at after about four seconds.

A graph such as the one in Figure A.1 provides a rough idea of the way a set of scores is distributed. In science, however, a rough idea is not sufficient; more precision is required. In particular, it would be useful to have an index of (1) the middle score of the distribution of scores (their **central tendency**) and (2) the extent to which the scores spread out around this point (their **dispersion**). Such measures are provided by **descriptive statistics.**

Measures of Central Tendency

You are already familiar with one important measure of central tendency: the **mean,** or average. We calculate a mean by adding all scores and then dividing by the total number of scores. The mean represents the typical score in a distribution and in this respect is often quite useful. Sometimes, though, it can be misleading. This is because the mean can be strongly affected by one or a few extreme scores. To see why this is so, consider the following example. Ten families live on a block. The number of children in each family is shown in Table A.2. Adding these numbers together and dividing by ten yields a mean of four. Yet, as you can see, not one family actually has four children. Most have none or two, but one has eight and another has nineteen.

In cases such as this one, it is better to refer to other measures of central tendency. One of these is the **mode**—the most frequently occurring score. As you can see, the mode of the data in Table A.2 is 2: More families have two children than have any other number. Another useful measure of central tendency is the **median**—the midpoint of the distribution. Fifty percent of the scores fall at or above the median, while 50 percent fall at or below this value. Returning to the data in Table A.2, the median also happens to be 2: Half the scores fall at or below this value, while half fall at or above it.

As you can readily see, both the mode and the median provide more accurate descriptions of the data than does the mean in this particular example. But please

Central Tendency: The middle area of a distribution of scores.

Dispersion: The extent to which scores in a distribution spread out or vary around the centre.

Descriptive Statistics: Statistics that summarize the major characteristics of an array of scores.

Mean: A measure of central tendency derived by adding all scores and dividing by the number of scores.

Mode: A measure of central tendency indicating the most frequent score in an array of scores.

Median: A measure of central tendency indicating the midpoint of an array of scores.

TABLE A.2

How the Mean Can Sometimes Be Misleading

Ten families have a total of forty children among them. The mean is 4.0, but, as you can see, not one family has this number of children. This illustrates the fact that the mean, while a useful measure of cen tral tendency, can be distorted by a few extreme scores.

	Number of Children
Family 1	0
Family 2	0
Family 3	2
Family 4	2
Family 5	2
Family 6	2
Family 7	2
Family 8	3
Family 9	19
Family 10	8

Total = 40 children

Mean = 40/10 = 4.0

Range: The difference between the highest and lowest scores in a distribution of scores.

Variance: A measure of dispersion reflecting the average squared distance between each score and the mean.

Standard Deviation: A measure of dispersion reflecting the average distance between each score and the mean.

Normal Curve: A symmetrical, bell-shaped frequency distribution. Most scores are found near the middle, and fewer and fewer occur toward the extremes. Most psychological characteristics are distributed in this manner.

note that this is not always or even usually the case. It is true only in instances where extreme scores distort the mean. In fact, there is no single rule for choosing among these measures. The decision to employ one over the others should be made only after careful study of frequency distributions such as the one shown in Figure A.1.

Measures of Dispersion

The mean, median, and mode each tell us something about the centre of a distribution, but they provide no indication of its shape. Are the scores bunched together? Do they spread out over a wide range? This issue is addressed by measures of dispersion.

The simplest measure of dispersion is the **range**—the difference between the highest and lowest scores. For example, the range for the data on number of children per family in Table A.2 is 19 (19 − 0 = 19). Although the range provides some idea of the extent to which scores vary, it suffers from one key drawback: It does not indicate how much the scores spread out around the centre. Information on this important question is provided by the **variance** and **standard deviation**.

The variance provides a measure of the average distance between scores in a distribution and the mean. It indicates the extent to which, on average, the scores depart from (vary around) the mean. Actually, the variance refers to the average squared distance of the scores from the mean; squaring eliminates negative numbers. The standard deviation then takes account of this operation of squaring by calculating the square root of the variance. So the standard deviation, which is widely used in psychology, represents the average distance between scores and the mean in any distribution. The larger the standard deviation, the more the scores are spread out around the centre of the distribution.

The Normal Curve

Despite the inclusion of several examples, this discussion so far has been somewhat abstract. As a result, it may have left you wondering what descriptive statistics have to do with understanding human behaviour or thinking like a psychologist. One important answer involves their relationship to a special type of frequency distribution known as the **normal curve.**

While you may never have encountered this term before, you are probably quite familiar with the concept it describes. Consider the following characteristics: height, size of vocabulary, and strength of motivation to attain success. Suppose you obtained measurements of each from thousands of individuals. What would be the shape of each of these distributions? If you guessed that they would all take the form shown in Figure A.2, you are correct. In fact, on each dimension most scores would pile up in the middle, and fewer and fewer scores would occur farther away from this value. In short, most people would be found to be average height, would have average vocabularies, and would show average desire for success; very few would be extremely high or low on these characteristics. We should add, by the way, that the normal curve applies to an amazingly wide range of human characteristics—everything from personality traits to cognitive abilities and physical attributes.

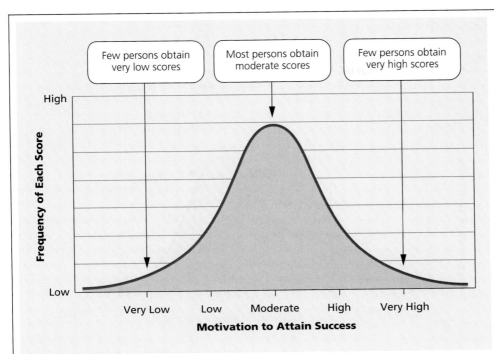

Figure A.2
The Normal Curve

On many dimensions relating to behaviour, scores show the kind of frequency distribution illustrated here: the normal curve. Most scores pile up in the middle, and fewer and fewer occur toward the extremes.

What does the normal curve have to do with the use of descriptive statistics? A great deal. One key property of the normal curve is as follows: Specific proportions of the scores within it are contained in certain areas of the curve; moreover, these portions can be defined in terms of the standard deviation of all of the scores. Therefore, once we know the mean of a normal distribution and its standard deviation, we can determine the relative standing of any specific score within it. Perhaps a concrete example will help clarify both the nature and the value of this relationship.

Figure A.3 presents a normal distribution with a mean of 5.0 and a standard deviation of 1.0. Let's assume that the scores shown are those on a test of desire for power. Suppose that we now encounter an individual with a score of 7.0. We know that she is high on this characteristic, but how high? On the basis of descriptive statistics—the mean and standard deviation—and of the properties of the normal curve, we can tell. Statisticians have found that 68 percent of the scores in a normal distribution fall within one standard deviation of the mean, either above or below it. Similarly, fully 96 percent of the scores fall within two standard deviations of the mean. Given this information, we can conclude that a score of 7 on this test is very high indeed: Only 2 percent of individuals taking the test attain a score equal to or higher than this one (refer to Figure A.3).

In a similar manner, descriptive statistics can be used to interpret scores in any other distribution, providing it approaches the normal curve in form. As noted above, a vast array of psychological characteristics and behaviours do seem to be distributed in this manner. As a result, we can readily determine an individual's relative standing on any of these dimensions from just two pieces of information: the mean of all scores in the distribution and the standard deviation. Little wonder, then, that the normal curve has sometimes been described as a statistician's or psychologist's delight.

Now imagine that your first psychology test contains fifty multiple-choice items. You obtain a score of 40. Did you do well or poorly? If your instructor provides two additional pieces of information—the mean of all the scores in the class

Figure A.3
Interpreting Scores by Means of the Normal Distribution

Sixty-eight percent of the scores in a normal distribution fall within one standard deviation of the mean (above or below it). Similarly, fully 96 percent of the scores fall within two standard deviations of the mean. Thus, on a test with a mean of 5.0 and a standard deviation of 1.0, only 2 percent of individuals attain a score of 7.0 or higher.

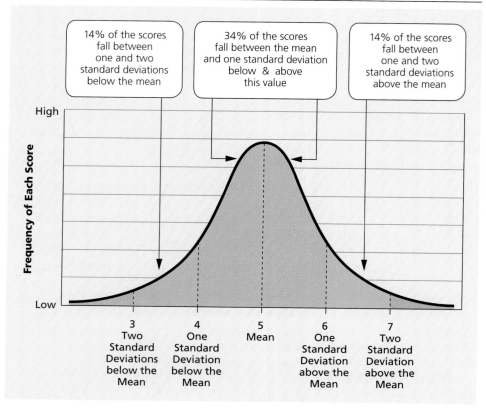

14% of the scores fall between one and two standard deviations below the mean

34% of the scores fall between the mean and one standard deviation below & above this value

14% of the scores fall between one and two standard deviations above the mean

and the standard deviation—you can tell. Suppose that the mean is 35 and the standard deviation is 2.50. The mean indicates that most people got a lower score than you did. The relatively small standard deviation indicates that most scores were quite close to the mean—only about twice this distance above the mean. Your score is two standard deviations above the mean, which indicates that only 2 percent of students fared better than you on the test. Further—and here is a key point—this conclusion would be accurate whether there were 30, 100, or 500 students in the class, assuming the mean and standard deviation remained unchanged. It is precisely this type of efficiency that makes descriptive statistics so useful for summarizing even large amounts of information.

K E Y *QUESTIONS*

- What tools do all scientists require in their research?
- What are the measures of central tendency?
- How is dispersion measured?

Inferential Statistics

Throughout this book, the results of many experiments have been described. When these studies were discussed, differences between various conditions or groups were often mentioned. For example, we saw that participants exposed to one set of conditions or one level of an independent variable behaved differently from participants exposed to another set of conditions or another level of an independent variable. How did we know that such differences were real ones rather than differences that might have occurred by chance alone? The answer involves the use of **inferential statistics.** These methods allow us to reach conclusions about just this issue: whether a difference we have actually observed is large enough for us to conclude (to infer) that it is indeed a real or significant one. The logic behind inferential statistics is complex, but some of its key points can be illustrated by the following example.

Suppose that a psychologist conducts an experiment to examine the impact of mood on memory. (As you may recall, such research was discussed in Chapter 6.) To do so, he exposes one group of participants to conditions designed to place them in a good mood: They watch a very funny videotape. A second group, in contrast, is exposed to a neutral tape—one that has little impact on their mood. Both groups are then asked to memorize lists of words, some of which refer to happy events, such as "party" and "success." Later, both groups are tested for recall of these words. Results indicate that those who watched the funny video remember more happy words than those who watched the neutral video; in fact, those in the first group remember twelve happy words, while those in the second remember only eight—a difference of 4.0. Is this difference a real one?

One way of answering this question would be to repeat the study over and over again. If a difference in favour of the happy group were obtained consistently, our confidence that it is indeed real (and perhaps due to differences in subjects' mood) would increase. As you can see, however, this would be a costly procedure. Is there any way of avoiding it? One answer is provided by inferential statistics. These methods assume that if we repeated the study over and over again, the size of the difference between the two groups obtained each time would vary; moreover, these differences would be normally distributed. Most would fall near the mean, and only a few would be quite large. When applying inferential statistics to the interpretation of psychological research, we make a very conservative assumption: We begin by assuming that there is no difference between the groups—that the mean of this distribution is zero. Through methods that are beyond the scope of this discussion, we then estimate the size of the standard deviation. Once we do, we can readily evaluate the difference obtained in an actual study. If an observed difference is large enough that it would occur by chance only 5 percent (or less) of the time, we can view it as significant. For example, assume that in the study we have been discussing, this standard deviation (a standard deviation of mean differences) is 2.0. This indicates that the difference we observed (4.0) is two standard deviations above the expected mean of zero (see Figure A.4). As you'll recall from our discussion of the normal curve, this means that the difference is quite large and would occur by chance less than 2 percent of the time. Our conclusion: The difference between the two groups in our study is probably real. Thus, mood does indeed seem to affect memory.

Please note that the word *probably* is being used here. Since the tails of the normal curve never entirely level off, there is always some chance—no matter how slight—that even a huge observed difference is due to chance. If we accept a difference that really occurred by chance as being real, we make what statisticians describe as a *Type I error.* If, in contrast, we interpret a real difference as being one that occurred by chance, we make a *Type II error.* Clearly, both kinds of errors can lead us to false conclusions about the findings of a research project.

Inferential Statistics: Statistical procedures that provide information on the probability that an observed event is due to chance, and that permit us to determine whether differences between individuals or groups are ones that are likely or unlikely to have occurred by chance.

KEY *QUESTIONS*

Why do psychologists use inferential statistics?

When is an observed difference viewed as significant?

Figure A.4
Using Inferential Statistics to Determine Whether an Observed Difference Is a Real One

Two groups in a study concerned with the effects of mood on memory attain mean scores of 12.0 and 8.0, respectively. Is this difference significant (real)? Through inferential statistics, we can tell. If the study were repeated over and over, and the two groups did not really differ, the mean difference in their scores would be zero. Assuming that the standard deviation is 2.0, we know that the probability of a difference this large is very small—less than 2 percent. In view of this fact, we conclude that this finding is indeed significant.

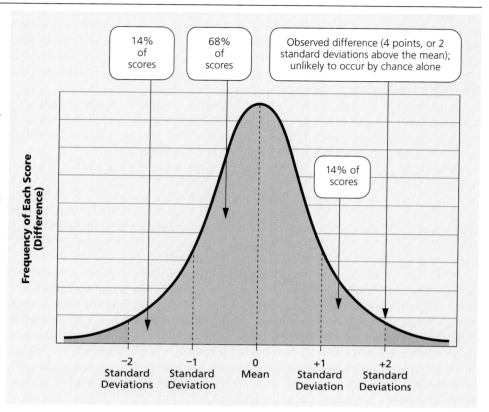

14% of scores

68% of scores

Observed difference (4 points, or 2 standard deviations above the mean); unlikely to occur by chance alone

14% of scores

Frequency of Each Score (Difference)

−2	−1	0	+1	+2
Standard Deviations	Standard Deviation	Mean	Standard Deviation	Standard Deviations

Correlation and Prediction

Does crime increase as temperatures rise? Does the chance of winning elections increase with a candidate's height? Does our ability to solve certain kinds of problems change with age? Psychologists are often interested in such questions. In short, they are concerned with whether two or more variables are related, so that changes in one are associated with changes in the other. Remember: This is quite different from the issue of whether changes in one variable *cause* changes in another. (If you're unclear about this distinction, refresh your memory by referring to Chapter 1.)

In order to answer such questions, we must gather information on each variable. For example, assume that we wanted to find out whether political fortunes are indeed related to height. To do so, we might obtain information on (1) the height of hundreds of candidates and (2) the percentage of votes they obtained in recent elections. Then we'd plot these two variables, height against votes, by entering a single point for each candidate on a graph such as the one in Figure A.5. As you can see, the first graph in this figure indicates that tallness is positively associated with political success. The second points to the opposite conclusion, and the third suggests that there is no relationship at all between height and political popularity.

While such graphs, known as scatterplots, are useful, they don't by themselves provide a precise index of the strength of the relationship between two or more variables. To obtain such an index, we often calculate a statistic known as a **correlation coefficient.** Such coefficients can range from −1.00 to +1.00. Positive numbers indicate that as one variable increases, so does the other. Negative numbers indicate that as one factor increases, the other decreases. The greater the departure from 0.00 in either direction, the stronger the relationship between the two variables. Thus, a correlation of +0.80 is stronger than one of +0.39. Similarly, a correlation of −0.76 is stronger than one of −0.51.

Correlation Coefficient: A statistic indicating the degree of relationship between two or more variables.

Figure A.5
Illustrating Relationships through Scatterplots

Is height related to success in politics? To find out, we measure the height of many candidates and obtain records of the percentage of votes they obtained. We then plot height against votes in a scatterplot. Plot A indicates a positive relationship between height and political success: The taller candidates are, the more votes they get. Plot B indicates a negative relationship between these variables. Plot C suggests that there is no relationship between these variables.

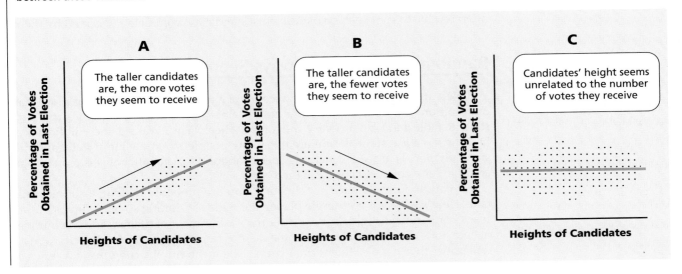

Once we've computed a correlation coefficient, we can test its significance: We can determine whether it is large enough to be viewed as unlikely to occur by chance alone. Further, we can also compare correlations to determine if, in fact, one is significantly larger or smaller than another. The methods used for completing these tasks are somewhat different from those used for comparing means, but the logic is much the same.

In addition to determining the extent to which two or more variables are related, statistical procedures also exist for determining the degree to which a specific variable can be predicted from one or more others. These methods of regression analysis are complex, but they are of great practical value. Knowing the extent to which performance can be predicted from currently available information—such as grades, past performance, or scores on psychological tests—can aid companies, schools, and many other organizations in selecting the best people for employment or educational opportunities.

KEY QUESTIONS

■ What is a correlation coefficient?

■ How are correlations used?

The Misuse of Statistics

A public figure once remarked, "There are lies, damned lies, and statistics!" By this, he meant that statistics are often used for purposes quite different from the ones we've discussed here. Instead of serving as a valuable basis for understanding scientific data, interpreting test scores, or making predictions about behaviour, statistics are sometimes employed to confuse, deceive, or mislead their intended victims. To make matters worse, in the wrong hands statistics can be quite effective in this role. The reason for such success lies in the fact that most of us firmly accept another popular saying: "Numbers don't lie." Thus, when confronted with what appear to be mathematical data and facts, we surrender our usual skepticism and readily accept what we are told. Since the costs of doing so can be quite high, let's conclude this brief discussion of statistics by examining some of the more common—and blatant—misuses of statistics. Here, too, thinking like a psychologist can be of considerable practical value. If you keep the principles outlined here firmly in mind, you'll often be able to spot such statistical abuses and can avoid being deceived by them.

Random Events Don't Always Seem Random

You pick up the paper and read an account of a young woman who won more than one million dollars at a gambling casino. She placed sixteen bets in a row at a roulette table and won on every spin of the wheel. Why? Was she incredibly lucky? Did she have a system? If you are like many people, you may jump to the conclusion that there is indeed something special about her. After all, how else can this incredible series of events be explained?

If you do jump to such conclusions, you are probably making a serious mistake. Here's why. For any single player, the odds of winning so many times in succession are indeed slight. But consider the vast number of players and the number of occasions on which they play; some casinos remain open around the clock. Also, remember the shape of the normal curve. The mean number of wins in a series of sixteen bets is indeed low—perhaps one or two. But the tails of the curve never level off, so there is some probability, however slight, of even sixteen wins occurring in a row. In short, even events that would not be expected to occur by chance *do* occur—albeit very rarely. The moral is clear: Don't overinterpret events that seem, at first glance, to border on impossible. They may actually be rare chance occurrences with no special significance of their own.

Large Samples Provide a Better Basis for Reaching Conclusions Than Small Ones

Many television commercials take the following form. A single consumer is asked to compare three unlabelled brands of facial tissue or to compare the whiteness of three loads of wash. The consumer then makes the "right" choice, selecting the sponsor's product as softest, brightest, or whitest. The commercial ends with a statement of the following type: "Here's proof. Our brand is the one most shoppers prefer." Should you take such evidence seriously? Caution is advised. In most cases, it is not possible to reach firm statistical conclusions on the basis of the reactions of a single individual, or even of several individuals. Rather, a much larger number of cooperative participants is necessary. After watching such a commercial, then, you should ask what would happen if the same procedures were repeated with 20, 50, or 500 shoppers. Would the sponsor's brand actually be chosen significantly more often than the others? The commercials leave the impression that it would; but, as you should realize by now, jumping to such conclusions is risky. So be skeptical of claims based on very small samples. They are on shaky grounds at best, and they may be designed to be purposely misleading.

Unbiased Samples Provide a Better Basis for Reaching Conclusions Than Biased Ones

Here's another popular type of commercial, and another common misuse of statistics. An announcer, usually dressed in a white coat, states: "Three out of four dentists surveyed recommend Jawbreak sugarless gum." At first glance, the meaning of this message seems clear: Most dentists prefer that their patients chew a specific brand of gum. But look more closely: There's an important catch. Notice that the announcer says, "Three out of four dentists surveyed...." Who were these people? A fair and representative sample of all dentists? Major stockholders in the Jawbreak company? Close relatives of the person holding the patent on this product? From the information given, it's impossible to tell. To the extent that these or many other possibilities are true, the dentists surveyed represent a biased sample; they are not representative of the population to which the sponsor wishes us to generalize—all dentists.

So whenever you encounter claims about the results of a survey, ask two questions: (1) Who were the people surveyed? (2) How were they chosen? If these questions can't be answered to your satisfaction, be on guard: Someone may be trying to mislead you.

Unexpressed Comparisons Are Often Meaningless

Another all-too-common misuse of statistics involves what might be described as "errors of omission." People using this tactic mention a comparison but then fail to specify all of the groups or items involved. For example, consider the following statement: "In recent laboratory tests, Plasti-spred was found to contain fully 82 percent less cholesterol! So, if you care about your family's health, buy Plasti-spred, the margarine for modern life." Impressive, right? After all, Plasti-spred seems to contain much less of a dangerous substance than—what? There, in fact, is the rub: We have no idea as to the identity of the other substances in the comparison. Were they other brands of margarine? Butter? A jar of bacon drippings? A beaker full of cholesterol?

The lesson offered by such claims is clear. Whenever you are told that a product, candidate, or anything else is better or superior in some way, always ask the following question: Better than what?

Some Differences Aren't Really There

Here's yet another type of commercial you've probably seen before. An announcer points to lines on a graph that diverge before your eyes and states, "Here's proof! Gasaway neutralizes stomach acid twice as fast as the other leading brand." And in fact, the line labelled Gasaway does seem to rise more quickly, leaving its poor competitor in the dust. Should you take such claims seriously? Again, the answer is no. First, such graphs are usually unlabelled. As a result, we have no idea as to what measure of neutralizing acids is being applied or how much time is involved. It is quite possible that the curves illustrate only the first few seconds after the medicine is taken and that beyond that period the advantage for the sponsor's product disappears.

Second, and even more important, there are no grounds for assuming that the differences shown are significant—that they could not have occurred by chance. Perhaps there is no difference whatsoever in the speed with which the two products neutralize acid, but the comparison was run over and over again until—by chance—a seemingly large difference in favour of the sponsor's brand occurred. This is not to say that all advertisers, or even most, engage in such practices. Perhaps the differences shown in some commercials are indeed real. Still, given the strong temptation companies face to stress the benefits of their own products, the following policy is probably best: Assume that all differences reported in ads and similar sources are not significant—that is, not real—unless specific information to the contrary is provided.

Graphs May Distort (or at Least Bend) Reality

The results of psychological research are often represented in graphs; graphs can communicate major findings efficiently and can readily present complex relationships that are difficult to describe verbally. Unfortunately, however, graphs are often used for another purpose: to alter the conclusions drawn from a given set of data. There are many ways to do this, but the most common involves altering the meaning of the axes—the horizontal or vertical boundaries of the graph. A specific example may help clarify this process.

Consider how two groups—one in favour of strong government actions to prevent teenagers from smoking and the other a lobbying group for the tobacco industry—might present data relating to the percentage of teenagers who smoke. The first group might make its case with the graph on the left of Figure A.6, while the second group would present its side with the graph on the right. As you can see, both charts show the same data: the proportion of teenagers smoking increased from 12 percent in the first year, to 16 percent in the third year. But this change seems much more dramatic—and potentially more important—in the graph on the left than in the one on the right. Why? Because of the different vertical axes used in the two versions. People looking at these graphs could easily be led to opposite conclusions about the scope of this problem if they don't pay careful attention to the numbers on the axis.

Sad to relate, such fine-tuning of graphs is common, and you will probably encounter it in magazines, political literature, and many other sources. The moral is clear: It is important to pay careful attention to the scale used in any graph, the precise quantities being measured, and all labels employed. If you overlook such factors, you may be a sitting duck for those who wish to lead you to the conclusions they favour.

K E Y QUESTIONS

- How can statistics be misused?

Figure A.6
Misleading Graphs: One Common Technique

By changing the scale on the vertical axis, the same trends can be made to seem small and trivial or large and impressive. In the graph on the left (A), the growth in teenage smoking seems tiny, while in the graph on the right (B) the growth rate seems very large. You should always be on guard against such tactics, which are designed to lead you to certain conclusions.

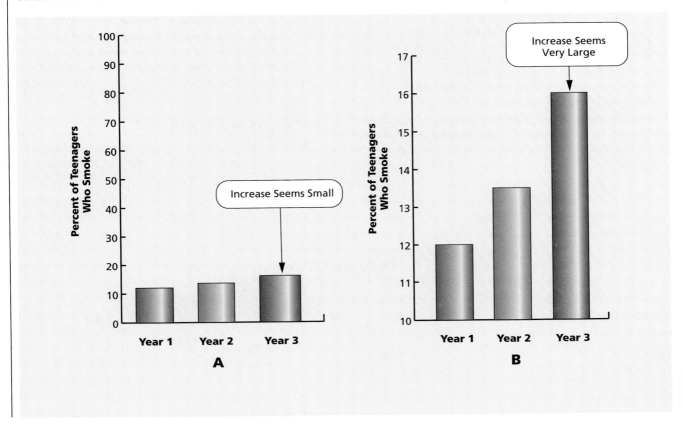

Summary and Review

Key Questions

Descriptive Statistics

What tools do all scientists require in their research? All scientists require equipment for collecting data and some means of interpreting their findings. In psychology, statistics are often used for the latter purpose.

What are the measures of central tendency? The measures of central tendency are the mean (the average of all scores), the mode (the most frequently occurring score), and the median (the midpoint of the distribution of scores).

■ **How is dispersion measured?** Dispersion is measured using range, variance, and standard deviation. Range measures the difference between the highest and lowest scores. Variance measures the average squared distance between each score and the mean score. Standard deviation measures the average distance between scores and the mean in any distribution.

Inferential Statistics

■ **Why do psychologists use inferential statistics?** Psychologists use inferential statistics to determine whether differences between individuals or groups are significant, or real. Inferential statistics assume that the mean difference in question is zero and that observed differences are distributed normally around this value.

■ **When is an observed difference viewed as significant?** If an observed difference is large enough that it would occur by chance only 5 percent of the time, it is viewed as significant.

Correlation and Prediction

■ **What is a correlation coefficient?** A correlation coefficient is a statistic indicating the degree of relationship between two variables. Such coefficients can range from -1.00 to $+1.00$. The larger the departure from 0.00, the stronger the correlation between the variables in question. A positive correlation coefficient indicates that as one variable increases, so does the other. A negative correlation coefficient indicates that as one variable increases, the other decreases.

■ **How are correlations used?** Correlations, and the statistics derived from them, can be used to predict future behaviour from current information. Such predictions are of great practical benefit to schools, companies, and others wishing to predict future performance from current behaviour.

The Misuse of Statistics

■ **How can statistics be misused?** Misuse of statistics can involve the use of extremely small or biased samples, unexpressed comparisons, and misleading graphs and presentations.

Key Terms

Central Tendency (p. 689)

Correlation Coefficient (p. 694)

Descriptive Statistics (p. 689)

Dispersion (p. 689)

Frequency Distribution (p. 688)

Inferential Statistics (p. 693)

Mean (p. 689)

Median (p. 689)

Mode (p. 689)

Normal Curve (p. 690)

Range (p. 690)

Standard Deviation (p. 690)

Statistics (p. 687)

Variance (p. 690)

GLOSSARY

A

Absolute Threshold: The smallest amount of a stimulus that we can detect 50 percent of the time.

Accommodation: In Piaget's theory, the modification of existing mental frameworks to take account of new information.

Achievement Motivation: The desire to accomplish difficult tasks and meet standards of excellence.

Acquisition: The process by which a conditioned stimulus acquires the ability to elicit a conditioned response through repeated pairings of an unconditioned stimulus with the conditioned stimulus.

Action Potential: A rapid shift in the electrical charge across the cell membrane of neurons. This disturbance along the membrane communicates information within neurons.

Adaptation: In Piaget's theory of cognitive development, the process through which individuals build mental representations of the world through interaction with it.

Adolescence: A period beginning with the onset of puberty and ending when individuals assume adult roles and responsibilities.

Adolescent Invulnerability: Adolescents' belief that they are immune from the potential harm of high-risk behaviours.

Adolescent Recklessness: The tendency for adolescents to engage in forms of behaviour that appear to adults to be dangerous or reckless.

Affect: A person's current mood/state.

Aggression: Behaviour directed toward the goal of harming another living being who wishes to avoid such treatment.

Aggression Machine: A device used in the laboratory study of human aggression.

Aggressive Motivation: The desire to inflict harm on others.

Agonist: A drug that mimics the action of a neurotransmitter.

Agoraphobia: Fear of losing control and experiencing a panic attack in specific situations, such as in open places, in a crowd, or on an airplane.

Agreeableness: One of the "big five" dimensions of personality; ranges from good-natured, cooperative, trusting at one end to irritable, suspicious, uncooperative at the other.

Alcohol: The most widely consumed drug in the world.

Algorithm: A rule that guarantees a solution to a specific type of problem.

Alpha Waves: Brain waves that occur when individuals are awake but relaxed.

Alzheimer's Disease: An illness primarily afflicting individuals over the age of sixty-five and involving severe mental deterioration, including anterograde and retrograde amnesia.

Amnesia: Loss of memory stemming from illness, accident, drug abuse, or other causes.

Amphetamines: Drugs that act as stimulants, increasing feelings of energy and activation.

Anal Stage: In Freud's theory, a psychosexual stage of development in which pleasure is focused primarily on the anal zone.

Analogy: A strategy for solving problems based on applying solutions that were previously successful to other problems similar in underlying structure.

Anchoring-and-Adjustment Heuristic: A cognitive rule of thumb for decision making in which existing information is accepted as a reference point but then adjusted in light of various factors.

Anima: According to Jung, the archetype representing the feminine side of males.

Animus: According to Jung, the archetype representing the masculine side of females.

Anorexia Nervosa: An eating disorder in which individuals starve themselves and often lose a dangerous amount of weight.

Antagonist: A drug that reduces the action of a neurotransmitter.

Anterograde Amnesia: The inability to store in long-term memory information that occurs after an amnesia-inducing event.

Antisocial Personality Disorder: A personality disorder involving a lack of conscience and sense of responsibility, impulsive behaviour, irritability, and aggressiveness.

Anxiety: In Freudian theory, unpleasant feelings of tension or worry experienced by individuals in reaction to unacceptable wishes or impulses; increased arousal accompanied by generalized feelings of fear or apprehension.

Anxiety Disorders: Psychological disorders that centre on the occurrence of anxiety and include generalized anxiety, phobias, and obsessive-compulsive disorders.

Archetypes: According to Jung, inherited images in the collective unconscious that shape our perceptions of the external world.

Arousal Process: A general activation or energization of brain and body systems.

Arousal Theory: A theory of motivation suggesting that human beings seek an optimal level of arousal.

Artificial Intelligence: A branch of science that studies the capacity of computers to demonstrate performance that, if it were produced by human beings, would be described as showing intelligence.

Assessment Interviews: Interviews conducted by psychologists in which they seek information about individuals' past and present behaviours, current problems, interpersonal relations, and personality.

Assimilation: In Piaget's theory, the tendency to understand new information in terms of existing mental frameworks.

Attachment: A strong affectional bond between infants and their caregivers.

Attention-Deficit/Hyperactivity Disorder: A psychological disorder in which children are unable to concentrate their attention on any task for more than a few minutes.

Attitudes: Mental representations and evaluations of features of the social or physical world.

Attribution: The processes through which we seek to determine the causes behind others' behaviour.

Autobiographical Memory: Memory for information about events in our own lives.

Automatic Processing: Processing of information with minimal conscious awareness.

Automatic Vigilance: The strong tendency to pay attention to negative social information.

Autonomic Nervous System: The part of the peripheral nervous system that connects internal organs, glands, and involuntary muscles to the central nervous system.

Availability Heuristic: A cognitive rule of thumb in which the importance or probability of various events is judged on the basis of how readily they come to mind.

Avoidant Attachment: A pattern of attachment in which infants don't cry when their mother leaves them alone during the strange situation test, and are slow to greet their mother when she returns.

Axon: The part of the neuron that conducts the action potential away from the cell body.

Axon Terminals: Structures at the end of axons that contain transmitter substances.

B

Babbling: An early stage of speech development in which infants emit virtually all known sounds of human speech.

Backward Conditioning: A type of conditioning in which the presentation of the unconditioned stimulus precedes and does not overlap with the presentation of the conditioned stimulus.

Barbiturates: Drugs that act as depressants, reducing activity in the nervous system and behaviour output.

Beck's Cognitive Behaviour Therapy: A form of cognitive therapy that focuses on changing illogical patterns of thought that underlie depression.

Behaviour Therapies: Forms of psychotherapy that focus on changing maladaptive patterns of behaviour through the use of basic principles of learning.

Behaviourism: The view that psychology should study only observable behaviour.

Bereavement: The process of grieving for the people we love who die.

Binocular Cues: Cues to depth or distance provided by the use of both eyes.

Biological Constraints on Learning: Tendencies of some species to acquire some forms of conditioning less readily than other species do.

Biological Rhythms: Cyclic changes in bodily processes.

Biologically Based Therapies: Forms of therapy that attempt to reduce psychological disorders through biological means such as drug therapy or surgery.

Bipolar Disorder: A mood disorder involving swings between depression and mania.

Bisexual: A sexual orientation in which individuals seek sexual relations with members of both their own and the other sex.

Blended Families: Families resulting from remarriage, consisting of biological parents, step-parents, and biological children of one or both spouses.

Blindsight: A rare condition resulting from damage to the primary visual cortex in which individuals report being blind, yet respond to certain aspects of visual stimuli as if they could see.

Blind Spot: The point in the back of the retina through which the optic nerve exits the eye. This exit point contains no rods or cones and is therefore insensitive to light.

Body Language: Non-verbal cues involving body posture or movement of body parts.

Brightness: The physical intensity of light.

Brightness Constancy: The tendency to perceive objects as having a constant brightness even when they are viewed under different conditions of illumination.

Bulimia: An eating disorder in which periods of binge eating alternate with periods of self-induced purging.

Bystander Effect: A reduced tendency of witnesses to an emergency to help when they believe that there are other potential helpers present.

C

Cancer: A group of illnesses in which abnormal cells are formed that are able to proliferate, invade, and overwhelm normal tissues, and to spread to distant sites in the body.

Cannon-Bard Theory: A theory of emotion suggesting that various emotion-provoking events simultaneously produce subjective reactions labelled as emotions and physiological arousal.

Cardinal Trait: According to Allport, a single trait that dominates an individual's entire personality.

Cardiovascular Disease: All diseases of the heart and blood vessels.

Case Method: A method of research in which detailed information about individuals is used to develop general principles about behaviour.

Catastrophic Thinking: Thoughts about impending disaster that may result in a full-blown panic attack.

Catatonic Type of Schizophrenia: A dramatic type of schizophrenia in which individuals show marked disturbances in motor behaviour. Many alternate between total immobility and wild, excited behaviour in which they rush madly about.

Central Executive Mechanism: A control process that regulates the operations of the phonological loop and the visuospatial sketchpad.

Central Nervous System: The brain and the spinal cord.

Central Route (to persuasion): Attitude change resulting from systematic processing of information contained in persuasive messages.

Central Tendency: The middle area of a distribution of scores.

Central Traits: According to Allport, the five or ten traits that best describe an individual's personality.

Cerebellum: A part of the brain concerned with the regulation and coordination of basic motor activities.

Cerebral Cortex: The outer covering of the cerebral hemispheres.

Chaining: A procedure that establishes a sequence of responses, which lead to a reward following the final response in the chain.

Charismatic Leaders: Leaders who exert profound effects on their followers and establish special types of relationships with them.

Choking under Pressure: The tendency to perform less well at times when pressures for excellent performance are especially high.

Chromosomes: Threadlike structures containing genetic material, found in every cell of the body.

Chunk: Stimuli perceived as a single unit or a meaningful grouping. Most people can retain seven to nine chunks of information in short-term memory at a given time.

Circadian Rhythms: Cyclic changes in bodily processes occurring within a single day.

Client-Centred Therapy: A form of psychotherapy that concentrates on eliminating irrational conditions of worth—conditions people believe they must meet in order to be loved or accepted.

Climacteric: A period during which the functioning of the reproductive system, and various aspects of sexual activity, change greatly.

Cocaine: A powerful stimulant that produces pleasurable sensations of increased energy and self-confidence.

Cochlea: A portion of the inner ear containing the sensory receptors for sound.

Cognition: The activities involved in thinking, reasoning, decision making, memory, problem solving, and all other forms of higher mental processes.

Cognitive Dissonance: The state experienced by individuals when they discover inconsistency between two attitudes they hold or between their attitudes and their behaviour.

Cognitive Perspective (on persuasion): An approach that seeks to understand persuasion by identifying the cognitive processes that play a role in it.

Cognitive Therapy: Psychotherapy that concentrates on altering faulty or distorted modes of thought so as to alleviate psychological disorders.

Cohort Effects: Differences between individuals of different ages stemming from the contrasting social or cultural conditions of the periods in which they grew up.

Collective Unconscious: In Jung's theory, a portion of the unconscious shared by all human beings.

Companionate Love: A form of love involving a high degree of commitment and deep concern for the well-being of the beloved.

Complex Cells: Neurons in the visual cortex that respond to stimuli moving in a particular direction and having a particular orientation.

Compliance: A form of social influence in which one or more individuals accept direct requests from one or more others.

Concepts: Mental categories for objects or events that are similar to one another in certain respects.

Concrete Operations: In Piaget's theory, a stage of cognitive development occurring roughly between the ages of seven and eleven. It is at this stage that children grasp such principles as conservation, and that the capacity for logical thought emerges.

Concurrent Schedule of Reinforcement: A situation in which behaviours having two or more different reinforcement schedules are simultaneously available.

Conditioned Response (CR): In classical conditioning, the response to the conditioned stimulus.

Conditioned Stimulus (CS): In classical conditioning, the stimulus that is repeatedly paired with an unconditioned stimulus.

Conditions of Worth: In Rogers's theory, individuals' beliefs that they must meet certain unrealistic conditions in order to be loved or accepted.

Cones: Sensory receptors in the eye that play a crucial role in sensations of colour.

Confirmation Bias: The tendency to pay attention primarily to information that confirms existing views or beliefs.

Confluence Approach: An approach suggesting that for creativity to occur, multiple components must converge.

Conformity: A type of social influence in which individuals experience pressure to adhere to existing social norms.

Conscientiousness: One of the "big five" dimensions of personality; this dimension ranges from well-organized, careful, responsible at one end to disorganized, careless, unscrupulous at the other.

Consensus: The extent to which behaviour by one person is shown by others as well.

Conservation: Principle that states that certain physical attributes of an object remain unchanged even though its outward appearance changes.

Consistency: The extent to which a given person responds in the same way to a given stimulus on separate occasions under the same circumstances.

Consolidation of Memory: The process of shifting new information from short-term to long-term storage.

Constancies: Our tendency to perceive physical objects as unchanging despite shifts in the pattern of sensations these objects induce.

Construct Validity: The extent to which a test measures a complex variable or concept described by a psychological theory.

Contact Hypothesis: The suggestion that increased contact between members of different social groups will reduce prejudice between them.

Content Validity: The extent to which the items on a test sample the skills or knowledge needed for achievement in a given field or task.

Context-Dependent Memory: The fact that information entered into memory in one context or setting is easier to recall in that context than in others.

Continuous Reinforcement Schedule: A schedule of reinforcement in which every occurrence of a particular behaviour is reinforced.

Control Theory of Self-Consciousness: A theory suggesting that people compare their current behaviour and states with important goals and values. They then alter their behaviour to close any gaps they observe.

Controlled Processing: Processing of information with relatively high levels of conscious awareness.

Conventional Level (of morality): According to Kohlberg, a stage of moral development during which individuals judge morality largely in terms of existing social norms or rules.

Conversion Disorder: Psychological disorder in which individuals experience real motor or sensory symptoms for which there is no known organic cause.

Convoy Model: A model of social networks suggesting that from mid-life on, we tend to maintain close relationships with only a small number of people.

Cornea: The curved, transparent layer through which light rays enter the eye.

Corpus Callosum: A band of nerve fibres connecting the two hemispheres of the brain.

Correlation Coefficient: A statistic indicating the degree of relationship between two or more variables.

Correlational Method of Research: A research method in which investigators observe two or more variables to determine whether, and to what extent, changes in one are accompanied by changes in the other.

Correlations: A tendency for one aspect of the world (or one variable) to change with another aspect of the world (or variable).

Counterfactual Thinking: The tendency to evaluate events by thinking about alternatives to them—"what might have been."

Crack: A cocaine derivative that can be smoked. It acts as a powerful stimulant.

Creativity: Cognitive activity resulting in new or novel ways of viewing or solving problems.

Criterion Measure: An independent index of performance that can serve to demonstrate the predictive validity of a test. For example, high school grades are an index of performance that should be highly correlated with scores on an intelligence test.

Critical Thinking: Careful assessment of available evidence in order to evaluate claims and statements in an objective and reasoned manner.

Cross-Sectional Research: Research comparing groups of individuals of different ages in order to determine how some aspect of behaviour or cognition changes with age.

Cross-Tolerance: Increased tolerance for one drug that develops as a result of taking another drug.

Crystallized Intelligence: Aspects of intelligence that draw on previously learned information to make decisions or solve problems.

Cultural Bias: The tendency of items on a test of intelligence to require specific cultural experience or knowledge.

D

Dark Adaptation: The process by which the visual system increases its sensitivity to light under low illumination.

Daydreams: Imaginary scenes or events that occur while a person is awake.

Debriefing: Providing participants in psychological research with complete and accurate information about a study after they have taken part in it.

Deception: Withholding information about a study from participants. Deception is used in situations in which the information that is withheld is likely to alter participants' behaviour.

Decision Making: The process of choosing among various courses of action or alternatives.

Deep Structure: Information that underlies the form of a sentence and is crucial to its meaning.

Defence Mechanisms: Techniques used by the ego to keep threatening and unacceptable material out of consciousness, and so to reduce anxiety.

Deinstitutionalization: Ending the practice of committing patients with many serious disorders to mental hospitals for long periods of time, made possible by new drug therapies introduced in the 1950s and 1960s that allowed control over the symptoms of these disorders.

Delayed Conditioning: A form of forward conditioning in which the presentation of the conditioned stimulus precedes, but overlaps with, the presentation of the unconditioned stimulus.

Delta Waves: High-amplitude, slow brain waves that occur during several stages of sleep, but especially during Stage 4.

Delusions: Irrational but firmly held beliefs about the world that have no basis in reality.

Demand-Withdraw Pattern: An interaction pattern in which one partner criticizes or blames, and the other partner responds by retreating and becoming silent.

Dendrites: The parts of neurons that conduct action potentials toward the cell body.

Dependence: Strong physiological or psychological need for particular drugs.

Dependent Variable: The aspect of behaviour that is measured in an experiment.

Depressants: Drugs that reduce activity in the nervous system and therefore slow many bodily and cognitive processes. Depressants include alcohol and barbiturates.

Depression: A psychological disorder involving intense feelings of sadness, lack of energy, and feelings of hopelessness and despair.

Descriptive Statistics: Statistics that summarize the major characteristics of an array of scores.

Developmental Psychology: The branch of psychology that studies all types of changes that occur throughout the lifespan.

Diagnostic and Statistical Manual of Mental Disorders-IV (DSM-IV): The latest version of a manual widely used for diagnosing various psychological disorders.

Diathesis–Stress Model: A model of schizophrenia suggesting that individuals with inherited dispositions to develop this disorder do so only when subjected to stressful environmental conditions.

Difference Threshold: The amount of change in a stimulus required before a person can detect the shift.

Discrimination: Negative actions toward the targets of prejudice.

Discriminative Stimulus: Stimulus that signals reinforcement will occur if a specific response is made.

Disorganized (or Disoriented) Attachment: A pattern of attachment in which infants show contradictory reactions to their mother after being reunited with her during the strange situation test.

Dispersion: The extent to which scores in a distribution spread out or vary around the centre.

Disruptive Behaviours: Childhood mental disorders involving poor control of impulses, conflict with other children and adults, and, in some cases, more serious forms of antisocial behaviour.

Dissociative Amnesia: Amnesia for which there is no organic cause.

Dissociative Disorder: Psychological disorder in which individuals experience profound and lengthy losses of identity or memory.

Dissociative Fugue: Form of dissociative amnesia in which individuals forget their identity and virtually all of their past life.

Dissociative Identity Disorder: A dissociative disorder in which a single individual seems to possess more than one personality.

Distinctiveness: The extent to which a given person reacts in the same manner to different stimuli or situations.

Door-in-the-Face Technique: A technique for gaining compliance in which a large request is followed by a smaller one.

Dopamine Hypothesis: The hypothesis that schizophrenia is associated with excess activity in those parts of the brain in which dopamine is the primary neurotransmitter.

Double-Blind Procedure: Procedure in which neither the people collecting data nor research participants have knowledge of the experimental or control conditions to which they have been assigned.

Down's Syndrome: A disorder caused by an extra chromosome and characterized by varying degrees of cognitive impairment and physical disorders.

Dreams: Cognitive events, often vivid but disconnected, that occur during sleep. Most dreams take place during REM sleep.

Dreams of Absent-Minded Transgression: Dreams in which people attempting to change their own behaviour, as in quitting smoking, see themselves unintentionally slipping into the unwanted behaviour, in an absent-minded or careless manner.

Drive Theory: A theory of motivation suggesting that behaviour is "pushed" from within by drives stemming from basic biological needs.

Drug Abuse: Instances in which individuals take drugs to change their moods, and in which they experience impaired behaviour or social functioning as a result of doing so.

Drug Therapy: Efforts to treat psychological disorders through administration of appropriate drugs.

Drugs: Chemical substances that change the structure or function of biological systems.

Dysfunctional Families: Families that do not meet the needs of children and in fact do them serious harm.

E

Eating Disorders: Serious disturbances in eating habits or patterns that pose a threat to individuals' physical health and well-being.

Effectiveness Studies: Studies designed to assess the degree to which psychotherapy is effective as it is practised in actual clinical settings.

Efficacy Study: Carefully controlled laboratory studies designed to determine whether a particular form of psychotherapy benefits those receiving it more than a comparable control group that does not receive psychotherapy.

Ego: In Freud's theory, the part of personality that takes rational account of external reality in the expression of instinctive sexual and aggressive urges.

Egocentrism: The inability of young children to distinguish their own perspective from that of others.

Elaboration Likelihood Model: A theory suggesting that there are two distinct routes to persuasion involving different amounts of cognitive elaboration in response to a persuasive message.

Elaborative Rehearsal: Rehearsal in which the meaning of information is considered and the information is related to other knowledge already present in memory.

Electroconvulsive Therapy (ECT): A treatment for depression that entails passing brief pulses of mild electric shock through the brain until a seizure ensues.

Electroencephalogram (EEG): A record of electrical activity within the brain. EEGs play an important role in the scientific study of sleep.

Electroencephalography: A technique for measuring the electrical activity of the brain via electrodes placed at specified locations on the skull.

Embryo: The developing child during the second through the eighth weeks of prenatal development.

Emotional Intelligence: A cluster of traits or abilities relating to the emotional side of life—abilities such as recognizing and managing one's own emotions, being able to motivate oneself and restrain impulses, recognizing and managing others' emotions, and handling interpersonal relationships in an effective manner.

Emotional Stability: One of the "big five" dimensions of personality; ranges from poised, calm, composed at one end to nervous, anxious, excitable at the other.

Emotions: Reactions consisting of physiological reactions, subjective cognitive states, and expressive behaviours.

Empathy: Our ability to recognize the emotions of others, to understand these reactions, and to experience them ourselves, at least to a degree

Empathy–Altruism Hypothesis: A view suggesting that when we encounter someone who needs help, we experience empathy, and as a result, are motivated to help them in an unselfish manner.

Empirically Validated Therapies: Therapies that have been scientifically demonstrated to be efficacious in treating particular problems or disorders.

Encoding: The process through which information is converted into a form that can be entered into memory.

Encounter Groups: A form of group therapy in which people are urged to tell other group members exactly how they feel; designed to foster personal growth through increased understanding of one's own behaviour and increased honesty and openness in personal relations.

Endocrine Glands: Glands that secrete hormones directly into the bloodstream.

Endogenously Controlled Attention: When attention is directed by inner goals or concerns.

Endorphins: Morphine-like substances produced by the body.

Environmental Psychology: The branch of psychology that investigates the effects of the physical environment on human behaviour and the effects of that behaviour on the environment.

Epidemiological Studies: Large-scale efforts to identify the risk factors that predict the development of certain diseases.

Episodic Memory: Memories of events that we have experienced personally (sometimes termed autobiographical memory).

Escalation of Commitment: The tendency to become increasingly committed to bad decisions even as losses associated with them increase.

Evolutionary Psychology: A branch of psychology that studies the adaptive problems humans have faced over the course of evolution and the behavioural mechanisms that have evolved in response to these environmental pressures.

Evolutionary Theory: A theory suggesting that sleep evolved to ensure that various species, including human beings, remain inactive during those times of day when they were not usually engaged in looking for food, eating, drinking, or mating—activities necessary for survival.

Exogenously Controlled Attention: When attention is directed by stimulus events in the external environment.

Expectancy Theory: A theory of motivation suggesting that behaviour is elicited by expectations of desirable outcomes.

Expected Utility: The product of the subjective value of an event and its predicted probability of occurrence.

Experimentation (the Experimental Method): A research method in which one variable is systematically changed to determine whether it has an effect on one or more other variables.

Experimenter Effects: Unintentional influence exerted by researchers on research participants.

Explicit (Declarative) Memory: A memory system that permits us to express the information it contains verbally. It includes both semantic and episodic memory.

External Locus of Control: Individuals are held to have an external locus of control if they believe that factors outside of their control largely determine the outcomes that they experience in life.

Extinction: The process through which a conditioned stimulus gradually loses the ability to elicit conditioned responses when it is no longer followed by the unconditioned stimulus.

Extrasensory Perception (ESP): Perception without a basis in sensory input.

Extraversion: One of the "big five" dimensions of personality; ranges from sociable, talkative, fun-loving at one end to sober, reserved, cautious at the other.

Extraverts: Individuals who are talkative and sociable, and who often give free rein to their impulses and feelings.

Eyewitness Testimony: Information provided by witnesses to crimes or accidents.

F

Facial Feedback Hypothesis: A hypothesis indicating that facial expressions can influence as well as reflect emotional states.

False Consensus Effect: The tendency to believe that other people share our attitudes to a greater extent than is true.

Family Systems Therapy: Therapy designed to change the relationships among family members in constructive ways.

Family Therapy: A form of psychotherapy that focuses on changing interactions or relations among family members.

Fantasies: Imaginary events or scenes that evoke emotions that a person experiences while awake.

Farsightedness: A condition in which the visual image of a nearby object is focused behind rather than directly on the retina. Therefore, close objects appear out of focus, while distant objects are seen clearly.

Fast-Approaching-Deadline Technique: A technique for gaining compliance in which a deadline is established after which it will be impossible to obtain something desired by the target person.

Feature Detectors: Neurons at various levels within the visual cortex that respond primarily to stimuli possessing certain features.

Fetus: The developing child during the last seven months of prenatal development.

Figure–Ground Relationship: Our tendency to divide the perceptual world into two distinct parts: discrete figures and the background against which they stand out.

Fixation: Excessive investment of psychic energy in a particular stage of psychosexual development, which results in various types of psychological disorders.

Fixed-Interval Schedule: A schedule of reinforcement in which a specific interval of time must elapse before a response will yield reinforcement.

Fixed-Ratio Schedule: A schedule of reinforcement in which reinforcement occurs only after a fixed number of responses have been emitted.

Flashbulb Memories: Vivid memories of what we were doing at the time of an emotion-provoking event.

Flooding: Procedure for eliminating conditioned fears based on principles of classical conditioning. During flooding, an individual is exposed to fear-inducing objects or events. Since no unconditioned stimulus then follows, extinction of fears eventually takes place.

Fluid Intelligence: Aspects of intelligence that involve forming concepts, reasoning, and identifying similarities.

Foot-in-the-Door Technique: A technique for gaining compliance in which a small request is followed by a larger one.

Forced Compliance: A situation in which we feel compelled to say or do things inconsistent with our true attitudes.

Formal Operations: In Piaget's theory, the final stage of cognitive development, during which individuals may acquire the capacity for deductive or propositional reasoning.

Fovea: The area in the centre of the retina in which cones are highly concentrated.

Framing: Presentation of information concerning potential outcomes in terms of gains or losses.

Free Association: A key procedure in psychoanalysis in which individuals spontaneously report all thoughts to the therapist.

Frequency Distribution: The frequency with which each score occurs within an entire distribution of scores.

Frequency Theory: A theory of pitch perception suggesting that sounds of different frequencies, heard as differences in pitch, induce different rates of neural activity in the hair cells of the inner ear.

Friendships: Relationships involving strong mutual affective (emotional) ties between two persons.

Frontal Lobe: The portion of the cerebral cortex that lies in front of the central fissure.

Frustration: The blocking of ongoing goal-directed behaviour.

Fully Functioning Persons: In Rogers's theory, psychologically healthy people who enjoy life to the fullest.

Functional Fixedness: The tendency to think of using objects only as they have been used in the past.

Functionalism: An early view of psychology suggesting that psychology should study the ways in which the ever-changing stream of conscious experience helps us adapt to a complex and challenging world.

Fundamental Attribution Error: The tendency to attribute behaviour to internal causes to a greater extent than is actually justified.

G

Gate-Control Theory: A theory suggesting that the spinal cord contains a mechanism that can block transmission of pain signals to the brain.

Gaze Following: Moving the eyes to where someone else is looking.

Gender: An individual's membership in one of the two sexes; all the attributes, behaviours, and expectancies associated with each sex in a given society.

Gender Identity Disorder: A disorder in which individuals believe that they were born with the wrong sexual identity.

Gender Stereotypes: Cultural beliefs about differences between women and men.

General Adaptation Syndrome: A three-phase model of how organisms respond to stress: (1) alarm or mobilization, (2) resistance, and (3) exhaustion.

Genes: Biological "blueprints" that shape development and all basic bodily processes.

Genetic Determinism Hypothesis: The view that we help other persons who are similar or related to us because this increases the likelihood of our genes, or related genes, being passed on to the next generation.

Genetic Hypothesis: The view that group differences in intelligence are due, at least in part, to genetic factors.

Genetic Theories of Aging: Theories that attribute physical aging primarily to genetic factors.

Genital Stage: In Freud's theory, the final psychosexual stage of development—one in which individuals acquire the adult capacity to combine lust with affection.

Gestalt Psychologists: German psychologists intrigued by our tendency to perceive sensory patterns as well-organized wholes rather than as separate, isolated parts.

Gestalt Therapy: A form of humanistic psychotherapy designed to increase individuals' awareness and understanding of their own feelings.

Gestures: Movements of various body parts that convey a specific meaning to others.

Glial Cells: Cells in the nervous system that surround, support, and protect neurons.

Goal-Setting Theory: A theory that explains why setting specific, challenging goals for a given task often leads to improvements in performance.

Gonads: The primary sex glands.

Graded Potential: A basic type of signal within neurons that results from external physical stimulation of the dendrite or cell body. Unlike the all-or-nothing nature of action potentials, graded potentials vary in proportion to the size of the stimulus that produced them.

Grammar: Rules within a given language indicating how words can be combined into meaningful sentences.

Group Therapies: Therapies conducted with groups of clients.

Groupthink: A set of conditions in a group that leads to bad decisions.

H

Hallucinations: Vivid sensory experiences that occur in the absence of external stimuli yet have the full force of impact of real events or stimuli.

Hallucinogens: Drugs that profoundly alter consciousness, such as LSD.

Health-Belief Model: A model predicting that whether a person practises a particular health behaviour depends on the degree to which the person believes in a personal health threat and believes that the behaviour will reduce that threat to their health.

Health Psychology: The study of the relation between psychological variables and health; reflects the view that both mind and body are important determinants of health and illness.

Heredity: Biologically inherited characteristics.

Heritability: The proportion of the variance in any trait within a given population that is attributable to genetic factors.

Heterosexual (sexual orientation): A sexual orientation in which individuals engage in sexual relations only with members of the other sex.

Heuristics: Mental rules of thumb that permit us to make decisions and judgments in a rapid and efficient manner.

Hierarchy of Needs: In Maslow's theory of motivation, an arrangement of needs from the most basic to those at the highest levels.

Hindsight Effect: The tendency to assume that we would have been better at predicting actual events than is really true.

Homeostasis: A state of physiological balance within the body.

Homosexual (sexual orientation): A sexual orientation in which individuals prefer sexual relations with members of their own sex.

Hormones: Substances secreted by endocrine glands that regulate a wide range of bodily processes.

Hue: The colour that we experience due to the dominant wavelength of a light.

Humanistic Theories: Theories of personality emphasizing personal responsibility and innate tendencies towards personal growth.

Humanistic Therapies: Forms of psychotherapy based on the assumption that psychological disorders stem from environmental conditions that block normal growth and development.

Hunger Motivation: The motivation to obtain and consume food.

Huntington's Disease: A genetically based fatal neuromuscular disorder characterized by the gradual onset of jerky, uncontrollable movements.

Hypercomplex Cells: Neurons in the visual cortex that respond to complex aspects of visual stimuli, such as width, length, and shape.

Hypersomnias: Disorders involving excessive amounts of sleep or an overwhelming urge to fall asleep.

Hypertension: High blood pressure, a condition in which the pressure within the blood vessels is abnormally high.

Hypnosis: An interaction between two persons in which one (the hypnotist) induces changes in the behaviour, feelings, or cognitions of the other (the subject) through suggestions. Hypnosis involves subjects' expectations and their attempts to conform to the role of the hypnotized person.

Hypochondriasis: A psychological disorder in which individuals convert anxiety into chronic preoccupations with their health and bodily functions.

Hypothalamus: A small structure deep within the brain that plays a key role in the regulation of the autonomic nervous system and of several forms of motivated behaviour such as eating and aggression.

Hypothesis: In psychology, a prediction about behaviour that is to be investigated in a research project.

Hypothetico-Deductive Reasoning: In Piaget's theory, a type of reasoning first shown during the stage of formal operations. It involves formulating a general theory and deducing specific hypotheses from it.

I

Id: In Freud's theory, the portion of personality concerned with immediate gratification of primitive needs.

Identity Fusion: A pattern in which bicultural children combine their two cultural identities into one.

Illusions: Instances in which perception yields false interpretations of physical reality.

Illusory-Knowledge Effect: Our tendency to assume we always knew information that we have only recently acquired.

Implicit Memory: A memory system that stores information that we cannot express verbally; sometimes termed procedural memory.

Inadequate Source Monitoring: The ability to remember factual information, but not the source whereby this information was acquired.

Incentives: Rewards individuals seek to attain.

Independent Variable: The variable that is systematically altered in an experiment.

Infantile Amnesia: Inability to remember events from the first two or three years of life.

Inferential Statistics: Statistical procedures that provide information on the probability that an observed event is due to chance, and that permit us to determine whether differences between individuals or groups are ones that are likely or unlikely to have occurred by chance.

Informed Consent: Participants' agreement to take part in a research project after they are provided with information about the nature of such participation.

Ingratiation: A technique of social influence based on inducing increased liking in the target person before influence is attempted.

Insomnia: Disorder involving the inability to fall asleep or remain asleep.

Inspection Time: The minimum amount of time a particular stimulus must be exposed for individuals to make a judgment about it that meets some pre-established criterion of accuracy.

Intelligence: The ability to think abstractly and to learn readily from experience.

Internal Locus of Control: Individuals are held to have internal locus of control if they believe their actions largely determine the outcomes that they experience in life.

Interpersonal Attraction: The extent to which we like or dislike other persons.

Intracranial Self-Stimulation: A procedure in which animals provide their own electrical brain stimulation.

Intrinsic Motivation: The desire to perform activities because they are rewarding in and of themselves.

Introverts: Individuals who are quiet, cautious, and reclusive, and who generally inhibit expression of their impulses and feelings.

IQ: A numerical value that reflects the extent to which an individual's score on an intelligence test departs from the average for other people of the same age.

Iris: The coloured part of the eye that adjusts the amount of light that enters by constricting or dilating the pupil.

J

James-Lange Theory: A theory of emotion suggesting that emotion-provoking events produce various physiological reactions and that recognition of these is responsible for subjective emotional experiences.

Just Noticeable Difference (jnd): The smallest amount of change in a physical stimulus necessary for an individual to notice a difference in the intensity of the stimulus.

K

Kinesthesia: The sense that gives us information about the location of our body parts with respect to each other and allows us to perform movements.

Korsakoff's Syndrome: An illness caused by long-term abuse of alcohol that often involves profound retrograde amnesia.

L

Language: A system of symbols, plus rules for combining them, used to communicate information.

Latency Stage: In Freud's theory, the psychosexual stage of development that follows resolution of the Oedipus complex. During this stage, sexual desires are relatively weak.

Lateral Thinking: A problem-solving approach that encourages early consideration of alternative ways of conceptualizing a problem.

Lateralization of Function: Specialization of the two hemispheres of the brain for the performance of different functions.

Laws of Grouping: Simple principles describing how we tend to group discrete stimuli together in the perceptual world.

Leadership: The process through which one member of a group (its leader) exerts influence over other group members with respect to the attainment of shared group goals.

Learned Helplessness: Feelings of helplessness that develop after exposure to situations in which no effort succeeds in changing outcomes. Learned helplessness appears to play a role in the occurrence of depression.

Learning: Any relatively permanent change in behaviour (or behaviour potential) resulting from experience.

Leniency Effects: Tendencies to assign higher ratings to persons being evaluated than they actually deserve.

Lens: A curved structure behind the pupil that bends light rays, focusing them on the retina.

Less-Leads-to-More Effect: The fact that rewards just barely sufficient to induce individuals to state positions contrary to their own views often generate more attitude change than larger rewards.

Levels of Processing View: A view of memory suggesting that the greater the effort expended in processing information, the more readily it will be recalled at later times.

Libido: According to Freud, the psychic energy that powers all mental activity.

Lifestyle: In the context of health psychology, the overall pattern of decisions and behaviours that determine health and quality of life.

Limbic System: Several structures deep within the brain that play a role in emotional responding and behaviour.

Linguistic Relativity Hypothesis: The view that language shapes thought.

Localization: The ability of our auditory system to determine the direction of a sound source.

Logical Concepts: Concepts that can be clearly defined by a set of rules or properties.

Longitudinal Research: Research in which the same individuals are studied over long intervals, such as years.

Longitudinal–Sequential Design: A research approach in which several groups of individuals of different ages are studied across time.

Long-Term Memory: A memory system for the retention of large amounts of information over long periods of time.

Lowball Procedure: A tactic for gaining compliance in which, after a deal or arrangement is made, it is changed by the person using this tactic.

LSD: A powerful hallucinogen that produces profound shifts in perception; many of these are frightening in nature.

M

Magnetic Resonance Imaging (MRI): A method for studying the intact brain in which images are obtained by exposure of the brain to a strong magnetic field.

Marital Therapy: Psychotherapy that attempts to improve relations and understanding in couples.

Mean: A measure of central tendency derived by adding all scores and dividing by the number of scores.

Median: A measure of central tendency indicating the midpoint of an array of scores.

Medical Perspective: The view that psychological disorders have a biological basis and should be viewed as treatable diseases.

Medulla: A brain structure concerned with the regulation of vital bodily functions such as breathing and heartbeat.

Memory: The capacity to retain and later retrieve information.

Menopause: Cessation of the menstrual cycle.

Mental Models: Knowledge structures that guide our interactions with objects and events in the world around us.

Mental Retardation: Considerably below-average intellectual functioning combined with varying degrees of difficulty in meeting the demands of everyday life.

Mental Set: The impact of past experience on present problem solving; specifically, the tendency to retain methods that were successful in the past even if better alternatives now exist.

Meta-Analysis: Statistical procedures for combining the results of many studies in order to determine whether their findings provide support for specific hypotheses.

Metacognition: Awareness and understanding of our own cognitive processes.

Metacognitive Processing: An expanded level of awareness that can be achieved by having a person monitor the steps that he or she is taking in attempting to solve a problem.

Midbrain: A part of the brain containing primitive centres for vision and hearing. It also plays a role in the regulation of visual reflexes.

Mitosis: Cell division in which chromosome pairs split and then replicate themselves so that the full number is restored in each of the cells produced by division.

MMPI: A widely used objective test of personality based on empirical keying.

Mode: A measure of central tendency indicating the most frequent score in an array of scores.

Monocular Cues: Cues to depth or distance provided by one eye.

Mood-Dependent Memory: The finding that what we remember while in a given mood may be determined, in part, by what we learned when previously in that same mood.

Mood Disorders: Psychological disorders involving intense and prolonged mood shifts.

Moral Development: Changes that occur with age in the capacity to reason about the rightness or wrongness of various actions.

Morphemes: The smallest units of speech that convey meaning.

Motivation: An inferred internal process that activates, guides, and maintains behaviour over time.

Multicultural Perspective: In modern psychology, a perspective that takes note of the fact that many aspects of behaviour are strongly influenced by factors related to culture and ethnic identity.

N

Narcolepsy: A sleep disorder in which individuals are overcome by uncontrollable periods of sleep during waking hours.

Natural Concepts: Concepts that are not based on a precise set of attributes or properties, do not have clear-cut boundaries, and are often defined by prototypes.

Naturalistic Decision Making: A movement toward studying decision making as it occurs in naturalistic settings.

Naturalistic Observation: A research method in which various aspects of behaviour are carefully observed in the settings where such behaviour naturally occurs.

Nearsightedness: A condition in which the visual image of a distant object is focused slightly in front of the retina rather than directly on it. Therefore, distant objects appear fuzzy or blurred, whereas near objects can be seen clearly.

Negative Afterimage: A sensation of complementary colour that we experience after staring at a stimulus of a given hue.

Negative Punisher: The loss of a desired outcome that occurs in order to suppress a target response.

Negative Reinforcers: Stimuli that strengthen responses that permit an organism to avoid or escape from their presence.

Negative-State Relief Hypothesis: A view suggesting that we sometimes help others in order to relieve the negative feelings that their plight arouses in us.

Neodissociation Theory: A theory of hypnosis suggesting that hypnotized individuals enter an altered state of consciousness in which consciousness is divided.

Neo-Freudians: Personality theorists who accepted basic portions of Freud's theory but rejected or modified other portions.

Nervous System: The complex structure that regulates bodily processes and is responsible, ultimately, for all aspects of conscious experience.

Neural Networks: Computer systems modelled after the brain and made up of highly interconnected elementary computational units that work together in parallel.

Neurons: Cells specialized for communicating information, the basic building blocks of the nervous system.

Neurotransmitters: Chemicals, released by axon terminals, that carry information across the synapse.

Nicotine: The addictive substance in tobacco.

Night Terrors: Extremely frightening dreamlike experiences that occur during non-REM sleep.

Nocturnal Myoclonus: A sleep disorder in which individuals endure periodic and repeated episodes of body twitching all through the night.

Nodes of Ranvier: Small gaps in the myelin sheath surrounding the axons of many neurons.

Non-verbal Cues: Outward signs of others' emotional states. Such cues involve facial expressions, eye contact, and body language.

Normal Curve: A symmetrical, bell-shaped frequency distribution. Most scores are found near the middle, and fewer and fewer occur toward the extremes. Most psychological characteristics are distributed in this manner.

O

Obedience: A form of social influence in which one individual issues orders to another to behave in a specific way.

Obesity: The state of being significantly overweight.

Object Permanence: An understanding of the fact that objects continue to exist when they are out of sight.

Observational Learning: The acquisition of new information, concepts, or forms of behaviour through observation of other people.

Obsessive-Compulsive Disorder: Anxiety disorder in which an individual is unable to stop thinking the same thoughts or performing the same ritualistic behaviours.

Occipital Lobe: The posterior portion of the cerebral cortex, involved in vision.

Oedipus Complex: In Freud's theory, a crisis of psychosexual development in which children must give up their sexual attraction to their opposite-sex parent.

Openness to Experience: One of the "big five" dimensions of personality; ranges from imaginative, sensitive, intellectual at one end to down-to-earth, insensitive, crude at the other.

Operant Conditioning: A process through which organisms learn to repeat behaviours that yield positive outcomes or permit them to avoid or escape from negative outcomes.

Operational Definition: A clear and precise statement of the procedures that are used to measure a psychological concept.

Opiates: Drugs that induce a dreamy, relaxed state and, in some persons, intense feelings of pleasure. Opiates exert their effects by stimulating special receptor sites within the brain.

Opponent-Process Theory: A theory that describes the processing of sensory information related to colour at levels above the retina. The theory suggests that we possess six types of neurons, each of which is either stimulated or inhibited by red, green, blue, yellow, black, or white.

Opponent-Process Theory of Emotion: A theory suggesting that an emotional reaction to a stimulus is followed automatically by an opposite reaction.

Optic Nerve: A bundle of nerve fibres that exit the back of the eye and carry visual information to the brain.

Oral Stage: In Freud's theory, a stage of psychosexual development during which pleasure is centred in the region of the mouth.

Overhelping: Help given to others when they really don't need it, in order to make them appear less competent than they really are.

P

Panic Attack Disorder: An anxiety disorder characterized by relatively brief periods during which individuals experience unbearably intense anxiety.

Paraphilias: Sexual disorders involving choices of inappropriate sexual objects, such as young children, or the inability to experience arousal except in the presence of specific objects or fantasies.

Parapsychologists: Individuals who study psi and other paranormal events.

Parasympathetic Nervous System: The division of the autonomic nervous system that readies the body for restoration of energy.

Parental Demandingness: The extent to which parents are strict or controlling, and confront their children (often angrily) when they do not meet the parents' expectations.

Parental Responsiveness: The extent to which parents are involved in and supportive of their children's activities

Parietal Lobe: A portion of the cerebral cortex, lying behind the central fissure, that plays a major role in the skin senses: touch, temperature, pressure.

Parkinson's Disease: A progressive and ultimately fatal nervous-system disorder, characterized by a gradual increase of tremors and muscle rigidity, followed by trouble maintaining balance and difficulty initiating movements.

Passionate Love: A form of love in which feelings of strong attraction and sexual desire toward another person are dominant.

Passive Smoking: Inhaling other people's cigarette smoke.

Peak Experiences: In Maslow's theory, intense emotional experiences during which individuals feel at one with the universe.

Perception: The process through which we select, organize, and interpret input from our sensory receptors.

Peripheral Nervous System: The division of the nervous system that connects internal organs and glands, as well as voluntary and involuntary muscles, to the central nervous system.

Peripheral Route (to persuasion): Attitude change resulting from peripheral persuasion cues—information concerning the expertise, status, or attractiveness of would-be persuaders.

Personality: Individuals' unique and relatively stable patterns of behaviour, thoughts, and feelings.

Personality Disorders: Extreme and inflexible personality traits that impair an individual's ability to enter into and maintain social relationships with others.

Personality Traits: Specific dimensions along which individuals' personalities differ in consistent, stable ways.

Person–Environment (P–E) Fit: The appropriateness of the match between a person and his or her work environment; a poor P–E fit may produce stress.

Persuasion: The process through which one or more persons attempt to alter the attitudes of one or more others.

Pervasive Development Disorders. Disorders that involve lifelong impairment in mental or physical functioning.

Phallic Stage: In Freud's theory, a psychosexual stage of development during which pleasure is centred in the genital region. It is during this stage that the Oedipus complex develops.

Phenylketonuria (PKU): A genetically based disorder in which a person lacks the enzyme to break down phenylalanine, a substance present in many foods. The gradual buildup of phenylalanine contributes to subsequent outcomes that include retardation.

Phobias: Intense, irrational fears of objects or events.

Phonemes: A set of sounds basic to a given language.

Phonological Development: Development of the ability to produce recognizable speech.

Phonological Store: A component of working memory that permits us to hold speech or speech-like material for about two seconds.

Physiological Dependence: Strong urges to continue using a drug based on biological factors such as changes in metabolism.

Pinna: The external portion of the ear.

Pitch: The characteristic of a sound that is described as high or low. Pitch is mediated by the frequency of a sound.

Pituitary Gland: An endocrine gland that releases hormones to regulate other glands and several basic biological processes.

Place Theory: A theory suggesting that sounds of different frequency stimulate different areas of the basilar membrane.

Placenta: A structure that surrounds, protects, and nourishes the developing fetus.

Playing Hard to Get: A tactic for gaining compliance in which individuals try to create the image that they are very popular or very much in demand.

Pleasure Principle: The principle on which the id operates—immediate pleasure with no attention to possible consequences.

Pons: A portion of the brain through which sensory and motor information passes, and which contains structures relating to sleep, arousal, and the regulation of muscle tone and cardiac reflexes.

Positive Punisher: An aversive consequence that is delivered in order to suppress a target response.

Positive Reinforcers: Stimuli that strengthen responses that precede them.

Positron Emission Tomography (PET): An imaging technique that detects the activity of the brain by measuring glucose utilization or blood flow.

Postconventional Level (of morality): According to Kohlberg, the final stage of moral development, in which individuals judge morality in terms of abstract principles.

Post-Traumatic Stress Disorder: Psychological disorder resulting from a very stressful experience; includes nightmares and flashbacks, distress at exposure to reminders of the event, irritability, difficulty concentrating, and a general unresponsiveness.

Power Motivation: Motivation to be in charge, have high status, and exert influence over others.

Practical Intelligence: Intelligence useful in solving everyday problems.

Preconventional Level (of morality): According to Kohlberg, the earliest stage of moral development, in which individuals judge morality in terms of the effects produced by various actions.

Predictive Validity: The extent to which scores on a test serve to predict future performance in a particular realm of behaviour.

Prejudice: Negative attitudes toward the members of some social group based on their membership in this group.

Premack Principle: The principle that a more preferred activity can be used to reinforce a less preferred activity.

Preoperational Stage: In Piaget's theory, a stage of cognitive development during which children become capable of mental representations of the external world.

Prevention Strategies: Techniques designed to reduce the occurrence of physical and psychological problems.

Primary Aging: Aging due to the passage of time and, to some extent, inherited biological factors.

Proactive Interference: Interference with the learning or storage of current information by information previously entered into memory.

Problem Solving: Efforts to develop or choose among various responses in order to attain desired goals.

Problem-Solving Therapy: A form of family therapy that focuses on instituting specific, well-defined changes within a family in order to eliminate specific problems.

Procedural Memory: A memory system that retains information we cannot readily express verbally—for example, information necessary to perform skilled motor activities such as riding a bicycle.

Processing Speed: The speed with which individuals can process information.

Propositions: Sentences that relate one concept to another and can stand as separate assertions.

Prosocial Behaviour: Actions that benefit others without necessarily providing any direct benefit to the persons who perform them.

Prosopagnosia: A rare condition in which brain damage impairs a person's ability to recognize faces.

Prototypes: Representations in memory of various objects or stimuli in the physical world; the best or clearest examples of various objects or stimuli in the physical world.

Psi: Unusual processes of information or energy transfer that are currently unexplained in terms of known physical or biological mechanisms. Included under the heading of psi are such supposed abilities as telepathy (reading others' thoughts) and clairvoyance (perceiving unseen objects or unknowable events).

Psychedelics: Drugs that alter sensory perception and so may be considered mind-expanding.

Psychiatry: A branch of medicine that focuses on the diagnosis and treatment of psychological disorders.

Psychoanalysis: A method of therapy based on Freud's theory of personality, in which the therapist attempts to bring repressed unconscious material into consciousness.

Psychodrama: A form of psychodynamic group therapy in which people act out their problems in front of fellow group members.

Psychodynamic Therapies: Therapies based on the assumption that psychological disorders stem primarily from hidden inner conflicts with repressed urges and impulses.

Psychological Dependence: Strong desires to continue using a drug even though it is not physiologically addicting.

Psychological Disorders: Behaviours or thoughts that are unusual in a given society, that are maladaptive, and that cause the persons who experience them considerable distress.

Psychology: The science of behaviour and cognitive processes.

Psychosexual Stages of Development: According to Freud, an innate sequence of stages through which all human beings pass. At each stage, pleasure is focused on a different region of the body.

Psychosurgery: Efforts to alleviate psychological disorders by performing surgery on the brain.

Psychotherapies: Procedures designed to eliminate or modify psychological disorders through the establishment of a special relationship between a client and a trained therapist.

Puberty: The period of rapid change during which individuals reach sexual maturity and become capable of reproduction.

Punishment: The application or removal of a stimulus so as to decrease the strength of a behaviour.

Pupil: An opening in the eye, just behind the cornea, through which light rays enter the eye.

R

Random Assignment of Participants to Experimental and Control Conditions: Assuring that all research participants have an equal chance of being assigned to each of the experimental and control conditions.

Range: The difference between the highest and lowest scores in a distribution of scores.

Rational–Emotive Therapy: A cognitive therapy that focuses on changing irrational beliefs.

Raven Progressive Matrices Test: One popular test of intelligence that was designed to be relatively free of cultural bias.

Reaction Time: The time that elapses between the presentation of a stimulus and a person's reaction to it.

Realistic Conflict Theory: A theory proposing that prejudice stems, at least in part, from economic competition between social groups.

Reality Principle: The principle on which the ego operates, according to which the external consequences of behaviour are considered in the regulation of expression of impulses from the id.

Reasoning: Cognitive activity that transforms information in order to reach specific conclusions.

Recategorization: Shifting the boundary between "us" and "them" so that persons previously seen as belonging to out-groups are now seen as belonging to the in-group.

Reconditioning: The rapid recovery of a conditioned response to a CS–UCS pairing following extinction.

Recuperative Theory: A theory suggesting that while repair of the body goes on during our waking hours, repair of the brain happens during sleep; therefore, sleep provides the rest we require to recover from the wear and tear of the previous day's activities.

Reinforcement: The application or removal of a stimulus so as to increase the strength of a behaviour.

Relative Size: A visual cue based on comparison of the size of an unknown object to one of known size.

Reliability: The extent to which any measuring device (including psychological tests) yields the same result each time it is applied to identical quantities.

REM (Rapid Eye Movement) Sleep: A state of sleep in which brain activity resembling waking restfulness is accompanied by deep muscle relaxation and movements of the eyes. Most dreams occur during periods of REM sleep.

Repeated Exposure Effect: The fact that the more frequently we are exposed to various stimuli (at least up to a point), the more we tend to like them.

Replication: A basic scientific principle requiring that the results of an experiment be repeated before they are accepted with confidence.

Representativeness Heuristic: A mental rule of thumb suggesting that the more closely an event or object resembles typical examples of some concept or category, the more likely it is to belong to that concept or category.

Repression: A theory of forgetting that suggests that memories of experiences or events we find threatening are sometimes pushed out of consciousness so that they can no longer be recalled.

Resilience in Development: Refers to the capacity of some adolescents raised in harmful environments to somehow rise above these disadvantages and achieve healthy development.

Resistance: Efforts by individuals undergoing psychoanalysis to prevent repressed impulses or conflicts from entering consciousness.

Resistant Attachment: A pattern of attachment in which infants reject their mother and refuse to be comforted by her after she leaves them alone during the strange situation test.

Reticular Activating System: A structure within the brain concerned with sleep, arousal, and the regulation of muscle tone and cardiac reflexes.

Retina: The surface at the back of the eye containing the rods and cones.

Retrieval: The process through which information stored in memory is located.

Retrieval Cues: Stimuli associated with information stored in memory that can aid in its retrieval.

Retroactive Interference: Interference with retention of information already present in memory by new information being entered into memory.

Retrograde Amnesia: The inability to store in long-term memory information that occurred before an amnesia-inducing event.

Revolving Door: An ineffective cycle of psychological treatment consisting of hospitalization, admission to treatment centres, and release.

Risk Factors: Aspects of our environment or behaviour that influence our chances of developing or contracting a disease, within the limits set by our genetic structure.

Rods: One of the two types of sensory receptors for vision found in the eye.

Rorschach Test: A widely used projective test of personality in which individuals are asked to describe what they see in a series of inkblots.

S

Saccadic Movements: Quick movements of the eyes from one point of fixation to another.

Sampling: With respect to the survey method, refers to how people who participate in a survey are selected.

Saturation: The degree of concentration of the hue of light. We experience saturation as the purity of a colour.

Savant Syndrome: A condition in which an individual has general cognitive impairment but nevertheless demonstrates normal or above-normal skills in one or more intellectual domains.

Schachter-Singer Theory (two-factor theory): A theory of emotion suggesting that our subjective emotional states are determined, at least in part, by the cognitive labels we attach to feelings of arousal.

Schedules of Reinforcement: Rules determining when and how reinforcements will be delivered.

Schemas: Cognitive frameworks representing our knowledge about aspects of the world.

Schizoid Personality Disorder: A personality disorder in which individuals become almost totally detached from the social world.

Schizophrenia: A group of serious psychological disorders characterized by severe distortions in thought and language, perceptions, and emotion.

Seasonal Affective Disorder (SAD): Depression typically experienced during the winter months, supposedly stemming from a lack of exposure to sunlight.

Secondary Aging: Aging due to the effects of disease, disuse, or abuse of the body.

Secondary Traits: According to Allport, traits that exert relatively specific and weak effects upon behaviour.

Secure Attachment: A pattern of attachment in which infants actively seek contact with their mother and take comfort from her presence when they are reunited with her during the strange situation test.

Selective Attention: Our ability to pay attention to only some aspects of the world around us while largely ignoring others.

Self-Actualization: A stage of personal development in which individuals reach their maximum potential.

Self-Concept: All the information and beliefs individuals have about their own characteristics and themselves.

Self-Consciousness: Increased awareness of oneself as a social object or of one's own values and attitudes.

Self-Determination Theory: Theory suggesting that motivation for health-promoting behaviours is highest when it is autonomous and lowest when it is prompted by others.

Self-Disclosure: The act of revealing information about oneself to another person.

Self-Efficacy: Individuals' expectations concerning their ability to perform various tasks.

Self-Esteem: The extent to which individuals have positive or negative feelings about themselves and their own worth.

Self-Help Groups: Groups of individuals experiencing the same kinds of difficulties that meet to discuss their shared problem and find solutions to it.

Self-Monitoring: A personality trait involving sensitivity to social situations and an ability to adapt one's behaviour to the demands of those situations in order to make favourable impressions on others.

Self-Reinforcement: A process in which individuals reward themselves for reaching their own goals.

Self-Serving Bias: The tendency to attribute positive outcomes to our own traits or characteristics but negative outcomes to factors beyond our control.

Self-System: In Bandura's social cognitive learning theory, the set of cognitive processes by which a person perceives, evaluates, and regulates his or her own behaviour.

Semantic Memory: The content of our general, abstract knowledge about the world.

Semicircular Canals: Fluid-filled structures that provide information about rotational acceleration of the head or body around three principal axes of rotation.

Sensation: Input about the physical world provided by our sensory receptors.

Sensation Seeking: The desire to seek out novel and intense experiences.

Sensitivity-Training Groups: A form of group therapy designed to foster personal growth through increased understanding of one's own behaviour and increased honesty and openness in personal relations.

Sensorimotor Stage: In Piaget's theory, the earliest stage of cognitive development.

Sensory Adaptation: Reduced sensitivity to unchanging stimuli over time.

Sensory Memory: A memory system that retains representations of sensory input for extremely brief periods of time.

Sensory Receptors: Cells specialized for the task of transduction—converting physical energy (light, sound) into neural impulses.

Serial Position Curve: The greater accuracy of recall of words or other information early and late in a list, than words or information in the middle of the list.

Serum Cholesterol: The amount of cholesterol in one's blood.

Sex-Category Constancy: Understanding of one's sexual identity, centring around a biologically based categorical distinction between males and females.

Sexual Abuse: Sexual contact or activities forced on children, adolescents, or adults by other persons, usually adults.

Sexual Arousal Disorders: Psychological disorders involving inability to attain an erection (males) or absence of vaginal swelling and lubrication (females).

Sexual Desire Disorders: Psychological disorders involving a lack of interest in sex or active aversion to sexual activities.

Sexual Jealousy: A negative state aroused by a perceived threat to one's sexual relationship with another person.

Sexual Motivation: Motivation to engage in various forms of sexual activity.

Shape Constancy: The tendency to perceive a physical object as having a constant shape even when the image it casts on the retina changes.

Shaping: A technique in which closer and closer approximations of desired behaviour are required for the delivery of positive reinforcement.

Signal Detection Theory: A theory suggesting that there are no absolute thresholds for sensations. Rather, detection of stimuli depends on their physical energy and on internal factors such as the relative costs and benefits associated with detecting their presence.

Simple Cells: Cells within the visual system that respond to linear shapes presented in certain orientations (horizontal, vertical, etc.).

Simultaneous Conditioning: A form of conditioning in which the conditioned stimulus and the unconditioned stimulus begin and end at the same time.

Situational Leadership Theory: A theory of leadership indicating that as their followers gain increasing experience, leaders should shift from a directive to a nondirective style of leadership.

Size Constancy: The tendency to perceive a physical object as having a constant size even when the size of the image it casts on the retina changes.

Sleep: A process in which important physiological changes (including shifts in brain activity and slowing of basic bodily functions) are accompanied by major shifts in consciousness.

Sleep Apnea: Cessation of breathing during sleep.

Social Age Clocks: Internalized calendars that tell us when certain events should occur in our lives and what we should be doing at certain ages.

Social Categorization: Our tendency to divide the social world into two distinct categories: "us" and "them."

Social Cognition: The processes through which we notice, interpret, remember, and later use social information.

Social Cognitive Theory: A theory of behaviour suggesting that human behaviour is influenced by many cognitive factors as well as by reinforcement contingencies, and that human beings have an impressive capacity to regulate their own actions.

Social Influence: Efforts by one or more individuals to change the attitudes or behaviour of one or more others.

Social Norms: Rules in a given group or society indicating how individuals ought to behave in specific situations.

Social Psychology: The branch of psychology that studies all aspects of social behaviour and social thought.

Social Referencing: Using others' reactions to appraise an uncertain situation or experience.

Somatic Nervous System: The portion of the peripheral nervous system that connects the brain and spinal cord to voluntary muscles.

Somatization Disorder: A psychological condition in which individuals report physical complaints and symptoms, including aches and pains, problems with their digestive systems, and sexual problems such as sexual indifference or irregular menstruation.

Somatoform Disorders: Category of disorders in which psychological conflicts or other problems take on a physical form.

Somnambulism: A sleep disorder in which individuals actually get up and move about while still asleep.

Source Traits: According to Cattell, key dimensions of personality that underlie many other traits.

Split-Half Reliability: The extent to which an individual attains equivalent scores on two halves of a psychological test.

Spontaneous Recovery: Following extinction, return of a conditioned response upon reinstatement of CS–UCS pairings.

SQUID (Superconducting Quantum Interference Device): An imaging device that captures images of the brain through its ability to detect tiny changes in magnetic fields in the brain.

Stage Theory: Any theory proposing that all human beings move through an orderly and predictable series of changes.

Standard Deviation: A measure of dispersion reflecting the average distance between each score and the mean.

Stanford-Binet Test: A popular test for measuring individual intelligence.

State-Dependent Retrieval: Information tends to be easier to recall when our internal state is similar to that which existed when the information was first entered into memory.

States of Consciousness: Varying degrees of awareness of ourselves and the external world.

Statistics: Mathematical procedures used to describe data and draw inferences from them.

Stereotypes: Cognitive frameworks in which all members of specific social groups share certain characteristics.

Stimulants: Drugs that increase activity in the nervous system, including amphetamines, caffeine, and nicotine.

Stimulus: A physical event capable of affecting behaviour.

Stimulus Control: Consistent occurrence of a behaviour in the presence of a discriminative stimulus.

Stimulus Discrimination: The process by which organisms learn to respond to certain stimuli but not to others.

Stimulus Generalization: The tendency of stimuli similar to a conditioned stimulus to elicit a conditioned response.

Stochastic Theories of Aging (also known as wear-tear theories of aging): Theories suggesting that we grow old because of cumulative damage to our bodies from both external and internal sources.

Storage: The process through which information is retained in memory.

Strange Situation Test: A procedure for studying attachment in which mothers leave their children alone with a stranger for several minutes and then return.

Stress: The process that occurs in response to events that disrupt, or threaten to disrupt, our physical or psychological functioning.

Stress Inoculation Training: A form of behaviour therapy dealing with anxiety problems.

Stressors: Events or situations in our environment that cause stress.

Striving for Superiority: Attempting to overcome feelings of inferiority. According to Adler, this is the primary motive for human behaviour.

Structuralism: An early view suggesting that psychology should focus on conscious experience and on the task of analyzing such experience into its basic parts.

Subjective Well-Being: Personal happiness.

Sublimation: A defense mechanism in which threatening unconscious impulses are channelled into socially acceptable forms of behaviour.

Subliminal Perception: The presumed ability to perceive a stimulus that is below the threshold for conscious experience.

Substance Abuse: Substance-related disorders involving one or more of the following: recurrent use resulting in a failure to fulfill major role obligations at work, school, or home; recurrent substance use in situations in which it is physically hazardous to do so; recurrent substance-related legal problems.

Substance Dependence: Substance-related disorders involving one or more of the following: the need for increasing amounts of the substance to achieve the desired effect, withdrawal symptoms when the substance isn't taken, an inability to cut down or control use of the substance, and spending a great deal of time in activities necessary to obtain the substance.

Substance-Related Disorders: Disorders involving maladaptive patterns of substance use leading to clinically significant impairment.

Suicide: The act of taking one's own life.

Superego: According to Freud, the portion of human personality representing the conscience.

Suprachiasmatic Nucleus: A portion of the hypothalamus that seems to play an important role in the regulation of circadian rhythms.

Surface Structure: The actual words of which sentences consist.

Survey Method: A research method in which large numbers of people answer questions about aspects of their views or their behaviour.

Symbolic Play: Play in which children pretend that one object is another object.

Sympathetic Nervous System: The division of the autonomic nervous system that readies the body for expenditure of energy.

Synapse: The gap between the axon of one neuron and other neurons, muscles, or glands.

Synaptic Vesicles: Structures in the axon terminals that contain neurotransmitters.

Syntax: Rules about how units of speech can be combined into sentences in a given language.

Systematic Desensitization: A form of behaviour therapy in which individuals imagine scenes or events that are increasingly anxiety-provoking and at the same time engage in procedures that induce feelings of relaxation.

Systematic Observation: A basic method of science in which the natural world, or various events or processes in it, are observed and measured in a very careful manner.

T

Tardive Dyskinesia: A side effect of prolonged exposure to antipsychotic drugs in which individuals experience involuntary muscular movements, especially of the face.

Temperament: Stable individual differences in the quality and intensity of emotional reactions.

Templates: Specific patterns stored in our memories for various visual stimuli that we encounter.

Temporal Lobe: The lobe of the cerebral cortex that is involved in audition.

Teratogens: Factors in the environment that can harm the developing fetus.

Test–Retest Reliability: The extent to which a psychological test yields similar scores when taken by the same person on different occasions.

Thalamus: A structure deep within the brain that receives sensory input from other portions of the nervous system and then transmits this information to the cerebral cortex and other parts of the brain.

That's-Not-All Technique: A technique for gaining compliance in which a small extra incentive is offered before the target person has agreed to or rejected a request.

Thematic Apperception Test (TAT): A psychological test used to assess individual differences in several motives, such as achievement motivation and power motivation.

Theories: Frameworks in science for explaining various phenomena. Theories consist of two major parts: basic concepts and assertions concerning relationships between these concepts.

Theory of Mind: Refers to children's growing understanding of their own mental states and those of others.

Therapeutic Alliance: The special relationship between therapist and client that contributes to the effectiveness of many forms of psychotherapy.

Timbre: The quality of a sound, resulting from the complex makeup of a sound wave; timbre helps us to distinguish the sound of a trumpet from that of a saxophone.

Token Economies: Forms of behaviour therapy based on operant conditioning, in which hospitalized patients earn tokens they can exchange for valued rewards when they behave in ways the hospital staff consider to be desirable.

Tolerance: Habituation to a drug, causing larger and larger doses to be required to produce effects of the same magnitude.

Trace Conditioning: A form of forward conditioning in which the presentation of the conditioned stimulus precedes and does not overlap with the presentation of the unconditioned stimulus.

Trace-Decay Hypothesis: A theory of forgetting that assumes information in long-term memory fades or decays with the passage of time.

Trait Theories: Theories of personality that focus on identifying the key dimensions along which people differ.

Transduction: The translation of a physical energy into electrical signals by specialized receptor cells.

Transference: Strong positive or negative feelings toward the therapist on the part of individuals undergoing psychoanalysis.

Trial and Error: A method of solving problems in which possible solutions are tried until one succeeds.

Triarchic Theory: A theory suggesting that there are actually three distinct kinds of intelligence.

Trichromatic Theory: A theory of colour perception suggesting that we have three types of cones, each primarily receptive to particular wavelengths of light.

Type A Behaviour Pattern: A cluster of traits (including competitiveness, aggressiveness, urgency, and hostility) related to important aspects of health, social behaviour, and task performance.

Type D Personality Type: A term used to describe a general tendency to cope with stress by keeping negative emotions to oneself. People who exhibit this behaviour pattern are more likely to experience suppressed immune systems and health-related problems.

U

Unconditional Positive Regard: In Rogers's theory, communicating to others that they will be respected or loved regardless of what they say or do.

Unconditioned Response (UCR): In classical conditioning, the response elicited by an unconditioned stimulus.

Unconditioned Stimulus (UCS): In classical conditioning, a stimulus that can elicit an unconditioned response the first time it is presented.

Universal Phonetic Sensitivity: The ability of infants at birth to discriminate contrasts between speech sound that occur in any human language.

V

Validity: The extent to which tests actually measure what they claim to measure.

Variable-Interval Schedule: A schedule of reinforcement in which a variable amount of time elapses before a response will yield reinforcement.

Variable-Ratio Schedule: A schedule of reinforcement in which reinforcement occurs after a variable number of responses have been performed.

Variance: A measure of dispersion reflecting the average squared distance between each score and the mean.

Vestibular Sacs: Fluid-filled sacs in our inner ear that provide information about the positions and changes in linear movement of our head and body.

Vestibular Sense: Our sense of balance.

Visual Images: Mental pictures or representations of objects or events.

Visuospatial Sketchpad: A component of working memory that allows us to hold important information about visual and spatial memory for a short period of time.

W

Wavelength: The peak-to-peak distance in a sound or light wave.

Wernicke-Geschwind Theory: A theory of how the brain processes information relating to speech and other verbal abilities.

Work Motivation: Motivation to perform and complete various tasks.

Working Memory: A memory system that holds limited amounts of information for relatively short periods of time.

REFERENCES

Aaronson, L.S., & MacNee, C.L. (1989). Tobacco, alcohol, and caffeine use during pregnancy. *Journal of Obstetrics, Gynecology, and Neonatal Nursing, 18,* 279–287.

Abbey, S. E., Hood, E., Young, L. T., & Malcolmson, S. A. (1993). Psychiatric Consultation in the Eastern Canadian Arctic III. Mental health issues in Inuit women in the Eastern Arctic. III. *Canadian Journal of Psychiatry, 38,* 32–35.

Aboud, F.E., & Doyle, A.B. (1996). Does talk of race foster prejudice or tolerance in children? *Canadian Journal of Behavioural Science, 28,* 161–170.

Aboud, F.E., & Doyle, A.B. (1996). Parental and peer influences on children's racial attitudes. *International Journal of Intercultural Relations, 20,* 371–383.

Aboud, F.E., & Mendelson, M.J. (1998). Determinants of friendship selection and quality: Developmental perspectives. In W.M. Bukowski, & A.F. Newcomb (Eds.), *The company they keep: Friendship in childhood and adolescence* (pp. 87–112). New York, NY: Cambridge University Press.

Abra, J. (1989). Changes in creativity with age: data, explanations, and further predictions. *International Journal of Aging and Human Development, 28(2),* 105–126.

Abramovitch, R., Freedman, J. L. Thoden, K., & Nicolick, C. (1991). Children's capacity to consent to participation in psychological research: Empirical findings. *Child Development, 62,* 1100–1109.

Abramowitz, S. I. (1986). Psychosocial outcomes of sexual reassignment surgery. *Journal of Consulting and Clinical Psychology, 54,* 183–189.

Absi-Semaan, N., Crombie, G., Freeman, C. (1993). Masculinity and femininity in middle childhood: Developmental and factor analyses. *Sex Roles, 28(3–4),* 187–206.

Adams, R.J. (1987). An evaluation of color preference in early infancy. *Infant Behavior and Development, 10(2),* 143–150.

Adams, R.J., Courage, M.L., Mercer, M.E. (1994). Systematic measurement of human neonatal color vision. *Vision Research, 34(13),* 1691–1701.

Addington, J. (1992). Separation group. *Journal for Specialists in Group Work, 17(1),* 20–28.

Addington, J.M. (1986). The development of children and adolescents from divorced homes. *Journal of Child Care, 2(5),* 83–97.

Adelstein, A. & Crowne, D.P. (1991). Visuospatial asymmetries and interocular transfer in the split-brain rat. *Behavioral Neuroscience, 105(3),* 459–469.

Ader, R., & Cohen, N. (1984). Behavior and the immune system. In W.D. Gentry (Ed.), *Handbook of behavioral medicine.* New York: Guilford.

Ader, R., & Cohen, N. (1993). Psychoneuroimmunology: Conditioning and stress. *Annual Review of Psychology, 44,* 53–85.

Adlaf, E.M. & Smart, R.G. (1995). Alcohol use, drug use, and well-being in older adults in Toronto. *International Journal of the Addictions, 30,* 1985–2016.

Adlaf, E.M., Smart, R.G., Walsh, G.W., & Ivis, F.J. (1994). Is the association between drug use and delinquency weakening? *Addiction, 89,* 1675–1681.

Adler, N.J., & Bartholomew, S. (1992). Managing globally competent people. *Academy of Management Executive, 6,* 52–65.

Adolphs, R. (in press). The human amygdala and emotion. *The Neuroscientist.*

Adolphs, R., Russell, J.A., & Tranel, D. (1999). A role for the human amygdala in recognizing emotional arousal from unpleasant stimuli. *Psychological Science, 10,* 167–171.

Adolphs, R., & Tranel, D. (1999). Intact recognition of emotional prosody following amygdala damage. *Neuropsychologia, 37,* 1285–1292.

Ahmed, S.M. & Mapletoft, S.J. (1989). A new approach to explain aggression. *Perceptual and Motor Skills, 69(2),* 403–408.

Ahmed, S.M. (1992). Fraisse's theory of emotion and aggression. *Journal of Social Psychology, 132(2),* 257–260.

Aiken, L. R. (1991). *Psychological testing and assessment* (7th ed.) Boston: Allyn & Bacon.

Ainsworth, M.D.S. (1969). Object relations, dependency, and attachment: A theoretical review of the infant-mother relationship. *Child Development, 40,* 969–1025.

Ainsworth, M.D.S. (1973). The development of infant-mother attachment. In B. Caldwell & H. Riciutti (Eds.), *Review of child development research* (vol. 3, pp. 1–94). Chicago: University of Chicago Press.

Ainsworth, M.D.S., Blehar, M.C., Waters, E., Wall, S. (1978). *Patterns of attachment.* Hillsdale, NJ: Erlbaum.

Akil, J., Watson, S. J., Young, E., Lewis, M. E., Kachaturian, H., & Walker, M. W. (1984). Endogenous opiates: Biology and function. *Annual Review of Neuroscience, 7,* 223–256.

Alberts-Corush, J., Firestone, P., Goodman, J.T., (1986). Attention and impulsivity characteristics of the biological and adoptive parents of hyperactive and normal control children. *American Journal of Orthopsychiatry, 56(3),* 413–423.

Aldridge, D., & Kimberly, St.J. (1991). Adolescent and pre-adolescent suicide in Newfoundland and Labrador. *Canadian Journal of Psychiatry, 36,* 432–436.

Algna, F.J., Whitcher, L.J., Fisher, J.D. (1979). Evaluative reactions to interpersonal touch in a counseling interview. *Journal of Counseling Psychology, 26,* 465–472.

Alicke, M.D., & Largo, E. (1995). The role of the self in the false consensus effect. *Journal of Experimental Social Psychology, 31,* 28–47.

Al-Issa, I. (1982). Does culture make a difference in psychopathology? In I. Al-Issa (Ed.), *Culture and psychopathology.* Baltimore: University Park Press.

Allan, L.G. and Siegel, S. (1993). McCollough effects as conditioned responses: Reply to Dodwell and Humphrey, *Psychological Review, 100.* 342–346.

Allen, M. G. (1976). Twin studies of affective illness. *Archives of General Psychiatry, 35,* 1476–1478.

Allgood-Merton, B., Lewinsohn, P.M. & Hops, H. (1990). Sex differences and adolescent depression. *Journal of Abnormal Psychology, 99(1),* 55–63.

Allodi, F.A. (1994). Post-traumatic stress disorder in hostages and victims of torture. *Psychiatric Clinics of North America, 17,* 279–288.

Alloy, L.B., Abramson, L.Y. & Dykman, B.M. (1990). Depressive realities and nondepressive optimistic illusions: The role of the self. In R.E. Ingram (Ed.)., *Contemporary psychological approaches to depression: Treatment, research, and theory.* New York: Plenum.

Allport, G. W. (1965). *Letters from Jenny.* New York: Harcourt, Brace & World.

Allport, G. W., & Odbert, H. S. (1936). Trait names: A psycholexical study. *Psychological Monographs, 47,* 211.

Aloise-Young, P.S., Graham, J.W., & Hnsen, W.B. (1994). Peer influence on smoking initiation during early adolescence: A comparison of group members and group outsiders. *Journal of Applied Psychology, 79,* 281–287.

Altemeyer, B. (1988). *Enemies of freedom: Understanding right-wing authoritarianism.* San Francisco: Jossey-Bass.

Altshuler, J.L., & Ruble, D.N., (1989). Developmental changes in children's awareness of strategies for coping with uncontrollable stress. *Child Development, 60(6),* 1337–1349.

Alvarez-Borda, B., Ramirez, A.V., Perez-Montfort, R., & Bermudez-Rattoni, F. (1995). Enhancement of antibody production by a learning paradigm. *Neurobiology of Learning and Memory, 64,* 103–105.

Amabile, T.M. (1983). *The social psychology of creativity.* New York: Springer-Verlag.

Amaro, H. (1995). Love, sex, and power: Considering women's realities in HIV prevention. 101st Annual Convention of the American Psychological Association (1993, Toronto, Canada). *American Psychologist, 50(6),* 437–447.

Amato, P.R. (1990). Parental divorce and attitudes toward marriage and family life. *Journal of Marriage and the Family, 50,* 453–461.

Ambuel, B. (1995). Adolescents, unintended pregnancy, and abortions: The struggle for a compassionate social policy. *Current Direction in Psychological Science, 4,* 1–5.

American Psychiatric Association (1993). DSM-IV Draft Criteria. Washington, DC: Author.

American Psychiatric Association. (1994). *Diagnostic and statistical manual of mental disorders* (4th ed.). Washington, DC: Author.

Amoore, J. (1970). *Molecular basis of odor.* Springfield, IL: Thomas.

Amoore, J. (1982). Odor theory and odor classification. In E. Theimer (Ed.), *Fragrance chemistry: The science of the sense of smell.* New York: Academic Press.

Amundson, N.E. (1993). Mattering: a foundation for employment counselling and training. Special issue: Employment counselling training. *Journal of Employment Counselling, 30(4),* 146–152.

Andersen, S.M., Klatzky, R.L., Murray, J. (1990). Traits and social stereotypes: Efficiency differences in social information processing. *Journal of Personality and Social Psychology, 59 (2),* 192–201.

Anderson, C.A. (1997). External validity of "trivial" experiments: The case of laboratory aggression. *Review of General Psychology, 1,* 19–41.

Anderson, C.A., Anderson, K.B., & Deuser, W.E. (1996). Examining an affective aggression framework: weapon and temperature effects on aggressive thoughts, affect, and attitudes. *Personality and Social Psychology Bulletin, 22,* 366–376.

Anderson, C.A., Deuser, W.E., & DeNeve, K.M. (1995). Hot temperatures, hostile affect, hostile cognition, and arousal: Tests of a general model of affective aggression. *Personality and Social Psychology Bulletin, 21,* 434–448.

Anderson, C.A., Lindsay, J.J., & Bushman, B.J. (1999). Research in the psychological laboratory: Truth or triviality? *Current Directions in Psychological Science, 8,* 3–9.

Anderson, J.L. & Crawford, C.B. (1992). Modeling costs and benefits of adolescent weight control as a mechanism for reproductive suppression. *Human Nature, 3(4),* 299–334.

Anderson, P.A., Bowman, L.L., Segrin, C., Buller, D.B., Street, R.L., Goleman, D., & Aune, R. K. (1999). Power, persuasion, and deception. In L.K. Guerrero, & J.A. DeVito (Eds.), *The nonverbal communication reader: Classic and contemporary readings* (2nd ed.) (pp. 317–376). Prospect Heights, IL: Waveland Press.

Anderson, R.C. & Pichert, J. W. (1978) Recall of previously unrecallabe information following a shift in perspective. *Journal of Verbal Learning and Verbal Behavior, 17,* 1–121.

Andreasen, N. C., Flaum, M., Swayze, V., II, O'Leary, D. S., Alliger, R., Cohen, G., Ehrhardt, J., & Yuhn, W. T. C. (1993). Intelligence and brain structure in normal individuals. *American Journal of Psychiatry, 150,* 130–134.

Andrews, G., & Harvey, R. (1981). Does psychotherapy benefit neurotic patients? A reanalysis of the Smith, Glass, and Miller data. *Archives of General Psychiatry, 38,* 1203–1208.

Angerspatch, D., Knauth, P., Darvonen, M.J., & Undeutsch, K. (1980). A retrospective cohort study comparing complaints and diseases in day and shift workers. *International Archives of Occupational and Environmental Health, 45,* 127–140.

Ankney, C.D. (1992). Sex differences in relative brain size: a mismeasure of woman, too? Special issue: biology and intelligence. *Intelligence, 16(3–4),* 329–336.

Anson, A.R., Cook, T.D., Habib, F., Grady, M.K., Haynes, N., Comer, P. (1991). The Comer school development program: A theoretical analysis. *Urban Education, 26,* 56–82.

Anstis, S. (1992). Adaptation to a negative, brightness-reversed world: Some preliminary observations. In G. A. Carpenter & S. Grossberg (Eds.), *Neural networks for vision and image processing.* Cambridge: MIT Press.

Anstis, S., & Hutahajan, P. (1991). Visual adaption to a negative, brightness-reversed world. Paper presented at the Association for Research in Vision and Opthalmology Conference, Sarasota, Florida.

Antrobus, J. (1991). Dreaming: Cognitive processes during cortical activation and high afferent thresholds. *Psychological Review, 98,* 96–212.

Antrobus, J.S., & Bertini, M. (Eds.). (1992). *The neuropsychology of eating and sleeping.* New York, NY: Lawrence Erlbaum Associates, Inc.

Arbuckle, T.Y. & Gold, D.P. (1993). Aging, inhibition, and verbosity. *Journal of Gerontology, 48(5),* 225–232.

Arbuckle, T.Y., Gold, D.P., Andres, D., Schwartzman, A., Chaikelson, J. (1992). The role of psychosocial context, age, and intelligence in memory performance of older men. *Psychology and Aging, 7(1),* 25–36.

Archer, L.A., Cunningham, C.E. & Whelan, D.T. (1988). Coping with dietary therapy in phenylketonuria: a case report. Special issue: child and adolescent health. *Canadian Journal of Behavioral Science, 20(4),* 461–466.

Arena, J.G., Bruno, G.M., Hannah, S.L., & Meador, J.K. (1995). A comparison of frontal electromyographic biofeedback training, trapezius electromyographic biofeedback training, and progressive muscle relaxation therapy in the treatment of tension headache. *Headache, 35,* 411–419.

Arendt, J., Skene, D.J., Middleton, B., Lockley, S.W., & Deacon, S. (1997). Efficacy of melatonin treatment in jet lag, shift work, and blindness. *Journal of Biological Rhythms, 12,* 604–617.

Arieti, S. (1974). *Interpretation of schizophrenia.* New York: Basic Books.

Arkes, H.R., Herren, L.T., Isen, A.M. (1988). The role of potential loss in the influence of affect on risk-taking behavior. *Organizational Behavior and Human Decision Processes, 42,* 181–193.

Arms, R.L., & Russell, G.W. (1997). Impulsivity, fight history, and camaradarie as predictors of a willingness to escalate a disturbance. *Current Psychology: Development, Learning, Personality, Social, 15,* 279–285.

Armstrong, C. (1991). Emotional changes following brain injury: Psychological and neurological components of depression, denial and anxiety. *Journal of Rehabilitation, 2,* 15–22.

Armstrong-Stassen, M. (1993). Production workers' reactions to a plant closing: The role of transfer, stress, and support. Special Issue: Stress and stress management at the workplace. *Anxiety, Stress and Coping: An International Journal, 6(3),* 201–214.

Armstrong, T. L., & Swartzman, L. C. (1999). Asian versus Western differences in satisfaction with Western medical care: The mediational effects of illness attributions. *Psychology and Health, 14,* 403–416.

Arnett, J. (1992). Reckless behavior in adolescence: A developmental perspective. *Developmental Review, 12,* 339–373.

Arnett, J. (1995). The young and the reckless: Adolescent reckless behavior. *Current Directions in Psychological Science, 4,* 67–70.

Arnett, J. J. (1998). Risk behavior and family role transitions during the twenties. *Journal of Youth and Adolescence, 27,* 301–320.

Arnoff, J., Woike, B.A., Hyman, L.M. (1992). Which are the stimuli in facial displays of anger and happiness? Configurational bases of emotional recognition. *Journal of Personality and Social Psychology, 62,* 1050–1066.

Aronoff, S.R., Spilka, B (1984–1985). Patterning of facial expressions among terminal cancer patients. *Omega, 15,* 101–108.

Arvey, R.D., Bouchard, T.J., Jr., Segal, N.L., Abraham, L.M. (1989). Job satisfaction: Genetic and environmental components. *Journal of Applied Psychology, 74,* 187–192.

Ashcraft, M. H. (1998). *Fundamentals of cognition.* New York: Addison-Wesley.

Ashmore, R.D., Solomon, M.R., & Longo, L.C. (1996). Thinking about fashion models' looks: A multidimensional approach to the structure of perceived physical attractiveness. *Personality and Social Psychology Bulletin, 22,* 1083–1104.

Ashton, M.C., & Esses, V.M. (1999). Stereotype accuracy: Estimating the academic performance of ethnic groups. *Personality and Social Psychology, 25,* 225–236.

Aspinwall, L.G., & Duran, R.E.F. (1999). Psychology applied to health. In A.M. Stec & D.A. Berstien (Eds.), *Psychology: Fields of application* (pp. 17–38). Boston, MA: Houghton Mifflin.

Assanand, S., Pinel, J.P.J., & Lehman, D.R. (1998). Personal theories of hunger and eating. *Journal of Applied Social Psychology, 28,* 998–1015.

Assanand, S., Pinel, J.P.J., & Lehman, D.R. (1998). Teaching theories of hunger and eating: Overcoming students' misconceptions. *Teaching of Psychology, 25,* 44–46.

Astington, J.W. (1995). Talking it over with my brain. In J. Flavell, F. Green, & E. Flavell, (Eds.), *Monographs of the Society for Research in Child Development, 60,* 104–113.

Astley, S.J., Claaren, S.K., Little, R.E., Sampson, P.D., Daling, J.R. (1992). Analysis of racial shape in children gestationally exposed to marijuana, alcohol, and/or cocaine. *Pediatrics, 89,* 67–77.

Astley, S. L., & Wasserman, E. A. (1992). Categorical discrimination and generalization in pigeons: All negative stimuli are not created equal. *Journal of Experimental Psychology: Animal Behavior Processes, 18,* 193–207.

Atkinson, J.W., & Litwin, G.H. (1960). Achievement motive and test anxiety conceived as motive to approach success and motive to avoid failure. *Journal of Abnormal and Social Psychology, 60,* 52–63.

Aube, J., Koestner, R. (1992). Gender characteristics and adjustment: A longitudinal study. *Journal of Personality and Social Psychology, 63,* 485–493.

Austin, J., Hatfield, D.B., Grindle, A.C., Bailey, J.S. (1993). Increasing recycling in office environments: The effects of specific, informative cues. *Journal of Applied Behavior Analysis, 26,* 247–253.

Austin, J.H. (1998). *Zen and the brain: Toward an understanding of meditation and consciousness.* Cambridge, MA: The Mit Press.

Avis, J. M. (1992). Where are all the family therapists? Abuse and violence within families and family therapy's response. *Journal of Marital and Family Therapy, 18,* 225–232.

Ayanian, J.Z., & Cleary, P.D. (1999). Perceived risks of heart disease and cancer among cigarette smokers. *Journal of the American Medical Association, 281,* 1019–1021.

Aycan, Z., & Kanungo, R. N. (1998). Impact of acculturation on socialization beliefs and behavioral occurrences among Indo-Canadian immigrants. *Journal of Comparative Family Studies, 29,* 451–467.

Ayed, N. (1998, March 29). Native health study reveals health concerns [Chiefs of Ontario] *Canadian Press Newswire.*

Azar, B. (1996). Why men lose keys—and women find them. *American Psychological Association Monitor,* August, p. 32.

Bachetti, P. (1990). Estimating the incubation period of AIDS by comparing population infection and diagnosis patterns. *Journal of the American Statistical Association, 85,* 1002–1008.

Bachman, J.G. (1987, February). An eye on the future. *Psychology Today,* pp. 6–7.

Backman, L., Hill, R.D., Forsell, Y. (1996). The influence of depressive symptomatology on episodic memory functioning among clinically non-depressed older adults. *Journal of Abnormal Psychology, 105,* 97–105.

Baddeley, A. (1990). *Human memory: Theory and practice.* Boston: Allyn & Bacon.

Baddeley, A. (1992). Working memory. *Science, 255,* 556–559.

Bagby, R.M., Schuller, D.R., Levitt, A.J., Joffe, R.T. et al. (1996). Seasonal and non-seasonal depression and the five-factor model of personality. *Journal of Affective Disorders, 38* (2–3), 89–95.

Bahrick, H. P. (1984). Memory for people. In J. E. Harris & P. E. Morris (Eds.), *Everyday memory actions and absent-mindedness* (19–34). London: Academic Press.

Bahrick, H. P., Bahrick, P.O., & Wittlinger, R. P. (1975). Fifty years of memory for names and faces: A cross-sectional approach. *Journal of Experimental Psychology: General, 104,* 54–75.

Bailey, M.J., & Pillard, R.C. (1991). A genetic study of male sexual orientation. *Archives of General Psychiatry, 48,* 1089–1096.

Bailey, M.J., Pillard, R.C., Neale, M.C., & Agyei, Y. (1993). Heritable factors influence sexual orientation in women. *Archives of General Psychiatry, 50,* 217–223.

Baillargeon, R. (1998). Infants' understanding of the physical world. In M. Sabourin, & F. Craik (Eds.), *Advances in psychological science, Vol. 2: Biological and cognitive aspects* (pp. 503–529). Hove, England UK: Psychology Press/Erlbaum (UK) Taylor & Francis.

Baker, A.G., & Mackintosh, N.J. (1977). Excitatory and inhibitory conditioning following uncorrelated presentations of CS and US. *Animal Learning and Behavior, 5(3),* 315–319.

Baker, B., Dorian, P., Woloshyn, N., Kazarian, S., Lanphier, C. (1991). Psychiatric treatment strategies for patients at risk of dying suddenly. *Psychotherapy and Psychsomatics, 56(4),* 242–246.

Baker, R.R., & Bellis, M.A. (1995). *Human sperm competition.* London: Chapman & Hall.

Baker-Ward, L., Ornstein, P.A., Holden, D.J., (1984). The expression of memorization in early childhood. *Journal of Experimental Child Psychology, 37(3),* 555–575.

Bakker, A.B. (1999). Persuasive communication about AIDS prevention: Need for cognition determines the impact of message format. *AIDS Education and Prevention, 11,* 150–162.

Baldwin, M.W. (1995). Relational schemas and cognition in close relationships. Special Section: Study of relationships. *Journal of Social and Personal Relationships, 12(4),* 547–552.

Baldwin, M.W., Keelan, J.P.R., Fehr, B., Enns, V. et al. (1996). Social-cognitive conceptualization of attachment working models: Availability and accessibility effects. *Journal of Personality and Social Psychology, 71,* 94–109.

Ball, S. A., & Zuckerman, M. (1992). Sensation seeking and selective attention: Focused and divided attention on a dichotic listening task. *Journal of Personality and Social Psychology, 63,* 825–831.

Balogh, R.D., & Porter, R.H. (1986). Olfactory preferences resulting from mere exposure in human neonates. *Infant Behavior and Development, 9,* 395–401.

Bandura, A. (1977). *Social learning theory.* Englewood Cliffs, NJ: Prentice-Hall.

Bandura, A. (1986). *Social foundations of thought and action: A social cognitive theory.* Englewood Cliffs, NJ: Prentice-Hall.

Bandura, A. (1992). Exercise of personal agency through the self-efficacy mechanism. In R. Schwarzer (Ed.), *Self-efficacy: Thought control of action* (pp. 3–38). Washington, DC: Hemisphere.

Bandura, A. (1997). *Self-efficacy: The exercise of control.* New York: Freeman.

Bandura, A., Ross, D., Ross, S. (1963). Imitation of film-mediated aggressive models. *Journal of Abnormal and Social Psychology, 66,* 3–11.

Banich, M.T., & Belger, A. (1990). Inter-hemispheric interaction: How do the hemispheres divide and conquer a task? *Cortex, 26,* 77–94.

Banks, A., & Gartrell, N.K. (1995). Hormones and sexual orientation: A questionable link. *Journal of Homosexuality, 3/4,* 247–268.

Banks, R.D., Salisbury, D.A., Ceresia, P.J. (1992). The Canadian Forces Airsickness Rehabilitation Program, 1981–1991. *Aviation, Space, and Environmental Medicine, 63(12),* 1098–1101.

Bar, M., & Biederman, I. (1998). Subliminal visual priming. *Psychological Science, 9,* 464–469.

Barabasz, A., & Barabasz, M. (1996). Neurotherapy and alert hypnosis in the treatment of attention deficit disorder. In S.J. Lynn, & I. Kirsch (Eds.), *Casebook of clinical hypnosis* (pp. 271–291). Washington, DC: American Psychological Association.

Barch, D.M., & Berenbaum, H. (1996). Language production and thought disorder in schizophrenia. *Journal of Abnormal Psychology, 105,* 81–88.

Bardach, A.L., & Park, B. (1996). The effect of ingroup / out-group status on memory for consistent and inconsistent behavior of an individual. *Personality and Social Psychology Bulletin, 22,* 169–178.

Bardwell, J.R., Cochran, S.W., Walker, S. (1986). Relationship of parental education, race, and gender to sex role stereotyping in five-year-old kindergarteners. *Sex Roles, 15,* 275–281.

Baressi, J., & Moore, C. (1996). Intentional relations and social understanding. *Behavioral and Brain Sciences, 19,* 107–154.

Barkley, R,.A., DuPaul, G.J., & McMurray, M.B. (1990). Comprehensive evaluation of attention deficit disorder with and without hyperactivity as defined by research criteria. *Journal of Consulting and Clinical Psychology, 58,* 775–789

Barlow, D. H. (1988) *Anxiety and its disorders: The nature and treatment of anxiety and panic* New York: Guilford Press.

Barlow, D. H. (1991). Introduction to the special issue on diagnoses, dimensions, and DSM-IV: The science of classification. *Journal of Abnormal Psychology, 100,* 243–244.

Barlow, D. H. (1992). An integrated model of panic. Described in Antony, M. M., Brown, T. A., & Barlow, D. H. Current perspectives on panic and panic disorder. *Journal of Abnormal Psychology, 100,* 79–82.

Baron, J. (1988). *Thinking and deciding.* Cambridge, England: Cambridge University Press.

Baron, J., Brown, R. (Eds.) (1991). *Teaching decision making to adolescents.* Hillsdale, NJ: Erlbaum.

Baron, R.A. (1970). Attraction toward the model and model's competence as determinants of adult imitative behavior. *Journal of Personality and Social Psychology, 14,* 335–344.

Baron, R.A. (1987). Mood of interviewer and the evaluation of job candidates. *Journal of Applied Social Psychology, 17,* 911–926.

Baron, R.A. (1993). Interviewers' moods and evaluations of job applicants: The role of applicant qualifications. *Journal of Applied Psychology, 23(4),* 253–271.

Baron, R.A. (1994). The physical environment of work settings: Effects on task performance, interpersonal relations, and job satisfaction. In B.M. Staw and L.L. Cummings (Eds.), *Research in organizational behavior* (vol. 16, pp. 1–46). Greenwich, CT: JAI Press.

Baron, R.A., & Byrne, D. (1994). *Social psychology: Understanding human interaction* (7th ed.). Boston: Allyn and Bacon.

Baron, R.A., & Kalsher, M.J. (1996). The sweet smell of... Safety? *Proceedings of the Human Factors and Ergonomics Society, 40.*

Baron, R.A. , & Neuman, J.H. (1996). Workplace violence and workplace aggression: Evidence on their relative frequency and potential causes. *Aggressive Behavior, 22,* 161–173.

Baron, R.A., Neuman, J.H., & Geddes, D. (1999). Social and personal determinants of workplace aggression: Evidence for the impact of perceived injustice and the Type A behavior pattern. *Aggressive Behavior, 25,* 281–296.

Baron, R.A., & Richardson, D.R. (1994). *Human aggression* (2nd ed.). New York: Plenum.

Baron, R.A., & Thomley, J. (1994). A whiff of reality: Positive affect as a potential mediator of the effects of pleasant fragrance son task performance and helping. *Environment and Behavior, 26,* 766–784.

Baron, R.A., & Richardson, D. (1994). *Human aggression* (2nd ed.). New York: Plenum.

Bar-Or, O., Foreyt, J., Couchard, C., Brownell, K.D., Dietz, W.H., Ravussin, E., Salbe, A.D., Schwenger, S., St-Jeor, S., & Torun, B. (1998). Physical activity, genetic, and nutritional considerations in childhood weight management. *Medicine and Science in Sports and Exercise, 30,* 2–10.

Barr, H.M., Streissguth, A.P., Darby, B.I., & Sampson, P.D. (1990). Prenatal exposure to alcohol, caffeine, tobacco and aspirin: Effects on fine and gross motor performance in 7–9 year old children. *Developmental Psychology, 26,* 339–348.

Barr, K., Hall, C. (1992). The use of imagery by rowers. *International Journal of Sport Psychology, 23,* 243–261.

Barrick, M.R., Mount, M.K. (1993). Autonomy as a moderator of the relationships between the big five personality dimensions and job performance. *Journal of Applied Psychology, 78,* 111–118.

Barth, R.J., Kinder, B.N. (1998). A theoretical analysis of sex differences in same-sex friendships. *Sex Roles, 19,* 343–363.

Bartholomew, K., & Shaver, P. R. (1998). Methods of assessing adult attachment: Do they converge? In J. Simpson, & W.S. Rholes (Eds*)., Attachment theory and close relationships.* New York: The Guilford Press.

Bartone, P.T., & Adler, A.B. (1999). Cohesion over time in a peacekeeping medical task force. *Military Psychology, 11,* 85–107.

Bartone, P.T., Adler, A.B., & Vaitkus, M.A. (1998). Dimensions in psychological stress in peacekeeping operations. *Military Medicine, 163,* 587–593.

Bashore, T. R., Ridderinkhof, K. R., & van der Molen, M. W. (1997). The decline of cognitive processing in old age. *Current Directions in Psychological Science, 6,* 163–169.

Batson, C.D. (1991). The altruism question: Toward a social-psychological answer. Hillsdale, NJ: Erlbaum.

Batson, C.D., & Weeks, J.L. (1996). Mood effects of unsuccessful helping: Another test of the empathy-altruism hypothesis. *Personality and Social Psychology Bulletin, 22 (2),* 148–157.

Baum, A., Fleming, I. (1993). Implications of psychological research on stress and technological accidents. *American Psychologist, 48,* 665–672.

Baum, A., & Posluszny, D. M. (1999). Health psychology: Mapping biobehavioral contributions to health and illness. *Annual Review of Psychology, 50,* 137–163.

Baumeister, R. F. (1990). Suicide as escape from self. *Psychological Review, 97,* 90–113.

Baumeister, R.F. (Ed.) (1993). *Self-esteem: The puzzle of low self-regard.* New York: Plenum.

Baumeister, R.F., & Leary, M.R. (1995). The need to belong: Desire for interpersonal attachments as a fundamental human motivation. *Psychological Bulletin, 117,* 497–529.

Baumeister, R.F., & Scher, S.J. (1988). Self-defeating behavior patterns among normal individuals: Review and analysis of common self-destructive tendencies. *Psychological Bulletin, 104,* 3–22.

Baumeister, R.F., & Steinhilber, A. (1984). Paradoxical effects of supportive audiences on performance under pressure: The home field disadvantage in sports championships. *Journal of Personality and Social Psychology, 47,* 85–93.

Baumrind, D. (1984). A developmental perspective on adolescent drug use. Unpublished manuscript, University of California, Berkley.

Baumrind, D. (1991) The influence of parenting style on adolescent competence and substance abuse. *Journal of Early Adolescence, 11,* 56–95.

Baumrind, D. (1993). The average expectable environment is not good enough: A response to Scarr. *Child Development, 64,* 1299–1317.

Beal, A.L. (1995). Post-traumatic stress disorder in prisoners of war and combat veterans of the Dieppe Raid: A 50-year follow-up. *Canadian Journal of Psychiatry, 40,* 177–184.

Beaumont, S.L. (1996). Adolescent girls' perceptions of conversations with mothers and friends. *Journal of Adolescent Research, 11,* 325–346.

Bebko, J.M., & McKinnon, E.E., (1990). The language experience of deaf children: Its relation to spontaneous rehearsal in a memory task. *Child Development, 61(6),* 1744–1752.

Beck, A. T. (1976). *Cognitive therapy and the emotional disorders.* New York: International Universities Press.

Beck, A. T. (1985). *Anxiety disorders and phobias: A cognitive perspective.* New York: Basic Books.

Beck, A. T., Rush, A. J., Shaw, B. F., & Emery, G. (1979). *Cognitive theory of depression.* New York: Guilford Press.

Becker, H.C., Randall, C.L., Salo, A.L., Saulnier, J.L., & Weathersby, R.T. (1994) Animal research: Charting the course for FAS. *Alcohol Health and Research World, 18,* 10–16.

Beckstead, J.W. (1991). Psychological factors influencing judgments and attitudes regarding animal research: An application of functional measurement and structural equation modeling. Unpublished doctoral dissertation, State University of New York, Albany.

Bedard, M.A., Montplaisir, J., Malo, J., & Richer, F. (1993). Persistent neuropsychological deficits and vigilance impairment in sleep apnea syndrome after treatment with continuous positive airways pressure (CPAP). *Journal of Clinical and Experimental Neuropsychology, 15,* 330–341.

Begg, I.M., Needham, D.R., & Bookbinder, M. (1993). Do backward messages unconsciously affect listeners? No. *Canadian Journal of Experimental Psychology, 47,* 1–14.

Begg, I. M., Robertson, R.K., Gruppuso, V. Anas, A., & Needham, D. R. (1996). *The illusory-knowledge effect. Journal of Memory and Language 35,* 410–433.

Behrend, D.A., Rosengren, K.S., & Perlmutter, M. (1992). The relation between private speech and parental interactive style. In R.M. Diaz & L.E. Berk (Eds.), *Private speech: From social interaction to self-regulation* (pp. 85–100). Hillsdale, NJ: Erlbaum.

Beiderman, I. (1987). Recognition by components: A theory of human image understanding. *Psychological Review, 94,* 115–147.

Beiser, M., Dion, R., Botowiec, A., Hyman, I., et al. (1995). Immigrant and refugee children in Canada. *Canadian Journal of Psychiatry, 40,* 67–72.

Bell, A.P., Weinberg, M.S., Hammersmith, S.K. (1981). *Sexual preference: Its development in men and women.* Bloomington: Indiana University Press.

Bell, D.W., Esses, V.M., & Maio, G.R. (1996). The utility of open-ended measures to assess intergroup ambivalence. *Canadian Journal of Behavioural Science, 28,* 12–18.

Bell, P.A. (1992). In defense of the negative affect escape model of heat and aggression. *Psychological Bulletin, 111,* 342–346.

Bell, S.T., Kuriloff, P.J., & Lottes, I. (1994). Understanding attributions of blame in stranger rape and date rape situations: An examination of gender, race, identification, and students' social perceptions of rape victims. *Journal of Applied Social Psychology, 24,* 171–1734.

Bellack, A.S., Morrison, R.L., Mueser, K.T., Wade, J.H., & Sayers, S.L. (1990). Role play for assessing the social competence of psychiatric patients. *Psychological Assessment: A Journal of Consulting and Clinical Psychology, 2,* 248–255.

Bellack, A.S., Sayers, M., Mueser, K.T., & Bennett, M. (1994). Evaluation of social problem solving in schizophrenia. *Journal of Abnormal Psychology, 103(2),* 371–378.

Bellak, L. (1994). The schizophrenic syndrome and attention deficit disorder. *American Psychologist, 49,* 25–29.

Belmore, S.M., & Hubbard, M.L. (1987). The role of advance expectancies in person memory. *Journal of Personality and Social Psychology, 53*, 61–70.

Belsky, J., & Braungart, J.M. (1991). Are insecure-avoidant infants with extensive day-care experience less stressed by and more independent in the Strange Situation? *Child Development, 62(3)*, 567–571.

Belsky, J., Cassidy, J. (1994). Attachment and close relationships: An individual difference perspective. *Psychological Inquiry, 5*, 27–30.

Belsky, J., Spritz, B., & Crnic, K. (1996). Infant attachment security and affective-cognitive information processing at age 3. *Psychological Science, 7*, 111–114.

Bem, D.J. (1996) Exotic becomes erotic: A developmental theory of sexual orientation. *Psychological Review, 103*, 320–335.

Bem, D. J., & Honorton, C. (1994). Does psi exist? Replicable evidence for an anomalous process of information transfer. *Psychological Bulletin, 115*, 4–18.

Bem, S.L. (1981). Gender schema theory: A cognitive account of sex typing. *Psychological Review, 88(4)*, 354–364.

Bem, S.L. (1984). Androgyny and gender schema theory: A conceptual and empirical integration. In R.A. Diesntsbier & T.B. Sondregger (Eds.), *Nebraska Symposium on Motivation* (vol. 34, pp. 179–226). Lincoln: University of Nebraska Press.

Bem, S.L. (1989). Genital knowledge and gender constancy in preschool children. *Child Development, 60*, 649–662.

Benesch, K.F. & Page, M.M. (1898). Self-construct systems and interpersonal congruence. *Journal of Personality, 57*, 139–173.

Beninger, R.J. (1992). D-1 receptor involvement in reward-related learning. *Journal of Psychopharmacology, 6*, 34–42.

Beninger, R.J., Wirsching, B.A., Jhamandas, K. & Boegman, R.J. (1989). Animal studies of brain acetylcholine and memory. Symposium: Memory and aging (1988, Lausanne, Switzerland). *Archives of Gerontology and Geriatrics*, supp 1, 71–89.

Benjamin, L.T., Jr., & Dixon, D.N. (1996). Dream analysis by mail: An American woman seeks Freud's advice. *Americal Psychologist, 51*, 461–468.

Benoit, D., Zeanah, C.H., & Barton, M.L., (1989). Maternal attachment disturbances in failure to thrive. Special Issue: Internal representations and parent-infant relationships. *Infant Mental Health Journal, 10(3)*, 185–202.

Benson, H., & Friedman, R. (1985). A rebuttal to the conclusions of David S. Holmes's article: "Meditation and somatic arousal reductions." *American Psychologist, 40*, 725–728.

Bentall, R.P. (1990). The illusion of reality: A review and integration of psychological research on hallucinations. *Psychological Bulletin, 107*, 82–95.

Bentley, K.M., & Li, A.K.F. (1995). Bully and victim problems in elementary schools and students' beliefs about aggression. *Canadian Journal of School Psychology, 11(2)*, 153–165.

Berardi-Coletta, B., Buyer, L.S., Dominowski, R.L., Rellinger, E.R. (1995). Metacognition and problem solving: A process-oriented approach. *Journal of Experimental Psychology: Learning, Memory, and Cognition, 21*, 205–223.

Berenbaum, S.A., Himes, M. (1992). Early androgens are related to childhood sex-types toy preferences. *Psychological Science, 3*, 203–206.

Bergeson, T. R., & Trehub, S. E. (1999). Mothers' singing to infants and preschool children. *Infant Behavior and Development, 22*, 51–64.

Bergin, A. E., & Lambert, M. J. (1978). The evaluation of therapeutic outcomes. In S. L. Garfield & A. E. Bergin (Eds.), *Handbook of psychotherapy and behavior change: An empirical analysis*, (2nd ed., pp. 139–190). New York: Wiley.

Berglas, S., & Jones, E.E. (1978). Drug choice as a self-handicapping strategy in response to noncontingent success. *Journal of Personality and Social Psychology, 36*, 405–417.

Berk, L.E. (1993). *Infants, children and adolescents.* Boston: Allyn and Bacon.

Berkowitz, L. (1984). Some effects of thought on anti- and pro-social influences of media events: A cognitive-neoassociation analysis. *Psychological Bulletin, 95*, 410–427.

Berkowitz, L. (1989). Frustration-aggression hypothesis: Examination and reformulation. *Psychological Bulletin, 106*, 59–73.

Berkowitz, L. (1993). *Aggression: Its causes, consequences, and control.* New York: McGraw-Hill.

Berlyne, D.E. (1967). Arousal and reinforcement. In D.Levine (Ed.), Nebraska Symposium on Motivation (Vol. 15, pp. 279–286.). Lincoln: University of Nebraska Press.

Berman, A. L., & Jobes, D. A. (1991). *Adolescent suicide: Assessment and intervention.* Washington, DC: American Psychological Association.

Berndt, T.J. (1992). Friendship and friends' influence in adolescence. *Current Directions in Psychological Sciences, 1*, 156–159.

Berndt, T.J., & Savin-Williams, R.C. (1993). Peer relations and friendships. In B. Tolan & B. Cohler (Eds.), *Handbook of clinical research and practice with adolescents* (pp. 203–219). New York: Wiley.

Bernstein, A. S. (1987). Orienting response research in schizophrenia: Where we have come and where we might go. *Schizophrenia Bulletin, 13*, 623–641.

Bernstein, I.L. (1978). Learned tasted aversion in children receiving chemotherapy. *Science, 200*, 1302–1303.

Berry, D.C., & Broadbent, D.E. (1984). On the relationship between task performance and associated verbal knowledge. *Quarterly Journal of Experimental Psychology, 36*, 209–231.

Berry, D.S. (1991). Attractive faces are not all created equal: Joint effects of facial babyishness and attractiveness on social perception. *Personality and Social Psychology Bulletin, 17*, 523–531.

Berry, D.S., & McArthur, L.Z. (1986). Perceiving character in faces: The impact of age-related craniofacial changes on social perception. *Psychological Bulletin, 100*, 3–18.

Berry, D.S., & Zebrowitz-McArthur, L. (1988). What's in a face? Facial maturity and the attribution of legal responsibility. *Personality and Social Psychology Bulletin, 14*, 23–33.

Berry, D.T.R., & Webb, W.B. (1985). Mood and sleep in aging women. *Journal of Personality and Social Psychology, 49*, 1724–1727.

Berry, J. W. (1999). Intercultural relations in plural societies. *Canadian Psychology, 40*, 12–21.

Bertelsen, A., Harvald, B., & Hauge, M. (1977). A Danish twin study of manic depressive disorders. *British Journal of Psychiatry, 130*, 330–351

Besseghini, V. H. (1997). Depression and suicide in children and adolescents. In G. Creatsas, & G. Mastorakos (Eds.), Adolescent gynecology and endocrinology: Basic and clinical aspects (pp.94–98). *Annals of the New York Academy of Sciences. 816*, New York: New York Academy of Sciences.

Besson, J., & Chaouch, A. (1987). Peripheral spinal mechanisms of nociception. *Psychological Review, 67*, 67–186

Best, D.L., Williams, J.E., Cloud, J.M., Davis, S.W., Robertson, L.S., Edwards, J.R., & Fowles, J. (1997). Development of sex-trait stereotypes among young children in the United States, England, and Ireland. *Child Development, 48*, 1375–1384.

Betz, A.L., & Krosnick, J.A. (1994). A test of the primacy affect: Does detection of the affective tone of a stimulus precede detection of stimulus presence or content? Manuscript submitted for publication, Ohio State University, (1993).

Betz, E.L. (1982). Need fulfillment in the career development of women. *Journal of Vocational Behavior, 20*, 53–66.

Beyerstein, B.L. (1999). Pseudoscience and the brain: Tuners and tonics for aspiring superhumans. In S.D. Sala (Ed.), *Mind myths: Exploring popular assumptions about the mind and brain* (pp. 59–82). Chichester, England: John Wiley & Sons Ltd.

Beyth-Marom, R., & Fischhoff, B. (1997). Adolescents' decisions about risks: A cognitive perspective. In J. Schulenberg, & J.L. Maggs (Eds.), *Health risks and developmental transitions during adolescence* (pp. 110–135). New York, NY: Cambridge University Press.

Beyth-Marom, R., Austin, L., Fischoff, B., Palmgren, C., & Quadrel, M. (1994). Perceived consequences of risky behaviors: Adolescents and adults. *Developmental Psychology*.

Bhatia, S., Hendricks, S. & Bhatia, S. (1993). Attitudes toward and beliefs about smoking in grade school children. *International Journal of the Addictions, 28(3)*, 271–280.

Bhatt, R. S., Wasserman, E. A., Reynolds, W. F., Jr., & Knauss, K. S. (1988). Conceptual behavior in pigeons: Categorization of both familiar and novel examples from four classes of natural and artificial stimuli. *Journal of Experimental Psychology: Animal Behavior Proccesses, 14*, 219–234.

Bienert, H., Schneider, B.H. (1995). Deficit specific social skills training with peer-nominated aggressive-disruptive and sensitive-isolated preadolescents. *Journal of Clinical Child Psychology, 24 (3)*, 287–299.

Bigler, R.S. (1995). The role of classification skill in moderating environmental influences on children's gender stereotyping: A study of the functional use of gender in the classroom. *Child Development, 66(4)*. 1072–1087.

Bini, L. (1938). Experimental researches on epileptic attacks induced by the electric current. *American Journal of Psychiatry* (Suppl. 94), 172–183.

The biology of obsessions and compulsions. *Scientific American*, 83–89

Birnbaum, I. M., & Parker, E. D. (Eds.). (1977). *Alcohol and human memory.* Hillsdale, NJ: Erlbaum.

Bishop, J.E. (1996). Sixth-sense therapy path to be reported. *Wall Street Journal*, April 11, B4.

Bisnaire, L.M., Firestone, P. & Rynard, D. (1990). Factors associated with academic achievement in children following parental separation. *American Journal of Orthopsychiatry, 60(1)*, 67–76.

Bivens, J.A., & Berk, L.E., (1990). A longitudinal study of the development of elementary school children's private speech. *Merrill-Palmer Quarterly, 36(4)*, 443–463.

Bixler, E.O., Kales, A., Soldatos, C.R., Kales, J.D., & Healey, S. (1979). Prevalence of sleep disorders in the Los Angeles metropolitan area. *American Journal of Psychiatry, 136*, 1257–1262.

Bjorklund, D.F., & Muir, J.E. (1988). Children's development of free recall memory: Remembering on their own. In R. Vasta (Ed.), *Annals of child development* (vol. 5, pp. 79–123). Greenwich, CT: JAI Press.

Bksy, G. von. (1960). *Experiments in hearing.* New York: McGraw Hill.

Black, J.S., & Mendenhall, M. (1990). Cross-cultural training effectiveness: A review and a theoretical framework for future research. *Academy of Management Review, 15*, 113–136.

Blackmore, S. (1986). A critical guide to parapsychology. *Skeptical Inquirer, 11(1)*, 97–102.

Blakemore, B., Shindler, S., & Conte, R., (1993). A problem solving training program for parents of children with attention deficit hyperactivity disorder. *Canadian Journal of School Psychology, 9(1)*, special issue 66–85.

Blakeslee, S. (1993). Human nose may hold an additional organ for a real sixth sense: Odorless skin chemical may draw or repel other people. *New York Times*, pp. C1, C3.

Bland, R. C., Newman, S. C., & Orn, H. (1988). Period prevalence of psychiatric disorders in Edmonton. *Acta Psychiatrica Scandinavica. 77*(suppl.388), 33–42. ® Munksgaard International Publishers Ltd., Copenhagen, Denmark.

Bland, R.C., Orn, H., & Newman, S.C. (1988). Lifetime prevalence of psychiatric disorders in Edmonton. *Acta Psychiatrica Scandinavica. 77*(suppl.388), 24–32.

Blashko, C.A. & Peterson, J.G. (1990). You and your heart: Promoting preventive health education through the mass media. *International Journal for the Advancement of Counselling, 13(1),* 49–59.

Blatt, S.J. (1995). The destructiveness of perfectionism: Implications for the treatment of depression. *American Psychologist, 50,* 1003–1020.

Blatt, S.J., Zuroff, D.C., Quinlan, D.M., & Pilkonis, P. (1996). Interpersonal factors in brief treatment of depression: Further analysis of the MINH Treatment of Depression Collaborative Research Program. *Journal of Consulting and Clinical Psychology,* in press.

Bless, H., Fiedler, K. (1995). Affective states and the influence of activated general knowledge. *Personality and Social Psychology Bulletin, 21(7),* 766–778.

Blessing, S.B., & Ross, B.H. (1996). Content effects in problem categorization and problem solving. *Journal of Experimental Psychology, Learning, Memory, and Cognition, 22,* 792–810.

Bliss, R.E., Garvey, A.J., Heinhold, J.W., & Hitchcock, J.L. (1989). The influence of situation and coping on relapse crisis outcomes after smoking cessation. *Journal of Consulting and Clinical Psychology, 57,* 443–449.

Block, J. (1995). A contrarian view of the five-factor approach to personality description. *Psychological Bulletin, 117,* 187–215.

Blood, A.J., Zatorre, R.J., Bermudez, P., & Evans, A.C. (1999). Emotional responses to pleasant and unpleasant music correlate with activity in paralimbic brain regions. *Nature Neuroscience, 2,* 382–387.

Blouin, A.G., & Goldfield, G.S. (1995). Body image and steroid use in male bodybuilders. *International Journal of Eating Disorders, 18(2),* 159–165.

Blyth, D.A., Bulcroft, R., & Simmons, R.G. (1991, August). The impact of puberty on adolescents: A longitudinal study. Paper presented at the annual meetings of the American Psychological Association, Los Angeles.

Bobo, L. (1983). Whites' opposition to busing: symbolic racism or realistic group conflict? *Journal of Personality and Social Psychology, 45,* 1196–1210.

Bodenhausen, G.V., Sheppard, L.A., & Kramer, G.P. (1994). Negative affect and social judgment: The differential impact of anger and sadness. Special Issue: Affect in social judgments and cognition. *European Journal of Social Psychology, 24(1),* 45–62.

Boehm, L.E. (1994). The validity effect: A search for mediating variables. *Personality and Social Psychology Bulletin, 20,* 285–293.

Bogard, N. (1990). Why we need gender to understand human violence. *Journal of Interpersonal Violence, 5,* 132–135.

Bogeart, A.F., & Fisher, W.A. (1995). Predictors of university men's number of sexual partners. *Journal of Sex Research, 32,* 119–130.

Bohannon, J., & Stanowicz, L. (1988). The issues of negative evidence: Adult responses to children's language errors. *Developmental Psychology, 24,* 684–689.

Boivin, M., & Hymel,. (1997). Peer expectations and social self-perceptions: A sequential model. *Developmental Psychology, 33,* 135–145.

Boles, D.B. (1992). Factor analysis and the cerebral hemispheres: Temporal, occipital and frontal functions. *Neuropsychologia, 30,* 963–988.

Bonardi, C., Honey, R.C., & Hall, G. (1990). Context specificity of conditioning in flavor-aversion learning: Extinction and blocking tests. *Animal Learning & Behavior, 18,* 229–237.

Bond, R., & Smith, P.B. (1996). Culture and conformity: A meta-analysis of studies using Asch's (1952b, 1956) line judgment task. *Psychological Bulletin, 119,* 111–137.

Bookstein, F.L., Sampson, P.D., Streissguth, A.P., & Barr, H.M. (1996). Exploiting redundant measurement of dose and developmental outcome: New methods from the behavioral teratology of alcohol. *Developmental Psychology, 32,* 404–415.

Bootzin, R. R., Acocella, J. R., & Alloy, L. B. (1993). *Abnormal psychology* (6th ed.). New York: McGraw-Hill.

Borbely, A. (1986). *Secrets of sleep.* New York: Basic Books.

Borbely, A., Achermann, P., Trqachsel, L., & Tobler, I. (1989). Sleep initiation and initial sleep intensity: Interaction of homeostatic and circadian mechanisms. *Journal of Biological Rhythms, 4,* 149–160.

Borges, G., & Rosovsky, H. (1996). Suicide attempts and alcohol consumption in an emergency room sample. *Journal of Studies on Alcohol, 57,* 543-548.

Bornstein, R.F. (1992). Subliminal mere exposure effects. In R.T.S. Pittman (Ed.), *Perception without awareness: cognitive, clinical and social perspectives* (pp. 191–210). New York: Guilford.

Bornstein, R.F. (1993, February). Personal communication.

Borod, J.C. (1993). Cerebral mechanisms underlying facial, prosodic, and lexical emotional expressions: A review of neuropsychological studies and methodological issues. *Neuropsychology, 7,* 445–463.

Borstein, M.H., & Tamis-LeMonda, C.S. (1997). Maternal responsiveness and infant mental abilities: Specific predictive relations. *Infant Behavior and Development, 20,* 283–296.

Bortolotti, S., D'Elia, P., & Whissell, C.M. (1993). When children talk about the causes of their emotions, how well do adults and other children understand which emotion they are talking about? *Perceptual and Motor Skills, 77(1),* 67–78.

Botha, R. P. (1998). Neo-Darwinian accounts of the evolution of language : 4. Questions about their comparative merit. *Language and Communication, 18,* 227–249.

Bouchard, T.J., Jr. (1987). Information about the Minnesota Center for Twin and Adoption Research. Minneapolis: University of Minnesota.

Bouchard, T.J., Jr. (1994). Genes, environment and personality. *Science, 264,* 1700–1701.

Bouchard, T. J., Jr. (1997). The genetics of personality. In K. Blum & E. P. Noble (Eds.), *The Handbook of psychiatric genetics* (pp. 273–296). Boca Raton, Fl: Crc Press Inc.

Bouchard, T.J., Jr. (1997). IQ similarity in twins reared apart: findings and responses to critics. In R.J. Sternberg & E.L. Girgorenko (Eds.), *Intelligence, Heredity, and Environment* (pp. 126–160). New York: Cambridge University Press.

Bouchard, T. J., Lykken, D. T., McGue, M., Segal, N. L., & Tellegen, A. (1990). Sources of human psychological differences: The Minnesota Study of Twins Reared Apart. *Science, 250,* 223–228.

Bouchard, T. J., & McGue, M. (1981). Familial studies of intelligence: A review. *Science, 212,* 1055–1059.

Boulos, Z. (1998). Bright light treatment for jet lag and shift work. In R.W. Lam (Ed.), *Seasonal affective disorder and beyond: Light treatment for SAD and non-SAD conditions* (pp. 253–287). Washington, DC: American Psychiatric Press, Inc.

Bowd, A. D. (1990). A decade of debate on animal research in psychology: Room for consensus? *Canadian Psychology, 31,* 74–82.

Bowd, A., & Brady, P. (1998). Note on preferred use of ethnic identity labels by aboriginal and non-aboriginal Canadians. *Psychological Reports, 82,* 1153–1154.

Bowen, B. (1986, September 18). Hong Kong students in Canada suffer high stress, study shows. *The Globe and Mail,* A23.

Bower, G. H., Clark, M. C., Lesgold, A. M., & Winzenz, D. (1969). Hierarchical retrieval schemes in recall of categorized word lists. *Journal of Verbal Learning and Verbal Behavior, 8,* 323–343.

Bowers, K.S. (1992). Imagination and dissociation in hypnotic responding. *International Journal of Clinical and Experimental Hypnosis, 40,* 253–275.

Bowers, K.S., Farvolden, P. (1996). Revisiting a century-old Freudian slip—From suggestion disavowed to the truth repressed. *Psychological Bulletin, 119,* 355–380.

Bowlby, J. (1969). *Attachment and loss: Vol. 1. Attachment.* New York: Basic Books.

Bowlby, J. (1973). *Attachment and loss: Vol. 2 separation.* New York: Basic Books.

Bowlby, J. (1988). *A secure base: Clinical applications of attachment theory.* London: Routledge.

Bowles, N., & Hynds, F. (1978). *Psy search: The comprehensive guide to psychic phenomena.* New York: Harper & Row.

Boyanowski, E.O. (1991). Grains of truth in a wasteland of fear. *Canadian Psychology, 32,* 188–189.

Boyes, M.C., Allen, S.G. (1993). Styles of parent-child interaction and moral reasoning in adolescence. *Merrill Palmer Quarterly, 39(4),* 551–570.

Boykin, A.W. (1994). Harvesting talent and culture: African-American children and educational reform. In R. Rossi (Ed.), *Schools and students at risk* (pp. 116–138). New York: Teachers College Press.

Boyle, P. (1993). The hazards of passive- and active-smoking. *New England Journal of Medicine, 328,* 1708–1709.

Bozarth, M.S. (1987). Intracranial self-administration procedures for the assessment of drug reinforcement. In M.A. Bozarth (Ed.), *Methods of assessing the reinforcing properties of abused drugs* (pp. 173–187). Berlin: Springer-Verlag.

Bradbury, T.N., Fincham, F.D. (1992). Attributions and behavior in marital interaction. *Journal of Personality and Social Psychology, 63,* 613–628.

Bradley, M.T., & Black, M.E. (1998). A control question test oriented towards students. *Perceptual and Motor Skills, 87,* 691–700.

Bradley, M.T., & Cullen M.C. (1993). Polygraph lie detection on real events in a laboratory setting. *Perceptual and Motor Skills, 76(3, Pt 1),* 1051–1058.

Bradley, M.T., MacLaren, V.V., Black, M.E. (1996). The control question test in polygraphic examinations with actual controls for truth. *Perceptual and Motor Skills, 83,* 755–762.

Bradley, M.T., MacLaren, V.V., Carle, S.B. (1996). Deception and nondeception in guilty knowledge and guilty actions polygraph tests. *Journal of Applied Psychology, 81(2),* 153–160.

Brady, P. (1996). Native dropouts and non-native dropouts in Canada: Two solitudes or a solitude shared? *Journal of American Indian Education, 35,* 10–20.

Braff, D. L. (1989). Sensory input deficits and negative symptoms in schizophrenic patients. *American Journal of Psychiatry, 146,* 1006–1011.

Braun, C.M. and Giroux, J. (1989). Arcade video games: Proxemic, cognitive and content analyses. *Journal of Leisure Research, 21,* 92–105.

Braverman, N.S., & Bronstein, P. (Eds.). (1985). Experimental assessments and clinical applications of conditioned food aversions. *Annals of the New York Academy of Sciences, 443,* 1–41.

Brean, H. (1958, March 31). What hidden sell is all about. *Life,* 104–114.

Breggin, P. R. (1979). *Electroshock: Its brain-disabling effects.* New York: Springer.

Bregman, A. (1990). *Auditory scene analysis.* Cambridge: MIT Press.

Bregman, A., & Campbell, J. (1971). Primary auditory stream segregation and perception of order in rapid sequence of tones. *Journal of Experimental Psychology, 89,* 244–249.

Brehm, J.W. (1998). Leon Festinger: Beyond the obvious. In G.A. Kimble, & M. Wertheimer (Eds.), *Portraits of pioneer in psychology* (pp. 329–344). Washington, DC: American Psychological Association.

Brehm, J.W., & Self, E.A. (1989). The intensity of motivation. *Annual Review of Psychology, 40,* 109–131.

Brennan, W.M., Ames, E.W., & Moore, R.W. (1966). Age differences in infants' attention to patterns of different complexities. *Science, 151,* 354–356.

Brewer, M.B. (1993). Social identity, distinctiveness, and in-group homogeneity. *Social Cognition, 11,* 150–154.

Breazeal (Ferrell), C., & Scallellati, B. (2000). Infantlike social interactions between a robot and a human caretaker. To appear in special issue of *Adaptive Behavior on Simulation Models of Social Agents,* guest editor Kerstin Dautenhahn.

Brickman, J. (1992). Female lives, feminist deaths: The relationship of the Montreal massacre to dissociation, incest, and violence against women. *Special Issue: Violence and its aftermath. Canadian Psychology, 33,* 128–143.

Brisson, C., Vezina, M., & Vinet, A. (1992). Health problems of women employed in jobs involving psychological and ergonomic stressors: The case of garment workers in Quebec. *Women and Health, 18(3),* 49–65.

Britt, T.W. (1992). The self-consciousness scale: On the stability of the three-factor structure. *Personality and Social Psychology Bulletin, 18,* 748–755.

Britt, T.W. (1998). Psychological ambiguities in peace-keeping. In H.J. Langholtz (Ed.), *The psychology of peacekeeping* (pp. 111–128). Westport, CT: Praeger Publishers/Greenwood Publishing Group, Inc.

Brockner, J., & Rubin, J. Z. (1985). *Entrapment in escalating conflicts.* New York: Springer-Verlag.

Brodbeck, D.R., Burack, O.R. & Shettleworth, S.J. (1992). One trial associative memory in black-capped chickadees. *Journal of Experimental Psychology: Animal Behaviour Processes, 18,* 12–21.

Brody, G. H., Neubaum, E., & Forehand, R. (1988). Serial marriage: A heuristic analysis of an emerging family form. *Psychological Bulletin, 103,* 211–222.

Brody, N. (1993). *Intelligence (2nd ed.).* San Diego, CA: Academic Press.

Broughton, R.J. (1992). Psychosocial impact of narcolepsy-cataplexy. *Loss, Grief and Care, 5,* 33–35.

Brown, J.D., & McGill, K.L. (1989). The cost of good fortune: When positive life events produce negative health consequences. *Journal of Personality and Social Psychology, 57,* 1103–1110.

Brown, J.D., & Rogers, R.J. (1991). Self-serving attributions: The role of physiological arousal. *Personality and Social Psychology Bulletin, 54,* 316–322.

Brown, R. (1973). *A first language: The early stages.* Cambridge, MA: Harvard University Press.

Brown, R. W., & Kulik, J. (1977). Flashbulb memories. *Cognition, 5,* 73–99.

Brown, R. W., & McNeill, D. (1966). The "tip of the tongue" phenomenon. *Journal of Verbal Learning and Verbal Behavior, 5,* 325–337.

Browne, M.W. (1992, April 14). Biologists tally generosity's rewards. *New York Times,* pp. C1, C8.

Brownell, K.D., & Cohen, L.R. (1995). Adherence to dietary regimens 1: An overview of research. *Behavioral Medicine, 20,* 149–154.

Bryden, M.P. & MacRae, L. (1988). Dichotic laterality effects obtained with emotional words. *Neuropsychiatry, Neuropsychology, and Behavioral Neurology, 1(3),* 171–176.

Bryden, M.P., Free, T., Gagne, S., & Groff, P. (1991). Handedness effects in the detection of dichotically-presented words and emotions. *Cortex, 27(2),* 229–235.

Bryden, M.P., Ley, R.G., & Sugarman, J.H. (1982). A left ear advantage for identifying the emotional quality of tonal sequences. *Neuropsychologia, 20,* 83–87.

Bujold, A., Ladouceur, R., Sylvain, C., Boisvert, J.M. (1994). Treatment of pathological gamblers: An experimental study. *Journal of Behavior Therapy and Experimental Psychiatry, 25(4),* 275–282.

Bullock, M. (1985). Animism in childhood thinking: A new look at an old question. *Developmental Psychology, 21,* 217–225.

Burger, J.M., & Palmer, M.L. (1992). Changes in and generalization of unrealistic optimism following experiences with stressful events: Reactions to the 1989 California earthquake. *Personality and Social Psychology Bulletin, 18,* 39–43.

Burish, T.G., & Carey, M.P. (1986). Conditioned aversive response in cancer chemotherapy patients: Theoretical and developmental analysis. *Journal of Consulting and Clinical Psychology, 54,* 593–600.

Burke, R.J., & Greenglass, E.R. (1995). A longitudinal examination of the Cherniss model of psychological burnout. *Social Science and Medicine, 40(10),* 1357–1363.

Burke, R.J., & Greenglass, E.R. (1995). A longitudinal study of psychological burnout in teachers. *Human Relations, 48(2),* 187–202.

Burns, B.D. (1996). Meta-analogical transfer: Transfer between episodes of analogical reasoning. *Journal of Experimental Psychology, Learning, Memory, and Cognition, 22,* 1032–1048.

Burnstein, E., Crandall, C., & Kitayama, S. (1994). Some neo-Darwinian rules for altruism: Weighing cues for inclusive fitness as a function of the biological importance of the decision. *Journal of Personality and Social Psychology, 67,* 773–789.

Burt, D.B., Zembar, M.J., Niederehe, G. (1995). Depression and memory impairment: A meta-analysis of the association, its pattern, and specificity. *Psychological Bulletin, 117,* 285–305.

Burton, I. (1990). Factors in urban stress. *Journal of Sociology and Social Welfare, 17(1),* 79–92.

Bush, A.J., Drebs, D.L., & Carpendale, J.I. (1993). The structural consistency of moral judgments about AIDS. *Journal of Genetic Psychology, 154(2),* 167–175.

Bushman, B.J. (1984). Perceived symbols of authority and their influence on compliance. Journal of Applied Psychology, 14 (6), 501–508.

Bushman, B.J. (1988). The effects of apparel on compliance: A field experiment with a female authority figure. *Personality and Social Psychology Bulletin, 14 (3),* 459–467.

Bushman, B.J. (1998), Effects of television violence on memory for commercial messages. *Journal of Experimental Psychology: Applied, 4,* 1–17.

Bushman, B.J., & Anderson, C.A. (1998). Methodology in the study of aggression: Integrating experimental and nonexperimental findings. In R.G. Geen, & E. Donnerstein (Eds.), *Human aggression: Theories, research, and implication for social policy* (pp. 23–49). San Diego, CA: Academic Press, Inc.

Buss, A.H. (1961). *The psychology of aggression.* New York, NY: John Wiley.

Buss, D.M. (1989). Sex differences in human mate preferences: Evolutionary hypotheses tested in 37 cultures. *Behavioral and Brain Sciences, 12,* 1–49.

Buss, D.M. (1990). Evolutionary social psychology: Prospects and pitfalls. *Motivation and Emotion, 14,* 265–286.

Buss, D.M. (1997). *Evolutionary psychology.* Boston: Allyn & Bacon.

Buss, D.M. (1999). *Evolutionary psychology: The new science of the mind.* Boston: Allyn & Bacon.

Buss, D.M., Larsen, R.J., Westen, D., & Semmelroth, J. (1992). Sex differences in jealousy: Evolution, physiology, and psychology. *Psychological Science, 3,* 251–258.

Buss, D.M., & Schackelford, T.K. (1997). Human aggression in evolutionary psychological perspective. *Clinical Psychology Review, 17,* 605–691.

Buss, D.M., & Schmitt, D.P. (1993). Sexual strategies theory: An evolutionary perspective on human mating. *Psychological Review, 100,* 204–232.

Butt, D.S. & Beiser, M. (1987). Successful aging: a theme for international psychology. *Psychology and Aging, 2(1),* 87–94.

Byers, E. S., Purdon, C., & Clark, D. A. (1998). Sexual intrusive thoughts of college students. *Journal of Sex Research, 35,* 359–369.

Byne, W. (1995). Science and belief: Psychobiological research on sexual orientation. *Journal of Homosexuality, 3/4,* 303–344.

Byne W. (1997). Why we cannot conclude that sexual orientation is primarily a biological phenomenon. *Journal of Homosexuality, 34,* 73–80.

Byrne, B. (1992). The Maslach Burnout Inventory: Validating factorial structure and invariance across intermediate, secondary, and university educators. *Multivariate Behavioral Research, 26,* 583–605.

Byrne, B.M. (1993). The Maslach Burnout Inventory: testing for factual validity and invariance across elementary, intermediate and secondary teachers. *Journal of Occupational and Organizational Psychology, 66(3),* 197–212.

Byrne, D. (1982). Predicting human sexual behavior. In A.G. Kraut (Ed.), *The G. Stanley Hall Lecture Series* (vol. 2, pp. 363–364, 368). Washington, DC: American Psychological Association.

Byrne, D., & Smeaton, G. (1998). The Feeling Scale: Positive and negative affective responses. In C.M. Davis, W.L. Yarger, R., Bauserman, G. Scheer, & S.L. Davis (Eds.), *Handbook of sexuality-related measures.* (pp. 50–52). Thousand Oaks, CA: Sage.

Cacioppo, J.T., Petty, R.E., & Quintanar, L.R. (1982). Individual differences in relative hemisphere alpha abundance and cognitive responses persuasive communications. *Journal of Personality and Social Psychology, 43,* 623–626.

Cacioppo, J.T., Priseter, J.R., & Berntson, G.G. (1993). Rudimentary determinants of attitude: II. Arm flexion and extension have differential effects on attitudes. *Journal of Personality and Social Psychology, 65,* 5–17.

Cain, W.S. (1988). Olfaction. In R.C. Atkinson, R.J. Herrnstein, G. Lindzey, & R.D. Luce (Eds.), *Stevens' handbook of experimental psychology: Vol. 1. Perception and motivation* (rev. ed., pp. 409–459). New York: Wiley.

Cairns, K.V., Woodward, J.B. & Hashizume, L.G. (1992). Employment counsellors' and youths' views of the transition to work: preparing to develop a work skills simulation. *Canadian Journal of Counselling, 26(4),* 222–239.

Came, B., Burke, D., Ferzoco, G., O'Farrell, B., & Wallace, B. (1989). *Montreal Massacre. Maclean's, 102,* 14–17.

Campbell, F.A., & Ramey, C.T. (1994). Effects of early intervention on intellectual and academic achievement: A follow-up study of children from low-income families. *Child Development, 65,* 694–698.

Campbell, J. N., & LaMotte, R. H. (1983). Latency to detection of first pain. *Brain Research, 266,* 203–208.

Campbell, P.E., Batsche, C.J., & Batsche, G.M. (1972). Spaced-trials reward magnitude effects in the rat: Single versus multiple food pellets. *Journal of Comparative and Physiological Psychology, 81,* 360–364.

Campbell, R.L., & Svenson, L.W. (1992). Drug use among university undergraduate students. *Psychological Reports, 70,* 1039–1042.

Campbell, S.C., Ewing, L.J., Breaux, A.M., & Szumowski, E.K. (1986). Problem three-year-olds: Follow-up at school entry. *Journal of Child Psychology and Psychiatry, 27,* 473–488.

Canadian Mental Health Association (2000). [WWW document]. URL www.ontario.cmha.ca/

Canadian Psychological Association (1991). Canadian Code of Ethics for Psychologists. Old Chelsea, Quebec: Author.

Canary, D.J., Stafford, L., Hause, K.S., & Wallace, L.A. (1993). An inductive analysis of relational maintenance strategies: Comparisons among lovers, relatives, friends, and others. *Communication Research Reports, 10,* 5–14.

Cannon, W.B., Lewis, J.T., & Britton, S.W. (1927). The dispensability of the sympathetic division of the autonomic nervous system. *Boston Medical Surgery Journal, 197,* 514.

Cannon-Bowers, J.A., Salas, E., & Pruitt, J.S. (1996). Establishing the boundaries of a paradigm for decision-making research. *Human Factors, 38,* 193–205.

Capaldi, E.J. (1978). Effects of schedule and delay of reinforcement on acquisition speed. *Animal learning and Behavior, 6,* 330–334.

Capaldi, E.J. (in press). The discriminative stimulus and response enhancing properties of reward produced memories.

Capaldi, E.J., Birmingham, K.M., & Alptekin, S. (1995). Memories of reward events and expectancies of reward events may work in tandem. *Animal Learning & Behavior, 23,* 40–48.

Carbonneau, P. (1988). Desengagement et reengagement social: la reinsertion par le travail en milieu rural. (Social disengagement and re-engagement: Resocialization through work in a rural environment.) *Revue Quebecoise de Psychologie, 9,* 136–144.

Carey, M.P., Morrison-Beedy, D., & Johnson B.T. (1997). The HIV-Knowledge Questionnaire: Development and evaluation of a reliable, valid, and practical self-administered questionnaire. *AIDS and Behavior, 1,* 61–74.

Carlson, N.R. (1994). *Physiology of behavior* (5th ed.). Boston: Allyn & Bacon.

Carlson, N.R. (1999). *Foundations of physiological psychology,* 4th ed. Boston: Allyn & Bacon.

Carmel, S., Shani, E., Rosenberg, L. (1994). The role of age and an expanded Health Belief Model on predicting skin cancer protective behavior. *Health Education Research, 9(4)*, 433–447.

Carpendale, J.I., & Chandler, M.J. (1996). On the distinction between false belief understanding and subscribing to an interpretive theory of mind. *Child Development, 67*, 1686–1706.

Carr, E.G. (1977). The motivation of self-injurious behavior: A review of some hypotheses. *Psychological Bulletin, 84*, 800–816.

Carr, M., & Robinson, G.E. (1990). The ethical and clinical dilemma of patient-therapist sex. *Canadian Journal of Psychiatry, 35*, 122–127.

Carrera, M.R.A., Ashley, J.A., Parsons, L.H., Wirsching, P., et al. (1995). Suppression of psychoactive effects of cocaine by active immunization. *Nature, 378(6558)*, 727–730.

Carrier, J., Dumont, M. (1995). Depression saisonniere et phototherapie: problematique et hypotheses. (Seasonal depression and phototherapy: Issues and hypotheses.). *Journal of Psychiatry and Neuroscience, 20(1)*, 67–79.

Carroll, J.M., & Russell, J.A. (1996). Do facial expressions signal specific emotions? Judging emotion from the face in context. *Journal of Personality and Social Psychology, 70*, 205–218.

Carson, R. C., Butcher, J. N., & Coleman, J. C. (1988). *Abnormal psychology and modern life* (8th ed.). Glenview, IL: Scott, Foresman.

Carstensen, L.I., & Charles, S.T. (1998). Emotion in the second half of life. *Current Directions in Psychological Science, 7*, 144–149.

Carstensen, L.I., Isaacowitz, D.M., & Charles, S.T. (1999). Taking time seriously: A life-span theory of social selectivity. *American Psychologist, 54*, 165–181.

Carstensen, L.I., Pasuapathi, M., & Mary, U. (1998). *Emotion experiences in the daily lives of older and younger adults.* Manuscript submitted for publication.

Carver, C.S. (1998). Resilience and thriving: Issues, models, and linkages. *Journal of Social Issues, 54*, 245–266.

Carver, C.S., Pozo, C., Harris, S.D., Noriega, V., Scheier, M.F., Robinson, D.S., Ketcham, A.S., Moffat, F.L., & Clark, K.C. (1993). How coping mediates the effect of optimism on distress: A study of women with early stage breast cancer. *Journal of Personality and Social Psychology, 65*, 375–390.

Carver, C.S., Reynolds, S.L., Scheier, M.F. (1994). The possible selves of optimists and pessimists. *Journal of Research in Personality, 28(2)*, 133–141.

Carver, C.S., & Scheier, M.F. (1981). *Attention and self-regulation: A control-theory approach to human behavior.* New York: Springer-Verlag.

Carver, C.S., & Scheier, M.F. (1990). Origins and functions of positive and negative affect: A control-process view. *Journal of Personality and Social Psychology, 97*, 19–35.

Case, R. (1991). *The mind's staircase: Exploring the conceptual underpinnings of children's thought and knowledge.* Hillsdale, NJ: Erlbaum.

Case, R. (1993). Theories of learning and theories of development. *Educational Psychologist, 28*, 219–233.

Casper, R.C. (1990). Personality features in women with good outcome from resticting anorexia nervosa. *Psychosomatic Medicine, 52(2)*, 156–170.

Catania, A.C. (1992). *Learning* (3rd ed.). Englewood Cliffs, NJ: Prentice-Hall, Inc.

Cattell, R. B. (1963). Theory of fluid and crystallized intelligence: A critical experiment. *Journal of Educational Psychology, 54*, 1–22.

Cattell, R. B. (1987). *Intelligence: Its structure, growth and action.* Amsterdam: North-Holland.

Cattell, R. B., & Dreger, R. M. (Eds.). (1977). *Handbook of modern personality theory.* Washington, DC: Hemisphere.

Ceci, S. J. (1991). How much does schooling influence general intelligence and its cognitive components? A resassessment of the evidence. *Developmental Psychology, 27*, 703–722.

Ceci, S.J. (1995). False beliefs: Some developmental and clinical considerations. In D.L.Schacter. (Ed.), *Memory distortion: How minds, brains, and societies reconstruct the past* (91–128). Cambridge: Harvard Press.

Ceci, S. J., Baker, J. E., & Bronfenbrenner, U. (1988). Prospective remembering, temporal calibration, and context. In M. M. Gruneberg, P. E. Morris, & R. N. Sykes (Eds.), *Practical aspects of memory: Current research and issues* (pp. 360–365). Chichester, England: Wiley.

Centerwall, B.S. (1989). Exposure to television as a cause of violence. In G. Comstock (Ed.), *Public communication and behavior* (Vol.2). San Diego: Academic Press.

Cerella, J., Poon, L. W., & Williams, D. M. (1980). Age and the complexity hypothesis. In L. Poon (Ed.), *Aging in the 1980s: Psychological Issues* (pp. 332–340). Washington, DC: American Psychological Association.

Cerelli, E. (1989). *Older drivers, the age factor in traffic safety* (DOT HS-807-402). Washington, DC: National Highway Traffic and Safety Administration.

Challis, G.B. and Stam, H.J. (1992). A longitudinal study of the development of anticipatory nausea and vomiting in cancer chemotherapy patients: The role of absorption and autonomic perception. *Health Psychology, 11*, 181–189.

Chambless, D. L. & Hollon, S. D. (1998). Defining empirically supported therapies. *Journal of Consulting and Clinical Psychology, 66*, 7–18.

Chambless, D. L., Baker, M. J., Baucom, D. H., Beutler, L. E. Calhoun, K. S., Crits-Christoph, P., Daiuto, A., DeRubeis, R., Detweiler, J., Faaga, D.A. F., Johnson, S. B. McCurry, S., Mueser, K. T., Pope, K. S., Sanderson W. C., Shoham, V. Stickle, T. Williams, D. A., & Woody, S. R. (1997). Update on empirically validated therapies, II. Retrieved from the World Wide Web: www.apa.org/divisions/div12/est/97REPORT.SS.html

Chandler, M.J., & Carpendale, J.I.M. (1998). Inching toward a mature theory of mind. In M.D. Ferrari, & R.J. Sternberg (Eds.), *Self-awareness: Its nature and development* (pp. 148–190). New York, NY: The Guilford Press.

Chang, E.C. (1998). Dispositional optimism and primary and secondary appraisal of a stressor: Controlling for confounding influences and relations to coping and psychological and physical adjustment. *Journal of Personality and Social Psychology, 74*, 1109–1120.

Chang, E.C. (1998). Dispositional optimism and primary and secondary appraisal of a stressor: Controlling for confounding influences and relations to coping and psychological and physical adjustment. *Journal of Personality and Social Psychology, 74*, 1109–1120.

Chapman, S., Wong, W.L. & Smith, W. (1993). Self-exempting beliefs about smoking and health: differences between smokers and ex-smokers. American *Journal of Public Health, 83(2)*, 215–219.

Charness, N., Clifton, J., & MacDonald, L. (1988). Case study of a musical "Mono-savant": A cognitive-psychological focus. In L. K. Obler & D. Fein (Eds.), *The Exceptional Brain.* New York: Guilford.

Chasnoff, I.J., Griffith, D.R., MacGregor, S., Dirkes, K., & Burns, K.S. (1989). Temporal patterns of cocaine use in pregnancy: Perinatal outcome. *Journal of the American medical Association, 261*, 1741–1744.

Chassin, L., Curran, P.J., Hussong, A.M., & Coldr C.R. (1996). The relation of parent alcoholism to adolescent substance use: a longitudinal follow-up study. *Journal of Abnormal Psychology, 105*, 70–80.

Chataway, C. J., & Berry, J. W. (1989). Acculturation experiences, appraisal, coping and adaptation: A comparison of Hong Kong Chinese, French, and English students in Canada. *Canadian Journal of Behavioral Science, 21*, 295–309.

Chaves, J. F., & Brown, J. M. (1987). Spontaneous cognitive strategies for the control of clinical pain and stress. *Journal of Behavioral Medicine, 10*, 263–276.

Chenard, J.R., Marchand, S., Charest, J., Li, J., et al. (1991). Evaluation d'un traitement comportemental de la lombalgie chronique: "l' ecole interactionelle du dos". (Evaluation of a behavioral intervention for chronic low-back pain: the "interactional back school".) Special issue: behavioral medicine. *Science et Comportement, 21(4)*, 225–239.

Cherek, D.R., Schnapp, W., Moeller, F.G., & Dougherty, D.M. (1996). Laboratory measures of aggressive responding in make parolees with violent and nonviolent histories. *Aggressive Behavior, 22*, 27–36.

Chess, S., & Thomas, A. (1984). *Origins and evolution of behavior disorders.* New York: Brunner/Mazel.

Chi, M.T.H., Feltovich, P.J., & Glaser, R. (1981). Categorization and representation of physics problems by experts and novices. *Cognitive Science, 5*, 121–152.

Chien, C. (1993). Ethnopsychopharmacology, In A.G. Gaw (Ed.), *Culture, ethnicity, and mental illness* (pp. 413–430). Washington, DC: American Psychiatric Association.

Chipperfield, J.G. (1993). Perceived barriers in coping with health problems: a twelve-year longitudinal study of survival among elderly individuals. *Journal of Aging and Health, 5(1)*, 123–139.

Chisholm, K., & Strayer, J. (1995). Verbal and facial measures of children's emotions and empathy. *Journal of Experimental Child Psychology, 59*, 299–316.

Chorney, M.J., Chorney, K., Seese, N., Owen, M.J., Daniels, J., McGuffin, P., Thompson, L.A., Detterman, D.K., Benbow, C., Lubinski, D., Eley, T., & Plomin, R. (1998). A quantitative trait locus associated with cognitive ability in children. *Psychological Science, 9*, 159–166.

Christensen, A., & Heavey, C.L., (1990). Gender and social structure in the demand/withdraw pattern of marital conflict. *Journal of Personality and Social Psychology, 59*, 73–81.

Christensen, A., & Jacobson, N. S. (1994). Who (or what) can do psychotherapy: The status and challenge of nonprofessional therapies. *Psychological Science, 5*, 8–14.

Christianson, S.-A., Goodman, J. & Loftus, E. F. (1992). Eyewitness memory for stressful events: Methodological quandaries and ethical dilemmas. In S. A. Christianson (Ed.), *The handbook of emotion and learning: Research and theory.* Hillsdale, NJ: Erlbaum.

Chuang, H.T., Devins, G.M., Hunsley, J., & Gill, M.J. (1989). Psychosocial distress and well-being among gay and bisexual men with human immunodeficiency virus infection. *American Journal of Psychiatry, 146(7)*, 876–880.

Chuang, H.T., Jason, G.W., Pajurkova, E.M., & Gill, M.J. (1992). Psychiatric morbidity in patients with HIV infection. *Canadian Journal of Psychiatry, 37(2)*, 109–115.

Chun, Z.F., Mitchell, J.E., Li, K., Yu, W.M., Lan, Y.D., Jun, Z, Rong, Z.Y., Huan, Z.Z., Filice, G.A., Pomeroy, C., Ryle, R.I. (1992). The prevalence of anorexia nervosa and bulimia nervosa among freshman medical college students in China. *International Journal of Eating Disorders, 12*, 209–214.

Church, R. M. (1993). Human models of animal behavior. *Psychological Science, 4.*

Cialdini, R.B. (1994). Interpersonal influence. In S. Shavitt & T.C. Brock (Eds.), *Persuasion* (pp. 195–218). Boston: Allyn & Bacon.

Cialdini, R.B. (1999). Of tricks and tumors: Some little-recognized costs of dishonest use of effective social influence. *Psychology and Marketing, 16*, 91–98.

Cialdini, R.B., Cacioppo, J.T., Bassett, R., & Miller, J.A. (1978). *Journal of Personality and Social Psychology, 36 (5)*, 463–476.

Cialdini, R.B., Eisenberg, N., Green, B.L., Rhoads, K., & Bator, R. (1998). Undermining the effect of reward on sustained interest. *Journal of Applied Social Psychology, 28*, 249–263.

Cialdini, R.B., Kallgren, C.A., & Reno, R.R. (1991). A focus theory of normative conduct. *Advances in Experimental Social Psychology, 24*, 201–234.

Cialdini, R.B., Schaller, M., Houlainhan, D., Arps, K., Fultz, J., & Beaman, A.L. (1987). Empathy-based helping; Is it selflessly or selfishly motivated? *Journal of Personality and Social Psychology, 52*, 749–758.

Claes, M.E. (1992). Friendship and personal adjustment during adolescence. *Journal of Adolescence, 15(1)*, 39–55.

Clark, D. A., Beck, A. T., & Brown, G. (1989). Cognitive mediation in general psychiatric outpatients: A test of the content-specificity hypothesis. *Journal of Personality and Social Psychology, 56*, 958–964.

Clark, D.A., & Oates, T. (1995). Daily hassles, major and minor life events, and their interaction with sociotropy and autonomy. *Behaviour Research and Therapy, 33(7)*, 819–823.

Clark, D.M., & Ehlers, A. (1993). An overview of the cognitive theory and treatment of panic disorder. *Applied and Preventative Psychology, 2(3)*, 131–139.

Clark, E. V. (1973). Nonlinguistic strategies and the acquisition of word meanings. *Cognition, 2*, 161–182.

Clark, H. H., & Chase, W. G. (1972). On the process of comparing sentences against pictures. *Cognitive Psychology, 3*, 472–517.

Clark, H., & Clark, E. (1977). *Psychology and language: An introduction to psycholinguistics.* New York: Harcourt Brace Jovanovich.

Clark, W., & Clark, S. (1980). Pain response in Nepalese porters. *Science, 209*, 410–412.

Clarke, J.N. (1992). Cancer, heart disease, and AIDS: What do the media tell us about these diseases? *Health Communication, 4(2)*, 105–120.

Clarke, J.T., Gates, R.D., Hogan, S.E., Barrett, M., et al (1987). Neuropsychological studies on adolescents with phenylketonuria returned to phenylalanine-restricted diets. *American Journal on Mental Retardation, 92 (3)*, 255–262.

Clarke-Steward, A., Friedman, S., & Koch, J. (1985). *Child development: A topical approach.* New York: Wiley.

Claxton-Oldfield, S., & Butler, B. (1998). Portrayal of stepparents in movie plot summaries. *Psychological Reports, 82*, 879–882.

Claxton-Oldfield, S., & Keefe, S.M. (1999). Assessing stereotypes about the Innu of Davis Inlet, Labrador. *Canadian Journal of Behavioural Science, 31*, 86–91.

Clum, G. A., & Bowers, T. G. (1990). Behavior therapy better than placebo treatments: Fact or artifact? *Psychological Bulletin, 107*, 110–113.

Cohen, A.J. (1990). Understanding musical soundtracks. *Empirical Studies of the Arts, 8*, 11–124.

Cohen, A.J. (in press). Film music: Perspectives from cognitive psychology. In D. Neumeyer, J.Buhler, & C.Flinn (Eds.), *Music and Cinema.* Middlebury: Wesleyan University Press.

Cohen, A.J. (in press). The functions of music in multimedia: A cognitive approach. In S.W.Y. (Ed.), *Music, Mind and Science* (pp. 57–69). Seoul: Seoul View Press.

Cohen, A.J., Thorpe, L.A., & Trehub, S.E. (1987). Infants' perception of musical relations in short transposed tome sequences. *Canadian Journal of Psychology, 41(1)*, 33–47.

Cohen, D. (Ed.). (1991). *Circle of Life: Rituals from the human family album.* Harper: San Francisco.

Cohen, D. (1997) A critique of the use of neuroleptic drugs in psychiatry. In S. Fischer & R. P. Greenberg (Eds.), *From placebo to panacea: Putting psychiatric drugs to the test* (pp.3173–228). New York: Wiley.

Cohen, D., & Strayer, J. (1996). Empathy in conduct-disordered and comparison youth. *Developmental Psychology, 32*, 988–998.

Cohen, D.B. (1999). *Stranger in the nest: Do parents really shape their child's personality, intelligence, or character?* New York: Wiley.

Cohen, J. (1993). AIDS research: The mood is uncertain. *Science, 260*, 1254–1265.

Cohen, N.J. (1994). The protective role of day care for mainstreamed high-risk infants and preschoolers. Special Issue: Prevention: Focus on children and youth. *Canadian Journal of Community Mental Health, 13*, 61–76.

Cohen, R. J., Montague, P., Nathanson, L. S., & Swerdlik, M. E. (1988). *Psychological testing: An introduction to test & measurement.* Mountain View, CA: Mayfield Publishing Company.

Cohen, R.L., & Griffiths, K., (1987). Release from PI in running memory: What does this tell us about developmental STM. *Intelligence, 11(4)*, 317–331.

Cohen, S., Frank, E., Doyle, W.J., Skoner, D.P., Rabin, B.S., & Gwaltney, J.M., Jr. (1998). Types of stressors that increase susceptibility to the common cold in healthy adults. *Health Psychology, 17*, 214–223.

Cohen, S., Kaplan, J.R., Cunnick, J.E., Manuck, S.B., & Rabin, B.S. (1992). Chronic social stress, affiliation, and cellular immune response in nonhuman primates. *Psychological Science, 3*, 301–304.

Cohen, S., Tyrrell, D.A., & Smith, A.P. (1993). Negative life events, perceived stress, negative affect, and susceptibility to the common cold. *Journal of Personality and Social Psychology, 64*, 131–140.

Cohen, S.R. & Mount, B.M. (1992). Quality of life in terminal illness: Defining and measuring subjective well-being in the dying. *Journal of Palliative Care, 8*, 40–45.

Cohen, S.R., Steiner, W., & Mount, B.M. (1994). Phototherapy in the treatment of depression in the terminally ill. *Journal of Pain and Symptom Management, 9*, 534–536.

Coie, J.D., & Jacobs, M.R. (1993). The role of social context in the preventions of conduct disorder. *Development and Psychopathology, 5*, 263–275.

Colby, A., Kohlberg, L., Feonton, E., Speicher-Dubin, B., & Lieberman, M. (1983). A longitudinal study of moral judgment. *Monographs of the Society for Research in Child Development, 48*, (1–2, Serial No. 200).

Colby, A., Kohlberg, L., Gibbs, J., Liegerman, M., (1983). A longitudinal study of moral judgement. *Monographs of the Society for Research in Child Development, 48(1–2)*, 124p.

Cole, W.A. & Bradford, J.M. (1992). Abduction during custody and access disputes. *Canadian Journal of Psychiatry, 37(4)*, 264–266.

Collager, M.L., Hines, M. (1995). Human behavioral sex differences: A role for gonadal hormones during early development? *Psychological Bulletin, 118*, 55–107.

Collier, A.C., Coombs, R.W., Schoenfeld, D.A., Bassett, R.L., Timpone, J., Baruch, A., Jones, M., Facey, K., Whitacre, C., McAuliffe, V.J., Friedman, H.M., & Merigan, T.C. Treatment of human immunodeficiency virus infection with saguinavir, zidovudine, and zalcitabine. AIDS Clinical Trials Group. *New England Journal of Medicine, 334 (16)*, 1011–1017.

Collier, G. (1994). *Social origins of mental ability.* New York: Wiley.

Collings, G.H. (1989). Stress containment through meditation. *Prevention in Human Services, 6*, 141–150.

Collins, M.A., & Zebrowitz, L.A. (1995). The contributions of appearance to occupational outcomes in civilian and military settings. *Journal of Applied Social Psychology, 25*, 129–163.

Colwill, R.M. (1993). An associative analysis of instrumental learning. *Current Directions in Psychological Science, 2*, 111–116.

Colwill, R.M., & Rescorla, R.A. (1985). Postconditioning devaluation of a reinforcer affects instrumental responding. *Journal of Experimental Psychology, 11*, 120–132.

Colwill, R.M., & Rescorla, R.A. (1988). Associations between the discriminative stimulus and the reinforcer in instrumental learning. *Journal of Experimental Psychology, 14*, 155–164.

Comer, R. J. (1992). *Abnormal psychology.* New York: Freeman & Co.

Compas, B. E., Haaga, D. A. F., Keefe, F. J., Leitenberg, H., & Williams, D. A. (1998). *Journal of Consulting & Clinical Psychology, 66*, 89–112.

Conger, J.A. (1991). Inspiring others: The language of leadership. *Academy of Management Executive, 5*, 31–45.

Contrada, R.J. (1989). Type A behavior, personality hardiness, and cardiovascular responses to stress. *Journal of Personality and Social Psychology, 57*, 895–903.

Conway, M. (1990). On bias in autobiographical recall: Retrospective adjustments following disconfirmed expectations. *Journal of Social Psychology, 130*, 183–189.

Conway, M., & Giannopoulos, C. (1993). Self-esteem and specificity in self-focused attention. *Journal of Social Psychology, 133*, 121–123.

Conway, M., Giannopoulos, C., Csank, P., & Mendelson, M. (1993). Dysphoria and specificity in self-focused attention. *Personality and Social Psychology Bulletin, 19*, 265–268.

Cook, R. G. (1993). The experimental analysis of cognition in animals. *Psychological Science, 4*, 174–178.

Cooper, B.A., Ward, M., Gowland, C.A. & McIntosh, J.M. (1991). The use of the Lanthony New Color Test in determining the effects of aging on color vision. *Journals of Gerontology, 46(6)*, 320–324.

Cooper, M., Corrado, R., Karlberg, A. M., & Adams, L. P.(1992). Aboriginal suicide in British Columbia: An overview. *Canada's Mental Health, 40*, 19–23.

Corballis, M.C. & Sergent, J. (1993). Judgements about numerosity by a commissurotomized subject. *Neuropsychologia, 30(10)*, 865–876.

Corbett, D. (1991). Cocaine enhances the reward value of medial prefrontal cortex self-stimulation. *Neuroreport: An International Journal for the Rapid Communication of Research in Neuroscience, 2(12)*, 215–218.

Coren, S. (1993). The lateral preference inventory for measurement of handedness, footedness, eyedness, and earedness: Norms for young adults. *Bulletin of the Psychnomic Society, 31(1)*, 1–3.

Coren, S., & Girgus, J. S. (1978). *Seeing is deceiving: The psychology of visual illusion.* Hillsdale, N.J.: Lawrence Erlbaum.

Coren, S., Girgus, J. S., Erlichman, H., & Hakstean, A. R. (1976). An empirical taxonomy of visual illusions. *Perception & Psychophysics, 20*, 129–137.

Coren, S., & Hewitt, P.L. (1998). Is anorexia nervosa associated with elevated rates of suicide? *American Journal of Public Health, 88*, 1206–1207.

Coren, S., & Mah, K.B. (1993). Prediction of physiological arousability: A validation of the Arousal Predisposition Scale. *Behavior Research and Therapy, 31(2)*, 215–219.

Coren, S., & Russel, J.A. (1992). The relative dominance of different facial expressions of emotion under conditions of perceptual ambiguity. *Cognition and Emotion, 6(5)*, 339–356.

Coren, S., & Ward, L. M. (1989). *Sensation and Perception* (3rd ed.). San Diego: Harcourt Brace Jovanovich.

Coren, S., Ward, L.M., & Enns, J.T. (1999). *Sensation and perception* (5th ed.). Fort Worth, TX: Harcourt Brace.

Corkum, V., & Moore, C. (1998). The origins of joint visual attention in infants. *Developmental Psychology, 34*, 28–38.

Corneil, W., Beaton, R., Murphy, S., Johnson, C., & Pike, K. (1999). Exposure to traumatic incidents and prevalence of posttraumatic stress symptomatology in urban firefighters in two countries. *Journal of Occupational Health Psychology, 4*, 131–141.

Cornelius, S.W., & Caspi, A. (1987). Everyday problem solving in adulthood and old age. *Psychology and Aging, 2*, 144–153.

Corrigall, W.A., & Coen, K.M. (1991). Cocaine self-administration is increased by both D1 and D2 dopamine antagonists. *Pharmacology, Biochemistry and Behavior, 39(3)*, 799–802.

Corso, J.F. (1977). Auditory perception and communication. In J.E. Birren & K.W. Schaie (Eds), *Handbook of the psychology of aging* (pp. 535–553). New York: Van Nostrand Reinhold.

Costa, P. T., Jr., & McCrae, R. R. (1994). The Revised NEO Personality Inventory (NEO-PI-R). In R. Briggs & J. M. Cheek (Eds.), *Personality measures: Development and evaluation* (Vol. 1). Greenwich, CT: JAI Press.

Cottrell, N., Eisenberg, R., & Speicher, H. (1992). Inhibiting effects of reciprocation wariness on interpersonal relationships. *Journal of Personality and Social Psychology, 62,* 658–668.

Cousins, S.O. & Burgess, A. (1992). Perspectives on older adults in physical activity and sports. Special Issue: Educational gerontology in Canada. *Educational Gerontology, 18*(5), 461–481.

Couture, R.T., Singh, M., Lee, W., Chahal, P., et al. (1994). The effect of mental training on the performance of military endurance tasks in the Canadian infantry. *International Journal of Sport Psychology, 25*(2), 144–157.

Covel, K. (1996). National and gender differences in adolescents' war attitudes. *International Journal of Behavioral Development, 19,* 871–883.

Covell, K., Grusec, J.E., & King. G. (1995). The intergenerational transmission of maternal discipline and standards for behavior. *Social Development, 4,* 32–43.

Covell, K., & Miles, B., (1992). Children's beliefs about strategies to reduce parental anger. *Child Development, 63*(2), 381–390.

Cowan, G., & Curtis, S.R. (1994). Predictors of rape occurrence and victim blame in the William Kennedy Smith case. *Journal of Applied Social Psychology, 24,* 12–20.

Cowan, N. (1984). On short and long auditory stores. *Psychological Bulletin, 96,* 341–370.

Cowan, N., Wood, N.L., & Borne, D.N. (1994). Reconfirmation of the short-term storage concept. *Psychological Science, 5*(2), 103–106.

Coyle, J. T. (1987). Alzheimer's disease. In G. Adelman (Ed.), *Encyclopedia of neuroscience* (pp. 29–31). Boston: Birkhauser.

Coyle, J.T., Price, D.L., & DeLong, M.R. (1983). Alzheimer's disease: A disorder of cortical cholinergic innervation. *Science, 219,* 1184–1190.

Crabbe, S. (2000, February 11). Stressed out...Mental health week recognizes daily stress as this year's theme. *Yellowknifer,* p. A6.

Craig, K.D., Grunau, R.V., & Aquan-Assee, J., (1988). Judgement of facial pain in newborns: Facial activity and cry as determinants. Special Issue: Child and adolescent health. *Canadian Journal of Behavioral Science, 20*(4), 442–451.

Craig, K.D., & Grunau, R.V.E. (1993). Neonatal pain perception and behavioral measurement. In K.J.S. Anand & P.J. McGrath (Eds.), *Neonatal pain and distress* (pp.67–105). Amsterdam: Elsevier.

Craig, K.D., Hill, M.L., & McCurty, B.W. (1999). Detecting deception and malingering. In A.R. Block, & E.F. Kremer (Eds.), *Handbook of pain syndromes: Biopsychosocial perspectives* (pp. 41–58). Mahwah, NJ: Lawrence Erlbaum Associates.

Craig, K.D., Whitfield, M.F., Grunau, R.V.E., Linton, J., & Hadjistavropoulos, H. (1993). Pain in the preterm neonate: behavioural and physiological indices. *Pain, 52,* 287–299.

Craik, F. I. M., & Lockhardt, R. S. (1972). Levels of processing: A framework for memory research. *Journal of Verbal Learning and Verbal Behavior, 11,* 671–684.

Craik, F.I.M., Moroz, T.M., Moscovitch, M., Stuss, D.T., Winocur, G., Tulving, E., & Kapur, S. (1999). In search of the self: A positron emission tomography study. *Psychological Science, 10,* 26–34.

Craik, F. I. M., & Tulving, E. (1975). Depth of processing and the retention of words in episodic memory. *Journal of Experimental Psychology: General, 104,* 268–294.

Cram, S. J., & Dobson, K. S. (1993). Confidentiality: Ethical and legal aspects for Canadian law. *Canadian Psychologist, 34,* 347–363.

Cramer, R.E., McMaster, M.R., Bartell, P.A., & Dragna, M. (1988). Subject competence and minimization of the bystander effect. *Journal of Personality and Social Psychology, 55,* 588–598.

Crawford, C., & Krebs, D. (1998). *Handbook of evolutionary psychology.* Mahwah, NJ: Lawrence Earlbaum Associates.

Crawford, H.J., Knebel, T., & Vendemia, J.M.C. (1998). The nature of hypnotic analgesia: Neurophysiological foundation and evidence. *Contemporary Hypnosis, 15,* 22–33.

Crespi, L.P. (1942). Quantitative variation of incentive and performance in the white rat. *American Journal of Psychology, 55,* 467–517.

Crews, F. C. (1998). *Unauthorized Freud: Doubters confront a legend.* New York, NY: Viking Penguin, Inc.

Crick, F., & Mitchisen, G. (1995). REM sleep and neural nets. *Behavioral Brain Research, 69,* 147-155

Criglington, A.J. (1998). Do professionals get jet lag?: A commentary on jet lag. *Aviation, Space, and Environmental Medicine, 69,* 810.

Crisp, J., Ungerer, J.A., & Goodnow, J.J. (1996). The impact of experience on children's understanding of illness. *Journal of Pediatric Psychology, 21,* 57–72.

Crocker, P.R. (1993). Sport and exercise psychology and research with individuals with disabilities: Using theory to advance knowledge. Special issue: Research with special populations: Part of an ongoing research program. *Adapted Physical Activity Quarterly, 10*(4), 324–335.

Crossman, J. & Eyjolfsson, K. (1991). Perceptions of participants regarding the long-term impact of an education and support program for heart attack and heart surgery patients and their partners. *Journal of Community Psychology, 19*(4), 333–336.

Crownshaw, S. F., & Ellis, R. J. (1991). A process investigation of self-monitoring and leaders emergence. *Small Group Research, 22,* 403–420.

Croyle, R.T. (1992). Appraisal of health threats: Cognition, motivation, and social comparison. *Cognitive Therapy and Research, 16,* 165-182.

Crusco, A.H., & Wetzel, C.G. (1984). The Midas touch: The effects of interpersonal touch on restaurant tipping. *Personality and Social Psychology Bulletin, 10,* 512–517.

Crutcher, R.J. (1994). Telling what we know: The use of verbal report methodologies in psychological research. *Psychological Science, 5,* 241–244.

Csikszentmihalyi, M., & Larson, R. (1984). *Being adolescent: Conflict and growth in the teenage years.* New York: Basic Books.

Cunningham, J.B. (1989) A compressed shift schedule: Dealing with some of the problems of shiftwork. *Journal of Organizational Behavior, 10,* 231–245.

Cunningham, M.R. (1979). Weather, mood, and helping behavior: Quasi experiments with the sunshine Samaritan. *Journal of Personality and Social Psychology, 37,* 1947–1956.

Cunningham, M.R. Roberts, A.R., Wu, C.-H., Barbee, A.Pl., & Druen, P.B. (1995). "Their ideas of beauty are, on the whole, the same as ours": Consistency and variability in the cross-cultural perception of female physical attractiveness. *Journal of Personality and Social Psychology, 68,* 261–279.

Cunningham, N. (2000, February 29). Clones and other science need not be feared. *Moncton Times and Transcript.*

Currie, D.H. (1997). Decoding femininity: Advertisements and their teenage readers. *Gender and Society, 11,* 453-477.

Czeisler, C.A. (1997). Commentary: Evidence for melatonin as a circadian phase-shifting agent. *Journal of Biological Rhythms, 12,* 618–623.

Czeisler, C.A., Moore-Ede, M.C., & Coleman, R.M. (1982). Rotating shift work schedules that disrupt sleep are improved by applying Circadian principles. *Science, 217,* 460–462.

Dabbs, J.M. (1992). Testosterone measurements in social and clinical psychology. Special issue: Social psychophysiology. *Journal of Social and Clinical Psychology, 11,* 302–321.

Dabbs, J.M., Carr, T.S., Frady, R.L., & Riad, J.K. (1995). Testosterone, crimes and misbehavior among 692 male prison inmates. *Personality and Individual Differences, 18,* 627–633.

Daniel, J., & Potasova, A. (1989). Oral temperature and performance in 8 hour and 12 hour shifts. *Ergonomics, 32,* 689–696.

Darou, W. G. (1992). Native Canadians and intelligence testing. *Canadian Journal of Counselling, 26,* 96–99.

Darwin, C. (1877). A biographical sketch of an infant. *Mind, 2,* 285–294.

Das, J. P. (1992). Beyond a unidimensional scale of merit. *Intelligence, 16,* 137–149.

Das, J. P., Naglieri, J. A., & Kirby, J. R. (1994). *Assessment of Cognitive Processes: The PASS Theory of Intelligence.* Needham Heights, MA: Allyn & Bacon.

DasGupta, B. (1992). Perceived control and examination stress. *Psychology—A Journal of Human Behavior, 29*(1), 31–34.

Datan, N., Antonovsky, A., & Moaz, B. (1984). Love, war, and the life cycle of the family. In K.A. McCluckey & H.W. Reese (Eds.), *Life-span developmental psychology: Historical and generational effects* (pp. 143–159). New York: Academic Press.

Daum, I., Ackermann, H., Schugens, M.M., Reimold, C., Dichgans, J., & Birbaumer, N. (1993). The cerebellum and cognitive functions in humans. *Behavioral Neuroscience, 104,* 411–419.

Daum, I., & Schugens, M.M. (1996). On the cerebellum and classical conditioning. *Current Directions in Psychological Science, 5,* 58–61.

Davey, G.C.L. (1992). Classical conditioning and the acquisition of human fears and phobias: A review and synthesis of the literature. *Advances in Behavior Research Therapy, 14,* 29–66.

Davey, V.A., & Biederman, G.B. (1991). Methodological issues in drug-drug conditioning in rats: Nonassociative factors in heart rate and avfail. *Behavioral Neuroscience, 105,* 850–859.

Davidson, K. W., Prkachin, K.M., & Mills, D.E. (1994). Comparison of three theories relating facial expressiveness to blood pressure in male and female undergraduates. *Health Psychology, 13,* 404–411.

Davidson, K., & Hopson, J. L. (1988). Gorilla business. *Image* (San Francisco Chronicle), 14–18.

Davidson, K., & Prkachin, K. (1997). Optimism and unrealistic optimism have an interacting impact on health-promoting behavior and knowledge changes. *Personality and Social Psychology Bulletin, 23,* 617–625.

Davidson, R.J. (1992). Emotion and affective style: Hemispheric substrates. *Psychological Science, 3,* 39–43.

Davidson, R.J., Finman, R., Straus, A, Kagan, J. (1991). Childhood temperament and frontal lobe activity: Patterns of asymmetry differentiate between wary and outgoing children. Manuscript submitted for publication.

Davidson, R.J., & Fox, N.A. (1988). Cerebral symmetry and emotion: Developmental and individual differences. In D.L. Molfese & S.J. Segalowitz (Eds.), *Brain lateralization in children: Developmental implications* (pp. 191–206). New York: Guilford Press.

Davies, M. F. (1987). Reduction of hindsight bias by restoration of foresight perspective. *Organizational Behavior & Human Decision Processes, 40,* 50–68.

Davis, C. (1994). Seventh International Congress on Obesity, as quoted in *The Globe and Mail,* August 24, (1994).

Davis, C., Brewer, H. & Weinstein, M. (1993). A study of appearance anxiety in young men. *Social Behavior and Personality, 21*(1), 63–74.

Davis, C., Katzman, D.K., Kaptein, S., Kirsh, C., Brewer, H., Kalmbach, K., Olmsted, M.P., Woodside, D.B., & Kaplan, A.S. (1997). The prevalence of high-level exercise in the eating disorders: Etiological implications. *Comprehensive Psychiatry, 38,* 321–326.

Davis, H. (1990). Cognitive style and nonsport imagery in elite ice hockey performance. *Perceptual and Motor Skills, 71*(3, Pt 1), 795–801.

Davis, J.R., & Tunks, E. (1990–91). Environments and addiction: A proposed taxonomy. *International Journal of the Addictions, 25,* 805–826.

Davison, G.C., Navarre, S.G., & Vogel, R.S. (1995). The articulated thoughts in simulated situations paradigm: A think-aloud approach to cognitive assessment. *Current Directions in Psychological Science, 4,* 29–33.

Dawson, N. V., Arkes, H. R., Siciliano, C., Blinkhorn, R., Lakshmanan, M., & Petrelli, M. (1988). Hindsight bias: An impediment to accurate probability estimation in clinicopathologic conferences. *Medical Decision Making, 8,* 259–264.

Day, H.I., & Chambers, J. (1991). Empathy and burnout in rehabilitation counsellors. *Canadian Journal of Rehabilitation, 5,* 33–44.

De Bono, E. (1990). *The mechanism of the mind.* New York: Penguin Books Inc.

De Bono, E. (1991). Lateral and vertical thinking. In Henry, J. (Ed.) *Creative management* (pp. 16–23). London, UK: Sage Publications Inc.

de Montigny, J. (1993). Distress, stress and solidarity in palliative care. Omega *Journal of Death and Dying, 27(1),* 5–15.

De Pascalis, V. (1999). Psychophysiological correlates of hypnosis and hypnotic susceptibility. *International Journal of Clinical and Experimental Hypnosis, 47,* 117–143.

De Villiers, J. G., & De Villiers, P. A. (1978). *Language acquisition.* Cambridge, MA: Harvard University Press.

de Vries, B., Bluck, S. & Birren, J.E. (1993). The understanding of death and dying in a life-span perspective. *Gerontologist, 33(3),* 366–372.

Deary, I.J. (1995). Auditory inspection time and intelligence: What is the direction of causation? *Developmental Psychology, 32,* 237–250.

Deary, I.J., & Stough, C. (1996). Intelligence and inspection time. *American Psychologist, 51,* 599–608.

Deaux, K. (1993). Commentary: Sorry, wrong number: A reply to Gentile's call. Special Section: Sex or gender. *Psychological Science, 4(2),* 125–126.

Deaux, K., & Lewis, L.L. (1986). The structure of gender stereotypes: Interrelationships among components and gender label. *Journal of Personality and Social Psychology, 46,* 991–1005.

DeBono, K.G. (1992). Pleasant scents and persuasion: An information processing approach. *Journal of Applied Social Psychology, 22,* 910–919.

deCantanzaro, D., & MacNiven, E. (1992). Psychogenic pregnancy disruptions in mammals. *Neuroscience and Behavioral Reviews, 16(1),* 43–53.

DeCasper, A.J., & Spence, M.J. (1986). Prenatal maternal speech influences newborns' perception of speech sounds. *Infant Behavior and Development, 9,* 133–150.

Deci, E.L. (1975). *Intrinsic motivation.* New York: Plenum Press.

Deci, E.L., & Ryan, R.M. (1985). *Intrinsic motivation and self-determination in human behavior.* New York: Plenum Press.

de-Koninck, J. (1991). Les rythmes biologiques lies au sommeil et l'adaptation physchologique, (Biological rhythms linked to sleep and psychological adaptiation.) *Journal of Psychiatry and Neuroscience, 16,* 115–122.

Delgado, P. L., Charney, D. S., Price, L. H., Aghajanian, G. K., Landis, H., & Heninger, G. R. (1990). Serotonin function and mechanism of antidepressant action: Reversal of antidepressant-induced remission by rapid depletion of plasma atryptophan. *Archives of General Psychiatry, 47,* 411–418.

DeLoache, J.S., Miller, K.F., & Rosengren, K.S. (1997). The credible shrinking room: Very young children's performance with symbolic and nonsymbolic relations. *Psychological Science, 8,* 308–313.

DeLoache, J.S., Pieroutsakos, S.L., Uttal, D.H., Rosengren, K.S., & Gottlieb, A. (1998). Grasping the nature of pictures. *Psychological Science, 9,* 205–210.

DeLongis, A., Folkman, S. & Lazarus, R.S. (1988). The impact of daily stress on health and mood: Psychological and social sources as mediators. *Journal of Personality and Social Psychology, 54(3),* 486–495.

Demare, D., Lips, H.M., & Briere, J. (1993). Sexually violent pornography, anti-women attitudes, and sexual agression: A structural equation model. *Journal of Research in Personality, 27,* 285–300.

Dembo, Y., Levin, I., & Siegler, R.S. (1997). A comparison of the geometric reasoning of students attending Israeli ultraorthodox and mainstream schools. *Developmental Psychology, 33,* 92–103.

Dembrowski, T.M., & Williams, R.B. (1989). Definition and assessment of coronary-prone behavior. In N. Schneiderman, P. Kaufmann, & S.M. Wiess (Eds.), *Handbook of research methods in cardiovascular behavioral medicine.* New York: Plenum.

Dement, W.C. (1975). *Some must watch while some must sleep.* San Francisco: W.H. Freeman.

Dement, W.C., & Kleitman, N. (1957). The relation of eye movement during sleep to dream activity: An objective method for the study of dreaming. *Journal of Experimental Psychology, 53,* 339–353.

DeMont, J. (1999). The tragedy of Andrew Rich: a teen suicide underscores the despair among the Innu of Labrador and northern Quebec. *Macleans, 112,* 36.

Dennett, D.C. (1995). *Darwin's dangerous idea.* New York: Simon & Schuster.

Denney, N.W., & Palmer, A.M. (1981). Adult age differences on traditional and practical problem-solving measures. *Journal of Gerontology, 36,* 323–328.

Denning, P. J. (1992). Neural networks. *American Scientist, 80,* 426–429.

Denollet, J. (1998). Personality and coronary heart disease: The Type-D Scale-16 (DS16). *Annals of Behavioral Medicine, 20,* 209–215.

DePaulo, B.M. (1992). Nonverbal behavior and self-presentation. *Psychological Bulletin, 111(2),* 203–243.

DePaulo, B.M., Kashy, D.A., Kiirkendol, S.E., Wyer, M.M., & Epstein, J.A. (1996). Lying in everyday life. *Journal of Personality and Social Psychology, 70,* 979–995.

Deppe, R.K., & Karackiewicz, J.M. (1996). Self-handicapping and intrinsic motivation: buffering intrinsic motivation from the threat of failure. *Journal of Personality and Social Psychology, 170,* 868–876.

Derksen, L., & Gartrell, J. (1993). The social context of recycling. *American Sociological Review, 58,* 434–442.

Dermer, M.L., & Jacobsen, E. (1986). Some potential negative social consequences of cigarette smoking: Marketing research in reverse. *Journal of Applied Social Psychology, 16(8),* 702–725.

Desimone, R. , & Ungerleider, L.G. (1989). Neural mechanisms of visual processing in monkeys. In F. Boller & J. Garfman (Eds.), *Handbook of neuropsychology* (pp. 267-299). New York: Elsevier.

Detchon, T., & Storm, C.L. (1987). Grabbing the brass ring: A study of referrals to family therapies by family physicians. *Family Systems Medicine, 5,* 504–511.

DeValois, R. L., & DeValois, K. K. (1975). Neural coding of color. In E. C. Carterette & M. P. Friedman (Eds.), *Handbook of perception* (pp. 117–166). New York: Academic Press.

Devins, G.M. (1992). Social cognitive analysis of recovery from a lapse after smoking cessation: comment on Haaga & Stewart (1992). *Journal of Consulting and Clinical Psychology, 60(1),* 29–31.

Dewit, D.J., & Beneteau, B. (1999). Predictors of the prevalence of tobacco use among Francophones and Anglophones in the province of Ontario. *Health Education Research, 14,* 209–221.

DeWit, D.J., Silverman, G., Goodstadt, M., & Stoduto, G. (1995). The construction of risk and protective factor indices for adolescent alcohol and other drug use. *Journal of Drug Issues, 25,* 837–863.

DewLoache, J.S. (1995). Early understanding and use of symbols: The model model. *Current Directions in Psychological Science, 4,* 109–113.

Diener, E., & Diener, C. (1996). Most people are happy. *Psychological Science, 7,* 181–185.

Diener, E., Wolsic, B., & Fujita, F. (1995). Physical attractiveness and subjective well-being. *Journal of Personality and Social Psychology, 69,* 120–129.

Dion, K. K., & Dion, K. L. (1991). Psychological individualism and romantic love. *Journal of Social Behavior and Personality, 6,* 17–33.

Dion, K. K., & Dion, K. L. (1993). Individualistic and collectivitist perspectives on gender and the cultural context of love and intimacy. *Journal of Social Issues, 49,* 53–69.

Dion, K.L., & Dion, K.K. (1987). Belief in a just world and physical attractiveness stereotyping. *Journal of Personality and Social Psychology, 52 (4),* 775–780.

Dion, K. L., Dion, K. K., & Pak, A. W.-P. (1992). Personality-based hardiness as a buffer for discrimination-related stress in members of Toronto's Chinese community. *Canadian Journal of Behavioral Science, 24,* 517–536.

Dion, K. L., & Giordano, C. (1990). Ethnicity and sex as correlates of depression symptoms in a Canadian university sample. *International Journal of Social Psychiatry, 36,* 30–41.

Dion, K.L., & Schuller, R.A. (1991). The Ms. Stereotype: Its generality and its relation to managerial and marital status stereotypes. *Canadian Journal of Behavioural Science, 23,* 25–40.

Dishman, R.K. (1988). *Exercise adherence: Its impact on public health.* Champaign, IL: Human Kinetic Books.

Dobson, K. S., & Craig, K. D. (Eds.). (1996). *Advances in cognitive-behavioral therapy.* (Vol. 2) , Thousand Oaks, CA: Sage.

Dohrenwend, B.P. (1998). *Adversity, stress, and psychopathology.* New York: Oxford University Press.

Dollard, J., Doob, L., Miller, N., Mowrer, O.H., & Sears, R.R. (1993). *Frustration and aggression.* New Haven, CT: Yale University Press.

Donald, M. (1991). *Origins of the modern mind: Three stages in the evolution of culture and cognition.* Cambridge, MA: Harvard University Press.

Dondi, M., Simion, F., & Caltran, G. (1999). Can newborns discriminate between their own cry and the cry of another newborn infant? *Developmental Psychology, 35,* 418–426.

Doob, A.N., & Climie, R.J. (1972). Delay of measurement and the effects of film violence. *Journal of Experimental Social Psychology, 8,* 136–142.

Douek, E. (1988). Olfaction and medicine. In S. Van Toller & G. Doll (Eds.), *Perfumery: The psychology and biology of fragrance.* London: Chapman Hall.

Dougherty, M. R .P., Gettys, C. F., & Ogden, E. E. (1999). MINERVA-DM: A memory processes model for judgments of likelihood. *Psychological Review, 106,* 180–209.

Dovidio, J.F., & Gaertner, S.L. (1986). Stereotype and evaluative intergroup bias. In D.M. Mackie & D.L. Hamilton (Eds.), *Affect, cognition, and stereotyping: Interactive processes in group perception.* Orlando, FL: Academic Press.

Dovidio, J.F., Gaertner, S.L., Isen, A.M., & Lowrance, R.E. (1995). Group representations and intergroup bias: Positive affect, similarity, and group size. *Personality and Social Psychology Bulletin, 21,* 856–865.

Dracup, K., Moser, D.K., Eisenberg, M., Meischke, H., et al. (1995). Causes of delay in seeking treatment for heart attack sympotms. *Social Science and Medicine, 40(3),* 379–392.

Dreher, N. (1995). Women and smoking. *Current Health, 21,* 16–19.

Dreidger, L. (1989).*The ethnic factor: Identity in diversity.* Toronto: McGraw-Hill Ryerson.

Dubbert, P.M. (1992). Exercise in behavioral medicine. *Journal of Consulting and Clinical Psychology, 60,* 613–618.

Dubbert, P.M. (1995). Behavioral (life-style) modification in the prevention and treatment of hypertension. *Clinical Psychology Review, 15,* 187–216.

Dudek, S.Z. & Hall, W.B. (1991). Personality consistency: Eminent architects 25 years later. *Creativity Research Journal, 4(3),* 213–231.

Dumas, C., Dore, F.Y., (1989). Cognitive development in kittens (Felis catus): A cross-sectional study of object permanence. *Journal of Comparative Psychology, 103(2),* 191–200.

Dumont, M., and Ladouceur, R. (1990). Evaluation of motivation among video-poker players. *Psychological Reports, 66,* 95–98.

Dumont, M., & Provost, M.A. (1999). Resilience in adolescents: Protective role of social support, coping strategies, self-esteem, and social activities on experience of stress and depression. *Journal of Youth and Adolescence, 28,* 343–363.

Duncan, L.E., & Agronick, G.S. (1995). The intersection of life stage and social events: Personality and life outcomes. *Journal of Personality and Social Psychology, 69 (3),* 558–568.

Duncker, K. (1945). On problem solving. *Psychological Monographs* (whole No. 270).

Dunn, K. (1991, October 17). City's homeless now top 15,000: Study. *The Gazette* (Montreal), A3.

Dunning, D., Leuenberger, A., & Sherman, D.A. (1995). A new look at motivated inference: Are self-serving theories of success a product of motivational forces? *Journal of Personality & Social Psychology, 69,* 58–68.

Dunning, D., & Sherman, D.A. (1997). Stereotypes and tacit inference. *Journal of Personality and Social Psychology, 73,* 459–471.

Duquette, A., Kerouac, S., Sandhu, B.K., Ducharme, F., et al. (1995). Psychosocial determinants of burnout in geriatric nursing. *International Journal of Nursing Studies, 32(5),* 443–456.

Durrant, J.E. (1993). Attributions for achievement outcomes among behavioral subgroups of children with learning disabilities. *Journal of Special Education, 27,* 306–320.

Dustin is a 'dummy' no longer. (2000, February 17). *Edmonton Journal,* p. 1.

Dutton, D.G., & Aron, A.P. (1974). Some evidence for heightened sexual attraction under conditions of high anxiety. *Journal of Personality and Social Psychology, 30(4),* 510–517.

Dutton, D.G., & Hart, S.D. (1992). Risk markers for family violence in a federally incarcerated population. *International Journal of Law and Psychiatry, 15,* 102–112.

Dwairy, M., & Van Sickle, T. D. (1996). Western psychotherapy in traditional Arabic societies. *Clinical Psychology Review. 16,* 231–249

Dweck, C.S., & Licht, B.G. (1980). Learned helplessness and intellectual achievement. In M.E.P. Seligman & J. Garber (Eds.), *Human helplessness: Theory and application.* New York: Academic Press.

Dwyer, W.O., Leeming, F.C., Cobern, M.K., Porter, B.E., & Jackson, J.M. (1993). Critical review of behavioral interventions to preserve the environment. *Environment and Behavior, 25,* 275–321.

Dyck, R. J., Bland, R. C., Newman, S. C., & Orn, H. (1988). Suicide attempts and psychiatric disorders in Edmonton. *Acta Psychiatrica Scandinavica, 77(suppl. 388),* 64–71.

Dywan, C.A., McGlone, J., & Fox, A. (1995). Do intracarotid barbiturate injections offer a way to investigate hemispheric models of anosognosia? *Journal of Clinical and Experimental Neuropsychology, 17,* 431–438.

Dywan, J. (1995). The illusion of familiarity: An alternative to the report-criterion account of hypnotic recall. *International Journal of Clinical and Experimental Hypnosis, 43(2),* 194–211.

Dywan, J. (1998). Toward a neuropsychological model of hypnotic memory effects. *American Journal of Clinical Hypnosis, 40,* 217–230.

Dywan, J., Segalowitz, S.J. (1996). Self- and family ratings of adaptive behavior after traumatic brain injury: Psychometric scores and frontally generated ERPs. *Journal of Head Trauma Rehabilitation, 11(2),* 79–95.

Dywan, J., Segalowitz, S.J., Henderson, D., & Jacoby, L.L. (1993). Memory for source after traumatic brain injury. *Brain and Cognition, 21,* 20–43.

Eagly, A.H. (1987). *Sex differences in social behavior: A social-role interpretation.* Hillsdale, NJ: Erlbaum.

Eagly, A.H., & Carli, L.L. (1981). Sex of researchers and sex-typed communications as determinants of sex differences in influenceability: A meta-analysis of social influence studies. *Psychological Bulletin, 90,* 1–20.

Eagly, A.H., & Chaiken, S. (1998). Attitude structure and function. In G. Lindsey, S.T, Fiske, & D.T. Gilbert (Eds.), *Handbook of social psychology* (4th ed.). New York: Oxford University Press and McGraw-Hill.

Eagly, A.H., & Wood, W. (1999). The origins of sex differences in human behavior. *American Psychologist, 54,* 408–423.

Eals, M., & Silverman, I. (1994). The hunter-gatherer theory of spatial sex differences: Proximate factors mediating the female advantage in recall of object arrays. *Ethology and Sociobiology, 15,* 95–105.

Earle, S.S. (1993). Assessing the needs of persons of advanced age: The Weston, Massachusetts Council on Aging "over 80" outreach survey. *Pride Institute Journal of Long Term Home Health Care, 12(3),* 33–36.

Eberhardt, C.A., & Schill, T. (1984). Differences in sexual attitudes and likeliness of sexual behavior of black lower-socioeconomic father-present vs. father-absent female adolescents. *Adolescence, 19,* 99–105.

Eden, D., & Aviram, A. (1993). Self-efficacy training to speed re-employment: Helping people to help themselves. *Journal of Applied Psychology, 78,* 352–360.

Education Quarterly Review (1996). Graduation rates and times to completion for doctoral programs in Canada (Statistics Canada, Catalogue No. 81-003-XPB, 3, p. 51.)

Edwards, J.R., & Harrison, R.V. (1993). Job demands and worker health: Three-dimensional reexamination of the relationship between person-environment fit and strain. *Journal of Applied Psychology, 78,* 628–648.

Edwards, K., & Bryan, T.S. (1997). Judgmental biases produced by instructions to disregard: The (paradoxical) case of emotional information. *Personality and Social Psychology Bulletin, 23,* 849–864.

Egeland, J. A., Gerhard, D. S., Pauls, D. L., Sussex, J. N., Kidd, K. K., Allen, C. R., Hostetter, A. M., & Housman, D. E. (1987). Bipolar affective disorders linked to DNA markers on chromosome 11. *Nature, 325,* 783–787.

Ehrlichman, H., & Bastone, L. (1990). Olfaction and emotion. In M. Serby & K. Chobor (Eds.), *Olfaction and the central nervous system.* Hillsdale, NJ: Erlbaum.

Ehrman, R.M., Robbins, S.J., Childress, A.R., & O'Brien, C.P. (1992). Conditioned responses to cocaine-related stimuli in cocaine abuse patients. *Psychopharmacology, 107,* 523–529.

Eich, E. (1995). Searching for mood dependent memory. *Psychological Science, 6,* 67–75.

Eich, E., Macaulay, D., & Lam W. R.W. (1997) Mania, depression, and mood-dependent memory. *Cognition and Emotion, 11,* 607–618.

Eich, E., Macaulay, D., & Ryan, L. (1994). Mood dependent memory for events of the personal past. *Journal of Experimental Psychology: Learning, Memory, and Cognition, 15,* 443–455.

Eich, J.E., Weingartner, H., Stillman, R.C., & Gillin, J.C. (1975). State-dependent acessibility of retrieval cues in the retention of a categorized list. *Journal of Verbal Learning and Verbal Behavior, 14(4),* 408–417.

Eimas, P.D., & Tarter, V.C. (1979). The development of speech perception. In H.W. Reese & L.P. Lipsitt (Eds.), *Advances in child development and behavior* (vol. 13, pp. 155–193). New York: Academic Press.

Ekman, P. (1992). Facial expressions of emotion: New findings, new question. *Psychological Science, 3,* 34–38.

Ekman, P. (1985, April 22). The fine art of catching liars. *Time,* p. 63.

Ekman, P., Davidson, R.J., & Friesen, W.V. (1990). The Duchenne smile: Emotional expression and brain physiology II. *Journal of Personality and Social Psychology, 58,* 231–242.

Ekman, P., & Friesen, W.V. (1975). *Unmasking the face: A guide to recognizing emotions from facial cues.* Englewood Cliffs, NJ: Prentice-Hall.

Eldridge, G.D., & Pear, J.J. (1987). Topographical variations in behavior during autoshaping, automaintenance, and omission training. *Journal of the Experimental Analysis of Behavior, 47,* 319–333.

Elkin, J., Shea, T., Watkins, J. T., Imber, S. D., Stotsky, S. M., Collins, J. F., Glass, D. R., Pilkonis, P. A., Leber, W. R., Docherty, J. P., Fiester, S. J., & Parloff, M. B. (1989). National Institutes of Mental Health treatment of depression and collaborative research program. *Archives of General Psychiatry, 46,* 971–982.

Elkind, D. (1967). Egocentrism in adolescence. *Child Development, 38,* 1025–1034.

Elkins, D.B., Dole, L.R., Maticka-Tyndale, E., & Stam, K.R. (1998). Relaying the message of safer sex: Condom races for community-based skills training. *Health Education Research, 13,* 357–370.

Elkins, I. J., Cromwell, R. L., & Asarnow, R. F. (1992). Span of apprehension in schizophrenic patients as a function of distracter masking and laterality. *Journal of Abnormal Psychology, 101,* 53–60.

Elkins, L.E., & Peterson, C. (1993). Gender differences in best friendships. *Sex Roles, 29,* 497–508.

Ellason, J.W., & Ross, C.A. (1997). Two year follow-up of inpatients with dissociative identity disorder. *American Journal of Psychiatry, 154,* 832–839.

Elliot, A.J. (1981). *Child language.* Cambridge, England: Cambridge University Press.

Elliott, A.J., & Devine, P.G. (1994). On the motivational nature of cognitive dissonance: Dissonance as psychological discomfort. *Journal of Personality and Social Psychology, 67,* 382–394.

Ellis, R.J. (1988). Self-monitoring and leadership emergence in groups. *Personality and Social Psychology, 14,* 681–693.

Ellsworth, C.P., Muir, D.W., Hains, S.M., (1993). Social competence and person-object differentiation: An analysis of the still-face effect. *Developmental Psychology, 29(1),* 63–73.

Ellsworth, P.C., & Carlsmith, J.M. (1973). Eye contact and gaze aversion in aggressive encounter. *Journal of Personality and Social Psychology, 33,* 117–122.

Elsmore, T.F., & McBride, S.A. (1994). An eight-alternative concurrent schedule: Foraging in a radial maze. *Journal of Applied Behavior Analysis, 28,* 236.

Emmons, K.M., Hammond, S.K., & Abrams, D.B. (1994). Smoking at home: The impact of smoking cessation on nonsmoker's exposure to environmental tobacco smoke. *Health Psychology, 13,* 516–520

Empson, J.A.C. (1984). Sleep and its disorders. In R. Stevens (Ed.), *Aspects of consciousness.* New York: Academic Press.

Empsom-Warner, S., & Krahn, H. (1992). Unemployment and occupational aspirations: a panel study of high school graduates. *Canadian Review of Sociology and Anthropology, 29(1),* 38–54.

Endler, N. S., & Persad, E. (1988). *Electroconvulsive therapy: The myths and the realities.* Toronto: Hans Huber.

Endler, N.S., Crooks, D.S., & Parker, J.D. (1992). The interaction model of anxiety: An empirical test in a parachute training situation. *Anxiety, Stress and Coping; An International Journal, 5(4),* 301–311.

Engel, G.L. (1980). The clinical application of a biopsychosocial model. *American Journal of Psychiatry, 137,* 535–544.

Engel, G.L. (1997). From biomedical to biopsychosocial: I. Being scientific in the human domain. *Psychotherapy and Psychosomatics, 66,* 57–62.

Engen, T. (1982). *The perception of odors.* New York: Academic Press.

Engen, T. (1986). *Remembering odors and their names.* Paper presented at the First International Conference on the Psychology of Perfumery, University of Warwick, England.

Engen, T. (1987). Remembering odors and their names. *American Scientist, 75,* 497–503.

Engen, T., & Ross, B. M. (1973). Long-term memory of odors with and without verbal descriptions. *Journal of Experimental Psychology, 100,* 221–227.

Enman, C. "2000 and Beyond," *Ottawa Citizen.*

Enns, M. W., & Reiss, J. P. R. (1992). Electroconvulsive therapy. *Canadian Journal of Psychiatry, 37,* 671–678.

Enns, M.W., Stein, M., & Kryger, M. (1995). Successful treatment of comorbid panic disorder and sleep apnea with continuous positive airway pressure. *Psychosomatics, 36(6),* 585–586.

Eppley, K.R., Abrams, A.I., & Shear, J. (1989). Differential effects of relaxation techniques on trait anxiety: A meta-analysis. *Journal of Clinical Psychology, 45,* 957–974.

Epstein, L.H. (1992). Role of behavior theory in behavioral medicine. Special Issue: Behavior medicine: An update for the 1990s. *Journal of Consulting and Clinical Psychology, 60,* 493–498.

Erblich, J., & Earleywine, M. (1995). Distraction does not impair memory during intoxication: Support for the attention-allocation model. *Journal of Studies on Alcohol, 56,* 444–448.

Erdelyi, M.H., & Kleinbard, J. (1978). Has Ebbinghaus decayed with time? The growth of recall (hypermnesia) over days. *Journal of Experimental psychology: Human Learning and Memory, 4,* 275–289.

Ericsson, K.A., Simon, H.A. (1993). *Protocol analysis: Verbal reports as data.* Cambridge, MA: MIT Press.

Erikson, E.H. (1950). *Childhood and society.* New York: Norton.

Erikson, E.H. (1987). *A way of looking at things: Selected papers from 1930–1980* (S. Schlein, Ed.). New York: Norton.

Erlenmeyer-Kimling, L., & Jarvik, L. F. (1963). Genetics and intelligence. *Science, 142,* 1477–1479.

Eron, L.D. (1987). The development of aggressive behavior from the perspective of a developing behaviorist. *American Psychologist, 42,* 435–442.

Esses, V.M., & Beaufoy, S.L. (1994). Determinants of attitudes toward people with disabilities. Special Issue: Psychosocial perspecitves on disability. *Journal of Social Behavior and Personality, 9(5),* 43–64.

Esses, V. M., & Zanna, M. P. (1995). Mood and the expression of ethnic stereotypes. *Journal of Personality and Social Psychology, 69,* 1052–1068.

Esterson, A. (1993). *Seductive mirage: An exploration of the work of Sigmund Freud.* Chicago, IL: Open Court Publishing Co.

Estrada, C.A., Isen, A.M., & Young, M.J. (1995). Positive affect improves creative problem solving and influences reported source of practice satisfaction in physicians. *Motivation and Emotion, 388,* 385–300.

Etaugh, C., & Liss, M.B. (1992). Home, school, and playroom: Training grounds for adult gender roles. *Sex Roles, 26,* 129–147.

Evans, B.K., & Fischer, D.G. (1993). The nature of burnout: a study of the three factor model of burnout in human service and non-human service samples. *Journal of Occupational and Organizational Psychology, 66(1),* 29–38.

Evans, D.R. (1997). Health promotion, wellness programs, quality of life and the marketing of psychology. *Canadian Psychology, 38,* 1–12.

Evans, K.R., & Vaccarino, F.J. (1990). Amphetamine- and morphine-induced feeding: Evidence for involvement of reward mechanisms. *Neuroscience and Biobehavioral Reviews, 14,* 9–22.

Evert, D. L., & Oscar-Berman, M. (1995). Alcohol-related cognitive impairments: An overview of how alcoholism may affect the workings of the brain. *Alcohol Health & Research World, 19,* 89–96.

Exner, J.E. (1993). *The Rorschach: A comprehensive system: Vol. 1. Basic Foundations* (34th ed.). New York: Wiley.

Eysenck, H. J. (1952). The effects of psychotherapy: An evaluation. *Journal of Consulting Psychology, 16,* 319–324.

Eysenck, H. J. (1967). *The biological basis of personality.* Springfield, IL: Charles C. Thomas.

Eysenck, H. J., & Eysenck, M. W. (1985). *Personality and individual differences.* New York: Plenum.

Fagot, B.I., & Kavanaugh, K. (1990). The prediction of antisocial behavior from avoidant attachment classification. *Child Development, 61(3),* 864–873.

Fallon, A.E. & Rozin, P. (1985). Sex differences in perceptions of desirable body shape. *Journal of Abnormal Psychology, 94(1),* 102–105.

Falomir, J.M., Mugny, G., & Perez, J.A. (2000). Social influence and identity conflict. In D.J. Terry, & M.A. Hogg (Eds.), *Attitudes, behavior, and social context: The role of norms and group membership* (pp.245–264). Mahwah, NJ: Lawrence Erlbaum.

Family, G. (1992). Projected image and observed behavior of physicians in terminal cancer care. *Omega Journal of Death and Dying, 26(2),* 129–136.

Fantz, R.L. (1961). The origin of form perception. *Scientific American, 204,* 66–72.

Farrales, L.L., & Chapman, G.E. (1999). Filipino women living in Canada: Constructing meanings of body, food, and health. *Health Care for Women International, 20,* 179–194.

Fazio, R.H., & Roskos-Ewoldsen, D.R. (1994). Acting as we feel: When and how attitudes guide behavior. In S. Shavitt & T.C. Brock (Eds.), *Persuasion* (pp. 71–93). Boston: Allyn & Bacon.

Feehan, G.G., & Enzle, M.E. (1991). Subjective control over rewards: Effects of percieved choice of reward schedule on intrinsic motivation and maintenance. *Perceptual and Motor Skills, 72(3, Pt 1),* 995–1006.

Fehr, B. (1994). Prototype-based assessment of laypeople's views of love. *Personal Relationships, 1,* 309–331.

Fehr, B. (1999). Laypeople's perceptions of commitment. *Journal of Personality and Social Psychology, 76,* 90–103.

Fehr, B., & Baldwin, M. (1995). Prototype and script analyses of laypeople's knowledge of anger. In G.J.O. Fletcher & J.Fitness (Eds.), *Knowledge structure in close relationships: A social psychological approach* (pp. 219–245). Mahwah, NJ: Erlbaum,.

Fehr, B., Baldwin, M., Collins, L., Patterson, S., & Benditt, R. (1999). Anger in close relationships: An interpersonal script analysis. *Personality and Social Psychology Bulletin, 25,* 299–312.

Fehr, B., & Russell, J.A. (1991). The concept of love viewed from a prototype perspective. *Journal of Personality and Social Psychology, 60 (3),* 425–438.

Feingold, A. (1990). Gender differences in effects of physical attractiveness on romantic attraction: A comparison across five research paradigms. *Journal of Personality and Social Psychology, 59 (5),* 981–993.

Feingold, A. (1992a). Gender differences in mate selection preferences: A test of the parental investment model. *Psychological Bulletin, 112,* 125–139.

Feingold, A. (1992b). Cognitive gender differences: A developmental perspective. *Sex Roles, 29,* 91–112.

Feldman, D.C., & Thompson, H.B. (1993). Entry shock, culture shock: Socializing the new breed of global managers. *Human Resource Management, 31,* 345–362.

Felleman, D.J., & vanEssen, D.C. (1991). Distributed hierarchical processing in the primate cerebral cortex. *Cerebral Cortex, 1,* 1–47.

Felmlee, D.H. (1995). Fatal attractions: Affection and disaffection in intimate relationships. *Journal of Social and Personal Relationships, 12 (2),* 295–311.

Fenton, W. S., & McGlashan, T. H. (1991). Natural history of schizophrenia subtypes: II. Positive and negative symptoms and long-term course. *Archives of General Psychiatry, 48,* 978–986.

Ferster, C.B., & Skinner, B.F. (1957). *Schedules of reinforcement.* New York: Appleton-Century-Crofts.

Fibiger, H. C., Murray, C. L., & Phillips, A. G. (1983). Lesions of the nucleus basalis magoncellularis impair long-term memory in rats. *Society for Neuroscience Abstracts, 9,* 332.

Fichten C.S., Creti, L., Amsel, R., Brender, W., et al. (1995). Poor sleepers who do not complain of insomnia: Myths and realities about psychological and lifestyle characteristics of older good and poor sleepers. *Journal of Behavioral Medicine, 18(2),* 189–223.

Fielder, F.E., Mitchell, T., & Triandis, H.C. (1971). The culture assimilator: An approach to cross-cultural training. *Journal of Applied Psychology, 55,* 95–102.

Fields, H.L., & Basbaum, A. (1984). Endogenous pain contro mechanisms. In P.D. Wall & R. Melzack (Eds.), *Textbook of pain* (pp. 142–152). Edinburgh: Churchill Livingstone.

Fierman, J. (1995, August 21). It's 2:00 A.M., let's go to work. *Fortune* , pp. 82–86.

Fiez, J.A., & Petersen, S.E. (1993). PET as part of an interdisciplinary approach to understanding processes involved in reading. *Psychological Science, 4,* 287–293.

Fincham, F.D., & Bradbury, T.N. (1992). Assessing attributions in marriage: the relationship attribution measure. *Journal of Personality and Social Psychology, 62,* 457–468.

Firth, D. D. (1979). Consciousness, information processing and schizophrenia. *British Journal of Psychiatry, 134,* 225–235.

Fischoff, B. (1975). Hindsight-foresight: The effect of outcome knowledge on judgment under uncertainty. *Journal of Experimental Psychology: Human Perception and Performance, 1,* 288–299.

Fischhoff, B. (1996). The real world: What good is it? *Organizational Behavior and Human Decision Processes, 65,* 232–248.

Fish, T.A., & Rye, B.J. (1991). Attitudes toward a homosexual or heterosexual person with AIDS. *Journal of Applied Social Psychology, 21(8),* 651–667.

Fisher J.D., & Misovich, S.J. (1989). Social influence and AIDS-preventive behavior. In J. Edwards (Ed.), *Applied social psychology annual* (Vol.9). New York: Plenum.

Fisher, E., Gainer, B., & Bristor, J. (1997). The sex of the service provider: Does it influence perceptions of service quality? *Journal of Retailing, 73,* 361–382.

Fisher, H. (1992). *Anatomy of love.* New York: Norton

Fisher, J.D., & Fisher, W.A. (1992). Changing AIDS-risk behavior. *Psychological Bulletin, 3,* 455–474.

Fisher, J.D., Fisher, W.A., Misovich, S.J., Kimble, D.L., & Malloy, T.E. (1996). Changing AIDS risk behavior: Effects of an intervention emphasizing AIDS risk reduction information, motivation, and behavioral skills in a college population. *Health Psychology, 15,* 114-123.

Fisher, J.D., Fisher, W.A., Williams, S.S., & Malloy, T.E. (1994). Empirical tests of an information-motivation-behavioral skills model of AIDS preventive behavior with gay men and heterosexual university students. *Health Psychology, 13,* 238–250.

Fisher, J.D., & Misovich, S.J. (1989). Social influence and AIDS-preventive behavior. In J. Edwards (Ed.), *Applied social psychology annual* (Vol. 9). New York: Plenum.

Fisher, R. P., & Geiselman, R. E. (1988). Enhancing eyewitness memory with the cognitive interview. In M. M. Gruneberg, P. E. Morris, & R. N. Sykes (Eds.), *Practical aspects of memory: Current research and issues: Vol. 1. Memory in everyday life* (pp. 34–39). Chichester, England: Wiley.

Fisher, R. P., Geiselman, R. E., & Amador, M. (1989). Field test of the cognitive interview: Enhancing the recollection of actual victims and witnesses of crime. *Journal of Applied Psychology, 75,* 722–727.

Fisher, S., & Greenberg, R. P. (1997). What are we to conclude about psychoactive drugs? Scanning the major findings. In S. Fischer & R. P. Greenberg (Eds.) *From placebo to panacea: Putting psychiatric drugs to the test* (pp.359–384). New York: Wiley.

Fiske, S.T. (1993). Social cognition and social perception. In L.W. Porter & M.R. Rosenzweig (Eds.), *Annual Review of Psychology 44,* 155–194.

Fiske, S.T., & Neuberg, S.L. (1990). A continuum model of impression formation, from category-based to individuating processes: Influence of information and motivation on attention and interpretation. In M.P. Zanna (Ed.)., *Advances in experimental social psychology* (Vol. 23), New York: Academic Press.

Fiske, S.T., & Taylor, S. (1991). *Social cognition* (2nd ed.). New York: Random House.

Fivusch, R., Gray, J. T., & Fromhoff, F. A. (1987). Two-year-olds talk about the past. *Cognitive Development, 2,* 393–409.

Flack, Laird, & Cavallaro (1999).

Flaherty, C.F., & Largen, J. (1975). Within-subjects positive and negative contrast effects in rats. *Journal of Comparative and Physiological Psycholgy, 88,* 653–664.

Flavell, J.H. (1973). The development of inferences about others. In T. Misebel (Ed.), *Understanding other persons.* Oxford: Blackwell, Basic, & Mott.

Flavell, J.H. (1982). Structures, stage and sequences in cognitive development. In W.A. Collins (Ed.), *Minnesota Symposia on Child Psychology* (Vol. 15, pp. 1–28). Hillsdale, NJ: Erlbaum.

Flavell, J.H. (1985). *Cognitive development* (2nd ed.). Englewood Cliffs, NJ: Prentice-Hall.

Fleming, A.S., & Corter, C. (1988). Factors influencing maternal responsiveness in humans: Usefulness of an animal model. *Psychoneuroendocrinology, 13,* 189–212.

Fleming, A.S., Corter, C., Franks, P., Surbey, M., et al., (1993). Postpartum factors related to mothers' attraction to newborn infant odors. *Developmental Psychology, 26(2),* 115–132.

Fleming, M.A., Wegener, D.T., & Petty, R.E. (1999). Procedural and legal motivations to correct for perceived judicial biases. *Journal of Experimental Social Psychology, 35*, 186–203.

Flemming, J.A. (1993). The difficult to treat insomniac patient. *Journal of Psychosomatic Research, 37*, 45–54.

Flessati, S.L., & Jamieson, J. (1991). Gender differences in mathematics anxiety: An artifact of response bias? *Anxiety Research, 3*, 303–312.

Flett, G.L., Blankstein, K.R., Hicken, D.J., & Watson, M.S. (1995). Social support and help-seeking in daily hassles versus major life events stress. *Journal of Applied Social Psychology, 25(1)*, 49–58.

Flett, G.L., Endler, N.S., & Fairlie, P. (1999). The interaction model of anxiety and the threat of Quebec's separation from Canada. *Journal of Personality and Social Psychology, 76*, 143–150.

Flett, G.L., Hewitt, P.L., Blankstein, K.R., & Gray, L. (1998). Psychological distress and the frequency of perfectionistic thinking. *Journal of Personality and Social Psychology, 75*, 1363–1381.

Flett, G.L., Hewitt, P.L., Blankstein, K.R. & Mosher, S.W. (1991). Perfectionism, self-actualization, and personal adjustment. Special issue: handbook of self-actualization. *Journal of Social Behavior and Personality, 6(5)*, 147–160.

Flin, R., Slaven, G., & Stewart, K. (1996). Emergency decision making in the offshore oil and gas industry. *Human Factors, 38*, 262–277.

Flynn, J. R. (1987). Massive IQ gains in 14 nations: What IQ tests really measure. *Psychological Bulletin, 101*, 171–191.

Foderaro, L. W. (1988, February 4). The fragrant house: An expanding market for every mood. *The New York Times*, pp. C1, C10.

Folger, R., & Baron, R.A. (in press). Violence and hostility at work: A model of reactions to perceived injustice. In C. VandenBos & E.Q. Bulato (eds.), *Workplace violence*. Washington, D.C.: American Psychological Association.

Folkman, S. (1997). Positive psychological states and coping with severe stress. *Social Science and Medicine, 45*, 1207–1221.

Folkman, S., Chesney, M., Collette, L., Boccellari, A., et al. (1996). Postbereavement depressive mood and its prebereavement predictors in HIV+ and HIV–gay men. *Journal of Personality and Social Psychology, 70*, 336–348.

Forest, M. (1992). La differenciation des affects: une nouvelle approche de la crise de rupture. (Differentiation of emotions: a new approach to the crisis of marital separation.) *Revue Quebecoise de Psychologie, 13(3)*, 119–145.

Forgas, J.P. (1991). Effective influences on partner choice: Role of mood in social decisions. *Journal of Personality and Social Psychology, 61(5)*, 708–720.

Forgas, J.P. (1995). Mood and judgment: The affect infusion model (AIM). *Psychological Bulletin, 21*, 747–765.

Forgas, J.P. (1998a). On being happy and mistaken: Mood effects on the fundamental attribution error. *Journal of Personality and Social Psychology, 75*, 318–331.

Forgas, J.P. (1998b). On feeling good and getting your way: Mood effects on negotiator cognition and bargaining strategies. *Journal of Personality and Social Psychology, 74*, 565–577.

Forgas, J.P., & Bower, G.H. (1988). Affect in social and personal judgments. In K. Fiedler & J.P. Forgas (Eds.), *Affect, cognition, and social behavior*. Toronto: Hogrefe.

Forgas, J.P., & Fiedler, K. (1996). Us and them: Mood effects on intergroup discrimination. *Journal of Personality and Social Psychology, 70*, 28–40.

Fortier, M.S., Vallerand, R.J., & Guay, F. (1995). Academic motivation and school performance: Toward a structural model. *Contemporary Educational Psychology, 20(3)*, 257–274.

Foss, K. (2000, March 10). Brains develop into puberty, study says. *The Globe and Mail*.

Foulkes, D. (1985). *Dreaming: A cognitive-psychological analysis*. Hillsdale, NJ: Erlbaum.

Fowler, B., & Lindeis, A.E. (1992). The effects of hypoxia on auditory reaction time and P300 latency. *Aviation, Space and Environmental Medicine, 63(11)*, 976–981.

Fowles, D.C. (1994). A motivation theory of psychopathology, In W. Spaulding (Ed.), *Nebraska symposium on motivation: Integrated views of motivation and emotion* (Vol. 41, pp. 181–238). Lincoln: University of Nebraska Press.

Fox, R., Aslin, R.N., Shea, S.L., & Dumais, S.T., (1980). Stereopsis in human infants. *Science 207 (4428)*, 323–324.

Francis, D. (2000, February 13). Opinion. *Montreal Gazette*.

Franken, R.E., Gibson, K.J., & Roland, G.L. (1992). Sensation seeking and the tendency to view the world as threatening. *Personality and Individual Differences*, 31–38.

Frederick, D., & Libby, R. (1986). Expertise and auditors' judgments of conjunctive events. *Journal of Accounting Research, 24*, 270–290.

Frese, M. (1985). Stress at work and psychosomatic complaints: A causal interpretation. *Journal of Applied Psychology, 70*, 314–328.

Frese, M. (1999). Social support as a moderator of the relationship between work stressors and psychological dysfunctioning. *Journal of Occupational Health Psychology, 4*, 179–192.

Fricko, M.A., & Beehr, T.A. (1992). A longitudinal investigation of interest congruence and gender concentration as predictors of job satisfaction. *Personnel Psychology, 45*, 99–117.

Fried, P.A., Watkinson, B., & Gray, R. (1992). A follow-up study of attentional behavior in 6-year-old children exposed prenatally to marijuana, cigarettes, and alcohol. *Neurotoxicology and Teratology, 14*, 299–311.

Fried, P.A., & Watkinson, B., (1990). 36 and 48 month neurobehavioral follow-up of children prenatally exposed to marijuana, cigarettes and alcohol. *Journal of Developmental and Behavioral Pediatrics, 11(2)*, 49–58.

Friedman, H., & Zebrowitz, L.A. (1992). The contribution of typical sex differences in facial maturity to sex role stereotypes. *Personality and Social Psychology Bulletin, 18*, 430–438.

Friedman, H.W., Hawley, P.H., & Tucker, J.S. (1994). Personality, health, and longevity. *Current Directions in Psychological Science, 3*, 37–41.

Friedman, H.W., Tucker, J.S., Schwartz, J.E., Tomlinson-Keasey, C., Martin, L.R., Wingart, D.L., & Criqui, M.H. (1995) Psychosocial and behavioral predictors of longevity: The aging and death of the "termites." *American Psychologist, 50*, 69–78.

Friedman, H.W., Tucker, J.S., Tomlinson-Keasey, C., Schwartz, J.E., Wingard, D.L., & Criqui, M. H. (1993). Does childhood personality predict longevity? *Journal of Personaltiy and Social Psychology, 65*, 176–185.

Friedrich, J., Featherstonhaugh, D., Casey, S., & Gallagher, D. (1996). Argument integration and attitude change: Suppression effects in the integration of one-sided arguments that vary in persuasiveness. *Personality and Social Psychology Bulletin, 22*, 176–185.

Friedrich, J., & Smith, P. (1998). Suppressive influence of weak arguments in mixed-quality messages: An exploration of mechanisms via argument rating, pretesting, and order effects. *Basic and Applied Social Psychology, 20*, 293–304.

Fry, P.S. (1995). Perfectionism, humor, and optimism as moderators of health outcomes and determinants of coping styles of women executives. *Genetic, Social and General Psychology Monographs, 121(2)*, 211–245.

Fuchs, I., Eisenberg, N., Hertz-Lazarowitz, R., & Sharabany, R., (1986). Kibbutz, Israeli city, and American children's moral reasoning about prosocial moral conflicts. *Merrill-Palmer Quarterly, 32(1)*, 37–50.

Fultz, J., Shaller, M., & Cialdini, R.B. (1988). Empathy, sadness, and distress: Three related but distant vicarious affective responses to another's suffering, *Personality and Social Psychology Bulletin, 14*, 312–325.

Funder, D. C., & Colvin, C. R. (1991). Explorations in behavioral consistency: Properties of persons, situations, and behavior. *Journal of Personaltiy and Social Psychology, 60*, 773–794.

Funder, D. C., & Sneed, C.D. (1993). Behavioral manifestations of personality: An ecological approach to judgmental accuracy. *Journal of Personality and Social Psychology, 64* 479–490.

Fung, H., Carstensen, L.I., & Lutz, A. (in press). the influence of time on social preferences: Implications for life-span development. *Psychology and Aging*.

Furedy, J.J. (1992). Reflections on human Pavlovian decelerative heart-rate conditiong with negative tilt as US: Alternative approaches. *Integrative Physiological and Behavioral Science, 27*, 347–355.

Gackenbach, J. (1992). Interhemispheric EEG coherence in REM sleep and meditation: The lucid dreaming connection. In J.S. Antrobus, & M. Bertini (Eds.), *The neuropsychology of sleep and dreaming* (pp. 265–288). Hillsdale, NJ: Lawrence Erlbaum Associates, Inc.

Gaertner, S.L., Mann, J.A., Dovidio, J.F., Murrell, A.J., et al. (1990). How does cooperation reduce intergroup bias? *Journal of Personality and Social Psychology, 59 (4)*, 692–704.

Gaines, J., Jermier, J.M. (1983). Emotional exhaustion in a high stress organization. *Academy of Management Journal, 26*, 567–586.

Galambos, N.L. (1992). Parent-adolescent relation. *Current Directions in Psychological Science, 1*, 146–149.

Galambos, N.L., & Almeida, D.M. (1992). Does parent-adolescent conflict increase in early adolescence? *Journal of Marriage and the Family, 54*, 737–747.

Galambos, N.L., Almeida, D.M., & Petersen, A.C. (1990). Masculinity, femininity, and sex role attitudes in early adolescence: Exploring gender intensification. *Child Development, 61*, 1905–1914.

Galambos, N.L., & Ehrenberg, M.F. (1997). The family as health risk and opportunity: A focus on divorce and working families. In J. Schulenberg, & J.L. Mags (Eds.), *Health risks and developmental transitions during adolescence* (pp. 139–160). New York, NY: Cambridge University Press.

Galambos, N.L., Kolaric, G.C., Sears, H.A., & Maggs, J.L. (1999). Adolescents' subjective age: An indicator of perceived maturity. *Journal of Research on Adolescence, 9*, 309–337.

Galambos, N.L., & Maggs, J.L. (1991). Out-of-school care of young adolescents and self-reported behavior. *Developmental Psychology, 27*, 644–655.

Galambos, N.L., & Tilton-Weaver, L.C. (1998). Multiple-risk behaviour in adolescents and young adults. *Health Reports, 10*, 9–20.

Galambos, N.L., Tilton-Weaver, L.C. (in press). Adolescents' psychosocial maturity, problem behavior, and subjective age: In search of the adultoid. *Applied Developmental Science*.

Galambos, N.L., & Walters, B.J. (1992). Work hours, schedule inflexibility and stress in dual-earner spouses. *Canadian Journal of Behavioral Science, 24(3)*, 290–302.

Galanter, E. (1962). Contemporary psychophysics. In R. Brown, E. Galnater, E. G. Hess, & G. Mandler (Eds.), *New directions in psychology*. New York: Holt, Rinehart, & Winston.

Galef, B.G. (1990). Necessary and sufficient conditions for communication of diet preferences by Norway rats. *Animal Learning and Behavior, 18*, 347–351.

Galef, B.G. (1993). Functions of social learning about food: A causal analysis of effects of diet novelty on preference transmission. *Animal Behaviour, 46(2)*, 257–265.

Galef, B.G. (1996). Food selection: Problems in understanding how we choose foods to eat. Special Issue: Society for the Study of Ingestive Behavior, Second Independent Meeting. *Neuroscience and the Biobehavioral Reviews, 20(1)*, 67–73.

Galef, B.G., McQuoid, L.M. and Whiskin, E.E. (1990). Further evidence that Norway rats do not socially transmit learned aversions to toxic baits. *Animal Learning and Behavior, 18*, 199–205.

Galef, B.G., & Whiskin, E.E. (1994). Passage of time reduces effects of familiarity on social learning: Functional implication. *Animal Behaviour, 48(5),* 1057–1062.

Gallo, L.C., & Eastman, C.I. (1993). Circadian rhythms during gradually delaying and advancing sleep and light schedules. *Physiology and Behavior, 53,* 119–126.

Gallop, R.M., Lancee, W.J., Taerk, G., Coates, R.A., et al. (1992). Fear of contagion and AIDS: Nurses' perception of risk. *AIDS Care, 4(1),* 103–109.

Gallop, R.M., Taerk, G., Lancee, W.J., Coates, R.A., et al. (1992). A randomized trial of group interventions for hospital staff caring for persons with AIDS. *AIDS Care, 4(2),* 117–185.

Galotti, K. (1989). Approaches to studying formal and everyday reasoning. *Psychological Bulletin, 105,* 331–351.

Galton, F. (1869). *Hereditary Genius: An inquiry into its laws and consequences.* London: Macmillan.

Galton, F. (1883). *Inquiries into human faculty and its development.* London: MacMillan.

Garb, J.L., & Stunkard, A.J. (1974). Taste aversion in man. *American Journal of Psychiatry, 131,* 1204–1207.

Garcia, J., Hankins, W.G., & Rusiniak, K.W. (1974). Behavioral regulation of the milieu interne in man and rat. *Science, 185,* 824–831.

Garcia, J., & Koelling, R.A. (1966). Relation of cue to consequence in avoidance learning. *Psychonomic Science, 4,* 123.

Garcia, J., Rusiniak, K.W., Brett, L.P. (1977). Conditioning food-illness aversions in wild animals: Caveat Canonici. In H. Davis & H.B. Hurwitz (Eds.), *Operant-Pavlovian interactions.* Hillsdale, NJ: Erlbaum.

Garcia, S.D. (1998). Appearance anxiety, health practices, metaperspectives and self-perception of physical attractiveness. *Journal of Social Behavior and Personality, 13,* 307–318.

Gardner, B. T., & Gardner, R. A. (1975). Evidence for sentence constituents in the early utterances of child and chimpanzee. *Journal of Experimental Psychology: General, 4,* 244–267.

Gardner, H. (1983). *Frames of mind: The theory of multiple intelligences.* New York: Basic Books.

Gardner, H. (1993). *Multiple intelligences: The theory in practice.* New York: Basic Books

Gardner, H. (1997). Reply to Perry D. Klein's "Multiplying the problems of intelligence by eight." *Canadian Journal of Education, 22,* 377–394.

Gardner, H. (1999). *Intelligence reframed: Multiple intelligences for the 21st century.* New York: Basic Books.

Gardner, R.C., MacIntyre, P.D., & Lalonde, R.N. (1995). The effects of multiple social categories on stereotyping. *Canadian Journal of Behavioural Science, 27* (4), 466–483.

Gardner, R.M., & Tockerman, Y.R. (1994). A computer-TV methodology for investigating the influence of somatotype on perceived personality traits. *Journal of Social Behavior and Personality, 9,* 555–563.

Garfield, S. L. (1995). *Psychotherapy: an eclectic—integrative approach.* New York: Wiley.

Garfield, S. L. (1998). Some comments on empirically supported treatments. *Journal of Consulting and Clinical Psychology, 66,* 121–125.

Garfinkel, P.E., Lin, E., Goering, P., Spegg, C., et al. (1995). Bulimia nervosa in a Canadian community sample: Prevalence and comparison of subgroups. *American Journal of Psychiatry, 152(7),* 1052–1058.

Garland, H., & Newport, S. (1991). Effects of absolute and relative sunk costs on the decision to persist with a course of action. *Organizational Behavior and Human Decision Processes, 48,* 55–69.

Garner, D.M., & Wooley, S.C. (1991). Confronting the failure of behavioral and dietary treatments for obesity. *Clinical Psychology Review, 11,* 729–780.

Garside, B. (1993). Physicians Mutual Aid Group: A response to AIDS-related burnout. *Health and Social Work, 18(4),* 259–267.

Gatchel, R.J., Baum, A., & Krantz, D.S. (1989). *An introduction to health psychology* (2nd ed.). New York: Random House.

Gauvain, M., & Rogoff, B. (1989). Collaborative problem solving and children's planning skills. *Developmental Psychology, 25,* 139–151.

Gauvin, L. (1990). An experiential perspective on the motivational features of exercise and lifestyle. *Canadian Journal of Sport Sciences, 15(1),* 51–58.

Gazzaniga, M.S. (1984). Right hemisphere language: Remaining problems. *American Psychologist, 39,* 1494–1495.

Ge, X., Conger, R.D., Lorenz, F.O., Shanahan, M., & Elder, G.H., Jr. (1995). Mutual influences in parent and adolescent psychological distress. *Developmental Psychology, 2,* 406–419.

Geary, D. C., & Widaman, K. F. (1992). Numerical cognition: on the convergence of componential and psychometric models. *Intelligence, 16,* 47–80.

Gee, E. (1991).The transition to grandmotherhood: A quantitative study. *Canadian Journal on Aging, 10,* 254–270.

Geen, R.G., Beatty, W.W., & Arkin, R.M. (1984). *Human motivation.* Boston: Allyn and Bacon.

Geiselman, R. E., Fisher, R. P., Mackinnon, D. P., & Holland, H. L. (1985). Eyewitness memory enhancement in the police interview: Cognitive retrieval mnemonics versus hypnosis. *Journal of Applied Psychology, 70,* 401–412.

Gelderloos, P., Walton, K.G., Orme, J.D.W., & Alexander, C.N. (1991). Effectiveness of the transcendental meditation program in preventing and treating substance misuse: A review. *International Journal of the Addictions, 26,* 293–325.

Geller, E.S. (1988). A behavioral science approach to transportation safety. *Bulletin of the New York Academy of Medicine, 64(7),* 632–661.

Geller, E.S. (1995). Integrating behaviorism and humanism for environmental protection. *Journal of Social Issues, 4,* 179–195.

Geller, E.S. (1996). Managing the human element of occupational health and safety. In R.W. Lack (Ed.), *Essentials of safety and health management.* Boca Raton, FL: Lewis.

Geller, E.S. (1996). *The psychology of safety: How to improve behaviors and attitudes on the job.* Radnor, PA: Chilton Book Company.

Geller, E.S., Winett, R.A., & Everett, P.B. (1982). *Preserving the environment: New strategies for behavior change.* New York: Pergamon Press.

Gentner, D. (1982). Why nouns are learned before verbs: Linguistic relativity versus natural partitioning. In S.A. Kuczaj (Ed.), *Language development* (Vol. 2, *Language, thought, and culture,* pp. 301–334). Hillsdale, NJ: Erlbaum.

George, J.T., & Hopkins, B.L. (1989). Multiple effects of performance-contingent pay for waitpersons. *Journal of Applied Behavior Analysis, 22,* 131–142.

Gerrard, M. (1986). Are men and women really different? In K. Kelley (Ed.), *Females, males, and sexuality.* Albany, NY: SUNY Press.

Geschwind, N. (1972). Language and the brain. *Scientific American, 226,* 76–83.

Giancola, P.R., Peterson, J.B. & Pihl, R.O. (1993). Risk for alcoholism, antisocial behavior, and response perseveration. *Journal of Clinical Psychology, 49(3),* 423–428.

Gibbons, B. (1986). The intimate sense of smell. *National Geographic, 170,* 324–361.

Gibbs, N.R. (1993, June 28). Bringing up father. *Time,* 53–61.

Gibson, E.J., & Rader, N. (1979). Attention: the perceiver as performer. In G.A. Hale, & M. Lewis (Eds.), *Attention and cognitive development.* New York: Plenum.

Gibson, E.J., & Walk, R.D. (1960). The "visual cliff." *Scientific American, 202,* 64–71.

Gibson, K.J., Zerbe, W.J. & Franken, R.E. (1992). Job search strategies for older job hunters: addressing employers' perceptions. *Canadian Journal of Counselling, 26(3),* 166–176.

Gidron, Y., & Davidson, K. (1996). Development and preliminary testing of a brief intervention for modifying CHD-predictive hostility components. *Journal of Behavioral Medicine, 19(3),* 203–220.

Gifford, R., & Hine, D.W. (1997). "I'm cooperative, but you're greedy": Some cognitive tendencies in a common dilemma. *Canadian Journal of Behavioural Science, 29,* 257–265.

Gilbert, A. N., & Wysocki, C. J. (1987). The smell survey results. *National Geographic, 172,* 514–525.

Gilbert, D.T., & Malone, P.S. (1995). The correspondence bias. *Psychological Bulletin, 117,* 21–38.

Gilbert, D.T., & Silvera, D.H. (1996). Overhelping. *Journal of Personality and Social Psychology, 70,* 678–690.

Gill, J. (1985, August, 22). Czechpoints. *Time Out,* p. 15.

Gillett, J. & White, P.G. (1992). Male bodybuilding and the reassertion of hegemonic masculinity: a critical feminist perspective. *Play and Culture, 5(4),* 358–369.

Gilligan, C.F. (1982). *In a different voice.* Cambridge, MA: Harvard University Press.

Gillis, K.J., & Hirdes, J.P. (1996). The quality of life implication of health practices among older adults: Evidence from the 1991 Canadian General Social Survey. *Canadian Journal on Aging, 15,* 299–314.

Gilovich, T., & Medvec, V.H. (1994). The temporal pattern of to the experience of regret. *Journal of Personality and Social Psychology, 69,* 357–365.

Gisiner, R., & Schusterman, R. J. (1992). Sequence, syntax, and semantics: Responses of a language-trained sea lion (*Zalophus californianus*) to novel sign combinations. *Journal of Comparative Psychology, 106,* 78–91.

Gist, M.E., & Mitchell, T.R. (1992). Self-efficacy: A theoretical analysis of its determinants and malleability. *Academy of Management Review, 17,* 183–211.

Gladue, B.A. (1991). Aggressive behavioral characteristics, hormones, and sexual orientation in men and women. *Aggressive Behavior, 17,* 313–326.

Gladwell, M. (1996, September 30). The new age of man. *The New Yorker,* 56–67.

Gladwell, M. (1998, February 2). The pima paradox. *The New Yorker,* 42–57.

Gleaves, D. H. (1996). The sociocognitive model of dissociative identity disorder: A reexamination of the evidence. *Psychological Bulletin, 120,* 42–59.

Glenn, N.D., & Kramer, K.B. (1987). The marriages and divorces of the children of divorce. *Journal of Marriage and the Family, 48,* 737–747.

Gliksman, L, McKenzie, D., Single, E., & Douglas, R. (1993). The role of alcohol provides in prevention: An evaluation of a server intervention programme. *Addiction, 88,* 1195–1203.

Gloor, P., Salanova, V., Oliver, A., & Quesney, L.F. (1993). The human dorsal hippocampal commissure. An anatomically identifiable and functional pathway. *Brain, 116, (pt 5),* 1249–1273.

Goddard, E. (1992). Why children start smoking. *British Journal of Addiction, 87(1),* 17–18.

Godden, D., & Baddeley, A. D. (1975). Context-dependent memory in two natural environments: On land and under water. *British Journal of Psychology, 66,* 325–331.

Godden, D., & Baddeley, A. D. (1980). When does context influence recognition memory? *British Journal of Psychology, 71,* 99–104.

Goethals, G.R. (1986). Social comparison theory: Psychology from the lost and found. American Psychological Association Convention (1984, Toronto, Canada). *Personality and Social Psychology Bulletin, 12* (3), 261–278.

Gold, D.P., & Arbuckle, T.Y. (1995). A longitudinal study of off-target verbosity. *Journal of Gerontology Series B Psychological Sciences and Social Sciences, 50B,* 307–315.

Gold, D.P., Andres, D., Etezadi, J., & Arbuckle, T.Y. (1995). Structural equation model of intellectual change and continuity and predictors of intelligence in older men. *Psychology and Aging, 10,* 294–303.

Goldberg, L.R., & Saucier, G. (1995). So what do you propose we use instead? A reply to Block. *Psychological Bulletin, 117,* 221–225.

Goldbloom, D.S. & Garfinkel, P.E. (1990). The serotonin hypothesis of bulimia nervosa: theory and evidence. *Canadian Journal of Psychiatry, 35(9),* 741–744.

Goldenring, J.M., & Purtell, E. (1984). Knowledge of testicular cancer risk and need for self-examination in college students: A call for equal time for men in teaching early cancer detection techniques. *Pediatrics, 74,* 1093–1096.

Goldfried, M.R., & Castonguay, L.C. (1992). The future of psychotherapy integration. *Psycholtherapy, 29,* 4–10.

Goldman, L.K., & Glantz, S.A. (1998). Evaluation of antismoking advertising campaigns. *Journal of the American Medical Association, 279,* 772–777.

Goldman, S.J., Herman, C.P. & Polivy, J. (1991). Is the effect of a social model on eating attenuated by hunger? *Appetite, 17(2),* 129–140.

Goldman-Rakic, P.S. (1994). Specification of higher cortical functions. In S.H. Broman & J. Grafman (Eds.), *Atypical cognitive deficits in developmental disorders* (pp. 3–17). Hillsdale, NJ: Erlbaum.

Goldman-Rakic, P.S. (1998). The prefrontal landscape: Implications of functional architecture for understanding human mentation and the central executive. In A.C. Roberts, & T.W. Robbins (Eds.), *The prefrontal cortex: Executive and cognitive functions* (pp. 87–102). New York: Oxford University Press.

Goldstein, D.S. (1995). Stress as a scientific idea: A homeostatic theory of stress and distress. CIANS/ISBM International Conference of Stress and Behavioral Medicine (1994, Prague, Czech Republic). *Homeostasis in Health and Disease, 36(4),* 177–215.

Goleman, D. (1993, June 11). Studies reveal suggestibility of very young as witnesses. *New York Times,* pp. A1, A23, A24.

Goleman, D. (1993, November 9). The secret of long life? Be dour and dependable. *New York Times,* p. C3.

Goleman, D. (1995). *Emotional intelligence.* New York: Bantam Books.

Goleman, D.R. (1998). *Working with emotional intelligence.* New York: Bantam Books.

Goleman, O. (1980, February). 1,528 little geniuses and how they grew. *Psychology Today,* 28–53.

Goodale, M.A. (Ed.) (1990). *Vision and action: The control of grasping.* Norwood, NJ: Ablex.

Goodale, M.A. & Milner, J.L. McClelland (Eds.), *Attention and Performance XVI: Information integration in Perception and Communications.* Cambridge: Branford.

Goodale, M.A. & Milner, A.D. (1992). Separate visual pathways for perception and action. *Trends in Neuroscience, 15(1) (163),* 20–25.

Goodale, M.A., Milner, A.D., Jacobson, L.S. & Carey, D.P. (1991). A neurological dissociation between percieving objects and grasping them. *Nature, 349(6305),* 154–156.

Goode, E. (1990). Getting slim. *U.S. News & World Report,* pp. 56–59.

Goodison, T., & Siegel, S. (1995). Learning and tolerance to the intake suppressive effect of cholecystokinin in rats. *Behavioral Neuroscience, 109(1),* 62–70.

Gopnik, A. (1996). The post-Piaget era. *Psychological Science, 7,* 221–225.

Gopnik, A., & Graf, P. (1988). Knowing how you know: Young children's ability to identify and remember the sources of their beliefs. *Child Development, 59,* 1366–1371.

Gorassinin, D.R., & Olson, J.M. (1995). Does self-perception change explaint the foot-in-the-door effect? *Journal of Personality and Social Psychology, 69,* 91–105.

Gordon, P. (1990). Learnability and feedback: A commentary on Bohannon and Stanowicz. *Developmental Psychology, 26,* 215–218.

Gordon, W.C. (1989). *Learning and memory.* Belmont, CA: Brooks/Cole.

Gotlieb, I.H., & McCabe, S.B. (1990). Marriage and psychopathology. In F.F. Fincham & T.N. Brabury (Eds.), *The psychology of marriage* (pp. 226–257). New York: Guilford Press.

Gotlib, I.H., & Whiffen, V.E. (1991). The interpersonal context of depression: Implications for theory and research. In W.H. Jones & D. Perlman (Eds.), *Advances in personal relationships* (Vol. 3, pp. 177–206). London, England: Jessica Kingsley.

Gottesman, I.I. (1993). Origins of schizophrenia: Past as a prologue. In R. Plomin & G.E. McClearn (Eds.), *Nature, nurture, and psychology,* (pp. 2231–2344). Washington, DC: American Psychological Association.

Gottfried, A.W. (Ed.). (1984). *Home environment and early cognitive development.* San Francisco: Academic.

Gottlieb, B.H. (1997). *Coping with chronic stress.* New York: Plenum Press.

Gottman, J.M. (1986). The observation of social process. In J.M. Gottman and J.G. Parker, *Conversations of Friends.* New York: Cambridge University Press.

Graf, P., Squire, L.R., & Mandler, G. (1984). The information the amnesic patients do not forget. *Journal of Experimental Psychology, Learning, Memory, and Cognition, 10,* 164–178.

Graffi, S. & Minnes, P. (1989). Stress and coping in caregivers of persons with traumatic head injuries. *Journal of Applied Social Sciences, 13(2),* 293–316.

Graham, C. H., & Hsia, Y. (1958). Color defect and color theory. *Science, 127,* 675–682.

Graham, S., & Folkes, V. (Eds.). (1990). *Attribution theory: applications to achievement, mental health, and interpersonal conflict.* Hillsdale, NJ: Erlbaum.

Granchrow, J.R., Steiner, J.E., & Daher, M. (1983). Neonatal facial expressions in response to different qualities and intensities of gustatory stimuli. *Infant Behavior and Development, 6(4),* 473–484.

Gray, T.A., & Morley, J.E. (1986). Minireview: Neuropeptide Y: Anatomical distribution and possible function in mammalian nervous system. *Life Sciences, 38,* 389–401.

Green, B.N., Johnson, C.D., & Maloney, A. (1999). Effects of altering cycling technique on gluteus medius syndrome. *Journal of Manipulative and Physiological Therapeutics, 22,* 108–113.

Green, L., Fry, A.F., & Myerson, J. (1994). Discounting of delayed rewards: A life-span comparison. *Psychological Science, 5,* 33-36.

Green, R., & Fleming, D. T. (1990). Transsexual surgery follow-up: Status in the 1990s. *Annual review of sex research, 1,* 163–174.

Green, R. G. (1984). Preferred stimulation levels in introverts and extraverts: Effects on arousal and performance. *Journal of Personality and Social Psychology, 46,* 1303–1312.

Green, R. G. (1997). Psychophysiological approaches to personality. In R. Hogan, J. Johnson & S. Briggs (Eds.), *Handbook of personality psychology* (pp. 387–413). New York: Academic Press.

Greenberg, C.I., Wang, Y., Dossett, D.L. (1982). Effects of work group size on observers' job characteristics ratings. *Basic and Applied Social Psychology, 3 ,* 53–66.

Greenberg, J., Baron, R.A. (1993). *Behavior in organizations* (5th Ed.). Boston: Allyn & Bacon.

Greenberg, J., & Baron, R.A. (1997). *Behavior in organizations* (6th ed.). Englewood Cliffs, NJ: Prentice-Hall.

Greenberg, J.S. (1991). *Comprehensive stress management* (3rd ed.). Madison, WI: William C. Brown.

Greenglass, E.R. (1990). Components of type A behavior in women and in men. In P.J.D. Drenth, J.A. Sergeant, & R.J. Takens (Eds.), *European perspectives in psychology, Vol.2: Clincal, health, stress, anxiety, neuropsychology, psychophysiology* (pp. 135–150). Chichester, England: Wiley.

Greenglass, E.R. (1995). Gender, work stress, and coping: Theoretical implications. Special Issue: Gender in the workplace. *Journal of Social Behavior and Personality, 10(6),* 121–134.

Greenglass, E.R., Burke, R.J., & Konarski, R. (1997). The impact of social support on the development of burnout in teachers: Examination of a model. *Work and Stress, 11,* 267–278.

Greenglass, E.R., Burke, R.J., & Konarski, R. (1998). Components of burnout, resources, and gender-related differences. *Journal of Applied Social Psychology, 28,* 1088–1106.

Greenglass, E.R., Fiksenbaum, L., & Burke, R.J. (1996). Components of social support, buffering effects and burnout: Implications for psychological functioning. *Anxiety, Stress and Coping: An International Journal, 9,* 185–197.

Greening, J., & Lynn, B. (1998). Vibration sense in the upper limb in patients with repetitive strain injury and a group of at-risk workers. *International Archives of Occupational and Environmental Health, 71,* 29–34.

Greenwald, A. G. (1992). New look 3: Unconscious cognition reclaimed. *American Psychologist, 47,* 766–779.

Greenwald, A.G., Draine, S.C., & Abrams, R.L. (1996). Three cognitive markers of unconscious semantic activation. *Science, 273,* 1699–1702.

Greenwald, A.G., & Pratkanis, A.R. (1988). On the use of "theory" and usefulness of theory. *Psycholical Review, 95,* 575–579.

Greenwald, A. G., Spangenberg, E. R., Pratkanis, A. R., & Eskenazi, J. (1991). Double-blind tests of subliminal self-help audiotapes. *Psychological Science, 2,* 119–122.

Gregg, W., Foote, A., Erfurt, J.C., & Heirich, M.A. (1990). Worksite follow-up and engagement strategies for initiating health risk behavior changes. *Health Education Quarterly, 17,* 455–478.

Greist-Bousquet, S., Watson, M., & Schiffman, H. R. (1990). *An examination of illusion decrement with inspection of wings-in and wings-out Müller-Lyer figures: The role of corrective and contextual information perception.* New York: Wiley.

Grillo, C.M., & Pogue-Geile, M.F. (1991). The nature of environmental influences on weight and obesity: A behavior genetic analysis. *Psychological Bulletin, 110,* 520–537.

Grillon, C., Courchesne, E., Ameli, R., Geyer, M. A., & Braff, D. L. (1990). Increased distractibility in schizophrenic patients: Electrophysiologic and behavioral evidence. *Archives of General Psychiatry, 47,* 171–179.

Grinspoon, L., & Bakalar, J.B. (1998). The use of cannabis as a mood stabilizer in bipolar disorder: Anecdotal evidence and the need for clinical research. *Journal of Psychoactive Drugs, 30,* 171–177.

Grobe, C. & Campbell, E. (1990). Who is using what in the public schools: the interrelationships among alcohol, drug and tobacco use by adolescents in New Brunswick classrooms. *Journal of Alcohol and Drug Education, 35(3),* 1–11.

Gross, P. (1986). Defining post-divorce remarriage families: A typology based on the subjective perceptions of children. Special Issue: The divorce process: A handbook for clinicians. *Journal of Divorce, 10(1-2),* 205–217.

Gruneberg, M. M. (1978). The feeling of knowing, memory blocks, and memory aids. In M. M. Greenberg & P. Morris (Eds.), *Aspects of memory.* London: Methuen.

Gruneberg, M. M., Morris, P., & Sykes, R. N. (1988). *Practical aspects of memory: Current research and issues* (Vols. 1, 2). Chichester, England: Wiley Interscience.

Grusec, J.E., & Goodnow, J.J. (1994). Impact of parental discipline methods on the child's internalization of values: A reconceptualization on current points of view. *Developmental Psychology, 30,* 4–19.

Guenther, R. K. (1998). *Human Cognition.* Upper Saddle River, N J: Prentice Hall.

Guidi, L., Tricerri, A., Vangeli, M., Frasca, D., Errani, A.R., Di Giovanni, A., Antico, L., Menini, E., Sciamanna, V., Magnavita, N., Doria, G., & Bartoloni, C. (1999). Neuropeptide Y plasma levels and immunological changes during academic stress. *Neuropsychology, 40,* 188–195.

Guilford, J. (1967). *The nature of human intelligence.* New York: McGraw-Hill.

Guilford, J. (1985). Cognitive psychology's ambiguities: Some suggested remedies. *Psychological Review, 89,* 48–59.

Guimond, S., & Dube, L. (1989). La representation des causes de l'inferiorite economique des quebecois francophones. (Representation of the causes of economic inferiority of French-speaking Canadians from Quebec.) *Canadian Journal of Behavioural Science, 21,* 28–39.

Gully, K.J., & Dengerink, H.A. (1983). The dyadic interaction of persons with violent and nonviolent histories. *Aggressive Behavior, 9,* 13–20.

Gully, K.J., Dengerink, H.A., Pepping, M., & Bergstrom, D.A. (1981). Research note: Sibling contribution to violent behavior. *Journal of Marriage and the Family, 43,* 333–337.

Gupta, R., & Derevensky, J. (1997). Familial and social influences on juvenile gambling behavior. *Journal of Gambling Studies, 13,* 179–192.

Gur, R.E., & Pearlson, G.D. (1993). Neuroimaging in schizophrenia research. *Schizophrenia 1993: Speical report* (pp. 163–179). Washington, DC: National Institute of Mental Health. Schizophrenia Research Branch.

Gurley, R.J., Aranow, R., & Katz, M. (1998). Medicinal marijuana: A comprehensive review. *Journal of Psychoactive Drugs, 30,* 137–147.

Gurman, A. S., Kniskern, D. P., & Pinsof, W. M. (1986). Research on marital and family therapies. In S. L. Garfield & A. E. Bergin (Eds.), *Handbook of psychotherapy and behavior change.* (pp. 565–626). New York: Wiley.

Gurstein, M. (1999). Leadership in the peacekeeping army of the future. In J.G. Hunt, & G.E. Dodge (Eds.), *Out-of-the-box leadership: Transforming the twenty-first-century army and other top-performing organizations. Monographs in leaderships and management, Vol. 1* (pp. 195–218). Stamford, CT: Jai Press.

Gustavson, C.R., Garcia, J., Hawkins, W.G., & Rusiniak, K.W. (1974). *Coyote predation control by aversive conditioning. Science, 184,* 581–583.

Gutek, B.A., & Winter, S.J. (1992). Consistency of job satisfaction across situations: Fact or framing artifact? *Journal of Vocational Behavior, 41,* 61–78.

Guthrie, J.P., Ash, R.A., & Bendapudi, V. (1995). Additional validity evidence for a measure of morningness. *Journal of Applied Psychology, 80,* 186–190.

Guttman, H.A. (1991). Parental death as a precipitant of marital conflict in middle age. *Journal of Marital and Family Therapy, 17(1),* 81–87.

Haas, K., & Haas, A. (1993). *Understanding sexuality.* St. Louis, MO: Mosby.

Hackett, R.D., Bycio, P., & Hausdorf, P.A. (1994). Further assessments of Meyer and Allen's (1991) three-component model of organizational commitment. *Journal of Applied Psychology, 79,* 15–23.

Haddock, G., & Zanna, M.P. (1998). Authoritarianism, values, and the favorability and structure of antigay attitudes. In G.M. Herek (Ed.), *Stigma and sexual orientation: Understanding prejudice against lesbians, gay men, and bisexuals* (pp. 82–107). Thousand Oaks, CA: Sage Publications.

Haddock, G., Zanna, M. P., & Esses, V. M. (1994). Mood and the expression of intergroup attitudes: The moderating role of affect intensity. *European Journal of Social Psychology, 24,* 189–205.

Hadjistavropoulos, T., & Genest, M. (1994). The underestimation of the role of physical attractiveness in dating preferences: Ignorance or taboo? *Canadian Journal of Behavioural Science, 26(2),* 298–318.

Hafer, C.L., Reynolds, K.L., & Obertynski, M.A. (1996). Message comprehensibility and persuasion: Effects of complex language in counterattitudinal appeals to laypeople. *Social Cognition, 14,* 317–337.

Hagan, J. & Wheaton, B. (1993). The search for adolescent role exits and the transition to adulthood. *Social Forces, 71(4),* 955–979.

Hagen, R. (1993). Clinical files, Florida State University. Quoted in R. R. Bootzin, J. R. Acocella, & L. B. Alloy, *Abnormal psychology* (6th ed.). New York: McGraw-Hill.

Haier, R. J., Siegel, B. V., Tang, C., Abel, L., & Buchsabum, M. S. (1992). Intelligence and changes in regional cerebral glucose metabolic rate following learning. *Intelligence, 16,* 415–526.

Hajek, P., & Belcher, M. (1991). Dream of absent-minded transgression: An empirical study of a cognitive withdrawal symptom. *Journal of Abnormal Psychology, 100,* 487–491.

Hall, J.A., Roter, D.L., & Katz, N.R. (1987). Task versus socioemotional behaviors in physicians. *Medical Care, 25,* 399–412.

Hall, J. A., Roter, D. L., & Milburn, M. A. (1999). Illness and satisfaction with medical care. *Current Directions in Psychological Science, 8,* 96–99.

Hall, J.A., & Veccia, E.M. (1990). More "touching" observations: New insights on men, women, and interpersonal touch. *Journal of Personality and Social Psychology, 59,* 1155–1162.

Halpern, A.R. (1989). Memory for the absolute pitch of familiar songs. *Memory and Cognition, 17,* 572–581.

Hamburg, S. (1998). Inherited hypohedonia leads to learned helplessness: A conjecture updated. *Review of General Psychology, 2,* 384–403.

Hamer, D.H., Hu, S., Magnuson, V.L., Hu, N., & Pattatucci, A.J. (1993). A linkage between DNA markers on the X chromosome and male sexual orientation. *Science, 261,* 321–327.

Hameroff, S.R., Kaszniak, A.W., & Scott, A.C. (Eds.). (1996). *Toward a science of consciousness: The first Tuscon discussions and debates.* Cambridge, MA: MIT Press.

Hammond, W. R., & Yung, B. (1993). Psychology's role in public health response to assaultive violence among young African-American men. *American Psychologist, 48,* 142–154.

Hampson, E., Rovet, J.F., & Altmann, D. (1994, August). *Spatial reasoning in children with congenital adrenal hyperplasia due to 21-hydroxylase deficiency.* Paper presented at the meeting of the International Society of Psychoneurendocrinology, Seattle, WA.

Hanisch, K.D. (1995). Behavioral families and multiple causes: Matching the complexity of responses to the complexity of antecedents. *Current Directions in Psychological Science, 4,* 156–161.

Hanly, C. (1978). Instincts and hostile affects. 30th International Psycho-Analytical Congress (1977, Jerusalem, Israel). *International Journal of Psycho-Analysis, 59(2-3),* 149–156.

Hardeman, W., Pierro, A., & Mannetti, L. (1997). Determinants of intentions to practise safe sex among 16-25 year-olds. *Journal of Community and Applied Social Psychology, 7,* 345–360.

Harder, L.D. (1988). Choice of individual flowers by bumble bees: Interaction of morphology time and energy. *Behaviour, 104,* 60–77.

Harlow, H.F., & Harlow, M.H. (1966). Learning to love. *American Scientist, 54,* 244–272.

Harpur, T. J., & Hare, R. D. (1990). Psychopathy and attention. In J. Enns (Ed.) *The development of attention: Research and theory* (pp. 429–444). New York: North Holland.

Harrel, W.A. (1992). Older motorist yielding to pedestrians: Are older inattentive and unwilling to stop? *International Journal of Aging and Human Development, 36(2),* 115–127.

Harrigan, T., Peredery, O., & Persinger, M.A. (1991). *Behavioral Neuroscience, 105,* 482–486.

Harrington, A. (1995). Unfinished business: Models of laterality in the nineteenth century. In R.J. Davidson & K. Hugdahl (Eds.), *Brain asymmetry* (pp. 34–27). Cambridge, MA: MIT Press.

Harris, J., & Wilkins, A. J. (1982). Remembering to do things: A theoretical framework and illustrative experiment. *Human Learning, 1,* 1–14.

Harris, M.B. (1992). Sex, race, and experiences of aggression. *Aggressive Behavior, 18,* 201–217.

Harris, P.L. (1991). The work of the imagination. In A. Whiten (Ed.), *Natural theories of mind* (pp. 283–304). Oxford: Blackwell.

Harris, P.R. (1979). Cultural awareness training for human resource development. *Training and Development Journal, 64–74.*

Harrison, J.K. (1992). Individual and combined effects of behavior modeling and the cultural assimilator in cross-cultural management training. *Journal of Applied Psychology, 77,* 952–962.

Harrison, R.V. (1985). The person–environment fit model and the study of job stress. In T.A. Beehr, R.S. Bhagat (Eds.), *Human stress and cognition in organizations* (pp. 23–55). New York: Wiley.

Hartmann, E.L. (1973). *The functions of sleep.* New Haven: Yale University Press.

Harvey, S.M. (1987). Female sexual behavior: Fluctuations dring the menstrual cycle. *Journal of Psychosomatic Research, 31,* 101–111.

Hassett, J. (1978). Sex and smell. *Psychology Today, 11,* 40, 42–45.

Hastings, P., & Grusec, J.E. (1997). Conflict outcome as a function of parental accuracy in perceiving child cognitions and affect. *Social Development, 6,* 76–90.

Hatfield, E. (1988). Passionate and companionate love. In R.J. Sternberg & M.K. Barnes (Eds.), *The psychology of love* (pp. 191–217). New Haven, CT: Yale University Press.

Hatfield, E.,& Rapson, R.L. (1993). *Love, sex, and intimacy: Their psychology, biology, and history.* New York: HarperCollins.

Haugaard, J. J., Repucci, N. D., Laurd, J., & Nauful, T. (1991). Children's definitions of the truth and their competency as witnesses in legal proceedings. *Law and Human Behavior, 15,* 253–273.

Hausenblas, H.A., & Carron, A.V. (1996). Group cohesion and self-handicapping in female and male athletes. *Journal of Sport and Exercise Psychology, 18,* 132–143.

Hauser, M.D. (1993). Right hemisphere dominance for the production of facial expression in monkeys. *Science, 264,* 475-477.

Hausfather, A., Toharia, A., LaRoche, C., & Engelsmann, F. (1997). Effects of age of entry, day-care quality, and family characteristics on preschool behavior. *Journal of Child Psychology and Psychiatry and Allied Disciplines, 38,* 441–448.

Hawkins, S. A., & Hastie, R. (1990). Hindsight: Biased judgments of past events after the outcomes are known. *Psychological Bulletin, 107,* 311-327.

Hawranik, P. (1991). A clinical possibility: preventing health problems after the age of 65. *Journal of Gerontological Nursing, 17(11),* 20-25.

Hay, J. F., & Jacoby, L. L. (1999). Separating habit and recollection in young and older adults: Effects of elaborative processing and distinctiveness. *Psychology and Aging, 14,* 122–134.

Hayward, P., Wardle, J., & Higgitt, A. (1989). Benzodiazepine research: Current findings and practical consequences. *British Journal of Psychiatry, 28,* 307–327.

Hazan, C., & Shaver, P. (1987). Romantic love conceptualized as an attachment process. *Journal of Personality and Social Psychology, 52 (3),* 511–524.

Hazelrigg, M. D., Cooper, H. M., & Borduin, C. M. (1987). Evaluating the effectiveness of family therapies: An integrative review and analysis. *Psychological Bulletin, 101,* 428–442.

Hearty, B. (1989). A further development of the relation between mourning and manic-depression. *Melanie Klien and Object Relations, 7(2),* 83–94.

Heatherton, T., & Weinberger, J.L. (1994). *Can personality change?* Washington, DC: American Psychological Association.

Hecht, M.L., Marston, P.J., & Larkey, L.K. (1994). Love ways and realtionship quality in heterosexual relationships. *Journal of Social and Personal Relationships, 11,* 25–43.

Heckhausen, J. (1997). Developmental regulation across adulthood: Primary and secondary control of age-related challenges. *Developmental Psychology, 33,* 176–187.

Heckhausen, J. (1999). *Developmental regulation in adulthood: Age-normative and sociostructural constraints as adaptive challenges.* New York: Cambridge University Press.

Heckhausen, J., & Schulz, R. (1995). A life-span theory of control. *Psychological Review, 102,* 284–304.

Heilman, M.E., Block, C.J., & Lucas, A. (1992). Presumed incompetent? Stigmatization and affirmative action efforts. *Journal of Applied Psychology, 77,* 536–544.

Heinrichs, R. W. (1993). Schizophrenia and the brain: Conditions for a neuropsychology of madness. *American Psychologist, 48,* 221–233.

Heller, W. (1997). Emotion. In M.T. Banich (Ed.), *Neuropsychology: The neural bases of mental function* (pp. 398–429). Boston: Houghton Mifflin.

Heller, W., Etienne, M.A., & Miller, G.A. (1995). Patterns of perceptual asymmetry in depression and anxiety: Implications for neuropsychological models of emotion and psychopathology. *Journal of Abnormal Psychology, 104,* 327–333.

Heller, W., Nitschke, J.B., & Miller, G.A. (1998). Lateralization in emotion and emotional disorders. *Current Directions in Psychological Science, 7,* 26–32.

Hellige, J.B. (1993). Unity of thought and action: varieties of interaction between the left and right cerebral hemispheres. *Current Directions in Psychological Science, 2(1),* 21–25.

Helms, J. E. (1989). Oral and literate traditions among black Americans living in poverty. *American Psychologist, 44,* 367–373.

Helms, J. E. (1992). Why is there no study of cultural equivalence in standardized cognitive ability testing? *American Psychologist, 47,* 1083–1101.

Hendrick, C. (Ed.). (1989). *Close relationships.* Newbury Park, CA: Sage.

Hendrick, C., & Hendrick S.S. (1993). Lovers as friends. *Journal of Social and Personal Relationship, 10,* 459–466.

Henggeler, S.W., Melton, G.B., & Smith, L.A. (1992). Family preservation using multisystemic therapy: An effective alternative to incarcerating serious juvenile offenders. *Journal of Consulting and Clinical Psychology, 60(6),* 953–961.

Henker, B., & Whalen, C.K., (1989). Hyperactivity and attention deficits. Special Issue: Children and their development: Knowledge base, research agenda, and social policy application. *American Psychologist, 44(2),* 216–223.

Henriques, J. B., & Davidson, R. J. (1990). Regional brain electrical asymmetries discriminate between previously depressed and healthy control subjects. *Journal of Abnormal Psychology, 99,* 22–31.

Henry, J. (1982). Circulating opiods: Possible physiological roles in central nervous function. *Neuroscience and Behavioral Reviews, 6(3),* 229–245.

Herdt, G.H., & Davidson, J. (1988). The Sambia "Turnim-Man": Sociocultural and clinical aspects of gender formation in male pesudohermaphrodites with 5-alpha-reductase deficiency in Papua New Guinea. *Archives of Sexual Behavior, 17,* 33–56.

Herman, L. M., Kuczaj, S. A., & Holder, M. D. (1993). Responses to anomalous gestural sequences by a language-trained dolphin: Evidence for processing of semantic relations and syntactic information. *Journal Experimental Psychology: General, 122,* 184–194.

Herman, L. M., Richards, D. G., & Wolz, J. P. (1984). Comprehension of sentences by bottlenosed dolphins. *Cognition, 16,* 129–219.

Hermann, C., Kim, M., & Blanchard, E.B. (1995). Behavioural and prophylactic pharmacological intervention studies of pediatric migraine: An exploratory meta-analysis. *Pain, 60,* 239–255.

Herold, E.S., Mewhinney, D.M.K. (1993). Gender differences in casual sex and AIDS prevention: A survey of dating bars. *Journal of Sex Research, 30(1),* 36–42.

Herold, E.S., Maticka-Tyndale, E., & Mewhinney, D. (1998). Predicting intentions to engage in casual sex. *Journal of Social and Personal Relationships, 15,* 502–516.

Herrmann, N., & Eryavec, G. (1994). Delayed onset port-traumatic stress disorder in World War II veterans. *Canadian Journal of Psychiatry, 39,* 439–441.

Herrnstein, R.J., & Murray, C. (1994). *The bell curve.* New York: The Free Press.

Hetzel, B., & McMichael, T. (1987). *The LS factor: Lifestyle and health.* Ringwood, Victoria: Penguin.

Hewitt, P.L., Flett, G.L., & Ediger, E. (1995). Perfectionism traits and perfectionistic self-presentation in eating disorder attitudes, characteristics, and symptoms. *International Journal of Eating Disorders, 18(4),* 317–326.

Hewstone, M., Bond, M.H., & Wan, K.C. (1983). Social factors and social attributions: The explanation of intergroup differences in Hong Kong. *Social cognition, 2,* 142–157.

Higginbottom, S.F., Barling, J., & Kelloway, E.K. (1993). Linking retirement experiences and marital satisfaction: A mediational model. *Psychology and Aging, 8(4),* 508–516.

Higgins, A.T., & Turnure, J.E. (1984). Distractibility and concentration of attention in children's development. *Child Development, 55,* 1799–1810.

Hillier, L.M., Hewitt, K.L., & Morrongiello, B.A., (1992). Infants' perception of illusions in sound localization: Reaching to sounds in the dark. *Journal of Experimental Child Psychology, 53(2),* 159–179.

Hilton, D.J. (1995). The social context of reasoning: Conversational inferences and rational judgment. *Psychological Bulletin, 118,* 248–271.

Hilton, J.L., Klein, J.G., & von Hippel, W. (1991). Attention allocation and impression formation. *Personality and Social Psychology Bulletin, 17,* 548–559.

Hilton, N.Z. (1993). Childhood sexual victimization and lack of empathy in child molesters: Explanation or excuse? *International Journal of Offender Therapy and Comparative Criminology, 37(4),* 287–296.

Hilts, P.J. (1996, July 2). In research scans, telltale signs sort false memories from true. *New York Times,* p. C3.

Hines, M., Chiu, L., McAdams, L.A., Bentler, P.M., & Lipcamon, J. (1992). Cognition and the corpus callosum: Verbal fluency, visuospatial ability, and language alteralization related to mid-sagittal surface areas of callosal subregions. *Behavioral Neuroscience, 106,* 3–14.

Hingson, R., Strunin, L., Berlin, B., & Heeren, T. (1990). Beliefs about AIDS, use of alcohol and drugs, and unprotected sex among Massachusetts adolescents. *American Journal of Public Health, 80,* 295–299.

Hinsz, L. D., & Williamson, D. A. (1987). Bulimia and depression: A review of the affective variant hypothesis. *Psychological Bulletin, 102,* 150–158.

Hinton, G. E., & Parsons, L. M. (1988). Scene based and viewer centered representations for comparing shapes. *Cognition, 30,* 1–35.

Hinton, G. E., & Shallice, T. (1991). Lesioning an attractor network: Investigations of acquired dyslexia. *Psychological Review, 98,* 74–95.

Hinz, L.D. & Williamson, D.A. (1987). Bulimia and depression: a review of the affective variant hypothesis. *Psychological Bulletin, 102(1),* 150–158.

Hixon, J.G., & Swann, W.B., Jr. (1993). When does introspection bear fruit? Self-reflection, self-insight, and interpersonal choices. *Journal of Personality and Social Psychology, 64,* 35–43.

Hoaken, P.N.S., Assaad, J., & Pihl, R.O. (1998). Cognitive functioning and the inhibition of alcohol-induced aggression. *Journal of Studies on Alcohol, 59,* 599–607.

Hoaken, P.N.S., Giancola, P.R., & Pihl, R.O. (1998). Executive cognitive functions as mediators of alcohol-related aggression. *Alcohol and Alcoholism, 33,* 47–54.

Hobfoll, S.E., Jackson, A.P., Lavin, J., Britton, P.J., & Shepard, J.B. (1994). Reducing inner-city women's AIDS risk activities: A study of single, pregnant women. *Health Psychology, 13,* 397–403.

Hobson, J.A. (1988). *The dreaming brain.* New York: Basic Books.

Hodben, K., & Pliner, P. (1995), Effects of a model on food neophobia in humans. *Appetite, 25(2),* 101–113.

Hodges, E.V.E., Boivin, M., Vitaro, F., & Bukowski, W.M. (1999). The power of friendship: Protection against an escalating cycle of peer victimization. *Developmental Psychology, 35,* 94–101.

Hodges, J., & Tizard, B., (1989). Social and family relationships of ex-institutional adolescents. *Journal of Child Psychology and Psychiatry and Allied Disciplines, 30(1),* 77–97.

Hogan, R., Hogan, J., & Roberts, B.W. (1996). Personality measurement and employment decisions: Questions and answers. *American Psychologist, 51,* 469–477.

Hollar, D.S., & Snizek, W.E. (1996). The influences of knowledge of HIV/AIDS and self-esteem on the sexual practices of college students. *Social Behavior and Personality, 24(1),* 75–86.

Hollon, S. D., DeRubeis, R. J., & Evans, M. D. (1987). Causal mediation of change in treatment for depression: Discriminating between nonspecificity and noncausality. *Psychological Bulletin, 102,* 139–149.

Hollon, S. D., Shelton, R. C., & Loosen, P. T. (1991). Cognitive therapy and pharmacotherapy for depression. *Journal of Consulting and Clinical Psychology, 59,* 88–99.

Hollon, S.D., & Beck, A.T. (1994). Cognitive and cognitive-behavioral therapies. In A.E. Bergin & S.L. Garfield (Eds.), *Handbook of psychotherapy and behavior change* (4th ed.). New York: Wiley.

Holmes, D. (1990). The evidence for repression: An examination of sixty years of research. In J. Singer (Ed.), *Repression and dissociation: Implications for personality theory, psychopathology, and health* (pp. 85–102). Chicago: University of Chicago Press.

Holmes, D.S. (1984). Meditation and somatic arousal reduction: A review of the experimental evidence. *American Pscyhologist, 39,* 1–10.

Holmes, T.H., & Masuda, M. (1974). Life change and illness susceptibility. In B.S. Dohrenwend and B.P. Dohrenwned (Eds.), *Stressful life events: Their nature and effects.* New York: Wiley.

Holmes, T.H., & Rahe, R.H. (1967). The social readjustment rating scale. *Journal of Psychosomatic Research, 11,* 213–218.

Holstein, C.B. (1976). Irreversible, stepwise sequence in the development of moral judgment: A longitudinal study of males and females. *Child Development, 47,* 51–61.

Homel, R., Hauritz, M., Wortley, R., McIlwain, G., & Carvolth, R. (1997). Preventing alcohol-related crime through community action: The Surfers Paradise Safety Action Project. *Crime Prevention Studies, 7,* 35–90.

Honig, W.K, & Staddon, J.E.R. (Eds.). (1977). *Handbook of operant behavior.* Englewood Cliffs, NJ: Prentice-Hall.

Honig, W.K., & Urcuioli, P.J. (1981). The legacy of Guttman and Kalish: Twenty-five years of research on stimulus generalization. *Journal of the Experimental Analysis of Behavior, 36,* 405–445.

Hoppe, R. B. (1988). In search of a phenomenon: Research in parapsychology. *Contemporary Psychology, 33,* 129–130.

Hopson, J., & Rosenfeld, A. (1984). PMS: Puzzling monthly symptoms. *Psychology Today,* 30–35.

Horgan, J. (1995). The new social darwinists. *Scientific American, 273,* 174–181.

Horne, J.A. (1988). Sleep loss and "divergent" thinking ability. *Sleep, 11,* 528–536.

Hornick, J.P., Devlin, M.C., Downey, M.K., & Baynham, T. (1985–1986). Successful and unsuccessful contraceptors: A multivariate typology. Special Issue: Social work practice in sexual problems. *Journal of Social Work and Human Sexuality 4(1-2),* 17–31.

Hornstein, G. A. (1992). The return of the repressed: Psychology's problematic relations with psychoanalysis, 1909–1960. *American Psychologist, 47,* 254–263.

Houfman, L. G., House, M., & Ryan, J. B. (1981). Dynamic visual acuity: A review. *Journal of the American Optometric Association, 52,* 883–887.

Houpt, T.A., Boulos, Z., & Moore-Ede, M.C. (1996). MidnightSun: Software for determining light exposure and phase-shifting schedules during global travel. *Physiology and Behavior, 59,* 561–568.

Houston, S., Archibald, C.P., Strike, C., & Sutherland, D. (1998). Factors associated with HIV testing among Canadians: Results of a population-based survey. *International Journal of STD and AIDS, 9,* 341–346.

Howard, K. I., Kopta, S. M., Krause, M. S., & Orlinsky, D. E. (1986). The dose-effect relationship in psychotherapy. *American Psychologist, 41,* 159–164.

Howe, B. & Poole, R. (1992). Goal proximity and achievement motivation of high school boys in a basketball shooting task. *Journal of Teaching in Physical Education, 11(3)*, 248–255.

Howe, M. L., & Courage, M. L. (1993). On resolving the enigma of infantile amnesia. *Psychological Bulletin. 113*, 305–326.

Howe, M.J.A., Davidson, J.W., Moore, D.G., & Sloboda, J.A. (1995). Are there early childhood signs of musical ability? *Psychology of Music, 23*, 162–176.

Howe, M.J.A., Davidson, J.W., & Sloboda, J.A. (1998). Innate talents: Reality or myth? *Behavioral and Brain Sciences, 21*, 399–442.

Howe, M.L., Courage, M.L., & Peterson, C. (1996). How can I remember when "I" wasn't there: Long-term retention of traumatic experiences and emergence of the cognitive self. In K. Pezdek, & W.P. Banks (Eds.), *The recovered memory/false memory debate* (pp. 121–149). San Diego, CA: Academic Press.

Howell, J.M., & Avolio, B.J. (1993). Transformational leadership, transactional leadership, locus of control, and support for innovation: Key predictors of consolidated-business-unit performance. Journal of Applied Psychology, 78 (6), 891–902.

Howell, J.M., & Avolio, B.J. (1998). The ethics of charismatic leadership: Submission or liberation? In G.R. Hickman (Ed.), *Leading organizations: Perspectives for a new era* (pp. 166–176). Thousand Oaks, CA: Sage.

Howell, J.M., & Frost, P.J. (1989). A laboratory study of charismatic leadership. *Organizational Behavior and Human Decision Processes, 43(2)*, 243–269.

Hubel, D. H., & Wiesel, T. N. (1979). Brain mechanisms of vision. *Scientific American, 241*, 150–162.

Huddleston, R.J. & Hawkins, L. (1993). The reaction of friends and family to divorce. *Journal of Divorce and Remarriage, 19(1-2)*, 195–207.

Hudiberg, R.A., & Necessary, J.R. (1996). Coping with computer stress. *Journal of Educational Computing Research, 15*, 113–124.

Hudiburg, R.A. (1995). Psychology of computer use: XXXIV. The Computer Hassles Scale: Subscales, norms, and reliability. *Psychological Reports, 77*, 779–782.

Hudiburg, R.A., Ahrens, P.K., & Jones, T.M. (1994). Psychology of computer use: XXXI. Relating computer users' stress, daily hassles, somatic complaints, and anxiety. *Psychological Reports, 75*, 1183–1186.

Hudiburg, R.A., Brown, S.R., & Jones, T.M. (1993). Psychology of computer use: XXIX. Measuring computer users' stress: The Computer Hassles Scale. *Psychological Reports, 73*, 923–929.

Hughes, J.R., Smith, T.W., Kosterlitz, H.W., Fothergill, L.A., Morgan, B.A., & Morris, H.R. (1975). Identification of two related pentapeptides from the brain with potent opiate agonist activity. *Nature, 258*, 577–581.

Hultsch, D.F., Hammer, M. & Small, B.J. (1993). Age differences in cognitive performance in later life: Relationships to self-reported health and activity life style. *Journals of Gerontology, 48(1)*, 1–11.

Hultsch, D.F., Hertzog, C. & Dixon, R.A. (1987). Age differences in metamemory: resolving the inconsistencies. Special issue: Aging and cognition. *Canadian Journal of Psychology, 41(2)*, 193–208.

Hume, K.M., & Crossman, J. (1992). Musical reinforcement of practice behaviors among competitive swimmers. *Journal of Applied Behavior Analysis, 25*, 665–670.

Hummell, J.E. (1994). Reference frames and relations in computational models of object recognition. *Current Directions in Psychological Science, 3*, 111–116.

Humphrey, F.J., Mayes, S.D., Bixler, E.O., & Good, C. (1989). Variables associated with frequency of rumination in a boy with profound mental retardation. *Journal of Autism and Developmental Disorders, 19*, 435–447.

Humphrey, G.K., & Humphrey, D.E. (1989). The role of structure in infant visual pattern perception. *Canadian Journal of Psychology, 43*, 165–182.

Hundleby, J.D., & Mercer, G.W. (1987). Family and friends as social environments and their relationship to young adolescents' use of alcohol, tobacco, and marijuana. *Journal of Marriage and the Family, 49(1)*, 151–164.

Hunsberger, B. (1995). Religion and prejudice: The role of religious fundamentalism, and right-wing authoritarianism. *Journal of Social Issues, 51*, 113–129.

Hunt, H.T. (1995). *On the nature of consciousness: Cognitive, phenomenological, and transpersonal perspectives*. New Haven, CT: Yale University Press.

Huntingford, F. A. (1976). The relationship between anti-predator behavior and aggression among conspecifics in the three-spined stickleback (Gasterosteus aculeatus). *Animal behavior, 24*, 245–260.

Hur, Y.M., Bouchard, T.J., Jr., & Lykken, D.T. (1998). Genetic and environmental influence on morningness-eveningness. *Personality and Individual Differences, 25*, 917–925.

Hura, S.L., & Echols, C.H. (1996). The role of stress and articulatory difficulty in children's early productions. *Developmental Psychology, 32*, 165–176.

Hurvich, L. M. (1981). *Color vision*. Sunderland, MA: Sinauer.

Husband, A.J., Lin, W., Madsen, G., & King, M.G. (1993). A conditioning model for immunostimulation: Enhancement of the antibody response to ovalbumin by behavioral conditioning in rats. In A.J. Husband (Ed.), *Psychoimmunology: CNS-Immune Interactions* (pp. 139–147). Boca Raton, FL: CRC Press.

Hyde, J.S., & Plant, E.A. (1995). Magnitude of psychological gender differences: Another side to the story. *American Psychologist, 3*, 159–161.

Hyde, J.S., Fennema, E., & Lamon, S.J. (1990). Gender differences in mathematics performance: A meta-analysis. *Psychological Bulletin, 107*, 130–155.

Hyman, R. (1994). Anomaly or artifact? Comments on Bem and Honorton. *Psychological Bulletin, 115*, 19–24.

Hymbaugh, K., & Garrett, J. (1974). Sensation seeking among skydivers. *Perceptual and Motor Skills, 38*, 118.

Hynie, M., & Lydon, J.E. (1995). Women's perceptions of female contraceptive behavior: Experimental evidence of the sexual double standard. *Psychology of Women Quarterly, 19 (4)*, 563–581.

Hynie, M., Lydon, J.E., Cote, S., & Wiener, S. (1998). Relational sexual scripts and women's condom use: The importance of internalized norms. *Journal of Sex Research, 35*, 370–380.

Hynie, M., Lydon, J.E., & Taradash, A. (1997). Commitment, intimacy, and women's perceptions of premarital sex and contraceptive readiness. *Psychology of Women Quarterly, 21*, 447–464.

Iacono, W.G., & Lykken, D.T. (1997). The validity of the lie detector: Two surveys of scientific opinion. *Journal of Applied Psychology, 82*, 426–433.

Idle, T., Wood, E., & Desmarais, S. (1993). Gender role socialization in toy play situations: Mothers and fathers with their sons and daughters. *Sex Roles, 28(11-12)*, 679–691.

Inglehart, R. (1990). *Culture shift in advanced industrial society*. Princeton, NJ: Princeton University Press.

Intons, P.M.J., Rocchi, P., West, T., McLellan, K., & Hackney, A. (1998). Aging, optimal testing times, and negative priming. *Journal of Experimental Psychology: Learning, Memory, and Cognition, 24*, 362–376.

Intons-Peterson, M. J., & Roskos-Ewoldsen, B. (1988). *Sensory/perceptual qualities of images*. Paper presented at the 29th annual meeting of the Psychonomics Society, Chicago.

Isabella, R.A., & Belsky, J., (1991). Interactional sychrony and the origins of infant-mother attachment: A replication study. *Child Development, 62(2)*, 373–384.

Isen, A. M., & Baron, R. A. (1991). Positive affect and organizational behavior. In B. M. Staw & L. L. Cummings (Eds.), *Research in organizational behavior* (Vol. 14, pp. 1–48). Greenwich, CT: JAI Press.

Isen, A.M. (1987). Positive affect, cognitive processes, and social behavior. In L. Berkowitz (Ed.), *Advances in experimental social psychology* (Vol. 20, pp. 203–253). New York: Academic Press.

Isen, A.M., Daubman, K.A., & Nowicki, G.P. (1987). Positive affect facilitates creative problem solving: When we are glad, we feel as if the light has increased. *Journal of Personality and Social Psychology, 52*, 1122–1131.

Isen, A.M., & Shalker, T.E. (1982). Do you "accentuate the positive, eliminate the negative" when you are in a good mood? *Social Psychology Quarterly, 41*, 345–349.

Ivkovich, D., Collins, K.L., Eckerman, C.O., Krasnegor, N.A., & Stanton, M.E. (1999). Classical delay eyeblink conditioning in 4- and 5-month-old human infants. *Psychological Science, 10*, 4–7.

Iwahashi, M. (1992). Scents and science. *Vogue*, 212–214.

Iwata, B.A., Dorsey, M.F., Slifer, K.J., Bauman, K.E., & Richman, G.S. (1982). Toward a functional analysis of self-injury. *Analysis and Intervention in Developmental Disabilities, 2*, 3–20.

Izard, C.E. (1992). *Human emotions* (2nd ed.). New York: Plenum.

Izard, C.E. (1992). *The psychology of emotion*. New York: Plenum.

Jaccard, J. (1992, November). Women and AIDS. Paper presented at the meetings of the Society for the Scientific Study of Sex, San Diego.

Jack S. J. & Ronan, K. R. (1998). Sensation seeking among high-and low-risk sports participants. *Personality and Individual Differences 25*, 1063–1068.

Jackson, A., & Haverkamp, B.E. (1991). Family response to traumatic brain injury. Special Issue: Disability and the family: Research, theory and practice. *Counselling Psychology Quarterly, 4*, 355–366.

Jackson, J. K. (1993). Human behavioral genetics, Scarr's theory, and her views on interventions: A critical review and commentary on their implications for African American children. *Child Development, 64*, 1318–1332.

Jackson, S.E., Schwab, R.L., Schuler, R.S. (1986). Toward an understanding of the burnout phenomenon. *Journal of Applied Psychology, 71*, 630–640.

Jacoby, L.L., Levy, B.A., & Steinbach, K. (1992). Episodic transfer: Automaticity: Integration of data-driven and conceptually-driven processing in rereading. *Journal of Experimental Psychology: Learning, Memory and Cognition, 18*, 15–24.

Jahnke, J. C., & Nowaczyk, R. H. (1998). *Cognition*. Upper Saddle River, NJ: Prentice Hall.

Jamal, M., & Baba, V.V. (1992). Shiftwork and department-type related to job stress, work attitudes and behavioral intentions: A study of nurses. *Journal of Organizational Behavior, 13(5)*, 449–464.

Jameson, D., & Hurvich, L. M. (1989). Essay concerning color constancy. *Annual Review of Psychology, 40*, 1–22.

Jamieson, D. W., Lydon, J. E., & Zanna, M. P. (1987). Attitude and activity preference similarity: Differential bases of interpersonal attraction for low and high self-monitors. *Journal of Personality and Social Psychology, 53*, 1052–1060.

Jan, J.E., & Espezed, H. (1995). Melatonin treatment of chronic sleep disorders. *Developmental Medicine and Child Neurology, 37(3)*, 279–280.

Jang, K.L., Lam, R.W., Harris, J.A., Vernon, P.A., & Livesley, W.J. (1998). Seasonal mood change and personality: An investigation of genetic comorbidity. *Psychiatry Research, 78*, 1–7.

Janzen, L.A., Nanson, J.L., & Block, G.W. (1995). Neuropsychological evaluation of preschoolers with fetal alcohol syndrome. *Neurotoxicology and Teratology, 17(3)*, 273–279.

Jarman, R.F., & Das, J.P. (1996). *Developmental Disabilities Bulletin, 24*, 3–17.

Jarvinen, D.W., & Nicholls, J.G. (1996). Adolescents' social goals, beliefs about the causes of social success, and satisfaction in peer relations. *Developmental Psychology, 32*, 434–441.

Jaschinski, W., Heuer, H., & Kylian, H. (1999). Procedure to determine the individually comfortable position of visual displays relative to the eyes. *Ergonomics, 42,* 535–549.

Jason, G.W., & Pajurkova, E.M. (1992). Failure of metacontrol: Breakdown in behavioural unity after lesion of the corpus callosum and inferomedial frontal lobes. *Cortex, 28(2),* 241–260.

Jefferson, D. J. (1993, August 12). Dr. Brown treats what ails the rides at amusement parks. *The Wall Street Journal,* p. 1.

Jemmott, J.B., III, Magloire, K. (1988). Academic stress, social support, and secretory immunoglobulin A. *Journal of Personality and Social Psychology, 55,* 803–810.

Jencks, D. (1972). *Inequality: A reassessment of the effect of family and school in America.* New York: Basic Books.

Jenike, M.A., Baer, L., Ballantine, H.T., Martuza, R.L., Tynes, S., Giriunas, I., Buttolph, M.L., & Cassem, N.H. (1991). Cingulotomy for refractory obsessive compulsive disorder: a long-term follow-up of 33 cases. *Archives of General Psychiatry, 48,* 548–557.

Jenkins, C.D., Zyzanski, S.J., & Rosenman, R.H. (1979). *Jenkins Activity Survey.* Cleveland, OH: Psychological Corp.

Jenkins, J. G., & Dallenbach, K. M. (1924). Obliviscence during sleep and waking. *American Journal of Psychology, 35,* 605–612.

Jenkins, J.M. & Smith, M.A. (1993). A prospective study of behavioral disturbance in children who subsequently experience parental divorce: A research note. *Journal of Divorce and Remarriage, 19(1-2),* 143–160.

Jennings, J. M., & Jacoby, L.L. (1993). Automatic versus intentional uses of memory: Aging, attention, and control. *Psychology and Aging, 8,* 283–293.

Jiujias, A., & Horvath, P. (1991). The evaluation of self-monitoring attributes. *Social Behavior and Personality, 19,* 204–215.

Joffe, R.T., Moul, D.E., Lam, R.W., & Levitt, A.J. (1993). Light visor treatment for seasonal affective disorder: A multicenter study. *Psychiatry Research, 46,* 29–39.

Joffe, R.T., Offord, D.R., & Boyle, M.H. (1988). Ontario child health study: Suicidal behavior in youth age 12–16 years. *American Journal of Psychiatry, 145,* 1420–1423

Johnson, B.T., Eagly, A.H. (1989). Effects of involvement on persuasion: A meta-analysis. *Psychological Bulletin, 106,* 290–314.

Johnson, D.F., & Pittenger, J.B. (1984). Attribution, the attractiveness stereotypes, and the elderly. *Developmental Psychology, 20,* 1168–1172.

Johnson, E. J. (1985). Expertise and decision under uncertainty: Performance and process. In M. Chi, R. Glasse, & M. Farr (Eds.), *The nature of expertise.* Columbus, OH: National Center for Research in Vocational Education.

Johnson-Laird, P.N., Byrne, R.M.J., & Shaeken, W. (1992). Propositional reasoning by model. *Psychological Review, 99,* 418–439.

Johnson-Laird, P. N., Byrne, R. M. J., & Tabossi, P. (1989). Reasoning by model: The case of multiple quantification. *Psychological Review, 96,* 658–673.

Johnston, C. (1996). Parent characteristics and parent-child interactions in families of nonproblem children and ADHD children with higher and lower levels of oppositional-defiant behavior. *Journal of Abnormal Child Psychology, 24,* 85–104.

Johnston, C.C., Stevens, B., Craig, K.D., & Grunau, R.V., (1993). Developmental changes in pain expression in premature, full-term, two-and four-month-old infants. *Pain, 52(2),* 201–208.

Johnston, J.C., McCann, R.S., & Remington, R.W. (1995). Chronometric evidence for two types of attention. *Psychological Science, 6,* 365–369.

Johnston, M.W., & Bell, A.P., (1995). Romantic emotional attachment: Additional factors in the development of the sexual orientation of men. *Journal of Counseling and Development, 73(6),* 621–625.

Johnston, W., & Dark, V. (1986). Selective attention. *Annual Review of Psychology, 37,* 43–75.

Joiner, T.E., Jr. (1994). The interplay of similarity and self-verification in relationship formation. *Social Behavior and Personality, 22,* 195–200.

Jones, I.L., & Hunter, F.M. (1993). Mutual sexual selection in a monogamous seabird. *Nature, 362(6417),* 238–239.

Jones, J.C., & Barlow, D.H. (1990). Self-reported frequency of sexual urges, fantasies, and masturbatory fantasies in heterosexual males and females. *Archives of Sexual Behavior, 19,* 269–279.

Jonides, J. (1995). Working memory and thinking. In E.E. Smith & F.N. Osherson (Eds.), *An invitation to cognitive science: Thinking* (Vol. 3, pp. 215–265). Cambridge, MA: MIT Press.

Joseph, J.A. (1992). The putative role of free radicals in the loss of neuronal functioning in senescence. *Intergrative Physiological and Behavioral Science, 27(3),* 216–227.

Journal of Addiction and Mental Health. (1998). Q&A: facts on homelessness [Homelessness crisis], 1, p. 14

Judd, C.M., Drake, R.A., Downing, J.W., & Krosnick, J.A. (1991). Some dynamic properties of attitude structures: Context-induced response facilitation and polarization. *Journal of Personality and Social Psychology, 60,* 193–202.

Judge, T.A., Martocchio, J.J., & Thoresn, C.J. (1998). Five-factor model of personality and employee absence. *Journal of Applied Psychology, 82,* 745–755.

Julien, R.M. (1995). *A primer of drug action* (7th ed.). New York: Freeman.

Jusczyk, P.W. (1993). From general to language-specific capacities: The WRAPSA model of how speech perception develops. Special Issue: Phonetic development. *Journal of Phonetics, 21(1–2),* 3–28.

Jussim, L. (1991). Interpersonal expectations and social reality: A reflection-construction model and reinterpretation of evidence. *Psychological Review, 98,* 54–73.

Just, M.A., & Carpenter, P. A. (1987). *The psychology of reading and language comprehension.* Newton, MA: Allyn & Bacon.

Kaempf, G.L., Klein, G.A., Thordsen, M.L., & Wolf, S. (1996). Decision making in complex naval command-and-control environments. *Human Factors, 38,* 220–231.

Kafer, R., Hodkin, B., Furrow, D., Landry, T. (1993). What do the Montreal murders mean? Attitudinal and demographic predictors of attribution. *Canadian Journal of Behavioral Science, 25,* 541–558.

Kagan, J., Reznick, J.S., & Snidman, N. (1988). Biological bases of childhood shyness. *Science, 240(4849),* 167–171.

Kagan, J., & Snidman, N. (1991). Temperamental factors in human development. *American Psychologist, 46,* 856–862.

Kagan, J., Snidman, N., & Arcus, D.M. (1992). Initial reactions to unfamiliarity. *Current Directions in Psychological Science, 1(6),* 171–174.

Kahneman, D., & Tversky, A. (1982). Judgment under uncertainty: Heuristics and biases. In D. Kahneman, P. Slovic, & A. Tversky (Eds.), *Judgment under uncertainty: Heuristics and biases* (pp. 3–22). Cambridge, England: Cambridge University Press.

Kahneman, D., Diener, E., & Schwarz, N. (1999). *Well-being: The foundations of hedonic psychology.* New York: Russell Sage Foundation.

Kahneman, D., & Miller, D.T. (1986). Norm theory: Comparing reality to its alternatives. *Psychological Review, 93(2),* 136–153.

Kako, E. (1999). Response to Pepperberg, Herman, Uyeyama, Shanker, Savage-Rumbaugh, and Taylor. *Animal Learning and Behavior, 27,* 26–27.

Kalin R., & Berry, J. W. (1996). Interethnic attitudes in Canada: Ethnocentrism, consensual hierarchy and reciprocity. *Canadian Journal of Behavioural Science, 28,* 253–261.

Kalivas, P.W., & Samson, H.H. (Eds.). (1992). The neurobiology of drug and allcohol addiction. *Annals of the New York Academy of Sciences,* Vol. 654. New York: Academy of Sciences.

Kallus, K.W., & Kellman, M. (2000). Burnout in athletes and coaches. In Y.L. Hanin (Ed.), *Emotions in sport* (pp. 209–230). Champaign, IL: Human Kinetics.

Kalsher, M.J., Clarke, S.W., & Wogalter, M.S. (1993). communication of alcohol facts and hazards by a warning poster. *Journal of Public Policy and Mrketing, 12,* 78-90.

Kamienska-Zyla, M., Prync-Skotniczny, K. (1996). Subjective fatigue symptons among computer systems operators in Poland. *Applied Ergonomics, 27(3),* 217–220.

Kamin, L.J. (1965). Temporal and intensity characteristics of the conditioned stimulus. In W.F. Prokasy (Ed.), *Classical conditioning: Symposium.* New York: Appleton-Century-Crofts.

Kaneda, M., Izuka, H., Ueno, H., Hiramatsu, M., Taguchi, J., & Tsukino, J. (1994, May). Development of a drowsiness warning system. Paper presented at the 14th International Technical Conference on the Enhanced Safety of Vehicles. Numich, Germany.

Kanner, A.D., Coyne, J.C., Schaefer, C., & Lazarus, R.S. (1981). Comparison of two modes of stress measurement: Daily hassles and uplifts versus major life events. *Journal of Behavioral Medicine, 4,* 1–39.

Kantrowitz, J.L., Katz, A.L., Greenman, D.A., Morris, H., et al. (1989). The patient-analyst match and the outcome of psychoanalysis: A pilot study. *Journal of the American Psychoanalytic Association, 37,* 893–919.

Kaplan, H. I., & Sadock, B. J. (1991). *Synopsis of psychiatry: Behavioral sciences, clinical psychiatry* (6th ed.). Baltimore: Williams & Wilkins.

Kaplan, R. E. (1982). The dynamics of injury in encounter groups: Power, splitting, and the mismanagement of resistance. *International Journal of Group Psychotherapy, 32,* 163–187.

Karasek, R., & Theorell, T. (1990). *Healthy work: Job stress, productivity, and the reconstruction of working life.* New York: Basic Books.

Katz, J. (1992). Psychophysiological contributions to phantom limbs. *Canadian Journal of Psychiatry, 37(5),* 282–298.

Katz, R.C., Meyers, K., & Walls, J. (1995). Cancer awareness and self-examination practices in young men and women. *Journal of Behavioral Medicine, 18(4),* 377–384.

Kaufman, A.S. (1983). Some questions and answers about the Kaufman Assessment Battery for Children (K-ABC). *Journal of Psychoeducational Assessment, 1,* 205–218.

Kaufman, A., Baron, A., Kopp, R.E. (1966). Some effects of instructions on human operant behavior. *Psychonomic Monographs Supplement, 1,* 243–250.

Kavanagh, R.D., Zimmerberg, B., Fein, S. (Eds.). (1996). *Emotion: Interdisciplinary perspectives.* Mawhah, NJ: Erlbaum.

Kawakami, K., Dion, K.L., & Dovidio, J.F. (1998). Racial prejudice and stereotype activation. *Personality and Social Psychology Bulletin, 24,* 407–416.

Kazdin, A.E. (1982). The token economy: A decade later. *Journal of Applied Behavior Analysis, 15,* 431–446.

Kazdin, A.E. (1993). Psychotherapy for children and adolescents: Current progress and future research directions. *American Psychologist, 48,* 644–657.

Kebbell, M. R. & Milne, R. (1998). Police officers' perceptions of eyewitness performance in forensic investigations. *Journal of Social Psychology, 138,* 323–330.

Keesling, B. & Friedman, H.S. (1987). Psychosocial factors in sunbathing and sunscreen use. *Health Psychology, 6(5),* 477–493.

Keinan, G. (1994). Effects of stress and tolerance of ambiguity on magical thinking. *Journal of Personality and Social Psychology, 67,* 48–55.

Kellar-Guenther, Y. (1999). The power of romance: Changing the focus of AIDS education messages. In W.N. Elwood (Ed.), *Power in the blood: A handbook on AIDS, politics, and communication* (pp. 215–229). Mahwah, NJ: Lawrence Erlbaum.

Kelley, K., & Byrne, D. (1992). *Exploring human sexuality.* Englewood Cliffs, NJ: Prentice Hall.

Kelley, K., & Byrne, D. (1992). *Human sexual behavior.* Englewood Cliffs, NJ: Prentice Hall.

Kelloway, E.K., Barling, J. & Shah, A. (1993). Industrial relations, stress and job satisfaction: concurrent effects and mediation. Special Issue: integrating domains of work stress and industrial relations: evidence from five countries. *Journal of Organizational Behavior, 14(5),* 447-457.

Kelly, J. A., & Kalichman, S. C. (1998). Reinforcement value of unsafe sex as a predictor of condom use and continued HIV/AIDS risk behavior among gay and bisexual men. *Health Psychology, 17,* 328–335.

Kelly, L., & Bielajew, C. (1991) Ventromedial hypothalamic regulation of brown adipose tissue. *Neuroreport An International Journal for the Rapid Communication of Research in Neuroscience, 2,* 41–44.

Kelly, W.L. (1972). Reliability assessments of the Group Kahn Test of Symbolic Arrangement. *International Journal of Symbology, 3(3),* 22–34.

Kelman, H.C., & Hamilton, V.L. (1989). *Crimes of obedience: Toward a social psychology of authority and responsibility.* Yale University Press: New Haven.

Kelner, M.J. & Bourgeault, I.L. (1993). Patient control over dying: Responses of health care professionals. *Social Science and Medicine, 36(6),* 757–765.

Kelsey, F.O. (1969). Drugs and pregnancy. *Mental Retardation, 7,* 7–10.

Kendall-Tackett, K.A. (1991). Characteristics of abuse that influence when adults molested as children seek treatment. *Journal of Interpersonal Violence, 6,* 486–493.

Kendall-Tackett, K.A., Williams, L.M., & Finkelhor, D. (1993). Impact of sexual abuse on children: A review and synthesis of recent empirical studies. *Psychological Bulletin, 113,* 164–180.

Kendler, K.S., Neale, M.C., Sullivan, P., Coreym L.A., Gardner, C.O., & Prescott, C.A. (1999). A population-based twin study in women of smoking initiation and nicotine dependence. *Psychological Medicine, 29,* 299–308.

Kendzierski, D., & Whitaker, D.J. (1997). The role of self-schema in linking intentions with behavior. *Personality and Social Psychology Bulletin, 23,* 139–147.

Kennedy, S.H. & Garfinkel, P.E. (1992). Advances in diagnosis and treatment of anorexia nervosa and bulimia nervosa. *Canadian Journal of Psychiatry, 37(5),* 309–315.

Kennett, D.J., & Miller, A. (1995). The successful job applicant: Understanding the pathway to employment. In M.V. Norman (Ed.), *Proceedings of the 21st national consultation on career development* (pp. 265–276). Toronto: University of Toronto Career Centre.

Kenny, E. (2000, May 1). Blind climber taking on Canada's highest peak. *Winnipeg Free Press.*

Kenrick, D.T., Groth, G.E., Trost, M.R., & Sadalla, E.K. (1993). Integrating evolutionary and social exchange perspectives on relationships: effects of gender, self-appraisal, and involvement level on mate selection criteria. *Journal of Personality and Social Psychology, 64,* 951–969.

Kerr, D., & Ram, B. (1994). *Focus on Canada: Population Dynamics in Canada.* Toronto: Prentice Hall.

Kerr, J.H. & Cox, T. (1991). Arousal and individual differences in sport. *Personality and Individual Differences, 12(10),* 1075–1085.

Kessler, C. R. (1994). Incidence of mental disorders in a non-institutionalized population. *Archives of General Psychiatry, 50.*

Kessler, R. C., McGonagle, K. A., Zhao, S., Nelson, C. B., Hughes, M., Eshleman, S., Witchen, H. U., & Kendler, K. S. (1994). Lifetime and 12-month prevalence of DSM-III-R psychiatric disorders in the United States. *Archives of General Psychiatry, 5,* 8–19.

Kiecolt-Glaser, J.K. & Glaser, R. (1992). Psychoneuroimmunology: Can psychological interventions modulate? Special issue: Behavioral medicine: An update for the 1990s. *Journal of Consulting and Clinical Psychology, 60(4),* 569–575.

Kiecolt-Glaser, J.K., Fisher, L., Ogrocki, P., Stout, J.C., Speicher, C.E., & Glaser, R. (1987). Marital quality, marital disruption, and immune function. *Psychosomatic Medicine, 49,* 13–34.

Kiecolt-Glaser, J.K., Kennedy, S., Malkoff, S., Fisher, L., Speicher, C.E., Glaser, R. (1988). Marital discord and immunity in males. *Psychosomatic Medicine, 50,* 213–229.

Kienker, P. K, Sejinowski, T. J. Hinton, G. E., & Scumacher, L. E. (1986). Separating figure from ground with a parallel network. *Perception, 15,* 197–216.

Kihlstrom, J. F., Tataryn, D. J., & Hoyt, I. P. (1993). Dissociative disorders. In P. B. Sutker & H. E. Adams. (Eds.), *Comprehensive handbook of psychopathology* (2nd ed.). New York: Plenum Press.

Kilduff, M., & Day, D.V. (1994). Do chameleons get ahead? The effects of self-monitoring on managerial careers. *Academy of Mangement Journal, 37,* 1047–1060.

Kilham, W., & Mann, L. (1974). Level of destructive obedience as a function of transmitter and executant roles in the Milgram obedience paradigm. *Journal of Personality and Social Psychology, 29* (5), 696-702.

Kim, C.K., Pinel, J.P., & Roese, N.R. (1992). *Pharmacology, Biochemistry, and Behavior, 4,* 127–132.

Kimball, M. M. (1986). Developing a feminist psychology of women: Past and future accomplishments. *Canadian Psychology, 27,* 248–259.

Kimura, D. (1987). Are men's and women's brains really different? Annual meeting of the Canadian Psychological Association (1986, Toronto). *Canadian Psychology, 28(2),* 133–147.

Kimura, D., Hampson, E. (1993). Neural and hormonal mechanisms mediating sex differences in cognition. In P.A. Vernon (Ed.), *Biological approaches to the study of human intelligence.* Norwood, NJ: Ablex.

Kimura, D., Hampson, E. (1994). Cognitive pattern in men and women is influenced by fluctuations in sex hormones. *Current Directions in Psychological Science, 3(2),* 57–61.

Kinsey, A.C., Pomeroy, W., & Martin, C. (1984). *Sexual behavior in the human male.* Philadelpia: W.B. Saunders.

Kinsey, A.C., Pomeroy, W., Martin, C., & Gebhard, P. (1953). *Sexual behavior in the human female.* Philadelphia: W.B. Saunders.

Kirby, J. R. & Das, J. P. (1990). A cognitive approach to intelligence: Attention, coding and planning. *Canadian Psychology, 31,* 320–333.

Kirby, J.R. (1995). Intelligence and social policy. *Alberta Journal of Educational Research, 41,* 322–334.

Kirby, K.N., & Herrnstein, R.J. (1995). Preference reversals due to myopic discounting of delayed reward. *Psychological Science, 6,* 83–89.

Kirchmeyer, C. (1990). A profile of managers active in office politics. *Basic and Applied Social Psychology, 11,* 339–356.

Kirkpatrick, S.A., & Locke, E.A. (1991). Leadership: Do traits matter? *Academy of Management Executive, 5,* 48–60.

Kirkpatrick, S.A., & Locke, E.A. (1996). Direct and indirect effects of three core charismatic leadership components on performance and attitudes. *Journal of Applied Psychology, 81,* 36–51.

Kirsch, I., & Lynn, S.J. (1998). Dissociation theories of hypnosis. *Psychological Bulletin, 123,* 100–115.

Kisilevsky, B.S., Muir, D.W., & Low, J.A., (1992). Maturation of human fetal responses to vibroacoustic stimulation. *Child Development, 63(6),* 1497–1508.

Kitchener, K.S. (1986). Teaching applied ethics in counselor education: An integration of psychological processes and philosophical analysis. *Journal of Counselling and Development, 64,* 306–310.

Klatzky, R.L., Lederman, S.J. (1995). Indentifying objects from a haptic glance. *Perception and Psychophysics, 37,* 1111–1123.

Klausner, J., Sweeney, J., Deck, M., Hass, G., & Kelly, A.B. (1992). Clinical correlates of cerebral ventricular enlargement on schizophrenia. Further evidence for frontal lobe disease. *Journal of Nervous and Mental Disease, 180,* 407–412.

Klayman, J., & Ha, Y. W. (1987). Confirmation, disconfirmation, and information in hypothesis testing. *Psychological Review, 94,* 211–228.

Klein, R., & Armitage, R. (1979). Rhythms in human performance: 1 1/2-hour oscillations in cognitive style. *Science, 204(4399),* 1326–1328.

Klein, S.B., & Loftus, J. (1988). The nature of self-reference encoding: The contributions of elaborative and organizational processes. *Journal of Personality and Social Psychology, 55,* 5–11.

Kleinke, C.L. (1986). Gaze and eye contact: A research review. *Psychological Bulletin, 100,* 78–100.

Kleinman, A. (1986). *Social origins of distress and disease.* New Haven, CT: Yale University Press.

Kline, D.W., Kline, T.J., Fozard, J.L., Kosnik, W., Shieber, F., & Sekuler, R. (1992). Vision, aging, and driving: The problems of older drivers. *Journals of Gerontology, 47(1),* 27–34.

Klinger, E. (1990). *Daydreaming: Using waking fantasy and imagery for self-knowledge and creativity.* Los Angeles: Tarcher.

Knowlton, B.J., Mangel, J.A., & Squire, L. (1996). A neostriatal habit learning system in humans. *Science, 273,* 1399–1402.

Kobasa, S.C. (1979). Stressful life events, Personality, and health: An inquiry into hardiness. *Journal of Personality and Social Psychology, 37,* 1–11.

Koestner, R., Bernieri, F., & Zuckerman, M. (1992). Self-regulation and consistency between attitudes, traits, and behaviors. *Personality and Social Psychology Bulletin, 18,* 52–59.

Koestner, R., Losier, G.F., Vallerand, R.J., & Carducci, D. (1996). Identified and introjected forms of political internalization: Extending self-determination theory. *Journal of Personality and Social Psychology, 70(5),* 1025–1036.

Kohlberg, L. (1984). *Essays on moral development: Vol. 2. The Psychology of moral development.* San Francisco: Harper & Row.

Kohler, I. (1962, May). Experiments with goggles. *Scientific American,* 62–72.

Kolaric, G.C., & Galambos, N. (1995). Face-to-face interactions in unacquainted female-male adolescent dyads: How do girls and boys behave? *Journal of Early Adolescence, 15,* 363–382.

Kolata, G. (1985). Obesity declared a disease. *Science, 227,* 1019–1020.

Kolata, G. B. (1986). Manic depression: Is it inherited? *Science 232,* 448–450.

Kolb, B. (1990). Recovery from occipital stroke: a self-report and an inquiry into visual processes. *Canadian Journal of Psychology, 44(2),* 130–147.

Kolb, B. (1999). Synaptic plasticity and the organization of behavior after early and late brain injury. *Canadian Journal of Experimental Psychology, 53,* 62–75.

Kolb., B., & Gibb, R. (1991). Environmental enrichment and cortical injury: Behavioral and anatomical consequences of frontal cortex lesions. *Cerebral Cortex, 1,* 189–198.

Kolb, B., & Gibb, R. (1993). Possible anatomical basis of recovery of function after neonatal frontal lesions in rats. *Behavioral Neuroscience, 107,* 799–811.

Kolb, B., Gibb, R., Gorny, G., & Whishaw, I.Q. (1998). Possible regeneration of rat medial frontal cortex following neonatal frontal lesions. *Behavioural Brain Research, 91,* 127–141.

Kolb, B., & Stewart, J. (1995). Changes in the neonatal gonadal homonal environment prevent behavioral sparing and alter cortical morphogenesis after early frontal cortes lesions in male and female rats. *Behavioral Neuroscience, 109(2),* 285–294.

Kolb, B, & Whishaw, I.Q. (1991). Mechanisms underlying behavioral sparing after neonatal retrplenial cingulate lesions in rats: Spatial navigation, cortical architecture, and electroencephalographic activity. *Brain Dysfunction, 4,* 75–92.

Kolb, B., Wilson, B., & Taylor, L. (1992). Developmental changes in the recognition and comprehension of facial expression: implications for frontal lobe function. Special issue: the role of frontal lobe maturation in cognitive and social development. *Brain and Cognition, 20(1),* 74–84.

Koloric, G.C., & Galambos, N.L. (1995). Face-to-face interactions in unacquainted female-male adolescent dyads: How do girls and boys behave? *Journal of Early Adolescence, 15,* 363–382.

Komaki, J.L. (1986). Toward effective supervision: An operant analysis and comparison of manager at work. *Journal of Applied Psychology, 36,* 271–279.

Konovsky, M.A., & Brockner, J. (1993). Managing victim and survivor layoff reactions: A procedural justice perspective. In R. Cropanzano (Ed.), *Justice in the workplace* (pp. 133–155). Hillsdale, NJ: Erlbaum.

Koss, M.P., & Harvey, M.R. (1991). *The rape victim: clinical and community interventions* (2nd ed.). Newbury Park, CA: Sage.

Kosslyn, S.M. (1980). *Image and mind.* Cambridge, MA: Harvard University Press.

Kosslyn, S.M. (1987). Seeing and imagining in the cerebral hemispheres: A computational approach. *Psychological Review, 14,* 148–175.

Koulack, D. (1991). *To catch a dream: Explorations of dreaming.* Albany: SUNY Press.

Kounious, J. (1996). On the continuity of thought and the representation of knowledge: electrophysiological and behavioral time-course measures reveal levels of structure in semantic memory. *Psychonomic Bulletin and Review, 3,* 265–286.

Kowhler, J.J. (1996). The base rate fallacy reconsidered: Descriptive, normative, and methodological challenges. *Behavioural and Brain Sciences, 19,* 1–53.

Krahn, H., & Lowe, G.S. (1999). School-to-work transitions and postmodern values: What's changing in Canada? In W.R. Heinz (Ed.), *From education to work: Cross-national perspectives* (pp. 260–283). New York: Cambridge University Press.

Krakoff, L.R., Dziedzic, S., Mann, S.J., Felton, K., & Yeager, K. (1985). Plasma epinephrine concentrations in healthy men: Correlation with systolic blood pressure and rate-pressure product. *Journal of American College of Cardiology, 5,* 352.

Krank, M.D., & Perkins, W.L. (1993). Conditioned withdrawal signs elicited by contextual cues for morphine administration. *Psychobiology, 21,* 113–119.

Kranzler, J., & Jensen, A.R. (1989). Inspection time and intelligence: A meta-analysis. *Intelligence, 13,* 329–247.

Krause, A.M. & Long, B.C. (1993). Predictors of coping for mothers of separated/ divorced offspring. *Canadian Journal on Aging, 12(1),* 50–66.

Krech, K.H. & Johnston, C. (1992). The relationship of depressed mood and life stress to materal perceptions of child behavior. *Journal of Clinical Child Psychology, 21(2),* 115–122.

Kritch, K.M., Bostow, D.E., & Dedrick, R.F. (1995). Level of interactivity of videodisc instruction on college students' recall of AIDS information. *Journal of Applied Behavior Analysis, 28,* 85–86.

Kroger, J. (2000). *Identity development: Adolescence through adulthood.* Thousand Oaks, CA: Sage.

Krosnick, J.A. (1993, March). Personal communication.

Krosnick, J.A., Betz, A.L., Jussim, L.J., & Lynn, A.R. (1992). Subliminal conditioning of attitudes. *Personality and Social Psychology Bulletin, 18(2),* 152–162.

Kruk, E. (1993). Promoting co-operative parenting after separation: a therapeutic/interventionist model of family mediation. *Journal of Family Therapy, 15(3),* 235–261.

Kruk, E. (1994). The disengaged noncustodial father: implications for social work practice with the divorced family. *Social Work, 39(1),* 15–25.

Kubany, E.S., Bauer, G.B., Muraoka, M.Y., Richard, D.C., & Read, P. (1995). Impact of labeled anger and blame in intimate relationships. *Journal of Social and Clinical Psychology, 14,* 53–60.

Kuczynski, L., & Kochanska, G. (1995). *Child Development, 66,* 616–628.

Kuhn, D., (1989). Children and adults as intuitive scientists. *Psychologial Review, 96(4),* 674–689.

Kuhn, L., Stein, Z.A., Thomas, P.A., Singh, T., & Tasai, W. (1994). Maternal-infant HIV transmission and circumstances of delivery. *American Journal of Public Health, 84,* 1110–11115.

Kuiper, N.A., & Martin, R.A. (1998). Laughter and stress in daily life: Relation to positive and negative affect. *Motivation and Emotion, 22,* 133–153.

Kuiper, N.A., Martin, R.A., & Olinger, L.J. (1993). Coping humour, stress and cognitive appraisals. *Canadian Journal of Behavioral Science, 25(1),* 81–96.

Kuiper, N.A., Martin, R.A., Olinger, L.J., Kazarian, S.S., & Jette, J.L. (1998). Sense of humor, self-concept, and psychological well-being in psychiatric inpatients. *Humor: International Journal of Humor Research, 11,* 357–381.

Kunda, Z., & Nisbett, R. E. (1986). The psychometrics of everyday life. *Cognitive Psychology, 18,* 195–224.

Kunda, Z., & Oleson, K.C. (1995). Maintaining stereotypes in the face of disconfirmation: Constructing ground for subtyping deviants. *Journal of Personality and Social Psychology, 68,* 565–579.

Kunda, Z., & Oleson, K.C. (1997). When exceptions prove the rule: How extremity of deviance determines the impact of deviant examples on stereotypes. *Journal of Personality and Social Psychology, 72,* 965–979.

Kunzinger, E.L., (1985). A short-term longitudinal study of memorial development during early grade school. *Developmental Psychology, 21(4),* 642–646.

Kupych, W.N., MacFalane, J.G., & Shapiro, C.M. (1993). A group approach for the management of insomnia. *Journal of Psychosomatic Research, 37,* 39–44.

Kurdek, L.A. (1993). Predicting marital dissolution: A 5-year longitudinal study of newlywed couples. *Journal of Personality and Social Psychology, 64,* 221–242.

Kurtz, L., & Derevensky, J.L. (1993). Stress and coping in adolescents: The effects of family configuration and environment on suicidality. Second International Conference for the Child of the Organization for the Protection of Children's Rights (1992, Montreal). *Canadian Journal of School Psychology, 9(2),* 204–216.

Kutcher, S., Williamson, P., Marton, P., & Szalai, J. (1992). REM latency in endogenously depressed adolescents. *British Journal of Psychiatry, 161,* 399–402.

Kutchinsky, B. (1992). The child sexual abuse panic. *Nordisk Sexologist, 10,* 30–42.

Kuykendall, D., & Keating, J.P. (1990). Mood and persuasion: Evidence for the differential influence of positive and negative states. *Psychology and Marketing, 7(1),* 1–9.

Labouvie-Vief, G.M., & Hakim-Larson, J. (1989). Developmental shifts in adult thought. In S. Hunter & M. Sundel (Eds.), *Midlife myths: Issues, findings, and practical implications* (pp. 690–696). Newbury Park, CA: Sage.

Lackie, L., & de Man, A.F. (1997). Correlates of sexual aggression among male university students. *Sex Roles, 37,* 451–457.

Ladavas, E., Umilta, C., & Ricci-Bitti, P.E. (1980). Evidence for sex differences in right-hemisphere dominance for emotions. *Neuropsychologia, 18,* 361–366.

Ladouceur, R. (1996). The prevalence of pathological gambling in Canada. *Journal of Gambling Studies, 12(2),* 129–142.

Ladouceur, R., Boisvert, J.M., & Dumont, J. (1994). Cognitive-behavioral treatment for adolescent pathological gamblers. *Behavior Modification, 18(2),* 230–242.

Ladouceur, R., Boisvert, J.M., Pepin, M., Loranger, M., et al. (1994). Social cost of pathological gambling. *Journal of Gambling Studies, 10(4),* 399–409.

Ladouceur, R., Dube, D., & Bujold, A. (1994). Gambling among primary school students. *Journal of Gambling Studies, 10(4),* 363–370.

Ladouceur, R., Dube, D., Bujold, A. (1994). Prevalence of pathological gambling and related problems abong college students in the Quebec metropolitan area. *Canadian Journal of Psychiatry, 39(5),* 289–293.

Ladouceur, R., Dube, D., Giroux, I., Legendre, N., & Gaudet, C. (1995). Cognitive Biases in Gambling: American Roulette and 6/49 Lottery. *Journal of Social Behavior and Personality, 10(2),* 473–479.

Ladouceur, R., & Walker, M. (1996). A cognitive perspective on gambling. *Trends in Cognitive and Behavioural Therapies,* 89–120.

Lagerspetz, K.M., Bjorkquixt, K., & Peitonen, T. (1988). Is indirect aggression typical of females? Gender differneces in aggressiveness in 11-12 year old children. *Aggressive Behavior, 14,* 403–414.

Lahey, B.B., Hart, E.L., Pliszka, S., Applegate, B., et al. (1993). Neurophysiological correlates of conduct disorder: A rationale and a review of research. Special Issue: The Neuropsychological basis of disorders affecting children and adolescents. *Journal of Clinical Child Psychology, 22 (2),* 141–153.

Laird, J.D. (1984). The real role of facial response in the experience of emotion: A reply to tourangeua and Ellsworth, and others. *Journal of Personality and Social Psycology, 47,* 909–917.

Lalande, S., Braun, C.M., Charlebois, N. & Whitaker, H.A. (1992). Effects of right and left hemisphere cerebrovascular lesions on the prosodic and semantic aspects of affect in sentences. *Brain and Language, 42(2),* 165–186.

Lalonde, M. (1974). *A new perspective on the health of Canadians.* Ottawa: Canadian Government Printing Office.

Lalonde, R., & Botez, M.I. (1990). The cerebellum and learning processes in animals. *Brain Research Reviews, 15(3),* 325–332.

Lalonde, R.N., Majumder, S., & Parris, R.D. (1995). Preferred responses to situations of housing and employment discrimination. *Journal of Applied Social Psychology, 25,* 1105–1119.

Lam, R.W. (Ed.). (1998). *Seasonal affective disorder and beyond: Light treatment for SAD and non-SAD conditions.* Washington, DC: American Psychiatric Press.

Lam, R.W., & Goldner, E.M. (1998). Seasonality of bulimia nervosa and treatment with light therapy. In R.W. Lam (Ed.), *Seasonal affective disorder and beyond: Light treatment for SAD and non-SAD conditions* (pp. 193–220). Washington, DC: American Psychiatric Press, Inc.

Lam, R.W., Gorman, C.P., Michalon, M., Steiner, M., et al. (1995). Multicenter, placebo-controlled study of fluoxetine in seasonal affective disorder. *American Journal of Psychiatry, 152(12),* 1765-1770.

Lam, R.W., Zis, A.P., Grewal, A., Delgado, P.L., et al. (1996). Effects of rapid tryptophan depletion in patients with seasonal affective disorder in remission after light therapy. *Archives of General Psychiatry, 53(1),* 41–44.

Lamb, M.E. (1977). Father-infant and mother-infant interaction in the first year of life. *Child Development, 48,* 167–181.

Lamb, M.R., London, B., Pond, H.M., & Whitt, K.A. (1998). Automatic and controlled processes in the analysis of hierarchical structure. *Psychological Science, 9,* 14–19.

Lambert, A.J. (1995). Stereotypes and social judgment: the consequences of group variability. *Journal of Personality and Social Psychology, 68,* 388–403.

Lambert, S.J. (1991). The combined effects of job and family characteristics on the job satisfaction, job involvement, and intrinsic motivation of men and women workers. *Journal of Organizational Behavior, 12(4),* 341–363.

Lambert, V., Lussier, Y., Sabourin, S., & Wright, J. (1995). Attachement, solitude et detresse psychologique chez des jeunes adultes. (Attachment style, loneliness, and psychological distress in young adults.) *International Journal of Psychology, 30,* 109–131.

Lambert, W.E. (1991). "And then add your two cent's worth" In A.G. Reynold (Ed.), *Bilingualism, multiculturalism, and second language learning: The McGill conference in honour of Wallace E. Lambert* (pp. 217–249). Hillsdale, NJ: Erlbaum,.

Lambert, W.E. (1992). Challenging established views on social issues: The power and limitations of research. *American Psychologist, 47,* 533–542.

Lamerson, C.D., & Kelloway, E.K. (1996). Towards a model of peacekeeping stress: Traumatic and contextual influences. *Canadian Psychology, 37,* 195–204.

Landau, S., Lorch, E.P., & Milich, R. (1992). Visual attention to and comprehension of television in attention deficit hyperactivity disordered and normal boys. *Child Development, 63(40),* 928–937.

Landry, S.H., Garner, P.W., Swank, P.R., & Baldwin, C.D. (1996). Effects of maternal scaffolding during joint toy play with preterm and full-term infants. *Merrill-Palmer Quarterly, 42,* 177–199.

Landsbergis, P.A., Schnall, P.L., Deitz, D., Friedman, R., & Pickering, T. (1992). The patterning of psychological atttributes and distress by job strain and social support in a sample of working men. *Journal of Behavioral Medicine, 15,* 379–405.

Lang, A., Gottlieb, L.N., & Amsel, R. (1996). Predictors of husbands' and wives' grief reactions following infant death: The role of marital intimacy. *Death Studies, 20,* 33–57.

Lange, J.D., Brown, W.A., Wincze, J.P., & Zwick, W. (1980). Serum testosterone concentration and penile tumescence changes in men. *Hormones and Behavior, 14,* 267–270.

Langholtz, H.J. (1998). The psychology of peacekeeping: Genesis, ethos, and application. *Peace and Conflict: Journal of Peace Psychology, 4,* 217–236.

Langlois, J.H., & Roggmann, L.A. (1990). Attractive faces are only average. *Psychological Science, 1,* 115–121.

Langlois, J.H., Roggman, L.A., & Rieser-Danner, L.A. (1990). Differential social responses to attractive and unattractive faces. *Developmental Psychology, 26,* 153–159.

Lanis, K., & Covell, K. (1995). Images of women in advertisements: Effects on attitudes related to sexual aggression. *Sex Roles, 32(9-10),* 639–649.

Lanken, D., & Vincent, M. (1999). Nunavut: On April 1, Canada's youngest population takes control of our largest territory. *Canadian Geographic, 119,* 35–46.

Larrick, R. P. (1993). Motivational factors in decision theories: The role of self-protection. *Psychological Bulletin, 113,* 440–450.

Larzelere, R. E., Sather, P. R., Schneider, W. N., Larson, D. B., & Pike, P. L. (1998). Punishment enhances reasoning's effectiveness as a disciplinary response to toddlers. *Journal of Marriage and the Family, 60,* 388–403.

Lassiter, G.D., Briggs, M.A., & Slaw, R.D. (1991). Need for cognition, causal processing, and memory for behavior. *Personality and Social Psychology Bulletin, 17,* 694–700.

Lassonde, M., Sauerwein, H.C., & Lepore, F. (1995). Extent and limits of callosal plasticity: Presence of disconnection symptoms in callosal aenesis. Symposium on Neuropsychological and Developmental Studies of the Corpus Callosum. *Neuropsychologia, 33,* 989–1007.

Latham, G.P. & Huber, V.L. (1992). Schedules of reinforcement: Lessons from the past and issues for the future. *Journal of Organizational Behavior Management, 12,* 125–149.

Lauer, J., & Lauer, R. (1985, June). Marriages made to last. *Psychology Today,* 22–26.

LaVecchia, C., Lucchini, F., Negri, E., Boyle, P., & Levi, F. (1993). Trends in cancer mortality in the Americas, 1955–1989. *European Journal of Cancer, 29,* 431–470.

LaVecchia, C., Lucchini, F., Negri, E., Boyle, P., Maisonneuve, P., & Levi, F. (1992). Trends of cancer mortality in Europe, 1955–1989: II, Respiratory tract, bone, connective and soft tissue sarcomas, and skin. *European Journal of Cancer, 23,* 514–599.

Law, D./J., Pellegrino, J. W., & Hunt, E. B. (1993). Comparing the tortoise and the hare: Gender differences and experience in dynamic spatial reasoning tasks. *Psychological Sciences, 4,* 35–40.

Lawless, H., & Engen, T. (1977). Associations to odors: Interference, mnemonics, and verbal labeling. *Journal of Experimental Psychology: Human Learning and Memory, 3,* 52–59.

Lay, C., & Nguyen, T. (1998). The role of acculturation-related and acculturation non-specific daily hassles: Vietnamese-Canadian students and psychological distress. *Canadian Journal of Behavioural Science, 30,* 172–181.

Lazarus, R. S., Opton, E. M., Nomikos, M. S., & Rankin, N. O. (1985). The principle of short-circuiting of threat: Further evidence. *Journal of Personality, 33,* 622–635.

Lazarus, R.S., & Folkman, S. (1984). *Stress, appraisal, and coping.* New York: Springer.

Lazurus, R.S., Opton, E.M., Nomikos, M.S., & Rankin, N.O. (1985). The principle of short-circuiting of threat: Further evidence. *Journal of Personality, 33,* 622–635.

Lazurus, A.A. (1989). Brief psychotherapy: The multimodal model. Special Issue: Counselling. *Psychology, A Journal of Human Behavior, 26,* 6–10.

Lecci, L., Kzroly, P., Suehlman, L.S., & Lanyon, R.I. (1996). Goal-relevant dimensions of hypochondriacal tendencies and their relation to symptom manifestation and psychological distress. *Journal of Abnormal Psychology, 105,* 42–52.

Ledingham, J., & Crombie, G. (1988). Promoting the mental health of children and youth: A critical review of recent literature. *Canada's Mental Health, 36(1),* 9û17.

Lee, G.R., Seccombe, K., & Shehan, C.L. (1991). Marital status and personal happiness: An analysis of trend data. *Journal of Marriage and the Family, 53,* 839–844.

Lee, J.A. (1998). Ideologies of lovestyle and sexstyle. In V.C. de Munck (Ed.), *Romantic love and sexual behavior: Perspectives from the social sciences* (pp. 33–76). Westport, CT: Praeger /Greenwood.

Lee, K., Cameron, C.A., Xu, F., Fu, G., & Board, J. (1997). Chinese and Canadian children's evaluations of lying and truth telling: Similarities and differences in the context of pro- and antisocial behaviors. *Child Development, 68,* 924–934.

Lee, P. C., Senders, C. W., Gantz, B. J., & Otto, S. R. (1985). Transient sensorineural hearing loss after overuse of portable headphone cassette radios. *Otolaryngology, 93,* 622–625.

Lee, R.T., & Ashforth, B.E. (1993). A longitudinal study of burnout among supervisors and managers: comparisons between the Lieter & Maslach (1988) and Golembiewski et al. (1986) models. *Organizational Behavior and Human Decision Processes, 54(3),* 369–398.

Lee, R.T., & Ashforth, B.E. (1996). A meta-analytic examination of the correlates of the three dimensions of job burnout. *Journal of Applied Psychology, 81,* 123–133.

Leenaars, A.A., & Lester, D. (1990). Suicide in adolescents: A comparison of Canada and the United States. *Psychological Reports, 67(3, pt 1),* 867–873.

Lefcourt, H.M., Davidson, K., Prkachin, K.M., & Mills, D.E. (1997). Humor as a stress moderator in the prediction of blood pressure obtained during five stresssful tasks. *Journal of Research in Personality, 31,* 523–542.

Lefebvre, L., & Giraldeau, L.A. (1994). Cultural transmission in pigeons is affected by the number of tutors and bystander present. *Animal Behaviour, 47(2),* 331–337.

LeFevre, J., Kulak, A.G., & Heymans, S.L. (1992). Factors influencing the selection of university majors varying in mathmatical content. *Canadian Journal of Behavioural Science, 24,* 276–289.

Legerstee, M. (1990). Infants use multimodal information to imitate speech sounds. *Infant Behavior and Development, 13(3),* 343–354.

Lehman, D.R., & Taylor, S.E. (1987). Date with an earthquake: Coping with a probable, unpredictable disaster. *Personality and Social Psychology Bulletin, 13(4),* 546–555.

Lehman, H.C. (1953). *Age and achievement.* Philadelphia: W.B. Saunders.

Leighton, A. H. (1959). *My name is legion: The Stirling County study of psychiatric disorder and social environment,* Vol. 1, New York: Basic Books.

Leitenberg, H., & Henning, K. (1995). Sexual fantasy. *Psychological Bulletin, 117,* 469–496.

Leiter, M.P., Clark, D., & Durup, J. (1994). Distinct models of burnout and commitment among men and women in the military. *Journal of Applied Behavioral Science, 30(1),* 63–82.

Leiter, M.P., & Durup, M.J. (1996). Work, home, and in-between: A longitudinal study of spillover. *Journal of Applied Behavioral Science, 32(1),* 29–47.

Leiter, M.P., Harvie, P., & Frizzel, C. (1998). The correspondence of patient satisfaction and nurse burnout. *Social Science and Medicine, 47,* 1611–1617.

Leiter, M.P., & Maslach, C. (1988). The impact of interpersonal environment on burnout and organizational commitment. *Journal of Organizational Behavior, 9(4),* 297–308.

Lemery, K.S., Goldsmith., H.H., Klinnert, M.D., & Mrazek, D.A. (1999). Developmental models of infant and childhood temperament. *Developmental Psychology, 35,* 189–204.

Lemme, B.H. (1999). *Development in adulthood* (2nd ed.). Boston: Allyn & Bacon.

Lepper, M., & Green, D. (1978). *The hidden costs of reward.* Hillsdale, NJ: Erlbaum.

Lepper, M.R., & Cordova, D.I. (1992). A desire to be taught: Instructional consequences of intrinsic motivation. *Motivation and Emotion, 16,* 187–208.

Lepper, M.R., & Hoddell, M. (1992). Instructional games: Effects of sex-typed fantasy contexts on boys' and girls' learning and instruction. Unpublished manuscript, Stanford University.

Lerman, C., Caporaso, N. E., Audrain, J., Main, D., Bowman, E. D., Lockshin, B., Boyd, N. R. & Shields, P. G. (1999). Evidence suggesting the role of specific genetic factors in cigarette smoking. *Health Psychology, 18,* 14–20.

Lerner, M.J. (1980). *The belief in a just world: a fundamental delusion.* New York: Plenum.

Lerner, R. M. (1990). Plasticity, person-context relations, and cognitive training in the aged years: A developmental contextual perspective. *Developmental Psychology, 26,* 911–915.

Lerner, R.M. (1993). The demise of the nature-nurture dichotomy. *Human Development, 36,* 119–124.

Lerner, R.M., & Galambos, N.L. (1998). Adolescent development: Challenges and opportunities for research, programs, and policies. *Annual Review of Psychology, 49,* 413–446.

Leung, A.K., & Robson, W.L. (1993). Nightmares. *Journal of the National Medical Association, 85,* 233–235.

LeVay, S. (1991). A difference in hypothalamic structure between heterosexual and homosexual men. *Science, 253,* 1034–1037.

Levenson, R.W. (1992). Autonomic nervous system differences among emotions. *Psychological Science, 3,* 23–27.

Levenson, R.W., Carstensen, L.L., Friesen, W.V., & Ekman, P. (1991). Emotion, physiology, and expression in old age. *Psychology and Aging, 6,* 28–35.

Levenstein, C. (1999). Economic losses from repetitive strain injuries. *Occupational Medicine, 14,* 149–161.

Leventhal, E.A., Hansell, S., Diefenbach, M., Leventhal, H., & Glass, D.C. (1996). Negative affect and self-report of physical symptoms: Two longitudinal studies of older adults. *Health Psychology, 15,* 193–199.

Levine, B., Black, S.E., Cabeza, R., Sinden, M., Mcintosh, A.R., Toth, J.P., Tulving, E., & Stuss, D.T. (1998). Episodic memory and the self in a case of isolated retrograde amnesia. *Brain, 121,* 1951–1973.

Levine, D.S. (1991). *Introduction to neural and cognitive modeling.* Hillsdale, NJ: Erlbaum.

Levine, J. M., & McBurney, D. H. (1982). *The role of olfaction in social perception and behavior.* Paper presented at the Third Ontario Symposium in Personality and Social Psychology, Toronto.

Levine, R.V., & Norenzayan, A. (1999). The pace of life in 31 countries. *Journal of Cross Cultural Psychology, 30,* 178–205.

Levine, R.V., Martinez, T.S., Brase, G., & Sorenson, K. (1994). Helping in 36 U.S. cities. *Journal of Personality and Social Psychology, 67,* 69–82.

Levine, S.V. (1987). The myths and needs of contemporary youth. *Adolescent Psychiatry, 14,* 48–62.

Levinger, G. (1988). Can we picture "love"? In R.J. Sternberg & M.I. Barnes (Eds.), *The psychology of love* (pp. 139–158). New Haven, CT: Yale University Press.

Levinson, D.J. (1986). A conception of adult development. *American Psychologist, 41*, 3–13.

Levinthal, C.F. (1999). *Drugs, behavior, and modern society*. Boston: Allyn & Bacon.

Levis, D. J. (1985). Implosive theory: A comprehensive extension of conditioning theory of fear/anxiety to psychology. In S. Reiss & R. R. Bootzin (Eds.), *Theoretical issues in behavior therapy*. New York: Academic Press.

Levitt, A.J. Joffe. R.T., Brecher, D., & MacDonald, C. (1993). Anxiety disorders and anxiety symptoms in a clinic sample of seasonal and non-seasonal depressives. *Journal of Affective Disorders, 28*, 51–56

Levitt, A.J., Joffe, R.T., Moul, D.E., Lam, R.W. Teicher, M.H., Lebegue, B., Murray, M.G., Oren, D.A., Schwartz, P., Buchanan, A., Glod, C.A., & Brown, J. (1993). Side effects of light therapy in seasonal affective disorder. *American Journal of Psychiatry, 150*, 650–652.

Levy, E.M., Cottrell, M.C., & Black, P.H. (1989). Psychological and immunological associations in men with AIDS pursuing a macrobiotic regimen as an alternative therapy: A pilot study. *Brain, Behavior and Immunity, 3* (2), 175–182.

Levy, S.M. (1990). Psychosocial risk factors and cancer progression: Mediating pathways linking behavior and disease. In K.D. Craig & S.M. Weiss (Eds.), *Health enhancement, disease prevention, and early intervention: Biobehavioral perspective*. New York: Springer.

Levy, S.M., Herberman, R.B., Maluish, A.M., Schlien, B., & Lippman, M. (1985). Prognostic risk assessment in primary breast cancer by behavioral and immunological parameters. *Health Psychology, 4(2)*, 99–113.

Lewkowics, D.J. (1996). Infants' response to the audible and visible properties of the human face 1. Role of lexical-syntactic content, temporal synchrony, gnder, and manner of speech. *Developmental Psychology, 32*, 347–366.

Lewy, A.J., Sack, R.L., Cutler, N.L., Bauer, V.K., & Hughes, R.J. (1998). Melatonin in circadian phase sleep and mood disorders. In M. Shafii & S.L. Shafii (Eds.), *Melatonin in psychiatric and neoplastic disorders* (pp. 81–104). Washington, DC: American Psychiatric Press, Inc.

Ley, P. (1988). *Communicating with patients*. London: Croom Helm.

Leyens, J.P., Yzerbyt, V., & Corneille, O. (1996). The role of applicability in the emergence of the over-attribution bias. *Journal of Personality and Social Psychology, 70*, 291–229.

Liddell, A. & Locker, D. (1993). Dental anxiety in the elderly. Special issue: dental health psychology. *Psychology and Health, 8(2–3)*, 175–183.

Liddell, A., & Gosse, V. (1998). Characteristics of early unpleasant dental experiences. *Journal of Behavior Therapy and Experimental Psychiatry, 29*, 227–237.

Liddell, F.D.K. (1982). Motor vehicle accidents (1973–6) in a cohort of Montreal drivers. *Journal of Epidemiological Community Health, 36*, 140–145.

Liden, R.C., & Mitchell, T.R. (1988). Ingratiatory behaviors in organizational settings. *Academy of Management Review, 13*, 572–587.

Lieberman, D.A. (1990). *Learning: Behavior and cognition*. Belmont, CA: Wadsworth.

Lieberman, J.A., & Koreen, A.R. (1993). Neurochemistry and neuroendocrinology of schizophrenia: A selective review. *Schizophrenia Bulletin, 19 (2)*, 371–429.

Lightdale, J.R., & Prentice, D.A. (1994). Rethinking sex differences aggression: Aggressive behavior in the absence of social roles. *Personality and Social Psychology Bulletin, 20*, 34–44.

Linden, E. (1993, March 22). Can animals think? *Time.*

Lindman, R.E., & Lang, A.R. (1994). The alcohol-aggression stereotype: A cross-cultural comparison of beliefs. *International Journal of the Addictions, 29*, 1–13.

Lindy, J.D., Green, B.L., & Grace, M.C. (1987). Commentary: The stressor criterion and post-traumatic stress disorder. *Journal of Nervous and Mental Disease, 175(5)*, 269–272.

Links, P.S., & Van Reekum, R. (1993). Childhood sexual abuse, parental impairment and the development of borderline personality disorder. *Canadian Journal of Psychiatry, 38(7)*, 472–474.

Linseman, M.A. (1989). Central versus peripheral mediation of opioid effects on alcohol consumption in free-feeding rats. *Pharmacology, Biochemistry and Behavior, 33(2)*, 407–413.

Linton, M. (1975). Memory for real-world events. In D. A. Norman & D. E. Rumelhart (Eds.), *Explorations in cognition*, Chapter 14. San Francisco: Freeman.

Linville, P.W., & Fischer, G.W. (1993). Exemplar and abstraction models of perceived group variability and stereotypicality. *Social Cognition, 11*, 92–125.

Lipshitz, R., & Bar-Ilan, O. (1996). How problems are solved: Reconsidering the phase theorem. *Organizational Behavior and Human Decision Processes, 65*, 48–60.

Litz, B.T., King, L.A., King, D.W., Orsillo, S.M., & Friedman, M.J. (1997). Warriors as peacekeepers: Features of the Somalia experience and PTSD. *Journal of Consulting and Clinical Psychology, 65*, 1001–1010.

Litz, B.T., Orsillo, S.M., Friedman, M. & Ehlich, P. (1997). Posttraumatic stress disorder associated with peacekeeping duty in Somalia for U.S. military personnel. *American Journal of Psychiatry, 154*, 178–184.

Lloyd, P., & Fernyhough, C. (Eds.). (1999). *Lev Vygotsky: Critical assessments: Vygotsky's theory*, Vol. I. New York, NY: Routledge.

Locke, B.Z., & Slaby, A.E. (1982). Preface. In D. Mechanic (Ed.), *Symptoms, illness behavior, and help-seeking* (pp. xi–xv). New York: Pordist.

Locke, E.A., & Latham, G.P. (1990). *A theory of goal setting and task performance*. Englewood Cliffs, NJ: Prentice Hall.

Locker, D., Shapiro, D., & Liddell, A. (1999). Variations in negative cognitions concerning dental treatment among dentally anxious and nonanxious individuals. *Cognitive Therapy and Research, 23*, 93–103.

Loehlin, J.C. (1992). *Genes and environment in personality development*. Newbury Park, CA: Sage.

Loehlin, J.C., Lindzey, G., & Spuhle, J.N. (1975). *Race differences in intelligence*. New York: Freeman.

Loftus, E. F. & Loftus, G. R. (1980). On the permanence of stored information in the human brain. *American Psychologist, 35*, 409–420.

Loftus, E.F. (1991). The glitter of everyday memory and the gold. *American Psychologist, 46*, 16–18.

Loftus, E.F. (1992). When a lie becomes memory's truth: Memory distortion after exposure to misinformation. *Current Directions in Psychological Science, 1*, 121–123.

Loftus, E.F. (1993). The reality of repressed memories. *American Psychologist, 48*, 518–537.

Loftus, E.F., & Coan, D. (in press). The construction of childhood memories. In D. Peters (Ed.), *The child in context: Cognitive, social and legal perspectives*. New York: Kluwer.

Loftus, E. F., & Herzog, C. (1991). Unpublished data, University of Washington.

Loftus, E., & Pickrell, J. E. (1995). The formation of false memories. *Psychiatric Annals, 25*, 720–725.

Loftus, E., Coan, J. A. & Pickrell, J. E. (1996). Manufacturing false memories using bits of reality. In L. M. Reder (Ed.) *Implicit memory and metacognition*. Mahwah, NJ: Earlbaum.

Logan, G.D. (1985). Skill and automaticity: Relations, implications, and future directions. *Canadian Journal of Psychology, 39*, 367–386.

Logan, G.D. (1988). Toward an instance theory of automotization. *Psychological Review, 95*, 492–527.

Logue, A.W. (1979). Taste aversion and the generaltiy of the laws of learning. *Psychological Bulletin, 86*, 27–296.

Logue, A.W. (1988). Research on self-control: An integrating framework. *Behavioral and Brain Sciences, 11*, 665–679.

Logue, A.W., Logue, K.R., & Strauss, K.E. (1983). The acquisition of taste aversion in humans with eating and drinking disorders. *Behavioral Research and Therapy, 21*, 275–289.

Logue, A.W., Ophir, I., & Strauss, K.E. (1981). The acquisition of taste aversion in humans. *Behavior Research and Therapy, 19*, 319–333.

Long, B.C., & Flood, K.R. (1993). Coping with work stress: Psychological benefits of exercise. Special Issue: Exercise, stress and health. *Work and Stress, 7(2)*, 109–119.

Long, B.C., Kahn, S.E. & Schutz, R.W. (1992). Causal model of stress and coping: women and management. *Journal of Counselling Psychology, 39(2)*, 227–239.

Long, G.M., & Crambert, R.F. (1990). The nature and basis of age-related change in dynamic visual acuity. *Psychology and Aging, 5*, 138–143.

Long, J.W., Rybacki, J.J. (1994). The essential guide to prescription drugs. New York: HarperCollins.

Longoni, A.M., Richardson, J.T., & Aiello, A. (1993). Atriculatory rehearsal and phonological storage in working memory. *Memory and Cognition, 21*, 11–22.

Lonner, W.J., & Malpass, R. (Eds.) (1994). *Psychology and Culture*. Boston: Allyn & Bacon.

Lou, H.C., Kjaer, T.W., Friberg, L., Wildschiodtz, G., Holm, S., & Nowak, M. (1999). A –sup-1-sup-5O-H-sub-2O PET study of meditation and the resting state of normal consciousness. *Human Brain Mapping, 7*, 98–105.

Louie, T. A. (1999). Decision makers' hindsight bias after receiving favorable and unfavorable feedback. *Journal of Applied Psychology, 84*, 29–41.

Lovass, O.I. (1982). Comments of self-destructive behaviors. *Analysis and Intervention in Developemental Disabilities, 2*, 115–124.

Lubart, T.I. (1994). Creativity. In R.J. Sternberg (Ed.), *Thinking problem solving* (pp. 289–332). San Diego, CA: Academic Press.

Lubart, T.T., & Sternberg, R.J. (1995). An investment approach to creativity: Theory and data. In S.M. Smith, T.B. Ward, & R.A. Finke (Eds.), *The creative cognition approach* (pp. 269–302). Cambridge, MA: MIT.

Luchins, A. S. (1942). Mechanization in problem solving. *Psychological Monographs, 54* (whole No. 248).

Lupker, S.J., Fleet, G.J. & Shelton, B.R. (1988). Callers' perceptions of post-dialing delays: The effects of new signaling technology. *Behaviour and Information Technology, 7*, 263–274.

Luria, A.R. (1973). The frontal lobes and the regulation of behavior. In K.H. Pribram & A.R. Luria (Eds.), *Psycholophysiology of the frontal lobes*. New York: Academic Press.

Luthans, F., Paul, R., & Baker, D. (1981). An experimental analysis of the impact of a contingent reinforcement intervention on salespersons' performance behaviors. *Journal of Applied Psychology, 66*, 314–323.

Lykken, D.T. (1957). A study of anxiety in the sociopathic personality. *Journal of Abnormal and Social Psychology, 55*, 6–10.

Lykken, D.T. (1985). The probity of polygraph. In S.M. Kassin & L.S. Wrightsman (Eds.), *The psychology of evidence and trial procedure*. Beverly Hills, CA: Sage.

Lykken, D.T. (1998). *A tremor in the blood: Uses and abuses of the lie detector*. New York, NY: Plenum Press.

Lykken, D.T. (1998). The genetics of genius. In A. Steptoe (Ed.), *Genius and mind: Studies of creativity and temperament* (pp. 15–37). New York: Oxford University Press.

Lykken, D.T., McGue, D. T., Tellegen, A., & Bouchard, T.J. (1992). Emergenesis: Genetic traits that may not run in families. *American Psychologist, 47*, 1565–1577.

Lyman, B. J., & McDaniel, M. A. (1986). Effects of encoding strategy on long-term memory for odours. *Quarterly Journal of Experimental Psychology, 38A*, 753–765.

Lyman, B. J., & McDaniel, M. A. (1987, April). Effects of experimenter and subject provided verbal and visual elaborations on long-term memory for odors. Paper presented at the annual meeting of the Eastern Psychological Association, Arlington, VA.

Lyness, S.A. (1993). Predictors of differences between Type A and B individuals in heart rate and blood pressure reactivity. *Psychological Bulletin, 114,* 226–295.

Lynn, S. J., & Rhue, J. W. (1986). The fantasy-prone person: Hypnosis, imagination, and creativity. *Journal of Personality and Social Psychology, 51,* 404–408.

Lynn, S. J., Rhue, J. W., & Weekes, J. R. (1990). Hypnotic involuntariness: A social cognitive analysis. *Psychological Review, 974,* 169–184.

Lytton, H. (1990). Child and parent effects in boys' conduct disorders. *Developmental Psychology, 26,* 683–697.

Lytton, H., & Romney, D.M. (1991). Parents' differential socialization of boys and girls: A meta-analysis. *Psychological Bulletin, 109(2),* 267–296.

Lyubimov, N.N. (1999). Changes in electroencephalogram and evoked potentials during application of the specific form of physiological training (meditation). *Human Physiology, 25,* 171–180.

Ma, K. O., & Hamid, P. N. (1998). The relationship between attachment prototypes, self-esteem, loneliness and casual attributions in Chinese trainee teachers. *Personality and Individual Differences, 24,* 357–371.

Maccoby, E., (1990). Gender and relationships: A development account. American Psychological Association: Distinguished Scientific Contributions Award Address (1989, New Orleans). *American Pshychologist, 45(4),* 513–520.

Maccoby, E.E., & Jacklin, C.N. (1987). Gender segregation in childhood. In H.W. Reese (Ed.), *Advances in child development and behavior* (Vol. 20, pp. 239–288). New York: Academic Press.

MacDonald, C., Chamberlain, K., Long, N., Pereira-Laird, J., & Mirfin, K. (1998). Mental health, physical health, and stressors reported by New Zealand Defense Force peacekeepers: A longitudinal study. *Military Medicine, 163,* 477–481.

MacDonald, T.K., Zanna, M.P., & Fong, G.T. (1995). Decision making in altered states: Effects of alcohol on attitudes toward drinking and driving. *Journal of Personality and Social Psychology, 68,* 973–985.

MacDonald, T.K., Zanna, M.P., & Fong, G.T. (1996). Why common sense goes out the window: Effects of alcohol on intentions to use condoms. *Personaltiy and Social Psychology Bulletin, 22,* 763–775.

MacDonald, T.K., Zanna, M.P., & Fong, G.T. (1998). Alcohol and intentions to engage in risky health-related behaviors: Experimental evidence for a causal relationship. In J.G. Adair, & D. Belanger (Eds.), *Advances in psychological science, Vol 1: Social, personal, and cultural aspects* (pp.407–428). Hove, England UK: Psychology Press/Erlbaum (UK) Taylor & Francis.

MacFarlane, M.M. (1999). Treating brain-injured clients and their families. *Family Therapy, 26,* 13–29.

Mackie, D.M., & Worth, L.T. (1989). Processing deficits and the mediation of positive affect in persuasion. *Journal of Personality and Social Psychology, 57,* 27–40.

Macmillan, M. (1992). Freud and his empirical evidence. *Australian Journal of Psychology, 44,* 171–175.

Macnamara, J., & Austin, G., (1993). Physics and plasticine. *Canadian Psychology, 34(3),* 225–232.

Macrae, C.N., N., Milne, A.B., & Bodenhausen, G.V. (1994). Stereotypes as energy-saving devices: A peek inside the cognitive toolbox. *Journal of Personality and Social Psychology, 66,* 37–47.

Maggs, J.L., Almeida, D.M., & Gambalos, N.L. (1995). Risky business: The paradoxical meaning of problem behavior for young adolescents. Special section: Canadian research. *Journal of Early Adolescence, 15,* 344–362.

Maher, B.A. (1974). Delusional thinking and perceptual disorder. *Journal of individual Psychology 30,* 98–113.

Maier, S.F., & Watkins, L.R. (1999). Bidirectional communication between the brain and the immune system: Implication for behaviour. *Animal Behaviour, 57,* 741–751.

Maier, S.F., & Jackson, R.L. (1979). Learned helplessness: All of us were right (and wrong): Inescapable shock has multiple effects. In G.H. Bower (Ed.), *The psychology of learning and motivation* (Vol. 13). New York: Academic Press.

Maio, G.R., & Olson, J.M. (1998). Attitude dissimulation and persuasion. *Journal of Experimental Social Psychology, 34,* 182–201.

Maio, G.R., Olson, J.M., & Bush, J.E. (1997). Telling jokes that disparage social groups: Effects on the joke teller's stereotypes. *Journal of Applied Social Psychology, 27,* 1986–2000.

Maio, G.R., Bell, D.W., & Esses, V.M. (1996). Ambivalence and persuasion: The processing of messages about immigrant groups. *Journal of Experimental Social Psychology, 32,* 513–536.

Malan, J. R., Norton, G. R., & Cox, B. J. (1993). Panic attacks and alcoholism: Primacy and frequency of attacks. *Alcoholism Treatment Quarterly, 10,* 95–105.

Malandro, L.A., Barker, L., & Barker, D.A. (1994). *Nonverbal communication* (3rd ed.). New York: Random House.

Malenfant, L. & Van Houten, R. (1990). Increasing the percentage of drivers yielding to pedestrians in three Canadian cities with a multifaceted safety program. *Health Education Research, 5,* 275–279.

Mallory, B.L., Schein, J.D. & Zingle, H.W. (1992). Hearing offspring as visual language mediators in deaf-parented families. *Sign Language Studies, 76,* 193–213.

Malpass, R. S., & Devine, P. G. (1981). Guided memory in eyewitness identification research. *Journal of Applied Psychology 66,* 343–350.

Man, K., & Hamid, P.N. (1998). The relationship between attachment prototypes, self-esteem, loneliness and casual attributions in Chinese trainee teachers. *Personality and Individual Differences, 24,* 357–371.

Mandel, D.R., Jusczyk, P.W., & Pisoni, D.B. (1995). Infants' recognition of the sound patterns of their own names. *Psychological Science, 6,* 314–317.

Mandler, J.M., Bauer, P.J., & McDonough, L. (1991). Separating the sheep from the goats: Differentiating global categories. *Cognitive Psychology, 23,* 263–298.

Mann, L.M., Chassin, L., & Sher, K.J. (1987). Alcohol, expectancies and risk for alcoholism. *Journal of Consulting and Clinical Psychology, 55,* 411–417.

Mann, T. (1994). Informed consent for psychological research: Do subjects comprehend consent forms and understand their legal rights? *Psychological Science, 5,* 140–143.

Mannuzza, S., Klein, R.G., Bessler, A., Mallory, P., et al. (1993). Adult outcome of hyperactive boys: Educational achievement, occupational rank, and psychiatric status. *Archives of General Psychiatry, 50* (7), 565–576.

Marche, T. A., & Howe, M. L. (1995). Preschoolers report misinformation despite accurate memory. *Developmental Psychology, 31,* 554–567.

Marcus, B.H., Owen, N., Forsyth, L.H., Cavill, N.A., & Fridinger, F. (1998). Physical activity interventions using mass media, print media, and information technology. *American Journal of Preventive Medicine, 15,* 362–378.

Mark, M. M., & Mellor, S. (1991). Effect of self-relevance of an event on hindsight bias: The foreseeability of a layoff. *Journal of Applied Psychology, 76,* 569–577.

Markowsky, A.J., & Pence, A.R. (1997). Looking back: Early adolescents' recollections of their preschool day care experiences. *Early Child Development and Care, 135,* 123–143.

Marks, I. (1994). Behavior therapy as an aid to self-care. Current *Directions in Psychological Science, 3,* 19–22.

Markus, H. M. & Nurius, P. (1986). Possible selves. *American Psychologist, 41,* 954–969.

Markus, H. R., & Kitayama, S. (1991). Culture and the self: Implications for cognition, emotion, and motivation. *Psychological Review, 98,* 224–253.

Markus, H.M., & Nurius, P. (1986). Possible selves. *American Psychologist, 41,* 954–969.

Marlatt, G.A., Baer, J.S., Donovan, D.M., & Kivlahan, D.R. (1988). Addictive behaviors: Etiology and treatment. *Annual Review of Psychology, 58,* 265–272.

Marr, D. (1982). *Vision: A computational investigation into the human representation and processing of visual information.* San Francisco: W. H. Freeman.

Marsh, H.W. (1993). Relations between global and specific domains of self: The importance of individual importance, certainty, and zeal. *Journal of Personality and Social Psychology 65,* 975–992.

Marshall, W.L., & Mazzucco, A. (1995). Self-esteem and parental attachments in child molesters. *Sexual Abuse Journal of Research and Treatment, 7(4),* 279–285.

Martin, C.L., & Little, J.K., (1990). The relation of gender understanding to children's sex-typed preferences and gender stereotypes. *Child Development, 61(5),* 1427–1439.

Martin, J.L., & Ross, H.S. (1995). The development of aggression within sibling conflict. Special Issue: Conflict resolution in early social development. *Early Education and Development. 6(4),* 335–358.

Martin, M. (1986). Individual differences in sensation seeking attentional ability. *Personality and Individual Differences, 6,* 637–649.

Marzetta, B.R., Benson, H., & Wallace, R.K. (1972). Combatting drug dependency in young people: A new approach. *Medical Counterpoint, 4,* 13–37.

Maslach, C. (1982). *Burnout: The cost of caring.* Englewood Cliffs, NJ: Prentice-Hall.

Maslach, C., & Leiter, M.P. (1999). Teacher burnout: A research guide. In R. Vandenberghe, & M.A. Huberman (Eds.), *Understanding and preventing teacher burnout: A sourcebook of international research and practice* (pp. 295–303). New York, NY: Cambridge University Press.

Maslach, C., & Jackson, S.E. (1984). Burnout in organizational settings. In S. Oskamp (Ed.), *Applied social psychology annual* (Vol. 5, pp. 135–154). Beverly Hills: Sage.

Maslow, A.H. (1970). *Motivation and personality,* (2nd ed.). New York: Harper & Row.

Mason, M.E., Graf, P. (1993). Introduction: Looking back and into the future. In P. Graf & E.J. Masson (Eds.), *Implicit memory: New directions in cognition, development, and neuropsychology* (pp. 1–11). Hillsdale, NJ: Erlbaum.

Matarazzo, J.D. (1980). Behavioral health and behavioral medicine: Frontiers for a new health psychology. *American Psychologist, 35,* 807–817.

Mather, J.A., & Anderson, R.C. (1993). Personalities of octopuses (Octopus rubescens). *Journal of Comparative Psychology, 107,* 336–340.

Mathews, F. (1996). Violent and aggressive girls. *Journal of Child and Youth Care, 11,* 1–23.

Mathews, G. & Amelang, M. (1993). Extraversion, arousal theory and performance: A study of individual differences in the EEG. *Personality and Individual Differences, 14,* 347–363.

Maticka-Tynedale, E. (1991). Sexual scripts and AIDS prevention: Variations in adherence to safer sex guidelines by heterosexual adolescents. *Journal of Sex Research, 28,* 45–66.

Matlin, M.W., & Foley, H.J. (1992). *Sensation and perception* (3rd ed.). Needham Heights, MA: Allyn & Bacon.

Matlin, M.W., & Foley, H.J. (1997). *Sensation and perception* (4th ed.). Needham Heights, MA: Allyn & Bacon.

Matthews, K.A. (1988). Coronary heart disease and Type A behaviors: Update on and alternative to the Booth-Kewley and Friedman (1987) quantitative review. *Psychological Bulletin, 104,* 373–380.

Maturi, R. (1992, July 20). Stress can be beaten. *Industry Week,* pp. 23–26.

Maurer, D., & Young, R.E. (1983). Newborns' following of natural and distorted arrangements of facial features. *Infant Behavior and Development,* 127–131.

Maurer, T.J., & Pierce, H.R. (1998). A comparison of Likert scale and traditional measures of self-efficacy. *Journal of Applied Psychology, 83,* 324–329.

Maurice, P., & Trudel, G. (1982). Self-injurious behavior prevalence and relationships to environmental events. In J.H. Hollis & C.E. Meyers (Eds.), *Life-threatening behavior: Analysis and intervention*. Washington, DC: American Association on Mental Deficiency, Monograph No. 5 , 81–103.

Mauzza, S., Klein, R.g., Bessler, A., Malloy, P.I., & LaPadula, A. (1993). Adult outcome of hyperactive boys: Educational achievement, occupational rank, and psychiatric status. *Archives of General Psychiatry, 50*, 565–576.

May, C.P., Hasher, L., & Stoltzfus, E.R. (1993). Optimal time of day and the magnitude of age differences in memory. *Psychological Science, 4*, 326–330.

Mayer, J.D., & Salovey, P. (1993). The intelligence of emotional intelligence. *Intelligence, 17*, 433–442.

Mayer, J.D., & Salovey, P. (in press). What is emotional intelligence? In P. Salovey & D. Suyter (Eds.), *Emotional development, emotional literacy, and emotional intelligence*. New York: Basic Books.

Mayer, R. E., Tajika, H., & Stanley, C. (1991). Mathematical problem solving in Japan and the United States: A controlled comparison. *Journal of Educational Psychology, 1*, 69–72.

Mayes, A.R. (1996). The functional deficits that underlie amnesia: Evidence from amnesic forgetting rate and item-specific implicit memory. In D.J. Herman, C., McEvoy, C. Hertzog, P. Hertel, & M.K. Johnson (Eds.), *Basic and applied memory research: Practical applications* (Vol. 2, pp. 391–405). Mahwah, NJ: Erlbaum.

Mazur, J.E. (1987). An adjusting procedure for studying delayed reinforcement. In M.L. Commons, J.E. Mazur, J.A. Nevin, & H. Rachlin (Eds.), *Quantitative analyses of behavior: Vol. 5. The effect of delay and of intervening events on reinforcement value* (pp. 44–73). Hillsdale, NJ: Erlbaum.

Mazur, J.E. (1996). Procrastination by pigeons: Preference for larger, more delayed work requirement. *Journal of the Experimental Analysis of Behavior, 65*, 159–171.

McAllister, T.W., & Flashman, L.A. (1999). Mild traumatic brain injury and mood disorders: Causal connections, assessment, and treatment. In N.R. Varney, & R.J. Roberts (Eds.), *The evaluation and treatment of mild traumatic brain injury* (pp. 347–373). Mahwah, NJ: Erlbaum.

McAlpine, L., & McGrath, P.J. (1999). Chronic and recurrent pain in children. In A.R. Block, & E.F. Kremer (Eds.), *Handbook of pain syndromes: Biopsychosocial perspectives* (pp. 529–549). Mahwah, NJ: Erlbaum.

McCall, R.B. (1994). Academic underachievers. *Current Directions in Psychological Science, 3*, 15–19.

McCanne, T.R., & Anderson, J.A. (1987). Emotional responding following experimental manipulation of facial electromyographic activity. *Journal of Personality and Social Psychology, 52*, 759–768.

McCarley, R.W., & Hobson, R.W. (1981). REM sleep dreams and the activation hypothesis. *American Journal of Psychiatry, 138*, 904–912.

McCarthy, B. & Hagan, J. (1991). Homelessness: A criminogenic situation? *British Journal of Criminology, 31(4)*, 393–410.

McClearn, G.E., Plomin, R., Gor-Maslak, G., & Crabbe, J.C. (1991). The gene chase in behavioral science. *Psychological Science, 2*, 222–229.

McClelland, D.C. (1961). *The achieving society*. Princeton, NJ: Van Nostrand.

McClelland, D.C. (1975). *Power: The inner experience*. New York: Invington.

McClelland, D.C. (1995). Achievement motivation in relation to achievement-related recall, performance, and urine flow, a marker associated with release of vasopressin. *Motivation and Emotion, 19*, 59–76.

McConkie, G.W., Kerr, P.W., Reddix, M.D., Zola, D., & Jacobs, A.M. (1989). Eye movement control during reading: II. Frequency of refixating a word. *Perception & Psychophysics, 46*, 245–253.

McConkie, G.W., & Zola, D. (1984). Eye movement control during reading. The effect of word units. In W. Prinz & A. F. Sanders (Eds.), *Cognition and motor processes* (pp. 63–74). Berlin: Springer-Verlag.

McCrae, R.R., & Costa, P.T. (1997). Personality trait structure as a human universal. *American Psychologist, 52*, 509–516.

McDaniel, M.A., & Frei, R.L. (1994). Validity of customer service measures in personnel selection: A review of creterion and construct evidence. Manuscript submitted for publication.

McDonald, H. E., & Hirt, E. R. (1997). When expectancy meets desire: Motivational effects in reconstructive memory. *Journal of Personality and Social Psychology, 72*, 5–23.

McDonald, J., & McKelvie, S.J. (1992). Playing safe: Helping rates for a dropped mitten and a box of condoms. *Psychological Reports, 71*, 113–114.

McDonald, R.J. & White, N.M. (1993). A triple dissociation of memory systems: Hippocampus, amygdala, and dorsal striatum. *Behavioral Neuroscience, 107(1)*, 3–22.

McFarland, C., Ross, M., & DeCourville, N. (1989). Women's theories of menstruation and biases in recall of menstrual symptoms. *Journal of Personality and Sosial Psychology, 576*, 522–531.

McGlone, J. & MacDonald, B.H. (1989). Reliability of the sodium amobarbital test for memory. *Journal of Epilepsy, 2(1)*, 31–39.

McGrath, J.E., & Cohen, D.B. (1978). REM sleep facilitation of adaptive waking behavior: A review of the literature. *Psychological Bulletin, 85*, 24–57.

McGrath, P.J. (1995). Aspects of pain in children and adolescents. *Journal of Child Psychology and Psychiatry and Allied Disciplines, 36(5)*, 717–730.

McGrath, P.J., & McAlpine, L. (1993). Psychologic perspectives on pediatric pain. *The Journal of Pediatrics, 122*, S2–S8.

McGregor, I., & Holmes, J.G. (1999). How storytelling shapes memory and impressions of relationship events over time. *Journal of Personality and Social Psychology, 76*, 403–419.

McGregor, I., Newby-Clark, I.R., & Zanna, M.P. (1999). "Remembering" dissonance: Simultaneous accessibility of inconsistent cognitive elements moderates epistemic discomfort. In E. Harmon-Jones, & J. Mills (Eds.), *Cognitive dissonance: Progress on a pivotal theory in social psychology* (pp. 325–353). Washington, DC: American Psychological Association.

McGue, M. (1999). The behavioral genetics of alcoholism. *Current Directions in Psychological Science, 8*, 109–115.

McGue, M., & Lykken, D.T. (1992). Genetic influence on risk of divorce. *Psychological Science, 3*, 368–373.

McGue, M., Sharma, A., & Benson, P. (1996). Parent and sibling influences on adolescent alcohol use and misuse: Evidence from a U.S. adoption cohort. *Journal of Studies on Alcohol, 57*, 8–18.

McGuire, P. A. (1999, June). Psychology and medicine connecting in war on cancer. *APA Monitor*, 8–9.

McKelvie, S.J. (1997). Perception of faces with and without spectacles. *Perceptual and Motor Skills, 84*, 497–498.

McKelvie, S.J., & Aikins, S. (1993). Why does coin head orientation tend to be misremembered? Tests of schema interference and handedness hypothesis. *British Journal of Psychology, 84*, 355–363.

McKenna, S.P., & Glendon, A.I. (1985). Occupational first aid training: Decay in cardiopulmonary resuscitation (CPR) skills. *Journal of Occupational Psychology, 58*, 109–117.

McKenry, P.C., Kotch, J.B., & Browne, D.H. (1991). Correlates of dysfunctional parenting attitudes among low-income adolescent mothers. *Journal of Adolescent Research, 6*, 212–234.

McKenzie, A. D., and Howe, B. L. (1997) The effect of imagery on self-efficacy for a motor skill. *International Journal of Sport Psychology, 28*, 196–210.

McLaren, J. & Bryson, S.E. (1987). Hemispheric asymmetries in the perception of emotional and neutral faces. *Cortex, 23(4)*, 645–654.

McLean, H.M., & Kalin, R. (1994). Congruence between self-image and occupational stereotypes in students entering gender-dominated occupations. *Canadian Journal of Behavioural Science, 26*, 142–162.

McLeod, P.J., (1993). What studies of communication with infants ask us about psychology: Baby-talk and other speech registers. *Canadian Psychology, 34(3)*, 282–292.

McNeal, E.T., & Cimbolic, P. (1986). Antidepressants and biochemical theories of depression. *Psychological Bulletin, 99*, 361–374.

McReynolds, W.T. (1980). Learned helplessness as a schedule-shift effect. *Journal of Research in Personality, 14*, 139–157.

Medcof, J.W., & Wegener, J.G. (1992). Work technology and the needs for achievement and nurturance among nurses. *Journal of Organizational Behavior, 13(4)*, 413–423.

Medin, D. L., & Ross, B. H. (1992). *Cognitive psychology*. Fort Worth, TX: Harcourt Brace Jovanovich.

Mednick, M.T., Mednick, S.A., & Mednick, E.V. (1964). Incubation of creative performance and specific associative priming. *Journal of Abnormal and Social Psychology, 69*, 84–88.

Meehan, P.J., Lamb, J.A., Saltzman, L.E., & O'Carroll, P.W. (1992). Attempted suicide among young adults: Progress towards a meaningful estimate of prevalence. *American Journal of Psychiatry, 149*, 41–44.

Meichenbaum, D.K., & Deffenbacher, J.L. (1988). Stress inoculation training. *Counseling Psychologist, 16*, 69–90.

Meier, S.T. (1991). Vocational behavior, 1988–1990: Vocational choice, decision-making, career development interventions, and assessment. *Journal of Vocational Behavior, 39*, 459–484.

Meijmann, T., van der Meer, O., & van Dormolen, M. (1993). The after-effects of night work on short-term memory performance. *Ergonomics, 36*, 37–42.

Melamed, S., Kushnir, T., & Shirom, A. (1992). Burnout and risk factors for cardiovascular diseases. *Behavioral Medicine, 18*, 53–60.

Meltzoff, A.N., & Moore, M.K. (1989). Imitation in newborn infants: Exploring the range of gestures imitated and the underlying mechanisms. *Developmental Psychology, 25*, 954–962.

Melzack, R. (1976). Pain: Past, present, and future. In M. Weisenberg & B. Tursky (Eds.), *Pain: New perspectives in therapy and research*. New York: Plenum.

Melzack, R. (1989). Phantom limbs, the self and the brain (the D. O. Hebb Memorial Lecture). *Canadian Psychology, 30(1)*, 1–16.

Melzack, R. (1990). The tragedy of needless pain. *Medicine* [Special Issue], 45–51.

Melzack, R. (1994). Folk medicine and the sensory modulation of pain. In P.D. Wall & R. Melzack (Eds.), *Textbook of pain* (pp. 1209–1217). Edinburgh: Churchill Livingstone.

Melzack, R. (1999). From the gate to the neuromatrix. *Pain*, S121–126.

Mendelson, B.K., White, D.R., & Mendelson, M.J. (1996). Self-esteem and body esteem: Effects of gender, age, and weight. *Journal of Applied Developmental Psychology, 17*, 321–346.

Mendolia, M., & Kleck, R.E. (1993). Effects of talking about a stressful event on arousal: Does what we talk about make a difference? *Journal of Personality and Social Psychology, 64*, 283–292.

Mento, A.J., Locke, E.A., & Klein, H.J. (1992). Relationship of goal level to valence and instrumentality. *Journal of Applied Psychology, 77*, 395–405.

Merikle, P.M. (1992). Perception without awareness. *American Psychologist, 47*, 792–795.

Merikle, P.M., & Daneman, M. (1998). Psychological investigations of unconscious perception. *Journal of Consciousness Studies, 5*, 5–18.

Mertens, T.E., & Low-Beer, D. (1996). HIV and AIDS: Where is the epidemic going? *WHO Bulletin OMS, 74*, 121–128.

Metcalfe, J., Funnell, M., & Gazzaniga, M.S., (1995). Right-hemisphere memory superiority: Studies of a split-brain patient. *Psychological Science, 6*, 157–163.

Metzger, A.M. (1980). A methodological study of the Kubler-Ross stage theory. *Omega, 10*, 291–301.

Meyer, T.P. (1972). The effects of verbally violent film content on aggressive behavior. *AV Communication Review, 20*, 160–169.

Miklowitz, D. J., Goldstein, M. J., Doane, J. A., Neuchterlein, K. H., Strachan, A. M., Snyder, K. S., & Magana-Amato, A. (1989). Is expressed emotion an index of a transactional process? I. Parents, affective style. *Family Process, 22*, 153–167.

Millan, M. J. (1986). Multiple opioid systems and pain. *Pain, 27*, 303–347.

Millar, W.J., & Hunter, L. (1990). Relationship between socioeconomic status and household smoking patterns in Canada. *American Journal of Health Promotion, 5(1)*, 36–43.

Millberger, S., Biederman, J., Faraone, S.V., & Jones, J. (1998). Further evidence of an association between maternal smoking during pregnancy and attention deficit hyperactivity disorder: Findings from a high-risk sample of siblings. *Journal of Clinical Child Psychology, 27*, 352–358.

Miller, A.G., Ashton, W.A., McHoskey, J.W., & Gimbel, J. (1990). What price attractiveness? Stereotype and risk factors in suntanning behavior. *Journal of Applied Social Psychology, 20(15, pt 1)*, 1272–1300.

Miller, B.L., & Cummings, J.L. (1999). *The human frontal lobes: Functions and disorders.* New York, NY: The Guilford Press.

Miller, B.L., Cummings, J., Mishkin, F., Boone, K., Prince, F., Ponton, M., & Cotman, C. (1998). Emergence of artistic talent in frontotemporal dementia. *Neurology, 51*, 978–982.

Miller, C.L., Miceli, P.J., Whitman, T.L., & Borkowski, J.G. (1996). *Developmental Psychology, 32*, 533–541.

Miller, C.T. (1998). What is lost by not losing: Losses related to body weight. In J.H. Harvey (Ed.), *Perspectives on loss: A sourcebook* (pp. 253–267). Philadelphia, PA: Brunner/Mazel.

Miller, D.T., & McFarland, C. (1987). Pluralistic ignorance: When similarity is interpreted as dissimilarity. *Journal of Personality and Social Psychology, 53(2)*, 298–305.

Miller, D.T., & Ross, M. (1975). Self-serving biases in the attribution of causality: Fact or fiction? *Psychological Bulletin, 82(2)*, 213–225.

Miller, G.A. (1956). The magic number seven plus or minus two. Some limits on our capacity for processing information. *Psychological Review, 63*, 81–97.

Miller, G. E., Dopp, J. M., Myers, H. F., Stevens, S. Y., & Fahey, J. L. (1999). Psychosocial predictors of natural killer cell mobilization during marital conflict. *Health Psychology, 18*, 262–271.

Miller, L. (1987). The emotional brain. *Psychology Today, 22*, 35–42.

Miller, L., Reesor, K., McCarrey, M., Leikin, L. (1995). Nursing burnout. *Employee Assistance Quarterly, 10(4)*, 29–52.

Miller, L.L., Cornelius, T., & McFarland, D. (1978). Marijuana: An analysis of storage and retrieval deficits in memory with the technique of restricted reminding. *Pharmacology, Biochemistry, and Behavior, 8*, 441–457.

Miller, M.E., & Bowers, K.S. (1993). Hypnotic analgesia: Dissociated experience or dissociated control? *Journal of Abnormal Psychology, 102*, 29–38.

Miller, N.E. (1985). The value of behavioral research on animals. *American Psychologist, 40*, 423–440.

Miller, P.H., & Zalenski, R., (1982). Preschooler's knowledge about attention. *Developmental Psychology, 18(6)*, 871–875.

Miller, R.S. (1991). On decorum in close relationships: Why aren't we polite to those we love? *Comtemporary Social Psychology, 15*, 63–65.

Miller, S.B. (1992). Affective moderators of the cardiovascular response to stress in offspring of hypertensives. *Journal of Psychosomatic Research, 36(2)*, 149–157.

Millon, T. (1991). Classification psychopathology: Rationale, alternatives, and standards. *Journal of Abnormal Psychology, 100*, 245–261.

Milner, B. (1974). Hemispheric specialization: Scope and limits. In F.O. Schmitt & F.G. Worden (Eds.), *The neurosciences: Third study program* (pp. 75–89). Cambridge, MA: MIT Press.

Minami, H., & Dallenbach, K.M. (1946). The effect of activity upon learning and retention in the cockroach. *American Journal of Psychology, 59*, 1–58.

Minkoff, H., Deepak, N., Menez, R., & Fikrig, S. (1987). Pregnancies resulting in infants with acquired immunodeficiency syndrome or AIDS-related complexes: Follow-up of mothers, children, and subsequently born siblings. *Obstetrics and Gynecology, 69*, 288–291.

Minor, T.R. (1990). Conditioned fear and neophobia following inescapable shock. *Animal Learning & Behavior, 18*, 212–226.

Minuchin, S., & Fishman, H. C. (1981). *Family therapy techniques.* Cambridge, MA: Harvard University Press.

Mischel, W. (1977). On the future of personality measurement. *American Psychologist, 32*, 246–254.

Mistlberger, R.E. (1991). Scheduled daily exercise or feeding alters the phase of photic entrainment in syrian hamsters. *Physiology and Behavior, 50*, 1257–1260.

Mistlberger, R.E. (1992). Nonphotic entrainment of circadian activity rhythms in suprachiasmatic nuclei-ablated hamsters. *Behavioral Neuroscience, 106*, 192–202.

Mistlberger, R.E. (1996). Circadian organization of locomotor activity in mammals. In P.R. Sanberg, & K. Ossenkopp (Eds.), *Motor activity and movement disorders: Research issues and applications* (pp. 81–109). Totowa, NJ: Humana Press, Inc.

Mistlberger, R.E., & Marchant, E.G. (1995). Computational and entrainment models of circadian food-anticipatory activity: Evidence from non-24-hr feeding schedules. *Behavioral Neuroscience, 109(4)*, 790–798.

Mistler-Lachman, J.L. (1975). Queer sentences, ambiguity, and levels of processing. *Memory and Cognition, 3*, 395–400.

Mistry, J., & Rogoff, B. (1994). Remembering in cultural context. In W.J. Lonner & R. Malpass (Eds.), *Psychology and culture* (pp. 139–144). Boston: Allyn & Bacon.

Mitchell, A. (1999, Sept. 11). The Canadian family is in the throes of profound change. *Globe and Mail*, p. A1.

Mitchell, D.J., Russo, J.E., & Pennington, N. (1989). Back to the future: Temporal perspective in the explanation of events. *Journal of Behavioral Decision Making. 2*, 25–38.

Mitchell, H. (1988, February). Why are women still dying of cervical cancer? *Australian Society, 34*–35.

Mitchell, T.R., & Larson, J.R., Jr., (1987). *People in organizations: An introduction to organizational behavior* (3rd ed.). New York: McGraw-Hill.

Mitler, M.M., Miller, J.C., Lipsitz, J.J., Walsh, J.K., & Wylie, C.D. (1997). The sleep of long haul truck drivers. *New England Journal of Medicine, 337*, 755–761.

Mittelstaetd, M. (1993, June 17). Ontario revamps psychiatric care. *The Globe and Mail*, p. A10.

Miura, I., & Okamoto, Y. (1989). Comparisons of U.S. and Japanese first graders' cognitive representation of number and understanding of place value. *Journal of Educational Psychology, 81*, 109–113.

Moffitt, A., Kramer, M., & Hoffmann, R. (Eds.). (1993). *The Functions of Dreaming.* Albany: SUNY Press.

Money, J., & Ehrhardt, A.A. (1972). *Man and woman, boy and girl.* Baltimore: Johns Hopkins University Press.

Monk, T.H., & Folkard, S. (1983). Circadian rhythms and shiftwork. In G.R.J. Hockey (Ed.), *Stress and fatigue in human performance* (pp. 97–121). New York: Wiley.

Montgomery, G., & Kirsch, I. (1996). Mechanisms of placebo pain reduction: An empirical investigation. *Psychological Science, 7*, 174–176.

Montepare, J., & Lachman, M. (1989) "You're only as old as you feel": Self-perceptions of age, fears of aging, and life satisfaction from essence to old age. *Psychology and Aging, 4*, 73–78.

Moon, (1997, February 17). Crees, soldiers unite against chill. *The Globe and Mail*, A1–A8.

Moon, C., Cooper, R. P., & Fifer, W. P. (1993). Two-day old infants prefer native language. *Infant Behavior Development, 16*, 495–500.

Moon, Y., & Nass, C. (1998). Are computers scapegoats? Attributions of responsibility in human-computer interaction. *International Journal of Human Computer Studies, 49*, 79–94.

Moore, A.D., & Stambrook, M. (1995). Cognitive moderators of outcome following traumatic brain injury: A conceptual model and implications for rehabilitation. *Brain Injury, 9*, 109–130.

Moore, A.D., Stambrook, M., Peters, L.C., & Lubusko, A. (1991). Family coping and marital adjustment after traumatic brain injury. *Journal of Head Trauma Rehabilitation, 6*, 83–89.

Moore, A.D., Stambrook, M., & Wilson, K.G. (1991). Cognitive moderators in adjustment to chronic illness: Locus of control beliefs following traumatic brain injury. *Neuropsychological Rehabilitation, 1*, 185–198.

Moore, B.C.J. (1982). *An introduction to the psychology of hearing* (2nd ed.). New York: Academic.

Moore, C. (1996). Theories of mind in infancy. *British Journal of Developmental Psychology, 14*, 19–40.

Moore, S.M., & Rosenthal, D.A. (1992). Australian adolescents' perceptions of health-related risks. *Journal of Adolescent Research, 7(2)*, 177–191.

Moore-Ede, M.C., Sulzman, F.M., & Fuller, C.A. (1982). *The clocks that time us.* Cambridge, MA: Havard University Press.

Moran, G., Pederson, D.R., Pettit, P., & Krupka, A., (1992). Maternal sensitivity and infant-mother attachment in a developmentally delayed sample. *Infant Behavior and Development, 15(4)*, 427–442.

Moray, N. (1959). Attention in dichotic listening: Affective cues and the influence of instruction. *Quarterly Journal of Experimental Psychology, 11*, 59–60.

Moreland, R.L., & Beach, S.R. (1992). Exposure effects in the classroom: The development of affinity among students. Journal of Experimental Social Psychology, 28 (3), 255–276.

Moreland, R.L., & Zajonc, R.B. (1982). Exposure effects in person perception: Familiarity, similarity, and attraction. *Journal of Experimental Social Psychology, 18 (5)*, 395–415.

Morgan, H.J., & Janoff-Bulman, R. (1994). Positive and negative self-complexity: Patterns of adjustment following traumatic versus non-traumatic life experiences. *Journal of Social and Clinical Psychology, 13*, 63–85.

Morganstern, K.P. (1973). Implosive therapy and flooding procedures: A critical review. *Psychological Bulletin, 79*, 318–334.

Morris, B., et al. (1993). In: Genetic Link to obesity could lead to therapy, by Chris Pritchard, *Medical Post*, February, 1993, p. 24.

Morrison, T.G., McLeod, L.D., Morrison, M.A., Anderson, D., & O'Connor, W.E. (1997). Gender stereotyping, homonegativity, and misconceptions about sexually coercive behavior among adolescents. *Youth and Society, 28*, 351–382.

Morrongiello, B.A., & Clifton, R.K., (1984). Effects of sound frequency on behavioral and cardiac orienting in newborn- and five-month-old-infants. *Journal of Experimental Child Psychology, 38(3)*, 429–446.

Morrow, K.B., & Sorrell, G.T. (1989). Factors affecting self-esteem, depression, and negative behaviors in sexually abused female adolescents. *Journal of Marriage and the Family, 51*, 677–686.

Morse, J. M., & Morse, R. M. (1988). Cultural variation in the inference of pain. *Journal of Cross Cultural Psychology, 19*, 232–242.

Moscarello, R. (1991). Posttraumatic stress disorder after sexual assault: Its psychodynamics and treatment. *Journal of the American Academy of Psychoanalysis, 19(2)*, 235–253.

Moscovitch, M. (1985). Memory from infancy to old age: Implications for theories of normal and pathological memory. *Annals of the New York Academy of Sciences, 444*, 79–96.

Motowidlo, S.J., Packard, J.S., & Manning, M.R. (1986). Occupational stress: Its causes and consequences for job performance. *Journal of Applied Psychology, 71*, 618–629.

Mottron, L., & Belleville, S. (1993). A study of perceptual analysis in a high-level autistic subjects with exceptional graphic ability. *Brain and Cognition, 23,* 279–309.

Mottron, L., & Belleville, S. (1995). Perspective production in a savant autistic draughtsman. *Psychological Medicine, 24,* 639-648.

Mrosovsky, N. (1986). Sleep researchers caught napping. *Nature, 319,* 536–537.

Mrosovsky, N. (1988). Seasonal affective disorder, hibernation, and annual cycles in animals: Chipmunks in the sky. *Journal of Biological Rhythms, 3,* 189–207.

Mueser, K.T., & Gingerich, S. (1994). *Coping with schizophrenia: A guide for families.* Oakland, CA: Harbinger.

Muir, D. W., & Mitchell, D. E. (1974) Behavioral deficits in cats following early selected visual exposure to contours of a single orientation. *Brain Research, 85,* 459–477.

Mullaney, D.J., Johnson, L.C., Naitoh, P., Friedman, J.K., & Globus, G.G. (1977). Sleep during and after gradual sleep reduction. *Psychophysiology, 14,* 237–244.

Mumby, D.G., Pinel, J.P. & Wood, E.R. (1990). Nonrecurring-items delayed nonmatching-to-sample in rats: A new paradigm for testing nonspatial working memory. *Psychobiology, 18,* 321–326.

Mumford, D.B., Whitehouse, A.M., & Choudry, I.Y. (1992). Survey of eating disorders in English-medium schools in Lahore, Pakistan. *International Journal of Eating Disorders, 11,* 173–184.

Munsinger, H.A. (1978). The adopted child's IQ: A crucial review. *Psychological Bulletin, 82,* 623–659.

Murdoch, D.D., & Pihl, R.O. (1988). The influence of beverage type on aggression in males in the natural setting. *Aggressive Behavior, 14,* 325–335.

Murdoch, D., Pihl, R.O., & Ross, D. (1990). Alcohol and crimes of violence: Present issues. *International Journal of the Addictions, 25(9),* 1065–1081.

Murphy, J. M. (1980). Continuities in community-based psychiatric epidemiology. *Archives of General Psychiatry, 37,* 1215–1223.

Murphy, S.T., & Zajonc, R.B. (1993). Affect, cognition, and awareness: Affective priming with suboptimal and optimal stimulus. *Journal of Personality and Social Psychology, 64,* 723–739.

Murray, S.L. (1999). The quest for conviction: Motivated cognition in romantic relationships. *Psychological Inquiry, 10,* 23–34.

Murray, S.L., & Holmes, J.G. (1993). Seeing virtues in faults: Negativity and the transformation of interpersonal narratives in close relationships. *Journal of Personality and Social Psychology, 65 (4),* 707–722.

Murray, S.L., & Holmes, J.G. (1994). Storytelling in close relationships: The construction of confidence. *Personality and Social Psychology Bulletin, 20,* 650–663.

Murray, S.L., & Holmes, J.G. (1997). A leap of faith? Positive illusions in romantic relationships. *Personality and Social Psychology Bulletin, 23,* 586–604.

Murray, S.L., Holmes, J.G., MacDonald, G., & Ellsworth, P.C. (1998). Through the looking glass darkly? When self-doubts turn into relationship insecurities. *Journal of Personality and Social Psychology, 75,* 1459–1480.

Murrey, G.J., Cross, H.J., & Whipple, J. (1992). Hypnotically created pseudomemories: Further investigation into the "memory distortion or response bias" question. *Journal of Abnormal Psychology, 101,* 75–77.

Mustonen, A., Arms, R.L., & Russell, G.W. (1996). Predictors of sports spectators' proclivity for riotous behaviour in Finland and Canada. *Personality and Individual Differences, 21,* 519–525.

Muter, P., Furedy, J.J., Vincent, A., & Pelcowitz, T. (1993). User-hostile systems and patterns of psychophysiological activity. *Computers in Human Activity, 9,* 105–111.

Muzi, M. J. (2000). *The experience of parenting.* New York: Prentice Hall Press.

Myers, C.E., Ermita, B.R., Harris, K., Hasselmo, M., Solomon, P., & Gluck, M.A. (1996). A computational model of cholinergic disruption of septo-hippocampal activity in classical eyeblink conditioning. *Neurobiology of Learning and Memory, 66,* 51–66.

Myers, D.G., & Diener, E. (1995). Who is happy? *Psychological Science, 6,* 10–19.

Myers, M.F. (1991). Marital therapy with HIV-infected men and their wives. *Psychiatric Annals, 21(8),* 466–470.

Myers, T., Orr, K.W., Locker, D., & Jackson, E.A. (1993). Factors affecting gay and bisexual men's decisions and intentions to seek HIV testing. *American Journal of Public Health, 83(5),* 701–704.

Nadis, S. (1992). The energy-efficient brain: PET scans reveal how the brain delegates mental tasks. *Omni,* February, p. 16.

Nadler, A. (1987) Determinants of help-seeking behaviour: The effects of helper's simliarity, task centrality, and recipient's self-esteem. *European Journal of Social Psychology, 17,* 57–67.

Naglieri, J.A., & Das, J.P. (1990). Planning, attention, simultaneous and successive (PASS) cognitive processes. *Journal of Psychoeducational Assessment, 8,* 303–337.

Nainzadeh, N., Malantic, L.A., Alvarez, M., & Loeser, A.C. (1999). Repetitive strain injury (cumulative trauma disorder): Causes and treatment. *Mount Sinai Journal of Medicine, 66,* 192–196.

Naito, M, Komatsu, S., & Fuke, T. (1994). Normal and autistic children's understanding of their own and others' false belief: A study from Japan. *British Journal of Developmental Psychology, 12,* 403–416.

Nakajima, S. (1986). Suppression of operant responding in the rat by dopamine D1 receptor blockade with SCH 23390. *Physiological Psychology, 14,* 111–114.

Nakajima, S., Kobayashi, Y., & Imada, H. (1995). Contextual control of taste aversion in rats: The effects of context extinction. *The Psychological Record, 45,* 309–318.

Nakajima, S., Liu, S., & Lau, C.L. (1993). Synergistic interaction of D1 and D2 dopamine receptors in the modulation of the reinforcing effect of brain stimulation. *Behavioral Neuroscience, 107(1),* 161–165.

Nakajima, S., & O'Regan, N.B. (1991). The effects of dopaminergic agonists and antagonists on the frequency-response function for hypothalamic self-stimulation in the rat. *Pharmacology, Biochemistry and Behavior, 39,* 465–468.

Nanson, J.L., & Hiscock, M., (1990). Attention deficits in children exposed to alcohol prenatally. *Alcoholism—Clinical and Experimental Research, 14(5),* 656–661.

Naranjo, C.A., & Bremner, K.E. (1993). Behavioral correlates of alcohol intoxication. *Addiction, 88(1),* 25–35.

Nasco, S.A., & Marsh, K.L. (1999). Gaining control through counterfactual thinking. *Personality and Social Psychology Bulletin, 25,* 556–568.

Nash, J.E., & Persaud, T.V.N. (1988). Embryopathic risks of cigarette smoking. *Experimental Pathology, 33,* 65–73.

Nathan, P.E. (1998). Practice guidelines: Not yet ideal. *American Psychologist, 53,* 290–299.

Nathans, J. (1989). The genes for color vision. *Scientific American, 260,* 42–49.

Nathans, J., Thomas, D., & Hogness, D. S. (1986). Molecular genetics of human color vision: The genes encoding blue, green, and red pigments. *Science, 232,* 193–202.

Navarro, R. (1990). *Sound pressure levels of portable stereo headphones.* Indianapolis: Ear Institute of Indiana.

Neale, J.H., Barker, J.L., Uhl, G.R., & Snyder, S.H. (1978). Enkephalin-containing neurons visualized in spinal cord cultures. *Science, 201,* 467–469.

Neale, M. A., & Bazerman, M.H. (1985). The effects of framing and negotiator overconfidence on bargaining behaviors and outcomes. *Academy of Management Journal, 28,* 34–49.

Necheff. J. (2000, May 27). Stormy weather cuts victory celebration short. *Winnipeg Free Press.*

Needleman, H.L., Schell, A., Bellinger, D, Leviton, A., & Allred, E.N. (1990). The long term effects of exposure to low dosages of lead in childhood: An 11-year follow-up report. *New England Journal of Medicine, 322,* 83–88.

Neher, A. (1991). Maslow's theory of motivation: A critique. *Journal of Humanistic Psychology, 31,* 89–112.

Neher, A. (1996). Jung's theory of archetypes: A critique. *Journal of Humanistic Psychology, 31,* 89–112.

Neisser, U. (1991). A case of misplaced nostalgia. *American Psychologist, 46,* 34–36.

Neisser, U., Boodoo, G., Bouchard, T.J.Jr., Bykin, A.W., Brody, N., Ceci, S.J., Halpern, D.F., Loehlin, J.C., Perloff, R., Sternberg, R.J., & Urbina, S. (1996). Intelligence: Knowns and unknowns. *American Psychologist, 51,* 77–101.

Nelson, G. (1996). The prevention of mental health problems in Canada: A survey of provincial policies, structures and programs. *Canadian Psychology, 37,* 161–172.

Nelson, M.J., Lamke, T.A., & French, J.L. (1973). *The Henmon-Nelson Tests of Mental Ability.* Riverside, CA: Riverside.

Nelson, T.M., Evelyn, B., & Taylor, R. (1992). Experimental intercomparisons of younger and older driver perception. *International Journal of Aging and Human Development, 36(3),* 239–253.

Netting, N.S. (1992). Sexuality in youth culture: Identity and change. *Adolescence, 27(108),* 961–976.

Neugarten, B.L. (1979). Time, age, and the life cycle. *American Journal of Psychiatry, 136,* 887–894.

Neugarten, B.L. (1987). The changing meaning of age. *Psychology Today, 21,* 29–33.

Newcomb, A.F., & Bagwell, C.L. (1995). Children's friendship relations: A meta-analytic review. *Psychological Bulletin, 117,* 306–347.

Newcombe, N., & Huttenlocher, J. (1992). Children's early ability to solve perspective-taking problems. *Developmental Psychology, 28,* 635–643.

Newell, A., & Rosenbloom, P.S. (1981). Mechanisms of skill acquisition and the law of practice. In J.R. Anderson (Ed.), *Cognitive skills and their acquisition* (pp.1–55). Hillsdale, NJ: Erlbaum.

Newman, J.P., Widom, C.S., & Nathan, S. (1985). Passive avoidance in syndromes of disinhibition: Psychopathy and extraversion. *Journal of Personality and Social Psychology, 48,* 1316–1327.

Newton, J., Toby, O., Spence, S.H., & Schotte, D. (1995). Cognitive behavioral therapy versus EMG biofeedback in the treatment of chronic low back pain. *Behaviour Research and Therapy, 33,* 691–697.

Ney, P.G., Fung, T. & Wickett, A.R. (1993). Child neglect: The precursor to child abuse. *Pre- and Perinatal Psychology Journal, 8(2),* 95–112.

Nicher & Parker. (1994, September/October). *Psychology Today, 9.*

Nicholls, A.L., & Kennedy, J.M., (1992). Drawing development: From similarity of features to direction. *Child Development, 63(1),* 227–241.

Nickerson, R. S. (1998). Confirmation bias: A ubiquitous phenomenon in many guises. *Review of General Psychology, 2,* 175–220.

Nicole, S.E., & Gottesman, I.I. (1983). Clues to the genetics and neurobiology of schizophrenia. *American Scientist, 71,* 398–404.

Nielsen, T.A. (1993). Changes in the kinesthetic content of dreams following somatosensory stimulation of leg muscles during REM sleep. *Dreaming Journal of the Association for the Study of Dreams, 3(2),* 99–113.

Nietzel, M.T., & Himelein, M.J. (1986). Prevention of crime and delinquency. In B. A. Edelstein & L. Mitchelson (Eds.), *Handbook of prevention.* New York: Plenum.

Nietzel, M.T., Speltz, M.L., McCauley, E.A., & Bernstein, D.A. (1998). *Abnormal psychology.* Boston: Allyn & Bacon.

Nilsson, L. G., & Cohen, R. L. (1988). Enrichment and generation in the recall of enacted and non-enacted instructions. In M. M. Gruneberg, P. E. Morris, & R. N. Sykes (Eds.), *Practical aspects of memory: Current research and issues: Vol. 1. Memory in everyday life* (pp. 427–432). Chichester, England: Wiley.

Nisan, M., & Kohlberg, L. (1982). Universality and variation in moral judement: A longitudinal and cross-sectional study in Turkey. *Child Development, 53*, 865–876.

Nixon, S. J. (1999). Neurocognitive performance in alcoholics: Is polysubstance abuse important? *Psychological Science, 10*, 181–185.

Nixon, S. J., Paul, R., & Phillips, M. (1998). Cognitive efficiency in alcoholics and polysubstance abusers. *Alcoholism: Clinical and Experimental Research, 22*, 1414–1420.

Noble, B.P. (1993, June, 13). *Staying bright-eyed in the wee hours.* New York Times, pp. F1, F11.

Noble, E.K., et al. (1994). In Big Brothers find gene blamed for obesity, by Susan Peterson, *Toronto Star,* March 15, 1994, p. C2.

Nolen-Hoeksema, S. (1990). *Sex differences in depression.* Stanford, CA: Stanford University Press.

Nopoulos, P.C., & Andreasen, N.C. (1999). Gender differences in neuroimaging findings. In E. Leibenluft (Ed.), *Gender differences in mood and anxiety disorders: From bench to bedside* (pp. 1–30). Washington, DC: American Psychiatric Press.

Norcross, J.C., Alford, B.A., & DeMichele, J.T. (1992). The future of psychotherapy: Delphi data and concluding observation. *Psychotherapy, 29*, 150–158.

Norman, D.A., & Shallice, T. (1985). Attention to action: Willed and automatic control of behavior. In R.J. Davidson, G.E. Schwartz & D. Shapiro (Eds.), *Consciousness and self-regulation: Vol. 4. Advances in research and theory* (pp. 2–18). New York: Plenum Press.

Norris, F.H., & Murrell, S.A. (1990). Social support, life events, and stress as modifiers of adjustment to bereavement by older adults. *Psychology and Aging, 5*, 429–436.

Northcraft, G.B., & Neale, M.A. (1987). Experts, amateurs, and real estate: An anchoring-and-adjustment perspective on property pricing in decision. *Organizational Behavior and Human Decision Processes, 39*, 94–97.

Norton, A., & Moorman, J.E. (1987). Current trends in marriage and divorce among American women. *Journal of Marriage and the Family, 49*, 3–14.

Novick, B.E. (1989). Pediatric AIDS: A medical overview. In J.M. Seibert & R.A. Olson (Eds.), *Children, adolescents, and AIDS* (pp. 1–23). Lincoln: University of Nebraska Press.

Novy, D..M., Nelson, D.V., Francis, D.J., & Turk, D.C. (1995). Perspectives of chronic pain: An evaluative comparison of restrictive and comprehensive models. *Psychological Bulletin, 118*, 238–247.

Nyhan, W.L. (1987). Phenylalanine and mental retardation (PKU). In G. Adelman (Ed.), *Encyclopedia of neuroscience* (Vol. 2, pp. 940–942). Boston: Birkhauser.

O'Brien, S.J., & Vertinsky, P.A. (1991). Unfit survivors: Exercise as a resource for aging women. *Gerontologist, 31(3)*, 347–357.

O'Connor, I., Gareau, D., & Borgeat, F. (1995). *Biofeedback and Self Regulation, 20*, 111–122.

O'Neill, D.K. (1996). Two-year-old children's sensitivity to a parent's knowledge state when making requests. *Child Development, 67(2)*, 659-677.

O'Sullivan, C.S., & Durso, F.T. (1984). Effects of schema-incongruent information on memory for stereotypical attributes. *Journal of Personality and Social Psychology, 47*, 55–70.

O'Sullivan, J.R., & Joy, R.M. (1994). If at first you don't succeed: Children's metacognition about reading problems. *Contemporary Educational Psychology, 19*, 118–127.

O'Sullivan, J.T., (1993). Preschooler's beliefs about effort, incentives, and recall. *Journal of Experimental Child Psychology, 53(3)*, 396–414.

O'Sullivan, J.T. (1997). Effort, interest, and recall: Beliefs and behaviors of preschoolers. *Journal of Experimental Child Psychology, 65*, 25–42.

O'Sullivan, J. T., & Howe, M. L. (1995). Metamemory and memory construction. *Consciousness and Cognition: An International Journal, 4*, 104–110.

O'Sullivan, J. T., & Howe, M. L. (1998). A different view of metamemory with illustrations from children's beliefs about long-term retention. *European Journal of Education, 13*, 9–28.

Oaksford, M., Morris, F., Grainger, B., & Williams, J.M.G. (1996). Mood, reasoning, and central executive processes. *Journal of Experimental Psychology: Learning, Memory and Cognition, 22*, 476–492.

Offord, D.R., Bolyl, M.H., Campbell, D., Goering, P., Lin, E., Wong, M., & Racine, Y.A. (1996). One-year prevalence of psychiatric disorder in Ontarians 15 to 64 years of age. *Canadian Journal of Psychiatry, 41*, 559–563.

Ofosu, H.B., Lafreniere, K.D., & Senn, C.Y. (1998). Body image perception among women of African descent: A normative context? *Feminism and Psychology, 8*, 303–323.

Ofshe, R.J. (1992). Inadvertent hypnosis during interrogation: False confession due to dissociative state, misidentified multiple personality, and the satanic cult hypothesis. *International Journal of Clinical and Experimental Hypnosis, 40*, 125–156.

Ogbu, J.U. (1994). From cultural differences to differences in cultural frames of references. In P.M. Greenfield, R.R. Cocking (Eds.), *Cross-cultural roots of minority child development* (pp. 365–391). Hillsdale, NJ: Erlbaum.

Ohlott, P.J. Ruderman, M.N., & McCauley, C.D. (1994). Gender differences in managers' developmental job experiences. *Academy of Management Journal, 37*, 46–67.

Olders, H. (1989). Mourning and grief as healing processes in psychotherapy. *Canadian Journal of Psychiatry, 34(4)*, 271–278.

Oldham, G.R., Cuings, A., Mischel, L.J., Schmidtke, J.M., & Zhou, J. (1995). Listen while you work? Quasi-experimental relations between personal-stereo headset use and employee work responses. *Journal of Applied Psychology, 80(5)*, 547–564.

Olff, M. (1999). Stress, depression and immunity: The role of defense and coping styles. *Psychiatry Research, 85*, 7–15.

Olson, J. M., Maio, G.R., & Hobden, K. L. (1999). The (null) effects of exposure to disparagement humor on stereotypes and attitudes. *Humor: International Journal of Humor Research,12*, 195–219.

Olson, J. M., & Zanna, M. P. (1993). Attitudes and attitude change. *Annual Review of Psychology, 44*, 117–154.

Olsson, P.A. (1989). Psychodrama and group therapy approaches to alexithymia. In D. A. Halperin (Ed.), *Group Psychodynamics: New paradigms and new perspectives.* Chicago: Year Book Medical.

One drinking binge may result in fetal brain damage. (2000, February 11). *Whitehorse Star,* p. 26.

Orbach, I., Kedem, P., Gorchover, O., Apter, A., & Tyano, S. (1993). Fears of death in suicidal and nonsuicidal adolescents. *Journal of Abnormal Psychology, 102*, 553–558.

Orlinsky, D.E., & Howard, K.E. (1987). The relation of process to outcome in psychotherapy. In S. L. Garfield & A. E. Bergin (Eds.), *Handbook of psychotherapy and behavior change* (3rd ed.). New York: Wiley.

Orsillo, S.M., Roemer, L., Litz, B.T., Ehlich, P., & Friedman, M.J. (1998). Psychiatric symptomatology associated with contemporary peacekeeping: An examination of post-mission functioning among peacekeepers in Somalia. *Journal of Traumatic Stress, 11*, 611–625.

Oscar-Berman, M., Shagrin, B., Evert, D. L., & Epstein, C. (1997). Impairments of brain and behavior: The neurological effects of alcohol. *Alcohol Health & Research World, 21*, 63–75.

Osterman, K., Bjorkqvist, K., Lagerspetz, K. Kaukianainen, A., Hauesmann, L.W., & Fraczek, A. (1994). Peer and self-estimated aggression and victimization in 8-year-old children from five ethnic groups. *Aggressive Behavior, 20*, 411–428.

Otis, A.S., & Lennon, R.T. (1967). *The Otis-Lennon Mental Ability Tests.* Los Angeles: Psychological Corp.

Ottati, V.C.., & Isbell, L.M. (1996). Effects of mood during exposure to target information on subsequently reported judgments: An on-line model of misattribution and correction. *Journal of Personality and Social Psychology, 71*, 39-53.

Oulette-Kobasa, S.C., & Puccetti, M.C. (1983). Personality and social resources in stress resistance. *Journal of Personality and Social Psychology, 45*, 836–850.

Ozier, M., & Morris, S. (1987). Judgement of morality: How men and women think about men and women. *Canadian Psychology, 28*, 448 (abstr.).

Padian, N.S., Shiboski, S., & Jewel, N. (1990)/ The effects of the number of exposures on the risk of heterosexual HIV transmission. *Journal of Infectious Diseases, 161*, 883–887.

Page, J.B., Fletcher, J., True, W.R. (1988). Psychosociocultural perspectives on chronic cannabis use: The Costa Rica follow-up. *Journal of Psychoactive Drugs, 20*, 57–65.

Paivio, A. (1983).The mind's eye in arts and science. *Poetics, 12*, 1–18

Paivio, A. (1990). *Mental representations: A dual coding approach.* New York: Oxford.

Paivio, A., Walsh, M., & Bons, T. (1994). Concreteness effects on memory: When and why? *Journal of Experimental Psychology: Learning, Memory, and Cognition, 20*, 1196–1204.

Palace, E.M. (1995). A cognitive-physiological process model of sexual arousal and response. *Clinical Psychology Science and Practice, 2*, 370–384.

Palmer, C.T. (1993). Anger, aggression, and humor in Newfoundland floor hockey: an evolutionary analysis. *Aggressive Behavior, 19(3)*, 167–173.

Palmer, S.E. (1992). Common region: A new principle of perceptual grouping. *Cognitive Psychology, 24*, 436–447.

Pancer, S.M., Brown, S.D., Gregor, P., & Claxton-Oldfield, S.P. (1992). Causal attributions and the perception of political figures. *Canadian Journal of Behavioural Science, 24(3)*, 371–381.

Paquette, C., Bourassa, M., & Peretz, I. (1996). Left ear advantage in pitch perception of complex tones without energy at the fundamental frequency. *Neuropsychologia, 34*, 153–157.

Parkin, A.J. (1993). *Memory: phenomena, experiment, and theory.* Oxford: Blackwell Publishers.

Parkin, A.J., & Walter, B.M. (1992). Recollective experience, normal aging, and frontal dysfunction. *Psychology and Aging, 7*, 290–298.

Passman, R.H., & Weisberg, P., (1975). Mothers and blankets as agents for promoting play and exploration by young children in a novel environment: The effects of social and nonsocial attachment objects. *Developmental Psychology, 11(2)*,170–177.

Patrick, C.J., Bradley, M.M., & Lang, P.J. (1993). Emotion in the criminal psychopath: Startle reflex modulation. *Journal of Abnormal Psychology, 102*, 83–92.

Patterson, F. (1978). Conversations with a gorilla. *National Geographic, 154*, 438–465.

Paul, G.L. (1982). *The development of a "transportable" system of behavioral assessment for chronic patients.* Invited address, University of Minnesota, Minneapolis.

Paul, G.L., & Lentz, R.J. (1977). *Psychosocial treatment of chronic mental patients: Milieu versus social-learning programs.* Cambridge, MA: Harvard University Press.

Paul, S.M. (1985). The Advanced Raven's Progressive Matrices: Normative data for an American university population and an examination of the relationship with Spearman's "g." *Journal of Experimental Education, 54*, 95–100.

Paulhus, D.L., Bruce, M.N., & Trapnell, P.D. (1995). Effects of self-presentation strategies on personality profiles and their structure. *Personality and Social Psychology Bulletin, 21(2)*, 100–108.

Pavlov, I.P. (1927). *Conditioned reflexes.* (G.V. Anrep, Trans.). London: Oxford University Press.

Payne, D.G. (1987). Hyperamnesia and reminiscence in recall: A historical and empirical review. *Psychological Bulletin, 101*, 5-27.

Payne, J.W. (1994). Thinking aloud: Insights into information processing. *Psychological Science, 5,* 241–248.

Peal, E., & Lambert, W.E. (1962). The relation of bilingualism to intelligence. *Psychological Monographs, 76,* 1–23.

Pearce, J.M. (1986). A model for stimulus generalization in Pavlovian conditioning. *Psychological Review, 94,* 61–73.

Pederson, D.R., Moran, K.G., Sitka, C., Compbell, K., Ghesquire, K., & Acton, H. (1990). Maternal sensitivity and the security of infant-mother attachment: A Q-sort study. *Child Development, 61(6),* 1974–1983.

Pegg, J.E., Werker, J.F., & McLeod, P.J., (1992). Preference for infant-directed over adult-directed speech: Evidence from 7-week-old infants. *Infant Behavior and Development, 15(3),* 325–345.

Pelletier, K.R. (1986). *What can centenarians teach us?* In K. Dychtwald (Ed.), *Wellness and health promotion for the elderly.* Rockville, MD: Aspen.

Pelletier, L.G., & Vallerand, R.J. (1990). L'Echelle Revisee de Conscience de Soi: Une traduction et une validitation Canadienne-Francaise due Revised Self-Consiousness Scale. (The Revised Self-Consciousness Scale: A translation and a French Canadian validation of the Revised Self-Consciousness scale.) *Canadian Journal of Behavioural Science, 22,* 191–206.

Pelletier, L.G., Fortier, M.S., Vallerand, R.J., Tuson, K.M., et al. (1995). Toward a new measure of intrinsic motiviation, extrinsic motiviation, and amotivation in sports: The Sport Motivation Scale (SMS). *Journal of Sport and Exercise Psychology, 17(1),* 35–53.

Penfield, W. & Milner, B. (1958). Memory deficit produced by bilateral lesions in the hippocampal zone. *Archives of Neurology & Psychiatry. 79,* 475–497.

Penhune, V.B., Zatorre, R.J., & Feindel, W.H. (1999). The role of auditory cortex in retention of rhythmic patterns as studied in patients with temporal lobe removals including Heschl's gyrus. *Neuropsychologica, 37,* 315–331.

Pennebaker, J.W. (1983). Accuracy of symptom perception. In A. Baum, S.E. Taylor, & J. Singer (Eds.), *Handbook of psychology and health* (Vol. 4, pp. 189–218). Hillsdale, NJ: Erlbaum.

Pennebaker, J.W. (2000). Psychological factors influencing the reporting of physical symptoms. In A.A. Stone, & J.S. Turkkan (Eds.), *The science of self-report: Implications for research and practice* (pp. 299–315). Mahwah, NJ: Lawrence Erlbaum Associates, Inc.

Pennington, N., & Hastle, R. (1993). A theory of explanation-based decision making. In G.A. Klein, J. Orasanu, R. Calderwood, & C.E. Zsambok (Eds.), *Decision making in action: Models and methods* (pp. 188–201). Norwood, NJ: Ablex.

Peplar, D.J., & Craig, W.M. (1995). A peek behind the fence: Naturalistic observations of aggressive children with remote audiovisual recording. *Developmental Psychology, 31,* 548–553.

Peretz, I. (in press, 1997). Can we lose memory for music? A case of music agnosia in a nonmusician. *Journal of Cognitive Neuroscience.*

Peretz, I., & Kolinsky, R. (1993). Boundaries of separability between melody and rhythm in music discrimination: A neuropsychological perspective. *Quarterly Journal of Experimental Psychology Human Experimental Psychology, 46A(2),* 301–325.

Peretz, I., Kolinsky, R., Tramo, M., Labrecque, R., et al. (1994). Functional dissociations following bilateral lesions of auditory cortex. *Brain, 117(6),* 1283–1301.

Perlini, A.H., Haley, A., & Buczel, A. (1998). Hypnosis and reporting biases: Telling the truth. *Journal of Research in Personality, 32,* 13–32.

Perls, F. S. (1969). *Gestalt therapy verbatim.* Lafayette, CA: Real People Press.

Perreault, Y. (1995). AIDS grief: "Out of the closet and into the boardrooms": The bereaved caregivers. *Journal of Palliative Care, 11(2),* 34–37.

Persad, S.M., & Polivy, J. (1993). Differences between depressed and nondepressed individuals in the recognition of and response to facial emotional cues. *Journal of Abnormal Psychology, 102(3),* 358–368.

Persinger, M.A. (1993) Transcendental Meditationsuper (TM) and general meditation are associated with enhanced complex partial epileptic-like signs: Evidence for "cognitive" kindling? *Perceptual and Motor Skills, 76,* 80–82.

Peters, J.F. (1987). Youth, family and employment. *Adolescence, 22(86),* 465–473.

Peters, M., & Ivanoff, J. (1999). Performance asymmetries in computer mouse control of right-handers, and left-handers with left- and right-handed mouse experience. *Journal of Motor Behavior, 31,* 86–94.

Petersen, S.E., Fox, P.T., Mintun, M.A., Posner, J.L., & Raichle, M.E. (1989). Studies of the processing of single words using averaged positron emission tomographic measurements of cerebral blood flow change. *Journal of Cognitive Neuroscience, 1,* 153–170.

Peterson, C. (1996). The preschool child witness: Error in accounts of traumatic injury. *Canadian Journal of Behavioural Science, 28,* 36–42.

Peterson, C., & Bell, M. (1996). Children's memory for traumatic injury. *Child Development, 67,* 3045–3070.

Peterson, C., & Biggs, M. (1997). Interviewing children about trauma: Problems with "specific" questions. *Journal of Traumatic Stress, 10,* 279–290.

Peterson, C., Parsons, T., & Dean, Myra. (2000). Providing misleading and reinstatement information a year after it happened: Effects on long-term memory. *Memory.* (In press).

Peterson, C., & Rideout, R. (1998). Memory for medical emergencies experienced by 1- and 2-year-olds. *Developmental Psychology, 34,* 1059–1072.

Peterson, D.W. (1981). Games in school psychology supervision. *School Psychology Review, 10* (4), 4450451.

Peterson, L. R., & Peterson, M. J. (1959). Short-term retention of individual verbal items. *Journal of Experimental Psychology, 58,* 193–198.

Petit, D., Montplaisir, J., Lorrain, D., & Gauthier, S. (1992). Spectral analysis of the rapid eye movement sleep electroencephalogram in right and left temporal regions: A biological marker of Alzheimer's disease. *Annals of Neurology, 32,* 172–176.

Petitto, L.A. (2000). The acquisition of natural signed languages: Lessons in the nature of human language and its biological foundations. In C. Chamberlain, & J.P. Morford (Eds.), *Language acquisition by eye* (pp. 41–50). Mahwah, NJ: Erlbaum.

Peto, R., Lopez, A.D., Boreham, J., Thum, M., & Heath, C. (1992). Mortality from tobacco in developed countries: Indirect estimation from national vital statistics. *Lancet, 339,* 1268–1278.

Petrie, A.J., & Davidson, I.F.W.K. (1995). Toward a grounded theory of parent preschool involvement. Special Issue: Focus on caregivers. *Early Child Development and Care, 111,* 5–17.

Petrie, R. (2000, February 28). Some anagram fun with Saskatchewan. Regina *Leader-Post.*

Pettigrew, T.F. (1997). Generalized intergroup contact effects on prejudice. *Personality and Social Psychology Bulletin, 23,* 173–185.

Petty, M.M., Singleton, B., & Connell, D.W. (1992). An experimental evlauation of an organizational incentive plan in the electric utility industry. *Journal of Applied Psychology, 77,* 427–436.

Petty, R.E., Cacioppo, J.T., Strathman, A.J.., & Priester, J.R. (1994). To think or not to think; Exploring two routes to persuasion. In S. Shavitt & T.C. Brock (Eds.), *Persuasion* (pp. 113–147). Boston: Allyn & Bacon.

Petty, R.E., Fleming, M.A., & White, P.H. (1999). Stigmatized sources and persuasion: Prejudice as a determinant of argument scrutiny. *Journal of Personality and Social Psychology, 76,* 19–34.

Petty, R.E., & Jarvis, B.G. (1996). An individual difference perspective on assessing cognitive processes. In N. Schwarz & S. Sudman (Eds.), *Answering questions: Methodology for determining cognitive and communicative processes in survey research* (pp. 221–257). San Francisco: Jossey-Bass.

Petty, R.E., Unnava, R., & Strathman, A.J. (1991). Theories of attitude change. In T.S. Robertson & H.H. Kassarjian (Eds.), *Handbook of consumer behavior* (pp. 241–280). Englewood Cliffs, NJ: Prentice Hall.

Petty, R.E., & Wegener, D.T. (1999). The elaboration likelihood model: Current status and controversies. In S. Chaiken, & Y. Trope (Eds.), *Dual-process theories in social psychology* (pp. 37–72). New York, NY: Guilford Press.

Pezdek, D., Finger, K, & Hodge, D. (1997) Planting false childhood memories: The role of event plausibility. *Psychological Science, 8,* 437–441.

Pfaffman, C. (1978). The vertebrate phylogyny, neural code, and integrative processess of taste. In E. C. Carterrette & M. P. Friedman (Eds.), *Handbook of perception* (Vol. 6A). New York: Academic.

Pfiffner, L.J., & O'Leary, S.G. (1993). School-based psychological treatment. In J.L. Matson (Ed.), *Handbook of hyperactivity in children* (pp. 234–255). Boston: Allyn & Bacon.

Phillips, A.G., & Fibiger, H.C. (1989). Neuroanatomical bases of intracranial self-stimulation: Untangling the Gordian knot. In J. M. Leibman & S.J. Cooper (Eds.), *The neuropharmacological bases of reward* (pp. 66–105). Oxford: Clarendon Press.

Phillips, A.G., & Fibiger, H.C. (1990). Role of reward and enhancement of conditioned reward in persistance of responding for cocaine. *Behavioral Pharmacology, 1 (4),* 269–282.

Phillips, D.P., & Brugge, J.F. (1985). Progress in neurophysiology of sound localization. *Annual Review of Psychology, 36,* 245–274.

Philpot, R.M., & Kirstein, C.L. (1999). Repeated cocaine exposure: Effects on catecholamines in the nucleus accumbens septi of periadolescent animals. *Pharmacology, Biochemistry and Behavior, 62,* 465–472.

Piaget, J. (1975). *The child's conception of the world.* Totowa, NJ: Littlefield, Adams. (Originally published in 1929).

Pierce, A.E. (1992). The acquisition of passives in Spanish and the question of A-chain maturation. *Language Acquisition A Journal of Developmental Linguistics, 2,* 55–81.

Pierce, J.P., Macaskill, P., & Hill, D. (1990). Long-term effectiveness of mass media led antismoking campaigns in Australia. *American Journal of Public Health, 80,* 565–569.

Pierce, P.F. (1996). When the patient chooses: Describing unaided decisions in health care. *Human Factors, 38,* 187–187.

Pierce, W.D., & Epling, W.F. (1994). The applied importance of research on the matching law. *Journal of Applied Behavior Analysis, 28,* 237–241.

Pihl, R.O. (1995). Violent behavior. *Journal of Psychiatry and Neuroscience, 20(2),* 101–103.

Pihl, R.O., Lau, M.L., & Assaad, J.M. (1997). Aggressive disposition, alcohol, and aggression. *Aggressive Behavior, 23,* 11–18.

Pihl, R.O., & Lemarquand, D. (1998). Serotonin and aggression and the alcohol-aggression relationship. *Alcohol and Alcoholism, 33,* 55–65.

Pihl, R.O., & Peterson, J. (1995). Drugs and aggression: Correlations, crime and human manipulative studies and some proposed mechanisms. *Journal of Psychiatry and Neuroscience, 20(2),* 141–149.

Pihl, R.O., Peterson, J.B., & Lau, M.A. (1993). A biosocial model of the alcohol-aggression relationship. *Journal of Studies of Alcohol, sep suppl 11,* 128–139.

Pihl, R.O., Young, S.N., Harden, P., Plotnick. S., et al. (1995). Acute effect of altered tryptophan levels and alcohol on aggression in normal human males. *Psychopharmacology, 119(4),* 353–360.

Pillow, D.R., Zatura, A.J., & Sandler, I., (1996). Major life events and minor stressors: Identifying mediational links in the stress process. *Journal of Personality and Social Psychology, 70,* 381–394.

Pinel, J.P.J. (1993). *Biopsychology* (2nd ed.). Boston: Allyn & Bacon.

Pines, A., & Aronson, E. (1988). *Career burnout: Causes and cures.* New York: Free Press.

Pinker, S. (1984). Visual cognition: An introduction. *Cognition: International Journal of Cognitive Science, 18,* 1–63.

Pinker, S. (1989). *Learnability and cognition.* Cambridge, MA: MIT Press.

Pinker, S. (1994). *The language instinct.* New York: HarperCollins.

Pinker, S. (1997). *How the mind works.* New York: Norton.

Pinker, S., & Bloom, P. (1990). Natural language and natural selection. *Behavioral and Brain Sciences, 13,* 707–784.

Piper, W.E., & McCallum, M. (1991). Group interventions for persons who have experienced loss: description and evaluative research. *Group Analysis, 24(4),* 363–373.

Plante, T.G., & Rodin, J. (1990). Physical fitness and enhanced psychological health. *Current Psychology: Research and Reviews, 9,* 3–24.

Plechaty, M. (1988). A conjugal curriculum vitae method: Behavioral assessment and treatment of marital problems. *Psychological Reports, 63(1),* 151–159.

Pliner, P. (1994). Development of measures of food neophobia in children. *Appetite, 23(2),* 147–163.

Pliner, P., & Chaiken, S. (1990). Eating, social motives, and self-presentation in women and men. *Journal of Experimental Social Psychology, 26(3),* 240–254.

Pliner, P., Pelchat, M., & Grabski, M. (1993). Reduction of neophobia in humans by exposure to novel foods. *Appetite, 20,* 111–123.

Plomin, R. (1989). Environment and genes: Determinants of behavior. *American Psychologist, 44,* 105–111.

Plomin, R. (1994) *Genetics and experience: The interplay between nature and nurture.* Thousand Oaks, CA: Sage.

Plomin, R., Fulker, D.W., Corley, R., & DeFries, J.C. (1997). Nature, nurture, and cognitive development from 1 to 16 years: A parent-offspring adoption study. *Psychological Science, 8,* 442–447

Plotkin, H. (1997). *Evolution in mind: An introduction to evolutionary psychology.* Cambridge, MA: Harvard University Press.

Plouffe, L., & Gravelle, F. (1989). Age, sex, and personality correlates of self-actualization in elderly adults. *Psychological Reports, 65(2),* 643–647.

Polich, J. (1993). Cognitive brain potentials. *Current Directions in Psychological Science, 3,* 175–178.

Polk, M., & Kertesz, A. (1993). Music and language in degenerative disease of the brain. *Brain and Cognition, 22,* 98–117.

Pomerleau, A., Bolduc, D., Malcuit, G., & Cossette, L., (1990). Pink or blue: Environmental gender stereotypes in the first two years of life. *Sex Roles, 22(5-6),* 359–367.

Pomerleau, A., Malcuit, G. Chamberland, C., Laurendeau, M.C., & Lamarre, G. (1992). Methodological problems in operant learning research with human infants. *International Journal of Psychology, 27(6),* 417–432.

Pomerleau, A., Malcuit, G., & Seguin, R. (1992). Five-month-old girls' and boys' exploratory behaviors in the presence of familiar and unfamiliar toys. *Journal of Genetic Psychology, 153,* 47–61.

Pomerleau, O. F. (1995). Individual differences in sensitivity to nicotine: Implications for genetic research on nicotine dependence. *Behavior Genetics, 25,* 161–177.

Pomerleau, O.F., & Kardia, S.L.R. (1999). Introduction to the featured selection: Genetic research on smoking. *Health Psychology, 18,* 3–6.

Pomerleau, O.F., & Pomerleau, C.S. (1984). Neuroregulators and the reinforcement of smoking: Towards a biobehavioral explanation. *Neuroscience and Biobehavioral Reviews, 8,* 503–513.

Poole, G.D., & Craig, K.D. (1992). Judgements of genuine, suppressed, and faked facial expressions of pain. *Journal of Personality and Social Psychology, 63(5),* 797–805.

Poon, L.W., & Fozard, J.L. (1980). Age and word frequency effects in continuous recognition memory. *Journal of Gerontology, 35,* 77–86.

Pope, A.W., & Bierman, K.L. (1999) Predicting adolescent peer problems and antisocial activities: The relative roles of aggression and dysregulation. *Developmental Psychology, 35,* 335–346.

Pope, K. S., & Vetter, V. A. (1992). Ethical dilemmas encountered by members of the American Psychological Association. *American Psychologist, 47,* 397–411.

Porac, B, & Buller, T. (1990). Overt attempts to change hand preference: A study of a group and individual characteristics. *Canadian Journal of Psychology, 44(4),* 512–521.

Porac, C. (1993). Hand preference and the incidence of accidental unilateral hand injury. *Neuropsychologia, 31(4),* 355–362.

Porter, J., & Weisberg, J. (1992). Overcoming destructive societal values in the treatment of anorexia nervosa: an intensive day treatment model. *Journal of Contemporary Psychotherapy, 22(2),* 77–88.

Porter, R. H., & Winberg, J. (1999). Unique salience for maternal breast odors for newborn infants. *Neuroscience and Biobehavioral reviews, 23,* 439–449.

Porter, S., Yuille, J.C., & Lehman, D.R. (1999). The nature of real, implanted, and fabricated memories for emotional childhood events: Implications for the recovered memory debate. *Law and Human Behaviour 23,* 517–538.

Posner, M.I., & McCandliss, B.D. (1993). Converging methods for investigating lexical access. *Psychological Science, 4,* 305–309.

Posner, M.I., & Petersen, S.E. (1990). The attention system of the human brain. *Annual Review of Neuroscience, 13,* 25–42.

Postman, L., & Phillips, L.W. (1965). Short-term temporal changes in free recall. *Quarterly Journal of Experimental Psychology, 17,* 132–138.

Poucet, B. (1993). Spatial cognitive maps in animals: New hypotheses on their structure and neural mechanisms. *Psychological Review, 100,* 163–182.

Powell, G.N., & Butterfield, D.A. (1994). Investigating the "glass ceiling" phenomenon: An empirical study of actual promotions to top management. *Academy of Management Journal, 37,* 68–86.

Powley, T.L., Opsahl, C.A., Cox, J.E., & Weingarten, H.P. (1980). The role of the hypothalamus in energy homeostasis. In P.J. Morgane & J. Panskepp (Eds.), *Handbook of the hypothalamus. 3A: Behavioral studies of the hypothalamus* (pp. 211–298). New York: Marcel Dekker.

Pranger, T., & Brown, G.T. (1992). Burnout: an issue for psychiatric occupational therapy personnel? *Occupational Therapy in Mental Health, 12(1),* 77–92.

Prapavessis, H., & Grove, J.R. (1998). Self-handicapping and self-esteem. *Journal of Applied Sport Psychology, 10,* 175–184.

Pratt, M.W., Golding, G., Hunter, W., & Norris, J., (1988). From inquiry to judgement: Age and sex differences in patterns of adult moral thinking and information seeking. *International Journal of Aging and Human Development, 27(2),* 109–124.

Pretty, G.M., McCarthy, M.E., & Catano, V.M. (1992). Psychological environments and burnout: Gender considerations within the corporation. *Journal of Organization Behavior, 13(7),* 701–711.

Priest, K. (1985). Adolescents' response to parents' alcoholism. *Social Casework, 66(9),* 533–539.

Priester, J., & Petty, R.E. (1995). Source attributions and pesuasion: Perceived honesty as a determinant of message scrutiny. *Personality and Social Psychology Bulletin, 21,* 637–654.

Prigatano, G.P. (2000). A brief overview of four principles of neuropsychological rehabilitation. In A. Christensen, & B.P. Uzzell (Eds.), *International handbook of neuropsychological rehabilitation* (pp. 115–125). New York: Kluwer Academic/Plenum.

Pritchard, R.M. (1961). Stabilized images on the retina. *Scientific American, 204,* 72–78.

Prkachin, G.C., & Prkachin, K.M. (1994). Adaptation to facial expressions of emotion. *Cognition and Emotion, 8,* 55–64.

Prkachin, K.M. (1992a). The consistency of facial expressions of pain: a comparison across modalities. *Pain, 51(3),* 297–306.

Prkachin, K.M. (1992b). Dissociating spontaneous and deliberate expressions of pain: Signal detection analysis. *Pain, 51(1),* 57–65.

Prkachin, K.M. (1997). The consistency of facial expressions of pain: A comparison across modalities. In P. Ekman, & E.L. Rosenberg (Eds.), *What the face reveals: Basic and Applied studies of spontaneous expression using the Facial Action Coding System (FACS)* (pp. 181–200). New York: Oxford University Press.

Prkachin, K.M., Berzins, S., & Mercer, S.R. (1994). Encoding and decoding of pain expressions: A judgment study. *Pain, 58(2),* 253–259.

Prkachin, K.M., & Craig, K.D. (1995). Expressing pain: The communication and interpretation of facial pain signals. *Journal of Nonverbal Behavior, 19(4),* 191–205.

Prkachin, K.M., Williams-Avery, R.M., Zwaal, C., & Mills, D.E. (1999). Cardiovascular changes during induced emotion: An application of Lang's theory of emotional imagery. *Journal of Psychosomatic Research, 47,* 255–267.

Pruitt, D.G., & Rubin, J.Z. (1986). *Social conflict: Escalation, stalemate, settlement.* New York: Random House.

Ptito, A., Crane, J., Leonard, G., Amsel, R., et. al (1995). Visual-spatial localization by patients with frontal-lobe lesions invading or sparing area 46. *Neuroreport: An International Journal for the Rapid Communication of Research in Neuroscience, 6,* 1781–1784.

Pulkinen, L. (1996). Female and male personality styles: A typological and developmental analysis. *Journal of Personality and Social Psychology, 708,* 1288–1306.

Purvis, A. (1993, December 6). Cursed, yet blessed. *Time, 67.*

Pyke, S.W. (1992). The more things change. *Canadian Psychology, 33,* 713–720.

Pyke, S.W., & Stark-Ademac, C. (1981). Canadian feminism and psychology: The first decade. *Canadian Psychology, 22,* 35–54.

Pylyshyn, Z.W. (1973). What the mind's eye tells the mind's brain: A critique of mental imagery. *Psychological Bulletin, 80,* 1–24.

Pylyshyn, Z.W. (1981). The imagery debate: Analogue media versus tacit knowledge. *Psychological Review, 88,* 16–45.

Pyryt, M.C. (1993). The fulfillment of promise revisited: A discriminant analysis of factors predicting success in the Terman study. *Roeper Review, 15,* 178–179

Quadrel, M.J. (1990). Elicitations of adolescents' risk perceptions: Qualitative and quantitative dimensions. Unpublished doctoral dissertation, Carnegie Mellon University.

Quadrel, M.J., Fischoff, B., & Davis, W. (1993). Adolescent in/vulnerability. *American Psychologist, 48,* 102–116.

Quirion, R. (1993). Colinergenic markers in Alzheimer disease and the autoregulation of acetylcholine release. *Journal of Psychiatry and Neuroscience, 18,* 226–234.

Quitsualik, R. A. (2000, February 25). Lost in translation: Part one. *Nunsiaq News.*

Rabin, M.D., & Cain, W.S. (1984). Determinants of measured olfactory sensitivity. *Perception & Psychophysics, 39,* 281–286.

Rachlin, J.J. (1996). The base rate fallacy reconsidered: Descriptive, normative, and methodological challenges. *Behavioral and Brain Sciences, 19,* 1–53.

Rachman, S. (1990). The determinants of treatment of simple phobias. *Advances in Behaviour Research and Therapy, 12,* 1–30.

Rachman, S.J. (1991) Neo-conditioning and the classical theory of fear acquisition. *Clinical Psychology Review, 11,* 155–173.

Rachman, S.J., & Hodgson, R.J. (1980). *Obsessions and compulsions.* Englewood Cliffs, NJ: Prentice Hall.

Rachman, S.J., & Wilson, G.T. (1980). *The effects of psychological therapy* (2nd ed.). New York, Pergamon Press.

Rae-Grant, Q., & Robson, B.E. (1988). Moderating the morbidity of divorce. *Canadian Journal of Psychiatry, 33(6),* 443–452.

Rainville, P., Hofbauer, R.K., Paus, T., Duncan, G.H., Bushnell, M.C., & Price, D.D. (1999). Cerebral mechanisms of hypnotic induction and suggestion. *Journal of Cognitive Neuroscience, 11,* 110–125.

Raphael, B., Cubis, J., Dunne, M., Lewin, T., & Kelly, B. (1990). The impact of parental loss on adolescents' psychosocial characteristics. *Adolescence, 25,* 689–700.

Rapoport, J.L. (1989). *The boy who couldn't stop washing: The experience and treatment of obsessive-compulsive disorder.* New York: Dutton.

Rapoport, J.L., Ryland, D.H., & Kriete, M. (1992). Drug treatment of canine acral lick: An animal model of obsessive-compulsive disorder. *Archives of General Psychiatry, 37,* 1075–1080.

Rasmussen, T., Milner, B. (1975). Excision of Broca's area without persistent aphasia. In K.J. Zulch, O. Creutzfeldt, & G.C. Gailbraith (Eds.), *Central localization* (pp. 258–263). New York: Springer-Verlag.

Raven, J.C. (1977). *Raven Progressive Matrices.* Los Angeles: Psychological Corp.

Ray, W.J. (1997). EEG complaints of hypnotic susceptibility. *International Journal of Clinical and Experimental Hypnosis, 45,* 301–313.

Raynor, J.O. (1970). Relationships between achievement-related motives, future orientation, and academic performance. *Journal of Personality and Social Psychology, 15,* 28–33.

Raz, S. (1993). Structural cerebral pathology in schizophrenia: Regional or diffuse? *Journal of Abnormal Psychology, 102,* 445–452.

Reason, J.T., & Lucas, D. (1984). Using cognitive diaries to investigate naturally occurring memory blocks. In J. E. Harris & P. E. Morris (Eds.), *Everyday memory actions and absent-mindedness* (pp. 53–70). London: Academic Press.

Rechtschaffen, A., Gilliland, M.A., Bergmann, B.M., & Winter, J.B. (1983). Physiological correlates of prolonged sleep deprivation in rats. *Science, 221,* 182–184.

Reed, S.B., Kirsch, I., Wickless, C., Moffitt, K.H., & Taren, P. (1996). Reporting biases in hypnosis: suggestion or compliance? *Journal of Abnormal Psychology, 105,* 142–145.

Reed, T.E. & Jensen, A.R., (1991). Arm nerve conduction velocity (NCV), brain NCV, reaction time, and intelligence. *Intelligence, 15 (1),* 33–47.

Reed, T.E., & Jensen, A.R. (1993). Conduction velocity in a brain nerve pathway of normal adults correlates with intelligence level. *Intelligence.*

Reeder, G.D., Fletcher, G.J.O., & Furman, K. (1989). The role of observers: Expectations in attitude attribution. *Journal of Experimental Social Psychology, 25,* 168–188.

Reese, H.W., & Rodeheaver, D. (1985). Problem solving and complex decision making, In J.E. Birren & K.W. Schaie (Eds.), *Handbook of the psychology of aging* (2nd ed., pp. 474–499). New York: Van Nostrand Reinhold.

Reeves, A., & Sperling, G. (1986). Attention gating in short-term retention of individual verbal items. *Psychological Review, 93,* 180–206.

Reichman, R.C., Hooper, C., & Corey, L. (1996). Treatment of human immunodeficiency virus infection with saquinavir, zidovudine, and zalcitabine. *New England Journal of Medicine, 334,* 1011–1017.

Reid, L.D. (1990). *Opioids, bulimia, and alcohol abuse and alcoholism.* New York: Springer-Verlag.

Reid, L.D. (1990). Rates of cocaine addiction among newborns. Personal communication, Rensselaer Polytechnic Institute.

Reid, L.D., & Carpenter, D.J. (1990). Alcohol-abuse and alcoholism. In L.D. Reid (Ed.), *Opioids, bulimia, and alcohol abuse and alcoholism* (pp. 23–48). New York: Springer-Verlag.

Reiman, E.M., Fusselman, M.J., Fox, P.T., & Raichle, M.E. (1989). Neuroanatomical correlates of anticipatory anxiety. *Science, 243,* 1071–1074.

Reinecke, J., Schmidt, P., & Ajzen, I. (1996). Application of the theory of planned behavior to adolescents' condom use: A panel study. *Journal of Applied Social Psychology, 26,* 749–772.

Reis, H.T., Senchak, M., & Solomon, B. (1985). Sex differences in the intimacy of social interaction: Further examination of potential explanations. *Journal of Personality and Social Psychology, 48(5),* 1204–1217.

Reissland, N. (1988). Neonatal imitation in the first hour of life: Observations in rural Nepal. *Developmental Psychology, 24,* 464–469.

Renaud, C. S., & Byers, E. S. (1999). Exploring the frequency, diversity and content of university students' positive and negative sexual cognitions. *Canadian Journal of Human Sexuality, 8,* 17–30.

Reneric, J.P., & Bouvard, M.P. (1998). Opiod receptor antagonists in psychiatry: Beyond drug addiction. *CNS Drugs, 10,* 365–382.

Reno, R.R., Cialdini, R.B., & Kallgren, C.A. (1993). The transsituational influence of social norms. *Journal of Personality and Social Psychology, 64,* 104–112.

Rensberger, B. (1993, May 3). The quest for machines that not only listen, but also understand. *Washington Post,* p. 3.

Rentsch, J.R., & Heffner, T.S. (1994). Assessing self-concept: A Gordon's coding scheme using "Whom am I?" responses. *Journal of Social Behavior and Personality, 9,* 283–300.

Repacholi, B.M., & Gopnik, A. (1997). Early reasoning about desires: Evidence from 14- and 18-month-olds. *Developmental Psychology, 33,* 12–21.

Rescorla, R.A. (1988). Pavlovian conditioning: It's not what you think it is. *American Psychologist, 43,* 151–160.

Rescorla, R.A., & Wagner, A.R. (1972). A theory of Pavlovian conditioning: Variations in the effectiveness of reinforcement and nonreinforcement. In A. Black & W.F. Prokasy (Eds.), *Classical conditioning: II. Current research and theory.* New York: Appleton.

Resnick, S.M. (1992). Positron emission tomography in psychiatric illness. *Current Directions in Psychological Science, 1,* 92–98.

Rest, J.R., & Thomas, S.J. (1985). Relation of moral judgment to formal education. *Developmental Psychology, 21,* 709–714.

Revusky, S., & Reilly, S. (1990). Dose effects on heart rate conditioning when phenobarbital is the CS and amphetamine is the US. *Pharmacology, Biochemistry and Behavior, 36,* 933–936.

Rhodewalt, F., & Fairfield, M. (1991). Claimed self-handicaps and the self-handicapper: The relations of reduction in intended effort to performance. *Journal for Research in Personality, 245,* 402–417.

Rice, C. G., Breslin, M., & Roper, R. G. (1987). Sound levels from personal cassette players. *British Journal of Audiology, 21,* 273–278.

Rice, F.P. (1992). *Intimate relationships, marriages, and families.* Mountain View, CA: Mayfield.

Richardson, G., Day, N., & Goldschmidt, L. (1995). *A longitudinal study of prenatal cocain exposure: Infant development at 12 months.* Paper presented at Biennial Meetings of the Society for Research in Child Development, Indianapolis, IN.

Richer, S., (1988). Schooling and the gendered subject: An exercise in planned social change. *Canadian Review of Sociology and Anthropolgy, 25(1),* 98–107.

Rigby, C.S., Deci, E.L., Patrick, B.C., & Ryan, R.M. (1992). Beyond the intrinsic-extrinsic dichotomy: Self-determination in motivation and learning. *Motivation and Emotion, 16,* 165–185.

Rigdon, I.S., Clayton, B.C., & Dimond, M. (1987). Toward a theory of helpfulness for the elderly bereaved: An invitation to a new life. *Advances in Nursing Science, 9,* 32–43.

Rind, B. (1996). Effect of beliefs about weather conditions on tipping. *Journal of Applied Social Psychology, 26(2),* 137–147.

Rind, B., & Bordia, P. (1995). Effect of server's "thank you" and personalization on restaurant tipping. *Journal of Applied Social Psychology, 25(9),* 745–751.

Rind, B., & Bordia, P. (1996). Effects of restaurant tipping of male and female servers drawing a happy, smiling face on the backs of customers' checks. *Journal of Applied Social Psychology, 26(3),* 218–225.

Rind, B., & Kipnis, D. (1999). Changes in self-perceptions as a result of successfully persuading others. *Journal of Social Issues, 55,* 141–156.

Rind, B., & Strohemtz, D. (1999). Effect on restaurant tipping of a helpful message written on the back of customers' checks. *Journal of Applied Social Psychology, 29,* 139–144.

Riskind, J.H., & Maddux, J.E. (1993). Loomingness, helplessness, and fearfulness: An integration of harm-looming and self-efficacy models of fear. *Journal of Social and Clinical Psychology, 12,* 73–89.

Rivers, M., Mullington, J., Stampi, C., & Broughton, R.J. (1994). A program for studies of altered sleep-wake schedules and performance. *Behavior Research Methods, Instruments and Computers, 26(3),* 323–330.

Robert, M. (1990). Observational learning in fish, birds, and mammals: A classified bibliography spanning over 100 years of research. *Psychological Record, 40,* 289–311.

Roberts, D.C., & Bennett, S.A. (1993). Heroin self-administration in rats under a progressive ratio schedule of reinforcement. *Psychopharmacology, 111 (2),* 215–218.

Roberts, D.C.S., & Ranaldi, R. (1995). Effect of dopaminergic drugs on cocaine reinforcement. Symposium: Dopamine receptor subtypes in neurological and psychiatric diseases (1994, Kalamazoo, Michigan). *Clinical Neuropharmacology, 18*(supplement 1), S84–S95.

Robin, A.L., & Foster, L. (1988). *Negotiating adolescence: A behavioral family systems approach to parent-teen conflict.* New York: Guilford Press.

Robins, L. N., & Regier, D. A. (1991). *Psychiatric disorders in America: The epidemiological catchment area.* New York: Free Press.

Robinson, L.A., Berman, J.S., & Neimeyer, R.A. (1990). Psychotherapy for the treatment of depression: A comprehensive review of controlled outcome research. *Psychological Bulletin, 108,* 30–49.

Robinson, R.G., Kubos, K.L., Starr, L.B., Rao, K., & Price, T.R. (1984). Mood disorders in stroke patients: Importance of location of lesion. *Brain, 107,* 81–93.

Rochefort, D.A. (1992). More lessons, of a different kind: Canadian mental health policy in comparative perspective. *Hospital and Community Psychiatry, 43,* 1083–1090.

Rochefort, D. A., & Portz, J. H. (1993). Different systems, shared challenges: Assessing Canadian mental health care from a U.S. perspective. *American Review of Canadian Studies, 23,* 65–82.

Rockman, G.E., Hall, A.M., & Markert, L. (1987). Early weaning effects on voluntary ethanol consumption and stress responsivity in rats. *Physiology and Behavior, 40,* 673–676.

Rodgers, C.D., Paterson, D.H., Cunningham, D.A., Noble, E.G., et al. (1995). Sleep deprivation: Effects on work capacity, self-paced walking, contractile properties and perceived exertion. *Sleep, 18(1),* 30–38.

Rodgers, W.M., & Brawley, L.R. (1991). The role of outcome expectancies in participation motivation. *Journal of Exercise and Sport Psychology, 13(4),* 411–427.

Rodin, J. (1984, April). A sense of control. *Psychology Today,* 38–45.

Rodin, J., & Plante, T. (1989). The psychological effects of exercise. In R.S. Williams & A. Wellece (Eds.), *Biological effects of physical activity.* Champaign, IL: Human Kinetics.

Rodin, J., & Salovey, P. (1989). Health psychology. *Annual Review of Psychology, 40,* 533–580.

Rodin, J., & Slochower, J. (1976). Externality in the nonobese: Effects of environmental responsiveness on weight. *Journal of Personality and Social Psychology, 33,* 338–344.

Roediger, H.L., III., & McDermott, K.B. (1996). False perceptions of false memories. *Journal of Experimental Psychology: Learning, Memory, and Cognition, 22,* 814–816.

Roediger, H. L., III, & Wheeler, M. A. (1993). Hypermnesia in episodic and semantic memory: Response to Bahrick and Hall. *Psychological Science, 4,* 207–208.

Roese, N.J. (1997). Counterfactual thinking. *Psychological Bulletin, 121,* 133–148.

Roese, N.J., Olsen, J.M., Borenstein, M.N., Martin, A., & Shores, A.L. (1992). Same-sex touching behavior: The moderating role of homophobic attitudes. *Journal of Nonverbal Behavior, 16(4),* 249–259.

Rogers, C.R. (1977). *Carl Rogers on personal power: Inner strength and its revolutionary impact.* New York: Delacorte.

Rogers, C. R. (1982, August). Nuclear war: A personal response. *American Psychological Association,* pp. 6–7.

Rogers, R. W. (1980). Subjects' reactions to experimental deception. Unpublished manuscript, University of Alabama.

Rogoff, B. (1990). *Apprenticeship in thinking: Cognitive development in social context.* Oxford, England: Oxford University Press.

Rogoff, B., & Mistry, J. (1985). Memory development in cultural contexts. In M. Pressley, C. Barinerd (Eds.), *The cognitive side of memory development.* New York: Springer-Verlag.

Roopnarine, J.L, Talukder, E., Jain, D., Joshi, P., & Srivastav, P. (1990). Characteristics of holding, patterns of play, and social behaviors between parents and infants in New Dehli, India. *Developmental Psychology, 26(4),* 667–673.

Rosch, E. H. (1973). Natural categories. *Cognitive Psychology, 4,* 328–349.

Rosch, E. H. (1975). The nature of mental codes for color categories. Journal of *Experimental Psychology: Human Perception and Performance, 1,* 303–322.

Rosebush, P.A. (1998). Psychological intervention with military personnel in Rwanda. *Military Medicine, 163,* 559–563.

Rosen, K.S., & Rothbaum, F. (1993). Quality of parental caregiving and security of attachment. *Developmental Psychology, 29,* 358–367.

Rosen, L.N., & Rosenthal, N.E. (1991). Seasonal variations in mood and behavior in the general population: A factor-analytic approach. *Psychiatry Research, 38,* 271–283.

Rosen, L.N., Targum, S.D., Terman, M., Bryant, M.J., Hoffman, H., Kasper, S.F., Hamovit, J.R., Docherty, J.P., Welch, B., & Rosenthal, N.E. (1990). Prevalence of seasonal affective disorder at four latitudes. *Psychiatry Research, 31,* 131–144.

Rosenberg, E.L., & Ekman, P. (1995). Conceptual and methodological issues in the judgment of facial expressions of emotion. *Motivation and Emotion, 19,* 111–138.

Rosenblith, J.F. (1992). *In the beginning: Development from conception to age two.* Newbury Park, CA: Sage.

Rosenfield, D., Folger, R., & Adelman, H.F. (1980). When rewards reflect competence: A qualification of the overjustification effect. *Journal of Personality and Social Psychology, 39,* 368–376.

Rosenman, R.H. (1988). The impact of certain emotions in cardiovascular disorders. In M.P. Janisse (Ed.), *Individual differences, stress, and health psychology* (pp. 1–23). New York: Springer-Verlag.

Rosenstein, D., & Oster, H. (1988). Differential facial responses to four basic tastes in newborns. *Child Development, 59,* 1555–1568.

Rosenstock, I.M. (1974). The health belief model and preventive health behavior. *Health Education Monographs, 2,* 354–386.

Rosenthal, C.J., Sulman, J. & Marshall, V.W. (1993). Depressive symptoms in family caregivers of long-stay patients. *Gerontologist, 33(2),* 249–257.

Rosenthal, D., Gifford, S., & Moore, S. (1998). Safe sex or safe love: Competing discourses? *AIDS Care, 10,* 35–47.

Rosenthal, G.T., Barlow, S., Folse, E.J., & Whipple, G.J. (1998). Role-play games and national guardsmen compared. *Psychological Reports, 82,* 169–170.

Rosenthal, R.R., & DePaulo, B.M. (1979). Sex differences in eaves-dropping on nonverbal cues. *Journal of Personality and Social Psychology, 37,* 273–285.

Roskies, E. (1987). *Stress management for the healthy Type A.* New York: Guilford Press.

Roskies, E. (1988). A new approach to managing stress. *Advances, 4,* 29–43.

Ross, C. A. (1994). *The Osiris complex: Case studies in multiple personality.* Toronto: University of Toronto Press.

Ross, C.A. (1997). Dissociative identity disorder: Diagnosis, clinical features, and treatment of multiple personality (2nd ed.). New York: Wiley.

Ross, C.A., & Anderson, G. (1988). Phenomenological overlap of multiple personality disorder and obsessive-compulsive disorder. *Journal of Nervous and Mental Disease, 176(5),* 295–299.

Ross, C. A., Miller, S. D., Bjornson, M. A., Reagor, P., Fraser, G. A., & Anderson G. (1991). Abuse histories in 102 cases of multiple personality. *Canadian Journal of Psychiatry, 36,* 97–101.

Ross, L.L., & McBean, D. (1995). A comparison of pacing contingencies in classes using a personalized system of instruction. *Journal of Applied Behavior Analysis, 28,* 87–88.

Ross, M., McFarland, C., Conway, M., & Zanna, M.P. (1983). Reciprocal relation between attitudes and behavior recall: Committing people to newly formed attitudes. *Journal of Personality and Social Psychology, 45 (2),* 257–267.

Ross, M., & Sicoly, F. (1979). Egocentric biases in availability and attribution. *Journal of Personality and Social Psychology, 37(3),* 322–336.

Rossberg-Gempton, I., & Poole, G.D. (1993). The effect of open and closed postures on pleasant and unpleasant emotions. Special issue: research in the creative arts therapies. *Arts in Psychotherapy, 20(1),* 75–82.

Rosselli, F., Skelly, J.J., & Mackie, D.M. (1995). Processing rational and emotional messages: The cognitive and affective mediation of persuasion. *Journal of Experimental Social Psychology, 31(2),* 163–190.

Roter, D.L., Ewart, C.K. (1992). Emotional inhibition in essential hypertension: Obstacle to communication dring medical visits? *Health Psychology, 11,* 163–169.

Roter, D.L., & Hall, J.A. (1989). Studies of doctor-patient interaction. *Annual Review of Public Health, 10,* 163–180.

Rothman, K.R., Cristina, I.C. Flanders., D., & Fried, M.P. (1980). Epidemology of laryngeal cancer. In P.E. Sartwell (Ed.), *Epidemological Reviews* (Vol. 2, pp. 195–209). Baltimore: Johns Hopkins University Press.

Rotter, J. B. (1982). *The development and applications of social learning theory: Selected papers.* New York: Praeger.

Rovee-Collier, C.K. (1987). Learning and memory. In J.D. Osofky (Ed.), *Handbook of infant development* (2nd ed., pp. 98–148). New York: Wiley.

Rowe, D. C. (1997). Genetics, temperament, and personality. In R. Hogan, J. Johnson & S. Briggs (Eds.), *Handbook of personality psychology* (pp. 369–386). New York: Academic Press.

Rowe, D.C., Vazsonyi, A.T., & Flannery, D.J. (1995). Ethnic and racial similarity in developmental process: A study of academic achievement. *Psychological Science, 6,* 33–38.

Rowland, D.L., Cooper, S.E., & Slob, A.K. (1996). Genital and psychoaffective response to erotic stimulation in sexually functional and dysfunctional men. *Journal of Abnormal Psychology, 105,* 194–203.

Rowlison, R.T., & Felner, R.D. (1988). Major life events, hassles, and adaptation in adolescence: Confounding in the conceptualization and measurement of life stress and adjustment revisited. *Journal of Personality and Social Psychology, 55,* 432–444.

Rozin, E.P., & Michener, L. (1996, April 8). Cited in "Is it the chocolate talking or are you really in love?" *Wall Street Journal,* p. B1.

Rozin, P. (1996). Toward a psychology of food and eating: From motivation to module to model to marker, morality, meaning, and metaphor. *Current Directions in Psychological Science, 6,* 18–20.

Rozin, P., Dow, S., Moscovitch, M ., & Rajaram, S. (1998). What causes humans to begin and end a meal? A role for memory for what has been eaten, as evidenced by a study of multiple meal eating in amnesic patients. *Psychological Science, 9,* 392–439.

Rozin, P., Markwith, M., & Nemeroff, C. (1992). Magical contagion beliefs and fear of AIDS. *Journal of Applied Social Psychology, 22,* 1081–1092.

Rubin, J. Z. (1985). Deceiving ourselves about deception: Comment on Smith and Richardson's "Amelioration of deception and harm in psychological research." *Journal of Personality and Social Psychology, 48,* 252–253.

Ruble, D.N., & Martin, C. (1998). Gender development. In W. Damon (Series Ed.)., & N. Eisenberg (Vol. Ed.), *Handbook of child psychology, Vol, 3, Social, emotional, and personality development* (5th ed., pp. 933–1016). New York: Wiley.

Rucker, N., & Greene, V. (1995). The myth of the invulnerable self of adolescence. *American Journal of Psychoanalysis, 55,* 369–379.

Ruggiero, K.M., & Marx, D.M. (1999). Less pain and more to gain: Why high status group members blame their failure on discrimination. *Journal of Personality and Social Psychology, 77,* 774–784.

Rumelhart, D. E., Hinton, G. E., & Williams, R. J. (1986). Learning representations by back propagating errors. *Nature, 323,* 533–536.

Rusak, B. (1990). Biological rhythms: From physiology to behavior. In J. Montplaisir & R. Godbout, (Eds.), *Sleep and biological rhythms: Basic mechanisms and applications to psychiatry.* New York: Oxford University Press.

Rushton, W. A. H. (1975). Visual pigments and color blindness. *Scientific American, 232,* 64–74.

Russell, G.W., & Arms, R.L. (1995). False consensus effect, physical aggression, anger, and a willingness to escalate a disturbance. *Aggressive Behavior, 21(5),* 381–386.

Russell, G.W., & Arms, R.L. (1998). Toward a social psychological profile of would-be rioters. *Aggressive Behavior, 24,* 219–226.

Russell, G.W., Arms, R.L., & Bibby, R.W. (1995). Canadians' beliefs in catharsis. *Social Behavior and Personality, 23(3),* 223–228.

Russell, G.W., Arms, R.L., Loaf, S.D., & Dwyer, R.S. (1996). Men's aggression toward women in a bungled procedure paradigm. *Journal of Social Behavior and Personality, 11,* 729–738.

Russell, G.W., Arms, R.L., & Mustonen, A. (1999). When cooler heads prevail: Peacemakers in a sports riot. *Scandinavian Journal of Psychology, 40,* 153–155.

Russell, J.A. (1994). Is there universal recognition of emotion from facial expressions? A review of the cross-cultural studies. *Psychological Bulletin, 115(1),* 102–141.

Rutter, D.R., Quine, L., & Chesham, D.J. (1995). Predicting safe riding behaviour and accidents: Demography, beliefs, and behaviour in motorcycling safety. *Psychology and Health, 10(5),* 369–386.

Rutter, M., Macdonald, H., LeCouteur, A., Harrington, R., Bolton, P., & Bailey, A. (1990). Genetic factors in child psychiatric disorders, II: empirical findings. *Journal of Child Psychology and Psychiatry, 31,* 39–83.

Ryan, C.S. (1996). Accuracy of black and white college students' in-group and out-group stereotypes. *Personality and Social Psychology Bulletin, 22,* 1114–1127.

Ryan, E.B. (1992). Beliefs about memory changes across the adult life span. *Journals of Gerontology, 47(1),* 41–46.

Ryan, E.B., & See, S.K. (1993). Age-based beliefs about memory changes for self and others across adulthood. *Journals of Gerontology, 48(4),* 199–201.

Ryan, R.M. (1982). Control and information in the intrapersonal sphere: An extension of cognitive evaluation theory. *Journal of Personality and Social Psychology, 43,* 450–561.

Ryckman, R.M. , Butler, J.C., Thornton, B., & Lindner, M.A. (1995, April). *Identification and assessment of physique subtype stereotypes.* Paper presented at the meeting of the Eastern Psychological Association, Boston.

Saarni, C. (1993). Socialization of emotion. In M. Lewis & J. Haviland (Eds.), *Handbook of emotions* (435–446).

Sabol, S. Z., Nelson, M. L., Fisher, C., Gunzerath, L., Brody, C. L., Hu, S., Sirota, L. A., Marcus, S. E., Greenberg, B. D., Lucas, F. R., Benjamin, J., Murphy, D. L. & Hamer, D. H. (1999). A genetic association for cigarette smoking behavior. *Health Psychology, 18*, 7–13.

Sackheim, H.A, & Gur, R.C. (1978). Lateral asymmetry in intensity of emotional expression. *Neuropsychologia, 16*, 473–482.

Sacks, O. (1990). *Seeing voices: A journey into the world of the deaf.* New York: Harperperennial

Sadava, S.W., & Weithe, H. (1985). Maintainance and attributions about smoking among smokers, nonsmokers and ex-smokers. *International Journal of the Addictions, 20(10)*, 1533–1544.

Salmon, J., Hall, C., & Haslam, I. (1994). The use of imagery by soccer players. *Journal of Applied Sport Psychology, 6*, 116–133.

Salovey, P. (1991). *The psychology of jealousy and envy.* New York: Guilford Press.

Salovey, P. (1992). Mood-induced self-focused attention. *Journal of Personality and Social Psychology, 62*, 699–707.

Salovey, P., & Birnbaum, D. (1989). Influence of mood on health-relevant cognitions. *Journal of Personality and Social Psychology, 57*, 539–551.

Samsom, D. & Rachman, S.J. (1992). A search for contrast effects with fear evoking stimuli. *British Journal of Clinical Psychology, 31*, 33–44.

Samson, L.F. (1988). Perinatal viral infections and neonates. *Journal of Perinatal and Neonatal Nursing, 1*, 56–65.

Samson, S., & Zatorre, R.J. (1991). Recognition memory for text and melody of songs after unilateral temporal lobe lesion: Evidence for dual encoding. *Journal of Experimental Psychology Learning, Memory, and Cognition, 17(4)*, 793–804.

Samson, S., & Zatorre, R.J. (1994). Contribution of the right temporal lobe to musical timbre discrimination. *Neuropsychologia, 32(2)*, 231–240.

Sande, G.N., Goethals, G.R., Ferrari, L., Worth, L.T. (1989). Value-guided attributions: Maintaining the moral self-image and the diabolical enemy-image. *Journal of Social Issues, 45(2)*, 91–118.

Sande, G. N., Goethals, G. R., & Radloff, C. E. (1988). Perceiving one's own traits and others': The multifaceted self. *Journal of Personality and Social Psychology, 54*, 13–20.

Sandell, M., & Sullivan, K. (1992). Teacher disillusionment and supervision as a part of professional development. *Alberta Journal of Educational Research, 38(2)*, 133–140.

Sanderson, C.A. (1999). Role of relationship context in influencing college students' responsiveness to HIV prevention videos. *Health Psychology, 18*, 295–300.

Sanna, L.J. (1997) Self-efficacy and counterfactual thinking: Up a creek with and without a paddle. *Personality and Social Psychology Bulletin, 23*, 654–666.

Sansavini, A., Bertoncini, J., & Giovanelli, G. (1997). Newborns discriminate the rhythm of multisyllabic stressed words. *Developmental Psychology, 33*, 3–11.

Santi, S., Best, J.A., Brown, K.S. & Cargo, M. 1990–91. Smoking environment and smoking initiation. Special issue: environmental factors in substance misuse and its treatment. *International Journal of the Addictions, 25(7A-8A)*, 881–903.

Sargent, C. (1984). Between death and shame: Dimensions in pain in Bariba culture. *Social Science Medicine, 19*, 1299–1304.

Savage-Rumbaugh, E. S., Sevcik, R. A., Brakke, K. E., & Rumbaugh, D. M. (1992). Symbols: Their communicative use, communication, and combination by bonobos (*Pan paniscus*). In L. P. Lipsitt & C. Rovee-Collier (Eds.), *Advances in infancy research* (Vol. 7, pp. 221–278). Norwood, NJ: Ablex.

Savitsky, K., Medvec, V.H., Charlton, A.E., & Giolvich, T. (1998). "What, me worry?": Arousal, misattribution, and the effect of temporal distance on confidence. *Personality and Social Psychology, 24*, 529–536.

Savoie, D., & Ladouceur, R. (1995). Evaluation and modification of misconceptions concerning lotteries. *Canadian Journal of Behavioural Science, 27*, 199–213.

Saxby, E. & Peniston, E.G. (1995). Alpha-theta brainwave neurofeedback training: An effective treatment for male and female alcoholics with depressive symptoms. *Journal of Clinical Psychology, 51*, 685–693.

Scarr, S. (1989). Protecting general intelligence: Constructs and consequences for interventions. In R.L. Linn (Ed.), *Intelligence: Measurement, theory and public policy.* Urbana: University of Illnois Press.

Scarr, S. (1997). The development of individual differences in intelligence and personality. In H.W. Rees & M. D. Franzen (Eds.), *Biological and neuropsychological mechanisms: Life-span development psychology* (pp. 1–22) Mahway, NJ: Lawrence Earlbaum.

Scarr, S., & Weinberg, R. A. (1976). IQ test performance of black children adopted by white families. *American Psychologist, 31*, 726–739.

Schab, F. R. (1991). Odor memory: Taking stock. *Psychological Bulletin, 109*, 242–251.

Schachter, D.L., & Kihlstrom, J.F. (1989). Functional amnesia. In F. Boller, & J. Grafman, (Eds.). *Handbook of neuropsychology* (Vol. 3, pp. 209–230). New York: Elsevier.

Schachter, S., & Singer, J.E. (1962). Cognitive, social, and physiological determinants of emotional states. *Psychological Review, 69*, 379–399.

Schaie, K.W. (1986). *Adult development and aging* (2nd ed.). Boston: Little, Brown.

Schaie, K.W. (1990). Intellectual development in adulthood. In J.E. Birren & K.W. Schaie (Eds.), *Handbook of the psychology of aging* (3rd ed., pp. 291–309). San Diego: Academic Press.

Schaie, K.W. (1993). The Seattle longitudinal sudies of adult intelligence. *Current Directions in Psychological Science, 2*, 171–175.

Schaller, G. G. (1986). Secrets of the wild panda. *National Geographic, 169*, 284–309.

Scharfe, E., & Bartholomew, K. (1998). Do you remember?: Recollections of adult attachments patterns. *Personal Relationships, 5*, 219–234.

Scheier, M.F., & Carver, C.S. (1986). A model of self-regulation: Translating intention into action. In L. Berkowitz (Ed.), *Advances in experimental social psychology* (Vol. 20). New York: Academic Press.

Scheier, M.F., & Carver, C.S. (1987). Dispositional optimism and physical well-being: The influence of generalized outcome expectancies in health. *Journal of Personality, 55*, 169–210.

Scheier, M.F., & Carver, C.S. (1988). *Perspectives on personality.* Boston: Allyn & Bacon.

Scheier, M.F., & Carver, C.S. (1992). Effects of optimism on psychological and physical well-being: Theoretical overview and empirical update. *Cognitive Therapy and Research, 16*, 201–228.

Scheier, M.F., Weintraub, J.K., & Carver, C.S. (1986). Coping with stress: Divergent strategies of optimists and pessimists. *Journal of Personality and Social Psychology, 51*, 1257–1264.

Schell, B.H., Paine-Mantha, V.A., Markham, M.E., & Morrison, K. (1992). Stress-coping styles and personality descriptors of ice arena workers: Indicators of "victims" or "copers" of an the job stressors? Special issue: Career decision making and career indecision. *Journal of Vocational Behaviour, 41(3)*, 270–281.

Schellenberg, E.G., & Trehub. S.E. (1996). Natural musical intervals: Evidence from infant listeners. *Psychological Science, 7*, 272–277.

Schellinck, H.M., & Anand, K.J.S. (1999). Consequences of early experience: Lessons for rodent models of newborn pain. *Progress in Pain Research and Management, 1*, 39–55.

Schiff, B.B., Esses, V.M., & Lamon, M. (1992). Unilateral facial contractions produce mood effects on social cognitive judgements. *Cognition and Emotion, 6(5)*, 357–368.

Schiff, B.B., & Lamon, M. (1989). Inducing emotion by unilateral contraction of facial muscles: A new look at hemispheric specialization and the experience of emotion. *Neuropsychologia, 27(7)*, 923–935.

Schiffman, H. R. (1990). *Sensation and perception: An integrated approach* (3rd ed). New York: Wiley.

Schiffman, S. E., Graham, B. G., Sattely-Miller, E. A., & Warwick, Z. S. (1998). Orosensory perception of sensory fat. *Current Directions in Psychological Science, 7*, 137–143.

Schlaug, G., Jancke, L., Huang, Y., & Steinmetz, H. (1995). In vivo evidence of structural brian asymmetry in musicians. *Science, 267(5198)*, 699–701.

Schliecker, E., White, D.R., & Jacobs, E. (1991). The role of day care quality in the prediction of children's vocabulary. *Canadian Journal of Behavioural Science, 23*, 12–24.

Schmidt, F.N., & Gifford, R. (1989). A dispositional approach to hazard perception: preliminary development of the Environmental Appraisal Inventory. *Journal of Environmental Psychology, 9(1)*, 57–67.

Schmidt-Wilk, J., Alexander, C.N., & Swanson, G.C. (1996). Developing consciousness in organizations: The transcendental meditation program in business. *Journal of Business and Psychology, 10*, 429–444.

Schneider, B. H. (1991). A comparison of skill-building and desensitization strategies for intervention with aggressive children. *Aggressive Behavior, 17*, 301–311.

Schneider, B. H., & Byrne, B. M. (1987). Individualizing social skills training for behaviour-disordered children. *Journal of Consulting and Clinical Psychology, 55*, 444–445.

Schneider, S. L. (1992). Framing and conflict: Aspiration level contingency, the status quo, and current theories of risky choice. *Journal of Experimental Psychology: Learning, Memory, and Cognition, 18*, 1040–1057.

Schneidereit, P. (2000, February 20). No known causes. *Halifax Chronicle Herald,* p. C5.

Schofield, W. (1964). *Psychotherapy: The purchase of friendship.* Englewood Cliffs, NJ: Prentice Hall.

Schroots, J.J.F., & Birren, J. (1990). Concept of time and aging in science. In J.E. Birren & K.W. Schaie (Eds.), *Handbook of the psychology of aging* (3rd ed., pp. 45–64). San Diego, CA: Academic Press.

Schulz, G., & Melzack, R. (1991). The Charles Bonnet syndrome: "Phantom visual images." *Perception, 20*, 809–825.

Schulze, C., Karie, T., & Dickens, W. (1996). *Does the bell curve ring true?* Washington, DC: Brookings Institution.

Schunn, C.D., & Dunbar, K. (1996). Priming, analogy, and awareness in complex reasoning. *Memory and Cognition, 24*, 271–284.

Schwartz, J. M., Stoessel, P. W., Baxter, L.R., Martin, K. M., & Phelps, M. E. (1996) Systematic changes in cerebral glucose metabolic rate after successful modification treatment of obsessive-compulsive disorder. *Archives of General Psychiatry, 53*, 109–113.

Schwartzman, A.E., Gold, D., Andres, D., Arbuckle, T.Y., & Chailelson, J. (1987). Stability of intelligence: A 40-year follow-up. Special issue: Aging and cognition. *Canadian Journal of Psychology, 41(2)*, 244–256.

Schweikert, R., Guentert, L., & Hersberger, L. (1990). Phonological similarity, pronunciation rate, and memory span. *Psychological Science, 1*, 74–77.

Schyns, P.G., & Oliva, A. (1994). From blobs to boundary edges: Evidence for time- and spatial-scale-dependent science recognition. *Psychological Science, 5*, 195–200.

Scott, J.P. (1992). Aggression: Functions and control in social systems. *Aggressive Behavior, 18*, 1–20.

Scribner, S. (1977). Recall of classical syllogisms: A cross-cultural investigation of error on logical problems. In R. J. Falmagne (Ed.), *Reasoning: Representation and process.* Hillsdale, NJ: Erlbaum.

Searle, J. (1980). Minds, brains, and programs. *Behavioral and Brain Science, 3*, 417–457.

Sedikides, C., & Skowronski. J.J. (1997). The symbolic self in evolutionary context. *Personality and Social Psychology Review, 1*, 80–102.

Segal, N.L., & Bouchard, T.J. (1993). Grief intensity following the loss of a twin and other relatives: Test of kinship-genetic hypotheses. *Human Biology, 65*, 87–105.

Segal, Z.V., & Ferguson, F.B. (1999). Mood disorders and suicide. In W. L Marshall & P. Firestone (Eds.), *Abnormal psychology perspectives* (pp. 315–343). Scarborough, ON: Prentice Hall Allyn & Bacon.

Segal, Z.V., Gemar, M., & Williams, S. (1999). Differential cognitive response to a mood challenge following successful cognitive therapy or pharmacotherapy for unipolar depression. *Journal of Abnormal Psychology, 108*, 5–10.

Segalowitz, S.J., Bernstein, D.M., & Lawson, S. (1996). P300 event-related potential decrements in well-functioning universtiy students with mild head injury 6 years post-injury. Submitted for publication.

Segalowitz, S.J., & Lawson, S. (1995). Subtle symptoms associated with self-reported mild head injury. *Journal of Learning Disabilities, 28(5)*, 309–319.

Segalowitz, S.J., Unsal, A., & Dywan, J. (1992). Cleverness and wisdom in 12-year-olds: Electrophysiological evidence for late maturation of the frontal lobe. *Developmental Neuropsychology, 8(2-3)*, 279–298.

Segerstrom, S.C., Taylor, S.E., Kemeny, M.E., & Fahey, J.L. (1998). Optimism is associated with mood, coping and immune change in response to stress. *Journal of Personality and Social Psychology, 74*, 1646–1655.

Seifer, R., Schiller, M., Sameroff, A.J., Resnick, S., & Riordan, K. (1996). Attachment, maternal sensitivity, and infant temperament during the first year of life. *Developmental Psychology, 32*, 12–25.

Seigel, S. (1984). Pavlovian conditioning and heroin overdose: Reports by overdose victims. *Bulletin of the Psychonomic Society, 22*, 428–430.

Sekuler, R., & Blake, R. (1990). *Perception.* New York: Knopf.

Self, D.W. (1998). Neural substrates of drug craving and relapse in drug addiction. *Annals of Medicine, 30*, 379–389.

Seligman, M.E.P. (1971). Phobias and preparedness. *Behavior Therapy, 2*, 307–320.

Seligman, M. E. P. (1975). *Helplessness: On depression, development, and death.* San Francisco: Freeman.

Seligman, M.E.P. (1995). The effectiveness of psychotherapy: The Consumer Reports study. *American Psychologist, 50*, 965–974.

Seligman, M. E. P., Castellon, C., Cacciola, J., Schulman, P., Luborsky, L., Ollove, M., & Downing, R. (1988). Explanatory style change during cognitive therapy for unipolar depression. *Journal of Abnormal Psychology, 97*, 13–18.

Seligman, M.E.P., & Hager, J.L. (1972). *Biological boundaries of learning.* New York: Appleton-Century-Crofts.

Seltzer, A. (1995). "Multiple personality: A psychiatric misadventure": Reply. *Canadian Journal of Psychiatry, 40*, 49–50.

Selye, H. (1973). The evolution of the stress concept. *American Scientist, 61(6)*, 692–699.

Senick, D. (2000, February 29). Chilling out the boomers. *Victoria Times Colonist,* p. B1.

Sergent, J. (1989). Image generation and processing of generated images in the cerebral hemispheres. *Journal of Experimental Psychology: Human Perception and Performance, 15(1)*, 170–178.

Sergent, J. (1990). The neuropsychology of visual image generation: Data, method, and theory. *Brain and Cognition, 13(1)*, 98–129.

Sergent, J. (1993). Music, the brain and Ravel. *Trends in Neurosciences, 16(5)*, 168–172.

Sergent, J., & Corballis, M.C. (1990). Generation of multipart images in the disconnected cerebral hemispheres. *Bulletin of the Psychonomic Society, 28(4)*, 309–311.

Seta, C.E., & Hayes, N. (1994). The influence of impression formation goals on the accuracy of social memory. *Personality and Social Psychology Bulletin, 20*, 93–101.

Seto, M.C., & Barbaree, H.E. (1995). The role of alcohol in sexual aggression. *Clinical Psychology Review, 15(6)*, 545–566.

Sewitch, D.E. (1987). Slow wave sleep deficiency insomnia: A problem in thermo-down regulation at sleep onset. *Psychophysiology, 24*, 200–215.

Sexton, M., Fox, N.L., & Hubel, H.J.R. (1990). Prenatal exposure to tobacco: II. Effects on cognitive functioning at age three. *International Journal of Epidemiology, 19*, 72–77.

Shaffer, D., Garland, A., Gould, M., Fisher, P., & Trautman, P. (1988). Preventing teenage suicide: a critical review. *Journal of the American Academy of Child and Adolescent Psychiatry, 27*, 675–687.

Shaffer, D., Garland, A., Vieland, V., Underwood, M., & Busner, C. (1991). The impact of curriculum-based suicide prevention programs for teenagers. *Journal of the American Academy of Child and Adolescent Psychiatry, 30*, 588–596.

Shaffer, D.R., & Graziano, W.G. (1983). Effects of positive and negative moods on helping tasks having pleasant of unpleasant consequences. *Motivation and Emotion, 7 (3)*, 269–278.

Shafir, E. (1993). Choosing versus rejecting: Why some options are both better and worse than others. *Memory and Cognition, 21*, 546–556.

Shaham, Y., & Stewart, J. (1995). Stress reinstates heroin-seeking in drug-free animals: An effect mimicking heroin, not withdrawal. *Psychopharmacology, 119(3)*, 334–341.

Shammi, P., & Stuss, D. T. (1999). Humour appreciation: A role of the right frontal lobe. *Brain, 122*, 657–666.

Shanab, M.E., & Spencer, R.E. (1978). Positive and negative contrast effects obtained following shifts in delayed water reward. *Bulletin of the Psychonomic Society, 12*, 199–202.

Shanab, M.E., & Yahhy, K.A. (1977). A behavioral study of obedience in children. *Journal of Personality and Social Psychology, 35 (7)*, 530–536.

Shantz, C.U., & Hartup, W.W. (Eds.) (1993). *Conflict in child and adolescent development.* Cambridge: Cambridge University Press.

Shapiro, C.M., MacFarland, J.G., & MacLean, A.W. (1993). Alleviating sleep-related disconinuance symptoms associated with benzodiazepine withdrawal: A new approach. *Journal of Psychosomatic Research, 37*, 55–57.

Shapiro, D.H. (1980). *Meditation: Self-regulation strategy and altered states of consciousness.* New York: Aldine.

Shapiro, R., Siegel, A.W., Scovill, L.C., & Hays, J. (1998). Risk-taking patterns of female adolescents: What they do and why. *Journal of Adolescence, 21*, 143–159.

Shapiro, S.L., Schwartz, G.E., & Bonner, G. (1998). Effects of mindfulness-based stress reduction on medical and premedical students. *Journal of Behavioral Medicine, 21*, 581–599.

Sharp, M.J., & Getz, J.G. (1996). Substance use as impression management. *Personality and Social Psychology Bulletin, 22*, 60–67.

Sharpe, D., Adair, J.G., & Roese, N.J. (1992). Twenty years of deception research: A decline in subjects' trust? *Personality and Social Psychology Bulletin, 18*, 585–590.

Shaver, P.R., & Brennan, K.A. (1992). Attachment styles and the "big five" personality traits: Their connections with each other and with romantic relationship outcomes. *Personality and Social Psychology Bulletin, 18*, 536–545.

Shaver, P.R., & Hazan, C. (1994). Attachment, In A.L. Weber & J.H. Harvey (Eds.), *Perspectives on close relationships* (pp. 110–130). Boston: Allyn & Bacon.

Shaver, P.R., Papalia, D., Clark, C.L., Koski, L.R., et al. (1996). Androgyny and attachment security: Two related models of optimal personality. *Personality and Social Psychology Bulletin, 22 (6)*, 582–597.

Shavitt, S., & Brock, T.C. (Eds.) (1994). *Persuasion.* Boston: Allyn & Bacon.

Shaw, L.L., Batson, C.D., & Todd, R.M. (1994). Empathy avoidance: Forestalling feeling for another in order to escape the motivational consequences. *Journal of Personality and Social Psychology, 67*, 879–887.

Shea, R., & Fisher, B.E. (1996). Self ratings of mood levels and mood variability as predictors of Junior 1–6 impulsivity and ADHD classroom behaviors. *Personality and Individual Differences, 20(2)*, 209–214.

Shear, J., & Jevning, R. (1999). Pure consciousness: Scientific exploration of meditation techniques. *Journal of Consciousness Studies, 6*, 189–209.

Shedler, J., & Block, J. (1990). Adolescent drug use and psychological health: A longitudinal inquiry. *American Psychologist, 45*, 612–630.

Shepard, R. N. (1964). Circularity in judgments of relative pitch. *Journal of the Acoustical Society of America, 36*, 2346–2353.

Shepard, R. N., & Metzler, J. (1971). Mental rotation of three-dimensional objects. *Science, 171*, 701–703.

Sher, K.J., & Trull, T.J. (1994). Personality and disinhibitory psychopathology: Alcoholism and antisocial personality disorder. *Journal of Abnormal Psychology, 103*, 92–102.

Sherif, M. (1935). A study of some social factors in perception. *Archives of Psychology, 27*, 187.

Sherman, S.L., Defries, J.C., Gottesman, L.I., Loehlin, J.C., Meyer, J.M., Pelias, M.Z., Rice, J., & Waldman, I. (1997). Behavioral genetics '97: ASHG Statement. Recent developments in human behavioral genetics: Past accomplishments and future directions. *American Journal of Human Genetics, 60*, 1265–1275.

Sherrick, C.E., & Cholewiak, R.W. (1986). Cutaneous sensitivity. In K.R. Boff, L. Kaufamn, & J.P. Thomas (Eds.), *Handbook of perception and human performance* (pp. 12.1–12.58). New York: Wiley.

Shettleworth, S. J. (1983). Memory in food-hoarding birds. *Scientific American, 248*, 102–110.

Shettleworth, S.J. (1993). Where is the comparison in comparative cognition? Alternative research programs. *Psychological Science, 4*, 179–184.

Shettleworth, S.J. (1998). *Cognition, evolution and behavior.* New York: Oxford University Press.

Shiffrin, R.M., & Dumais, S.T. (1981). The development of automatism, In J.R. Anderson (Ed.), *Cognitive skills and their acquisition.* Hillsdale, NJ: Erlbaum.

Shiffrin, R.M., & Schneider, W. (1977). Controlled and automatic human information processing. II: Perceptual learning, automatic attending, and a general theory. *Psychological Review, 84*, 127–190.

Shimamura, A.P., & Jurica, P.J. (1994). Memory interference effects and aging: Findings from a test of frontal lobe function. *Neuropsychology, 8*, 408–412.

Shimamura, A.P., Berry, J.M., Mangela, J.A., Rusting, C.L., & Jurica, P.J. (1995). Memory and cognitive abilities in university professors: Evidence for successful aging. *Psychological Science, 6*, 271–277.

Shin, W.S. (1993). Self-actualization and wilderness attitudes: A replication. *Journal of Social Behavior and Personality, 8(2)*, 241–256.

Shiota, M., Sudou, M., & Ohshima, M. (1996). Using outdoor exercise to decrease jet lag in airline crewmembers. *Aviation, Space, and Environmental Medicine, 67*, 1155–1160.

Shoda, Y., Mischel, W., & Peake, P.K. (1990). Predicting adolescent cognitive and self-regulatory competencies from preschool delay of gratification. *Developmental Psychology, 26*, 978–986.

Shore, D. (1993). *Special report: Schizophrenia* (1993). Rockville, MD: US Department of Health and Human Services.

Shu, A. (1995). Toronto psychiatrists make house calls to Baffin. *Medical Post,* March 28, p.36.

Sicard, G., & Holley, A. (1984). Receptor cell responses to odorants: Similarities and differences among odorants. *Brain Research, 292*, 282–296.

Siegal, M., & Peterson, C. C. (1996). Breaking the mold: A fresh look at children's understanding of questions about lies and mistakes. *Developmental Psychology, 32*, 322–334.

Siegel, S. (1975). Evidence from rats that morphine tolerance is a learned response. *Journal of Comparative and Physiological Psychology, 89,* 598–606.

Siegel, S. (1983). Classical condtitioning, drug tolerance, and drug dependence. In R.G. Smart, F.B. Glaser, Y. Israel, H. Kalant, R.E. Popham & W. Schmidt (Eds.), *Research advances in alcohol and drug problems* (Vol. 7). New York: Plenum.

Siegel, S., Hinson, R.E., Krank, M.D., & McCully, J. (1982). Heroin "overdose" death: Contribution of drug-associated environmental cues. *Science, 216,* 436–437.

Siegle, L.S., (1993). Amazing new discovery: Piaget was wrong. *Canadian Psychology, 34(3),* 239–245.

Siegler, R.S. (1994). Cognitive variability: A key to understanding cognitive development. *Current Directions in Psychological Science, 3,* 1–5.

Siegler, R.S. (1996). *Emerging minds: The process of change in children's thinking.* New York: Oxford University Press.

Siegler, R.S., & Jenkins, E., (1989). *How children discover new strategies.* Hillsdale, NJ: Erlbaum.

Sigman, M. (1995). Nutrition and child development: More food for thought. *Current Directions in Psychological Science, 4,* 52–55.

Sigurdson, E., Stanley, D., Matas, M., Hildahl, K., & Squair, K. (1994). A five year review of youth suicide in Manitoba. *Canadian Journal of Psychiatry, 39,* 397–403.

Sigvardsson, S, Bohman, M., & Cloninger, R.C. (1996). Replication of the Stockholm adoption study of alcoholism. *Archives of General Psychiatry, 53,* 681–687.

Silagy, C., Mant, D., Fowler, G., & Lodge, M. (1994). Meta-analysis of efficacy of nicotine replacement therapies in smoking cessation. *Lancet, 343,* 139–142.

Silva, C.E., & Kirsch, I. (1992). Interpretive sets, expectancy, fantasy proneness, and dissociation as predictors of hypnotic response. *Journal of Personality and Social Psychology, 63,* 847–856.

Silver, S., Mitchell, R.M., & Gist, B. (1997). Responses to successful and unsuccessful performance: The relationship between self-efficacy and causal attributions. *Organizational Behavior and Human Decision Processes.*

Silverman, I., & Eals, M. (1992). Sex differences in spatial abilities: Evolutionary theory and data. In J. H. Barkow, L. Cosmides, & J. Tooby (Eds.), *The adapted mind* (pp. 533–549). New York: Oxford University Press.

Silverman, I., & Phillips, K. (1998). The evolutionary psychology of spatial sex differences. In C. Crawford & D. L Krebs (Eds.), *Handbook of evolutionary psychology* (pp. 595–612). Mahwah: NJ: Erlbaum.

Simeon, J.G., & Wiggins, D.M., (1993). Pharmacotherapy of attention deficit hyperactivity disorder. *Canadian Journal of Psychiatry, 38(6),* 443–448.

Simon, L., Greenberg, J., & Brehm, J. (1995). Trivialization: The forgotten mode of dissonance reduction. *Journal of Personality and Social Psychology, 68,* 247–260.

Simonton, D. K. (1990). Creativity and wisdom in aging. In J. E. Birren & K. W. Schaie (Eds.), *Handbook of the psychology of aging* (3rd ed., pp. 320–329). San Diego: Academic Press.

Simpson, E. (1974). Moral development research: A case study of scientific cultural bias. *Human Development, 17,* 81–105.

Sinclair, R.C., & Mark, M.M. (1995). The effects of mood state on judgemental accuracy: Processing strategy as a mechanism. *Cognition and Emotion, 9(5),* 417–438.

Singer, J.L. (1975). Navigating the stream of consciousness: Research in daydreaming and related inner experience. *American Psychologist, 30,* 727–738.

Singer, J.L., Singer, D.G., & Rapaczynski, W.S. (1984). Children's imagination as predicted by family patterns and television viewing: A longitudinal study. *Genetic Psychology Monographs, 110,* 43–69.

Singer, P.A., Choudhry, S., & Armstrong, J. (1993). Public opinion regarding consent to treatment. *Journal of the American Geriatrics Society, 41(2),* 112–116.

Singh, D. (1993). Adaptive significance of female's physical attractiveness: Role of waist-to-hip ratio. *Journal of Personality and Social Psychology, 65,* 293–307.

Sinnott, J.D. (1986). Prospective/intentional and incidental everyday memory: Effects of age and passage of time. *Psychology and Aging, 1,* 110–116.

Siquelande, E.R., & Lipsitt, L. P. (1966). Conditioned head-turning in human newborns. *Journal of Experimental Child Psychology, 3,* 356–376.

Skeels, H. M. (1938). Mental development of children in foster homes. *Journal of Consulting Psychology, 2,* 33–43.

Skeels, H. M. (1966). Ability status of children with contrasting early life experience. *Society for Research in Child Development Monographs, 31(3),* 1–65.

Skene, D.J., Deacon, S., & Arendt, J. (1996). Use of melatonin in circadian rhythm disorders and following phase shifts. *Acta Neurobiologiae Experimentalis, 56,* 359–362.

Skinner, B.F. (1938). *The behavior of organisms.* New York: Appleton-Century-Crofts.

Skinner, B. F. (1974). *About behaviorism.* New York: Vintage Books.

Skinner, B.F. (1969). *Contingencies of reinforcement.* New York: Appleton-Century-Crofts.

Sladen-Dew, N., Bigelow, D. A., Buckley, R., & Bornemann, S. (1993). The Greater Vancouver Mental Health Service Society: 20 years' experience in urban community mental health. *Canadian Journal of Psychiatry, 38,* 308–314.

Sloan, E.P., Hauri, P., Bootzin, R., & Morin, C. et al., (1993). The nuts and bolts of behavioral therapy for insomnia. *Journal of Psychosomatic Research, 37,* 19–37.

Slobin, D. I. (1979). *Psycholinguistics* (2nd ed.). Glenview, IL: Scott, Foresman.

Sloboda, J.A. (1991). Music structure and emotional response: Some empirical findings. *Psychology of Music, 19(2),* 110–120.

Slovic, P., Fischoff, B., & Lichtenstein, S. (1977). Behavioral decision theory. *Annual Review of Psychology, 28,* 1–39.

Small, B.J., Dixon, R.A., Hultsch, D.F., & Hertzog, C. (1999). Longitudinal changes in quantitative and qualitative indicators of word and story recall in young-old and old-old adults. *Journal of Gerontology: Psychological Sciences, 54B,* 107–115.

Smart, R.G. (1991). Crack cocaine use: A review of prevalence and adverse effects. *American Journal of Drug and Alcohol Abuse, 17,* 13–26.

Smart, R.G., & Adlaf, E.M. (1992). Recent studies of cocaine use and abuse in Canada. *Canadian Journal of Criminology, 34,* 1–13.

Smart, R.G., & Walsh, G.W. (1993). Predictors of depression in street youth. *Adolescence, 28(109),* 41–53.

Smith, B. D., Wilson, R. J., & Davidson, R. (1984). Electordermal activity and extraversion: Caffeine, preparatory signal and stimulus intensity effects. *Personality and Individual Differences, 5,* 59–65.

Smith, C. (1995). Sleep states and memory processes. Special Issue: The function of sleep. *Behavioural Brain Research, 69(1–2),* 137–145.

Smith, C.T., Conway, J.M., & Rose, G.M. (1998). Brief paradoxical sleep deprivation impairs reference, but not working, memory in the radial arm maze task. *Neurobiology of Learning and Memory, 69,* 211–217.

Smith, C.T., & Rose, G.M. (1996). Evidence for a paradoxical sleep window for place learning in the Morris water maze. *Physiology and Behavior, 59,* 93–97.

Smith, C.T., & Rose, G.M. (1997). Posttraining paradoxical sleep in rats is increased after spatial learning in the Morris water maze. *Behavioral Neuroscience, 111,* 1197–1204.

Smith, d.E., Gier, J.A., & Willis, F.N. (1982). Interpersonal touch and compliance with a marketing request. *Basic and Applied Social Psychology, 3,* 35–38.

Smith, E.R., & Henry, S. (1996). An in-group becomes part of the self; response time evidence. *Personality and Social Psychology Bulletin, 22,* 635–642.

Smith, J., & Baltes, P.B. (1990). Wisdom-related knowledge: Age/cohort differences in response to life-planning problems. *Developmental Psychology, 26,* 494–505.

Smith, M.L., Minden, D., & Lefevbre, A. (1993). Knowledge and attitudes about AIDS and AIDS education in elementary school students and their parents. *Journal of School Psychology, 31(2),* 281–292.

Smith, P. B., & Bond, N. H. (1993). *Social psychology across cultures.* Boston: Allyn & Bacon.

Smith, S. M. (1979). Remembering in and out of context. *Journal of Experimental Psychology: Human Learning and Memory, 5,* 460–471.

Smith, S.M., & Shaffer, D.R. (1991). The effects of good moods on systematic processing: "Willing but not able, able but not willing?" *Motivation and Emotion, 15(4),* 243–279.

Smith, S.M., & Shaffer, D.R. (1991). Celerity and cajolery: Rapid speech may promote or inhibit persuasion through its impact of message elaboration. *Personality and Social Psychology Bulletin, 17(6),* 663–669.

Smith, S.M., & Shaffer, D.R. (1995). Speed of speech and persuasion: Evidence for multiple effects. *Personality and Social Psychology Bulletin, 21(10),* 1051–1060.

Smith, S. S., & Richardson, D. (1985). On deceiving ourselves about deception: Reply to Rubin. *Journal of Personality and Social Psychology, 48,* 254–255.

Snowden, L. R., & Cheung, F. K. (1990). Use of inpatient mental health services by members of ethnic minority groups. *American Psychologist, 45,* 347–355.

Snyder, M. (1987). *Public appearances/private realities: The psychology of self-monitoring.* New York: W. H. Freeman.

Snyder, M., & Gangestad, S. (1986). On the nature of self-monitoring: Matters of assessment, matters of validity. *Journal of Personality and Social Psychology, 51,* 125–139.

Snyder, S. (1991). Movies and juvenile delinquency: An overview. *Adolescence, 26,* 121–132.

Snyder, S. H. (1977). The brain's own opiates. *Chemical & Engineering News, 55,* 26–35.

Sobell, L.C., Sobell, M.B., Kozlowski, L.T., & Toneatto, T. (1990). Alcohol or tobacco research versus alcohol and tobacco research. *British Journal of Addiction, 85(2),* 263–269.

Solomon, R.L. (1982). The opponent-process in acquired motivation. In D.W. Pfaff (Ed.), *The physiological mechanisms of motivation.* New York: Springer-Verlag.

Sorrentino, R.M., Hewitt, E.C. & Raso-Knott, P.A. (1992). Risk-taking in games of games of chance and skill: Informational and affective influences on choice behavior. *Journal of Personality and Social Psychology, 62(3),* 522–533.

Spanos, N. P. (1994). Multiple identity enactments and multiple personality disorder: A sociocognitive perspective. *Psychological Bulletin, 116,* 1432–165.

Spanos, N. P. (1996). *Multiple identities and false memories: A sociocognitive perceptive.* Washington: American Psychological Association.

Spanos, N.P., Burgess, C.A., Cross, P., & McCleod, G. (1992). Hypnosis, reporting bias and negative hallucinations. *Journal of Abnormal Psychology 101,* 192–199.

Spanos, N.P., Burgess, C.A., & Perlini, A.H. (1992). Compliance and suggested deafness in hypnotic and nonhypnotic subjects. *Imagination, Cognition and Personality, 11,* 211–223.

Spanos, N.P., DuBreuil, S.C., & Gabora, N.J. (1991). Four-month follow-up of skill-training-induced enhancements in hypnotizability. *Contemporary Hypnosis, 8,* 25–32.

Spanos, N.P., Flynn, D.M.., & Gabora, N.J. (1989). Suggestive negative visual hallucinations in hypnotic subjects: When no means yes. *British Journal of Experimental and Clinical Hypnosis, 6,* 63–67.

Spanos, N.P., Menary, E., Gabora, N.J., DuBreuil, S.C., & Dewhirst, B. (1991). Secondary identity enactments during hypnotic past-life regression: A sociocognitive perspective. *Journal of Personality and Social Psychology, 61,* 308–320.

Spanos, N.P., Perlini, A.H., Patrick, L., Bell, S., & Gwynn, M.I. (1990). The role of compliance and hypnotic and nonhypnotic analgesia. *Journal of Research in Personality, 24,* 433–453.

Spearman, C. E. (1927). *The abilities of man.* London: Macmillan.

Spence, A.P. (1989). *Biology of human aging.* Englewood Cliffs, NJ: Prentice Hall.

Sperling, G. (1960). The information available in brief visual presentations. *Psychological Monographs: General and Applied, 74,* 1–29.

Sperry, R.W. (1968). Hemisphere deconnection and unity of conscious experience. *American Psychologist, 29,* 723–733.

Spetch, M.L. (1995). Overshadowing in landmark learning: Touch-screen studies with pigeons and humans. *Journal of Experimental Psychology: Animal Behavior Processes, 21(2),* 166–181.

Spetch, M.L., Cheng, K., & MacDonald, S.E. (1996). Learning the configuration of a landmark array: I. Touch-screen studies with pigeons and humans. *Journal of Comparative Psychology, 110(1),* 55–68.

Spetch, M.L., & Grant, D.S. (1993). Pigeons' memory for event duration in choice and successive matching-to-sample tasks. *Learning and Motivation, 24,* 156–174.

Spetch, M.L., Grant, D.S., & Kelly, R. (1996). Procedural determinants of coding processes in pigeons' memory for duration. *Learning and Motivation, 27(2),* 179–199.

Spetch, M.L., & Wilkie, D.M. (1994). Pigeons' use of landmarks presented in digitized images. *Learning and Motivation, 25,* in press.

Spirduso, W.W., & MacRae, P.G. (1990). Motor performance and aging. In J.E. Birren & K.W. Schaie (Eds.), *Handbook of the psychology of aging* (3rd ed., pp. 184–200). San Diego: Academic Press.

Spitzer, M. (1999). *The mind within the net: Models of learning, thinking, and acting.* Cambridge, MA: MIT Press.

Sprecher, S., & Duck, S. (1994). Sweet talk: The importance of perceived communication for romantic and friendship attraction experienced during a get-acquainted date. *Personality and Social Psychology Bulletin, 20 (4),* 391–400.

Springer, S.P., & Deutsch, G. (1985). *Left brain, right brain.* San Francisco: Freeman.

Squire, L.R. (1991). Closing remarks. In L. R. Squire & E. Lindenlaub (Eds.), *The biology of memory* (pp. 643–64). Stuttgart, Germany: Schattauer Verlag.

Squire, L.R. (1995). Biological foundations of accuracy and inaccuracy of memory. In D.L. Schachter (Ed.)., *Memory distortions* (pp. 197–225). Cambridge, MA: Harvard University Press.

Squire, L.R., & Spanis, C.W. (1984). Long gradient of retrograde amnesia in mice: Continuity with the findings in humans. *Behavioral Neuroscience, 98,* 345–348.

St. George-Hyslop, P. H., & Westaway, D. A. (1999). Alzheimer's disease: Antibody clears senile plaques. *Nature, 400,* 116–117.

Stack, D.M., & Muir, D.W., (1992). Adult tactile stimulation during face-to-face interactions modulates five-month-olds' affect and attention. *Child Development, 63(6),* 1509–1525.

Stafford-Clark, D. (1997). *What Freud really said.* New York: Schocken Books.

Stam, H.J., Lubek, I., & Radtke, H.L. (1998). Repopulating social psychology texts: Disembodied "subjects" and embodied subjectivity. In B.M. Bayer, & J. Shotter (Eds.), *Reconstructing the psychological subject: Bodies, practices and technologies* (pp. 153–186). London, England: Sage.

Stambrook, M., Peters, L.C., & Moore, A.D. (1989). Issues in the rehabilitation of severe tramatic brain injury: A focus on the neuropsychologist's role. *Canadian Journal of Rehabilitation, 3,* 87–98.

Standing, L. G. (1973). Learning 10,000 pictures. *Quarterly Journal of Experimental Psychology, 25,* 207–222.

Stanger, C., & Ruble, D.N. (1989). Strength of expectancies and memory for social information: What we remember depends on how much we know. *Journal of Experimental Social Psychology, 39,* 1408–1423.

Stanton, W.R., Mahalski, P.A., McGee, R. & Silva, P.A. (1993). Reasons for smoking and not smoking in early adolescence. *Addictive Behaviors, 18(3),* 321–329.

Staw, B. M., & Ross, J. (1987). Behavior in escalation situations: Antecedents, prototypes, and solutions. In L. L. Cummings & B. M. Staw (Eds.), *Research in organizational behavior* (Vol. 9, pp. 29–78). Greenwich, CT: JAI Press.

Staw, B. M., & Ross, J. (1989). Understanding behavior in escalation situations. *Science, 246,* 216–220.

Stearns, G.M. & Moore, R.J. (1993). The physical and psychological correlates of job burnout in the Royal Canadian Mounted Police. *Canadian Journal of Criminology, 35(2),* 127–147.

Steele, C.M. (1988). The psychology of self-affirmation: sustaining the integrity of the self. In L. Berkowitz (Ed.), *Advances in experimental social pscyhology* (pp. 261–302). Hillsdale, NJ: Erlbaum.

Steele, C.M., & Josephs, R.A. (1990). Alcohol myopia: Its prized and dangerous effects. *American Psychologist, 45,* 921–933.

Steers, R.M. (1984). *Organizational behavior* (2nd ed.). Glenview, IL: Scott Foresman.

Steffen, V.J. (1990). Men's motivation to perform the testicular self-exam: Effect of prior knowledge and an educational brochure. *Journal of Applied Social Psychology, 20,* 681–702.

Steger, M.A., Pierce, J.C., Steel, B.S., & Lovrich, N.P. (1989). Political culture, postmaterial values, and the new environmental paradigm: A comparative analysis of Canada and the United States. *Political Behavior, 11,* 233–254.

Stein, B.A., Golombek, H., Marton, P. & Korenblum, M. (1991). Consistency and change in personality characteristics and affect from middle to late adolescence. *Canadian Journal of Psychiatry, 36(1),* 16–20.

Steinmetz, J.E. (1999). A renewed interest in human classical conditioning. *Psychological Science, 10,* 24–25.

Stellar, E. (1985). Hunger in animals and humans. Lecture to the Eastern Psychological Association, Boston.

Stemberger, R.T., Turner, S.M., Beidel, D.C., Calhoun, K.S. (1995). Social phobia; An analysis of possible developmental factors. *Journal of Abnormal Psychology, 104,* 526–531.

Stenson, P., & Anderson, C. (1987). Treating juvenile sex offenders and preventing the cycle of abuse. *Journal of Child Care, 3(2),* 91–102.

Stephan, R.A. (1987). Audiotape instruction of face-washing skills for an adult with mental retardation. *American Journal of Occupational Therapy, 41* (3), 184–185.

Sternberg, R. J. (1985). *Beyond IQ.* Cambridge: Cambridge University Press.

Sternberg, R. J. (1988). Mental self-government: A theory of intellectual styles and their development. *Human Development, 31,* 197–224.

Sternberg, R.J. (1988). *The triangle of love.* New York: Basic Books.

Sternberg, R.J. (1995). For whom the bell curve tolls: A review of the Bell Curve. *Psychological Science, 6,* 257–261.

Sternberg, R. J., & Kaufman, J. C. (1998), Human abilities. *Annual Review of Psychology, 49,* 479–502.

Sternberg, R.J., & Lubart, T.I. (1995). *Defying the crowd: Cultivating creativity in a culture of conformity.* New York: Free Press.

Sternberg, R.J., & Lubart, T.I. (1996). Investing in creativity. *American Psychologist, 51,* 677–688.

Sternberg, R.J., Wagner, R.K., Williams, W.M., & Horvath, J.A. (1995). Testing common sense. *American Psychologist, 50,* 912–927.

Sternberg, R.J., & Williams, M.W. (1997). *How to develop student creativity.* Alexandria, VA: Association for Supervision and Curriculum Development.

Stevenson-Hinde, J., Stillwell-Barnes, R., & Sunz, M. (1980). Subjective assessments of rhesus monkeys over four successive years. *Primates, 21,* 66–82.

Stewart, D.E., Boydell, K.M., Derzko, C., & Marshall, V. (1992). Psychological distress during the menopausal years in women attending a menopause clinic. *International Journal of Psychiatry in Medicine, 22(3),* 213–220.

Stewart, S., Zeitlin, S.B., & Samoluk, S.B. (1996). Examination of a three-dimensional drinking motives questionnaire in a young adult university student sample. *Behavior Research and Therapy, 34,* 61-71.

Stice, E., & Barrera, M., Jr. (1995). A longitudinal examination of the reciprocal relations between perceived parenting and adolescents' substance use and externalizing behaviors. *Developmental Psychology, 31,* 332–334.

Stickels, T. (1998). *Mind bending puzzles 2.* Rohnert Park, CA: Pomegranate Communications.

Stiff, J.B., Miller, G.R., Sleight, C., & Mongeau, P. (1989). Explanations for visual cue primacy in judgments of honesty and deceit. *Journal of Personality and Social Psychology, 56,* 555–564.

Stifter, C.A., & Fox, N.A. (1990). Infant reactivity: Physiological correlates of newborn and 5-month temperament. *Developmental Psychology 2,* 582–588.

Stiles, W.B., Shapiro, D. A., & Elliot, R. "Are all psychotherapies equivalent." *American Psychologist, 41,* 165–180.

Stipp, D. (1990, May 17). Einstein bird has scientists atwitter over mental feats. *Wall Street Journal,* pp. 1, 7.

Stoduto, G., Adlaf, E.M., & Mann, R.E. (1998). Adolescents, bush parties, and drinking-driving. *Journal of Studies on Alcohol, 59,* 544–548.

Stone, J., Aronson, E., Crain, A.L., Winslow, M.P., et al. (1994). Inducing hypocrisy as a means of encouraging young adults to use condoms. *Personality and Social Psychology Bulletin, 20,* 116–128.

Stoppard, J.M., & Gruchy, C.G. (1993). Gender, context, and expression of positive emotion. *Personality and Social Psychology Bulletin, 19(2),* 143–150.

Storm, C., & Storm, T. (1987). A taxonomic study of the vocabulary of emotions. *Journal of Personality and Social Psychology, 53,* 805–816.

Stoutjesdyk, D., & Jevne, R. (1993). Eating disorders among high performance athletes. *Journal of Youth and Adolescence, 22(3),* 271–282.

Strachan, H. J., Johansen, H., Nair, C., & Nargundkar, M. (1990). Canadian suicide mortality rates: First-generation immigrants versus Canadian-born. *Health Reports, 2,* 327–341.

Strauss, E., Wada, J.A., & Goldwater, B. (1992). Sex differences in interhemispheric reorganization of speech. *Neuropsychologia, 30(4),* 353–359.

Strayer, J., (1985). Current research in diffective development. Special Issue: The feeling child: Affective development reconsidered. *Journal of Children in Contemporary Society, 17(4),* 37–55.

Strayer, J. (1993). Children's concordant emotions and cognitions in response to observed emotions. *Child Development, 64,* 188–201.

Strayer, J., & Roberts, W. (1997). Facial and verbal measures of children's emotions and empathy. *International Journal of Behavioral Development, 20,* 627–649.

Strean, H. S. (1985). *Resolving resistances in psychotherapy.* New York: Wiley Interscience.

Strecher, V.J., Champion, V.L., & Rosenstock, I.M. (1997). The health belief model and health behavior. In D.S. Gochman (Ed.), *Handbook of health behavior research 1: Personal and social determinants* (pp.71–91). New York: Plenum Press.

Streigel-Moore, R.H., Silberstein, L.R. & Rodin, J. (1993). The social self in bulimia nervosa: public self-consciousness, social anxiety, and perceived fraudulence. *Journal of Abnormal Psychology, 102(2),* 297–303.

Stretch, R.H. (1990). Post-traumatic stress disorder and the Canadian Vietnam veteran. *Journal of Traumatic Stress, 3,* 239–254.

Strickland, B. R. (1992). Women and depression. *Current Directions in Psychological Science, 1,* 132–135.

Stroessner, S.J., & Mackie, D.M. (1992). The impact of induced affect on the perception of variability in social groups. *Personality and Social Psychology Bulletin, 18(5),* 546–554.

Stroop, J.R. (1935). Studies of interference in serial verbal reactions. *Journal of Experimental Psychology, 18,* 643–662.

Stuss, D.T., & Benson, D.F. (1984). Neuropsychological studies of the frontal lobes. *Psychological Bulletin, 95(1),* 3–28.

Stuss, D.T., & Buckle, L. (1992). Traumatic brain injury: Neuropsychological deficits and evaluation at different stages of recovery and in different pathological subtypes. *Journal of Head Trauma Rehabilitation, 7,* 40–49.

Stuss, D.T., Gow, C.A., & Hetherington, C.R. (1992). "No longer gage": Frontal lobe dysfunction and emotional changes. Special section: The emotional concomitants of brain damage. *Journal of Consulting and Clinical Psychology, 60(3),* 349–359.

Stuss, D.T., Stethem, L.L., Hugenholtz, H., Picton, T., et al. (1989). Reaction time after head injury: Fatigue, divided and focused attention, and consistency of performance. *Journal of Neurology, Neurosurgery and Psychiatry, 52,* 742–748.

Stuss, D.T., Stetham, L.L., Hugenholtz, H., & Richard, M.T. (1989). Traumatic brain injury: A comparison of three clinical tests, and analysis of recovery. *Clinical Neuropsychologist, 3,* 145–156.

Sullivan, M.J., Reesor, K., Mikail, S., & Fisher, R. (1992). The treatment of depression in chronic low back pain: Review and recommendations. *Pain, 50(1),* 5–13.

Sullivan, M.J.L., Bishop, S.R., & Pivik, J. (1995). The pain catastrophizing scale: Development and validation. *Psychological Assessment, 7,* 524–532.

Sulloway, F. J. (1992). *Freud, biologist of the mind: Beyond the psychoanalytic legend.* Cambridge, MA: Harvard University Press.

Suls, J., Wan, C.K., & Sanders, G.S. (1988). False consensus and false uniqueness in estimating the prevalence of health-protective behaviors. *Journal of Applied Social Psychology, 18,* 66–79.

Sundstrom, E., & Sundstrom, M. G. (1986). *Work places: The psychology of the physical environment in offices and factories.* Cambridge, England: Cambridge University Press.

Surridge, D.M., MacLean, A., Coulter, M.E., & Knowles, J.B. (1987). Mood change following an acute delay of sleep. *Psychiatry Research, 22,* 149–158.

Sussman, S. (1998). The first asylums in Canada: A response to neglectful community care and current trends. *Canadian Journal of Psychiatry, 43,* 260–264.

Swaab, D.F., Gooren, L.J.G., & Hofman, M.A. (1995). Brain research, gender, and sexual orientation. Special Issue: Sex, cell, and same-sex desire: The biology of sexual preference: II. *Journal of Homosexuality, 28(3-4),* 283–301.

Swaan, W.B., Jr., Stein-Seroussi, A., & Giesler, R.B. (1992). Why people self-verify. *Journal of Personality and Social Psychology, 62,* 392–401.

Swartzentruber, D. (1991). Blocking between occasion setters and contextual stimuli. *Journal of Experimental Psychology: Animal Behavior Processes, 12,* 163–173.

Swets, J. A. (1992). The science of choosing the right decision threshold in high-stakes diagnostics. *American Psychologist, 47,* 522–532.

Swift, D. (1998). *Medical Post, 34,* 24.

Sylvain, C., & Ladouceur, R. (1992). Correction cognitive et habitudes de jue chez les joueurs de poker video. (Corrective cognition and gambling habits of players of video poker.) *Canadian Journal of Behavioural Science, 24,* 479–489.

Symons, D.K., & McLeod, P.J. (1994). Maternal, infant, and occupational characteristics that predict postpartum employment patterns. *Infant Behavior and Development, 17,* 71–82.

Szkrybalo, J., & Ruble, D.N. (1999). "God made me a girl": Sex-category constancy judgments and explanations revisited. *Developmental Psychology, 35,* 392–402.

Szmajke, A. (1998). Self-handicapping as a tactic of impression management: Is it effective? *Polish Psychological Bulletin, 29,* 165–179.

Taerk, G., Gallop, R.M., Lancee, W.J., Coates, R.A., et al. (1993). Recurrent themes of concern in groups for health care professionals. *AIDS Care, 5(2),* 215–222.

Taggart, H.M., & Connor, S.E. (1995). The relation of exercise habits to health beliefs and knowledge about osteoporosis. *Journal of American College Health, 44(3),* 127–130.

Takanishi, R. (1993). The opportunities of adolescence—research, intervention, and policy. *American Psychologist, 48,* 85–87.

Talaga, T. (2000, March 24). Rethinking the Brain. The *Toronto Star.*

Tam, E.M., Lam, R.W., & Levitt, A.J. (1995). Treatment of seasonal affective disorder: A review. *Canadian Journal of Psychiatry, 40(8),* 457–466.

Tang, J. L., Law, M., & Wald, N. (1994). How effective is nicotine replacement therapy in helping people to stop smoking? *British Medical Journal, 308,* 21–26.

Tannock, R., Purvis, K.L., & Schachar, R.J. (1993). Narrative abilities in children with attention deficit hyperactivity disorder and normal peers. *Journal of Abnormal Psychology, 21(1),* 103–117.

Tanouye, E. (1999, August 25). For drug makers, high-stakes race inside the brain. *Wall Street Journal,* pp. B1, B8.

Tarabulsy, G.M., Tessier, R., Gagnon, J., & Piche, C. (1996). Attachment classification and infant responsiveness during interaction. *Infant Behavior and Development, 19,* 131–143.

Tardiff, T. (1996). Nouns are not always learned before verbs: Evidence from Mandarin speakers' early vocabularies. *Developmental Psychology, 32,* 492–504.

Tate, R.L., & Broe G.A. (1999). Psychosocial adjustment after traumatic brain injury: What are the important variables? *Psychological Medicine, 29,* 713–725.

Taylor, S., & Todd, P. (1995). An integrated model of waste management bahavior: A test of household recycling and composting intentions. *Environment and Behavior, 27(5),* 603–630.

Taylor, S.E. (1991). *Health psychology* (2nd ed.). New York: McGraw-Hill.

Taylor, S. E. (1999). *Health psychology* (4th ed.). New York: McGraw-Hill.

Taylor, S.E., & Brown, J. (1988). Illusion and well-being: A social psychological perspective on mental health. *Psychological Bulletin, 103,* 193–210.

Teasley, S.D. (1995). The role of talk in children's peer collaborations. *Developmental Psychology, 31,* 207–220.

Teicher, M.H., Glod, C., & Cole, J.O. (1990). Emergence of intense suicidal preoccupation during fluoxetine treatment. *American Journal of Psychiatry, 147(2),* 207–210.

Teichman, M., Barnea, Z., & Rahav, G. (1989). Sensation seeking, state and trait anxiety, and depressive mood in adolescent substance abusers. *International Journal of the Addictions, 24,* 87–99.

Tellegan, A., Lykken, D.T., Bouchard, T.J., Wilcox, K.J., Segal, N.L., & Rich, S. (1988). Personality similarity in twins reared apart and together. *Journal of Personality and Social Psychology, 54,* 1031–1039.

Tennen, H., & Eller, S.J. (1977). Attributional components of learned helplessness. *Journal of Personality and Social Psychology, 35,* 265–271.

Terman, L. M. (1954). The discovery and encouragement of exceptional talent. *American Psychologist, 9,* 221–230.

Terrace, H. S. (1985). In the beginning was the "name." *American Psychologist, 40,* 1011–1028.

Terrace, H. S. (1993). The phylogeny and ontogeny of serial memory: List learning by pigeons and monkeys. *Psychological Science, 4,* 162–169.

Terry, D.J., Mayocchi, L., & Hynes, G.J. (1996). Depressive symptomatology in new mothers: A stress and coping perspective. *Journal of Abnormal Psychology, 105,* 220–231.

Teyler, T. J., & DiScenna, P. (1984). Long-term potentiation as a candidate mnemonic device. *Brain Research Reviews, 7,* 15–28.

Thibault, C. (1992). Preventing suicide in young people—it's a matter of life. *Canada's Mental Health, 40,* 2–7.

Thiessen, I. (1993). The impact of divorce on children. Special issue: Enhancing young children's lives. *Early Child Development and Care, 96,* 19–26.

Thimpson, R.F., & Krupa, D.J. (1994). Organization of memory traces in the mammalian brain. *Annual Review of Neuroscience, 17,* 519–549.

Thoma, S.J. (1986). Estimating gender differences in the comprehension and preference of moral issues. *Developmental Review, 6,* 165–180.

Thomas, A., & Chess, S. (1989). Temperament and development. In G.A. Kohnstamm, J.E. Bates, & M.K. Rothbart (Eds.), *Temperament in childhood.* New York: Wiley.

Thomas, J.L. (1992). *Adulthood and aging.* Boston: Allyn & Bacon.

Thomas, M.H. (1982). Physiological arousal, exposure to a relatively lengthy aggressive film, and aggressive behavior. *Journal of Research in Personality, 16,* 72–181.

Thomas-Stonell, N., Johnson, P., Schuller, R., & Jutai, J. (1994). Evaluation of a computer-based program for remediation of cognitive-communication skills. *Journal of Head Trauma Rehabilitation, 9,* 25–37.

Thompson, J. K. (1992). Body image: Extent of disturbance, associated features, theoretical models, assessment methodologies, intervention strategies, and a proposal for a new DSM-IV diagnostic category—Body Image Disorder. In M. Hesen, R. M. Eisler, & P. M. Miller (Eds.), *Progress in behavior modification* (pp. 3–54). Sycamore, IL: Sycamore.

Thompson, R.A. (1988). The effects of infant day care through the prism of attachment theory: A critical appraisal. *Early Childhood Research Quarterly, 3,* 273–283.

Thompson, R. F. (1989). A model system approach to memory. In P. R. Solomon, G. R. Goethals, C. M., Kelley, & B. R. Stephens (Eds.), *Memory: Interdisciplinary approaches.* New York: Springer-Verlag.

Thorndike, R. L., & Hagen, E. (1982). *Ten thousand careers.* New York: Wiley.

Thurstone, E. L. (1938). *Primary mental abilities.* Chicago: University of Chicago Press.

Tice, D. M. (1989). Metatraits: Interited variance as personality assessment. In D. M. Buss & N. Cantor (Eds.), *Personality psychology: Recent trends and emerging directions* (pp. 194–200). New York: Springer-Verlag.

Tice, D.M., & Baumeister, R.F. (1993). Anger control. In D. Wagner & J. Pennebaker (Eds.), *Handbook of mental control.* Englewood Cliffs, NJ: Prentice Hall.

Tice, D.M., & Baumeister, R.F. (1997). Longitudinal study of procrastination, performance, stress, and health: The costs and benefits of dawdling. *Psychological Science, 8,* 454–458.

Tiffany, S.T. (1990). A cognitive model of drug urges and drug-use behavior: Role of automatic and nonautomatic prosesses. *Psychological Review, 97,* 147–168.

Tim Hortons thief leaves workers' tips (2000, February 28). The Prince Edward Island *Guardian,* p. B8.

Timney, B., (1990). Effects of brief monocular deprivation on binocular depth perception in the cat: A sensitive period for the loss of stereopsis. *Visual Neuroscience, 5(3),* 273–280.

Ting-Toomey, S. (1991). Intimacy expressions in three cultures: France, Japan, and the United States. *International Journal of Intercultural Relations, 15,* 29–46.

Tobin, D.L., Johnson, C. Steinberg, S., Staats, M., & Dennis, A.M. (1991). Multifactorial assessment of bulimia nervosa. *Journal of Abnormal Psychology, 100(1),* 14–21.

Tolman, E. C., & Honzik, C. H. (1930). Introduction and removal of reward, and maze performance in rats. *University of California Publications in Psychology, 4,* 257–275.

Tomaka, J., Blascovich, J., Kelsey, R.M., & Leitten, C.L. (1993). Subjective, physiological, and behavioral effects of threat and challenge appraisal. *Journal of Personality and Social Psychology, 65*, 248–260.

Tomaka, J., Palacios, R., Schneider, K.T., Colota, M., Concha, J.B., & Herrald, M.M. (1999). Assertiveness predicts threat and challenge reactions to potential stress among women. *Journal of Personality and Social Psychology, 76*, 1008–1021.

Tomarken, A.J., Davidson, R.J., & Henriques, J.B. (1990). Resting frontal brain asymmetry predicts affective responses to films. *Journal of Personality and Social Psychology, 59*, 791–801.

Tomasell, M. & Call, J. (1997). *Primate cognition.* New York: Oxford University Press.

Toneatto, T. (1995). The regulation of cognitive states: A cognitive model of psychoactive substance abuse. *Journal of Cognitive Psychotherapy, 9(2),* 93–104.

Tonkin, R.S. (1997). Evaluation of a summer camp for adolescents with eating disorders. *Journal of Adolescent Health, 20,* 412–413.

Totterdell, P., Spelten, E., Smith, L., Barton, J., & Folkard, S. (1995). Recovery from work shifts: How long does it take? *Journal of Applied Psychology, 80,* 43–57.

Toufexis, A. (1993). The right chemistry. *Time,* pp. 49–51.

Tousignant, M., Bastien, M.F. & Hamel, S. (1993). Suicidal attempts and the ideations among adolescents and young adults: The contribution of the father's and mother's care and of parental separation. *Social Psychiatry and Psychiatric Epidemiology, 28(5),* 256–261.

Towson, S.M.J., & Zanna, M.P. (1982). Toward a situational analysis of gender differences in aggression. *Sex Roles, 8,* 903–914.

Tracy, J., Ghose, S.S., Stecher, T., McFall, R.M., & Steinmetz, J.E. (1999). *Psychological Science, 10,* 9–13.

Trapnell, P.D., & Campbell, J.D. (1999). Private self-conscious and the five-factor model of personality: Distinguishing rumination from reflection. *Journal of Personality and Social Psychology, 76,* 284–304.

Treffert, D. A. (1989). *Extraordinary people.* New York: Harper & Row.

Trehub, S.E. (1987). Infants' perception of musical patterns. *Perception and Psychophysics, 41,* 635–641.

Trehub, S.E. (1996). The world of infants: A world of music. *Early Childhood Connections,* 27–34.

Trehub, S.E., Schellenberg, E., & Hill, D. (1997). The origins of music perception and cognition: A developmental perspective. In I. Deliege & J. Sloboda (Eds.), *Music perception and cognition* (pp. 107–132). East Sussex, UK: Erlbaum (UK), Taylor & Francis.

Trehub, S.E., Unyk, A.M., & Henderson, J.L. (1994). Children's songs to infant siblings: Parallels with speech. *Journal of Child Language, 21(3),* 735–744.

Trehub, S.E., Unyk, A.M., Kamenetsky, S.B., & Hill, D.S. (1997). Mothers' and fathers' singing to infants. *Developmental Psychology, 33,* 500–507.

Trehub, S.E., Unyk, A.M., & Trainor, L.J., (1993). Adults identify infant directed music across cultures. *Infant Behavior and Development, 16(2),* 193–211.

Trehub, S.E., Unyk, A.M., & Trainor, L.J., (1993). Maternal singing in cross-cultural perspective. *Infant Behavior and Development, 16(3),* 285–295.

Tremblay, S. (1992). Le counseling prenuptial: Une invitation a intervenir. (Prenuptial counseling: An invitation for intervention.) *Revue Quebecoise de Psychologie, 13(1),* 43–57.

Trick, L.R. (1993). Patient compliance: Don't count on it. *Journal of the American Optometric Association, 64(4),* 264–270.

Trinder, J. (1988). Subjective insomnia without objective findings: A pseudo diagnostic classification? *Psychlogical Bulletin, 103,* 87–94.

Trinke, S.J., & Bartholomew, K. (1997). Hierarchies of attachment relationships in young adulthood. *Journal of Social and Personal Relationships, 14,* 603–625.

Tripp, D. A., Catano, V., & Sullivan, M.J. L. (1997). The contributions of attributional style, expectancies, depression, and self-esteem in a cognition based depression model. *Canadian Journal of Behavioural Science, 29,* 101–111.

Trudeau, M., Overbury, O., & Conrod, B. (1990). Perceptual training and figure-ground performance in low vision. *Journal of Visual Impairment and Blindness, 84(5),* 204–206.

Truscott, D. (1992). Intergenerational transmission of violent behavior in adolescent males. *Aggressive Behavior, 18(5),* 327–335.

Tschann, J.M., Johnston, J.R., & Wallerstein, J.S. (1989). Resources, stressors, and attachment as predictors of adult adjustment after divorce: A longitudinal study. *Journal of Marriage and the Family, 51,* 1033–1046.

Tudiver, F., Hilditch, J., Permaul, J.A., & McKendree, D.J. (1992). Does mutual help facilitate newly bereaved widowers? Report of a randomized controlled trial. *Evaluation and the Health Professions, 15(2),* 147–162.

Tudiver, F., Myers, T., Kurtz, R.G., Orr, K., et al. (1992). The talking sex project. *Evaluation and the Health Professions, 15(1),* 26–42.

Tudiver, F., & Talbot, Y. (1999). Why don't men seek help? Family physicians' perspectives on help-seeking behavior in men. *Journal of Family Practice, 48,* 47–52.

Tulving , E. (1989). Remembering and knowing the past. *American Scientist, 77,* 361–367

Tulving, E. (1993). What is episodic memory? *Current Directions in Psychological Science, 2,* 67–70.

Tulving, E., & Psotka, L. (1971). Retroactive inhibition in free recall: Inaccessibility of information available in the memory store. *Journal of Experimental Psychology, 87,* 1–8.

Tulving, E., Schacter, D. L. McLachlan, D. R. & Moscovitch, M. (1988). Priming of semantic autobiographical memory: A case study of retrograde amnesia. *Brain and Cognition, 8,* 3–20.

Turban, D.B., & Keon, T.O. (1993). Organizational attractiveness: A interactionist perspective. *Journal of Applied Psychology 78,* 184–193.

Turban, D.B., & Dougherty, T.M. (1994). Role of protégé personality in receipt of mentoring and career success. *Academy of Management Journal, 378,* 688–702.

Turk, D.C. (1994). Perspectives on chronic pain: The role of psychological factors. *Current Directions in Psychological Science, 3,* 45–48.

Turk, D. C., & Rudy, T. E. (1992). Cognitive factors and persistent pain: A glimpse into Pandora's box. *Cognitive Therapy and Research, 16,* 99–122.

Turkheimer, E. (1998). Heritability and biological explanation. *Psychological Review, 105,* 782–791.

Turner, J. A., & Clancy, S. (1986). Strategies for coping with chronic low back pain: Relationship to pain and disability. *Pain. 24,* 355–362

Turner, W.J. (1995). Type 1: An Xq28 phenomenon. *Archive of Sexual Behavior, 24,* 109–134.

Turtle, J. W., & Yuille, J. C. (1994). Lost but not forgotten details: Repeated eyewitness recall leads to reminiscence but not hypermnesia. *Journal of Applied Psychology, 79,* 260–271.

Tversky, A., & Kahneman, D. (1974). Judgment under uncertainty: Heuristics and biases. *Science, 185,* 1124–1131.

Tversky, A., & Kahneman, D. (1981). The framing of decisions and the psychology of choice. *Science, 211,* 453–458.

Tyler, T. R., & Cook, F. L. (1984). The mass media and judgment of risk: Distinguishing impact on personal and societal level judgments. *Journal of Personality and Social Psychology, 47,* 693–708.

Tyrer, S.P. (1999). Repetitive strain injury. *Pain Reviews, 6,* 155–166.

Uhrbock, R.S. (1961). Music on the job: Its influence on worker morale and production. *Personnel Psychology, 14,* 9–38.

Unger, R.K., & Crawford, M. (1992). *Women and gender: A feminist psychology.* Philadelphia: Temple University Press.

Unyk, A. M. (1990). An information-processing analysis of expectancy in music cognition. *Psychomusicology, 9,* 229–240.

Urban, M. J. (1992) Auditory subliminal stimulation: A reexamination. *Perceptual and Motor Skills, 74,* 515–541.

Urberg, K.A., Degirmencioglu, S.M., & Tolson, J.M. (1995). The structure of adolescent peer networks. *Developmental Psychology, 31,* 540–547.

Urberg, K.A., Degirmencioglu, S.M., Tolson, J.M., & Halliday-Scher, K. (1995). The structure of adolescent peer networks. *Developmental Psychology, 31,* 540–547.

Usher, J. A., & Neisser, U. (1993). Childhood amnesia and the beginnings of memory for four early life events. *Journal of Experimental Psychology: General, 122,* 155–165.

Uttl, B., & Graf, P. (1993). Episodic spatial memory in adulthood. *Psychology and Aging, 8(2),* 257–273.

Vaccarino et al. (1993). As quoted by Leo Charbonneau in the *Medical Post,* June 22, 1993, p. 34.

Vaccarino, F.J., Kennedy, S.H., Ralevski, E., & Black, R. (1994). The effects of growth hormone-releasing factor on food consumption in anorexia nervosa patients and normals. *Biological Psychiatry, 35(7),* 446–451.

Valenza, E., Simion, F., Cassia, V.M., & Umilta, C. (1996). Face preference at birth. *Journal of Experimental Psychology, 22,* 892–903.

Valkenburg, P.M., & van der Voort, T.H.A. (1994). Influence of TV on daydreaming and creative imagination: A review of research. *Psychological Bulletin, 116,* 316–339.

Vallerand, R.J., & Bissonnette, R. (1992). Intrinsic, extrinsic, and amotivational styles as predictors of behavior: A prospective study. *Journal of Personality, 60(3),* 599–620.

Vallerand, R.J., & O'Connor, B.P. (1989). Motivation in the elderly: A theoretical framework and some promising findings. Special Issue: Psychology of aging and gerontology. *Canadian Psychology, 30(3),* 538–550.

Valleroy, L.A., Harris, J.R., & Way, P.O. (1990). The impact of HIV infection on child survival in the developing world. *AIDS, 4,* 667–672.

Van Houten, R. (1993). The use of wrist weights to reduce self-injury maintained by sensory reinforcement. *Journal of Applied Behavior Analysis, 26,* 197–203.

Van Roosmalen, E.H., & McDaniel, S.A. (1992). Adolescent smoking intentions: Gender difference in peer context. *Adolescence, 27(105),* 87–105.

Van Velsor, E., & Hughes, M.W. (1990). *Gender differences in the development of managers: How women managers learn from experience.* Technical report no. 145, Center for Creative Leadership, Greensboro, N.C.

Vance, J., et al. v. Judas Priest et al., No. 86-5844 (2nd Dist. Ct. Nev. 1990).

Vauclair, J., Fagot, J., & Hopkins, W. D. (1993). Rotation of mental images in baboons when the visual input is directed to the cerebral hemisphere. *Psychological Science, 4,* 99–103.

Veenhoven, R. (1993). *Happiness in nations.* Rotterdam, Netherlands: Risbo.

Velicer, W. F., & Prochaska, J. O. (1999). An expert system intervention for smoking cessation. *Patient Education & Counseling, 36,* 119–129

Verby, C., & Herold, E.S. (1992). Parents and AIDS education. *AIDS Education and Prevention, 4(3),* 187–196.

Vermeire, B.A., & Hamilton, C.R. (1998). Inversion effect for faces in split-brain monkeys. *Neuropsychologica, 36,* 1003–1014.

Vernberg, E.M., LaGreca, A.M., Silverman, W.K., & Prinstein, M.J. (1996). Prediction of posttraumatic stress symptoms in children after hurricane Andrew. *Journal of Abnormal Psychology, 105,* 237–248.

Vernon, P.A. (1991). Studying intelligence the hard way. *Intelligence, 15,* 389–395.

Vernon, P.A. (1994). *The neuropsychology of individual differences.* San Diego: Academic.

Vernon, P.A., & Jang, K.L. (1993). Self-rated vs. "actual" personality similarity in monozygotic and dizygotic twins and non-twin siblings. *Personality and Individual Differences, 15*(2), 219–220.

Vernon, P.A., & Mori, M. (1992). Intelligence, reaction times, and peripheral nerve conduction velocity. *Intelligence, 16,* 273–288.

Viemero, V., & Paajanen, S. (1992). The role of fantasies and dreams in the TV viewing-aggression relationship. *Aggressive-Behavior, 18,* 109–116.

Vincente, K. J., & Brewer, W. F. (1993). Reconstructive remembering of the scientific literature. *Cognition, 46,* 101–128.

Violanti, J.M., & Paton, D. (1999). *Police trauma: Psychological aftermath of civilian combat.* Springfield, IL: Charles C. Thomas Publisher.

Vogel, L.Z., & Savva, S. (1993). Atlas personality. *British Journal of Medical Psychology, 66,* 323–330.

Volpe, J.J. (1992). The effect of cocaine use on the fetus. *New England Journal of Medicine, 327,* 399–407.

Volpicelli, J.R., Alterman, A.I., Hayashida, M., & O'Brien, C.P. (1992). Naltrexone in the treatment of alcohol dependence. *Archives of General Psychiatry, 49,* 876–880.

Von Senden, M. (1960). *Space and sign.* Trans. by P. Heath. New York: Free Press.

Vorauer, J.D., & Miller, D.T. (1997). Failure to recognize the effect of implicit social influence in the presentation of self. *Journal of Personality and Social Psychology, 73,* 281–295.

Voyer, D., & Bryden, M.P. (1990). Gender, level of spatial ability, and lateralization of mental rotation. *Brain and Cognition, 13*(1), 18–29.

Voyer, D., Voyer, S., & Bryden, M.P. (1995). Magnitude of sex differences in spatial abilities: A meta-analysis and consideration of critical variables. *Psychological Bulletin, 117*(2), 250–270.

Vygotsky, L.S. (1987). Thinking and speech. In R.W. Rieber, A.S. Carton (Eds.) & N. Minick (Trans.), *The collected works of L.S. Vygotsky: Vol 1. Problems of general psychology* (pp. 37–285). New York: Plenum. (Original work published 1934).

Wagenaar, W. A., (1986). My memory: A study of autobiographical memory over six years. *Cognitive Psychology, 18,* 225–522.

Wahlsten, D. (1999). Single-gene influences on brain and behavior. *Annual Review of Psychology, 50,* 599–624.

Waitzkin, H. (1984). Doctor–patient communication: Clinical implications of social scientific research. *Journal of the American Medical Association, 252,* 2441–2446.

Walden, T.A., & Ogan, T.A., (1988). The development of social referencing. *Child Development, 59*(5), 1230–1240.

Waldholz, M. (1996, July 8). Combined-drug therapy being hailed as promising weapon in AIDS battle. *The Wall Street Journal.*

Walker, L.J. (1989). A longitudinal study of moral reasoning. *Child Development, 60,* 157–166.

Walker, L.J. (1991). Sex differences in moral reasoning. In W.M. Kurines & J.L. Gewirtz (Eds.), *Handbook of moral behavior and development, Vol 2,* Hillsdale NJ: Erlbaum.

Walker, L.J., & Taylor, J.H., (1991). Family interactions and the development of moral reasoning. *Child Development, 62*(2), 264–283.

Walker, L.J., Taylor, J.H., (1991). Stage transitions in moral reasoning: A longitudinal study of developmental processes. *Developmental Psychology, 27*(2), 330–337.

Walker, P.W., Cole, J.O., Gardner, E.A., Hughes, A.R., Johnston, J.A., & Batey, S.R. (1993). Improvement in fluoxetine-associated sexual dysfunction in patients switched to bupropion. *Journal of Clinical Psychiatry, 54,* 549–565.

Wall, A.M., Hinson, R.E., Schmidt, E., Johnson, C., et al. (1990). Place conditioning with d–amphetamine: The effect of the CS–UCS interval and evidence of a place avoidance. *Animal Learning and Memory, 18,* 393–400.

Wallace, B. (1993). Day persons, night persons, and variability in hypnotic susceptibility. *Journal of Personality and Social Psychology, 64,* 827–833.

Wallace, R.K., & Benson, H. (1972). The physiology of meditation. *Scientific American, 236,* 84–90.

Wallace, R.K., & Fisher, L.E. (1987). *Consciousness and behavior* (2nd ed.). Boston: Allyn & Bacon.

Wallman, J. (1992). *Aping Language.* New York: Cambridge.

Walsh, S. (1993). Cited in Toufexis, A. (1993, February 15), *Time,* 49–51.

Walters, D. (1995). Mandatory reporting of child abuse: Legal ethical, and clinical implications within a Canadian context. *Canadian Psychology, 36,* 163–182.

Walters, G., & Grusec, J. E. (1977). *Punishment.* San Francisco: Freeman.

Wankel, L.M. (1993). The importance of enjoyment to adherence and psychological benefits from physical activity. Special issue: Exercise and psychological well being. *International Journal of Sport Psychology, 24*(2), 151–169.

Ward, W. (1997). Psychiatric morbidity in Australian veterans of the United Nations peacekeeping force in Somalia. *Australian and New Zealand Journal of Psychiatry, 31,* 184–193.

Wark, G.R., & Krebs, D.L. (1996). Gender and dilemma differences in real-life moral judgment. *Developmental Psychology, 32,* 220–230.

Warwick, Z.S., Hall, W.G., Pappas, T.N., & Schiffman, S.S. (1993). Taste and smell sensations enhance the satiating effect of both a high-carbohydrate and a high-fat meal in humans. *Physiology and Behavior, 53*(3), 553–563.

Warwick, Z. S., & Schiffman, S. S. (1992). Role of dietary fat in calorie intake and weight gain. *Neuroscience & Biobehavioral Reviews, 16,* 585–596.

Wasserman, E. A. (1993). Comparative cognition: Toward a general understanding of cognition in behavior. *Psychological Science, 4,* 156–161.

Wasserman, E. A., Kiedinger, R. E., & Bhatt, R. S. (1988). Conceptual behavior in pigeons: Categories, subcategories, and pseudocategories. *Journal of Experimental Psychology: Animal Behavior Processes, 14,* 235–246.

Wasylenki, D. A., Goering, P. N., Lemire, D., Lindsey, S., & Lancee, W. (1993). The hostel outreach program: Assertive case management for homeless mentally ill persons. *Hospital and Community Psychiatry, 44,* 848–853.

Waters, L.K., & Zakarajsek, T. (1990). Correlates of need for cognition total and subscale scores. *Education and Psychological Measurement, 50,* 21–217.

Watkins, P.C., Vache, K., Verney, S.P., Mathews, A., & Muller, S. (1996). Unconscious mood-congruent memory bias in depression. *Journal of Abnormal Psychology, 105,* 34–41.

Watson, A.C., Nixon, C.L., Wilson, A., & Capage, L. (1999). Social interaction skills and theory of mind in young children. *Developmental Psychology, 35,* 386–391.

Watson, C., Anderson, F., Gloor, P., Jones-Gotman, M., Peters, T., Evans, A., Oliver, A., Melanson, D., & Leroux, G. (1992). Anatomic basis of amygdaloid and hippocampal volume measurement by magnetic resonance imaging. *Neurology, 42*(9), 1743–1750.

Watson, D. (1989). Strangers' ratings of the five robust personality factors: Evidence of a surprising convergence with self-report. *Journal of Personality and Social Psychology, 57,* 120–128.

Watson, J. B. (1924). The unverbalized in human behavior. *Psychological Review, 31,* 273–280.

Watson, J. B., & Raynor, R. (1920). Conditioned emotional reactions. *Journal of Experimental Psychology, 3,* 1–14.

Watson, T.S. (1996). A prompt pulse delayed contingency procedure for reducing bathroom graffiti. *Journal of Applied Behavior Analysis, 29,* 121–124.

Watts, B.L. (1982)l. Individual differences in circadian activity rhythms and their effects on roommate relationships. *Journal of Personality, 50,* 374–384.

Wayne, S.J., & Liden, R.C. (1995). Effects of impression management on performance ratings: A longitudinal study. *Academy of Management Journal, 38,* 232–260.

Webb, W. (1975). *Sleep: The gentle tyrant.* Englewood Cliffs, NJ: Prentice-Hall.

Webb, W., & Agnew, H.W. (1967). Sleep cycling within the twenty-four hour period. *Journal of Experimental Psychology, 74,* 167–169.

Webster, J.D., & Cappeliez, P. (1993). Reminiscence and autobiographical memory: Complementary context for cognitive aging research. *Developmental Review, 13*(1), 54–91.

Wehner, R., & Menzel, R. (1990). Do insects have cognitive maps? *Annual Review of Neuroscience, 13,* 403–414.

Wehr, T.A. (1997). Melatonin and seasonal rhythms. *Journal of Biological Rhythms, 12,* 518–527.

Wehr, T.A., Giesen, H.A., Schulz, P.M., Anderson, J.L., Joseph-Vanderpool, J.R., Kelly, K., Kasper, S., & Rosenthal, N.E. (1991). Contrasts between symptoms of summer depression and winter depression. *Journal of Affective Disorders, 23,* 173–183.

Weigel, R.H., Kim, E.L., & Frost, J.L. (1995). Race relations on prime time television reconsidered: Patterns of continuity and change. *Journal of Applied Social Psychology, 25,* 223–236.

Weinberg, R. A. (1989). Landmark issues and great debates. *American Psychologist, 44*(2), 98–104.

Weinberger, A. (1989). Ethics: Code value and application. *Canadian Psychology, 30,* 77–85.

Weinberger, D.R. (1994). Bilogical basis of schizophrenia: Structural/functional considerations relevant to potential for antipsychotic drug resons. *Journal of Clincial Psychiatry, Monograph Series, 12,* 4–7.

Weiner, B. (1989). *Human motivation.* Hillsdale, NJ: Erlbaum.

Weisberg, R., & Suls, J. M. (1973). An information-processing model of Duncker's candle problem. *Cognitive Psychology, 4,* 255–276.

Weisner, T.S., & Wilson-Mitchell, J.E. (1990). Nonconventional family life-styles and sex typing in six-year-olds. *Child Development, 61,* 1915–1933.

Weiss, R.A. (1993). How does HIV cause AIDS? *Science, 260,* 1273–1278.

Weisz, J. R., Weiss, B., & Donenberg, G. R. (1992). The lab versus the clinic: Effects of child and adolescent psychotherapy. *American Psychologist, 47,* 1578–1585.

Weisz, J. R., Weiss, B., Morton, T., Granger, D., & Han, S. (1992). *Meta-analysis of psychotherapy outcome research with children and adolescents.* Unpublished manuscript, University of California, Los Angeles.

Wellman, H.M., Ritter, K., & Flavell, J.H. (1975). Deliberate memory behavior in the delayed reactions of very young children. *Developmental Psychology, 11,* 780–787.

Wellman, H.M., Somerville, S.C., & Haake, R.J. (1979). Development of search procedures in real-life spatial environments. *Developmental Psychology, 15,* 530–542.

Wells, G. L. (1993). What do we know about eyewitness identification? *American Psychologist, 48,* 553–571.

Wells, S., Graham, K., & West, P. (1998). "The good, the bad, and the ugly": Responses by security staff to aggressive incidents in public drinking settings. *Journal of Drug Issues, 28,* 817–836.

Weltzl-Fairchild, A., Dufresne-Tasse, C., & Dube, L. (1997). Aesthetic experience and different typologies of dissonance. *Visual Arts Research, 158–167.*

Werker, J. F. (1989). Becoming a native listener. *American Scientist, 77,* 54–59.

Werker, J. F., & Tees, R. C. (1999). Influences on infant speech processing: Toward a new synthesis. *Annual Review of Psychology, 50.* 509–535.

Werner, C., & Parmelee, P. (1979). Similarity of activity preferences among friends: Those who play together stay together. *Social Psychology Quarterly, 42,* 62–66.

Werner, E.E. (1995). Resilience in development. *Current Directions in Psychological Science, 4,* 81–85.

Werts, M.G., Caldwell, N.K., & Wolery, M. (1996). Peer modeling of response chains: Observational learning by students with disabilities. *Journal of Applied Behavior Analysis, 29,* 53–66.

West, R. (1993). Beneficial effects of nicotine: Fact or fiction. *Addiction, 88*(5), 589–590.

Whaley, B.B. (2000). *Explaining illness: Research, theory, and strategies.* Mahwah, NJ: Erlbaum.

Whalsten, D. (1995). Increasing the raw intelligence of a nation is constrained by ignorance, not its citizens' genes. *Alberta Journal of Educational Research, 41,* 257–264.

Wheaton, B. (1990). Life transitions, role histories and mental health. *American Sociological Review, 55(2),* 209–223.

Wheaton, B. (1999). Social stress. In C.S. Aneshensel & J.C. Phelan (Eds.), *Handbook of sociology of mental health* (pp. 277–300). New York, NY: Kluwer Academic/Plenum.

Wheaton, B. (1999). The nature of stressors. In A.V. Horwitz, & T.L. Scheid (Eds.), *A handbook for the study of mental health: Social contexts, theories, and systems* (pp. 176–197). New York: Cambridge University Press.

Whiffen, V.E., & Gotlib, I.H. (1993). Comparison of postpartum and nonpostpartum depression: Clinical presentation, psychiatric history, and psychosocial functioning. *Journal of Consulting and Clinical Psychology, 61(3),* 485–494.

Whishaw, I.Q., Pellis, S.M., & Gorny, B.P. (1992). Medial frontal cortex lesions impair the aiming component of rat reaching. *Behavioral Brain Research, 50(1–2),* 93–104.

White, D.J., & Bennett, G., Jr. (1998). Social influence on avoidance of dangerous stimuli by rats. *Animal Learning and Behavior, 26,* 433–438.

White, D. J., & Galef, B. G., Jr. (1998). Social influence on avoidance of dangerous stimuli by rats. *Animal Learning and Behavior, 26,* 433–438.

White, G.L., & Mullen, P.E. (1990). *Jealousy: Theory, research, and clinical strategies.* New York: Guilford Press.

Whorf, B. L. (1956). Science and linguistics. In J. B. Carroll (Ed.), *Language, thought, and reality: Selected writings of Benjamin Whorf.* Cambridge, MA: MIT Press.

Whyte, G. (1991). Diffusion of responsibility: Effects on the escalation tendency. *Journal of Applied Psychology, 76,* 408–415.

Whyte, K. (1992). A community in crisis: Will mental health services respond to AIDS? *Canada's Mental Health, 40(4),* 2–5.

Wickett, J. C., & Vernon, P. A. (1994). Peripheral nerve conduction velocity, reaction time, and intelligence: An attempt to replicate Vernon and Mori (1992). *Intelligence, 18,* 127–131.

Wiegman, O., & van Schie, E.G.M. (1998). Video game playing and its relations with aggressive and prosocial behaviour. *British Journal of Social Psychology, 37,* 367–378.

Wielkiewicz, R. M., & Calvert, C. R. X. (1989). *Training and habilitating developmentally disabled people: An introduction.* Newbury Park, CA: Sage.

Wiesel, T. N. (1982). Postnatal development of the visual cortex and the influence of environment. *Nature, 299,* 583–591.

Wiggins, J. S., & Pincus, A. L. (1992). Personality, structure and assessment. *Annual Review of Psychology, 43,* 473–504.

Wilcoxon, H.C., Dragoin, W.B., & Dral, P.A. (1971). Illness-induced aversions in rats and quail: Relative salience of visual and gustatory cues. *Science, 171,* 826–828.

Wild, T.C., Enzle, M.E., & Hawkins, W.L. (1992). Effects if perceived extrinsic versus intrinsic teacher motivation on student reactions to skill acquisition. *Personality and Social Psychology Bulletin, 18,* 245–251.

Wiley, J.A., & Camacho, T.C. (1980). Life-style and future health: Evidence from the Alameda County study. *Preventive Medicine, 9,* 1–21.

Wilgosh, L. & Mueller, H.H. (1993). Work skills for disadvantaged and unprepared youth and adults. *International Journal for the Advancement of Counselling, 16(2),* 99–105.

Wilhelm, K., & Parker, G. (1994). Sex differences in lifetime depression rates: Fact or artifact? *Psychological Medicine, 24,* 97–111.

Willet, W.C., & MacMahon, B. (1984). Diet and cancer—an overview. *New England Journal of Medicine, 310,* 633–638.

Williams, D.E., & Page, M.M. (1989). A multi-dimensional measure of Maslow's hierarchy of needs. *Journal of Research in Personality, 23,* 192–213.

Williams, G.C., Grow, V.M., Freedman, Z.R., Ryan, R.M., & Deci, E.I. (1996). Motivational predictors of weight loss and weight-loss maintenance. *Journal of Personality and Social Psychology, 70,* 115–126.

Williams, K.B., Radefled, P.A. Binning J.F., & Suadk, J.R. (1993). When job candidates are "hard" versus "easy-to-get": Effects of candidate availability on employment decisions. *Journal of Applied Social Psychology, 23,* 169–198.

Williams, R., Zyzanski, S.J., & Wright, A.L. (1992). Life events and daily hassles and uplifts and predictors of hospitalization and out-patient visitation. *Social Science Medicine, 34,* 763–768.

Williams, T., & Clarke, V.A. (1997). Optimistic bias in beliefs about smoking. *Australian Journal of Psychology, 49,* 106–112.

Williamson, D. A., Cubic, B. A., & Gleaves, D. H. (1993). Equivalence of body image disturbances in anorexia and bulimia nervosa. *Journal of Abnormal Psychology, 102(1),* 177–180.

Williamson, D.A. (1990). *Assessment of eating disorders: Obesity, anorexia, and bulimia nervosa.* New York: Pergamon Press.

Williamson, D.A., Cubic, B.A., & Gleaves, D.H. (1993). Equivalence of body image disturbances in anorexia and bulimia nervosa. *Journal of Abnormal Psychology, 102(1),* 177–180.

Willis, S. L., & Nesselroade, C. S. (1990). Long-term effects of fluid ability training in old-old age. *Developmental Psychology, 26,* 905–910.

Willis, W. D. (1985). *The pain system. The neural basis of nociceptive transmission in the mammalian nervous system.* Basel: Karger.

Wills, T.A., McNamara, G., Vaccaro, D., & Hirky, A.E. (1996). Escalated substance use: A longitudinal grouping analysis from early to middle adolescence. *Journal of Abnormal Psycholgy, 105,* 166–180.

Wilson, D.W. (1981). Is helping a laughing matter? *Psychology, 18,* 6–9.

Wilson, G.T., Nathan, P.E., O'Leary, K.D., & Clark, L.A. (1996). *Abnormal psychology: Integrating perspectives.* Boston: Allyn & Bacon.

Wilson, M.I., & Daly, M. (1996). Male sexual proprietariness and violence against wives. *Current Directions in Psychological Science, 5,* 2–7.

Wilson, T.D., & Klaaren, K.J. (1992). Effects of affective expectations on willingness to relive pleasant and unpleasant events. Unpublished data. Cited in Wilson, T.D. & Klaaren, K.J., "Expectation whirls me round": The role of affective expectations in affective experience. In M.S. Clark (Ed.), *Emotion and social behavior* (pp. 1–31). Newbury Park, CA: Sage.

Wilson, T.D., Lisle, D.J., Draft, D., & Wetzel, C.G. (1989). Preferences as expectation-driven inferences: Effects of affective expectations on affective experience. *Journal of Personality and Social Psychology, 56,* 519–530.

Wilson, T.D., & Schooner, J. (1991). Thinking too much: Introspection can reduce the quality of preferences and decisions. *Journal of Personality and Social Psychology, 60,* 181–192.

Winefield, A.H., & Tiggemann, M. (1991). Employment status and psychological well-being: A longitudinal study. *Journal of Applied Psychology, 75,* 455–459.

Winett, R.A. (1995). A framework for health promotion and disease prevention programs. *American Psychologist, 50,* 341–350.

Winn, P. (1995). The lateral hypothalamus and motivated behavior: An old syndrome reassessed and a new perspective gained. *Current Directions in Psychological Science, 4,* 182–187.

Winocur, G. (1992). A comparison of normal old rats and young adult rats with lesions to the hippocampus or prefrontal cortex on a test of matching-to-sample. *Neuropsychologia, 30(9),* 769–781.

Winograd, E. (1988). Some observations on prospective remembering. In M. M. Gruneberg, P. E. Morris, & R. N. Sykes (Eds.), *Practical aspects of memory: Current research and issues* (Vol. 1, pp. 348–353). Chichester, England: Wiley.

Winter, D.G. (1983). Development of an integrated system for scoring motives in verbal running text. Unpublished manuscript, Wesleyan University.

Wise, R.A. (1998). Drug activation of brain reward pathways. *Drug and Alcohol Dependence, 51,* 13–22.

Wise, R.A., & Bozarth, M.A. (1987). A psychomotor stimulation theory of addiction. *Psychological Review, 94,* 469–492.

Wisniewski, H.M., & Terry, R.D. (1976). Neuropathology of the aging brain. In R.D. Terry & S. Gershod (Eds.), *Neurobiology of aging* (pp. 65–78). New York: Reven.

Witelson, S.F. (1991). Neural sexual mosaicism: Sexual differentiation of the human temporo-parietal region for functional assymetry. Special Issue: neuroendocrine effects on brain development and cognition. *Psychoneuroendocrinology, 16(1–3),* 131–153.

Witelson, S.F., & McCulloch, P.B. (1991). Premortem and postmortem measurement to study structure with function: A human brain collection. *Schizophrenia Bulletin, 17(4),* 583–591.

Wolberg, L. R. (1977). *The technique of psychotherapy.* New York: Grune & Stratton.

Wolfe, B.M., & Baron, R.A. (1971). Laboratory aggression related to aggression in naturalistic social situations: Effects of an aggressive model on the behavior of college student and prisoner observers. *Psychonomic Science, 24,* 193–194.

Wolfe, D. A., Sandler, J., & Kaufman, K. (1981). Competency-based parent training program for child abusers. *Journal of Consulting and Clinical Psychology, 49,* 633–640.

Wolfson, C., Handfield-Jones, R., Glass, K.C., McClaren, J., & Keyserlingk, E. (1993). Adult children's perceptions of their responsibility to provide care for dependent elderly parents. *Gerontologist, 33(3),* 315–323.

Wolpe, J. (1958). *Psychotherapy by reciprocal inhibition.* Stanford, CA: Standord University Press.

Wolpe, J. (1969). *The practice of behavior therapy.* Oxford: Pergamon Press.

Wong, P.T.P. (1998). *The human quest for meaning: A handbook of psychological research and clinical applications.* Mahwah, NJ: Erlbaum.

Wong, R., & McBride, C.B. (1993). Flavour neophobia in gerbils (Meriones unguiculatus) and hamsters (Mesocricetus auratus). *Quarterly Journal of Experimental Psychology: Comparative and Physiological Psychology, 46B,* 129–143.

Wood, J.M., Nezworski, M.T., & Stejskal, W.J. (1996). The comprehensive system for the Rorschach: A critical examination. *Psychological Science, 7,* 3–10.

Wood, R.A., & Locke, E.A. (1990). Goal setting and strategy effects on complex tasks. In B.M. Staw & L.L. Cummings (Eds.), *Research in organizational behavior* (Vol. 12, pp. 73–110). Greenwich, CT: JAI Press.

Wood, W., Wong, F.Y., & Chachere, J.G. (1991). Effects of media violence on viewers' aggression in unconstrained social interaction. *Psychological Bulletin, 109,* 373–383.

Woodall, K. L., & Matthews, K. A. (1993). Changes in and stability of hostile characteristics: Results from a 4-year longitudinal study of children. *Journal of Personality and Social Psychology, 64,* 491–499.

Woodruff-Pak, D. S. (1999). New directions for a classical paradigm: Human eyeblink conditioning. *Psychological Science, 10,* 1–3.

Woody, E.Z., & Bowers, K.S. (1994). A frontal assault on dissociated control. In S.J. Lynn & J.W. Rhue (Eds.)., *Dissociation: Theoretical and clinical perspectives* (pp. 52–79). New York: Guilford Press.

Worden, J.W. (1989). As in the *Toronto Star,* January 14, 1989, p. H4.

Wortman, C.B., Carnelley, K.B., & Kessler, R.C. (1994). *Impact of widowhood on depression: Findings from a prospective national survey.* Manuscript submitted for publication.

Wortman, C. B., & Linsenmeier, H. A. W. (1977). Interpersonal attraction and techniques of ingratiation in organizational settings. In B.N. Staw & G. R. Salancik (Eds.), *New directions in organizational behavior* (pp. 133–178). Chicago: St. Clair Press.

Wright, E.F., Rule, B.G., Ferguson, T.J., McGuire, G.R., & Wells, G.L. (1992). Misattribution of dissonance and behaviour-consistent attitude change. *Canadian Journal of Behavioural Science, 24(4)*, 456–464.

Wright, M. J. & Myers, R. C. (1982). *History of academic psychology in Canada.* Toronto: C. J. Hogrefe, Inc.

Wright, P.M., O'Leary-Kelly, A.M., Cortinak, J.M., Klein, H.J. & Hollenbeck, J.R. (1994) On the meaning and measurement of goal commitment. *Journal of Applied Psychology, 79*, 795–803.

Wright, R. (1995, March 13). The biology of violence. *New Yorker,* 68–77.

Wright, S.C., Aron, A., McLaughlin-Volpe, T., & Ropp, S.A. (1997). The extended contact effect: Knowledge of cross-group friendships and prejudice. *Journal of Personality and Social Psychology, 73*, 73-90.

Wright, W. (1999). *Born that way: Genes—behavior—personality.* New York: Knopf,.

Wrightsman, L.S. (1981). Personal documents as data in conceptualizing adult personality development. *Personality and Social Psychology Bulletin, 7*, 367–385.

Wyer, R.S., Jr., & Srull, T.K. (Eds.). (1994). *Handbook of social cognition.* (2nd ed., Vol. 1). Hillsdale, NJ: Erlbaum.

Yankner, J., Johnson, S. T., Menerdo, T., Cordell, B., & Firth, C. L. (1990). Relations of neural APP-751/APP-695 in RNA ratio and neuritic plaque density in Alzheimer's disease. *Science, 248*, 854–856.

Yates, S. (1992). Lay attributions about distress after a natural disaster. *Personality and Social Psychology Bulletin, 18*, 217–222.

Yogman, M.W. (1981). Development of the father-infant relationship. In H. Fitzgerald, B. Lester, & M.W. Yogman (Eds.), *Theory and research in behavioral pediatrics* (Vol. 1, pp. 221–279). New York: Plenum.

Yonas, A., Arterberry, M.E., & Granrud, C.E. (1987). Four-month-old infants' sensitivity to binocular and kinetic information for three-dimensional-object shape. *Child Development, 58(4)*, 910–917.

You smell iSmell (2000, March 4). *The Telegram,* p. 25.

Young, A.M., & Herling, S. (1986). Drugs as reinforcers: Studies in laboratory animals. In S.R. Goldberg & I.P. Stolerman (Eds.), *Behavioral analysis of drug dependence* (pp. 9–67). New York: Academic Press.

Young, L. T. , Hood, E., Abbey, S. E., & Malcolmson, S. A. (1993). Psychiatric Consultation in the Eastern Canadian Arctic. II. Referral patterns, diagnosis and treatment. *Canadian Journal of Psychiatry, 38*, 28–31.

Yudofsky, S., Hales, R.E., & Ferguson, T. (1991). *What you need to know about psychiatric drugs.* New York: Grove Weidenfeld.

Yuen, S.A., & Kuiper, N.A. (1992). Type A and self-evaluations: A social comparison perspective. *Personality and Individual Differences, 13*, 549–562.

Yuille, J. C., & Tollestrup, P. A. (1992). A model of the diverse effects of emotion on eyewitness memory. In S.-A. Christianson (Ed.), *The handbook of emotion and learning: Research and theory.* Hillsdale, NJ: Erlbaum.

Zaccaro, S.J., Foti, R.J., & Kenny, D.A. (1991). Self-monitoring and trait-based variance in leadership: An investigation of leader flexibility across multiple group situations. *Journal of Applied Psychology, 76*, 308–315.

Zaccaro, S.J., Gilbert, J.A., Thor, K.K., & Mumford, M.D. (1991). Leadership and social intelligence: Linking social perspectives and behavioral flexibility to leader effectiveness. Special Issue: Individual differences and leadership: I. *Leadership Quarterly, 2 (4)*, 317–342.

Zahn-Waxler, C., Radke-Yarrow, M., Wagner, E., & Chapman, M. (1992). Development of concern for others. *Developmental Psychology, 28*, 126–136.

Zaidel, D.W. (1994). Worlds apart: Pictorial semantics in the left and right cerebral hemispheres. *Current Directions in Psycholgical Science, 3*, 5-8.

Zajonc, R.B., & McIntosh, D.N. (1992). Emotions research: Some promising questions and some qestionable promises. *Psychological Science, 3*, 70–74.

Zapf, M.K. (1993). Remote practice and culture shock: Social workers moving to isolated northern regions. *Social Work, 38(6)*, 694–704.

Zatorre, R.J. (1983). Category-boundary effects and speeded sorting with a harmonic musical-interval continuum: Evidence for dual processing. *Journal of Experimental Psychology: Human Perception and Performance, 9*, 739–752.

Zatorre, R.J. (1989). Intact absolute pitch ability after left temporal lobectomy. *Cortex, 25*, 567–580.

Zatorre, R.J., Evans, A.C., & Meyer, E. (1994). Neural mechanisms underlying melodic perception and memory for pitch. *Journal of Neuroscience, 14*, 1908û1919.

Zatorre, R.J., & Halpern, A.R. (1993). Effect of unilateral temporal-lobe excision on perception and imagery of songs. *Neuropsychologia, 31(3)*, 221–232.

Zatorre, R.J., Halpern, A.R., Perry, D.W., Meyer, E., & Evans, A.C. (1996). Hearing in the mind's ear: A PET investigation of musical imagery and perception. *Journal of Cognitive Neuroscience, 8(1)*, 29–46.

Zatzick, D. F., & Dimsdale, J. E. (1990). *Psychosomatic Medicine, 52*, 544–557.

Zeki, S. (1992, September). The visual image in mind and brain. *Scientific American,* pp. 69–76.

Zeki, S. (1993). *A vision of the brain.* London: Blackwell Scientific.

Zelazo, N.A., Zelazo, P.R., Cohen, K.M., & Zelazo, P.D. (1993). Specificity of practice effects on elementary neuromotor patterns. *Developmental Psychology, 29(4)*, 686–691.

Zeman, J., & Shipman, K. (1996). Children's expression of negative affect: Reasons and method. *Developmental Psychology, 32*, 842–849.

Zihl, J., von Cramon, D., Mai, N. (1983). Selective disturbance of movement vision after bilateral brain damage. *Brain, 106*, 313–340.

Zillman, D., & Bryant, J. (1984). Effects of massive exposure to pornography. In N.M. Malamuth & E. Donnerstein (Eds.), *Pornography and sexual aggression.* New York: Academic Press.

Zillman, D., & Bryant, J. (1988). Pornography's impact on sexual satisfaction. *Journal of Applied Social Pschology, 18*, 438–453.

Zimbardo, P.G. (1977). *Shyness: What it is and what you can do about it.* Reading, MA: Addison-Wesley.

Zuckerman, M. (1990). The psychophysiology of sensation seeking. *Journal of Personality, 58*, 313–345.

Zuckerman, M. (1994). *Behavioral expressions and biosocial bases of sensation seeking.* New York: Cambridge University Press.

Zuckerman, M. (1995). Good and bad humors: Biochemical bases of personality and its disorders. *Psychological Science, 6*, 325–332.

Zuckerman, M. (1996). Psychobiological model for impulsive unsocialized sensation seeking: A comparative approach. *Neuropsychobiology, 34*, 125–129.

Zuckerman, M., DePaulo, B.M., & Rosenthal, R. (1981). Verbal and nonverbal communication of deception. In L. Berkowitz (Ed.), *Advances in experimental social psychology* (Vol. 14, pp. 1–59). New York: Academic Press.

Zuckerman, M., & Neeb, M. (1980). Demographic influences in sensation seeking and expression of sensation seeking in religion, smoking, and driving habits. *Personality and Individual Differences, 1*, 197–206.

Zuckerman, M., Simons, R. F., & Como, P. (1988). Sensation seeking and stimulus intensity as modulators of cortical, cardiovascular, and electrodermal responses: A cross-modality study. *Personality and Individual Differences, 9*, 361–372.

Zuroff, D.C., Blatt, S.J., Sanislow, C.A., Bondi, C.M., & Pilkonis, P.A. (1999). Vulnerability to depression: reexamining state dependence and relative stability. *Journal of Abnormal Psychology, 108*, 76–89.

Zusne, L., & Jones, W.H. (1989). *Anomalistic psychology: A study of magical thinking* (2nd ed.). Hillsdale, NJ: Erlbaum.

Zuwerink, J.R., & Devine, P.G. (1996). Attitude importance and resistance to persuasion: It's not just the thought that counts. *Journal of Personality and Social Psychology, 70*, 931–944.

NAME INDEX

Beneteau, B., 537
Benjamin, L.T., Jr., 481
Benoit, D., 334
Benson, D.F., 65
Benson, H., 173
Bentall, R.P., 169
Bentley, K.M., 408
Berardi-Coletta, B., 278
Berenbaum, H., 588
Berenbaun, S.A., 78
Bergeson, 309
Bergin, A.E., 620
Berk, L.E., 306, 316
Berkowitz, L., 216, 407, 408, 410
Berlyne, D.E., 529
Bernays, Martha, 476
Berndt, T.J., 353, 356
Bernieri, F., 475
Bernstein, 566
Bernstein, I.L., 188
Berntson, G.G., 648
Berry, 661
Berry, D.S., 349
Berry, D.T.R., 148
Berry, J.W., 505
Bertelsen, A., 572
Bertini, M., 145
Besseghini, V.H., 574
Besson, J., 109
Betz, A.L., 648
Betz, E.L., 397
Beyerstein, B.L., 174
Beyth-Marom, R., 351
Bhatia, S., 535
Bhatt, R.S., 283
Biddy, 216
Biederman, G.B., 184
Biederman, I., 94
Biederman, J., 569, 570
Bierman, K.L., 353
Biggs, M., 319
Bigler, R.S., 339
Binet, Alfred, 440, 441, 442
Bini, L., 625
Birnbaum, I.M., 233
Birren, J., 367
Bishop, J.E., 405
Bishop, S.R., 110
Bisnaire, L.M., 361
Bissonnette, R., 416
Bivens, J.A., 316
Bixler, E.O., 150
Bjorklund, D.F., 317
Bjorkqvist, K., 408
Black, J.S., 217
Black, M.E., 427
Blackmore, S., 130
Blake, R., 121, 123
Blakemore, B., 570
Blakeslee, S., 405
Bland, R.C., 567, 575, 591
Blashko, C.A., 547
Blatt, S.J., 611
Blinn-Pike, 362
Bliss, R.E., 161
Block, 156
Block, J., 491
Blood, A.J., 422
Bloom, P., 293
Blouin, A.G., 403

Blyth, D.A., 349
Boaert, 401
Bobo, L., 654
Bobocel, 273
Bodenhausen, G.V., 659
Bodenstein, 521
Bogeart, A.F., 493
Bohannon, J., 287
Bohman, M., 163
Boivin, M., 338
Boldrey, 65
Boles, D.B., 74
Bonardi, C., 189
Bond, 170
Bond, N.H., 13
Bond, R., 32
Bonnet, Charles, 91
Bons, T., 262
Bookstein, F.L., 304
Bootzin, R.R., 605
Bordia, P., 426
Borges, G., 540
Bornstein, R.F., 482, 673
Borod, J.C., 421
Borstein, M.H., 330
Bortolotti, S., 423
Botez, M.I., 62
Botha, R.P., 293
Bouchard, T.J., 79, 455
Bouchard, T.J., Jr., 81, 494
Bouchard, T.J.Jr., 496
Boulos, Z., 144
Bourhis, 655, 656
Bouvard, M.P., 55
Bowd, A., 657
Bowd, A.D., 35
Bowen, B., 505, 656
Bower, G.H., 170, 235
Bowers, K.S., 157, 240
Bowers, T.G., 620
Bowlby, J., 332, 335
Bowles, N., 129
Boyanowski, E.O., 413
Boyes, 314
Boyes, M.C., 326
Boykin, A.W., 459, 460
Boyle, 418
Bozarth, M.A., 53, 160
Bradbury, T.N., 677
Bradley, M.M., 586
Bradley, M.T., 427
Brady, P., 657, 662
Braff, D.L., 590
Brainerd, 316
Braun, C.M., 204
Braverman, N.S., 187
Brawley, L.R., 395
Brean, H., 93
Breazeal (Ferrell), C., 281
Breggin, P.R., 626
Bregman, A., 119
Brehm, J.W., 393
Brehms, 650
Breland, K., 201
Breland, M., 201
Brennan, K.A., 329
Brent, 372
Brett, L.P., 189
Breuer, Joseph, 477
Brewer, W.F., 245

Brickman, J., 413
Brisson, C., 551
Britt, T.W., 171, 524
Broca, Paul, 72
Brockner, J., 273, 377
Brodbeck, D.R., 210
Brody, 452
Brody, G.H., 615
Broe G.A., 83
Bronstein, P., 187
Broughton, R.J., 151
Brown, J.D., 517, 643
Brown, J.M., 110
Brown, R., 351
Brown, R.W., 242
Browne, M.W., 671
Brownell, K.D., 539
Bruck, 246
Bruder, 611
Brugge, J.F., 107
Bryan, T.S., 428
Bryant, J., 405
Bryden, M.P., 69
Buckle, L., 83
Bullock, M., 315
Bunk, 677
Burger, J.M., 498
Burgess, C.A., 157
Burish, T.G., 188
Burns, B.D., 278
Burnstein, E., 671
Burt, D.B., 233
Burton, L., 515
Bush, A.J., 546
Bushman, B.J., 408, 409, 668
Buss, A.H., 409, 410
Buss, D.M., 10, 11, 405, 406, 407, 496, 675, 676
Butler, 318
Butler, B., 656
Butt, D.S., 380
Buyer, L.S., 278
Byers, E.S., 170, 543, 544, 653
Byl, N.N., 552
Byne, W., 82
Byrne, 673
Byrne, B., 405
Byrne, D., 181, 354, 393, 403, 406, 672, 674
Byrne, R.M.J., 260

Cacioppo, J.T., 68, 648, 649
Cain, W.S., 114, 405
Call, J., 283
Calvert, C.R.X., 443
Camacho, T.C., 516
Camancho, 516
Cameron, 640
Campbell, E., 540
Campbell, F.A., 458
Campbell, J., 119
Campbell, J.D., 172
Campbell, J.N., 109
Campbell, P.E., 201
Campbell, R.L., 164
Campbell, S.C., 569
Canadian Cancer Society, 535
Canadian Mental health Association, 600
Canadian Psychological Association, 13
Canary, D.J., 678
Cannon-Bowers, J.A., 274
Cantor, 378

SUBJECT INDEX

PHOTO CREDITS

p. 7 Danny Abriel/Dalhousie University; p. 8 Fred Chartrand/The Canadian Press; p. 13 Jeff Greenberg/PhotoEdit; p. 17 Alex Mares-Manton/Stone; p. 23 Robert Harbison; p. 24 ©1993 Gamma; p. 27 Bruce Ayres/Stone, Nick Vedros/ Stone; p. 34 Steve Winter/Black Star; p. 52 © Kevin Morris/Allstock; p. 56 (Fig. 2.7) Custom Medical Stock Photo; p. 58 The Harvard Medical Library in the F.A. Countway Library of Medicine, Boston; p. 59 ©1993 Strange/Porter; p. 60 Peter Menzel; p. 65 (top) Dan McCoy/Rainbow, (middle) Montreal Neurological Institute; p. 71 Ryan Remiorz/The Canadian Press; p. 79 Science Photo Library/Photo Researchers, Inc.; p. 80 Porter/The Image Works; p. 83 Dick Hemingway; p. 95 Peter Menzel/Stock Boston; p. 116 © Gerard Vandystad/Photo Researchers, Inc.; p. 120 Bill Ross/Stone; p. 122 (top left) Tommy L. Thompson/Black Star, (top right) Steve Mats/Stone, (bottom) Rob Pretzer; p. 126 DigiRule Inc.; p. 130 PhotoDisc, Inc.; p. 139 Jeff Greenberg,/Photo researchers, Inc.; p. 146 Michael Heron/Woodfin Camp & Assoc.; p. 159 Dave Starrett; p. 166 M. Ferri/The Stock Market, Allan Tannenbaum/Sygma, Monkmeyer Press, The Stock Market; p. 172 Kevin Frayer/The Canadian Press; p. 173 Marco Shark; p. 187 Ian O'Leary/Stone; p. 189 © Stan Wayman/Photo Researchers, Inc.; p. 191 (Fig. 5.6) data from Kamin (1969, p. 283) with permission of the author, calculated by Vin Lolordo; p. 192 Dr. Benjamin Harris; p. 193 David Weintraub/Science Source/Photo Researchers, Inc.; p. 199 (left) © Stephen Frisch/Stock Boston, (right) Marco Shark.; p. 204 Nina Leen/Time Warner Inc.; p. 211 Edward Regan/The Globe and Mail; p. 215 Robert Harbison; p. 227 PhotoFest; p. 229 ©1989 Kent Wood/Allstock; p. 233 Brian Smith; p. 239 Shahn Kermani/Gamma-Liason; p. 241 Steven Peters; p. 243 ©1989 Kent Wood/Allstock, Steven Underwood Photography, Photofest; p. 252 Stephen Marks; p. 271 Toronto Sun, Japanese Tourist and Information Centre, Angelika Baur; p. 276 Bridgeman Art Library; p. 285 Gallaudet University; p. 286 © Peter Pearson/Stone; p. 291 ©1994 Michael Goldman/The Pace Gallery; p. 292 CNN; p. 295 Robert Harbison; p. 302, Will Faller; p. 303 Francis Leroy/Biocosmos–Science Photo Library, Photo Researchers Inc., © Lennart Nilsson/Bonniers; p. 315 Dr. Reissland-Burghart; p. 308 courtesy of Janet Werker; p. 309 courtesy of J. Campos, B. Bertenthal, and R. Kermoian; p. 313 Tom McCarthy/Stock South; p. 316 Andy Sacks/Stone; p. 325 Randy Wells/Stone; p. 336 Will Faller; p. 337 (left) Martin Rogers/Woodfin Camp and Assoc., (right) Martin Rogers/Stone; p. 340 (left) Robert Harbison, (right)

Kagan/Monkmeyer; p. 348 Robert A. Baron; p. 349 J. Gerard Smith/Monkmeyer Press; p. 352 © Nathan Benn/Stock Boston; p. 361 Culver Pictures; p. 363 Wendy Holonen/Northern News Service; p. 376 David Young-Wolff/Stone; p. 383 (top) Natsuko Utsumi/Gamma-Liason; p. 393 Shahn Kermani/Gamma-Liason; p. 397 Stephen Marks, K. Reininger/Black Star; p. 398 Steven Underwood Photography, © Donovan Reese/Stone; p. 407 Chuck Stoody/The Canadian Press; p. 409 courtesy of Robert A. Baron; p. 420 Shaun Best/The Canadian Press, Toronto Sun; p. 426 Jon Riley/The Stock Shop; p. 437 Canadian Olympic Association; p. 439 Jim Pickerell, Laima Druskis/Stock Boston, F. Baldwin/Photo Researchers, Inc.; p. 441 Danny Abriel/Dalhousie University; p. 442 Merrim/Monkmeyer Press; p. 443 Mario Ruiz/Picture Group; p. 449 (top left) Paul Chesley/Stone, (bottom left) UPI/Corbis-Bettmann, (top right) RobertE. Daemmrich/Stock boston, (bottom right) Culver Pictures; p. 464 Michael Newman/PhotoEdit; p. 478 The Granger Collection; p. 480 Underwood Photo Archives; p. 487 Toronto Sun; p. 484 Photofest; p. 489 Corbis; p. 491 Dave Buston/The Canadian Press; p. 492 Praeger Publishers; p. 493 ©1987 Joel W. Rogers; p. 497 Stanford University News Service; p. 500 (middle) Corbis, (bottom) Stanford University News Service; p. 514 Elena Dorfman; p. 517 AP/Worldwide Photos; p. 520 ©1992 David Madison; p. 522 Robert Harbison; p. 524 Andre Forget/The Canadian Press; p. 541 Jeff Persons/Stock Boston; p. 542 Defleur/Photo Researchers, Inc.; p. 538 Prentice Hall Inc./Pearson Education; p. 58 Baum/Monkmeyer Press; p. 560 Northwind Photo Archives; p. 561 © Anis Hamdani/ Gamma-Liason; p. 562 The Granger Collection, © James Wilson/Woodfin Camp & Assoc.; p. 565 Michael Newman/PhotoEdit; p. 581 UPI/Bettmann; p. 590 Grunnitus/Monkmeyer Press; p. 601 AP/Worldwide Photos; p. 607 Bernama/The Canadian Press–AP Photo; p. 614 (top) Mary Evans/Sigmund Freud Copyrights, (second row) Michael Newman/PhotoEdit, (third row) Bernama/The Canadian Press–AP Photo; p. 616 Robert E. Daemmrich/Stock Boston; p. 625 Robert A. Baron; p. 626 James Wilson/Woodfin Camp & Assoc.; p. 627 Adam Hart-Davis/Science Photo Library/Photo Researchers, Inc; p. 631 © Peter Southwick/Stock Boston; p. 632 Lyn Hancock; p. 634 © Louis Benze/Allstock; p. 646 Sanford/Toronto Sun; p. 648 Halifax Mail Star; p. 655 Bob Carroll; p. 656 Paul Conklin/PhotoEdit; p. 661 Bob Carroll; p. 676 Marcia Ozier; p. 681 Johnson Space Center/NASA.